I0010816

The GNU C Library Reference Manual

The GNU C Library
Reference Manual

Sandra Loosemore
with
Richard M. Stallman, Roland McGrath, Andrew Oram, and Ulrich Drepper

for version 2.26

This file documents the GNU C Library.

This is *The GNU C Library Reference Manual*, for version 2.26.

Copyright © 1993–2017 Free Software Foundation, Inc.

Permission is granted to copy, distribute and/or modify this document under the terms of the GNU Free Documentation License, Version 1.3 or any later version published by the Free Software Foundation; with the Invariant Sections being "Free Software Needs Free Documentation" and "GNU Lesser General Public License", the Front-Cover texts being "A GNU Manual", and with the Back-Cover Texts as in (a) below. A copy of the license is included in the section entitled "GNU Free Documentation License".

(a) The FSF's Back-Cover Text is: "You have the freedom to copy and modify this GNU manual. Buying copies from the FSF supports it in developing GNU and promoting software freedom."

Changes to original document: Pages numbers were moved to the bottom of each page.

Short Contents

Table of Contents

1 Introduction

The C language provides no built-in facilities for performing such common operations as input/output, memory management, string manipulation, and the like. Instead, these facilities are defined in a standard *library*, which you compile and link with your programs.

The GNU C Library, described in this document, defines all of the library functions that are specified by the ISO C standard, as well as additional features specific to POSIX and other derivatives of the Unix operating system, and extensions specific to GNU systems.

The purpose of this manual is to tell you how to use the facilities of the GNU C Library. We have mentioned which features belong to which standards to help you identify things that are potentially non-portable to other systems. But the emphasis in this manual is not on strict portability.

1.1 Getting Started

This manual is written with the assumption that you are at least somewhat familiar with the C programming language and basic programming concepts. Specifically, familiarity with ISO standard C (see Section 1.2.1 [ISO C], page 2), rather than "traditional" pre-ISO C dialects, is assumed.

The GNU C Library includes several *header files*, each of which provides definitions and declarations for a group of related facilities; this information is used by the C compiler when processing your program. For example, the header file `stdio.h` declares facilities for performing input and output, and the header file `string.h` declares string processing utilities. The organization of this manual generally follows the same division as the header files.

If you are reading this manual for the first time, you should read all of the introductory material and skim the remaining chapters. There are a *lot* of functions in the GNU C Library and it's not realistic to expect that you will be able to remember exactly *how* to use each and every one of them. It's more important to become generally familiar with the kinds of facilities that the library provides, so that when you are writing your programs you can recognize *when* to make use of library functions, and *where* in this manual you can find more specific information about them.

1.2 Standards and Portability

This section discusses the various standards and other sources that the GNU C Library is based upon. These sources include the ISO C and POSIX standards, and the System V and Berkeley Unix implementations.

The primary focus of this manual is to tell you how to make effective use of the GNU C Library facilities. But if you are concerned about making your programs compatible with these standards, or portable to operating systems other than GNU, this can affect how you use the library. This section gives you an overview of these standards, so that you will know what they are when they are mentioned in other parts of the manual.

See Appendix B [Summary of Library Facilities], page 925, for an alphabetical list of the functions and other symbols provided by the library. This list also states which standards each function or symbol comes from.

1.2.1 ISO C

The GNU C Library is compatible with the C standard adopted by the American National Standards Institute (ANSI): *American National Standard X3.159-1989—"ANSI C"* and later by the International Standardization Organization (ISO): *ISO/IEC 9899:1990, "Programming languages—C"*. We here refer to the standard as ISO C since this is the more general standard in respect of ratification. The header files and library facilities that make up the GNU C Library are a superset of those specified by the ISO C standard.

If you are concerned about strict adherence to the ISO C standard, you should use the '-ansi' option when you compile your programs with the GNU C compiler. This tells the compiler to define *only* ISO standard features from the library header files, unless you explicitly ask for additional features. See Section 1.3.4 [Feature Test Macros], page 15, for information on how to do this.

Being able to restrict the library to include only ISO C features is important because ISO C puts limitations on what names can be defined by the library implementation, and the GNU extensions don't fit these limitations. See Section 1.3.3 [Reserved Names], page 14, for more information about these restrictions.

This manual does not attempt to give you complete details on the differences between ISO C and older dialects. It gives advice on how to write programs to work portably under multiple C dialects, but does not aim for completeness.

1.2.2 POSIX (The Portable Operating System Interface)

The GNU C Library is also compatible with the ISO *POSIX* family of standards, known more formally as the *Portable Operating System Interface for Computer Environments* (ISO/IEC 9945). They were also published as ANSI/IEEE Std 1003. POSIX is derived mostly from various versions of the Unix operating system.

The library facilities specified by the POSIX standards are a superset of those required by ISO C; POSIX specifies additional features for ISO C functions, as well as specifying new additional functions. In general, the additional requirements and functionality defined by the POSIX standards are aimed at providing lower-level support for a particular kind of operating system environment, rather than general programming language support which can run in many diverse operating system environments.

The GNU C Library implements all of the functions specified in *ISO/IEC 9945-1:1996, the POSIX System Application Program Interface*, commonly referred to as POSIX.1. The primary extensions to the ISO C facilities specified by this standard include file system interface primitives (see Chapter 14 [File System Interface], page 390), device-specific terminal control functions (see Chapter 17 [Low-Level Terminal Interface], page 490), and process control functions (see Chapter 26 [Processes], page 773).

Some facilities from *ISO/IEC 9945-2:1993, the POSIX Shell and Utilities standard* (POSIX.2) are also implemented in the GNU C Library. These include utilities for dealing with regular expressions and other pattern matching facilities (see Chapter 10 [Pattern Matching], page 230).

1.2.2.1 POSIX Safety Concepts

This manual documents various safety properties of GNU C Library functions, in lines that follow their prototypes and look like:

Preliminary: | MT-Safe | AS-Safe | AC-Safe |

The properties are assessed according to the criteria set forth in the POSIX standard for such safety contexts as Thread-, Async-Signal- and Async-Cancel- -Safety. Intuitive definitions of these properties, attempting to capture the meaning of the standard definitions, follow.

- `MT-Safe` or Thread-Safe functions are safe to call in the presence of other threads. MT, in MT-Safe, stands for Multi Thread.

  Being MT-Safe does not imply a function is atomic, nor that it uses any of the memory synchronization mechanisms POSIX exposes to users. It is even possible that calling MT-Safe functions in sequence does not yield an MT-Safe combination. For example, having a thread call two MT-Safe functions one right after the other does not guarantee behavior equivalent to atomic execution of a combination of both functions, since concurrent calls in other threads may interfere in a destructive way.

  Whole-program optimizations that could inline functions across library interfaces may expose unsafe reordering, and so performing inlining across the GNU C Library interface is not recommended. The documented MT-Safety status is not guaranteed under whole-program optimization. However, functions defined in user-visible headers are designed to be safe for inlining.

- `AS-Safe` or Async-Signal-Safe functions are safe to call from asynchronous signal handlers. AS, in AS-Safe, stands for Asynchronous Signal.

  Many functions that are AS-Safe may set `errno`, or modify the floating-point environment, because their doing so does not make them unsuitable for use in signal handlers. However, programs could misbehave should asynchronous signal handlers modify this thread-local state, and the signal handling machinery cannot be counted on to preserve it. Therefore, signal handlers that call functions that may set `errno` or modify the floating-point environment *must* save their original values, and restore them before returning.

- `AC-Safe` or Async-Cancel-Safe functions are safe to call when asynchronous cancellation is enabled. AC in AC-Safe stands for Asynchronous Cancellation.

  The POSIX standard defines only three functions to be AC-Safe, namely `pthread_cancel`, `pthread_setcancelstate`, and `pthread_setcanceltype`. At present the GNU C Library provides no guarantees beyond these three functions, but does document which functions are presently AC-Safe. This documentation is provided for use by the GNU C Library developers.

  Just like signal handlers, cancellation cleanup routines must configure the floating point environment they require. The routines cannot assume a floating point environment, particularly when asynchronous cancellation is enabled. If the configuration of the floating point environment cannot be performed atomically then it is also possible that the environment encountered is internally inconsistent.

- `MT-Unsafe`, `AS-Unsafe`, `AC-Unsafe` functions are not safe to call within the safety contexts described above. Calling them within such contexts invokes undefined behavior.

  Functions not explicitly documented as safe in a safety context should be regarded as Unsafe.

- `Preliminary` safety properties are documented, indicating these properties may *not* be counted on in future releases of the GNU C Library.

Such preliminary properties are the result of an assessment of the properties of our current implementation, rather than of what is mandated and permitted by current and future standards.

Although we strive to abide by the standards, in some cases our implementation is safe even when the standard does not demand safety, and in other cases our implementation does not meet the standard safety requirements. The latter are most likely bugs; the former, when marked as `Preliminary`, should not be counted on: future standards may require changes that are not compatible with the additional safety properties afforded by the current implementation.

Furthermore, the POSIX standard does not offer a detailed definition of safety. We assume that, by "safe to call", POSIX means that, as long as the program does not invoke undefined behavior, the "safe to call" function behaves as specified, and does not cause other functions to deviate from their specified behavior. We have chosen to use its loose definitions of safety, not because they are the best definitions to use, but because choosing them harmonizes this manual with POSIX.

Please keep in mind that these are preliminary definitions and annotations, and certain aspects of the definitions are still under discussion and might be subject to clarification or change.

Over time, we envision evolving the preliminary safety notes into stable commitments, as stable as those of our interfaces. As we do, we will remove the `Preliminary` keyword from safety notes. As long as the keyword remains, however, they are not to be regarded as a promise of future behavior.

Other keywords that appear in safety notes are defined in subsequent sections.

1.2.2.2 Unsafe Features

Functions that are unsafe to call in certain contexts are annotated with keywords that document their features that make them unsafe to call. AS-Unsafe features in this section indicate the functions are never safe to call when asynchronous signals are enabled. AC-Unsafe features indicate they are never safe to call when asynchronous cancellation is enabled. There are no MT-Unsafe marks in this section.

- `lock`

  Functions marked with `lock` as an AS-Unsafe feature may be interrupted by a signal while holding a non-recursive lock. If the signal handler calls another such function that takes the same lock, the result is a deadlock.

  Functions annotated with `lock` as an AC-Unsafe feature may, if cancelled asynchronously, fail to release a lock that would have been released if their execution had not been interrupted by asynchronous thread cancellation. Once a lock is left taken, attempts to take that lock will block indefinitely.

- `corrupt`

  Functions marked with `corrupt` as an AS-Unsafe feature may corrupt data structures and misbehave when they interrupt, or are interrupted by, another such function. Unlike functions marked with `lock`, these take recursive locks to avoid MT-Safety problems, but this is not enough to stop a signal handler from observing a partially-updated data structure. Further corruption may arise from the interrupted function's failure to notice updates made by signal handlers.

Functions marked with `corrupt` as an AC-Unsafe feature may leave data structures in a corrupt, partially updated state. Subsequent uses of the data structure may misbehave.

- `heap`

  Functions marked with `heap` may call heap memory management functions from the `malloc`/`free` family of functions and are only as safe as those functions. This note is thus equivalent to:

  | AS-Unsafe lock | AC-Unsafe lock fd mem |

- `dlopen`

  Functions marked with `dlopen` use the dynamic loader to load shared libraries into the current execution image. This involves opening files, mapping them into memory, allocating additional memory, resolving symbols, applying relocations and more, all of this while holding internal dynamic loader locks.

  The locks are enough for these functions to be AS- and AC-Unsafe, but other issues may arise. At present this is a placeholder for all potential safety issues raised by `dlopen`.

- `plugin`

  Functions annotated with `plugin` may run code from plugins that may be external to the GNU C Library. Such plugin functions are assumed to be MT-Safe, AS-Unsafe and AC-Unsafe. Examples of such plugins are stack unwinding libraries, name service switch (NSS) and character set conversion (iconv) back-ends.

  Although the plugins mentioned as examples are all brought in by means of dlopen, the `plugin` keyword does not imply any direct involvement of the dynamic loader or the `libdl` interfaces, those are covered by `dlopen`. For example, if one function loads a module and finds the addresses of some of its functions, while another just calls those already-resolved functions, the former will be marked with `dlopen`, whereas the latter will get the `plugin`. When a single function takes all of these actions, then it gets both marks.

- `i18n`

  Functions marked with `i18n` may call internationalization functions of the `gettext` family and will be only as safe as those functions. This note is thus equivalent to:

  | MT-Safe env | AS-Unsafe corrupt heap dlopen | AC-Unsafe corrupt |

- `timer`

  Functions marked with `timer` use the `alarm` function or similar to set a time-out for a system call or a long-running operation. In a multi-threaded program, there is a risk that the time-out signal will be delivered to a different thread, thus failing to interrupt the intended thread. Besides being MT-Unsafe, such functions are always AS-Unsafe, because calling them in signal handlers may interfere with timers set in the interrupted code, and AC-Unsafe, because there is no safe way to guarantee an earlier timer will be reset in case of asynchronous cancellation.

1.2.2.3 Conditionally Safe Features

For some features that make functions unsafe to call in certain contexts, there are known ways to avoid the safety problem other than refraining from calling the function altogether. The keywords that follow refer to such features, and each of their definitions indicate how the whole program needs to be constrained in order to remove the safety problem indicated by the keyword. Only when all the reasons that make a function unsafe are observed and addressed, by applying the documented constraints, does the function become safe to call in a context.

- `init`

  Functions marked with `init` as an MT-Unsafe feature perform MT-Unsafe initialization when they are first called.

  Calling such a function at least once in single-threaded mode removes this specific cause for the function to be regarded as MT-Unsafe. If no other cause for that remains, the function can then be safely called after other threads are started.

  Functions marked with `init` as an AS- or AC-Unsafe feature use the internal `libc_once` machinery or similar to initialize internal data structures.

  If a signal handler interrupts such an initializer, and calls any function that also performs `libc_once` initialization, it will deadlock if the thread library has been loaded.

  Furthermore, if an initializer is partially complete before it is canceled or interrupted by a signal whose handler requires the same initialization, some or all of the initialization may be performed more than once, leaking resources or even resulting in corrupt internal data.

  Applications that need to call functions marked with `init` as an AS- or AC-Unsafe feature should ensure the initialization is performed before configuring signal handlers or enabling cancellation, so that the AS- and AC-Safety issues related with `libc_once` do not arise.

- `race`

  Functions annotated with `race` as an MT-Safety issue operate on objects in ways that may cause data races or similar forms of destructive interference out of concurrent execution. In some cases, the objects are passed to the functions by users; in others, they are used by the functions to return values to users; in others, they are not even exposed to users.

  We consider access to objects passed as (indirect) arguments to functions to be data race free. The assurance of data race free objects is the caller's responsibility. We will not mark a function as MT-Unsafe or AS-Unsafe if it misbehaves when users fail to take the measures required by POSIX to avoid data races when dealing with such objects. As a general rule, if a function is documented as reading from an object passed (by reference) to it, or modifying it, users ought to use memory synchronization primitives to avoid data races just as they would should they perform the accesses themselves rather than by calling the library function. `FILE` streams are the exception to the general rule, in that POSIX mandates the library to guard against data races in many functions that manipulate objects of this specific opaque type. We regard this as a convenience provided to users, rather than as a general requirement whose expectations should extend to other types.

  In order to remind users that guarding certain arguments is their responsibility, we will annotate functions that take objects of certain types as arguments. We draw the line for objects passed by users as follows: objects whose types are exposed to users, and that users are expected to access directly, such as memory buffers, strings, and various user-visible `struct` types, do *not* give reason for functions to be annotated with `race`. It would be noisy and redundant with the general requirement, and not many would be surprised by the library's lack of internal guards when accessing objects that can be accessed directly by users.

As for objects that are opaque or opaque-like, in that they are to be manipulated only by passing them to library functions (e.g., `FILE`, `DIR`, `obstack`, `iconv_t`), there might be additional expectations as to internal coordination of access by the library. We will annotate, with `race` followed by a colon and the argument name, functions that take such objects but that do not take care of synchronizing access to them by default. For example, `FILE` stream `unlocked` functions will be annotated, but those that perform implicit locking on `FILE` streams by default will not, even though the implicit locking may be disabled on a per-stream basis.

In either case, we will not regard as MT-Unsafe functions that may access user-supplied objects in unsafe ways should users fail to ensure the accesses are well defined. The notion prevails that users are expected to safeguard against data races any user-supplied objects that the library accesses on their behalf.

This user responsibility does not apply, however, to objects controlled by the library itself, such as internal objects and static buffers used to return values from certain calls. When the library doesn't guard them against concurrent uses, these cases are regarded as MT-Unsafe and AS-Unsafe (although the `race` mark under AS-Unsafe will be omitted as redundant with the one under MT-Unsafe). As in the case of user-exposed objects, the mark may be followed by a colon and an identifier. The identifier groups all functions that operate on a certain unguarded object; users may avoid the MT-Safety issues related with unguarded concurrent access to such internal objects by creating a non-recursive mutex related with the identifier, and always holding the mutex when calling any function marked as racy on that identifier, as they would have to should the identifier be an object under user control. The non-recursive mutex avoids the MT-Safety issue, but it trades one AS-Safety issue for another, so use in asynchronous signals remains undefined.

When the identifier relates to a static buffer used to hold return values, the mutex must be held for as long as the buffer remains in use by the caller. Many functions that return pointers to static buffers offer reentrant variants that store return values in caller-supplied buffers instead. In some cases, such as `tmpname`, the variant is chosen not by calling an alternate entry point, but by passing a non-`NULL` pointer to the buffer in which the returned values are to be stored. These variants are generally preferable in multi-threaded programs, although some of them are not MT-Safe because of other internal buffers, also documented with `race` notes.

- `const`

  Functions marked with `const` as an MT-Safety issue non-atomically modify internal objects that are better regarded as constant, because a substantial portion of the GNU C Library accesses them without synchronization. Unlike `race`, that causes both readers and writers of internal objects to be regarded as MT-Unsafe and AS-Unsafe, this mark is applied to writers only. Writers remain equally MT- and AS-Unsafe to call, but the then-mandatory constness of objects they modify enables readers to be regarded as MT-Safe and AS-Safe (as long as no other reasons for them to be unsafe remain), since the lack of synchronization is not a problem when the objects are effectively constant.

The identifier that follows the `const` mark will appear by itself as a safety note in readers. Programs that wish to work around this safety issue, so as to call writers, may use a non-recursve `rwlock` associated with the identifier, and guard *all* calls to functions marked with `const` followed by the identifier with a write lock, and *all* calls to functions marked with the identifier by itself with a read lock. The non-recursive locking removes the MT-Safety problem, but it trades one AS-Safety problem for another, so use in asynchronous signals remains undefined.

- `sig`

  Functions marked with `sig` as a MT-Safety issue (that implies an identical AS-Safety issue, omitted for brevity) may temporarily install a signal handler for internal purposes, which may interfere with other uses of the signal, identified after a colon.

  This safety problem can be worked around by ensuring that no other uses of the signal will take place for the duration of the call. Holding a non-recursive mutex while calling all functions that use the same temporary signal; blocking that signal before the call and resetting its handler afterwards is recommended.

  There is no safe way to guarantee the original signal handler is restored in case of asynchronous cancellation, therefore so-marked functions are also AC-Unsafe.

  Besides the measures recommended to work around the MT- and AS-Safety problem, in order to avert the cancellation problem, disabling asynchronous cancellation *and* installing a cleanup handler to restore the signal to the desired state and to release the mutex are recommended.

- `term`

  Functions marked with `term` as an MT-Safety issue may change the terminal settings in the recommended way, namely: call `tcgetattr`, modify some flags, and then call `tcsetattr`; this creates a window in which changes made by other threads are lost. Thus, functions marked with `term` are MT-Unsafe. The same window enables changes made by asynchronous signals to be lost. These functions are also AS-Unsafe, but the corresponding mark is omitted as redundant.

  It is thus advisable for applications using the terminal to avoid concurrent and reentrant interactions with it, by not using it in signal handlers or blocking signals that might use it, and holding a lock while calling these functions and interacting with the terminal. This lock should also be used for mutual exclusion with functions marked with `race:tcattr(fd)`, where *fd* is a file descriptor for the controlling terminal. The caller may use a single mutex for simplicity, or use one mutex per terminal, even if referenced by different file descriptors.

  Functions marked with `term` as an AC-Safety issue are supposed to restore terminal settings to their original state, after temporarily changing them, but they may fail to do so if cancelled.

  Besides the measures recommended to work around the MT- and AS-Safety problem, in order to avert the cancellation problem, disabling asynchronous cancellation *and* installing a cleanup handler to restore the terminal settings to the original state and to release the mutex are recommended.

1.2.2.4 Other Safety Remarks

Additional keywords may be attached to functions, indicating features that do not make a function unsafe to call, but that may need to be taken into account in certain classes of programs:

- `locale`

  Functions annotated with `locale` as an MT-Safety issue read from the locale object without any form of synchronization. Functions annotated with `locale` called concurrently with locale changes may behave in ways that do not correspond to any of the locales active during their execution, but an unpredictable mix thereof.

  We do not mark these functions as MT- or AS-Unsafe, however, because functions that modify the locale object are marked with `const:locale` and regarded as unsafe. Being unsafe, the latter are not to be called when multiple threads are running or asynchronous signals are enabled, and so the locale can be considered effectively constant in these contexts, which makes the former safe.

- `env`

  Functions marked with `env` as an MT-Safety issue access the environment with `getenv` or similar, without any guards to ensure safety in the presence of concurrent modifications.

  We do not mark these functions as MT- or AS-Unsafe, however, because functions that modify the environment are all marked with `const:env` and regarded as unsafe. Being unsafe, the latter are not to be called when multiple threads are running or asynchronous signals are enabled, and so the environment can be considered effectively constant in these contexts, which makes the former safe.

- `hostid`

  The function marked with `hostid` as an MT-Safety issue reads from the system-wide data structures that hold the "host ID" of the machine. These data structures cannot generally be modified atomically. Since it is expected that the "host ID" will not normally change, the function that reads from it (`gethostid`) is regarded as safe, whereas the function that modifies it (`sethostid`) is marked with `const:hostid`, indicating it may require special care if it is to be called. In this specific case, the special care amounts to system-wide (not merely intra-process) coordination.

- `sigintr`

  Functions marked with `sigintr` as an MT-Safety issue access the `_sigintr` internal data structure without any guards to ensure safety in the presence of concurrent modifications.

  We do not mark these functions as MT- or AS-Unsafe, however, because functions that modify the this data structure are all marked with `const:sigintr` and regarded as unsafe. Being unsafe, the latter are not to be called when multiple threads are running or asynchronous signals are enabled, and so the data structure can be considered effectively constant in these contexts, which makes the former safe.

- `fd`

  Functions annotated with `fd` as an AC-Safety issue may leak file descriptors if asynchronous thread cancellation interrupts their execution.

Functions that allocate or deallocate file descriptors will generally be marked as such. Even if they attempted to protect the file descriptor allocation and deallocation with cleanup regions, allocating a new descriptor and storing its number where the cleanup region could release it cannot be performed as a single atomic operation. Similarly, releasing the descriptor and taking it out of the data structure normally responsible for releasing it cannot be performed atomically. There will always be a window in which the descriptor cannot be released because it was not stored in the cleanup handler argument yet, or it was already taken out before releasing it. It cannot be taken out after release: an open descriptor could mean either that the descriptor still has to be closed, or that it already did so but the descriptor was reallocated by another thread or signal handler.

Such leaks could be internally avoided, with some performance penalty, by temporarily disabling asynchronous thread cancellation. However, since callers of allocation or deallocation functions would have to do this themselves, to avoid the same sort of leak in their own layer, it makes more sense for the library to assume they are taking care of it than to impose a performance penalty that is redundant when the problem is solved in upper layers, and insufficient when it is not.

This remark by itself does not cause a function to be regarded as AC-Unsafe. However, cumulative effects of such leaks may pose a problem for some programs. If this is the case, suspending asynchronous cancellation for the duration of calls to such functions is recommended.

- `mem`

  Functions annotated with `mem` as an AC-Safety issue may leak memory if asynchronous thread cancellation interrupts their execution.

  The problem is similar to that of file descriptors: there is no atomic interface to allocate memory and store its address in the argument to a cleanup handler, or to release it and remove its address from that argument, without at least temporarily disabling asynchronous cancellation, which these functions do not do.

  This remark does not by itself cause a function to be regarded as generally AC-Unsafe. However, cumulative effects of such leaks may be severe enough for some programs that disabling asynchronous cancellation for the duration of calls to such functions may be required.

- `cwd`

  Functions marked with `cwd` as an MT-Safety issue may temporarily change the current working directory during their execution, which may cause relative pathnames to be resolved in unexpected ways in other threads or within asynchronous signal or cancellation handlers.

  This is not enough of a reason to mark so-marked functions as MT- or AS-Unsafe, but when this behavior is optional (e.g., `nftw` with `FTW_CHDIR`), avoiding the option may be a good alternative to using full pathnames or file descriptor-relative (e.g. `openat`) system calls.

- `!posix`

  This remark, as an MT-, AS- or AC-Safety note to a function, indicates the safety status of the function is known to differ from the specified status in the POSIX standard. For example, POSIX does not require a function to be Safe, but our implementation is, or vice-versa.

For the time being, the absence of this remark does not imply the safety properties we documented are identical to those mandated by POSIX for the corresponding functions.

- `:identifier`

  Annotations may sometimes be followed by identifiers, intended to group several functions that e.g. access the data structures in an unsafe way, as in `race` and `const`, or to provide more specific information, such as naming a signal in a function marked with `sig`. It is envisioned that it may be applied to `lock` and `corrupt` as well in the future.

  In most cases, the identifier will name a set of functions, but it may name global objects or function arguments, or identifiable properties or logical components associated with them, with a notation such as e.g. `:buf(arg)` to denote a buffer associated with the argument *arg*, or `:tcattr(fd)` to denote the terminal attributes of a file descriptor *fd*.

  The most common use for identifiers is to provide logical groups of functions and arguments that need to be protected by the same synchronization primitive in order to ensure safe operation in a given context.

- `/condition`

  Some safety annotations may be conditional, in that they only apply if a boolean expression involving arguments, global variables or even the underlying kernel evaluates to true. Such conditions as `/hurd` or `/!linux!bsd` indicate the preceding marker only applies when the underlying kernel is the HURD, or when it is neither Linux nor a BSD kernel, respectively. `/!ps` and `/one_per_line` indicate the preceding marker only applies when argument *ps* is NULL, or global variable *one_per_line* is nonzero.

  When all marks that render a function unsafe are adorned with such conditions, and none of the named conditions hold, then the function can be regarded as safe.

1.2.3 Berkeley Unix

The GNU C Library defines facilities from some versions of Unix which are not formally standardized, specifically from the 4.2 BSD, 4.3 BSD, and 4.4 BSD Unix systems (also known as *Berkeley Unix*) and from *SunOS* (a popular 4.2 BSD derivative that includes some Unix System V functionality). These systems support most of the ISO C and POSIX facilities, and 4.4 BSD and newer releases of SunOS in fact support them all.

The BSD facilities include symbolic links (see Section 14.5 [Symbolic Links], page 406), the `select` function (see Section 13.8 [Waiting for Input or Output], page 355), the BSD signal functions (see Section 24.10 [BSD Signal Handling], page 727), and sockets (see Chapter 16 [Sockets], page 442).

1.2.4 SVID (The System V Interface Description)

The *System V Interface Description* (SVID) is a document describing the AT&T Unix System V operating system. It is to some extent a superset of the POSIX standard (see Section 1.2.2 [POSIX (The Portable Operating System Interface)], page 2).

The GNU C Library defines most of the facilities required by the SVID that are not also required by the ISO C or POSIX standards, for compatibility with System V Unix and other Unix systems (such as SunOS) which include these facilities. However, many of the more obscure and less generally useful facilities required by the SVID are not included. (In fact, Unix System V itself does not provide them all.)

The supported facilities from System V include the methods for inter-process communication and shared memory, the `hsearch` and `drand48` families of functions, `fmtmsg` and several of the mathematical functions.

1.2.5 XPG (The X/Open Portability Guide)

The X/Open Portability Guide, published by the X/Open Company, Ltd., is a more general standard than POSIX. X/Open owns the Unix copyright and the XPG specifies the requirements for systems which are intended to be a Unix system.

The GNU C Library complies to the X/Open Portability Guide, Issue 4.2, with all extensions common to XSI (X/Open System Interface) compliant systems and also all X/Open UNIX extensions.

The additions on top of POSIX are mainly derived from functionality available in System V and BSD systems. Some of the really bad mistakes in System V systems were corrected, though. Since fulfilling the XPG standard with the Unix extensions is a precondition for getting the Unix brand chances are good that the functionality is available on commercial systems.

1.3 Using the Library

This section describes some of the practical issues involved in using the GNU C Library.

1.3.1 Header Files

Libraries for use by C programs really consist of two parts: *header files* that define types and macros and declare variables and functions; and the actual library or *archive* that contains the definitions of the variables and functions.

(Recall that in C, a *declaration* merely provides information that a function or variable exists and gives its type. For a function declaration, information about the types of its arguments might be provided as well. The purpose of declarations is to allow the compiler to correctly process references to the declared variables and functions. A *definition*, on the other hand, actually allocates storage for a variable or says what a function does.)

In order to use the facilities in the GNU C Library, you should be sure that your program source files include the appropriate header files. This is so that the compiler has declarations of these facilities available and can correctly process references to them. Once your program has been compiled, the linker resolves these references to the actual definitions provided in the archive file.

Header files are included into a program source file by the '`#include`' preprocessor directive. The C language supports two forms of this directive; the first,

```
#include "header"
```

is typically used to include a header file *header* that you write yourself; this would contain definitions and declarations describing the interfaces between the different parts of your particular application. By contrast,

```
#include <file.h>
```

is typically used to include a header file `file.h` that contains definitions and declarations for a standard library. This file would normally be installed in a standard place by your system administrator. You should use this second form for the C library header files.

Typically, '`#include`' directives are placed at the top of the C source file, before any other code. If you begin your source files with some comments explaining what the code in the file does (a good idea), put the '`#include`' directives immediately afterwards, following the feature test macro definition (see Section 1.3.4 [Feature Test Macros], page 15).

For more information about the use of header files and '`#include`' directives, see Section "Header Files" in *The GNU C Preprocessor Manual*.

The GNU C Library provides several header files, each of which contains the type and macro definitions and variable and function declarations for a group of related facilities. This means that your programs may need to include several header files, depending on exactly which facilities you are using.

Some library header files include other library header files automatically. However, as a matter of programming style, you should not rely on this; it is better to explicitly include all the header files required for the library facilities you are using. The GNU C Library header files have been written in such a way that it doesn't matter if a header file is accidentally included more than once; including a header file a second time has no effect. Likewise, if your program needs to include multiple header files, the order in which they are included doesn't matter.

Compatibility Note: Inclusion of standard header files in any order and any number of times works in any ISO C implementation. However, this has traditionally not been the case in many older C implementations.

Strictly speaking, you don't *have to* include a header file to use a function it declares; you could declare the function explicitly yourself, according to the specifications in this manual. But it is usually better to include the header file because it may define types and macros that are not otherwise available and because it may define more efficient macro replacements for some functions. It is also a sure way to have the correct declaration.

1.3.2 Macro Definitions of Functions

If we describe something as a function in this manual, it may have a macro definition as well. This normally has no effect on how your program runs—the macro definition does the same thing as the function would. In particular, macro equivalents for library functions evaluate arguments exactly once, in the same way that a function call would. The main reason for these macro definitions is that sometimes they can produce an inline expansion that is considerably faster than an actual function call.

Taking the address of a library function works even if it is also defined as a macro. This is because, in this context, the name of the function isn't followed by the left parenthesis that is syntactically necessary to recognize a macro call.

You might occasionally want to avoid using the macro definition of a function—perhaps to make your program easier to debug. There are two ways you can do this:

- You can avoid a macro definition in a specific use by enclosing the name of the function in parentheses. This works because the name of the function doesn't appear in a syntactic context where it is recognizable as a macro call.

- You can suppress any macro definition for a whole source file by using the '#undef' preprocessor directive, unless otherwise stated explicitly in the description of that facility.

For example, suppose the header file stdlib.h declares a function named abs with

```
extern int abs (int);
```

and also provides a macro definition for abs. Then, in:

```
#include <stdlib.h>
int f (int *i) { return abs (++*i); }
```

the reference to abs might refer to either a macro or a function. On the other hand, in each of the following examples the reference is to a function and not a macro.

```
#include <stdlib.h>
int g (int *i) { return (abs) (++*i); }
```

```
#undef abs
int h (int *i) { return abs (++*i); }
```

Since macro definitions that double for a function behave in exactly the same way as the actual function version, there is usually no need for any of these methods. In fact, removing macro definitions usually just makes your program slower.

1.3.3 Reserved Names

The names of all library types, macros, variables and functions that come from the ISO C standard are reserved unconditionally; your program **may not** redefine these names. All other library names are reserved if your program explicitly includes the header file that defines or declares them. There are several reasons for these restrictions:

- Other people reading your code could get very confused if you were using a function named exit to do something completely different from what the standard exit function does, for example. Preventing this situation helps to make your programs easier to understand and contributes to modularity and maintainability.

- It avoids the possibility of a user accidentally redefining a library function that is called by other library functions. If redefinition were allowed, those other functions would not work properly.

- It allows the compiler to do whatever special optimizations it pleases on calls to these functions, without the possibility that they may have been redefined by the user. Some library facilities, such as those for dealing with variadic arguments (see Section A.2 [Variadic Functions], page 910) and non-local exits (see Chapter 23 [Non-Local Exits], page 676), actually require a considerable amount of cooperation on the part of the C compiler, and with respect to the implementation, it might be easier for the compiler to treat these as built-in parts of the language.

In addition to the names documented in this manual, reserved names include all external identifiers (global functions and variables) that begin with an underscore ('_') and all identifiers regardless of use that begin with either two underscores or an underscore followed by a capital letter are reserved names. This is so that the library and header files can define functions, variables, and macros for internal purposes without risk of conflict with names in user programs.

Some additional classes of identifier names are reserved for future extensions to the C language or the POSIX.1 environment. While using these names for your own purposes right now might not cause a problem, they do raise the possibility of conflict with future versions of the C or POSIX standards, so you should avoid these names.

- Names beginning with a capital 'E' followed a digit or uppercase letter may be used for additional error code names. See Chapter 2 [Error Reporting], page 22.

- Names that begin with either 'is' or 'to' followed by a lowercase letter may be used for additional character testing and conversion functions. See Chapter 4 [Character Handling], page 81.

- Names that begin with 'LC_' followed by an uppercase letter may be used for additional macros specifying locale attributes. See Chapter 7 [Locales and Internationalization], page 176.

- Names of all existing mathematics functions (see Chapter 19 [Mathematics], page 525) suffixed with 'f' or 'l' are reserved for corresponding functions that operate on float and long double arguments, respectively.

- Names that begin with 'SIG' followed by an uppercase letter are reserved for additional signal names. See Section 24.2 [Standard Signals], page 687.

- Names that begin with 'SIG_' followed by an uppercase letter are reserved for additional signal actions. See Section 24.3.1 [Basic Signal Handling], page 696.

- Names beginning with 'str', 'mem', or 'wcs' followed by a lowercase letter are reserved for additional string and array functions. See Chapter 5 [String and Array Utilities], page 91.

- Names that end with '_t' are reserved for additional type names.

In addition, some individual header files reserve names beyond those that they actually define. You only need to worry about these restrictions if your program includes that particular header file.

- The header file dirent.h reserves names prefixed with 'd_'.
- The header file fcntl.h reserves names prefixed with 'l_', 'F_', 'O_', and 'S_'.
- The header file grp.h reserves names prefixed with 'gr_'.
- The header file limits.h reserves names suffixed with '_MAX'.
- The header file pwd.h reserves names prefixed with 'pw_'.
- The header file signal.h reserves names prefixed with 'sa_' and 'SA_'.
- The header file sys/stat.h reserves names prefixed with 'st_' and 'S_'.
- The header file sys/times.h reserves names prefixed with 'tms_'.
- The header file termios.h reserves names prefixed with 'c_', 'V', 'I', 'O', and 'TC'; and names prefixed with 'B' followed by a digit.

1.3.4 Feature Test Macros

The exact set of features available when you compile a source file is controlled by which *feature test macros* you define.

If you compile your programs using 'gcc -ansi', you get only the ISO C library features, unless you explicitly request additional features by defining one or more of the feature macros. See Section "GNU CC Command Options" in *The GNU CC Manual*, for more information about GCC options.

You should define these macros by using '#define' preprocessor directives at the top of your source code files. These directives *must* come before any #include of a system header file. It is best to make them the very first thing in the file, preceded only by comments. You could also use the '-D' option to GCC, but it's better if you make the source files indicate their own meaning in a self-contained way.

This system exists to allow the library to conform to multiple standards. Although the different standards are often described as supersets of each other, they are usually incompatible because larger standards require functions with names that smaller ones reserve to the user program. This is not mere pedantry — it has been a problem in practice. For instance, some non-GNU programs define functions named getline that have nothing to do with this library's getline. They would not be compilable if all features were enabled indiscriminately.

This should not be used to verify that a program conforms to a limited standard. It is insufficient for this purpose, as it will not protect you from including header files outside the standard, or relying on semantics undefined within the standard.

_POSIX_SOURCE   [Macro]

> If you define this macro, then the functionality from the POSIX.1 standard (IEEE Standard 1003.1) is available, as well as all of the ISO C facilities.
>
> The state of _POSIX_SOURCE is irrelevant if you define the macro _POSIX_C_SOURCE to a positive integer.

_POSIX_C_SOURCE   [Macro]

> Define this macro to a positive integer to control which POSIX functionality is made available. The greater the value of this macro, the more functionality is made available.
>
> If you define this macro to a value greater than or equal to 1, then the functionality from the 1990 edition of the POSIX.1 standard (IEEE Standard 1003.1-1990) is made available.
>
> If you define this macro to a value greater than or equal to 2, then the functionality from the 1992 edition of the POSIX.2 standard (IEEE Standard 1003.2-1992) is made available.
>
> If you define this macro to a value greater than or equal to 199309L, then the functionality from the 1993 edition of the POSIX.1b standard (IEEE Standard 1003.1b-1993) is made available.
>
> Greater values for _POSIX_C_SOURCE will enable future extensions. The POSIX standards process will define these values as necessary, and the GNU C Library should support them some time after they become standardized. The 1996 edition of POSIX.1 (ISO/IEC 9945-1: 1996) states that if you define _POSIX_C_SOURCE to a value greater than or equal to 199506L, then the functionality from the 1996 edition is made available.

_XOPEN_SOURCE   [Macro]
_XOPEN_SOURCE_EXTENDED   [Macro]

> If you define this macro, functionality described in the X/Open Portability Guide is included. This is a superset of the POSIX.1 and POSIX.2 functionality and in fact _POSIX_SOURCE and _POSIX_C_SOURCE are automatically defined.

As the unification of all Unices, functionality only available in BSD and SVID is also included.

If the macro `_XOPEN_SOURCE_EXTENDED` is also defined, even more functionality is available. The extra functions will make all functions available which are necessary for the X/Open Unix brand.

If the macro `_XOPEN_SOURCE` has the value 500 this includes all functionality described so far plus some new definitions from the Single Unix Specification, version 2.

`_LARGEFILE_SOURCE`   [Macro]

If this macro is defined some extra functions are available which rectify a few shortcomings in all previous standards. Specifically, the functions `fseeko` and `ftello` are available. Without these functions the difference between the ISO C interface (`fseek`, `ftell`) and the low-level POSIX interface (`lseek`) would lead to problems.

This macro was introduced as part of the Large File Support extension (LFS).

`_LARGEFILE64_SOURCE`   [Macro]

If you define this macro an additional set of functions is made available which enables 32 bit systems to use files of sizes beyond the usual limit of 2GB. This interface is not available if the system does not support files that large. On systems where the natural file size limit is greater than 2GB (i.e., on 64 bit systems) the new functions are identical to the replaced functions.

The new functionality is made available by a new set of types and functions which replace the existing ones. The names of these new objects contain `64` to indicate the intention, e.g., `off_t` vs. `off64_t` and `fseeko` vs. `fseeko64`.

This macro was introduced as part of the Large File Support extension (LFS). It is a transition interface for the period when 64 bit offsets are not generally used (see `_FILE_OFFSET_BITS`).

`_FILE_OFFSET_BITS`   [Macro]

This macro determines which file system interface shall be used, one replacing the other. Whereas `_LARGEFILE64_SOURCE` makes the 64 bit interface available as an additional interface, `_FILE_OFFSET_BITS` allows the 64 bit interface to replace the old interface.

If `_FILE_OFFSET_BITS` is undefined, or if it is defined to the value 32, nothing changes. The 32 bit interface is used and types like `off_t` have a size of 32 bits on 32 bit systems.

If the macro is defined to the value 64, the large file interface replaces the old interface. I.e., the functions are not made available under different names (as they are with `_LARGEFILE64_SOURCE`). Instead the old function names now reference the new functions, e.g., a call to `fseeko` now indeed calls `fseeko64`.

This macro should only be selected if the system provides mechanisms for handling large files. On 64 bit systems this macro has no effect since the `*64` functions are identical to the normal functions.

This macro was introduced as part of the Large File Support extension (LFS).

`_ISOC99_SOURCE` [Macro]

Until the revised ISO C standard is widely adopted the new features are not automatically enabled. The GNU C Library nevertheless has a complete implementation of the new standard and to enable the new features the macro `_ISOC99_SOURCE` should be defined.

`__STDC_WANT_LIB_EXT2__` [Macro]

If you define this macro to the value 1, features from ISO/IEC TR 24731-2:2010 (Dynamic Allocation Functions) are enabled. Only some of the features from this TR are supported by the GNU C Library.

`__STDC_WANT_IEC_60559_BFP_EXT__` [Macro]

If you define this macro, features from ISO/IEC TS 18661-1:2014 (Floating-point extensions for C: Binary floating-point arithmetic) are enabled. Only some of the features from this TS are supported by the GNU C Library.

`__STDC_WANT_IEC_60559_FUNCS_EXT__` [Macro]

If you define this macro, features from ISO/IEC TS 18661-4:2015 (Floating-point extensions for C: Supplementary functions) are enabled. Only some of the features from this TS are supported by the GNU C Library.

`__STDC_WANT_IEC_60559_TYPES_EXT__` [Macro]

If you define this macro, features from ISO/IEC TS 18661-3:2015 (Floating-point extensions for C: Interchange and extended types) are enabled. Only some of the features from this TS are supported by the GNU C Library.

`_GNU_SOURCE` [Macro]

If you define this macro, everything is included: ISO C89, ISO C99, POSIX.1, POSIX.2, BSD, SVID, X/Open, LFS, and GNU extensions. In the cases where POSIX.1 conflicts with BSD, the POSIX definitions take precedence.

`_DEFAULT_SOURCE` [Macro]

If you define this macro, most features are included apart from X/Open, LFS and GNU extensions: the effect is to enable features from the 2008 edition of POSIX, as well as certain BSD and SVID features without a separate feature test macro to control them. Defining this macro, on its own and without using compiler options such as `-ansi` or `-std=c99`, has the same effect as not defining any feature test macros; defining it together with other feature test macros, or when options such as `-ansi` are used, enables those features even when the other options would otherwise cause them to be disabled.

`_REENTRANT` [Macro]
`_THREAD_SAFE` [Macro]

These macros are obsolete. They have the same effect as defining `_POSIX_C_SOURCE` with the value `199506L`.

Some very old C libraries required one of these macros to be defined for basic functionality (e.g. `getchar`) to be thread-safe.

We recommend you use _GNU_SOURCE in new programs. If you don't specify the '-ansi' option to GCC, or other conformance options such as -std=c99, and don't define any of these macros explicitly, the effect is the same as defining _DEFAULT_SOURCE to 1.

When you define a feature test macro to request a larger class of features, it is harmless to define in addition a feature test macro for a subset of those features. For example, if you define _POSIX_C_SOURCE, then defining _POSIX_SOURCE as well has no effect. Likewise, if you define _GNU_SOURCE, then defining either _POSIX_SOURCE or _POSIX_C_SOURCE as well has no effect.

1.4 Roadmap to the Manual

Here is an overview of the contents of the remaining chapters of this manual.

- Chapter 2 [Error Reporting], page 22, describes how errors detected by the library are reported.

- Chapter 3 [Virtual Memory Allocation And Paging], page 41, describes the GNU C Library's facilities for managing and using virtual and real memory, including dynamic allocation of virtual memory. If you do not know in advance how much memory your program needs, you can allocate it dynamically instead, and manipulate it via pointers.

- Chapter 4 [Character Handling], page 81, contains information about character classification functions (such as isspace) and functions for performing case conversion.

- Chapter 5 [String and Array Utilities], page 91, has descriptions of functions for manipulating strings (null-terminated character arrays) and general byte arrays, including operations such as copying and comparison.

- Chapter 6 [Character Set Handling], page 134, contains information about manipulating characters and strings using character sets larger than will fit in the usual char data type.

- Chapter 7 [Locales and Internationalization], page 176, describes how selecting a particular country or language affects the behavior of the library. For example, the locale affects collation sequences for strings and how monetary values are formatted.

- Chapter 9 [Searching and Sorting], page 220, contains information about functions for searching and sorting arrays. You can use these functions on any kind of array by providing an appropriate comparison function.

- Chapter 10 [Pattern Matching], page 230, presents functions for matching regular expressions and shell file name patterns, and for expanding words as the shell does.

- Chapter 11 [Input/Output Overview], page 252, gives an overall look at the input and output facilities in the library, and contains information about basic concepts such as file names.

- Chapter 12 [Input/Output on Streams], page 257, describes I/O operations involving streams (or FILE * objects). These are the normal C library functions from stdio.h.

- Chapter 13 [Low-Level Input/Output], page 333, contains information about I/O operations on file descriptors. File descriptors are a lower-level mechanism specific to the Unix family of operating systems.

- Chapter 14 [File System Interface], page 390, has descriptions of operations on entire files, such as functions for deleting and renaming them and for creating new directories.

This chapter also contains information about how you can access the attributes of a file, such as its owner and file protection modes.

- Chapter 15 [Pipes and FIFOs], page 437, contains information about simple interprocess communication mechanisms. Pipes allow communication between two related processes (such as between a parent and child), while FIFOs allow communication between processes sharing a common file system on the same machine.

- Chapter 16 [Sockets], page 442, describes a more complicated interprocess communication mechanism that allows processes running on different machines to communicate over a network. This chapter also contains information about Internet host addressing and how to use the system network databases.

- Chapter 17 [Low-Level Terminal Interface], page 490, describes how you can change the attributes of a terminal device. If you want to disable echo of characters typed by the user, for example, read this chapter.

- Chapter 19 [Mathematics], page 525, contains information about the math library functions. These include things like random-number generators and remainder functions on integers as well as the usual trigonometric and exponential functions on floating-point numbers.

- Chapter 20 [Low-Level Arithmetic Functions], page 575, describes functions for simple arithmetic, analysis of floating-point values, and reading numbers from strings.

- Chapter 21 [Date and Time], page 619, describes functions for measuring both calendar time and CPU time, as well as functions for setting alarms and timers.

- Chapter 23 [Non-Local Exits], page 676, contains descriptions of the `setjmp` and `longjmp` functions. These functions provide a facility for `goto`-like jumps which can jump from one function to another.

- Chapter 24 [Signal Handling], page 685, tells you all about signals—what they are, how to establish a handler that is called when a particular kind of signal is delivered, and how to prevent signals from arriving during critical sections of your program.

- Chapter 25 [The Basic Program/System Interface], page 729, tells how your programs can access their command-line arguments and environment variables.

- Chapter 26 [Processes], page 773, contains information about how to start new processes and run programs.

- Chapter 28 [Job Control], page 786, describes functions for manipulating process groups and the controlling terminal. This material is probably only of interest if you are writing a shell or other program which handles job control specially.

- Chapter 29 [System Databases and Name Service Switch], page 805, describes the services which are available for looking up names in the system databases, how to determine which service is used for which database, and how these services are implemented so that contributors can design their own services.

- Section 30.13 [User Database], page 834, and Section 30.14 [Group Database], page 838, tell you how to access the system user and group databases.

- Chapter 31 [System Management], page 845, describes functions for controlling and getting information about the hardware and software configuration your program is executing under.

- Chapter 32 [System Configuration Parameters], page 862, tells you how you can get information about various operating system limits. Most of these parameters are provided for compatibility with POSIX.

- Appendix A [C Language Facilities in the Library], page 909, contains information about library support for standard parts of the C language, including things like the `sizeof` operator and the symbolic constant `NULL`, how to write functions accepting variable numbers of arguments, and constants describing the ranges and other properties of the numerical types. There is also a simple debugging mechanism which allows you to put assertions in your code, and have diagnostic messages printed if the tests fail.

- Appendix B [Summary of Library Facilities], page 925, gives a summary of all the functions, variables, and macros in the library, with complete data types and function prototypes, and says what standard or system each is derived from.

- Appendix C [Installing the GNU C Library], page 1043, explains how to build and install the GNU C Library on your system, and how to report any bugs you might find.

- Appendix D [Library Maintenance], page 1053, explains how to add new functions or port the library to a new system.

If you already know the name of the facility you are interested in, you can look it up in Appendix B [Summary of Library Facilities], page 925. This gives you a summary of its syntax and a pointer to where you can find a more detailed description. This appendix is particularly useful if you just want to verify the order and type of arguments to a function, for example. It also tells you what standard or system each function, variable, or macro is derived from.

2 Error Reporting

Many functions in the GNU C Library detect and report error conditions, and sometimes your programs need to check for these error conditions. For example, when you open an input file, you should verify that the file was actually opened correctly, and print an error message or take other appropriate action if the call to the library function failed.

This chapter describes how the error reporting facility works. Your program should include the header file `errno.h` to use this facility.

2.1 Checking for Errors

Most library functions return a special value to indicate that they have failed. The special value is typically -1, a null pointer, or a constant such as `EOF` that is defined for that purpose. But this return value tells you only that an error has occurred. To find out what kind of error it was, you need to look at the error code stored in the variable `errno`. This variable is declared in the header file `errno.h`.

`volatile int errno`   [Variable]

> The variable `errno` contains the system error number. You can change the value of `errno`.
>
> Since `errno` is declared `volatile`, it might be changed asynchronously by a signal handler; see Section 24.4 [Defining Signal Handlers], page 702. However, a properly written signal handler saves and restores the value of `errno`, so you generally do not need to worry about this possibility except when writing signal handlers.
>
> The initial value of `errno` at program startup is zero. Many library functions are guaranteed to set it to certain nonzero values when they encounter certain kinds of errors. These error conditions are listed for each function. These functions do not change `errno` when they succeed; thus, the value of `errno` after a successful call is not necessarily zero, and you should not use `errno` to determine *whether* a call failed. The proper way to do that is documented for each function. *If* the call failed, you can examine `errno`.
>
> Many library functions can set `errno` to a nonzero value as a result of calling other library functions which might fail. You should assume that any library function might alter `errno` when the function returns an error.
>
> **Portability Note:** ISO C specifies `errno` as a "modifiable lvalue" rather than as a variable, permitting it to be implemented as a macro. For example, its expansion might involve a function call, like `*__errno_location ()`. In fact, that is what it is on GNU/Linux and GNU/Hurd systems. The GNU C Library, on each system, does whatever is right for the particular system.
>
> There are a few library functions, like `sqrt` and `atan`, that return a perfectly legitimate value in case of an error, but also set `errno`. For these functions, if you want to check to see whether an error occurred, the recommended method is to set `errno` to zero before calling the function, and then check its value afterward.

All the error codes have symbolic names; they are macros defined in `errno.h`. The names start with 'E' and an upper-case letter or digit; you should consider names of this form to be reserved names. See Section 1.3.3 [Reserved Names], page 14.

The error code values are all positive integers and are all distinct, with one exception: EWOULDBLOCK and EAGAIN are the same. Since the values are distinct, you can use them as labels in a switch statement; just don't use both EWOULDBLOCK and EAGAIN. Your program should not make any other assumptions about the specific values of these symbolic constants.

The value of errno doesn't necessarily have to correspond to any of these macros, since some library functions might return other error codes of their own for other situations. The only values that are guaranteed to be meaningful for a particular library function are the ones that this manual lists for that function.

Except on GNU/Hurd systems, almost any system call can return EFAULT if it is given an invalid pointer as an argument. Since this could only happen as a result of a bug in your program, and since it will not happen on GNU/Hurd systems, we have saved space by not mentioning EFAULT in the descriptions of individual functions.

In some Unix systems, many system calls can also return EFAULT if given as an argument a pointer into the stack, and the kernel for some obscure reason fails in its attempt to extend the stack. If this ever happens, you should probably try using statically or dynamically allocated memory instead of stack memory on that system.

2.2 Error Codes

The error code macros are defined in the header file errno.h. All of them expand into integer constant values. Some of these error codes can't occur on GNU systems, but they can occur using the GNU C Library on other systems.

int EPERM   [Macro]
    "Operation not permitted." Only the owner of the file (or other resource) or processes with special privileges can perform the operation.

int ENOENT   [Macro]
    "No such file or directory." This is a "file doesn't exist" error for ordinary files that are referenced in contexts where they are expected to already exist.

int ESRCH   [Macro]
    "No such process." No process matches the specified process ID.

int EINTR   [Macro]
    "Interrupted system call." An asynchronous signal occurred and prevented completion of the call. When this happens, you should try the call again.

    You can choose to have functions resume after a signal that is handled, rather than failing with EINTR; see Section 24.5 [Primitives Interrupted by Signals], page 711.

int EIO   [Macro]
    "Input/output error." Usually used for physical read or write errors.

int ENXIO   [Macro]
    "No such device or address." The system tried to use the device represented by a file you specified, and it couldn't find the device. This can mean that the device file was installed incorrectly, or that the physical device is missing or not correctly attached to the computer.

`int E2BIG`   [Macro]

"Argument list too long." Used when the arguments passed to a new program being executed with one of the `exec` functions (see Section 26.5 [Executing a File], page 776) occupy too much memory space. This condition never arises on GNU/Hurd systems.

`int ENOEXEC`   [Macro]

"Exec format error." Invalid executable file format. This condition is detected by the `exec` functions; see Section 26.5 [Executing a File], page 776.

`int EBADF`   [Macro]

"Bad file descriptor." For example, I/O on a descriptor that has been closed or reading from a descriptor open only for writing (or vice versa).

`int ECHILD`   [Macro]

"No child processes." This error happens on operations that are supposed to manipulate child processes, when there aren't any processes to manipulate.

`int EDEADLK`   [Macro]

"Resource deadlock avoided." Allocating a system resource would have resulted in a deadlock situation. The system does not guarantee that it will notice all such situations. This error means you got lucky and the system noticed; it might just hang. See Section 13.15 [File Locks], page 380, for an example.

`int ENOMEM`   [Macro]

"Cannot allocate memory." The system cannot allocate more virtual memory because its capacity is full.

`int EACCES`   [Macro]

"Permission denied." The file permissions do not allow the attempted operation.

`int EFAULT`   [Macro]

"Bad address." An invalid pointer was detected. On GNU/Hurd systems, this error never happens; you get a signal instead.

`int ENOTBLK`   [Macro]

"Block device required." A file that isn't a block special file was given in a situation that requires one. For example, trying to mount an ordinary file as a file system in Unix gives this error.

`int EBUSY`   [Macro]

"Device or resource busy." A system resource that can't be shared is already in use. For example, if you try to delete a file that is the root of a currently mounted filesystem, you get this error.

`int EEXIST`   [Macro]

"File exists." An existing file was specified in a context where it only makes sense to specify a new file.

`int EXDEV`   [Macro]

"Invalid cross-device link." An attempt to make an improper link across file systems was detected. This happens not only when you use `link` (see Section 14.4 [Hard Links], page 405) but also when you rename a file with `rename` (see Section 14.7 [Renaming Files], page 410).

`int` `ENODEV`   [Macro]

"No such device." The wrong type of device was given to a function that expects a particular sort of device.

`int` `ENOTDIR`   [Macro]

"Not a directory." A file that isn't a directory was specified when a directory is required.

`int` `EISDIR`   [Macro]

"Is a directory." You cannot open a directory for writing, or create or remove hard links to it.

`int` `EINVAL`   [Macro]

"Invalid argument." This is used to indicate various kinds of problems with passing the wrong argument to a library function.

`int` `EMFILE`   [Macro]

"Too many open files." The current process has too many files open and can't open any more. Duplicate descriptors do count toward this limit.

In BSD and GNU, the number of open files is controlled by a resource limit that can usually be increased. If you get this error, you might want to increase the `RLIMIT_NOFILE` limit or make it unlimited; see Section 22.2 [Limiting Resource Usage], page 656.

`int` `ENFILE`   [Macro]

"Too many open files in system." There are too many distinct file openings in the entire system. Note that any number of linked channels count as just one file opening; see Section 13.5.1 [Linked Channels], page 347. This error never occurs on GNU/Hurd systems.

`int` `ENOTTY`   [Macro]

"Inappropriate ioctl for device." Inappropriate I/O control operation, such as trying to set terminal modes on an ordinary file.

`int` `ETXTBSY`   [Macro]

"Text file busy." An attempt to execute a file that is currently open for writing, or write to a file that is currently being executed. Often using a debugger to run a program is considered having it open for writing and will cause this error. (The name stands for "text file busy".) This is not an error on GNU/Hurd systems; the text is copied as necessary.

`int` `EFBIG`   [Macro]

"File too large." The size of a file would be larger than allowed by the system.

`int` `ENOSPC`   [Macro]

"No space left on device." Write operation on a file failed because the disk is full.

`int` `ESPIPE`   [Macro]

"Illegal seek." Invalid seek operation (such as on a pipe).

`int` `EROFS` [Macro]

"Read-only file system." An attempt was made to modify something on a read-only file system.

`int` `EMLINK` [Macro]

"Too many links." The link count of a single file would become too large. `rename` can cause this error if the file being renamed already has as many links as it can take (see Section 14.7 [Renaming Files], page 410).

`int` `EPIPE` [Macro]

"Broken pipe." There is no process reading from the other end of a pipe. Every library function that returns this error code also generates a `SIGPIPE` signal; this signal terminates the program if not handled or blocked. Thus, your program will never actually see `EPIPE` unless it has handled or blocked `SIGPIPE`.

`int` `EDOM` [Macro]

"Numerical argument out of domain." Used by mathematical functions when an argument value does not fall into the domain over which the function is defined.

`int` `ERANGE` [Macro]

"Numerical result out of range." Used by mathematical functions when the result value is not representable because of overflow or underflow.

`int` `EAGAIN` [Macro]

"Resource temporarily unavailable." The call might work if you try again later. The macro `EWOULDBLOCK` is another name for `EAGAIN`; they are always the same in the GNU C Library.

This error can happen in a few different situations:

- An operation that would block was attempted on an object that has non-blocking mode selected. Trying the same operation again will block until some external condition makes it possible to read, write, or connect (whatever the operation). You can use `select` to find out when the operation will be possible; see Section 13.8 [Waiting for Input or Output], page 355.

  Portability Note: In many older Unix systems, this condition was indicated by `EWOULDBLOCK`, which was a distinct error code different from `EAGAIN`. To make your program portable, you should check for both codes and treat them the same.

- A temporary resource shortage made an operation impossible. `fork` can return this error. It indicates that the shortage is expected to pass, so your program can try the call again later and it may succeed. It is probably a good idea to delay for a few seconds before trying it again, to allow time for other processes to release scarce resources. Such shortages are usually fairly serious and affect the whole system, so usually an interactive program should report the error to the user and return to its command loop.

`int` `EWOULDBLOCK` [Macro]

"Operation would block." In the GNU C Library, this is another name for `EAGAIN` (above). The values are always the same, on every operating system.

C libraries in many older Unix systems have `EWOULDBLOCK` as a separate error code.

`int` `EINPROGRESS`   [Macro]

"Operation now in progress." An operation that cannot complete immediately was initiated on an object that has non-blocking mode selected. Some functions that must always block (such as `connect`; see Section 16.9.1 [Making a Connection], page 469) never return `EAGAIN`. Instead, they return `EINPROGRESS` to indicate that the operation has begun and will take some time. Attempts to manipulate the object before the call completes return `EALREADY`. You can use the `select` function to find out when the pending operation has completed; see Section 13.8 [Waiting for Input or Output], page 355.

`int` `EALREADY`   [Macro]

"Operation already in progress." An operation is already in progress on an object that has non-blocking mode selected.

`int` `ENOTSOCK`   [Macro]

"Socket operation on non-socket." A file that isn't a socket was specified when a socket is required.

`int` `EMSGSIZE`   [Macro]

"Message too long." The size of a message sent on a socket was larger than the supported maximum size.

`int` `EPROTOTYPE`   [Macro]

"Protocol wrong type for socket." The socket type does not support the requested communications protocol.

`int` `ENOPROTOOPT`   [Macro]

"Protocol not available." You specified a socket option that doesn't make sense for the particular protocol being used by the socket. See Section 16.12 [Socket Options], page 485.

`int` `EPROTONOSUPPORT`   [Macro]

"Protocol not supported." The socket domain does not support the requested communications protocol (perhaps because the requested protocol is completely invalid). See Section 16.8.1 [Creating a Socket], page 466.

`int` `ESOCKTNOSUPPORT`   [Macro]

"Socket type not supported." The socket type is not supported.

`int` `EOPNOTSUPP`   [Macro]

"Operation not supported." The operation you requested is not supported. Some socket functions don't make sense for all types of sockets, and others may not be implemented for all communications protocols. On GNU/Hurd systems, this error can happen for many calls when the object does not support the particular operation; it is a generic indication that the server knows nothing to do for that call.

`int` `EPFNOSUPPORT`   [Macro]

"Protocol family not supported." The socket communications protocol family you requested is not supported.

`int` `EAFNOSUPPORT`   [Macro]
> "Address family not supported by protocol." The address family specified for a socket is not supported; it is inconsistent with the protocol being used on the socket. See Chapter 16 [Sockets], page 442.

`int` `EADDRINUSE`   [Macro]
> "Address already in use." The requested socket address is already in use. See Section 16.3 [Socket Addresses], page 444.

`int` `EADDRNOTAVAIL`   [Macro]
> "Cannot assign requested address." The requested socket address is not available; for example, you tried to give a socket a name that doesn't match the local host name. See Section 16.3 [Socket Addresses], page 444.

`int` `ENETDOWN`   [Macro]
> "Network is down." A socket operation failed because the network was down.

`int` `ENETUNREACH`   [Macro]
> "Network is unreachable." A socket operation failed because the subnet containing the remote host was unreachable.

`int` `ENETRESET`   [Macro]
> "Network dropped connection on reset." A network connection was reset because the remote host crashed.

`int` `ECONNABORTED`   [Macro]
> "Software caused connection abort." A network connection was aborted locally.

`int` `ECONNRESET`   [Macro]
> "Connection reset by peer." A network connection was closed for reasons outside the control of the local host, such as by the remote machine rebooting or an unrecoverable protocol violation.

`int` `ENOBUFS`   [Macro]
> "No buffer space available." The kernel's buffers for I/O operations are all in use. In GNU, this error is always synonymous with `ENOMEM`; you may get one or the other from network operations.

`int` `EISCONN`   [Macro]
> "Transport endpoint is already connected." You tried to connect a socket that is already connected. See Section 16.9.1 [Making a Connection], page 469.

`int` `ENOTCONN`   [Macro]
> "Transport endpoint is not connected." The socket is not connected to anything. You get this error when you try to transmit data over a socket, without first specifying a destination for the data. For a connectionless socket (for datagram protocols, such as UDP), you get `EDESTADDRREQ` instead.

`int` `EDESTADDRREQ`   [Macro]
> "Destination address required." No default destination address was set for the socket. You get this error when you try to transmit data over a connectionless socket, without first specifying a destination for the data with `connect`.

`int` `ESHUTDOWN`   [Macro]

"Cannot send after transport endpoint shutdown." The socket has already been shut down.

`int` `ETOOMANYREFS`   [Macro]

"Too many references: cannot splice."

`int` `ETIMEDOUT`   [Macro]

"Connection timed out." A socket operation with a specified timeout received no response during the timeout period.

`int` `ECONNREFUSED`   [Macro]

"Connection refused." A remote host refused to allow the network connection (typically because it is not running the requested service).

`int` `ELOOP`   [Macro]

"Too many levels of symbolic links." Too many levels of symbolic links were encountered in looking up a file name. This often indicates a cycle of symbolic links.

`int` `ENAMETOOLONG`   [Macro]

"File name too long." Filename too long (longer than `PATH_MAX`; see Section 32.6 [Limits on File System Capacity], page 874) or host name too long (in `gethostname` or `sethostname`; see Section 31.1 [Host Identification], page 845).

`int` `EHOSTDOWN`   [Macro]

"Host is down." The remote host for a requested network connection is down.

`int` `EHOSTUNREACH`   [Macro]

"No route to host." The remote host for a requested network connection is not reachable.

`int` `ENOTEMPTY`   [Macro]

"Directory not empty." Directory not empty, where an empty directory was expected. Typically, this error occurs when you are trying to delete a directory.

`int` `EPROCLIM`   [Macro]

"Too many processes." This means that the per-user limit on new process would be exceeded by an attempted `fork`. See Section 22.2 [Limiting Resource Usage], page 656, for details on the `RLIMIT_NPROC` limit.

`int` `EUSERS`   [Macro]

"Too many users." The file quota system is confused because there are too many users.

`int` `EDQUOT`   [Macro]

"Disk quota exceeded." The user's disk quota was exceeded.

`int` `ESTALE`   [Macro]

"Stale file handle." This indicates an internal confusion in the file system which is due to file system rearrangements on the server host for NFS file systems or corruption in other file systems. Repairing this condition usually requires unmounting, possibly repairing and remounting the file system.

int EREMOTE   [Macro]

> "Object is remote." An attempt was made to NFS-mount a remote file system with a file name that already specifies an NFS-mounted file. (This is an error on some operating systems, but we expect it to work properly on GNU/Hurd systems, making this error code impossible.)

int EBADRPC   [Macro]

> "RPC struct is bad."

int ERPCMISMATCH   [Macro]

> "RPC version wrong."

int EPROGUNAVAIL   [Macro]

> "RPC program not available."

int EPROGMISMATCH   [Macro]

> "RPC program version wrong."

int EPROCUNAVAIL   [Macro]

> "RPC bad procedure for program."

int ENOLCK   [Macro]

> "No locks available." This is used by the file locking facilities; see Section 13.15 [File Locks], page 380. This error is never generated by GNU/Hurd systems, but it can result from an operation to an NFS server running another operating system.

int EFTYPE   [Macro]

> "Inappropriate file type or format." The file was the wrong type for the operation, or a data file had the wrong format.

> On some systems chmod returns this error if you try to set the sticky bit on a non-directory file; see Section 14.9.7 [Assigning File Permissions], page 423.

int EAUTH   [Macro]

> "Authentication error."

int ENEEDAUTH   [Macro]

> "Need authenticator."

int ENOSYS   [Macro]

> "Function not implemented." This indicates that the function called is not implemented at all, either in the C library itself or in the operating system. When you get this error, you can be sure that this particular function will always fail with ENOSYS unless you install a new version of the C library or the operating system.

int ENOTSUP   [Macro]

> "Not supported." A function returns this error when certain parameter values are valid, but the functionality they request is not available. This can mean that the function does not implement a particular command or option value or flag bit at all. For functions that operate on some object given in a parameter, such as a file descriptor or a port, it might instead mean that only *that specific object* (file descriptor,

port, etc.) is unable to support the other parameters given; different file descriptors might support different ranges of parameter values.

If the entire function is not available at all in the implementation, it returns `ENOSYS` instead.

`int EILSEQ`   [Macro]

"Invalid or incomplete multibyte or wide character." While decoding a multibyte character the function came along an invalid or an incomplete sequence of bytes or the given wide character is invalid.

`int EBACKGROUND`   [Macro]

"Inappropriate operation for background process." On GNU/Hurd systems, servers supporting the `term` protocol return this error for certain operations when the caller is not in the foreground process group of the terminal. Users do not usually see this error because functions such as `read` and `write` translate it into a `SIGTTIN` or `SIGTTOU` signal. See Chapter 28 [Job Control], page 786, for information on process groups and these signals.

`int EDIED`   [Macro]

"Translator died." On GNU/Hurd systems, opening a file returns this error when the file is translated by a program and the translator program dies while starting up, before it has connected to the file.

`int ED`   [Macro]

"?." The experienced user will know what is wrong.

`int EGREGIOUS`   [Macro]

"You really blew it this time." You did **what**?

`int EIEIO`   [Macro]

"Computer bought the farm." Go home and have a glass of warm, dairy-fresh milk.

`int EGRATUITOUS`   [Macro]

"Gratuitous error." This error code has no purpose.

`int EBADMSG`   [Macro]

"Bad message."

`int EIDRM`   [Macro]

"Identifier removed."

`int EMULTIHOP`   [Macro]

"Multihop attempted."

`int ENODATA`   [Macro]

"No data available."

`int ENOLINK`   [Macro]

"Link has been severed."

`int ENOMSG`   [Macro]

"No message of desired type."

int **ENOSR** [Macro]
> "Out of streams resources."

int **ENOSTR** [Macro]
> "Device not a stream."

int **EOVERFLOW** [Macro]
> "Value too large for defined data type."

int **EPROTO** [Macro]
> "Protocol error."

int **ETIME** [Macro]
> "Timer expired."

int **ECANCELED** [Macro]
> "Operation canceled." An asynchronous operation was canceled before it completed. See Section 13.10 [Perform I/O Operations in Parallel], page 359. When you call `aio_cancel`, the normal result is for the operations affected to complete with this error; see Section 13.10.4 [Cancellation of AIO Operations], page 369.

The following error codes are defined by the Linux/i386 kernel. They are not yet documented.

int **ERESTART** [Macro]
> "Interrupted system call should be restarted."

int **ECHRNG** [Macro]
> "Channel number out of range."

int **EL2NSYNC** [Macro]
> "Level 2 not synchronized."

int **EL3HLT** [Macro]
> "Level 3 halted."

int **EL3RST** [Macro]
> "Level 3 reset."

int **ELNRNG** [Macro]
> "Link number out of range."

int **EUNATCH** [Macro]
> "Protocol driver not attached."

int **ENOCSI** [Macro]
> "No CSI structure available."

int **EL2HLT** [Macro]
> "Level 2 halted."

int **EBADE** [Macro]
> "Invalid exchange."

int **EBADR**   [Macro]
> "Invalid request descriptor."

int **EXFULL**   [Macro]
> "Exchange full."

int **ENOANO**   [Macro]
> "No anode."

int **EBADRQC**   [Macro]
> "Invalid request code."

int **EBADSLT**   [Macro]
> "Invalid slot."

int **EDEADLOCK**   [Macro]
> "File locking deadlock error."

int **EBFONT**   [Macro]
> "Bad font file format."

int **ENONET**   [Macro]
> "Machine is not on the network."

int **ENOPKG**   [Macro]
> "Package not installed."

int **EADV**   [Macro]
> "Advertise error."

int **ESRMNT**   [Macro]
> "Srmount error."

int **ECOMM**   [Macro]
> "Communication error on send."

int **EDOTDOT**   [Macro]
> "RFS specific error."

int **ENOTUNIQ**   [Macro]
> "Name not unique on network."

int **EBADFD**   [Macro]
> "File descriptor in bad state."

int **EREMCHG**   [Macro]
> "Remote address changed."

int **ELIBACC**   [Macro]
> "Can not access a needed shared library."

int **ELIBBAD**   [Macro]
> "Accessing a corrupted shared library."

`int` `ELIBSCN`   [Macro]
: ".lib section in a.out corrupted."

`int` `ELIBMAX`   [Macro]
: "Attempting to link in too many shared libraries."

`int` `ELIBEXEC`   [Macro]
: "Cannot exec a shared library directly."

`int` `ESTRPIPE`   [Macro]
: "Streams pipe error."

`int` `EUCLEAN`   [Macro]
: "Structure needs cleaning."

`int` `ENOTNAM`   [Macro]
: "Not a XENIX named type file."

`int` `ENAVAIL`   [Macro]
: "No XENIX semaphores available."

`int` `EISNAM`   [Macro]
: "Is a named type file."

`int` `EREMOTEIO`   [Macro]
: "Remote I/O error."

`int` `ENOMEDIUM`   [Macro]
: "No medium found."

`int` `EMEDIUMTYPE`   [Macro]
: "Wrong medium type."

`int` `ENOKEY`   [Macro]
: "Required key not available."

`int` `EKEYEXPIRED`   [Macro]
: "Key has expired."

`int` `EKEYREVOKED`   [Macro]
: "Key has been revoked."

`int` `EKEYREJECTED`   [Macro]
: "Key was rejected by service."

`int` `EOWNERDEAD`   [Macro]
: "Owner died."

`int` `ENOTRECOVERABLE`   [Macro]
: "State not recoverable."

`int` `ERFKILL`   [Macro]
: "Operation not possible due to RF-kill."

`int` `EHWPOISON`   [Macro]
: "Memory page has hardware error."

2.3 Error Messages

The library has functions and variables designed to make it easy for your program to report informative error messages in the customary format about the failure of a library call. The functions `strerror` and `perror` give you the standard error message for a given error code; the variable `program_invocation_short_name` gives you convenient access to the name of the program that encountered the error.

char * strerror (*int errnum*)   [Function]
    Preliminary: | MT-Unsafe race:strerror | AS-Unsafe heap i18n | AC-Unsafe mem | See Section 1.2.2.1 [POSIX Safety Concepts], page 2.

    The `strerror` function maps the error code (see Section 2.1 [Checking for Errors], page 22) specified by the *errnum* argument to a descriptive error message string. The return value is a pointer to this string.

    The value *errnum* normally comes from the variable `errno`.

    You should not modify the string returned by `strerror`. Also, if you make subsequent calls to `strerror`, the string might be overwritten. (But it's guaranteed that no library function ever calls `strerror` behind your back.)

    The function `strerror` is declared in `string.h`.

char * strerror_r (*int errnum, char *buf, size_t n*)   [Function]
    Preliminary: | MT-Safe | AS-Unsafe i18n | AC-Unsafe | See Section 1.2.2.1 [POSIX Safety Concepts], page 2.

    The `strerror_r` function works like `strerror` but instead of returning the error message in a statically allocated buffer shared by all threads in the process, it returns a private copy for the thread. This might be either some permanent global data or a message string in the user supplied buffer starting at *buf* with the length of *n* bytes.

    At most *n* characters are written (including the NUL byte) so it is up to the user to select a buffer large enough.

    This function should always be used in multi-threaded programs since there is no way to guarantee the string returned by `strerror` really belongs to the last call of the current thread.

    The function `strerror_r` is a GNU extension and it is declared in `string.h`.

void perror (*const char *message*)   [Function]
    Preliminary: | MT-Safe race:stderr | AS-Unsafe corrupt i18n heap lock | AC-Unsafe corrupt lock mem fd | See Section 1.2.2.1 [POSIX Safety Concepts], page 2.

    This function prints an error message to the stream `stderr`; see Section 12.2 [Standard Streams], page 257. The orientation of `stderr` is not changed.

    If you call `perror` with a *message* that is either a null pointer or an empty string, `perror` just prints the error message corresponding to `errno`, adding a trailing newline.

    If you supply a non-null *message* argument, then `perror` prefixes its output with this string. It adds a colon and a space character to separate the *message* from the error string corresponding to `errno`.

    The function `perror` is declared in `stdio.h`.

`strerror` and `perror` produce the exact same message for any given error code; the precise text varies from system to system. With the GNU C Library, the messages are fairly short; there are no multi-line messages or embedded newlines. Each error message begins with a capital letter and does not include any terminating punctuation.

Many programs that don't read input from the terminal are designed to exit if any system call fails. By convention, the error message from such a program should start with the program's name, sans directories. You can find that name in the variable `program_invocation_short_name`; the full file name is stored the variable `program_invocation_name`.

`char * program_invocation_name`   [Variable]

>   This variable's value is the name that was used to invoke the program running in the current process. It is the same as `argv[0]`. Note that this is not necessarily a useful file name; often it contains no directory names. See Section 25.1 [Program Arguments], page 729.

>   This variable is a GNU extension and is declared in `errno.h`.

`char * program_invocation_short_name`   [Variable]

>   This variable's value is the name that was used to invoke the program running in the current process, with directory names removed. (That is to say, it is the same as `program_invocation_name` minus everything up to the last slash, if any.)

>   This variable is a GNU extension and is declared in `errno.h`.

The library initialization code sets up both of these variables before calling `main`.

Portability Note: If you want your program to work with non-GNU libraries, you must save the value of `argv[0]` in `main`, and then strip off the directory names yourself. We added these extensions to make it possible to write self-contained error-reporting subroutines that require no explicit cooperation from `main`.

Here is an example showing how to handle failure to open a file correctly. The function `open_sesame` tries to open the named file for reading and returns a stream if successful. The `fopen` library function returns a null pointer if it couldn't open the file for some reason. In that situation, `open_sesame` constructs an appropriate error message using the `strerror` function, and terminates the program. If we were going to make some other library calls before passing the error code to `strerror`, we'd have to save it in a local variable instead, because those other library functions might overwrite `errno` in the meantime.

```
#define _GNU_SOURCE

#include <errno.h>
#include <stdio.h>
#include <stdlib.h>
#include <string.h>

FILE *
open_sesame (char *name)
{
  FILE *stream;

  errno = 0;
  stream = fopen (name, "r");
```

```
    if (stream == NULL)
      {
        fprintf (stderr, "%s: Couldn't open file %s; %s\n",
                 program_invocation_short_name, name, strerror (errno));
        exit (EXIT_FAILURE);
      }
    else
      return stream;
}
```

Using `perror` has the advantage that the function is portable and available on all systems implementing ISO C. But often the text `perror` generates is not what is wanted and there is no way to extend or change what `perror` does. The GNU coding standard, for instance, requires error messages to be preceded by the program name and programs which read some input files should provide information about the input file name and the line number in case an error is encountered while reading the file. For these occasions there are two functions available which are widely used throughout the GNU project. These functions are declared in `error.h`.

---

void error (*int status*, *int errnum*, *const char *format*, ...)   [Function]
    Preliminary: | MT-Safe locale | AS-Unsafe corrupt heap i18n | AC-Safe | See
    Section 1.2.2.1 [POSIX Safety Concepts], page 2.

    The `error` function can be used to report general problems during program execution. The *format* argument is a format string just like those given to the `printf` family of functions. The arguments required for the format can follow the *format* parameter. Just like `perror`, `error` also can report an error code in textual form. But unlike `perror` the error value is explicitly passed to the function in the *errnum* parameter. This eliminates the problem mentioned above that the error reporting function must be called immediately after the function causing the error since otherwise `errno` might have a different value.

    `error` prints first the program name. If the application defined a global variable `error_print_progname` and points it to a function this function will be called to print the program name. Otherwise the string from the global variable `program_name` is used. The program name is followed by a colon and a space which in turn is followed by the output produced by the format string. If the *errnum* parameter is non-zero the format string output is followed by a colon and a space, followed by the error message for the error code *errnum*. In any case is the output terminated with a newline.

    The output is directed to the `stderr` stream. If the `stderr` wasn't oriented before the call it will be narrow-oriented afterwards.

    The function will return unless the *status* parameter has a non-zero value. In this case the function will call `exit` with the *status* value for its parameter and therefore never return. If `error` returns, the global variable `error_message_count` is incremented by one to keep track of the number of errors reported.

void error_at_line (*int* **status**, *int* **errnum**, *const char* ***fname**,   [Function]
        unsigned int **lineno**, *const char* ***format**, ...)
>   Preliminary: | MT-Unsafe race:error_at_line/error_one_per_line locale | AS-Unsafe
>   corrupt heap i18n | AC-Unsafe corrupt/error_one_per_line | See Section 1.2.2.1
>   [POSIX Safety Concepts], page 2.
>
>   The error_at_line function is very similar to the error function. The only dif-
>   ferences are the additional parameters *fname* and *lineno*. The handling of the other
>   parameters is identical to that of error except that between the program name and
>   the string generated by the format string additional text is inserted.
>
>   Directly following the program name a colon, followed by the file name pointed to by
>   *fname*, another colon, and the value of *lineno* is printed.
>
>   This additional output of course is meant to be used to locate an error in an input
>   file (like a programming language source code file etc).
>
>   If the global variable error_one_per_line is set to a non-zero value error_at_line
>   will avoid printing consecutive messages for the same file and line. Repetition which
>   are not directly following each other are not caught.
>
>   Just like error this function only returns if *status* is zero. Otherwise exit is called
>   with the non-zero value. If error returns, the global variable error_message_count
>   is incremented by one to keep track of the number of errors reported.

As mentioned above, the error and error_at_line functions can be customized by
defining a variable named error_print_progname.

void (*error_print_progname) (void)   [Variable]
>   If the error_print_progname variable is defined to a non-zero value the function
>   pointed to is called by error or error_at_line. It is expected to print the program
>   name or do something similarly useful.
>
>   The function is expected to print to the stderr stream and must be able to handle
>   whatever orientation the stream has.
>
>   The variable is global and shared by all threads.

unsigned int error_message_count   [Variable]
>   The error_message_count variable is incremented whenever one of the functions
>   error or error_at_line returns. The variable is global and shared by all threads.

int error_one_per_line   [Variable]
>   The error_one_per_line variable influences only error_at_line. Normally the
>   error_at_line function creates output for every invocation. If error_one_per_
>   line is set to a non-zero value error_at_line keeps track of the last file name and
>   line number for which an error was reported and avoids directly following messages
>   for the same file and line. This variable is global and shared by all threads.

A program which read some input file and reports errors in it could look like this:

```
{
  char *line = NULL;
  size_t len = 0;
  unsigned int lineno = 0;
```

```
      error_message_count = 0;
      while (! feof_unlocked (fp))
        {
          ssize_t n = getline (&line, &len, fp);
          if (n <= 0)
            /* End of file or error.  */
            break;
          ++lineno;

          /* Process the line.  */
          ...

          if (Detect error in line)
            error_at_line (0, errval, filename, lineno,
                           "some error text %s", some_variable);
        }

    if (error_message_count != 0)
      error (EXIT_FAILURE, 0, "%u errors found", error_message_count);
  }
```

error and error_at_line are clearly the functions of choice and enable the programmer to write applications which follow the GNU coding standard. The GNU C Library additionally contains functions which are used in BSD for the same purpose. These functions are declared in err.h. It is generally advised to not use these functions. They are included only for compatibility.

void **warn** (*const char *format, ...*)   [Function]
    Preliminary: | MT-Safe locale | AS-Unsafe corrupt heap i18n | AC-Unsafe corrupt lock mem | See Section 1.2.2.1 [POSIX Safety Concepts], page 2.

    The **warn** function is roughly equivalent to a call like

```
            error (0, errno, format, the parameters)
```

    except that the global variables **error** respects and modifies are not used.

void **vwarn** (*const char *format, va_list ap*)   [Function]
    Preliminary: | MT-Safe locale | AS-Unsafe corrupt heap i18n | AC-Unsafe corrupt lock mem | See Section 1.2.2.1 [POSIX Safety Concepts], page 2.

    The **vwarn** function is just like **warn** except that the parameters for the handling of the format string *format* are passed in as a value of type **va_list**.

void **warnx** (*const char *format, ...*)   [Function]
    Preliminary: | MT-Safe locale | AS-Unsafe corrupt heap | AC-Unsafe corrupt lock mem | See Section 1.2.2.1 [POSIX Safety Concepts], page 2.

    The **warnx** function is roughly equivalent to a call like

```
            error (0, 0, format, the parameters)
```

    except that the global variables **error** respects and modifies are not used. The difference to **warn** is that no error number string is printed.

void **vwarnx** (*const char *format, va_list ap*)   [Function]
    Preliminary: | MT-Safe locale | AS-Unsafe corrupt heap | AC-Unsafe corrupt lock mem | See Section 1.2.2.1 [POSIX Safety Concepts], page 2.

    The **vwarnx** function is just like **warnx** except that the parameters for the handling of the format string *format* are passed in as a value of type **va_list**.

void **err** (*int* **status**, *const char* ***format**, ...)   [Function]
> Preliminary: | MT-Safe locale | AS-Unsafe corrupt heap i18n | AC-Unsafe corrupt
> lock mem | See Section 1.2.2.1 [POSIX Safety Concepts], page 2.
>
> The **err** function is roughly equivalent to a call like
>
>   error (status, errno, format, the parameters)
>
> except that the global variables **error** respects and modifies are not used and that
> the program is exited even if *status* is zero.

void **verr** (*int* **status**, *const char* ***format**, *va_list* **ap**)   [Function]
> Preliminary: | MT-Safe locale | AS-Unsafe corrupt heap i18n | AC-Unsafe corrupt
> lock mem | See Section 1.2.2.1 [POSIX Safety Concepts], page 2.
>
> The **verr** function is just like **err** except that the parameters for the handling of the
> format string *format* are passed in as a value of type **va_list**.

void **errx** (*int* **status**, *const char* ***format**, ...)   [Function]
> Preliminary: | MT-Safe locale | AS-Unsafe corrupt heap | AC-Unsafe corrupt lock
> mem | See Section 1.2.2.1 [POSIX Safety Concepts], page 2.
>
> The **errx** function is roughly equivalent to a call like
>
>   error (status, 0, format, the parameters)
>
> except that the global variables **error** respects and modifies are not used and that
> the program is exited even if *status* is zero. The difference to **err** is that no error
> number string is printed.

void **verrx** (*int* **status**, *const char* ***format**, *va_list* **ap**)   [Function]
> Preliminary: | MT-Safe locale | AS-Unsafe corrupt heap | AC-Unsafe corrupt lock
> mem | See Section 1.2.2.1 [POSIX Safety Concepts], page 2.
>
> The **verrx** function is just like **errx** except that the parameters for the handling of
> the format string *format* are passed in as a value of type **va_list**.

3 Virtual Memory Allocation And Paging

This chapter describes how processes manage and use memory in a system that uses the GNU C Library.

The GNU C Library has several functions for dynamically allocating virtual memory in various ways. They vary in generality and in efficiency. The library also provides functions for controlling paging and allocation of real memory.

Memory mapped I/O is not discussed in this chapter. See Section 13.7 [Memory-mapped I/O], page 350.

3.1 Process Memory Concepts

One of the most basic resources a process has available to it is memory. There are a lot of different ways systems organize memory, but in a typical one, each process has one linear virtual address space, with addresses running from zero to some huge maximum. It need not be contiguous; i.e., not all of these addresses actually can be used to store data.

The virtual memory is divided into pages (4 kilobytes is typical). Backing each page of virtual memory is a page of real memory (called a *frame*) or some secondary storage, usually disk space. The disk space might be swap space or just some ordinary disk file. Actually, a page of all zeroes sometimes has nothing at all backing it – there's just a flag saying it is all zeroes.

The same frame of real memory or backing store can back multiple virtual pages belonging to multiple processes. This is normally the case, for example, with virtual memory occupied by GNU C Library code. The same real memory frame containing the `printf` function backs a virtual memory page in each of the existing processes that has a `printf` call in its program.

In order for a program to access any part of a virtual page, the page must at that moment be backed by ("connected to") a real frame. But because there is usually a lot more virtual memory than real memory, the pages must move back and forth between real memory and backing store regularly, coming into real memory when a process needs to access them and then retreating to backing store when not needed anymore. This movement is called *paging*.

When a program attempts to access a page which is not at that moment backed by real memory, this is known as a *page fault*. When a page fault occurs, the kernel suspends the process, places the page into a real page frame (this is called "paging in" or "faulting in"), then resumes the process so that from the process' point of view, the page was in real memory all along. In fact, to the process, all pages always seem to be in real memory. Except for one thing: the elapsed execution time of an instruction that would normally be a few nanoseconds is suddenly much, much, longer (because the kernel normally has to do I/O to complete the page-in). For programs sensitive to that, the functions described in Section 3.4 [Locking Pages], page 76, can control it.

Within each virtual address space, a process has to keep track of what is at which addresses, and that process is called memory allocation. Allocation usually brings to mind meting out scarce resources, but in the case of virtual memory, that's not a major goal, because there is generally much more of it than anyone needs. Memory allocation within a process is mainly just a matter of making sure that the same byte of memory isn't used to store two different things.

Processes allocate memory in two major ways: by exec and programmatically. Actually, forking is a third way, but it's not very interesting. See Section 26.4 [Creating a Process], page 775.

Exec is the operation of creating a virtual address space for a process, loading its basic program into it, and executing the program. It is done by the "exec" family of functions (e.g. `execl`). The operation takes a program file (an executable), it allocates space to load all the data in the executable, loads it, and transfers control to it. That data is most notably the instructions of the program (the *text*), but also literals and constants in the program and even some variables: C variables with the static storage class (see Section 3.2.1 [Memory Allocation in C Programs], page 43).

Once that program begins to execute, it uses programmatic allocation to gain additional memory. In a C program with the GNU C Library, there are two kinds of programmatic allocation: automatic and dynamic. See Section 3.2.1 [Memory Allocation in C Programs], page 43.

Memory-mapped I/O is another form of dynamic virtual memory allocation. Mapping memory to a file means declaring that the contents of certain range of a process' addresses shall be identical to the contents of a specified regular file. The system makes the virtual memory initially contain the contents of the file, and if you modify the memory, the system writes the same modification to the file. Note that due to the magic of virtual memory and page faults, there is no reason for the system to do I/O to read the file, or allocate real memory for its contents, until the program accesses the virtual memory. See Section 13.7 [Memory-mapped I/O], page 350.

Just as it programmatically allocates memory, the program can programmatically deal-locate (*free*) it. You can't free the memory that was allocated by exec. When the program exits or execs, you might say that all its memory gets freed, but since in both cases the address space ceases to exist, the point is really moot. See Section 25.7 [Program Termination], page 768.

A process' virtual address space is divided into segments. A segment is a contiguous range of virtual addresses. Three important segments are:

-
    The *text segment* contains a program's instructions and literals and static constants. It is allocated by exec and stays the same size for the life of the virtual address space.

- The *data segment* is working storage for the program. It can be preallocated and preloaded by exec and the process can extend or shrink it by calling functions as described in See Section 3.3 [Resizing the Data Segment], page 76. Its lower end is fixed.

- The *stack segment* contains a program stack. It grows as the stack grows, but doesn't shrink when the stack shrinks.

3.2 Allocating Storage For Program Data

This section covers how ordinary programs manage storage for their data, including the famous `malloc` function and some fancier facilities special to the GNU C Library and GNU Compiler.

3.2.1 Memory Allocation in C Programs

The C language supports two kinds of memory allocation through the variables in C programs:

- *Static allocation* is what happens when you declare a static or global variable. Each static or global variable defines one block of space, of a fixed size. The space is allocated once, when your program is started (part of the exec operation), and is never freed.

- *Automatic allocation* happens when you declare an automatic variable, such as a function argument or a local variable. The space for an automatic variable is allocated when the compound statement containing the declaration is entered, and is freed when that compound statement is exited.

  In GNU C, the size of the automatic storage can be an expression that varies. In other C implementations, it must be a constant.

A third important kind of memory allocation, *dynamic allocation*, is not supported by C variables but is available via GNU C Library functions.

3.2.1.1 Dynamic Memory Allocation

Dynamic memory allocation is a technique in which programs determine as they are running where to store some information. You need dynamic allocation when the amount of memory you need, or how long you continue to need it, depends on factors that are not known before the program runs.

For example, you may need a block to store a line read from an input file; since there is no limit to how long a line can be, you must allocate the memory dynamically and make it dynamically larger as you read more of the line.

Or, you may need a block for each record or each definition in the input data; since you can't know in advance how many there will be, you must allocate a new block for each record or definition as you read it.

When you use dynamic allocation, the allocation of a block of memory is an action that the program requests explicitly. You call a function or macro when you want to allocate space, and specify the size with an argument. If you want to free the space, you do so by calling another function or macro. You can do these things whenever you want, as often as you want.

Dynamic allocation is not supported by C variables; there is no storage class "dynamic", and there can never be a C variable whose value is stored in dynamically allocated space. The only way to get dynamically allocated memory is via a system call (which is generally via a GNU C Library function call), and the only way to refer to dynamically allocated space is through a pointer. Because it is less convenient, and because the actual process of dynamic allocation requires more computation time, programmers generally use dynamic allocation only when neither static nor automatic allocation will serve.

For example, if you want to allocate dynamically some space to hold a `struct foobar`, you cannot declare a variable of type `struct foobar` whose contents are the dynamically allocated space. But you can declare a variable of pointer type `struct foobar *` and assign it the address of the space. Then you can use the operators '`*`' and '`->`' on this pointer variable to refer to the contents of the space:

```
{
```

```
    struct foobar *ptr
        = (struct foobar *) malloc (sizeof (struct foobar));
    ptr->name = x;
    ptr->next = current_foobar;
    current_foobar = ptr;
}
```

3.2.2 The GNU Allocator

The `malloc` implementation in the GNU C Library is derived from ptmalloc (pthreads malloc), which in turn is derived from dlmalloc (Doug Lea malloc). This malloc may allocate memory in two different ways depending on their size and certain parameters that may be controlled by users. The most common way is to allocate portions of memory (called chunks) from a large contiguous area of memory and manage these areas to optimize their use and reduce wastage in the form of unusable chunks. Traditionally the system heap was set up to be the one large memory area but the GNU C Library `malloc` implementation maintains multiple such areas to optimize their use in multi-threaded applications. Each such area is internally referred to as an *arena*.

As opposed to other versions, the `malloc` in the GNU C Library does not round up chunk sizes to powers of two, neither for large nor for small sizes. Neighboring chunks can be coalesced on a `free` no matter what their size is. This makes the implementation suitable for all kinds of allocation patterns without generally incurring high memory waste through fragmentation. The presence of multiple arenas allows multiple threads to allocate memory simultaneously in separate arenas, thus improving performance.

The other way of memory allocation is for very large blocks, i.e. much larger than a page. These requests are allocated with `mmap` (anonymous or via `/dev/zero`; see Section 13.7 [Memory-mapped I/O], page 350)). This has the great advantage that these chunks are returned to the system immediately when they are freed. Therefore, it cannot happen that a large chunk becomes "locked" in between smaller ones and even after calling `free` wastes memory. The size threshold for `mmap` to be used is dynamic and gets adjusted according to allocation patterns of the program. `mallopt` can be used to statically adjust the threshold using `M_MMAP_THRESHOLD` and the use of `mmap` can be disabled completely with `M_MMAP_MAX`; see Section 3.2.3.7 [Malloc Tunable Parameters], page 50.

A more detailed technical description of the GNU Allocator is maintained in the GNU C Library wiki. See `https://sourceware.org/glibc/wiki/MallocInternals`.

It is possible to use your own custom `malloc` instead of the built-in allocator provided by the GNU C Library. See Section 3.2.5 [Replacing `malloc`], page 61.

3.2.3 Unconstrained Allocation

The most general dynamic allocation facility is `malloc`. It allows you to allocate blocks of memory of any size at any time, make them bigger or smaller at any time, and free the blocks individually at any time (or never).

3.2.3.1 Basic Memory Allocation

To allocate a block of memory, call `malloc`. The prototype for this function is in `stdlib.h`.

void * malloc (*size_t size*) [Function]

> Preliminary: | MT-Safe | AS-Unsafe lock | AC-Unsafe lock fd mem | See Section 1.2.2.1 [POSIX Safety Concepts], page 2.
>
> This function returns a pointer to a newly allocated block *size* bytes long, or a null pointer if the block could not be allocated.

The contents of the block are undefined; you must initialize it yourself (or use `calloc` instead; see Section 3.2.3.5 [Allocating Cleared Space], page 48). Normally you would cast the value as a pointer to the kind of object that you want to store in the block. Here we show an example of doing so, and of initializing the space with zeros using the library function `memset` (see Section 5.4 [Copying Strings and Arrays], page 95):

```
struct foo *ptr;
...
ptr = (struct foo *) malloc (sizeof (struct foo));
if (ptr == 0) abort ();
memset (ptr, 0, sizeof (struct foo));
```

You can store the result of `malloc` into any pointer variable without a cast, because ISO C automatically converts the type `void *` to another type of pointer when necessary. But the cast is necessary in contexts other than assignment operators or if you might want your code to run in traditional C.

Remember that when allocating space for a string, the argument to `malloc` must be one plus the length of the string. This is because a string is terminated with a null character that doesn't count in the "length" of the string but does need space. For example:

```
char *ptr;
...
ptr = (char *) malloc (length + 1);
```

See Section 5.1 [Representation of Strings], page 91, for more information about this.

3.2.3.2 Examples of `malloc`

If no more space is available, `malloc` returns a null pointer. You should check the value of *every* call to `malloc`. It is useful to write a subroutine that calls `malloc` and reports an error if the value is a null pointer, returning only if the value is nonzero. This function is conventionally called `xmalloc`. Here it is:

```
void *
xmalloc (size_t size)
{
  void *value = malloc (size);
  if (value == 0)
    fatal ("virtual memory exhausted");
  return value;
}
```

Here is a real example of using `malloc` (by way of `xmalloc`). The function `savestring` will copy a sequence of characters into a newly allocated null-terminated string:

```
char *
savestring (const char *ptr, size_t len)
{
  char *value = (char *) xmalloc (len + 1);
  value[len] = '\0';
  return (char *) memcpy (value, ptr, len);
}
```

The block that `malloc` gives you is guaranteed to be aligned so that it can hold any type of data. On GNU systems, the address is always a multiple of eight on 32-bit systems, and a multiple of 16 on 64-bit systems. Only rarely is any higher boundary (such as a page boundary) necessary; for those cases, use `aligned_alloc` or `posix_memalign` (see Section 3.2.3.6 [Allocating Aligned Memory Blocks], page 48).

Note that the memory located after the end of the block is likely to be in use for something else; perhaps a block already allocated by another call to `malloc`. If you attempt to treat the block as longer than you asked for it to be, you are liable to destroy the data that `malloc` uses to keep track of its blocks, or you may destroy the contents of another block. If you have already allocated a block and discover you want it to be bigger, use `realloc` (see Section 3.2.3.4 [Changing the Size of a Block], page 47).

3.2.3.3 Freeing Memory Allocated with `malloc`

When you no longer need a block that you got with `malloc`, use the function `free` to make the block available to be allocated again. The prototype for this function is in `stdlib.h`.

void free (*void *ptr*)   [Function]
> Preliminary: | MT-Safe | AS-Unsafe lock | AC-Unsafe lock fd mem | See Section 1.2.2.1 [POSIX Safety Concepts], page 2.

> The `free` function deallocates the block of memory pointed at by *ptr*.

Freeing a block alters the contents of the block. **Do not expect to find any data (such as a pointer to the next block in a chain of blocks) in the block after freeing it.** Copy whatever you need out of the block before freeing it! Here is an example of the proper way to free all the blocks in a chain, and the strings that they point to:

```
struct chain
  {
    struct chain *next;
    char *name;
  }

void
free_chain (struct chain *chain)
{
  while (chain != 0)
    {
      struct chain *next = chain->next;
      free (chain->name);
      free (chain);
      chain = next;
    }
}
```

Occasionally, `free` can actually return memory to the operating system and make the process smaller. Usually, all it can do is allow a later call to `malloc` to reuse the space. In the meantime, the space remains in your program as part of a free-list used internally by `malloc`.

There is no point in freeing blocks at the end of a program, because all of the program's space is given back to the system when the process terminates.

3.2.3.4 Changing the Size of a Block

Often you do not know for certain how big a block you will ultimately need at the time you must begin to use the block. For example, the block might be a buffer that you use to hold a line being read from a file; no matter how long you make the buffer initially, you may encounter a line that is longer.

You can make the block longer by calling **realloc** or **reallocarray**. These functions are declared in **stdlib.h**.

void * realloc (*void *ptr, size_t newsize*) [Function]

> Preliminary: | MT-Safe | AS-Unsafe lock | AC-Unsafe lock fd mem | See Section 1.2.2.1 [POSIX Safety Concepts], page 2.
>
> The **realloc** function changes the size of the block whose address is *ptr* to be *newsize*.
>
> Since the space after the end of the block may be in use, **realloc** may find it necessary to copy the block to a new address where more free space is available. The value of **realloc** is the new address of the block. If the block needs to be moved, **realloc** copies the old contents.
>
> If you pass a null pointer for *ptr*, **realloc** behaves just like '**malloc (*newsize*)**'. This can be convenient, but beware that older implementations (before ISO C) may not support this behavior, and will probably crash when **realloc** is passed a null pointer.

void * reallocarray (*void *ptr, size_t nmemb, size_t size*) [Function]

> Preliminary: | MT-Safe | AS-Unsafe lock | AC-Unsafe lock fd mem | See Section 1.2.2.1 [POSIX Safety Concepts], page 2.
>
> The **reallocarray** function changes the size of the block whose address is *ptr* to be long enough to contain a vector of *nmemb* elements, each of size *size*. It is equivalent to '**realloc (*ptr, nmemb * size*)**', except that **reallocarray** fails safely if the multiplication overflows, by setting **errno** to **ENOMEM**, returning a null pointer, and leaving the original block unchanged.
>
> **reallocarray** should be used instead of **realloc** when the new size of the allocated block is the result of a multiplication that might overflow.
>
> **Portability Note:** This function is not part of any standard. It was first introduced in OpenBSD 5.6.

Like **malloc**, **realloc** and **reallocarray** may return a null pointer if no memory space is available to make the block bigger. When this happens, the original block is untouched; it has not been modified or relocated.

In most cases it makes no difference what happens to the original block when **realloc** fails, because the application program cannot continue when it is out of memory, and the only thing to do is to give a fatal error message. Often it is convenient to write and use a subroutine, conventionally called **xrealloc**, that takes care of the error message as **xmalloc** does for **malloc**:

```
void *
xrealloc (void *ptr, size_t size)
{
  void *value = realloc (ptr, size);
  if (value == 0)
    fatal ("Virtual memory exhausted");
```

```
    return value;
  }
```

You can also use `realloc` or `reallocarray` to make a block smaller. The reason you would do this is to avoid tying up a lot of memory space when only a little is needed. In several allocation implementations, making a block smaller sometimes necessitates copying it, so it can fail if no other space is available.

If the new size you specify is the same as the old size, `realloc` and `reallocarray` are guaranteed to change nothing and return the same address that you gave.

3.2.3.5 Allocating Cleared Space

The function `calloc` allocates memory and clears it to zero. It is declared in `stdlib.h`.

void * calloc (*size_t count*, *size_t eltsize*)   [Function]
> Preliminary: | MT-Safe | AS-Unsafe lock | AC-Unsafe lock fd mem | See Section 1.2.2.1 [POSIX Safety Concepts], page 2.
>
> This function allocates a block long enough to contain a vector of *count* elements, each of size *eltsize*. Its contents are cleared to zero before `calloc` returns.
>
> You could define `calloc` as follows:
>
> ```
> void *
> calloc (size_t count, size_t eltsize)
> {
>   size_t size = count * eltsize;
>   void *value = malloc (size);
>   if (value != 0)
>     memset (value, 0, size);
>   return value;
> }
> ```

But in general, it is not guaranteed that `calloc` calls `malloc` internally. Therefore, if an application provides its own `malloc/realloc/free` outside the C library, it should always define `calloc`, too.

3.2.3.6 Allocating Aligned Memory Blocks

The address of a block returned by `malloc` or `realloc` in GNU systems is always a multiple of eight (or sixteen on 64-bit systems). If you need a block whose address is a multiple of a higher power of two than that, use `aligned_alloc` or `posix_memalign`. `aligned_alloc` and `posix_memalign` are declared in `stdlib.h`.

void * aligned_alloc (*size_t alignment*, *size_t size*)   [Function]
> Preliminary: | MT-Safe | AS-Unsafe lock | AC-Unsafe lock fd mem | See Section 1.2.2.1 [POSIX Safety Concepts], page 2.
>
> The `aligned_alloc` function allocates a block of *size* bytes whose address is a multiple of *alignment*. The *alignment* must be a power of two and *size* must be a multiple of *alignment*.
>
> The `aligned_alloc` function returns a null pointer on error and sets `errno` to one of the following values:
>
> ENOMEM   There was insufficient memory available to satisfy the request.

EINVAL   *alignment* is not a power of two.

This function was introduced in ISO C11 and hence may have better portability to modern non-POSIX systems than `posix_memalign`.

---

void * memalign (*size_t boundary*, *size_t size*)   [Function]

Preliminary: | MT-Safe | AS-Unsafe lock | AC-Unsafe lock fd mem | See Section 1.2.2.1 [POSIX Safety Concepts], page 2.

The `memalign` function allocates a block of *size* bytes whose address is a multiple of *boundary*. The *boundary* must be a power of two! The function `memalign` works by allocating a somewhat larger block, and then returning an address within the block that is on the specified boundary.

The `memalign` function returns a null pointer on error and sets `errno` to one of the following values:

ENOMEM   There was insufficient memory available to satisfy the request.

EINVAL   *boundary* is not a power of two.

The `memalign` function is obsolete and `aligned_alloc` or `posix_memalign` should be used instead.

---

int posix_memalign (*void **memptr*, *size_t alignment*, *size_t size*)   [Function]

Preliminary: | MT-Safe | AS-Unsafe lock | AC-Unsafe lock fd mem | See Section 1.2.2.1 [POSIX Safety Concepts], page 2.

The `posix_memalign` function is similar to the `memalign` function in that it returns a buffer of *size* bytes aligned to a multiple of *alignment*. But it adds one requirement to the parameter *alignment*: the value must be a power of two multiple of `sizeof (void *)`.

If the function succeeds in allocation memory a pointer to the allocated memory is returned in `*memptr` and the return value is zero. Otherwise the function returns an error value indicating the problem. The possible error values returned are:

ENOMEM   There was insufficient memory available to satisfy the request.

EINVAL   *alignment* is not a power of two multiple of `sizeof (void *)`.

This function was introduced in POSIX 1003.1d. Although this function is superseded by `aligned_alloc`, it is more portable to older POSIX systems that do not support ISO C11.

---

void * valloc (*size_t size*)   [Function]

Preliminary: | MT-Unsafe init | AS-Unsafe init lock | AC-Unsafe init lock fd mem | See Section 1.2.2.1 [POSIX Safety Concepts], page 2.

Using `valloc` is like using `memalign` and passing the page size as the value of the first argument. It is implemented like this:

```
void *
valloc (size_t size)
{
  return memalign (getpagesize (), size);
}
```

Section 22.4.2 [How to get information about the memory subsystem?], page 672, for more information about the memory subsystem.

The `valloc` function is obsolete and `aligned_alloc` or `posix_memalign` should be used instead.

3.2.3.7 Malloc Tunable Parameters

You can adjust some parameters for dynamic memory allocation with the `mallopt` function. This function is the general SVID/XPG interface, defined in `malloc.h`.

`int mallopt (int param, int value)` [Function]

> Preliminary: | MT-Unsafe init const:mallopt | AS-Unsafe init lock | AC-Unsafe init lock | See Section 1.2.2.1 [POSIX Safety Concepts], page 2.
>
> When calling `mallopt`, the *param* argument specifies the parameter to be set, and *value* the new value to be set. Possible choices for *param*, as defined in `malloc.h`, are:
>
> `M_MMAP_MAX`
> > The maximum number of chunks to allocate with `mmap`. Setting this to zero disables all use of `mmap`.
> >
> > The default value of this parameter is `65536`.
> >
> > This parameter can also be set for the process at startup by setting the environment variable `MALLOC_MMAP_MAX_` to the desired value.
>
> `M_MMAP_THRESHOLD`
> > All chunks larger than this value are allocated outside the normal heap, using the `mmap` system call. This way it is guaranteed that the memory for these chunks can be returned to the system on `free`. Note that requests smaller than this threshold might still be allocated via `mmap`.
> >
> > If this parameter is not set, the default value is set as 128 KiB and the threshold is adjusted dynamically to suit the allocation patterns of the program. If the parameter is set, the dynamic adjustment is disabled and the value is set statically to the input value.
> >
> > This parameter can also be set for the process at startup by setting the environment variable `MALLOC_MMAP_THRESHOLD_` to the desired value.
>
> `M_PERTURB`
> > If non-zero, memory blocks are filled with values depending on some low order bits of this parameter when they are allocated (except when allocated by `calloc`) and freed. This can be used to debug the use of uninitialized or freed heap memory. Note that this option does not guarantee that the freed block will have any specific values. It only guarantees that the content the block had before it was freed will be overwritten.
> >
> > The default value of this parameter is `0`.
> >
> > This parameter can also be set for the process at startup by setting the environment variable `MALLOC_MMAP_PERTURB_` to the desired value.
>
> `M_TOP_PAD`
> > This parameter determines the amount of extra memory to obtain from the system when an arena needs to be extended. It also specifies the

number of bytes to retain when shrinking an arena. This provides the necessary hysteresis in heap size such that excessive amounts of system calls can be avoided.

The default value of this parameter is 0.

This parameter can also be set for the process at startup by setting the environment variable `MALLOC_TOP_PAD_` to the desired value.

M_TRIM_THRESHOLD

This is the minimum size (in bytes) of the top-most, releasable chunk that will trigger a system call in order to return memory to the system.

If this parameter is not set, the default value is set as 128 KiB and the threshold is adjusted dynamically to suit the allocation patterns of the program. If the parameter is set, the dynamic adjustment is disabled and the value is set statically to the provided input.

This parameter can also be set for the process at startup by setting the environment variable `MALLOC_TRIM_THRESHOLD_` to the desired value.

M_ARENA_TEST

This parameter specifies the number of arenas that can be created before the test on the limit to the number of arenas is conducted. The value is ignored if `M_ARENA_MAX` is set.

The default value of this parameter is 2 on 32-bit systems and 8 on 64-bit systems.

This parameter can also be set for the process at startup by setting the environment variable `MALLOC_ARENA_TEST` to the desired value.

M_ARENA_MAX

This parameter sets the number of arenas to use regardless of the number of cores in the system.

The default value of this tunable is 0, meaning that the limit on the number of arenas is determined by the number of CPU cores online. For 32-bit systems the limit is twice the number of cores online and on 64-bit systems, it is eight times the number of cores online. Note that the default value is not derived from the default value of M_ARENA_TEST and is computed independently.

This parameter can also be set for the process at startup by setting the environment variable `MALLOC_ARENA_MAX` to the desired value.

3.2.3.8 Heap Consistency Checking

You can ask `malloc` to check the consistency of dynamic memory by using the `mcheck` function. This function is a GNU extension, declared in `mcheck.h`.

int mcheck (*void* (*abortfn*) (*enum mcheck_status* **status**))   [Function]

Preliminary: | MT-Unsafe race:mcheck const:malloc_hooks | AS-Unsafe corrupt | AC-Unsafe corrupt | See Section 1.2.2.1 [POSIX Safety Concepts], page 2.

Calling `mcheck` tells `malloc` to perform occasional consistency checks. These will catch things such as writing past the end of a block that was allocated with `malloc`.

The *abortfn* argument is the function to call when an inconsistency is found. If you supply a null pointer, then `mcheck` uses a default function which prints a message and calls `abort` (see Section 25.7.4 [Aborting a Program], page 771). The function you supply is called with one argument, which says what sort of inconsistency was detected; its type is described below.

It is too late to begin allocation checking once you have allocated anything with `malloc`. So `mcheck` does nothing in that case. The function returns −1 if you call it too late, and 0 otherwise (when it is successful).

The easiest way to arrange to call `mcheck` early enough is to use the option '−lmcheck' when you link your program; then you don't need to modify your program source at all. Alternatively you might use a debugger to insert a call to `mcheck` whenever the program is started, for example these gdb commands will automatically call `mcheck` whenever the program starts:

```
(gdb) break main
Breakpoint 1, main (argc=2, argv=0xbffff964) at whatever.c:10
(gdb) command 1
Type commands for when breakpoint 1 is hit, one per line.
End with a line saying just "end".
>call mcheck(0)
>continue
>end
(gdb) ...
```

This will however only work if no initialization function of any object involved calls any of the `malloc` functions since `mcheck` must be called before the first such function.

---

enum mcheck_status mprobe (*void *pointer*) [Function]

Preliminary: | MT-Unsafe race:mcheck const:malloc_hooks | AS-Unsafe corrupt | AC-Unsafe corrupt | See Section 1.2.2.1 [POSIX Safety Concepts], page 2.

The `mprobe` function lets you explicitly check for inconsistencies in a particular allocated block. You must have already called `mcheck` at the beginning of the program, to do its occasional checks; calling `mprobe` requests an additional consistency check to be done at the time of the call.

The argument *pointer* must be a pointer returned by `malloc` or `realloc`. `mprobe` returns a value that says what inconsistency, if any, was found. The values are described below.

---

enum mcheck_status [Data Type]

This enumerated type describes what kind of inconsistency was detected in an allocated block, if any. Here are the possible values:

MCHECK_DISABLED

> `mcheck` was not called before the first allocation. No consistency checking can be done.

MCHECK_OK

> No inconsistency detected.

MCHECK_HEAD

> The data immediately before the block was modified. This commonly happens when an array index or pointer is decremented too far.

MCHECK_TAIL

>The data immediately after the block was modified. This commonly happens when an array index or pointer is incremented too far.

MCHECK_FREE

>The block was already freed.

Another possibility to check for and guard against bugs in the use of `malloc`, `realloc` and `free` is to set the environment variable `MALLOC_CHECK_`. When `MALLOC_CHECK_` is set, a special (less efficient) implementation is used which is designed to be tolerant against simple errors, such as double calls of `free` with the same argument, or overruns of a single byte (off-by-one bugs). Not all such errors can be protected against, however, and memory leaks can result. If `MALLOC_CHECK_` is set to 0, any detected heap corruption is silently ignored; if set to 1, a diagnostic is printed on `stderr`; if set to 2, `abort` is called immediately. This can be useful because otherwise a crash may happen much later, and the true cause for the problem is then very hard to track down.

There is one problem with `MALLOC_CHECK_`: in SUID or SGID binaries it could possibly be exploited since diverging from the normal programs behavior it now writes something to the standard error descriptor. Therefore the use of `MALLOC_CHECK_` is disabled by default for SUID and SGID binaries. It can be enabled again by the system administrator by adding a file `/etc/suid-debug` (the content is not important it could be empty).

So, what's the difference between using `MALLOC_CHECK_` and linking with '`-lmcheck`'? `MALLOC_CHECK_` is orthogonal with respect to '`-lmcheck`'. '`-lmcheck`' has been added for backward compatibility. Both `MALLOC_CHECK_` and '`-lmcheck`' should uncover the same bugs - but using `MALLOC_CHECK_` you don't need to recompile your application.

3.2.3.9 Memory Allocation Hooks

The GNU C Library lets you modify the behavior of `malloc`, `realloc`, and `free` by specifying appropriate hook functions. You can use these hooks to help you debug programs that use dynamic memory allocation, for example.

The hook variables are declared in `malloc.h`.

`__malloc_hook` [Variable]

>The value of this variable is a pointer to the function that `malloc` uses whenever it is called. You should define this function to look like `malloc`; that is, like:

>```
void *function (size_t size, const void *caller)
>```

>The value of *caller* is the return address found on the stack when the `malloc` function was called. This value allows you to trace the memory consumption of the program.

`__realloc_hook` [Variable]

>The value of this variable is a pointer to function that `realloc` uses whenever it is called. You should define this function to look like `realloc`; that is, like:

>```
void *function (void *ptr, size_t size, const void *caller)
>```

>The value of *caller* is the return address found on the stack when the `realloc` function was called. This value allows you to trace the memory consumption of the program.

__free_hook   [Variable]

The value of this variable is a pointer to function that **free** uses whenever it is called. You should define this function to look like **free**; that is, like:

    void *function* (void *ptr, const void *caller)

The value of *caller* is the return address found on the stack when the **free** function was called. This value allows you to trace the memory consumption of the program.

__memalign_hook   [Variable]

The value of this variable is a pointer to function that **aligned_alloc**, **memalign**, **posix_memalign** and **valloc** use whenever they are called. You should define this function to look like **aligned_alloc**; that is, like:

    void **function* (size_t *alignment*, size_t *size*, const void *caller)

The value of *caller* is the return address found on the stack when the **aligned_alloc**, **memalign**, **posix_memalign** or **valloc** functions are called. This value allows you to trace the memory consumption of the program.

You must make sure that the function you install as a hook for one of these functions does not call that function recursively without restoring the old value of the hook first! Otherwise, your program will get stuck in an infinite recursion. Before calling the function recursively, one should make sure to restore all the hooks to their previous value. When coming back from the recursive call, all the hooks should be resaved since a hook might modify itself.

An issue to look out for is the time at which the malloc hook functions can be safely installed. If the hook functions call the malloc-related functions recursively, it is necessary that malloc has already properly initialized itself at the time when __malloc_hook etc. is assigned to. On the other hand, if the hook functions provide a complete malloc implementation of their own, it is vital that the hooks are assigned to *before* the very first **malloc** call has completed, because otherwise a chunk obtained from the ordinary, un-hooked malloc may later be handed to __free_hook, for example.

Here is an example showing how to use __malloc_hook and __free_hook properly. It installs a function that prints out information every time **malloc** or **free** is called. We just assume here that **realloc** and **memalign** are not used in our program.

```
/* Prototypes for __malloc_hook, __free_hook */
#include <malloc.h>

/* Prototypes for our hooks.  */
static void my_init_hook (void);
static void *my_malloc_hook (size_t, const void *);
static void my_free_hook (void*, const void *);

static void
my_init (void)
{
  old_malloc_hook = __malloc_hook;
  old_free_hook = __free_hook;
  __malloc_hook = my_malloc_hook;
  __free_hook = my_free_hook;
}

static void *
```

```
my_malloc_hook (size_t size, const void *caller)
{
  void *result;
  /* Restore all old hooks */
  __malloc_hook = old_malloc_hook;
  __free_hook = old_free_hook;
  /* Call recursively */
  result = malloc (size);
  /* Save underlying hooks */
  old_malloc_hook = __malloc_hook;
  old_free_hook = __free_hook;
  /* printf might call malloc, so protect it too. */
  printf ("malloc (%u) returns %p\n", (unsigned int) size, result);
  /* Restore our own hooks */
  __malloc_hook = my_malloc_hook;
  __free_hook = my_free_hook;
  return result;
}

static void
my_free_hook (void *ptr, const void *caller)
{
  /* Restore all old hooks */
  __malloc_hook = old_malloc_hook;
  __free_hook = old_free_hook;
  /* Call recursively */
  free (ptr);
  /* Save underlying hooks */
  old_malloc_hook = __malloc_hook;
  old_free_hook = __free_hook;
  /* printf might call free, so protect it too. */
  printf ("freed pointer %p\n", ptr);
  /* Restore our own hooks */
  __malloc_hook = my_malloc_hook;
  __free_hook = my_free_hook;
}

main ()
{
  my_init ();
  ...
}
```

The mcheck function (see Section 3.2.3.8 [Heap Consistency Checking], page 51) works by installing such hooks.

3.2.3.10 Statistics for Memory Allocation with malloc

You can get information about dynamic memory allocation by calling the mallinfo function. This function and its associated data type are declared in malloc.h; they are an extension of the standard SVID/XPG version.

struct mallinfo   [Data Type]

This structure type is used to return information about the dynamic memory allocator. It contains the following members:

int arena   This is the total size of memory allocated with sbrk by malloc, in bytes.

int ordblks

> This is the number of chunks not in use. (The memory allocator internally gets chunks of memory from the operating system, and then carves them up to satisfy individual `malloc` requests; see Section 3.2.2 [The GNU Allocator], page 44.)

int smblks

> This field is unused.

int hblks   This is the total number of chunks allocated with `mmap`.

int hblkhd

> This is the total size of memory allocated with `mmap`, in bytes.

int usmblks

> This field is unused and always 0.

int fsmblks

> This field is unused.

int uordblks

> This is the total size of memory occupied by chunks handed out by `malloc`.

int fordblks

> This is the total size of memory occupied by free (not in use) chunks.

int keepcost

> This is the size of the top-most releasable chunk that normally borders the end of the heap (i.e., the high end of the virtual address space's data segment).

struct mallinfo mallinfo (*void*)   [Function]

> Preliminary: | MT-Unsafe init const:mallopt | AS-Unsafe init lock | AC-Unsafe init lock | See Section 1.2.2.1 [POSIX Safety Concepts], page 2.

> This function returns information about the current dynamic memory usage in a structure of type `struct mallinfo`.

3.2.3.11 Summary of `malloc`-Related Functions

Here is a summary of the functions that work with `malloc`:

void *malloc (size_t *size*)

> Allocate a block of *size* bytes. See Section 3.2.3.1 [Basic Memory Allocation], page 44.

void free (void *addr*)

> Free a block previously allocated by `malloc`. See Section 3.2.3.3 [Freeing Memory Allocated with `malloc`], page 46.

void *realloc (void *addr*, size_t *size*)

> Make a block previously allocated by `malloc` larger or smaller, possibly by copying it to a new location. See Section 3.2.3.4 [Changing the Size of a Block], page 47.

`void *reallocarray (void *ptr, size_t nmemb, size_t size)`
> Change the size of a block previously allocated by `malloc` to *nmemb * size* bytes as with `realloc`. See Section 3.2.3.4 [Changing the Size of a Block], page 47.

`void *calloc (size_t count, size_t eltsize)`
> Allocate a block of *count * eltsize* bytes using `malloc`, and set its contents to zero. See Section 3.2.3.5 [Allocating Cleared Space], page 48.

`void *valloc (size_t size)`
> Allocate a block of *size* bytes, starting on a page boundary. See Section 3.2.3.6 [Allocating Aligned Memory Blocks], page 48.

`void *aligned_alloc (size_t size, size_t alignment)`
> Allocate a block of *size* bytes, starting on an address that is a multiple of *alignment*. See Section 3.2.3.6 [Allocating Aligned Memory Blocks], page 48.

`int posix_memalign (void **memptr, size_t alignment, size_t size)`
> Allocate a block of *size* bytes, starting on an address that is a multiple of *alignment*. See Section 3.2.3.6 [Allocating Aligned Memory Blocks], page 48.

`void *memalign (size_t size, size_t boundary)`
> Allocate a block of *size* bytes, starting on an address that is a multiple of *boundary*. See Section 3.2.3.6 [Allocating Aligned Memory Blocks], page 48.

`int mallopt (int param, int value)`
> Adjust a tunable parameter. See Section 3.2.3.7 [Malloc Tunable Parameters], page 50.

`int mcheck (void (*abortfn) (void))`
> Tell `malloc` to perform occasional consistency checks on dynamically allocated memory, and to call *abortfn* when an inconsistency is found. See Section 3.2.3.8 [Heap Consistency Checking], page 51.

`void *(*__malloc_hook) (size_t size, const void *caller)`
> A pointer to a function that `malloc` uses whenever it is called.

`void *(*__realloc_hook) (void *ptr, size_t size, const void *caller)`
> A pointer to a function that `realloc` uses whenever it is called.

`void (*__free_hook) (void *ptr, const void *caller)`
> A pointer to a function that `free` uses whenever it is called.

`void (*__memalign_hook) (size_t size, size_t alignment, const void *caller)`
> A pointer to a function that `aligned_alloc`, `memalign`, `posix_memalign` and `valloc` use whenever they are called.

`struct mallinfo mallinfo (void)`
> Return information about the current dynamic memory usage. See Section 3.2.3.10 [Statistics for Memory Allocation with `malloc`], page 55.

3.2.4 Allocation Debugging

A complicated task when programming with languages which do not use garbage collected dynamic memory allocation is to find memory leaks. Long running programs must ensure that dynamically allocated objects are freed at the end of their lifetime. If this does not happen the system runs out of memory, sooner or later.

The `malloc` implementation in the GNU C Library provides some simple means to detect such leaks and obtain some information to find the location. To do this the application must be started in a special mode which is enabled by an environment variable. There are no speed penalties for the program if the debugging mode is not enabled.

3.2.4.1 How to install the tracing functionality

void mtrace (*void*)   [Function]

> Preliminary: | MT-Unsafe env race:mtrace const:malloc_hooks init | AS-Unsafe init heap corrupt lock | AC-Unsafe init corrupt lock fd mem | See Section 1.2.2.1 [POSIX Safety Concepts], page 2.
>
> When the `mtrace` function is called it looks for an environment variable named `MALLOC_TRACE`. This variable is supposed to contain a valid file name. The user must have write access. If the file already exists it is truncated. If the environment variable is not set or it does not name a valid file which can be opened for writing nothing is done. The behavior of `malloc` etc. is not changed. For obvious reasons this also happens if the application is installed with the SUID or SGID bit set.
>
> If the named file is successfully opened, `mtrace` installs special handlers for the functions `malloc`, `realloc`, and `free` (see Section 3.2.3.9 [Memory Allocation Hooks], page 53). From then on, all uses of these functions are traced and protocolled into the file. There is now of course a speed penalty for all calls to the traced functions so tracing should not be enabled during normal use.
>
> This function is a GNU extension and generally not available on other systems. The prototype can be found in `mcheck.h`.

void muntrace (*void*)   [Function]

> Preliminary: | MT-Unsafe race:mtrace const:malloc_hooks locale | AS-Unsafe corrupt heap | AC-Unsafe corrupt mem lock fd | See Section 1.2.2.1 [POSIX Safety Concepts], page 2.
>
> The `muntrace` function can be called after `mtrace` was used to enable tracing the `malloc` calls. If no (successful) call of `mtrace` was made `muntrace` does nothing.
>
> Otherwise it deinstalls the handlers for `malloc`, `realloc`, and `free` and then closes the protocol file. No calls are protocolled anymore and the program runs again at full speed.
>
> This function is a GNU extension and generally not available on other systems. The prototype can be found in `mcheck.h`.

3.2.4.2 Example program excerpts

Even though the tracing functionality does not influence the runtime behavior of the program it is not a good idea to call `mtrace` in all programs. Just imagine that you debug a program using `mtrace` and all other programs used in the debugging session also trace their `malloc` calls. The output file would be the same for all programs and thus is unusable. Therefore one should call `mtrace` only if compiled for debugging. A program could therefore start like this:

```
#include <mcheck.h>
```

```
int
main (int argc, char *argv[])
{
#ifdef DEBUGGING
  mtrace ();
#endif
  ...
}
```

This is all that is needed if you want to trace the calls during the whole runtime of the program. Alternatively you can stop the tracing at any time with a call to `muntrace`. It is even possible to restart the tracing again with a new call to `mtrace`. But this can cause unreliable results since there may be calls of the functions which are not called. Please note that not only the application uses the traced functions, also libraries (including the C library itself) use these functions.

This last point is also why it is not a good idea to call `muntrace` before the program terminates. The libraries are informed about the termination of the program only after the program returns from `main` or calls `exit` and so cannot free the memory they use before this time.

So the best thing one can do is to call `mtrace` as the very first function in the program and never call `muntrace`. So the program traces almost all uses of the `malloc` functions (except those calls which are executed by constructors of the program or used libraries).

3.2.4.3 Some more or less clever ideas

You know the situation. The program is prepared for debugging and in all debugging sessions it runs well. But once it is started without debugging the error shows up. A typical example is a memory leak that becomes visible only when we turn off the debugging. If you foresee such situations you can still win. Simply use something equivalent to the following little program:

```
#include <mcheck.h>
#include <signal.h>

static void
enable (int sig)
{
  mtrace ();
  signal (SIGUSR1, enable);
}

static void
disable (int sig)
{
  muntrace ();
  signal (SIGUSR2, disable);
}
```

```
int
main (int argc, char *argv[])
{
  ...

  signal (SIGUSR1, enable);
  signal (SIGUSR2, disable);


  ...
}
```

I.e., the user can start the memory debugger any time s/he wants if the program was started with `MALLOC_TRACE` set in the environment. The output will of course not show the allocations which happened before the first signal but if there is a memory leak this will show up nevertheless.

3.2.4.4 Interpreting the traces

If you take a look at the output it will look similar to this:

```
= Start
[0x8048209] - 0x8064cc8
[0x8048209] - 0x8064ce0
[0x8048209] - 0x8064cf8
[0x80481eb] + 0x8064c48 0x14
[0x80481eb] + 0x8064c60 0x14
[0x80481eb] + 0x8064c78 0x14
[0x80481eb] + 0x8064c90 0x14
= End
```

What this all means is not really important since the trace file is not meant to be read by a human. Therefore no attention is given to readability. Instead there is a program which comes with the GNU C Library which interprets the traces and outputs a summary in an user-friendly way. The program is called `mtrace` (it is in fact a Perl script) and it takes one or two arguments. In any case the name of the file with the trace output must be specified. If an optional argument precedes the name of the trace file this must be the name of the program which generated the trace.

```
drepper$ mtrace tst-mtrace log
No memory leaks.
```

In this case the program `tst-mtrace` was run and it produced a trace file `log`. The message printed by `mtrace` shows there are no problems with the code, all allocated memory was freed afterwards.

If we call `mtrace` on the example trace given above we would get a different outout:

```
drepper$ mtrace errlog
- 0x08064cc8 Free 2 was never alloc'd 0x8048209
- 0x08064ce0 Free 3 was never alloc'd 0x8048209
- 0x08064cf8 Free 4 was never alloc'd 0x8048209

Memory not freed:
```

```
    -----------------
    Address     Size      Caller
    0x08064c48  0x14   at 0x80481eb
    0x08064c60  0x14   at 0x80481eb
    0x08064c78  0x14   at 0x80481eb
    0x08064c90  0x14   at 0x80481eb
```

We have called `mtrace` with only one argument and so the script has no chance to find out what is meant with the addresses given in the trace. We can do better:

```
drepper$ mtrace tst errlog
 - 0x08064cc8 Free 2 was never alloc'd /home/drepper/tst.c:39
 - 0x08064ce0 Free 3 was never alloc'd /home/drepper/tst.c:39
 - 0x08064cf8 Free 4 was never alloc'd /home/drepper/tst.c:39

Memory not freed:
-----------------
    Address     Size      Caller
    0x08064c48  0x14   at /home/drepper/tst.c:33
    0x08064c60  0x14   at /home/drepper/tst.c:33
    0x08064c78  0x14   at /home/drepper/tst.c:33
    0x08064c90  0x14   at /home/drepper/tst.c:33
```

Suddenly the output makes much more sense and the user can see immediately where the function calls causing the trouble can be found.

Interpreting this output is not complicated. There are at most two different situations being detected. First, `free` was called for pointers which were never returned by one of the allocation functions. This is usually a very bad problem and what this looks like is shown in the first three lines of the output. Situations like this are quite rare and if they appear they show up very drastically: the program normally crashes.

The other situation which is much harder to detect are memory leaks. As you can see in the output the `mtrace` function collects all this information and so can say that the program calls an allocation function from line 33 in the source file **/home/drepper/tst-mtrace.c** four times without freeing this memory before the program terminates. Whether this is a real problem remains to be investigated.

3.2.5 Replacing `malloc`

The GNU C Library supports replacing the built-in `malloc` implementation with a different allocator with the same interface. For dynamically linked programs, this happens through ELF symbol interposition, either using shared object dependencies or `LD_PRELOAD`. For static linking, the `malloc` replacement library must be linked in before linking against `libc.a` (explicitly or implicitly).

Note: Failure to provide a complete set of replacement functions (that is, all the functions used by the application, the GNU C Library, and other linked-in libraries) can lead to static linking failures, and, at run time, to heap corruption and application crashes.

The minimum set of functions which has to be provided by a custom `malloc` is given in the table below.

`malloc`

```
free
```

```
calloc
```

```
realloc
```

These `malloc`-related functions are required for the GNU C Library to work.[1]

The `malloc` implementation in the GNU C Library provides additional functionality not used by the library itself, but which is often used by other system libraries and applications. A general-purpose replacement `malloc` implementation should provide definitions of these functions, too. Their names are listed in the following table.

```
aligned_alloc
malloc_usable_size
memalign
```

```
posix_memalign
pvalloc
```

```
valloc
```

In addition, very old applications may use the obsolete `cfree` function.

Further `malloc`-related functions such as `mallopt` or `mallinfo` will not have any effect or return incorrect statistics when a replacement `malloc` is in use. However, failure to replace these functions typically does not result in crashes or other incorrect application behavior, but may result in static linking failures.

3.2.6 Obstacks

An *obstack* is a pool of memory containing a stack of objects. You can create any number of separate obstacks, and then allocate objects in specified obstacks. Within each obstack, the last object allocated must always be the first one freed, but distinct obstacks are independent of each other.

Aside from this one constraint of order of freeing, obstacks are totally general: an obstack can contain any number of objects of any size. They are implemented with macros, so allocation is usually very fast as long as the objects are usually small. And the only space overhead per object is the padding needed to start each object on a suitable boundary.

3.2.6.1 Creating Obstacks

The utilities for manipulating obstacks are declared in the header file `obstack.h`.

`struct obstack`   [Data Type]

An obstack is represented by a data structure of type `struct obstack`. This structure has a small fixed size; it records the status of the obstack and how to find the space in which objects are allocated. It does not contain any of the objects themselves. You should not try to access the contents of the structure directly; use only the functions described in this chapter.

---

[1] Versions of the GNU C Library before 2.25 required that a custom `malloc` defines `__libc_memalign` (with the same interface as the `memalign` function).

You can declare variables of type **struct obstack** and use them as obstacks, or you can allocate obstacks dynamically like any other kind of object. Dynamic allocation of obstacks allows your program to have a variable number of different stacks. (You can even allocate an obstack structure in another obstack, but this is rarely useful.)

All the functions that work with obstacks require you to specify which obstack to use. You do this with a pointer of type **struct obstack ***. In the following, we often say "an obstack" when strictly speaking the object at hand is such a pointer.

The objects in the obstack are packed into large blocks called *chunks*. The **struct obstack** structure points to a chain of the chunks currently in use.

The obstack library obtains a new chunk whenever you allocate an object that won't fit in the previous chunk. Since the obstack library manages chunks automatically, you don't need to pay much attention to them, but you do need to supply a function which the obstack library should use to get a chunk. Usually you supply a function which uses **malloc** directly or indirectly. You must also supply a function to free a chunk. These matters are described in the following section.

3.2.6.2 Preparing for Using Obstacks

Each source file in which you plan to use the obstack functions must include the header file **obstack.h**, like this:

```
#include <obstack.h>
```

Also, if the source file uses the macro **obstack_init**, it must declare or define two functions or macros that will be called by the obstack library. One, **obstack_chunk_alloc**, is used to allocate the chunks of memory into which objects are packed. The other, **obstack_chunk_free**, is used to return chunks when the objects in them are freed. These macros should appear before any use of obstacks in the source file.

Usually these are defined to use **malloc** via the intermediary **xmalloc** (see Section 3.2.3 [Unconstrained Allocation], page 44). This is done with the following pair of macro definitions:

```
#define obstack_chunk_alloc xmalloc
#define obstack_chunk_free free
```

Though the memory you get using obstacks really comes from **malloc**, using obstacks is faster because **malloc** is called less often, for larger blocks of memory. See Section 3.2.6.10 [Obstack Chunks], page 71, for full details.

At run time, before the program can use a **struct obstack** object as an obstack, it must initialize the obstack by calling **obstack_init**.

int obstack_init (*struct obstack *obstack-ptr*)   [Function]
>   Preliminary: | MT-Safe race:obstack-ptr | AS-Safe | AC-Safe mem | See Section 1.2.2.1 [POSIX Safety Concepts], page 2.
>
>   Initialize obstack *obstack-ptr* for allocation of objects. This function calls the obstack's **obstack_chunk_alloc** function. If allocation of memory fails, the function pointed to by **obstack_alloc_failed_handler** is called. The **obstack_init** function always returns 1 (Compatibility notice: Former versions of obstack returned 0 if allocation failed).

Here are two examples of how to allocate the space for an obstack and initialize it. First, an obstack that is a static variable:

```
static struct obstack myobstack;
...
obstack_init (&myobstack);
```

Second, an obstack that is itself dynamically allocated:

```
struct obstack *myobstack_ptr
  = (struct obstack *) xmalloc (sizeof (struct obstack));

obstack_init (myobstack_ptr);
```

`obstack_alloc_failed_handler`   [Variable]

> The value of this variable is a pointer to a function that `obstack` uses when `obstack_chunk_alloc` fails to allocate memory. The default action is to print a message and abort. You should supply a function that either calls `exit` (see Section 25.7 [Program Termination], page 768) or `longjmp` (see Chapter 23 [Non-Local Exits], page 676) and doesn't return.
>
> ```
> void my_obstack_alloc_failed (void)
> ...
> obstack_alloc_failed_handler = &my_obstack_alloc_failed;
> ```

3.2.6.3 Allocation in an Obstack

The most direct way to allocate an object in an obstack is with `obstack_alloc`, which is invoked almost like `malloc`.

`void * obstack_alloc (struct obstack *obstack-ptr, int size)`   [Function]

> Preliminary: | MT-Safe race:obstack-ptr | AS-Safe | AC-Unsafe corrupt mem | See Section 1.2.2.1 [POSIX Safety Concepts], page 2.
>
> This allocates an uninitialized block of *size* bytes in an obstack and returns its address. Here *obstack-ptr* specifies which obstack to allocate the block in; it is the address of the `struct obstack` object which represents the obstack. Each obstack function or macro requires you to specify an *obstack-ptr* as the first argument.
>
> This function calls the obstack's `obstack_chunk_alloc` function if it needs to allocate a new chunk of memory; it calls `obstack_alloc_failed_handler` if allocation of memory by `obstack_chunk_alloc` failed.

For example, here is a function that allocates a copy of a string *str* in a specific obstack, which is in the variable `string_obstack`:

```
struct obstack string_obstack;

char *
copystring (char *string)
{
  size_t len = strlen (string) + 1;
  char *s = (char *) obstack_alloc (&string_obstack, len);
  memcpy (s, string, len);
  return s;
}
```

To allocate a block with specified contents, use the function `obstack_copy`, declared like this:

void * obstack_copy (*struct obstack *obstack-ptr*, *void*   [Function]
        **address*, *int size*)

> Preliminary: | MT-Safe race:obstack-ptr | AS-Safe | AC-Unsafe corrupt mem | See Section 1.2.2.1 [POSIX Safety Concepts], page 2.

> This allocates a block and initializes it by copying *size* bytes of data starting at *address*. It calls `obstack_alloc_failed_handler` if allocation of memory by `obstack_chunk_alloc` failed.

void * obstack_copy0 (*struct obstack *obstack-ptr*, *void*   [Function]
        **address*, *int size*)

> Preliminary: | MT-Safe race:obstack-ptr | AS-Safe | AC-Unsafe corrupt mem | See Section 1.2.2.1 [POSIX Safety Concepts], page 2.

> Like `obstack_copy`, but appends an extra byte containing a null character. This extra byte is not counted in the argument *size*.

The `obstack_copy0` function is convenient for copying a sequence of characters into an obstack as a null-terminated string. Here is an example of its use:

```
char *
obstack_savestring (char *addr, int size)
{
  return obstack_copy0 (&myobstack, addr, size);
}
```

Contrast this with the previous example of `savestring` using `malloc` (see Section 3.2.3.1 [Basic Memory Allocation], page 44).

3.2.6.4 Freeing Objects in an Obstack

To free an object allocated in an obstack, use the function `obstack_free`. Since the obstack is a stack of objects, freeing one object automatically frees all other objects allocated more recently in the same obstack.

void obstack_free (*struct obstack *obstack-ptr*, *void *object*)   [Function]

> Preliminary: | MT-Safe race:obstack-ptr | AS-Safe | AC-Unsafe corrupt | See Section 1.2.2.1 [POSIX Safety Concepts], page 2.

> If *object* is a null pointer, everything allocated in the obstack is freed. Otherwise, *object* must be the address of an object allocated in the obstack. Then *object* is freed, along with everything allocated in *obstack-ptr* since *object*.

Note that if *object* is a null pointer, the result is an uninitialized obstack. To free all memory in an obstack but leave it valid for further allocation, call `obstack_free` with the address of the first object allocated on the obstack:

```
obstack_free (obstack_ptr, first_object_allocated_ptr);
```

Recall that the objects in an obstack are grouped into chunks. When all the objects in a chunk become free, the obstack library automatically frees the chunk (see Section 3.2.6.2 [Preparing for Using Obstacks], page 63). Then other obstacks, or non-obstack allocation, can reuse the space of the chunk.

3.2.6.5 Obstack Functions and Macros

The interfaces for using obstacks may be defined either as functions or as macros, depending on the compiler. The obstack facility works with all C compilers, including both ISO C and traditional C, but there are precautions you must take if you plan to use compilers other than GNU C.

If you are using an old-fashioned non-ISO C compiler, all the obstack "functions" are actually defined only as macros. You can call these macros like functions, but you cannot use them in any other way (for example, you cannot take their address).

Calling the macros requires a special precaution: namely, the first operand (the obstack pointer) may not contain any side effects, because it may be computed more than once. For example, if you write this:

```
obstack_alloc (get_obstack (), 4);
```

you will find that **get_obstack** may be called several times. If you use ***obstack_list_ptr++** as the obstack pointer argument, you will get very strange results since the incrementation may occur several times.

In ISO C, each function has both a macro definition and a function definition. The function definition is used if you take the address of the function without calling it. An ordinary call uses the macro definition by default, but you can request the function definition instead by writing the function name in parentheses, as shown here:

```
char *x;
void *(*funcp) ();
/* Use the macro.  */
x = (char *) obstack_alloc (obptr, size);
/* Call the function.  */
x = (char *) (obstack_alloc) (obptr, size);
/* Take the address of the function.  */
funcp = obstack_alloc;
```

This is the same situation that exists in ISO C for the standard library functions. See Section 1.3.2 [Macro Definitions of Functions], page 13.

Warning: When you do use the macros, you must observe the precaution of avoiding side effects in the first operand, even in ISO C.

If you use the GNU C compiler, this precaution is not necessary, because various language extensions in GNU C permit defining the macros so as to compute each argument only once.

3.2.6.6 Growing Objects

Because memory in obstack chunks is used sequentially, it is possible to build up an object step by step, adding one or more bytes at a time to the end of the object. With this technique, you do not need to know how much data you will put in the object until you come to the end of it. We call this the technique of *growing objects*. The special functions for adding data to the growing object are described in this section.

You don't need to do anything special when you start to grow an object. Using one of the functions to add data to the object automatically starts it. However, it is necessary to say explicitly when the object is finished. This is done with the function **obstack_finish**.

The actual address of the object thus built up is not known until the object is finished. Until then, it always remains possible that you will add so much data that the object must be copied into a new chunk.

While the obstack is in use for a growing object, you cannot use it for ordinary allocation of another object. If you try to do so, the space already added to the growing object will become part of the other object.

void obstack_blank (*struct obstack *obstack-ptr, int size*) [Function]
> Preliminary: | MT-Safe race:obstack-ptr | AS-Safe | AC-Unsafe corrupt mem | See Section 1.2.2.1 [POSIX Safety Concepts], page 2.
>
> The most basic function for adding to a growing object is `obstack_blank`, which adds space without initializing it.

void obstack_grow (*struct obstack *obstack-ptr, void *data, int size*) [Function]
> Preliminary: | MT-Safe race:obstack-ptr | AS-Safe | AC-Unsafe corrupt mem | See Section 1.2.2.1 [POSIX Safety Concepts], page 2.
>
> To add a block of initialized space, use `obstack_grow`, which is the growing-object analogue of `obstack_copy`. It adds *size* bytes of data to the growing object, copying the contents from *data*.

void obstack_grow0 (*struct obstack *obstack-ptr, void *data, int size*) [Function]
> Preliminary: | MT-Safe race:obstack-ptr | AS-Safe | AC-Unsafe corrupt mem | See Section 1.2.2.1 [POSIX Safety Concepts], page 2.
>
> This is the growing-object analogue of `obstack_copy0`. It adds *size* bytes copied from *data*, followed by an additional null character.

void obstack_1grow (*struct obstack *obstack-ptr, char c*) [Function]
> Preliminary: | MT-Safe race:obstack-ptr | AS-Safe | AC-Unsafe corrupt mem | See Section 1.2.2.1 [POSIX Safety Concepts], page 2.
>
> To add one character at a time, use the function `obstack_1grow`. It adds a single byte containing *c* to the growing object.

void obstack_ptr_grow (*struct obstack *obstack-ptr, void *data*) [Function]
> Preliminary: | MT-Safe race:obstack-ptr | AS-Safe | AC-Unsafe corrupt mem | See Section 1.2.2.1 [POSIX Safety Concepts], page 2.
>
> Adding the value of a pointer one can use the function `obstack_ptr_grow`. It adds `sizeof (void *)` bytes containing the value of *data*.

void obstack_int_grow (*struct obstack *obstack-ptr, int data*) [Function]
> Preliminary: | MT-Safe race:obstack-ptr | AS-Safe | AC-Unsafe corrupt mem | See Section 1.2.2.1 [POSIX Safety Concepts], page 2.
>
> A single value of type `int` can be added by using the `obstack_int_grow` function. It adds `sizeof (int)` bytes to the growing object and initializes them with the value of *data*.

void * obstack_finish (*struct obstack *obstack-ptr*) [Function]
> Preliminary: | MT-Safe race:obstack-ptr | AS-Safe | AC-Unsafe corrupt | See Section 1.2.2.1 [POSIX Safety Concepts], page 2.

When you are finished growing the object, use the function `obstack_finish` to close it off and return its final address.

Once you have finished the object, the obstack is available for ordinary allocation or for growing another object.

This function can return a null pointer under the same conditions as `obstack_alloc` (see Section 3.2.6.3 [Allocation in an Obstack], page 64).

When you build an object by growing it, you will probably need to know afterward how long it became. You need not keep track of this as you grow the object, because you can find out the length from the obstack just before finishing the object with the function `obstack_object_size`, declared as follows:

`int obstack_object_size (struct obstack *obstack-ptr)`   [Function]
> Preliminary: | MT-Safe race:obstack-ptr | AS-Safe | AC-Safe | See Section 1.2.2.1 [POSIX Safety Concepts], page 2.
>
> This function returns the current size of the growing object, in bytes. Remember to call this function *before* finishing the object. After it is finished, `obstack_object_size` will return zero.

If you have started growing an object and wish to cancel it, you should finish it and then free it, like this:

```
obstack_free (obstack_ptr, obstack_finish (obstack_ptr));
```

This has no effect if no object was growing.

You can use `obstack_blank` with a negative size argument to make the current object smaller. Just don't try to shrink it beyond zero length—there's no telling what will happen if you do that.

3.2.6.7 Extra Fast Growing Objects

The usual functions for growing objects incur overhead for checking whether there is room for the new growth in the current chunk. If you are frequently constructing objects in small steps of growth, this overhead can be significant.

You can reduce the overhead by using special "fast growth" functions that grow the object without checking. In order to have a robust program, you must do the checking yourself. If you do this checking in the simplest way each time you are about to add data to the object, you have not saved anything, because that is what the ordinary growth functions do. But if you can arrange to check less often, or check more efficiently, then you make the program faster.

The function `obstack_room` returns the amount of room available in the current chunk. It is declared as follows:

`int obstack_room (struct obstack *obstack-ptr)`   [Function]
> Preliminary: | MT-Safe race:obstack-ptr | AS-Safe | AC-Safe | See Section 1.2.2.1 [POSIX Safety Concepts], page 2.
>
> This returns the number of bytes that can be added safely to the current growing object (or to an object about to be started) in obstack *obstack-ptr* using the fast growth functions.

While you know there is room, you can use these fast growth functions for adding data to a growing object:

---

void **obstack_1grow_fast** (*struct obstack *obstack-ptr*, *char c*)   [Function]
    Preliminary: | MT-Safe race:obstack-ptr | AS-Safe | AC-Unsafe corrupt mem | See Section 1.2.2.1 [POSIX Safety Concepts], page 2.

    The function **obstack_1grow_fast** adds one byte containing the character *c* to the growing object in obstack *obstack-ptr*.

---

void **obstack_ptr_grow_fast** (*struct obstack *obstack-ptr*, *void*   [Function]
    *data)
    Preliminary: | MT-Safe race:obstack-ptr | AS-Safe | AC-Safe | See Section 1.2.2.1 [POSIX Safety Concepts], page 2.

    The function **obstack_ptr_grow_fast** adds **sizeof (void *)** bytes containing the value of *data* to the growing object in obstack *obstack-ptr*.

---

void **obstack_int_grow_fast** (*struct obstack *obstack-ptr*, *int*   [Function]
    data)
    Preliminary: | MT-Safe race:obstack-ptr | AS-Safe | AC-Safe | See Section 1.2.2.1 [POSIX Safety Concepts], page 2.

    The function **obstack_int_grow_fast** adds **sizeof (int)** bytes containing the value of *data* to the growing object in obstack *obstack-ptr*.

---

void **obstack_blank_fast** (*struct obstack *obstack-ptr*, *int size*)   [Function]
    Preliminary: | MT-Safe race:obstack-ptr | AS-Safe | AC-Safe | See Section 1.2.2.1 [POSIX Safety Concepts], page 2.

    The function **obstack_blank_fast** adds *size* bytes to the growing object in obstack *obstack-ptr* without initializing them.

When you check for space using **obstack_room** and there is not enough room for what you want to add, the fast growth functions are not safe. In this case, simply use the corresponding ordinary growth function instead. Very soon this will copy the object to a new chunk; then there will be lots of room available again.

So, each time you use an ordinary growth function, check afterward for sufficient space using **obstack_room**. Once the object is copied to a new chunk, there will be plenty of space again, so the program will start using the fast growth functions again.

Here is an example:

```
void
add_string (struct obstack *obstack, const char *ptr, int len)
{
  while (len > 0)
    {
      int room = obstack_room (obstack);
      if (room == 0)
        {
          /* Not enough room.  Add one character slowly,
             which may copy to a new chunk and make room.  */
          obstack_1grow (obstack, *ptr++);
          len--;
        }
      else
        {
          if (room > len)
            room = len;
          /* Add fast as much as we have room for. */
          len -= room;
          while (room-- > 0)
            obstack_1grow_fast (obstack, *ptr++);
        }
    }
}
```

3.2.6.8 Status of an Obstack

Here are functions that provide information on the current status of allocation in an obstack. You can use them to learn about an object while still growing it.

void * obstack_base (*struct obstack *obstack-ptr*) [Function]
> Preliminary: | MT-Safe | AS-Unsafe corrupt | AC-Safe | See Section 1.2.2.1 [POSIX Safety Concepts], page 2.
>
> This function returns the tentative address of the beginning of the currently growing object in *obstack-ptr*. If you finish the object immediately, it will have that address. If you make it larger first, it may outgrow the current chunk—then its address will change!
>
> If no object is growing, this value says where the next object you allocate will start (once again assuming it fits in the current chunk).

void * obstack_next_free (*struct obstack *obstack-ptr*) [Function]
> Preliminary: | MT-Safe | AS-Unsafe corrupt | AC-Safe | See Section 1.2.2.1 [POSIX Safety Concepts], page 2.
>
> This function returns the address of the first free byte in the current chunk of obstack *obstack-ptr*. This is the end of the currently growing object. If no object is growing, **obstack_next_free** returns the same value as **obstack_base**.

int obstack_object_size (*struct obstack *obstack-ptr*) [Function]
> Preliminary: | MT-Safe race:obstack-ptr | AS-Safe | AC-Safe | See Section 1.2.2.1 [POSIX Safety Concepts], page 2.
>
> This function returns the size in bytes of the currently growing object. This is equivalent to
>
> ```
> obstack_next_free (obstack-ptr) - obstack_base (obstack-ptr)
> ```

3.2.6.9 Alignment of Data in Obstacks

Each obstack has an *alignment boundary*; each object allocated in the obstack automatically starts on an address that is a multiple of the specified boundary. By default, this boundary is aligned so that the object can hold any type of data.

To access an obstack's alignment boundary, use the macro `obstack_alignment_mask`, whose function prototype looks like this:

int obstack_alignment_mask (*struct obstack *obstack-ptr*)   [Macro]
> Preliminary: | MT-Safe | AS-Safe | AC-Safe | See Section 1.2.2.1 [POSIX Safety Concepts], page 2.
>
> The value is a bit mask; a bit that is 1 indicates that the corresponding bit in the address of an object should be 0. The mask value should be one less than a power of 2; the effect is that all object addresses are multiples of that power of 2. The default value of the mask is a value that allows aligned objects to hold any type of data: for example, if its value is 3, any type of data can be stored at locations whose addresses are multiples of 4. A mask value of 0 means an object can start on any multiple of 1 (that is, no alignment is required).
>
> The expansion of the macro `obstack_alignment_mask` is an lvalue, so you can alter the mask by assignment. For example, this statement:
>
> ```
> obstack_alignment_mask (obstack_ptr) = 0;
> ```
>
> has the effect of turning off alignment processing in the specified obstack.

Note that a change in alignment mask does not take effect until *after* the next time an object is allocated or finished in the obstack. If you are not growing an object, you can make the new alignment mask take effect immediately by calling `obstack_finish`. This will finish a zero-length object and then do proper alignment for the next object.

3.2.6.10 Obstack Chunks

Obstacks work by allocating space for themselves in large chunks, and then parceling out space in the chunks to satisfy your requests. Chunks are normally 4096 bytes long unless you specify a different chunk size. The chunk size includes 8 bytes of overhead that are not actually used for storing objects. Regardless of the specified size, longer chunks will be allocated when necessary for long objects.

The obstack library allocates chunks by calling the function `obstack_chunk_alloc`, which you must define. When a chunk is no longer needed because you have freed all the objects in it, the obstack library frees the chunk by calling `obstack_chunk_free`, which you must also define.

These two must be defined (as macros) or declared (as functions) in each source file that uses `obstack_init` (see Section 3.2.6.1 [Creating Obstacks], page 62). Most often they are defined as macros like this:

```
#define obstack_chunk_alloc malloc
#define obstack_chunk_free free
```

Note that these are simple macros (no arguments). Macro definitions with arguments will not work! It is necessary that `obstack_chunk_alloc` or `obstack_chunk_free`, alone, expand into a function name if it is not itself a function name.

If you allocate chunks with `malloc`, the chunk size should be a power of 2. The default chunk size, 4096, was chosen because it is long enough to satisfy many typical requests on the obstack yet short enough not to waste too much memory in the portion of the last chunk not yet used.

`int obstack_chunk_size (struct obstack *obstack-ptr)`   [Macro]
> Preliminary: | MT-Safe | AS-Safe | AC-Safe | See Section 1.2.2.1 [POSIX Safety Concepts], page 2.
>
> This returns the chunk size of the given obstack.

Since this macro expands to an lvalue, you can specify a new chunk size by assigning it a new value. Doing so does not affect the chunks already allocated, but will change the size of chunks allocated for that particular obstack in the future. It is unlikely to be useful to make the chunk size smaller, but making it larger might improve efficiency if you are allocating many objects whose size is comparable to the chunk size. Here is how to do so cleanly:

```
if (obstack_chunk_size (obstack_ptr) < new-chunk-size)
  obstack_chunk_size (obstack_ptr) = new-chunk-size;
```

3.2.6.11 Summary of Obstack Functions

Here is a summary of all the functions associated with obstacks. Each takes the address of an obstack (`struct obstack *`) as its first argument.

`void obstack_init (struct obstack *obstack-ptr)`
> Initialize use of an obstack. See Section 3.2.6.1 [Creating Obstacks], page 62.

`void *obstack_alloc (struct obstack *obstack-ptr, int size)`
> Allocate an object of size uninitialized bytes. See Section 3.2.6.3 [Allocation in an Obstack], page 64.

`void *obstack_copy (struct obstack *obstack-ptr, void *address, int size)`
> Allocate an object of size bytes, with contents copied from address. See Section 3.2.6.3 [Allocation in an Obstack], page 64.

`void *obstack_copy0 (struct obstack *obstack-ptr, void *address, int size)`
> Allocate an object of size+1 bytes, with size of them copied from address, followed by a null character at the end. See Section 3.2.6.3 [Allocation in an Obstack], page 64.

`void obstack_free (struct obstack *obstack-ptr, void *object)`
> Free object (and everything allocated in the specified obstack more recently than object). See Section 3.2.6.4 [Freeing Objects in an Obstack], page 65.

`void obstack_blank (struct obstack *obstack-ptr, int size)`
> Add size uninitialized bytes to a growing object. See Section 3.2.6.6 [Growing Objects], page 66.

`void obstack_grow (struct obstack *obstack-ptr, void *address, int size)`
> Add size bytes, copied from address, to a growing object. See Section 3.2.6.6 [Growing Objects], page 66.

`void obstack_grow0 (struct obstack *obstack-ptr, void *address, int size)`

> Add *size* bytes, copied from *address*, to a growing object, and then add another byte containing a null character. See Section 3.2.6.6 [Growing Objects], page 66.

`void obstack_1grow (struct obstack *obstack-ptr, char data-char)`

> Add one byte containing *data-char* to a growing object. See Section 3.2.6.6 [Growing Objects], page 66.

`void *obstack_finish (struct obstack *obstack-ptr)`

> Finalize the object that is growing and return its permanent address. See Section 3.2.6.6 [Growing Objects], page 66.

`int obstack_object_size (struct obstack *obstack-ptr)`

> Get the current size of the currently growing object. See Section 3.2.6.6 [Growing Objects], page 66.

`void obstack_blank_fast (struct obstack *obstack-ptr, int size)`

> Add *size* uninitialized bytes to a growing object without checking that there is enough room. See Section 3.2.6.7 [Extra Fast Growing Objects], page 68.

`void obstack_1grow_fast (struct obstack *obstack-ptr, char data-char)`

> Add one byte containing *data-char* to a growing object without checking that there is enough room. See Section 3.2.6.7 [Extra Fast Growing Objects], page 68.

`int obstack_room (struct obstack *obstack-ptr)`

> Get the amount of room now available for growing the current object. See Section 3.2.6.7 [Extra Fast Growing Objects], page 68.

`int obstack_alignment_mask (struct obstack *obstack-ptr)`

> The mask used for aligning the beginning of an object. This is an lvalue. See Section 3.2.6.9 [Alignment of Data in Obstacks], page 71.

`int obstack_chunk_size (struct obstack *obstack-ptr)`

> The size for allocating chunks. This is an lvalue. See Section 3.2.6.10 [Obstack Chunks], page 71.

`void *obstack_base (struct obstack *obstack-ptr)`

> Tentative starting address of the currently growing object. See Section 3.2.6.8 [Status of an Obstack], page 70.

`void *obstack_next_free (struct obstack *obstack-ptr)`

> Address just after the end of the currently growing object. See Section 3.2.6.8 [Status of an Obstack], page 70.

3.2.7 Automatic Storage with Variable Size

The function `alloca` supports a kind of half-dynamic allocation in which blocks are allocated dynamically but freed automatically.

Allocating a block with `alloca` is an explicit action; you can allocate as many blocks as you wish, and compute the size at run time. But all the blocks are freed when you exit the function that `alloca` was called from, just as if they were automatic variables declared in that function. There is no way to free the space explicitly.

The prototype for `alloca` is in `stdlib.h`. This function is a BSD extension.

void * alloca (*size_t size*)   [Function]
> Preliminary: | MT-Safe | AS-Safe | AC-Safe | See Section 1.2.2.1 [POSIX Safety
> Concepts], page 2.
>
> The return value of `alloca` is the address of a block of *size* bytes of memory, allocated
> in the stack frame of the calling function.

Do not use `alloca` inside the arguments of a function call—you will get unpredictable results, because the stack space for the `alloca` would appear on the stack in the middle of the space for the function arguments. An example of what to avoid is `foo (x, alloca (4), y)`.

3.2.7.1 `alloca` Example

As an example of the use of `alloca`, here is a function that opens a file name made from concatenating two argument strings, and returns a file descriptor or minus one signifying failure:

```
int
open2 (char *str1, char *str2, int flags, int mode)
{
  char *name = (char *) alloca (strlen (str1) + strlen (str2) + 1);
  stpcpy (stpcpy (name, str1), str2);
  return open (name, flags, mode);
}
```

Here is how you would get the same results with `malloc` and `free`:

```
int
open2 (char *str1, char *str2, int flags, int mode)
{
  char *name = (char *) malloc (strlen (str1) + strlen (str2) + 1);
  int desc;
  if (name == 0)
    fatal ("virtual memory exceeded");
  stpcpy (stpcpy (name, str1), str2);
  desc = open (name, flags, mode);
  free (name);
  return desc;
}
```

As you can see, it is simpler with `alloca`. But `alloca` has other, more important advantages, and some disadvantages.

3.2.7.2 Advantages of `alloca`

Here are the reasons why `alloca` may be preferable to `malloc`:

- Using `alloca` wastes very little space and is very fast. (It is open-coded by the GNU C compiler.)

- Since `alloca` does not have separate pools for different sizes of blocks, space used for any size block can be reused for any other size. `alloca` does not cause memory fragmentation.

- Nonlocal exits done with `longjmp` (see Chapter 23 [Non-Local Exits], page 676) automatically free the space allocated with `alloca` when they exit through the function that called `alloca`. This is the most important reason to use `alloca`.

To illustrate this, suppose you have a function `open_or_report_error` which returns a descriptor, like `open`, if it succeeds, but does not return to its caller if it fails. If the file cannot be opened, it prints an error message and jumps out to the command level of your program using `longjmp`. Let's change `open2` (see Section 3.2.7.1 [`alloca` Example], page 74) to use this subroutine:

```
int
open2 (char *str1, char *str2, int flags, int mode)
{
  char *name = (char *) alloca (strlen (str1) + strlen (str2) + 1);
  stpcpy (stpcpy (name, str1), str2);
  return open_or_report_error (name, flags, mode);
}
```

Because of the way `alloca` works, the memory it allocates is freed even when an error occurs, with no special effort required.

By contrast, the previous definition of `open2` (which uses `malloc` and `free`) would develop a memory leak if it were changed in this way. Even if you are willing to make more changes to fix it, there is no easy way to do so.

3.2.7.3 Disadvantages of `alloca`

These are the disadvantages of `alloca` in comparison with `malloc`:

- If you try to allocate more memory than the machine can provide, you don't get a clean error message. Instead you get a fatal signal like the one you would get from an infinite recursion; probably a segmentation violation (see Section 24.2.1 [Program Error Signals], page 687).

- Some non-GNU systems fail to support `alloca`, so it is less portable. However, a slower emulation of `alloca` written in C is available for use on systems with this deficiency.

3.2.7.4 GNU C Variable-Size Arrays

In GNU C, you can replace most uses of `alloca` with an array of variable size. Here is how `open2` would look then:

```
int open2 (char *str1, char *str2, int flags, int mode)
{
  char name[strlen (str1) + strlen (str2) + 1];
  stpcpy (stpcpy (name, str1), str2);
  return open (name, flags, mode);
}
```

But `alloca` is not always equivalent to a variable-sized array, for several reasons:

- A variable size array's space is freed at the end of the scope of the name of the array. The space allocated with `alloca` remains until the end of the function.

- It is possible to use `alloca` within a loop, allocating an additional block on each iteration. This is impossible with variable-sized arrays.

NB: If you mix use of `alloca` and variable-sized arrays within one function, exiting a scope in which a variable-sized array was declared frees all blocks allocated with `alloca` during the execution of that scope.

3.3 Resizing the Data Segment

The symbols in this section are declared in `unistd.h`.

You will not normally use the functions in this section, because the functions described in Section 3.2 [Allocating Storage For Program Data], page 42, are easier to use. Those are interfaces to a GNU C Library memory allocator that uses the functions below itself. The functions below are simple interfaces to system calls.

int brk (*void *addr*)   [Function]

> Preliminary: | MT-Safe | AS-Safe | AC-Safe | See Section 1.2.2.1 [POSIX Safety Concepts], page 2.

> `brk` sets the high end of the calling process' data segment to *addr*.

> The address of the end of a segment is defined to be the address of the last byte in the segment plus 1.

> The function has no effect if *addr* is lower than the low end of the data segment. (This is considered success, by the way.)

> The function fails if it would cause the data segment to overlap another segment or exceed the process' data storage limit (see Section 22.2 [Limiting Resource Usage], page 656).

> The function is named for a common historical case where data storage and the stack are in the same segment. Data storage allocation grows upward from the bottom of the segment while the stack grows downward toward it from the top of the segment and the curtain between them is called the *break*.

> The return value is zero on success. On failure, the return value is `-1` and `errno` is set accordingly. The following `errno` values are specific to this function:

> ENOMEM   The request would cause the data segment to overlap another segment or exceed the process' data storage limit.

void *sbrk (*ptrdiff_t delta*)   [Function]

> Preliminary: | MT-Safe | AS-Safe | AC-Safe | See Section 1.2.2.1 [POSIX Safety Concepts], page 2.

> This function is the same as `brk` except that you specify the new end of the data segment as an offset *delta* from the current end and on success the return value is the address of the resulting end of the data segment instead of zero.

> This means you can use 'sbrk(0)' to find out what the current end of the data segment is.

3.4 Locking Pages

You can tell the system to associate a particular virtual memory page with a real page frame and keep it that way — i.e., cause the page to be paged in if it isn't already and mark it so it will never be paged out and consequently will never cause a page fault. This is called *locking* a page.

The functions in this chapter lock and unlock the calling process' pages.

3.4.1 Why Lock Pages

Because page faults cause paged out pages to be paged in transparently, a process rarely needs to be concerned about locking pages. However, there are two reasons people sometimes are:

- Speed. A page fault is transparent only insofar as the process is not sensitive to how long it takes to do a simple memory access. Time-critical processes, especially realtime processes, may not be able to wait or may not be able to tolerate variance in execution speed.

  A process that needs to lock pages for this reason probably also needs priority among other processes for use of the CPU. See Section 22.3 [Process CPU Priority And Scheduling], page 660.

  In some cases, the programmer knows better than the system's demand paging allocator which pages should remain in real memory to optimize system performance. In this case, locking pages can help.

- Privacy. If you keep secrets in virtual memory and that virtual memory gets paged out, that increases the chance that the secrets will get out. If a password gets written out to disk swap space, for example, it might still be there long after virtual and real memory have been wiped clean.

Be aware that when you lock a page, that's one fewer page frame that can be used to back other virtual memory (by the same or other processes), which can mean more page faults, which means the system runs more slowly. In fact, if you lock enough memory, some programs may not be able to run at all for lack of real memory.

3.4.2 Locked Memory Details

A memory lock is associated with a virtual page, not a real frame. The paging rule is: If a frame backs at least one locked page, don't page it out.

Memory locks do not stack. I.e., you can't lock a particular page twice so that it has to be unlocked twice before it is truly unlocked. It is either locked or it isn't.

A memory lock persists until the process that owns the memory explicitly unlocks it. (But process termination and exec cause the virtual memory to cease to exist, which you might say means it isn't locked any more).

Memory locks are not inherited by child processes. (But note that on a modern Unix system, immediately after a fork, the parent's and the child's virtual address space are backed by the same real page frames, so the child enjoys the parent's locks). See Section 26.4 [Creating a Process], page 775.

Because of its ability to impact other processes, only the superuser can lock a page. Any process can unlock its own page.

The system sets limits on the amount of memory a process can have locked and the amount of real memory it can have dedicated to it. See Section 22.2 [Limiting Resource Usage], page 656.

In Linux, locked pages aren't as locked as you might think. Two virtual pages that are not shared memory can nonetheless be backed by the same real frame. The kernel does this in the name of efficiency when it knows both virtual pages contain identical data, and does it even if one or both of the virtual pages are locked.

But when a process modifies one of those pages, the kernel must get it a separate frame and fill it with the page's data. This is known as a *copy-on-write page fault*. It takes a small amount of time and in a pathological case, getting that frame may require I/O.

To make sure this doesn't happen to your program, don't just lock the pages. Write to them as well, unless you know you won't write to them ever. And to make sure you have pre-allocated frames for your stack, enter a scope that declares a C automatic variable larger than the maximum stack size you will need, set it to something, then return from its scope.

3.4.3 Functions To Lock And Unlock Pages

The symbols in this section are declared in **sys/mman.h**. These functions are defined by POSIX.1b, but their availability depends on your kernel. If your kernel doesn't allow these functions, they exist but always fail. They *are* available with a Linux kernel.

Portability Note: POSIX.1b requires that when the **mlock** and **munlock** functions are available, the file **unistd.h** define the macro **_POSIX_MEMLOCK_RANGE** and the file **limits.h** define the macro **PAGESIZE** to be the size of a memory page in bytes. It requires that when the **mlockall** and **munlockall** functions are available, the **unistd.h** file define the macro **_POSIX_MEMLOCK**. The GNU C Library conforms to this requirement.

int mlock (*const void *addr*, *size_t* len) [Function]
> Preliminary: | MT-Safe | AS-Safe | AC-Safe | See Section 1.2.2.1 [POSIX Safety Concepts], page 2.
>
> **mlock** locks a range of the calling process' virtual pages.
>
> The range of memory starts at address *addr* and is *len* bytes long. Actually, since you must lock whole pages, it is the range of pages that include any part of the specified range.
>
> When the function returns successfully, each of those pages is backed by (connected to) a real frame (is resident) and is marked to stay that way. This means the function may cause page-ins and have to wait for them.
>
> When the function fails, it does not affect the lock status of any pages.
>
> The return value is zero if the function succeeds. Otherwise, it is **-1** and **errno** is set accordingly. **errno** values specific to this function are:
>
> ENOMEM
> > - At least some of the specified address range does not exist in the calling process' virtual address space.
> > - The locking would cause the process to exceed its locked page limit.
>
> EPERM   The calling process is not superuser.
>
> EINVAL   *len* is not positive.
>
> ENOSYS   The kernel does not provide **mlock** capability.
>
> You can lock *all* a process' memory with **mlockall**. You unlock memory with **munlock** or **munlockall**.
>
> To avoid all page faults in a C program, you have to use **mlockall**, because some of the memory a program uses is hidden from the C code, e.g. the stack and automatic variables, and you wouldn't know what address to tell **mlock**.

int munlock (*const void *addr, size_t len*)   [Function]
> Preliminary: | MT-Safe | AS-Safe | AC-Safe | See Section 1.2.2.1 [POSIX Safety Concepts], page 2.
>
> `munlock` unlocks a range of the calling process' virtual pages.
>
> `munlock` is the inverse of `mlock` and functions completely analogously to `mlock`, except that there is no `EPERM` failure.

int mlockall (*int flags*)   [Function]
> Preliminary: | MT-Safe | AS-Safe | AC-Safe | See Section 1.2.2.1 [POSIX Safety Concepts], page 2.
>
> `mlockall` locks all the pages in a process' virtual memory address space, and/or any that are added to it in the future. This includes the pages of the code, data and stack segment, as well as shared libraries, user space kernel data, shared memory, and memory mapped files.
>
> *flags* is a string of single bit flags represented by the following macros. They tell `mlockall` which of its functions you want. All other bits must be zero.
>
> `MCL_CURRENT`
>> Lock all pages which currently exist in the calling process' virtual address space.
>
> `MCL_FUTURE`
>> Set a mode such that any pages added to the process' virtual address space in the future will be locked from birth. This mode does not affect future address spaces owned by the same process so exec, which replaces a process' address space, wipes out `MCL_FUTURE`. See Section 26.5 [Executing a File], page 776.
>
> When the function returns successfully, and you specified `MCL_CURRENT`, all of the process' pages are backed by (connected to) real frames (they are resident) and are marked to stay that way. This means the function may cause page-ins and have to wait for them.
>
> When the process is in `MCL_FUTURE` mode because it successfully executed this function and specified `MCL_CURRENT`, any system call by the process that requires space be added to its virtual address space fails with `errno` = `ENOMEM` if locking the additional space would cause the process to exceed its locked page limit. In the case that the address space addition that can't be accommodated is stack expansion, the stack expansion fails and the kernel sends a `SIGSEGV` signal to the process.
>
> When the function fails, it does not affect the lock status of any pages or the future locking mode.
>
> The return value is zero if the function succeeds. Otherwise, it is `-1` and `errno` is set accordingly. `errno` values specific to this function are:
>
> `ENOMEM`
>> - At least some of the specified address range does not exist in the calling process' virtual address space.
>> - The locking would cause the process to exceed its locked page limit.

EPERM   The calling process is not superuser.

EINVAL   Undefined bits in *flags* are not zero.

ENOSYS   The kernel does not provide `mlockall` capability.

You can lock just specific pages with `mlock`. You unlock pages with `munlockall` and `munlock`.

`int munlockall (`*void*`)`   [Function]

Preliminary: | MT-Safe | AS-Safe | AC-Safe | See Section 1.2.2.1 [POSIX Safety Concepts], page 2.

`munlockall` unlocks every page in the calling process' virtual address space and turns off `MCL_FUTURE` future locking mode.

The return value is zero if the function succeeds. Otherwise, it is `-1` and `errno` is set accordingly. The only way this function can fail is for generic reasons that all functions and system calls can fail, so there are no specific `errno` values.

4 Character Handling

Programs that work with characters and strings often need to classify a character—is it alphabetic, is it a digit, is it whitespace, and so on—and perform case conversion operations on characters. The functions in the header file `ctype.h` are provided for this purpose.

Since the choice of locale and character set can alter the classifications of particular character codes, all of these functions are affected by the current locale. (More precisely, they are affected by the locale currently selected for character classification—the `LC_CTYPE` category; see Section 7.3 [Locale Categories], page 177.)

The ISO C standard specifies two different sets of functions. The one set works on `char` type characters, the other one on `wchar_t` wide characters (see Section 6.1 [Introduction to Extended Characters], page 134).

4.1 Classification of Characters

This section explains the library functions for classifying characters. For example, `isalpha` is the function to test for an alphabetic character. It takes one argument, the character to test, and returns a nonzero integer if the character is alphabetic, and zero otherwise. You would use it like this:

```
if (isalpha (c))
  printf ("The character `%c' is alphabetic.\n", c);
```

Each of the functions in this section tests for membership in a particular class of characters; each has a name starting with 'is'. Each of them takes one argument, which is a character to test, and returns an `int` which is treated as a boolean value. The character argument is passed as an `int`, and it may be the constant value `EOF` instead of a real character.

The attributes of any given character can vary between locales. See Chapter 7 [Locales and Internationalization], page 176, for more information on locales.

These functions are declared in the header file `ctype.h`.

`int islower` (*int c*)   [Function]
> Preliminary: | MT-Safe | AS-Safe | AC-Safe | See Section 1.2.2.1 [POSIX Safety Concepts], page 2.
>
> Returns true if *c* is a lower-case letter. The letter need not be from the Latin alphabet, any alphabet representable is valid.

`int isupper` (*int c*)   [Function]
> Preliminary: | MT-Safe | AS-Safe | AC-Safe | See Section 1.2.2.1 [POSIX Safety Concepts], page 2.
>
> Returns true if *c* is an upper-case letter. The letter need not be from the Latin alphabet, any alphabet representable is valid.

`int isalpha` (*int c*)   [Function]
> Preliminary: | MT-Safe | AS-Safe | AC-Safe | See Section 1.2.2.1 [POSIX Safety Concepts], page 2.
>
> Returns true if *c* is an alphabetic character (a letter). If `islower` or `isupper` is true of a character, then `isalpha` is also true.

In some locales, there may be additional characters for which `isalpha` is true—letters which are neither upper case nor lower case. But in the standard "C" locale, there are no such additional characters.

int isdigit (*int c*) [Function]
> Preliminary: | MT-Safe | AS-Safe | AC-Safe | See Section 1.2.2.1 [POSIX Safety Concepts], page 2.
>
> Returns true if *c* is a decimal digit ('0' through '9').

int isalnum (*int c*) [Function]
> Preliminary: | MT-Safe | AS-Safe | AC-Safe | See Section 1.2.2.1 [POSIX Safety Concepts], page 2.
>
> Returns true if *c* is an alphanumeric character (a letter or number); in other words, if either `isalpha` or `isdigit` is true of a character, then `isalnum` is also true.

int isxdigit (*int c*) [Function]
> Preliminary: | MT-Safe | AS-Safe | AC-Safe | See Section 1.2.2.1 [POSIX Safety Concepts], page 2.
>
> Returns true if *c* is a hexadecimal digit. Hexadecimal digits include the normal decimal digits '0' through '9' and the letters 'A' through 'F' and 'a' through 'f'.

int ispunct (*int c*) [Function]
> Preliminary: | MT-Safe | AS-Safe | AC-Safe | See Section 1.2.2.1 [POSIX Safety Concepts], page 2.
>
> Returns true if *c* is a punctuation character. This means any printing character that is not alphanumeric or a space character.

int isspace (*int c*) [Function]
> Preliminary: | MT-Safe | AS-Safe | AC-Safe | See Section 1.2.2.1 [POSIX Safety Concepts], page 2.
>
> Returns true if *c* is a *whitespace* character. In the standard "C" locale, `isspace` returns true for only the standard whitespace characters:
>
> | | |
> |---|---|
> | `' '` | space |
> | `'\f'` | formfeed |
> | `'\n'` | newline |
> | `'\r'` | carriage return |
> | `'\t'` | horizontal tab |
> | `'\v'` | vertical tab |

int isblank (*int c*) [Function]
> Preliminary: | MT-Safe | AS-Safe | AC-Safe | See Section 1.2.2.1 [POSIX Safety Concepts], page 2.
>
> Returns true if *c* is a blank character; that is, a space or a tab. This function was originally a GNU extension, but was added in ISO C99.

int isgraph (*int c*)   [Function]
> Preliminary: | MT-Safe | AS-Safe | AC-Safe | See Section 1.2.2.1 [POSIX Safety Concepts], page 2.
>
> Returns true if *c* is a graphic character; that is, a character that has a glyph associated with it. The whitespace characters are not considered graphic.

int isprint (*int c*)   [Function]
> Preliminary: | MT-Safe | AS-Safe | AC-Safe | See Section 1.2.2.1 [POSIX Safety Concepts], page 2.
>
> Returns true if *c* is a printing character. Printing characters include all the graphic characters, plus the space (' ') character.

int iscntrl (*int c*)   [Function]
> Preliminary: | MT-Safe | AS-Safe | AC-Safe | See Section 1.2.2.1 [POSIX Safety Concepts], page 2.
>
> Returns true if *c* is a control character (that is, a character that is not a printing character).

int isascii (*int c*)   [Function]
> Preliminary: | MT-Safe | AS-Safe | AC-Safe | See Section 1.2.2.1 [POSIX Safety Concepts], page 2.
>
> Returns true if *c* is a 7-bit `unsigned char` value that fits into the US/UK ASCII character set. This function is a BSD extension and is also an SVID extension.

4.2 Case Conversion

This section explains the library functions for performing conversions such as case mappings on characters. For example, `toupper` converts any character to upper case if possible. If the character can't be converted, `toupper` returns it unchanged.

These functions take one argument of type `int`, which is the character to convert, and return the converted character as an `int`. If the conversion is not applicable to the argument given, the argument is returned unchanged.

Compatibility Note: In pre-ISO C dialects, instead of returning the argument unchanged, these functions may fail when the argument is not suitable for the conversion. Thus for portability, you may need to write `islower(c) ? toupper(c) : c` rather than just `toupper(c)`.

These functions are declared in the header file `ctype.h`.

int tolower (*int c*)   [Function]
> Preliminary: | MT-Safe | AS-Safe | AC-Safe | See Section 1.2.2.1 [POSIX Safety Concepts], page 2.
>
> If *c* is an upper-case letter, `tolower` returns the corresponding lower-case letter. If *c* is not an upper-case letter, *c* is returned unchanged.

int toupper (*int c*)   [Function]
> Preliminary: | MT-Safe | AS-Safe | AC-Safe | See Section 1.2.2.1 [POSIX Safety Concepts], page 2.

If *c* is a lower-case letter, `toupper` returns the corresponding upper-case letter. Otherwise *c* is returned unchanged.

`int toascii (`*int c*`)` [Function]
> Preliminary: | MT-Safe | AS-Safe | AC-Safe | See Section 1.2.2.1 [POSIX Safety Concepts], page 2.
>
> This function converts *c* to a 7-bit `unsigned char` value that fits into the US/UK ASCII character set, by clearing the high-order bits. This function is a BSD extension and is also an SVID extension.

`int _tolower (`*int c*`)` [Function]
> Preliminary: | MT-Safe | AS-Safe | AC-Safe | See Section 1.2.2.1 [POSIX Safety Concepts], page 2.
>
> This is identical to `tolower`, and is provided for compatibility with the SVID. See Section 1.2.4 [SVID (The System V Interface Description)], page 11.

`int _toupper (`*int c*`)` [Function]
> Preliminary: | MT-Safe | AS-Safe | AC-Safe | See Section 1.2.2.1 [POSIX Safety Concepts], page 2.
>
> This is identical to `toupper`, and is provided for compatibility with the SVID.

4.3 Character class determination for wide characters

Amendment 1 to ISO C90 defines functions to classify wide characters. Although the original ISO C90 standard already defined the type `wchar_t`, no functions operating on them were defined.

The general design of the classification functions for wide characters is more general. It allows extensions to the set of available classifications, beyond those which are always available. The POSIX standard specifies how extensions can be made, and this is already implemented in the GNU C Library implementation of the `localedef` program.

The character class functions are normally implemented with bitsets, with a bitset per character. For a given character, the appropriate bitset is read from a table and a test is performed as to whether a certain bit is set. Which bit is tested for is determined by the class.

For the wide character classification functions this is made visible. There is a type classification type defined, a function to retrieve this value for a given class, and a function to test whether a given character is in this class, using the classification value. On top of this the normal character classification functions as used for `char` objects can be defined.

`wctype_t` [Data type]
> The `wctype_t` can hold a value which represents a character class. The only defined way to generate such a value is by using the `wctype` function.
>
> This type is defined in `wctype.h`.

`wctype_t wctype (`*const char *property*`)` [Function]
> Preliminary: | MT-Safe locale | AS-Safe | AC-Safe | See Section 1.2.2.1 [POSIX Safety Concepts], page 2.

wctype returns a value representing a class of wide characters which is identified by the string *property*. Besides some standard properties each locale can define its own ones. In case no property with the given name is known for the current locale selected for the LC_CTYPE category, the function returns zero.

The properties known in every locale are:

"alnum"	"alpha"	"cntrl"	"digit"
"graph"	"lower"	"print"	"punct"
"space"	"upper"	"xdigit"	

This function is declared in wctype.h.

To test the membership of a character to one of the non-standard classes the ISO C standard defines a completely new function.

int iswctype (*wint_t wc, wctype_t desc*) [Function]
> Preliminary: | MT-Safe | AS-Safe | AC-Safe | See Section 1.2.2.1 [POSIX Safety Concepts], page 2.
>
> This function returns a nonzero value if *wc* is in the character class specified by *desc*. *desc* must previously be returned by a successful call to wctype.
>
> This function is declared in wctype.h.

To make it easier to use the commonly-used classification functions, they are defined in the C library. There is no need to use wctype if the property string is one of the known character classes. In some situations it is desirable to construct the property strings, and then it is important that wctype can also handle the standard classes.

int iswalnum (*wint_t wc*) [Function]
> Preliminary: | MT-Safe locale | AS-Safe | AC-Safe | See Section 1.2.2.1 [POSIX Safety Concepts], page 2.
>
> This function returns a nonzero value if *wc* is an alphanumeric character (a letter or number); in other words, if either iswalpha or iswdigit is true of a character, then iswalnum is also true.
>
> This function can be implemented using
> ```
> iswctype (wc, wctype ("alnum"))
> ```
> It is declared in wctype.h.

int iswalpha (*wint_t wc*) [Function]
> Preliminary: | MT-Safe locale | AS-Safe | AC-Safe | See Section 1.2.2.1 [POSIX Safety Concepts], page 2.
>
> Returns true if *wc* is an alphabetic character (a letter). If iswlower or iswupper is true of a character, then iswalpha is also true.
>
> In some locales, there may be additional characters for which iswalpha is true— letters which are neither upper case nor lower case. But in the standard "C" locale, there are no such additional characters.
>
> This function can be implemented using
> ```
> iswctype (wc, wctype ("alpha"))
> ```
> It is declared in wctype.h.

int **iswcntrl** (*wint_t wc*) [Function]

Preliminary: | MT-Safe locale | AS-Safe | AC-Safe | See Section 1.2.2.1 [POSIX Safety Concepts], page 2.

Returns true if *wc* is a control character (that is, a character that is not a printing character).

This function can be implemented using

```
iswctype (wc, wctype ("cntrl"))
```

It is declared in `wctype.h`.

int **iswdigit** (*wint_t wc*) [Function]

Preliminary: | MT-Safe locale | AS-Safe | AC-Safe | See Section 1.2.2.1 [POSIX Safety Concepts], page 2.

Returns true if *wc* is a digit (e.g., '0' through '9'). Please note that this function does not only return a nonzero value for *decimal* digits, but for all kinds of digits. A consequence is that code like the following will **not** work unconditionally for wide characters:

```
n = 0;
while (iswdigit (*wc))
  {
    n *= 10;
    n += *wc++ - L'0';
  }
```

This function can be implemented using

```
iswctype (wc, wctype ("digit"))
```

It is declared in `wctype.h`.

int **iswgraph** (*wint_t wc*) [Function]

Preliminary: | MT-Safe locale | AS-Safe | AC-Safe | See Section 1.2.2.1 [POSIX Safety Concepts], page 2.

Returns true if *wc* is a graphic character; that is, a character that has a glyph associated with it. The whitespace characters are not considered graphic.

This function can be implemented using

```
iswctype (wc, wctype ("graph"))
```

It is declared in `wctype.h`.

int **iswlower** (*wint_t wc*) [Function]

Preliminary: | MT-Safe locale | AS-Safe | AC-Safe | See Section 1.2.2.1 [POSIX Safety Concepts], page 2.

Returns true if *wc* is a lower-case letter. The letter need not be from the Latin alphabet, any alphabet representable is valid.

This function can be implemented using

```
iswctype (wc, wctype ("lower"))
```

It is declared in `wctype.h`.

`int iswprint (`*wint_t wc*`)` [Function]

Preliminary: | MT-Safe locale | AS-Safe | AC-Safe | See Section 1.2.2.1 [POSIX Safety Concepts], page 2.

Returns true if *wc* is a printing character. Printing characters include all the graphic characters, plus the space (' ') character.

This function can be implemented using

```
iswctype (wc, wctype ("print"))
```

It is declared in `wctype.h`.

`int iswpunct (`*wint_t wc*`)` [Function]

Preliminary: | MT-Safe locale | AS-Safe | AC-Safe | See Section 1.2.2.1 [POSIX Safety Concepts], page 2.

Returns true if *wc* is a punctuation character. This means any printing character that is not alphanumeric or a space character.

This function can be implemented using

```
iswctype (wc, wctype ("punct"))
```

It is declared in `wctype.h`.

`int iswspace (`*wint_t wc*`)` [Function]

Preliminary: | MT-Safe locale | AS-Safe | AC-Safe | See Section 1.2.2.1 [POSIX Safety Concepts], page 2.

Returns true if *wc* is a *whitespace* character. In the standard `"C"` locale, `iswspace` returns true for only the standard whitespace characters:

`L' '` space

`L'\f'` formfeed

`L'\n'` newline

`L'\r'` carriage return

`L'\t'` horizontal tab

`L'\v'` vertical tab

This function can be implemented using

```
iswctype (wc, wctype ("space"))
```

It is declared in `wctype.h`.

`int iswupper (`*wint_t wc*`)` [Function]

Preliminary: | MT-Safe locale | AS-Safe | AC-Safe | See Section 1.2.2.1 [POSIX Safety Concepts], page 2.

Returns true if *wc* is an upper-case letter. The letter need not be from the Latin alphabet, any alphabet representable is valid.

This function can be implemented using

```
iswctype (wc, wctype ("upper"))
```

It is declared in `wctype.h`.

int iswxdigit (*wint_t wc*)   [Function]

> Preliminary: | MT-Safe locale | AS-Safe | AC-Safe | See Section 1.2.2.1 [POSIX Safety Concepts], page 2.
>
> Returns true if *wc* is a hexadecimal digit. Hexadecimal digits include the normal decimal digits '0' through '9' and the letters 'A' through 'F' and 'a' through 'f'.
>
> This function can be implemented using
>
> ```
> iswctype (wc, wctype ("xdigit"))
> ```
>
> It is declared in `wctype.h`.

The GNU C Library also provides a function which is not defined in the ISO C standard but which is available as a version for single byte characters as well.

int iswblank (*wint_t wc*)   [Function]

> Preliminary: | MT-Safe locale | AS-Safe | AC-Safe | See Section 1.2.2.1 [POSIX Safety Concepts], page 2.
>
> Returns true if *wc* is a blank character; that is, a space or a tab. This function was originally a GNU extension, but was added in ISO C99. It is declared in `wchar.h`.

4.4 Notes on using the wide character classes

The first note is probably not astonishing but still occasionally a cause of problems. The *iswXXX* functions can be implemented using macros and in fact, the GNU C Library does this. They are still available as real functions but when the `wctype.h` header is included the macros will be used. This is the same as the `char` type versions of these functions.

The second note covers something new. It can be best illustrated by a (real-world) example. The first piece of code is an excerpt from the original code. It is truncated a bit but the intention should be clear.

```
int
is_in_class (int c, const char *class)
{
  if (strcmp (class, "alnum") == 0)
    return isalnum (c);
  if (strcmp (class, "alpha") == 0)
    return isalpha (c);
  if (strcmp (class, "cntrl") == 0)
    return iscntrl (c);
  ...
  return 0;
}
```

Now, with the `wctype` and `iswctype` you can avoid the `if` cascades, but rewriting the code as follows is wrong:

```
int
is_in_class (int c, const char *class)
{
  wctype_t desc = wctype (class);
  return desc ? iswctype ((wint_t) c, desc) : 0;
}
```

The problem is that it is not guaranteed that the wide character representation of a single-byte character can be found using casting. In fact, usually this fails miserably. The correct solution to this problem is to write the code as follows:

```
int
```

```
is_in_class (int c, const char *class)
{
  wctype_t desc = wctype (class);
  return desc ? iswctype (btowc (c), desc) : 0;
}
```

See Section 6.3.3 [Converting Single Characters], page 140, for more information on btowc. Note that this change probably does not improve the performance of the program a lot since the wctype function still has to make the string comparisons. It gets really interesting if the is_in_class function is called more than once for the same class name. In this case the variable *desc* could be computed once and reused for all the calls. Therefore the above form of the function is probably not the final one.

4.5 Mapping of wide characters.

The classification functions are also generalized by the ISO C standard. Instead of just allowing the two standard mappings, a locale can contain others. Again, the localedef program already supports generating such locale data files.

wctrans_t   [Data Type]
> This data type is defined as a scalar type which can hold a value representing the locale-dependent character mapping. There is no way to construct such a value apart from using the return value of the wctrans function.
>
> This type is defined in wctype.h.

wctrans_t wctrans (*const char *property*)   [Function]
> Preliminary: | MT-Safe locale | AS-Safe | AC-Safe | See Section 1.2.2.1 [POSIX Safety Concepts], page 2.
>
> The wctrans function has to be used to find out whether a named mapping is defined in the current locale selected for the LC_CTYPE category. If the returned value is non-zero, you can use it afterwards in calls to towctrans. If the return value is zero no such mapping is known in the current locale.
>
> Beside locale-specific mappings there are two mappings which are guaranteed to be available in every locale:
>
> "tolower"   "toupper"
>
> These functions are declared in wctype.h.

wint_t towctrans (*wint_t wc, wctrans_t desc*)   [Function]
> Preliminary: | MT-Safe | AS-Safe | AC-Safe | See Section 1.2.2.1 [POSIX Safety Concepts], page 2.
>
> towctrans maps the input character *wc* according to the rules of the mapping for which *desc* is a descriptor, and returns the value it finds. *desc* must be obtained by a successful call to wctrans.
>
> This function is declared in wctype.h.

For the generally available mappings, the ISO C standard defines convenient shortcuts so that it is not necessary to call wctrans for them.

wint_t towlower (*wint_t wc*)   [Function]

> Preliminary: | MT-Safe locale | AS-Safe | AC-Safe | See Section 1.2.2.1 [POSIX Safety Concepts], page 2.
>
> If *wc* is an upper-case letter, `towlower` returns the corresponding lower-case letter. If *wc* is not an upper-case letter, *wc* is returned unchanged.
>
> `towlower` can be implemented using
>
> ```
> towctrans (wc, wctrans ("tolower"))
> ```
>
> This function is declared in `wctype.h`.

wint_t towupper (*wint_t wc*)   [Function]

> Preliminary: | MT-Safe locale | AS-Safe | AC-Safe | See Section 1.2.2.1 [POSIX Safety Concepts], page 2.
>
> If *wc* is a lower-case letter, `towupper` returns the corresponding upper-case letter. Otherwise *wc* is returned unchanged.
>
> `towupper` can be implemented using
>
> ```
> towctrans (wc, wctrans ("toupper"))
> ```
>
> This function is declared in `wctype.h`.

The same warnings given in the last section for the use of the wide character classification functions apply here. It is not possible to simply cast a `char` type value to a `wint_t` and use it as an argument to `towctrans` calls.

5 String and Array Utilities

Operations on strings (null-terminated byte sequences) are an important part of many programs. The GNU C Library provides an extensive set of string utility functions, including functions for copying, concatenating, comparing, and searching strings. Many of these functions can also operate on arbitrary regions of storage; for example, the `memcpy` function can be used to copy the contents of any kind of array.

It's fairly common for beginning C programmers to "reinvent the wheel" by duplicating this functionality in their own code, but it pays to become familiar with the library functions and to make use of them, since this offers benefits in maintenance, efficiency, and portability.

For instance, you could easily compare one string to another in two lines of C code, but if you use the built-in `strcmp` function, you're less likely to make a mistake. And, since these library functions are typically highly optimized, your program may run faster too.

5.1 Representation of Strings

This section is a quick summary of string concepts for beginning C programmers. It describes how strings are represented in C and some common pitfalls. If you are already familiar with this material, you can skip this section.

A *string* is a null-terminated array of bytes of type `char`, including the terminating null byte. String-valued variables are usually declared to be pointers of type `char *`. Such variables do not include space for the text of a string; that has to be stored somewhere else— in an array variable, a string constant, or dynamically allocated memory (see Section 3.2 [Allocating Storage For Program Data], page 42). It's up to you to store the address of the chosen memory space into the pointer variable. Alternatively you can store a *null pointer* in the pointer variable. The null pointer does not point anywhere, so attempting to reference the string it points to gets an error.

A *multibyte character* is a sequence of one or more bytes that represents a single character using the locale's encoding scheme; a null byte always represents the null character. A *multibyte string* is a string that consists entirely of multibyte characters. In contrast, a *wide string* is a null-terminated sequence of `wchar_t` objects. A wide-string variable is usually declared to be a pointer of type `wchar_t *`, by analogy with string variables and `char *`. See Section 6.1 [Introduction to Extended Characters], page 134.

By convention, the *null byte*, `'\0'`, marks the end of a string and the *null wide character*, `L'\0'`, marks the end of a wide string. For example, in testing to see whether the `char *` variable p points to a null byte marking the end of a string, you can write `!*p` or `*p == '\0'`.

A null byte is quite different conceptually from a null pointer, although both are represented by the integer constant `0`.

A *string literal* appears in C program source as a multibyte string between double-quote characters ('"'). If the initial double-quote character is immediately preceded by a capital 'L' (ell) character (as in `L"foo"`), it is a wide string literal. String literals can also contribute to *string concatenation*: `"a" "b"` is the same as `"ab"`. For wide strings one can use either `L"a"` `L"b"` or `L"a" "b"`. Modification of string literals is not allowed by the GNU C compiler, because literals are placed in read-only storage.

Arrays that are declared `const` cannot be modified either. It's generally good style to declare non-modifiable string pointers to be of type `const char *`, since this often allows the C compiler to detect accidental modifications as well as providing some amount of documentation about what your program intends to do with the string.

The amount of memory allocated for a byte array may extend past the null byte that marks the end of the string that the array contains. In this document, the term *allocated size* is always used to refer to the total amount of memory allocated for an array, while the term *length* refers to the number of bytes up to (but not including) the terminating null byte. Wide strings are similar, except their sizes and lengths count wide characters, not bytes.

A notorious source of program bugs is trying to put more bytes into a string than fit in its allocated size. When writing code that extends strings or moves bytes into a pre-allocated array, you should be very careful to keep track of the length of the text and make explicit checks for overflowing the array. Many of the library functions *do not* do this for you! Remember also that you need to allocate an extra byte to hold the null byte that marks the end of the string.

Originally strings were sequences of bytes where each byte represented a single character. This is still true today if the strings are encoded using a single-byte character encoding. Things are different if the strings are encoded using a multibyte encoding (for more information on encodings see Section 6.1 [Introduction to Extended Characters], page 134). There is no difference in the programming interface for these two kind of strings; the programmer has to be aware of this and interpret the byte sequences accordingly.

But since there is no separate interface taking care of these differences the byte-based string functions are sometimes hard to use. Since the count parameters of these functions specify bytes a call to `memcpy` could cut a multibyte character in the middle and put an incomplete (and therefore unusable) byte sequence in the target buffer.

To avoid these problems later versions of the ISO C standard introduce a second set of functions which are operating on *wide characters* (see Section 6.1 [Introduction to Extended Characters], page 134). These functions don't have the problems the single-byte versions have since every wide character is a legal, interpretable value. This does not mean that cutting wide strings at arbitrary points is without problems. It normally is for alphabet-based languages (except for non-normalized text) but languages based on syllables still have the problem that more than one wide character is necessary to complete a logical unit. This is a higher level problem which the C library functions are not designed to solve. But it is at least good that no invalid byte sequences can be created. Also, the higher level functions can also much more easily operate on wide characters than on multibyte characters so that a common strategy is to use wide characters internally whenever text is more than simply copied.

The remaining of this chapter will discuss the functions for handling wide strings in parallel with the discussion of strings since there is almost always an exact equivalent available.

5.2 String and Array Conventions

This chapter describes both functions that work on arbitrary arrays or blocks of memory, and functions that are specific to strings and wide strings.

Functions that operate on arbitrary blocks of memory have names beginning with 'mem' and 'wmem' (such as memcpy and wmemcpy) and invariably take an argument which specifies the size (in bytes and wide characters respectively) of the block of memory to operate on. The array arguments and return values for these functions have type void * or wchar_t. As a matter of style, the elements of the arrays used with the 'mem' functions are referred to as "bytes". You can pass any kind of pointer to these functions, and the sizeof operator is useful in computing the value for the size argument. Parameters to the 'wmem' functions must be of type wchar_t *. These functions are not really usable with anything but arrays of this type.

In contrast, functions that operate specifically on strings and wide strings have names beginning with 'str' and 'wcs' respectively (such as strcpy and wcscpy) and look for a terminating null byte or null wide character instead of requiring an explicit size argument to be passed. (Some of these functions accept a specified maximum length, but they also check for premature termination.) The array arguments and return values for these functions have type char * and wchar_t * respectively, and the array elements are referred to as "bytes" and "wide characters".

In many cases, there are both 'mem' and 'str'/'wcs' versions of a function. The one that is more appropriate to use depends on the exact situation. When your program is manipulating arbitrary arrays or blocks of storage, then you should always use the 'mem' functions. On the other hand, when you are manipulating strings it is usually more convenient to use the 'str'/'wcs' functions, unless you already know the length of the string in advance. The 'wmem' functions should be used for wide character arrays with known size.

Some of the memory and string functions take single characters as arguments. Since a value of type char is automatically promoted into a value of type int when used as a parameter, the functions are declared with int as the type of the parameter in question. In case of the wide character functions the situation is similar: the parameter type for a single wide character is wint_t and not wchar_t. This would for many implementations not be necessary since wchar_t is large enough to not be automatically promoted, but since the ISO C standard does not require such a choice of types the wint_t type is used.

5.3 String Length

You can get the length of a string using the strlen function. This function is declared in the header file string.h.

size_t strlen (*const char *s*)   [Function]

> Preliminary: | MT-Safe | AS-Safe | AC-Safe | See Section 1.2.2.1 [POSIX Safety Concepts], page 2.
>
> The strlen function returns the length of the string s in bytes. (In other words, it returns the offset of the terminating null byte within the array.)
>
> For example,
>
> ```
>     strlen ("hello, world")
>         ⇒ 12
> ```
>
> When applied to an array, the strlen function returns the length of the string stored there, not its allocated size. You can get the allocated size of the array that holds a string using the sizeof operator:
>
> ```
>     char string[32] = "hello, world";
> ```

```
sizeof (string)
    ⇒ 32
strlen (string)
    ⇒ 12
```

But beware, this will not work unless *string* is the array itself, not a pointer to it. For example:

```
char string[32] = "hello, world";
char *ptr = string;
sizeof (string)
    ⇒ 32
sizeof (ptr)
    ⇒ 4  /* (on a machine with 4 byte pointers) */
```

This is an easy mistake to make when you are working with functions that take string arguments; those arguments are always pointers, not arrays.

It must also be noted that for multibyte encoded strings the return value does not have to correspond to the number of characters in the string. To get this value the string can be converted to wide characters and `wcslen` can be used or something like the following code can be used:

```
/* The input is in string.
   The length is expected in n.  */
{
  mbstate_t t;
  char *scopy = string;
  /* In initial state.  */
  memset (&t, '\0', sizeof (t));
  /* Determine number of characters.  */
  n = mbsrtowcs (NULL, &scopy, strlen (scopy), &t);
}
```

This is cumbersome to do so if the number of characters (as opposed to bytes) is needed often it is better to work with wide characters.

The wide character equivalent is declared in `wchar.h`.

`size_t wcslen` (*const wchar_t *ws*)   [Function]
> Preliminary: | MT-Safe | AS-Safe | AC-Safe | See Section 1.2.2.1 [POSIX Safety Concepts], page 2.
>
> The `wcslen` function is the wide character equivalent to `strlen`. The return value is the number of wide characters in the wide string pointed to by *ws* (this is also the offset of the terminating null wide character of *ws*).
>
> Since there are no multi wide character sequences making up one wide character the return value is not only the offset in the array, it is also the number of wide characters.
>
> This function was introduced in Amendment 1 to ISO C90.

`size_t strnlen` (*const char *s, size_t maxlen*)   [Function]
> Preliminary: | MT-Safe | AS-Safe | AC-Safe | See Section 1.2.2.1 [POSIX Safety Concepts], page 2.
>
> If the array *s* of size *maxlen* contains a null byte, the `strnlen` function returns the length of the string *s* in bytes. Otherwise it returns *maxlen*. Therefore this function is equivalent to (`strlen (s)` < *maxlen* ? `strlen (s)` : *maxlen*) but it is more efficient

and works even if *s* is not null-terminated so long as *maxlen* does not exceed the size of *s*'s array.

```
char string[32] = "hello, world";
strnlen (string, 32)
    ⇒ 12
strnlen (string, 5)
    ⇒ 5
```

This function is a GNU extension and is declared in `string.h`.

size_t wcsnlen (*const wchar_t *ws, size_t* `maxlen`)   [Function]
> Preliminary: | MT-Safe | AS-Safe | AC-Safe | See Section 1.2.2.1 [POSIX Safety Concepts], page 2.
>
> `wcsnlen` is the wide character equivalent to `strnlen`. The *maxlen* parameter specifies the maximum number of wide characters.
>
> This function is a GNU extension and is declared in `wchar.h`.

5.4 Copying Strings and Arrays

You can use the functions described in this section to copy the contents of strings, wide strings, and arrays. The 'str' and 'mem' functions are declared in `string.h` while the 'w' functions are declared in `wchar.h`.

A helpful way to remember the ordering of the arguments to the functions in this section is that it corresponds to an assignment expression, with the destination array specified to the left of the source array. Most of these functions return the address of the destination array; a few return the address of the destination's terminating null, or of just past the destination.

Most of these functions do not work properly if the source and destination arrays overlap. For example, if the beginning of the destination array overlaps the end of the source array, the original contents of that part of the source array may get overwritten before it is copied. Even worse, in the case of the string functions, the null byte marking the end of the string may be lost, and the copy function might get stuck in a loop trashing all the memory allocated to your program.

All functions that have problems copying between overlapping arrays are explicitly identified in this manual. In addition to functions in this section, there are a few others like `sprintf` (see Section 12.12.7 [Formatted Output Functions], page 287) and `scanf` (see Section 12.14.8 [Formatted Input Functions], page 309).

void * memcpy (*void *restrict* `to`, *const void *restrict* `from`, *size_t*   [Function]
    `size`)
> Preliminary: | MT-Safe | AS-Safe | AC-Safe | See Section 1.2.2.1 [POSIX Safety Concepts], page 2.
>
> The `memcpy` function copies *size* bytes from the object beginning at *from* into the object beginning at *to*. The behavior of this function is undefined if the two arrays *to* and *from* overlap; use `memmove` instead if overlapping is possible.
>
> The value returned by `memcpy` is the value of *to*.
>
> Here is an example of how you might use `memcpy` to copy the contents of an array:
>
> ```
> struct foo *oldarray, *newarray;
> ```

```
int arraysize;
...
memcpy (new, old, arraysize * sizeof (struct foo));
```

wchar_t * wmemcpy (*wchar_t *restrict* `wto`, *const wchar_t *restrict*   [Function]
    `wfrom`, *size_t* `size`)

Preliminary: | MT-Safe | AS-Safe | AC-Safe | See Section 1.2.2.1 [POSIX Safety
Concepts], page 2.

The `wmemcpy` function copies *size* wide characters from the object beginning at *wfrom*
into the object beginning at *wto*. The behavior of this function is undefined if the
two arrays *wto* and *wfrom* overlap; use `wmemmove` instead if overlapping is possible.

The following is a possible implementation of `wmemcpy` but there are more optimizations possible.

```
wchar_t *
wmemcpy (wchar_t *restrict wto, const wchar_t *restrict wfrom,
        size_t size)
{
  return (wchar_t *) memcpy (wto, wfrom, size * sizeof (wchar_t));
}
```

The value returned by `wmemcpy` is the value of *wto*.

This function was introduced in Amendment 1 to ISO C90.

void * mempcpy (*void *restrict* `to`, *const void *restrict* `from`, *size_t*   [Function]
    `size`)

Preliminary: | MT-Safe | AS-Safe | AC-Safe | See Section 1.2.2.1 [POSIX Safety
Concepts], page 2.

The `mempcpy` function is nearly identical to the `memcpy` function. It copies *size* bytes
from the object beginning at *from* into the object pointed to by *to*. But instead of
returning the value of *to* it returns a pointer to the byte following the last written byte
in the object beginning at *to*. I.e., the value is ((void *) ((char *) `to` + `size`)).

This function is useful in situations where a number of objects shall be copied to
consecutive memory positions.

```
void *
combine (void *o1, size_t s1, void *o2, size_t s2)
{
  void *result = malloc (s1 + s2);
  if (result != NULL)
    mempcpy (mempcpy (result, o1, s1), o2, s2);
  return result;
}
```

This function is a GNU extension.

wchar_t * wmempcpy (*wchar_t *restrict* `wto`, *const wchar_t *restrict*   [Function]
    `wfrom`, *size_t* `size`)

Preliminary: | MT-Safe | AS-Safe | AC-Safe | See Section 1.2.2.1 [POSIX Safety
Concepts], page 2.

The `wmempcpy` function is nearly identical to the `wmemcpy` function. It copies *size*
wide characters from the object beginning at `wfrom` into the object pointed to by
wto. But instead of returning the value of *wto* it returns a pointer to the wide

character following the last written wide character in the object beginning at *wto*. I.e., the value is `wto + size`.

This function is useful in situations where a number of objects shall be copied to consecutive memory positions.

The following is a possible implementation of `wmemcpy` but there are more optimizations possible.

```
wchar_t *
wmempcpy (wchar_t *restrict wto, const wchar_t *restrict wfrom,
          size_t size)
{
  return (wchar_t *) mempcpy (wto, wfrom, size * sizeof (wchar_t));
}
```

This function is a GNU extension.

void * memmove (*void *to, const void *from, size_t size*)   [Function]
Preliminary: | MT-Safe | AS-Safe | AC-Safe | See Section 1.2.2.1 [POSIX Safety Concepts], page 2.

`memmove` copies the *size* bytes at *from* into the *size* bytes at *to*, even if those two blocks of space overlap. In the case of overlap, `memmove` is careful to copy the original values of the bytes in the block at *from*, including those bytes which also belong to the block at *to*.

The value returned by `memmove` is the value of *to*.

wchar_t * wmemmove (*wchar_t *wto, const wchar_t *wfrom, size_t*   [Function]
size)
Preliminary: | MT-Safe | AS-Safe | AC-Safe | See Section 1.2.2.1 [POSIX Safety Concepts], page 2.

`wmemmove` copies the *size* wide characters at *wfrom* into the *size* wide characters at *wto*, even if those two blocks of space overlap. In the case of overlap, `wmemmove` is careful to copy the original values of the wide characters in the block at *wfrom*, including those wide characters which also belong to the block at *wto*.

The following is a possible implementation of `wmemcpy` but there are more optimizations possible.

```
wchar_t *
wmempcpy (wchar_t *restrict wto, const wchar_t *restrict wfrom,
          size_t size)
{
  return (wchar_t *) mempcpy (wto, wfrom, size * sizeof (wchar_t));
}
```

The value returned by `wmemmove` is the value of *wto*.

This function is a GNU extension.

void * memccpy (*void *restrict to, const void *restrict from, int c,*   [Function]
size_t size)
Preliminary: | MT-Safe | AS-Safe | AC-Safe | See Section 1.2.2.1 [POSIX Safety Concepts], page 2.

This function copies no more than *size* bytes from *from* to *to*, stopping if a byte matching *c* is found. The return value is a pointer into *to* one byte past where *c* was copied, or a null pointer if no byte matching *c* appeared in the first *size* bytes of *from*.

void * memset (*void *block*, *int c*, *size_t size*) [Function]

Preliminary: | MT-Safe | AS-Safe | AC-Safe | See Section 1.2.2.1 [POSIX Safety Concepts], page 2.

This function copies the value of *c* (converted to an **unsigned char**) into each of the first *size* bytes of the object beginning at *block*. It returns the value of *block*.

wchar_t * wmemset (*wchar_t *block*, *wchar_t wc*, *size_t size*) [Function]

Preliminary: | MT-Safe | AS-Safe | AC-Safe | See Section 1.2.2.1 [POSIX Safety Concepts], page 2.

This function copies the value of *wc* into each of the first *size* wide characters of the object beginning at *block*. It returns the value of *block*.

char * strcpy (*char *restrict to*, *const char *restrict from*) [Function]

Preliminary: | MT-Safe | AS-Safe | AC-Safe | See Section 1.2.2.1 [POSIX Safety Concepts], page 2.

This copies bytes from the string *from* (up to and including the terminating null byte) into the string *to*. Like **memcpy**, this function has undefined results if the strings overlap. The return value is the value of *to*.

wchar_t * wcscpy (*wchar_t *restrict wto*, *const wchar_t *restrict wfrom*) [Function]

Preliminary: | MT-Safe | AS-Safe | AC-Safe | See Section 1.2.2.1 [POSIX Safety Concepts], page 2.

This copies wide characters from the wide string *wfrom* (up to and including the terminating null wide character) into the string *wto*. Like **wmemcpy**, this function has undefined results if the strings overlap. The return value is the value of *wto*.

char * strdup (*const char *s*) [Function]

Preliminary: | MT-Safe | AS-Unsafe heap | AC-Unsafe mem | See Section 1.2.2.1 [POSIX Safety Concepts], page 2.

This function copies the string *s* into a newly allocated string. The string is allocated using **malloc**; see Section 3.2.3 [Unconstrained Allocation], page 44. If **malloc** cannot allocate space for the new string, **strdup** returns a null pointer. Otherwise it returns a pointer to the new string.

wchar_t * wcsdup (*const wchar_t *ws*) [Function]

Preliminary: | MT-Safe | AS-Unsafe heap | AC-Unsafe mem | See Section 1.2.2.1 [POSIX Safety Concepts], page 2.

This function copies the wide string *ws* into a newly allocated string. The string is allocated using **malloc**; see Section 3.2.3 [Unconstrained Allocation], page 44. If **malloc** cannot allocate space for the new string, **wcsdup** returns a null pointer. Otherwise it returns a pointer to the new wide string.

This function is a GNU extension.

char * stpcpy (*char *restrict to*, *const char *restrict from*) [Function]

Preliminary: | MT-Safe | AS-Safe | AC-Safe | See Section 1.2.2.1 [POSIX Safety Concepts], page 2.

This function is like `strcpy`, except that it returns a pointer to the end of the string *to* (that is, the address of the terminating null byte `to + strlen (from)`) rather than the beginning.

For example, this program uses `stpcpy` to concatenate 'foo' and 'bar' to produce 'foobar', which it then prints.

```
#include <string.h>
#include <stdio.h>

int
main (void)
{
  char buffer[10];
  char *to = buffer;
  to = stpcpy (to, "foo");
  to = stpcpy (to, "bar");
  puts (buffer);
  return 0;
}
```

This function is part of POSIX.1-2008 and later editions, but was available in the GNU C Library and other systems as an extension long before it was standardized.

Its behavior is undefined if the strings overlap. The function is declared in `string.h`.

`wchar_t * wcpcpy` (*wchar_t *restrict* `wto`, *const wchar_t *restrict*   [Function]
    `wfrom`)
Preliminary: | MT-Safe | AS-Safe | AC-Safe | See Section 1.2.2.1 [POSIX Safety Concepts], page 2.

This function is like `wcscpy`, except that it returns a pointer to the end of the string *wto* (that is, the address of the terminating null wide character `wto + wcslen (wfrom)`) rather than the beginning.

This function is not part of ISO or POSIX but was found useful while developing the GNU C Library itself.

The behavior of `wcpcpy` is undefined if the strings overlap.

`wcpcpy` is a GNU extension and is declared in `wchar.h`.

`char * strdupa` (*const char *s*)   [Macro]
Preliminary: | MT-Safe | AS-Safe | AC-Safe | See Section 1.2.2.1 [POSIX Safety Concepts], page 2.

This macro is similar to `strdup` but allocates the new string using `alloca` instead of `malloc` (see Section 3.2.7 [Automatic Storage with Variable Size], page 73). This means of course the returned string has the same limitations as any block of memory allocated using `alloca`.

For obvious reasons `strdupa` is implemented only as a macro; you cannot get the address of this function. Despite this limitation it is a useful function. The following code shows a situation where using `malloc` would be a lot more expensive.

```
#include <paths.h>
#include <string.h>
#include <stdio.h>
```

```
const char path[] = _PATH_STDPATH;

int
main (void)
{
  char *wr_path = strdupa (path);
  char *cp = strtok (wr_path, ":");

  while (cp != NULL)
    {
      puts (cp);
      cp = strtok (NULL, ":");
    }
  return 0;
}
```

Please note that calling **strtok** using *path* directly is invalid. It is also not allowed to call **strdupa** in the argument list of **strtok** since **strdupa** uses **alloca** (see Section 3.2.7 [Automatic Storage with Variable Size], page 73) can interfere with the parameter passing.

This function is only available if GNU CC is used.

void **bcopy** (*const void *from, void *to, size_t size*)   [Function]
Preliminary: | MT-Safe | AS-Safe | AC-Safe | See Section 1.2.2.1 [POSIX Safety Concepts], page 2.

This is a partially obsolete alternative for **memmove**, derived from BSD. Note that it is not quite equivalent to **memmove**, because the arguments are not in the same order and there is no return value.

void **bzero** (*void *block, size_t size*)   [Function]
Preliminary: | MT-Safe | AS-Safe | AC-Safe | See Section 1.2.2.1 [POSIX Safety Concepts], page 2.

This is a partially obsolete alternative for **memset**, derived from BSD. Note that it is not as general as **memset**, because the only value it can store is zero.

5.5 Concatenating Strings

The functions described in this section concatenate the contents of a string or wide string to another. They follow the string-copying functions in their conventions. See Section 5.4 [Copying Strings and Arrays], page 95. 'strcat' is declared in the header file **string.h** while 'wcscat' is declared in **wchar.h**.

char * **strcat** (*char *restrict to, const char *restrict from*)   [Function]
Preliminary: | MT-Safe | AS-Safe | AC-Safe | See Section 1.2.2.1 [POSIX Safety Concepts], page 2.

The **strcat** function is similar to **strcpy**, except that the bytes from *from* are concatenated or appended to the end of *to*, instead of overwriting it. That is, the first byte from *from* overwrites the null byte marking the end of *to*.

An equivalent definition for **strcat** would be:

```
char *
```

```
strcat (char *restrict to, const char *restrict from)
{
  strcpy (to + strlen (to), from);
  return to;
}
```

This function has undefined results if the strings overlap.

As noted below, this function has significant performance issues.

wchar_t * wcscat (*wchar_t *restrict* **wto**, *const wchar_t *restrict*   [Function]
    wfrom)
Preliminary: | MT-Safe | AS-Safe | AC-Safe | See Section 1.2.2.1 [POSIX Safety
Concepts], page 2.

The wcscat function is similar to wcscpy, except that the wide characters from *wfrom*
are concatenated or appended to the end of *wto*, instead of overwriting it. That is,
the first wide character from *wfrom* overwrites the null wide character marking the
end of *wto*.

An equivalent definition for wcscat would be:

```
wchar_t *
wcscat (wchar_t *wto, const wchar_t *wfrom)
{
  wcscpy (wto + wcslen (wto), wfrom);
  return wto;
}
```

This function has undefined results if the strings overlap.

As noted below, this function has significant performance issues.

Programmers using the strcat or wcscat function (or the strncat or wcsncat functions
defined in a later section, for that matter) can easily be recognized as lazy and reckless.
In almost all situations the lengths of the participating strings are known (it better should
be since how can one otherwise ensure the allocated size of the buffer is sufficient?) Or at
least, one could know them if one keeps track of the results of the various function calls.
But then it is very inefficient to use strcat/wcscat. A lot of time is wasted finding the end
of the destination string so that the actual copying can start. This is a common example:

```
/* This function concatenates arbitrarily many strings.  The last
   parameter must be NULL.  */
char *
concat (const char *str, ...)
{
  va_list ap, ap2;
  size_t total = 1;
  const char *s;
  char *result;

  va_start (ap, str);
  va_copy (ap2, ap);

  /* Determine how much space we need.  */
  for (s = str; s != NULL; s = va_arg (ap, const char *))
    total += strlen (s);

  va_end (ap);
```

```
  result = (char *) malloc (total);
  if (result != NULL)
    {
      result[0] = '\0';

      /* Copy the strings.  */
      for (s = str; s != NULL; s = va_arg (ap2, const char *))
        strcat (result, s);
    }

  va_end (ap2);

  return result;
}
```

This looks quite simple, especially the second loop where the strings are actually copied. But these innocent lines hide a major performance penalty. Just imagine that ten strings of 100 bytes each have to be concatenated. For the second string we search the already stored 100 bytes for the end of the string so that we can append the next string. For all strings in total the comparisons necessary to find the end of the intermediate results sums up to 5500! If we combine the copying with the search for the allocation we can write this function more efficiently:

```
char *
concat (const char *str, ...)
{
  va_list ap;
  size_t allocated = 100;
  char *result = (char *) malloc (allocated);

  if (result != NULL)
    {
      char *newp;
      char *wp;
      const char *s;

      va_start (ap, str);

      wp = result;
      for (s = str; s != NULL; s = va_arg (ap, const char *))
        {
          size_t len = strlen (s);

          /* Resize the allocated memory if necessary.  */
          if (wp + len + 1 > result + allocated)
            {
              allocated = (allocated + len) * 2;
              newp = (char *) realloc (result, allocated);
              if (newp == NULL)
                {
                  free (result);
                  return NULL;
                }
              wp = newp + (wp - result);
              result = newp;
            }

          wp = mempcpy (wp, s, len);
```

```
      }

      /* Terminate the result string.  */
      *wp++ = '\0';

      /* Resize memory to the optimal size.  */
      newp = realloc (result, wp - result);
      if (newp != NULL)
        result = newp;

      va_end (ap);
    }

  return result;
}
```

With a bit more knowledge about the input strings one could fine-tune the memory allocation. The difference we are pointing to here is that we don't use `strcat` anymore. We always keep track of the length of the current intermediate result so we can save ourselves the search for the end of the string and use `mempcpy`. Please note that we also don't use `stpcpy` which might seem more natural since we are handling strings. But this is not necessary since we already know the length of the string and therefore can use the faster memory copying function. The example would work for wide characters the same way.

Whenever a programmer feels the need to use `strcat` she or he should think twice and look through the program to see whether the code cannot be rewritten to take advantage of already calculated results. Again: it is almost always unnecessary to use `strcat`.

5.6 Truncating Strings while Copying

The functions described in this section copy or concatenate the possibly-truncated contents of a string or array to another, and similarly for wide strings. They follow the string-copying functions in their header conventions. See Section 5.4 [Copying Strings and Arrays], page 95. The 'str' functions are declared in the header file `string.h` and the 'wc' functions are declared in the file `wchar.h`.

char * strncpy (char *restrict *to*, const char *restrict *from*, size_t [Function]
    size)

    Preliminary: | MT-Safe | AS-Safe | AC-Safe | See Section 1.2.2.1 [POSIX Safety Concepts], page 2.

    This function is similar to `strcpy` but always copies exactly *size* bytes into *to*.

    If *from* does not contain a null byte in its first *size* bytes, `strncpy` copies just the first *size* bytes. In this case no null terminator is written into *to*.

    Otherwise *from* must be a string with length less than *size*. In this case `strncpy` copies all of *from*, followed by enough null bytes to add up to *size* bytes in all.

    The behavior of `strncpy` is undefined if the strings overlap.

    This function was designed for now-rarely-used arrays consisting of non-null bytes followed by zero or more null bytes. It needs to set all *size* bytes of the destination, even when *size* is much greater than the length of *from*. As noted below, this function is generally a poor choice for processing text.

wchar_t * wcsncpy (*wchar_t *restrict wto, const wchar_t *restrict*   [Function]
> *wfrom, size_t size*)
> Preliminary: | MT-Safe | AS-Safe | AC-Safe | See Section 1.2.2.1 [POSIX Safety Concepts], page 2.
>
> This function is similar to wcscpy but always copies exactly *size* wide characters into *wto*.
>
> If *wfrom* does not contain a null wide character in its first *size* wide characters, then wcsncpy copies just the first *size* wide characters. In this case no null terminator is written into *wto*.
>
> Otherwise *wfrom* must be a wide string with length less than *size*. In this case wcsncpy copies all of *wfrom*, followed by enough null wide characters to add up to *size* wide characters in all.
>
> The behavior of wcsncpy is undefined if the strings overlap.
>
> This function is the wide-character counterpart of strncpy and suffers from most of the problems that strncpy does. For example, as noted below, this function is generally a poor choice for processing text.

char * strndup (*const char *s, size_t size*)   [Function]
> Preliminary: | MT-Safe | AS-Unsafe heap | AC-Unsafe mem | See Section 1.2.2.1 [POSIX Safety Concepts], page 2.
>
> This function is similar to strdup but always copies at most *size* bytes into the newly allocated string.
>
> If the length of *s* is more than *size*, then strndup copies just the first *size* bytes and adds a closing null byte. Otherwise all bytes are copied and the string is terminated.
>
> This function differs from strncpy in that it always terminates the destination string.
>
> As noted below, this function is generally a poor choice for processing text.
>
> strndup is a GNU extension.

char * strndupa (*const char *s, size_t size*)   [Macro]
> Preliminary: | MT-Safe | AS-Safe | AC-Safe | See Section 1.2.2.1 [POSIX Safety Concepts], page 2.
>
> This function is similar to strndup but like strdupa it allocates the new string using alloca see Section 3.2.7 [Automatic Storage with Variable Size], page 73. The same advantages and limitations of strdupa are valid for strndupa, too.
>
> This function is implemented only as a macro, just like strdupa. Just as strdupa this macro also must not be used inside the parameter list in a function call.
>
> As noted below, this function is generally a poor choice for processing text.
>
> strndupa is only available if GNU CC is used.

char * stpncpy (*char *restrict to, const char *restrict from, size_t*   [Function]
> *size*)
> Preliminary: | MT-Safe | AS-Safe | AC-Safe | See Section 1.2.2.1 [POSIX Safety Concepts], page 2.
>
> This function is similar to stpcpy but copies always exactly *size* bytes into *to*.

If the length of *from* is more than *size*, then `stpncpy` copies just the first *size* bytes and returns a pointer to the byte directly following the one which was copied last. Note that in this case there is no null terminator written into *to*.

If the length of *from* is less than *size*, then `stpncpy` copies all of *from*, followed by enough null bytes to add up to *size* bytes in all. This behavior is rarely useful, but it is implemented to be useful in contexts where this behavior of the `strncpy` is used. `stpncpy` returns a pointer to the *first* written null byte.

This function is not part of ISO or POSIX but was found useful while developing the GNU C Library itself.

Its behavior is undefined if the strings overlap. The function is declared in `string.h`.

As noted below, this function is generally a poor choice for processing text.

wchar_t * **wcpncpy** (*wchar_t *restrict* `wto`, *const wchar_t *restrict*   [Function]
    `wfrom`, *size_t* `size`)

Preliminary: | MT-Safe | AS-Safe | AC-Safe | See Section 1.2.2.1 [POSIX Safety Concepts], page 2.

This function is similar to `wcpcpy` but copies always exactly *wsize* wide characters into *wto*.

If the length of *wfrom* is more than *size*, then `wcpncpy` copies just the first *size* wide characters and returns a pointer to the wide character directly following the last non-null wide character which was copied last. Note that in this case there is no null terminator written into *wto*.

If the length of *wfrom* is less than *size*, then `wcpncpy` copies all of *wfrom*, followed by enough null wide characters to add up to *size* wide characters in all. This behavior is rarely useful, but it is implemented to be useful in contexts where this behavior of the `wcsncpy` is used. `wcpncpy` returns a pointer to the *first* written null wide character.

This function is not part of ISO or POSIX but was found useful while developing the GNU C Library itself.

Its behavior is undefined if the strings overlap.

As noted below, this function is generally a poor choice for processing text.

`wcpncpy` is a GNU extension.

char * **strncat** (*char *restrict* `to`, *const char *restrict* `from`, *size_t*   [Function]
    `size`)

Preliminary: | MT-Safe | AS-Safe | AC-Safe | See Section 1.2.2.1 [POSIX Safety Concepts], page 2.

This function is like `strcat` except that not more than *size* bytes from *from* are appended to the end of *to*, and *from* need not be null-terminated. A single null byte is also always appended to *to*, so the total allocated size of *to* must be at least `size` + 1 bytes longer than its initial length.

The `strncat` function could be implemented like this:

```
char *
strncat (char *to, const char *from, size_t size)
{
  size_t len = strlen (to);
  memcpy (to + len, from, strnlen (from, size));
  to[len + strnlen (from, size)] = '\0';
  return to;
}
```

The behavior of `strncat` is undefined if the strings overlap.

As a companion to `strncpy`, `strncat` was designed for now-rarely-used arrays consisting of non-null bytes followed by zero or more null bytes. As noted below, this function is generally a poor choice for processing text. Also, this function has significant performance issues. See Section 5.5 [Concatenating Strings], page 100.

wchar_t * wcsncat (*wchar_t *restrict wto, const wchar_t *restrict*   [Function]
    wfrom, size_t size)

Preliminary: | MT-Safe | AS-Safe | AC-Safe | See Section 1.2.2.1 [POSIX Safety Concepts], page 2.

This function is like `wcscat` except that not more than *size* wide characters from *from* are appended to the end of *to*, and *from* need not be null-terminated. A single null wide character is also always appended to *to*, so the total allocated size of *to* must be at least `wcsnlen (`*wfrom*`, `*size*`)` + 1 wide characters longer than its initial length.

The `wcsncat` function could be implemented like this:

```
wchar_t *
wcsncat (wchar_t *restrict wto, const wchar_t *restrict wfrom,
        size_t size)
{
  size_t len = wcslen (wto);
  memcpy (wto + len, wfrom, wcsnlen (wfrom, size) * sizeof (wchar_t));
  wto[len + wcsnlen (wfrom, size)] = L'\0';
  return wto;
}
```

The behavior of `wcsncat` is undefined if the strings overlap.

As noted below, this function is generally a poor choice for processing text. Also, this function has significant performance issues. See Section 5.5 [Concatenating Strings], page 100.

Because these functions can abruptly truncate strings or wide strings, they are generally poor choices for processing text. When coping or concatening multibyte strings, they can truncate within a multibyte character so that the result is not a valid multibyte string. When combining or concatenating multibyte or wide strings, they may truncate the output after a combining character, resulting in a corrupted grapheme. They can cause bugs even when processing single-byte strings: for example, when calculating an ASCII-only user name, a truncated name can identify the wrong user.

Although some buffer overruns can be prevented by manually replacing calls to copying functions with calls to truncation functions, there are often easier and safer automatic techniques that cause buffer overruns to reliably terminate a program, such as GCC's `-fcheck-pointer-bounds` and `-fsanitize=address` options. See Section "Options for Debugging Your Program or GCC" in *Using GCC*. Because truncation functions can mask application bugs that would otherwise be caught by the automatic techniques, these functions should be used only when the application's underlying logic requires truncation.

Note: GNU programs should not truncate strings or wide strings to fit arbitrary size limits. See Section "Writing Robust Programs" in *The GNU Coding Standards*. Instead of string-truncation functions, it is usually better to use dynamic memory allocation (see Section 3.2.3 [Unconstrained Allocation], page 44) and functions such as `strdup` or `asprintf` to construct strings.

5.7 String/Array Comparison

You can use the functions in this section to perform comparisons on the contents of strings and arrays. As well as checking for equality, these functions can also be used as the ordering functions for sorting operations. See Chapter 9 [Searching and Sorting], page 220, for an example of this.

Unlike most comparison operations in C, the string comparison functions return a nonzero value if the strings are *not* equivalent rather than if they are. The sign of the value indicates the relative ordering of the first part of the strings that are not equivalent: a negative value indicates that the first string is "less" than the second, while a positive value indicates that the first string is "greater".

The most common use of these functions is to check only for equality. This is canonically done with an expression like '`! strcmp (s1, s2)`'.

All of these functions are declared in the header file `string.h`.

`int memcmp (const void *a1, const void *a2, size_t size)` [Function]

> Preliminary: | MT-Safe | AS-Safe | AC-Safe | See Section 1.2.2.1 [POSIX Safety Concepts], page 2.
>
> The function `memcmp` compares the *size* bytes of memory beginning at *a1* against the *size* bytes of memory beginning at *a2*. The value returned has the same sign as the difference between the first differing pair of bytes (interpreted as `unsigned char` objects, then promoted to `int`).
>
> If the contents of the two blocks are equal, `memcmp` returns 0.

`int wmemcmp (const wchar_t *a1, const wchar_t *a2, size_t size)` [Function]

> Preliminary: | MT-Safe | AS-Safe | AC-Safe | See Section 1.2.2.1 [POSIX Safety Concepts], page 2.
>
> The function `wmemcmp` compares the *size* wide characters beginning at *a1* against the *size* wide characters beginning at *a2*. The value returned is smaller than or larger than zero depending on whether the first differing wide character is *a1* is smaller or larger than the corresponding wide character in *a2*.
>
> If the contents of the two blocks are equal, `wmemcmp` returns 0.

On arbitrary arrays, the `memcmp` function is mostly useful for testing equality. It usually isn't meaningful to do byte-wise ordering comparisons on arrays of things other than bytes. For example, a byte-wise comparison on the bytes that make up floating-point numbers isn't likely to tell you anything about the relationship between the values of the floating-point numbers.

wmemcmp is really only useful to compare arrays of type `wchar_t` since the function looks at `sizeof (wchar_t)` bytes at a time and this number of bytes is system dependent.

You should also be careful about using `memcmp` to compare objects that can contain "holes", such as the padding inserted into structure objects to enforce alignment requirements, extra space at the end of unions, and extra bytes at the ends of strings whose length is less than their allocated size. The contents of these "holes" are indeterminate and may cause strange behavior when performing byte-wise comparisons. For more predictable results, perform an explicit component-wise comparison.

For example, given a structure type definition like:

```
struct foo
  {
    unsigned char tag;
    union
      {
        double f;
        long i;
        char *p;
      } value;
  };
```

you are better off writing a specialized comparison function to compare `struct foo` objects instead of comparing them with `memcmp`.

---

int strcmp (*const char *s1, const char *s2*)   [Function]
Preliminary: | MT-Safe | AS-Safe | AC-Safe | See Section 1.2.2.1 [POSIX Safety Concepts], page 2.

The `strcmp` function compares the string *s1* against *s2*, returning a value that has the same sign as the difference between the first differing pair of bytes (interpreted as `unsigned char` objects, then promoted to `int`).

If the two strings are equal, `strcmp` returns 0.

A consequence of the ordering used by `strcmp` is that if *s1* is an initial substring of *s2*, then *s1* is considered to be "less than" *s2*.

`strcmp` does not take sorting conventions of the language the strings are written in into account. To get that one has to use `strcoll`.

---

int wcscmp (*const wchar_t *ws1, const wchar_t *ws2*)   [Function]
Preliminary: | MT-Safe | AS-Safe | AC-Safe | See Section 1.2.2.1 [POSIX Safety Concepts], page 2.

The `wcscmp` function compares the wide string *ws1* against *ws2*. The value returned is smaller than or larger than zero depending on whether the first differing wide character is *ws1* is smaller or larger than the corresponding wide character in *ws2*.

If the two strings are equal, `wcscmp` returns 0.

A consequence of the ordering used by `wcscmp` is that if *ws1* is an initial substring of *ws2*, then *ws1* is considered to be "less than" *ws2*.

`wcscmp` does not take sorting conventions of the language the strings are written in into account. To get that one has to use `wcscoll`.

`int strcasecmp` (*const char *s1, const char *s2*) [Function]
Preliminary: | MT-Safe locale | AS-Safe | AC-Safe | See Section 1.2.2.1 [POSIX Safety Concepts], page 2.

This function is like `strcmp`, except that differences in case are ignored, and its arguments must be multibyte strings. How uppercase and lowercase characters are related is determined by the currently selected locale. In the standard `"C"` locale the characters Ä and ä do not match but in a locale which regards these characters as parts of the alphabet they do match.

`strcasecmp` is derived from BSD.

`int wcscasecmp` (*const wchar_t *ws1, const wchar_t *ws2*) [Function]
Preliminary: | MT-Safe locale | AS-Safe | AC-Safe | See Section 1.2.2.1 [POSIX Safety Concepts], page 2.

This function is like `wcscmp`, except that differences in case are ignored. How uppercase and lowercase characters are related is determined by the currently selected locale. In the standard `"C"` locale the characters Ä and ä do not match but in a locale which regards these characters as parts of the alphabet they do match.

`wcscasecmp` is a GNU extension.

`int strncmp` (*const char *s1, const char *s2, size_t size*) [Function]
Preliminary: | MT-Safe | AS-Safe | AC-Safe | See Section 1.2.2.1 [POSIX Safety Concepts], page 2.

This function is the similar to `strcmp`, except that no more than *size* bytes are compared. In other words, if the two strings are the same in their first *size* bytes, the return value is zero.

`int wcsncmp` (*const wchar_t *ws1, const wchar_t *ws2, size_t size*) [Function]
Preliminary: | MT-Safe | AS-Safe | AC-Safe | See Section 1.2.2.1 [POSIX Safety Concepts], page 2.

This function is similar to `wcscmp`, except that no more than *size* wide characters are compared. In other words, if the two strings are the same in their first *size* wide characters, the return value is zero.

`int strncasecmp` (*const char *s1, const char *s2, size_t n*) [Function]
Preliminary: | MT-Safe locale | AS-Safe | AC-Safe | See Section 1.2.2.1 [POSIX Safety Concepts], page 2.

This function is like `strncmp`, except that differences in case are ignored, and the compared parts of the arguments should consist of valid multibyte characters. Like `strcasecmp`, it is locale dependent how uppercase and lowercase characters are related.

`strncasecmp` is a GNU extension.

`int wcsncasecmp` (*const wchar_t *ws1, const wchar_t *s2, size_t n*) [Function]
Preliminary: | MT-Safe locale | AS-Safe | AC-Safe | See Section 1.2.2.1 [POSIX Safety Concepts], page 2.

This function is like `wcsncmp`, except that differences in case are ignored. Like `wcscasecmp`, it is locale dependent how uppercase and lowercase characters are related.

`wcsncasecmp` is a GNU extension.

Here are some examples showing the use of **strcmp** and **strncmp** (equivalent examples can be constructed for the wide character functions). These examples assume the use of the ASCII character set. (If some other character set—say, EBCDIC—is used instead, then the glyphs are associated with different numeric codes, and the return values and ordering may differ.)

```
strcmp ("hello", "hello")
    ⇒ 0      /* These two strings are the same. */
strcmp ("hello", "Hello")
    ⇒ 32     /* Comparisons are case-sensitive. */
strcmp ("hello", "world")
    ⇒ -15    /* The byte 'h' comes before 'w'. */
strcmp ("hello", "hello, world")
    ⇒ -44    /* Comparing a null byte against a comma. */
strncmp ("hello", "hello, world", 5)
    ⇒ 0      /* The initial 5 bytes are the same. */
strncmp ("hello, world", "hello, stupid world!!!", 5)
    ⇒ 0      /* The initial 5 bytes are the same. */
```

`int strverscmp` (*const char *s1, const char *s2*)   [Function]
Preliminary: | MT-Safe locale | AS-Safe | AC-Safe | See Section 1.2.2.1 [POSIX Safety Concepts], page 2.

The `strverscmp` function compares the string *s1* against *s2*, considering them as holding indices/version numbers. The return value follows the same conventions as found in the `strcmp` function. In fact, if *s1* and *s2* contain no digits, `strverscmp` behaves like `strcmp` (in the sense that the sign of the result is the same).

The comparison algorithm which the `strverscmp` function implements differs slightly from other version-comparison algorithms. The implementation is based on a finite-state machine, whose behavior is approximated below.

- The input strings are each split into sequences of non-digits and digits. These sequences can be empty at the beginning and end of the string. Digits are determined by the `isdigit` function and are thus subject to the current locale.

- Comparison starts with a (possibly empty) non-digit sequence. The first non-equal sequences of non-digits or digits determines the outcome of the comparison.

- Corresponding non-digit sequences in both strings are compared lexicographically if their lengths are equal. If the lengths differ, the shorter non-digit sequence is extended with the input string character immediately following it (which may be the null terminator), the other sequence is truncated to be of the same (extended) length, and these two sequences are compared lexicographically. In the last case, the sequence comparison determines the result of the function because the extension character (or some character before it) is necessarily different from the character at the same offset in the other input string.

- For two sequences of digits, the number of leading zeros is counted (which can be zero). If the count differs, the string with more leading zeros in the digit sequence is considered smaller than the other string.

- If the two sequences of digits have no leading zeros, they are compared as integers, that is, the string with the longer digit sequence is deemed larger, and if both sequences are of equal length, they are compared lexicographically.

- If both digit sequences start with a zero and have an equal number of leading zeros, they are compared lexicographically if their lengths are the same. If the lengths differ, the shorter sequence is extended with the following character in its input string, and the other sequence is truncated to the same length, and both sequences are compared lexicographically (similar to the non-digit sequence case above).

The treatment of leading zeros and the tie-breaking extension characters (which in effect propagate across non-digit/digit sequence boundaries) differs from other version-comparison algorithms.

```
strverscmp ("no digit", "no digit")
    ⇒ 0     /* same behavior as strcmp. */
strverscmp ("item#99", "item#100")
    ⇒ <0     /* same prefix, but 99 < 100. */
strverscmp ("alpha1", "alpha001")
    ⇒ >0     /* different number of leading zeros (0 and 2). */
strverscmp ("part1_f012", "part1_f01")
    ⇒ >0     /* lexicographical comparison with leading zeros. */
strverscmp ("foo.009", "foo.0")
    ⇒ <0     /* different number of leading zeros (2 and 1). */
```

strverscmp is a GNU extension.

int bcmp (*const void *a1, const void *a2, size_t size*)   [Function]
Preliminary: | MT-Safe | AS-Safe | AC-Safe | See Section 1.2.2.1 [POSIX Safety Concepts], page 2.

This is an obsolete alias for memcmp, derived from BSD.

5.8 Collation Functions

In some locales, the conventions for lexicographic ordering differ from the strict numeric ordering of character codes. For example, in Spanish most glyphs with diacritical marks such as accents are not considered distinct letters for the purposes of collation. On the other hand, the two-character sequence 'll' is treated as a single letter that is collated immediately after 'l'.

You can use the functions strcoll and strxfrm (declared in the headers file string.h) and wcscoll and wcsxfrm (declared in the headers file wchar) to compare strings using a collation ordering appropriate for the current locale. The locale used by these functions in particular can be specified by setting the locale for the LC_COLLATE category; see Chapter 7 [Locales and Internationalization], page 176.

In the standard C locale, the collation sequence for strcoll is the same as that for strcmp. Similarly, wcscoll and wcscmp are the same in this situation.

Effectively, the way these functions work is by applying a mapping to transform the characters in a multibyte string to a byte sequence that represents the string's position in the collating sequence of the current locale. Comparing two such byte sequences in a simple fashion is equivalent to comparing the strings with the locale's collating sequence.

The functions `strcoll` and `wcscoll` perform this translation implicitly, in order to do one comparison. By contrast, `strxfrm` and `wcsxfrm` perform the mapping explicitly. If you are making multiple comparisons using the same string or set of strings, it is likely to be more efficient to use `strxfrm` or `wcsxfrm` to transform all the strings just once, and subsequently compare the transformed strings with `strcmp` or `wcscmp`.

int strcoll (*const char *s1, const char *s2*)   [Function]
  Preliminary: | MT-Safe locale | AS-Unsafe heap | AC-Unsafe mem | See Section 1.2.2.1 [POSIX Safety Concepts], page 2.

  The `strcoll` function is similar to `strcmp` but uses the collating sequence of the current locale for collation (the `LC_COLLATE` locale). The arguments are multibyte strings.

int wcscoll (*const wchar_t *ws1, const wchar_t *ws2*)   [Function]
  Preliminary: | MT-Safe locale | AS-Unsafe heap | AC-Unsafe mem | See Section 1.2.2.1 [POSIX Safety Concepts], page 2.

  The `wcscoll` function is similar to `wcscmp` but uses the collating sequence of the current locale for collation (the `LC_COLLATE` locale).

Here is an example of sorting an array of strings, using `strcoll` to compare them. The actual sort algorithm is not written here; it comes from `qsort` (see Section 9.3 [Array Sort Function], page 221). The job of the code shown here is to say how to compare the strings while sorting them. (Later on in this section, we will show a way to do this more efficiently using `strxfrm`.)

```
/* This is the comparison function used with qsort. */

int
compare_elements (const void *v1, const void *v2)
{
  char * const *p1 = v1;
  char * const *p2 = v2;

  return strcoll (*p1, *p2);
}

/* This is the entry point—the function to sort
   strings using the localefls collating sequence. */

void
sort_strings (char **array, int nstrings)
{
  /* Sort temp_array by comparing the strings. */
  qsort (array, nstrings,
         sizeof (char *), compare_elements);
}
```

size_t strxfrm (*char *restrict to, const char *restrict from, size_t* [Function]
    size)
  Preliminary: | MT-Safe locale | AS-Unsafe heap | AC-Unsafe mem | See Section 1.2.2.1 [POSIX Safety Concepts], page 2.

  The function `strxfrm` transforms the multibyte string *from* using the collation transformation determined by the locale currently selected for collation, and stores the transformed string in the array *to*. Up to *size* bytes (including a terminating null byte) are stored.

The behavior is undefined if the strings *to* and *from* overlap; see Section 5.4 [Copying Strings and Arrays], page 95.

The return value is the length of the entire transformed string. This value is not affected by the value of *size*, but if it is greater or equal than *size*, it means that the transformed string did not entirely fit in the array *to*. In this case, only as much of the string as actually fits was stored. To get the whole transformed string, call `strxfrm` again with a bigger output array.

The transformed string may be longer than the original string, and it may also be shorter.

If *size* is zero, no bytes are stored in *to*. In this case, `strxfrm` simply returns the number of bytes that would be the length of the transformed string. This is useful for determining what size the allocated array should be. It does not matter what *to* is if *size* is zero; *to* may even be a null pointer.

`size_t wcsxfrm` (*wchar_t* *restrict *wto*, *const wchar_t* *wfrom, *size_t*   [Function] *size*)

Preliminary: | MT-Safe locale | AS-Unsafe heap | AC-Unsafe mem | See Section 1.2.2.1 [POSIX Safety Concepts], page 2.

The function `wcsxfrm` transforms wide string *wfrom* using the collation transformation determined by the locale currently selected for collation, and stores the transformed string in the array *wto*. Up to *size* wide characters (including a terminating null wide character) are stored.

The behavior is undefined if the strings *wto* and *wfrom* overlap; see Section 5.4 [Copying Strings and Arrays], page 95.

The return value is the length of the entire transformed wide string. This value is not affected by the value of *size*, but if it is greater or equal than *size*, it means that the transformed wide string did not entirely fit in the array *wto*. In this case, only as much of the wide string as actually fits was stored. To get the whole transformed wide string, call `wcsxfrm` again with a bigger output array.

The transformed wide string may be longer than the original wide string, and it may also be shorter.

If *size* is zero, no wide characters are stored in *to*. In this case, `wcsxfrm` simply returns the number of wide characters that would be the length of the transformed wide string. This is useful for determining what size the allocated array should be (remember to multiply with `sizeof (wchar_t)`). It does not matter what *wto* is if *size* is zero; *wto* may even be a null pointer.

Here is an example of how you can use `strxfrm` when you plan to do many comparisons. It does the same thing as the previous example, but much faster, because it has to transform each string only once, no matter how many times it is compared with other strings. Even the time needed to allocate and free storage is much less than the time we save, when there are many strings.

```
struct sorter { char *input; char *transformed; };
```

```
/* This is the comparison function used with qsort
   to sort an array of struct sorter. */

int
compare_elements (const void *v1, const void *v2)
{
  const struct sorter *p1 = v1;
  const struct sorter *p2 = v2;

  return strcmp (p1->transformed, p2->transformed);
}


/* This is the entry point—the function to sort
   strings using the localefls collating sequence. */

void
sort_strings_fast (char **array, int nstrings)
{
  struct sorter temp_array[nstrings];
  int i;

  /* Set up temp_array. Each element contains
     one input string and its transformed string. */
  for (i = 0; i < nstrings; i++)
    {
      size_t length = strlen (array[i]) * 2;
      char *transformed;
      size_t transformed_length;

      temp_array[i].input = array[i];

      /* First try a buffer perhaps big enough.  */
      transformed = (char *) xmalloc (length);

      /* Transform array[i].  */
      transformed_length = strxfrm (transformed, array[i], length);

      /* If the buffer was not large enough, resize it
         and try again.  */
      if (transformed_length >= length)
        {
          /* Allocate the needed space. +1 for terminating
             '\0' byte.  */
          transformed = (char *) xrealloc (transformed,
                                           transformed_length + 1);

          /* The return value is not interesting because we know
             how long the transformed string is.  */
          (void) strxfrm (transformed, array[i],
                          transformed_length + 1);
        }

      temp_array[i].transformed = transformed;
    }

  /* Sort temp_array by comparing transformed strings. */
  qsort (temp_array, nstrings,
         sizeof (struct sorter), compare_elements);
```

```
    /* Put the elements back in the permanent array
       in their sorted order. */
    for (i = 0; i < nstrings; i++)
      array[i] = temp_array[i].input;

    /* Free the strings we allocated. */
    for (i = 0; i < nstrings; i++)
      free (temp_array[i].transformed);
  }
```

The interesting part of this code for the wide character version would look like this:

```
void
sort_strings_fast (wchar_t **array, int nstrings)
{
  ...
    /* Transform array[i]. */
    transformed_length = wcsxfrm (transformed, array[i], length);

    /* If the buffer was not large enough, resize it
       and try again.  */
    if (transformed_length >= length)
      {
        /* Allocate the needed space. +1 for terminating
           L'\0' wide character.  */
        transformed = (wchar_t *) xrealloc (transformed,
                                            (transformed_length + 1)
                                            * sizeof (wchar_t));

        /* The return value is not interesting because we know
           how long the transformed string is.  */
        (void) wcsxfrm (transformed, array[i],
                    transformed_length + 1);
      }
  ...
}
```

Note the additional multiplication with `sizeof (wchar_t)` in the `realloc` call.

Compatibility Note: The string collation functions are a new feature of ISO C90. Older C dialects have no equivalent feature. The wide character versions were introduced in Amendment 1 to ISO C90.

5.9 Search Functions

This section describes library functions which perform various kinds of searching operations on strings and arrays. These functions are declared in the header file `string.h`.

void * memchr (*const void *block, int c, size_t size*)   [Function]
    Preliminary: | MT-Safe | AS-Safe | AC-Safe | See Section 1.2.2.1 [POSIX Safety Concepts], page 2.

    This function finds the first occurrence of the byte c (converted to an unsigned char) in the initial *size* bytes of the object beginning at *block*. The return value is a pointer to the located byte, or a null pointer if no match was found.

wchar_t * wmemchr (*const wchar_t *block, wchar_t wc, size_t size*)   [Function]
    Preliminary: | MT-Safe | AS-Safe | AC-Safe | See Section 1.2.2.1 [POSIX Safety Concepts], page 2.

This function finds the first occurrence of the wide character *wc* in the initial *size* wide characters of the object beginning at *block*. The return value is a pointer to the located wide character, or a null pointer if no match was found.

void * rawmemchr (*const void *block, int c*)   [Function]
Preliminary: | MT-Safe | AS-Safe | AC-Safe | See Section 1.2.2.1 [POSIX Safety Concepts], page 2.

Often the `memchr` function is used with the knowledge that the byte *c* is available in the memory block specified by the parameters. But this means that the *size* parameter is not really needed and that the tests performed with it at runtime (to check whether the end of the block is reached) are not needed.

The `rawmemchr` function exists for just this situation which is surprisingly frequent. The interface is similar to `memchr` except that the *size* parameter is missing. The function will look beyond the end of the block pointed to by *block* in case the programmer made an error in assuming that the byte *c* is present in the block. In this case the result is unspecified. Otherwise the return value is a pointer to the located byte.

This function is of special interest when looking for the end of a string. Since all strings are terminated by a null byte a call like

        rawmemchr (str, '\0')

will never go beyond the end of the string.

This function is a GNU extension.

void * memrchr (*const void *block, int c, size_t size*)   [Function]
Preliminary: | MT-Safe | AS-Safe | AC-Safe | See Section 1.2.2.1 [POSIX Safety Concepts], page 2.

The function `memrchr` is like `memchr`, except that it searches backwards from the end of the block defined by *block* and *size* (instead of forwards from the front).

This function is a GNU extension.

char * strchr (*const char *string, int c*)   [Function]
Preliminary: | MT-Safe | AS-Safe | AC-Safe | See Section 1.2.2.1 [POSIX Safety Concepts], page 2.

The `strchr` function finds the first occurrence of the byte *c* (converted to a `char`) in the string beginning at *string*. The return value is a pointer to the located byte, or a null pointer if no match was found.

For example,

        strchr ("hello, world", 'l')
            ⇒ "llo, world"
        strchr ("hello, world", '?')
            ⇒ NULL

The terminating null byte is considered to be part of the string, so you can use this function get a pointer to the end of a string by specifying zero as the value of the *c* argument.

When `strchr` returns a null pointer, it does not let you know the position of the terminating null byte it has found. If you need that information, it is better (but less portable) to use `strchrnul` than to search for it a second time.

wchar_t * wcschr (const wchar_t *wstring, int wc)   [Function]
> Preliminary: | MT-Safe | AS-Safe | AC-Safe | See Section 1.2.2.1 [POSIX Safety
> Concepts], page 2.
>
> The wcschr function finds the first occurrence of the wide character wc in the wide
> string beginning at wstring. The return value is a pointer to the located wide char-
> acter, or a null pointer if no match was found.
>
> The terminating null wide character is considered to be part of the wide string, so
> you can use this function get a pointer to the end of a wide string by specifying a
> null wide character as the value of the wc argument. It would be better (but less
> portable) to use wcschrnul in this case, though.

char * strchrnul (const char *string, int c)   [Function]
> Preliminary: | MT-Safe | AS-Safe | AC-Safe | See Section 1.2.2.1 [POSIX Safety
> Concepts], page 2.
>
> strchrnul is the same as strchr except that if it does not find the byte, it returns
> a pointer to string's terminating null byte rather than a null pointer.
>
> This function is a GNU extension.

wchar_t * wcschrnul (const wchar_t *wstring, wchar_t wc)   [Function]
> Preliminary: | MT-Safe | AS-Safe | AC-Safe | See Section 1.2.2.1 [POSIX Safety
> Concepts], page 2.
>
> wcschrnul is the same as wcschr except that if it does not find the wide character,
> it returns a pointer to the wide string's terminating null wide character rather than
> a null pointer.
>
> This function is a GNU extension.

One useful, but unusual, use of the strchr function is when one wants to have a pointer
pointing to the null byte terminating a string. This is often written in this way:

```
s += strlen (s);
```

This is almost optimal but the addition operation duplicated a bit of the work already done
in the strlen function. A better solution is this:

```
s = strchr (s, '\0');
```

There is no restriction on the second parameter of strchr so it could very well also be
zero. Those readers thinking very hard about this might now point out that the strchr
function is more expensive than the strlen function since we have two abort criteria. This
is right. But in the GNU C Library the implementation of strchr is optimized in a special
way so that strchr actually is faster.

char * strrchr (const char *string, int c)   [Function]
> Preliminary: | MT-Safe | AS-Safe | AC-Safe | See Section 1.2.2.1 [POSIX Safety
> Concepts], page 2.
>
> The function strrchr is like strchr, except that it searches backwards from the end
> of the string string (instead of forwards from the front).
>
> For example,
>
> ```
> strrchr ("hello, world", 'l')
>     ⇒ "ld"
> ```

wchar_t * **wcsrchr** (*const wchar_t *wstring, wchar_t c*)   [Function]
> Preliminary: | MT-Safe | AS-Safe | AC-Safe | See Section 1.2.2.1 [POSIX Safety Concepts], page 2.

> The function **wcsrchr** is like **wcschr**, except that it searches backwards from the end of the string *wstring* (instead of forwards from the front).

char * **strstr** (*const char *haystack, const char *needle*)   [Function]
> Preliminary: | MT-Safe | AS-Safe | AC-Safe | See Section 1.2.2.1 [POSIX Safety Concepts], page 2.

> This is like **strchr**, except that it searches *haystack* for a substring *needle* rather than just a single byte. It returns a pointer into the string *haystack* that is the first byte of the substring, or a null pointer if no match was found. If *needle* is an empty string, the function returns *haystack*.

> For example,

```
strstr ("hello, world", "l")
    ⇒ "llo, world"
strstr ("hello, world", "wo")
    ⇒ "world"
```

wchar_t * **wcsstr** (*const wchar_t *haystack, const wchar_t *needle*)   [Function]
> Preliminary: | MT-Safe | AS-Safe | AC-Safe | See Section 1.2.2.1 [POSIX Safety Concepts], page 2.

> This is like **wcschr**, except that it searches *haystack* for a substring *needle* rather than just a single wide character. It returns a pointer into the string *haystack* that is the first wide character of the substring, or a null pointer if no match was found. If *needle* is an empty string, the function returns *haystack*.

wchar_t * **wcswcs** (*const wchar_t *haystack, const wchar_t *needle*)   [Function]
> Preliminary: | MT-Safe | AS-Safe | AC-Safe | See Section 1.2.2.1 [POSIX Safety Concepts], page 2.

> **wcswcs** is a deprecated alias for **wcsstr**. This is the name originally used in the X/Open Portability Guide before the Amendment 1 to ISO C90 was published.

char * **strcasestr** (*const char *haystack, const char *needle*)   [Function]
> Preliminary: | MT-Safe locale | AS-Safe | AC-Safe | See Section 1.2.2.1 [POSIX Safety Concepts], page 2.

> This is like **strstr**, except that it ignores case in searching for the substring. Like **strcasecmp**, it is locale dependent how uppercase and lowercase characters are related, and arguments are multibyte strings.

> For example,

```
strcasestr ("hello, world", "L")
    ⇒ "llo, world"
strcasestr ("hello, World", "wo")
    ⇒ "World"
```

void * memmem (*const void *haystack, size_t haystack-len,*   [Function]
        const void *needle, size_t needle-len)

> Preliminary: | MT-Safe | AS-Safe | AC-Safe | See Section 1.2.2.1 [POSIX Safety Concepts], page 2.
>
> This is like `strstr`, but *needle* and *haystack* are byte arrays rather than strings. *needle-len* is the length of *needle* and *haystack-len* is the length of *haystack*.
>
> This function is a GNU extension.

size_t strspn (*const char *string, const char *skipset*)   [Function]

> Preliminary: | MT-Safe | AS-Safe | AC-Safe | See Section 1.2.2.1 [POSIX Safety Concepts], page 2.
>
> The `strspn` ("string span") function returns the length of the initial substring of *string* that consists entirely of bytes that are members of the set specified by the string *skipset*. The order of the bytes in *skipset* is not important.
>
> For example,
>
> ```
> strspn ("hello, world", "abcdefghijklmnopqrstuvwxyz")
>     ⇒ 5
> ```
>
> In a multibyte string, characters consisting of more than one byte are not treated as single entities. Each byte is treated separately. The function is not locale-dependent.

size_t wcsspn (*const wchar_t *wstring, const wchar_t *skipset*)   [Function]

> Preliminary: | MT-Safe | AS-Safe | AC-Safe | See Section 1.2.2.1 [POSIX Safety Concepts], page 2.
>
> The `wcsspn` ("wide character string span") function returns the length of the initial substring of *wstring* that consists entirely of wide characters that are members of the set specified by the string *skipset*. The order of the wide characters in *skipset* is not important.

size_t strcspn (*const char *string, const char *stopset*)   [Function]

> Preliminary: | MT-Safe | AS-Safe | AC-Safe | See Section 1.2.2.1 [POSIX Safety Concepts], page 2.
>
> The `strcspn` ("string complement span") function returns the length of the initial substring of *string* that consists entirely of bytes that are *not* members of the set specified by the string *stopset*. (In other words, it returns the offset of the first byte in *string* that is a member of the set *stopset*.)
>
> For example,
>
> ```
> strcspn ("hello, world", " \t\n,.;!?")
>     ⇒ 5
> ```
>
> In a multibyte string, characters consisting of more than one byte are not treated as a single entities. Each byte is treated separately. The function is not locale-dependent.

size_t wcscspn (*const wchar_t *wstring, const wchar_t *stopset*)   [Function]

> Preliminary: | MT-Safe | AS-Safe | AC-Safe | See Section 1.2.2.1 [POSIX Safety Concepts], page 2.
>
> The `wcscspn` ("wide character string complement span") function returns the length of the initial substring of *wstring* that consists entirely of wide characters that are *not* members of the set specified by the string *stopset*. (In other words, it returns the offset of the first wide character in *string* that is a member of the set *stopset*.)

char * strpbrk (*const char *string, const char *stopset*)   [Function]
> Preliminary: | MT-Safe | AS-Safe | AC-Safe | See Section 1.2.2.1 [POSIX Safety Concepts], page 2.
>
> The strpbrk ("string pointer break") function is related to strcspn, except that it returns a pointer to the first byte in *string* that is a member of the set *stopset* instead of the length of the initial substring. It returns a null pointer if no such byte from *stopset* is found.
>
> For example,
>
>   strpbrk ("hello, world", " \t\n,.;!?")
>   ⇒ ", world"
>
> In a multibyte string, characters consisting of more than one byte are not treated as single entities. Each byte is treated separately. The function is not locale-dependent.

wchar_t * wcspbrk (*const wchar_t *wstring, const wchar_t *stopset*)   [Function]
> Preliminary: | MT-Safe | AS-Safe | AC-Safe | See Section 1.2.2.1 [POSIX Safety Concepts], page 2.
>
> The wcspbrk ("wide character string pointer break") function is related to wcscspn, except that it returns a pointer to the first wide character in *wstring* that is a member of the set *stopset* instead of the length of the initial substring. It returns a null pointer if no such wide character from *stopset* is found.

5.9.1 Compatibility String Search Functions

char * index (*const char *string, int c*)   [Function]
> Preliminary: | MT-Safe | AS-Safe | AC-Safe | See Section 1.2.2.1 [POSIX Safety Concepts], page 2.
>
> index is another name for strchr; they are exactly the same. New code should always use strchr since this name is defined in ISO C while index is a BSD invention which never was available on System V derived systems.

char * rindex (*const char *string, int c*)   [Function]
> Preliminary: | MT-Safe | AS-Safe | AC-Safe | See Section 1.2.2.1 [POSIX Safety Concepts], page 2.
>
> rindex is another name for strrchr; they are exactly the same. New code should always use strrchr since this name is defined in ISO C while rindex is a BSD invention which never was available on System V derived systems.

5.10 Finding Tokens in a String

It's fairly common for programs to have a need to do some simple kinds of lexical analysis and parsing, such as splitting a command string up into tokens. You can do this with the strtok function, declared in the header file string.h.

char * strtok (*char *restrict newstring, const char *restrict delimiters*)   [Function]
> Preliminary: | MT-Unsafe race:strtok | AS-Unsafe | AC-Safe | See Section 1.2.2.1 [POSIX Safety Concepts], page 2.

A string can be split into tokens by making a series of calls to the function `strtok`.

The string to be split up is passed as the *newstring* argument on the first call only. The `strtok` function uses this to set up some internal state information. Subsequent calls to get additional tokens from the same string are indicated by passing a null pointer as the *newstring* argument. Calling `strtok` with another non-null *newstring* argument reinitializes the state information. It is guaranteed that no other library function ever calls `strtok` behind your back (which would mess up this internal state information).

The *delimiters* argument is a string that specifies a set of delimiters that may surround the token being extracted. All the initial bytes that are members of this set are discarded. The first byte that is *not* a member of this set of delimiters marks the beginning of the next token. The end of the token is found by looking for the next byte that is a member of the delimiter set. This byte in the original string *newstring* is overwritten by a null byte, and the pointer to the beginning of the token in *newstring* is returned.

On the next call to `strtok`, the searching begins at the next byte beyond the one that marked the end of the previous token. Note that the set of delimiters *delimiters* do not have to be the same on every call in a series of calls to `strtok`.

If the end of the string *newstring* is reached, or if the remainder of string consists only of delimiter bytes, `strtok` returns a null pointer.

In a multibyte string, characters consisting of more than one byte are not treated as single entities. Each byte is treated separately. The function is not locale-dependent.

`wchar_t * wcstok` (*wchar_t *newstring, const wchar_t *delimiters, wchar_t **save_ptr*)   [Function]

Preliminary: | MT-Safe | AS-Safe | AC-Safe | See Section 1.2.2.1 [POSIX Safety Concepts], page 2.

A string can be split into tokens by making a series of calls to the function `wcstok`.

The string to be split up is passed as the *newstring* argument on the first call only. The `wcstok` function uses this to set up some internal state information. Subsequent calls to get additional tokens from the same wide string are indicated by passing a null pointer as the *newstring* argument, which causes the pointer previously stored in *save_ptr* to be used instead.

The *delimiters* argument is a wide string that specifies a set of delimiters that may surround the token being extracted. All the initial wide characters that are members of this set are discarded. The first wide character that is *not* a member of this set of delimiters marks the beginning of the next token. The end of the token is found by looking for the next wide character that is a member of the delimiter set. This wide character in the original wide string *newstring* is overwritten by a null wide character, the pointer past the overwritten wide character is saved in *save_ptr*, and the pointer to the beginning of the token in *newstring* is returned.

On the next call to `wcstok`, the searching begins at the next wide character beyond the one that marked the end of the previous token. Note that the set of delimiters *delimiters* do not have to be the same on every call in a series of calls to `wcstok`.

If the end of the wide string *newstring* is reached, or if the remainder of string consists only of delimiter wide characters, `wcstok` returns a null pointer.

Warning: Since `strtok` and `wcstok` alter the string they is parsing, you should always copy the string to a temporary buffer before parsing it with `strtok`/`wcstok` (see Section 5.4 [Copying Strings and Arrays], page 95). If you allow `strtok` or `wcstok` to modify a string that came from another part of your program, you are asking for trouble; that string might be used for other purposes after `strtok` or `wcstok` has modified it, and it would not have the expected value.

The string that you are operating on might even be a constant. Then when `strtok` or `wcstok` tries to modify it, your program will get a fatal signal for writing in read-only memory. See Section 24.2.1 [Program Error Signals], page 687. Even if the operation of `strtok` or `wcstok` would not require a modification of the string (e.g., if there is exactly one token) the string can (and in the GNU C Library case will) be modified.

This is a special case of a general principle: if a part of a program does not have as its purpose the modification of a certain data structure, then it is error-prone to modify the data structure temporarily.

The function `strtok` is not reentrant, whereas `wcstok` is. See Section 24.4.6 [Signal Handling and Nonreentrant Functions], page 708, for a discussion of where and why reentrancy is important.

Here is a simple example showing the use of `strtok`.

```
#include <string.h>
#include <stddef.h>

…

const char string[] = "words separated by spaces -- and, punctuation!";
const char delimiters[] = " .,;:!-";
char *token, *cp;

…

cp = strdupa (string);               /* Make writable copy.  */
token = strtok (cp, delimiters);     /* token => "words" */
token = strtok (NULL, delimiters);   /* token => "separated" */
token = strtok (NULL, delimiters);   /* token => "by" */
token = strtok (NULL, delimiters);   /* token => "spaces" */
token = strtok (NULL, delimiters);   /* token => "and" */
token = strtok (NULL, delimiters);   /* token => "punctuation" */
token = strtok (NULL, delimiters);   /* token => NULL */
```

The GNU C Library contains two more functions for tokenizing a string which overcome the limitation of non-reentrancy. They are not available available for wide strings.

`char * strtok_r (char *newstring, const char *delimiters, char **save_ptr)` [Function]

Preliminary: | MT-Safe | AS-Safe | AC-Safe | See Section 1.2.2.1 [POSIX Safety Concepts], page 2.

Just like `strtok`, this function splits the string into several tokens which can be accessed by successive calls to `strtok_r`. The difference is that, as in `wcstok`, the information about the next token is stored in the space pointed to by the third argument, *save_ptr*, which is a pointer to a string pointer. Calling `strtok_r` with a null pointer for *newstring* and leaving *save_ptr* between the calls unchanged does the job without hindering reentrancy.

This function is defined in POSIX.1 and can be found on many systems which support multi-threading.

char * strsep (*char **string_ptr, const char *delimiter*)   [Function]
Preliminary: | MT-Safe | AS-Safe | AC-Safe | See Section 1.2.2.1 [POSIX Safety Concepts], page 2.

This function has a similar functionality as **strtok_r** with the *newstring* argument replaced by the *save_ptr* argument. The initialization of the moving pointer has to be done by the user. Successive calls to **strsep** move the pointer along the tokens separated by *delimiter*, returning the address of the next token and updating *string_ptr* to point to the beginning of the next token.

One difference between **strsep** and **strtok_r** is that if the input string contains more than one byte from *delimiter* in a row **strsep** returns an empty string for each pair of bytes from *delimiter*. This means that a program normally should test for **strsep** returning an empty string before processing it.

This function was introduced in 4.3BSD and therefore is widely available.

Here is how the above example looks like when **strsep** is used.

```
#include <string.h>
#include <stddef.h>

...

const char string[] = "words separated by spaces -- and, punctuation!";
const char delimiters[] = " .,;:!-";
char *running;
char *token;

...

running = strdupa (string);
token = strsep (&running, delimiters);    /* token => "words" */
token = strsep (&running, delimiters);    /* token => "separated" */
token = strsep (&running, delimiters);    /* token => "by" */
token = strsep (&running, delimiters);    /* token => "spaces" */
token = strsep (&running, delimiters);    /* token => "" */
token = strsep (&running, delimiters);    /* token => "" */
token = strsep (&running, delimiters);    /* token => "" */
token = strsep (&running, delimiters);    /* token => "and" */
token = strsep (&running, delimiters);    /* token => "" */
token = strsep (&running, delimiters);    /* token => "punctuation" */
token = strsep (&running, delimiters);    /* token => "" */
token = strsep (&running, delimiters);    /* token => NULL */
```

char * basename (*const char *filename*)   [Function]
Preliminary: | MT-Safe | AS-Safe | AC-Safe | See Section 1.2.2.1 [POSIX Safety Concepts], page 2.

The GNU version of the **basename** function returns the last component of the path in *filename*. This function is the preferred usage, since it does not modify the argument, *filename*, and respects trailing slashes. The prototype for **basename** can be found in **string.h**. Note, this function is overridden by the XPG version, if **libgen.h** is included.

Example of using GNU `basename`:

```
#include <string.h>

int
main (int argc, char *argv[])
{
  char *prog = basename (argv[0]);

  if (argc < 2)
    {
      fprintf (stderr, "Usage %s <arg>\n", prog);
      exit (1);
    }

  ...
}
```

Portability Note: This function may produce different results on different systems.

char * **basename** (*char *path*)   [Function]
> Preliminary: | MT-Safe | AS-Safe | AC-Safe | See Section 1.2.2.1 [POSIX Safety Concepts], page 2.
>
> This is the standard XPG defined `basename`. It is similar in spirit to the GNU version, but may modify the *path* by removing trailing '/' bytes. If the *path* is made up entirely of '/' bytes, then "/" will be returned. Also, if *path* is `NULL` or an empty string, then "." is returned. The prototype for the XPG version can be found in `libgen.h`.
>
> Example of using XPG `basename`:
>
> ```
> #include <libgen.h>
>
> int
> main (int argc, char *argv[])
> {
>   char *prog;
>   char *path = strdupa (argv[0]);
>
>   prog = basename (path);
>
>   if (argc < 2)
>     {
>       fprintf (stderr, "Usage %s <arg>\n", prog);
>       exit (1);
>     }
>
>   ...
>
> }
> ```

char * **dirname** (*char *path*)   [Function]
> Preliminary: | MT-Safe | AS-Safe | AC-Safe | See Section 1.2.2.1 [POSIX Safety Concepts], page 2.
>
> The `dirname` function is the compliment to the XPG version of `basename`. It returns the parent directory of the file specified by *path*. If *path* is `NULL`, an empty string, or contains no '/' bytes, then "." is returned. The prototype for this function can be found in `libgen.h`.

5.11 Erasing Sensitive Data

Sensitive data, such as cryptographic keys, should be erased from memory after use, to reduce the risk that a bug will expose it to the outside world. However, compiler optimizations may determine that an erasure operation is "unnecessary," and remove it from the generated code, because no *correct* program could access the variable or heap object containing the sensitive data after it's deallocated. Since erasure is a precaution against bugs, this optimization is inappropriate.

The function `explicit_bzero` erases a block of memory, and guarantees that the compiler will not remove the erasure as "unnecessary."

```
#include <string.h>

extern void encrypt (const char *key, const char *in,
                     char *out, size_t n);
extern void genkey (const char *phrase, char *key);

void encrypt_with_phrase (const char *phrase, const char *in,
                          char *out, size_t n)
{
  char key[16];
  genkey (phrase, key);
  encrypt (key, in, out, n);
  explicit_bzero (key, 16);
}
```

In this example, if `memset`, `bzero`, or a hand-written loop had been used, the compiler might remove them as "unnecessary."

Warning: `explicit_bzero` does not guarantee that sensitive data is *completely* erased from the computer's memory. There may be copies in temporary storage areas, such as registers and "scratch" stack space; since these are invisible to the source code, a library function cannot erase them.

Also, `explicit_bzero` only operates on RAM. If a sensitive data object never needs to have its address taken other than to call `explicit_bzero`, it might be stored entirely in CPU registers *until* the call to `explicit_bzero`. Then it will be copied into RAM, the copy will be erased, and the original will remain intact. Data in RAM is more likely to be exposed by a bug than data in registers, so this creates a brief window where the data is at greater risk of exposure than it would have been if the program didn't try to erase it at all.

Declaring sensitive variables as `volatile` will make both the above problems *worse*; a `volatile` variable will be stored in memory for its entire lifetime, and the compiler will make *more* copies of it than it would otherwise have. Attempting to erase a normal variable "by hand" through a `volatile`-qualified pointer doesn't work at all—because the variable itself is not `volatile`, some compilers will ignore the qualification on the pointer and remove the erasure anyway.

Having said all that, in most situations, using `explicit_bzero` is better than not using it. At present, the only way to do a more thorough job is to write the entire sensitive operation in assembly language. We anticipate that future compilers will recognize calls to `explicit_bzero` and take appropriate steps to erase all the copies of the affected data, whereever they may be.

void **explicit_bzero** (*void *block, size_t* `len`)   [Function]
> Preliminary: | MT-Safe | AS-Safe | AC-Safe | See Section 1.2.2.1 [POSIX Safety Concepts], page 2.
>
> `explicit_bzero` writes zero into *len* bytes of memory beginning at *block*, just as `bzero` would. The zeroes are always written, even if the compiler could determine that this is "unnecessary" because no correct program could read them back.
>
> **Note:** The *only* optimization that `explicit_bzero` disables is removal of "unnecessary" writes to memory. The compiler can perform all the other optimizations that it could for a call to `memset`. For instance, it may replace the function call with inline memory writes, and it may assume that *block* cannot be a null pointer.
>
> **Portability Note:** This function first appeared in OpenBSD 5.5 and has not been standardized. Other systems may provide the same functionality under a different name, such as `explicit_memset`, `memset_s`, or `SecureZeroMemory`.
>
> The GNU C Library declares this function in `string.h`, but on other systems it may be in `strings.h` instead.

5.12 strfry

The function below addresses the perennial programming quandary: "How do I take good data in string form and painlessly turn it into garbage?" This is actually a fairly simple task for C programmers who do not use the GNU C Library string functions, but for programs based on the GNU C Library, the `strfry` function is the preferred method for destroying string data.

The prototype for this function is in `string.h`.

char * **strfry** (*char *string*)   [Function]
> Preliminary: | MT-Safe | AS-Safe | AC-Safe | See Section 1.2.2.1 [POSIX Safety Concepts], page 2.
>
> `strfry` creates a pseudorandom anagram of a string, replacing the input with the anagram in place. For each position in the string, `strfry` swaps it with a position in the string selected at random (from a uniform distribution). The two positions may be the same.
>
> The return value of `strfry` is always *string*.
>
> **Portability Note:** This function is unique to the GNU C Library.

5.13 Trivial Encryption

The `memfrob` function converts an array of data to something unrecognizable and back again. It is not encryption in its usual sense since it is easy for someone to convert the encrypted data back to clear text. The transformation is analogous to Usenet's "Rot13" encryption method for obscuring offensive jokes from sensitive eyes and such. Unlike Rot13, `memfrob` works on arbitrary binary data, not just text.

For true encryption, See Chapter 33 [DES Encryption and Password Handling], page 883.

This function is declared in `string.h`.

void * memfrob (*void *mem, size_t* `length`)   [Function]
>   Preliminary: | MT-Safe | AS-Safe | AC-Safe | See Section 1.2.2.1 [POSIX Safety
>   Concepts], page 2.
>
>   `memfrob` transforms (frobnicates) each byte of the data structure at *mem*, which is
>   *length* bytes long, by bitwise exclusive oring it with binary 00101010. It does the
>   transformation in place and its return value is always *mem*.
>
>   Note that `memfrob` a second time on the same data structure returns it to its original
>   state.
>
>   This is a good function for hiding information from someone who doesn't want to see
>   it or doesn't want to see it very much. To really prevent people from retrieving the
>   information, use stronger encryption such as that described in See Chapter 33 [DES
>   Encryption and Password Handling], page 883.
>
>   **Portability Note:** This function is unique to the GNU C Library.

5.14 Encode Binary Data

To store or transfer binary data in environments which only support text one has to encode
the binary data by mapping the input bytes to bytes in the range allowed for storing
or transferring. SVID systems (and nowadays XPG compliant systems) provide minimal
support for this task.

char * l64a (*long int n*)   [Function]
>   Preliminary: | MT-Unsafe race:l64a | AS-Unsafe | AC-Safe | See Section 1.2.2.1
>   [POSIX Safety Concepts], page 2.
>
>   This function encodes a 32-bit input value using bytes from the basic character set.
>   It returns a pointer to a 7 byte buffer which contains an encoded version of *n*. To
>   encode a series of bytes the user must copy the returned string to a destination buffer.
>   It returns the empty string if *n* is zero, which is somewhat bizarre but mandated by
>   the standard.
>
>   **Warning:** Since a static buffer is used this function should not be used in multi-
>   threaded programs. There is no thread-safe alternative to this function in the C
>   library.
>
>   **Compatibility Note:** The XPG standard states that the return value of `l64a` is un-
>   defined if *n* is negative. In the GNU implementation, `l64a` treats its argument as
>   unsigned, so it will return a sensible encoding for any nonzero *n*; however, portable
>   programs should not rely on this.
>
>   To encode a large buffer `l64a` must be called in a loop, once for each 32-bit word of
>   the buffer. For example, one could do something like this:

```
char *
encode (const void *buf, size_t len)
{
  /* We know in advance how long the buffer has to be. */
  unsigned char *in = (unsigned char *) buf;
  char *out = malloc (6 + ((len + 3) / 4) * 6 + 1);
  char *cp = out, *p;

  /* Encode the length. */
  /* Using `htonlfl is necessary so that the data can be
```

decoded even on machines with different byte order.
`l64afl can return a string shorter than 6 bytes, so
we pad it with encoding of 0 ('.') at the end by
hand. */

```
p = stpcpy (cp, l64a (htonl (len)));
cp = mempcpy (p, "......", 6 - (p - cp));

while (len > 3)
  {
    unsigned long int n = *in++;
    n = (n << 8) | *in++;
    n = (n << 8) | *in++;
    n = (n << 8) | *in++;
    len -= 4;
    p = stpcpy (cp, l64a (htonl (n)));
    cp = mempcpy (p, "......", 6 - (p - cp));
  }
if (len > 0)
  {
    unsigned long int n = *in++;
    if (--len > 0)
      {
        n = (n << 8) | *in++;
        if (--len > 0)
          n = (n << 8) | *in;
      }
    cp = stpcpy (cp, l64a (htonl (n)));
  }
*cp = '\0';
return out;
}
```

It is strange that the library does not provide the complete functionality needed but
so be it.

To decode data produced with `l64a` the following function should be used.

long int a64l (*const char *string*)   [Function]
    Preliminary: | MT-Safe | AS-Safe | AC-Safe | See Section 1.2.2.1 [POSIX Safety
    Concepts], page 2.

    The parameter *string* should contain a string which was produced by a call to `l64a`.
    The function processes at least 6 bytes of this string, and decodes the bytes it finds
    according to the table below. It stops decoding when it finds a byte not in the table,
    rather like `atoi`; if you have a buffer which has been broken into lines, you must be
    careful to skip over the end-of-line bytes.

    The decoded number is returned as a `long int` value.

The `l64a` and `a64l` functions use a base 64 encoding, in which each byte of an encoded
string represents six bits of an input word. These symbols are used for the base 64 digits:

	0	1	2	3	4	5	6	7
0	.	/	0	1	2	3	4	5
8	6	7	8	9	A	B	C	D
16	E	F	G	H	I	J	K	L

24	M	N	O	P	Q	R	S	T
32	U	V	W	X	Y	Z	a	b
40	c	d	e	f	g	h	i	j
48	k	l	m	n	o	p	q	r
56	s	t	u	v	w	x	y	z

This encoding scheme is not standard. There are some other encoding methods which are much more widely used (UU encoding, MIME encoding). Generally, it is better to use one of these encodings.

5.15 Argz and Envz Vectors

argz vectors are vectors of strings in a contiguous block of memory, each element separated from its neighbors by null bytes (`'\0'`).

Envz vectors are an extension of argz vectors where each element is a name-value pair, separated by a `'='` byte (as in a Unix environment).

5.15.1 Argz Functions

Each argz vector is represented by a pointer to the first element, of type `char *`, and a size, of type `size_t`, both of which can be initialized to 0 to represent an empty argz vector. All argz functions accept either a pointer and a size argument, or pointers to them, if they will be modified.

The argz functions use `malloc/realloc` to allocate/grow argz vectors, and so any argz vector created using these functions may be freed by using `free`; conversely, any argz function that may grow a string expects that string to have been allocated using `malloc` (those argz functions that only examine their arguments or modify them in place will work on any sort of memory). See Section 3.2.3 [Unconstrained Allocation], page 44.

All argz functions that do memory allocation have a return type of `error_t`, and return 0 for success, and `ENOMEM` if an allocation error occurs.

These functions are declared in the standard include file `argz.h`.

error_t argz_create (*char *const* **argv**[], *char* **argz**, *size_t*   [Function]
        argz_len)

Preliminary: | MT-Safe | AS-Unsafe heap | AC-Unsafe mem | See Section 1.2.2.1 [POSIX Safety Concepts], page 2.

The **argz_create** function converts the Unix-style argument vector *argv* (a vector of pointers to normal C strings, terminated by (`char *`)0; see Section 25.1 [Program Arguments], page 729) into an argz vector with the same elements, which is returned in *argz* and *argz_len*.

error_t argz_create_sep (*const char *string*, *int sep*, *char*   [Function]
        ***argz*, *size_t *argz_len*)

Preliminary: | MT-Safe | AS-Unsafe heap | AC-Unsafe mem | See Section 1.2.2.1 [POSIX Safety Concepts], page 2.

The **argz_create_sep** function converts the string *string* into an argz vector (returned in *argz* and *argz_len*) by splitting it into elements at every occurrence of the byte *sep*.

`size_t argz_count (`*const char* `*argz,` *size_t* `argz_len)` [Function]
> Preliminary: | MT-Safe | AS-Safe | AC-Safe | See Section 1.2.2.1 [POSIX Safety Concepts], page 2.

> Returns the number of elements in the argz vector *argz* and *argz_len*.

`void argz_extract (`*const char* `*argz,` *size_t* `argz_len,` *char* `**argv)` [Function]
> Preliminary: | MT-Safe | AS-Safe | AC-Safe | See Section 1.2.2.1 [POSIX Safety Concepts], page 2.

> The `argz_extract` function converts the argz vector *argz* and *argz_len* into a Unix-style argument vector stored in *argv*, by putting pointers to every element in *argz* into successive positions in *argv*, followed by a terminator of 0. *Argv* must be pre-allocated with enough space to hold all the elements in *argz* plus the terminating `(char *)0` (`(argz_count (argz, argz_len) + 1) * sizeof (char *)` bytes should be enough). Note that the string pointers stored into *argv* point into *argz*—they are not copies—and so *argz* must be copied if it will be changed while *argv* is still active. This function is useful for passing the elements in *argz* to an exec function (see Section 26.5 [Executing a File], page 776).

`void argz_stringify (`*char* `*argz,` *size_t* `len,` *int* `sep)` [Function]
> Preliminary: | MT-Safe | AS-Safe | AC-Safe | See Section 1.2.2.1 [POSIX Safety Concepts], page 2.

> The `argz_stringify` converts *argz* into a normal string with the elements separated by the byte *sep*, by replacing each `'\0'` inside *argz* (except the last one, which terminates the string) with *sep*. This is handy for printing *argz* in a readable manner.

`error_t argz_add (`*char* `**argz,` *size_t* `*argz_len,` *const char* `*str)` [Function]
> Preliminary: | MT-Safe | AS-Unsafe heap | AC-Unsafe mem | See Section 1.2.2.1 [POSIX Safety Concepts], page 2.

> The `argz_add` function adds the string *str* to the end of the argz vector `*argz`, and updates `*argz` and `*argz_len` accordingly.

`error_t argz_add_sep (`*char* `**argz,` *size_t* `*argz_len,` *const char* `*str,` *int* `delim)` [Function]
> Preliminary: | MT-Safe | AS-Unsafe heap | AC-Unsafe mem | See Section 1.2.2.1 [POSIX Safety Concepts], page 2.

> The `argz_add_sep` function is similar to `argz_add`, but *str* is split into separate elements in the result at occurrences of the byte *delim*. This is useful, for instance, for adding the components of a Unix search path to an argz vector, by using a value of `':'` for *delim*.

`error_t argz_append (`*char* `**argz,` *size_t* `*argz_len,` *const char* `*buf,` *size_t* `buf_len)` [Function]
> Preliminary: | MT-Safe | AS-Unsafe heap | AC-Unsafe mem | See Section 1.2.2.1 [POSIX Safety Concepts], page 2.

> The `argz_append` function appends *buf_len* bytes starting at *buf* to the argz vector `*argz`, reallocating `*argz` to accommodate it, and adding *buf_len* to `*argz_len`.

void **argz_delete** (*char **argz, size_t *argz_len, char *entry*)　　　[Function]
Preliminary: | MT-Safe | AS-Unsafe heap | AC-Unsafe mem | See Section 1.2.2.1 [POSIX Safety Concepts], page 2.

If *entry* points to the beginning of one of the elements in the argz vector *argz, the **argz_delete** function will remove this entry and reallocate *argz, modifying *argz and *argz_len accordingly. Note that as destructive argz functions usually reallocate their argz argument, pointers into argz vectors such as *entry* will then become invalid.

error_t **argz_insert** (*char **argz, size_t *argz_len, char*　　　[Function]
　　　*before, const char *entry)
Preliminary: | MT-Safe | AS-Unsafe heap | AC-Unsafe mem | See Section 1.2.2.1 [POSIX Safety Concepts], page 2.

The **argz_insert** function inserts the string *entry* into the argz vector *argz at a point just before the existing element pointed to by *before*, reallocating *argz and updating *argz and *argz_len. If *before* is 0, *entry* is added to the end instead (as if by **argz_add**). Since the first element is in fact the same as *argz, passing in *argz as the value of *before* will result in *entry* being inserted at the beginning.

char * **argz_next** (*const char *argz, size_t argz_len, const char*　　　[Function]
　　　*entry)
Preliminary: | MT-Safe | AS-Safe | AC-Safe | See Section 1.2.2.1 [POSIX Safety Concepts], page 2.

The **argz_next** function provides a convenient way of iterating over the elements in the argz vector *argz*. It returns a pointer to the next element in *argz* after the element *entry*, or 0 if there are no elements following *entry*. If *entry* is 0, the first element of *argz* is returned.

This behavior suggests two styles of iteration:

```
char *entry = 0;
while ((entry = argz_next (argz, argz_len, entry)))
  action;
```

(the double parentheses are necessary to make some C compilers shut up about what they consider a questionable **while**-test) and:

```
char *entry;
for (entry = argz;
     entry;
     entry = argz_next (argz, argz_len, entry))
  action;
```

Note that the latter depends on *argz* having a value of 0 if it is empty (rather than a pointer to an empty block of memory); this invariant is maintained for argz vectors created by the functions here.

error_t **argz_replace** (*char **argz, size_t *argz_len,*　　　[Function]
　　　const char *str, const char *with, unsigned *replace_count)
Preliminary: | MT-Safe | AS-Unsafe heap | AC-Unsafe mem | See Section 1.2.2.1 [POSIX Safety Concepts], page 2.

Replace any occurrences of the string *str* in *argz* with *with*, reallocating *argz* as necessary. If *replace_count* is non-zero, *replace_count will be incremented by the number of replacements performed.

5.15.2 Envz Functions

Envz vectors are just argz vectors with additional constraints on the form of each element; as such, argz functions can also be used on them, where it makes sense.

Each element in an envz vector is a name-value pair, separated by a '=' byte; if multiple '=' bytes are present in an element, those after the first are considered part of the value, and treated like all other non-'\0' bytes.

If *no* '=' bytes are present in an element, that element is considered the name of a "null" entry, as distinct from an entry with an empty value: `envz_get` will return 0 if given the name of null entry, whereas an entry with an empty value would result in a value of ""; `envz_entry` will still find such entries, however. Null entries can be removed with the `envz_strip` function.

As with argz functions, envz functions that may allocate memory (and thus fail) have a return type of `error_t`, and return either 0 or `ENOMEM`.

These functions are declared in the standard include file `envz.h`.

char * **envz_entry** (*const char *envz, size_t* `envz_len`, *const char*   [Function]
    *name)

> Preliminary: | MT-Safe | AS-Safe | AC-Safe | See Section 1.2.2.1 [POSIX Safety Concepts], page 2.

> The `envz_entry` function finds the entry in *envz* with the name *name*, and returns a pointer to the whole entry—that is, the argz element which begins with *name* followed by a '=' byte. If there is no entry with that name, 0 is returned.

char * **envz_get** (*const char *envz, size_t* `envz_len`, *const char*   [Function]
    *name)

> Preliminary: | MT-Safe | AS-Safe | AC-Safe | See Section 1.2.2.1 [POSIX Safety Concepts], page 2.

> The `envz_get` function finds the entry in *envz* with the name *name* (like `envz_entry`), and returns a pointer to the value portion of that entry (following the '='). If there is no entry with that name (or only a null entry), 0 is returned.

error_t **envz_add** (*char **envz, size_t* `*envz_len`, *const char*   [Function]
    *name, const char *value)

> Preliminary: | MT-Safe | AS-Unsafe heap | AC-Unsafe mem | See Section 1.2.2.1 [POSIX Safety Concepts], page 2.

> The `envz_add` function adds an entry to **envz* (updating **envz* and **envz_len*) with the name *name*, and value *value*. If an entry with the same name already exists in *envz*, it is removed first. If *value* is 0, then the new entry will be the special null type of entry (mentioned above).

error_t **envz_merge** (*char **envz, size_t* `*envz_len`, *const char*   [Function]
    *envz2, size_t `envz2_len`, *int* `override`)

> Preliminary: | MT-Safe | AS-Unsafe heap | AC-Unsafe mem | See Section 1.2.2.1 [POSIX Safety Concepts], page 2.

> The `envz_merge` function adds each entry in *envz2* to *envz*, as if with `envz_add`, updating **envz* and **envz_len*. If *override* is true, then values in *envz2* will supersede those with the same name in *envz*, otherwise not.

Null entries are treated just like other entries in this respect, so a null entry in *envz* can prevent an entry of the same name in *envz2* from being added to *envz*, if *override* is false.

void **envz_strip** (*char** **envz, size_t *envz_len*) [Function]

Preliminary: | MT-Safe | AS-Safe | AC-Safe | See Section 1.2.2.1 [POSIX Safety Concepts], page 2.

The **envz_strip** function removes any null entries from *envz*, updating ***envz** and ***envz_len**.

void **envz_remove** (*char** **envz, size_t *envz_len, const char *name*) [Function]

Preliminary: | MT-Safe | AS-Unsafe heap | AC-Unsafe mem | See Section 1.2.2.1 [POSIX Safety Concepts], page 2.

The **envz_remove** function removes an entry named *name* from *envz*, updating ***envz** and ***envz_len**.

6 Character Set Handling

Character sets used in the early days of computing had only six, seven, or eight bits for each character: there was never a case where more than eight bits (one byte) were used to represent a single character. The limitations of this approach became more apparent as more people grappled with non-Roman character sets, where not all the characters that make up a language's character set can be represented by 2^8 choices. This chapter shows the functionality that was added to the C library to support multiple character sets.

6.1 Introduction to Extended Characters

A variety of solutions are available to overcome the differences between character sets with a 1:1 relation between bytes and characters and character sets with ratios of 2:1 or 4:1. The remainder of this section gives a few examples to help understand the design decisions made while developing the functionality of the C library.

A distinction we have to make right away is between internal and external representation. *Internal representation* means the representation used by a program while keeping the text in memory. External representations are used when text is stored or transmitted through some communication channel. Examples of external representations include files waiting in a directory to be read and parsed.

Traditionally there has been no difference between the two representations. It was equally comfortable and useful to use the same single-byte representation internally and externally. This comfort level decreases with more and larger character sets.

One of the problems to overcome with the internal representation is handling text that is externally encoded using different character sets. Assume a program that reads two texts and compares them using some metric. The comparison can be usefully done only if the texts are internally kept in a common format.

For such a common format (= character set) eight bits are certainly no longer enough. So the smallest entity will have to grow: *wide characters* will now be used. Instead of one byte per character, two or four will be used instead. (Three are not good to address in memory and more than four bytes seem not to be necessary).

As shown in some other part of this manual, a completely new family has been created of functions that can handle wide character texts in memory. The most commonly used character sets for such internal wide character representations are Unicode and ISO 10646 (also known as UCS for Universal Character Set). Unicode was originally planned as a 16-bit character set; whereas, ISO 10646 was designed to be a 31-bit large code space. The two standards are practically identical. They have the same character repertoire and code table, but Unicode specifies added semantics. At the moment, only characters in the first `0x10000` code positions (the so-called Basic Multilingual Plane, BMP) have been assigned, but the assignment of more specialized characters outside this 16-bit space is already in progress. A number of encodings have been defined for Unicode and ISO 10646 characters: UCS-2 is a 16-bit word that can only represent characters from the BMP, UCS-4 is a 32-bit word than can represent any Unicode and ISO 10646 character, UTF-8 is an ASCII compatible encoding where ASCII characters are represented by ASCII bytes and non-ASCII characters by sequences of 2-6 non-ASCII bytes, and finally UTF-16 is an extension of UCS-2 in which pairs of certain UCS-2 words can be used to encode non-BMP characters up to `0x10ffff`.

To represent wide characters the `char` type is not suitable. For this reason the ISO C standard introduces a new type that is designed to keep one character of a wide character string. To maintain the similarity there is also a type corresponding to `int` for those functions that take a single wide character.

`wchar_t`   [Data type]

> This data type is used as the base type for wide character strings. In other words, arrays of objects of this type are the equivalent of `char[]` for multibyte character strings. The type is defined in `stddef.h`.
>
> The ISO C90 standard, where `wchar_t` was introduced, does not say anything specific about the representation. It only requires that this type is capable of storing all elements of the basic character set. Therefore it would be legitimate to define `wchar_t` as `char`, which might make sense for embedded systems.
>
> But in the GNU C Library `wchar_t` is always 32 bits wide and, therefore, capable of representing all UCS-4 values and, therefore, covering all of ISO 10646. Some Unix systems define `wchar_t` as a 16-bit type and thereby follow Unicode very strictly. This definition is perfectly fine with the standard, but it also means that to represent all characters from Unicode and ISO 10646 one has to use UTF-16 surrogate characters, which is in fact a multi-wide-character encoding. But resorting to multi-wide-character encoding contradicts the purpose of the `wchar_t` type.

`wint_t`   [Data type]

> `wint_t` is a data type used for parameters and variables that contain a single wide character. As the name suggests this type is the equivalent of `int` when using the normal `char` strings. The types `wchar_t` and `wint_t` often have the same representation if their size is 32 bits wide but if `wchar_t` is defined as `char` the type `wint_t` must be defined as `int` due to the parameter promotion.
>
> This type is defined in `wchar.h` and was introduced in Amendment 1 to ISO C90.

As there are for the `char` data type macros are available for specifying the minimum and maximum value representable in an object of type `wchar_t`.

`wint_t WCHAR_MIN`   [Macro]

> The macro `WCHAR_MIN` evaluates to the minimum value representable by an object of type `wint_t`.
>
> This macro was introduced in Amendment 1 to ISO C90.

`wint_t WCHAR_MAX`   [Macro]

> The macro `WCHAR_MAX` evaluates to the maximum value representable by an object of type `wint_t`.
>
> This macro was introduced in Amendment 1 to ISO C90.

Another special wide character value is the equivalent to `EOF`.

`wint_t WEOF`   [Macro]

> The macro `WEOF` evaluates to a constant expression of type `wint_t` whose value is different from any member of the extended character set.

`WEOF` need not be the same value as `EOF` and unlike `EOF` it also need *not* be negative. In other words, sloppy code like

```
{
    int c;
    ...
    while ((c = getc (fp)) < 0)
        ...
}
```

has to be rewritten to use `WEOF` explicitly when wide characters are used:

```
{
    wint_t c;
    ...
    while ((c = wgetc (fp)) != WEOF)
        ...
}
```

This macro was introduced in Amendment 1 to ISO C90 and is defined in `wchar.h`.

These internal representations present problems when it comes to storage and transmittal. Because each single wide character consists of more than one byte, they are affected by byte-ordering. Thus, machines with different endianesses would see different values when accessing the same data. This byte ordering concern also applies for communication protocols that are all byte-based and therefore require that the sender has to decide about splitting the wide character in bytes. A last (but not least important) point is that wide characters often require more storage space than a customized byte-oriented character set.

For all the above reasons, an external encoding that is different from the internal encoding is often used if the latter is UCS-2 or UCS-4. The external encoding is byte-based and can be chosen appropriately for the environment and for the texts to be handled. A variety of different character sets can be used for this external encoding (information that will not be exhaustively presented here–instead, a description of the major groups will suffice). All of the ASCII-based character sets fulfill one requirement: they are "filesystem safe." This means that the character '/' is used in the encoding *only* to represent itself. Things are a bit different for character sets like EBCDIC (Extended Binary Coded Decimal Interchange Code, a character set family used by IBM), but if the operating system does not understand EBCDIC directly the parameters-to-system calls have to be converted first anyhow.

- The simplest character sets are single-byte character sets. There can be only up to 256 characters (for 8 bit character sets), which is not sufficient to cover all languages but might be sufficient to handle a specific text. Handling of a 8 bit character sets is simple. This is not true for other kinds presented later, and therefore, the application one uses might require the use of 8 bit character sets.

- The ISO 2022 standard defines a mechanism for extended character sets where one character *can* be represented by more than one byte. This is achieved by associating a state with the text. Characters that can be used to change the state can be embedded in the text. Each byte in the text might have a different interpretation in each state. The state might even influence whether a given byte stands for a character on its own or whether it has to be combined with some more bytes.

  In most uses of ISO 2022 the defined character sets do not allow state changes that cover more than the next character. This has the big advantage that whenever one can identify the beginning of the byte sequence of a character one can interpret a text correctly. Examples of character sets using this policy are the various EUC character sets (used by Sun's operating systems, EUC-JP, EUC-KR, EUC-TW, and EUC-CN) or Shift_JIS (SJIS, a Japanese encoding).

But there are also character sets using a state that is valid for more than one character and has to be changed by another byte sequence. Examples for this are ISO-2022-JP, ISO-2022-KR, and ISO-2022-CN.

- Early attempts to fix 8 bit character sets for other languages using the Roman alphabet lead to character sets like ISO 6937. Here bytes representing characters like the acute accent do not produce output themselves: one has to combine them with other characters to get the desired result. For example, the byte sequence `0xc2 0x61` (non-spacing acute accent, followed by lower-case 'a') to get the "small a with acute" character. To get the acute accent character on its own, one has to write `0xc2 0x20` (the non-spacing acute followed by a space).

  Character sets like ISO 6937 are used in some embedded systems such as teletex.

- Instead of converting the Unicode or ISO 10646 text used internally, it is often also sufficient to simply use an encoding different than UCS-2/UCS-4. The Unicode and ISO 10646 standards even specify such an encoding: UTF-8. This encoding is able to represent all of ISO 10646 31 bits in a byte string of length one to six.

  There were a few other attempts to encode ISO 10646 such as UTF-7, but UTF-8 is today the only encoding that should be used. In fact, with any luck UTF-8 will soon be the only external encoding that has to be supported. It proves to be universally usable and its only disadvantage is that it favors Roman languages by making the byte string representation of other scripts (Cyrillic, Greek, Asian scripts) longer than necessary if using a specific character set for these scripts. Methods like the Unicode compression scheme can alleviate these problems.

The question remaining is: how to select the character set or encoding to use. The answer: you cannot decide about it yourself, it is decided by the developers of the system or the majority of the users. Since the goal is interoperability one has to use whatever the other people one works with use. If there are no constraints, the selection is based on the requirements the expected circle of users will have. In other words, if a project is expected to be used in only, say, Russia it is fine to use KOI8-R or a similar character set. But if at the same time people from, say, Greece are participating one should use a character set that allows all people to collaborate.

The most widely useful solution seems to be: go with the most general character set, namely ISO 10646. Use UTF-8 as the external encoding and problems about users not being able to use their own language adequately are a thing of the past.

One final comment about the choice of the wide character representation is necessary at this point. We have said above that the natural choice is using Unicode or ISO 10646. This is not required, but at least encouraged, by the ISO C standard. The standard defines at least a macro `__STDC_ISO_10646__` that is only defined on systems where the `wchar_t` type encodes ISO 10646 characters. If this symbol is not defined one should avoid making assumptions about the wide character representation. If the programmer uses only the functions provided by the C library to handle wide character strings there should be no compatibility problems with other systems.

6.2 Overview about Character Handling Functions

A Unix C library contains three different sets of functions in two families to handle character set conversion. One of the function families (the most commonly used) is specified in the ISO C90 standard and, therefore, is portable even beyond the Unix world. Unfortunately this family is the least useful one. These functions should be avoided whenever possible, especially when developing libraries (as opposed to applications).

The second family of functions got introduced in the early Unix standards (XPG2) and is still part of the latest and greatest Unix standard: Unix 98. It is also the most powerful and useful set of functions. But we will start with the functions defined in Amendment 1 to ISO C90.

6.3 Restartable Multibyte Conversion Functions

The ISO C standard defines functions to convert strings from a multibyte representation to wide character strings. There are a number of peculiarities:

- The character set assumed for the multibyte encoding is not specified as an argument to the functions. Instead the character set specified by the LC_CTYPE category of the current locale is used; see Section 7.3 [Locale Categories], page 177.

- The functions handling more than one character at a time require NUL terminated strings as the argument (i.e., converting blocks of text does not work unless one can add a NUL byte at an appropriate place). The GNU C Library contains some extensions to the standard that allow specifying a size, but basically they also expect terminated strings.

Despite these limitations the ISO C functions can be used in many contexts. In graphical user interfaces, for instance, it is not uncommon to have functions that require text to be displayed in a wide character string if the text is not simple ASCII. The text itself might come from a file with translations and the user should decide about the current locale, which determines the translation and therefore also the external encoding used. In such a situation (and many others) the functions described here are perfect. If more freedom while performing the conversion is necessary take a look at the iconv functions (see Section 6.5 [Generic Charset Conversion], page 155).

6.3.1 Selecting the conversion and its properties

We already said above that the currently selected locale for the LC_CTYPE category decides the conversion that is performed by the functions we are about to describe. Each locale uses its own character set (given as an argument to localedef) and this is the one assumed as the external multibyte encoding. The wide character set is always UCS-4 in the GNU C Library.

A characteristic of each multibyte character set is the maximum number of bytes that can be necessary to represent one character. This information is quite important when writing code that uses the conversion functions (as shown in the examples below). The ISO C standard defines two macros that provide this information.

int MB_LEN_MAX   [Macro]

> MB_LEN_MAX specifies the maximum number of bytes in the multibyte sequence for a
> single character in any of the supported locales. It is a compile-time constant and is
> defined in limits.h.

int MB_CUR_MAX   [Macro]

> MB_CUR_MAX expands into a positive integer expression that is the maximum number
> of bytes in a multibyte character in the current locale. The value is never greater than
> MB_LEN_MAX. Unlike MB_LEN_MAX this macro need not be a compile-time constant, and
> in the GNU C Library it is not.
>
> MB_CUR_MAX is defined in stdlib.h.

Two different macros are necessary since strictly ISO C90 compilers do not allow variable
length array definitions, but still it is desirable to avoid dynamic allocation. This incomplete
piece of code shows the problem:

```
{
  char buf[MB_LEN_MAX];
  ssize_t len = 0;

  while (! feof (fp))
    {
      fread (&buf[len], 1, MB_CUR_MAX - len, fp);
      /* ... process buf */
      len -= used;
    }
}
```

The code in the inner loop is expected to have always enough bytes in the array *buf*
to convert one multibyte character. The array *buf* has to be sized statically since many
compilers do not allow a variable size. The fread call makes sure that MB_CUR_MAX bytes
are always available in *buf*. Note that it isn't a problem if MB_CUR_MAX is not a compile-time
constant.

6.3.2 Representing the state of the conversion

In the introduction of this chapter it was said that certain character sets use a *stateful*
encoding. That is, the encoded values depend in some way on the previous bytes in the
text.

Since the conversion functions allow converting a text in more than one step we must
have a way to pass this information from one call of the functions to another.

mbstate_t   [Data type]

> A variable of type mbstate_t can contain all the information about the *shift state*
> needed from one call to a conversion function to another.
>
> mbstate_t is defined in wchar.h. It was introduced in Amendment 1 to ISO C90.

To use objects of type mbstate_t the programmer has to define such objects (normally
as local variables on the stack) and pass a pointer to the object to the conversion functions.
This way the conversion function can update the object if the current multibyte character
set is stateful.

There is no specific function or initializer to put the state object in any specific state. The rules are that the object should always represent the initial state before the first use, and this is achieved by clearing the whole variable with code such as follows:

```
{
  mbstate_t state;
  memset (&state, '\0', sizeof (state));
  /* from now on state can be used.  */
  ...
}
```

When using the conversion functions to generate output it is often necessary to test whether the current state corresponds to the initial state. This is necessary, for example, to decide whether to emit escape sequences to set the state to the initial state at certain sequence points. Communication protocols often require this.

int mbsinit (const mbstate_t *ps)   [Function]
> Preliminary: | MT-Safe | AS-Safe | AC-Safe | See Section 1.2.2.1 [POSIX Safety Concepts], page 2.
>
> The mbsinit function determines whether the state object pointed to by ps is in the initial state. If ps is a null pointer or the object is in the initial state the return value is nonzero. Otherwise it is zero.
>
> mbsinit was introduced in Amendment 1 to ISO C90 and is declared in wchar.h.

Code using mbsinit often looks similar to this:

```
{
  mbstate_t state;
  memset (&state, '\0', sizeof (state));
  /* Use state.  */
  ...
  if (! mbsinit (&state))
    {
      /* Emit code to return to initial state.  */
      const wchar_t empty[] = L"";
      const wchar_t *srcp = empty;
      wcsrtombs (outbuf, &srcp, outbuflen, &state);
    }
  ...
}
```

The code to emit the escape sequence to get back to the initial state is interesting. The wcsrtombs function can be used to determine the necessary output code (see Section 6.3.4 [Converting Multibyte and Wide Character Strings], page 146). Please note that with the GNU C Library it is not necessary to perform this extra action for the conversion from multibyte text to wide character text since the wide character encoding is not stateful. But there is nothing mentioned in any standard that prohibits making wchar_t use a stateful encoding.

6.3.3 Converting Single Characters

The most fundamental of the conversion functions are those dealing with single characters. Please note that this does not always mean single bytes. But since there is very often a subset of the multibyte character set that consists of single byte sequences, there are functions to help with converting bytes. Frequently, ASCII is a subset of the multibyte character set. In such a scenario, each ASCII character stands for itself, and all other characters have at least a first byte that is beyond the range 0 to 127.

wint_t btowc (*int* c) [Function]
> Preliminary: | MT-Safe | AS-Unsafe corrupt heap lock dlopen | AC-Unsafe corrupt lock mem fd | See Section 1.2.2.1 [POSIX Safety Concepts], page 2.
>
> The `btowc` function ("byte to wide character") converts a valid single byte character c in the initial shift state into the wide character equivalent using the conversion rules from the currently selected locale of the `LC_CTYPE` category.
>
> If (`unsigned char`) c is no valid single byte multibyte character or if c is `EOF`, the function returns `WEOF`.
>
> Please note the restriction of c being tested for validity only in the initial shift state. No `mbstate_t` object is used from which the state information is taken, and the function also does not use any static state.
>
> The `btowc` function was introduced in Amendment 1 to ISO C90 and is declared in `wchar.h`.

Despite the limitation that the single byte value is always interpreted in the initial state, this function is actually useful most of the time. Most characters are either entirely single-byte character sets or they are extensions to ASCII. But then it is possible to write code like this (not that this specific example is very useful):

```
wchar_t *
itow (unsigned long int val)
{
  static wchar_t buf[30];
  wchar_t *wcp = &buf[29];
  *wcp = L'\0';
  while (val != 0)
    {
      *--wcp = btowc ('0' + val % 10);
      val /= 10;
    }
  if (wcp == &buf[29])
    *--wcp = L'0';
  return wcp;
}
```

Why is it necessary to use such a complicated implementation and not simply cast `'0' + val % 10` to a wide character? The answer is that there is no guarantee that one can perform this kind of arithmetic on the character of the character set used for `wchar_t` representation. In other situations the bytes are not constant at compile time and so the compiler cannot do the work. In situations like this, using `btowc` is required.

There is also a function for the conversion in the other direction.

int wctob (*wint_t* c) [Function]
> Preliminary: | MT-Safe | AS-Unsafe corrupt heap lock dlopen | AC-Unsafe corrupt lock mem fd | See Section 1.2.2.1 [POSIX Safety Concepts], page 2.
>
> The `wctob` function ("wide character to byte") takes as the parameter a valid wide character. If the multibyte representation for this character in the initial state is

exactly one byte long, the return value of this function is this character. Otherwise the return value is EOF.

wctob was introduced in Amendment 1 to ISO C90 and is declared in wchar.h.

There are more general functions to convert single characters from multibyte representation to wide characters and vice versa. These functions pose no limit on the length of the multibyte representation and they also do not require it to be in the initial state.

size_t mbrtowc (*wchar_t* *restrict *pwc*, *const char* *restrict *s*, *size_t*   [Function]
    n, *mbstate_t* *restrict *ps*)

Preliminary: | MT-Unsafe race:mbrtowc/!ps | AS-Unsafe corrupt heap lock dlopen | AC-Unsafe corrupt lock mem fd | See Section 1.2.2.1 [POSIX Safety Concepts], page 2.

The mbrtowc function ("multibyte restartable to wide character") converts the next multibyte character in the string pointed to by *s* into a wide character and stores it in the wide character string pointed to by *pwc*. The conversion is performed according to the locale currently selected for the LC_CTYPE category. If the conversion for the character set used in the locale requires a state, the multibyte string is interpreted in the state represented by the object pointed to by *ps*. If *ps* is a null pointer, a static, internal state variable used only by the mbrtowc function is used.

If the next multibyte character corresponds to the NUL wide character, the return value of the function is 0 and the state object is afterwards in the initial state. If the next *n* or fewer bytes form a correct multibyte character, the return value is the number of bytes starting from *s* that form the multibyte character. The conversion state is updated according to the bytes consumed in the conversion. In both cases the wide character (either the L'\0' or the one found in the conversion) is stored in the string pointed to by *pwc* if *pwc* is not null.

If the first *n* bytes of the multibyte string possibly form a valid multibyte character but there are more than *n* bytes needed to complete it, the return value of the function is (size_t) -2 and no value is stored. Please note that this can happen even if *n* has a value greater than or equal to MB_CUR_MAX since the input might contain redundant shift sequences.

If the first *n* bytes of the multibyte string cannot possibly form a valid multibyte character, no value is stored, the global variable errno is set to the value EILSEQ, and the function returns (size_t) -1. The conversion state is afterwards undefined.

mbrtowc was introduced in Amendment 1 to ISO C90 and is declared in wchar.h.

Use of mbrtowc is straightforward. A function that copies a multibyte string into a wide character string while at the same time converting all lowercase characters into uppercase could look like this (this is not the final version, just an example; it has no error checking, and sometimes leaks memory):

```
wchar_t *
mbstouwcs (const char *s)
{
  size_t len = strlen (s);
  wchar_t *result = malloc ((len + 1) * sizeof (wchar_t));
  wchar_t *wcp = result;
  wchar_t tmp[1];
```

```
      mbstate_t state;
      size_t nbytes;

      memset (&state, '\0', sizeof (state));
      while ((nbytes = mbrtowc (tmp, s, len, &state)) > 0)
        {
          if (nbytes >= (size_t) -2)
            /* Invalid input string.  */
            return NULL;
          *wcp++ = towupper (tmp[0]);
          len -= nbytes;
          s += nbytes;
        }
      return result;
    }
```

The use of `mbrtowc` should be clear. A single wide character is stored in *tmp*[0], and the number of consumed bytes is stored in the variable *nbytes*. If the conversion is successful, the uppercase variant of the wide character is stored in the *result* array and the pointer to the input string and the number of available bytes is adjusted.

The only non-obvious thing about `mbrtowc` might be the way memory is allocated for the result. The above code uses the fact that there can never be more wide characters in the converted result than there are bytes in the multibyte input string. This method yields a pessimistic guess about the size of the result, and if many wide character strings have to be constructed this way or if the strings are long, the extra memory required to be allocated because the input string contains multibyte characters might be significant. The allocated memory block can be resized to the correct size before returning it, but a better solution might be to allocate just the right amount of space for the result right away. Unfortunately there is no function to compute the length of the wide character string directly from the multibyte string. There is, however, a function that does part of the work.

size_t mbrlen (*const char *restrict s, size_t n, mbstate_t *ps*)   [Function]
    Preliminary: | MT-Unsafe race:mbrlen/!ps | AS-Unsafe corrupt heap lock dlopen | AC-Unsafe corrupt lock mem fd | See Section 1.2.2.1 [POSIX Safety Concepts], page 2.

    The `mbrlen` function ("multibyte restartable length") computes the number of at most *n* bytes starting at *s*, which form the next valid and complete multibyte character.

    If the next multibyte character corresponds to the NUL wide character, the return value is 0. If the next *n* bytes form a valid multibyte character, the number of bytes belonging to this multibyte character byte sequence is returned.

    If the first *n* bytes possibly form a valid multibyte character but the character is incomplete, the return value is (`size_t`) -2. Otherwise the multibyte character sequence is invalid and the return value is (`size_t`) -1.

    The multibyte sequence is interpreted in the state represented by the object pointed to by *ps*. If *ps* is a null pointer, a state object local to `mbrlen` is used.

    `mbrlen` was introduced in Amendment 1 to ISO C90 and is declared in `wchar.h`.

The attentive reader now will note that `mbrlen` can be implemented as

```
mbrtowc (NULL, s, n, ps != NULL ? ps : &internal)
```

This is true and in fact is mentioned in the official specification. How can this function be used to determine the length of the wide character string created from a multibyte character string? It is not directly usable, but we can define a function `mbslen` using it:

```
size_t
mbslen (const char *s)
{
  mbstate_t state;
  size_t result = 0;
  size_t nbytes;
  memset (&state, '\0', sizeof (state));
  while ((nbytes = mbrlen (s, MB_LEN_MAX, &state)) > 0)
    {
      if (nbytes >= (size_t) -2)
        /* Something is wrong.  */
        return (size_t) -1;
      s += nbytes;
      ++result;
    }
  return result;
}
```

This function simply calls `mbrlen` for each multibyte character in the string and counts the number of function calls. Please note that we here use `MB_LEN_MAX` as the size argument in the `mbrlen` call. This is acceptable since a) this value is larger than the length of the longest multibyte character sequence and b) we know that the string *s* ends with a NUL byte, which cannot be part of any other multibyte character sequence but the one representing the NUL wide character. Therefore, the `mbrlen` function will never read invalid memory.

Now that this function is available (just to make this clear, this function is *not* part of the GNU C Library) we can compute the number of wide characters required to store the converted multibyte character string *s* using

```
wcs_bytes = (mbslen (s) + 1) * sizeof (wchar_t);
```

Please note that the `mbslen` function is quite inefficient. The implementation of `mbstouwcs` with `mbslen` would have to perform the conversion of the multibyte character input string twice, and this conversion might be quite expensive. So it is necessary to think about the consequences of using the easier but imprecise method before doing the work twice.

`size_t wcrtomb` (*char *restrict s, wchar_t wc, mbstate_t *restrict ps*)   [Function]
Preliminary: | MT-Unsafe race:wcrtomb/!ps | AS-Unsafe corrupt heap lock dlopen | AC-Unsafe corrupt lock mem fd | See Section 1.2.2.1 [POSIX Safety Concepts], page 2.

The `wcrtomb` function ("wide character restartable to multibyte") converts a single wide character into a multibyte string corresponding to that wide character.

If *s* is a null pointer, the function resets the state stored in the object pointed to by *ps* (or the internal `mbstate_t` object) to the initial state. This can also be achieved by a call like this:

```
wcrtombs (temp_buf, L'\0', ps)
```

since, if *s* is a null pointer, `wcrtomb` performs as if it writes into an internal buffer, which is guaranteed to be large enough.

If *wc* is the NUL wide character, `wcrtomb` emits, if necessary, a shift sequence to get the state *ps* into the initial state followed by a single NUL byte, which is stored in the string *s*.

Otherwise a byte sequence (possibly including shift sequences) is written into the string *s*. This only happens if *wc* is a valid wide character (i.e., it has a multibyte representation in the character set selected by locale of the `LC_CTYPE` category). If *wc* is no valid wide character, nothing is stored in the strings *s*, `errno` is set to `EILSEQ`, the conversion state in *ps* is undefined and the return value is (`size_t`) `-1`.

If no error occurred the function returns the number of bytes stored in the string *s*. This includes all bytes representing shift sequences.

One word about the interface of the function: there is no parameter specifying the length of the array *s*. Instead the function assumes that there are at least `MB_CUR_MAX` bytes available since this is the maximum length of any byte sequence representing a single character. So the caller has to make sure that there is enough space available, otherwise buffer overruns can occur.

`wcrtomb` was introduced in Amendment 1 to ISO C90 and is declared in `wchar.h`.

Using `wcrtomb` is as easy as using `mbrtowc`. The following example appends a wide character string to a multibyte character string. Again, the code is not really useful (or correct), it is simply here to demonstrate the use and some problems.

```
char *
mbscatwcs (char *s, size_t len, const wchar_t *ws)
{
  mbstate_t state;
  /* Find the end of the existing string.  */
  char *wp = strchr (s, '\0');
  len -= wp - s;
  memset (&state, '\0', sizeof (state));
  do
    {
      size_t nbytes;
      if (len < MB_CUR_LEN)
        {
          /* We cannot guarantee that the next
             character fits into the buffer, so
             return an error.  */
          errno = E2BIG;
          return NULL;
        }
      nbytes = wcrtomb (wp, *ws, &state);
      if (nbytes == (size_t) -1)
        /* Error in the conversion.  */
        return NULL;
      len -= nbytes;
      wp += nbytes;
    }
  while (*ws++ != L'\0');
  return s;
}
```

First the function has to find the end of the string currently in the array *s*. The `strchr` call does this very efficiently since a requirement for multibyte character representations is that the NUL byte is never used except to represent itself (and in this context, the end of the string).

After initializing the state object the loop is entered where the first task is to make sure there is enough room in the array *s*. We abort if there are not at least `MB_CUR_LEN` bytes available. This is not always optimal but we have no other choice. We might have less than `MB_CUR_LEN` bytes available but the next multibyte character might also be only one byte long. At the time the `wcrtomb` call returns it is too late to decide whether the buffer was large enough. If this solution is unsuitable, there is a very slow but more accurate solution.

```
      ...
  if (len < MB_CUR_LEN)
    {
      mbstate_t temp_state;
      memcpy (&temp_state, &state, sizeof (state));
      if (wcrtomb (NULL, *ws, &temp_state) > len)
        {
          /* We cannot guarantee that the next
             character fits into the buffer, so
             return an error.   */
          errno = E2BIG;
          return NULL;
        }
    }
      ...
```

Here we perform the conversion that might overflow the buffer so that we are afterwards in the position to make an exact decision about the buffer size. Please note the `NULL` argument for the destination buffer in the new `wcrtomb` call; since we are not interested in the converted text at this point, this is a nice way to express this. The most unusual thing about this piece of code certainly is the duplication of the conversion state object, but if a change of the state is necessary to emit the next multibyte character, we want to have the same shift state change performed in the real conversion. Therefore, we have to preserve the initial shift state information.

There are certainly many more and even better solutions to this problem. This example is only provided for educational purposes.

6.3.4 Converting Multibyte and Wide Character Strings

The functions described in the previous section only convert a single character at a time. Most operations to be performed in real-world programs include strings and therefore the ISO C standard also defines conversions on entire strings. However, the defined set of functions is quite limited; therefore, the GNU C Library contains a few extensions that can help in some important situations.

`size_t mbsrtowcs (wchar_t *restrict dst, const char **restrict src,`   [Function]
      `size_t len, mbstate_t *restrict ps)`

    Preliminary: | MT-Unsafe race:mbsrtowcs/!ps | AS-Unsafe corrupt heap lock dlopen | AC-Unsafe corrupt lock mem fd | See Section 1.2.2.1 [POSIX Safety Concepts], page 2.

    The `mbsrtowcs` function ("multibyte string restartable to wide character string") converts the NUL-terminated multibyte character string at `*src` into an equivalent wide character string, including the NUL wide character at the end. The conversion is started using the state information from the object pointed to by *ps* or from an internal object of `mbsrtowcs` if *ps* is a null pointer. Before returning, the state object is updated to match the state after the last converted character. The state is the initial state if the terminating NUL byte is reached and converted.

If *dst* is not a null pointer, the result is stored in the array pointed to by *dst*; otherwise, the conversion result is not available since it is stored in an internal buffer.

If *len* wide characters are stored in the array *dst* before reaching the end of the input string, the conversion stops and *len* is returned. If *dst* is a null pointer, *len* is never checked.

Another reason for a premature return from the function call is if the input string contains an invalid multibyte sequence. In this case the global variable `errno` is set to `EILSEQ` and the function returns `(size_t) -1`.

In all other cases the function returns the number of wide characters converted during this call. If *dst* is not null, `mbsrtowcs` stores in the pointer pointed to by *src* either a null pointer (if the NUL byte in the input string was reached) or the address of the byte following the last converted multibyte character.

`mbsrtowcs` was introduced in Amendment 1 to ISO C90 and is declared in `wchar.h`.

The definition of the `mbsrtowcs` function has one important limitation. The requirement that *dst* has to be a NUL-terminated string provides problems if one wants to convert buffers with text. A buffer is not normally a collection of NUL-terminated strings but instead a continuous collection of lines, separated by newline characters. Now assume that a function to convert one line from a buffer is needed. Since the line is not NUL-terminated, the source pointer cannot directly point into the unmodified text buffer. This means, either one inserts the NUL byte at the appropriate place for the time of the `mbsrtowcs` function call (which is not doable for a read-only buffer or in a multi-threaded application) or one copies the line in an extra buffer where it can be terminated by a NUL byte. Note that it is not in general possible to limit the number of characters to convert by setting the parameter *len* to any specific value. Since it is not known how many bytes each multibyte character sequence is in length, one can only guess.

There is still a problem with the method of NUL-terminating a line right after the newline character, which could lead to very strange results. As said in the description of the `mbsrtowcs` function above, the conversion state is guaranteed to be in the initial shift state after processing the NUL byte at the end of the input string. But this NUL byte is not really part of the text (i.e., the conversion state after the newline in the original text could be something different than the initial shift state and therefore the first character of the next line is encoded using this state). But the state in question is never accessible to the user since the conversion stops after the NUL byte (which resets the state). Most stateful character sets in use today require that the shift state after a newline be the initial state–but this is not a strict guarantee. Therefore, simply NUL-terminating a piece of a running text is not always an adequate solution and, therefore, should never be used in generally used code.

The generic conversion interface (see Section 6.5 [Generic Charset Conversion], page 155) does not have this limitation (it simply works on buffers, not strings), and the GNU C Library contains a set of functions that take additional parameters specifying the maximal number of bytes that are consumed from the input string. This way the problem of `mbsrtowcs`'s example above could be solved by determining the line length and passing this length to the function.

`size_t wcsrtombs` (*char *restrict **dst**, const wchar_t **restrict **src**,*   [Function]
*size_t **len**, mbstate_t *restrict **ps***)

Preliminary: | MT-Unsafe race:wcsrtombs/!ps | AS-Unsafe corrupt heap lock dlopen | AC-Unsafe corrupt lock mem fd | See Section 1.2.2.1 [POSIX Safety Concepts], page 2.

The `wcsrtombs` function ("wide character string restartable to multibyte string") converts the NUL-terminated wide character string at *src* into an equivalent multibyte character string and stores the result in the array pointed to by *dst*. The NUL wide character is also converted. The conversion starts in the state described in the object pointed to by *ps* or by a state object local to `wcsrtombs` in case *ps* is a null pointer. If *dst* is a null pointer, the conversion is performed as usual but the result is not available. If all characters of the input string were successfully converted and if *dst* is not a null pointer, the pointer pointed to by *src* gets assigned a null pointer.

If one of the wide characters in the input string has no valid multibyte character equivalent, the conversion stops early, sets the global variable `errno` to `EILSEQ`, and returns `(size_t) -1`.

Another reason for a premature stop is if *dst* is not a null pointer and the next converted character would require more than *len* bytes in total to the array *dst*. In this case (and if *dst* is not a null pointer) the pointer pointed to by *src* is assigned a value pointing to the wide character right after the last one successfully converted.

Except in the case of an encoding error the return value of the `wcsrtombs` function is the number of bytes in all the multibyte character sequences stored in *dst*. Before returning, the state in the object pointed to by *ps* (or the internal object in case *ps* is a null pointer) is updated to reflect the state after the last conversion. The state is the initial shift state in case the terminating NUL wide character was converted.

The `wcsrtombs` function was introduced in Amendment 1 to ISO C90 and is declared in `wchar.h`.

The restriction mentioned above for the `mbsrtowcs` function applies here also. There is no possibility of directly controlling the number of input characters. One has to place the NUL wide character at the correct place or control the consumed input indirectly via the available output array size (the *len* parameter).

`size_t mbsnrtowcs` (*wchar_t *restrict **dst**, const char **restrict **src**,*   [Function]
*size_t **nmc**, size_t **len**, mbstate_t *restrict **ps***)

Preliminary: | MT-Unsafe race:mbsnrtowcs/!ps | AS-Unsafe corrupt heap lock dlopen | AC-Unsafe corrupt lock mem fd | See Section 1.2.2.1 [POSIX Safety Concepts], page 2.

The `mbsnrtowcs` function is very similar to the `mbsrtowcs` function. All the parameters are the same except for *nmc*, which is new. The return value is the same as for `mbsrtowcs`.

This new parameter specifies how many bytes at most can be used from the multibyte character string. In other words, the multibyte character string *src* need not be

NUL-terminated. But if a NUL byte is found within the *nmc* first bytes of the string, the conversion stops there.

This function is a GNU extension. It is meant to work around the problems mentioned above. Now it is possible to convert a buffer with multibyte character text piece by piece without having to care about inserting NUL bytes and the effect of NUL bytes on the conversion state.

A function to convert a multibyte string into a wide character string and display it could be written like this (this is not a really useful example):

```
void
showmbs (const char *src, FILE *fp)
{
  mbstate_t state;
  int cnt = 0;
  memset (&state, '\0', sizeof (state));
  while (1)
    {
      wchar_t linebuf[100];
      const char *endp = strchr (src, '\n');
      size_t n;

      /* Exit if there is no more line.  */
      if (endp == NULL)
        break;

      n = mbsnrtowcs (linebuf, &src, endp - src, 99, &state);
      linebuf[n] = L'\0';
      fprintf (fp, "line %d: \"%S\"\n", linebuf);
    }
}
```

There is no problem with the state after a call to `mbsnrtowcs`. Since we don't insert characters in the strings that were not in there right from the beginning and we use *state* only for the conversion of the given buffer, there is no problem with altering the state.

`size_t wcsnrtombs` (*char *restrict* **dst**, *const wchar_t **restrict* **src**,   [Function]
      size_t **nwc**, *size_t* **len**, *mbstate_t *restrict* **ps**)
Preliminary: | MT-Unsafe race:wcsnrtombs/!ps | AS-Unsafe corrupt heap lock dlopen | AC-Unsafe corrupt lock mem fd | See Section 1.2.2.1 [POSIX Safety Concepts], page 2.

The `wcsnrtombs` function implements the conversion from wide character strings to multibyte character strings. It is similar to `wcsrtombs` but, just like `mbsnrtowcs`, it takes an extra parameter, which specifies the length of the input string.

No more than *nwc* wide characters from the input string **src* are converted. If the input string contains a NUL wide character in the first *nwc* characters, the conversion stops at this place.

The `wcsnrtombs` function is a GNU extension and just like `mbsnrtowcs` helps in situations where no NUL-terminated input strings are available.

6.3.5 A Complete Multibyte Conversion Example

The example programs given in the last sections are only brief and do not contain all the error checking, etc. Presented here is a complete and documented example. It features the `mbrtowc` function but it should be easy to derive versions using the other functions.

```
int
file_mbsrtowcs (int input, int output)
{
  /* Note the use of MB_LEN_MAX.
     MB_CUR_MAX cannot portably be used here.   */
  char buffer[BUFSIZ + MB_LEN_MAX];
  mbstate_t state;
  int filled = 0;
  int eof = 0;

  /* Initialize the state.  */
  memset (&state, '\0', sizeof (state));

  while (!eof)
    {
      ssize_t nread;
      ssize_t nwrite;
      char *inp = buffer;
      wchar_t outbuf[BUFSIZ];
      wchar_t *outp = outbuf;

      /* Fill up the buffer from the input file.   */
      nread = read (input, buffer + filled, BUFSIZ);
      if (nread < 0)
        {
          perror ("read");
          return 0;
        }
      /* If we reach end of file, make a note to read no more. */
      if (nread == 0)
        eof = 1;

      /* filled is now the number of bytes in buffer. */
      filled += nread;

      /* Convert those bytes to wide characters–as many as we can. */
      while (1)
        {
          size_t thislen = mbrtowc (outp, inp, filled, &state);
          /* Stop converting at invalid character;
             this can mean we have read just the first part
             of a valid character.  */
          if (thislen == (size_t) -1)
            break;
          /* We want to handle embedded NUL bytes
             but the return value is 0.  Correct this.  */
          if (thislen == 0)
            thislen = 1;
          /* Advance past this character. */
          inp += thislen;
          filled -= thislen;
          ++outp;
        }
```

```
    /* Write the wide characters we just made.  */
    nwrite = write (output, outbuf,
                      (outp - outbuf) * sizeof (wchar_t));
    if (nwrite < 0)
      {
        perror ("write");
        return 0;
      }

    /* See if we have a real invalid character. */
    if ((eof && filled > 0) || filled >= MB_CUR_MAX)
      {
        error (0, 0, "invalid multibyte character");
        return 0;
      }

    /* If any characters must be carried forward,
       put them at the beginning of buffer. */
    if (filled > 0)
      memmove (buffer, inp, filled);
  }

  return 1;
}
```

6.4 Non-reentrant Conversion Function

The functions described in the previous chapter are defined in Amendment 1 to ISO C90, but the original ISO C90 standard also contained functions for character set conversion. The reason that these original functions are not described first is that they are almost entirely useless.

The problem is that all the conversion functions described in the original ISO C90 use a local state. Using a local state implies that multiple conversions at the same time (not only when using threads) cannot be done, and that you cannot first convert single characters and then strings since you cannot tell the conversion functions which state to use.

These original functions are therefore usable only in a very limited set of situations. One must complete converting the entire string before starting a new one, and each string/text must be converted with the same function (there is no problem with the library itself; it is guaranteed that no library function changes the state of any of these functions). **For the above reasons it is highly requested that the functions described in the previous section be used in place of non-reentrant conversion functions.**

6.4.1 Non-reentrant Conversion of Single Characters

int mbtowc (*wchar_t *restrict **result**, const char *restrict **string**,*   [Function]
       *size_t **size**)*

> Preliminary: | MT-Unsafe race | AS-Unsafe corrupt heap lock dlopen | AC-Unsafe corrupt lock mem fd | See Section 1.2.2.1 [POSIX Safety Concepts], page 2.
>
> The mbtowc ("multibyte to wide character") function when called with non-null *string* converts the first multibyte character beginning at *string* to its corresponding wide character code. It stores the result in *result*.

`mbtowc` never examines more than *size* bytes. (The idea is to supply for *size* the number of bytes of data you have in hand.)

`mbtowc` with non-null *string* distinguishes three possibilities: the first *size* bytes at *string* start with valid multibyte characters, they start with an invalid byte sequence or just part of a character, or *string* points to an empty string (a null character).

For a valid multibyte character, `mbtowc` converts it to a wide character and stores that in **result*, and returns the number of bytes in that character (always at least 1 and never more than *size*).

For an invalid byte sequence, `mbtowc` returns −1. For an empty string, it returns 0, also storing `'\0'` in **result*.

If the multibyte character code uses shift characters, then `mbtowc` maintains and updates a shift state as it scans. If you call `mbtowc` with a null pointer for *string*, that initializes the shift state to its standard initial value. It also returns nonzero if the multibyte character code in use actually has a shift state. See Section 6.4.3 [States in Non-reentrant Functions], page 154.

`int wctomb (`*char *string, wchar_t wchar*`)`   [Function]
Preliminary: | MT-Unsafe race | AS-Unsafe corrupt heap lock dlopen | AC-Unsafe corrupt lock mem fd | See Section 1.2.2.1 [POSIX Safety Concepts], page 2.

The `wctomb` ("wide character to multibyte") function converts the wide character code *wchar* to its corresponding multibyte character sequence, and stores the result in bytes starting at *string*. At most `MB_CUR_MAX` characters are stored.

`wctomb` with non-null *string* distinguishes three possibilities for *wchar*: a valid wide character code (one that can be translated to a multibyte character), an invalid code, and `L'\0'`.

Given a valid code, `wctomb` converts it to a multibyte character, storing the bytes starting at *string*. Then it returns the number of bytes in that character (always at least 1 and never more than `MB_CUR_MAX`).

If *wchar* is an invalid wide character code, `wctomb` returns −1. If *wchar* is `L'\0'`, it returns 0, also storing `'\0'` in **string*.

If the multibyte character code uses shift characters, then `wctomb` maintains and updates a shift state as it scans. If you call `wctomb` with a null pointer for *string*, that initializes the shift state to its standard initial value. It also returns nonzero if the multibyte character code in use actually has a shift state. See Section 6.4.3 [States in Non-reentrant Functions], page 154.

Calling this function with a *wchar* argument of zero when *string* is not null has the side-effect of reinitializing the stored shift state *as well as* storing the multibyte character `'\0'` and returning 0.

Similar to `mbrlen` there is also a non-reentrant function that computes the length of a multibyte character. It can be defined in terms of `mbtowc`.

`int mblen (`*const char *string, size_t size*`)`   [Function]
Preliminary: | MT-Unsafe race | AS-Unsafe corrupt heap lock dlopen | AC-Unsafe corrupt lock mem fd | See Section 1.2.2.1 [POSIX Safety Concepts], page 2.

The `mblen` function with a non-null *string* argument returns the number of bytes that make up the multibyte character beginning at *string*, never examining more than *size* bytes. (The idea is to supply for *size* the number of bytes of data you have in hand.)

The return value of `mblen` distinguishes three possibilities: the first *size* bytes at *string* start with valid multibyte characters, they start with an invalid byte sequence or just part of a character, or *string* points to an empty string (a null character).

For a valid multibyte character, `mblen` returns the number of bytes in that character (always at least 1 and never more than *size*). For an invalid byte sequence, `mblen` returns −1. For an empty string, it returns 0.

If the multibyte character code uses shift characters, then `mblen` maintains and updates a shift state as it scans. If you call `mblen` with a null pointer for *string*, that initializes the shift state to its standard initial value. It also returns a nonzero value if the multibyte character code in use actually has a shift state. See Section 6.4.3 [States in Non-reentrant Functions], page 154.

The function `mblen` is declared in `stdlib.h`.

6.4.2 Non-reentrant Conversion of Strings

For convenience the ISO C90 standard also defines functions to convert entire strings instead of single characters. These functions suffer from the same problems as their reentrant counterparts from Amendment 1 to ISO C90; see Section 6.3.4 [Converting Multibyte and Wide Character Strings], page 146.

`size_t mbstowcs (`*wchar_t *wstring, const char *`string`*, size_t*   [Function]
    `size`*)*

Preliminary: | MT-Safe | AS-Unsafe corrupt heap lock dlopen | AC-Unsafe corrupt lock mem fd | See Section 1.2.2.1 [POSIX Safety Concepts], page 2.

The `mbstowcs` ("multibyte string to wide character string") function converts the null-terminated string of multibyte characters *string* to an array of wide character codes, storing not more than *size* wide characters into the array beginning at *wstring*. The terminating null character counts towards the size, so if *size* is less than the actual number of wide characters resulting from *string*, no terminating null character is stored.

The conversion of characters from *string* begins in the initial shift state.

If an invalid multibyte character sequence is found, the `mbstowcs` function returns a value of −1. Otherwise, it returns the number of wide characters stored in the array *wstring*. This number does not include the terminating null character, which is present if the number is less than *size*.

Here is an example showing how to convert a string of multibyte characters, allocating enough space for the result.

```
wchar_t *
mbstowcs_alloc (const char *string)
{
  size_t size = strlen (string) + 1;
  wchar_t *buf = xmalloc (size * sizeof (wchar_t));

  size = mbstowcs (buf, string, size);
  if (size == (size_t) -1)
```

```
          return NULL;
        buf = xrealloc (buf, (size + 1) * sizeof (wchar_t));
        return buf;
      }
```

size_t wcstombs (*char *string, const wchar_t *wstring, size_t*   [Function]
    size)

> Preliminary: | MT-Safe | AS-Unsafe corrupt heap lock dlopen | AC-Unsafe corrupt lock mem fd | See Section 1.2.2.1 [POSIX Safety Concepts], page 2.
>
> The `wcstombs` ("wide character string to multibyte string") function converts the null-terminated wide character array *wstring* into a string containing multibyte characters, storing not more than *size* bytes starting at *string*, followed by a terminating null character if there is room. The conversion of characters begins in the initial shift state.
>
> The terminating null character counts towards the size, so if *size* is less than or equal to the number of bytes needed in *wstring*, no terminating null character is stored.
>
> If a code that does not correspond to a valid multibyte character is found, the `wcstombs` function returns a value of -1. Otherwise, the return value is the number of bytes stored in the array *string*. This number does not include the terminating null character, which is present if the number is less than *size*.

6.4.3 States in Non-reentrant Functions

In some multibyte character codes, the *meaning* of any particular byte sequence is not fixed; it depends on what other sequences have come earlier in the same string. Typically there are just a few sequences that can change the meaning of other sequences; these few are called *shift sequences* and we say that they set the *shift state* for other sequences that follow.

To illustrate shift state and shift sequences, suppose we decide that the sequence 0200 (just one byte) enters Japanese mode, in which pairs of bytes in the range from 0240 to 0377 are single characters, while 0201 enters Latin-1 mode, in which single bytes in the range from 0240 to 0377 are characters, and interpreted according to the ISO Latin-1 character set. This is a multibyte code that has two alternative shift states ("Japanese mode" and "Latin-1 mode"), and two shift sequences that specify particular shift states.

When the multibyte character code in use has shift states, then `mblen`, `mbtowc`, and `wctomb` must maintain and update the current shift state as they scan the string. To make this work properly, you must follow these rules:

- Before starting to scan a string, call the function with a null pointer for the multibyte character address—for example, `mblen (NULL, 0)`. This initializes the shift state to its standard initial value.

- Scan the string one character at a time, in order. Do not "back up" and rescan characters already scanned, and do not intersperse the processing of different strings.

Here is an example of using `mblen` following these rules:

```
void
scan_string (char *s)
{
  int length = strlen (s);

  /* Initialize shift state.  */
```

```
mblen (NULL, 0);

while (1)
  {
    int thischar = mblen (s, length);
    /* Deal with end of string and invalid characters.  */
    if (thischar == 0)
      break;
    if (thischar == -1)
      {
        error ("invalid multibyte character");
        break;
      }
    /* Advance past this character.  */
    s += thischar;
    length -= thischar;
  }
}
```

The functions `mblen`, `mbtowc` and `wctomb` are not reentrant when using a multibyte code that uses a shift state. However, no other library functions call these functions, so you don't have to worry that the shift state will be changed mysteriously.

6.5 Generic Charset Conversion

The conversion functions mentioned so far in this chapter all had in common that they operate on character sets that are not directly specified by the functions. The multibyte encoding used is specified by the currently selected locale for the `LC_CTYPE` category. The wide character set is fixed by the implementation (in the case of the GNU C Library it is always UCS-4 encoded ISO 10646).

This has of course several problems when it comes to general character conversion:

- For every conversion where neither the source nor the destination character set is the character set of the locale for the `LC_CTYPE` category, one has to change the `LC_CTYPE` locale using `setlocale`.

  Changing the `LC_CTYPE` locale introduces major problems for the rest of the programs since several more functions (e.g., the character classification functions, see Section 4.1 [Classification of Characters], page 81) use the `LC_CTYPE` category.

- Parallel conversions to and from different character sets are not possible since the `LC_CTYPE` selection is global and shared by all threads.

- If neither the source nor the destination character set is the character set used for `wchar_t` representation, there is at least a two-step process necessary to convert a text using the functions above. One would have to select the source character set as the multibyte encoding, convert the text into a `wchar_t` text, select the destination character set as the multibyte encoding, and convert the wide character text to the multibyte (= destination) character set.

  Even if this is possible (which is not guaranteed) it is a very tiring work. Plus it suffers from the other two raised points even more due to the steady changing of the locale.

The XPG2 standard defines a completely new set of functions, which has none of these limitations. They are not at all coupled to the selected locales, and they have no constraints on the character sets selected for source and destination. Only the set of available conversions limits them. The standard does not specify that any conversion at all must be available. Such availability is a measure of the quality of the implementation.

In the following text first the interface to `iconv` and then the conversion function, will be described. Comparisons with other implementations will show what obstacles stand in the way of portable applications. Finally, the implementation is described in so far as might interest the advanced user who wants to extend conversion capabilities.

6.5.1 Generic Character Set Conversion Interface

This set of functions follows the traditional cycle of using a resource: open–use–close. The interface consists of three functions, each of which implements one step.

Before the interfaces are described it is necessary to introduce a data type. Just like other open–use–close interfaces the functions introduced here work using handles and the `iconv.h` header defines a special type for the handles used.

`iconv_t`   [Data Type]

> This data type is an abstract type defined in `iconv.h`. The user must not assume anything about the definition of this type; it must be completely opaque.
>
> Objects of this type can be assigned handles for the conversions using the `iconv` functions. The objects themselves need not be freed, but the conversions for which the handles stand for have to.

The first step is the function to create a handle.

`iconv_t iconv_open (const char *tocode, const char *fromcode)`   [Function]

> Preliminary: | MT-Safe locale | AS-Unsafe corrupt heap lock dlopen | AC-Unsafe corrupt lock mem fd | See Section 1.2.2.1 [POSIX Safety Concepts], page 2.
>
> The `iconv_open` function has to be used before starting a conversion. The two parameters this function takes determine the source and destination character set for the conversion, and if the implementation has the possibility to perform such a conversion, the function returns a handle.
>
> If the wanted conversion is not available, the `iconv_open` function returns (`iconv_t`) `-1`. In this case the global variable `errno` can have the following values:
>
> EMFILE   The process already has `OPEN_MAX` file descriptors open.
>
> ENFILE   The system limit of open files is reached.
>
> ENOMEM   Not enough memory to carry out the operation.
>
> EINVAL   The conversion from *fromcode* to *tocode* is not supported.
>
> It is not possible to use the same descriptor in different threads to perform independent conversions. The data structures associated with the descriptor include information about the conversion state. This must not be messed up by using it in different conversions.
>
> An `iconv` descriptor is like a file descriptor as for every use a new descriptor must be created. The descriptor does not stand for all of the conversions from *fromset* to *toset*.

The GNU C Library implementation of `iconv_open` has one significant extension to other implementations. To ease the extension of the set of available conversions, the implementation allows storing the necessary files with data and code in an arbitrary number of directories. How this extension must be written will be explained below (see Section 6.5.4 [The `iconv` Implementation in the GNU C Library], page 162). Here it is only important to say that all directories mentioned in the `GCONV_PATH` environment variable are considered only if they contain a file `gconv-modules`. These directories need not necessarily be created by the system administrator. In fact, this extension is introduced to help users writing and using their own, new conversions. Of course, this does not work for security reasons in SUID binaries; in this case only the system directory is considered and this normally is *prefix*/lib/gconv. The `GCONV_PATH` environment variable is examined exactly once at the first call of the `iconv_open` function. Later modifications of the variable have no effect.

The `iconv_open` function was introduced early in the X/Open Portability Guide, version 2. It is supported by all commercial Unices as it is required for the Unix branding. However, the quality and completeness of the implementation varies widely. The `iconv_open` function is declared in `iconv.h`.

The `iconv` implementation can associate large data structure with the handle returned by `iconv_open`. Therefore, it is crucial to free all the resources once all conversions are carried out and the conversion is not needed anymore.

`int iconv_close` (*iconv_t cd*)   [Function]
    Preliminary: | MT-Safe | AS-Unsafe corrupt heap lock dlopen | AC-Unsafe corrupt lock mem | See Section 1.2.2.1 [POSIX Safety Concepts], page 2.

    The `iconv_close` function frees all resources associated with the handle *cd*, which must have been returned by a successful call to the `iconv_open` function.

    If the function call was successful the return value is 0. Otherwise it is −1 and `errno` is set appropriately. Defined errors are:

    EBADF   The conversion descriptor is invalid.

    The `iconv_close` function was introduced together with the rest of the `iconv` functions in XPG2 and is declared in `iconv.h`.

The standard defines only one actual conversion function. This has, therefore, the most general interface: it allows conversion from one buffer to another. Conversion from a file to a buffer, vice versa, or even file to file can be implemented on top of it.

`size_t iconv` (*iconv_t cd, char **inbuf, size_t *inbytesleft, char*   [Function]
        ***outbuf, size_t *outbytesleft*)
    Preliminary: | MT-Safe race:cd | AS-Safe | AC-Unsafe corrupt | See Section 1.2.2.1 [POSIX Safety Concepts], page 2.

    The `iconv` function converts the text in the input buffer according to the rules associated with the descriptor *cd* and stores the result in the output buffer. It is possible to call the function for the same text several times in a row since for stateful character sets the necessary state information is kept in the data structures associated with the descriptor.

The input buffer is specified by *inbuf* and it contains *inbytesleft* bytes. The extra indirection is necessary for communicating the used input back to the caller (see below). It is important to note that the buffer pointer is of type char and the length is measured in bytes even if the input text is encoded in wide characters.

The output buffer is specified in a similar way. *outbuf* points to the beginning of the buffer with at least *outbytesleft* bytes room for the result. The buffer pointer again is of type char and the length is measured in bytes. If *outbuf* or *outbuf* is a null pointer, the conversion is performed but no output is available.

If *inbuf* is a null pointer, the iconv function performs the necessary action to put the state of the conversion into the initial state. This is obviously a no-op for non-stateful encodings, but if the encoding has a state, such a function call might put some byte sequences in the output buffer, which perform the necessary state changes. The next call with *inbuf* not being a null pointer then simply goes on from the initial state. It is important that the programmer never makes any assumption as to whether the conversion has to deal with states. Even if the input and output character sets are not stateful, the implementation might still have to keep states. This is due to the implementation chosen for the GNU C Library as it is described below. Therefore an iconv call to reset the state should always be performed if some protocol requires this for the output text.

The conversion stops for one of three reasons. The first is that all characters from the input buffer are converted. This actually can mean two things: either all bytes from the input buffer are consumed or there are some bytes at the end of the buffer that possibly can form a complete character but the input is incomplete. The second reason for a stop is that the output buffer is full. And the third reason is that the input contains invalid characters.

In all of these cases the buffer pointers after the last successful conversion, for the input and output buffers, are stored in *inbuf* and *outbuf*, and the available room in each buffer is stored in *inbytesleft* and *outbytesleft*.

Since the character sets selected in the iconv_open call can be almost arbitrary, there can be situations where the input buffer contains valid characters, which have no identical representation in the output character set. The behavior in this situation is undefined. The *current* behavior of the GNU C Library in this situation is to return with an error immediately. This certainly is not the most desirable solution; therefore, future versions will provide better ones, but they are not yet finished.

If all input from the input buffer is successfully converted and stored in the output buffer, the function returns the number of non-reversible conversions performed. In all other cases the return value is (size_t) -1 and errno is set appropriately. In such cases the value pointed to by *inbytesleft* is nonzero.

EILSEQ   The conversion stopped because of an invalid byte sequence in the input. After the call, *inbuf* points at the first byte of the invalid byte sequence.

E2BIG   The conversion stopped because it ran out of space in the output buffer.

EINVAL   The conversion stopped because of an incomplete byte sequence at the end of the input buffer.

EBADF   The *cd* argument is invalid.

The `iconv` function was introduced in the XPG2 standard and is declared in the `iconv.h` header.

The definition of the `iconv` function is quite good overall. It provides quite flexible functionality. The only problems lie in the boundary cases, which are incomplete byte sequences at the end of the input buffer and invalid input. A third problem, which is not really a design problem, is the way conversions are selected. The standard does not say anything about the legitimate names, a minimal set of available conversions. We will see how this negatively impacts other implementations, as demonstrated below.

6.5.2 A complete `iconv` example

The example below features a solution for a common problem. Given that one knows the internal encoding used by the system for `wchar_t` strings, one often is in the position to read text from a file and store it in wide character buffers. One can do this using `mbsrtowcs`, but then we run into the problems discussed above.

```
int
file2wcs (int fd, const char *charset, wchar_t *outbuf, size_t avail)
{
  char inbuf[BUFSIZ];
  size_t insize = 0;
  char *wrptr = (char *) outbuf;
  int result = 0;
  iconv_t cd;

  cd = iconv_open ("WCHAR_T", charset);
  if (cd == (iconv_t) -1)
    {
      /* Something went wrong.  */
      if (errno == EINVAL)
        error (0, 0, "conversion from '%s' to wchar_t not available",
               charset);
      else
        perror ("iconv_open");

      /* Terminate the output string.  */
      *outbuf = L'\0';

      return -1;
    }

  while (avail > 0)
    {
      size_t nread;
      size_t nconv;
      char *inptr = inbuf;

      /* Read more input.  */
      nread = read (fd, inbuf + insize, sizeof (inbuf) - insize);
      if (nread == 0)
        {
          /* When we come here the file is completely read.
             This still could mean there are some unused
             characters in the inbuf. Put them back.  */
          if (lseek (fd, -insize, SEEK_CUR) == -1)
            result = -1;
```

```
            /* Now write out the byte sequence to get into the
               initial state if this is necessary.  */
            iconv (cd, NULL, NULL, &wrptr, &avail);

            break;
          }
        insize += nread;

        /* Do the conversion.  */
        nconv = iconv (cd, &inptr, &insize, &wrptr, &avail);
        if (nconv == (size_t) -1)
          {
            /* Not everything went right.  It might only be
               an unfinished byte sequence at the end of the
               buffer.  Or it is a real problem.  */
            if (errno == EINVAL)
              /* This is harmless.  Simply move the unused
                 bytes to the beginning of the buffer so that
                 they can be used in the next round.  */
              memmove (inbuf, inptr, insize);
            else
              {
                /* It is a real problem.  Maybe we ran out of
                   space in the output buffer or we have invalid
                   input.  In any case back the file pointer to
                   the position of the last processed byte.  */
                lseek (fd, -insize, SEEK_CUR);
                result = -1;
                break;
              }
          }
      }

    /* Terminate the output string.  */
    if (avail >= sizeof (wchar_t))
      *((wchar_t *) wrptr) = L'\0';

    if (iconv_close (cd) != 0)
      perror ("iconv_close");

    return (wchar_t *) wrptr - outbuf;
  }
```

This example shows the most important aspects of using the `iconv` functions. It shows how successive calls to `iconv` can be used to convert large amounts of text. The user does not have to care about stateful encodings as the functions take care of everything.

An interesting point is the case where `iconv` returns an error and **errno** is set to `EINVAL`. This is not really an error in the transformation. It can happen whenever the input character set contains byte sequences of more than one byte for some character and texts are not processed in one piece. In this case there is a chance that a multibyte sequence is cut. The caller can then simply read the remainder of the takes and feed the offending bytes together with new character from the input to `iconv` and continue the work. The internal state kept in the descriptor is *not* unspecified after such an event as is the case with the conversion functions from the ISO C standard.

The example also shows the problem of using wide character strings with `iconv`. As explained in the description of the `iconv` function above, the function always takes a pointer to a `char` array and the available space is measured in bytes. In the example, the output buffer is a wide character buffer; therefore, we use a local variable *wrptr* of type `char *`, which is used in the `iconv` calls.

This looks rather innocent but can lead to problems on platforms that have tight restriction on alignment. Therefore the caller of `iconv` has to make sure that the pointers passed are suitable for access of characters from the appropriate character set. Since, in the above case, the input parameter to the function is a `wchar_t` pointer, this is the case (unless the user violates alignment when computing the parameter). But in other situations, especially when writing generic functions where one does not know what type of character set one uses and, therefore, treats text as a sequence of bytes, it might become tricky.

6.5.3 Some Details about other `iconv` Implementations

This is not really the place to discuss the `iconv` implementation of other systems but it is necessary to know a bit about them to write portable programs. The above mentioned problems with the specification of the `iconv` functions can lead to portability issues.

The first thing to notice is that, due to the large number of character sets in use, it is certainly not practical to encode the conversions directly in the C library. Therefore, the conversion information must come from files outside the C library. This is usually done in one or both of the following ways:

- The C library contains a set of generic conversion functions that can read the needed conversion tables and other information from data files. These files get loaded when necessary.

  This solution is problematic as it requires a great deal of effort to apply to all character sets (potentially an infinite set). The differences in the structure of the different character sets is so large that many different variants of the table-processing functions must be developed. In addition, the generic nature of these functions make them slower than specifically implemented functions.

- The C library only contains a framework that can dynamically load object files and execute the conversion functions contained therein.

  This solution provides much more flexibility. The C library itself contains only very little code and therefore reduces the general memory footprint. Also, with a documented interface between the C library and the loadable modules it is possible for third parties to extend the set of available conversion modules. A drawback of this solution is that dynamic loading must be available.

Some implementations in commercial Unices implement a mixture of these possibilities; the majority implement only the second solution. Using loadable modules moves the code out of the library itself and keeps the door open for extensions and improvements, but this design is also limiting on some platforms since not many platforms support dynamic loading in statically linked programs. On platforms without this capability it is therefore not possible to use this interface in statically linked programs. The GNU C Library has, on ELF platforms, no problems with dynamic loading in these situations; therefore, this point is moot. The danger is that one gets acquainted with this situation and forgets about the restrictions on other systems.

A second thing to know about other `iconv` implementations is that the number of available conversions is often very limited. Some implementations provide, in the standard release (not special international or developer releases), at most 100 to 200 conversion possibilities. This does not mean 200 different character sets are supported; for example, conversions from one character set to a set of 10 others might count as 10 conversions. Together with the other direction this makes 20 conversion possibilities used up by one character set. One can imagine the thin coverage these platforms provide. Some Unix vendors even provide only a handful of conversions, which renders them useless for almost all uses.

This directly leads to a third and probably the most problematic point. The way the `iconv` conversion functions are implemented on all known Unix systems and the availability of the conversion functions from character set $\mathcal{A}$ to $\mathcal{B}$ and the conversion from $\mathcal{B}$ to $\mathcal{C}$ does *not* imply that the conversion from $\mathcal{A}$ to $\mathcal{C}$ is available.

This might not seem unreasonable and problematic at first, but it is a quite big problem as one will notice shortly after hitting it. To show the problem we assume to write a program that has to convert from $\mathcal{A}$ to $\mathcal{C}$. A call like

```
cd = iconv_open ("C", "A");
```

fails according to the assumption above. But what does the program do now? The conversion is necessary; therefore, simply giving up is not an option.

This is a nuisance. The `iconv` function should take care of this. But how should the program proceed from here on? If it tries to convert to character set $\mathcal{B}$, first the two `iconv_open` calls

```
cd1 = iconv_open ("B", "A");
```

and

```
cd2 = iconv_open ("C", "B");
```

will succeed, but how to find $\mathcal{B}$?

Unfortunately, the answer is: there is no general solution. On some systems guessing might help. On those systems most character sets can convert to and from UTF-8 encoded ISO 10646 or Unicode text. Besides this only some very system-specific methods can help. Since the conversion functions come from loadable modules and these modules must be stored somewhere in the filesystem, one *could* try to find them and determine from the available file which conversions are available and whether there is an indirect route from $\mathcal{A}$ to $\mathcal{C}$.

This example shows one of the design errors of `iconv` mentioned above. It should at least be possible to determine the list of available conversions programmatically so that if `iconv_open` says there is no such conversion, one could make sure this also is true for indirect routes.

6.5.4 The `iconv` Implementation in the GNU C Library

After reading about the problems of `iconv` implementations in the last section it is certainly good to note that the implementation in the GNU C Library has none of the problems mentioned above. What follows is a step-by-step analysis of the points raised above. The evaluation is based on the current state of the development (as of January 1999). The development of the `iconv` functions is not complete, but basic functionality has solidified.

The GNU C Library's `iconv` implementation uses shared loadable modules to implement the conversions. A very small number of conversions are built into the library itself but these are only rather trivial conversions.

All the benefits of loadable modules are available in the GNU C Library implementation. This is especially appealing since the interface is well documented (see below), and it, therefore, is easy to write new conversion modules. The drawback of using loadable objects is not a problem in the GNU C Library, at least on ELF systems. Since the library is able to load shared objects even in statically linked binaries, static linking need not be forbidden in case one wants to use `iconv`.

The second mentioned problem is the number of supported conversions. Currently, the GNU C Library supports more than 150 character sets. The way the implementation is designed the number of supported conversions is greater than 22350 (150 times 149). If any conversion from or to a character set is missing, it can be added easily.

Particularly impressive as it may be, this high number is due to the fact that the GNU C Library implementation of `iconv` does not have the third problem mentioned above (i.e., whenever there is a conversion from a character set $\mathcal{A}$ to $\mathcal{B}$ and from $\mathcal{B}$ to $\mathcal{C}$ it is always possible to convert from $\mathcal{A}$ to $\mathcal{C}$ directly). If the `iconv_open` returns an error and sets `errno` to `EINVAL`, there is no known way, directly or indirectly, to perform the wanted conversion.

Triangulation is achieved by providing for each character set a conversion from and to UCS-4 encoded ISO 10646. Using ISO 10646 as an intermediate representation it is possible to *triangulate* (i.e., convert with an intermediate representation).

There is no inherent requirement to provide a conversion to ISO 10646 for a new character set, and it is also possible to provide other conversions where neither source nor destination character set is ISO 10646. The existing set of conversions is simply meant to cover all conversions that might be of interest.

All currently available conversions use the triangulation method above, making conversion run unnecessarily slow. If, for example, somebody often needs the conversion from ISO-2022-JP to EUC-JP, a quicker solution would involve direct conversion between the two character sets, skipping the input to ISO 10646 first. The two character sets of interest are much more similar to each other than to ISO 10646.

In such a situation one easily can write a new conversion and provide it as a better alternative. The GNU C Library `iconv` implementation would automatically use the module implementing the conversion if it is specified to be more efficient.

6.5.4.1 Format of `gconv-modules` files

All information about the available conversions comes from a file named `gconv-modules`, which can be found in any of the directories along the `GCONV_PATH`. The `gconv-modules` files are line-oriented text files, where each of the lines has one of the following formats:

- If the first non-whitespace character is a `#` the line contains only comments and is ignored.

- Lines starting with `alias` define an alias name for a character set. Two more words are expected on the line. The first word defines the alias name, and the second defines the original name of the character set. The effect is that it is possible to use the alias name in the *fromset* or *toset* parameters of `iconv_open` and achieve the same result as when using the real character set name.

This is quite important as a character set has often many different names. There is normally an official name but this need not correspond to the most popular name. Besides this many character sets have special names that are somehow constructed. For example, all character sets specified by the ISO have an alias of the form `ISO-IR-nnn` where *nnn* is the registration number. This allows programs that know about the registration number to construct character set names and use them in `iconv_open` calls. More on the available names and aliases follows below.

- Lines starting with `module` introduce an available conversion module. These lines must contain three or four more words.

  The first word specifies the source character set, the second word the destination character set of conversion implemented in this module, and the third word is the name of the loadable module. The filename is constructed by appending the usual shared object suffix (normally `.so`) and this file is then supposed to be found in the same directory the `gconv-modules` file is in. The last word on the line, which is optional, is a numeric value representing the cost of the conversion. If this word is missing, a cost of 1 is assumed. The numeric value itself does not matter that much; what counts are the relative values of the sums of costs for all possible conversion paths. Below is a more precise description of the use of the cost value.

Returning to the example above where one has written a module to directly convert from ISO-2022-JP to EUC-JP and back. All that has to be done is to put the new module, let its name be ISO2022JP-EUCJP.so, in a directory and add a file `gconv-modules` with the following content in the same directory:

```
module  ISO-2022-JP//   EUC-JP//        ISO2022JP-EUCJP    1
module  EUC-JP//         ISO-2022-JP//   ISO2022JP-EUCJP    1
```

To see why this is sufficient, it is necessary to understand how the conversion used by `iconv` (and described in the descriptor) is selected. The approach to this problem is quite simple.

At the first call of the `iconv_open` function the program reads all available `gconv-modules` files and builds up two tables: one containing all the known aliases and another that contains the information about the conversions and which shared object implements them.

6.5.4.2 Finding the conversion path in `iconv`

The set of available conversions form a directed graph with weighted edges. The weights on the edges are the costs specified in the `gconv-modules` files. The `iconv_open` function uses an algorithm suitable for search for the best path in such a graph and so constructs a list of conversions that must be performed in succession to get the transformation from the source to the destination character set.

Explaining why the above `gconv-modules` files allows the `iconv` implementation to resolve the specific ISO-2022-JP to EUC-JP conversion module instead of the conversion coming with the library itself is straightforward. Since the latter conversion takes two steps (from ISO-2022-JP to ISO 10646 and then from ISO 10646 to EUC-JP), the cost is $1 + 1 = 2$. The above `gconv-modules` file, however, specifies that the new conversion modules can perform this conversion with only the cost of 1.

A mysterious item about the `gconv-modules` file above (and also the file coming with the GNU C Library) are the names of the character sets specified in the `module` lines. Why do almost all the names end in //? And this is not all: the names can actually be regular expressions. At this point in time this mystery should not be revealed, unless you have the relevant spell-casting materials: ashes from an original DOS 6.2 boot disk burnt in effigy, a crucifix blessed by St. Emacs, assorted herbal roots from Central America, sand from Cebu, etc. Sorry! **The part of the implementation where this is used is not yet finished. For now please simply follow the existing examples. It'll become clearer once it is. –drepper**

A last remark about the `gconv-modules` is about the names not ending with //. A character set named `INTERNAL` is often mentioned. From the discussion above and the chosen name it should have become clear that this is the name for the representation used in the intermediate step of the triangulation. We have said that this is UCS-4 but actually that is not quite right. The UCS-4 specification also includes the specification of the byte ordering used. Since a UCS-4 value consists of four bytes, a stored value is affected by byte ordering. The internal representation is *not* the same as UCS-4 in case the byte ordering of the processor (or at least the running process) is not the same as the one required for UCS-4. This is done for performance reasons as one does not want to perform unnecessary byte-swapping operations if one is not interested in actually seeing the result in UCS-4. To avoid trouble with endianness, the internal representation consistently is named `INTERNAL` even on big-endian systems where the representations are identical.

6.5.4.3 `iconv` module data structures

So far this section has described how modules are located and considered to be used. What remains to be described is the interface of the modules so that one can write new ones. This section describes the interface as it is in use in January 1999. The interface will change a bit in the future but, with luck, only in an upwardly compatible way.

The definitions necessary to write new modules are publicly available in the non-standard header `gconv.h`. The following text, therefore, describes the definitions from this header file. First, however, it is necessary to get an overview.

From the perspective of the user of `iconv` the interface is quite simple: the `iconv_open` function returns a handle that can be used in calls to `iconv`, and finally the handle is freed with a call to `iconv_close`. The problem is that the handle has to be able to represent the possibly long sequences of conversion steps and also the state of each conversion since the handle is all that is passed to the `iconv` function. Therefore, the data structures are really the elements necessary to understanding the implementation.

We need two different kinds of data structures. The first describes the conversion and the second describes the state etc. There are really two type definitions like this in `gconv.h`.

`struct __gconv_step` [Data type]
> This data structure describes one conversion a module can perform. For each function in a loaded module with conversion functions there is exactly one object of this type. This object is shared by all users of the conversion (i.e., this object does not contain any information corresponding to an actual conversion; it only describes the conversion itself).

```
struct __gconv_loaded_object *__shlib_handle
const char *__modname
int __counter
```
> All these elements of the structure are used internally in the C library to coordinate loading and unloading the shared object. One must not expect any of the other elements to be available or initialized.

```
const char *__from_name
const char *__to_name
```
> `__from_name` and `__to_name` contain the names of the source and destination character sets. They can be used to identify the actual conversion to be carried out since one module might implement conversions for more than one character set and/or direction.

```
gconv_fct __fct
gconv_init_fct __init_fct
gconv_end_fct __end_fct
```
> These elements contain pointers to the functions in the loadable module. The interface will be explained below.

```
int __min_needed_from
int __max_needed_from
int __min_needed_to
int __max_needed_to;
```
> These values have to be supplied in the init function of the module. The `__min_needed_from` value specifies how many bytes a character of the source character set at least needs. The `__max_needed_from` specifies the maximum value that also includes possible shift sequences.
>
> The `__min_needed_to` and `__max_needed_to` values serve the same purpose as `__min_needed_from` and `__max_needed_from` but this time for the destination character set.
>
> It is crucial that these values be accurate since otherwise the conversion functions will have problems or not work at all.

```
int __stateful
```
> This element must also be initialized by the init function. `int __stateful` is nonzero if the source character set is stateful. Otherwise it is zero.

```
void *__data
```
> This element can be used freely by the conversion functions in the module. `void *__data` can be used to communicate extra information from one call to another. `void *__data` need not be initialized if not needed at all. If `void *__data` element is assigned a pointer to dynamically allocated memory (presumably in the init function) it has to be made sure that the end function deallocates the memory. Otherwise the application will leak memory.
>
> It is important to be aware that this data structure is shared by all users of this specification conversion and therefore the `__data` element must not contain data specific to one specific use of the conversion function.

`struct __gconv_step_data`   [Data type]

> This is the data structure that contains the information specific to each use of the conversion functions.

> `char *__outbuf`
> `char *__outbufend`

>> These elements specify the output buffer for the conversion step. The `__outbuf` element points to the beginning of the buffer, and `__outbufend` points to the byte following the last byte in the buffer. The conversion function must not assume anything about the size of the buffer but it can be safely assumed there is room for at least one complete character in the output buffer.

>> Once the conversion is finished, if the conversion is the last step, the `__outbuf` element must be modified to point after the last byte written into the buffer to signal how much output is available. If this conversion step is not the last one, the element must not be modified. The `__outbufend` element must not be modified.

> `int __is_last`

>> This element is nonzero if this conversion step is the last one. This information is necessary for the recursion. See the description of the conversion function internals below. This element must never be modified.

> `int __invocation_counter`

>> The conversion function can use this element to see how many calls of the conversion function already happened. Some character sets require a certain prolog when generating output, and by comparing this value with zero, one can find out whether it is the first call and whether, therefore, the prolog should be emitted. This element must never be modified.

> `int __internal_use`

>> This element is another one rarely used but needed in certain situations. It is assigned a nonzero value in case the conversion functions are used to implement `mbsrtowcs` et.al. (i.e., the function is not used directly through the `iconv` interface).

>> This sometimes makes a difference as it is expected that the `iconv` functions are used to translate entire texts while the `mbsrtowcs` functions are normally used only to convert single strings and might be used multiple times to convert entire texts.

>> But in this situation we would have problem complying with some rules of the character set specification. Some character sets require a prolog, which must appear exactly once for an entire text. If a number of `mbsrtowcs` calls are used to convert the text, only the first call must add the prolog. However, because there is no communication between the different calls of `mbsrtowcs`, the conversion functions have no possibility to find this out. The situation is different for sequences of `iconv` calls since the handle allows access to the needed information.

>> The `int __internal_use` element is mostly used together with `__invocation_counter` as follows:

```
if (!data->__internal_use
    && data->__invocation_counter == 0)
  /* Emit prolog.  */
  ...
```

This element must never be modified.

mbstate_t *__statep

> The __statep element points to an object of type mbstate_t (see Section 6.3.2 [Representing the state of the conversion], page 139). The conversion of a stateful character set must use the object pointed to by __statep to store information about the conversion state. The __statep element itself must never be modified.

mbstate_t __state

> This element must *never* be used directly. It is only part of this structure to have the needed space allocated.

6.5.4.4 iconv module interfaces

With the knowledge about the data structures we now can describe the conversion function itself. To understand the interface a bit of knowledge is necessary about the functionality in the C library that loads the objects with the conversions.

It is often the case that one conversion is used more than once (i.e., there are several iconv_open calls for the same set of character sets during one program run). The mbsrtowcs et.al. functions in the GNU C Library also use the iconv functionality, which increases the number of uses of the same functions even more.

Because of this multiple use of conversions, the modules do not get loaded exclusively for one conversion. Instead a module once loaded can be used by an arbitrary number of iconv or mbsrtowcs calls at the same time. The splitting of the information between conversion- function-specific information and conversion data makes this possible. The last section showed the two data structures used to do this.

This is of course also reflected in the interface and semantics of the functions that the modules must provide. There are three functions that must have the following names:

gconv_init

> The gconv_init function initializes the conversion function specific data structure. This very same object is shared by all conversions that use this conversion and, therefore, no state information about the conversion itself must be stored in here. If a module implements more than one conversion, the gconv_init function will be called multiple times.

gconv_end

> The gconv_end function is responsible for freeing all resources allocated by the gconv_init function. If there is nothing to do, this function can be missing. Special care must be taken if the module implements more than one conversion and the gconv_init function does not allocate the same resources for all conversions.

gconv

> This is the actual conversion function. It is called to convert one block of text. It gets passed the conversion step information initialized by gconv_init and the conversion data, specific to this use of the conversion functions.

There are three data types defined for the three module interface functions and these define the interface.

int (*__gconv_init_fct) (*struct __gconv_step* *)   [Data type]
    This specifies the interface of the initialization function of the module. It is called exactly once for each conversion the module implements.

    As explained in the description of the **struct __gconv_step** data structure above the initialization function has to initialize parts of it.

__min_needed_from
__max_needed_from
__min_needed_to
__max_needed_to
        These elements must be initialized to the exact numbers of the minimum and maximum number of bytes used by one character in the source and destination character sets, respectively. If the characters all have the same size, the minimum and maximum values are the same.

__stateful
        This element must be initialized to a nonzero value if the source character set is stateful. Otherwise it must be zero.

If the initialization function needs to communicate some information to the conversion function, this communication can happen using the **__data** element of the **__gconv_step** structure. But since this data is shared by all the conversions, it must not be modified by the conversion function. The example below shows how this can be used.

```
#define MIN_NEEDED_FROM      1
#define MAX_NEEDED_FROM      4
#define MIN_NEEDED_TO        4
#define MAX_NEEDED_TO        4

int
gconv_init (struct __gconv_step *step)
{
  /* Determine which direction.  */
  struct iso2022jp_data *new_data;
  enum direction dir = illegal_dir;
  enum variant var = illegal_var;
  int result;

  if (__strcasecmp (step->__from_name, "ISO-2022-JP//") == 0)
    {
      dir = from_iso2022jp;
      var = iso2022jp;
    }
  else if (__strcasecmp (step->__to_name, "ISO-2022-JP//") == 0)
    {
      dir = to_iso2022jp;
      var = iso2022jp;
    }
  else if (__strcasecmp (step->__from_name, "ISO-2022-JP-2//") == 0)
    {
      dir = from_iso2022jp;
      var = iso2022jp2;
```

```
        }
      else if (__strcasecmp (step->__to_name, "ISO-2022-JP-2//") == 0)
        {
          dir = to_iso2022jp;
          var = iso2022jp2;
        }

      result = __GCONV_NOCONV;
      if (dir != illegal_dir)
        {
          new_data = (struct iso2022jp_data *)
            malloc (sizeof (struct iso2022jp_data));

          result = __GCONV_NOMEM;
          if (new_data != NULL)
            {
              new_data->dir = dir;
              new_data->var = var;
              step->__data = new_data;

              if (dir == from_iso2022jp)
                {
                  step->__min_needed_from = MIN_NEEDED_FROM;
                  step->__max_needed_from = MAX_NEEDED_FROM;
                  step->__min_needed_to = MIN_NEEDED_TO;
                  step->__max_needed_to = MAX_NEEDED_TO;
                }
              else
                {
                  step->__min_needed_from = MIN_NEEDED_TO;
                  step->__max_needed_from = MAX_NEEDED_TO;
                  step->__min_needed_to = MIN_NEEDED_FROM;
                  step->__max_needed_to = MAX_NEEDED_FROM + 2;
                }

              /* Yes, this is a stateful encoding.  */
              step->__stateful = 1;

              result = __GCONV_OK;
            }
        }

    return result;
}
```

The function first checks which conversion is wanted. The module from which this function is taken implements four different conversions; which one is selected can be determined by comparing the names. The comparison should always be done without paying attention to the case.

Next, a data structure, which contains the necessary information about which conversion is selected, is allocated. The data structure struct iso2022jp_data is locally defined since, outside the module, this data is not used at all. Please note that if all four conversions this module supports are requested there are four data blocks.

One interesting thing is the initialization of the __min_ and __max_ elements of the step data object. A single ISO-2022-JP character can consist of one to four bytes. Therefore the MIN_NEEDED_FROM and MAX_NEEDED_FROM macros are defined this way.

The output is always the INTERNAL character set (aka UCS-4) and therefore each character consists of exactly four bytes. For the conversion from INTERNAL to ISO-2022-JP we have to take into account that escape sequences might be necessary to switch the character sets. Therefore the __max_needed_to element for this direction gets assigned MAX_NEEDED_FROM + 2. This takes into account the two bytes needed for the escape sequences to signal the switching. The asymmetry in the maximum values for the two directions can be explained easily: when reading ISO-2022-JP text, escape sequences can be handled alone (i.e., it is not necessary to process a real character since the effect of the escape sequence can be recorded in the state information). The situation is different for the other direction. Since it is in general not known which character comes next, one cannot emit escape sequences to change the state in advance. This means the escape sequences have to be emitted together with the next character. Therefore one needs more room than only for the character itself.

The possible return values of the initialization function are:

__GCONV_OK

> The initialization succeeded

__GCONV_NOCONV

> The requested conversion is not supported in the module. This can happen if the gconv-modules file has errors.

__GCONV_NOMEM

> Memory required to store additional information could not be allocated.

The function called before the module is unloaded is significantly easier. It often has nothing at all to do; in which case it can be left out completely.

void (*__gconv_end_fct) (struct gconv_step *)   [Data type]
> The task of this function is to free all resources allocated in the initialization function. Therefore only the __data element of the object pointed to by the argument is of interest. Continuing the example from the initialization function, the finalization function looks like this:
>
> ```
> void
> gconv_end (struct __gconv_step *data)
> {
>   free (data->__data);
> }
> ```

The most important function is the conversion function itself, which can get quite complicated for complex character sets. But since this is not of interest here, we will only describe a possible skeleton for the conversion function.

int (*__gconv_fct) (struct __gconv_step *, struct   [Data type]
__gconv_step_data *, const char **, const char *, size_t *, int)
> The conversion function can be called for two basic reasons: to convert text or to reset the state. From the description of the iconv function it can be seen why the flushing mode is necessary. What mode is selected is determined by the sixth argument, an integer. This argument being nonzero means that flushing is selected.
>
> Common to both modes is where the output buffer can be found. The information about this buffer is stored in the conversion step data. A pointer to this information

is passed as the second argument to this function. The description of the `struct __gconv_step_data` structure has more information on the conversion step data.

What has to be done for flushing depends on the source character set. If the source character set is not stateful, nothing has to be done. Otherwise the function has to emit a byte sequence to bring the state object into the initial state. Once this all happened the other conversion modules in the chain of conversions have to get the same chance. Whether another step follows can be determined from the `__is_last` element of the step data structure to which the first parameter points.

The more interesting mode is when actual text has to be converted. The first step in this case is to convert as much text as possible from the input buffer and store the result in the output buffer. The start of the input buffer is determined by the third argument, which is a pointer to a pointer variable referencing the beginning of the buffer. The fourth argument is a pointer to the byte right after the last byte in the buffer.

The conversion has to be performed according to the current state if the character set is stateful. The state is stored in an object pointed to by the `__statep` element of the step data (second argument). Once either the input buffer is empty or the output buffer is full the conversion stops. At this point, the pointer variable referenced by the third parameter must point to the byte following the last processed byte (i.e., if all of the input is consumed, this pointer and the fourth parameter have the same value).

What now happens depends on whether this step is the last one. If it is the last step, the only thing that has to be done is to update the `__outbuf` element of the step data structure to point after the last written byte. This update gives the caller the information on how much text is available in the output buffer. In addition, the variable pointed to by the fifth parameter, which is of type `size_t`, must be incremented by the number of characters (*not bytes*) that were converted in a non-reversible way. Then, the function can return.

In case the step is not the last one, the later conversion functions have to get a chance to do their work. Therefore, the appropriate conversion function has to be called. The information about the functions is stored in the conversion data structures, passed as the first parameter. This information and the step data are stored in arrays, so the next element in both cases can be found by simple pointer arithmetic:

```
int
gconv (struct __gconv_step *step, struct __gconv_step_data *data,
       const char **inbuf, const char *inbufend, size_t *written,
       int do_flush)
{
  struct __gconv_step *next_step = step + 1;
  struct __gconv_step_data *next_data = data + 1;
  ...
```

The `next_step` pointer references the next step information and `next_data` the next data record. The call of the next function therefore will look similar to this:

```
next_step->__fct (next_step, next_data, &outerr, outbuf,
                  written, 0)
```

But this is not yet all. Once the function call returns the conversion function might have some more to do. If the return value of the function is `__GCONV_EMPTY_INPUT`, more room is available in the output buffer. Unless the input buffer is empty, the conversion functions start all over again and process the rest of the input buffer. If the return value is not `__GCONV_EMPTY_INPUT`, something went wrong and we have to recover from this.

A requirement for the conversion function is that the input buffer pointer (the third argument) always point to the last character that was put in converted form into the output buffer. This is trivially true after the conversion performed in the current step, but if the conversion functions deeper downstream stop prematurely, not all characters from the output buffer are consumed and, therefore, the input buffer pointers must be backed off to the right position.

Correcting the input buffers is easy to do if the input and output character sets have a fixed width for all characters. In this situation we can compute how many characters are left in the output buffer and, therefore, can correct the input buffer pointer appropriately with a similar computation. Things are getting tricky if either character set has characters represented with variable length byte sequences, and it gets even more complicated if the conversion has to take care of the state. In these cases the conversion has to be performed once again, from the known state before the initial conversion (i.e., if necessary the state of the conversion has to be reset and the conversion loop has to be executed again). The difference now is that it is known how much input must be created, and the conversion can stop before converting the first unused character. Once this is done the input buffer pointers must be updated again and the function can return.

One final thing should be mentioned. If it is necessary for the conversion to know whether it is the first invocation (in case a prolog has to be emitted), the conversion function should increment the `__invocation_counter` element of the step data structure just before returning to the caller. See the description of the `struct __gconv_step_data` structure above for more information on how this can be used.

The return value must be one of the following values:

`__GCONV_EMPTY_INPUT`

> All input was consumed and there is room left in the output buffer.

`__GCONV_FULL_OUTPUT`

> No more room in the output buffer. In case this is not the last step this value is propagated down from the call of the next conversion function in the chain.

`__GCONV_INCOMPLETE_INPUT`

> The input buffer is not entirely empty since it contains an incomplete character sequence.

The following example provides a framework for a conversion function. In case a new conversion has to be written the holes in this implementation have to be filled and that is it.

```
int
gconv (struct __gconv_step *step, struct __gconv_step_data *data,
       const char **inbuf, const char *inbufend, size_t *written,
       int do_flush)
{
```

```
struct __gconv_step *next_step = step + 1;
struct __gconv_step_data *next_data = data + 1;
gconv_fct fct = next_step->__fct;
int status;

/* If the function is called with no input this means we have
   to reset to the initial state.  The possibly partly
   converted input is dropped.  */
if (do_flush)
  {
    status = __GCONV_OK;

    /* Possible emit a byte sequence which put the state object
       into the initial state.  */

    /* Call the steps down the chain if there are any but only
       if we successfully emitted the escape sequence.  */
    if (status == __GCONV_OK && ! data->__is_last)
      status = fct (next_step, next_data, NULL, NULL,
                    written, 1);
  }
else
  {
    /* We preserve the initial values of the pointer variables.  */
    const char *inptr = *inbuf;
    char *outbuf = data->__outbuf;
    char *outend = data->__outbufend;
    char *outptr;

    do
      {
        /* Remember the start value for this round.  */
        inptr = *inbuf;
        /* The outbuf buffer is empty.  */
        outptr = outbuf;

        /* For stateful encodings the state must be safe here.  */

        /* Run the conversion loop.  status is set
           appropriately afterwards.  */

        /* If this is the last step, leave the loop.  There is
           nothing we can do.  */
        if (data->__is_last)
          {
            /* Store information about how many bytes are
               available.  */
            data->__outbuf = outbuf;

            /* If any non-reversible conversions were performed,
               add the number to *written.  */

            break;
          }

        /* Write out all output that was produced.  */
        if (outbuf > outptr)
          {
```

```
                    const char *outerr = data->__outbuf;
                    int result;

                    result = fct (next_step, next_data, &outerr,
                                  outbuf, written, 0);

                    if (result != __GCONV_EMPTY_INPUT)
                      {
                        if (outerr != outbuf)
                          {
                            /* Reset the input buffer pointer.  We
                               document here the complex case.   */
                            size_t nstatus;

                            /* Reload the pointers.   */
                            *inbuf = inptr;
                            outbuf = outptr;

                            /* Possibly reset the state.   */

                            /* Redo the conversion, but this time
                               the end of the output buffer is at
                               outerr.   */
                          }

                        /* Change the status.   */
                        status = result;
                      }
                    else
                      /* All the output is consumed, we can make
                         another run if everything was ok.   */
                      if (status == __GCONV_FULL_OUTPUT)
                        status = __GCONV_OK;
                  }
              }
            while (status == __GCONV_OK);

            /* We finished one use of this step.   */
            ++data->__invocation_counter;
          }

      return status;
    }
```

This information should be sufficient to write new modules. Anybody doing so should also take a look at the available source code in the GNU C Library sources. It contains many examples of working and optimized modules.

7 Locales and Internationalization

Different countries and cultures have varying conventions for how to communicate. These conventions range from very simple ones, such as the format for representing dates and times, to very complex ones, such as the language spoken.

Internationalization of software means programming it to be able to adapt to the user's favorite conventions. In ISO C, internationalization works by means of *locales*. Each locale specifies a collection of conventions, one convention for each purpose. The user chooses a set of conventions by specifying a locale (via environment variables).

All programs inherit the chosen locale as part of their environment. Provided the programs are written to obey the choice of locale, they will follow the conventions preferred by the user.

7.1 What Effects a Locale Has

Each locale specifies conventions for several purposes, including the following:

- What multibyte character sequences are valid, and how they are interpreted (see Chapter 6 [Character Set Handling], page 134).

- Classification of which characters in the local character set are considered alphabetic, and upper- and lower-case conversion conventions (see Chapter 4 [Character Handling], page 81).

- The collating sequence for the local language and character set (see Section 5.8 [Collation Functions], page 111).

- Formatting of numbers and currency amounts (see Section 7.7.1.1 [Generic Numeric Formatting Parameters], page 182).

- Formatting of dates and times (see Section 21.4.5 [Formatting Calendar Time], page 632).

- What language to use for output, including error messages (see Chapter 8 [Message Translation], page 195).

- What language to use for user answers to yes-or-no questions (see Section 7.9 [Yes-or-No Questions], page 194).

- What language to use for more complex user input. (The C library doesn't yet help you implement this.)

Some aspects of adapting to the specified locale are handled automatically by the library subroutines. For example, all your program needs to do in order to use the collating sequence of the chosen locale is to use `strcoll` or `strxfrm` to compare strings.

Other aspects of locales are beyond the comprehension of the library. For example, the library can't automatically translate your program's output messages into other languages. The only way you can support output in the user's favorite language is to program this more or less by hand. The C library provides functions to handle translations for multiple languages easily.

This chapter discusses the mechanism by which you can modify the current locale. The effects of the current locale on specific library functions are discussed in more detail in the descriptions of those functions.

7.2 Choosing a Locale

The simplest way for the user to choose a locale is to set the environment variable `LANG`. This specifies a single locale to use for all purposes. For example, a user could specify a hypothetical locale named 'espana-castellano' to use the standard conventions of most of Spain.

The set of locales supported depends on the operating system you are using, and so do their names, except that the standard locale called 'C' or 'POSIX' always exist. See Section 7.6 [Locale Names], page 180.

In order to force the system to always use the default locale, the user can set the `LC_ALL` environment variable to 'C'.

A user also has the option of specifying different locales for different purposes—in effect, choosing a mixture of multiple locales. See Section 7.3 [Locale Categories], page 177.

For example, the user might specify the locale 'espana-castellano' for most purposes, but specify the locale 'usa-english' for currency formatting. This might make sense if the user is a Spanish-speaking American, working in Spanish, but representing monetary amounts in US dollars.

Note that both locales 'espana-castellano' and 'usa-english', like all locales, would include conventions for all of the purposes to which locales apply. However, the user can choose to use each locale for a particular subset of those purposes.

7.3 Locale Categories

The purposes that locales serve are grouped into *categories*, so that a user or a program can choose the locale for each category independently. Here is a table of categories; each name is both an environment variable that a user can set, and a macro name that you can use as the first argument to `setlocale`.

The contents of the environment variable (or the string in the second argument to `setlocale`) has to be a valid locale name. See Section 7.6 [Locale Names], page 180.

LC_COLLATE
This category applies to collation of strings (functions `strcoll` and `strxfrm`); see Section 5.8 [Collation Functions], page 111.

LC_CTYPE This category applies to classification and conversion of characters, and to multibyte and wide characters; see Chapter 4 [Character Handling], page 81, and Chapter 6 [Character Set Handling], page 134.

LC_MONETARY
This category applies to formatting monetary values; see Section 7.7.1.1 [Generic Numeric Formatting Parameters], page 182.

LC_NUMERIC
This category applies to formatting numeric values that are not monetary; see Section 7.7.1.1 [Generic Numeric Formatting Parameters], page 182.

LC_TIME This category applies to formatting date and time values; see Section 21.4.5 [Formatting Calendar Time], page 632.

LC_MESSAGES

> This category applies to selecting the language used in the user interface for message translation (see Section 8.2 [The Uniforum approach to Message Translation], page 204; see Section 8.1 [X/Open Message Catalog Handling], page 195) and contains regular expressions for affirmative and negative responses.

LC_ALL   This is not a category; it is only a macro that you can use with `setlocale` to set a single locale for all purposes. Setting this environment variable overwrites all selections by the other LC_* variables or `LANG`.

LANG   If this environment variable is defined, its value specifies the locale to use for all purposes except as overridden by the variables above.

When developing the message translation functions it was felt that the functionality provided by the variables above is not sufficient. For example, it should be possible to specify more than one locale name. Take a Swedish user who better speaks German than English, and a program whose messages are output in English by default. It should be possible to specify that the first choice of language is Swedish, the second German, and if this also fails to use English. This is possible with the variable `LANGUAGE`. For further description of this GNU extension see Section 8.2.1.6 [User influence on `gettext`], page 216.

7.4 How Programs Set the Locale

A C program inherits its locale environment variables when it starts up. This happens automatically. However, these variables do not automatically control the locale used by the library functions, because ISO C says that all programs start by default in the standard 'C' locale. To use the locales specified by the environment, you must call `setlocale`. Call it as follows:

```
setlocale (LC_ALL, "");
```

to select a locale based on the user choice of the appropriate environment variables.

You can also use `setlocale` to specify a particular locale, for general use or for a specific category.

The symbols in this section are defined in the header file `locale.h`.

char * setlocale (*int category*, *const char *locale*)   [Function]
> Preliminary: | MT-Unsafe const:locale env | AS-Unsafe init lock heap corrupt | AC-Unsafe init corrupt lock mem fd | See Section 1.2.2.1 [POSIX Safety Concepts], page 2.
>
> The function `setlocale` sets the current locale for category *category* to *locale*.
>
> If *category* is LC_ALL, this specifies the locale for all purposes. The other possible values of *category* specify a single purpose (see Section 7.3 [Locale Categories], page 177).
>
> You can also use this function to find out the current locale by passing a null pointer as the *locale* argument. In this case, `setlocale` returns a string that is the name of the locale currently selected for category *category*.
>
> The string returned by `setlocale` can be overwritten by subsequent calls, so you should make a copy of the string (see Section 5.4 [Copying Strings and Arrays],

page 95) if you want to save it past any further calls to `setlocale`. (The standard library is guaranteed never to call `setlocale` itself.)

You should not modify the string returned by `setlocale`. It might be the same string that was passed as an argument in a previous call to `setlocale`. One requirement is that the *category* must be the same in the call the string was returned and the one when the string is passed in as *locale* parameter.

When you read the current locale for category `LC_ALL`, the value encodes the entire combination of selected locales for all categories. If you specify the same "locale name" with `LC_ALL` in a subsequent call to `setlocale`, it restores the same combination of locale selections.

To be sure you can use the returned string encoding the currently selected locale at a later time, you must make a copy of the string. It is not guaranteed that the returned pointer remains valid over time.

When the *locale* argument is not a null pointer, the string returned by `setlocale` reflects the newly-modified locale.

If you specify an empty string for *locale*, this means to read the appropriate environment variable and use its value to select the locale for *category*.

If a nonempty string is given for *locale*, then the locale of that name is used if possible.

The effective locale name (either the second argument to `setlocale`, or if the argument is an empty string, the name obtained from the process environment) must be a valid locale name. See Section 7.6 [Locale Names], page 180.

If you specify an invalid locale name, `setlocale` returns a null pointer and leaves the current locale unchanged.

Here is an example showing how you might use `setlocale` to temporarily switch to a new locale.

```
#include <stddef.h>
#include <locale.h>
#include <stdlib.h>
#include <string.h>

void
with_other_locale (char *new_locale,
                   void (*subroutine) (int),
                   int argument)
{
  char *old_locale, *saved_locale;

  /* Get the name of the current locale.  */
  old_locale = setlocale (LC_ALL, NULL);

  /* Copy the name so it wonflt be clobbered by setlocale. */
  saved_locale = strdup (old_locale);
  if (saved_locale == NULL)
    fatal ("Out of memory");

  /* Now change the locale and do some stuff with it. */
  setlocale (LC_ALL, new_locale);
  (*subroutine) (argument);
```

```
    /* Restore the original locale. */
    setlocale (LC_ALL, saved_locale);
    free (saved_locale);
}
```

Portability Note: Some ISO C systems may define additional locale categories, and future versions of the library will do so. For portability, assume that any symbol beginning with 'LC_' might be defined in `locale.h`.

7.5 Standard Locales

The only locale names you can count on finding on all operating systems are these three standard ones:

"C"　　　 This is the standard C locale. The attributes and behavior it provides are specified in the ISO C standard. When your program starts up, it initially uses this locale by default.

"POSIX"　 This is the standard POSIX locale. Currently, it is an alias for the standard C locale.

""　　　　 The empty name says to select a locale based on environment variables. See Section 7.3 [Locale Categories], page 177.

Defining and installing named locales is normally a responsibility of the system administrator at your site (or the person who installed the GNU C Library). It is also possible for the user to create private locales. All this will be discussed later when describing the tool to do so.

If your program needs to use something other than the 'C' locale, it will be more portable if you use whatever locale the user specifies with the environment, rather than trying to specify some non-standard locale explicitly by name. Remember, different machines might have different sets of locales installed.

7.6 Locale Names

The following command prints a list of locales supported by the system:

```
    locale -a
```

Portability Note: With the notable exception of the standard locale names 'C' and 'POSIX', locale names are system-specific.

Most locale names follow XPG syntax and consist of up to four parts:

```
    language[_territory[.codeset]][@modifier]
```

Beside the first part, all of them are allowed to be missing. If the full specified locale is not found, less specific ones are looked for. The various parts will be stripped off, in the following order:

1. codeset

2. normalized codeset

3. territory

4. modifier

For example, the locale name 'de_AT.iso885915@euro' denotes a German-language locale for use in Austria, using the ISO-8859-15 (Latin-9) character set, and with the Euro as the currency symbol.

In addition to locale names which follow XPG syntax, systems may provide aliases such as 'german'. Both categories of names must not contain the slash character '/'.

If the locale name starts with a slash '/', it is treated as a path relative to the configured locale directories; see LOCPATH below. The specified path must not contain a component '..', or the name is invalid, and setlocale will fail.

Portability Note: POSIX suggests that if a locale name starts with a slash '/', it is resolved as an absolute path. However, the GNU C Library treats it as a relative path under the directories listed in LOCPATH (or the default locale directory if LOCPATH is unset).

Locale names which are longer than an implementation-defined limit are invalid and cause setlocale to fail.

As a special case, locale names used with LC_ALL can combine several locales, reflecting different locale settings for different categories. For example, you might want to use a U.S. locale with ISO A4 paper format, so you set LANG to 'en_US.UTF-8', and LC_PAPER to 'de_DE.UTF-8'. In this case, the LC_ALL-style combined locale name is

```
LC_CTYPE=en_US.UTF-8;LC_TIME=en_US.UTF-8;LC_PAPER=de_DE.UTF-8; ...
```

followed by other category settings not shown here.

The path used for finding locale data can be set using the LOCPATH environment variable. This variable lists the directories in which to search for locale definitions, separated by a colon ':'.

The default path for finding locale data is system specific. A typical value for the LOCPATH default is:

```
/usr/share/locale
```

The value of LOCPATH is ignored by privileged programs for security reasons, and only the default directory is used.

7.7 Accessing Locale Information

There are several ways to access locale information. The simplest way is to let the C library itself do the work. Several of the functions in this library implicitly access the locale data, and use what information is provided by the currently selected locale. This is how the locale model is meant to work normally.

As an example take the strftime function, which is meant to nicely format date and time information (see Section 21.4.5 [Formatting Calendar Time], page 632). Part of the standard information contained in the LC_TIME category is the names of the months. Instead of requiring the programmer to take care of providing the translations the strftime function does this all by itself. %A in the format string is replaced by the appropriate weekday name of the locale currently selected by LC_TIME. This is an easy example, and wherever possible functions do things automatically in this way.

But there are quite often situations when there is simply no function to perform the task, or it is simply not possible to do the work automatically. For these cases it is necessary to access the information in the locale directly. To do this the C library provides two functions: localeconv and nl_langinfo. The former is part of ISO C and therefore portable, but has a brain-damaged interface. The second is part of the Unix interface and is portable in as far as the system follows the Unix standards.

7.7.1 `localeconv`: **It is portable but . . .**

Together with the `setlocale` function the ISO C people invented the `localeconv` function. It is a masterpiece of poor design. It is expensive to use, not extensible, and not generally usable as it provides access to only `LC_MONETARY` and `LC_NUMERIC` related information. Nevertheless, if it is applicable to a given situation it should be used since it is very portable. The function `strfmon` formats monetary amounts according to the selected locale using this information.

`struct lconv * localeconv (`*void*`)` [Function]

> Preliminary: | MT-Unsafe race:localeconv locale | AS-Unsafe | AC-Safe | See Section 1.2.2.1 [POSIX Safety Concepts], page 2.

> The `localeconv` function returns a pointer to a structure whose components contain information about how numeric and monetary values should be formatted in the current locale.

> You should not modify the structure or its contents. The structure might be overwritten by subsequent calls to `localeconv`, or by calls to `setlocale`, but no other function in the library overwrites this value.

`struct lconv` [Data Type]

> `localeconv`'s return value is of this data type. Its elements are described in the following subsections.

If a member of the structure `struct lconv` has type `char`, and the value is `CHAR_MAX`, it means that the current locale has no value for that parameter.

7.7.1.1 Generic Numeric Formatting Parameters

These are the standard members of `struct lconv`; there may be others.

`char *decimal_point`
`char *mon_decimal_point`

> These are the decimal-point separators used in formatting non-monetary and monetary quantities, respectively. In the 'C' locale, the value of `decimal_point` is `"."`, and the value of `mon_decimal_point` is `""`.

`char *thousands_sep`
`char *mon_thousands_sep`

> These are the separators used to delimit groups of digits to the left of the decimal point in formatting non-monetary and monetary quantities, respectively. In the 'C' locale, both members have a value of `""` (the empty string).

`char *grouping`
`char *mon_grouping`

> These are strings that specify how to group the digits to the left of the decimal point. `grouping` applies to non-monetary quantities and `mon_grouping` applies to monetary quantities. Use either `thousands_sep` or `mon_thousands_sep` to separate the digit groups.

Each member of these strings is to be interpreted as an integer value of type `char`. Successive numbers (from left to right) give the sizes of successive groups (from right to left, starting at the decimal point.) The last member is either 0, in which case the previous member is used over and over again for all the remaining groups, or `CHAR_MAX`, in which case there is no more grouping—or, put another way, any remaining digits form one large group without separators.

For example, if `grouping` is `"\04\03\02"`, the correct grouping for the number `123456787654321` is '12', '34', '56', '78', '765', '4321'. This uses a group of 4 digits at the end, preceded by a group of 3 digits, preceded by groups of 2 digits (as many as needed). With a separator of ',', the number would be printed as '12,34,56,78,765,4321'.

A value of `"\03"` indicates repeated groups of three digits, as normally used in the U.S.

In the standard 'C' locale, both `grouping` and `mon_grouping` have a value of `""`. This value specifies no grouping at all.

`char int_frac_digits`
`char frac_digits`

These are small integers indicating how many fractional digits (to the right of the decimal point) should be displayed in a monetary value in international and local formats, respectively. (Most often, both members have the same value.)

In the standard 'C' locale, both of these members have the value `CHAR_MAX`, meaning "unspecified". The ISO standard doesn't say what to do when you find this value; we recommend printing no fractional digits. (This locale also specifies the empty string for `mon_decimal_point`, so printing any fractional digits would be confusing!)

7.7.1.2 Printing the Currency Symbol

These members of the `struct lconv` structure specify how to print the symbol to identify a monetary value—the international analog of '$' for US dollars.

Each country has two standard currency symbols. The *local currency symbol* is used commonly within the country, while the *international currency symbol* is used internationally to refer to that country's currency when it is necessary to indicate the country unambiguously.

For example, many countries use the dollar as their monetary unit, and when dealing with international currencies it's important to specify that one is dealing with (say) Canadian dollars instead of U.S. dollars or Australian dollars. But when the context is known to be Canada, there is no need to make this explicit—dollar amounts are implicitly assumed to be in Canadian dollars.

`char *currency_symbol`

The local currency symbol for the selected locale.

In the standard 'C' locale, this member has a value of `""` (the empty string), meaning "unspecified". The ISO standard doesn't say what to do when you find this value; we recommend you simply print the empty string as you would print any other string pointed to by this variable.

`char *int_curr_symbol`

> The international currency symbol for the selected locale.
>
> The value of `int_curr_symbol` should normally consist of a three-letter abbreviation determined by the international standard *ISO 4217 Codes for the Representation of Currency and Funds*, followed by a one-character separator (often a space).
>
> In the standard 'C' locale, this member has a value of `""` (the empty string), meaning "unspecified". We recommend you simply print the empty string as you would print any other string pointed to by this variable.

`char p_cs_precedes`
`char n_cs_precedes`
`char int_p_cs_precedes`
`char int_n_cs_precedes`

> These members are 1 if the `currency_symbol` or `int_curr_symbol` strings should precede the value of a monetary amount, or 0 if the strings should follow the value. The `p_cs_precedes` and `int_p_cs_precedes` members apply to positive amounts (or zero), and the `n_cs_precedes` and `int_n_cs_precedes` members apply to negative amounts.
>
> In the standard 'C' locale, all of these members have a value of `CHAR_MAX`, meaning "unspecified". The ISO standard doesn't say what to do when you find this value. We recommend printing the currency symbol before the amount, which is right for most countries. In other words, treat all nonzero values alike in these members.
>
> The members with the `int_` prefix apply to the `int_curr_symbol` while the other two apply to `currency_symbol`.

`char p_sep_by_space`
`char n_sep_by_space`
`char int_p_sep_by_space`
`char int_n_sep_by_space`

> These members are 1 if a space should appear between the `currency_symbol` or `int_curr_symbol` strings and the amount, or 0 if no space should appear. The `p_sep_by_space` and `int_p_sep_by_space` members apply to positive amounts (or zero), and the `n_sep_by_space` and `int_n_sep_by_space` members apply to negative amounts.
>
> In the standard 'C' locale, all of these members have a value of `CHAR_MAX`, meaning "unspecified". The ISO standard doesn't say what you should do when you find this value; we suggest you treat it as 1 (print a space). In other words, treat all nonzero values alike in these members.
>
> The members with the `int_` prefix apply to the `int_curr_symbol` while the other two apply to `currency_symbol`. There is one specialty with the `int_curr_symbol`, though. Since all legal values contain a space at the end of the string one either prints this space (if the currency symbol must appear in front and must be separated) or one has to avoid printing this character at all (especially when at the end of the string).

7.7.1.3 Printing the Sign of a Monetary Amount

These members of the **struct lconv** structure specify how to print the sign (if any) of a monetary value.

```
char *positive_sign
char *negative_sign
```

>These are strings used to indicate positive (or zero) and negative monetary quantities, respectively.
>
>In the standard 'C' locale, both of these members have a value of "" (the empty string), meaning "unspecified".
>
>The ISO standard doesn't say what to do when you find this value; we recommend printing **positive_sign** as you find it, even if it is empty. For a negative value, print **negative_sign** as you find it unless both it and **positive_sign** are empty, in which case print '-' instead. (Failing to indicate the sign at all seems rather unreasonable.)

```
char p_sign_posn
char n_sign_posn
char int_p_sign_posn
char int_n_sign_posn
```

>These members are small integers that indicate how to position the sign for nonnegative and negative monetary quantities, respectively. (The string used for the sign is what was specified with **positive_sign** or **negative_sign**.) The possible values are as follows:
>
>| | |
>|---|---|
>| 0 | The currency symbol and quantity should be surrounded by parentheses. |
>| 1 | Print the sign string before the quantity and currency symbol. |
>| 2 | Print the sign string after the quantity and currency symbol. |
>| 3 | Print the sign string right before the currency symbol. |
>| 4 | Print the sign string right after the currency symbol. |
>| CHAR_MAX | "Unspecified". Both members have this value in the standard 'C' locale. |
>
>The ISO standard doesn't say what you should do when the value is **CHAR_MAX**. We recommend you print the sign after the currency symbol.
>
>The members with the **int_** prefix apply to the **int_curr_symbol** while the other two apply to **currency_symbol**.

7.7.2 Pinpoint Access to Locale Data

When writing the X/Open Portability Guide the authors realized that the **localeconv** function is not enough to provide reasonable access to locale information. The information which was meant to be available in the locale (as later specified in the POSIX.1 standard) requires more ways to access it. Therefore the **nl_langinfo** function was introduced.

char * nl_langinfo (*nl_item item*)   [Function]
> Preliminary: | MT-Safe locale | AS-Safe | AC-Safe | See Section 1.2.2.1 [POSIX Safety Concepts], page 2.

The `nl_langinfo` function can be used to access individual elements of the locale categories. Unlike the `localeconv` function, which returns all the information, `nl_langinfo` lets the caller select what information it requires. This is very fast and it is not a problem to call this function multiple times.

A second advantage is that in addition to the numeric and monetary formatting information, information from the `LC_TIME` and `LC_MESSAGES` categories is available.

The type `nl_type` is defined in `nl_types.h`. The argument *item* is a numeric value defined in the header `langinfo.h`. The X/Open standard defines the following values:

CODESET
: `nl_langinfo` returns a string with the name of the coded character set used in the selected locale.

ABDAY_1
ABDAY_2
ABDAY_3
ABDAY_4
ABDAY_5
ABDAY_6
ABDAY_7
: `nl_langinfo` returns the abbreviated weekday name. `ABDAY_1` corresponds to Sunday.

DAY_1
DAY_2
DAY_3
DAY_4
DAY_5
DAY_6
DAY_7
: Similar to `ABDAY_1` etc., but here the return value is the unabbreviated weekday name.

ABMON_1
ABMON_2
ABMON_3
ABMON_4
ABMON_5
ABMON_6
ABMON_7
ABMON_8
ABMON_9
ABMON_10
ABMON_11
ABMON_12
: The return value is abbreviated name of the month. `ABMON_1` corresponds to January.

`MON_1`
`MON_2`
`MON_3`
`MON_4`
`MON_5`
`MON_6`
`MON_7`
`MON_8`
`MON_9`
`MON_10`
`MON_11`
`MON_12`   Similar to `ABMON_1` etc., but here the month names are not abbreviated. Here the first value `MON_1` also corresponds to January.

`AM_STR`
`PM_STR`   The return values are strings which can be used in the representation of time as an hour from 1 to 12 plus an am/pm specifier.

Note that in locales which do not use this time representation these strings might be empty, in which case the am/pm format cannot be used at all.

`D_T_FMT`   The return value can be used as a format string for **strftime** to represent time and date in a locale-specific way.

`D_FMT`   The return value can be used as a format string for **strftime** to represent a date in a locale-specific way.

`T_FMT`   The return value can be used as a format string for **strftime** to represent time in a locale-specific way.

`T_FMT_AMPM`

The return value can be used as a format string for **strftime** to represent time in the am/pm format.

Note that if the am/pm format does not make any sense for the selected locale, the return value might be the same as the one for `T_FMT`.

`ERA`   The return value represents the era used in the current locale.

Most locales do not define this value. An example of a locale which does define this value is the Japanese one. In Japan, the traditional representation of dates includes the name of the era corresponding to the then-emperor's reign.

Normally it should not be necessary to use this value directly. Specifying the E modifier in their format strings causes the **strftime** functions to use this information. The format of the returned string is not specified, and therefore you should not assume knowledge of it on different systems.

`ERA_YEAR`   The return value gives the year in the relevant era of the locale. As for `ERA` it should not be necessary to use this value directly.

`ERA_D_T_FMT`

This return value can be used as a format string for **strftime** to represent dates and times in a locale-specific era-based way.

ERA_D_FMT

>This return value can be used as a format string for `strftime` to represent a date in a locale-specific era-based way.

ERA_T_FMT

>This return value can be used as a format string for `strftime` to represent time in a locale-specific era-based way.

ALT_DIGITS

>The return value is a representation of up to 100 values used to represent the values 0 to 99. As for `ERA` this value is not intended to be used directly, but instead indirectly through the `strftime` function. When the modifier `O` is used in a format which would otherwise use numerals to represent hours, minutes, seconds, weekdays, months, or weeks, the appropriate value for the locale is used instead.

INT_CURR_SYMBOL

>The same as the value returned by `localeconv` in the `int_curr_symbol` element of the `struct lconv`.

CURRENCY_SYMBOL
CRNCYSTR The same as the value returned by `localeconv` in the `currency_symbol` element of the `struct lconv`.

>`CRNCYSTR` is a deprecated alias still required by Unix98.

MON_DECIMAL_POINT

>The same as the value returned by `localeconv` in the `mon_decimal_point` element of the `struct lconv`.

MON_THOUSANDS_SEP

>The same as the value returned by `localeconv` in the `mon_thousands_sep` element of the `struct lconv`.

MON_GROUPING

>The same as the value returned by `localeconv` in the `mon_grouping` element of the `struct lconv`.

POSITIVE_SIGN

>The same as the value returned by `localeconv` in the `positive_sign` element of the `struct lconv`.

NEGATIVE_SIGN

>The same as the value returned by `localeconv` in the `negative_sign` element of the `struct lconv`.

INT_FRAC_DIGITS

>The same as the value returned by `localeconv` in the `int_frac_digits` element of the `struct lconv`.

FRAC_DIGITS

>The same as the value returned by `localeconv` in the `frac_digits` element of the `struct lconv`.

P_CS_PRECEDES

>The same as the value returned by localeconv in the p_cs_precedes element of the **struct lconv**.

P_SEP_BY_SPACE

>The same as the value returned by localeconv in the p_sep_by_space element of the **struct lconv**.

N_CS_PRECEDES

>The same as the value returned by localeconv in the n_cs_precedes element of the **struct lconv**.

N_SEP_BY_SPACE

>The same as the value returned by localeconv in the n_sep_by_space element of the **struct lconv**.

P_SIGN_POSN

>The same as the value returned by localeconv in the p_sign_posn element of the **struct lconv**.

N_SIGN_POSN

>The same as the value returned by localeconv in the n_sign_posn element of the **struct lconv**.

INT_P_CS_PRECEDES

>The same as the value returned by localeconv in the int_p_cs_precedes element of the **struct lconv**.

INT_P_SEP_BY_SPACE

>The same as the value returned by localeconv in the int_p_sep_by_space element of the **struct lconv**.

INT_N_CS_PRECEDES

>The same as the value returned by localeconv in the int_n_cs_precedes element of the **struct lconv**.

INT_N_SEP_BY_SPACE

>The same as the value returned by localeconv in the int_n_sep_by_space element of the **struct lconv**.

INT_P_SIGN_POSN

>The same as the value returned by localeconv in the int_p_sign_posn element of the **struct lconv**.

INT_N_SIGN_POSN

>The same as the value returned by localeconv in the int_n_sign_posn element of the **struct lconv**.

DECIMAL_POINT
RADIXCHAR

>The same as the value returned by localeconv in the decimal_point element of the **struct lconv**.

>The name **RADIXCHAR** is a deprecated alias still used in Unix98.

THOUSANDS_SEP

THOUSEP   The same as the value returned by `localeconv` in the `thousands_sep` element of the `struct lconv`.

                 The name `THOUSEP` is a deprecated alias still used in Unix98.

GROUPING   The same as the value returned by `localeconv` in the `grouping` element of the `struct lconv`.

YESEXPR   The return value is a regular expression which can be used with the `regex` function to recognize a positive response to a yes/no question. The GNU C Library provides the `rpmatch` function for easier handling in applications.

NOEXPR   The return value is a regular expression which can be used with the `regex` function to recognize a negative response to a yes/no question.

YESSTR   The return value is a locale-specific translation of the positive response to a yes/no question.

                 Using this value is deprecated since it is a very special case of message translation, and is better handled by the message translation functions (see Chapter 8 [Message Translation], page 195).

                 The use of this symbol is deprecated. Instead message translation should be used.

NOSTR   The return value is a locale-specific translation of the negative response to a yes/no question. What is said for `YESSTR` is also true here.

                 The use of this symbol is deprecated. Instead message translation should be used.

The file `langinfo.h` defines a lot more symbols but none of them are official. Using them is not portable, and the format of the return values might change. Therefore we recommended you not use them.

Note that the return value for any valid argument can be used in all situations (with the possible exception of the am/pm time formatting codes). If the user has not selected any locale for the appropriate category, `nl_langinfo` returns the information from the "C" locale. It is therefore possible to use this function as shown in the example below.

If the argument *item* is not valid, a pointer to an empty string is returned.

An example of `nl_langinfo` usage is a function which has to print a given date and time in a locale-specific way. At first one might think that, since `strftime` internally uses the locale information, writing something like the following is enough:

```
size_t
i18n_time_n_data (char *s, size_t len, const struct tm *tp)
{
  return strftime (s, len, "%X %D", tp);
}
```

The format contains no weekday or month names and therefore is internationally usable. Wrong! The output produced is something like `"hh:mm:ss MM/DD/YY"`. This format is only recognizable in the USA. Other countries use different formats. Therefore the function should be rewritten like this:

```
size_t
i18n_time_n_data (char *s, size_t len, const struct tm *tp)
{
  return strftime (s, len, nl_langinfo (D_T_FMT), tp);
}
```

Now it uses the date and time format of the locale selected when the program runs. If the user selects the locale correctly there should never be a misunderstanding over the time and date format.

7.8 A dedicated function to format numbers

We have seen that the structure returned by `localeconv` as well as the values given to `nl_langinfo` allow you to retrieve the various pieces of locale-specific information to format numbers and monetary amounts. We have also seen that the underlying rules are quite complex.

Therefore the X/Open standards introduce a function which uses such locale information, making it easier for the user to format numbers according to these rules.

ssize_t strfmon (*char *s, size_t maxsize, const char *format, . . .*)   [Function]
Preliminary: | MT-Safe locale | AS-Unsafe heap | AC-Unsafe mem | See Section 1.2.2.1 [POSIX Safety Concepts], page 2.

The `strfmon` function is similar to the `strftime` function in that it takes a buffer, its size, a format string, and values to write into the buffer as text in a form specified by the format string. Like `strftime`, the function also returns the number of bytes written into the buffer.

There are two differences: `strfmon` can take more than one argument, and, of course, the format specification is different. Like `strftime`, the format string consists of normal text, which is output as is, and format specifiers, which are indicated by a '%'. Immediately after the '%', you can optionally specify various flags and formatting information before the main formatting character, in a similar way to `printf`:

- Immediately following the '%' there can be one or more of the following flags:

    '=*f*'   The single byte character *f* is used for this field as the numeric fill character. By default this character is a space character. Filling with this character is only performed if a left precision is specified. It is not just to fill to the given field width.

    '^'   The number is printed without grouping the digits according to the rules of the current locale. By default grouping is enabled.

    '+', '('   At most one of these flags can be used. They select which format to represent the sign of a currency amount. By default, and if '+' is given, the locale equivalent of $+/-$ is used. If '(' is given, negative amounts are enclosed in parentheses. The exact format is determined by the values of the `LC_MONETARY` category of the locale selected at program runtime.

    '!'   The output will not contain the currency symbol.

'-'   The output will be formatted left-justified instead of right-justified if it does not fill the entire field width.

The next part of the specification is an optional field width. If no width is specified 0 is taken. During output, the function first determines how much space is required. If it requires at least as many characters as given by the field width, it is output using as much space as necessary. Otherwise, it is extended to use the full width by filling with the space character. The presence or absence of the '-' flag determines the side at which such padding occurs. If present, the spaces are added at the right making the output left-justified, and vice versa.

So far the format looks familiar, being similar to the `printf` and `strftime` formats. However, the next two optional fields introduce something new. The first one is a '#' character followed by a decimal digit string. The value of the digit string specifies the number of *digit* positions to the left of the decimal point (or equivalent). This does *not* include the grouping character when the '^' flag is not given. If the space needed to print the number does not fill the whole width, the field is padded at the left side with the fill character, which can be selected using the '=' flag and by default is a space. For example, if the field width is selected as 6 and the number is 123, the fill character is '*' the result will be '***123'.

The second optional field starts with a '.' (period) and consists of another decimal digit string. Its value describes the number of characters printed after the decimal point. The default is selected from the current locale (`frac_digits`, `int_frac_digits`, see see Section 7.7.1.1 [Generic Numeric Formatting Parameters], page 182). If the exact representation needs more digits than given by the field width, the displayed value is rounded. If the number of fractional digits is selected to be zero, no decimal point is printed.

As a GNU extension, the `strfmon` implementation in the GNU C Library allows an optional 'L' next as a format modifier. If this modifier is given, the argument is expected to be a `long double` instead of a `double` value.

Finally, the last component is a format specifier. There are three specifiers defined:

'i'   Use the locale's rules for formatting an international currency value.

'n'   Use the locale's rules for formatting a national currency value.

'%'   Place a '%' in the output. There must be no flag, width specifier or modifier given, only '%%' is allowed.

As for `printf`, the function reads the format string from left to right and uses the values passed to the function following the format string. The values are expected to be either of type `double` or `long double`, depending on the presence of the modifier 'L'. The result is stored in the buffer pointed to by *s*. At most *maxsize* characters are stored.

The return value of the function is the number of characters stored in *s*, including the terminating `NULL` byte. If the number of characters stored would exceed *maxsize*, the function returns −1 and the content of the buffer *s* is unspecified. In this case `errno` is set to `E2BIG`.

A few examples should make clear how the function works. It is assumed that all the following pieces of code are executed in a program which uses the USA locale (en_US). The simplest form of the format is this:

```
strfmon (buf, 100, "@%n@%n@%n@", 123.45, -567.89, 12345.678);
```

The output produced is

```
"@$123.45@-$567.89@$12,345.68@"
```

We can notice several things here. First, the widths of the output numbers are different. We have not specified a width in the format string, and so this is no wonder. Second, the third number is printed using thousands separators. The thousands separator for the en_US locale is a comma. The number is also rounded. .678 is rounded to .68 since the format does not specify a precision and the default value in the locale is 2. Finally, note that the national currency symbol is printed since '%n' was used, not 'i'. The next example shows how we can align the output.

```
strfmon (buf, 100, "@%=*11n@%=*11n@%=*11n@", 123.45, -567.89, 12345.678);
```

The output this time is:

```
"@    $123.45@   -$567.89@ $12,345.68@"
```

Two things stand out. Firstly, all fields have the same width (eleven characters) since this is the width given in the format and since no number required more characters to be printed. The second important point is that the fill character is not used. This is correct since the white space was not used to achieve a precision given by a '#' modifier, but instead to fill to the given width. The difference becomes obvious if we now add a width specification.

```
strfmon (buf, 100, "@%=*11#5n@%=*11#5n@%=*11#5n@",
         123.45, -567.89, 12345.678);
```

The output is

```
"@ $***123.45@-$***567.89@ $12,456.68@"
```

Here we can see that all the currency symbols are now aligned, and that the space between the currency sign and the number is filled with the selected fill character. Note that although the width is selected to be 5 and 123.45 has three digits left of the decimal point, the space is filled with three asterisks. This is correct since, as explained above, the width does not include the positions used to store thousands separators. One last example should explain the remaining functionality.

```
strfmon (buf, 100, "@%=0(16#5.3i@%=0(16#5.3i@%=0(16#5.3i@",
         123.45, -567.89, 12345.678);
```

This rather complex format string produces the following output:

```
"@ USD 000123,450 @(USD 000567.890)@ USD 12,345.678 @"
```

The most noticeable change is the alternative way of representing negative numbers. In financial circles this is often done using parentheses, and this is what the '(' flag selected. The fill character is now '0'. Note that this '0' character is not regarded as a numeric zero, and therefore the first and second numbers are not printed using a thousands separator. Since we used the format specifier 'i' instead of 'n', the international form of the currency symbol is used. This is a four letter string, in this case "USD ". The last point is that since the precision right of the decimal point is selected to be three, the first and second numbers are printed with an extra zero at the end and the third number is printed without rounding.

7.9 Yes-or-No Questions

Some non GUI programs ask a yes-or-no question. If the messages (especially the questions) are translated into foreign languages, be sure that you localize the answers too. It would be very bad habit to ask a question in one language and request the answer in another, often English.

The GNU C Library contains `rpmatch` to give applications easy access to the corresponding locale definitions.

int rpmatch (*const char *response*)   [Function]
> Preliminary: | MT-Safe locale | AS-Unsafe corrupt heap lock dlopen | AC-Unsafe corrupt lock mem fd | See Section 1.2.2.1 [POSIX Safety Concepts], page 2.
>
> The function `rpmatch` checks the string in *response* for whether or not it is a correct yes-or-no answer and if yes, which one. The check uses the `YESEXPR` and `NOEXPR` data in the `LC_MESSAGES` category of the currently selected locale. The return value is as follows:
>
> 1   The user entered an affirmative answer.
>
> 0   The user entered a negative answer.
>
> −1   The answer matched neither the `YESEXPR` nor the `NOEXPR` regular expression.
>
> This function is not standardized but available beside in the GNU C Library at least also in the IBM AIX library.

This function would normally be used like this:

```
...
/* Use a safe default.  */
_Bool doit = false;

fputs (gettext ("Do you really want to do this? "), stdout);
fflush (stdout);
/* Prepare the getline call.  */
line = NULL;
len = 0;
while (getline (&line, &len, stdin) >= 0)
  {
    /* Check the response.  */
    int res = rpmatch (line);
    if (res >= 0)
      {
        /* We got a definitive answer.  */
        if (res > 0)
          doit = true;
        break;
      }
  }
/* Free what getline allocated.  */
free (line);
```

Note that the loop continues until a read error is detected or until a definitive (positive or negative) answer is read.

8 Message Translation

The program's interface with the user should be designed to ease the user's task. One way to ease the user's task is to use messages in whatever language the user prefers.

Printing messages in different languages can be implemented in different ways. One could add all the different languages in the source code and choose among the variants every time a message has to be printed. This is certainly not a good solution since extending the set of languages is cumbersome (the code must be changed) and the code itself can become really big with dozens of message sets.

A better solution is to keep the message sets for each language in separate files which are loaded at runtime depending on the language selection of the user.

The GNU C Library provides two different sets of functions to support message translation. The problem is that neither of the interfaces is officially defined by the POSIX standard. The `catgets` family of functions is defined in the X/Open standard but this is derived from industry decisions and therefore not necessarily based on reasonable decisions.

As mentioned above, the message catalog handling provides easy extendability by using external data files which contain the message translations. I.e., these files contain for each of the messages used in the program a translation for the appropriate language. So the tasks of the message handling functions are

- locate the external data file with the appropriate translations
- load the data and make it possible to address the messages
- map a given key to the translated message

The two approaches mainly differ in the implementation of this last step. Decisions made in the last step influence the rest of the design.

8.1 X/Open Message Catalog Handling

The `catgets` functions are based on the simple scheme:

> Associate every message to translate in the source code with a unique identifier.
> To retrieve a message from a catalog file solely the identifier is used.

This means for the author of the program that s/he will have to make sure the meaning of the identifier in the program code and in the message catalogs is always the same.

Before a message can be translated the catalog file must be located. The user of the program must be able to guide the responsible function to find whatever catalog the user wants. This is separated from what the programmer had in mind.

All the types, constants and functions for the `catgets` functions are defined/declared in the `nl_types.h` header file.

8.1.1 The `catgets` function family

`nl_catd catopen` (*const char* *cat_name, *int* flag)   [Function]
      Preliminary: | MT-Safe env | AS-Unsafe heap | AC-Unsafe mem | See Section 1.2.2.1
      [POSIX Safety Concepts], page 2.

The `catopen` function tries to locate the message data file named *cat_name* and loads it when found. The return value is of an opaque type and can be used in calls to the other functions to refer to this loaded catalog.

The return value is `(nl_catd) -1` in case the function failed and no catalog was loaded. The global variable *errno* contains a code for the error causing the failure. But even if the function call succeeded this does not mean that all messages can be translated.

Locating the catalog file must happen in a way which lets the user of the program influence the decision. It is up to the user to decide about the language to use and sometimes it is useful to use alternate catalog files. All this can be specified by the user by setting some environment variables.

The first problem is to find out where all the message catalogs are stored. Every program could have its own place to keep all the different files but usually the catalog files are grouped by languages and the catalogs for all programs are kept in the same place.

To tell the `catopen` function where the catalog for the program can be found the user can set the environment variable `NLSPATH` to a value which describes her/his choice. Since this value must be usable·for different languages and locales it cannot be a simple string. Instead it is a format string (similar to `printf`'s). An example is

> `/usr/share/locale/%L/%N:/usr/share/locale/%L/LC_MESSAGES/%N`

First one can see that more than one directory can be specified (with the usual syntax of separating them by colons). The next things to observe are the format string, `%L` and `%N` in this case. The `catopen` function knows about several of them and the replacement for all of them is of course different.

`%N`   This format element is substituted with the name of the catalog file. This is the value of the *cat_name* argument given to `catgets`.

`%L`   This format element is substituted with the name of the currently selected locale for translating messages. How this is determined is explained below.

`%l`   (This is the lowercase ell.) This format element is substituted with the language element of the locale name. The string describing the selected locale is expected to have the form *lang[_terr[.codeset]]* and this format uses the first part *lang*.

`%t`   This format element is substituted by the territory part *terr* of the name of the currently selected locale. See the explanation of the format above.

`%c`   This format element is substituted by the codeset part *codeset* of the name of the currently selected locale. See the explanation of the format above.

`%%`   Since `%` is used as a meta character there must be a way to express the `%` character in the result itself. Using `%%` does this just like it works for `printf`.

Using NLSPATH allows arbitrary directories to be searched for message catalogs while still allowing different languages to be used. If the NLSPATH environment variable is not set, the default value is

```
prefix/share/locale/%L/%N:prefix/share/locale/%L/LC_MESSAGES/%N
```

where *prefix* is given to configure while installing the GNU C Library (this value is in many cases /usr or the empty string).

The remaining problem is to decide which must be used. The value decides about the substitution of the format elements mentioned above. First of all the user can specify a path in the message catalog name (i.e., the name contains a slash character). In this situation the NLSPATH environment variable is not used. The catalog must exist as specified in the program, perhaps relative to the current working directory. This situation in not desirable and catalogs names never should be written this way. Beside this, this behavior is not portable to all other platforms providing the catgets interface.

Otherwise the values of environment variables from the standard environment are examined (see Section 25.4.2 [Standard Environment Variables], page 765). Which variables are examined is decided by the *flag* parameter of catopen. If the value is NL_CAT_LOCALE (which is defined in nl_types.h) then the catopen function uses the name of the locale currently selected for the LC_MESSAGES category.

If *flag* is zero the LANG environment variable is examined. This is a left-over from the early days when the concept of locales had not even reached the level of POSIX locales.

The environment variable and the locale name should have a value of the form *lang[_terr[.codeset]]* as explained above. If no environment variable is set the "C" locale is used which prevents any translation.

The return value of the function is in any case a valid string. Either it is a translation from a message catalog or it is the same as the *string* parameter. So a piece of code to decide whether a translation actually happened must look like this:

```
{
  char *trans = catgets (desc, set, msg, input_string);
  if (trans == input_string)
    {
      /* Something went wrong.  */
    }
}
```

When an error occurs the global variable *errno* is set to

EBADF   The catalog does not exist.

ENOMSG   The set/message tuple does not name an existing element in the message catalog.

While it sometimes can be useful to test for errors programs normally will avoid any test. If the translation is not available it is no big problem if the original, untranslated message is printed. Either the user understands this as well or s/he will look for the reason why the messages are not translated.

Please note that the currently selected locale does not depend on a call to the setlocale function. It is not necessary that the locale data files for this locale exist and calling `setlocale` succeeds. The `catopen` function directly reads the values of the environment variables.

char * catgets (*nl_catd* `catalog_desc`, *int* `set`, *int* `message`, *const*   [Function]
     char `*string`)

Preliminary: | MT-Safe | AS-Safe | AC-Safe | See Section 1.2.2.1 [POSIX Safety Concepts], page 2.

The function `catgets` has to be used to access the message catalog previously opened using the `catopen` function. The *catalog_desc* parameter must be a value previously returned by `catopen`.

The next two parameters, *set* and *message*, reflect the internal organization of the message catalog files. This will be explained in detail below. For now it is interesting to know that a catalog can consist of several sets and the messages in each thread are individually numbered using numbers. Neither the set number nor the message number must be consecutive. They can be arbitrarily chosen. But each message (unless equal to another one) must have its own unique pair of set and message numbers.

Since it is not guaranteed that the message catalog for the language selected by the user exists the last parameter *string* helps to handle this case gracefully. If no matching string can be found *string* is returned. This means for the programmer that

- the *string* parameters should contain reasonable text (this also helps to understand the program seems otherwise there would be no hint on the string which is expected to be returned.

- all *string* arguments should be written in the same language.

It is somewhat uncomfortable to write a program using the `catgets` functions if no supporting functionality is available. Since each set/message number tuple must be unique the programmer must keep lists of the messages at the same time the code is written. And the work between several people working on the same project must be coordinated. We will see how some of these problems can be relaxed a bit (see Section 8.1.4 [How to use the `catgets` interface], page 202).

int catclose (*nl_catd* `catalog_desc`)   [Function]

Preliminary: | MT-Safe | AS-Unsafe heap | AC-Unsafe corrupt mem | See Section 1.2.2.1 [POSIX Safety Concepts], page 2.

The `catclose` function can be used to free the resources associated with a message catalog which previously was opened by a call to `catopen`. If the resources can be successfully freed the function returns 0. Otherwise it returns −1 and the global variable *errno* is set. Errors can occur if the catalog descriptor *catalog_desc* is not valid in which case *errno* is set to `EBADF`.

8.1.2 Format of the message catalog files

The only reasonable way to translate all the messages of a function and store the result in a message catalog file which can be read by the `catopen` function is to write all the message text to the translator and let her/him translate them all. I.e., we must have a file with entries which associate the set/message tuple with a specific translation. This file format is specified in the X/Open standard and is as follows:

- Lines containing only whitespace characters or empty lines are ignored.

- Lines which contain as the first non-whitespace character a $ followed by a whitespace character are comment and are also ignored.

- If a line contains as the first non-whitespace characters the sequence $set followed by a whitespace character an additional argument is required to follow. This argument can either be:

  - a number. In this case the value of this number determines the set to which the following messages are added.

  - an identifier consisting of alphanumeric characters plus the underscore character. In this case the set get automatically a number assigned. This value is one added to the largest set number which so far appeared.

    How to use the symbolic names is explained in section Section 8.1.4 [How to use the `catgets` interface], page 202.

    It is an error if a symbol name appears more than once. All following messages are placed in a set with this number.

- If a line contains as the first non-whitespace characters the sequence $delset followed by a whitespace character an additional argument is required to follow. This argument can either be:

  - a number. In this case the value of this number determines the set which will be deleted.

  - an identifier consisting of alphanumeric characters plus the underscore character. This symbolic identifier must match a name for a set which previously was defined. It is an error if the name is unknown.

  In both cases all messages in the specified set will be removed. They will not appear in the output. But if this set is later again selected with a $set command again messages could be added and these messages will appear in the output.

- If a line contains after leading whitespaces the sequence $quote, the quoting character used for this input file is changed to the first non-whitespace character following $quote. If no non-whitespace character is present before the line ends quoting is disabled.

  By default no quoting character is used. In this mode strings are terminated with the first unescaped line break. If there is a $quote sequence present newline need not be escaped. Instead a string is terminated with the first unescaped appearance of the quote character.

  A common usage of this feature would be to set the quote character to ". Then any appearance of the " in the strings must be escaped using the backslash (i.e., \" must be written).

- Any other line must start with a number or an alphanumeric identifier (with the underscore character included). The following characters (starting after the first whitespace character) will form the string which gets associated with the currently selected set and the message number represented by the number and identifier respectively.

  If the start of the line is a number the message number is obvious. It is an error if the same message number already appeared for this set.

If the leading token was an identifier the message number gets automatically assigned. The value is the current maximum message number for this set plus one. It is an error if the identifier was already used for a message in this set. It is OK to reuse the identifier for a message in another thread. How to use the symbolic identifiers will be explained below (see Section 8.1.4 [How to use the `catgets` interface], page 202). There is one limitation with the identifier: it must not be `Set`. The reason will be explained below.

The text of the messages can contain escape characters. The usual bunch of characters known from the ISO C language are recognized (`\n`, `\t`, `\v`, `\b`, `\r`, `\f`, `\\`, and `\`*nnn*, where *nnn* is the octal coding of a character code).

Important: The handling of identifiers instead of numbers for the set and messages is a GNU extension. Systems strictly following the X/Open specification do not have this feature. An example for a message catalog file is this:

```
$ This is a leading comment.
$quote "

$set SetOne
1 Message with ID 1.
two "  Message with ID \"two\", which gets the value 2 assigned"

$set SetTwo
$ Since the last set got the number 1 assigned this set has number 2.
4000 "The numbers can be arbitrary, they need not start at one."
```

This small example shows various aspects:

- Lines 1 and 9 are comments since they start with `$` followed by a whitespace.

- The quoting character is set to `"`. Otherwise the quotes in the message definition would have to be omitted and in this case the message with the identifier `two` would lose its leading whitespace.

- Mixing numbered messages with messages having symbolic names is no problem and the numbering happens automatically.

While this file format is pretty easy it is not the best possible for use in a running program. The `catopen` function would have to parse the file and handle syntactic errors gracefully. This is not so easy and the whole process is pretty slow. Therefore the `catgets` functions expect the data in another more compact and ready-to-use file format. There is a special program `gencat` which is explained in detail in the next section.

Files in this other format are not human readable. To be easy to use by programs it is a binary file. But the format is byte order independent so translation files can be shared by systems of arbitrary architecture (as long as they use the GNU C Library).

Details about the binary file format are not important to know since these files are always created by the `gencat` program. The sources of the GNU C Library also provide the sources for the `gencat` program and so the interested reader can look through these source files to learn about the file format.

8.1.3 Generate Message Catalogs files

The `gencat` program is specified in the X/Open standard and the GNU implementation follows this specification and so processes all correctly formed input files. Additionally some extension are implemented which help to work in a more reasonable way with the `catgets` functions.

The `gencat` program can be invoked in two ways:

> `` `gencat [Option ...] [Output-File [Input-File ...]]` ``

This is the interface defined in the X/Open standard. If no *Input-File* parameter is given, input will be read from standard input. Multiple input files will be read as if they were concatenated. If *Output-File* is also missing, the output will be written to standard output. To provide the interface one is used to from other programs a second interface is provided.

> `` `gencat [Option ...] -o Output-File [Input-File ...]` ``

The option '`-o`' is used to specify the output file and all file arguments are used as input files.

Beside this one can use – or `/dev/stdin` for *Input-File* to denote the standard input. Corresponding one can use – and `/dev/stdout` for *Output-File* to denote standard output. Using – as a file name is allowed in X/Open while using the device names is a GNU extension.

The `gencat` program works by concatenating all input files and then **merging** the resulting collection of message sets with a possibly existing output file. This is done by removing all messages with set/message number tuples matching any of the generated messages from the output file and then adding all the new messages. To regenerate a catalog file while ignoring the old contents therefore requires removing the output file if it exists. If the output is written to standard output no merging takes place.

The following table shows the options understood by the `gencat` program. The X/Open standard does not specify any options for the program so all of these are GNU extensions.

'`-V`'
'`--version`'
> Print the version information and exit.

'`-h`'
'`--help`' Print a usage message listing all available options, then exit successfully.

'`--new`' Do not merge the new messages from the input files with the old content of the output file. The old content of the output file is discarded.

'`-H`'
'`--header=name`'
> This option is used to emit the symbolic names given to sets and messages in the input files for use in the program. Details about how to use this are given in the next section. The *name* parameter to this option specifies the name of the output file. It will contain a number of C preprocessor **#define**s to associate a name with a number.
>
> Please note that the generated file only contains the symbols from the input files. If the output is merged with the previous content of the output file the possibly existing symbols from the file(s) which generated the old output files are not in the generated header file.

8.1.4 How to use the `catgets` interface

The `catgets` functions can be used in two different ways. By following slavishly the X/Open specs and not relying on the extension and by using the GNU extensions. We will take a look at the former method first to understand the benefits of extensions.

8.1.4.1 Not using symbolic names

Since the X/Open format of the message catalog files does not allow symbol names we have to work with numbers all the time. When we start writing a program we have to replace all appearances of translatable strings with something like

```
catgets (catdesc, set, msg, "string")
```

catgets is retrieved from a call to **catopen** which is normally done once at the program start. The `"string"` is the string we want to translate. The problems start with the set and message numbers.

In a bigger program several programmers usually work at the same time on the program and so coordinating the number allocation is crucial. Though no two different strings must be indexed by the same tuple of numbers it is highly desirable to reuse the numbers for equal strings with equal translations (please note that there might be strings which are equal in one language but have different translations due to difference contexts).

The allocation process can be relaxed a bit by different set numbers for different parts of the program. So the number of developers who have to coordinate the allocation can be reduced. But still lists must be keep track of the allocation and errors can easily happen. These errors cannot be discovered by the compiler or the **catgets** functions. Only the user of the program might see wrong messages printed. In the worst cases the messages are so irritating that they cannot be recognized as wrong. Think about the translations for `"true"` and `"false"` being exchanged. This could result in a disaster.

8.1.4.2 Using symbolic names

The problems mentioned in the last section derive from the fact that:

1. the numbers are allocated once and due to the possibly frequent use of them it is difficult to change a number later.

2. the numbers do not allow guessing anything about the string and therefore collisions can easily happen.

By constantly using symbolic names and by providing a method which maps the string content to a symbolic name (however this will happen) one can prevent both problems above. The cost of this is that the programmer has to write a complete message catalog file while s/he is writing the program itself.

This is necessary since the symbolic names must be mapped to numbers before the program sources can be compiled. In the last section it was described how to generate a header containing the mapping of the names. E.g., for the example message file given in the last section we could call the **gencat** program as follows (assume **ex.msg** contains the sources).

```
gencat -H ex.h -o ex.cat ex.msg
```

This generates a header file with the following content:

```
#define SetTwoSet 0x2   /* ex.msg:8 */
```

```
#define SetOneSet 0x1    /* ex.msg:4 */
#define SetOnetwo 0x2    /* ex.msg:6 */
```

As can be seen the various symbols given in the source file are mangled to generate unique identifiers and these identifiers get numbers assigned. Reading the source file and knowing about the rules will allow to predict the content of the header file (it is deterministic) but this is not necessary. The `gencat` program can take care for everything. All the programmer has to do is to put the generated header file in the dependency list of the source files of her/his project and add a rule to regenerate the header if any of the input files change.

One word about the symbol mangling. Every symbol consists of two parts: the name of the message set plus the name of the message or the special string `Set`. So `SetOnetwo` means this macro can be used to access the translation with identifier `two` in the message set `SetOne`.

The other names denote the names of the message sets. The special string `Set` is used in the place of the message identifier.

If in the code the second string of the set `SetOne` is used the C code should look like this:

```
catgets (catdesc, SetOneSet, SetOnetwo,
         "  Message with ID \"two\", which gets the value 2 assigned")
```

Writing the function this way will allow to change the message number and even the set number without requiring any change in the C source code. (The text of the string is normally not the same; this is only for this example.)

8.1.4.3 How does to this allow to develop

To illustrate the usual way to work with the symbolic version numbers here is a little example. Assume we want to write the very complex and famous greeting program. We start by writing the code as usual:

```
#include <stdio.h>
int
main (void)
{
  printf ("Hello, world!\n");
  return 0;
}
```

Now we want to internationalize the message and therefore replace the message with whatever the user wants.

```
#include <nl_types.h>
#include <stdio.h>
#include "msgnrs.h"
int
main (void)
{
  nl_catd catdesc = catopen ("hello.cat", NL_CAT_LOCALE);
  printf (catgets (catdesc, SetMainSet, SetMainHello,
                   "Hello, world!\n"));
  catclose (catdesc);
  return 0;
}
```

We see how the catalog object is opened and the returned descriptor used in the other function calls. It is not really necessary to check for failure of any of the functions since even in these situations the functions will behave reasonable. They simply will be return a translation.

What remains unspecified here are the constants `SetMainSet` and `SetMainHello`. These are the symbolic names describing the message. To get the actual definitions which match the information in the catalog file we have to create the message catalog source file and process it using the `gencat` program.

```
$ Messages for the famous greeting program.
$quote "

$set Main
Hello "Hallo, Welt!\n"
```

Now we can start building the program (assume the message catalog source file is named `hello.msg` and the program source file `hello.c`):

```
% gencat -H msgnrs.h -o hello.cat hello.msg
% cat msgnrs.h
#define MainSet 0x1      /* hello.msg:4 */
#define MainHello 0x1    /* hello.msg:5 */
% gcc -o hello hello.c -I.
% cp hello.cat /usr/share/locale/de/LC_MESSAGES
% echo $LC_ALL
de
% ./hello
Hallo, Welt!
%
```

The call of the `gencat` program creates the missing header file `msgnrs.h` as well as the message catalog binary. The former is used in the compilation of `hello.c` while the later is placed in a directory in which the `catopen` function will try to locate it. Please check the `LC_ALL` environment variable and the default path for `catopen` presented in the description above.

8.2 The Uniforum approach to Message Translation

Sun Microsystems tried to standardize a different approach to message translation in the Uniforum group. There never was a real standard defined but still the interface was used in Sun's operating systems. Since this approach fits better in the development process of free software it is also used throughout the GNU project and the GNU `gettext` package provides support for this outside the GNU C Library.

The code of the `libintl` from GNU `gettext` is the same as the code in the GNU C Library. So the documentation in the GNU `gettext` manual is also valid for the functionality here. The following text will describe the library functions in detail. But the numerous helper programs are not described in this manual. Instead people should read the GNU `gettext` manual (see Section "GNU gettext utilities" in *Native Language Support Library and Tools*). We will only give a short overview.

Though the `catgets` functions are available by default on more systems the `gettext` interface is at least as portable as the former. The GNU `gettext` package can be used wherever the functions are not available.

8.2.1 The gettext family of functions

The paradigms underlying the gettext approach to message translations is different from that of the catgets functions the basic functionally is equivalent. There are functions of the following categories:

8.2.1.1 What has to be done to translate a message?

The gettext functions have a very simple interface. The most basic function just takes the string which shall be translated as the argument and it returns the translation. This is fundamentally different from the catgets approach where an extra key is necessary and the original string is only used for the error case.

If the string which has to be translated is the only argument this of course means the string itself is the key. I.e., the translation will be selected based on the original string. The message catalogs must therefore contain the original strings plus one translation for any such string. The task of the gettext function is to compare the argument string with the available strings in the catalog and return the appropriate translation. Of course this process is optimized so that this process is not more expensive than an access using an atomic key like in catgets.

The gettext approach has some advantages but also some disadvantages. Please see the GNU gettext manual for a detailed discussion of the pros and cons.

All the definitions and declarations for gettext can be found in the libintl.h header file. On systems where these functions are not part of the C library they can be found in a separate library named libintl.a (or accordingly different for shared libraries).

char * gettext (*const char *msgid*)   [Function]
> Preliminary: | MT-Safe env | AS-Unsafe corrupt heap lock dlopen | AC-Unsafe corrupt lock fd mem | See Section 1.2.2.1 [POSIX Safety Concepts], page 2.
>
> The gettext function searches the currently selected message catalogs for a string which is equal to *msgid*. If there is such a string available it is returned. Otherwise the argument string *msgid* is returned.
>
> Please note that although the return value is char * the returned string must not be changed. This broken type results from the history of the function and does not reflect the way the function should be used.
>
> Please note that above we wrote "message catalogs" (plural). This is a specialty of the GNU implementation of these functions and we will say more about this when we talk about the ways message catalogs are selected (see Section 8.2.1.2 [How to determine which catalog to be used], page 207).
>
> The gettext function does not modify the value of the global *errno* variable. This is necessary to make it possible to write something like
>
> ```
>       printf (gettext ("Operation failed: %m\n"));
> ```
>
> Here the *errno* value is used in the printf function while processing the %m format element and if the gettext function would change this value (it is called before printf is called) we would get a wrong message.
>
> So there is no easy way to detect a missing message catalog besides comparing the argument string with the result. But it is normally the task of the user to react on missing catalogs. The program cannot guess when a message catalog is really

necessary since for a user who speaks the language the program was developed in, the message does not need any translation.

The remaining two functions to access the message catalog add some functionality to select a message catalog which is not the default one. This is important if parts of the program are developed independently. Every part can have its own message catalog and all of them can be used at the same time. The C library itself is an example: internally it uses the `gettext` functions but since it must not depend on a currently selected default message catalog it must specify all ambiguous information.

char * dgettext (*const char *domainname, const char *msgid*)   [Function]
Preliminary: | MT-Safe env | AS-Unsafe corrupt heap lock dlopen | AC-Unsafe corrupt lock fd mem | See Section 1.2.2.1 [POSIX Safety Concepts], page 2.

> The `dgettext` function acts just like the `gettext` function. It only takes an additional first argument *domainname* which guides the selection of the message catalogs which are searched for the translation. If the *domainname* parameter is the null pointer the `dgettext` function is exactly equivalent to `gettext` since the default value for the domain name is used.
>
> As for `gettext` the return value type is `char *` which is an anachronism. The returned string must never be modified.

char * dcgettext (*const char *domainname, const char *msgid, int* [Function]
    category)
Preliminary: | MT-Safe env | AS-Unsafe corrupt heap lock dlopen | AC-Unsafe corrupt lock fd mem | See Section 1.2.2.1 [POSIX Safety Concepts], page 2.

> The `dcgettext` adds another argument to those which `dgettext` takes. This argument *category* specifies the last piece of information needed to localize the message catalog. I.e., the domain name and the locale category exactly specify which message catalog has to be used (relative to a given directory, see below).
>
> The `dgettext` function can be expressed in terms of `dcgettext` by using
>
>   dcgettext (domain, string, LC_MESSAGES)
>
> instead of
>
>   dgettext (domain, string)
>
> This also shows which values are expected for the third parameter. One has to use the available selectors for the categories available in `locale.h`. Normally the available values are LC_CTYPE, LC_COLLATE, LC_MESSAGES, LC_MONETARY, LC_NUMERIC, and LC_TIME. Please note that LC_ALL must not be used and even though the names might suggest this, there is no relation to the environment variable of this name.
>
> The `dcgettext` function is only implemented for compatibility with other systems which have `gettext` functions. There is not really any situation where it is necessary (or useful) to use a different value than LC_MESSAGES for the *category* parameter. We are dealing with messages here and any other choice can only be irritating.
>
> As for `gettext` the return value type is `char *` which is an anachronism. The returned string must never be modified.

When using the three functions above in a program it is a frequent case that the *msgid* argument is a constant string. So it is worthwhile to optimize this case. Thinking shortly about this one will realize that as long as no new message catalog is loaded the translation of a message will not change. This optimization is actually implemented by the `gettext`, `dgettext` and `dcgettext` functions.

8.2.1.2 How to determine which catalog to be used

The functions to retrieve the translations for a given message have a remarkable simple interface. But to provide the user of the program still the opportunity to select exactly the translation s/he wants and also to provide the programmer the possibility to influence the way to locate the search for catalogs files there is a quite complicated underlying mechanism which controls all this. The code is complicated the use is easy.

Basically we have two different tasks to perform which can also be performed by the `catgets` functions:

1. Locate the set of message catalogs. There are a number of files for different languages which all belong to the package. Usually they are all stored in the filesystem below a certain directory.

   There can be arbitrarily many packages installed and they can follow different guidelines for the placement of their files.

2. Relative to the location specified by the package the actual translation files must be searched, based on the wishes of the user. I.e., for each language the user selects the program should be able to locate the appropriate file.

This is the functionality required by the specifications for `gettext` and this is also what the `catgets` functions are able to do. But there are some problems unresolved:

- The language to be used can be specified in several different ways. There is no generally accepted standard for this and the user always expects the program to understand what s/he means. E.g., to select the German translation one could write `de`, `german`, or `deutsch` and the program should always react the same.

- Sometimes the specification of the user is too detailed. If s/he, e.g., specifies `de_DE.ISO-8859-1` which means German, spoken in Germany, coded using the ISO 8859-1 character set there is the possibility that a message catalog matching this exactly is not available. But there could be a catalog matching `de` and if the character set used on the machine is always ISO 8859-1 there is no reason why this later message catalog should not be used. (We call this *message inheritance*.)

- If a catalog for a wanted language is not available it is not always the second best choice to fall back on the language of the developer and simply not translate any message. Instead a user might be better able to read the messages in another language and so the user of the program should be able to define a precedence order of languages.

We can divide the configuration actions in two parts: the one is performed by the programmer, the other by the user. We will start with the functions the programmer can use since the user configuration will be based on this.

As the functions described in the last sections already mention separate sets of messages can be selected by a *domain name*. This is a simple string which should be unique for each program part that uses a separate domain. It is possible to use in one program arbitrarily many domains at the same time. E.g., the GNU C Library itself uses a domain named `libc` while the program using the C Library could use a domain named `foo`. The important point is that at any time exactly one domain is active. This is controlled with the following function.

char * textdomain (*const char *domainname*)   [Function]

> Preliminary: | MT-Safe | AS-Unsafe lock heap | AC-Unsafe lock mem | See Section 1.2.2.1 [POSIX Safety Concepts], page 2.
>
> The `textdomain` function sets the default domain, which is used in all future `gettext` calls, to *domainname*. Please note that `dgettext` and `dcgettext` calls are not influenced if the *domainname* parameter of these functions is not the null pointer.
>
> Before the first call to `textdomain` the default domain is `messages`. This is the name specified in the specification of the `gettext` API. This name is as good as any other name. No program should ever really use a domain with this name since this can only lead to problems.
>
> The function returns the value which is from now on taken as the default domain. If the system went out of memory the returned value is `NULL` and the global variable *errno* is set to `ENOMEM`. Despite the return value type being `char *` the return string must not be changed. It is allocated internally by the `textdomain` function.
>
> If the *domainname* parameter is the null pointer no new default domain is set. Instead the currently selected default domain is returned.
>
> If the *domainname* parameter is the empty string the default domain is reset to its initial value, the domain with the name `messages`. This possibility is questionable to use since the domain `messages` really never should be used.

char * bindtextdomain (*const char *domainname, const char*   [Function]
  *dirname)

> Preliminary: | MT-Safe | AS-Unsafe heap | AC-Unsafe mem | See Section 1.2.2.1 [POSIX Safety Concepts], page 2.
>
> The `bindtextdomain` function can be used to specify the directory which contains the message catalogs for domain *domainname* for the different languages. To be correct, this is the directory where the hierarchy of directories is expected. Details are explained below.
>
> For the programmer it is important to note that the translations which come with the program have to be placed in a directory hierarchy starting at, say, `/foo/bar`. Then the program should make a `bindtextdomain` call to bind the domain for the current program to this directory. So it is made sure the catalogs are found. A correctly running program does not depend on the user setting an environment variable.
>
> The `bindtextdomain` function can be used several times and if the *domainname* argument is different the previously bound domains will not be overwritten.
>
> If the program which wish to use `bindtextdomain` at some point of time use the `chdir` function to change the current working directory it is important that the *dirname* strings ought to be an absolute pathname. Otherwise the addressed directory might vary with the time.
>
> If the *dirname* parameter is the null pointer `bindtextdomain` returns the currently selected directory for the domain with the name *domainname*.

The `bindtextdomain` function returns a pointer to a string containing the name of the selected directory name. The string is allocated internally in the function and must not be changed by the user. If the system went out of core during the execution of `bindtextdomain` the return value is `NULL` and the global variable *errno* is set accordingly.

8.2.1.3 Additional functions for more complicated situations

The functions of the `gettext` family described so far (and all the `catgets` functions as well) have one problem in the real world which has been neglected completely in all existing approaches. What is meant here is the handling of plural forms.

Looking through Unix source code before the time anybody thought about internationalization (and, sadly, even afterwards) one can often find code similar to the following:

```
printf ("%d file%s deleted", n, n == 1 ? "" : "s");
```

After the first complaints from people internationalizing the code people either completely avoided formulations like this or used strings like `"file(s)"`. Both look unnatural and should be avoided. First tries to solve the problem correctly looked like this:

```
if (n == 1)
  printf ("%d file deleted", n);
else
  printf ("%d files deleted", n);
```

But this does not solve the problem. It helps languages where the plural form of a noun is not simply constructed by adding an 's' but that is all. Once again people fell into the trap of believing the rules their language uses are universal. But the handling of plural forms differs widely between the language families. There are two things we can differ between (and even inside language families);

- The form how plural forms are build differs. This is a problem with language which have many irregularities. German, for instance, is a drastic case. Though English and German are part of the same language family (Germanic), the almost regular forming of plural noun forms (appending an 's') is hardly found in German.

- The number of plural forms differ. This is somewhat surprising for those who only have experiences with Romanic and Germanic languages since here the number is the same (there are two).

  But other language families have only one form or many forms. More information on this in an extra section.

The consequence of this is that application writers should not try to solve the problem in their code. This would be localization since it is only usable for certain, hardcoded language environments. Instead the extended `gettext` interface should be used.

These extra functions are taking instead of the one key string two strings and a numerical argument. The idea behind this is that using the numerical argument and the first string as a key, the implementation can select using rules specified by the translator the right plural form. The two string arguments then will be used to provide a return value in case no message catalog is found (similar to the normal `gettext` behavior). In this case the rules for Germanic language are used and it is assumed that the first string argument is the singular form, the second the plural form.

This has the consequence that programs without language catalogs can display the correct strings only if the program itself is written using a Germanic language. This is a limitation but since the GNU C Library (as well as the GNU `gettext` package) is written as part of the GNU package and the coding standards for the GNU project require programs to be written in English, this solution nevertheless fulfills its purpose.

char * ngettext (*const char *msgid1, const char *msgid2, unsigned*   [Function]
      long int n)

> Preliminary: | MT-Safe env | AS-Unsafe corrupt heap lock dlopen | AC-Unsafe corrupt lock fd mem | See Section 1.2.2.1 [POSIX Safety Concepts], page 2.

> The `ngettext` function is similar to the `gettext` function as it finds the message catalogs in the same way. But it takes two extra arguments. The *msgid1* parameter must contain the singular form of the string to be converted. It is also used as the key for the search in the catalog. The *msgid2* parameter is the plural form. The parameter *n* is used to determine the plural form. If no message catalog is found *msgid1* is returned if `n == 1`, otherwise `msgid2`.

> An example for the use of this function is:

```
printf (ngettext ("%d file removed", "%d files removed", n), n);
```

> Please note that the numeric value *n* has to be passed to the `printf` function as well. It is not sufficient to pass it only to `ngettext`.

char * dngettext (*const char *domain, const char *msgid1, const*   [Function]
      char *msgid2, unsigned long int n)

> Preliminary: | MT-Safe env | AS-Unsafe corrupt heap lock dlopen | AC-Unsafe corrupt lock fd mem | See Section 1.2.2.1 [POSIX Safety Concepts], page 2.

> The `dngettext` is similar to the `dgettext` function in the way the message catalog is selected. The difference is that it takes two extra parameters to provide the correct plural form. These two parameters are handled in the same way `ngettext` handles them.

char * dcngettext (*const char *domain, const char *msgid1, const*   [Function]
      char *msgid2, unsigned long int n, int `category`)

> Preliminary: | MT-Safe env | AS-Unsafe corrupt heap lock dlopen | AC-Unsafe corrupt lock fd mem | See Section 1.2.2.1 [POSIX Safety Concepts], page 2.

> The `dcngettext` is similar to the `dcgettext` function in the way the message catalog is selected. The difference is that it takes two extra parameters to provide the correct plural form. These two parameters are handled in the same way `ngettext` handles them.

The problem of plural forms

A description of the problem can be found at the beginning of the last section. Now there is the question how to solve it. Without the input of linguists (which was not available) it was not possible to determine whether there are only a few different forms in which plural forms are formed or whether the number can increase with every new supported language.

Therefore the solution implemented is to allow the translator to specify the rules of how to select the plural form. Since the formula varies with every language this is the only viable solution except for hardcoding the information in the code (which still would require the possibility of extensions to not prevent the use of new languages). The details are explained in the GNU `gettext` manual. Here only a bit of information is provided.

The information about the plural form selection has to be stored in the header entry (the one with the empty `msgid` string). It looks like this:

```
Plural-Forms: nplurals=2; plural=n == 1 ? 0 : 1;
```

The `nplurals` value must be a decimal number which specifies how many different plural forms exist for this language. The string following `plural` is an expression using the C language syntax. Exceptions are that no negative numbers are allowed, numbers must be decimal, and the only variable allowed is `n`. This expression will be evaluated whenever one of the functions `ngettext`, `dngettext`, or `dcngettext` is called. The numeric value passed to these functions is then substituted for all uses of the variable `n` in the expression. The resulting value then must be greater or equal to zero and smaller than the value given as the value of `nplurals`.

The following rules are known at this point. The language with families are listed. But this does not necessarily mean the information can be generalized for the whole family (as can be easily seen in the table below).[1]

Only one form:

> Some languages only require one single form. There is no distinction between the singular and plural form. An appropriate header entry would look like this:
>
> ```
> Plural-Forms: nplurals=1; plural=0;
> ```

Languages with this property include:

Finno-Ugric family
> Hungarian

Asian family
> Japanese, Korean

Turkic/Altaic family
> Turkish

Two forms, singular used for one only

> This is the form used in most existing programs since it is what English uses. A header entry would look like this:
>
> ```
> Plural-Forms: nplurals=2; plural=n != 1;
> ```

(Note: this uses the feature of C expressions that boolean expressions have to value zero or one.)

Languages with this property include:

Germanic family
> Danish, Dutch, English, German, Norwegian, Swedish

Finno-Ugric family
> Estonian, Finnish

Latin/Greek family
> Greek

Semitic family
> Hebrew

---

[1] Additions are welcome. Send appropriate information to `bug-glibc-manual@gnu.org`.

Romance family
Italian, Portuguese, Spanish

Artificial   Esperanto

Two forms, singular used for zero and one
Exceptional case in the language family. The header entry would be:
```
Plural-Forms: nplurals=2; plural=n>1;
```
Languages with this property include:

Romanic family
French, Brazilian Portuguese

Three forms, special case for zero
The header entry would be:
```
Plural-Forms: nplurals=3; plural=n%10==1 && n%100!=11 ? 0 : n != 0 ? 1 : 2;
```
Languages with this property include:

Baltic family
Latvian

Three forms, special cases for one and two
The header entry would be:
```
Plural-Forms: nplurals=3; plural=n==1 ? 0 : n==2 ? 1 : 2;
```
Languages with this property include:

Celtic   Gaeilge (Irish)

Three forms, special case for numbers ending in 1[2-9]
The header entry would look like this:
```
Plural-Forms: nplurals=3; \
    plural=n%10==1 && n%100!=11 ? 0 : \
        n%10>=2 && (n%100<10 || n%100>=20) ? 1 : 2;
```
Languages with this property include:

Baltic family
Lithuanian

Three forms, special cases for numbers ending in 1 and 2, 3, 4, except those ending in 1[1-4]
The header entry would look like this:
```
Plural-Forms: nplurals=3; \
    plural=n%100/10==1 ? 2 : n%10==1 ? 0 : (n+9)%10>3 ? 2 : 1;
```
Languages with this property include:

Slavic family
Croatian, Czech, Russian, Ukrainian

Three forms, special cases for 1 and 2, 3, 4
The header entry would look like this:
```
Plural-Forms: nplurals=3; \
    plural=(n==1) ? 1 : (n>=2 && n<=4) ? 2 : 0;
```

Languages with this property include:

Slavic family
Slovak

Three forms, special case for one and some numbers ending in 2, 3, or 4

The header entry would look like this:

```
Plural-Forms: nplurals=3; \
    plural=n==1 ? 0 : \
            n%10>=2 && n%10<=4 && (n%100<10 || n%100>=20) ? 1 : 2;
```

Languages with this property include:

Slavic family
Polish

Four forms, special case for one and all numbers ending in 02, 03, or 04

The header entry would look like this:

```
Plural-Forms: nplurals=4; \
    plural=n%100==1 ? 0 : n%100==2 ? 1 : n%100==3 || n%100==4 ? 2 : 3;
```

Languages with this property include:

Slavic family
Slovenian

8.2.1.4 How to specify the output character set gettext uses

gettext not only looks up a translation in a message catalog, it also converts the translation on the fly to the desired output character set. This is useful if the user is working in a different character set than the translator who created the message catalog, because it avoids distributing variants of message catalogs which differ only in the character set.

The output character set is, by default, the value of nl_langinfo (CODESET), which depends on the LC_CTYPE part of the current locale. But programs which store strings in a locale independent way (e.g. UTF-8) can request that gettext and related functions return the translations in that encoding, by use of the bind_textdomain_codeset function.

Note that the *msgid* argument to gettext is not subject to character set conversion. Also, when gettext does not find a translation for *msgid*, it returns *msgid* unchanged – independently of the current output character set. It is therefore recommended that all *msgid*s be US-ASCII strings.

char * bind_textdomain_codeset (*const char *domainname, const*   [Function]
    *char *codeset*)

Preliminary: | MT-Safe | AS-Unsafe heap | AC-Unsafe mem | See Section 1.2.2.1 [POSIX Safety Concepts], page 2.

The bind_textdomain_codeset function can be used to specify the output character set for message catalogs for domain *domainname*. The *codeset* argument must be a valid codeset name which can be used for the iconv_open function, or a null pointer.

If the *codeset* parameter is the null pointer, bind_textdomain_codeset returns the currently selected codeset for the domain with the name *domainname*. It returns NULL if no codeset has yet been selected.

The `bind_textdomain_codeset` function can be used several times. If used multiple times with the same *domainname* argument, the later call overrides the settings made by the earlier one.

The `bind_textdomain_codeset` function returns a pointer to a string containing the name of the selected codeset. The string is allocated internally in the function and must not be changed by the user. If the system went out of core during the execution of `bind_textdomain_codeset`, the return value is `NULL` and the global variable *errno* is set accordingly.

8.2.1.5 How to use `gettext` in GUI programs

One place where the `gettext` functions, if used normally, have big problems is within programs with graphical user interfaces (GUIs). The problem is that many of the strings which have to be translated are very short. They have to appear in pull-down menus which restricts the length. But strings which are not containing entire sentences or at least large fragments of a sentence may appear in more than one situation in the program but might have different translations. This is especially true for the one-word strings which are frequently used in GUI programs.

As a consequence many people say that the `gettext` approach is wrong and instead `catgets` should be used which indeed does not have this problem. But there is a very simple and powerful method to handle these kind of problems with the `gettext` functions.

As an example consider the following fictional situation. A GUI program has a menu bar with the following entries:

```
+------------+------------+------------------------------------------+
| File       | Printer    |                                          |
+------------+------------+------------------------------------------+
| Open       | | Select   |
| New        | | Open     |
+----------+ | Connect  |
             +----------+
```

To have the strings `File`, `Printer`, `Open`, `New`, `Select`, and `Connect` translated there has to be at some point in the code a call to a function of the `gettext` family. But in two places the string passed into the function would be `Open`. The translations might not be the same and therefore we are in the dilemma described above.

One solution to this problem is to artificially extend the strings to make them unambiguous. But what would the program do if no translation is available? The extended string is not what should be printed. So we should use a slightly modified version of the functions.

To extend the strings a uniform method should be used. E.g., in the example above, the strings could be chosen as

```
Menu|File
Menu|Printer
Menu|File|Open
Menu|File|New
Menu|Printer|Select
Menu|Printer|Open
Menu|Printer|Connect
```

Now all the strings are different and if now instead of `gettext` the following little wrapper function is used, everything works just fine:

```
char *
```

```
sgettext (const char *msgid)
{
  char *msgval = gettext (msgid);
  if (msgval == msgid)
    msgval = strrchr (msgid, '|') + 1;
  return msgval;
}
```

What this little function does is to recognize the case when no translation is available. This can be done very efficiently by a pointer comparison since the return value is the input value. If there is no translation we know that the input string is in the format we used for the Menu entries and therefore contains a | character. We simply search for the last occurrence of this character and return a pointer to the character following it. That's it!

If one now consistently uses the extended string form and replaces the **gettext** calls with calls to **sgettext** (this is normally limited to very few places in the GUI implementation) then it is possible to produce a program which can be internationalized.

With advanced compilers (such as GNU C) one can write the **sgettext** functions as an inline function or as a macro like this:

```
#define sgettext(msgid) \
  ({ const char *__msgid = (msgid);            \
     char *__msgstr = gettext (__msgid);       \
     if (__msgval == __msgid)                  \
       __msgval = strrchr (__msgid, '|') + 1;  \
     __msgval; })
```

The other **gettext** functions (**dgettext**, **dcgettext** and the **ngettext** equivalents) can and should have corresponding functions as well which look almost identical, except for the parameters and the call to the underlying function.

Now there is of course the question why such functions do not exist in the GNU C Library? There are two parts of the answer to this question.

- They are easy to write and therefore can be provided by the project they are used in. This is not an answer by itself and must be seen together with the second part which is:

- There is no way the C library can contain a version which can work everywhere. The problem is the selection of the character to separate the prefix from the actual string in the extended string. The examples above used | which is a quite good choice because it resembles a notation frequently used in this context and it also is a character not often used in message strings.

  But what if the character is used in message strings. Or if the chose character is not available in the character set on the machine one compiles (e.g., | is not required to exist for ISO C; this is why the **iso646.h** file exists in ISO C programming environments).

There is only one more comment to make left. The wrapper function above requires that the translations strings are not extended themselves. This is only logical. There is no need to disambiguate the strings (since they are never used as keys for a search) and one also saves quite some memory and disk space by doing this.

8.2.1.6 User influence on `gettext`

The last sections described what the programmer can do to internationalize the messages of the program. But it is finally up to the user to select the message s/he wants to see. S/He must understand them.

The POSIX locale model uses the environment variables `LC_COLLATE`, `LC_CTYPE`, `LC_MESSAGES`, `LC_MONETARY`, `LC_NUMERIC`, and `LC_TIME` to select the locale which is to be used. This way the user can influence lots of functions. As we mentioned above, the **gettext** functions also take advantage of this.

To understand how this happens it is necessary to take a look at the various components of the filename which gets computed to locate a message catalog. It is composed as follows:

> `dir_name/locale/LC_category/domain_name.mo`

The default value for *dir_name* is system specific. It is computed from the value given as the prefix while configuring the C library. This value normally is `/usr` or `/`. For the former the complete *dir_name* is:

> `/usr/share/locale`

We can use `/usr/share` since the `.mo` files containing the message catalogs are system independent, so all systems can use the same files. If the program executed the **bindtextdomain** function for the message domain that is currently handled, the `dir_name` component is exactly the value which was given to the function as the second parameter. I.e., **bindtextdomain** allows overwriting the only system dependent and fixed value to make it possible to address files anywhere in the filesystem.

The *category* is the name of the locale category which was selected in the program code. For **gettext** and **dgettext** this is always `LC_MESSAGES`, for **dcgettext** this is selected by the value of the third parameter. As said above it should be avoided to ever use a category other than `LC_MESSAGES`.

The *locale* component is computed based on the category used. Just like for the **setlocale** function here comes the user selection into the play. Some environment variables are examined in a fixed order and the first environment variable set determines the return value of the lookup process. In detail, for the category `LC_xxx` the following variables in this order are examined:

`LANGUAGE`

`LC_ALL`

`LC_xxx`

`LANG`

This looks very familiar. With the exception of the `LANGUAGE` environment variable this is exactly the lookup order the **setlocale** function uses. But why introduce the `LANGUAGE` variable?

The reason is that the syntax of the values these variables can have is different to what is expected by the **setlocale** function. If we would set `LC_ALL` to a value following the extended syntax that would mean the **setlocale** function will never be able to use the value of this variable as well. An additional variable removes this problem plus we can select the language independently of the locale setting which sometimes is useful.

While for the `LC_xxx` variables the value should consist of exactly one specification of a locale the `LANGUAGE` variable's value can consist of a colon separated list of locale names. The attentive reader will realize that this is the way we manage to implement one of our additional demands above: we want to be able to specify an ordered list of languages.

Back to the constructed filename we have only one component missing. The *domain_name* part is the name which was either registered using the `textdomain` function or which was given to `dgettext` or `dcgettext` as the first parameter. Now it becomes obvious that a good choice for the domain name in the program code is a string which is closely related to the program/package name. E.g., for the GNU C Library the domain name is `libc`.

A limited piece of example code should show how the program is supposed to work:

```
{
  setlocale (LC_ALL, "");
  textdomain ("test-package");
  bindtextdomain ("test-package", "/usr/local/share/locale");
  puts (gettext ("Hello, world!"));
}
```

At the program start the default domain is `messages`, and the default locale is `"C"`. The `setlocale` call sets the locale according to the user's environment variables; remember that correct functioning of `gettext` relies on the correct setting of the `LC_MESSAGES` locale (for looking up the message catalog) and of the `LC_CTYPE` locale (for the character set conversion). The `textdomain` call changes the default domain to `test-package`. The `bindtextdomain` call specifies that the message catalogs for the domain `test-package` can be found below the directory `/usr/local/share/locale`.

If the user sets in her/his environment the variable `LANGUAGE` to `de` the `gettext` function will try to use the translations from the file

```
/usr/local/share/locale/de/LC_MESSAGES/test-package.mo
```

From the above descriptions it should be clear which component of this filename is determined by which source.

In the above example we assumed the `LANGUAGE` environment variable to be `de`. This might be an appropriate selection but what happens if the user wants to use `LC_ALL` because of the wider usability and here the required value is `de_DE.ISO-8859-1`? We already mentioned above that a situation like this is not infrequent. E.g., a person might prefer reading a dialect and if this is not available fall back on the standard language.

The `gettext` functions know about situations like this and can handle them gracefully. The functions recognize the format of the value of the environment variable. It can split the value is different pieces and by leaving out the only or the other part it can construct new values. This happens of course in a predictable way. To understand this one must know the format of the environment variable value. There is one more or less standardized form, originally from the X/Open specification:

```
language[_territory[.codeset]][@modifier]
```

Less specific locale names will be stripped in the order of the following list:

1. `codeset`

2. `normalized codeset`

3. `territory`

4. `modifier`

The `language` field will never be dropped for obvious reasons.

The only new thing is the `normalized codeset` entry. This is another goodie which is introduced to help reduce the chaos which derives from the inability of people to standardize the names of character sets. Instead of ISO-8859-1 one can often see 8859-1, 88591, iso8859-1, or iso_8859-1. The `normalized codeset` value is generated from the user-provided character set name by applying the following rules:

1. Remove all characters besides numbers and letters.

2. Fold letters to lowercase.

3. If the same only contains digits prepend the string `"iso"`.

So all of the above names will be normalized to `iso88591`. This allows the program user much more freedom in choosing the locale name.

Even this extended functionality still does not help to solve the problem that completely different names can be used to denote the same locale (e.g., `de` and `german`). To be of help in this situation the locale implementation and also the `gettext` functions know about aliases.

The file `/usr/share/locale/locale.alias` (replace `/usr` with whatever prefix you used for configuring the C library) contains a mapping of alternative names to more regular names. The system manager is free to add new entries to fill her/his own needs. The selected locale from the environment is compared with the entries in the first column of this file ignoring the case. If they match, the value of the second column is used instead for the further handling.

In the description of the format of the environment variables we already mentioned the character set as a factor in the selection of the message catalog. In fact, only catalogs which contain text written using the character set of the system/program can be used (directly; there will come a solution for this some day). This means for the user that s/he will always have to take care of this. If in the collection of the message catalogs there are files for the same language but coded using different character sets the user has to be careful.

8.2.2 Programs to handle message catalogs for `gettext`

The GNU C Library does not contain the source code for the programs to handle message catalogs for the `gettext` functions. As part of the GNU project the GNU gettext package contains everything the developer needs. The functionality provided by the tools in this package by far exceeds the abilities of the `gencat` program described above for the `catgets` functions.

There is a program `msgfmt` which is the equivalent program to the `gencat` program. It generates from the human-readable and -editable form of the message catalog a binary file which can be used by the `gettext` functions. But there are several more programs available.

The `xgettext` program can be used to automatically extract the translatable messages from a source file. I.e., the programmer need not take care of the translations and the list of messages which have to be translated. S/He will simply wrap the translatable string in calls to `gettext` et.al and the rest will be done by `xgettext`. This program has a lot of options which help to customize the output or help to understand the input better.

Other programs help to manage the development cycle when new messages appear in the source files or when a new translation of the messages appears. Here it should only be noted that using all the tools in GNU gettext it is possible to *completely* automate the handling of message catalogs. Besides marking the translatable strings in the source code and generating the translations the developers do not have anything to do themselves.

9 Searching and Sorting

This chapter describes functions for searching and sorting arrays of arbitrary objects. You pass the appropriate comparison function to be applied as an argument, along with the size of the objects in the array and the total number of elements.

9.1 Defining the Comparison Function

In order to use the sorted array library functions, you have to describe how to compare the elements of the array.

To do this, you supply a comparison function to compare two elements of the array. The library will call this function, passing as arguments pointers to two array elements to be compared. Your comparison function should return a value the way `strcmp` (see Section 5.7 [String/Array Comparison], page 107) does: negative if the first argument is "less" than the second, zero if they are "equal", and positive if the first argument is "greater".

Here is an example of a comparison function which works with an array of numbers of type `double`:

```
int
compare_doubles (const void *a, const void *b)
{
  const double *da = (const double *) a;
  const double *db = (const double *) b;

  return (*da > *db) - (*da < *db);
}
```

The header file `stdlib.h` defines a name for the data type of comparison functions. This type is a GNU extension.

```
int comparison_fn_t (const void *, const void *);
```

9.2 Array Search Function

Generally searching for a specific element in an array means that potentially all elements must be checked. The GNU C Library contains functions to perform linear search. The prototypes for the following two functions can be found in `search.h`.

void * lfind (*const void *key, const void *base, size_t *nmemb,*   [Function]
     size_t size, comparison_fn_t compar)

Preliminary: | MT-Safe | AS-Safe | AC-Safe | See Section 1.2.2.1 [POSIX Safety Concepts], page 2.

The `lfind` function searches in the array with *nmemb* elements of *size* bytes pointed to by *base* for an element which matches the one pointed to by *key*. The function pointed to by *compar* is used to decide whether two elements match.

The return value is a pointer to the matching element in the array starting at *base* if it is found. If no matching element is available `NULL` is returned.

The mean runtime of this function is *nmemb*/2. This function should only be used if elements often get added to or deleted from the array in which case it might not be useful to sort the array before searching.

void * lsearch (*const void *key, void *base, size_t *nmemb, size_t*   [Function]
      size, comparison_fn_t compar)

> Preliminary: | MT-Safe | AS-Safe | AC-Safe | See Section 1.2.2.1 [POSIX Safety Concepts], page 2.
>
> The lsearch function is similar to the lfind function. It searches the given array for an element and returns it if found. The difference is that if no matching element is found the lsearch function adds the object pointed to by *key* (with a size of *size* bytes) at the end of the array and it increments the value of *nmemb* to reflect this addition.
>
> This means for the caller that if it is not sure that the array contains the element one is searching for the memory allocated for the array starting at *base* must have room for at least *size* more bytes. If one is sure the element is in the array it is better to use lfind so having more room in the array is always necessary when calling lsearch.

To search a sorted array for an element matching the key, use the bsearch function. The prototype for this function is in the header file stdlib.h.

void * bsearch (*const void *key, const void *array, size_t* count,   [Function]
      size_t size, *comparison_fn_t* compare)

> Preliminary: | MT-Safe | AS-Safe | AC-Safe | See Section 1.2.2.1 [POSIX Safety Concepts], page 2.
>
> The bsearch function searches the sorted array *array* for an object that is equivalent to *key*. The array contains *count* elements, each of which is of size *size* bytes.
>
> The *compare* function is used to perform the comparison. This function is called with two pointer arguments and should return an integer less than, equal to, or greater than zero corresponding to whether its first argument is considered less than, equal to, or greater than its second argument. The elements of the *array* must already be sorted in ascending order according to this comparison function.
>
> The return value is a pointer to the matching array element, or a null pointer if no match is found. If the array contains more than one element that matches, the one that is returned is unspecified.
>
> This function derives its name from the fact that it is implemented using the binary search algorithm.

9.3 Array Sort Function

To sort an array using an arbitrary comparison function, use the qsort function. The prototype for this function is in stdlib.h.

void qsort (*void *array, size_t* count, *size_t* size, *comparison_fn_t*   [Function]
      compare)

> Preliminary: | MT-Safe | AS-Safe | AC-Unsafe corrupt | See Section 1.2.2.1 [POSIX Safety Concepts], page 2.
>
> The qsort function sorts the array *array*. The array contains *count* elements, each of which is of size *size*.
>
> The *compare* function is used to perform the comparison on the array elements. This function is called with two pointer arguments and should return an integer less than,

equal to, or greater than zero corresponding to whether its first argument is considered less than, equal to, or greater than its second argument.

Warning: If two objects compare as equal, their order after sorting is unpredictable. That is to say, the sorting is not stable. This can make a difference when the comparison considers only part of the elements. Two elements with the same sort key may differ in other respects.

Although the object addresses passed to the comparison function lie within the array, they need not correspond with the original locations of those objects because the sorting algorithm may swap around objects in the array before making some comparisons. The only way to perform a stable sort with **qsort** is to first augment the objects with a monotonic counter of some kind.

Here is a simple example of sorting an array of doubles in numerical order, using the comparison function defined above (see Section 9.1 [Defining the Comparison Function], page 220):

```
{
  double *array;
  int size;
  ...
  qsort (array, size, sizeof (double), compare_doubles);
}
```

The **qsort** function derives its name from the fact that it was originally implemented using the "quick sort" algorithm.

The implementation of **qsort** in this library might not be an in-place sort and might thereby use an extra amount of memory to store the array.

9.4 Searching and Sorting Example

Here is an example showing the use of **qsort** and **bsearch** with an array of structures. The objects in the array are sorted by comparing their **name** fields with the **strcmp** function. Then, we can look up individual objects based on their names.

```
#include <stdlib.h>
#include <stdio.h>
#include <string.h>

/* Define an array of critters to sort. */

struct critter
  {
    const char *name;
    const char *species;
  };

struct critter muppets[] =
  {
    {"Kermit", "frog"},
    {"Piggy", "pig"},
    {"Gonzo", "whatever"},
    {"Fozzie", "bear"},
    {"Sam", "eagle"},
    {"Robin", "frog"},
```

```
      {"Animal", "animal"},
      {"Camilla", "chicken"},
      {"Sweetums", "monster"},
      {"Dr. Strangepork", "pig"},
      {"Link Hogthrob", "pig"},
      {"Zoot", "human"},
      {"Dr. Bunsen Honeydew", "human"},
      {"Beaker", "human"},
      {"Swedish Chef", "human"}
  };

int count = sizeof (muppets) / sizeof (struct critter);



/* This is the comparison function used for sorting and searching. */

int
critter_cmp (const void *v1, const void *v2)
{
  const struct critter *c1 = v1;
  const struct critter *c2 = v2;

  return strcmp (c1->name, c2->name);
}



/* Print information about a critter. */

void
print_critter (const struct critter *c)
{
  printf ("%s, the %s\n", c->name, c->species);
}



/* Do the lookup into the sorted array. */

void
find_critter (const char *name)
{
  struct critter target, *result;
  target.name = name;
  result = bsearch (&target, muppets, count, sizeof (struct critter),
                    critter_cmp);
  if (result)
    print_critter (result);
  else
    printf ("Couldn't find %s.\n", name);
}

/* Main program. */

int
main (void)
{
  int i;
```

```
    for (i = 0; i < count; i++)
      print_critter (&muppets[i]);
    printf ("\n");

    qsort (muppets, count, sizeof (struct critter), critter_cmp);

    for (i = 0; i < count; i++)
      print_critter (&muppets[i]);
    printf ("\n");

    find_critter ("Kermit");
    find_critter ("Gonzo");
    find_critter ("Janice");

    return 0;
  }
```

The output from this program looks like:

```
Kermit, the frog
Piggy, the pig
Gonzo, the whatever
Fozzie, the bear
Sam, the eagle
Robin, the frog
Animal, the animal
Camilla, the chicken
Sweetums, the monster
Dr. Strangepork, the pig
Link Hogthrob, the pig
Zoot, the human
Dr. Bunsen Honeydew, the human
Beaker, the human
Swedish Chef, the human

Animal, the animal
Beaker, the human
Camilla, the chicken
Dr. Bunsen Honeydew, the human
Dr. Strangepork, the pig
Fozzie, the bear
Gonzo, the whatever
Kermit, the frog
Link Hogthrob, the pig
Piggy, the pig
Robin, the frog
Sam, the eagle
Swedish Chef, the human
Sweetums, the monster
Zoot, the human

Kermit, the frog
Gonzo, the whatever
Couldn't find Janice.
```

9.5 The hsearch function.

The functions mentioned so far in this chapter are for searching in a sorted or unsorted array. There are other methods to organize information which later should be searched.

The costs of insert, delete and search differ. One possible implementation is using hashing tables. The following functions are declared in the header file `search.h`.

int hcreate (*size_t nel*)   [Function]
> Preliminary: | MT-Unsafe race:hsearch | AS-Unsafe heap | AC-Unsafe corrupt mem | See Section 1.2.2.1 [POSIX Safety Concepts], page 2.
>
> The `hcreate` function creates a hashing table which can contain at least *nel* elements. There is no possibility to grow this table so it is necessary to choose the value for *nel* wisely. The method used to implement this function might make it necessary to make the number of elements in the hashing table larger than the expected maximal number of elements. Hashing tables usually work inefficiently if they are filled 80% or more. The constant access time guaranteed by hashing can only be achieved if few collisions exist. See Knuth's "The Art of Computer Programming, Part 3: Searching and Sorting" for more information.
>
> The weakest aspect of this function is that there can be at most one hashing table used through the whole program. The table is allocated in local memory out of control of the programmer. As an extension the GNU C Library provides an additional set of functions with a reentrant interface which provides a similar interface but which allows keeping arbitrarily many hashing tables.
>
> It is possible to use more than one hashing table in the program run if the former table is first destroyed by a call to `hdestroy`.
>
> The function returns a non-zero value if successful. If it returns zero, something went wrong. This could either mean there is already a hashing table in use or the program ran out of memory.

void hdestroy (*void*)   [Function]
> Preliminary: | MT-Unsafe race:hsearch | AS-Unsafe heap | AC-Unsafe corrupt mem | See Section 1.2.2.1 [POSIX Safety Concepts], page 2.
>
> The `hdestroy` function can be used to free all the resources allocated in a previous call of `hcreate`. After a call to this function it is again possible to call `hcreate` and allocate a new table with possibly different size.
>
> It is important to remember that the elements contained in the hashing table at the time `hdestroy` is called are *not* freed by this function. It is the responsibility of the program code to free those strings (if necessary at all). Freeing all the element memory is not possible without extra, separately kept information since there is no function to iterate through all available elements in the hashing table. If it is really necessary to free a table and all elements the programmer has to keep a list of all table elements and before calling `hdestroy` s/he has to free all element's data using this list. This is a very unpleasant mechanism and it also shows that this kind of hashing table is mainly meant for tables which are created once and used until the end of the program run.

Entries of the hashing table and keys for the search are defined using this type:

struct ENTRY   [Data type]
> Both elements of this structure are pointers to zero-terminated strings. This is a limiting restriction of the functionality of the `hsearch` functions. They can only be

used for data sets which use the NUL character always and solely to terminate the records. It is not possible to handle general binary data.

char *key   Pointer to a zero-terminated string of characters describing the key for the search or the element in the hashing table.

char *data

Pointer to a zero-terminated string of characters describing the data. If the functions will be called only for searching an existing entry this element might stay undefined since it is not used.

ENTRY * hsearch (*ENTRY item, ACTION action*)   [Function]
Preliminary: | MT-Unsafe race:hsearch | AS-Unsafe | AC-Unsafe corrupt/action==ENTER | See   Section   1.2.2.1   [POSIX   Safety   Concepts], page 2.

To search in a hashing table created using **hcreate** the **hsearch** function must be used. This function can perform a simple search for an element (if *action* has the value **FIND**) or it can alternatively insert the key element into the hashing table. Entries are never replaced.

The key is denoted by a pointer to an object of type **ENTRY**. For locating the corresponding position in the hashing table only the **key** element of the structure is used.

If an entry with a matching key is found the *action* parameter is irrelevant. The found entry is returned. If no matching entry is found and the *action* parameter has the value **FIND** the function returns a **NULL** pointer. If no entry is found and the *action* parameter has the value **ENTER** a new entry is added to the hashing table which is initialized with the parameter *item*. A pointer to the newly added entry is returned.

As mentioned before, the hashing table used by the functions described so far is global and there can be at any time at most one hashing table in the program. A solution is to use the following functions which are a GNU extension. All have in common that they operate on a hashing table which is described by the content of an object of the type **struct hsearch_data**. This type should be treated as opaque, none of its members should be changed directly.

int hcreate_r (*size_t nel*, *struct hsearch_data *htab*)   [Function]
Preliminary: | MT-Safe race:htab | AS-Unsafe heap | AC-Unsafe corrupt mem | See Section 1.2.2.1 [POSIX Safety Concepts], page 2.

The **hcreate_r** function initializes the object pointed to by *htab* to contain a hashing table with at least *nel* elements. So this function is equivalent to the **hcreate** function except that the initialized data structure is controlled by the user.

This allows having more than one hashing table at one time. The memory necessary for the **struct hsearch_data** object can be allocated dynamically. It must be initialized with zero before calling this function.

The return value is non-zero if the operation was successful. If the return value is zero, something went wrong, which probably means the program ran out of memory.

void hdestroy_r (*struct hsearch_data *htab*) [Function]

> Preliminary: | MT-Safe race:htab | AS-Unsafe heap | AC-Unsafe corrupt mem | See Section 1.2.2.1 [POSIX Safety Concepts], page 2.

> The **hdestroy_r** function frees all resources allocated by the **hcreate_r** function for this very same object *htab*. As for **hdestroy** it is the program's responsibility to free the strings for the elements of the table.

int hsearch_r (*ENTRY item, ACTION action, ENTRY **retval, struct hsearch_data *htab*) [Function]

> Preliminary: | MT-Safe race:htab | AS-Safe | AC-Unsafe corrupt/action==ENTER | See Section 1.2.2.1 [POSIX Safety Concepts], page 2.

> The **hsearch_r** function is equivalent to **hsearch**. The meaning of the first two arguments is identical. But instead of operating on a single global hashing table the function works on the table described by the object pointed to by *htab* (which is initialized by a call to **hcreate_r**).

> Another difference to **hcreate** is that the pointer to the found entry in the table is not the return value of the function. It is returned by storing it in a pointer variable pointed to by the *retval* parameter. The return value of the function is an integer value indicating success if it is non-zero and failure if it is zero. In the latter case the global variable *errno* signals the reason for the failure.

> ENOMEM   The table is filled and **hsearch_r** was called with a so far unknown key and *action* set to **ENTER**.

> ESRCH   The *action* parameter is **FIND** and no corresponding element is found in the table.

9.6 The tsearch function.

Another common form to organize data for efficient search is to use trees. The **tsearch** function family provides a nice interface to functions to organize possibly large amounts of data by providing a mean access time proportional to the logarithm of the number of elements. The GNU C Library implementation even guarantees that this bound is never exceeded even for input data which cause problems for simple binary tree implementations.

The functions described in the chapter are all described in the System V and X/Open specifications and are therefore quite portable.

In contrast to the **hsearch** functions the **tsearch** functions can be used with arbitrary data and not only zero-terminated strings.

The **tsearch** functions have the advantage that no function to initialize data structures is necessary. A simple pointer of type **void *** initialized to **NULL** is a valid tree and can be extended or searched. The prototypes for these functions can be found in the header file **search.h**.

void * tsearch (*const void *key, void **rootp, comparison_fn_t compar*) [Function]

> Preliminary: | MT-Safe race:rootp | AS-Unsafe heap | AC-Unsafe corrupt mem | See Section 1.2.2.1 [POSIX Safety Concepts], page 2.

The `tsearch` function searches in the tree pointed to by *`rootp`* for an element matching *key*. The function pointed to by *compar* is used to determine whether two elements match. See Section 9.1 [Defining the Comparison Function], page 220, for a specification of the functions which can be used for the *compar* parameter.

If the tree does not contain a matching entry the *key* value will be added to the tree. `tsearch` does not make a copy of the object pointed to by *key* (how could it since the size is unknown). Instead it adds a reference to this object which means the object must be available as long as the tree data structure is used.

The tree is represented by a pointer to a pointer since it is sometimes necessary to change the root node of the tree. So it must not be assumed that the variable pointed to by *rootp* has the same value after the call. This also shows that it is not safe to call the `tsearch` function more than once at the same time using the same tree. It is no problem to run it more than once at a time on different trees.

The return value is a pointer to the matching element in the tree. If a new element was created the pointer points to the new data (which is in fact *key*). If an entry had to be created and the program ran out of space `NULL` is returned.

void * **tfind** (*const void *`key`, void *const *`rootp`, comparison_fn_t*   [Function]
    compar)
Preliminary: | MT-Safe race:rootp | AS-Safe | AC-Safe | See Section 1.2.2.1 [POSIX Safety Concepts], page 2.

The `tfind` function is similar to the `tsearch` function. It locates an element matching the one pointed to by *key* and returns a pointer to this element. But if no matching element is available no new element is entered (note that the *rootp* parameter points to a constant pointer). Instead the function returns `NULL`.

Another advantage of the `tsearch` functions in contrast to the `hsearch` functions is that there is an easy way to remove elements.

void * **tdelete** (*const void *`key`, void **`rootp`, comparison_fn_t*   [Function]
    compar)
Preliminary: | MT-Safe race:rootp | AS-Unsafe heap | AC-Unsafe corrupt mem | See Section 1.2.2.1 [POSIX Safety Concepts], page 2.

To remove a specific element matching *key* from the tree `tdelete` can be used. It locates the matching element using the same method as `tfind`. The corresponding element is then removed and a pointer to the parent of the deleted node is returned by the function. If there is no matching entry in the tree nothing can be deleted and the function returns `NULL`. If the root of the tree is deleted `tdelete` returns some unspecified value not equal to `NULL`.

void **tdestroy** (*void *`vroot`, __free_fn_t `freefct`*)   [Function]
Preliminary: | MT-Safe | AS-Unsafe heap | AC-Unsafe mem | See Section 1.2.2.1 [POSIX Safety Concepts], page 2.

If the complete search tree has to be removed one can use `tdestroy`. It frees all resources allocated by the `tsearch` functions to generate the tree pointed to by *vroot*.

For the data in each tree node the function *freefct* is called. The pointer to the data is passed as the argument to the function. If no such work is necessary *freefct* must point to a function doing nothing. It is called in any case.

This function is a GNU extension and not covered by the System V or X/Open specifications.

In addition to the functions to create and destroy the tree data structure, there is another function which allows you to apply a function to all elements of the tree. The function must have this type:

```
void __action_fn_t (const void *nodep, VISIT value, int level);
```

The *nodep* is the data value of the current node (once given as the *key* argument to `tsearch`). *level* is a numeric value which corresponds to the depth of the current node in the tree. The root node has the depth 0 and its children have a depth of 1 and so on. The `VISIT` type is an enumeration type.

`VISIT`   [Data Type]

The `VISIT` value indicates the status of the current node in the tree and how the function is called. The status of a node is either 'leaf' or 'internal node'. For each leaf node the function is called exactly once, for each internal node it is called three times: before the first child is processed, after the first child is processed and after both children are processed. This makes it possible to handle all three methods of tree traversal (or even a combination of them).

preorder   The current node is an internal node and the function is called before the first child was processed.

postorder
            The current node is an internal node and the function is called after the first child was processed.

endorder   The current node is an internal node and the function is called after the second child was processed.

leaf   The current node is a leaf.

`void twalk (const void *root, __action_fn_t action)`   [Function]
Preliminary: | MT-Safe race:root | AS-Safe | AC-Safe | See Section 1.2.2.1 [POSIX Safety Concepts], page 2.

For each node in the tree with a node pointed to by *root*, the `twalk` function calls the function provided by the parameter *action*. For leaf nodes the function is called exactly once with *value* set to `leaf`. For internal nodes the function is called three times, setting the *value* parameter or *action* to the appropriate value. The *level* argument for the *action* function is computed while descending the tree by increasing the value by one for each descent to a child, starting with the value 0 for the root node.

Since the functions used for the *action* parameter to `twalk` must not modify the tree data, it is safe to run `twalk` in more than one thread at the same time, working on the same tree. It is also safe to call `tfind` in parallel. Functions which modify the tree must not be used, otherwise the behavior is undefined.

10 Pattern Matching

The GNU C Library provides pattern matching facilities for two kinds of patterns: regular expressions and file-name wildcards. The library also provides a facility for expanding variable and command references and parsing text into words in the way the shell does.

10.1 Wildcard Matching

This section describes how to match a wildcard pattern against a particular string. The result is a yes or no answer: does the string fit the pattern or not. The symbols described here are all declared in `fnmatch.h`.

int fnmatch (*const char *pattern, const char *string, int flags*) [Function]
> Preliminary: | MT-Safe env locale | AS-Unsafe heap | AC-Unsafe mem | See Section 1.2.2.1 [POSIX Safety Concepts], page 2.
>
> This function tests whether the string *string* matches the pattern *pattern*. It returns 0 if they do match; otherwise, it returns the nonzero value `FNM_NOMATCH`. The arguments *pattern* and *string* are both strings.
>
> The argument *flags* is a combination of flag bits that alter the details of matching. See below for a list of the defined flags.
>
> In the GNU C Library, `fnmatch` might sometimes report "errors" by returning nonzero values that are not equal to `FNM_NOMATCH`.

These are the available flags for the *flags* argument:

`FNM_FILE_NAME`
> Treat the '/' character specially, for matching file names. If this flag is set, wildcard constructs in *pattern* cannot match '/' in *string*. Thus, the only way to match '/' is with an explicit '/' in *pattern*.

`FNM_PATHNAME`
> This is an alias for `FNM_FILE_NAME`; it comes from POSIX.2. We don't recommend this name because we don't use the term "pathname" for file names.

`FNM_PERIOD`
> Treat the '.' character specially if it appears at the beginning of *string*. If this flag is set, wildcard constructs in *pattern* cannot match '.' as the first character of *string*.
>
> If you set both `FNM_PERIOD` and `FNM_FILE_NAME`, then the special treatment applies to '.' following '/' as well as to '.' at the beginning of *string*. (The shell uses the `FNM_PERIOD` and `FNM_FILE_NAME` flags together for matching file names.)

`FNM_NOESCAPE`
> Don't treat the '\' character specially in patterns. Normally, '\' quotes the following character, turning off its special meaning (if any) so that it matches only itself. When quoting is enabled, the pattern '\?' matches only the string '?', because the question mark in the pattern acts like an ordinary character.
>
> If you use `FNM_NOESCAPE`, then '\' is an ordinary character.

FNM_LEADING_DIR

> Ignore a trailing sequence of characters starting with a '/' in *string*; that is to say, test whether *string* starts with a directory name that *pattern* matches.
>
> If this flag is set, either 'foo*' or 'foobar' as a pattern would match the string 'foobar/frobozz'.

FNM_CASEFOLD

> Ignore case in comparing *string* to *pattern*.

FNM_EXTMATCH

> Besides the normal patterns, also recognize the extended patterns introduced in **ksh**. The patterns are written in the form explained in the following table where *pattern-list* is a | separated list of patterns.

> `?(pattern-list)`
>
> > The pattern matches if zero or one occurrences of any of the patterns in the *pattern-list* allow matching the input string.

> `*(pattern-list)`
>
> > The pattern matches if zero or more occurrences of any of the patterns in the *pattern-list* allow matching the input string.

> `+(pattern-list)`
>
> > The pattern matches if one or more occurrences of any of the patterns in the *pattern-list* allow matching the input string.

> `@(pattern-list)`
>
> > The pattern matches if exactly one occurrence of any of the patterns in the *pattern-list* allows matching the input string.

> `!(pattern-list)`
>
> > The pattern matches if the input string cannot be matched with any of the patterns in the *pattern-list*.

10.2 Globbing

The archetypal use of wildcards is for matching against the files in a directory, and making a list of all the matches. This is called *globbing*.

You could do this using **fnmatch**, by reading the directory entries one by one and testing each one with **fnmatch**. But that would be slow (and complex, since you would have to handle subdirectories by hand).

The library provides a function **glob** to make this particular use of wildcards convenient. **glob** and the other symbols in this section are declared in **glob.h**.

10.2.1 Calling glob

The result of globbing is a vector of file names (strings). To return this vector, **glob** uses a special data type, **glob_t**, which is a structure. You pass **glob** the address of the structure, and it fills in the structure's fields to tell you about the results.

glob_t   [Data Type]

This data type holds a pointer to a word vector. More precisely, it records both the address of the word vector and its size. The GNU implementation contains some more fields which are non-standard extensions.

gl_pathc   The number of elements in the vector, excluding the initial null entries if the GLOB_DOOFFS flag is used (see gl_offs below).

gl_pathv   The address of the vector. This field has type char **.

gl_offs   The offset of the first real element of the vector, from its nominal address in the gl_pathv field. Unlike the other fields, this is always an input to glob, rather than an output from it.

If you use a nonzero offset, then that many elements at the beginning of the vector are left empty. (The glob function fills them with null pointers.)

The gl_offs field is meaningful only if you use the GLOB_DOOFFS flag. Otherwise, the offset is always zero regardless of what is in this field, and the first real element comes at the beginning of the vector.

gl_closedir

The address of an alternative implementation of the closedir function. It is used if the GLOB_ALTDIRFUNC bit is set in the flag parameter. The type of this field is void (*) (void *).

This is a GNU extension.

gl_readdir

The address of an alternative implementation of the readdir function used to read the contents of a directory. It is used if the GLOB_ALTDIRFUNC bit is set in the flag parameter. The type of this field is struct dirent *(*) (void *).

An implementation of gl_readdir needs to initialize the following members of the struct dirent object:

d_type   This member should be set to the file type of the entry if it is known. Otherwise, the value DT_UNKNOWN can be used. The glob function may use the specified file type to avoid callbacks in cases where the file type indicates that the data is not required.

d_ino   This member needs to be non-zero, otherwise glob may skip the current entry and call the gl_readdir callback function again to retrieve another entry.

d_name   This member must be set to the name of the entry. It must be null-terminated.

The example below shows how to allocate a struct dirent object containing a given name.

```
#include <dirent.h>
```

```
#include <errno.h>
#include <stddef.h>
#include <stdlib.h>
#include <string.h>

struct dirent *
mkdirent (const char *name)
{
  size_t dirent_size = offsetof (struct dirent, d_name) + 1;
  size_t name_length = strlen (name);
  size_t total_size = dirent_size + name_length;
  if (total_size < dirent_size)
    {
      errno = ENOMEM;
      return NULL;
    }
  struct dirent *result = malloc (total_size);
  if (result == NULL)
    return NULL;
  result->d_type = DT_UNKNOWN;
  result->d_ino = 1;                 /* Do not skip this entry. */
  memcpy (result->d_name, name, name_length + 1);
  return result;
}
```

The `glob` function reads the **struct dirent** members listed above and makes a copy of the file name in the **d_name** member immediately after the **gl_readdir** callback function returns. Future invocations of any of the callback functions may dealloacte or reuse the buffer. It is the responsibility of the caller of the **glob** function to allocate and deallocate the buffer, around the call to **glob** or using the callback functions. For example, an application could allocate the buffer in the **gl_readdir** callback function, and deallocate it in the **gl_closedir** callback function.

The **gl_readdir** member is a GNU extension.

gl_opendir

> The address of an alternative implementation of the **opendir** function. It is used if the GLOB_ALTDIRFUNC bit is set in the flag parameter. The type of this field is **void *(*) (const char *)**.
>
> This is a GNU extension.

gl_stat   The address of an alternative implementation of the **stat** function to get information about an object in the filesystem. It is used if the GLOB_ALTDIRFUNC bit is set in the flag parameter. The type of this field is **int (*) (const char *, struct stat *)**.

> This is a GNU extension.

gl_lstat   The address of an alternative implementation of the **lstat** function to get information about an object in the filesystems, not following symbolic links. It is used if the GLOB_ALTDIRFUNC bit is set in the flag parameter. The type of this field is **int (*) (const char *, struct stat *)**.

> This is a GNU extension.

gl_flags The flags used when `glob` was called. In addition, `GLOB_MAGCHAR` might be set. See Section 10.2.2 [Flags for Globbing], page 236, for more details.

This is a GNU extension.

For use in the `glob64` function `glob.h` contains another definition for a very similar type. `glob64_t` differs from `glob_t` only in the types of the members `gl_readdir`, `gl_stat`, and `gl_lstat`.

`glob64_t`   [Data Type]

This data type holds a pointer to a word vector. More precisely, it records both the address of the word vector and its size. The GNU implementation contains some more fields which are non-standard extensions.

gl_pathc The number of elements in the vector, excluding the initial null entries if the GLOB_DOOFFS flag is used (see gl_offs below).

gl_pathv The address of the vector. This field has type `char **`.

gl_offs The offset of the first real element of the vector, from its nominal address in the `gl_pathv` field. Unlike the other fields, this is always an input to `glob`, rather than an output from it.

If you use a nonzero offset, then that many elements at the beginning of the vector are left empty. (The `glob` function fills them with null pointers.)

The `gl_offs` field is meaningful only if you use the `GLOB_DOOFFS` flag. Otherwise, the offset is always zero regardless of what is in this field, and the first real element comes at the beginning of the vector.

gl_closedir
 The address of an alternative implementation of the `closedir` function. It is used if the `GLOB_ALTDIRFUNC` bit is set in the flag parameter. The type of this field is `void (*) (void *)`.

This is a GNU extension.

gl_readdir
 The address of an alternative implementation of the `readdir64` function used to read the contents of a directory. It is used if the `GLOB_ALTDIRFUNC` bit is set in the flag parameter. The type of this field is `struct dirent64 *(*) (void *)`.

This is a GNU extension.

gl_opendir
 The address of an alternative implementation of the `opendir` function. It is used if the `GLOB_ALTDIRFUNC` bit is set in the flag parameter. The type of this field is `void *(*) (const char *)`.

This is a GNU extension.

gl_stat The address of an alternative implementation of the `stat64` function to get information about an object in the filesystem. It is used if the `GLOB_ALTDIRFUNC` bit is set in the flag parameter. The type of this field is `int (*) (const char *, struct stat64 *)`.

This is a GNU extension.

gl_lstat   The address of an alternative implementation of the lstat64 function to
              get information about an object in the filesystems, not following symbolic
              links. It is used if the GLOB_ALTDIRFUNC bit is set in the flag parameter.
              The type of this field is int (*) (const char *, struct stat64 *).

              This is a GNU extension.

gl_flags   The flags used when glob was called. In addition, GLOB_MAGCHAR might
              be set. See Section 10.2.2 [Flags for Globbing], page 236, for more details.

              This is a GNU extension.

int glob (const char *pattern, int flags, int (*errfunc) (const   [Function]
      char *filename, int error-code), glob_t *vector-ptr)
Preliminary: | MT-Unsafe race:utent env sig:ALRM timer locale | AS-Unsafe dlopen
plugin corrupt heap lock | AC-Unsafe corrupt lock fd mem | See Section 1.2.2.1
[POSIX Safety Concepts], page 2.

The function glob does globbing using the pattern *pattern* in the current directory.
It puts the result in a newly allocated vector, and stores the size and address of
this vector into *vector-ptr*. The argument *flags* is a combination of bit flags; see
Section 10.2.2 [Flags for Globbing], page 236, for details of the flags.

The result of globbing is a sequence of file names. The function glob allocates a string
for each resulting word, then allocates a vector of type char ** to store the addresses
of these strings. The last element of the vector is a null pointer. This vector is called
the *word vector*.

To return this vector, glob stores both its address and its length (number of elements,
not counting the terminating null pointer) into *vector-ptr*.

Normally, glob sorts the file names alphabetically before returning them. You can
turn this off with the flag GLOB_NOSORT if you want to get the information as fast
as possible. Usually it's a good idea to let glob sort them—if you process the files
in alphabetical order, the users will have a feel for the rate of progress that your
application is making.

If glob succeeds, it returns 0. Otherwise, it returns one of these error codes:

GLOB_ABORTED
              There was an error opening a directory, and you used the flag GLOB_ERR
              or your specified *errfunc* returned a nonzero value. See below for an
              explanation of the GLOB_ERR flag and *errfunc*.

GLOB_NOMATCH
              The pattern didn't match any existing files. If you use the GLOB_NOCHECK
              flag, then you never get this error code, because that flag tells glob to
              pretend that the pattern matched at least one file.

GLOB_NOSPACE
              It was impossible to allocate memory to hold the result.

In the event of an error, glob stores information in *vector-ptr* about all the matches
it has found so far.

It is important to notice that the `glob` function will not fail if it encounters directories or files which cannot be handled without the LFS interfaces. The implementation of `glob` is supposed to use these functions internally. This at least is the assumption made by the Unix standard. The GNU extension of allowing the user to provide their own directory handling and `stat` functions complicates things a bit. If these callback functions are used and a large file or directory is encountered `glob` *can* fail.

`int glob64` (*const char *pattern*, *int flags*, *int (*errfunc)* (*const*   [Function]
        *char *filename*, *int error-code*), *glob64_t *vector-ptr*)
Preliminary: | MT-Unsafe race:utent env sig:ALRM timer locale | AS-Unsafe dlopen corrupt heap lock | AC-Unsafe corrupt lock fd mem | See Section 1.2.2.1 [POSIX Safety Concepts], page 2.

The `glob64` function was added as part of the Large File Summit extensions but is not part of the original LFS proposal. The reason for this is simple: it is not necessary. The necessity for a `glob64` function is added by the extensions of the GNU `glob` implementation which allows the user to provide their own directory handling and `stat` functions. The `readdir` and `stat` functions do depend on the choice of `_FILE_OFFSET_BITS` since the definition of the types `struct dirent` and `struct stat` will change depending on the choice.

Besides this difference, `glob64` works just like `glob` in all aspects.

This function is a GNU extension.

10.2.2 Flags for Globbing

This section describes the standard flags that you can specify in the *flags* argument to `glob`. Choose the flags you want, and combine them with the C bitwise OR operator |.

Note that there are Section 10.2.3 [More Flags for Globbing], page 237, available as GNU extensions.

GLOB_APPEND
            Append the words from this expansion to the vector of words produced by previous calls to `glob`. This way you can effectively expand several words as if they were concatenated with spaces between them.

            In order for appending to work, you must not modify the contents of the word vector structure between calls to `glob`. And, if you set `GLOB_DOOFFS` in the first call to `glob`, you must also set it when you append to the results.

            Note that the pointer stored in `gl_pathv` may no longer be valid after you call `glob` the second time, because `glob` might have relocated the vector. So always fetch `gl_pathv` from the `glob_t` structure after each `glob` call; **never** save the pointer across calls.

GLOB_DOOFFS
            Leave blank slots at the beginning of the vector of words. The `gl_offs` field says how many slots to leave. The blank slots contain null pointers.

GLOB_ERR   Give up right away and report an error if there is any difficulty reading the directories that must be read in order to expand *pattern* fully. Such difficulties might include a directory in which you don't have the requisite access. Normally, `glob` tries its best to keep on going despite any errors, reading whatever directories it can.

You can exercise even more control than this by specifying an error-handler function *errfunc* when you call `glob`. If *errfunc* is not a null pointer, then `glob` doesn't give up right away when it can't read a directory; instead, it calls *errfunc* with two arguments, like this:

```
(*errfunc) (filename, error-code)
```

The argument *filename* is the name of the directory that `glob` couldn't open or couldn't read, and *error-code* is the `errno` value that was reported to `glob`.

If the error handler function returns nonzero, then `glob` gives up right away. Otherwise, it continues.

GLOB_MARK

> If the pattern matches the name of a directory, append '/' to the directory's name when returning it.

GLOB_NOCHECK

> If the pattern doesn't match any file names, return the pattern itself as if it were a file name that had been matched. (Normally, when the pattern doesn't match anything, `glob` returns that there were no matches.)

GLOB_NOESCAPE

> Don't treat the '\' character specially in patterns. Normally, '\' quotes the following character, turning off its special meaning (if any) so that it matches only itself. When quoting is enabled, the pattern '\?' matches only the string '?', because the question mark in the pattern acts like an ordinary character.

> If you use GLOB_NOESCAPE, then '\' is an ordinary character.

> `glob` does its work by calling the function `fnmatch` repeatedly. It handles the flag GLOB_NOESCAPE by turning on the FNM_NOESCAPE flag in calls to `fnmatch`.

GLOB_NOSORT

> Don't sort the file names; return them in no particular order. (In practice, the order will depend on the order of the entries in the directory.) The only reason *not* to sort is to save time.

10.2.3 More Flags for Globbing

Beside the flags described in the last section, the GNU implementation of `glob` allows a few more flags which are also defined in the `glob.h` file. Some of the extensions implement functionality which is available in modern shell implementations.

GLOB_PERIOD

> The . character (period) is treated special. It cannot be matched by wildcards. See Section 10.1 [Wildcard Matching], page 230, FNM_PERIOD.

GLOB_MAGCHAR

> The GLOB_MAGCHAR value is not to be given to `glob` in the *flags* parameter. Instead, `glob` sets this bit in the *gl_flags* element of the *glob_t* structure provided as the result if the pattern used for matching contains any wildcard character.

GLOB_ALTDIRFUNC

Instead of using the normal functions for accessing the filesystem the `glob` implementation uses the user-supplied functions specified in the structure pointed to by *pglob* parameter. For more information about the functions refer to the sections about directory handling see Section 14.2 [Accessing Directories], page 392, and Section 14.9.2 [Reading the Attributes of a File], page 416.

GLOB_BRACE

If this flag is given, the handling of braces in the pattern is changed. It is now required that braces appear correctly grouped. I.e., for each opening brace there must be a closing one. Braces can be used recursively. So it is possible to define one brace expression in another one. It is important to note that the range of each brace expression is completely contained in the outer brace expression (if there is one).

The string between the matching braces is separated into single expressions by splitting at , (comma) characters. The commas themselves are discarded. Please note what we said above about recursive brace expressions. The commas used to separate the subexpressions must be at the same level. Commas in brace subexpressions are not matched. They are used during expansion of the brace expression of the deeper level. The example below shows this

```
glob ("{foo/{,bar,biz},baz}", GLOB_BRACE, NULL, &result)
```

is equivalent to the sequence

```
glob ("foo/", GLOB_BRACE, NULL, &result)
glob ("foo/bar", GLOB_BRACE|GLOB_APPEND, NULL, &result)
glob ("foo/biz", GLOB_BRACE|GLOB_APPEND, NULL, &result)
glob ("baz", GLOB_BRACE|GLOB_APPEND, NULL, &result)
```

if we leave aside error handling.

GLOB_NOMAGIC

If the pattern contains no wildcard constructs (it is a literal file name), return it as the sole "matching" word, even if no file exists by that name.

GLOB_TILDE

If this flag is used the character ~ (tilde) is handled specially if it appears at the beginning of the pattern. Instead of being taken verbatim it is used to represent the home directory of a known user.

If ~ is the only character in pattern or it is followed by a / (slash), the home directory of the process owner is substituted. Using `getlogin` and `getpwnam` the information is read from the system databases. As an example take user `bart` with his home directory at `/home/bart`. For him a call like

```
glob ("~/bin/*", GLOB_TILDE, NULL, &result)
```

would return the contents of the directory `/home/bart/bin`. Instead of referring to the own home directory it is also possible to name the home directory of other users. To do so one has to append the user name after the tilde character. So the contents of user `homer`'s `bin` directory can be retrieved by

```
glob ("~homer/bin/*", GLOB_TILDE, NULL, &result)
```

If the user name is not valid or the home directory cannot be determined for some reason the pattern is left untouched and itself used as the result.

I.e., if in the last example `home` is not available the tilde expansion yields to `"~homer/bin/*"` and `glob` is not looking for a directory named `~homer`.

This functionality is equivalent to what is available in C-shells if the `nonomatch` flag is set.

`GLOB_TILDE_CHECK`

If this flag is used `glob` behaves as if `GLOB_TILDE` is given. The only difference is that if the user name is not available or the home directory cannot be determined for other reasons this leads to an error. `glob` will return `GLOB_NOMATCH` instead of using the pattern itself as the name.

This functionality is equivalent to what is available in C-shells if the `nonomatch` flag is not set.

`GLOB_ONLYDIR`

If this flag is used the globbing function takes this as a **hint** that the caller is only interested in directories matching the pattern. If the information about the type of the file is easily available non-directories will be rejected but no extra work will be done to determine the information for each file. I.e., the caller must still be able to filter directories out.

This functionality is only available with the GNU `glob` implementation. It is mainly used internally to increase the performance but might be useful for a user as well and therefore is documented here.

Calling **glob** will in most cases allocate resources which are used to represent the result of the function call. If the same object of type `glob_t` is used in multiple call to `glob` the resources are freed or reused so that no leaks appear. But this does not include the time when all **glob** calls are done.

void **globfree** (*glob_t *pglob*)   [Function]
Preliminary: | MT-Safe | AS-Unsafe corrupt heap | AC-Unsafe corrupt mem | See Section 1.2.2.1 [POSIX Safety Concepts], page 2.

The **globfree** function frees all resources allocated by previous calls to **glob** associated with the object pointed to by *pglob*. This function should be called whenever the currently used `glob_t` typed object isn't used anymore.

void **globfree64** (*glob64_t *pglob*)   [Function]
Preliminary: | MT-Safe | AS-Unsafe corrupt lock | AC-Unsafe corrupt lock fd mem | See Section 1.2.2.1 [POSIX Safety Concepts], page 2.

This function is equivalent to **globfree** but it frees records of type `glob64_t` which were allocated by **glob64**.

10.3 Regular Expression Matching

The GNU C Library supports two interfaces for matching regular expressions. One is the standard POSIX.2 interface, and the other is what the GNU C Library has had for many years.

Both interfaces are declared in the header file `regex.h`. If you define `_POSIX_C_SOURCE`, then only the POSIX.2 functions, structures, and constants are declared.

10.3.1 POSIX Regular Expression Compilation

Before you can actually match a regular expression, you must *compile* it. This is not true compilation—it produces a special data structure, not machine instructions. But it is like ordinary compilation in that its purpose is to enable you to "execute" the pattern fast. (See Section 10.3.3 [Matching a Compiled POSIX Regular Expression], page 242, for how to use the compiled regular expression for matching.)

There is a special data type for compiled regular expressions:

`regex_t` [Data Type]

This type of object holds a compiled regular expression. It is actually a structure. It has just one field that your programs should look at:

`re_nsub`   This field holds the number of parenthetical subexpressions in the regular expression that was compiled.

There are several other fields, but we don't describe them here, because only the functions in the library should use them.

After you create a `regex_t` object, you can compile a regular expression into it by calling `regcomp`.

`int regcomp` (*regex_t *restrict `compiled`, const char *restrict* [Function]
    `pattern`, int `cflags`)

Preliminary: | MT-Safe locale | AS-Unsafe corrupt heap lock dlopen | AC-Unsafe corrupt lock mem fd | See Section 1.2.2.1 [POSIX Safety Concepts], page 2.

The function `regcomp` "compiles" a regular expression into a data structure that you can use with `regexec` to match against a string. The compiled regular expression format is designed for efficient matching. `regcomp` stores it into *`compiled`.

It's up to you to allocate an object of type `regex_t` and pass its address to `regcomp`.

The argument *cflags* lets you specify various options that control the syntax and semantics of regular expressions. See Section 10.3.2 [Flags for POSIX Regular Expressions], page 241.

If you use the flag `REG_NOSUB`, then `regcomp` omits from the compiled regular expression the information necessary to record how subexpressions actually match. In this case, you might as well pass 0 for the *matchptr* and *nmatch* arguments when you call `regexec`.

If you don't use `REG_NOSUB`, then the compiled regular expression does have the capacity to record how subexpressions match. Also, `regcomp` tells you how many subexpressions *pattern* has, by storing the number in *compiled->re_nsub*. You can use that value to decide how long an array to allocate to hold information about subexpression matches.

`regcomp` returns 0 if it succeeds in compiling the regular expression; otherwise, it returns a nonzero error code (see the table below). You can use `regerror` to produce an error message string describing the reason for a nonzero value; see Section 10.3.6 [POSIX Regexp Matching Cleanup], page 244.

Here are the possible nonzero values that `regcomp` can return:

REG_BADBR

> There was an invalid '\{...\}' construct in the regular expression. A valid '\{...\}' construct must contain either a single number, or two numbers in increasing order separated by a comma.

REG_BADPAT

> There was a syntax error in the regular expression.

REG_BADRPT

> A repetition operator such as '?' or '*' appeared in a bad position (with no preceding subexpression to act on).

REG_ECOLLATE

> The regular expression referred to an invalid collating element (one not defined in the current locale for string collation). See Section 7.3 [Locale Categories], page 177.

REG_ECTYPE

> The regular expression referred to an invalid character class name.

REG_EESCAPE

> The regular expression ended with '\'.

REG_ESUBREG

> There was an invalid number in the '\\$digit$' construct.

REG_EBRACK

> There were unbalanced square brackets in the regular expression.

REG_EPAREN

> An extended regular expression had unbalanced parentheses, or a basic regular expression had unbalanced '\(' and '\)'.

REG_EBRACE

> The regular expression had unbalanced '\{' and '\}'.

REG_ERANGE

> One of the endpoints in a range expression was invalid.

REG_ESPACE

> `regcomp` ran out of memory.

10.3.2 Flags for POSIX Regular Expressions

These are the bit flags that you can use in the *cflags* operand when compiling a regular expression with `regcomp`.

REG_EXTENDED

> Treat the pattern as an extended regular expression, rather than as a basic regular expression.

REG_ICASE

> Ignore case when matching letters.

`REG_NOSUB`

> Don't bother storing the contents of the *matchptr* array.

`REG_NEWLINE`

> Treat a newline in *string* as dividing *string* into multiple lines, so that '$' can match before the newline and '^' can match after. Also, don't permit '.' to match a newline, and don't permit '[^...]' to match a newline.

> Otherwise, newline acts like any other ordinary character.

10.3.3 Matching a Compiled POSIX Regular Expression

Once you have compiled a regular expression, as described in Section 10.3.1 [POSIX Regular Expression Compilation], page 240, you can match it against strings using `regexec`. A match anywhere inside the string counts as success, unless the regular expression contains anchor characters ('^' or '$').

`int regexec` (*const regex_t *restrict* `compiled`, *const char *restrict*   [Function]
      `string`, *size_t* `nmatch`, *regmatch_t* `matchptr`[*restrict*], *int* `eflags`)

> Preliminary: | MT-Safe locale | AS-Unsafe corrupt heap lock dlopen | AC-Unsafe corrupt lock mem fd | See Section 1.2.2.1 [POSIX Safety Concepts], page 2.

> This function tries to match the compiled regular expression **compiled* against *string*.

> `regexec` returns 0 if the regular expression matches; otherwise, it returns a nonzero value. See the table below for what nonzero values mean. You can use `regerror` to produce an error message string describing the reason for a nonzero value; see Section 10.3.6 [POSIX Regexp Matching Cleanup], page 244.

> The argument *eflags* is a word of bit flags that enable various options.

> If you want to get information about what part of *string* actually matched the regular expression or its subexpressions, use the arguments *matchptr* and *nmatch*. Otherwise, pass 0 for *nmatch*, and `NULL` for *matchptr*. See Section 10.3.4 [Match Results with Subexpressions], page 243.

You must match the regular expression with the same set of current locales that were in effect when you compiled the regular expression.

The function `regexec` accepts the following flags in the *eflags* argument:

`REG_NOTBOL`

> Do not regard the beginning of the specified string as the beginning of a line; more generally, don't make any assumptions about what text might precede it.

`REG_NOTEOL`

> Do not regard the end of the specified string as the end of a line; more generally, don't make any assumptions about what text might follow it.

Here are the possible nonzero values that `regexec` can return:

`REG_NOMATCH`

> The pattern didn't match the string. This isn't really an error.

`REG_ESPACE`

> `regexec` ran out of memory.

10.3.4 Match Results with Subexpressions

When `regexec` matches parenthetical subexpressions of *pattern*, it records which parts of *string* they match. It returns that information by storing the offsets into an array whose elements are structures of type `regmatch_t`. The first element of the array (index 0) records the part of the string that matched the entire regular expression. Each other element of the array records the beginning and end of the part that matched a single parenthetical subexpression.

`regmatch_t`   [Data Type]

> This is the data type of the *matchptr* array that you pass to `regexec`. It contains two structure fields, as follows:
>
> > `rm_so`   The offset in *string* of the beginning of a substring. Add this value to *string* to get the address of that part.
> >
> > `rm_eo`   The offset in *string* of the end of the substring.

`regoff_t`   [Data Type]

> `regoff_t` is an alias for another signed integer type. The fields of `regmatch_t` have type `regoff_t`.

The `regmatch_t` elements correspond to subexpressions positionally; the first element (index 1) records where the first subexpression matched, the second element records the second subexpression, and so on. The order of the subexpressions is the order in which they begin.

When you call `regexec`, you specify how long the *matchptr* array is, with the *nmatch* argument. This tells `regexec` how many elements to store. If the actual regular expression has more than *nmatch* subexpressions, then you won't get offset information about the rest of them. But this doesn't alter whether the pattern matches a particular string or not.

If you don't want `regexec` to return any information about where the subexpressions matched, you can either supply 0 for *nmatch*, or use the flag `REG_NOSUB` when you compile the pattern with `regcomp`.

10.3.5 Complications in Subexpression Matching

Sometimes a subexpression matches a substring of no characters. This happens when 'f\(o*\)' matches the string 'fum'. (It really matches just the 'f'.) In this case, both of the offsets identify the point in the string where the null substring was found. In this example, the offsets are both 1.

Sometimes the entire regular expression can match without using some of its subexpressions at all—for example, when 'ba\(na\)*' matches the string 'ba', the parenthetical subexpression is not used. When this happens, `regexec` stores −1 in both fields of the element for that subexpression.

Sometimes matching the entire regular expression can match a particular subexpression more than once—for example, when 'ba\(na\)*' matches the string 'bananana', the parenthetical subexpression matches three times. When this happens, `regexec` usually stores the offsets of the last part of the string that matched the subexpression. In the case of 'bananana', these offsets are 6 and 8.

But the last match is not always the one that is chosen. It's more accurate to say that the last *opportunity* to match is the one that takes precedence. What this means is that when one subexpression appears within another, then the results reported for the inner subexpression reflect whatever happened on the last match of the outer subexpression. For an example, consider '`\(ba\(na\)*s \)*`' matching the string '`bananas bas `'. The last time the inner expression actually matches is near the end of the first word. But it is *considered* again in the second word, and fails to match there. `regexec` reports nonuse of the "na" subexpression.

Another place where this rule applies is when the regular expression

```
\(ba\(na\)*s \|nefer\(ti\)* \)*
```

matches '`bananas nefertiti`'. The "na" subexpression does match in the first word, but it doesn't match in the second word because the other alternative is used there. Once again, the second repetition of the outer subexpression overrides the first, and within that second repetition, the "na" subexpression is not used. So `regexec` reports nonuse of the "na" subexpression.

10.3.6 POSIX Regexp Matching Cleanup

When you are finished using a compiled regular expression, you can free the storage it uses by calling `regfree`.

void regfree (*regex_t *compiled***)** [Function]

    Preliminary: | MT-Safe | AS-Unsafe heap | AC-Unsafe mem | See Section 1.2.2.1 [POSIX Safety Concepts], page 2.

    Calling `regfree` frees all the storage that **compiled* points to. This includes various internal fields of the `regex_t` structure that aren't documented in this manual.

    `regfree` does not free the object **compiled* itself.

You should always free the space in a `regex_t` structure with `regfree` before using the structure to compile another regular expression.

When `regcomp` or `regexec` reports an error, you can use the function `regerror` to turn it into an error message string.

size_t regerror (*int errcode, const regex_t *restrict compiled,*** [Function]**
      char *restrict buffer, size_t length)

    Preliminary: | MT-Safe env | AS-Unsafe corrupt heap lock dlopen | AC-Unsafe corrupt lock fd mem | See Section 1.2.2.1 [POSIX Safety Concepts], page 2.

    This function produces an error message string for the error code *errcode*, and stores the string in *length* bytes of memory starting at *buffer*. For the *compiled* argument, supply the same compiled regular expression structure that `regcomp` or `regexec` was working with when it got the error. Alternatively, you can supply NULL for *compiled*; you will still get a meaningful error message, but it might not be as detailed.

    If the error message can't fit in *length* bytes (including a terminating null character), then `regerror` truncates it. The string that `regerror` stores is always null-terminated even if it has been truncated.

    The return value of `regerror` is the minimum length needed to store the entire error message. If this is less than *length*, then the error message was not truncated, and you can use it. Otherwise, you should call `regerror` again with a larger buffer.

Here is a function which uses `regerror`, but always dynamically allocates a buffer for the error message:

```
char *get_regerror (int errcode, regex_t *compiled)
{
  size_t length = regerror (errcode, compiled, NULL, 0);
  char *buffer = xmalloc (length);
  (void) regerror (errcode, compiled, buffer, length);
  return buffer;
}
```

10.4 Shell-Style Word Expansion

Word expansion means the process of splitting a string into *words* and substituting for variables, commands, and wildcards just as the shell does.

For example, when you write '`ls -l foo.c`', this string is split into three separate words—'`ls`', '`-l`' and '`foo.c`'. This is the most basic function of word expansion.

When you write '`ls *.c`', this can become many words, because the word '`*.c`' can be replaced with any number of file names. This is called *wildcard expansion*, and it is also a part of word expansion.

When you use '`echo $PATH`' to print your path, you are taking advantage of *variable substitution*, which is also part of word expansion.

Ordinary programs can perform word expansion just like the shell by calling the library function `wordexp`.

10.4.1 The Stages of Word Expansion

When word expansion is applied to a sequence of words, it performs the following transformations in the order shown here:

1. *Tilde expansion*: Replacement of '`~foo`' with the name of the home directory of '`foo`'.

2. Next, three different transformations are applied in the same step, from left to right:

   - *Variable substitution*: Environment variables are substituted for references such as '`$foo`'.

   - *Command substitution*: Constructs such as '``cat foo``' and the equivalent '`$(cat foo)`' are replaced with the output from the inner command.

   - *Arithmetic expansion*: Constructs such as '`$(($x-1))`' are replaced with the result of the arithmetic computation.

3. *Field splitting*: subdivision of the text into *words*.

4. *Wildcard expansion*: The replacement of a construct such as '`*.c`' with a list of '`.c`' file names. Wildcard expansion applies to an entire word at a time, and replaces that word with 0 or more file names that are themselves words.

5. *Quote removal*: The deletion of string-quotes, now that they have done their job by inhibiting the above transformations when appropriate.

For the details of these transformations, and how to write the constructs that use them, see *The BASH Manual* (to appear).

10.4.2 Calling `wordexp`

All the functions, constants and data types for word expansion are declared in the header file `wordexp.h`.

Word expansion produces a vector of words (strings). To return this vector, `wordexp` uses a special data type, `wordexp_t`, which is a structure. You pass `wordexp` the address of the structure, and it fills in the structure's fields to tell you about the results.

`wordexp_t`   [Data Type]

This data type holds a pointer to a word vector. More precisely, it records both the address of the word vector and its size.

`we_wordc`   The number of elements in the vector.

`we_wordv`   The address of the vector. This field has type `char **`.

`we_offs`   The offset of the first real element of the vector, from its nominal address in the `we_wordv` field. Unlike the other fields, this is always an input to `wordexp`, rather than an output from it.

If you use a nonzero offset, then that many elements at the beginning of the vector are left empty. (The `wordexp` function fills them with null pointers.)

The `we_offs` field is meaningful only if you use the `WRDE_DOOFFS` flag. Otherwise, the offset is always zero regardless of what is in this field, and the first real element comes at the beginning of the vector.

`int wordexp (const char *words, wordexp_t *word-vector-ptr, int`   [Function]
`     flags)`

Preliminary: | MT-Unsafe race:utent const:env env sig:ALRM timer locale | AS-Unsafe dlopen plugin i18n heap corrupt lock | AC-Unsafe corrupt lock fd mem | See Section 1.2.2.1 [POSIX Safety Concepts], page 2.

Perform word expansion on the string *words*, putting the result in a newly allocated vector, and store the size and address of this vector into *word-vector-ptr*. The argument *flags* is a combination of bit flags; see Section 10.4.3 [Flags for Word Expansion], page 247, for details of the flags.

You shouldn't use any of the characters '`|&;<>`' in the string *words* unless they are quoted; likewise for newline. If you use these characters unquoted, you will get the `WRDE_BADCHAR` error code. Don't use parentheses or braces unless they are quoted or part of a word expansion construct. If you use quotation characters '`'"``', they should come in pairs that balance.

The results of word expansion are a sequence of words. The function `wordexp` allocates a string for each resulting word, then allocates a vector of type `char **` to store the addresses of these strings. The last element of the vector is a null pointer. This vector is called the *word vector*.

To return this vector, `wordexp` stores both its address and its length (number of elements, not counting the terminating null pointer) into *word-vector-ptr*.

If `wordexp` succeeds, it returns 0. Otherwise, it returns one of these error codes:

WRDE_BADCHAR

> The input string *words* contains an unquoted invalid character such as '|'.

WRDE_BADVAL

> The input string refers to an undefined shell variable, and you used the flag WRDE_UNDEF to forbid such references.

WRDE_CMDSUB

> The input string uses command substitution, and you used the flag WRDE_NOCMD to forbid command substitution.

WRDE_NOSPACE

> It was impossible to allocate memory to hold the result. In this case, wordexp can store part of the results—as much as it could allocate room for.

WRDE_SYNTAX

> There was a syntax error in the input string. For example, an unmatched quoting character is a syntax error. This error code is also used to signal division by zero and overflow in arithmetic expansion.

void **wordfree** (*wordexp_t *word-vector-ptr*)   [Function]
Preliminary: | MT-Safe | AS-Unsafe corrupt heap | AC-Unsafe corrupt mem | See Section 1.2.2.1 [POSIX Safety Concepts], page 2.

Free the storage used for the word-strings and vector that **word-vector-ptr* points to. This does not free the structure **word-vector-ptr* itself—only the other data it points to.

10.4.3 Flags for Word Expansion

This section describes the flags that you can specify in the *flags* argument to wordexp. Choose the flags you want, and combine them with the C operator |.

WRDE_APPEND

> Append the words from this expansion to the vector of words produced by previous calls to wordexp. This way you can effectively expand several words as if they were concatenated with spaces between them.
>
> In order for appending to work, you must not modify the contents of the word vector structure between calls to wordexp. And, if you set WRDE_DOOFFS in the first call to wordexp, you must also set it when you append to the results.

WRDE_DOOFFS

> Leave blank slots at the beginning of the vector of words. The we_offs field says how many slots to leave. The blank slots contain null pointers.

WRDE_NOCMD

> Don't do command substitution; if the input requests command substitution, report an error.

WRDE_REUSE

> Reuse a word vector made by a previous call to **wordexp**. Instead of allocating a new vector of words, this call to **wordexp** will use the vector that already exists (making it larger if necessary).

> Note that the vector may move, so it is not safe to save an old pointer and use it again after calling **wordexp**. You must fetch **we_pathv** anew after each call.

WRDE_SHOWERR

> Do show any error messages printed by commands run by command substitution. More precisely, allow these commands to inherit the standard error output stream of the current process. By default, **wordexp** gives these commands a standard error stream that discards all output.

WRDE_UNDEF

> If the input refers to a shell variable that is not defined, report an error.

10.4.4 `wordexp` Example

Here is an example of using **wordexp** to expand several strings and use the results to run a shell command. It also shows the use of **WRDE_APPEND** to concatenate the expansions and of **wordfree** to free the space allocated by **wordexp**.

```
int
expand_and_execute (const char *program, const char **options)
{
  wordexp_t result;
  pid_t pid
  int status, i;

  /* Expand the string for the program to run.  */
  switch (wordexp (program, &result, 0))
    {
    case 0:  /* Successful.  */
      break;
    case WRDE_NOSPACE:
      /* If the error was WRDE_NOSPACE,
         then perhaps part of the result was allocated.  */
      wordfree (&result);
    default:                        /* Some other error.  */
      return -1;
    }

  /* Expand the strings specified for the arguments.  */
  for (i = 0; options[i] != NULL; i++)
    {
      if (wordexp (options[i], &result, WRDE_APPEND))
        {
          wordfree (&result);
          return -1;
        }
    }

  pid = fork ();
  if (pid == 0)
    {
      /* This is the child process.  Execute the command. */
      execv (result.we_wordv[0], result.we_wordv);
```

```
      exit (EXIT_FAILURE);
    }
  else if (pid < 0)
    /* The fork failed.  Report failure.  */
    status = -1;
  else
    /* This is the parent process.  Wait for the child to complete.  */
    if (waitpid (pid, &status, 0) != pid)
      status = -1;

  wordfree (&result);
  return status;
}
```

10.4.5 Details of Tilde Expansion

It's a standard part of shell syntax that you can use '~' at the beginning of a file name to stand for your own home directory. You can use '~*user*' to stand for *user*'s home directory.

Tilde expansion is the process of converting these abbreviations to the directory names that they stand for.

Tilde expansion applies to the '~' plus all following characters up to whitespace or a slash. It takes place only at the beginning of a word, and only if none of the characters to be transformed is quoted in any way.

Plain '~' uses the value of the environment variable HOME as the proper home directory name. '~' followed by a user name uses getpwname to look up that user in the user database, and uses whatever directory is recorded there. Thus, '~' followed by your own name can give different results from plain '~', if the value of HOME is not really your home directory.

10.4.6 Details of Variable Substitution

Part of ordinary shell syntax is the use of '$*variable*' to substitute the value of a shell variable into a command. This is called *variable substitution*, and it is one part of doing word expansion.

There are two basic ways you can write a variable reference for substitution:

${*variable*}

> If you write braces around the variable name, then it is completely unambiguous where the variable name ends. You can concatenate additional letters onto the end of the variable value by writing them immediately after the close brace. For example, '${foo}s' expands into 'tractors'.

$*variable*

> If you do not put braces around the variable name, then the variable name consists of all the alphanumeric characters and underscores that follow the '$'. The next punctuation character ends the variable name. Thus, '$foo-bar' refers to the variable foo and expands into 'tractor-bar'.

When you use braces, you can also use various constructs to modify the value that is substituted, or test it in various ways.

${*variable*:-*default*}

> Substitute the value of *variable*, but if that is empty or undefined, use *default* instead.

`${variable:=default}`

> Substitute the value of *variable*, but if that is empty or undefined, use *default* instead and set the variable to *default*.

`${variable:?message}`

> If *variable* is defined and not empty, substitute its value.
>
> Otherwise, print *message* as an error message on the standard error stream, and consider word expansion a failure.

`${variable:+replacement}`

> Substitute *replacement*, but only if *variable* is defined and nonempty. Otherwise, substitute nothing for this construct.

`${#variable}`

> Substitute a numeral which expresses in base ten the number of characters in the value of *variable*. '`${#foo}`' stands for '7', because '`tractor`' is seven characters.

These variants of variable substitution let you remove part of the variable's value before substituting it. The *prefix* and *suffix* are not mere strings; they are wildcard patterns, just like the patterns that you use to match multiple file names. But in this context, they match against parts of the variable value rather than against file names.

`${variable%%suffix}`

> Substitute the value of *variable*, but first discard from that variable any portion at the end that matches the pattern *suffix*.
>
> If there is more than one alternative for how to match against *suffix*, this construct uses the longest possible match.
>
> Thus, '`${foo%%r*}`' substitutes 't', because the largest match for '`r*`' at the end of '`tractor`' is '`ractor`'.

`${variable%suffix}`

> Substitute the value of *variable*, but first discard from that variable any portion at the end that matches the pattern *suffix*.
>
> If there is more than one alternative for how to match against *suffix*, this construct uses the shortest possible alternative.
>
> Thus, '`${foo%r*}`' substitutes '`tracto`', because the shortest match for '`r*`' at the end of '`tractor`' is just '`r`'.

`${variable##prefix}`

> Substitute the value of *variable*, but first discard from that variable any portion at the beginning that matches the pattern *prefix*.
>
> If there is more than one alternative for how to match against *prefix*, this construct uses the longest possible match.
>
> Thus, '`${foo##*t}`' substitutes '`or`', because the largest match for '`*t`' at the beginning of '`tractor`' is '`tract`'.

`${variable#prefix}`

> Substitute the value of *variable*, but first discard from that variable any portion at the beginning that matches the pattern *prefix*.

If there is more than one alternative for how to match against *prefix*, this construct uses the shortest possible alternative.

Thus, '`${foo#*t}`' substitutes '`ractor`', because the shortest match for '`*t`' at the beginning of '`tractor`' is just '`t`'.

11 Input/Output Overview

Most programs need to do either input (reading data) or output (writing data), or most frequently both, in order to do anything useful. The GNU C Library provides such a large selection of input and output functions that the hardest part is often deciding which function is most appropriate!

This chapter introduces concepts and terminology relating to input and output. Other chapters relating to the GNU I/O facilities are:

- Chapter 12 [Input/Output on Streams], page 257, which covers the high-level functions that operate on streams, including formatted input and output.
- Chapter 13 [Low-Level Input/Output], page 333, which covers the basic I/O and control functions on file descriptors.
- Chapter 14 [File System Interface], page 390, which covers functions for operating on directories and for manipulating file attributes such as access modes and ownership.
- Chapter 15 [Pipes and FIFOs], page 437, which includes information on the basic interprocess communication facilities.
- Chapter 16 [Sockets], page 442, which covers a more complicated interprocess communication facility with support for networking.
- Chapter 17 [Low-Level Terminal Interface], page 490, which covers functions for changing how input and output to terminals or other serial devices are processed.

11.1 Input/Output Concepts

Before you can read or write the contents of a file, you must establish a connection or communications channel to the file. This process is called *opening* the file. You can open a file for reading, writing, or both.

The connection to an open file is represented either as a stream or as a file descriptor. You pass this as an argument to the functions that do the actual read or write operations, to tell them which file to operate on. Certain functions expect streams, and others are designed to operate on file descriptors.

When you have finished reading to or writing from the file, you can terminate the connection by *closing* the file. Once you have closed a stream or file descriptor, you cannot do any more input or output operations on it.

11.1.1 Streams and File Descriptors

When you want to do input or output to a file, you have a choice of two basic mechanisms for representing the connection between your program and the file: file descriptors and streams. File descriptors are represented as objects of type `int`, while streams are represented as `FILE *` objects.

File descriptors provide a primitive, low-level interface to input and output operations. Both file descriptors and streams can represent a connection to a device (such as a terminal), or a pipe or socket for communicating with another process, as well as a normal file. But, if you want to do control operations that are specific to a particular kind of device, you must use a file descriptor; there are no facilities to use streams in this way. You must also use file descriptors if your program needs to do input or output in special modes, such as nonblocking (or polled) input (see Section 13.14 [File Status Flags], page 375).

Streams provide a higher-level interface, layered on top of the primitive file descriptor facilities. The stream interface treats all kinds of files pretty much alike—the sole exception being the three styles of buffering that you can choose (see Section 12.20 [Stream Buffering], page 319).

The main advantage of using the stream interface is that the set of functions for performing actual input and output operations (as opposed to control operations) on streams is much richer and more powerful than the corresponding facilities for file descriptors. The file descriptor interface provides only simple functions for transferring blocks of characters, but the stream interface also provides powerful formatted input and output functions (`printf` and `scanf`) as well as functions for character- and line-oriented input and output.

Since streams are implemented in terms of file descriptors, you can extract the file descriptor from a stream and perform low-level operations directly on the file descriptor. You can also initially open a connection as a file descriptor and then make a stream associated with that file descriptor.

In general, you should stick with using streams rather than file descriptors, unless there is some specific operation you want to do that can only be done on a file descriptor. If you are a beginning programmer and aren't sure what functions to use, we suggest that you concentrate on the formatted input functions (see Section 12.14 [Formatted Input], page 301) and formatted output functions (see Section 12.12 [Formatted Output], page 279).

If you are concerned about portability of your programs to systems other than GNU, you should also be aware that file descriptors are not as portable as streams. You can expect any system running ISO C to support streams, but non-GNU systems may not support file descriptors at all, or may only implement a subset of the GNU functions that operate on file descriptors. Most of the file descriptor functions in the GNU C Library are included in the POSIX.1 standard, however.

11.1.2 File Position

One of the attributes of an open file is its *file position* that keeps track of where in the file the next character is to be read or written. On GNU systems, and all POSIX.1 systems, the file position is simply an integer representing the number of bytes from the beginning of the file.

The file position is normally set to the beginning of the file when it is opened, and each time a character is read or written, the file position is incremented. In other words, access to the file is normally *sequential*.

Ordinary files permit read or write operations at any position within the file. Some other kinds of files may also permit this. Files which do permit this are sometimes referred to as *random-access* files. You can change the file position using the `fseek` function on a stream (see Section 12.18 [File Positioning], page 314) or the `lseek` function on a file descriptor (see Section 13.2 [Input and Output Primitives], page 336). If you try to change the file position on a file that doesn't support random access, you get the `ESPIPE` error.

Streams and descriptors that are opened for *append access* are treated specially for output: output to such files is *always* appended sequentially to the *end* of the file, regardless of the file position. However, the file position is still used to control where in the file reading is done.

If you think about it, you'll realize that several programs can read a given file at the same time. In order for each program to be able to read the file at its own pace, each program must have its own file pointer, which is not affected by anything the other programs do.

In fact, each opening of a file creates a separate file position. Thus, if you open a file twice even in the same program, you get two streams or descriptors with independent file positions.

By contrast, if you open a descriptor and then duplicate it to get another descriptor, these two descriptors share the same file position: changing the file position of one descriptor will affect the other.

11.2 File Names

In order to open a connection to a file, or to perform other operations such as deleting a file, you need some way to refer to the file. Nearly all files have names that are strings—even files which are actually devices such as tape drives or terminals. These strings are called *file names*. You specify the file name to say which file you want to open or operate on.

This section describes the conventions for file names and how the operating system works with them.

11.2.1 Directories

In order to understand the syntax of file names, you need to understand how the file system is organized into a hierarchy of directories.

A *directory* is a file that contains information to associate other files with names; these associations are called *links* or *directory entries*. Sometimes, people speak of "files in a directory", but in reality, a directory only contains pointers to files, not the files themselves.

The name of a file contained in a directory entry is called a *file name component*. In general, a file name consists of a sequence of one or more such components, separated by the slash character ('/'). A file name which is just one component names a file with respect to its directory. A file name with multiple components names a directory, and then a file in that directory, and so on.

Some other documents, such as the POSIX standard, use the term *pathname* for what we call a file name, and either *filename* or *pathname component* for what this manual calls a file name component. We don't use this terminology because a "path" is something completely different (a list of directories to search), and we think that "pathname" used for something else will confuse users. We always use "file name" and "file name component" (or sometimes just "component", where the context is obvious) in GNU documentation. Some macros use the POSIX terminology in their names, such as `PATH_MAX`. These macros are defined by the POSIX standard, so we cannot change their names.

You can find more detailed information about operations on directories in Chapter 14 [File System Interface], page 390.

11.2.2 File Name Resolution

A file name consists of file name components separated by slash ('/') characters. On the systems that the GNU C Library supports, multiple successive '/' characters are equivalent to a single '/' character.

The process of determining what file a file name refers to is called *file name resolution*. This is performed by examining the components that make up a file name in left-to-right order, and locating each successive component in the directory named by the previous component. Of course, each of the files that are referenced as directories must actually exist, be directories instead of regular files, and have the appropriate permissions to be accessible by the process; otherwise the file name resolution fails.

If a file name begins with a '/', the first component in the file name is located in the *root directory* of the process (usually all processes on the system have the same root directory). Such a file name is called an *absolute file name*.

Otherwise, the first component in the file name is located in the current working directory (see Section 14.1 [Working Directory], page 390). This kind of file name is called a *relative file name*.

The file name components . ("dot") and .. ("dot-dot") have special meanings. Every directory has entries for these file name components. The file name component . refers to the directory itself, while the file name component .. refers to its *parent directory* (the directory that contains the link for the directory in question). As a special case, .. in the root directory refers to the root directory itself, since it has no parent; thus /.. is the same as /.

Here are some examples of file names:

/a   The file named a, in the root directory.

/a/b   The file named b, in the directory named a in the root directory.

a   The file named a, in the current working directory.

/a/./b   This is the same as /a/b.

./a   The file named a, in the current working directory.

../a   The file named a, in the parent directory of the current working directory.

A file name that names a directory may optionally end in a '/'. You can specify a file name of / to refer to the root directory, but the empty string is not a meaningful file name. If you want to refer to the current working directory, use a file name of . or ./.

Unlike some other operating systems, GNU systems don't have any built-in support for file types (or extensions) or file versions as part of its file name syntax. Many programs and utilities use conventions for file names—for example, files containing C source code usually have names suffixed with '.c'—but there is nothing in the file system itself that enforces this kind of convention.

11.2.3 File Name Errors

Functions that accept file name arguments usually detect these **errno** error conditions relating to the file name syntax or trouble finding the named file. These errors are referred to throughout this manual as the *usual file name errors*.

EACCES   The process does not have search permission for a directory component of the file name.

ENAMETOOLONG

This error is used when either the total length of a file name is greater than `PATH_MAX`, or when an individual file name component has a length greater than `NAME_MAX`. See Section 32.6 [Limits on File System Capacity], page 874.

On GNU/Hurd systems, there is no imposed limit on overall file name length, but some file systems may place limits on the length of a component.

ENOENT   This error is reported when a file referenced as a directory component in the file name doesn't exist, or when a component is a symbolic link whose target file does not exist. See Section 14.5 [Symbolic Links], page 406.

ENOTDIR   A file that is referenced as a directory component in the file name exists, but it isn't a directory.

ELOOP   Too many symbolic links were resolved while trying to look up the file name. The system has an arbitrary limit on the number of symbolic links that may be resolved in looking up a single file name, as a primitive way to detect loops. See Section 14.5 [Symbolic Links], page 406.

11.2.4 Portability of File Names

The rules for the syntax of file names discussed in Section 11.2 [File Names], page 254, are the rules normally used by GNU systems and by other POSIX systems. However, other operating systems may use other conventions.

There are two reasons why it can be important for you to be aware of file name portability issues:

- If your program makes assumptions about file name syntax, or contains embedded literal file name strings, it is more difficult to get it to run under other operating systems that use different syntax conventions.

- Even if you are not concerned about running your program on machines that run other operating systems, it may still be possible to access files that use different naming conventions. For example, you may be able to access file systems on another computer running a different operating system over a network, or read and write disks in formats used by other operating systems.

The ISO C standard says very little about file name syntax, only that file names are strings. In addition to varying restrictions on the length of file names and what characters can validly appear in a file name, different operating systems use different conventions and syntax for concepts such as structured directories and file types or extensions. Some concepts such as file versions might be supported in some operating systems and not by others.

The POSIX.1 standard allows implementations to put additional restrictions on file name syntax, concerning what characters are permitted in file names and on the length of file name and file name component strings. However, on GNU systems, any character except the null character is permitted in a file name string, and on GNU/Hurd systems there are no limits on the length of file name strings.

12 Input/Output on Streams

This chapter describes the functions for creating streams and performing input and output operations on them. As discussed in Chapter 11 [Input/Output Overview], page 252, a stream is a fairly abstract, high-level concept representing a communications channel to a file, device, or process.

12.1 Streams

For historical reasons, the type of the C data structure that represents a stream is called FILE rather than "stream". Since most of the library functions deal with objects of type FILE *, sometimes the term *file pointer* is also used to mean "stream". This leads to unfortunate confusion over terminology in many books on C. This manual, however, is careful to use the terms "file" and "stream" only in the technical sense.

The FILE type is declared in the header file stdio.h.

FILE   [Data Type]

> This is the data type used to represent stream objects. A FILE object holds all of the internal state information about the connection to the associated file, including such things as the file position indicator and buffering information. Each stream also has error and end-of-file status indicators that can be tested with the ferror and feof functions; see Section 12.15 [End-Of-File and Errors], page 311.

FILE objects are allocated and managed internally by the input/output library functions. Don't try to create your own objects of type FILE; let the library do it. Your programs should deal only with pointers to these objects (that is, FILE * values) rather than the objects themselves.

12.2 Standard Streams

When the main function of your program is invoked, it already has three predefined streams open and available for use. These represent the "standard" input and output channels that have been established for the process.

These streams are declared in the header file stdio.h.

FILE * stdin   [Variable]

> The *standard input* stream, which is the normal source of input for the program.

FILE * stdout   [Variable]

> The *standard output* stream, which is used for normal output from the program.

FILE * stderr   [Variable]

> The *standard error* stream, which is used for error messages and diagnostics issued by the program.

On GNU systems, you can specify what files or processes correspond to these streams using the pipe and redirection facilities provided by the shell. (The primitives shells use to implement these facilities are described in Chapter 14 [File System Interface], page 390.)

Most other operating systems provide similar mechanisms, but the details of how to use them can vary.

In the GNU C Library, `stdin`, `stdout`, and `stderr` are normal variables which you can set just like any others. For example, to redirect the standard output to a file, you could do:

```
fclose (stdout);
stdout = fopen ("standard-output-file", "w");
```

Note however, that in other systems `stdin`, `stdout`, and `stderr` are macros that you cannot assign to in the normal way. But you can use `freopen` to get the effect of closing one and reopening it. See Section 12.3 [Opening Streams], page 258.

The three streams `stdin`, `stdout`, and `stderr` are not unoriented at program start (see Section 12.6 [Streams in Internationalized Applications], page 266).

12.3 Opening Streams

Opening a file with the `fopen` function creates a new stream and establishes a connection between the stream and a file. This may involve creating a new file.

Everything described in this section is declared in the header file `stdio.h`.

FILE * fopen (*const char *filename, const char *opentype*)   [Function]
> Preliminary: | MT-Safe | AS-Unsafe heap lock | AC-Unsafe mem fd lock | See Section 1.2.2.1 [POSIX Safety Concepts], page 2.
>
> The `fopen` function opens a stream for I/O to the file *filename*, and returns a pointer to the stream.
>
> The *opentype* argument is a string that controls how the file is opened and specifies attributes of the resulting stream. It must begin with one of the following sequences of characters:
>
> 'r'   Open an existing file for reading only.
>
> 'w'   Open the file for writing only. If the file already exists, it is truncated to zero length. Otherwise a new file is created.
>
> 'a'   Open a file for append access; that is, writing at the end of file only. If the file already exists, its initial contents are unchanged and output to the stream is appended to the end of the file. Otherwise, a new, empty file is created.
>
> 'r+'   Open an existing file for both reading and writing. The initial contents of the file are unchanged and the initial file position is at the beginning of the file.
>
> 'w+'   Open a file for both reading and writing. If the file already exists, it is truncated to zero length. Otherwise, a new file is created.
>
> 'a+'   Open or create file for both reading and appending. If the file exists, its initial contents are unchanged. Otherwise, a new file is created. The initial file position for reading is at the beginning of the file, but output is always appended to the end of the file.

As you can see, '+' requests a stream that can do both input and output. When using such a stream, you must call **fflush** (see Section 12.20 [Stream Buffering], page 319) or a file positioning function such as **fseek** (see Section 12.18 [File Positioning], page 314) when switching from reading to writing or vice versa. Otherwise, internal buffers might not be emptied properly.

Additional characters may appear after these to specify flags for the call. Always put the mode ('r', 'w+', etc.) first; that is the only part you are guaranteed will be understood by all systems.

The GNU C Library defines additional characters for use in *opentype*:

'c'   The file is opened with cancellation in the I/O functions disabled.

'e'   The underlying file descriptor will be closed if you use any of the **exec...** functions (see Section 26.5 [Executing a File], page 776). (This is equivalent to having set **FD_CLOEXEC** on that descriptor. See Section 13.13 [File Descriptor Flags], page 374.)

'm'   The file is opened and accessed using **mmap**. This is only supported with files opened for reading.

'x'   Insist on creating a new file—if a file *filename* already exists, **fopen** fails rather than opening it. If you use 'x' you are guaranteed that you will not clobber an existing file. This is equivalent to the **O_EXCL** option to the **open** function (see Section 13.1 [Opening and Closing Files], page 333).

            The 'x' modifier is part of ISO C11.

The character 'b' in *opentype* has a standard meaning; it requests a binary stream rather than a text stream. But this makes no difference in POSIX systems (including GNU systems). If both '+' and 'b' are specified, they can appear in either order. See Section 12.17 [Text and Binary Streams], page 313.

If the *opentype* string contains the sequence ,ccs=*STRING* then *STRING* is taken as the name of a coded character set and **fopen** will mark the stream as wide-oriented with appropriate conversion functions in place to convert from and to the character set *STRING*. Any other stream is opened initially unoriented and the orientation is decided with the first file operation. If the first operation is a wide character operation, the stream is not only marked as wide-oriented, also the conversion functions to convert to the coded character set used for the current locale are loaded. This will not change anymore from this point on even if the locale selected for the **LC_CTYPE** category is changed.

Any other characters in *opentype* are simply ignored. They may be meaningful in other systems.

If the open fails, **fopen** returns a null pointer.

When the sources are compiled with **_FILE_OFFSET_BITS == 64** on a 32 bit machine this function is in fact **fopen64** since the LFS interface replaces transparently the old interface.

You can have multiple streams (or file descriptors) pointing to the same file open at the same time. If you do only input, this works straightforwardly, but you must be careful if any output streams are included. See Section 13.5 [Dangers of Mixing Streams and Descriptors], page 347. This is equally true whether the streams are in one program (not usual) or in several programs (which can easily happen). It may be advantageous to use the file locking facilities to avoid simultaneous access. See Section 13.15 [File Locks], page 380.

FILE * fopen64 (*const char *filename, const char *opentype*) [Function]

Preliminary: | MT-Safe | AS-Unsafe heap lock | AC-Unsafe mem fd lock | See Section 1.2.2.1 [POSIX Safety Concepts], page 2.

This function is similar to `fopen` but the stream it returns a pointer for is opened using `open64`. Therefore this stream can be used even on files larger than 2^{31} bytes on 32 bit machines.

Please note that the return type is still `FILE *`. There is no special `FILE` type for the LFS interface.

If the sources are compiled with `_FILE_OFFSET_BITS == 64` on a 32 bits machine this function is available under the name `fopen` and so transparently replaces the old interface.

---

int FOPEN_MAX [Macro]

The value of this macro is an integer constant expression that represents the minimum number of streams that the implementation guarantees can be open simultaneously. You might be able to open more than this many streams, but that is not guaranteed. The value of this constant is at least eight, which includes the three standard streams `stdin`, `stdout`, and `stderr`. In POSIX.1 systems this value is determined by the `OPEN_MAX` parameter; see Section 32.1 [General Capacity Limits], page 862. In BSD and GNU, it is controlled by the `RLIMIT_NOFILE` resource limit; see Section 22.2 [Limiting Resource Usage], page 656.

FILE * freopen (*const char *filename, const char *opentype,* [Function]
     FILE *stream)

Preliminary: | MT-Safe | AS-Unsafe corrupt | AC-Unsafe corrupt fd | See Section 1.2.2.1 [POSIX Safety Concepts], page 2.

This function is like a combination of `fclose` and `fopen`. It first closes the stream referred to by *stream*, ignoring any errors that are detected in the process. (Because errors are ignored, you should not use `freopen` on an output stream if you have actually done any output using the stream.) Then the file named by *filename* is opened with mode *opentype* as for `fopen`, and associated with the same stream object *stream*.

If the operation fails, a null pointer is returned; otherwise, `freopen` returns *stream*. On Linux, `freopen` may also fail and set `errno` to `EBUSY` when the kernel structure for the old file descriptor was not initialized completely before `freopen` was called. This can only happen in multi-threaded programs, when two threads race to allocate the same file descriptor number. To avoid the possibility of this race, do not use `close` to close the underlying file descriptor for a `FILE`; either use `freopen` while the file is still open, or use `open` and then `dup2` to install the new file descriptor.

`freopen` has traditionally been used to connect a standard stream such as `stdin` with a file of your own choice. This is useful in programs in which use of a standard stream for certain purposes is hard-coded. In the GNU C Library, you can simply close the standard streams and open new ones with `fopen`. But other systems lack this ability, so using `freopen` is more portable.

When the sources are compiled with `_FILE_OFFSET_BITS == 64` on a 32 bit machine this function is in fact `freopen64` since the LFS interface replaces transparently the old interface.

`FILE * freopen64` (*const char *filename, const char *opentype,*   [Function]
    *FILE *stream*)

Preliminary: | MT-Safe | AS-Unsafe corrupt | AC-Unsafe corrupt fd | See Section 1.2.2.1 [POSIX Safety Concepts], page 2.

This function is similar to `freopen`. The only difference is that on 32 bit machine the stream returned is able to read beyond the 2^{31} bytes limits imposed by the normal interface. It should be noted that the stream pointed to by *stream* need not be opened using `fopen64` or `freopen64` since its mode is not important for this function.

If the sources are compiled with `_FILE_OFFSET_BITS == 64` on a 32 bits machine this function is available under the name `freopen` and so transparently replaces the old interface.

In some situations it is useful to know whether a given stream is available for reading or writing. This information is normally not available and would have to be remembered separately. Solaris introduced a few functions to get this information from the stream descriptor and these functions are also available in the GNU C Library.

`int __freadable` (*FILE *stream*)   [Function]

Preliminary: | MT-Safe | AS-Safe | AC-Safe | See Section 1.2.2.1 [POSIX Safety Concepts], page 2.

The `__freadable` function determines whether the stream *stream* was opened to allow reading. In this case the return value is nonzero. For write-only streams the function returns zero.

This function is declared in `stdio_ext.h`.

`int __fwritable` (*FILE *stream*)   [Function]

Preliminary: | MT-Safe | AS-Safe | AC-Safe | See Section 1.2.2.1 [POSIX Safety Concepts], page 2.

The `__fwritable` function determines whether the stream *stream* was opened to allow writing. In this case the return value is nonzero. For read-only streams the function returns zero.

This function is declared in `stdio_ext.h`.

For slightly different kinds of problems there are two more functions. They provide even finer-grained information.

`int __freading` (*FILE *stream*)   [Function]

Preliminary: | MT-Safe | AS-Safe | AC-Safe | See Section 1.2.2.1 [POSIX Safety Concepts], page 2.

The `__freading` function determines whether the stream *stream* was last read from or whether it is opened read-only. In this case the return value is nonzero, otherwise it is zero. Determining whether a stream opened for reading and writing was last used for writing allows to draw conclusions about the content about the buffer, among other things.

This function is declared in `stdio_ext.h`.

int `__fwriting` (*FILE *stream*)   [Function]
    Preliminary: | MT-Safe | AS-Safe | AC-Safe | See Section 1.2.2.1 [POSIX Safety Concepts], page 2.

    The `__fwriting` function determines whether the stream *stream* was last written to or whether it is opened write-only. In this case the return value is nonzero, otherwise it is zero.

    This function is declared in `stdio_ext.h`.

12.4 Closing Streams

When a stream is closed with `fclose`, the connection between the stream and the file is canceled. After you have closed a stream, you cannot perform any additional operations on it.

int `fclose` (*FILE *stream*)   [Function]
    Preliminary: | MT-Safe | AS-Unsafe heap lock | AC-Unsafe lock mem fd | See Section 1.2.2.1 [POSIX Safety Concepts], page 2.

    This function causes *stream* to be closed and the connection to the corresponding file to be broken. Any buffered output is written and any buffered input is discarded. The `fclose` function returns a value of 0 if the file was closed successfully, and `EOF` if an error was detected.

    It is important to check for errors when you call `fclose` to close an output stream, because real, everyday errors can be detected at this time. For example, when `fclose` writes the remaining buffered output, it might get an error because the disk is full. Even if you know the buffer is empty, errors can still occur when closing a file if you are using NFS.

    The function `fclose` is declared in `stdio.h`.

To close all streams currently available the GNU C Library provides another function.

int `fcloseall` (*void*)   [Function]
    Preliminary: | MT-Unsafe race:streams | AS-Unsafe | AC-Safe | See Section 1.2.2.1 [POSIX Safety Concepts], page 2.

    This function causes all open streams of the process to be closed and the connections to corresponding files to be broken. All buffered data is written and any buffered input is discarded. The `fcloseall` function returns a value of 0 if all the files were closed successfully, and `EOF` if an error was detected.

    This function should be used only in special situations, e.g., when an error occurred and the program must be aborted. Normally each single stream should be closed separately so that problems with individual streams can be identified. It is also problematic since the standard streams (see Section 12.2 [Standard Streams], page 257) will also be closed.

The function `fcloseall` is declared in `stdio.h`.

If the `main` function to your program returns, or if you call the `exit` function (see Section 25.7.1 [Normal Termination], page 769), all open streams are automatically closed properly. If your program terminates in any other manner, such as by calling the `abort` function (see Section 25.7.4 [Aborting a Program], page 771) or from a fatal signal (see Chapter 24 [Signal Handling], page 685), open streams might not be closed properly. Buffered output might not be flushed and files may be incomplete. For more information on buffering of streams, see Section 12.20 [Stream Buffering], page 319.

12.5 Streams and Threads

Streams can be used in multi-threaded applications in the same way they are used in single-threaded applications. But the programmer must be aware of the possible complications. It is important to know about these also if the program one writes never use threads since the design and implementation of many stream functions are heavily influenced by the requirements added by multi-threaded programming.

The POSIX standard requires that by default the stream operations are atomic. I.e., issuing two stream operations for the same stream in two threads at the same time will cause the operations to be executed as if they were issued sequentially. The buffer operations performed while reading or writing are protected from other uses of the same stream. To do this each stream has an internal lock object which has to be (implicitly) acquired before any work can be done.

But there are situations where this is not enough and there are also situations where this is not wanted. The implicit locking is not enough if the program requires more than one stream function call to happen atomically. One example would be if an output line a program wants to generate is created by several function calls. The functions by themselves would ensure only atomicity of their own operation, but not atomicity over all the function calls. For this it is necessary to perform the stream locking in the application code.

void flockfile (*FILE *stream*)   [Function]
> Preliminary: | MT-Safe | AS-Safe | AC-Unsafe lock | See Section 1.2.2.1 [POSIX Safety Concepts], page 2.
>
> The `flockfile` function acquires the internal locking object associated with the stream *stream*. This ensures that no other thread can explicitly through `flockfile/ftrylockfile` or implicitly through the call of a stream function lock the stream. The thread will block until the lock is acquired. An explicit call to `funlockfile` has to be used to release the lock.

int ftrylockfile (*FILE *stream*)   [Function]
> Preliminary: | MT-Safe | AS-Safe | AC-Unsafe lock | See Section 1.2.2.1 [POSIX Safety Concepts], page 2.
>
> The `ftrylockfile` function tries to acquire the internal locking object associated with the stream *stream* just like `flockfile`. But unlike `flockfile` this function

does not block if the lock is not available. `ftrylockfile` returns zero if the lock was successfully acquired. Otherwise the stream is locked by another thread.

void funlockfile (*FILE *stream*) [Function]

Preliminary: | MT-Safe | AS-Safe | AC-Unsafe lock | See Section 1.2.2.1 [POSIX Safety Concepts], page 2.

The `funlockfile` function releases the internal locking object of the stream *stream*. The stream must have been locked before by a call to `flockfile` or a successful call of `ftrylockfile`. The implicit locking performed by the stream operations do not count. The `funlockfile` function does not return an error status and the behavior of a call for a stream which is not locked by the current thread is undefined.

The following example shows how the functions above can be used to generate an output line atomically even in multi-threaded applications (yes, the same job could be done with one `fprintf` call but it is sometimes not possible):

```
FILE *fp;
{
    ...
    flockfile (fp);
    fputs ("This is test number ", fp);
    fprintf (fp, "%d\n", test);
    funlockfile (fp)
}
```

Without the explicit locking it would be possible for another thread to use the stream *fp* after the `fputs` call returns and before `fprintf` was called with the result that the number does not follow the word 'number'.

From this description it might already be clear that the locking objects in streams are no simple mutexes. Since locking the same stream twice in the same thread is allowed the locking objects must be equivalent to recursive mutexes. These mutexes keep track of the owner and the number of times the lock is acquired. The same number of `funlockfile` calls by the same threads is necessary to unlock the stream completely. For instance:

```
void
foo (FILE *fp)
{
  ftrylockfile (fp);
  fputs ("in foo\n", fp);
  /* This is very wrong!!!  */
  funlockfile (fp);
}
```

It is important here that the `funlockfile` function is only called if the `ftrylockfile` function succeeded in locking the stream. It is therefore always wrong to ignore the result of `ftrylockfile`. And it makes no sense since otherwise one would use `flockfile`. The result of code like that above is that either `funlockfile` tries to free a stream that hasn't been locked by the current thread or it frees the stream prematurely. The code should look like this:

```
void
foo (FILE *fp)
{
  if (ftrylockfile (fp) == 0)
    {
```

```
        fputs ("in foo\n", fp);
        funlockfile (fp);
      }
  }
```

Now that we covered why it is necessary to have locking it is necessary to talk about situations when locking is unwanted and what can be done. The locking operations (explicit or implicit) don't come for free. Even if a lock is not taken the cost is not zero. The operations which have to be performed require memory operations that are safe in multi-processor environments. With the many local caches involved in such systems this is quite costly. So it is best to avoid the locking completely if it is not needed – because the code in question is never used in a context where two or more threads may use a stream at a time. This can be determined most of the time for application code; for library code which can be used in many contexts one should default to be conservative and use locking.

There are two basic mechanisms to avoid locking. The first is to use the `_unlocked` variants of the stream operations. The POSIX standard defines quite a few of those and the GNU C Library adds a few more. These variants of the functions behave just like the functions with the name without the suffix except that they do not lock the stream. Using these functions is very desirable since they are potentially much faster. This is not only because the locking operation itself is avoided. More importantly, functions like `putc` and `getc` are very simple and traditionally (before the introduction of threads) were implemented as macros which are very fast if the buffer is not empty. With the addition of locking requirements these functions are no longer implemented as macros since they would expand to too much code. But these macros are still available with the same functionality under the new names `putc_unlocked` and `getc_unlocked`. This possibly huge difference of speed also suggests the use of the `_unlocked` functions even if locking is required. The difference is that the locking then has to be performed in the program:

```
    void
    foo (FILE *fp, char *buf)
    {
      flockfile (fp);
      while (*buf != '/')
        putc_unlocked (*buf++, fp);
      funlockfile (fp);
    }
```

If in this example the `putc` function would be used and the explicit locking would be missing the `putc` function would have to acquire the lock in every call, potentially many times depending on when the loop terminates. Writing it the way illustrated above allows the `putc_unlocked` macro to be used which means no locking and direct manipulation of the buffer of the stream.

A second way to avoid locking is by using a non-standard function which was introduced in Solaris and is available in the GNU C Library as well.

`int __fsetlocking (FILE *stream, int type)` [Function]

   Preliminary: | MT-Safe race:stream | AS-Unsafe lock | AC-Safe | See Section 1.2.2.1 [POSIX Safety Concepts], page 2.

   The `__fsetlocking` function can be used to select whether the stream operations will implicitly acquire the locking object of the stream *stream*. By default this is done but it can be disabled and reinstated using this function. There are three values defined for the *type* parameter.

FSETLOCKING_INTERNAL

> The stream **stream** will from now on use the default internal locking. Every stream operation with exception of the **_unlocked** variants will implicitly lock the stream.

FSETLOCKING_BYCALLER

> After the **__fsetlocking** function returns, the user is responsible for locking the stream. None of the stream operations will implicitly do this anymore until the state is set back to FSETLOCKING_INTERNAL.

FSETLOCKING_QUERY

> **__fsetlocking** only queries the current locking state of the stream. The return value will be FSETLOCKING_INTERNAL or FSETLOCKING_BYCALLER depending on the state.

The return value of **__fsetlocking** is either FSETLOCKING_INTERNAL or FSETLOCKING_BYCALLER depending on the state of the stream before the call.

This function and the values for the *type* parameter are declared in **stdio_ext.h**.

This function is especially useful when program code has to be used which is written without knowledge about the **_unlocked** functions (or if the programmer was too lazy to use them).

12.6 Streams in Internationalized Applications

ISO C90 introduced the new type **wchar_t** to allow handling larger character sets. What was missing was a possibility to output strings of **wchar_t** directly. One had to convert them into multibyte strings using **mbstowcs** (there was no **mbsrtowcs** yet) and then use the normal stream functions. While this is doable it is very cumbersome since performing the conversions is not trivial and greatly increases program complexity and size.

The Unix standard early on (I think in XPG4.2) introduced two additional format specifiers for the **printf** and **scanf** families of functions. Printing and reading of single wide characters was made possible using the %C specifier and wide character strings can be handled with %S. These modifiers behave just like %c and %s only that they expect the corresponding argument to have the wide character type and that the wide character and string are transformed into/from multibyte strings before being used.

This was a beginning but it is still not good enough. Not always is it desirable to use **printf** and **scanf**. The other, smaller and faster functions cannot handle wide characters. Second, it is not possible to have a format string for **printf** and **scanf** consisting of wide characters. The result is that format strings would have to be generated if they have to contain non-basic characters.

In the Amendment 1 to ISO C90 a whole new set of functions was added to solve the problem. Most of the stream functions got a counterpart which take a wide character or wide character string instead of a character or string respectively. The new functions operate on the same streams (like **stdout**). This is different from the model of the C++ runtime library where separate streams for wide and normal I/O are used.

Being able to use the same stream for wide and normal operations comes with a restriction: a stream can be used either for wide operations or for normal operations. Once it is decided there is no way back. Only a call to `freopen` or `freopen64` can reset the *orientation*. The orientation can be decided in three ways:

- If any of the normal character functions are used (this includes the `fread` and `fwrite` functions) the stream is marked as not wide oriented.

- If any of the wide character functions are used the stream is marked as wide oriented.

- The `fwide` function can be used to set the orientation either way.

It is important to never mix the use of wide and not wide operations on a stream. There are no diagnostics issued. The application behavior will simply be strange or the application will simply crash. The `fwide` function can help avoid this.

`int fwide (`*FILE *stream, int mode*`)` [Function]
> Preliminary: | MT-Safe | AS-Unsafe corrupt | AC-Unsafe lock | See Section 1.2.2.1 [POSIX Safety Concepts], page 2.
>
> The `fwide` function can be used to set and query the state of the orientation of the stream *stream*. If the *mode* parameter has a positive value the streams get wide oriented, for negative values narrow oriented. It is not possible to overwrite previous orientations with `fwide`. I.e., if the stream *stream* was already oriented before the call nothing is done.
>
> If *mode* is zero the current orientation state is queried and nothing is changed.
>
> The `fwide` function returns a negative value, zero, or a positive value if the stream is narrow, not at all, or wide oriented respectively.
>
> This function was introduced in Amendment 1 to ISO C90 and is declared in `wchar.h`.

It is generally a good idea to orient a stream as early as possible. This can prevent surprise especially for the standard streams `stdin`, `stdout`, and `stderr`. If some library function in some situations uses one of these streams and this use orients the stream in a different way the rest of the application expects it one might end up with hard to reproduce errors. Remember that no errors are signal if the streams are used incorrectly. Leaving a stream unoriented after creation is normally only necessary for library functions which create streams which can be used in different contexts.

When writing code which uses streams and which can be used in different contexts it is important to query the orientation of the stream before using it (unless the rules of the library interface demand a specific orientation). The following little, silly function illustrates this.

```
void
print_f (FILE *fp)
{
  if (fwide (fp, 0) > 0)
    /* Positive return value means wide orientation.  */
    fputwc (L'f', fp);
  else
    fputc ('f', fp);
}
```

Note that in this case the function `print_f` decides about the orientation of the stream if it was unoriented before (will not happen if the advice above is followed).

The encoding used for the `wchar_t` values is unspecified and the user must not make any assumptions about it. For I/O of `wchar_t` values this means that it is impossible to write these values directly to the stream. This is not what follows from the ISO C locale model either. What happens instead is that the bytes read from or written to the underlying media are first converted into the internal encoding chosen by the implementation for `wchar_t`. The external encoding is determined by the `LC_CTYPE` category of the current locale or by the 'ccs' part of the mode specification given to `fopen`, `fopen64`, `freopen`, or `freopen64`. How and when the conversion happens is unspecified and it happens invisibly to the user.

Since a stream is created in the unoriented state it has at that point no conversion associated with it. The conversion which will be used is determined by the `LC_CTYPE` category selected at the time the stream is oriented. If the locales are changed at the runtime this might produce surprising results unless one pays attention. This is just another good reason to orient the stream explicitly as soon as possible, perhaps with a call to `fwide`.

12.7 Simple Output by Characters or Lines

This section describes functions for performing character- and line-oriented output.

These narrow stream functions are declared in the header file `stdio.h` and the wide stream functions in `wchar.h`.

---

int fputc (*int c, FILE *stream*)   [Function]

Preliminary: | MT-Safe | AS-Unsafe corrupt | AC-Unsafe corrupt lock | See Section 1.2.2.1 [POSIX Safety Concepts], page 2.

The `fputc` function converts the character *c* to type `unsigned char`, and writes it to the stream *stream*. `EOF` is returned if a write error occurs; otherwise the character *c* is returned.

---

wint_t fputwc (*wchar_t wc, FILE *stream*)   [Function]

Preliminary: | MT-Safe | AS-Unsafe corrupt | AC-Unsafe corrupt lock | See Section 1.2.2.1 [POSIX Safety Concepts], page 2.

The `fputwc` function writes the wide character *wc* to the stream *stream*. `WEOF` is returned if a write error occurs; otherwise the character *wc* is returned.

---

int fputc_unlocked (*int c, FILE *stream*)   [Function]

Preliminary: | MT-Safe race:stream | AS-Unsafe corrupt | AC-Unsafe corrupt | See Section 1.2.2.1 [POSIX Safety Concepts], page 2.

The `fputc_unlocked` function is equivalent to the `fputc` function except that it does not implicitly lock the stream.

---

wint_t fputwc_unlocked (*wchar_t wc, FILE *stream*)   [Function]

Preliminary: | MT-Safe race:stream | AS-Unsafe corrupt | AC-Unsafe corrupt | See Section 1.2.2.1 [POSIX Safety Concepts], page 2.

The `fputwc_unlocked` function is equivalent to the `fputwc` function except that it does not implicitly lock the stream.

This function is a GNU extension.

int putc (*int c, FILE *stream*)   [Function]
Preliminary: | MT-Safe | AS-Unsafe corrupt | AC-Unsafe corrupt lock | See Section 1.2.2.1 [POSIX Safety Concepts], page 2.

This is just like `fputc`, except that most systems implement it as a macro, making it faster. One consequence is that it may evaluate the *stream* argument more than once, which is an exception to the general rule for macros. `putc` is usually the best function to use for writing a single character.

wint_t putwc (*wchar_t wc, FILE *stream*)   [Function]
Preliminary: | MT-Safe | AS-Unsafe corrupt | AC-Unsafe corrupt lock | See Section 1.2.2.1 [POSIX Safety Concepts], page 2.

This is just like `fputwc`, except that it can be implement as a macro, making it faster. One consequence is that it may evaluate the *stream* argument more than once, which is an exception to the general rule for macros. `putwc` is usually the best function to use for writing a single wide character.

int putc_unlocked (*int c, FILE *stream*)   [Function]
Preliminary: | MT-Safe race:stream | AS-Unsafe corrupt | AC-Unsafe corrupt | See Section 1.2.2.1 [POSIX Safety Concepts], page 2.

The `putc_unlocked` function is equivalent to the `putc` function except that it does not implicitly lock the stream.

wint_t putwc_unlocked (*wchar_t wc, FILE *stream*)   [Function]
Preliminary: | MT-Safe race:stream | AS-Unsafe corrupt | AC-Unsafe corrupt | See Section 1.2.2.1 [POSIX Safety Concepts], page 2.

The `putwc_unlocked` function is equivalent to the `putwc` function except that it does not implicitly lock the stream.

This function is a GNU extension.

int putchar (*int c*)   [Function]
Preliminary: | MT-Safe | AS-Unsafe corrupt | AC-Unsafe corrupt lock | See Section 1.2.2.1 [POSIX Safety Concepts], page 2.

The `putchar` function is equivalent to `putc` with `stdout` as the value of the *stream* argument.

wint_t putwchar (*wchar_t wc*)   [Function]
Preliminary: | MT-Safe | AS-Unsafe corrupt | AC-Unsafe corrupt lock | See Section 1.2.2.1 [POSIX Safety Concepts], page 2.

The `putwchar` function is equivalent to `putwc` with `stdout` as the value of the *stream* argument.

int putchar_unlocked (*int c*)   [Function]
Preliminary: | MT-Unsafe race:stdout | AS-Unsafe corrupt | AC-Unsafe corrupt | See Section 1.2.2.1 [POSIX Safety Concepts], page 2.

The `putchar_unlocked` function is equivalent to the `putchar` function except that it does not implicitly lock the stream.

wint_t putwchar_unlocked (*wchar_t wc*)   [Function]

> Preliminary: | MT-Unsafe race:stdout | AS-Unsafe corrupt | AC-Unsafe corrupt |
> See Section 1.2.2.1 [POSIX Safety Concepts], page 2.

> The `putwchar_unlocked` function is equivalent to the `putwchar` function except that
> it does not implicitly lock the stream.

> This function is a GNU extension.

int fputs (*const char *s, FILE *stream*)   [Function]

> Preliminary: | MT-Safe | AS-Unsafe corrupt | AC-Unsafe corrupt lock | See
> Section 1.2.2.1 [POSIX Safety Concepts], page 2.

> The function `fputs` writes the string *s* to the stream *stream*. The terminating null
> character is not written. This function does *not* add a newline character, either. It
> outputs only the characters in the string.

> This function returns `EOF` if a write error occurs, and otherwise a non-negative value.

> For example:

```
fputs ("Are ", stdout);
fputs ("you ", stdout);
fputs ("hungry?\n", stdout);
```

> outputs the text 'Are you hungry?' followed by a newline.

int fputws (*const wchar_t *ws, FILE *stream*)   [Function]

> Preliminary: | MT-Safe | AS-Unsafe corrupt | AC-Unsafe corrupt lock | See
> Section 1.2.2.1 [POSIX Safety Concepts], page 2.

> The function `fputws` writes the wide character string *ws* to the stream *stream*. The
> terminating null character is not written. This function does *not* add a newline
> character, either. It outputs only the characters in the string.

> This function returns `WEOF` if a write error occurs, and otherwise a non-negative value.

int fputs_unlocked (*const char *s, FILE *stream*)   [Function]

> Preliminary: | MT-Safe race:stream | AS-Unsafe corrupt | AC-Unsafe corrupt | See
> Section 1.2.2.1 [POSIX Safety Concepts], page 2.

> The `fputs_unlocked` function is equivalent to the `fputs` function except that it does
> not implicitly lock the stream.

> This function is a GNU extension.

int fputws_unlocked (*const wchar_t *ws, FILE *stream*)   [Function]

> Preliminary: | MT-Safe race:stream | AS-Unsafe corrupt | AC-Unsafe corrupt | See
> Section 1.2.2.1 [POSIX Safety Concepts], page 2.

> The `fputws_unlocked` function is equivalent to the `fputws` function except that it
> does not implicitly lock the stream.

> This function is a GNU extension.

int puts (*const char *s*)   [Function]

> Preliminary: | MT-Safe | AS-Unsafe corrupt | AC-Unsafe lock corrupt | See
> Section 1.2.2.1 [POSIX Safety Concepts], page 2.

The `puts` function writes the string *s* to the stream `stdout` followed by a newline. The terminating null character of the string is not written. (Note that `fputs` does *not* write a newline as this function does.)

`puts` is the most convenient function for printing simple messages. For example:

```
puts ("This is a message.");
```

outputs the text 'This is a message.' followed by a newline.

---

int putw (*int w, FILE *stream*)   [Function]

Preliminary: | MT-Safe | AS-Unsafe corrupt | AC-Unsafe lock corrupt | See Section 1.2.2.1 [POSIX Safety Concepts], page 2.

This function writes the word *w* (that is, an `int`) to *stream*. It is provided for compatibility with SVID, but we recommend you use `fwrite` instead (see Section 12.11 [Block Input/Output], page 278).

12.8 Character Input

This section describes functions for performing character-oriented input. These narrow stream functions are declared in the header file `stdio.h` and the wide character functions are declared in `wchar.h`.

These functions return an `int` or `wint_t` value (for narrow and wide stream functions respectively) that is either a character of input, or the special value EOF/WEOF (usually -1). For the narrow stream functions it is important to store the result of these functions in a variable of type `int` instead of `char`, even when you plan to use it only as a character. Storing EOF in a `char` variable truncates its value to the size of a character, so that it is no longer distinguishable from the valid character '(char) -1'. So always use an `int` for the result of `getc` and friends, and check for EOF after the call; once you've verified that the result is not EOF, you can be sure that it will fit in a 'char' variable without loss of information.

---

int fgetc (*FILE *stream*)   [Function]

Preliminary: | MT-Safe | AS-Unsafe corrupt | AC-Unsafe lock corrupt | See Section 1.2.2.1 [POSIX Safety Concepts], page 2.

This function reads the next character as an **unsigned char** from the stream *stream* and returns its value, converted to an `int`. If an end-of-file condition or read error occurs, EOF is returned instead.

---

wint_t fgetwc (*FILE *stream*)   [Function]

Preliminary: | MT-Safe | AS-Unsafe corrupt | AC-Unsafe lock corrupt | See Section 1.2.2.1 [POSIX Safety Concepts], page 2.

This function reads the next wide character from the stream *stream* and returns its value. If an end-of-file condition or read error occurs, WEOF is returned instead.

---

int fgetc_unlocked (*FILE *stream*)   [Function]

Preliminary: | MT-Safe race:stream | AS-Unsafe corrupt | AC-Unsafe corrupt | See Section 1.2.2.1 [POSIX Safety Concepts], page 2.

The `fgetc_unlocked` function is equivalent to the `fgetc` function except that it does not implicitly lock the stream.

`wint_t fgetwc_unlocked (FILE *stream)`   [Function]
 Preliminary: | MT-Safe race:stream | AS-Unsafe corrupt | AC-Unsafe corrupt | See
 Section 1.2.2.1 [POSIX Safety Concepts], page 2.

 The `fgetwc_unlocked` function is equivalent to the `fgetwc` function except that it
 does not implicitly lock the stream.

 This function is a GNU extension.

`int getc (FILE *stream)`   [Function]
 Preliminary: | MT-Safe | AS-Unsafe corrupt | AC-Unsafe lock corrupt | See
 Section 1.2.2.1 [POSIX Safety Concepts], page 2.

 This is just like `fgetc`, except that it is permissible (and typical) for it to be implemented as a macro that evaluates the *stream* argument more than once. `getc` is often
 highly optimized, so it is usually the best function to use to read a single character.

`wint_t getwc (FILE *stream)`   [Function]
 Preliminary: | MT-Safe | AS-Unsafe corrupt | AC-Unsafe lock corrupt | See
 Section 1.2.2.1 [POSIX Safety Concepts], page 2.

 This is just like `fgetwc`, except that it is permissible for it to be implemented as
 a macro that evaluates the *stream* argument more than once. `getwc` can be highly
 optimized, so it is usually the best function to use to read a single wide character.

`int getc_unlocked (FILE *stream)`   [Function]
 Preliminary: | MT-Safe race:stream | AS-Unsafe corrupt | AC-Unsafe corrupt | See
 Section 1.2.2.1 [POSIX Safety Concepts], page 2.

 The `getc_unlocked` function is equivalent to the `getc` function except that it does
 not implicitly lock the stream.

`wint_t getwc_unlocked (FILE *stream)`   [Function]
 Preliminary: | MT-Safe race:stream | AS-Unsafe corrupt | AC-Unsafe corrupt | See
 Section 1.2.2.1 [POSIX Safety Concepts], page 2.

 The `getwc_unlocked` function is equivalent to the `getwc` function except that it does
 not implicitly lock the stream.

 This function is a GNU extension.

`int getchar (void)`   [Function]
 Preliminary: | MT-Safe | AS-Unsafe corrupt | AC-Unsafe lock corrupt | See
 Section 1.2.2.1 [POSIX Safety Concepts], page 2.

 The `getchar` function is equivalent to `getc` with `stdin` as the value of the *stream*
 argument.

`wint_t getwchar (void)`   [Function]
 Preliminary: | MT-Safe | AS-Unsafe corrupt | AC-Unsafe lock corrupt | See
 Section 1.2.2.1 [POSIX Safety Concepts], page 2.

 The `getwchar` function is equivalent to `getwc` with `stdin` as the value of the *stream*
 argument.

int getchar_unlocked (*void*)   [Function]

Preliminary: | MT-Unsafe race:stdin | AS-Unsafe corrupt | AC-Unsafe corrupt | See Section 1.2.2.1 [POSIX Safety Concepts], page 2.

The `getchar_unlocked` function is equivalent to the `getchar` function except that it does not implicitly lock the stream.

wint_t getwchar_unlocked (*void*)   [Function]

Preliminary: | MT-Unsafe race:stdin | AS-Unsafe corrupt | AC-Unsafe corrupt | See Section 1.2.2.1 [POSIX Safety Concepts], page 2.

The `getwchar_unlocked` function is equivalent to the `getwchar` function except that it does not implicitly lock the stream.

This function is a GNU extension.

Here is an example of a function that does input using `fgetc`. It would work just as well using `getc` instead, or using `getchar ()` instead of `fgetc (stdin)`. The code would also work the same for the wide character stream functions.

```
int
y_or_n_p (const char *question)
{
  fputs (question, stdout);
  while (1)
    {
      int c, answer;
      /* Write a space to separate answer from question. */
      fputc (' ', stdout);
      /* Read the first character of the line.
 This should be the answer character, but might not be. */
      c = tolower (fgetc (stdin));
      answer = c;
      /* Discard rest of input line. */
      while (c != '\n' && c != EOF)
c = fgetc (stdin);
      /* Obey the answer if it was valid. */
      if (answer == 'y')
return 1;
      if (answer == 'n')
return 0;
      /* Answer was invalid: ask for valid answer. */
      fputs ("Please answer y or n:", stdout);
    }
}
```

int getw (*FILE *stream*)   [Function]

Preliminary: | MT-Safe | AS-Unsafe corrupt | AC-Unsafe lock corrupt | See Section 1.2.2.1 [POSIX Safety Concepts], page 2.

This function reads a word (that is, an `int`) from *stream*. It's provided for compatibility with SVID. We recommend you use `fread` instead (see Section 12.11 [Block Input/Output], page 278). Unlike `getc`, any `int` value could be a valid result. `getw` returns `EOF` when it encounters end-of-file or an error, but there is no way to distinguish this from an input word with value -1.

12.9 Line-Oriented Input

Since many programs interpret input on the basis of lines, it is convenient to have functions to read a line of text from a stream.

Standard C has functions to do this, but they aren't very safe: null characters and even (for `gets`) long lines can confuse them. So the GNU C Library provides the nonstandard `getline` function that makes it easy to read lines reliably.

Another GNU extension, `getdelim`, generalizes `getline`. It reads a delimited record, defined as everything through the next occurrence of a specified delimiter character.

All these functions are declared in `stdio.h`.

`ssize_t getline (char **lineptr, size_t *n, FILE *stream)`   [Function]
>   Preliminary: | MT-Safe | AS-Unsafe corrupt heap | AC-Unsafe lock corrupt mem | See Section 1.2.2.1 [POSIX Safety Concepts], page 2.
>
>   This function reads an entire line from *stream*, storing the text (including the newline and a terminating null character) in a buffer and storing the buffer address in *`lineptr`*.
>
>   Before calling `getline`, you should place in *`lineptr`* the address of a buffer *`n`* bytes long, allocated with `malloc`. If this buffer is long enough to hold the line, `getline` stores the line in this buffer. Otherwise, `getline` makes the buffer bigger using `realloc`, storing the new buffer address back in *`lineptr`* and the increased size back in *`n`*. See Section 3.2.3 [Unconstrained Allocation], page 44.
>
>   If you set *`lineptr`* to a null pointer, and *`n`* to zero, before the call, then `getline` allocates the initial buffer for you by calling `malloc`. This buffer remains allocated even if `getline` encounters errors and is unable to read any bytes.
>
>   In either case, when `getline` returns, *`lineptr`* is a `char *` which points to the text of the line.
>
>   When `getline` is successful, it returns the number of characters read (including the newline, but not including the terminating null). This value enables you to distinguish null characters that are part of the line from the null character inserted as a terminator.
>
>   This function is a GNU extension, but it is the recommended way to read lines from a stream. The alternative standard functions are unreliable.
>
>   If an error occurs or end of file is reached without any bytes read, `getline` returns -1.

`ssize_t getdelim (char **lineptr, size_t *n, int delimiter, FILE *stream)`   [Function]
>   Preliminary: | MT-Safe | AS-Unsafe corrupt heap | AC-Unsafe lock corrupt mem | See Section 1.2.2.1 [POSIX Safety Concepts], page 2.
>
>   This function is like `getline` except that the character which tells it to stop reading is not necessarily newline. The argument *delimiter* specifies the delimiter character; `getdelim` keeps reading until it sees that character (or end of file).
>
>   The text is stored in *lineptr*, including the delimiter character and a terminating null. Like `getline`, `getdelim` makes *lineptr* bigger if it isn't big enough.

getline is in fact implemented in terms of getdelim, just like this:

```
ssize_t
getline (char **lineptr, size_t *n, FILE *stream)
{
  return getdelim (lineptr, n, '\n', stream);
}
```

char * fgets (char *s, int count, FILE *stream)   [Function]
Preliminary: | MT-Safe | AS-Unsafe corrupt | AC-Unsafe lock corrupt | See
Section 1.2.2.1 [POSIX Safety Concepts], page 2.

The fgets function reads characters from the stream stream up to and including a
newline character and stores them in the string s, adding a null character to mark
the end of the string. You must supply count characters worth of space in s, but the
number of characters read is at most count − 1. The extra character space is used to
hold the null character at the end of the string.

If the system is already at end of file when you call fgets, then the contents of the
array s are unchanged and a null pointer is returned. A null pointer is also returned
if a read error occurs. Otherwise, the return value is the pointer s.

Warning: If the input data has a null character, you can't tell. So don't use fgets
unless you know the data cannot contain a null. Don't use it to read files edited by the
user because, if the user inserts a null character, you should either handle it properly
or print a clear error message. We recommend using getline instead of fgets.

wchar_t * fgetws (wchar_t *ws, int count, FILE *stream)   [Function]
Preliminary: | MT-Safe | AS-Unsafe corrupt | AC-Unsafe lock corrupt | See
Section 1.2.2.1 [POSIX Safety Concepts], page 2.

The fgetws function reads wide characters from the stream stream up to and including a newline character and stores them in the string ws, adding a null wide character
to mark the end of the string. You must supply count wide characters worth of space
in ws, but the number of characters read is at most count − 1. The extra character
space is used to hold the null wide character at the end of the string.

If the system is already at end of file when you call fgetws, then the contents of the
array ws are unchanged and a null pointer is returned. A null pointer is also returned
if a read error occurs. Otherwise, the return value is the pointer ws.

Warning: If the input data has a null wide character (which are null bytes in the
input stream), you can't tell. So don't use fgetws unless you know the data cannot
contain a null. Don't use it to read files edited by the user because, if the user inserts
a null character, you should either handle it properly or print a clear error message.

char * fgets_unlocked (char *s, int count, FILE *stream)   [Function]
Preliminary: | MT-Safe race:stream | AS-Unsafe corrupt | AC-Unsafe corrupt | See
Section 1.2.2.1 [POSIX Safety Concepts], page 2.

The fgets_unlocked function is equivalent to the fgets function except that it does
not implicitly lock the stream.

This function is a GNU extension.

`wchar_t * fgetws_unlocked (wchar_t *ws, int count, FILE`   [Function]
      `*stream)`

> Preliminary: | MT-Safe race:stream | AS-Unsafe corrupt | AC-Unsafe corrupt | See Section 1.2.2.1 [POSIX Safety Concepts], page 2.
>
> The `fgetws_unlocked` function is equivalent to the `fgetws` function except that it does not implicitly lock the stream.
>
> This function is a GNU extension.

`char * gets (char *s)`   [Deprecated function]

> Preliminary: | MT-Safe | AS-Unsafe corrupt | AC-Unsafe lock corrupt | See Section 1.2.2.1 [POSIX Safety Concepts], page 2.
>
> The function `gets` reads characters from the stream `stdin` up to the next newline character, and stores them in the string *s*. The newline character is discarded (note that this differs from the behavior of `fgets`, which copies the newline character into the string). If `gets` encounters a read error or end-of-file, it returns a null pointer; otherwise it returns *s*.
>
> **Warning:** The `gets` function is **very dangerous** because it provides no protection against overflowing the string *s*. The GNU C Library includes it for compatibility only. You should **always** use `fgets` or `getline` instead. To remind you of this, the linker (if using GNU `ld`) will issue a warning whenever you use `gets`.

12.10 Unreading

In parser programs it is often useful to examine the next character in the input stream without removing it from the stream. This is called "peeking ahead" at the input because your program gets a glimpse of the input it will read next.

Using stream I/O, you can peek ahead at input by first reading it and then *unreading* it (also called *pushing it back* on the stream). Unreading a character makes it available to be input again from the stream, by the next call to `fgetc` or other input function on that stream.

12.10.1 What Unreading Means

Here is a pictorial explanation of unreading. Suppose you have a stream reading a file that contains just six characters, the letters 'foobar'. Suppose you have read three characters so far. The situation looks like this:

```
f o o b a r
      ^
```

so the next input character will be 'b'.

If instead of reading 'b' you unread the letter 'o', you get a situation like this:

```
f o o b a r
 |
    o--
      ^
```

so that the next input characters will be 'o' and 'b'.

If you unread '9' instead of 'o', you get this situation:

```
f o o b a r
```

```
    |
        9--
        ^
```

so that the next input characters will be '9' and 'b'.

12.10.2 Using `ungetc` To Do Unreading

The function to unread a character is called `ungetc`, because it reverses the action of `getc`.

`int ungetc` (*int c, FILE *stream*) [Function]

> Preliminary: | MT-Safe | AS-Unsafe corrupt | AC-Unsafe lock corrupt | See Section 1.2.2.1 [POSIX Safety Concepts], page 2.
>
> The `ungetc` function pushes back the character *c* onto the input stream *stream*. So the next input from *stream* will read *c* before anything else.
>
> If *c* is `EOF`, `ungetc` does nothing and just returns `EOF`. This lets you call `ungetc` with the return value of `getc` without needing to check for an error from `getc`.
>
> The character that you push back doesn't have to be the same as the last character that was actually read from the stream. In fact, it isn't necessary to actually read any characters from the stream before unreading them with `ungetc`! But that is a strange way to write a program; usually `ungetc` is used only to unread a character that was just read from the same stream. The GNU C Library supports this even on files opened in binary mode, but other systems might not.
>
> The GNU C Library only supports one character of pushback—in other words, it does not work to call `ungetc` twice without doing input in between. Other systems might let you push back multiple characters; then reading from the stream retrieves the characters in the reverse order that they were pushed.
>
> Pushing back characters doesn't alter the file; only the internal buffering for the stream is affected. If a file positioning function (such as `fseek`, `fseeko` or `rewind`; see Section 12.18 [File Positioning], page 314) is called, any pending pushed-back characters are discarded.
>
> Unreading a character on a stream that is at end of file clears the end-of-file indicator for the stream, because it makes the character of input available. After you read that character, trying to read again will encounter end of file.

`wint_t ungetwc` (*wint_t wc, FILE *stream*) [Function]

> Preliminary: | MT-Safe | AS-Unsafe corrupt | AC-Unsafe lock corrupt | See Section 1.2.2.1 [POSIX Safety Concepts], page 2.
>
> The `ungetwc` function behaves just like `ungetc` just that it pushes back a wide character.

Here is an example showing the use of `getc` and `ungetc` to skip over whitespace characters. When this function reaches a non-whitespace character, it unreads that character to be seen again on the next read operation on the stream.

```
#include <stdio.h>
#include <ctype.h>

void
skip_whitespace (FILE *stream)
```

```
{
  int c;
  do
    /* No need to check for EOF because it is not
        isspace, and ungetc ignores EOF.  */
    c = getc (stream);
  while (isspace (c));
  ungetc (c, stream);
}
```

12.11 Block Input/Output

This section describes how to do input and output operations on blocks of data. You can use these functions to read and write binary data, as well as to read and write text in fixed-size blocks instead of by characters or lines.

Binary files are typically used to read and write blocks of data in the same format as is used to represent the data in a running program. In other words, arbitrary blocks of memory—not just character or string objects—can be written to a binary file, and meaningfully read in again by the same program.

Storing data in binary form is often considerably more efficient than using the formatted I/O functions. Also, for floating-point numbers, the binary form avoids possible loss of precision in the conversion process. On the other hand, binary files can't be examined or modified easily using many standard file utilities (such as text editors), and are not portable between different implementations of the language, or different kinds of computers.

These functions are declared in `stdio.h`.

size_t fread (*void *data, size_t size, size_t count, FILE *stream*)   [Function]
> Preliminary: | MT-Safe | AS-Unsafe corrupt | AC-Unsafe lock corrupt | See Section 1.2.2.1 [POSIX Safety Concepts], page 2.
>
> This function reads up to *count* objects of size *size* into the array *data*, from the stream *stream*. It returns the number of objects actually read, which might be less than *count* if a read error occurs or the end of the file is reached. This function returns a value of zero (and doesn't read anything) if either *size* or *count* is zero.
>
> If `fread` encounters end of file in the middle of an object, it returns the number of complete objects read, and discards the partial object. Therefore, the stream remains at the actual end of the file.

size_t fread_unlocked (*void *data, size_t size, size_t count,*   [Function]
   *FILE *stream*)
> Preliminary: | MT-Safe race:stream | AS-Unsafe corrupt | AC-Unsafe corrupt | See Section 1.2.2.1 [POSIX Safety Concepts], page 2.
>
> The `fread_unlocked` function is equivalent to the `fread` function except that it does not implicitly lock the stream.
>
> This function is a GNU extension.

size_t fwrite (*const void *data, size_t size, size_t count, FILE*   [Function]
   stream)
> Preliminary: | MT-Safe | AS-Unsafe corrupt | AC-Unsafe lock corrupt | See Section 1.2.2.1 [POSIX Safety Concepts], page 2.

This function writes up to *count* objects of size *size* from the array *data*, to the stream *stream*. The return value is normally *count*, if the call succeeds. Any other value indicates some sort of error, such as running out of space.

`size_t fwrite_unlocked (const void *data, size_t size, size_t`   [Function]
     `count, FILE *stream)`

Preliminary: | MT-Safe race:stream | AS-Unsafe corrupt | AC-Unsafe corrupt | See Section 1.2.2.1 [POSIX Safety Concepts], page 2.

The `fwrite_unlocked` function is equivalent to the `fwrite` function except that it does not implicitly lock the stream.

This function is a GNU extension.

12.12 Formatted Output

The functions described in this section (`printf` and related functions) provide a convenient way to perform formatted output. You call `printf` with a *format string* or *template string* that specifies how to format the values of the remaining arguments.

Unless your program is a filter that specifically performs line- or character-oriented processing, using `printf` or one of the other related functions described in this section is usually the easiest and most concise way to perform output. These functions are especially useful for printing error messages, tables of data, and the like.

12.12.1 Formatted Output Basics

The `printf` function can be used to print any number of arguments. The template string argument you supply in a call provides information not only about the number of additional arguments, but also about their types and what style should be used for printing them.

Ordinary characters in the template string are simply written to the output stream as-is, while *conversion specifications* introduced by a '%' character in the template cause subsequent arguments to be formatted and written to the output stream. For example,

```
int pct = 37;
char filename[] = "foo.txt";
printf ("Processing of `%s' is %d%% finished.\nPlease be patient.\n",
filename, pct);
```

produces output like

```
Processing of `foo.txt' is 37% finished.
Please be patient.
```

This example shows the use of the '%d' conversion to specify that an `int` argument should be printed in decimal notation, the '%s' conversion to specify printing of a string argument, and the '%%' conversion to print a literal '%' character.

There are also conversions for printing an integer argument as an unsigned value in octal, decimal, or hexadecimal radix ('%o', '%u', or '%x', respectively); or as a character value ('%c').

Floating-point numbers can be printed in normal, fixed-point notation using the '%f' conversion or in exponential notation using the '%e' conversion. The '%g' conversion uses either '%e' or '%f' format, depending on what is more appropriate for the magnitude of the particular number.

You can control formatting more precisely by writing *modifiers* between the '%' and the character that indicates which conversion to apply. These slightly alter the ordinary behavior of the conversion. For example, most conversion specifications permit you to specify a minimum field width and a flag indicating whether you want the result left- or right-justified within the field.

The specific flags and modifiers that are permitted and their interpretation vary depending on the particular conversion. They're all described in more detail in the following sections. Don't worry if this all seems excessively complicated at first; you can almost always get reasonable free-format output without using any of the modifiers at all. The modifiers are mostly used to make the output look "prettier" in tables.

12.12.2 Output Conversion Syntax

This section provides details about the precise syntax of conversion specifications that can appear in a `printf` template string.

Characters in the template string that are not part of a conversion specification are printed as-is to the output stream. Multibyte character sequences (see Chapter 6 [Character Set Handling], page 134) are permitted in a template string.

The conversion specifications in a `printf` template string have the general form:

> `% [ param-no $] flags width [ . precision ] type conversion`

or

> `% [ param-no $] flags width . * [ param-no $] type conversion`

For example, in the conversion specifier '`%-10.8ld`', the '`-`' is a flag, '`10`' specifies the field width, the precision is '`8`', the letter '`l`' is a type modifier, and '`d`' specifies the conversion style. (This particular type specifier says to print a `long int` argument in decimal notation, with a minimum of 8 digits left-justified in a field at least 10 characters wide.)

In more detail, output conversion specifications consist of an initial '%' character followed in sequence by:

- An optional specification of the parameter used for this format. Normally the parameters to the `printf` function are assigned to the formats in the order of appearance in the format string. But in some situations (such as message translation) this is not desirable and this extension allows an explicit parameter to be specified.

  The *param-no* parts of the format must be integers in the range of 1 to the maximum number of arguments present to the function call. Some implementations limit this number to a certain upper bound. The exact limit can be retrieved by the following constant.

`NL_ARGMAX`   [Macro]

> The value of `NL_ARGMAX` is the maximum value allowed for the specification of a positional parameter in a `printf` call. The actual value in effect at runtime can be retrieved by using `sysconf` using the `_SC_NL_ARGMAX` parameter see Section 32.4.1 [Definition of `sysconf`], page 865.

> Some systems have a quite low limit such as 9 for System V systems. The GNU C Library has no real limit.

If any of the formats has a specification for the parameter position all of them in the format string shall have one. Otherwise the behavior is undefined.

- Zero or more *flag characters* that modify the normal behavior of the conversion specification.

- An optional decimal integer specifying the *minimum field width*. If the normal conversion produces fewer characters than this, the field is padded with spaces to the specified width. This is a *minimum* value; if the normal conversion produces more characters than this, the field is *not* truncated. Normally, the output is right-justified within the field.

  You can also specify a field width of '*'. This means that the next argument in the argument list (before the actual value to be printed) is used as the field width. The value must be an `int`. If the value is negative, this means to set the '-' flag (see below) and to use the absolute value as the field width.

- An optional *precision* to specify the number of digits to be written for the numeric conversions. If the precision is specified, it consists of a period ('.') followed optionally by a decimal integer (which defaults to zero if omitted).

  You can also specify a precision of '*'. This means that the next argument in the argument list (before the actual value to be printed) is used as the precision. The value must be an `int`, and is ignored if it is negative. If you specify '*' for both the field width and precision, the field width argument precedes the precision argument. Other C library versions may not recognize this syntax.

- An optional *type modifier character*, which is used to specify the data type of the corresponding argument if it differs from the default type. (For example, the integer conversions assume a type of `int`, but you can specify 'h', 'l', or 'L' for other integer types.)

- A character that specifies the conversion to be applied.

The exact options that are permitted and how they are interpreted vary between the different conversion specifiers. See the descriptions of the individual conversions for information about the particular options that they use.

With the '-Wformat' option, the GNU C compiler checks calls to `printf` and related functions. It examines the format string and verifies that the correct number and types of arguments are supplied. There is also a GNU C syntax to tell the compiler that a function you write uses a `printf`-style format string. See Section "Declaring Attributes of Functions" in *Using GNU CC*, for more information.

12.12.3 Table of Output Conversions

Here is a table summarizing what all the different conversions do:

'%d', '%i'   Print an integer as a signed decimal number. See Section 12.12.4 [Integer Conversions], page 282, for details. '%d' and '%i' are synonymous for output, but are different when used with `scanf` for input (see Section 12.14.3 [Table of Input Conversions], page 303).

'%o'   Print an integer as an unsigned octal number. See Section 12.12.4 [Integer Conversions], page 282, for details.

'%u'   Print an integer as an unsigned decimal number. See Section 12.12.4 [Integer Conversions], page 282, for details.

'%x', '%X' Print an integer as an unsigned hexadecimal number. '%x' uses lower-case letters and '%X' uses upper-case. See Section 12.12.4 [Integer Conversions], page 282, for details.

'%f' Print a floating-point number in normal (fixed-point) notation. See Section 12.12.5 [Floating-Point Conversions], page 284, for details.

'%e', '%E' Print a floating-point number in exponential notation. '%e' uses lower-case letters and '%E' uses upper-case. See Section 12.12.5 [Floating-Point Conversions], page 284, for details.

'%g', '%G' Print a floating-point number in either normal or exponential notation, whichever is more appropriate for its magnitude. '%g' uses lower-case letters and '%G' uses upper-case. See Section 12.12.5 [Floating-Point Conversions], page 284, for details.

'%a', '%A' Print a floating-point number in a hexadecimal fractional notation with the exponent to base 2 represented in decimal digits. '%a' uses lower-case letters and '%A' uses upper-case. See Section 12.12.5 [Floating-Point Conversions], page 284, for details.

'%c' Print a single character. See Section 12.12.6 [Other Output Conversions], page 286.

'%C' This is an alias for '%lc' which is supported for compatibility with the Unix standard.

'%s' Print a string. See Section 12.12.6 [Other Output Conversions], page 286.

'%S' This is an alias for '%ls' which is supported for compatibility with the Unix standard.

'%p' Print the value of a pointer. See Section 12.12.6 [Other Output Conversions], page 286.

'%n' Get the number of characters printed so far. See Section 12.12.6 [Other Output Conversions], page 286. Note that this conversion specification never produces any output.

'%m' Print the string corresponding to the value of **errno**. (This is a GNU extension.) See Section 12.12.6 [Other Output Conversions], page 286.

'%%' Print a literal '%' character. See Section 12.12.6 [Other Output Conversions], page 286.

If the syntax of a conversion specification is invalid, unpredictable things will happen, so don't do this. If there aren't enough function arguments provided to supply values for all the conversion specifications in the template string, or if the arguments are not of the correct types, the results are unpredictable. If you supply more arguments than conversion specifications, the extra argument values are simply ignored; this is sometimes useful.

12.12.4 Integer Conversions

This section describes the options for the '%d', '%i', '%o', '%u', '%x', and '%X' conversion specifications. These conversions print integers in various formats.

The '%d' and '%i' conversion specifications both print an `int` argument as a signed decimal number; while '%o', '%u', and '%x' print the argument as an unsigned octal, decimal, or hexadecimal number (respectively). The '%X' conversion specification is just like '%x' except that it uses the characters 'ABCDEF' as digits instead of 'abcdef'.

The following flags are meaningful:

'-'   Left-justify the result in the field (instead of the normal right-justification).

'+'   For the signed '%d' and '%i' conversions, print a plus sign if the value is positive.

' '   For the signed '%d' and '%i' conversions, if the result doesn't start with a plus or minus sign, prefix it with a space character instead. Since the '+' flag ensures that the result includes a sign, this flag is ignored if you supply both of them.

'#'   For the '%o' conversion, this forces the leading digit to be '0', as if by increasing the precision. For '%x' or '%X', this prefixes a leading '0x' or '0X' (respectively) to the result. This doesn't do anything useful for the '%d', '%i', or '%u' conversions. Using this flag produces output which can be parsed by the `strtoul` function (see Section 20.11.1 [Parsing of Integers], page 608) and `scanf` with the '%i' conversion (see Section 12.14.4 [Numeric Input Conversions], page 305).

' '   Separate the digits into groups as specified by the locale specified for the `LC_NUMERIC` category; see Section 7.7.1.1 [Generic Numeric Formatting Parameters], page 182. This flag is a GNU extension.

'0'   Pad the field with zeros instead of spaces. The zeros are placed after any indication of sign or base. This flag is ignored if the '-' flag is also specified, or if a precision is specified.

If a precision is supplied, it specifies the minimum number of digits to appear; leading zeros are produced if necessary. If you don't specify a precision, the number is printed with as many digits as it needs. If you convert a value of zero with an explicit precision of zero, then no characters at all are produced.

Without a type modifier, the corresponding argument is treated as an `int` (for the signed conversions '%i' and '%d') or `unsigned int` (for the unsigned conversions '%o', '%u', '%x', and '%X'). Recall that since `printf` and friends are variadic, any `char` and `short` arguments are automatically converted to `int` by the default argument promotions. For arguments of other integer types, you can use these modifiers:

'hh'   Specifies that the argument is a `signed char` or `unsigned char`, as appropriate. A `char` argument is converted to an `int` or `unsigned int` by the default argument promotions anyway, but the 'hh' modifier says to convert it back to a `char` again.

        This modifier was introduced in ISO C99.

'h'   Specifies that the argument is a `short int` or `unsigned short int`, as appropriate. A `short` argument is converted to an `int` or `unsigned int` by the default argument promotions anyway, but the 'h' modifier says to convert it back to a `short` again.

'j'   Specifies that the argument is a `intmax_t` or `uintmax_t`, as appropriate.

        This modifier was introduced in ISO C99.

'l' Specifies that the argument is a `long int` or `unsigned long int`, as appropriate. Two 'l' characters are like the 'L' modifier, below.

If used with '%c' or '%s' the corresponding parameter is considered as a wide character or wide character string respectively. This use of 'l' was introduced in Amendment 1 to ISO C90.

'L'
'll'
'q' Specifies that the argument is a `long long int`. (This type is an extension supported by the GNU C compiler. On systems that don't support extra-long integers, this is the same as `long int`.)

The 'q' modifier is another name for the same thing, which comes from 4.4 BSD; a `long long int` is sometimes called a "quad" `int`.

't' Specifies that the argument is a `ptrdiff_t`.

This modifier was introduced in ISO C99.

'z'
'Z' Specifies that the argument is a `size_t`.

'z' was introduced in ISO C99. 'Z' is a GNU extension predating this addition and should not be used in new code.

Here is an example. Using the template string:

```
"|%5d|%-5d|%+5d|%+-5d|% 5d|%05d|%5.0d|%5.2d|%d|\n"
```

to print numbers using the different options for the '%d' conversion gives results like:

```
|    0|0    |   +0|+0   |    0|00000|     |   00|0    |
|    1|1    |   +1|+1   |    1|00001|    1|   01|1    |
|   -1|-1   |   -1|-1   |   -1|-0001|   -1|  -01|-1   |
|100000|100000|+100000|+100000| 100000|100000|100000|100000|100000|
```

In particular, notice what happens in the last case where the number is too large to fit in the minimum field width specified.

Here are some more examples showing how unsigned integers print under various format options, using the template string:

```
"|%5u|%5o|%5x|%5X|%#5o|%#5x|%#5X|%#10.8x|\n"
```

```
|    0|    0|    0|    0|    0|    0|    0|  00000000|
|    1|    1|    1|    1|   01|  0x1|  0X1|0x00000001|
|100000|303240|186a0|186A0|0303240|0x186a0|0X186A0|0x000186a0|
```

12.12.5 Floating-Point Conversions

This section discusses the conversion specifications for floating-point numbers: the '%f', '%e', '%E', '%g', and '%G' conversions.

The '%f' conversion prints its argument in fixed-point notation, producing output of the form [-]*ddd*.*ddd*, where the number of digits following the decimal point is controlled by the precision you specify.

The '%e' conversion prints its argument in exponential notation, producing output of the form [-]*d*.*ddd*e[+|-]*dd*. Again, the number of digits following the decimal point is controlled by the precision. The exponent always contains at least two digits. The '%E' conversion is similar but the exponent is marked with the letter 'E' instead of 'e'.

The '%g' and '%G' conversions print the argument in the style of '%e' or '%E' (respectively) if the exponent would be less than -4 or greater than or equal to the precision; otherwise they use the '%f' style. A precision of 0, is taken as 1. Trailing zeros are removed from the fractional portion of the result and a decimal-point character appears only if it is followed by a digit.

The '%a' and '%A' conversions are meant for representing floating-point numbers exactly in textual form so that they can be exchanged as texts between different programs and/or machines. The numbers are represented in the form $[-]0xh.hhhp[+|-]dd$. At the left of the decimal-point character exactly one digit is print. This character is only 0 if the number is denormalized. Otherwise the value is unspecified; it is implementation dependent how many bits are used. The number of hexadecimal digits on the right side of the decimal-point character is equal to the precision. If the precision is zero it is determined to be large enough to provide an exact representation of the number (or it is large enough to distinguish two adjacent values if the **FLT_RADIX** is not a power of 2, see Section A.5.3.2 [Floating Point Parameters], page 921). For the '%a' conversion lower-case characters are used to represent the hexadecimal number and the prefix and exponent sign are printed as 0x and p respectively. Otherwise upper-case characters are used and 0X and P are used for the representation of prefix and exponent string. The exponent to the base of two is printed as a decimal number using at least one digit but at most as many digits as necessary to represent the value exactly.

If the value to be printed represents infinity or a NaN, the output is [-]inf or nan respectively if the conversion specifier is '%a', '%e', '%f', or '%g' and it is [-]INF or NAN respectively if the conversion is '%A', '%E', or '%G'.

The following flags can be used to modify the behavior:

'-'   Left-justify the result in the field. Normally the result is right-justified.

'+'   Always include a plus or minus sign in the result.

' '   If the result doesn't start with a plus or minus sign, prefix it with a space instead. Since the '+' flag ensures that the result includes a sign, this flag is ignored if you supply both of them.

'#'   Specifies that the result should always include a decimal point, even if no digits follow it. For the '%g' and '%G' conversions, this also forces trailing zeros after the decimal point to be left in place where they would otherwise be removed.

'''   Separate the digits of the integer part of the result into groups as specified by the locale specified for the **LC_NUMERIC** category; see Section 7.7.1.1 [Generic Numeric Formatting Parameters], page 182. This flag is a GNU extension.

'0'   Pad the field with zeros instead of spaces; the zeros are placed after any sign. This flag is ignored if the '-' flag is also specified.

The precision specifies how many digits follow the decimal-point character for the '%f', '%e', and '%E' conversions. For these conversions, the default precision is 6. If the precision is explicitly 0, this suppresses the decimal point character entirely. For the '%g' and '%G' conversions, the precision specifies how many significant digits to print. Significant digits are the first digit before the decimal point, and all the digits after it. If the precision is 0 or not specified for '%g' or '%G', it is treated like a value of 1. If the value being printed cannot be expressed accurately in the specified number of digits, the value is rounded to the nearest number that fits.

Without a type modifier, the floating-point conversions use an argument of type `double`. (By the default argument promotions, any `float` arguments are automatically converted to `double`.) The following type modifier is supported:

'L'   An uppercase 'L' specifies that the argument is a `long double`.

Here are some examples showing how numbers print using the various floating-point conversions. All of the numbers were printed using this template string:

```
"|%13.4a|%13.4f|%13.4e|%13.4g|\n"
```

Here is the output:

```
|   0x0.0000p+0|       0.0000|   0.0000e+00|            0|
|   0x1.0000p-1|       0.5000|   5.0000e-01|          0.5|
|   0x1.0000p+0|       1.0000|   1.0000e+00|            1|
|  -0x1.0000p+0|      -1.0000|  -1.0000e+00|           -1|
|   0x1.9000p+6|     100.0000|   1.0000e+02|          100|
|   0x1.f400p+9|    1000.0000|   1.0000e+03|         1000|
|  0x1.3880p+13|   10000.0000|   1.0000e+04|        1e+04|
|  0x1.81c8p+13|   12345.0000|   1.2345e+04|    1.234e+04|
|  0x1.86a0p+16|  100000.0000|   1.0000e+05|        1e+05|
|  0x1.e240p+16|  123456.0000|   1.2346e+05|    1.235e+05|
```

Notice how the '%g' conversion drops trailing zeros.

12.12.6 Other Output Conversions

This section describes miscellaneous conversions for `printf`.

The '%c' conversion prints a single character. In case there is no 'l' modifier the `int` argument is first converted to an `unsigned char`. Then, if used in a wide stream function, the character is converted into the corresponding wide character. The '-' flag can be used to specify left-justification in the field, but no other flags are defined, and no precision or type modifier can be given. For example:

```
printf ("%c%c%c%c%c", 'h', 'e', 'l', 'l', 'o');
```

prints 'hello'.

If there is an 'l' modifier present the argument is expected to be of type `wint_t`. If used in a multibyte function the wide character is converted into a multibyte character before being added to the output. In this case more than one output byte can be produced.

The '%s' conversion prints a string. If no 'l' modifier is present the corresponding argument must be of type `char *` (or `const char *`). If used in a wide stream function the string is first converted to a wide character string. A precision can be specified to indicate the maximum number of characters to write; otherwise characters in the string up to but not including the terminating null character are written to the output stream. The '-' flag can be used to specify left-justification in the field, but no other flags or type modifiers are defined for this conversion. For example:

```
printf ("%3s%-6s", "no", "where");
```

prints ' no where '.

If there is an 'l' modifier present, the argument is expected to be of type `wchar_t` (or `const wchar_t *`).

If you accidentally pass a null pointer as the argument for a '%s' conversion, the GNU C Library prints it as '(null)'. We think this is more useful than crashing. But it's not good practice to pass a null argument intentionally.

The '%m' conversion prints the string corresponding to the error code in errno. See Section 2.3 [Error Messages], page 35. Thus:

```
fprintf (stderr, "can't open `%s': %m\n", filename);
```

is equivalent to:

```
fprintf (stderr, "can't open `%s': %s\n", filename, strerror (errno));
```

The '%m' conversion is a GNU C Library extension.

The '%p' conversion prints a pointer value. The corresponding argument must be of type void *. In practice, you can use any type of pointer.

In the GNU C Library, non-null pointers are printed as unsigned integers, as if a '%#x' conversion were used. Null pointers print as '(nil)'. (Pointers might print differently in other systems.)

For example:

```
printf ("%p", "testing");
```

prints '0x' followed by a hexadecimal number—the address of the string constant "testing". It does not print the word 'testing'.

You can supply the '-' flag with the '%p' conversion to specify left-justification, but no other flags, precision, or type modifiers are defined.

The '%n' conversion is unlike any of the other output conversions. It uses an argument which must be a pointer to an int, but instead of printing anything it stores the number of characters printed so far by this call at that location. The 'h' and 'l' type modifiers are permitted to specify that the argument is of type short int * or long int * instead of int *, but no flags, field width, or precision are permitted.

For example,

```
int nchar;
printf ("%d %s%n\n", 3, "bears", &nchar);
```

prints:

```
3 bears
```

and sets nchar to 7, because '3 bears' is seven characters.

The '%%' conversion prints a literal '%' character. This conversion doesn't use an argument, and no flags, field width, precision, or type modifiers are permitted.

12.12.7 Formatted Output Functions

This section describes how to call printf and related functions. Prototypes for these functions are in the header file stdio.h. Because these functions take a variable number of arguments, you *must* declare prototypes for them before using them. Of course, the easiest way to make sure you have all the right prototypes is to just include stdio.h.

int printf (const char *template, ...)   [Function]
    Preliminary: | MT-Safe locale | AS-Unsafe corrupt heap | AC-Unsafe mem lock
    corrupt | See Section 1.2.2.1 [POSIX Safety Concepts], page 2.

The `printf` function prints the optional arguments under the control of the template string *template* to the stream `stdout`. It returns the number of characters printed, or a negative value if there was an output error.

int wprintf (*const wchar_t *template, . . .*)   [Function]
    Preliminary: | MT-Safe locale | AS-Unsafe corrupt heap | AC-Unsafe mem lock corrupt | See Section 1.2.2.1 [POSIX Safety Concepts], page 2.

    The `wprintf` function prints the optional arguments under the control of the wide template string *template* to the stream `stdout`. It returns the number of wide characters printed, or a negative value if there was an output error.

int fprintf (*FILE *stream, const char *template, . . .*)   [Function]
    Preliminary: | MT-Safe locale | AS-Unsafe corrupt heap | AC-Unsafe mem lock corrupt | See Section 1.2.2.1 [POSIX Safety Concepts], page 2.

    This function is just like `printf`, except that the output is written to the stream *stream* instead of `stdout`.

int fwprintf (*FILE *stream, const wchar_t *template, . . .*)   [Function]
    Preliminary: | MT-Safe locale | AS-Unsafe corrupt heap | AC-Unsafe mem lock corrupt | See Section 1.2.2.1 [POSIX Safety Concepts], page 2.

    This function is just like `wprintf`, except that the output is written to the stream *stream* instead of `stdout`.

int sprintf (*char *s, const char *template, . . .*)   [Function]
    Preliminary: | MT-Safe locale | AS-Unsafe heap | AC-Unsafe mem | See Section 1.2.2.1 [POSIX Safety Concepts], page 2.

    This is like `printf`, except that the output is stored in the character array *s* instead of written to a stream. A null character is written to mark the end of the string.

    The `sprintf` function returns the number of characters stored in the array *s*, not including the terminating null character.

    The behavior of this function is undefined if copying takes place between objects that overlap—for example, if *s* is also given as an argument to be printed under control of the '%s' conversion. See Section 5.4 [Copying Strings and Arrays], page 95.

    Warning: The `sprintf` function can be **dangerous** because it can potentially output more characters than can fit in the allocation size of the string *s*. Remember that the field width given in a conversion specification is only a *minimum* value.

    To avoid this problem, you can use `snprintf` or `asprintf`, described below.

int swprintf (*wchar_t *ws, size_t size, const wchar_t *template,*   [Function]
        . . .)
    Preliminary: | MT-Safe locale | AS-Unsafe heap | AC-Unsafe mem | See Section 1.2.2.1 [POSIX Safety Concepts], page 2.

    This is like `wprintf`, except that the output is stored in the wide character array *ws* instead of written to a stream. A null wide character is written to mark the end of the string. The *size* argument specifies the maximum number of characters to produce. The trailing null character is counted towards this limit, so you should allocate at least *size* wide characters for the string *ws*.

The return value is the number of characters generated for the given input, excluding the trailing null. If not all output fits into the provided buffer a negative value is returned. You should try again with a bigger output string. *Note:* this is different from how `snprintf` handles this situation.

Note that the corresponding narrow stream function takes fewer parameters. `swprintf` in fact corresponds to the `snprintf` function. Since the `sprintf` function can be dangerous and should be avoided the ISO C committee refused to make the same mistake again and decided to not define a function exactly corresponding to `sprintf`.

---

int **snprintf** (*char *s, size_t size, const char *template, . . .*) [Function]
Preliminary: | MT-Safe locale | AS-Unsafe heap | AC-Unsafe mem | See Section 1.2.2.1 [POSIX Safety Concepts], page 2.

The `snprintf` function is similar to `sprintf`, except that the *size* argument specifies the maximum number of characters to produce. The trailing null character is counted towards this limit, so you should allocate at least *size* characters for the string *s*. If *size* is zero, nothing, not even the null byte, shall be written and *s* may be a null pointer.

The return value is the number of characters which would be generated for the given input, excluding the trailing null. If this value is greater than or equal to *size*, not all characters from the result have been stored in *s*. You should try again with a bigger output string. Here is an example of doing this:

```
/* Construct a message describing the value of a variable
   whose name is name and whose value is value. */
char *
make_message (char *name, char *value)
{
  /* Guess we need no more than 100 chars of space. */
  int size = 100;
  char *buffer = (char *) xmalloc (size);
  int nchars;
  if (buffer == NULL)
    return NULL;

  /* Try to print in the allocated space. */
  nchars = snprintf (buffer, size, "value of %s is %s",
    name, value);
  if (nchars >= size)
    {
      /* Reallocate buffer now that we know
how much space is needed. */
        size = nchars + 1;
        buffer = (char *) xrealloc (buffer, size);

        if (buffer != NULL)
/* Try again. */
snprintf (buffer, size, "value of %s is %s",
  name, value);
    }
    /* The last call worked, return the string. */
    return buffer;
}
```

In practice, it is often easier just to use `asprintf`, below.

Attention: In versions of the GNU C Library prior to 2.1 the return value is the number of characters stored, not including the terminating null; unless there was not enough space in *s* to store the result in which case `-1` is returned. This was changed in order to comply with the ISO C99 standard.

12.12.8 Dynamically Allocating Formatted Output

The functions in this section do formatted output and place the results in dynamically allocated memory.

`int asprintf` (*char **ptr, const char *template, ...*)　　　　[Function]
Preliminary: | MT-Safe locale | AS-Unsafe heap | AC-Unsafe mem | See Section 1.2.2.1 [POSIX Safety Concepts], page 2.

This function is similar to `sprintf`, except that it dynamically allocates a string (as with `malloc`; see Section 3.2.3 [Unconstrained Allocation], page 44) to hold the output, instead of putting the output in a buffer you allocate in advance. The *ptr* argument should be the address of a `char *` object, and a successful call to `asprintf` stores a pointer to the newly allocated string at that location.

The return value is the number of characters allocated for the buffer, or less than zero if an error occurred. Usually this means that the buffer could not be allocated.

Here is how to use `asprintf` to get the same result as the `snprintf` example, but more easily:

```
/* Construct a message describing the value of a variable
   whose name is name and whose value is value. */
char *
make_message (char *name, char *value)
{
  char *result;
  if (asprintf (&result, "value of %s is %s", name, value) < 0)
    return NULL;
  return result;
}
```

`int obstack_printf` (*struct obstack *obstack, const char*　　[Function]
　　*template, ...)
Preliminary: | MT-Safe race:obstack locale | AS-Unsafe corrupt heap | AC-Unsafe corrupt mem | See Section 1.2.2.1 [POSIX Safety Concepts], page 2.

This function is similar to `asprintf`, except that it uses the obstack *obstack* to allocate the space. See Section 3.2.6 [Obstacks], page 62.

The characters are written onto the end of the current object. To get at them, you must finish the object with `obstack_finish` (see Section 3.2.6.6 [Growing Objects], page 66).

12.12.9 Variable Arguments Output Functions

The functions `vprintf` and friends are provided so that you can define your own variadic `printf`-like functions that make use of the same internals as the built-in formatted output functions.

The most natural way to define such functions would be to use a language construct to say, "Call `printf` and pass this template plus all of my arguments after the first five." But there is no way to do this in C, and it would be hard to provide a way, since at the C language level there is no way to tell how many arguments your function received.

Since that method is impossible, we provide alternative functions, the `vprintf` series, which lets you pass a `va_list` to describe "all of my arguments after the first five."

When it is sufficient to define a macro rather than a real function, the GNU C compiler provides a way to do this much more easily with macros. For example:

```
#define myprintf(a, b, c, d, e, rest...) \
    printf (mytemplate , ## rest)
```

See Section "Variadic Macros" in *The C preprocessor*, for details. But this is limited to macros, and does not apply to real functions at all.

Before calling `vprintf` or the other functions listed in this section, you *must* call `va_start` (see Section A.2 [Variadic Functions], page 910) to initialize a pointer to the variable arguments. Then you can call `va_arg` to fetch the arguments that you want to handle yourself. This advances the pointer past those arguments.

Once your `va_list` pointer is pointing at the argument of your choice, you are ready to call `vprintf`. That argument and all subsequent arguments that were passed to your function are used by `vprintf` along with the template that you specified separately.

Portability Note: The value of the `va_list` pointer is undetermined after the call to `vprintf`, so you must not use `va_arg` after you call `vprintf`. Instead, you should call `va_end` to retire the pointer from service. You can call `va_start` again and begin fetching the arguments from the start of the variable argument list. (Alternatively, you can use `va_copy` to make a copy of the `va_list` pointer before calling `vfprintf`.) Calling `vprintf` does not destroy the argument list of your function, merely the particular pointer that you passed to it.

Prototypes for these functions are declared in `stdio.h`.

int vprintf (*const char *template, va_list ap*)   [Function]
> Preliminary: | MT-Safe locale | AS-Unsafe corrupt heap | AC-Unsafe mem lock corrupt | See Section 1.2.2.1 [POSIX Safety Concepts], page 2.
>
> This function is similar to `printf` except that, instead of taking a variable number of arguments directly, it takes an argument list pointer *ap*.

int vwprintf (*const wchar_t *template, va_list ap*)   [Function]
> Preliminary: | MT-Safe locale | AS-Unsafe corrupt heap | AC-Unsafe mem lock corrupt | See Section 1.2.2.1 [POSIX Safety Concepts], page 2.
>
> This function is similar to `wprintf` except that, instead of taking a variable number of arguments directly, it takes an argument list pointer *ap*.

int vfprintf (*FILE *stream, const char *template, va_list ap*)   [Function]
> Preliminary: | MT-Safe locale | AS-Unsafe corrupt heap | AC-Unsafe mem lock corrupt | See Section 1.2.2.1 [POSIX Safety Concepts], page 2.
>
> This is the equivalent of `fprintf` with the variable argument list specified directly as for `vprintf`.

int vfwprintf (*FILE *stream*, *const wchar_t *template*, *va_list* ap)   [Function]
> Preliminary: | MT-Safe locale | AS-Unsafe corrupt heap | AC-Unsafe mem lock corrupt | See Section 1.2.2.1 [POSIX Safety Concepts], page 2.
>
> This is the equivalent of `fwprintf` with the variable argument list specified directly as for `vwprintf`.

int vsprintf (*char *s*, *const char *template*, *va_list* ap)   [Function]
> Preliminary: | MT-Safe locale | AS-Unsafe heap | AC-Unsafe mem | See Section 1.2.2.1 [POSIX Safety Concepts], page 2.
>
> This is the equivalent of `sprintf` with the variable argument list specified directly as for `vprintf`.

int vswprintf (*wchar_t *ws*, *size_t* size, *const wchar_t *template*,   [Function]
    va_list ap)
> Preliminary: | MT-Safe locale | AS-Unsafe heap | AC-Unsafe mem | See Section 1.2.2.1 [POSIX Safety Concepts], page 2.
>
> This is the equivalent of `swprintf` with the variable argument list specified directly as for `vwprintf`.

int vsnprintf (*char *s*, *size_t* size, *const char *template*, *va_list*   [Function]
    ap)
> Preliminary: | MT-Safe locale | AS-Unsafe heap | AC-Unsafe mem | See Section 1.2.2.1 [POSIX Safety Concepts], page 2.
>
> This is the equivalent of `snprintf` with the variable argument list specified directly as for `vprintf`.

int vasprintf (*char **ptr*, *const char *template*, *va_list* ap)   [Function]
> Preliminary: | MT-Safe locale | AS-Unsafe heap | AC-Unsafe mem | See Section 1.2.2.1 [POSIX Safety Concepts], page 2.
>
> The `vasprintf` function is the equivalent of `asprintf` with the variable argument list specified directly as for `vprintf`.

int obstack_vprintf (*struct obstack *obstack*, *const char*   [Function]
    template, *va_list* ap)
> Preliminary: | MT-Safe race:obstack locale | AS-Unsafe corrupt heap | AC-Unsafe corrupt mem | See Section 1.2.2.1 [POSIX Safety Concepts], page 2.
>
> The `obstack_vprintf` function is the equivalent of `obstack_printf` with the variable argument list specified directly as for `vprintf`.

Here's an example showing how you might use **vfprintf**. This is a function that prints error messages to the stream **stderr**, along with a prefix indicating the name of the program (see Section 2.3 [Error Messages], page 35, for a description of `program_invocation_short_name`).

```
#include <stdio.h>
#include <stdarg.h>

void
eprintf (const char *template, ...)
{
  va_list ap;
  extern char *program_invocation_short_name;

  fprintf (stderr, "%s: ", program_invocation_short_name);
  va_start (ap, template);
  vfprintf (stderr, template, ap);
  va_end (ap);
}
```

You could call `eprintf` like this:

```
eprintf ("file `%s' does not exist\n", filename);
```

In GNU C, there is a special construct you can use to let the compiler know that a function uses a `printf`-style format string. Then it can check the number and types of arguments in each call to the function, and warn you when they do not match the format string. For example, take this declaration of `eprintf`:

```
void eprintf (const char *template, ...)
__attribute__ ((format (printf, 1, 2)));
```

This tells the compiler that `eprintf` uses a format string like `printf` (as opposed to `scanf`; see Section 12.14 [Formatted Input], page 301); the format string appears as the first argument; and the arguments to satisfy the format begin with the second. See Section "Declaring Attributes of Functions" in *Using GNU CC*, for more information.

12.12.10 Parsing a Template String

You can use the function `parse_printf_format` to obtain information about the number and types of arguments that are expected by a given template string. This function permits interpreters that provide interfaces to `printf` to avoid passing along invalid arguments from the user's program, which could cause a crash.

All the symbols described in this section are declared in the header file `printf.h`.

`size_t parse_printf_format` (*const char *template, size_t n, int*   [Function]
    *argtypes)

Preliminary: | MT-Safe locale | AS-Safe | AC-Safe | See Section 1.2.2.1 [POSIX Safety Concepts], page 2.

This function returns information about the number and types of arguments expected by the `printf` template string *template*. The information is stored in the array *argtypes*; each element of this array describes one argument. This information is encoded using the various 'PA_' macros, listed below.

The argument *n* specifies the number of elements in the array *argtypes*. This is the maximum number of elements that `parse_printf_format` will try to write.

`parse_printf_format` returns the total number of arguments required by *template*. If this number is greater than *n*, then the information returned describes only the first *n* arguments. If you want information about additional arguments, allocate a bigger array and call `parse_printf_format` again.

The argument types are encoded as a combination of a basic type and modifier flag bits.

`int PA_FLAG_MASK`   [Macro]

> This macro is a bitmask for the type modifier flag bits. You can write the expression `(argtypes[i] & PA_FLAG_MASK)` to extract just the flag bits for an argument, or `(argtypes[i] & ~PA_FLAG_MASK)` to extract just the basic type code.

Here are symbolic constants that represent the basic types; they stand for integer values.

`PA_INT`   This specifies that the base type is `int`.

`PA_CHAR`   This specifies that the base type is `int`, cast to `char`.

`PA_STRING`

> This specifies that the base type is `char *`, a null-terminated string.

`PA_POINTER`

> This specifies that the base type is `void *`, an arbitrary pointer.

`PA_FLOAT`   This specifies that the base type is `float`.

`PA_DOUBLE`

> This specifies that the base type is `double`.

`PA_LAST`   You can define additional base types for your own programs as offsets from `PA_LAST`. For example, if you have data types 'foo' and 'bar' with their own specialized `printf` conversions, you could define encodings for these types as:

```
#define PA_FOO  PA_LAST
#define PA_BAR  (PA_LAST + 1)
```

Here are the flag bits that modify a basic type. They are combined with the code for the basic type using inclusive-or.

`PA_FLAG_PTR`

> If this bit is set, it indicates that the encoded type is a pointer to the base type, rather than an immediate value. For example, 'PA_INT|PA_FLAG_PTR' represents the type 'int *'.

`PA_FLAG_SHORT`

> If this bit is set, it indicates that the base type is modified with `short`. (This corresponds to the 'h' type modifier.)

`PA_FLAG_LONG`

> If this bit is set, it indicates that the base type is modified with `long`. (This corresponds to the 'l' type modifier.)

`PA_FLAG_LONG_LONG`

> If this bit is set, it indicates that the base type is modified with `long long`. (This corresponds to the 'L' type modifier.)

`PA_FLAG_LONG_DOUBLE`

> This is a synonym for `PA_FLAG_LONG_LONG`, used by convention with a base type of `PA_DOUBLE` to indicate a type of `long double`.

12.12.11 Example of Parsing a Template String

Here is an example of decoding argument types for a format string. We assume this is part of an interpreter which contains arguments of type NUMBER, CHAR, STRING and STRUCTURE (and perhaps others which are not valid here).

```
/* Test whether the nargs specified objects
   in the vector args are valid
   for the format string format:
   if so, return 1.
   If not, return 0 after printing an error message.  */

int
validate_args (char *format, int nargs, OBJECT *args)
{
  int *argtypes;
  int nwanted;

  /* Get the information about the arguments.
     Each conversion specification must be at least two characters
     long, so there cannot be more specifications than half the
     length of the string.  */

  argtypes = (int *) alloca (strlen (format) / 2 * sizeof (int));
  nwanted = parse_printf_format (string, nelts, argtypes);

  /* Check the number of arguments.  */
  if (nwanted > nargs)
    {
      error ("too few arguments (at least %d required)", nwanted);
      return 0;
    }

  /* Check the C type wanted for each argument
     and see if the object given is suitable.  */
  for (i = 0; i < nwanted; i++)
    {
      int wanted;

      if (argtypes[i] & PA_FLAG_PTR)
wanted = STRUCTURE;
      else
switch (argtypes[i] & ~PA_FLAG_MASK)
  {
  case PA_INT:
  case PA_FLOAT:
  case PA_DOUBLE:
    wanted = NUMBER;
    break;
  case PA_CHAR:
    wanted = CHAR;
    break;
  case PA_STRING:
    wanted = STRING;
    break;
  case PA_POINTER:
    wanted = STRUCTURE;
    break;
  }
```

```
        if (TYPE (args[i]) != wanted)
  {
    error ("type mismatch for arg number %d", i);
    return 0;
  }
      }
    return 1;
  }
```

12.13 Customizing `printf`

The GNU C Library lets you define your own custom conversion specifiers for `printf` template strings, to teach `printf` clever ways to print the important data structures of your program.

The way you do this is by registering the conversion with the function `register_printf_function`; see Section 12.13.1 [Registering New Conversions], page 296. One of the arguments you pass to this function is a pointer to a handler function that produces the actual output; see Section 12.13.3 [Defining the Output Handler], page 298, for information on how to write this function.

You can also install a function that just returns information about the number and type of arguments expected by the conversion specifier. See Section 12.12.10 [Parsing a Template String], page 293, for information about this.

The facilities of this section are declared in the header file `printf.h`.

Portability Note: The ability to extend the syntax of `printf` template strings is a GNU extension. ISO standard C has nothing similar.

12.13.1 Registering New Conversions

The function to register a new output conversion is `register_printf_function`, declared in `printf.h`.

int register_printf_function (*int* `spec`, *printf_function*   [Function]
      handler-function, *printf_arginfo_function* `arginfo-function`)

Preliminary: | MT-Unsafe const:printfext | AS-Unsafe heap lock | AC-Unsafe mem lock | See Section 1.2.2.1 [POSIX Safety Concepts], page 2.

This function defines the conversion specifier character *spec*. Thus, if *spec* is `'Y'`, it defines the conversion '`%Y`'. You can redefine the built-in conversions like '`%s`', but flag characters like '`#`' and type modifiers like '`l`' can never be used as conversions; calling `register_printf_function` for those characters has no effect. It is advisable not to use lowercase letters, since the ISO C standard warns that additional lowercase letters may be standardized in future editions of the standard.

The *handler-function* is the function called by `printf` and friends when this conversion appears in a template string. See Section 12.13.3 [Defining the Output Handler], page 298, for information about how to define a function to pass as this argument. If you specify a null pointer, any existing handler function for *spec* is removed.

The *arginfo-function* is the function called by `parse_printf_format` when this conversion appears in a template string. See Section 12.12.10 [Parsing a Template String], page 293, for information about this.

Attention: In the GNU C Library versions before 2.0 the *arginfo-function* function did not need to be installed unless the user used the `parse_printf_format` function. This has changed. Now a call to any of the `printf` functions will call this function when this format specifier appears in the format string.

The return value is 0 on success, and -1 on failure (which occurs if *spec* is out of range).

You can redefine the standard output conversions, but this is probably not a good idea because of the potential for confusion. Library routines written by other people could break if you do this.

12.13.2 Conversion Specifier Options

If you define a meaning for '%A', what if the template contains '%+23A' or '%-#A'? To implement a sensible meaning for these, the handler when called needs to be able to get the options specified in the template.

Both the *handler-function* and *arginfo-function* accept an argument that points to a `struct printf_info`, which contains information about the options appearing in an instance of the conversion specifier. This data type is declared in the header file `printf.h`.

`struct printf_info`   [Type]

This structure is used to pass information about the options appearing in an instance of a conversion specifier in a `printf` template string to the handler and arginfo functions for that specifier. It contains the following members:

int prec   This is the precision specified. The value is -1 if no precision was specified. If the precision was given as '*', the `printf_info` structure passed to the handler function contains the actual value retrieved from the argument list. But the structure passed to the arginfo function contains a value of `INT_MIN`, since the actual value is not known.

int width   This is the minimum field width specified. The value is 0 if no width was specified. If the field width was given as '*', the `printf_info` structure passed to the handler function contains the actual value retrieved from the argument list. But the structure passed to the arginfo function contains a value of `INT_MIN`, since the actual value is not known.

wchar_t spec

This is the conversion specifier character specified. It's stored in the structure so that you can register the same handler function for multiple characters, but still have a way to tell them apart when the handler function is called.

unsigned int is_long_double

This is a boolean that is true if the 'L', 'll', or 'q' type modifier was specified. For integer conversions, this indicates **long long int**, as opposed to **long double** for floating point conversions.

unsigned int is_char

This is a boolean that is true if the 'hh' type modifier was specified.

unsigned int is_short
> This is a boolean that is true if the 'h' type modifier was specified.

unsigned int is_long
> This is a boolean that is true if the 'l' type modifier was specified.

unsigned int alt
> This is a boolean that is true if the '#' flag was specified.

unsigned int space
> This is a boolean that is true if the ' ' flag was specified.

unsigned int left
> This is a boolean that is true if the '-' flag was specified.

unsigned int showsign
> This is a boolean that is true if the '+' flag was specified.

unsigned int group
> This is a boolean that is true if the ''' flag was specified.

unsigned int extra
> This flag has a special meaning depending on the context. It could be used freely by the user-defined handlers but when called from the `printf` function this variable always contains the value 0.

unsigned int wide
> This flag is set if the stream is wide oriented.

wchar_t pad
> This is the character to use for padding the output to the minimum field width. The value is '0' if the '0' flag was specified, and ' ' otherwise.

12.13.3 Defining the Output Handler

Now let's look at how to define the handler and arginfo functions which are passed as arguments to `register_printf_function`.

Compatibility Note: The interface changed in the GNU C Library version 2.0. Previously the third argument was of type `va_list *`.

You should define your handler functions with a prototype like:

```
int function (FILE *stream, const struct printf_info *info,
    const void *const *args)
```

The *stream* argument passed to the handler function is the stream to which it should write output.

The *info* argument is a pointer to a structure that contains information about the various options that were included with the conversion in the template string. You should not modify this structure inside your handler function. See Section 12.13.2 [Conversion Specifier Options], page 297, for a description of this data structure.

The *args* is a vector of pointers to the arguments data. The number of arguments was determined by calling the argument information function provided by the user.

Your handler function should return a value just like `printf` does: it should return the number of characters it has written, or a negative value to indicate an error.

printf_function   [Data Type]

This is the data type that a handler function should have.

If you are going to use **parse_printf_format** in your application, you must also define a function to pass as the *arginfo-function* argument for each new conversion you install with **register_printf_function**.

You have to define these functions with a prototype like:

```
int function (const struct printf_info *info,
    size_t n, int *argtypes)
```

The return value from the function should be the number of arguments the conversion expects. The function should also fill in no more than *n* elements of the *argtypes* array with information about the types of each of these arguments. This information is encoded using the various 'PA_' macros. (You will notice that this is the same calling convention **parse_printf_format** itself uses.)

printf_arginfo_function   [Data Type]

This type is used to describe functions that return information about the number and type of arguments used by a conversion specifier.

12.13.4 printf Extension Example

Here is an example showing how to define a **printf** handler function. This program defines a data structure called a **Widget** and defines the '%W' conversion to print information about **Widget *** arguments, including the pointer value and the name stored in the data structure. The '%W' conversion supports the minimum field width and left-justification options, but ignores everything else.

```
#include <stdio.h>
#include <stdlib.h>
#include <printf.h>

typedef struct
{
  char *name;
}
Widget;

int
print_widget (FILE *stream,
              const struct printf_info *info,
              const void *const *args)
{
  const Widget *w;
  char *buffer;
  int len;

  /* Format the output into a string. */
  w = *((const Widget **) (args[0]));
  len = asprintf (&buffer, "<Widget %p: %s>", w, w->name);
  if (len == -1)
    return -1;

  /* Pad to the minimum field width and print to the stream. */
  len = fprintf (stream, "%*s",
```

```
                        (info->left ? -info->width : info->width),
                        buffer);

    /* Clean up and return. */
    free (buffer);
    return len;
  }


  int
  print_widget_arginfo (const struct printf_info *info, size_t n,
                        int *argtypes)
  {
    /* We always take exactly one argument and this is a pointer to the
       structure.. */
    if (n > 0)
      argtypes[0] = PA_POINTER;
    return 1;
  }


  int
  main (void)
  {
    /* Make a widget to print. */
    Widget mywidget;
    mywidget.name = "mywidget";

    /* Register the print function for widgets. */
    register_printf_function ('W', print_widget, print_widget_arginfo);

    /* Now print the widget. */
    printf ("|%W|\n", &mywidget);
    printf ("|%35W|\n", &mywidget);
    printf ("|%-35W|\n", &mywidget);

    return 0;
  }
```

The output produced by this program looks like:

```
|<Widget 0xffeffb7c: mywidget>|
|      <Widget 0xffeffb7c: mywidget>|
|<Widget 0xffeffb7c: mywidget>      |
```

12.13.5 Predefined `printf` Handlers

The GNU C Library also contains a concrete and useful application of the `printf` handler extension. There are two functions available which implement a special way to print floating-point numbers.

int `printf_size` (*FILE *fp, const struct printf_info *info, const*   [Function]
    void *const *args)

    Preliminary: | MT-Safe race:fp locale | AS-Unsafe corrupt heap | AC-Unsafe mem corrupt | See Section 1.2.2.1 [POSIX Safety Concepts], page 2.

    Print a given floating point number as for the format `%f` except that there is a postfix character indicating the divisor for the number to make this less than 1000. There are two possible divisors: powers of 1024 or powers of 1000. Which one is used depends on the format character specified while registered this handler. If the character is of lower case, 1024 is used. For upper case characters, 1000 is used.

The postfix tag corresponds to bytes, kilobytes, megabytes, gigabytes, etc. The full table is:

low	Multiplier	From	Upper	Multiplier
␣	1		␣	1
k	$2^{10} = 1024$	kilo	K	$10^3 = 1000$
m	2^{20}	mega	M	10^6
g	2^{30}	giga	G	10^9
t	2^{40}	tera	T	10^{12}
p	2^{50}	peta	P	10^{15}
e	2^{60}	exa	E	10^{18}
z	2^{70}	zetta	Z	10^{21}
y	2^{80}	yotta	Y	10^{24}

The default precision is 3, i.e., 1024 is printed with a lower-case format character as if it were `%.3fk` and will yield `1.000k`.

Due to the requirements of `register_printf_function` we must also provide the function which returns information about the arguments.

int `printf_size_info` (*const struct printf_info *info, size_t n, int*   [Function]
    *argtypes)

Preliminary: | MT-Safe | AS-Safe | AC-Safe | See Section 1.2.2.1 [POSIX Safety Concepts], page 2.

This function will return in *argtypes* the information about the used parameters in the way the `vfprintf` implementation expects it. The format always takes one argument.

To use these functions both functions must be registered with a call like

```
register_printf_function ('B', printf_size, printf_size_info);
```

Here we register the functions to print numbers as powers of 1000 since the format character `'B'` is an upper-case character. If we would additionally use `'b'` in a line like

```
register_printf_function ('b', printf_size, printf_size_info);
```

we could also print using a power of 1024. Please note that all that is different in these two lines is the format specifier. The `printf_size` function knows about the difference between lower and upper case format specifiers.

The use of `'B'` and `'b'` is no coincidence. Rather it is the preferred way to use this functionality since it is available on some other systems which also use format specifiers.

12.14 Formatted Input

The functions described in this section (`scanf` and related functions) provide facilities for formatted input analogous to the formatted output facilities. These functions provide a mechanism for reading arbitrary values under the control of a *format string* or *template string*.

12.14.1 Formatted Input Basics

Calls to scanf are superficially similar to calls to printf in that arbitrary arguments are read under the control of a template string. While the syntax of the conversion specifications in the template is very similar to that for printf, the interpretation of the template is oriented more towards free-format input and simple pattern matching, rather than fixed-field formatting. For example, most scanf conversions skip over any amount of "white space" (including spaces, tabs, and newlines) in the input file, and there is no concept of precision for the numeric input conversions as there is for the corresponding output conversions. Ordinarily, non-whitespace characters in the template are expected to match characters in the input stream exactly, but a matching failure is distinct from an input error on the stream.

Another area of difference between scanf and printf is that you must remember to supply pointers rather than immediate values as the optional arguments to scanf; the values that are read are stored in the objects that the pointers point to. Even experienced programmers tend to forget this occasionally, so if your program is getting strange errors that seem to be related to scanf, you might want to double-check this.

When a *matching failure* occurs, scanf returns immediately, leaving the first non-matching character as the next character to be read from the stream. The normal return value from scanf is the number of values that were assigned, so you can use this to determine if a matching error happened before all the expected values were read.

The scanf function is typically used for things like reading in the contents of tables. For example, here is a function that uses scanf to initialize an array of double:

```
void
readarray (double *array, int n)
{
  int i;
  for (i=0; i<n; i++)
    if (scanf (" %lf", &(array[i])) != 1)
      invalid_input_error ();
}
```

The formatted input functions are not used as frequently as the formatted output functions. Partly, this is because it takes some care to use them properly. Another reason is that it is difficult to recover from a matching error.

If you are trying to read input that doesn't match a single, fixed pattern, you may be better off using a tool such as Flex to generate a lexical scanner, or Bison to generate a parser, rather than using scanf. For more information about these tools, see *Flex: The Lexical Scanner Generator*, and *The Bison Reference Manual*.

12.14.2 Input Conversion Syntax

A scanf template string is a string that contains ordinary multibyte characters interspersed with conversion specifications that start with '%'.

Any whitespace character (as defined by the isspace function; see Section 4.1 [Classification of Characters], page 81) in the template causes any number of whitespace characters in the input stream to be read and discarded. The whitespace characters that are matched need not be exactly the same whitespace characters that appear in the template string. For example, write ' , ' in the template to recognize a comma with optional whitespace before and after.

Other characters in the template string that are not part of conversion specifications must match characters in the input stream exactly; if this is not the case, a matching failure occurs.

The conversion specifications in a `scanf` template string have the general form:

`% flags width type conversion`

In more detail, an input conversion specification consists of an initial '`%`' character followed in sequence by:

- An optional *flag character* '`*`', which says to ignore the text read for this specification. When `scanf` finds a conversion specification that uses this flag, it reads input as directed by the rest of the conversion specification, but it discards this input, does not use a pointer argument, and does not increment the count of successful assignments.

- An optional flag character '`a`' (valid with string conversions only) which requests allocation of a buffer long enough to store the string in. (This is a GNU extension.) See Section 12.14.6 [Dynamically Allocating String Conversions], page 308.

- An optional decimal integer that specifies the *maximum field width*. Reading of characters from the input stream stops either when this maximum is reached or when a non-matching character is found, whichever happens first. Most conversions discard initial whitespace characters (those that don't are explicitly documented), and these discarded characters don't count towards the maximum field width. String input conversions store a null character to mark the end of the input; the maximum field width does not include this terminator.

- An optional *type modifier character*. For example, you can specify a type modifier of '`l`' with integer conversions such as '`%d`' to specify that the argument is a pointer to a `long int` rather than a pointer to an `int`.

- A character that specifies the conversion to be applied.

The exact options that are permitted and how they are interpreted vary between the different conversion specifiers. See the descriptions of the individual conversions for information about the particular options that they allow.

With the '`-Wformat`' option, the GNU C compiler checks calls to `scanf` and related functions. It examines the format string and verifies that the correct number and types of arguments are supplied. There is also a GNU C syntax to tell the compiler that a function you write uses a `scanf`-style format string. See Section "Declaring Attributes of Functions" in *Using GNU CC*, for more information.

12.14.3 Table of Input Conversions

Here is a table that summarizes the various conversion specifications:

'`%d`'   Matches an optionally signed integer written in decimal. See Section 12.14.4 [Numeric Input Conversions], page 305.

'`%i`'   Matches an optionally signed integer in any of the formats that the C language defines for specifying an integer constant. See Section 12.14.4 [Numeric Input Conversions], page 305.

'`%o`'   Matches an unsigned integer written in octal radix. See Section 12.14.4 [Numeric Input Conversions], page 305.

'%u'   Matches an unsigned integer written in decimal radix. See Section 12.14.4
            [Numeric Input Conversions], page 305.

'%x', '%X' Matches an unsigned integer written in hexadecimal radix. See Section 12.14.4
            [Numeric Input Conversions], page 305.

'%e', '%f', '%g', '%E', '%G'
            Matches an optionally signed floating-point number. See Section 12.14.4 [Numeric Input Conversions], page 305.

'%s'

            Matches a string containing only non-whitespace characters. See Section 12.14.5
            [String Input Conversions], page 306. The presence of the 'l' modifier determines whether the output is stored as a wide character string or a multibyte
            string. If '%s' is used in a wide character function the string is converted as
            with multiple calls to `wcrtomb` into a multibyte string. This means that the
            buffer must provide room for `MB_CUR_MAX` bytes for each wide character read.
            In case '%ls' is used in a multibyte function the result is converted into wide
            characters as with multiple calls of `mbrtowc` before being stored in the user
            provided buffer.

'%S'   This is an alias for '%ls' which is supported for compatibility with the Unix
            standard.

'%['   Matches a string of characters that belong to a specified set. See Section 12.14.5
            [String Input Conversions], page 306. The presence of the 'l' modifier determines whether the output is stored as a wide character string or a multibyte
            string. If '%[' is used in a wide character function the string is converted as
            with multiple calls to `wcrtomb` into a multibyte string. This means that the
            buffer must provide room for `MB_CUR_MAX` bytes for each wide character read.
            In case '%l[' is used in a multibyte function the result is converted into wide
            characters as with multiple calls of `mbrtowc` before being stored in the user
            provided buffer.

'%c'   Matches a string of one or more characters; the number of characters read is controlled by the maximum field width given for the conversion. See Section 12.14.5
            [String Input Conversions], page 306.

            If '%c' is used in a wide stream function the read value is converted from a
            wide character to the corresponding multibyte character before storing it. Note
            that this conversion can produce more than one byte of output and therefore
            the provided buffer must be large enough for up to `MB_CUR_MAX` bytes for each
            character. If '%lc' is used in a multibyte function the input is treated as a
            multibyte sequence (and not bytes) and the result is converted as with calls to
            `mbrtowc`.

'%C'   This is an alias for '%lc' which is supported for compatibility with the Unix
            standard.

'%p'   Matches a pointer value in the same implementation-defined format used by
            the '%p' output conversion for `printf`. See Section 12.14.7 [Other Input Conversions], page 308.

'%n'	This conversion doesn't read any characters; it records the number of characters read so far by this call. See Section 12.14.7 [Other Input Conversions], page 308.

'%%'	This matches a literal '%' character in the input stream. No corresponding argument is used. See Section 12.14.7 [Other Input Conversions], page 308.

If the syntax of a conversion specification is invalid, the behavior is undefined. If there aren't enough function arguments provided to supply addresses for all the conversion specifications in the template strings that perform assignments, or if the arguments are not of the correct types, the behavior is also undefined. On the other hand, extra arguments are simply ignored.

12.14.4 Numeric Input Conversions

This section describes the `scanf` conversions for reading numeric values.

The '%d' conversion matches an optionally signed integer in decimal radix. The syntax that is recognized is the same as that for the `strtol` function (see Section 20.11.1 [Parsing of Integers], page 608) with the value 10 for the *base* argument.

The '%i' conversion matches an optionally signed integer in any of the formats that the C language defines for specifying an integer constant. The syntax that is recognized is the same as that for the `strtol` function (see Section 20.11.1 [Parsing of Integers], page 608) with the value 0 for the *base* argument. (You can print integers in this syntax with `printf` by using the '#' flag character with the '%x', '%o', or '%d' conversion. See Section 12.12.4 [Integer Conversions], page 282.)

For example, any of the strings '10', '0xa', or '012' could be read in as integers under the '%i' conversion. Each of these specifies a number with decimal value 10.

The '%o', '%u', and '%x' conversions match unsigned integers in octal, decimal, and hexadecimal radices, respectively. The syntax that is recognized is the same as that for the `strtoul` function (see Section 20.11.1 [Parsing of Integers], page 608) with the appropriate value (8, 10, or 16) for the *base* argument.

The '%X' conversion is identical to the '%x' conversion. They both permit either uppercase or lowercase letters to be used as digits.

The default type of the corresponding argument for the %d and %i conversions is `int *`, and `unsigned int *` for the other integer conversions. You can use the following type modifiers to specify other sizes of integer:

'hh'	Specifies that the argument is a `signed char *` or `unsigned char *`.
	This modifier was introduced in ISO C99.

'h'	Specifies that the argument is a `short int *` or `unsigned short int *`.

'j'	Specifies that the argument is a `intmax_t *` or `uintmax_t *`.
	This modifier was introduced in ISO C99.

'l'	Specifies that the argument is a `long int *` or `unsigned long int *`. Two 'l' characters is like the 'L' modifier, below.

	If used with '%c' or '%s' the corresponding parameter is considered as a pointer to a wide character or wide character string respectively. This use of 'l' was introduced in Amendment 1 to ISO C90.

'll'

'L'

'q'   Specifies that the argument is a `long long int *` or `unsigned long long int` `*`. (The `long long` type is an extension supported by the GNU C compiler. For systems that don't provide extra-long integers, this is the same as `long int`.)

The 'q' modifier is another name for the same thing, which comes from 4.4 BSD; a `long long int` is sometimes called a "quad" `int`.

't'   Specifies that the argument is a `ptrdiff_t *`.

This modifier was introduced in ISO C99.

'z'   Specifies that the argument is a `size_t *`.

This modifier was introduced in ISO C99.

All of the '%e', '%f', '%g', '%E', and '%G' input conversions are interchangeable. They all match an optionally signed floating point number, in the same syntax as for the `strtod` function (see Section 20.11.2 [Parsing of Floats], page 613).

For the floating-point input conversions, the default argument type is `float *`. (This is different from the corresponding output conversions, where the default type is `double`; remember that `float` arguments to `printf` are converted to `double` by the default argument promotions, but `float *` arguments are not promoted to `double *`.) You can specify other sizes of float using these type modifiers:

'l'   Specifies that the argument is of type `double *`.

'L'   Specifies that the argument is of type `long double *`.

For all the above number parsing formats there is an additional optional flag ' '. When this flag is given the `scanf` function expects the number represented in the input string to be formatted according to the grouping rules of the currently selected locale (see Section 7.7.1.1 [Generic Numeric Formatting Parameters], page 182).

If the `"C"` or `"POSIX"` locale is selected there is no difference. But for a locale which specifies values for the appropriate fields in the locale the input must have the correct form in the input. Otherwise the longest prefix with a correct form is processed.

12.14.5 String Input Conversions

This section describes the `scanf` input conversions for reading string and character values: '%s', '%S', '%[', '%c', and '%C'.

You have two options for how to receive the input from these conversions:

- Provide a buffer to store it in. This is the default. You should provide an argument of type `char *` or `wchar_t *` (the latter if the 'l' modifier is present).

    Warning: To make a robust program, you must make sure that the input (plus its terminating null) cannot possibly exceed the size of the buffer you provide. In general, the only way to do this is to specify a maximum field width one less than the buffer size. **If you provide the buffer, always specify a maximum field width to prevent overflow.**

- Ask `scanf` to allocate a big enough buffer, by specifying the 'a' flag character. This is a GNU extension. You should provide an argument of type `char **` for the buffer address to be stored in. See Section 12.14.6 [Dynamically Allocating String Conversions], page 308.

The '%c' conversion is the simplest: it matches a fixed number of characters, always. The maximum field width says how many characters to read; if you don't specify the maximum, the default is 1. This conversion doesn't append a null character to the end of the text it reads. It also does not skip over initial whitespace characters. It reads precisely the next n characters, and fails if it cannot get that many. Since there is always a maximum field width with '%c' (whether specified, or 1 by default), you can always prevent overflow by making the buffer long enough.

If the format is '%lc' or '%C' the function stores wide characters which are converted using the conversion determined at the time the stream was opened from the external byte stream. The number of bytes read from the medium is limited by MB_CUR_LEN * n but at most n wide characters get stored in the output string.

The '%s' conversion matches a string of non-whitespace characters. It skips and discards initial whitespace, but stops when it encounters more whitespace after having read something. It stores a null character at the end of the text that it reads.

For example, reading the input:

```
hello, world
```

with the conversion '%10c' produces " hello, wo", but reading the same input with the conversion '%10s' produces "hello,".

Warning: If you do not specify a field width for '%s', then the number of characters read is limited only by where the next whitespace character appears. This almost certainly means that invalid input can make your program crash—which is a bug.

The '%ls' and '%S' format are handled just like '%s' except that the external byte sequence is converted using the conversion associated with the stream to wide characters with their own encoding. A width or precision specified with the format do not directly determine how many bytes are read from the stream since they measure wide characters. But an upper limit can be computed by multiplying the value of the width or precision by MB_CUR_MAX.

To read in characters that belong to an arbitrary set of your choice, use the '%[' conversion. You specify the set between the '[' character and a following ']' character, using the same syntax used in regular expressions for explicit sets of characters. As special cases:

- A literal ']' character can be specified as the first character of the set.

- An embedded '-' character (that is, one that is not the first or last character of the set) is used to specify a range of characters.

- If a caret character '^' immediately follows the initial '[', then the set of allowed input characters is everything *except* the characters listed.

The '%[' conversion does not skip over initial whitespace characters.

Note that the *character class* syntax available in character sets that appear inside regular expressions (such as '[:alpha:]') is *not* available in the '%[' conversion.

Here are some examples of '%[' conversions and what they mean:

'%25[1234567890]'
> Matches a string of up to 25 digits.

'%25[][]'   Matches a string of up to 25 square brackets.

'%25[^ \f\n\r\t\v]'

> Matches a string up to 25 characters long that doesn't contain any of the standard whitespace characters. This is slightly different from '%s', because if the input begins with a whitespace character, '%[' reports a matching failure while '%s' simply discards the initial whitespace.

'%25[a-z]'

> Matches up to 25 lowercase characters.

As for '%c' and '%s' the '%[' format is also modified to produce wide characters if the 'l' modifier is present. All what is said about '%ls' above is true for '%l['.

One more reminder: the '%s' and '%[' conversions are **dangerous** if you don't specify a maximum width or use the 'a' flag, because input too long would overflow whatever buffer you have provided for it. No matter how long your buffer is, a user could supply input that is longer. A well-written program reports invalid input with a comprehensible error message, not with a crash.

12.14.6 Dynamically Allocating String Conversions

A GNU extension to formatted input lets you safely read a string with no maximum size. Using this feature, you don't supply a buffer; instead, scanf allocates a buffer big enough to hold the data and gives you its address. To use this feature, write 'a' as a flag character, as in '%as' or '%a[0-9a-z]'.

The pointer argument you supply for where to store the input should have type char **. The scanf function allocates a buffer and stores its address in the word that the argument points to. You should free the buffer with free when you no longer need it.

Here is an example of using the 'a' flag with the '%[...]' conversion specification to read a "variable assignment" of the form 'variable = value'.

```
{
  char *variable, *value;

  if (2 > scanf ("%a[a-zA-Z0-9] = %a[^\n]\n",
&variable, &value))
    {
      invalid_input_error ();
      return 0;
    }

  ...
}
```

12.14.7 Other Input Conversions

This section describes the miscellaneous input conversions.

The '%p' conversion is used to read a pointer value. It recognizes the same syntax used by the '%p' output conversion for printf (see Section 12.12.6 [Other Output Conversions], page 286); that is, a hexadecimal number just as the '%x' conversion accepts. The corresponding argument should be of type void **; that is, the address of a place to store a pointer.

The resulting pointer value is not guaranteed to be valid if it was not originally written during the same program execution that reads it in.

The '%n' conversion produces the number of characters read so far by this call. The corresponding argument should be of type `int *`. This conversion works in the same way as the '%n' conversion for `printf`; see Section 12.12.6 [Other Output Conversions], page 286, for an example.

The '%n' conversion is the only mechanism for determining the success of literal matches or conversions with suppressed assignments. If the '%n' follows the locus of a matching failure, then no value is stored for it since `scanf` returns before processing the '%n'. If you store -1 in that argument slot before calling `scanf`, the presence of -1 after `scanf` indicates an error occurred before the '%n' was reached.

Finally, the '%%' conversion matches a literal '%' character in the input stream, without using an argument. This conversion does not permit any flags, field width, or type modifier to be specified.

12.14.8 Formatted Input Functions

Here are the descriptions of the functions for performing formatted input. Prototypes for these functions are in the header file `stdio.h`.

int scanf (*const char *template, ...*)   [Function]
> Preliminary: | MT-Safe locale | AS-Unsafe corrupt heap | AC-Unsafe mem lock corrupt | See Section 1.2.2.1 [POSIX Safety Concepts], page 2.
>
> The `scanf` function reads formatted input from the stream `stdin` under the control of the template string *template*. The optional arguments are pointers to the places which receive the resulting values.
>
> The return value is normally the number of successful assignments. If an end-of-file condition is detected before any matches are performed, including matches against whitespace and literal characters in the template, then `EOF` is returned.

int wscanf (*const wchar_t *template, ...*)   [Function]
> Preliminary: | MT-Safe locale | AS-Unsafe corrupt heap | AC-Unsafe mem lock corrupt | See Section 1.2.2.1 [POSIX Safety Concepts], page 2.
>
> The `wscanf` function reads formatted input from the stream `stdin` under the control of the template string *template*. The optional arguments are pointers to the places which receive the resulting values.
>
> The return value is normally the number of successful assignments. If an end-of-file condition is detected before any matches are performed, including matches against whitespace and literal characters in the template, then `WEOF` is returned.

int fscanf (*FILE *stream, const char *template, ...*)   [Function]
> Preliminary: | MT-Safe locale | AS-Unsafe corrupt heap | AC-Unsafe mem lock corrupt | See Section 1.2.2.1 [POSIX Safety Concepts], page 2.
>
> This function is just like `scanf`, except that the input is read from the stream *stream* instead of `stdin`.

int fwscanf (*FILE *stream, const wchar_t *template, ...*)   [Function]
> Preliminary: | MT-Safe locale | AS-Unsafe corrupt heap | AC-Unsafe mem lock corrupt | See Section 1.2.2.1 [POSIX Safety Concepts], page 2.

This function is just like `wscanf`, except that the input is read from the stream *stream* instead of `stdin`.

---

int sscanf (*const char *s, const char *template*, ...) [Function]
Preliminary: | MT-Safe locale | AS-Unsafe heap | AC-Unsafe mem | See Section 1.2.2.1 [POSIX Safety Concepts], page 2.

This is like `scanf`, except that the characters are taken from the null-terminated string *s* instead of from a stream. Reaching the end of the string is treated as an end-of-file condition.

The behavior of this function is undefined if copying takes place between objects that overlap—for example, if *s* is also given as an argument to receive a string read under control of the '`%s`', '`%S`', or '`%[`' conversion.

---

int swscanf (*const wchar_t *ws, const wchar_t *template*, ...) [Function]
Preliminary: | MT-Safe locale | AS-Unsafe heap | AC-Unsafe mem | See Section 1.2.2.1 [POSIX Safety Concepts], page 2.

This is like `wscanf`, except that the characters are taken from the null-terminated string *ws* instead of from a stream. Reaching the end of the string is treated as an end-of-file condition.

The behavior of this function is undefined if copying takes place between objects that overlap—for example, if *ws* is also given as an argument to receive a string read under control of the '`%s`', '`%S`', or '`%[`' conversion.

12.14.9 Variable Arguments Input Functions

The functions `vscanf` and friends are provided so that you can define your own variadic `scanf`-like functions that make use of the same internals as the built-in formatted output functions. These functions are analogous to the `vprintf` series of output functions. See Section 12.12.9 [Variable Arguments Output Functions], page 290, for important information on how to use them.

Portability Note: The functions listed in this section were introduced in ISO C99 and were before available as GNU extensions.

---

int vscanf (*const char *template*, va_list ap) [Function]
Preliminary: | MT-Safe locale | AS-Unsafe corrupt heap | AC-Unsafe mem lock corrupt | See Section 1.2.2.1 [POSIX Safety Concepts], page 2.

This function is similar to `scanf`, but instead of taking a variable number of arguments directly, it takes an argument list pointer *ap* of type `va_list` (see Section A.2 [Variadic Functions], page 910).

---

int vwscanf (*const wchar_t *template*, va_list ap) [Function]
Preliminary: | MT-Safe locale | AS-Unsafe corrupt heap | AC-Unsafe mem lock corrupt | See Section 1.2.2.1 [POSIX Safety Concepts], page 2.

This function is similar to `wscanf`, but instead of taking a variable number of arguments directly, it takes an argument list pointer *ap* of type `va_list` (see Section A.2 [Variadic Functions], page 910).

int **vfscanf** (*FILE *stream, const char *template, va_list ap*)   [Function]
> Preliminary: | MT-Safe locale | AS-Unsafe corrupt heap | AC-Unsafe mem lock corrupt | See Section 1.2.2.1 [POSIX Safety Concepts], page 2.
>
> This is the equivalent of **fscanf** with the variable argument list specified directly as for **vscanf**.

int **vfwscanf** (*FILE *stream, const wchar_t *template, va_list ap*)   [Function]
> Preliminary: | MT-Safe locale | AS-Unsafe corrupt heap | AC-Unsafe mem lock corrupt | See Section 1.2.2.1 [POSIX Safety Concepts], page 2.
>
> This is the equivalent of **fwscanf** with the variable argument list specified directly as for **vwscanf**.

int **vsscanf** (*const char *s, const char *template, va_list ap*)   [Function]
> Preliminary: | MT-Safe locale | AS-Unsafe heap | AC-Unsafe mem | See Section 1.2.2.1 [POSIX Safety Concepts], page 2.
>
> This is the equivalent of **sscanf** with the variable argument list specified directly as for **vscanf**.

int **vswscanf** (*const wchar_t *s, const wchar_t *template, va_list ap*)   [Function]
> Preliminary: | MT-Safe locale | AS-Unsafe heap | AC-Unsafe mem | See Section 1.2.2.1 [POSIX Safety Concepts], page 2.
>
> This is the equivalent of **swscanf** with the variable argument list specified directly as for **vwscanf**.

In GNU C, there is a special construct you can use to let the compiler know that a function uses a **scanf**-style format string. Then it can check the number and types of arguments in each call to the function, and warn you when they do not match the format string. For details, see Section "Declaring Attributes of Functions" in *Using GNU CC*.

12.15 End-Of-File and Errors

Many of the functions described in this chapter return the value of the macro EOF to indicate unsuccessful completion of the operation. Since EOF is used to report both end of file and random errors, it's often better to use the **feof** function to check explicitly for end of file and **ferror** to check for errors. These functions check indicators that are part of the internal state of the stream object, indicators set if the appropriate condition was detected by a previous I/O operation on that stream.

int **EOF**   [Macro]
> This macro is an integer value that is returned by a number of narrow stream functions to indicate an end-of-file condition, or some other error situation. With the GNU C Library, EOF is -1. In other libraries, its value may be some other negative number.
>
> This symbol is declared in **stdio.h**.

int **WEOF**   [Macro]
> This macro is an integer value that is returned by a number of wide stream functions to indicate an end-of-file condition, or some other error situation. With the GNU C Library, WEOF is -1. In other libraries, its value may be some other negative number.

This symbol is declared in `wchar.h`.

`int feof (FILE *stream)` [Function]

Preliminary: | MT-Safe | AS-Safe | AC-Unsafe lock | See Section 1.2.2.1 [POSIX Safety Concepts], page 2.

The `feof` function returns nonzero if and only if the end-of-file indicator for the stream *stream* is set.

This symbol is declared in `stdio.h`.

`int feof_unlocked (FILE *stream)` [Function]

Preliminary: | MT-Safe | AS-Safe | AC-Safe | See Section 1.2.2.1 [POSIX Safety Concepts], page 2.

The `feof_unlocked` function is equivalent to the `feof` function except that it does not implicitly lock the stream.

This function is a GNU extension.

This symbol is declared in `stdio.h`.

`int ferror (FILE *stream)` [Function]

Preliminary: | MT-Safe | AS-Safe | AC-Unsafe lock | See Section 1.2.2.1 [POSIX Safety Concepts], page 2.

The `ferror` function returns nonzero if and only if the error indicator for the stream *stream* is set, indicating that an error has occurred on a previous operation on the stream.

This symbol is declared in `stdio.h`.

`int ferror_unlocked (FILE *stream)` [Function]

Preliminary: | MT-Safe | AS-Safe | AC-Safe | See Section 1.2.2.1 [POSIX Safety Concepts], page 2.

The `ferror_unlocked` function is equivalent to the `ferror` function except that it does not implicitly lock the stream.

This function is a GNU extension.

This symbol is declared in `stdio.h`.

In addition to setting the error indicator associated with the stream, the functions that operate on streams also set `errno` in the same way as the corresponding low-level functions that operate on file descriptors. For example, all of the functions that perform output to a stream—such as `fputc`, `printf`, and `fflush`—are implemented in terms of `write`, and all of the `errno` error conditions defined for `write` are meaningful for these functions. For more information about the descriptor-level I/O functions, see Chapter 13 [Low-Level Input/Output], page 333.

12.16 Recovering from errors

You may explicitly clear the error and EOF flags with the `clearerr` function.

void clearerr (*FILE *stream*)   [Function]
> Preliminary: | MT-Safe | AS-Safe | AC-Unsafe lock | See Section 1.2.2.1 [POSIX Safety Concepts], page 2.
>
> This function clears the end-of-file and error indicators for the stream *stream*.
>
> The file positioning functions (see Section 12.18 [File Positioning], page 314) also clear the end-of-file indicator for the stream.

void clearerr_unlocked (*FILE *stream*)   [Function]
> Preliminary: | MT-Safe race:stream | AS-Safe | AC-Safe | See Section 1.2.2.1 [POSIX Safety Concepts], page 2.
>
> The `clearerr_unlocked` function is equivalent to the `clearerr` function except that it does not implicitly lock the stream.
>
> This function is a GNU extension.

Note that it is *not* correct to just clear the error flag and retry a failed stream operation. After a failed write, any number of characters since the last buffer flush may have been committed to the file, while some buffered data may have been discarded. Merely retrying can thus cause lost or repeated data.

A failed read may leave the file pointer in an inappropriate position for a second try. In both cases, you should seek to a known position before retrying.

Most errors that can happen are not recoverable — a second try will always fail again in the same way. So usually it is best to give up and report the error to the user, rather than install complicated recovery logic.

One important exception is `EINTR` (see Section 24.5 [Primitives Interrupted by Signals], page 711). Many stream I/O implementations will treat it as an ordinary error, which can be quite inconvenient. You can avoid this hassle by installing all signals with the `SA_RESTART` flag.

For similar reasons, setting nonblocking I/O on a stream's file descriptor is not usually advisable.

12.17 Text and Binary Streams

GNU systems and other POSIX-compatible operating systems organize all files as uniform sequences of characters. However, some other systems make a distinction between files containing text and files containing binary data, and the input and output facilities of ISO C provide for this distinction. This section tells you how to write programs portable to such systems.

When you open a stream, you can specify either a *text stream* or a *binary stream*. You indicate that you want a binary stream by specifying the 'b' modifier in the *opentype* argument to `fopen`; see Section 12.3 [Opening Streams], page 258. Without this option, `fopen` opens the file as a text stream.

Text and binary streams differ in several ways:

- The data read from a text stream is divided into *lines* which are terminated by newline ('\n') characters, while a binary stream is simply a long series of characters. A text stream might on some systems fail to handle lines more than 254 characters long (including the terminating newline character).

- On some systems, text files can contain only printing characters, horizontal tab characters, and newlines, and so text streams may not support other characters. However, binary streams can handle any character value.

- Space characters that are written immediately preceding a newline character in a text stream may disappear when the file is read in again.

- More generally, there need not be a one-to-one mapping between characters that are read from or written to a text stream, and the characters in the actual file.

Since a binary stream is always more capable and more predictable than a text stream, you might wonder what purpose text streams serve. Why not simply always use binary streams? The answer is that on these operating systems, text and binary streams use different file formats, and the only way to read or write "an ordinary file of text" that can work with other text-oriented programs is through a text stream.

In the GNU C Library, and on all POSIX systems, there is no difference between text streams and binary streams. When you open a stream, you get the same kind of stream regardless of whether you ask for binary. This stream can handle any file content, and has none of the restrictions that text streams sometimes have.

12.18 File Positioning

The *file position* of a stream describes where in the file the stream is currently reading or writing. I/O on the stream advances the file position through the file. On GNU systems, the file position is represented as an integer, which counts the number of bytes from the beginning of the file. See Section 11.1.2 [File Position], page 253.

During I/O to an ordinary disk file, you can change the file position whenever you wish, so as to read or write any portion of the file. Some other kinds of files may also permit this. Files which support changing the file position are sometimes referred to as *random-access* files.

You can use the functions in this section to examine or modify the file position indicator associated with a stream. The symbols listed below are declared in the header file `stdio.h`.

`long int ftell` (*FILE *stream*)   [Function]
    Preliminary: | MT-Safe | AS-Unsafe corrupt | AC-Unsafe lock corrupt | See Section 1.2.2.1 [POSIX Safety Concepts], page 2.

    This function returns the current file position of the stream *stream*.

    This function can fail if the stream doesn't support file positioning, or if the file position can't be represented in a `long int`, and possibly for other reasons as well. If a failure occurs, a value of `-1` is returned.

`off_t ftello (FILE *stream)`   [Function]
> Preliminary: | MT-Safe | AS-Unsafe corrupt | AC-Unsafe lock corrupt | See
> Section 1.2.2.1 [POSIX Safety Concepts], page 2.
>
> The `ftello` function is similar to `ftell`, except that it returns a value of type `off_`
> `t`. Systems which support this type use it to describe all file positions, unlike the
> POSIX specification which uses a long int. The two are not necessarily the same size.
> Therefore, using ftell can lead to problems if the implementation is written on top
> of a POSIX compliant low-level I/O implementation, and using `ftello` is preferable
> whenever it is available.
>
> If this function fails it returns `(off_t) -1`. This can happen due to missing support
> for file positioning or internal errors. Otherwise the return value is the current file
> position.
>
> The function is an extension defined in the Unix Single Specification version 2.
>
> When the sources are compiled with `_FILE_OFFSET_BITS == 64` on a 32 bit system
> this function is in fact `ftello64`. I.e., the LFS interface transparently replaces the
> old interface.

`off64_t ftello64 (FILE *stream)`   [Function]
> Preliminary: | MT-Safe | AS-Unsafe corrupt | AC-Unsafe lock corrupt | See
> Section 1.2.2.1 [POSIX Safety Concepts], page 2.
>
> This function is similar to `ftello` with the only difference that the return value is
> of type `off64_t`. This also requires that the stream *stream* was opened using either
> `fopen64`, `freopen64`, or `tmpfile64` since otherwise the underlying file operations to
> position the file pointer beyond the 2^{31} bytes limit might fail.
>
> If the sources are compiled with `_FILE_OFFSET_BITS == 64` on a 32 bits machine this
> function is available under the name `ftello` and so transparently replaces the old
> interface.

`int fseek (FILE *stream, long int offset, int whence)`   [Function]
> Preliminary: | MT-Safe | AS-Unsafe corrupt | AC-Unsafe lock corrupt | See
> Section 1.2.2.1 [POSIX Safety Concepts], page 2.
>
> The `fseek` function is used to change the file position of the stream *stream*. The
> value of *whence* must be one of the constants `SEEK_SET`, `SEEK_CUR`, or `SEEK_END`,
> to indicate whether the *offset* is relative to the beginning of the file, the current file
> position, or the end of the file, respectively.
>
> This function returns a value of zero if the operation was successful, and a nonzero
> value to indicate failure. A successful call also clears the end-of-file indicator of *stream*
> and discards any characters that were "pushed back" by the use of `ungetc`.
>
> `fseek` either flushes any buffered output before setting the file position or else re-
> members it so it will be written later in its proper place in the file.

`int fseeko (FILE *stream, off_t offset, int whence)`   [Function]
> Preliminary: | MT-Safe | AS-Unsafe corrupt | AC-Unsafe lock corrupt | See
> Section 1.2.2.1 [POSIX Safety Concepts], page 2.

This function is similar to `fseek` but it corrects a problem with `fseek` in a system with POSIX types. Using a value of type `long int` for the offset is not compatible with POSIX. `fseeko` uses the correct type `off_t` for the *offset* parameter.

For this reason it is a good idea to prefer `ftello` whenever it is available since its functionality is (if different at all) closer the underlying definition.

The functionality and return value are the same as for `fseek`.

The function is an extension defined in the Unix Single Specification version 2.

When the sources are compiled with `_FILE_OFFSET_BITS == 64` on a 32 bit system this function is in fact `fseeko64`. I.e., the LFS interface transparently replaces the old interface.

`int fseeko64 (`*`FILE *stream`*`, `*`off64_t offset`*`, `*`int whence`*`)` [Function]
    Preliminary: | MT-Safe | AS-Unsafe corrupt | AC-Unsafe lock corrupt | See Section 1.2.2.1 [POSIX Safety Concepts], page 2.

This function is similar to `fseeko` with the only difference that the *offset* parameter is of type `off64_t`. This also requires that the stream *stream* was opened using either `fopen64`, `freopen64`, or `tmpfile64` since otherwise the underlying file operations to position the file pointer beyond the 2^{31} bytes limit might fail.

If the sources are compiled with `_FILE_OFFSET_BITS == 64` on a 32 bits machine this function is available under the name `fseeko` and so transparently replaces the old interface.

Portability Note: In non-POSIX systems, `ftell`, `ftello`, `fseek` and `fseeko` might work reliably only on binary streams. See Section 12.17 [Text and Binary Streams], page 313.

The following symbolic constants are defined for use as the *whence* argument to `fseek`. They are also used with the `lseek` function (see Section 13.2 [Input and Output Primitives], page 336) and to specify offsets for file locks (see Section 13.11 [Control Operations on Files], page 371).

`int SEEK_SET` [Macro]
    This is an integer constant which, when used as the *whence* argument to the `fseek` or `fseeko` functions, specifies that the offset provided is relative to the beginning of the file.

`int SEEK_CUR` [Macro]
    This is an integer constant which, when used as the *whence* argument to the `fseek` or `fseeko` functions, specifies that the offset provided is relative to the current file position.

`int SEEK_END` [Macro]
    This is an integer constant which, when used as the *whence* argument to the `fseek` or `fseeko` functions, specifies that the offset provided is relative to the end of the file.

`void rewind (`*`FILE *stream`*`)` [Function]
    Preliminary: | MT-Safe | AS-Unsafe corrupt | AC-Unsafe lock corrupt | See Section 1.2.2.1 [POSIX Safety Concepts], page 2.

The `rewind` function positions the stream *stream* at the beginning of the file. It is equivalent to calling `fseek` or `fseeko` on the *stream* with an *offset* argument of 0L and a *whence* argument of `SEEK_SET`, except that the return value is discarded and the error indicator for the stream is reset.

These three aliases for the 'SEEK_...' constants exist for the sake of compatibility with older BSD systems. They are defined in two different header files: `fcntl.h` and `sys/file.h`.

L_SET   An alias for `SEEK_SET`.

L_INCR   An alias for `SEEK_CUR`.

L_XTND   An alias for `SEEK_END`.

12.19 Portable File-Position Functions

On GNU systems, the file position is truly a character count. You can specify any character count value as an argument to `fseek` or `fseeko` and get reliable results for any random access file. However, some ISO C systems do not represent file positions in this way.

On some systems where text streams truly differ from binary streams, it is impossible to represent the file position of a text stream as a count of characters from the beginning of the file. For example, the file position on some systems must encode both a record offset within the file, and a character offset within the record.

As a consequence, if you want your programs to be portable to these systems, you must observe certain rules:

- The value returned from `ftell` on a text stream has no predictable relationship to the number of characters you have read so far. The only thing you can rely on is that you can use it subsequently as the *offset* argument to `fseek` or `fseeko` to move back to the same file position.

- In a call to `fseek` or `fseeko` on a text stream, either the *offset* must be zero, or *whence* must be `SEEK_SET` and the *offset* must be the result of an earlier call to `ftell` on the same stream.

- The value of the file position indicator of a text stream is undefined while there are characters that have been pushed back with `ungetc` that haven't been read or discarded. See Section 12.10 [Unreading], page 276.

But even if you observe these rules, you may still have trouble for long files, because `ftell` and `fseek` use a `long int` value to represent the file position. This type may not have room to encode all the file positions in a large file. Using the `ftello` and `fseeko` functions might help here since the `off_t` type is expected to be able to hold all file position values but this still does not help to handle additional information which must be associated with a file position.

So if you do want to support systems with peculiar encodings for the file positions, it is better to use the functions `fgetpos` and `fsetpos` instead. These functions represent the file position using the data type `fpos_t`, whose internal representation varies from system to system.

These symbols are declared in the header file `stdio.h`.

fpos_t [Data Type]

This is the type of an object that can encode information about the file position of a stream, for use by the functions `fgetpos` and `fsetpos`.

In the GNU C Library, `fpos_t` is an opaque data structure that contains internal data to represent file offset and conversion state information. In other systems, it might have a different internal representation.

When compiling with _FILE_OFFSET_BITS == 64 on a 32 bit machine this type is in fact equivalent to `fpos64_t` since the LFS interface transparently replaces the old interface.

fpos64_t [Data Type]

This is the type of an object that can encode information about the file position of a stream, for use by the functions `fgetpos64` and `fsetpos64`.

In the GNU C Library, `fpos64_t` is an opaque data structure that contains internal data to represent file offset and conversion state information. In other systems, it might have a different internal representation.

int fgetpos (FILE *stream, fpos_t *position) [Function]

Preliminary: | MT-Safe | AS-Unsafe corrupt | AC-Unsafe lock corrupt | See Section 1.2.2.1 [POSIX Safety Concepts], page 2.

This function stores the value of the file position indicator for the stream *stream* in the `fpos_t` object pointed to by *position*. If successful, `fgetpos` returns zero; otherwise it returns a nonzero value and stores an implementation-defined positive value in `errno`.

When the sources are compiled with _FILE_OFFSET_BITS == 64 on a 32 bit system the function is in fact `fgetpos64`. I.e., the LFS interface transparently replaces the old interface.

int fgetpos64 (FILE *stream, fpos64_t *position) [Function]

Preliminary: | MT-Safe | AS-Unsafe corrupt | AC-Unsafe lock corrupt | See Section 1.2.2.1 [POSIX Safety Concepts], page 2.

This function is similar to `fgetpos` but the file position is returned in a variable of type `fpos64_t` to which *position* points.

If the sources are compiled with _FILE_OFFSET_BITS == 64 on a 32 bits machine this function is available under the name `fgetpos` and so transparently replaces the old interface.

int fsetpos (FILE *stream, const fpos_t *position) [Function]

Preliminary: | MT-Safe | AS-Unsafe corrupt | AC-Unsafe lock corrupt | See Section 1.2.2.1 [POSIX Safety Concepts], page 2.

This function sets the file position indicator for the stream *stream* to the position *position*, which must have been set by a previous call to `fgetpos` on the same stream. If successful, `fsetpos` clears the end-of-file indicator on the stream, discards any characters that were "pushed back" by the use of `ungetc`, and returns a value of zero. Otherwise, `fsetpos` returns a nonzero value and stores an implementation-defined positive value in `errno`.

When the sources are compiled with `_FILE_OFFSET_BITS` == 64 on a 32 bit system the function is in fact `fsetpos64`. I.e., the LFS interface transparently replaces the old interface.

`int fsetpos64` (*FILE *stream, const fpos64_t *position*)   [Function]
Preliminary: | MT-Safe | AS-Unsafe corrupt | AC-Unsafe lock corrupt | See Section 1.2.2.1 [POSIX Safety Concepts], page 2.

This function is similar to `fsetpos` but the file position used for positioning is provided in a variable of type `fpos64_t` to which *position* points.

If the sources are compiled with `_FILE_OFFSET_BITS` == 64 on a 32 bits machine this function is available under the name `fsetpos` and so transparently replaces the old interface.

12.20 Stream Buffering

Characters that are written to a stream are normally accumulated and transmitted asynchronously to the file in a block, instead of appearing as soon as they are output by the application program. Similarly, streams often retrieve input from the host environment in blocks rather than on a character-by-character basis. This is called *buffering*.

If you are writing programs that do interactive input and output using streams, you need to understand how buffering works when you design the user interface to your program. Otherwise, you might find that output (such as progress or prompt messages) doesn't appear when you intended it to, or displays some other unexpected behavior.

This section deals only with controlling when characters are transmitted between the stream and the file or device, and *not* with how things like echoing, flow control, and the like are handled on specific classes of devices. For information on common control operations on terminal devices, see Chapter 17 [Low-Level Terminal Interface], page 490.

You can bypass the stream buffering facilities altogether by using the low-level input and output functions that operate on file descriptors instead. See Chapter 13 [Low-Level Input/Output], page 333.

12.20.1 Buffering Concepts

There are three different kinds of buffering strategies:

- Characters written to or read from an *unbuffered* stream are transmitted individually to or from the file as soon as possible.
- Characters written to a *line buffered* stream are transmitted to the file in blocks when a newline character is encountered.
- Characters written to or read from a *fully buffered* stream are transmitted to or from the file in blocks of arbitrary size.

Newly opened streams are normally fully buffered, with one exception: a stream connected to an interactive device such as a terminal is initially line buffered. See Section 12.20.3 [Controlling Which Kind of Buffering], page 321, for information on how to select a different kind of buffering. Usually the automatic selection gives you the most convenient kind of buffering for the file or device you open.

The use of line buffering for interactive devices implies that output messages ending in a newline will appear immediately—which is usually what you want. Output that doesn't end in a newline might or might not show up immediately, so if you want them to appear immediately, you should flush buffered output explicitly with `fflush`, as described in Section 12.20.2 [Flushing Buffers], page 320.

12.20.2 Flushing Buffers

Flushing output on a buffered stream means transmitting all accumulated characters to the file. There are many circumstances when buffered output on a stream is flushed automatically:

- When you try to do output and the output buffer is full.
- When the stream is closed. See Section 12.4 [Closing Streams], page 262.
- When the program terminates by calling `exit`. See Section 25.7.1 [Normal Termination], page 769.
- When a newline is written, if the stream is line buffered.
- Whenever an input operation on *any* stream actually reads data from its file.

If you want to flush the buffered output at another time, call `fflush`, which is declared in the header file `stdio.h`.

int fflush (*FILE *stream*)   [Function]
> Preliminary: | MT-Safe | AS-Unsafe corrupt | AC-Unsafe lock corrupt | See Section 1.2.2.1 [POSIX Safety Concepts], page 2.
>
> This function causes any buffered output on *stream* to be delivered to the file. If *stream* is a null pointer, then `fflush` causes buffered output on *all* open output streams to be flushed.
>
> This function returns `EOF` if a write error occurs, or zero otherwise.

int fflush_unlocked (*FILE *stream*)   [Function]
> Preliminary: | MT-Safe race:stream | AS-Unsafe corrupt | AC-Unsafe corrupt | See Section 1.2.2.1 [POSIX Safety Concepts], page 2.
>
> The `fflush_unlocked` function is equivalent to the `fflush` function except that it does not implicitly lock the stream.

The `fflush` function can be used to flush all streams currently opened. While this is useful in some situations it does often more than necessary since it might be done in situations when terminal input is required and the program wants to be sure that all output is visible on the terminal. But this means that only line buffered streams have to be flushed. Solaris introduced a function especially for this. It was always available in the GNU C Library in some form but never officially exported.

void _flushlbf (*void*)   [Function]
> Preliminary: | MT-Safe | AS-Unsafe corrupt | AC-Unsafe lock corrupt | See Section 1.2.2.1 [POSIX Safety Concepts], page 2.
>
> The `_flushlbf` function flushes all line buffered streams currently opened.
>
> This function is declared in the `stdio_ext.h` header.

Compatibility Note: Some brain-damaged operating systems have been known to be so thoroughly fixated on line-oriented input and output that flushing a line buffered stream causes a newline to be written! Fortunately, this "feature" seems to be becoming less common. You do not need to worry about this with the GNU C Library.

In some situations it might be useful to not flush the output pending for a stream but instead simply forget it. If transmission is costly and the output is not needed anymore this is valid reasoning. In this situation a non-standard function introduced in Solaris and available in the GNU C Library can be used.

void __fpurge (*FILE *stream*)   [Function]
>   Preliminary: | MT-Safe race:stream | AS-Unsafe corrupt | AC-Unsafe corrupt | See Section 1.2.2.1 [POSIX Safety Concepts], page 2.
>
>   The __fpurge function causes the buffer of the stream *stream* to be emptied. If the stream is currently in read mode all input in the buffer is lost. If the stream is in output mode the buffered output is not written to the device (or whatever other underlying storage) and the buffer is cleared.
>
>   This function is declared in stdio_ext.h.

12.20.3 Controlling Which Kind of Buffering

After opening a stream (but before any other operations have been performed on it), you can explicitly specify what kind of buffering you want it to have using the setvbuf function.

The facilities listed in this section are declared in the header file stdio.h.

int setvbuf (*FILE *stream, char *buf, int mode, size_t size*)   [Function]
>   Preliminary: | MT-Safe | AS-Unsafe corrupt | AC-Unsafe lock corrupt | See Section 1.2.2.1 [POSIX Safety Concepts], page 2.
>
>   This function is used to specify that the stream *stream* should have the buffering mode *mode*, which can be either _IOFBF (for full buffering), _IOLBF (for line buffering), or _IONBF (for unbuffered input/output).
>
>   If you specify a null pointer as the *buf* argument, then setvbuf allocates a buffer itself using malloc. This buffer will be freed when you close the stream.
>
>   Otherwise, *buf* should be a character array that can hold at least *size* characters. You should not free the space for this array as long as the stream remains open and this array remains its buffer. You should usually either allocate it statically, or malloc (see Section 3.2.3 [Unconstrained Allocation], page 44) the buffer. Using an automatic array is not a good idea unless you close the file before exiting the block that declares the array.
>
>   While the array remains a stream buffer, the stream I/O functions will use the buffer for their internal purposes. You shouldn't try to access the values in the array directly while the stream is using it for buffering.
>
>   The setvbuf function returns zero on success, or a nonzero value if the value of *mode* is not valid or if the request could not be honored.

int _IOFBF   [Macro]

> The value of this macro is an integer constant expression that can be used as the *mode* argument to the setvbuf function to specify that the stream should be fully buffered.

int _IOLBF   [Macro]

> The value of this macro is an integer constant expression that can be used as the *mode* argument to the setvbuf function to specify that the stream should be line buffered.

int _IONBF   [Macro]

> The value of this macro is an integer constant expression that can be used as the *mode* argument to the setvbuf function to specify that the stream should be unbuffered.

int BUFSIZ   [Macro]

> The value of this macro is an integer constant expression that is good to use for the *size* argument to setvbuf. This value is guaranteed to be at least 256.
>
> The value of BUFSIZ is chosen on each system so as to make stream I/O efficient. So it is a good idea to use BUFSIZ as the size for the buffer when you call setvbuf.
>
> Actually, you can get an even better value to use for the buffer size by means of the fstat system call: it is found in the st_blksize field of the file attributes. See Section 14.9.1 [The meaning of the File Attributes], page 412.
>
> Sometimes people also use BUFSIZ as the allocation size of buffers used for related purposes, such as strings used to receive a line of input with fgets (see Section 12.8 [Character Input], page 271). There is no particular reason to use BUFSIZ for this instead of any other integer, except that it might lead to doing I/O in chunks of an efficient size.

void setbuf (*FILE *stream, char *buf*)   [Function]

> Preliminary: | MT-Safe | AS-Unsafe corrupt | AC-Unsafe lock corrupt | See Section 1.2.2.1 [POSIX Safety Concepts], page 2.
>
> If *buf* is a null pointer, the effect of this function is equivalent to calling setvbuf with a *mode* argument of _IONBF. Otherwise, it is equivalent to calling setvbuf with *buf*, and a *mode* of _IOFBF and a *size* argument of BUFSIZ.
>
> The setbuf function is provided for compatibility with old code; use setvbuf in all new programs.

void setbuffer (*FILE *stream, char *buf, size_t size*)   [Function]

> Preliminary: | MT-Safe | AS-Unsafe corrupt | AC-Unsafe lock corrupt | See Section 1.2.2.1 [POSIX Safety Concepts], page 2.
>
> If *buf* is a null pointer, this function makes *stream* unbuffered. Otherwise, it makes *stream* fully buffered using *buf* as the buffer. The *size* argument specifies the length of *buf*.
>
> This function is provided for compatibility with old BSD code. Use setvbuf instead.

void setlinebuf (*FILE *stream*)   [Function]

> Preliminary: | MT-Safe | AS-Unsafe corrupt | AC-Unsafe lock corrupt | See Section 1.2.2.1 [POSIX Safety Concepts], page 2.

This function makes *stream* be line buffered, and allocates the buffer for you.

This function is provided for compatibility with old BSD code. Use `setvbuf` instead.

It is possible to query whether a given stream is line buffered or not using a non-standard function introduced in Solaris and available in the GNU C Library.

`int __flbf (FILE *stream)` [Function]
> Preliminary: | MT-Safe | AS-Safe | AC-Safe | See Section 1.2.2.1 [POSIX Safety Concepts], page 2.
>
> The `__flbf` function will return a nonzero value in case the stream *stream* is line buffered. Otherwise the return value is zero.
>
> This function is declared in the `stdio_ext.h` header.

Two more extensions allow to determine the size of the buffer and how much of it is used. These functions were also introduced in Solaris.

`size_t __fbufsize (FILE *stream)` [Function]
> Preliminary: | MT-Safe race:stream | AS-Unsafe corrupt | AC-Safe | See Section 1.2.2.1 [POSIX Safety Concepts], page 2.
>
> The `__fbufsize` function return the size of the buffer in the stream *stream*. This value can be used to optimize the use of the stream.
>
> This function is declared in the `stdio_ext.h` header.

`size_t __fpending (FILE *stream)` [Function]
> Preliminary: | MT-Safe race:stream | AS-Unsafe corrupt | AC-Safe | See Section 1.2.2.1 [POSIX Safety Concepts], page 2.
>
> The `__fpending` function returns the number of bytes currently in the output buffer. For wide-oriented streams the measuring unit is wide characters. This function should not be used on buffers in read mode or opened read-only.
>
> This function is declared in the `stdio_ext.h` header.

12.21 Other Kinds of Streams

The GNU C Library provides ways for you to define additional kinds of streams that do not necessarily correspond to an open file.

One such type of stream takes input from or writes output to a string. These kinds of streams are used internally to implement the `sprintf` and `sscanf` functions. You can also create such a stream explicitly, using the functions described in Section 12.21.1 [String Streams], page 324.

More generally, you can define streams that do input/output to arbitrary objects using functions supplied by your program. This protocol is discussed in Section 12.21.2 [Programming Your Own Custom Streams], page 326.

Portability Note: The facilities described in this section are specific to GNU. Other systems or C implementations might or might not provide equivalent functionality.

12.21.1 String Streams

The `fmemopen` and `open_memstream` functions allow you to do I/O to a string or memory buffer. These facilities are declared in `stdio.h`.

`FILE * fmemopen (`*void *buf*, *size_t* `size`, *const char *opentype*)`   [Function]
Preliminary: | MT-Safe | AS-Unsafe heap lock | AC-Unsafe mem lock | See Section 1.2.2.1 [POSIX Safety Concepts], page 2.

> This function opens a stream that allows the access specified by the *opentype* argument, that reads from or writes to the buffer specified by the argument *buf*. This array must be at least *size* bytes long.

> If you specify a null pointer as the *buf* argument, `fmemopen` dynamically allocates an array *size* bytes long (as with `malloc`; see Section 3.2.3 [Unconstrained Allocation], page 44). This is really only useful if you are going to write things to the buffer and then read them back in again, because you have no way of actually getting a pointer to the buffer (for this, try `open_memstream`, below). The buffer is freed when the stream is closed.

> The argument *opentype* is the same as in `fopen` (see Section 12.3 [Opening Streams], page 258). If the *opentype* specifies append mode, then the initial file position is set to the first null character in the buffer. Otherwise the initial file position is at the beginning of the buffer.

> When a stream open for writing is flushed or closed, a null character (zero byte) is written at the end of the buffer if it fits. You should add an extra byte to the *size* argument to account for this. Attempts to write more than *size* bytes to the buffer result in an error.

> For a stream open for reading, null characters (zero bytes) in the buffer do not count as "end of file". Read operations indicate end of file only when the file position advances past *size* bytes. So, if you want to read characters from a null-terminated string, you should supply the length of the string as the *size* argument.

Here is an example of using `fmemopen` to create a stream for reading from a string:

```
#include <stdio.h>

static char buffer[] = "foobar";

int
main (void)
{
  int ch;
  FILE *stream;

  stream = fmemopen (buffer, strlen (buffer), "r");
  while ((ch = fgetc (stream)) != EOF)
    printf ("Got %c\n", ch);
  fclose (stream);

  return 0;
}
```

This program produces the following output:

```
Got f
```

324

```
Got o
Got o
Got b
Got a
Got r
```

FILE * open_memstream (*char **ptr*, *size_t *sizeloc*)   [Function]
Preliminary: | MT-Safe | AS-Unsafe heap | AC-Unsafe mem | See Section 1.2.2.1
[POSIX Safety Concepts], page 2.

This function opens a stream for writing to a buffer. The buffer is allocated dynamically and grown as necessary, using **malloc**. After you've closed the stream, this buffer is your responsibility to clean up using **free** or **realloc**. See Section 3.2.3 [Unconstrained Allocation], page 44.

When the stream is closed with **fclose** or flushed with **fflush**, the locations *ptr* and *sizeloc* are updated to contain the pointer to the buffer and its size. The values thus stored remain valid only as long as no further output on the stream takes place. If you do more output, you must flush the stream again to store new values before you use them again.

A null character is written at the end of the buffer. This null character is *not* included in the size value stored at *sizeloc*.

You can move the stream's file position with **fseek** or **fseeko** (see Section 12.18 [File Positioning], page 314). Moving the file position past the end of the data already written fills the intervening space with zeroes.

Here is an example of using **open_memstream**:

```c
#include <stdio.h>

int
main (void)
{
  char *bp;
  size_t size;
  FILE *stream;

  stream = open_memstream (&bp, &size);
  fprintf (stream, "hello");
  fflush (stream);
  printf ("buf = `%s', size = %zu\n", bp, size);
  fprintf (stream, ", world");
  fclose (stream);
  printf ("buf = `%s', size = %zu\n", bp, size);

  return 0;
}
```

This program produces the following output:

```
buf = `hello', size = 5
buf = `hello, world', size = 12
```

12.21.2 Programming Your Own Custom Streams

This section describes how you can make a stream that gets input from an arbitrary data source or writes output to an arbitrary data sink programmed by you. We call these *custom streams*. The functions and types described here are all GNU extensions.

12.21.2.1 Custom Streams and Cookies

Inside every custom stream is a special object called the *cookie*. This is an object supplied by you which records where to fetch or store the data read or written. It is up to you to define a data type to use for the cookie. The stream functions in the library never refer directly to its contents, and they don't even know what the type is; they record its address with type void *.

To implement a custom stream, you must specify *how* to fetch or store the data in the specified place. You do this by defining *hook functions* to read, write, change "file position", and close the stream. All four of these functions will be passed the stream's cookie so they can tell where to fetch or store the data. The library functions don't know what's inside the cookie, but your functions will know.

When you create a custom stream, you must specify the cookie pointer, and also the four hook functions stored in a structure of type cookie_io_functions_t.

These facilities are declared in stdio.h.

cookie_io_functions_t   [Data Type]
> This is a structure type that holds the functions that define the communications protocol between the stream and its cookie. It has the following members:

> cookie_read_function_t *read
>> This is the function that reads data from the cookie. If the value is a null pointer instead of a function, then read operations on this stream always return EOF.

> cookie_write_function_t *write
>> This is the function that writes data to the cookie. If the value is a null pointer instead of a function, then data written to the stream is discarded.

> cookie_seek_function_t *seek
>> This is the function that performs the equivalent of file positioning on the cookie. If the value is a null pointer instead of a function, calls to fseek or fseeko on this stream can only seek to locations within the buffer; any attempt to seek outside the buffer will return an ESPIPE error.

> cookie_close_function_t *close
>> This function performs any appropriate cleanup on the cookie when closing the stream. If the value is a null pointer instead of a function, nothing special is done to close the cookie when the stream is closed.

FILE * fopencookie (*void *cookie, const char *opentype,*   [Function]
        cookie_io_functions_t io-functions)
> Preliminary: | MT-Safe | AS-Unsafe heap lock | AC-Unsafe mem lock | See Section 1.2.2.1 [POSIX Safety Concepts], page 2.

This function actually creates the stream for communicating with the *cookie* using the functions in the *io-functions* argument. The *opentype* argument is interpreted as for `fopen`; see Section 12.3 [Opening Streams], page 258. (But note that the "truncate on open" option is ignored.) The new stream is fully buffered.

The `fopencookie` function returns the newly created stream, or a null pointer in case of an error.

12.21.2.2 Custom Stream Hook Functions

Here are more details on how you should define the four hook functions that a custom stream needs.

You should define the function to read data from the cookie as:

```
ssize_t reader (void *cookie, char *buffer, size_t size)
```

This is very similar to the `read` function; see Section 13.2 [Input and Output Primitives], page 336. Your function should transfer up to *size* bytes into the *buffer*, and return the number of bytes read, or zero to indicate end-of-file. You can return a value of -1 to indicate an error.

You should define the function to write data to the cookie as:

```
ssize_t writer (void *cookie, const char *buffer, size_t size)
```

This is very similar to the `write` function; see Section 13.2 [Input and Output Primitives], page 336. Your function should transfer up to *size* bytes from the buffer, and return the number of bytes written. You can return a value of 0 to indicate an error. You must not return any negative value.

You should define the function to perform seek operations on the cookie as:

```
int seeker (void *cookie, off64_t *position, int whence)
```

For this function, the *position* and *whence* arguments are interpreted as for `fgetpos`; see Section 12.19 [Portable File-Position Functions], page 317.

After doing the seek operation, your function should store the resulting file position relative to the beginning of the file in *position*. Your function should return a value of 0 on success and -1 to indicate an error.

You should define the function to do cleanup operations on the cookie appropriate for closing the stream as:

```
int cleaner (void *cookie)
```

Your function should return -1 to indicate an error, and 0 otherwise.

`cookie_read_function_t`   [Data Type]
    This is the data type that the read function for a custom stream should have. If you declare the function as shown above, this is the type it will have.

`cookie_write_function_t`   [Data Type]
    The data type of the write function for a custom stream.

`cookie_seek_function_t`   [Data Type]
    The data type of the seek function for a custom stream.

`cookie_close_function_t`   [Data Type]
    The data type of the close function for a custom stream.

12.22 Formatted Messages

On systems which are based on System V messages of programs (especially the system tools) are printed in a strict form using the **fmtmsg** function. The uniformity sometimes helps the user to interpret messages and the strictness tests of the **fmtmsg** function ensure that the programmer follows some minimal requirements.

12.22.1 Printing Formatted Messages

Messages can be printed to standard error and/or to the console. To select the destination the programmer can use the following two values, bitwise OR combined if wanted, for the *classification* parameter of **fmtmsg**:

MM_PRINT   Display the message in standard error.

MM_CONSOLE
          Display the message on the system console.

The erroneous piece of the system can be signalled by exactly one of the following values which also is bitwise ORed with the *classification* parameter to **fmtmsg**:

MM_HARD   The source of the condition is some hardware.

MM_SOFT   The source of the condition is some software.

MM_FIRM   The source of the condition is some firmware.

A third component of the *classification* parameter to **fmtmsg** can describe the part of the system which detects the problem. This is done by using exactly one of the following values:

MM_APPL   The erroneous condition is detected by the application.

MM_UTIL   The erroneous condition is detected by a utility.

MM_OPSYS   The erroneous condition is detected by the operating system.

A last component of *classification* can signal the results of this message. Exactly one of the following values can be used:

MM_RECOVER
          It is a recoverable error.

MM_NRECOV
          It is a non-recoverable error.

int fmtmsg (*long int* **classification**, *const char* ***label**, *int*   [Function]
      severity, *const char* ***text**, *const char* ***action**, *const char* ***tag**)
      Preliminary: | MT-Safe | AS-Unsafe lock | AC-Safe | See Section 1.2.2.1 [POSIX Safety Concepts], page 2.

      Display a message described by its parameters on the device(s) specified in the *classification* parameter. The *label* parameter identifies the source of the message. The string should consist of two colon separated parts where the first part has not more than 10 and the second part not more than 14 characters. The *text* parameter describes the condition of the error, the *action* parameter possible steps to recover from the error and the *tag* parameter is a reference to the online documentation where more information can be found. It should contain the *label* value and a unique identification number.

Each of the parameters can be a special value which means this value is to be omitted. The symbolic names for these values are:

MM_NULLLBL

>Ignore *label* parameter.

MM_NULLSEV

>Ignore *severity* parameter.

MM_NULLMC

>Ignore *classification* parameter. This implies that nothing is actually printed.

MM_NULLTXT

>Ignore *text* parameter.

MM_NULLACT

>Ignore *action* parameter.

MM_NULLTAG

>Ignore *tag* parameter.

There is another way certain fields can be omitted from the output to standard error. This is described below in the description of environment variables influencing the behavior.

The *severity* parameter can have one of the values in the following table:

MM_NOSEV Nothing is printed, this value is the same as MM_NULLSEV.

MM_HALT This value is printed as HALT.

MM_ERROR This value is printed as ERROR.

MM_WARNING

>This value is printed as WARNING.

MM_INFO This value is printed as INFO.

The numeric value of these five macros are between 0 and 4. Using the environment variable SEV_LEVEL or using the **addseverity** function one can add more severity levels with their corresponding string to print. This is described below (see Section 12.22.2 [Adding Severity Classes], page 330).

If no parameter is ignored the output looks like this:

```
label: severity-string: text
TO FIX: action tag
```

The colons, new line characters and the **TO FIX** string are inserted if necessary, i.e., if the corresponding parameter is not ignored.

This function is specified in the X/Open Portability Guide. It is also available on all systems derived from System V.

The function returns the value MM_OK if no error occurred. If only the printing to standard error failed, it returns MM_NOMSG. If printing to the console fails, it returns MM_NOCON. If nothing is printed MM_NOTOK is returned. Among situations where all outputs fail this last value is also returned if a parameter value is incorrect.

There are two environment variables which influence the behavior of **fmtmsg**. The first is MSGVERB. It is used to control the output actually happening on standard error (*not* the console output). Each of the five fields can explicitly be enabled. To do this the user has to put the MSGVERB variable with a format like the following in the environment before calling the **fmtmsg** function the first time:

```
MSGVERB=keyword[:keyword[:...]]
```

Valid *keyword*s are **label**, **severity**, **text**, **action**, and **tag**. If the environment variable is not given or is the empty string, a not supported keyword is given or the value is somehow else invalid, no part of the message is masked out.

The second environment variable which influences the behavior of **fmtmsg** is SEV_LEVEL. This variable and the change in the behavior of **fmtmsg** is not specified in the X/Open Portability Guide. It is available in System V systems, though. It can be used to introduce new severity levels. By default, only the five severity levels described above are available. Any other numeric value would make **fmtmsg** print nothing.

If the user puts SEV_LEVEL with a format like

```
SEV_LEVEL=[description[:description[:...]]]
```

in the environment of the process before the first call to **fmtmsg**, where *description* has a value of the form

```
severity-keyword,level,printstring
```

The *severity-keyword* part is not used by **fmtmsg** but it has to be present. The *level* part is a string representation of a number. The numeric value must be a number greater than 4. This value must be used in the *severity* parameter of **fmtmsg** to select this class. It is not possible to overwrite any of the predefined classes. The *printstring* is the string printed when a message of this class is processed by **fmtmsg** (see above, **fmtsmg** does not print the numeric value but instead the string representation).

12.22.2 Adding Severity Classes

There is another possibility to introduce severity classes besides using the environment variable SEV_LEVEL. This simplifies the task of introducing new classes in a running program. One could use the **setenv** or **putenv** function to set the environment variable, but this is toilsome.

int addseverity (*int* **severity**, *const char* ***string**)   [Function]
    Preliminary: | MT-Safe | AS-Unsafe heap lock | AC-Unsafe lock mem | See Section 1.2.2.1 [POSIX Safety Concepts], page 2.

    This function allows the introduction of new severity classes which can be addressed by the *severity* parameter of the **fmtmsg** function. The *severity* parameter of **addseverity** must match the value for the parameter with the same name of **fmtmsg**, and *string* is the string printed in the actual messages instead of the numeric value.

    If *string* is NULL the severity class with the numeric value according to *severity* is removed.

    It is not possible to overwrite or remove one of the default severity classes. All calls to **addseverity** with *severity* set to one of the values for the default classes will fail.

The return value is `MM_OK` if the task was successfully performed. If the return value is `MM_NOTOK` something went wrong. This could mean that no more memory is available or a class is not available when it has to be removed.

This function is not specified in the X/Open Portability Guide although the `fmtsmg` function is. It is available on System V systems.

12.22.3 How to use `fmtmsg` and `addseverity`

Here is a simple example program to illustrate the use of both functions described in this section.

```
#include <fmtmsg.h>

int
main (void)
{
  addseverity (5, "NOTE2");
  fmtmsg (MM_PRINT, "only1field", MM_INFO, "text2", "action2", "tag2");
  fmtmsg (MM_PRINT, "UX:cat", 5, "invalid syntax", "refer to manual",
          "UX:cat:001");
  fmtmsg (MM_PRINT, "label:foo", 6, "text", "action", "tag");
  return 0;
}
```

The second call to `fmtmsg` illustrates a use of this function as it usually occurs on System V systems, which heavily use this function. It seems worthwhile to give a short explanation here of how this system works on System V. The value of the *label* field (`UX:cat`) says that the error occurred in the Unix program `cat`. The explanation of the error follows and the value for the *action* parameter is `"refer to manual"`. One could be more specific here, if necessary. The *tag* field contains, as proposed above, the value of the string given for the *label* parameter, and additionally a unique ID (`001` in this case). For a GNU environment this string could contain a reference to the corresponding node in the Info page for the program.

Running this program without specifying the `MSGVERB` and `SEV_LEVEL` function produces the following output:

```
UX:cat: NOTE2: invalid syntax
TO FIX: refer to manual UX:cat:001
```

We see the different fields of the message and how the extra glue (the colons and the `TO FIX` string) is printed. But only one of the three calls to `fmtmsg` produced output. The first call does not print anything because the *label* parameter is not in the correct form. The string must contain two fields, separated by a colon (see Section 12.22.1 [Printing Formatted Messages], page 328). The third `fmtmsg` call produced no output since the class with the numeric value 6 is not defined. Although a class with numeric value 5 is also not defined by default, the call to `addseverity` introduces it and the second call to `fmtmsg` produces the above output.

When we change the environment of the program to contain `SEV_LEVEL=XXX,6,NOTE` when running it we get a different result:

```
UX:cat: NOTE2: invalid syntax
TO FIX: refer to manual UX:cat:001
label:foo: NOTE: text
TO FIX: action tag
```

Now the third call to `fmtmsg` produced some output and we see how the string `NOTE` from the environment variable appears in the message.

Now we can reduce the output by specifying which fields we are interested in. If we additionally set the environment variable `MSGVERB` to the value `severity:label:action` we get the following output:

```
UX:cat: NOTE2
TO FIX: refer to manual
label:foo: NOTE
TO FIX: action
```

I.e., the output produced by the *text* and the *tag* parameters to `fmtmsg` vanished. Please also note that now there is no colon after the `NOTE` and `NOTE2` strings in the output. This is not necessary since there is no more output on this line because the text is missing.

13 Low-Level Input/Output

This chapter describes functions for performing low-level input/output operations on file descriptors. These functions include the primitives for the higher-level I/O functions described in Chapter 12 [Input/Output on Streams], page 257, as well as functions for performing low-level control operations for which there are no equivalents on streams.

Stream-level I/O is more flexible and usually more convenient; therefore, programmers generally use the descriptor-level functions only when necessary. These are some of the usual reasons:

- For reading binary files in large chunks.

- For reading an entire file into core before parsing it.

- To perform operations other than data transfer, which can only be done with a descriptor. (You can use `fileno` to get the descriptor corresponding to a stream.)

- To pass descriptors to a child process. (The child can create its own stream to use a descriptor that it inherits, but cannot inherit a stream directly.)

13.1 Opening and Closing Files

This section describes the primitives for opening and closing files using file descriptors. The `open` and `creat` functions are declared in the header file `fcntl.h`, while `close` is declared in `unistd.h`.

int **open** (*const char *filename, int flags*[, *mode_t mode*]) [Function]
Preliminary: | MT-Safe | AS-Safe | AC-Safe fd | See Section 1.2.2.1 [POSIX Safety Concepts], page 2.

The `open` function creates and returns a new file descriptor for the file named by *filename*. Initially, the file position indicator for the file is at the beginning of the file. The argument *mode* (see Section 14.9.5 [The Mode Bits for Access Permission], page 421) is used only when a file is created, but it doesn't hurt to supply the argument in any case.

The *flags* argument controls how the file is to be opened. This is a bit mask; you create the value by the bitwise OR of the appropriate parameters (using the '|' operator in C). See Section 13.14 [File Status Flags], page 375, for the parameters available.

The normal return value from `open` is a non-negative integer file descriptor. In the case of an error, a value of −1 is returned instead. In addition to the usual file name errors (see Section 11.2.3 [File Name Errors], page 255), the following `errno` error conditions are defined for this function:

EACCES   The file exists but is not readable/writable as requested by the *flags* argument, or the file does not exist and the directory is unwritable so it cannot be created.

EEXIST   Both `O_CREAT` and `O_EXCL` are set, and the named file already exists.

EINTR   The `open` operation was interrupted by a signal. See Section 24.5 [Primitives Interrupted by Signals], page 711.

EISDIR   The *flags* argument specified write access, and the file is a directory.

EMFILE   The process has too many files open. The maximum number of file descriptors is controlled by the `RLIMIT_NOFILE` resource limit; see Section 22.2 [Limiting Resource Usage], page 656.

ENFILE   The entire system, or perhaps the file system which contains the directory, cannot support any additional open files at the moment. (This problem cannot happen on GNU/Hurd systems.)

ENOENT   The named file does not exist, and `O_CREAT` is not specified.

ENOSPC   The directory or file system that would contain the new file cannot be extended, because there is no disk space left.

ENXIO   `O_NONBLOCK` and `O_WRONLY` are both set in the *flags* argument, the file named by *filename* is a FIFO (see Chapter 15 [Pipes and FIFOs], page 437), and no process has the file open for reading.

EROFS   The file resides on a read-only file system and any of `O_WRONLY`, `O_RDWR`, and `O_TRUNC` are set in the *flags* argument, or `O_CREAT` is set and the file does not already exist.

If on a 32 bit machine the sources are translated with `_FILE_OFFSET_BITS == 64` the function **open** returns a file descriptor opened in the large file mode which enables the file handling functions to use files up to 2^{63} bytes in size and offset from -2^{63} to 2^{63}. This happens transparently for the user since all of the low-level file handling functions are equally replaced.

This function is a cancellation point in multi-threaded programs. This is a problem if the thread allocates some resources (like memory, file descriptors, semaphores or whatever) at the time **open** is called. If the thread gets canceled these resources stay allocated until the program ends. To avoid this calls to **open** should be protected using cancellation handlers.

The **open** function is the underlying primitive for the **fopen** and **freopen** functions, that create streams.

int **open64** (*const char *filename, int flags*[, *mode_t mode*])   [Function]
Preliminary: | MT-Safe | AS-Safe | AC-Safe fd | See Section 1.2.2.1 [POSIX Safety Concepts], page 2.

This function is similar to **open**. It returns a file descriptor which can be used to access the file named by *filename*. The only difference is that on 32 bit systems the file is opened in the large file mode. I.e., file length and file offsets can exceed 31 bits.

When the sources are translated with `_FILE_OFFSET_BITS == 64` this function is actually available under the name **open**. I.e., the new, extended API using 64 bit file sizes and offsets transparently replaces the old API.

int **creat** (*const char *filename, mode_t mode*)   [Obsolete function]
Preliminary: | MT-Safe | AS-Safe | AC-Safe fd | See Section 1.2.2.1 [POSIX Safety Concepts], page 2.

This function is obsolete. The call:

```
creat (filename, mode)
```

is equivalent to:

```
open (filename, O_WRONLY | O_CREAT | O_TRUNC, mode)
```

If on a 32 bit machine the sources are translated with `_FILE_OFFSET_BITS == 64` the function `creat` returns a file descriptor opened in the large file mode which enables the file handling functions to use files up to 2^{63} in size and offset from -2^{63} to 2^{63}. This happens transparently for the user since all of the low-level file handling functions are equally replaced.

`int creat64 (const char *filename, mode_t mode)` [Obsolete function]
Preliminary: | MT-Safe | AS-Safe | AC-Safe fd | See Section 1.2.2.1 [POSIX Safety Concepts], page 2.

This function is similar to `creat`. It returns a file descriptor which can be used to access the file named by *filename*. The only difference is that on 32 bit systems the file is opened in the large file mode. I.e., file length and file offsets can exceed 31 bits.

To use this file descriptor one must not use the normal operations but instead the counterparts named *64, e.g., `read64`.

When the sources are translated with `_FILE_OFFSET_BITS == 64` this function is actually available under the name `open`. I.e., the new, extended API using 64 bit file sizes and offsets transparently replaces the old API.

`int close (int filedes)` [Function]
Preliminary: | MT-Safe | AS-Safe | AC-Safe fd | See Section 1.2.2.1 [POSIX Safety Concepts], page 2.

The function `close` closes the file descriptor *filedes*. Closing a file has the following consequences:

- The file descriptor is deallocated.

- Any record locks owned by the process on the file are unlocked.

- When all file descriptors associated with a pipe or FIFO have been closed, any unread data is discarded.

This function is a cancellation point in multi-threaded programs. This is a problem if the thread allocates some resources (like memory, file descriptors, semaphores or whatever) at the time `close` is called. If the thread gets canceled these resources stay allocated until the program ends. To avoid this, calls to `close` should be protected using cancellation handlers.

The normal return value from `close` is 0; a value of −1 is returned in case of failure. The following `errno` error conditions are defined for this function:

EBADF   The *filedes* argument is not a valid file descriptor.

EINTR   The `close` call was interrupted by a signal. See Section 24.5 [Primitives Interrupted by Signals], page 711. Here is an example of how to handle EINTR properly:

```
TEMP_FAILURE_RETRY (close (desc));
```

```
ENOSPC
EIO
EDQUOT      When the file is accessed by NFS, these errors from write can some-
            times not be detected until close. See Section 13.2 [Input and Output
            Primitives], page 336, for details on their meaning.
```

Please note that there is *no* separate `close64` function. This is not necessary since this function does not determine nor depend on the mode of the file. The kernel which performs the `close` operation knows which mode the descriptor is used for and can handle this situation.

To close a stream, call `fclose` (see Section 12.4 [Closing Streams], page 262) instead of trying to close its underlying file descriptor with `close`. This flushes any buffered output and updates the stream object to indicate that it is closed.

13.2 Input and Output Primitives

This section describes the functions for performing primitive input and output operations on file descriptors: `read`, `write`, and `lseek`. These functions are declared in the header file `unistd.h`.

`ssize_t`   [Data Type]
> This data type is used to represent the sizes of blocks that can be read or written in a single operation. It is similar to `size_t`, but must be a signed type.

`ssize_t read` (*int filedes, void *buffer, size_t size*)   [Function]
> Preliminary: | MT-Safe | AS-Safe | AC-Safe | See Section 1.2.2.1 [POSIX Safety Concepts], page 2.
>
> The `read` function reads up to *size* bytes from the file with descriptor *filedes*, storing the results in the *buffer*. (This is not necessarily a character string, and no terminating null character is added.)
>
> The return value is the number of bytes actually read. This might be less than *size*; for example, if there aren't that many bytes left in the file or if there aren't that many bytes immediately available. The exact behavior depends on what kind of file it is. Note that reading less than *size* bytes is not an error.
>
> A value of zero indicates end-of-file (except if the value of the *size* argument is also zero). This is not considered an error. If you keep calling `read` while at end-of-file, it will keep returning zero and doing nothing else.
>
> If `read` returns at least one character, there is no way you can tell whether end-of-file was reached. But if you did reach the end, the next read will return zero.
>
> In case of an error, `read` returns −1. The following `errno` error conditions are defined for this function:
>
> `EAGAIN`   Normally, when no input is immediately available, `read` waits for some input. But if the `O_NONBLOCK` flag is set for the file (see Section 13.14 [File Status Flags], page 375), `read` returns immediately without reading any data, and reports this error.

Compatibility Note: Most versions of BSD Unix use a different error code for this: `EWOULDBLOCK`. In the GNU C Library, `EWOULDBLOCK` is an alias for `EAGAIN`, so it doesn't matter which name you use.

On some systems, reading a large amount of data from a character special file can also fail with `EAGAIN` if the kernel cannot find enough physical memory to lock down the user's pages. This is limited to devices that transfer with direct memory access into the user's memory, which means it does not include terminals, since they always use separate buffers inside the kernel. This problem never happens on GNU/Hurd systems.

Any condition that could result in `EAGAIN` can instead result in a successful `read` which returns fewer bytes than requested. Calling `read` again immediately would result in `EAGAIN`.

EBADF
: The *filedes* argument is not a valid file descriptor, or is not open for reading.

EINTR
: `read` was interrupted by a signal while it was waiting for input. See Section 24.5 [Primitives Interrupted by Signals], page 711. A signal will not necessarily cause `read` to return `EINTR`; it may instead result in a successful `read` which returns fewer bytes than requested.

EIO
: For many devices, and for disk files, this error code indicates a hardware error.

    `EIO` also occurs when a background process tries to read from the controlling terminal, and the normal action of stopping the process by sending it a `SIGTTIN` signal isn't working. This might happen if the signal is being blocked or ignored, or because the process group is orphaned. See Chapter 28 [Job Control], page 786, for more information about job control, and Chapter 24 [Signal Handling], page 685, for information about signals.

EINVAL
: In some systems, when reading from a character or block device, position and size offsets must be aligned to a particular block size. This error indicates that the offsets were not properly aligned.

Please note that there is no function named `read64`. This is not necessary since this function does not directly modify or handle the possibly wide file offset. Since the kernel handles this state internally, the `read` function can be used for all cases.

This function is a cancellation point in multi-threaded programs. This is a problem if the thread allocates some resources (like memory, file descriptors, semaphores or whatever) at the time `read` is called. If the thread gets canceled these resources stay allocated until the program ends. To avoid this, calls to `read` should be protected using cancellation handlers.

The `read` function is the underlying primitive for all of the functions that read from streams, such as `fgetc`.

ssize_t pread (*int filedes, void *buffer, size_t size, off_t offset*)   [Function]

Preliminary: | MT-Safe | AS-Safe | AC-Safe | See Section 1.2.2.1 [POSIX Safety Concepts], page 2.

The **pread** function is similar to the **read** function. The first three arguments are identical, and the return values and error codes also correspond.

The difference is the fourth argument and its handling. The data block is not read from the current position of the file descriptor **filedes**. Instead the data is read from the file starting at position *offset*. The position of the file descriptor itself is not affected by the operation. The value is the same as before the call.

When the source file is compiled with _FILE_OFFSET_BITS == 64 the **pread** function is in fact **pread64** and the type **off_t** has 64 bits, which makes it possible to handle files up to 2^{63} bytes in length.

The return value of **pread** describes the number of bytes read. In the error case it returns -1 like **read** does and the error codes are also the same, with these additions:

EINVAL The value given for *offset* is negative and therefore illegal.

ESPIPE The file descriptor *filedes* is associated with a pipe or a FIFO and this device does not allow positioning of the file pointer.

The function is an extension defined in the Unix Single Specification version 2.

ssize_t **pread64** (*int* `filedes`, *void* `*buffer`, *size_t* `size`, *off64_t*   [Function]
  `offset`)
Preliminary: | MT-Safe | AS-Safe | AC-Safe | See Section 1.2.2.1 [POSIX Safety Concepts], page 2.

This function is similar to the **pread** function. The difference is that the *offset* parameter is of type **off64_t** instead of **off_t** which makes it possible on 32 bit machines to address files larger than 2^{31} bytes and up to 2^{63} bytes. The file descriptor **filedes** must be opened using **open64** since otherwise the large offsets possible with **off64_t** will lead to errors with a descriptor in small file mode.

When the source file is compiled with _FILE_OFFSET_BITS == 64 on a 32 bit machine this function is actually available under the name **pread** and so transparently replaces the 32 bit interface.

ssize_t **write** (*int* `filedes`, *const void* `*buffer`, *size_t* `size`)   [Function]
Preliminary: | MT-Safe | AS-Safe | AC-Safe | See Section 1.2.2.1 [POSIX Safety Concepts], page 2.

The **write** function writes up to *size* bytes from *buffer* to the file with descriptor *filedes*. The data in *buffer* is not necessarily a character string and a null character is output like any other character.

The return value is the number of bytes actually written. This may be *size*, but can always be smaller. Your program should always call **write** in a loop, iterating until all the data is written.

Once **write** returns, the data is enqueued to be written and can be read back right away, but it is not necessarily written out to permanent storage immediately. You can use **fsync** when you need to be sure your data has been permanently stored before continuing. (It is more efficient for the system to batch up consecutive writes and do them all at once when convenient. Normally they will always be written to disk within a minute or less.) Modern systems provide another function **fdatasync** which guarantees integrity only for the file data and is therefore faster. You can use the `O_FSYNC` open mode to make `write` always store the data to disk before returning; see Section 13.14.3 [I/O Operating Modes], page 378.

In the case of an error, `write` returns −1. The following `errno` error conditions are defined for this function:

`EAGAIN`   Normally, `write` blocks until the write operation is complete. But if the `O_NONBLOCK` flag is set for the file (see Section 13.11 [Control Operations on Files], page 371), it returns immediately without writing any data and reports this error. An example of a situation that might cause the process to block on output is writing to a terminal device that supports flow control, where output has been suspended by receipt of a STOP character.

   Compatibility Note: Most versions of BSD Unix use a different error code for this: EWOULDBLOCK. In the GNU C Library, EWOULDBLOCK is an alias for `EAGAIN`, so it doesn't matter which name you use.

   On some systems, writing a large amount of data from a character special file can also fail with `EAGAIN` if the kernel cannot find enough physical memory to lock down the user's pages. This is limited to devices that transfer with direct memory access into the user's memory, which means it does not include terminals, since they always use separate buffers inside the kernel. This problem does not arise on GNU/Hurd systems.

`EBADF`   The *filedes* argument is not a valid file descriptor, or is not open for writing.

`EFBIG`   The size of the file would become larger than the implementation can support.

`EINTR`   The `write` operation was interrupted by a signal while it was blocked waiting for completion. A signal will not necessarily cause `write` to return EINTR; it may instead result in a successful `write` which writes fewer bytes than requested. See Section 24.5 [Primitives Interrupted by Signals], page 711.

`EIO`   For many devices, and for disk files, this error code indicates a hardware error.

`ENOSPC`   The device containing the file is full.

`EPIPE`   This error is returned when you try to write to a pipe or FIFO that isn't open for reading by any process. When this happens, a `SIGPIPE` signal is also sent to the process; see Chapter 24 [Signal Handling], page 685.

`EINVAL`   In some systems, when writing to a character or block device, position and size offsets must be aligned to a particular block size. This error indicates that the offsets were not properly aligned.

Unless you have arranged to prevent `EINTR` failures, you should check `errno` after each failing call to `write`, and if the error was `EINTR`, you should simply repeat the call. See Section 24.5 [Primitives Interrupted by Signals], page 711. The easy way to do this is with the macro TEMP_FAILURE_RETRY, as follows:

```
nbytes = TEMP_FAILURE_RETRY (write (desc, buffer, count));
```

Please note that there is no function named write64. This is not necessary since this function does not directly modify or handle the possibly wide file offset. Since the kernel handles this state internally the write function can be used for all cases.

This function is a cancellation point in multi-threaded programs. This is a problem if the thread allocates some resources (like memory, file descriptors, semaphores or whatever) at the time write is called. If the thread gets canceled these resources stay allocated until the program ends. To avoid this, calls to write should be protected using cancellation handlers.

The write function is the underlying primitive for all of the functions that write to streams, such as fputc.

ssize_t pwrite (*int filedes*, *const void *buffer*, *size_t size*, *off_t*   [Function]
    offset)
Preliminary: | MT-Safe | AS-Safe | AC-Safe | See Section 1.2.2.1 [POSIX Safety Concepts], page 2.

The pwrite function is similar to the write function. The first three arguments are identical, and the return values and error codes also correspond.

The difference is the fourth argument and its handling. The data block is not written to the current position of the file descriptor filedes. Instead the data is written to the file starting at position *offset*. The position of the file descriptor itself is not affected by the operation. The value is the same as before the call.

However, on Linux, if a file is opened with O_APPEND, pwrite appends data to the end of the file, regardless of the value of offset.

When the source file is compiled with _FILE_OFFSET_BITS == 64 the pwrite function is in fact pwrite64 and the type off_t has 64 bits, which makes it possible to handle files up to 2^{63} bytes in length.

The return value of pwrite describes the number of written bytes. In the error case it returns -1 like write does and the error codes are also the same, with these additions:

EINVAL   The value given for *offset* is negative and therefore illegal.

ESPIPE   The file descriptor *filedes* is associated with a pipe or a FIFO and this device does not allow positioning of the file pointer.

The function is an extension defined in the Unix Single Specification version 2.

ssize_t pwrite64 (*int filedes*, *const void *buffer*, *size_t size*,   [Function]
    off64_t offset)
Preliminary: | MT-Safe | AS-Safe | AC-Safe | See Section 1.2.2.1 [POSIX Safety Concepts], page 2.

This function is similar to the pwrite function. The difference is that the *offset* parameter is of type off64_t instead of off_t which makes it possible on 32 bit machines to address files larger than 2^{31} bytes and up to 2^{63} bytes. The file descriptor filedes must be opened using open64 since otherwise the large offsets possible with off64_t will lead to errors with a descriptor in small file mode.

When the source file is compiled using _FILE_OFFSET_BITS == 64 on a 32 bit machine this function is actually available under the name pwrite and so transparently replaces the 32 bit interface.

ssize_t preadv (*int* **fd**, *const struct iovec* ***iov**, *int* **iovcnt**, *off_t*   [Function]
     offset)

Preliminary: | MT-Safe | AS-Safe | AC-Safe | See Section 1.2.2.1 [POSIX Safety Concepts], page 2.

This function is similar to the **readv** function, with the difference it adds an extra *offset* parameter of type off_t similar to **pread**. The data is written to the file starting at position *offset*. The position of the file descriptor itself is not affected by the operation. The value is the same as before the call.

When the source file is compiled with _FILE_OFFSET_BITS == 64 the **preadv** function is in fact **preadv64** and the type off_t has 64 bits, which makes it possible to handle files up to 2^{63} bytes in length.

The return value is a count of bytes (*not* buffers) read, 0 indicating end-of-file, or -1 indicating an error. The possible errors are the same as in **readv** and **pread**.

ssize_t preadv64 (*int* **fd**, *const struct iovec* ***iov**, *int* **iovcnt**,   [Function]
     off64_t **offset**)

Preliminary: | MT-Safe | AS-Safe | AC-Safe | See Section 1.2.2.1 [POSIX Safety Concepts], page 2.

This function is similar to the **preadv** function with the difference is that the *offset* parameter is of type off64_t instead of off_t. It makes it possible on 32 bit machines to address files larger than 2^{31} bytes and up to 2^{63} bytes. The file descriptor filedes must be opened using open64 since otherwise the large offsets possible with off64_t will lead to errors with a descriptor in small file mode.

When the source file is compiled using _FILE_OFFSET_BITS == 64 on a 32 bit machine this function is actually available under the name **preadv** and so transparently replaces the 32 bit interface.

ssize_t pwritev (*int* **fd**, *const struct iovec* ***iov**, *int* **iovcnt**, *off_t*   [Function]
     offset)

Preliminary: | MT-Safe | AS-Safe | AC-Safe | See Section 1.2.2.1 [POSIX Safety Concepts], page 2.

This function is similar to the **writev** function, with the difference it adds an extra *offset* parameter of type off_t similar to **pwrite**. The data is written to the file starting at position *offset*. The position of the file descriptor itself is not affected by the operation. The value is the same as before the call.

However, on Linux, if a file is opened with O_APPEND, **pwrite** appends data to the end of the file, regardless of the value of offset.

When the source file is compiled with _FILE_OFFSET_BITS == 64 the **pwritev** function is in fact **pwritev64** and the type off_t has 64 bits, which makes it possible to handle files up to 2^{63} bytes in length.

The return value is a count of bytes (*not* buffers) written, 0 indicating end-of-file, or -1 indicating an error. The possible errors are the same as in writev and pwrite.

ssize_t pwritev64 (*int fd, const struct iovec *iov, int iovcnt,*   [Function]
    off64_t offset)

Preliminary: | MT-Safe | AS-Safe | AC-Safe | See Section 1.2.2.1 [POSIX Safety Concepts], page 2.

This function is similar to the pwritev function with the difference is that the *offset* parameter is of type off64_t instead of off_t. It makes it possible on 32 bit machines to address files larger than 2^{31} bytes and up to 2^{63} bytes. The file descriptor filedes must be opened using open64 since otherwise the large offsets possible with off64_t will lead to errors with a descriptor in small file mode.

When the source file is compiled using _FILE_OFFSET_BITS == 64 on a 32 bit machine this function is actually available under the name pwritev and so transparently replaces the 32 bit interface.

ssize_t preadv2 (*int fd, const struct iovec *iov, int iovcnt, off_t*   [Function]
    offset, int flags)

Preliminary: | MT-Safe | AS-Safe | AC-Safe | See Section 1.2.2.1 [POSIX Safety Concepts], page 2.

This function is similar to the preadv function, with the difference it adds an extra *flags* parameter of type int. The supported *flags* are dependent of the underlying system. For Linux it supports:

RWF_HIPRI
>High priority request. This adds a flag that tells the file system that this is a high priority request for which it is worth to poll the hardware. The flag is purely advisory and can be ignored if not supported. The *fd* must be opened using O_DIRECT.

RWF_DSYNC
>Per-IO synchronization as if the file was opened with O_DSYNC flag.

RWF_SYNC   Per-IO synchronization as if the file was opened with O_SYNC flag.

RWF_NOWAIT
>Use nonblocking mode for this operation; that is, this call to preadv2 will fail and set errno to EAGAIN if the operation would block.

When the source file is compiled with _FILE_OFFSET_BITS == 64 the preadv2 function is in fact preadv64v2 and the type off_t has 64 bits, which makes it possible to handle files up to 2^{63} bytes in length.

The return value is a count of bytes (*not* buffers) read, 0 indicating end-of-file, or -1 indicating an error. The possible errors are the same as in preadv with the addition of:

EOPNOTSUPP
>An unsupported *flags* was used.

`ssize_t preadv64v2 (int fd, const struct iovec *iov, int iovcnt,` [Function]
    `off64_t offset, int flags)`

Preliminary: | MT-Safe | AS-Safe | AC-Safe | See Section 1.2.2.1 [POSIX Safety Concepts], page 2.

This function is similar to the `preadv2` function with the difference is that the *offset* parameter is of type `off64_t` instead of `off_t`. It makes it possible on 32 bit machines to address files larger than 2^{31} bytes and up to 2^{63} bytes. The file descriptor `filedes` must be opened using `open64` since otherwise the large offsets possible with `off64_t` will lead to errors with a descriptor in small file mode.

When the source file is compiled using `_FILE_OFFSET_BITS == 64` on a 32 bit machine this function is actually available under the name `preadv2` and so transparently replaces the 32 bit interface.

`ssize_t pwritev2 (int fd, const struct iovec *iov, int iovcnt, off_t` [Function]
    `offset, int flags)`

Preliminary: | MT-Safe | AS-Safe | AC-Safe | See Section 1.2.2.1 [POSIX Safety Concepts], page 2.

This function is similar to the `pwritev` function, with the difference it adds an extra *flags* parameter of type `int`. The supported *flags* are dependent of the underlying system and for Linux it supports the same ones as for `preadv2`.

When the source file is compiled with `_FILE_OFFSET_BITS == 64` the `pwritev2` function is in fact `pwritev64v2` and the type `off_t` has 64 bits, which makes it possible to handle files up to 2^{63} bytes in length.

The return value is a count of bytes (*not* buffers) write, 0 indicating end-of-file, or −1 indicating an error. The possible errors are the same as in `preadv2`.

`ssize_t pwritev64v2 (int fd, const struct iovec *iov, int iovcnt,` [Function]
    `off64_t offset, int flags)`

Preliminary: | MT-Safe | AS-Safe | AC-Safe | See Section 1.2.2.1 [POSIX Safety Concepts], page 2.

This function is similar to the `pwritev2` function with the difference is that the *offset* parameter is of type `off64_t` instead of `off_t`. It makes it possible on 32 bit machines to address files larger than 2^{31} bytes and up to 2^{63} bytes. The file descriptor `filedes` must be opened using `open64` since otherwise the large offsets possible with `off64_t` will lead to errors with a descriptor in small file mode.

When the source file is compiled using `_FILE_OFFSET_BITS == 64` on a 32 bit machine this function is actually available under the name `pwritev2` and so transparently replaces the 32 bit interface.

13.3 Setting the File Position of a Descriptor

Just as you can set the file position of a stream with `fseek`, you can set the file position of a descriptor with `lseek`. This specifies the position in the file for the next `read` or `write` operation. See Section 12.18 [File Positioning], page 314, for more information on the file position and what it means.

To read the current file position value from a descriptor, use `lseek (desc, 0, SEEK_CUR)`.

`off_t lseek (int filedes, off_t offset, int whence)` [Function]

Preliminary: | MT-Safe | AS-Safe | AC-Safe | See Section 1.2.2.1 [POSIX Safety Concepts], page 2.

The `lseek` function is used to change the file position of the file with descriptor *filedes*.

The *whence* argument specifies how the *offset* should be interpreted, in the same way as for the `fseek` function, and it must be one of the symbolic constants `SEEK_SET`, `SEEK_CUR`, or `SEEK_END`.

`SEEK_SET`   Specifies that *offset* is a count of characters from the beginning of the file.

`SEEK_CUR`   Specifies that *offset* is a count of characters from the current file position. This count may be positive or negative.

`SEEK_END`   Specifies that *offset* is a count of characters from the end of the file. A negative count specifies a position within the current extent of the file; a positive count specifies a position past the current end. If you set the position past the current end, and actually write data, you will extend the file with zeros up to that position.

The return value from `lseek` is normally the resulting file position, measured in bytes from the beginning of the file. You can use this feature together with `SEEK_CUR` to read the current file position.

If you want to append to the file, setting the file position to the current end of file with `SEEK_END` is not sufficient. Another process may write more data after you seek but before you write, extending the file so the position you write onto clobbers their data. Instead, use the `O_APPEND` operating mode; see Section 13.14.3 [I/O Operating Modes], page 378.

You can set the file position past the current end of the file. This does not by itself make the file longer; `lseek` never changes the file. But subsequent output at that position will extend the file. Characters between the previous end of file and the new position are filled with zeros. Extending the file in this way can create a "hole": the blocks of zeros are not actually allocated on disk, so the file takes up less space than it appears to; it is then called a "sparse file".

If the file position cannot be changed, or the operation is in some way invalid, `lseek` returns a value of −1. The following `errno` error conditions are defined for this function:

`EBADF`   The *filedes* is not a valid file descriptor.

`EINVAL`   The *whence* argument value is not valid, or the resulting file offset is not valid. A file offset is invalid.

`ESPIPE`   The *filedes* corresponds to an object that cannot be positioned, such as a pipe, FIFO or terminal device. (POSIX.1 specifies this error only for pipes and FIFOs, but on GNU systems, you always get `ESPIPE` if the object is not seekable.)

When the source file is compiled with `_FILE_OFFSET_BITS == 64` the `lseek` function is in fact `lseek64` and the type `off_t` has 64 bits which makes it possible to handle files up to 2^{63} bytes in length.

This function is a cancellation point in multi-threaded programs. This is a problem if the thread allocates some resources (like memory, file descriptors, semaphores or whatever) at the time `lseek` is called. If the thread gets canceled these resources stay allocated until the program ends. To avoid this calls to `lseek` should be protected using cancellation handlers.

The `lseek` function is the underlying primitive for the `fseek`, `fseeko`, `ftell`, `ftello` and `rewind` functions, which operate on streams instead of file descriptors.

off64_t lseek64 (*int filedes, off64_t offset, int whence*)   [Function]
Preliminary: | MT-Safe | AS-Safe | AC-Safe | See Section 1.2.2.1 [POSIX Safety Concepts], page 2.

This function is similar to the `lseek` function. The difference is that the *offset* parameter is of type `off64_t` instead of `off_t` which makes it possible on 32 bit machines to address files larger than 2^{31} bytes and up to 2^{63} bytes. The file descriptor `filedes` must be opened using `open64` since otherwise the large offsets possible with `off64_t` will lead to errors with a descriptor in small file mode.

When the source file is compiled with `_FILE_OFFSET_BITS == 64` on a 32 bits machine this function is actually available under the name `lseek` and so transparently replaces the 32 bit interface.

You can have multiple descriptors for the same file if you open the file more than once, or if you duplicate a descriptor with `dup`. Descriptors that come from separate calls to `open` have independent file positions; using `lseek` on one descriptor has no effect on the other. For example,

```
{
  int d1, d2;
  char buf[4];
  d1 = open ("foo", O_RDONLY);
  d2 = open ("foo", O_RDONLY);
  lseek (d1, 1024, SEEK_SET);
  read (d2, buf, 4);
}
```

will read the first four characters of the file `foo`. (The error-checking code necessary for a real program has been omitted here for brevity.)

By contrast, descriptors made by duplication share a common file position with the original descriptor that was duplicated. Anything which alters the file position of one of the duplicates, including reading or writing data, affects all of them alike. Thus, for example,

```
{
  int d1, d2, d3;
  char buf1[4], buf2[4];
  d1 = open ("foo", O_RDONLY);
  d2 = dup (d1);
  d3 = dup (d2);
  lseek (d3, 1024, SEEK_SET);
  read (d1, buf1, 4);
  read (d2, buf2, 4);
}
```

will read four characters starting with the 1024'th character of `foo`, and then four more characters starting with the 1028'th character.

`off_t`   [Data Type]

> This is a signed integer type used to represent file sizes. In the GNU C Library, this type is no narrower than `int`.
>
> If the source is compiled with `_FILE_OFFSET_BITS == 64` this type is transparently replaced by `off64_t`.

`off64_t`   [Data Type]

> This type is used similar to `off_t`. The difference is that even on 32 bit machines, where the `off_t` type would have 32 bits, `off64_t` has 64 bits and so is able to address files up to 2^{63} bytes in length.
>
> When compiling with `_FILE_OFFSET_BITS == 64` this type is available under the name `off_t`.

These aliases for the 'SEEK_...' constants exist for the sake of compatibility with older BSD systems. They are defined in two different header files: `fcntl.h` and `sys/file.h`.

`L_SET`   An alias for `SEEK_SET`.

`L_INCR`   An alias for `SEEK_CUR`.

`L_XTND`   An alias for `SEEK_END`.

13.4 Descriptors and Streams

Given an open file descriptor, you can create a stream for it with the `fdopen` function. You can get the underlying file descriptor for an existing stream with the `fileno` function. These functions are declared in the header file `stdio.h`.

`FILE * fdopen (int filedes, const char *opentype)`   [Function]

> Preliminary: | MT-Safe | AS-Unsafe heap lock | AC-Unsafe mem lock | See Section 1.2.2.1 [POSIX Safety Concepts], page 2.
>
> The `fdopen` function returns a new stream for the file descriptor *filedes*.
>
> The *opentype* argument is interpreted in the same way as for the `fopen` function (see Section 12.3 [Opening Streams], page 258), except that the 'b' option is not permitted; this is because GNU systems make no distinction between text and binary files. Also, `"w"` and `"w+"` do not cause truncation of the file; these have an effect only when opening a file, and in this case the file has already been opened. You must make sure that the *opentype* argument matches the actual mode of the open file descriptor.
>
> The return value is the new stream. If the stream cannot be created (for example, if the modes for the file indicated by the file descriptor do not permit the access specified by the *opentype* argument), a null pointer is returned instead.
>
> In some other systems, `fdopen` may fail to detect that the modes for file descriptors do not permit the access specified by `opentype`. The GNU C Library always checks for this.

For an example showing the use of the `fdopen` function, see Section 15.1 [Creating a Pipe], page 437.

`int fileno (FILE *stream)` [Function]

> Preliminary: | MT-Safe | AS-Safe | AC-Safe | See Section 1.2.2.1 [POSIX Safety Concepts], page 2.
>
> This function returns the file descriptor associated with the stream *stream*. If an error is detected (for example, if the *stream* is not valid) or if *stream* does not do I/O to a file, `fileno` returns −1.

`int fileno_unlocked (FILE *stream)` [Function]

> Preliminary: | MT-Safe | AS-Safe | AC-Safe | See Section 1.2.2.1 [POSIX Safety Concepts], page 2.
>
> The `fileno_unlocked` function is equivalent to the `fileno` function except that it does not implicitly lock the stream if the state is `FSETLOCKING_INTERNAL`.
>
> This function is a GNU extension.

There are also symbolic constants defined in `unistd.h` for the file descriptors belonging to the standard streams `stdin`, `stdout`, and `stderr`; see Section 12.2 [Standard Streams], page 257.

`STDIN_FILENO`

> This macro has value 0, which is the file descriptor for standard input.

`STDOUT_FILENO`

> This macro has value 1, which is the file descriptor for standard output.

`STDERR_FILENO`

> This macro has value 2, which is the file descriptor for standard error output.

13.5 Dangers of Mixing Streams and Descriptors

You can have multiple file descriptors and streams (let's call both streams and descriptors "channels" for short) connected to the same file, but you must take care to avoid confusion between channels. There are two cases to consider: *linked* channels that share a single file position value, and *independent* channels that have their own file positions.

It's best to use just one channel in your program for actual data transfer to any given file, except when all the access is for input. For example, if you open a pipe (something you can only do at the file descriptor level), either do all I/O with the descriptor, or construct a stream from the descriptor with `fdopen` and then do all I/O with the stream.

13.5.1 Linked Channels

Channels that come from a single opening share the same file position; we call them *linked* channels. Linked channels result when you make a stream from a descriptor using `fdopen`, when you get a descriptor from a stream with `fileno`, when you copy a descriptor with `dup` or `dup2`, and when descriptors are inherited during `fork`. For files that don't support random access, such as terminals and pipes, *all* channels are effectively linked. On random-access files, all append-type output streams are effectively linked to each other.

If you have been using a stream for I/O (or have just opened the stream), and you want to do I/O using another channel (either a stream or a descriptor) that is linked to it, you must first *clean up* the stream that you have been using. See Section 13.5.3 [Cleaning Streams], page 348.

Terminating a process, or executing a new program in the process, destroys all the streams in the process. If descriptors linked to these streams persist in other processes, their file positions become undefined as a result. To prevent this, you must clean up the streams before destroying them.

13.5.2 Independent Channels

When you open channels (streams or descriptors) separately on a seekable file, each channel has its own file position. These are called *independent channels*.

The system handles each channel independently. Most of the time, this is quite predictable and natural (especially for input): each channel can read or write sequentially at its own place in the file. However, if some of the channels are streams, you must take these precautions:

- You should clean an output stream after use, before doing anything else that might read or write from the same part of the file.

- You should clean an input stream before reading data that may have been modified using an independent channel. Otherwise, you might read obsolete data that had been in the stream's buffer.

If you do output to one channel at the end of the file, this will certainly leave the other independent channels positioned somewhere before the new end. You cannot reliably set their file positions to the new end of file before writing, because the file can always be extended by another process between when you set the file position and when you write the data. Instead, use an append-type descriptor or stream; they always output at the current end of the file. In order to make the end-of-file position accurate, you must clean the output channel you were using, if it is a stream.

It's impossible for two channels to have separate file pointers for a file that doesn't support random access. Thus, channels for reading or writing such files are always linked, never independent. Append-type channels are also always linked. For these channels, follow the rules for linked channels; see Section 13.5.1 [Linked Channels], page 347.

13.5.3 Cleaning Streams

You can use `fflush` to clean a stream in most cases.

You can skip the `fflush` if you know the stream is already clean. A stream is clean whenever its buffer is empty. For example, an unbuffered stream is always clean. An input stream that is at end-of-file is clean. A line-buffered stream is clean when the last character output was a newline. However, a just-opened input stream might not be clean, as its input buffer might not be empty.

There is one case in which cleaning a stream is impossible on most systems. This is when the stream is doing input from a file that is not random-access. Such streams typically read ahead, and when the file is not random access, there is no way to give back the excess data already read. When an input stream reads from a random-access file, `fflush` does clean the stream, but leaves the file pointer at an unpredictable place; you must set the file pointer before doing any further I/O.

Closing an output-only stream also does `fflush`, so this is a valid way of cleaning an output stream.

You need not clean a stream before using its descriptor for control operations such as setting terminal modes; these operations don't affect the file position and are not affected by it. You can use any descriptor for these operations, and all channels are affected simultaneously. However, text already "output" to a stream but still buffered by the stream will be subject to the new terminal modes when subsequently flushed. To make sure "past" output is covered by the terminal settings that were in effect at the time, flush the output streams for that terminal before setting the modes. See Section 17.4 [Terminal Modes], page 492.

13.6 Fast Scatter-Gather I/O

Some applications may need to read or write data to multiple buffers, which are separated in memory. Although this can be done easily enough with multiple calls to `read` and `write`, it is inefficient because there is overhead associated with each kernel call.

Instead, many platforms provide special high-speed primitives to perform these *scatter-gather* operations in a single kernel call. The GNU C Library will provide an emulation on any system that lacks these primitives, so they are not a portability threat. They are defined in `sys/uio.h`.

These functions are controlled with arrays of `iovec` structures, which describe the location and size of each buffer.

`struct iovec`   [Data Type]
>   The `iovec` structure describes a buffer. It contains two fields:
>
>   `void *iov_base`
>>   Contains the address of a buffer.
>
>   `size_t iov_len`
>>   Contains the length of the buffer.

`ssize_t readv (int filedes, const struct iovec *vector, int count)`   [Function]
>   Preliminary: | MT-Safe | AS-Unsafe heap | AC-Unsafe mem | See Section 1.2.2.1 [POSIX Safety Concepts], page 2.
>
>   The `readv` function reads data from *filedes* and scatters it into the buffers described in *vector*, which is taken to be *count* structures long. As each buffer is filled, data is sent to the next.
>
>   Note that `readv` is not guaranteed to fill all the buffers. It may stop at any point, for the same reasons `read` would.
>
>   The return value is a count of bytes (*not* buffers) read, 0 indicating end-of-file, or −1 indicating an error. The possible errors are the same as in `read`.

`ssize_t writev (int filedes, const struct iovec *vector, int count)`   [Function]
>   Preliminary: | MT-Safe | AS-Unsafe heap | AC-Unsafe mem | See Section 1.2.2.1 [POSIX Safety Concepts], page 2.
>
>   The `writev` function gathers data from the buffers described in *vector*, which is taken to be *count* structures long, and writes them to *filedes*. As each buffer is written, it moves on to the next.
>
>   Like `readv`, `writev` may stop midstream under the same conditions `write` would.
>
>   The return value is a count of bytes written, or −1 indicating an error. The possible errors are the same as in `write`.

Note that if the buffers are small (under about 1kB), high-level streams may be easier to use than these functions. However, `readv` and `writev` are more efficient when the individual buffers themselves (as opposed to the total output), are large. In that case, a high-level stream would not be able to cache the data efficiently.

13.7 Memory-mapped I/O

On modern operating systems, it is possible to *mmap* (pronounced "em-map") a file to a region of memory. When this is done, the file can be accessed just like an array in the program.

This is more efficient than `read` or `write`, as only the regions of the file that a program actually accesses are loaded. Accesses to not-yet-loaded parts of the mmapped region are handled in the same way as swapped out pages.

Since mmapped pages can be stored back to their file when physical memory is low, it is possible to mmap files orders of magnitude larger than both the physical memory *and* swap space. The only limit is address space. The theoretical limit is 4GB on a 32-bit machine - however, the actual limit will be smaller since some areas will be reserved for other purposes. If the LFS interface is used the file size on 32-bit systems is not limited to 2GB (offsets are signed which reduces the addressable area of 4GB by half); the full 64-bit are available.

Memory mapping only works on entire pages of memory. Thus, addresses for mapping must be page-aligned, and length values will be rounded up. To determine the size of a page the machine uses one should use

```
size_t page_size = (size_t) sysconf (_SC_PAGESIZE);
```

These functions are declared in `sys/mman.h`.

---

void * mmap (*void *address, size_t length, int protect, int flags,*   [Function]
    int filedes, off_t offset)

Preliminary: | MT-Safe | AS-Safe | AC-Safe | See Section 1.2.2.1 [POSIX Safety Concepts], page 2.

The `mmap` function creates a new mapping, connected to bytes (*offset*) to (*offset* + *length* - 1) in the file open on *filedes*. A new reference for the file specified by *filedes* is created, which is not removed by closing the file.

address gives a preferred starting address for the mapping. `NULL` expresses no preference. Any previous mapping at that address is automatically removed. The address you give may still be changed, unless you use the `MAP_FIXED` flag.

protect contains flags that control what kind of access is permitted. They include `PROT_READ`, `PROT_WRITE`, and `PROT_EXEC`, which permit reading, writing, and execution, respectively. Inappropriate access will cause a segfault (see Section 24.2.1 [Program Error Signals], page 687).

Note that most hardware designs cannot support write permission without read permission, and many do not distinguish read and execute permission. Thus, you may receive wider permissions than you ask for, and mappings of write-only files may be denied even if you do not use `PROT_READ`.

flags contains flags that control the nature of the map. One of `MAP_SHARED` or `MAP_PRIVATE` must be specified.

They include:

MAP_PRIVATE

> This specifies that writes to the region should never be written back to the attached file. Instead, a copy is made for the process, and the region will be swapped normally if memory runs low. No other process will see the changes.

> Since private mappings effectively revert to ordinary memory when written to, you must have enough virtual memory for a copy of the entire mmapped region if you use this mode with PROT_WRITE.

MAP_SHARED

> This specifies that writes to the region will be written back to the file. Changes made will be shared immediately with other processes mmaping the same file.

> Note that actual writing may take place at any time. You need to use msync, described below, if it is important that other processes using conventional I/O get a consistent view of the file.

MAP_FIXED

> This forces the system to use the exact mapping address specified in *address* and fail if it can't.

MAP_ANONYMOUS
MAP_ANON   This flag tells the system to create an anonymous mapping, not connected to a file. *filedes* and *offset* are ignored, and the region is initialized with zeros.

> Anonymous maps are used as the basic primitive to extend the heap on some systems. They are also useful to share data between multiple tasks without creating a file.

> On some systems using private anonymous mmaps is more efficient than using malloc for large blocks. This is not an issue with the GNU C Library, as the included malloc automatically uses mmap where appropriate.

mmap returns the address of the new mapping, or MAP_FAILED for an error.

Possible errors include:

EINVAL

> Either *address* was unusable, or inconsistent *flags* were given.

EACCES

> *filedes* was not open for the type of access specified in *protect*.

ENOMEM

> Either there is not enough memory for the operation, or the process is out of address space.

ENODEV

> This file is of a type that doesn't support mapping.

ENOEXEC

> The file is on a filesystem that doesn't support mapping.

void * mmap64 (*void *address*, *size_t length*, *int protect*, *int*   [Function]
      flags, *int filedes*, *off64_t offset*)
Preliminary: | MT-Safe | AS-Safe | AC-Safe | See Section 1.2.2.1 [POSIX Safety
Concepts], page 2.

The mmap64 function is equivalent to the mmap function but the *offset* parameter is
of type off64_t. On 32-bit systems this allows the file associated with the *filedes*
descriptor to be larger than 2GB. *filedes* must be a descriptor returned from a call to
open64 or fopen64 and freopen64 where the descriptor is retrieved with fileno.

When the sources are translated with _FILE_OFFSET_BITS == 64 this function is actually available under the name mmap. I.e., the new, extended API using 64 bit file
sizes and offsets transparently replaces the old API.

int munmap (*void *addr*, *size_t length*)   [Function]
Preliminary: | MT-Safe | AS-Safe | AC-Safe | See Section 1.2.2.1 [POSIX Safety
Concepts], page 2.

munmap removes any memory maps from (*addr*) to (*addr* + *length*). *length* should be
the length of the mapping.

It is safe to unmap multiple mappings in one command, or include unmapped space
in the range. It is also possible to unmap only part of an existing mapping. However,
only entire pages can be removed. If *length* is not an even number of pages, it will
be rounded up.

It returns 0 for success and −1 for an error.

One error is possible:

EINVAL   The memory range given was outside the user mmap range or wasn't page
          aligned.

int msync (*void *address*, *size_t length*, *int flags*)   [Function]
Preliminary: | MT-Safe | AS-Safe | AC-Safe | See Section 1.2.2.1 [POSIX Safety
Concepts], page 2.

When using shared mappings, the kernel can write the file at any time before the
mapping is removed. To be certain data has actually been written to the file and will
be accessible to non-memory-mapped I/O, it is necessary to use this function.

It operates on the region *address* to (*address* + *length*). It may be used on part of
a mapping or multiple mappings, however the region given should not contain any
unmapped space.

flags can contain some options:

MS_SYNC

> This flag makes sure the data is actually written *to disk*. Normally msync
> only makes sure that accesses to a file with conventional I/O reflect the
> recent changes.

MS_ASYNC

> This tells msync to begin the synchronization, but not to wait for it to complete.

msync returns 0 for success and −1 for error. Errors include:

EINVAL   An invalid region was given, or the *flags* were invalid.

EFAULT   There is no existing mapping in at least part of the given region.

void * mremap (*void *address, size_t length, size_t new_length,*   [Function]
     int flag)

Preliminary: | MT-Safe | AS-Safe | AC-Safe | See Section 1.2.2.1 [POSIX Safety Concepts], page 2.

This function can be used to change the size of an existing memory area. *address* and *length* must cover a region entirely mapped in the same mmap statement. A new mapping with the same characteristics will be returned with the length *new_length*.

One option is possible, MREMAP_MAYMOVE. If it is given in *flags*, the system may remove the existing mapping and create a new one of the desired length in another location.

The address of the resulting mapping is returned, or −1. Possible error codes include:

EFAULT   There is no existing mapping in at least part of the original region, or the region covers two or more distinct mappings.

EINVAL   The address given is misaligned or inappropriate.

EAGAIN   The region has pages locked, and if extended it would exceed the process's resource limit for locked pages. See Section 22.2 [Limiting Resource Usage], page 656.

ENOMEM   The region is private writable, and insufficient virtual memory is available to extend it. Also, this error will occur if MREMAP_MAYMOVE is not given and the extension would collide with another mapped region.

This function is only available on a few systems. Except for performing optional optimizations one should not rely on this function.

Not all file descriptors may be mapped. Sockets, pipes, and most devices only allow sequential access and do not fit into the mapping abstraction. In addition, some regular files may not be mmapable, and older kernels may not support mapping at all. Thus, programs using mmap should have a fallback method to use should it fail. See Section "Mmap" in *GNU Coding Standards*.

int madvise (*void *addr, size_t length, int advice*)   [Function]
Preliminary: | MT-Safe | AS-Safe | AC-Safe | See Section 1.2.2.1 [POSIX Safety Concepts], page 2.

This function can be used to provide the system with *advice* about the intended usage patterns of the memory region starting at *addr* and extending *length* bytes.

The valid BSD values for *advice* are:

MADV_NORMAL

> The region should receive no further special treatment.

MADV_RANDOM

> The region will be accessed via random page references. The kernel should page-in the minimal number of pages for each page fault.

MADV_SEQUENTIAL

> The region will be accessed via sequential page references. This may cause the kernel to aggressively read-ahead, expecting further sequential references after any page fault within this region.

MADV_WILLNEED

> The region will be needed. The pages within this region may be pre-faulted in by the kernel.

MADV_DONTNEED

> The region is no longer needed. The kernel may free these pages, causing any changes to the pages to be lost, as well as swapped out pages to be discarded.

The POSIX names are slightly different, but with the same meanings:

POSIX_MADV_NORMAL

> This corresponds with BSD's MADV_NORMAL.

POSIX_MADV_RANDOM

> This corresponds with BSD's MADV_RANDOM.

POSIX_MADV_SEQUENTIAL

> This corresponds with BSD's MADV_SEQUENTIAL.

POSIX_MADV_WILLNEED

> This corresponds with BSD's MADV_WILLNEED.

POSIX_MADV_DONTNEED

> This corresponds with BSD's MADV_DONTNEED.

madvise returns 0 for success and −1 for error. Errors include:

EINVAL   An invalid region was given, or the *advice* was invalid.

EFAULT   There is no existing mapping in at least part of the given region.

int shm_open (const char *name, int oflag, mode_t mode)   [Function]
> Preliminary: | MT-Safe locale | AS-Unsafe init heap lock | AC-Unsafe lock mem fd | See Section 1.2.2.1 [POSIX Safety Concepts], page 2.

> This function returns a file descriptor that can be used to allocate shared memory via mmap. Unrelated processes can use same *name* to create or open existing shared memory objects.

> A *name* argument specifies the shared memory object to be opened. In the GNU C Library it must be a string smaller than NAME_MAX bytes starting with an optional slash but containing no other slashes.

> The semantics of *oflag* and *mode* arguments is same as in open.

> shm_open returns the file descriptor on success or −1 on error. On failure errno is set.

`int shm_unlink (const char *name)` [Function]

> Preliminary: | MT-Safe locale | AS-Unsafe init heap lock | AC-Unsafe lock mem fd
> | See Section 1.2.2.1 [POSIX Safety Concepts], page 2.
>
> This function is the inverse of `shm_open` and removes the object with the given *name*
> previously created by `shm_open`.
>
> `shm_unlink` returns 0 on success or −1 on error. On failure `errno` is set.

13.8 Waiting for Input or Output

Sometimes a program needs to accept input on multiple input channels whenever input arrives. For example, some workstations may have devices such as a digitizing tablet, function button box, or dial box that are connected via normal asynchronous serial interfaces; good user interface style requires responding immediately to input on any device. Another example is a program that acts as a server to several other processes via pipes or sockets.

You cannot normally use `read` for this purpose, because this blocks the program until input is available on one particular file descriptor; input on other channels won't wake it up. You could set nonblocking mode and poll each file descriptor in turn, but this is very inefficient.

A better solution is to use the `select` function. This blocks the program until input or output is ready on a specified set of file descriptors, or until a timer expires, whichever comes first. This facility is declared in the header file `sys/types.h`.

In the case of a server socket (see Section 16.9.2 [Listening for Connections], page 470), we say that "input" is available when there are pending connections that could be accepted (see Section 16.9.3 [Accepting Connections], page 470). `accept` for server sockets blocks and interacts with `select` just as `read` does for normal input.

The file descriptor sets for the `select` function are specified as `fd_set` objects. Here is the description of the data type and some macros for manipulating these objects.

`fd_set` [Data Type]

> The `fd_set` data type represents file descriptor sets for the `select` function. It is
> actually a bit array.

`int FD_SETSIZE` [Macro]

> The value of this macro is the maximum number of file descriptors that a `fd_set`
> object can hold information about. On systems with a fixed maximum number, `FD_`
> `SETSIZE` is at least that number. On some systems, including GNU, there is no
> absolute limit on the number of descriptors open, but this macro still has a constant
> value which controls the number of bits in an `fd_set`; if you get a file descriptor with
> a value as high as `FD_SETSIZE`, you cannot put that descriptor into an `fd_set`.

`void FD_ZERO (fd_set *set)` [Macro]

> Preliminary: | MT-Safe race:set | AS-Safe | AC-Safe | See Section 1.2.2.1 [POSIX
> Safety Concepts], page 2.
>
> This macro initializes the file descriptor set *set* to be the empty set.

`void FD_SET (int filedes, fd_set *set)` [Macro]

> Preliminary: | MT-Safe race:set | AS-Safe | AC-Safe | See Section 1.2.2.1 [POSIX
> Safety Concepts], page 2.

This macro adds *filedes* to the file descriptor set *set*.

The *filedes* parameter must not have side effects since it is evaluated more than once.

void **FD_CLR** (*int* **filedes**, *fd_set* ***set***)   [Macro]
Preliminary: | MT-Safe race:set | AS-Safe | AC-Safe | See Section 1.2.2.1 [POSIX Safety Concepts], page 2.

This macro removes *filedes* from the file descriptor set *set*.

The *filedes* parameter must not have side effects since it is evaluated more than once.

int **FD_ISSET** (*int* **filedes**, *const fd_set* ***set***)   [Macro]
Preliminary: | MT-Safe race:set | AS-Safe | AC-Safe | See Section 1.2.2.1 [POSIX Safety Concepts], page 2.

This macro returns a nonzero value (true) if *filedes* is a member of the file descriptor set *set*, and zero (false) otherwise.

The *filedes* parameter must not have side effects since it is evaluated more than once.

Next, here is the description of the **select** function itself.

int **select** (*int* **nfds**, *fd_set* ***read-fds***, *fd_set* ***write-fds***, *fd_set*   [Function]
    except-fds, *struct timeval* ***timeout***)
Preliminary: | MT-Safe race:read-fds race:write-fds race:except-fds | AS-Safe | AC-Safe | See Section 1.2.2.1 [POSIX Safety Concepts], page 2.

The **select** function blocks the calling process until there is activity on any of the specified sets of file descriptors, or until the timeout period has expired.

The file descriptors specified by the *read-fds* argument are checked to see if they are ready for reading; the *write-fds* file descriptors are checked to see if they are ready for writing; and the *except-fds* file descriptors are checked for exceptional conditions. You can pass a null pointer for any of these arguments if you are not interested in checking for that kind of condition.

A file descriptor is considered ready for reading if a **read** call will not block. This usually includes the read offset being at the end of the file or there is an error to report. A server socket is considered ready for reading if there is a pending connection which can be accepted with **accept**; see Section 16.9.3 [Accepting Connections], page 470. A client socket is ready for writing when its connection is fully established; see Section 16.9.1 [Making a Connection], page 469.

"Exceptional conditions" does not mean errors—errors are reported immediately when an erroneous system call is executed, and do not constitute a state of the descriptor. Rather, they include conditions such as the presence of an urgent message on a socket. (See Chapter 16 [Sockets], page 442, for information on urgent messages.)

The **select** function checks only the first *nfds* file descriptors. The usual thing is to pass **FD_SETSIZE** as the value of this argument.

The *timeout* specifies the maximum time to wait. If you pass a null pointer for this argument, it means to block indefinitely until one of the file descriptors is ready. Otherwise, you should provide the time in **struct timeval** format; see Section 21.4.2 [High-Resolution Calendar], page 624. Specify zero as the time (a **struct timeval** containing all zeros) if you want to find out which descriptors are ready without waiting if none are ready.

The normal return value from `select` is the total number of ready file descriptors in all of the sets. Each of the argument sets is overwritten with information about the descriptors that are ready for the corresponding operation. Thus, to see if a particular descriptor *desc* has input, use `FD_ISSET (desc, read-fds)` after `select` returns.

If `select` returns because the timeout period expires, it returns a value of zero.

Any signal will cause `select` to return immediately. So if your program uses signals, you can't rely on `select` to keep waiting for the full time specified. If you want to be sure of waiting for a particular amount of time, you must check for `EINTR` and repeat the `select` with a newly calculated timeout based on the current time. See the example below. See also Section 24.5 [Primitives Interrupted by Signals], page 711.

If an error occurs, `select` returns -1 and does not modify the argument file descriptor sets. The following `errno` error conditions are defined for this function:

EBADF   One of the file descriptor sets specified an invalid file descriptor.

EINTR   The operation was interrupted by a signal. See Section 24.5 [Primitives Interrupted by Signals], page 711.

EINVAL   The *timeout* argument is invalid; one of the components is negative or too large.

Portability Note: The `select` function is a BSD Unix feature.

Here is an example showing how you can use `select` to establish a timeout period for reading from a file descriptor. The `input_timeout` function blocks the calling process until input is available on the file descriptor, or until the timeout period expires.

```
#include <errno.h>
#include <stdio.h>
#include <unistd.h>
#include <sys/types.h>
#include <sys/time.h>

int
input_timeout (int filedes, unsigned int seconds)
{
  fd_set set;
  struct timeval timeout;

  /* Initialize the file descriptor set. */
  FD_ZERO (&set);
  FD_SET (filedes, &set);

  /* Initialize the timeout data structure. */
  timeout.tv_sec = seconds;
  timeout.tv_usec = 0;

  /* select returns 0 if timeout, 1 if input available, -1 if error. */
  return TEMP_FAILURE_RETRY (select (FD_SETSIZE,
                                     &set, NULL, NULL,
                                     &timeout));
}
```

```
int
main (void)
{
  fprintf (stderr, "select returned %d.\n",
           input_timeout (STDIN_FILENO, 5));
  return 0;
}
```

There is another example showing the use of **select** to multiplex input from multiple sockets in Section 16.9.7 [Byte Stream Connection Server Example], page 475.

13.9 Synchronizing I/O operations

In most modern operating systems, the normal I/O operations are not executed synchronously. I.e., even if a **write** system call returns, this does not mean the data is actually written to the media, e.g., the disk.

In situations where synchronization points are necessary, you can use special functions which ensure that all operations finish before they return.

void sync (*void*)   [Function]
> Preliminary: | MT-Safe | AS-Safe | AC-Safe | See Section 1.2.2.1 [POSIX Safety Concepts], page 2.
>
> A call to this function will not return as long as there is data which has not been written to the device. All dirty buffers in the kernel will be written and so an overall consistent system can be achieved (if no other process in parallel writes data).
>
> A prototype for **sync** can be found in **unistd.h**.

Programs more often want to ensure that data written to a given file is committed, rather than all data in the system. For this, **sync** is overkill.

int fsync (*int fildes*)   [Function]
> Preliminary: | MT-Safe | AS-Safe | AC-Safe | See Section 1.2.2.1 [POSIX Safety Concepts], page 2.
>
> The **fsync** function can be used to make sure all data associated with the open file *fildes* is written to the device associated with the descriptor. The function call does not return unless all actions have finished.
>
> A prototype for **fsync** can be found in **unistd.h**.
>
> This function is a cancellation point in multi-threaded programs. This is a problem if the thread allocates some resources (like memory, file descriptors, semaphores or whatever) at the time **fsync** is called. If the thread gets canceled these resources stay allocated until the program ends. To avoid this, calls to **fsync** should be protected using cancellation handlers.
>
> The return value of the function is zero if no error occurred. Otherwise it is −1 and the global variable *errno* is set to the following values:
>
> **EBADF**   The descriptor *fildes* is not valid.
>
> **EINVAL**   No synchronization is possible since the system does not implement this.

Sometimes it is not even necessary to write all data associated with a file descriptor. E.g., in database files which do not change in size it is enough to write all the file content data to the device. Meta-information, like the modification time etc., are not that important and leaving such information uncommitted does not prevent a successful recovery of the file in case of a problem.

int fdatasync (*int fildes*)   [Function]

> Preliminary: | MT-Safe | AS-Safe | AC-Safe | See Section 1.2.2.1 [POSIX Safety Concepts], page 2.
>
> When a call to the **fdatasync** function returns, it is ensured that all of the file data is written to the device. For all pending I/O operations, the parts guaranteeing data integrity finished.
>
> Not all systems implement the **fdatasync** operation. On systems missing this functionality **fdatasync** is emulated by a call to **fsync** since the performed actions are a superset of those required by **fdatasync**.
>
> The prototype for **fdatasync** is in **unistd.h**.
>
> The return value of the function is zero if no error occurred. Otherwise it is −1 and the global variable *errno* is set to the following values:
>
> **EBADF**   The descriptor *fildes* is not valid.
>
> **EINVAL**   No synchronization is possible since the system does not implement this.

13.10 Perform I/O Operations in Parallel

The POSIX.1b standard defines a new set of I/O operations which can significantly reduce the time an application spends waiting for I/O. The new functions allow a program to initiate one or more I/O operations and then immediately resume normal work while the I/O operations are executed in parallel. This functionality is available if the **unistd.h** file defines the symbol **_POSIX_ASYNCHRONOUS_IO**.

These functions are part of the library with realtime functions named **librt**. They are not actually part of the **libc** binary. The implementation of these functions can be done using support in the kernel (if available) or using an implementation based on threads at userlevel. In the latter case it might be necessary to link applications with the thread library **libpthread** in addition to **librt**.

All AIO operations operate on files which were opened previously. There might be arbitrarily many operations running for one file. The asynchronous I/O operations are controlled using a data structure named **struct aiocb** (*AIO control block*). It is defined in **aio.h** as follows.

struct aiocb   [Data Type]

> The POSIX.1b standard mandates that the **struct aiocb** structure contains at least the members described in the following table. There might be more elements which are used by the implementation, but depending upon these elements is not portable and is highly deprecated.
>
> **int aio_fildes**
>
> > This element specifies the file descriptor to be used for the operation. It must be a legal descriptor, otherwise the operation will fail.

The device on which the file is opened must allow the seek operation. I.e., it is not possible to use any of the AIO operations on devices like terminals where an `lseek` call would lead to an error.

`off_t aio_offset`

This element specifies the offset in the file at which the operation (input or output) is performed. Since the operations are carried out in arbitrary order and more than one operation for one file descriptor can be started, one cannot expect a current read/write position of the file descriptor.

`volatile void *aio_buf`

This is a pointer to the buffer with the data to be written or the place where the read data is stored.

`size_t aio_nbytes`

This element specifies the length of the buffer pointed to by `aio_buf`.

`int aio_reqprio`

If the platform has defined `_POSIX_PRIORITIZED_IO` and `_POSIX_PRIORITY_SCHEDULING`, the AIO requests are processed based on the current scheduling priority. The `aio_reqprio` element can then be used to lower the priority of the AIO operation.

`struct sigevent aio_sigevent`

This element specifies how the calling process is notified once the operation terminates. If the `sigev_notify` element is `SIGEV_NONE`, no notification is sent. If it is `SIGEV_SIGNAL`, the signal determined by `sigev_signo` is sent. Otherwise, `sigev_notify` must be `SIGEV_THREAD`. In this case, a thread is created which starts executing the function pointed to by `sigev_notify_function`.

`int aio_lio_opcode`

This element is only used by the `lio_listio` and `lio_listio64` functions. Since these functions allow an arbitrary number of operations to start at once, and each operation can be input or output (or nothing), the information must be stored in the control block. The possible values are:

LIO_READ   Start a read operation. Read from the file at position `aio_offset` and store the next `aio_nbytes` bytes in the buffer pointed to by `aio_buf`.

LIO_WRITE

Start a write operation. Write `aio_nbytes` bytes starting at `aio_buf` into the file starting at position `aio_offset`.

LIO_NOP   Do nothing for this control block. This value is useful sometimes when an array of `struct aiocb` values contains holes, i.e., some of the values must not be handled although the whole array is presented to the `lio_listio` function.

When the sources are compiled using _FILE_OFFSET_BITS == 64 on a 32 bit machine, this type is in fact struct aiocb64, since the LFS interface transparently replaces the struct aiocb definition.

For use with the AIO functions defined in the LFS, there is a similar type defined which replaces the types of the appropriate members with larger types but otherwise is equivalent to struct aiocb. Particularly, all member names are the same.

struct aiocb64   [Data Type]

> int aio_fildes
>
>> This element specifies the file descriptor which is used for the operation. It must be a legal descriptor since otherwise the operation fails for obvious reasons.
>>
>> The device on which the file is opened must allow the seek operation. I.e., it is not possible to use any of the AIO operations on devices like terminals where an lseek call would lead to an error.
>
> off64_t aio_offset
>
>> This element specifies at which offset in the file the operation (input or output) is performed. Since the operation are carried in arbitrary order and more than one operation for one file descriptor can be started, one cannot expect a current read/write position of the file descriptor.
>
> volatile void *aio_buf
>
>> This is a pointer to the buffer with the data to be written or the place where the read data is stored.
>
> size_t aio_nbytes
>
>> This element specifies the length of the buffer pointed to by aio_buf.
>
> int aio_reqprio
>
>> If for the platform _POSIX_PRIORITIZED_IO and _POSIX_PRIORITY_ SCHEDULING are defined the AIO requests are processed based on the current scheduling priority. The aio_reqprio element can then be used to lower the priority of the AIO operation.
>
> struct sigevent aio_sigevent
>
>> This element specifies how the calling process is notified once the operation terminates. If the sigev_notify element is SIGEV_NONE no notification is sent. If it is SIGEV_SIGNAL, the signal determined by sigev_signo is sent. Otherwise, sigev_notify must be SIGEV_THREAD in which case a thread is created which starts executing the function pointed to by sigev_notify_function.
>
> int aio_lio_opcode
>
>> This element is only used by the lio_listio and lio_listio64 functions. Since these functions allow an arbitrary number of operations to start at once, and since each operation can be input or output (or nothing), the information must be stored in the control block. See the description of struct aiocb for a description of the possible values.

When the sources are compiled using _FILE_OFFSET_BITS == 64 on a 32 bit machine, this type is available under the name struct aiocb64, since the LFS transparently replaces the old interface.

13.10.1 Asynchronous Read and Write Operations

int aio_read (*struct aiocb *aiocbp*)   [Function]
> Preliminary: | MT-Safe | AS-Unsafe lock heap | AC-Unsafe lock mem | See Section 1.2.2.1 [POSIX Safety Concepts], page 2.
>
> This function initiates an asynchronous read operation. It immediately returns after the operation was enqueued or when an error was encountered.
>
> The first aiocbp->aio_nbytes bytes of the file for which aiocbp->aio_fildes is a descriptor are written to the buffer starting at aiocbp->aio_buf. Reading starts at the absolute position aiocbp->aio_offset in the file.
>
> If prioritized I/O is supported by the platform the aiocbp->aio_reqprio value is used to adjust the priority before the request is actually enqueued.
>
> The calling process is notified about the termination of the read request according to the aiocbp->aio_sigevent value.
>
> When aio_read returns, the return value is zero if no error occurred that can be found before the process is enqueued. If such an early error is found, the function returns −1 and sets errno to one of the following values:
>
> EAGAIN   The request was not enqueued due to (temporarily) exceeded resource limitations.
>
> ENOSYS   The aio_read function is not implemented.
>
> EBADF   The aiocbp->aio_fildes descriptor is not valid. This condition need not be recognized before enqueueing the request and so this error might also be signaled asynchronously.
>
> EINVAL   The aiocbp->aio_offset or aiocbp->aio_reqpiro value is invalid. This condition need not be recognized before enqueueing the request and so this error might also be signaled asynchronously.
>
> If aio_read returns zero, the current status of the request can be queried using aio_error and aio_return functions. As long as the value returned by aio_error is EINPROGRESS the operation has not yet completed. If aio_error returns zero, the operation successfully terminated, otherwise the value is to be interpreted as an error code. If the function terminated, the result of the operation can be obtained using a call to aio_return. The returned value is the same as an equivalent call to read would have returned. Possible error codes returned by aio_error are:
>
> EBADF   The aiocbp->aio_fildes descriptor is not valid.
>
> ECANCELED
>   The operation was canceled before the operation was finished (see Section 13.10.4 [Cancellation of AIO Operations], page 369)
>
> EINVAL   The aiocbp->aio_offset value is invalid.

When the sources are compiled with `_FILE_OFFSET_BITS == 64` this function is in fact `aio_read64` since the LFS interface transparently replaces the normal implementation.

`int aio_read64` (*struct aiocb64 *aiocbp*)   [Function]
> Preliminary: | MT-Safe | AS-Unsafe lock heap | AC-Unsafe lock mem | See Section 1.2.2.1 [POSIX Safety Concepts], page 2.
>
> This function is similar to the `aio_read` function. The only difference is that on 32 bit machines, the file descriptor should be opened in the large file mode. Internally, `aio_read64` uses functionality equivalent to `lseek64` (see Section 13.3 [Setting the File Position of a Descriptor], page 343) to position the file descriptor correctly for the reading, as opposed to the `lseek` functionality used in `aio_read`.
>
> When the sources are compiled with `_FILE_OFFSET_BITS == 64`, this function is available under the name `aio_read` and so transparently replaces the interface for small files on 32 bit machines.

To write data asynchronously to a file, there exists an equivalent pair of functions with a very similar interface.

`int aio_write` (*struct aiocb *aiocbp*)   [Function]
> Preliminary: | MT-Safe | AS-Unsafe lock heap | AC-Unsafe lock mem | See Section 1.2.2.1 [POSIX Safety Concepts], page 2.
>
> This function initiates an asynchronous write operation. The function call immediately returns after the operation was enqueued or if before this happens an error was encountered.
>
> The first `aiocbp->aio_nbytes` bytes from the buffer starting at `aiocbp->aio_buf` are written to the file for which `aiocbp->aio_fildes` is a descriptor, starting at the absolute position `aiocbp->aio_offset` in the file.
>
> If prioritized I/O is supported by the platform, the `aiocbp->aio_reqprio` value is used to adjust the priority before the request is actually enqueued.
>
> The calling process is notified about the termination of the read request according to the `aiocbp->aio_sigevent` value.
>
> When `aio_write` returns, the return value is zero if no error occurred that can be found before the process is enqueued. If such an early error is found the function returns −1 and sets `errno` to one of the following values.
>
> `EAGAIN`   The request was not enqueued due to (temporarily) exceeded resource limitations.
>
> `ENOSYS`   The `aio_write` function is not implemented.
>
> `EBADF`   The `aiocbp->aio_fildes` descriptor is not valid. This condition may not be recognized before enqueueing the request, and so this error might also be signaled asynchronously.
>
> `EINVAL`   The `aiocbp->aio_offset` or `aiocbp->aio_reqprio` value is invalid. This condition may not be recognized before enqueueing the request and so this error might also be signaled asynchronously.

In the case `aio_write` returns zero, the current status of the request can be queried using the `aio_error` and `aio_return` functions. As long as the value returned by `aio_error` is `EINPROGRESS` the operation has not yet completed. If `aio_error` returns zero, the operation successfully terminated, otherwise the value is to be interpreted as an error code. If the function terminated, the result of the operation can be obtained using a call to `aio_return`. The returned value is the same as an equivalent call to `read` would have returned. Possible error codes returned by `aio_error` are:

EBADF The `aiocbp->aio_fildes` descriptor is not valid.

ECANCELED

    The operation was canceled before the operation was finished. (see Section 13.10.4 [Cancellation of AIO Operations], page 369)

EINVAL The `aiocbp->aio_offset` value is invalid.

When the sources are compiled with `_FILE_OFFSET_BITS == 64`, this function is in fact `aio_write64` since the LFS interface transparently replaces the normal implementation.

`int aio_write64 (struct aiocb64 *aiocbp)`   [Function]
Preliminary: | MT-Safe | AS-Unsafe lock heap | AC-Unsafe lock mem | See Section 1.2.2.1 [POSIX Safety Concepts], page 2.

This function is similar to the `aio_write` function. The only difference is that on 32 bit machines the file descriptor should be opened in the large file mode. Internally `aio_write64` uses functionality equivalent to `lseek64` (see Section 13.3 [Setting the File Position of a Descriptor], page 343) to position the file descriptor correctly for the writing, as opposed to the `lseek` functionality used in `aio_write`.

When the sources are compiled with `_FILE_OFFSET_BITS == 64`, this function is available under the name `aio_write` and so transparently replaces the interface for small files on 32 bit machines.

Besides these functions with the more or less traditional interface, POSIX.1b also defines a function which can initiate more than one operation at a time, and which can handle freely mixed read and write operations. It is therefore similar to a combination of `readv` and `writev`.

`int lio_listio (int mode, struct aiocb *const list[], int nent,`   [Function]
   `struct sigevent *sig)`
Preliminary: | MT-Safe | AS-Unsafe lock heap | AC-Unsafe lock mem | See Section 1.2.2.1 [POSIX Safety Concepts], page 2.

The `lio_listio` function can be used to enqueue an arbitrary number of read and write requests at one time. The requests can all be meant for the same file, all for different files or every solution in between.

`lio_listio` gets the *nent* requests from the array pointed to by *list*. The operation to be performed is determined by the `aio_lio_opcode` member in each element of *list*. If this field is `LIO_READ` a read operation is enqueued, similar to a call of `aio_read` for this element of the array (except that the way the termination is signalled is different, as we will see below). If the `aio_lio_opcode` member is `LIO_WRITE` a write operation is enqueued. Otherwise the `aio_lio_opcode` must be `LIO_NOP` in which case this element of *list* is simply ignored. This "operation" is useful in situations where one has a fixed array of `struct aiocb` elements from which only a few need to be handled at a time. Another situation is where the `lio_listio` call was canceled before all requests are processed (see Section 13.10.4 [Cancellation of AIO Operations], page 369) and the remaining requests have to be reissued.

The other members of each element of the array pointed to by `list` must have values suitable for the operation as described in the documentation for `aio_read` and `aio_write` above.

The *mode* argument determines how `lio_listio` behaves after having enqueued all the requests. If *mode* is `LIO_WAIT` it waits until all requests terminated. Otherwise *mode* must be `LIO_NOWAIT` and in this case the function returns immediately after having enqueued all the requests. In this case the caller gets a notification of the termination of all requests according to the *sig* parameter. If *sig* is `NULL` no notification is sent. Otherwise a signal is sent or a thread is started, just as described in the description for `aio_read` or `aio_write`.

If *mode* is `LIO_WAIT`, the return value of `lio_listio` is 0 when all requests completed successfully. Otherwise the function returns −1 and `errno` is set accordingly. To find out which request or requests failed one has to use the `aio_error` function on all the elements of the array *list*.

In case *mode* is `LIO_NOWAIT`, the function returns 0 if all requests were enqueued correctly. The current state of the requests can be found using `aio_error` and `aio_return` as described above. If `lio_listio` returns −1 in this mode, the global variable `errno` is set accordingly. If a request did not yet terminate, a call to `aio_error` returns `EINPROGRESS`. If the value is different, the request is finished and the error value (or 0) is returned and the result of the operation can be retrieved using `aio_return`.

Possible values for `errno` are:

EAGAIN   The resources necessary to queue all the requests are not available at the moment. The error status for each element of *list* must be checked to determine which request failed.

Another reason could be that the system wide limit of AIO requests is exceeded. This cannot be the case for the implementation on GNU systems since no arbitrary limits exist.

EINVAL   The *mode* parameter is invalid or *nent* is larger than `AIO_LISTIO_MAX`.

EIO   One or more of the request's I/O operations failed. The error status of each request should be checked to determine which one failed.

ENOSYS   The `lio_listio` function is not supported.

If the *mode* parameter is `LIO_NOWAIT` and the caller cancels a request, the error status for this request returned by `aio_error` is `ECANCELED`.

When the sources are compiled with `_FILE_OFFSET_BITS == 64`, this function is in fact `lio_listio64` since the LFS interface transparently replaces the normal implementation.

int lio_listio64 (*int mode, struct aiocb64 *const list[], int nent,*   [Function]
        struct sigevent *sig)
    Preliminary: | MT-Safe | AS-Unsafe lock heap | AC-Unsafe lock mem | See
    Section 1.2.2.1 [POSIX Safety Concepts], page 2.

    This function is similar to the `lio_listio` function. The only difference is that on
    32 bit machines, the file descriptor should be opened in the large file mode. Internally,
    `lio_listio64` uses functionality equivalent to `lseek64` (see Section 13.3 [Setting the
    File Position of a Descriptor], page 343) to position the file descriptor correctly for
    the reading or writing, as opposed to the `lseek` functionality used in `lio_listio`.

    When the sources are compiled with `_FILE_OFFSET_BITS == 64`, this function is avail-
    able under the name `lio_listio` and so transparently replaces the interface for small
    files on 32 bit machines.

13.10.2 Getting the Status of AIO Operations

As already described in the documentation of the functions in the last section, it must be
possible to get information about the status of an I/O request. When the operation is
performed truly asynchronously (as with `aio_read` and `aio_write` and with `lio_listio`
when the mode is `LIO_NOWAIT`), one sometimes needs to know whether a specific request
already terminated and if so, what the result was. The following two functions allow you
to get this kind of information.

int aio_error (*const struct aiocb *aiocbp*)   [Function]
    Preliminary: | MT-Safe | AS-Safe | AC-Safe | See Section 1.2.2.1 [POSIX Safety
    Concepts], page 2.

    This function determines the error state of the request described by the **struct aiocb**
    variable pointed to by *aiocbp*. If the request has not yet terminated the value returned
    is always `EINPROGRESS`. Once the request has terminated the value `aio_error` returns
    is either 0 if the request completed successfully or it returns the value which would be
    stored in the **errno** variable if the request would have been done using **read**, **write**,
    or **fsync**.

    The function can return `ENOSYS` if it is not implemented. It could also return `EINVAL`
    if the *aiocbp* parameter does not refer to an asynchronous operation whose return
    status is not yet known.

    When the sources are compiled with `_FILE_OFFSET_BITS == 64` this function is in
    fact `aio_error64` since the LFS interface transparently replaces the normal imple-
    mentation.

int aio_error64 (*const struct aiocb64 *aiocbp*)   [Function]
    Preliminary: | MT-Safe | AS-Safe | AC-Safe | See Section 1.2.2.1 [POSIX Safety
    Concepts], page 2.

    This function is similar to `aio_error` with the only difference that the argument is a
    reference to a variable of type **struct aiocb64**.

    When the sources are compiled with `_FILE_OFFSET_BITS == 64` this function is avail-
    able under the name `aio_error` and so transparently replaces the interface for small
    files on 32 bit machines.

`ssize_t aio_return (struct aiocb *aiocbp)` [Function]
> Preliminary: | MT-Safe | AS-Safe | AC-Safe | See Section 1.2.2.1 [POSIX Safety Concepts], page 2.
>
> This function can be used to retrieve the return status of the operation carried out by the request described in the variable pointed to by *aiocbp*. As long as the error status of this request as returned by `aio_error` is `EINPROGRESS` the return value of this function is undefined.
>
> Once the request is finished this function can be used exactly once to retrieve the return value. Following calls might lead to undefined behavior. The return value itself is the value which would have been returned by the `read`, `write`, or `fsync` call.
>
> The function can return `ENOSYS` if it is not implemented. It could also return `EINVAL` if the *aiocbp* parameter does not refer to an asynchronous operation whose return status is not yet known.
>
> When the sources are compiled with `_FILE_OFFSET_BITS == 64` this function is in fact `aio_return64` since the LFS interface transparently replaces the normal implementation.

`ssize_t aio_return64 (struct aiocb64 *aiocbp)` [Function]
> Preliminary: | MT-Safe | AS-Safe | AC-Safe | See Section 1.2.2.1 [POSIX Safety Concepts], page 2.
>
> This function is similar to `aio_return` with the only difference that the argument is a reference to a variable of type `struct aiocb64`.
>
> When the sources are compiled with `_FILE_OFFSET_BITS == 64` this function is available under the name `aio_return` and so transparently replaces the interface for small files on 32 bit machines.

13.10.3 Getting into a Consistent State

When dealing with asynchronous operations it is sometimes necessary to get into a consistent state. This would mean for AIO that one wants to know whether a certain request or a group of requests were processed. This could be done by waiting for the notification sent by the system after the operation terminated, but this sometimes would mean wasting resources (mainly computation time). Instead POSIX.1b defines two functions which will help with most kinds of consistency.

The `aio_fsync` and `aio_fsync64` functions are only available if the symbol `_POSIX_SYNCHRONIZED_IO` is defined in `unistd.h`.

`int aio_fsync (int op, struct aiocb *aiocbp)` [Function]
> Preliminary: | MT-Safe | AS-Unsafe lock heap | AC-Unsafe lock mem | See Section 1.2.2.1 [POSIX Safety Concepts], page 2.
>
> Calling this function forces all I/O operations queued at the time of the function call operating on the file descriptor `aiocbp->aio_fildes` into the synchronized I/O completion state (see Section 13.9 [Synchronizing I/O operations], page 358). The `aio_fsync` function returns immediately but the notification through the method described in `aiocbp->aio_sigevent` will happen only after all requests for this file descriptor have terminated and the file is synchronized. This also means that requests

for this very same file descriptor which are queued after the synchronization request are not affected.

If *op* is `O_DSYNC` the synchronization happens as with a call to `fdatasync`. Otherwise *op* should be `O_SYNC` and the synchronization happens as with `fsync`.

As long as the synchronization has not happened, a call to `aio_error` with the reference to the object pointed to by *aiocbp* returns `EINPROGRESS`. Once the synchronization is done `aio_error` return 0 if the synchronization was not successful. Otherwise the value returned is the value to which the `fsync` or `fdatasync` function would have set the `errno` variable. In this case nothing can be assumed about the consistency of the data written to this file descriptor.

The return value of this function is 0 if the request was successfully enqueued. Otherwise the return value is −1 and `errno` is set to one of the following values:

EAGAIN   The request could not be enqueued due to temporary lack of resources.

EBADF   The file descriptor *aiocbp->aio_fildes* is not valid.

EINVAL   The implementation does not support I/O synchronization or the *op* parameter is other than `O_DSYNC` and `O_SYNC`.

ENOSYS   This function is not implemented.

When the sources are compiled with `_FILE_OFFSET_BITS == 64` this function is in fact `aio_fsync64` since the LFS interface transparently replaces the normal implementation.

int **aio_fsync64** (*int op, struct aiocb64 *`aiocbp`*)   [Function]
Preliminary: | MT-Safe | AS-Unsafe lock heap | AC-Unsafe lock mem | See Section 1.2.2.1 [POSIX Safety Concepts], page 2.

This function is similar to `aio_fsync` with the only difference that the argument is a reference to a variable of type `struct aiocb64`.

When the sources are compiled with `_FILE_OFFSET_BITS == 64` this function is available under the name `aio_fsync` and so transparently replaces the interface for small files on 32 bit machines.

Another method of synchronization is to wait until one or more requests of a specific set terminated. This could be achieved by the `aio_*` functions to notify the initiating process about the termination but in some situations this is not the ideal solution. In a program which constantly updates clients somehow connected to the server it is not always the best solution to go round robin since some connections might be slow. On the other hand letting the `aio_*` functions notify the caller might also be not the best solution since whenever the process works on preparing data for a client it makes no sense to be interrupted by a notification since the new client will not be handled before the current client is served. For situations like this `aio_suspend` should be used.

int **aio_suspend** (*const struct aiocb *const `list`[], int `nent`, const*   [Function]
        struct timespec *`timeout`)
Preliminary: | MT-Safe | AS-Unsafe lock | AC-Unsafe lock | See Section 1.2.2.1 [POSIX Safety Concepts], page 2.

When calling this function, the calling thread is suspended until at least one of the requests pointed to by the *nent* elements of the array *list* has completed. If any of the requests has already completed at the time `aio_suspend` is called, the function returns immediately. Whether a request has terminated or not is determined by comparing the error status of the request with `EINPROGRESS`. If an element of *list* is `NULL`, the entry is simply ignored.

If no request has finished, the calling process is suspended. If *timeout* is `NULL`, the process is not woken until a request has finished. If *timeout* is not `NULL`, the process remains suspended at least as long as specified in *timeout*. In this case, `aio_suspend` returns with an error.

The return value of the function is 0 if one or more requests from the *list* have terminated. Otherwise the function returns −1 and `errno` is set to one of the following values:

EAGAIN   None of the requests from the *list* completed in the time specified by *timeout*.

EINTR   A signal interrupted the `aio_suspend` function. This signal might also be sent by the AIO implementation while signalling the termination of one of the requests.

ENOSYS   The `aio_suspend` function is not implemented.

When the sources are compiled with `_FILE_OFFSET_BITS == 64` this function is in fact `aio_suspend64` since the LFS interface transparently replaces the normal implementation.

int `aio_suspend64` (*const struct aiocb64 *const* `list`[], *int* `nent`,   [Function]
    *const struct timespec *`timeout`)
Preliminary: | MT-Safe | AS-Unsafe lock | AC-Unsafe lock | See Section 1.2.2.1 [POSIX Safety Concepts], page 2.

This function is similar to `aio_suspend` with the only difference that the argument is a reference to a variable of type `struct aiocb64`.

When the sources are compiled with `_FILE_OFFSET_BITS == 64` this function is available under the name `aio_suspend` and so transparently replaces the interface for small files on 32 bit machines.

13.10.4 Cancellation of AIO Operations

When one or more requests are asynchronously processed, it might be useful in some situations to cancel a selected operation, e.g., if it becomes obvious that the written data is no longer accurate and would have to be overwritten soon. As an example, assume an application, which writes data in files in a situation where new incoming data would have to be written in a file which will be updated by an enqueued request. The POSIX AIO implementation provides such a function, but this function is not capable of forcing the cancellation of the request. It is up to the implementation to decide whether it is possible to cancel the operation or not. Therefore using this function is merely a hint.

int `aio_cancel` (*int* `fildes`, *struct aiocb *`aiocbp`)   [Function]
    Preliminary: | MT-Safe | AS-Unsafe lock heap | AC-Unsafe lock mem | See Section 1.2.2.1 [POSIX Safety Concepts], page 2.

The `aio_cancel` function can be used to cancel one or more outstanding requests. If the *aiocbp* parameter is NULL, the function tries to cancel all of the outstanding requests which would process the file descriptor *fildes* (i.e., whose `aio_fildes` member is *fildes*). If *aiocbp* is not NULL, `aio_cancel` attempts to cancel the specific request pointed to by *aiocbp*.

For requests which were successfully canceled, the normal notification about the termination of the request should take place. I.e., depending on the `struct sigevent` object which controls this, nothing happens, a signal is sent or a thread is started. If the request cannot be canceled, it terminates the usual way after performing the operation.

After a request is successfully canceled, a call to `aio_error` with a reference to this request as the parameter will return ECANCELED and a call to `aio_return` will return −1. If the request wasn't canceled and is still running the error status is still EINPROGRESS.

The return value of the function is AIO_CANCELED if there were requests which haven't terminated and which were successfully canceled. If there is one or more requests left which couldn't be canceled, the return value is AIO_NOTCANCELED. In this case `aio_error` must be used to find out which of the, perhaps multiple, requests (if *aiocbp* is NULL) weren't successfully canceled. If all requests already terminated at the time `aio_cancel` is called the return value is AIO_ALLDONE.

If an error occurred during the execution of `aio_cancel` the function returns −1 and sets `errno` to one of the following values.

EBADF   The file descriptor *fildes* is not valid.

ENOSYS   `aio_cancel` is not implemented.

When the sources are compiled with `_FILE_OFFSET_BITS == 64`, this function is in fact `aio_cancel64` since the LFS interface transparently replaces the normal implementation.

int aio_cancel64 (*int fildes*, *struct aiocb64 *aiocbp*)   [Function]
Preliminary: | MT-Safe | AS-Unsafe lock heap | AC-Unsafe lock mem | See Section 1.2.2.1 [POSIX Safety Concepts], page 2.

This function is similar to `aio_cancel` with the only difference that the argument is a reference to a variable of type `struct aiocb64`.

When the sources are compiled with `_FILE_OFFSET_BITS == 64`, this function is available under the name `aio_cancel` and so transparently replaces the interface for small files on 32 bit machines.

13.10.5 How to optimize the AIO implementation

The POSIX standard does not specify how the AIO functions are implemented. They could be system calls, but it is also possible to emulate them at userlevel.

At the time of writing, the available implementation is a user-level implementation which uses threads for handling the enqueued requests. While this implementation requires making some decisions about limitations, hard limitations are something best avoided in the GNU C Library. Therefore, the GNU C Library provides a means for tuning the AIO implementation according to the individual use.

`struct aioinit`   [Data Type]

> This data type is used to pass the configuration or tunable parameters to the implementation. The program has to initialize the members of this struct and pass it to the implementation using the `aio_init` function.

> `int aio_threads`
>> This member specifies the maximal number of threads which may be used at any one time.

> `int aio_num`
>> This number provides an estimate on the maximal number of simultaneously enqueued requests.

> `int aio_locks`
>> Unused.

> `int aio_usedba`
>> Unused.

> `int aio_debug`
>> Unused.

> `int aio_numusers`
>> Unused.

> `int aio_reserved[2]`
>> Unused.

`void aio_init (const struct aioinit *init)`   [Function]

> Preliminary: | MT-Safe | AS-Unsafe lock | AC-Unsafe lock | See Section 1.2.2.1 [POSIX Safety Concepts], page 2.

> This function must be called before any other AIO function. Calling it is completely voluntary, as it is only meant to help the AIO implementation perform better.

> Before calling `aio_init`, the members of a variable of type `struct aioinit` must be initialized. Then a reference to this variable is passed as the parameter to `aio_init` which itself may or may not pay attention to the hints.

> The function has no return value and no error cases are defined. It is an extension which follows a proposal from the SGI implementation in Irix 6. It is not covered by POSIX.1b or Unix98.

13.11 Control Operations on Files

This section describes how you can perform various other operations on file descriptors, such as inquiring about or setting flags describing the status of the file descriptor, manipulating record locks, and the like. All of these operations are performed by the function `fcntl`.

The second argument to the `fcntl` function is a command that specifies which operation to perform. The function and macros that name various flags that are used with it are declared in the header file `fcntl.h`. Many of these flags are also used by the `open` function; see Section 13.1 [Opening and Closing Files], page 333.

`int fcntl (int filedes, int command, ...)`   [Function]

Preliminary: | MT-Safe | AS-Safe | AC-Safe | See Section 1.2.2.1 [POSIX Safety Concepts], page 2.

The `fcntl` function performs the operation specified by *command* on the file descriptor *filedes*. Some commands require additional arguments to be supplied. These additional arguments and the return value and error conditions are given in the detailed descriptions of the individual commands.

Briefly, here is a list of what the various commands are.

F_DUPFD   Duplicate the file descriptor (return another file descriptor pointing to the same open file). See Section 13.12 [Duplicating Descriptors], page 373.

F_GETFD   Get flags associated with the file descriptor. See Section 13.13 [File Descriptor Flags], page 374.

F_SETFD   Set flags associated with the file descriptor. See Section 13.13 [File Descriptor Flags], page 374.

F_GETFL   Get flags associated with the open file. See Section 13.14 [File Status Flags], page 375.

F_SETFL   Set flags associated with the open file. See Section 13.14 [File Status Flags], page 375.

F_GETLK   Test a file lock. See Section 13.15 [File Locks], page 380.

F_SETLK   Set or clear a file lock. See Section 13.15 [File Locks], page 380.

F_SETLKW   Like `F_SETLK`, but wait for completion. See Section 13.15 [File Locks], page 380.

F_OFD_GETLK
            Test an open file description lock. See Section 13.16 [Open File Description Locks], page 384. Specific to Linux.

F_OFD_SETLK
            Set or clear an open file description lock. See Section 13.16 [Open File Description Locks], page 384. Specific to Linux.

F_OFD_SETLKW
            Like `F_OFD_SETLK`, but block until lock is acquired. See Section 13.16 [Open File Description Locks], page 384. Specific to Linux.

F_GETOWN   Get process or process group ID to receive `SIGIO` signals. See Section 13.18 [Interrupt-Driven Input], page 387.

F_SETOWN   Set process or process group ID to receive `SIGIO` signals. See Section 13.18 [Interrupt-Driven Input], page 387.

This function is a cancellation point in multi-threaded programs. This is a problem if the thread allocates some resources (like memory, file descriptors, semaphores or whatever) at the time `fcntl` is called. If the thread gets canceled these resources stay allocated until the program ends. To avoid this calls to `fcntl` should be protected using cancellation handlers.

13.12 Duplicating Descriptors

You can *duplicate* a file descriptor, or allocate another file descriptor that refers to the same open file as the original. Duplicate descriptors share one file position and one set of file status flags (see Section 13.14 [File Status Flags], page 375), but each has its own set of file descriptor flags (see Section 13.13 [File Descriptor Flags], page 374).

The major use of duplicating a file descriptor is to implement *redirection* of input or output: that is, to change the file or pipe that a particular file descriptor corresponds to.

You can perform this operation using the `fcntl` function with the `F_DUPFD` command, but there are also convenient functions `dup` and `dup2` for duplicating descriptors.

The `fcntl` function and flags are declared in `fcntl.h`, while prototypes for `dup` and `dup2` are in the header file `unistd.h`.

int dup (*int old*)   [Function]
> Preliminary: | MT-Safe | AS-Safe | AC-Safe | See Section 1.2.2.1 [POSIX Safety Concepts], page 2.
>
> This function copies descriptor *old* to the first available descriptor number (the first number not currently open). It is equivalent to `fcntl (old, F_DUPFD, 0)`.

int dup2 (*int old, int new*)   [Function]
> Preliminary: | MT-Safe | AS-Safe | AC-Safe | See Section 1.2.2.1 [POSIX Safety Concepts], page 2.
>
> This function copies the descriptor *old* to descriptor number *new*.
>
> If *old* is an invalid descriptor, then `dup2` does nothing; it does not close *new*. Otherwise, the new duplicate of *old* replaces any previous meaning of descriptor *new*, as if *new* were closed first.
>
> If *old* and *new* are different numbers, and *old* is a valid descriptor number, then `dup2` is equivalent to:
>
> ```
> close (new);
> fcntl (old, F_DUPFD, new)
> ```
>
> However, `dup2` does this atomically; there is no instant in the middle of calling `dup2` at which *new* is closed and not yet a duplicate of *old*.

int F_DUPFD   [Macro]
> This macro is used as the *command* argument to `fcntl`, to copy the file descriptor given as the first argument.
>
> The form of the call in this case is:
>
> ```
> fcntl (old, F_DUPFD, next-filedes)
> ```
>
> The *next-filedes* argument is of type `int` and specifies that the file descriptor returned should be the next available one greater than or equal to this value.
>
> The return value from `fcntl` with this command is normally the value of the new file descriptor. A return value of −1 indicates an error. The following `errno` error conditions are defined for this command:

EBADF   The *old* argument is invalid.

EINVAL   The *next-filedes* argument is invalid.

EMFILE   There are no more file descriptors available—your program is already using the maximum. In BSD and GNU, the maximum is controlled by a resource limit that can be changed; see Section 22.2 [Limiting Resource Usage], page 656, for more information about the `RLIMIT_NOFILE` limit.

`ENFILE` is not a possible error code for `dup2` because `dup2` does not create a new opening of a file; duplicate descriptors do not count toward the limit which `ENFILE` indicates. `EMFILE` is possible because it refers to the limit on distinct descriptor numbers in use in one process.

Here is an example showing how to use `dup2` to do redirection. Typically, redirection of the standard streams (like `stdin`) is done by a shell or shell-like program before calling one of the `exec` functions (see Section 26.5 [Executing a File], page 776) to execute a new program in a child process. When the new program is executed, it creates and initializes the standard streams to point to the corresponding file descriptors, before its `main` function is invoked.

So, to redirect standard input to a file, the shell could do something like:

```
pid = fork ();
if (pid == 0)
  {
    char *filename;
    char *program;
    int file;
    ...
    file = TEMP_FAILURE_RETRY (open (filename, O_RDONLY));
    dup2 (file, STDIN_FILENO);
    TEMP_FAILURE_RETRY (close (file));
    execv (program, NULL);
  }
```

There is also a more detailed example showing how to implement redirection in the context of a pipeline of processes in Section 28.6.3 [Launching Jobs], page 791.

13.13 File Descriptor Flags

File descriptor flags are miscellaneous attributes of a file descriptor. These flags are associated with particular file descriptors, so that if you have created duplicate file descriptors from a single opening of a file, each descriptor has its own set of flags.

Currently there is just one file descriptor flag: `FD_CLOEXEC`, which causes the descriptor to be closed if you use any of the `exec...` functions (see Section 26.5 [Executing a File], page 776).

The symbols in this section are defined in the header file `fcntl.h`.

int F_GETFD   [Macro]
     This macro is used as the *command* argument to `fcntl`, to specify that it should return the file descriptor flags associated with the *filedes* argument.

     The normal return value from `fcntl` with this command is a nonnegative number which can be interpreted as the bitwise OR of the individual flags (except that currently there is only one flag to use).

In case of an error, `fcntl` returns −1. The following `errno` error conditions are defined for this command:

EBADF   The *filedes* argument is invalid.

int F_SETFD [Macro]

This macro is used as the *command* argument to `fcntl`, to specify that it should set the file descriptor flags associated with the *filedes* argument. This requires a third `int` argument to specify the new flags, so the form of the call is:

    `fcntl (filedes, F_SETFD, new-flags)`

The normal return value from `fcntl` with this command is an unspecified value other than −1, which indicates an error. The flags and error conditions are the same as for the `F_GETFD` command.

The following macro is defined for use as a file descriptor flag with the `fcntl` function. The value is an integer constant usable as a bit mask value.

int FD_CLOEXEC [Macro]

This flag specifies that the file descriptor should be closed when an `exec` function is invoked; see Section 26.5 [Executing a File], page 776. When a file descriptor is allocated (as with `open` or `dup`), this bit is initially cleared on the new file descriptor, meaning that descriptor will survive into the new program after `exec`.

If you want to modify the file descriptor flags, you should get the current flags with `F_GETFD` and modify the value. Don't assume that the flags listed here are the only ones that are implemented; your program may be run years from now and more flags may exist then. For example, here is a function to set or clear the flag `FD_CLOEXEC` without altering any other flags:

```
/* Set the FD_CLOEXEC flag of desc if value is nonzero,
   or clear the flag if value is 0.
   Return 0 on success, or -1 on error with errno set. */

int
set_cloexec_flag (int desc, int value)
{
  int oldflags = fcntl (desc, F_GETFD, 0);
  /* If reading the flags failed, return error indication now. */
  if (oldflags < 0)
    return oldflags;
  /* Set just the flag we want to set. */
  if (value != 0)
    oldflags |= FD_CLOEXEC;
  else
    oldflags &= ~FD_CLOEXEC;
  /* Store modified flag word in the descriptor. */
  return fcntl (desc, F_SETFD, oldflags);
}
```

13.14 File Status Flags

File status flags are used to specify attributes of the opening of a file. Unlike the file descriptor flags discussed in Section 13.13 [File Descriptor Flags], page 374, the file status flags are shared by duplicated file descriptors resulting from a single opening of the file. The file status flags are specified with the *flags* argument to open; see Section 13.1 [Opening and Closing Files], page 333.

File status flags fall into three categories, which are described in the following sections.

- Section 13.14.1 [File Access Modes], page 376, specify what type of access is allowed to the file: reading, writing, or both. They are set by open and are returned by fcntl, but cannot be changed.

- Section 13.14.2 [Open-time Flags], page 377, control details of what open will do. These flags are not preserved after the open call.

- Section 13.14.3 [I/O Operating Modes], page 378, affect how operations such as read and write are done. They are set by open, and can be fetched or changed with fcntl.

The symbols in this section are defined in the header file fcntl.h.

13.14.1 File Access Modes

The file access modes allow a file descriptor to be used for reading, writing, or both. (On GNU/Hurd systems, they can also allow none of these, and allow execution of the file as a program.) The access modes are chosen when the file is opened, and never change.

int O_RDONLY   [Macro]
> Open the file for read access.

int O_WRONLY   [Macro]
> Open the file for write access.

int O_RDWR   [Macro]
> Open the file for both reading and writing.

On GNU/Hurd systems (and not on other systems), O_RDONLY and O_WRONLY are independent bits that can be bitwise-ORed together, and it is valid for either bit to be set or clear. This means that O_RDWR is the same as O_RDONLY|O_WRONLY. A file access mode of zero is permissible; it allows no operations that do input or output to the file, but does allow other operations such as fchmod. On GNU/Hurd systems, since "read-only" or "write-only" is a misnomer, fcntl.h defines additional names for the file access modes. These names are preferred when writing GNU-specific code. But most programs will want to be portable to other POSIX.1 systems and should use the POSIX.1 names above instead.

int O_READ   [Macro]
> Open the file for reading. Same as O_RDONLY; only defined on GNU.

int O_WRITE   [Macro]
> Open the file for writing. Same as O_WRONLY; only defined on GNU.

int O_EXEC   [Macro]
> Open the file for executing. Only defined on GNU.

To determine the file access mode with fcntl, you must extract the access mode bits from the retrieved file status flags. On GNU/Hurd systems, you can just test the O_READ and O_WRITE bits in the flags word. But in other POSIX.1 systems, reading and writing access modes are not stored as distinct bit flags. The portable way to extract the file access mode bits is with O_ACCMODE.

`int O_ACCMODE` [Macro]

> This macro stands for a mask that can be bitwise-ANDed with the file status flag value to produce a value representing the file access mode. The mode will be `O_RDONLY`, `O_WRONLY`, or `O_RDWR`. (On GNU/Hurd systems it could also be zero, and it never includes the `O_EXEC` bit.)

13.14.2 Open-time Flags

The open-time flags specify options affecting how **open** will behave. These options are not preserved once the file is open. The exception to this is `O_NONBLOCK`, which is also an I/O operating mode and so it *is* saved. See Section 13.1 [Opening and Closing Files], page 333, for how to call **open**.

There are two sorts of options specified by open-time flags.

- *File name translation flags* affect how **open** looks up the file name to locate the file, and whether the file can be created.

- *Open-time action flags* specify extra operations that **open** will perform on the file once it is open.

Here are the file name translation flags.

`int O_CREAT` [Macro]

> If set, the file will be created if it doesn't already exist.

`int O_EXCL` [Macro]

> If both `O_CREAT` and `O_EXCL` are set, then **open** fails if the specified file already exists. This is guaranteed to never clobber an existing file.

`int O_NONBLOCK` [Macro]

> This prevents **open** from blocking for a "long time" to open the file. This is only meaningful for some kinds of files, usually devices such as serial ports; when it is not meaningful, it is harmless and ignored. Often, opening a port to a modem blocks until the modem reports carrier detection; if `O_NONBLOCK` is specified, **open** will return immediately without a carrier.
>
> Note that the `O_NONBLOCK` flag is overloaded as both an I/O operating mode and a file name translation flag. This means that specifying `O_NONBLOCK` in **open** also sets nonblocking I/O mode; see Section 13.14.3 [I/O Operating Modes], page 378. To open the file without blocking but do normal I/O that blocks, you must call **open** with `O_NONBLOCK` set and then call `fcntl` to turn the bit off.

`int O_NOCTTY` [Macro]

> If the named file is a terminal device, don't make it the controlling terminal for the process. See Chapter 28 [Job Control], page 786, for information about what it means to be the controlling terminal.
>
> On GNU/Hurd systems and 4.4 BSD, opening a file never makes it the controlling terminal and `O_NOCTTY` is zero. However, GNU/Linux systems and some other systems use a nonzero value for `O_NOCTTY` and set the controlling terminal when you open a file that is a terminal device; so to be portable, use `O_NOCTTY` when it is important to avoid this.

The following three file name translation flags exist only on GNU/Hurd systems.

int O_IGNORE_CTTY [Macro]

Do not recognize the named file as the controlling terminal, even if it refers to the process's existing controlling terminal device. Operations on the new file descriptor will never induce job control signals. See Chapter 28 [Job Control], page 786.

int O_NOLINK [Macro]

If the named file is a symbolic link, open the link itself instead of the file it refers to. (`fstat` on the new file descriptor will return the information returned by `lstat` on the link's name.)

int O_NOTRANS [Macro]

If the named file is specially translated, do not invoke the translator. Open the bare file the translator itself sees.

The open-time action flags tell **open** to do additional operations which are not really related to opening the file. The reason to do them as part of **open** instead of in separate calls is that **open** can do them *atomically*.

int O_TRUNC [Macro]

Truncate the file to zero length. This option is only useful for regular files, not special files such as directories or FIFOs. POSIX.1 requires that you open the file for writing to use `O_TRUNC`. In BSD and GNU you must have permission to write the file to truncate it, but you need not open for write access.

This is the only open-time action flag specified by POSIX.1. There is no good reason for truncation to be done by **open**, instead of by calling `ftruncate` afterwards. The `O_TRUNC` flag existed in Unix before `ftruncate` was invented, and is retained for backward compatibility.

The remaining operating modes are BSD extensions. They exist only on some systems. On other systems, these macros are not defined.

int O_SHLOCK [Macro]

Acquire a shared lock on the file, as with `flock`. See Section 13.15 [File Locks], page 380.

If `O_CREAT` is specified, the locking is done atomically when creating the file. You are guaranteed that no other process will get the lock on the new file first.

int O_EXLOCK [Macro]

Acquire an exclusive lock on the file, as with `flock`. See Section 13.15 [File Locks], page 380. This is atomic like `O_SHLOCK`.

13.14.3 I/O Operating Modes

The operating modes affect how input and output operations using a file descriptor work. These flags are set by **open** and can be fetched and changed with `fcntl`.

int O_APPEND [Macro]

The bit that enables append mode for the file. If set, then all **write** operations write the data at the end of the file, extending it, regardless of the current file position.

This is the only reliable way to append to a file. In append mode, you are guaranteed that the data you write will always go to the current end of the file, regardless of other processes writing to the file. Conversely, if you simply set the file position to the end of file and write, then another process can extend the file after you set the file position but before you write, resulting in your data appearing someplace before the real end of file.

int O_NONBLOCK [Macro]

The bit that enables nonblocking mode for the file. If this bit is set, `read` requests on the file can return immediately with a failure status if there is no input immediately available, instead of blocking. Likewise, `write` requests can also return immediately with a failure status if the output can't be written immediately.

Note that the `O_NONBLOCK` flag is overloaded as both an I/O operating mode and a file name translation flag; see Section 13.14.2 [Open-time Flags], page 377.

int O_NDELAY [Macro]

This is an obsolete name for `O_NONBLOCK`, provided for compatibility with BSD. It is not defined by the POSIX.1 standard.

The remaining operating modes are BSD and GNU extensions. They exist only on some systems. On other systems, these macros are not defined.

int O_ASYNC [Macro]

The bit that enables asynchronous input mode. If set, then `SIGIO` signals will be generated when input is available. See Section 13.18 [Interrupt-Driven Input], page 387.

Asynchronous input mode is a BSD feature.

int O_FSYNC [Macro]

The bit that enables synchronous writing for the file. If set, each `write` call will make sure the data is reliably stored on disk before returning.

Synchronous writing is a BSD feature.

int O_SYNC [Macro]

This is another name for `O_FSYNC`. They have the same value.

int O_NOATIME [Macro]

If this bit is set, `read` will not update the access time of the file. See Section 14.9.9 [File Times], page 426. This is used by programs that do backups, so that backing a file up does not count as reading it. Only the owner of the file or the superuser may use this bit.

This is a GNU extension.

13.14.4 Getting and Setting File Status Flags

The `fcntl` function can fetch or change file status flags.

int F_GETFL [Macro]

This macro is used as the *command* argument to `fcntl`, to read the file status flags for the open file with descriptor *filedes*.

The normal return value from `fcntl` with this command is a nonnegative number which can be interpreted as the bitwise OR of the individual flags. Since the file access modes are not single-bit values, you can mask off other bits in the returned flags with `O_ACCMODE` to compare them.

In case of an error, `fcntl` returns −1. The following **errno** error conditions are defined for this command:

EBADF   The *filedes* argument is invalid.

`int F_SETFL`   [Macro]

This macro is used as the *command* argument to `fcntl`, to set the file status flags for the open file corresponding to the *filedes* argument. This command requires a third `int` argument to specify the new flags, so the call looks like this:

>   fcntl (*filedes*, F_SETFL, *new-flags*)

You can't change the access mode for the file in this way; that is, whether the file descriptor was opened for reading or writing.

The normal return value from `fcntl` with this command is an unspecified value other than −1, which indicates an error. The error conditions are the same as for the `F_GETFL` command.

If you want to modify the file status flags, you should get the current flags with `F_GETFL` and modify the value. Don't assume that the flags listed here are the only ones that are implemented; your program may be run years from now and more flags may exist then. For example, here is a function to set or clear the flag `O_NONBLOCK` without altering any other flags:

```
/* Set the O_NONBLOCK flag of desc if value is nonzero,
   or clear the flag if value is 0.
   Return 0 on success, or -1 on error with errno set. */

int
set_nonblock_flag (int desc, int value)
{
  int oldflags = fcntl (desc, F_GETFL, 0);
  /* If reading the flags failed, return error indication now. */
  if (oldflags == -1)
    return -1;
  /* Set just the flag we want to set. */
  if (value != 0)
    oldflags |= O_NONBLOCK;
  else
    oldflags &= ~O_NONBLOCK;
  /* Store modified flag word in the descriptor. */
  return fcntl (desc, F_SETFL, oldflags);
}
```

13.15 File Locks

This section describes record locks that are associated with the process. There is also a different type of record lock that is associated with the open file description instead of the process. See Section 13.16 [Open File Description Locks], page 384.

The remaining `fcntl` commands are used to support *record locking*, which permits multiple cooperating programs to prevent each other from simultaneously accessing parts of a file in error-prone ways.

An *exclusive* or *write* lock gives a process exclusive access for writing to the specified part of the file. While a write lock is in place, no other process can lock that part of the file.

A *shared* or *read* lock prohibits any other process from requesting a write lock on the specified part of the file. However, other processes can request read locks.

The `read` and `write` functions do not actually check to see whether there are any locks in place. If you want to implement a locking protocol for a file shared by multiple processes, your application must do explicit `fcntl` calls to request and clear locks at the appropriate points.

Locks are associated with processes. A process can only have one kind of lock set for each byte of a given file. When any file descriptor for that file is closed by the process, all of the locks that process holds on that file are released, even if the locks were made using other descriptors that remain open. Likewise, locks are released when a process exits, and are not inherited by child processes created using `fork` (see Section 26.4 [Creating a Process], page 775).

When making a lock, use a `struct flock` to specify what kind of lock and where. This data type and the associated macros for the `fcntl` function are declared in the header file `fcntl.h`.

`struct flock`   [Data Type]

> This structure is used with the `fcntl` function to describe a file lock. It has these members:

> `short int l_type`
>
> > Specifies the type of the lock; one of `F_RDLCK`, `F_WRLCK`, or `F_UNLCK`.

> `short int l_whence`
>
> > This corresponds to the *whence* argument to `fseek` or `lseek`, and specifies what the offset is relative to. Its value can be one of `SEEK_SET`, `SEEK_CUR`, or `SEEK_END`.

> `off_t l_start`
>
> > This specifies the offset of the start of the region to which the lock applies, and is given in bytes relative to the point specified by the `l_whence` member.

> `off_t l_len`
>
> > This specifies the length of the region to be locked. A value of 0 is treated specially; it means the region extends to the end of the file.

> `pid_t l_pid`
>
> > This field is the process ID (see Section 26.2 [Process Creation Concepts], page 774) of the process holding the lock. It is filled in by calling `fcntl` with the `F_GETLK` command, but is ignored when making a lock. If the conflicting lock is an open file description lock (see Section 13.16 [Open File Description Locks], page 384), then this field will be set to −1.

int F_GETLK   [Macro]

> This macro is used as the *command* argument to `fcntl`, to specify that it should
> get information about a lock. This command requires a third argument of type
> `struct flock *` to be passed to `fcntl`, so that the form of the call is:
>
>> `fcntl (filedes, F_GETLK, lockp)`
>
> If there is a lock already in place that would block the lock described by the *lockp*
> argument, information about that lock overwrites **lockp*. Existing locks are not
> reported if they are compatible with making a new lock as specified. Thus, you
> should specify a lock type of `F_WRLCK` if you want to find out about both read and
> write locks, or `F_RDLCK` if you want to find out about write locks only.
>
> There might be more than one lock affecting the region specified by the *lockp* argu-
> ment, but `fcntl` only returns information about one of them. The `l_whence` member
> of the *lockp* structure is set to `SEEK_SET` and the `l_start` and `l_len` fields set to
> identify the locked region.
>
> If no lock applies, the only change to the *lockp* structure is to update the `l_type` to
> a value of `F_UNLCK`.
>
> The normal return value from `fcntl` with this command is an unspecified value other
> than −1, which is reserved to indicate an error. The following `errno` error conditions
> are defined for this command:
>
> EBADF   The *filedes* argument is invalid.
>
> EINVAL   Either the *lockp* argument doesn't specify valid lock information, or the
>   file associated with *filedes* doesn't support locks.

int F_SETLK   [Macro]

> This macro is used as the *command* argument to `fcntl`, to specify that it should set
> or clear a lock. This command requires a third argument of type `struct flock *` to
> be passed to `fcntl`, so that the form of the call is:
>
>> `fcntl (filedes, F_SETLK, lockp)`
>
> If the process already has a lock on any part of the region, the old lock on that part
> is replaced with the new lock. You can remove a lock by specifying a lock type of
> `F_UNLCK`.
>
> If the lock cannot be set, `fcntl` returns immediately with a value of −1. This function
> does not block while waiting for other processes to release locks. If `fcntl` succeeds,
> it returns a value other than −1.
>
> The following `errno` error conditions are defined for this function:
>
> EAGAIN
> EACCES   The lock cannot be set because it is blocked by an existing lock on the
>   file. Some systems use `EAGAIN` in this case, and other systems use `EACCES`;
>   your program should treat them alike, after `F_SETLK`. (GNU/Linux and
>   GNU/Hurd systems always use `EAGAIN`.)
>
> EBADF   Either: the *filedes* argument is invalid; you requested a read lock but the
>   *filedes* is not open for read access; or, you requested a write lock but the
>   *filedes* is not open for write access.

EINVAL   Either the *lockp* argument doesn't specify valid lock information, or the file associated with *filedes* doesn't support locks.

ENOLCK   The system has run out of file lock resources; there are already too many file locks in place.

> Well-designed file systems never report this error, because they have no limitation on the number of locks. However, you must still take account of the possibility of this error, as it could result from network access to a file system on another machine.

int F_SETLKW [Macro]

This macro is used as the *command* argument to `fcntl`, to specify that it should set or clear a lock. It is just like the `F_SETLK` command, but causes the process to block (or wait) until the request can be specified.

This command requires a third argument of type **struct flock ***, as for the `F_SETLK` command.

The `fcntl` return values and errors are the same as for the `F_SETLK` command, but these additional `errno` error conditions are defined for this command:

EINTR   The function was interrupted by a signal while it was waiting. See Section 24.5 [Primitives Interrupted by Signals], page 711.

EDEADLK   The specified region is being locked by another process. But that process is waiting to lock a region which the current process has locked, so waiting for the lock would result in deadlock. The system does not guarantee that it will detect all such conditions, but it lets you know if it notices one.

The following macros are defined for use as values for the `l_type` member of the `flock` structure. The values are integer constants.

F_RDLCK   This macro is used to specify a read (or shared) lock.

F_WRLCK   This macro is used to specify a write (or exclusive) lock.

F_UNLCK   This macro is used to specify that the region is unlocked.

As an example of a situation where file locking is useful, consider a program that can be run simultaneously by several different users, that logs status information to a common file. One example of such a program might be a game that uses a file to keep track of high scores. Another example might be a program that records usage or accounting information for billing purposes.

Having multiple copies of the program simultaneously writing to the file could cause the contents of the file to become mixed up. But you can prevent this kind of problem by setting a write lock on the file before actually writing to the file.

If the program also needs to read the file and wants to make sure that the contents of the file are in a consistent state, then it can also use a read lock. While the read lock is set, no other process can lock that part of the file for writing.

Remember that file locks are only an *advisory* protocol for controlling access to a file. There is still potential for access to the file by programs that don't use the lock protocol.

13.16 Open File Description Locks

In contrast to process-associated record locks (see Section 13.15 [File Locks], page 380), open file description record locks are associated with an open file description rather than a process.

Using `fcntl` to apply an open file description lock on a region that already has an existing open file description lock that was created via the same file descriptor will never cause a lock conflict.

Open file description locks are also inherited by child processes across `fork`, or `clone` with `CLONE_FILES` set (see Section 26.4 [Creating a Process], page 775), along with the file descriptor.

It is important to distinguish between the open file *description* (an instance of an open file, usually created by a call to `open`) and an open file *descriptor*, which is a numeric value that refers to the open file description. The locks described here are associated with the open file *description* and not the open file *descriptor*.

Using `dup` (see Section 13.12 [Duplicating Descriptors], page 373) to copy a file descriptor does not give you a new open file description, but rather copies a reference to an existing open file description and assigns it to a new file descriptor. Thus, open file description locks set on a file descriptor cloned by `dup` will never conflict with open file description locks set on the original descriptor since they refer to the same open file description. Depending on the range and type of lock involved, the original lock may be modified by a `F_OFD_SETLK` or `F_OFD_SETLKW` command in this situation however.

Open file description locks always conflict with process-associated locks, even if acquired by the same process or on the same open file descriptor.

Open file description locks use the same `struct flock` as process-associated locks as an argument (see Section 13.15 [File Locks], page 380) and the macros for the `command` values are also declared in the header file `fcntl.h`. To use them, the macro `_GNU_SOURCE` must be defined prior to including any header file.

In contrast to process-associated locks, any `struct flock` used as an argument to open file description lock commands must have the `l_pid` value set to 0. Also, when returning information about an open file description lock in a `F_GETLK` or `F_OFD_GETLK` request, the `l_pid` field in `struct flock` will be set to −1 to indicate that the lock is not associated with a process.

When the same `struct flock` is reused as an argument to a `F_OFD_SETLK` or `F_OFD_SETLKW` request after being used for an `F_OFD_GETLK` request, it is necessary to inspect and reset the `l_pid` field to 0.

int F_OFD_GETLK   [Macro]
> This macro is used as the *command* argument to `fcntl`, to specify that it should get information about a lock. This command requires a third argument of type `struct flock *` to be passed to `fcntl`, so that the form of the call is:
>
>   fcntl (filedes, F_OFD_GETLK, lockp)
>
> If there is a lock already in place that would block the lock described by the *lockp* argument, information about that lock is written to **lockp*. Existing locks are not reported if they are compatible with making a new lock as specified. Thus, you should

specify a lock type of F_WRLCK if you want to find out about both read and write locks, or F_RDLCK if you want to find out about write locks only.

There might be more than one lock affecting the region specified by the *lockp* argument, but **fcntl** only returns information about one of them. Which lock is returned in this situation is undefined.

The l_whence member of the *lockp* structure are set to SEEK_SET and the l_start and l_len fields are set to identify the locked region.

If no conflicting lock exists, the only change to the *lockp* structure is to update the l_type field to the value F_UNLCK.

The normal return value from **fcntl** with this command is either 0 on success or −1, which indicates an error. The following **errno** error conditions are defined for this command:

EBADF The *filedes* argument is invalid.

EINVAL Either the *lockp* argument doesn't specify valid lock information, the operating system kernel doesn't support open file description locks, or the file associated with *filedes* doesn't support locks.

int F_OFD_SETLK   [Macro]

This macro is used as the *command* argument to **fcntl**, to specify that it should set or clear a lock. This command requires a third argument of type **struct flock *** to be passed to **fcntl**, so that the form of the call is:

```
fcntl (filedes, F_OFD_SETLK, lockp)
```

If the open file already has a lock on any part of the region, the old lock on that part is replaced with the new lock. You can remove a lock by specifying a lock type of F_UNLCK.

If the lock cannot be set, **fcntl** returns immediately with a value of −1. This command does not wait for other tasks to release locks. If **fcntl** succeeds, it returns 0.

The following **errno** error conditions are defined for this command:

EAGAIN The lock cannot be set because it is blocked by an existing lock on the file.

EBADF Either: the *filedes* argument is invalid; you requested a read lock but the *filedes* is not open for read access; or, you requested a write lock but the *filedes* is not open for write access.

EINVAL Either the *lockp* argument doesn't specify valid lock information, the operating system kernel doesn't support open file description locks, or the file associated with *filedes* doesn't support locks.

ENOLCK The system has run out of file lock resources; there are already too many file locks in place.

      Well-designed file systems never report this error, because they have no limitation on the number of locks. However, you must still take account of the possibility of this error, as it could result from network access to a file system on another machine.

`int F_OFD_SETLKW`   [Macro]

> This macro is used as the *command* argument to `fcntl`, to specify that it should set or clear a lock. It is just like the `F_OFD_SETLK` command, but causes the process to wait until the request can be completed.
>
> This command requires a third argument of type `struct flock *`, as for the `F_OFD_SETLK` command.
>
> The `fcntl` return values and errors are the same as for the `F_OFD_SETLK` command, but these additional `errno` error conditions are defined for this command:
>
> `EINTR`   The function was interrupted by a signal while it was waiting. See Section 24.5 [Primitives Interrupted by Signals], page 711.

Open file description locks are useful in the same sorts of situations as process-associated locks. They can also be used to synchronize file access between threads within the same process by having each thread perform its own `open` of the file, to obtain its own open file description.

Because open file description locks are automatically freed only upon closing the last file descriptor that refers to the open file description, this locking mechanism avoids the possibility that locks are inadvertently released due to a library routine opening and closing a file without the application being aware.

As with process-associated locks, open file description locks are advisory.

13.17 Open File Description Locks Example

Here is an example of using open file description locks in a threaded program. If this program used process-associated locks, then it would be subject to data corruption because process-associated locks are shared by the threads inside a process, and thus cannot be used by one thread to lock out another thread in the same process.

Proper error handling has been omitted in the following program for brevity.

```
#define _GNU_SOURCE
#include <stdio.h>
#include <sys/types.h>
#include <sys/stat.h>
#include <unistd.h>
#include <fcntl.h>
#include <pthread.h>

#define FILENAME      "/tmp/foo"
#define NUM_THREADS   3
#define ITERATIONS    5

void *
thread_start (void *arg)
{
  int i, fd, len;
  long tid = (long) arg;
  char buf[256];
  struct flock lck = {
    .l_whence = SEEK_SET,
    .l_start = 0,
```

```
      .l_len = 1,
    };

    fd = open ("/tmp/foo", O_RDWR | O_CREAT, 0666);

    for (i = 0; i < ITERATIONS; i++)
      {
        lck.l_type = F_WRLCK;
        fcntl (fd, F_OFD_SETLKW, &lck);

        len = sprintf (buf, "%d: tid=%ld fd=%d\n", i, tid, fd);

        lseek (fd, 0, SEEK_END);
        write (fd, buf, len);
        fsync (fd);

        lck.l_type = F_UNLCK;
        fcntl (fd, F_OFD_SETLK, &lck);

        /* sleep to ensure lock is yielded to another thread */
        usleep (1);
      }
    pthread_exit (NULL);
}

int
main (int argc, char **argv)
{
  long i;
  pthread_t threads[NUM_THREADS];

  truncate (FILENAME, 0);

  for (i = 0; i < NUM_THREADS; i++)
    pthread_create (&threads[i], NULL, thread_start, (void *) i);

  pthread_exit (NULL);
  return 0;
}
```

This example creates three threads each of which loops five times, appending to the file. Access to the file is serialized via open file description locks. If we compile and run the above program, we'll end up with /tmp/foo that has 15 lines in it.

If we, however, were to replace the **F_OFD_SETLK** and **F_OFD_SETLKW** commands with their process-associated lock equivalents, the locking essentially becomes a noop since it is all done within the context of the same process. That leads to data corruption (typically manifested as missing lines) as some threads race in and overwrite the data written by others.

13.18 Interrupt-Driven Input

If you set the **O_ASYNC** status flag on a file descriptor (see Section 13.14 [File Status Flags], page 375), a **SIGIO** signal is sent whenever input or output becomes possible on that file descriptor. The process or process group to receive the signal can be selected by using the **F_SETOWN** command to the **fcntl** function. If the file descriptor is a socket, this also selects the recipient of SIGURG signals that are delivered when out-of-band data arrives on that socket; see Section 16.9.8 [Out-of-Band Data], page 477. (SIGURG is sent in any situation where select would report the socket as having an "exceptional condition". See Section 13.8 [Waiting for Input or Output], page 355.)

If the file descriptor corresponds to a terminal device, then SIGIO signals are sent to the foreground process group of the terminal. See Chapter 28 [Job Control], page 786.

The symbols in this section are defined in the header file fcntl.h.

---

int F_GETOWN   [Macro]

This macro is used as the *command* argument to fcntl, to specify that it should get information about the process or process group to which SIGIO signals are sent. (For a terminal, this is actually the foreground process group ID, which you can get using tcgetpgrp; see Section 28.7.3 [Functions for Controlling Terminal Access], page 803.)

The return value is interpreted as a process ID; if negative, its absolute value is the process group ID.

The following errno error condition is defined for this command:

EBADF   The *filedes* argument is invalid.

---

int F_SETOWN   [Macro]

This macro is used as the *command* argument to fcntl, to specify that it should set the process or process group to which SIGIO signals are sent. This command requires a third argument of type pid_t to be passed to fcntl, so that the form of the call is:

    fcntl (*filedes*, F_SETOWN, *pid*)

The *pid* argument should be a process ID. You can also pass a negative number whose absolute value is a process group ID.

The return value from fcntl with this command is −1 in case of error and some other value if successful. The following errno error conditions are defined for this command:

EBADF   The *filedes* argument is invalid.

ESRCH   There is no process or process group corresponding to *pid*.

13.19 Generic I/O Control operations

GNU systems can handle most input/output operations on many different devices and objects in terms of a few file primitives - read, write and lseek. However, most devices also have a few peculiar operations which do not fit into this model. Such as:

- Changing the character font used on a terminal.
- Telling a magnetic tape system to rewind or fast forward. (Since they cannot move in byte increments, lseek is inapplicable).
- Ejecting a disk from a drive.
- Playing an audio track from a CD-ROM drive.
- Maintaining routing tables for a network.

Although some such objects such as sockets and terminals[1] have special functions of their own, it would not be practical to create functions for all these cases.

Instead these minor operations, known as *IOCTLs*, are assigned code numbers and multiplexed through the `ioctl` function, defined in `sys/ioctl.h`. The code numbers themselves are defined in many different headers.

int ioctl (*int filedes*, *int command*, ...)   [Function]

> Preliminary: | MT-Safe | AS-Safe | AC-Safe | See Section 1.2.2.1 [POSIX Safety Concepts], page 2.
>
> The `ioctl` function performs the generic I/O operation *command* on *filedes*.
>
> A third argument is usually present, either a single number or a pointer to a structure. The meaning of this argument, the returned value, and any error codes depends upon the command used. Often −1 is returned for a failure.

On some systems, IOCTLs used by different devices share the same numbers. Thus, although use of an inappropriate IOCTL *usually* only produces an error, you should not attempt to use device-specific IOCTLs on an unknown device.

Most IOCTLs are OS-specific and/or only used in special system utilities, and are thus beyond the scope of this document. For an example of the use of an IOCTL, see Section 16.9.8 [Out-of-Band Data], page 477.

---

[1] Actually, the terminal-specific functions are implemented with IOCTLs on many platforms.

14 File System Interface

This chapter describes the GNU C Library's functions for manipulating files. Unlike the input and output functions (see Chapter 12 [Input/Output on Streams], page 257; see Chapter 13 [Low-Level Input/Output], page 333), these functions are concerned with operating on the files themselves rather than on their contents.

Among the facilities described in this chapter are functions for examining or modifying directories, functions for renaming and deleting files, and functions for examining and setting file attributes such as access permissions and modification times.

14.1 Working Directory

Each process has associated with it a directory, called its *current working directory* or simply *working directory*, that is used in the resolution of relative file names (see Section 11.2.2 [File Name Resolution], page 255).

When you log in and begin a new session, your working directory is initially set to the home directory associated with your login account in the system user database. You can find any user's home directory using the `getpwuid` or `getpwnam` functions; see Section 30.13 [User Database], page 834.

Users can change the working directory using shell commands like `cd`. The functions described in this section are the primitives used by those commands and by other programs for examining and changing the working directory.

Prototypes for these functions are declared in the header file `unistd.h`.

char * getcwd (*char *buffer*, *size_t size*)   [Function]
> Preliminary: | MT-Safe | AS-Unsafe heap | AC-Unsafe mem fd | See Section 1.2.2.1 [POSIX Safety Concepts], page 2.
>
> The `getcwd` function returns an absolute file name representing the current working directory, storing it in the character array *buffer* that you provide. The *size* argument is how you tell the system the allocation size of *buffer*.
>
> The GNU C Library version of this function also permits you to specify a null pointer for the *buffer* argument. Then `getcwd` allocates a buffer automatically, as with `malloc` (see Section 3.2.3 [Unconstrained Allocation], page 44). If the *size* is greater than zero, then the buffer is that large; otherwise, the buffer is as large as necessary to hold the result.
>
> The return value is *buffer* on success and a null pointer on failure. The following `errno` error conditions are defined for this function:
>
> EINVAL   The *size* argument is zero and *buffer* is not a null pointer.
>
> ERANGE   The *size* argument is less than the length of the working directory name. You need to allocate a bigger array and try again.
>
> EACCES   Permission to read or search a component of the file name was denied.

You could implement the behavior of GNU's `getcwd (NULL, 0)` using only the standard behavior of `getcwd`:

```
char *
```

```
gnu_getcwd ()
{
  size_t size = 100;

  while (1)
    {
      char *buffer = (char *) xmalloc (size);
      if (getcwd (buffer, size) == buffer)
        return buffer;
      free (buffer);
      if (errno != ERANGE)
        return 0;
      size *= 2;
    }
}
```

See Section 3.2.3.2 [Examples of malloc], page 45, for information about xmalloc, which is not a library function but is a customary name used in most GNU software.

char * getwd (char *buffer)   [Deprecated Function]
    Preliminary: | MT-Safe | AS-Unsafe heap i18n | AC-Unsafe mem fd | See Section 1.2.2.1 [POSIX Safety Concepts], page 2.

    This is similar to getcwd, but has no way to specify the size of the buffer. The GNU C Library provides getwd only for backwards compatibility with BSD.

    The buffer argument should be a pointer to an array at least PATH_MAX bytes long (see Section 32.6 [Limits on File System Capacity], page 874). On GNU/Hurd systems there is no limit to the size of a file name, so this is not necessarily enough space to contain the directory name. That is why this function is deprecated.

char * get_current_dir_name (void)   [Function]
    Preliminary: | MT-Safe env | AS-Unsafe heap | AC-Unsafe mem fd | See Section 1.2.2.1 [POSIX Safety Concepts], page 2.

    This get_current_dir_name function is basically equivalent to getcwd (NULL, 0). The only difference is that the value of the PWD variable is returned if this value is correct. This is a subtle difference which is visible if the path described by the PWD value is using one or more symbol links in which case the value returned by getcwd can resolve the symbol links and therefore yield a different result.

    This function is a GNU extension.

int chdir (const char *filename)   [Function]
    Preliminary: | MT-Safe | AS-Safe | AC-Safe | See Section 1.2.2.1 [POSIX Safety Concepts], page 2.

    This function is used to set the process's working directory to filename.

    The normal, successful return value from chdir is 0. A value of -1 is returned to indicate an error. The errno error conditions defined for this function are the usual file name syntax errors (see Section 11.2.3 [File Name Errors], page 255), plus ENOTDIR if the file filename is not a directory.

int fchdir (int filedes)   [Function]
    Preliminary: | MT-Safe | AS-Safe | AC-Safe | See Section 1.2.2.1 [POSIX Safety Concepts], page 2.

This function is used to set the process's working directory to directory associated with the file descriptor *filedes*.

The normal, successful return value from `fchdir` is 0. A value of `-1` is returned to indicate an error. The following `errno` error conditions are defined for this function:

EACCES   Read permission is denied for the directory named by `dirname`.

EBADF   The *filedes* argument is not a valid file descriptor.

ENOTDIR   The file descriptor *filedes* is not associated with a directory.

EINTR   The function call was interrupt by a signal.

EIO   An I/O error occurred.

14.2 Accessing Directories

The facilities described in this section let you read the contents of a directory file. This is useful if you want your program to list all the files in a directory, perhaps as part of a menu.

The `opendir` function opens a *directory stream* whose elements are directory entries. Alternatively `fdopendir` can be used which can have advantages if the program needs to have more control over the way the directory is opened for reading. This allows, for instance, to pass the `O_NOATIME` flag to `open`.

You use the `readdir` function on the directory stream to retrieve these entries, represented as `struct dirent` objects. The name of the file for each entry is stored in the `d_name` member of this structure. There are obvious parallels here to the stream facilities for ordinary files, described in Chapter 12 [Input/Output on Streams], page 257.

14.2.1 Format of a Directory Entry

This section describes what you find in a single directory entry, as you might obtain it from a directory stream. All the symbols are declared in the header file `dirent.h`.

`struct dirent`   [Data Type]

> This is a structure type used to return information about directory entries. It contains the following fields:
>
> `char d_name[]`
>> This is the null-terminated file name component. This is the only field you can count on in all POSIX systems.
>
> `ino_t d_fileno`
>> This is the file serial number. For BSD compatibility, you can also refer to this member as `d_ino`. On GNU/Linux and GNU/Hurd systems and most POSIX systems, for most files this the same as the `st_ino` member that `stat` will return for the file. See Section 14.9 [File Attributes], page 412.
>
> `unsigned char d_namlen`
>> This is the length of the file name, not including the terminating null character. Its type is `unsigned char` because that is the integer type of the appropriate size. This member is a BSD extension. The symbol `_DIRENT_HAVE_D_NAMLEN` is defined if this member is available.

`unsigned char d_type`

> This is the type of the file, possibly unknown. The following constants are defined for its value:

`DT_UNKNOWN`

> > The type is unknown. Only some filesystems have full support to return the type of the file, others might always return this value.

`DT_REG`   A regular file.

`DT_DIR`   A directory.

`DT_FIFO` A named pipe, or FIFO. See Section 15.3 [FIFO Special Files], page 440.

`DT_SOCK` A local-domain socket.

`DT_CHR`   A character device.

`DT_BLK`   A block device.

`DT_LNK`   A symbolic link.

> This member is a BSD extension. The symbol `_DIRENT_HAVE_D_TYPE` is defined if this member is available. On systems where it is used, it corresponds to the file type bits in the `st_mode` member of `struct stat`. If the value cannot be determined the member value is DT_UNKNOWN. These two macros convert between `d_type` values and `st_mode` values:

`int IFTODT (`*`mode_t mode`*`)`   [Function]

> Preliminary: | MT-Safe | AS-Safe | AC-Safe | See Section 1.2.2.1 [POSIX Safety Concepts], page 2.
>
> This returns the `d_type` value corresponding to *mode*.

`mode_t DTTOIF (`*`int dtype`*`)`   [Function]

> Preliminary: | MT-Safe | AS-Safe | AC-Safe | See Section 1.2.2.1 [POSIX Safety Concepts], page 2.
>
> This returns the `st_mode` value corresponding to *dtype*.

This structure may contain additional members in the future. Their availability is always announced in the compilation environment by a macro named `_DIRENT_HAVE_D_xxx` where *xxx* is replaced by the name of the new member. For instance, the member `d_reclen` available on some systems is announced through the macro `_DIRENT_HAVE_D_RECLEN`.

When a file has multiple names, each name has its own directory entry. The only way you can tell that the directory entries belong to a single file is that they have the same value for the `d_fileno` field.

File attributes such as size, modification times etc., are part of the file itself, not of any particular directory entry. See Section 14.9 [File Attributes], page 412.

14.2.2 Opening a Directory Stream

This section describes how to open a directory stream. All the symbols are declared in the header file `dirent.h`.

DIR [Data Type]

> The `DIR` data type represents a directory stream.

You shouldn't ever allocate objects of the `struct dirent` or `DIR` data types, since the directory access functions do that for you. Instead, you refer to these objects using the pointers returned by the following functions.

DIR * opendir (*const char *dirname*) [Function]

> Preliminary: | MT-Safe | AS-Unsafe heap | AC-Unsafe mem fd | See Section 1.2.2.1 [POSIX Safety Concepts], page 2.
>
> The `opendir` function opens and returns a directory stream for reading the directory whose file name is *dirname*. The stream has type `DIR *`.
>
> If unsuccessful, `opendir` returns a null pointer. In addition to the usual file name errors (see Section 11.2.3 [File Name Errors], page 255), the following `errno` error conditions are defined for this function:
>
> > **EACCES** Read permission is denied for the directory named by `dirname`.
> >
> > **EMFILE** The process has too many files open.
> >
> > **ENFILE** The entire system, or perhaps the file system which contains the directory, cannot support any additional open files at the moment. (This problem cannot happen on GNU/Hurd systems.)
> >
> > **ENOMEM** Not enough memory available.
>
> The `DIR` type is typically implemented using a file descriptor, and the `opendir` function in terms of the `open` function. See Chapter 13 [Low-Level Input/Output], page 333. Directory streams and the underlying file descriptors are closed on `exec` (see Section 26.5 [Executing a File], page 776).

The directory which is opened for reading by `opendir` is identified by the name. In some situations this is not sufficient. Or the way `opendir` implicitly creates a file descriptor for the directory is not the way a program might want it. In these cases an alternative interface can be used.

DIR * fdopendir (*int fd*) [Function]

> Preliminary: | MT-Safe | AS-Unsafe heap | AC-Unsafe mem fd | See Section 1.2.2.1 [POSIX Safety Concepts], page 2.
>
> The `fdopendir` function works just like `opendir` but instead of taking a file name and opening a file descriptor for the directory the caller is required to provide a file descriptor. This file descriptor is then used in subsequent uses of the returned directory stream object.
>
> The caller must make sure the file descriptor is associated with a directory and it allows reading.

If the `fdopendir` call returns successfully the file descriptor is now under the control of the system. It can be used in the same way the descriptor implicitly created by `opendir` can be used but the program must not close the descriptor.

In case the function is unsuccessful it returns a null pointer and the file descriptor remains to be usable by the program. The following `errno` error conditions are defined for this function:

`EBADF`   The file descriptor is not valid.

`ENOTDIR`   The file descriptor is not associated with a directory.

`EINVAL`   The descriptor does not allow reading the directory content.

`ENOMEM`   Not enough memory available.

In some situations it can be desirable to get hold of the file descriptor which is created by the `opendir` call. For instance, to switch the current working directory to the directory just read the `fchdir` function could be used. Historically the `DIR` type was exposed and programs could access the fields. This does not happen in the GNU C Library. Instead a separate function is provided to allow access.

`int dirfd (DIR *dirstream)`   [Function]
> Preliminary: | MT-Safe | AS-Safe | AC-Safe | See Section 1.2.2.1 [POSIX Safety Concepts], page 2.
>
> The function `dirfd` returns the file descriptor associated with the directory stream *dirstream*. This descriptor can be used until the directory is closed with `closedir`. If the directory stream implementation is not using file descriptors the return value is `-1`.

14.2.3 Reading and Closing a Directory Stream

This section describes how to read directory entries from a directory stream, and how to close the stream when you are done with it. All the symbols are declared in the header file `dirent.h`.

`struct dirent * readdir (DIR *dirstream)`   [Function]
> Preliminary: | MT-Safe | AS-Unsafe lock | AC-Unsafe lock | See Section 1.2.2.1 [POSIX Safety Concepts], page 2.
>
> This function reads the next entry from the directory. It normally returns a pointer to a structure containing information about the file. This structure is associated with the *dirstream* handle and can be rewritten by a subsequent call.
>
> **Portability Note:** On some systems `readdir` may not return entries for . and .., even though these are always valid file names in any directory. See Section 11.2.2 [File Name Resolution], page 255.
>
> If there are no more entries in the directory or an error is detected, `readdir` returns a null pointer. The following `errno` error conditions are defined for this function:
>
> `EBADF`   The *dirstream* argument is not valid.
>
> To distinguish between an end-of-directory condition or an error, you must set `errno` to zero before calling `readdir`. To avoid entering an infinite loop, you should stop reading from the directory after the first error.

Caution: The pointer returned by `readdir` points to a buffer within the `DIR` object. The data in that buffer will be overwritten by the next call to `readdir`. You must take care, for instance, to copy the `d_name` string if you need it later.

Because of this, it is not safe to share a `DIR` object among multiple threads, unless you use your own locking to ensure that no thread calls `readdir` while another thread is still using the data from the previous call. In the GNU C Library, it is safe to call `readdir` from multiple threads as long as each thread uses its own `DIR` object. POSIX.1-2008 does not require this to be safe, but we are not aware of any operating systems where it does not work.

`readdir_r` allows you to provide your own buffer for the `struct dirent`, but it is less portable than `readdir`, and has problems with very long filenames (see below). We recommend you use `readdir`, but do not share DIR objects.

`int readdir_r` (*DIR *dirstream, struct dirent *entry, struct dirent*   [Function]
   **result)

Preliminary: | MT-Safe | AS-Unsafe lock | AC-Unsafe lock | See Section 1.2.2.1 [POSIX Safety Concepts], page 2.

This function is a version of `readdir` which performs internal locking. Like `readdir` it returns the next entry from the directory. To prevent conflicts between simultaneously running threads the result is stored inside the *entry* object.

Portability Note: `readdir_r` is deprecated. It is recommended to use `readdir` instead of `readdir_r` for the following reasons:

- On systems which do not define `NAME_MAX`, it may not be possible to use `readdir_r` safely because the caller does not specify the length of the buffer for the directory entry.

- On some systems, `readdir_r` cannot read directory entries with very long names. If such a name is encountered, the GNU C Library implementation of `readdir_r` returns with an error code of `ENAMETOOLONG` after the final directory entry has been read. On other systems, `readdir_r` may return successfully, but the `d_name` member may not be NUL-terminated or may be truncated.

- POSIX-1.2008 does not guarantee that `readdir` is thread-safe, even when access to the same *dirstream* is serialized. But in current implementations (including the GNU C Library), it is safe to call `readdir` concurrently on different *dirstreams*, so there is no need to use `readdir_r` in most multi-threaded programs. In the rare case that multiple threads need to read from the same *dirstream*, it is still better to use `readdir` and external synchronization.

- It is expected that future versions of POSIX will obsolete `readdir_r` and mandate the level of thread safety for `readdir` which is provided by the GNU C Library and other implementations today.

Normally `readdir_r` returns zero and sets **result* to *entry*. If there are no more entries in the directory or an error is detected, `readdir_r` sets **result* to a null pointer and returns a nonzero error code, also stored in `errno`, as described for `readdir`.

It is also important to look at the definition of the `struct dirent` type. Simply passing a pointer to an object of this type for the second parameter of `readdir_r` might not be enough. Some systems don't define the **d_name** element sufficiently long. In this case the user has to provide additional space. There must be room for at least **NAME_MAX + 1** characters in the **d_name** array. Code to call **readdir_r** could look like this:

```
union
{
  struct dirent d;
  char b[offsetof (struct dirent, d_name) + NAME_MAX + 1];
} u;

if (readdir_r (dir, &u.d, &res) == 0)
  ...
```

To support large filesystems on 32-bit machines there are LFS variants of the last two functions.

struct dirent64 * readdir64 (*DIR *dirstream*)   [Function]

Preliminary: | MT-Safe | AS-Unsafe lock | AC-Unsafe lock | See Section 1.2.2.1 [POSIX Safety Concepts], page 2.

The **readdir64** function is just like the **readdir** function except that it returns a pointer to a record of type **struct dirent64**. Some of the members of this data type (notably **d_ino**) might have a different size to allow large filesystems.

In all other aspects this function is equivalent to **readdir**.

int readdir64_r (*DIR *dirstream*, *struct dirent64 *entry*, *struct*   [Function]
    ***dirent64 **result*)**

Preliminary: | MT-Safe | AS-Unsafe lock | AC-Unsafe lock | See Section 1.2.2.1 [POSIX Safety Concepts], page 2.

The deprecated **readdir64_r** function is equivalent to the **readdir_r** function except that it takes parameters of base type **struct dirent64** instead of **struct dirent** in the second and third position. The same precautions mentioned in the documentation of **readdir_r** also apply here.

int closedir (*DIR *dirstream*)   [Function]

Preliminary: | MT-Safe | AS-Unsafe heap lock/hurd | AC-Unsafe mem fd lock/hurd | See Section 1.2.2.1 [POSIX Safety Concepts], page 2.

This function closes the directory stream *dirstream*. It returns 0 on success and −1 on failure.

The following **errno** error conditions are defined for this function:

EBADF   The *dirstream* argument is not valid.

14.2.4 Simple Program to List a Directory

Here's a simple program that prints the names of the files in the current working directory:

```
#include <stdio.h>
#include <sys/types.h>
#include <dirent.h>

int
```

```
main (void)
{
  DIR *dp;
  struct dirent *ep;

  dp = opendir ("./");
  if (dp != NULL)
    {
      while (ep = readdir (dp))
        puts (ep->d_name);
      (void) closedir (dp);
    }
  else
    perror ("Couldn't open the directory");

  return 0;
}
```

The order in which files appear in a directory tends to be fairly random. A more useful program would sort the entries (perhaps by alphabetizing them) before printing them; see Section 14.2.6 [Scanning the Content of a Directory], page 399, and Section 9.3 [Array Sort Function], page 221.

14.2.5 Random Access in a Directory Stream

This section describes how to reread parts of a directory that you have already read from an open directory stream. All the symbols are declared in the header file dirent.h.

void rewinddir (*DIR *dirstream*)   [Function]

Preliminary: | MT-Safe | AS-Unsafe lock | AC-Unsafe lock | See Section 1.2.2.1 [POSIX Safety Concepts], page 2.

The rewinddir function is used to reinitialize the directory stream *dirstream*, so that if you call readdir it returns information about the first entry in the directory again. This function also notices if files have been added or removed to the directory since it was opened with opendir. (Entries for these files might or might not be returned by readdir if they were added or removed since you last called opendir or rewinddir.)

long int telldir (*DIR *dirstream*)   [Function]

Preliminary: | MT-Safe | AS-Unsafe heap/bsd lock/bsd | AC-Unsafe mem/bsd lock/bsd | See Section 1.2.2.1 [POSIX Safety Concepts], page 2.

The telldir function returns the file position of the directory stream *dirstream*. You can use this value with seekdir to restore the directory stream to that position.

void seekdir (*DIR *dirstream, long int pos*)   [Function]

Preliminary: | MT-Safe | AS-Unsafe heap/bsd lock/bsd | AC-Unsafe mem/bsd lock/bsd | See Section 1.2.2.1 [POSIX Safety Concepts], page 2.

The seekdir function sets the file position of the directory stream *dirstream* to *pos*. The value *pos* must be the result of a previous call to telldir on this particular stream; closing and reopening the directory can invalidate values returned by telldir.

14.2.6 Scanning the Content of a Directory

A higher-level interface to the directory handling functions is the `scandir` function. With its help one can select a subset of the entries in a directory, possibly sort them and get a list of names as the result.

int scandir (*const char *dir, struct dirent ***namelist, int*   [Function]
    (**selector*) (*const struct dirent **), *int (*cmp) (const struct dirent **,*
    const struct dirent **))

    Preliminary: | MT-Safe | AS-Unsafe heap | AC-Unsafe mem fd | See Section 1.2.2.1 [POSIX Safety Concepts], page 2.

    The `scandir` function scans the contents of the directory selected by *dir*. The result in **namelist* is an array of pointers to structures of type `struct dirent` which describe all selected directory entries and which is allocated using `malloc`. Instead of always getting all directory entries returned, the user supplied function *selector* can be used to decide which entries are in the result. Only the entries for which *selector* returns a non-zero value are selected.

    Finally the entries in **namelist* are sorted using the user-supplied function *cmp*. The arguments passed to the *cmp* function are of type `struct dirent **`, therefore one cannot directly use the `strcmp` or `strcoll` functions; instead see the functions `alphasort` and `versionsort` below.

    The return value of the function is the number of entries placed in **namelist*. If it is `-1` an error occurred (either the directory could not be opened for reading or the malloc call failed) and the global variable `errno` contains more information on the error.

As described above, the fourth argument to the `scandir` function must be a pointer to a sorting function. For the convenience of the programmer the GNU C Library contains implementations of functions which are very helpful for this purpose.

int alphasort (*const struct dirent **a, const struct dirent **b*)   [Function]
    Preliminary: | MT-Safe locale | AS-Unsafe heap | AC-Unsafe mem | See Section 1.2.2.1 [POSIX Safety Concepts], page 2.

    The `alphasort` function behaves like the `strcoll` function (see Section 5.7 [String/Array Comparison], page 107). The difference is that the arguments are not string pointers but instead they are of type `struct dirent **`.

    The return value of `alphasort` is less than, equal to, or greater than zero depending on the order of the two entries *a* and *b*.

int versionsort (*const struct dirent **a, const struct dirent **b*)   [Function]
    Preliminary: | MT-Safe locale | AS-Safe | AC-Safe | See Section 1.2.2.1 [POSIX Safety Concepts], page 2.

    The `versionsort` function is like `alphasort` except that it uses the `strverscmp` function internally.

If the filesystem supports large files we cannot use the `scandir` anymore since the `dirent` structure might not able to contain all the information. The LFS provides the new type `struct dirent64`. To use this we need a new function.

int scandir64 (*const char *dir, struct dirent64 ***namelist, int*   [Function]
    (**selector*) (*const struct dirent64 **), int (**cmp*) (*const struct dirent64
    , const struct dirent64 *))
> Preliminary: | MT-Safe | AS-Unsafe heap | AC-Unsafe mem fd | See Section 1.2.2.1
> [POSIX Safety Concepts], page 2.
>
> The `scandir64` function works like the `scandir` function except that the directory
> entries it returns are described by elements of type `struct dirent64`. The function
> pointed to by *selector* is again used to select the desired entries, except that *selector*
> now must point to a function which takes a `struct dirent64 *` parameter.
>
> Similarly the *cmp* function should expect its two arguments to be of type `struct
> dirent64 **`.

As *cmp* is now a function of a different type, the functions `alphasort` and `versionsort`
cannot be supplied for that argument. Instead we provide the two replacement functions
below.

int alphasort64 (*const struct dirent64 **a, const struct dirent **b*)   [Function]
> Preliminary: | MT-Safe locale | AS-Unsafe heap | AC-Unsafe mem | See
> Section 1.2.2.1 [POSIX Safety Concepts], page 2.
>
> The `alphasort64` function behaves like the `strcoll` function (see Section 5.7
> [String/Array Comparison], page 107). The difference is that the arguments are not
> string pointers but instead they are of type `struct dirent64 **`.
>
> Return value of `alphasort64` is less than, equal to, or greater than zero depending
> on the order of the two entries *a* and *b*.

int versionsort64 (*const struct dirent64 **a, const struct dirent64*   [Function]
    **b)
> Preliminary: | MT-Safe locale | AS-Safe | AC-Safe | See Section 1.2.2.1 [POSIX
> Safety Concepts], page 2.
>
> The `versionsort64` function is like `alphasort64`, excepted that it uses the
> `strverscmp` function internally.

It is important not to mix the use of `scandir` and the 64-bit comparison functions or
vice versa. There are systems on which this works but on others it will fail miserably.

14.2.7 Simple Program to List a Directory, Mark II

Here is a revised version of the directory lister found above (see Section 14.2.4 [Simple
Program to List a Directory], page 397). Using the `scandir` function we can avoid the
functions which work directly with the directory contents. After the call the returned
entries are available for direct use.

```
#include <stdio.h>
#include <dirent.h>

static int
one (const struct dirent *unused)
{
  return 1;
```

```
}

int
main (void)
{
  struct dirent **eps;
  int n;

  n = scandir ("./", &eps, one, alphasort);
  if (n >= 0)
    {
      int cnt;
      for (cnt = 0; cnt < n; ++cnt)
        puts (eps[cnt]->d_name);
    }
  else
    perror ("Couldn't open the directory");

  return 0;
}
```

Note the simple selector function in this example. Since we want to see all directory entries we always return 1.

14.3 Working with Directory Trees

The functions described so far for handling the files in a directory have allowed you to either retrieve the information bit by bit, or to process all the files as a group (see scandir). Sometimes it is useful to process whole hierarchies of directories and their contained files. The X/Open specification defines two functions to do this. The simpler form is derived from an early definition in System V systems and therefore this function is available on SVID-derived systems. The prototypes and required definitions can be found in the ftw.h header.

There are four functions in this family: ftw, nftw and their 64-bit counterparts ftw64 and nftw64. These functions take as one of their arguments a pointer to a callback function of the appropriate type.

__ftw_func_t   [Data Type]
       int (*) (const char *, const struct stat *, int)

The type of callback functions given to the ftw function. The first parameter points to the file name, the second parameter to an object of type struct stat which is filled in for the file named in the first parameter.

The last parameter is a flag giving more information about the current file. It can have the following values:

FTW_F   The item is either a normal file or a file which does not fit into one of the following categories. This could be special files, sockets etc.

FTW_D   The item is a directory.

FTW_NS   The stat call failed and so the information pointed to by the second parameter is invalid.

FTW_DNR   The item is a directory which cannot be read.

FTW_SL   The item is a symbolic link. Since symbolic links are normally followed seeing this value in a `ftw` callback function means the referenced file does not exist. The situation for `nftw` is different.

         This value is only available if the program is compiled with `_XOPEN_ EXTENDED` defined before including the first header. The original SVID systems do not have symbolic links.

If the sources are compiled with `_FILE_OFFSET_BITS == 64` this type is in fact `__ ftw64_func_t` since this mode changes `struct stat` to be `struct stat64`.

For the LFS interface and for use in the function `ftw64`, the header `ftw.h` defines another function type.

`__ftw64_func_t`   [Data Type]
         `int (*) (const char *, const struct stat64 *, int)`

This type is used just like `__ftw_func_t` for the callback function, but this time is called from `ftw64`. The second parameter to the function is a pointer to a variable of type `struct stat64` which is able to represent the larger values.

`__nftw_func_t`   [Data Type]
         `int (*) (const char *, const struct stat *, int, struct FTW *)`

The first three arguments are the same as for the `__ftw_func_t` type. However for the third argument some additional values are defined to allow finer differentiation:

FTW_DP   The current item is a directory and all subdirectories have already been visited and reported. This flag is returned instead of `FTW_D` if the `FTW_ DEPTH` flag is passed to `nftw` (see below).

FTW_SLN   The current item is a stale symbolic link. The file it points to does not exist.

The last parameter of the callback function is a pointer to a structure with some extra information as described below.

If the sources are compiled with `_FILE_OFFSET_BITS == 64` this type is in fact `__ nftw64_func_t` since this mode changes `struct stat` to be `struct stat64`.

For the LFS interface there is also a variant of this data type available which has to be used with the `nftw64` function.

`__nftw64_func_t`   [Data Type]
         `int (*) (const char *, const struct stat64 *, int, struct FTW *)`

This type is used just like `__nftw_func_t` for the callback function, but this time is called from `nftw64`. The second parameter to the function is this time a pointer to a variable of type `struct stat64` which is able to represent the larger values.

`struct FTW`   [Data Type]
The information contained in this structure helps in interpreting the name parameter and gives some information about the current state of the traversal of the directory hierarchy.

     `int base`   The value is the offset into the string passed in the first parameter to the callback function of the beginning of the file name. The rest of the string is the path of the file. This information is especially important if the FTW_CHDIR flag was set in calling nftw since then the current directory is the one the current item is found in.

int level   Whilst processing, the code tracks how many directories down it has gone to find the current file. This nesting level starts at 0 for files in the initial directory (or is zero for the initial file if a file was passed).

int ftw (*const char *filename*, __ftw_func_t *func*, int *descriptors*)   [Function]
Preliminary: | MT-Safe | AS-Unsafe heap | AC-Unsafe mem fd | See Section 1.2.2.1 [POSIX Safety Concepts], page 2.

The ftw function calls the callback function given in the parameter *func* for every item which is found in the directory specified by *filename* and all directories below. The function follows symbolic links if necessary but does not process an item twice. If *filename* is not a directory then it itself is the only object returned to the callback function.

The file name passed to the callback function is constructed by taking the *filename* parameter and appending the names of all passed directories and then the local file name. So the callback function can use this parameter to access the file. ftw also calls stat for the file and passes that information on to the callback function. If this stat call is not successful the failure is indicated by setting the third argument of the callback function to FTW_NS. Otherwise it is set according to the description given in the account of __ftw_func_t above.

The callback function is expected to return 0 to indicate that no error occurred and that processing should continue. If an error occurred in the callback function or it wants ftw to return immediately, the callback function can return a value other than 0. This is the only correct way to stop the function. The program must not use setjmp or similar techniques to continue from another place. This would leave resources allocated by the ftw function unfreed.

The *descriptors* parameter to ftw specifies how many file descriptors it is allowed to consume. The function runs faster the more descriptors it can use. For each level in the directory hierarchy at most one descriptor is used, but for very deep ones any limit on open file descriptors for the process or the system may be exceeded. Moreover, file descriptor limits in a multi-threaded program apply to all the threads as a group, and therefore it is a good idea to supply a reasonable limit to the number of open descriptors.

The return value of the ftw function is 0 if all callback function calls returned 0 and all actions performed by the ftw succeeded. If a function call failed (other than calling stat on an item) the function returns −1. If a callback function returns a value other than 0 this value is returned as the return value of ftw.

When the sources are compiled with _FILE_OFFSET_BITS == 64 on a 32-bit system this function is in fact ftw64, i.e., the LFS interface transparently replaces the old interface.

int·ftw64 (*const char* `*filename`, `__ftw64_func_t func`, *int*   [Function]
    descriptors)

Preliminary: | MT-Safe | AS-Unsafe heap | AC-Unsafe mem fd | See Section 1.2.2.1 [POSIX Safety Concepts], page 2.

This function is similar to `ftw` but it can work on filesystems with large files. File information is reported using a variable of type `struct stat64` which is passed by reference to the callback function.

When the sources are compiled with `_FILE_OFFSET_BITS == 64` on a 32-bit system this function is available under the name `ftw` and transparently replaces the old implementation.

int nftw (*const char* `*filename`, `__nftw_func_t func`, *int*   [Function]
    descriptors, *int* `flag`)

Preliminary: | MT-Safe cwd | AS-Unsafe heap | AC-Unsafe mem fd cwd | See Section 1.2.2.1 [POSIX Safety Concepts], page 2.

The `nftw` function works like the `ftw` functions. They call the callback function *func* for all items found in the directory *filename* and below. At most *descriptors* file descriptors are consumed during the `nftw` call.

One difference is that the callback function is of a different type. It is of type `struct FTW *` and provides the callback function with the extra information described above.

A second difference is that `nftw` takes a fourth argument, which is 0 or a bitwise-OR combination of any of the following values.

FTW_PHYS   While traversing the directory symbolic links are not followed. Instead symbolic links are reported using the `FTW_SL` value for the type parameter to the callback function. If the file referenced by a symbolic link does not exist `FTW_SLN` is returned instead.

FTW_MOUNT

    The callback function is only called for items which are on the same mounted filesystem as the directory given by the *filename* parameter to `nftw`.

FTW_CHDIR

    If this flag is given the current working directory is changed to the directory of the reported object before the callback function is called. When `ntfw` finally returns the current directory is restored to its original value.

FTW_DEPTH

    If this option is specified then all subdirectories and files within them are processed before processing the top directory itself (depth-first processing). This also means the type flag given to the callback function is `FTW_DP` and not `FTW_D`.

FTW_ACTIONRETVAL

    If this option is specified then return values from callbacks are handled differently. If the callback returns `FTW_CONTINUE`, walking continues normally. `FTW_STOP` means walking stops and `FTW_STOP` is returned to the caller. If `FTW_SKIP_SUBTREE` is returned by the callback with `FTW_D` argument, the subtree is skipped and walking continues with next sibling of the directory. If `FTW_SKIP_SIBLINGS` is returned by the callback, all siblings of the current entry are skipped and walking continues in its parent. No other return values should be returned from the callbacks if this option is set. This option is a GNU extension.

The return value is computed in the same way as for `ftw`. `nftw` returns 0 if no failures occurred and all callback functions returned 0. In case of internal errors, such as memory problems, the return value is −1 and *errno* is set accordingly. If the return value of a callback invocation was non-zero then that value is returned.

When the sources are compiled with `_FILE_OFFSET_BITS == 64` on a 32-bit system this function is in fact `nftw64`, i.e., the LFS interface transparently replaces the old interface.

int nftw64 *(const char *filename, __nftw64_func_t func, int*   [Function]
    descriptors, int flag)

Preliminary: | MT-Safe cwd | AS-Unsafe heap | AC-Unsafe mem fd cwd | See Section 1.2.2.1 [POSIX Safety Concepts], page 2.

This function is similar to `nftw` but it can work on filesystems with large files. File information is reported using a variable of type `struct stat64` which is passed by reference to the callback function.

When the sources are compiled with `_FILE_OFFSET_BITS == 64` on a 32-bit system this function is available under the name `nftw` and transparently replaces the old implementation.

14.4 Hard Links

In POSIX systems, one file can have many names at the same time. All of the names are equally real, and no one of them is preferred to the others.

To add a name to a file, use the `link` function. (The new name is also called a *hard link* to the file.) Creating a new link to a file does not copy the contents of the file; it simply makes a new name by which the file can be known, in addition to the file's existing name or names.

One file can have names in several directories, so the organization of the file system is not a strict hierarchy or tree.

In most implementations, it is not possible to have hard links to the same file in multiple file systems. `link` reports an error if you try to make a hard link to the file from another file system when this cannot be done.

The prototype for the `link` function is declared in the header file `unistd.h`.

int link *(const char *oldname, const char *newname)*   [Function]

Preliminary: | MT-Safe | AS-Safe | AC-Safe | See Section 1.2.2.1 [POSIX Safety Concepts], page 2.

The `link` function makes a new link to the existing file named by *oldname*, under the new name *newname*.

This function returns a value of 0 if it is successful and -1 on failure. In addition to the usual file name errors (see Section 11.2.3 [File Name Errors], page 255) for both *oldname* and *newname*, the following `errno` error conditions are defined for this function:

EACCES   You are not allowed to write to the directory in which the new link is to be written.

EEXIST   There is already a file named *newname*. If you want to replace this link with a new link, you must remove the old link explicitly first.

EMLINK   There are already too many links to the file named by *oldname*. (The maximum number of links to a file is `LINK_MAX`; see Section 32.6 [Limits on File System Capacity], page 874.)

ENOENT   The file named by *oldname* doesn't exist. You can't make a link to a file that doesn't exist.

ENOSPC   The directory or file system that would contain the new link is full and cannot be extended.

EPERM   On GNU/Linux and GNU/Hurd systems and some others, you cannot make links to directories. Many systems allow only privileged users to do so. This error is used to report the problem.

EROFS   The directory containing the new link can't be modified because it's on a read-only file system.

EXDEV   The directory specified in *newname* is on a different file system than the existing file.

EIO   A hardware error occurred while trying to read or write the to filesystem.

14.5 Symbolic Links

GNU systems support *soft links* or *symbolic links*. This is a kind of "file" that is essentially a pointer to another file name. Unlike hard links, symbolic links can be made to directories or across file systems with no restrictions. You can also make a symbolic link to a name which is not the name of any file. (Opening this link will fail until a file by that name is created.) Likewise, if the symbolic link points to an existing file which is later deleted, the symbolic link continues to point to the same file name even though the name no longer names any file.

The reason symbolic links work the way they do is that special things happen when you try to open the link. The `open` function realizes you have specified the name of a link, reads the file name contained in the link, and opens that file name instead. The `stat` function likewise operates on the file that the symbolic link points to, instead of on the link itself.

By contrast, other operations such as deleting or renaming the file operate on the link itself. The functions `readlink` and `lstat` also refrain from following symbolic links, because their purpose is to obtain information about the link. `link`, the function that makes a hard link, does too. It makes a hard link to the symbolic link, which one rarely wants.

Some systems have, for some functions operating on files, a limit on how many symbolic links are followed when resolving a path name. The limit if it exists is published in the `sys/param.h` header file.

`int MAXSYMLINKS` [Macro]

> The macro `MAXSYMLINKS` specifies how many symlinks some function will follow before returning `ELOOP`. Not all functions behave the same and this value is not the same as that returned for `_SC_SYMLOOP` by `sysconf`. In fact, the `sysconf` result can indicate that there is no fixed limit although `MAXSYMLINKS` exists and has a finite value.

Prototypes for most of the functions listed in this section are in `unistd.h`.

`int symlink (const char *oldname, const char *newname)` [Function]

> Preliminary: | MT-Safe | AS-Safe | AC-Safe | See Section 1.2.2.1 [POSIX Safety Concepts], page 2.
>
> The `symlink` function makes a symbolic link to *oldname* named *newname*.
>
> The normal return value from `symlink` is 0. A return value of −1 indicates an error. In addition to the usual file name syntax errors (see Section 11.2.3 [File Name Errors], page 255), the following `errno` error conditions are defined for this function:
>
> `EEXIST`   There is already an existing file named *newname*.
>
> `EROFS`   The file *newname* would exist on a read-only file system.
>
> `ENOSPC`   The directory or file system cannot be extended to make the new link.
>
> `EIO`   A hardware error occurred while reading or writing data on the disk.

`ssize_t readlink (const char *filename, char *buffer, size_t` [Function]
` size)`

> Preliminary: | MT-Safe | AS-Safe | AC-Safe | See Section 1.2.2.1 [POSIX Safety Concepts], page 2.
>
> The `readlink` function gets the value of the symbolic link *filename*. The file name that the link points to is copied into *buffer*. This file name string is *not* null-terminated; `readlink` normally returns the number of characters copied. The *size* argument specifies the maximum number of characters to copy, usually the allocation size of *buffer*.
>
> If the return value equals *size*, you cannot tell whether or not there was room to return the entire name. So make a bigger buffer and call `readlink` again. Here is an example:

```
char *
readlink_malloc (const char *filename)
{
  int size = 100;
  char *buffer = NULL;

  while (1)
    {
      buffer = (char *) xrealloc (buffer, size);
      int nchars = readlink (filename, buffer, size);
      if (nchars < 0)
        {
          free (buffer);
          return NULL;
        }
      if (nchars < size)
```

```
            return buffer;
          size *= 2;
      }
  }
```

A value of −1 is returned in case of error. In addition to the usual file name errors (see Section 11.2.3 [File Name Errors], page 255), the following **errno** error conditions are defined for this function:

EINVAL   The named file is not a symbolic link.

EIO   A hardware error occurred while reading or writing data on the disk.

In some situations it is desirable to resolve all the symbolic links to get the real name of a file where no prefix names a symbolic link which is followed and no filename in the path is . or . . . This is for instance desirable if files have to be compared in which case different names can refer to the same inode.

char * canonicalize_file_name (*const char *name*)   [Function]
     Preliminary: | MT-Safe | AS-Unsafe heap | AC-Unsafe mem fd | See Section 1.2.2.1
     [POSIX Safety Concepts], page 2.

     The **canonicalize_file_name** function returns the absolute name of the file named by *name* which contains no ., . . components nor any repeated path separators (/) or symlinks. The result is passed back as the return value of the function in a block of memory allocated with **malloc**. If the result is not used anymore the memory should be freed with a call to **free**.

     If any of the path components are missing the function returns a NULL pointer. This is also what is returned if the length of the path reaches or exceeds **PATH_MAX** characters. In any case **errno** is set accordingly.

     ENAMETOOLONG
               The resulting path is too long. This error only occurs on systems which have a limit on the file name length.

     EACCES   At least one of the path components is not readable.

     ENOENT   The input file name is empty.

     ENOENT   At least one of the path components does not exist.

     ELOOP   More than **MAXSYMLINKS** many symlinks have been followed.

     This function is a GNU extension and is declared in **stdlib.h**.

The Unix standard includes a similar function which differs from **canonicalize_file_name** in that the user has to provide the buffer where the result is placed in.

char * realpath (*const char *restrict **name**, char *restrict*   [Function]
     resolved)
     Preliminary: | MT-Safe | AS-Unsafe heap | AC-Unsafe mem fd | See Section 1.2.2.1
     [POSIX Safety Concepts], page 2.

     A call to **realpath** where the *resolved* parameter is NULL behaves exactly like **canonicalize_file_name**. The function allocates a buffer for the file name and returns a pointer to it. If *resolved* is not NULL it points to a buffer into which the result is copied. It is the callers responsibility to allocate a buffer which is large enough. On systems which define PATH_MAX this means the buffer must be large enough for a pathname of this size. For systems without limitations on the pathname length the requirement cannot be met and programs should not call realpath with anything but NULL for the second parameter.

One other difference is that the buffer *resolved* (if nonzero) will contain the part of the path component which does not exist or is not readable if the function returns NULL and errno is set to EACCES or ENOENT.

This function is declared in stdlib.h.

The advantage of using this function is that it is more widely available. The drawback is that it reports failures for long paths on systems which have no limits on the file name length.

14.6 Deleting Files

You can delete a file with unlink or remove.

Deletion actually deletes a file name. If this is the file's only name, then the file is deleted as well. If the file has other remaining names (see Section 14.4 [Hard Links], page 405), it remains accessible under those names.

int unlink (*const char *filename*)   [Function]
    Preliminary: | MT-Safe | AS-Safe | AC-Safe | See Section 1.2.2.1 [POSIX Safety Concepts], page 2.

    The unlink function deletes the file name *filename*. If this is a file's sole name, the file itself is also deleted. (Actually, if any process has the file open when this happens, deletion is postponed until all processes have closed the file.)

    The function unlink is declared in the header file unistd.h.

    This function returns 0 on successful completion, and −1 on error. In addition to the usual file name errors (see Section 11.2.3 [File Name Errors], page 255), the following errno error conditions are defined for this function:

    EACCES   Write permission is denied for the directory from which the file is to be removed, or the directory has the sticky bit set and you do not own the file.

    EBUSY   This error indicates that the file is being used by the system in such a way that it can't be unlinked. For example, you might see this error if the file name specifies the root directory or a mount point for a file system.

    ENOENT   The file name to be deleted doesn't exist.

    EPERM   On some systems unlink cannot be used to delete the name of a directory, or at least can only be used this way by a privileged user. To avoid such problems, use rmdir to delete directories. (On GNU/Linux and GNU/Hurd systems unlink can never delete the name of a directory.)

    EROFS   The directory containing the file name to be deleted is on a read-only file system and can't be modified.

int rmdir (*const char *filename*)   [Function]
>   Preliminary: | MT-Safe | AS-Safe | AC-Safe | See Section 1.2.2.1 [POSIX Safety
>   Concepts], page 2.
>
>   The `rmdir` function deletes a directory. The directory must be empty before it can
>   be removed; in other words, it can only contain entries for . and ...
>
>   In most other respects, `rmdir` behaves like `unlink`. There are two additional `errno`
>   error conditions defined for `rmdir`:
>
>   ENOTEMPTY
>   EEXIST   The directory to be deleted is not empty.
>
>   These two error codes are synonymous; some systems use one, and some use the other.
>   GNU/Linux and GNU/Hurd systems always use `ENOTEMPTY`.
>
>   The prototype for this function is declared in the header file `unistd.h`.

int remove (*const char *filename*)   [Function]
>   Preliminary: | MT-Safe | AS-Safe | AC-Safe | See Section 1.2.2.1 [POSIX Safety
>   Concepts], page 2.
>
>   This is the ISO C function to remove a file. It works like `unlink` for files and like
>   `rmdir` for directories. `remove` is declared in `stdio.h`.

14.7 Renaming Files

The `rename` function is used to change a file's name.

int rename (*const char *oldname, const char *newname*)   [Function]
>   Preliminary: | MT-Safe | AS-Safe | AC-Safe | See Section 1.2.2.1 [POSIX Safety
>   Concepts], page 2.
>
>   The `rename` function renames the file *oldname* to *newname*. The file formerly acces-
>   sible under the name *oldname* is afterwards accessible as *newname* instead. (If the
>   file had any other names aside from *oldname*, it continues to have those names.)
>
>   The directory containing the name *newname* must be on the same file system as the
>   directory containing the name *oldname*.
>
>   One special case for `rename` is when *oldname* and *newname* are two names for the
>   same file. The consistent way to handle this case is to delete *oldname*. However,
>   in this case POSIX requires that `rename` do nothing and report success—which is
>   inconsistent. We don't know what your operating system will do.
>
>   If *oldname* is not a directory, then any existing file named *newname* is removed during
>   the renaming operation. However, if *newname* is the name of a directory, `rename` fails
>   in this case.
>
>   If *oldname* is a directory, then either *newname* must not exist or it must name a
>   directory that is empty. In the latter case, the existing directory named *newname* is
>   deleted first. The name *newname* must not specify a subdirectory of the directory
>   `oldname` which is being renamed.
>
>   One useful feature of `rename` is that the meaning of *newname* changes "atomically"
>   from any previously existing file by that name to its new meaning (i.e., the file that
>   was called *oldname*). There is no instant at which *newname* is non-existent "in

between" the old meaning and the new meaning. If there is a system crash during the operation, it is possible for both names to still exist; but *newname* will always be intact if it exists at all.

If `rename` fails, it returns -1. In addition to the usual file name errors (see Section 11.2.3 [File Name Errors], page 255), the following `errno` error conditions are defined for this function:

EACCES One of the directories containing *newname* or *oldname* refuses write permission; or *newname* and *oldname* are directories and write permission is refused for one of them.

EBUSY   A directory named by *oldname* or *newname* is being used by the system in a way that prevents the renaming from working. This includes directories that are mount points for filesystems, and directories that are the current working directories of processes.

ENOTEMPTY
EEXIST The directory *newname* isn't empty. GNU/Linux and GNU/Hurd systems always return ENOTEMPTY for this, but some other systems return EEXIST.

EINVAL *oldname* is a directory that contains *newname*.

EISDIR *newname* is a directory but the *oldname* isn't.

EMLINK The parent directory of *newname* would have too many links (entries).

ENOENT The file *oldname* doesn't exist.

ENOSPC The directory that would contain *newname* has no room for another entry, and there is no space left in the file system to expand it.

EROFS   The operation would involve writing to a directory on a read-only file system.

EXDEV   The two file names *newname* and *oldname* are on different file systems.

14.8 Creating Directories

Directories are created with the `mkdir` function. (There is also a shell command `mkdir` which does the same thing.)

int mkdir (*const char *filename, mode_t mode*)   [Function]
    Preliminary: | MT-Safe | AS-Safe | AC-Safe | See Section 1.2.2.1 [POSIX Safety Concepts], page 2.

    The `mkdir` function creates a new, empty directory with name *filename*.

    The argument *mode* specifies the file permissions for the new directory file. See Section 14.9.5 [The Mode Bits for Access Permission], page 421, for more information about this.

    A return value of 0 indicates successful completion, and -1 indicates failure. In addition to the usual file name syntax errors (see Section 11.2.3 [File Name Errors], page 255), the following `errno` error conditions are defined for this function:

    EACCES Write permission is denied for the parent directory in which the new directory is to be added.

EEXIST   A file named *filename* already exists.

EMLINK   The parent directory has too many links (entries).

> Well-designed file systems never report this error, because they permit more links than your disk could possibly hold. However, you must still take account of the possibility of this error, as it could result from network access to a file system on another machine.

ENOSPC   The file system doesn't have enough room to create the new directory.

EROFS   The parent directory of the directory being created is on a read-only file system and cannot be modified.

To use this function, your program should include the header file `sys/stat.h`.

14.9 File Attributes

When you issue an '`ls -l`' shell command on a file, it gives you information about the size of the file, who owns it, when it was last modified, etc. These are called the *file attributes*, and are associated with the file itself and not a particular one of its names.

This section contains information about how you can inquire about and modify the attributes of a file.

14.9.1 The meaning of the File Attributes

When you read the attributes of a file, they come back in a structure called `struct stat`. This section describes the names of the attributes, their data types, and what they mean. For the functions to read the attributes of a file, see Section 14.9.2 [Reading the Attributes of a File], page 416.

The header file `sys/stat.h` declares all the symbols defined in this section.

`struct stat`   [Data Type]

> The `stat` structure type is used to return information about the attributes of a file. It contains at least the following members:

> `mode_t st_mode`

> > Specifies the mode of the file. This includes file type information (see Section 14.9.3 [Testing the Type of a File], page 417) and the file permission bits (see Section 14.9.5 [The Mode Bits for Access Permission], page 421).

> `ino_t st_ino`

> > The file serial number, which distinguishes this file from all other files on the same device.

> `dev_t st_dev`

> > Identifies the device containing the file. The `st_ino` and `st_dev`, taken together, uniquely identify the file. The `st_dev` value is not necessarily consistent across reboots or system crashes, however.

> `nlink_t st_nlink`

> > The number of hard links to the file. This count keeps track of how many directories have entries for this file. If the count is ever decremented to

zero, then the file itself is discarded as soon as no process still holds it open. Symbolic links are not counted in the total.

`uid_t st_uid`

> The user ID of the file's owner. See Section 14.9.4 [File Owner], page 420.

`gid_t st_gid`

> The group ID of the file. See Section 14.9.4 [File Owner], page 420.

`off_t st_size`

> This specifies the size of a regular file in bytes. For files that are really devices this field isn't usually meaningful. For symbolic links this specifies the length of the file name the link refers to.

`time_t st_atime`

> This is the last access time for the file. See Section 14.9.9 [File Times], page 426.

`unsigned long int st_atime_usec`

> This is the fractional part of the last access time for the file. See Section 14.9.9 [File Times], page 426.

`time_t st_mtime`

> This is the time of the last modification to the contents of the file. See Section 14.9.9 [File Times], page 426.

`unsigned long int st_mtime_usec`

> This is the fractional part of the time of the last modification to the contents of the file. See Section 14.9.9 [File Times], page 426.

`time_t st_ctime`

> This is the time of the last modification to the attributes of the file. See Section 14.9.9 [File Times], page 426.

`unsigned long int st_ctime_usec`

> This is the fractional part of the time of the last modification to the attributes of the file. See Section 14.9.9 [File Times], page 426.

`blkcnt_t st_blocks`

> This is the amount of disk space that the file occupies, measured in units of 512-byte blocks.
>
> The number of disk blocks is not strictly proportional to the size of the file, for two reasons: the file system may use some blocks for internal record keeping; and the file may be sparse—it may have "holes" which contain zeros but do not actually take up space on the disk.
>
> You can tell (approximately) whether a file is sparse by comparing this value with `st_size`, like this:
>
>   (st.st_blocks * 512 < st.st_size)
>
> This test is not perfect because a file that is just slightly sparse might not be detected as sparse at all. For practical applications, this is not a problem.

unsigned int st_blksize

> The optimal block size for reading or writing this file, in bytes. You might use this size for allocating the buffer space for reading or writing the file. (This is unrelated to st_blocks.)

The extensions for the Large File Support (LFS) require, even on 32-bit machines, types which can handle file sizes up to 2^{63}. Therefore a new definition of struct stat is necessary.

struct stat64   [Data Type]

> The members of this type are the same and have the same names as those in struct stat. The only difference is that the members st_ino, st_size, and st_blocks have a different type to support larger values.

mode_t st_mode

> Specifies the mode of the file. This includes file type information (see Section 14.9.3 [Testing the Type of a File], page 417) and the file permission bits (see Section 14.9.5 [The Mode Bits for Access Permission], page 421).

ino64_t st_ino

> The file serial number, which distinguishes this file from all other files on the same device.

dev_t st_dev

> Identifies the device containing the file. The st_ino and st_dev, taken together, uniquely identify the file. The st_dev value is not necessarily consistent across reboots or system crashes, however.

nlink_t st_nlink

> The number of hard links to the file. This count keeps track of how many directories have entries for this file. If the count is ever decremented to zero, then the file itself is discarded as soon as no process still holds it open. Symbolic links are not counted in the total.

uid_t st_uid

> The user ID of the file's owner. See Section 14.9.4 [File Owner], page 420.

gid_t st_gid

> The group ID of the file. See Section 14.9.4 [File Owner], page 420.

off64_t st_size

> This specifies the size of a regular file in bytes. For files that are really devices this field isn't usually meaningful. For symbolic links this specifies the length of the file name the link refers to.

time_t st_atime

> This is the last access time for the file. See Section 14.9.9 [File Times], page 426.

unsigned long int st_atime_usec

> This is the fractional part of the last access time for the file. See Section 14.9.9 [File Times], page 426.

time_t st_mtime

> This is the time of the last modification to the contents of the file. See Section 14.9.9 [File Times], page 426.

unsigned long int st_mtime_usec

> This is the fractional part of the time of the last modification to the contents of the file. See Section 14.9.9 [File Times], page 426.

time_t st_ctime

> This is the time of the last modification to the attributes of the file. See Section 14.9.9 [File Times], page 426.

unsigned long int st_ctime_usec

> This is the fractional part of the time of the last modification to the attributes of the file. See Section 14.9.9 [File Times], page 426.

blkcnt64_t st_blocks

> This is the amount of disk space that the file occupies, measured in units of 512-byte blocks.

unsigned int st_blksize

> The optimal block size for reading of writing this file, in bytes. You might use this size for allocating the buffer space for reading of writing the file. (This is unrelated to st_blocks.)

Some of the file attributes have special data type names which exist specifically for those attributes. (They are all aliases for well-known integer types that you know and love.) These typedef names are defined in the header file sys/types.h as well as in sys/stat.h. Here is a list of them.

mode_t   [Data Type]
> This is an integer data type used to represent file modes. In the GNU C Library, this is an unsigned type no narrower than unsigned int.

ino_t   [Data Type]
> This is an unsigned integer type used to represent file serial numbers. (In Unix jargon, these are sometimes called *inode numbers*.) In the GNU C Library, this type is no narrower than unsigned int.
>
> If the source is compiled with _FILE_OFFSET_BITS == 64 this type is transparently replaced by ino64_t.

ino64_t   [Data Type]
> This is an unsigned integer type used to represent file serial numbers for the use in LFS. In the GNU C Library, this type is no narrower than unsigned int.
>
> When compiling with _FILE_OFFSET_BITS == 64 this type is available under the name ino_t.

dev_t   [Data Type]
> This is an arithmetic data type used to represent file device numbers. In the GNU C Library, this is an integer type no narrower than int.

nlink_t   [Data Type]

> This is an integer type used to represent file link counts.

blkcnt_t   [Data Type]

> This is a signed integer type used to represent block counts. In the GNU C Library, this type is no narrower than **int**.
>
> If the source is compiled with **_FILE_OFFSET_BITS == 64** this type is transparently replaced by **blkcnt64_t**.

blkcnt64_t   [Data Type]

> This is a signed integer type used to represent block counts for the use in LFS. In the GNU C Library, this type is no narrower than **int**.
>
> When compiling with **_FILE_OFFSET_BITS == 64** this type is available under the name **blkcnt_t**.

14.9.2 Reading the Attributes of a File

To examine the attributes of files, use the functions **stat**, **fstat** and **lstat**. They return the attribute information in a **struct stat** object. All three functions are declared in the header file **sys/stat.h**.

int stat (*const char *filename*, *struct stat *buf*)   [Function]

> Preliminary: | MT-Safe | AS-Safe | AC-Safe | See Section 1.2.2.1 [POSIX Safety Concepts], page 2.
>
> The **stat** function returns information about the attributes of the file named by *filename* in the structure pointed to by *buf*.
>
> If *filename* is the name of a symbolic link, the attributes you get describe the file that the link points to. If the link points to a nonexistent file name, then **stat** fails reporting a nonexistent file.
>
> The return value is 0 if the operation is successful, or -1 on failure. In addition to the usual file name errors (see Section 11.2.3 [File Name Errors], page 255, the following **errno** error conditions are defined for this function:
>
> ENOENT   The file named by *filename* doesn't exist.
>
> When the sources are compiled with **_FILE_OFFSET_BITS == 64** this function is in fact **stat64** since the LFS interface transparently replaces the normal implementation.

int stat64 (*const char *filename*, *struct stat64 *buf*)   [Function]

> Preliminary: | MT-Safe | AS-Safe | AC-Safe | See Section 1.2.2.1 [POSIX Safety Concepts], page 2.
>
> This function is similar to **stat** but it is also able to work on files larger than 2^{31} bytes on 32-bit systems. To be able to do this the result is stored in a variable of type **struct stat64** to which *buf* must point.
>
> When the sources are compiled with **_FILE_OFFSET_BITS == 64** this function is available under the name **stat** and so transparently replaces the interface for small files on 32-bit machines.

int fstat (int *filedes*, struct stat *buf)   [Function]
> Preliminary: | MT-Safe | AS-Safe | AC-Safe | See Section 1.2.2.1 [POSIX Safety Concepts], page 2.
>
> The fstat function is like stat, except that it takes an open file descriptor as an argument instead of a file name. See Chapter 13 [Low-Level Input/Output], page 333.
>
> Like stat, fstat returns 0 on success and -1 on failure. The following errno error conditions are defined for fstat:
>
> EBADF   The *filedes* argument is not a valid file descriptor.
>
> When the sources are compiled with _FILE_OFFSET_BITS == 64 this function is in fact fstat64 since the LFS interface transparently replaces the normal implementation.

int fstat64 (int *filedes*, struct stat64 *buf)   [Function]
> Preliminary: | MT-Safe | AS-Safe | AC-Safe | See Section 1.2.2.1 [POSIX Safety Concepts], page 2.
>
> This function is similar to fstat but is able to work on large files on 32-bit platforms. For large files the file descriptor *filedes* should be obtained by open64 or creat64. The *buf* pointer points to a variable of type struct stat64 which is able to represent the larger values.
>
> When the sources are compiled with _FILE_OFFSET_BITS == 64 this function is available under the name fstat and so transparently replaces the interface for small files on 32-bit machines.

int lstat (const char *filename*, struct stat *buf)   [Function]
> Preliminary: | MT-Safe | AS-Safe | AC-Safe | See Section 1.2.2.1 [POSIX Safety Concepts], page 2.
>
> The lstat function is like stat, except that it does not follow symbolic links. If *filename* is the name of a symbolic link, lstat returns information about the link itself; otherwise lstat works like stat. See Section 14.5 [Symbolic Links], page 406.
>
> When the sources are compiled with _FILE_OFFSET_BITS == 64 this function is in fact lstat64 since the LFS interface transparently replaces the normal implementation.

int lstat64 (const char *filename*, struct stat64 *buf)   [Function]
> Preliminary: | MT-Safe | AS-Safe | AC-Safe | See Section 1.2.2.1 [POSIX Safety Concepts], page 2.
>
> This function is similar to lstat but it is also able to work on files larger than 2^{31} bytes on 32-bit systems. To be able to do this the result is stored in a variable of type struct stat64 to which *buf* must point.
>
> When the sources are compiled with _FILE_OFFSET_BITS == 64 this function is available under the name lstat and so transparently replaces the interface for small files on 32-bit machines.

14.9.3 Testing the Type of a File

The *file mode*, stored in the st_mode field of the file attributes, contains two kinds of information: the file type code, and the access permission bits. This section discusses only the type code, which you can use to tell whether the file is a directory, socket, symbolic link, and so on. For details about access permissions see Section 14.9.5 [The Mode Bits for Access Permission], page 421.

There are two ways you can access the file type information in a file mode. Firstly, for each file type there is a *predicate macro* which examines a given file mode and returns whether it is of that type or not. Secondly, you can mask out the rest of the file mode to leave just the file type code, and compare this against constants for each of the supported file types.

All of the symbols listed in this section are defined in the header file sys/stat.h.

The following predicate macros test the type of a file, given the value m which is the st_mode field returned by stat on that file:

int S_ISDIR (*mode_t m*)   [Macro]
>   Preliminary: | MT-Safe | AS-Safe | AC-Safe | See Section 1.2.2.1 [POSIX Safety Concepts], page 2.
>
>   This macro returns non-zero if the file is a directory.

int S_ISCHR (*mode_t m*)   [Macro]
>   Preliminary: | MT-Safe | AS-Safe | AC-Safe | See Section 1.2.2.1 [POSIX Safety Concepts], page 2.
>
>   This macro returns non-zero if the file is a character special file (a device like a terminal).

int S_ISBLK (*mode_t m*)   [Macro]
>   Preliminary: | MT-Safe | AS-Safe | AC-Safe | See Section 1.2.2.1 [POSIX Safety Concepts], page 2.
>
>   This macro returns non-zero if the file is a block special file (a device like a disk).

int S_ISREG (*mode_t m*)   [Macro]
>   Preliminary: | MT-Safe | AS-Safe | AC-Safe | See Section 1.2.2.1 [POSIX Safety Concepts], page 2.
>
>   This macro returns non-zero if the file is a regular file.

int S_ISFIFO (*mode_t m*)   [Macro]
>   Preliminary: | MT-Safe | AS-Safe | AC-Safe | See Section 1.2.2.1 [POSIX Safety Concepts], page 2.
>
>   This macro returns non-zero if the file is a FIFO special file, or a pipe. See Chapter 15 [Pipes and FIFOs], page 437.

int S_ISLNK (*mode_t m*)   [Macro]
>   Preliminary: | MT-Safe | AS-Safe | AC-Safe | See Section 1.2.2.1 [POSIX Safety Concepts], page 2.
>
>   This macro returns non-zero if the file is a symbolic link. See Section 14.5 [Symbolic Links], page 406.

int S_ISSOCK (*mode_t m*)   [Macro]
>   Preliminary: | MT-Safe | AS-Safe | AC-Safe | See Section 1.2.2.1 [POSIX Safety Concepts], page 2.
>
>   This macro returns non-zero if the file is a socket. See Chapter 16 [Sockets], page 442.

An alternate non-POSIX method of testing the file type is supported for compatibility with BSD. The mode can be bitwise AND-ed with `S_IFMT` to extract the file type code, and compared to the appropriate constant. For example,

```
S_ISCHR (mode)
```

is equivalent to:

```
((mode & S_IFMT) == S_IFCHR)
```

`int S_IFMT`   [Macro]

This is a bit mask used to extract the file type code from a mode value.

These are the symbolic names for the different file type codes:

`S_IFDIR`   This is the file type constant of a directory file.

`S_IFCHR`   This is the file type constant of a character-oriented device file.

`S_IFBLK`   This is the file type constant of a block-oriented device file.

`S_IFREG`   This is the file type constant of a regular file.

`S_IFLNK`   This is the file type constant of a symbolic link.

`S_IFSOCK`   This is the file type constant of a socket.

`S_IFIFO`   This is the file type constant of a FIFO or pipe.

The POSIX.1b standard introduced a few more objects which possibly can be implemented as objects in the filesystem. These are message queues, semaphores, and shared memory objects. To allow differentiating these objects from other files the POSIX standard introduced three new test macros. But unlike the other macros they do not take the value of the `st_mode` field as the parameter. Instead they expect a pointer to the whole **struct stat** structure.

`int S_TYPEISMQ (struct stat *s)`   [Macro]

Preliminary: | MT-Safe | AS-Safe | AC-Safe | See Section 1.2.2.1 [POSIX Safety Concepts], page 2.

If the system implements POSIX message queues as distinct objects and the file is a message queue object, this macro returns a non-zero value. In all other cases the result is zero.

`int S_TYPEISSEM (struct stat *s)`   [Macro]

Preliminary: | MT-Safe | AS-Safe | AC-Safe | See Section 1.2.2.1 [POSIX Safety Concepts], page 2.

If the system implements POSIX semaphores as distinct objects and the file is a semaphore object, this macro returns a non-zero value. In all other cases the result is zero.

`int S_TYPEISSHM (struct stat *s)`   [Macro]

Preliminary: | MT-Safe | AS-Safe | AC-Safe | See Section 1.2.2.1 [POSIX Safety Concepts], page 2.

If the system implements POSIX shared memory objects as distinct objects and the file is a shared memory object, this macro returns a non-zero value. In all other cases the result is zero.

14.9.4 File Owner

Every file has an *owner* which is one of the registered user names defined on the system. Each file also has a *group* which is one of the defined groups. The file owner can often be useful for showing you who edited the file (especially when you edit with GNU Emacs), but its main purpose is for access control.

The file owner and group play a role in determining access because the file has one set of access permission bits for the owner, another set that applies to users who belong to the file's group, and a third set of bits that applies to everyone else. See Section 14.9.6 [How Your Access to a File is Decided], page 423, for the details of how access is decided based on this data.

When a file is created, its owner is set to the effective user ID of the process that creates it (see Section 30.2 [The Persona of a Process], page 815). The file's group ID may be set to either the effective group ID of the process, or the group ID of the directory that contains the file, depending on the system where the file is stored. When you access a remote file system, it behaves according to its own rules, not according to the system your program is running on. Thus, your program must be prepared to encounter either kind of behavior no matter what kind of system you run it on.

You can change the owner and/or group owner of an existing file using the `chown` function. This is the primitive for the `chown` and `chgrp` shell commands.

The prototype for this function is declared in **unistd.h.**

---

int **chown** (*const char *filename, uid_t owner, gid_t group*) [Function]
    Preliminary: | MT-Safe | AS-Safe | AC-Safe | See Section 1.2.2.1 [POSIX Safety Concepts], page 2.

The **chown** function changes the owner of the file *filename* to *owner*, and its group owner to *group*.

Changing the owner of the file on certain systems clears the set-user-ID and set-group-ID permission bits. (This is because those bits may not be appropriate for the new owner.) Other file permission bits are not changed.

The return value is 0 on success and -1 on failure. In addition to the usual file name errors (see Section 11.2.3 [File Name Errors], page 255), the following **errno** error conditions are defined for this function:

EPERM   This process lacks permission to make the requested change.

        Only privileged users or the file's owner can change the file's group. On most file systems, only privileged users can change the file owner; some file systems allow you to change the owner if you are currently the owner. When you access a remote file system, the behavior you encounter is determined by the system that actually holds the file, not by the system your program is running on.

        See Section 32.7 [Optional Features in File Support], page 875, for information about the **_POSIX_CHOWN_RESTRICTED** macro.

EROFS   The file is on a read-only file system.

`int fchown (int filedes, uid_t owner, gid_t group)`   [Function]

> Preliminary: | MT-Safe | AS-Safe | AC-Safe | See Section 1.2.2.1 [POSIX Safety Concepts], page 2.
>
> This is like `chown`, except that it changes the owner of the open file with descriptor *filedes*.
>
> The return value from `fchown` is 0 on success and -1 on failure. The following `errno` error codes are defined for this function:
>
> EBADF
> > The *filedes* argument is not a valid file descriptor.
>
> EINVAL
> > The *filedes* argument corresponds to a pipe or socket, not an ordinary file.
>
> EPERM
> > This process lacks permission to make the requested change. For details see `chmod` above.
>
> EROFS
> > The file resides on a read-only file system.

14.9.5 The Mode Bits for Access Permission

The *file mode*, stored in the `st_mode` field of the file attributes, contains two kinds of information: the file type code, and the access permission bits. This section discusses only the access permission bits, which control who can read or write the file. See Section 14.9.3 [Testing the Type of a File], page 417, for information about the file type code.

All of the symbols listed in this section are defined in the header file `sys/stat.h`.

These symbolic constants are defined for the file mode bits that control access permission for the file:

S_IRUSR

S_IREAD
> Read permission bit for the owner of the file. On many systems this bit is 0400. `S_IREAD` is an obsolete synonym provided for BSD compatibility.

S_IWUSR

S_IWRITE
> Write permission bit for the owner of the file. Usually 0200. `S_IWRITE` is an obsolete synonym provided for BSD compatibility.

S_IXUSR

S_IEXEC
> Execute (for ordinary files) or search (for directories) permission bit for the owner of the file. Usually 0100. `S_IEXEC` is an obsolete synonym provided for BSD compatibility.

S_IRWXU
> This is equivalent to '(S_IRUSR | S_IWUSR | S_IXUSR)'.

S_IRGRP
> Read permission bit for the group owner of the file. Usually 040.

S_IWGRP
> Write permission bit for the group owner of the file. Usually 020.

S_IXGRP
> Execute or search permission bit for the group owner of the file. Usually 010.

S_IRWXG
> This is equivalent to '(S_IRGRP | S_IWGRP | S_IXGRP)'.

S_IROTH
> Read permission bit for other users. Usually 04.

S_IWOTH
> Write permission bit for other users. Usually 02.

`S_IXOTH`   Execute or search permission bit for other users. Usually 01.

`S_IRWXO`   This is equivalent to '(`S_IROTH | S_IWOTH | S_IXOTH`)'.

`S_ISUID`   This is the set-user-ID on execute bit, usually 04000. See Section 30.4 [How an Application Can Change Persona], page 816.

`S_ISGID`   This is the set-group-ID on execute bit, usually 02000. See Section 30.4 [How an Application Can Change Persona], page 816.

`S_ISVTX`   This is the *sticky* bit, usually 01000.

For a directory it gives permission to delete a file in that directory only if you own that file. Ordinarily, a user can either delete all the files in a directory or cannot delete any of them (based on whether the user has write permission for the directory). The same restriction applies—you must have both write permission for the directory and own the file you want to delete. The one exception is that the owner of the directory can delete any file in the directory, no matter who owns it (provided the owner has given himself write permission for the directory). This is commonly used for the /tmp directory, where anyone may create files but not delete files created by other users.

Originally the sticky bit on an executable file modified the swapping policies of the system. Normally, when a program terminated, its pages in core were immediately freed and reused. If the sticky bit was set on the executable file, the system kept the pages in core for a while as if the program were still running. This was advantageous for a program likely to be run many times in succession. This usage is obsolete in modern systems. When a program terminates, its pages always remain in core as long as there is no shortage of memory in the system. When the program is next run, its pages will still be in core if no shortage arose since the last run.

On some modern systems where the sticky bit has no useful meaning for an executable file, you cannot set the bit at all for a non-directory. If you try, `chmod` fails with `EFTYPE`; see Section 14.9.7 [Assigning File Permissions], page 423.

Some systems (particularly SunOS) have yet another use for the sticky bit. If the sticky bit is set on a file that is *not* executable, it means the opposite: never cache the pages of this file at all. The main use of this is for the files on an NFS server machine which are used as the swap area of diskless client machines. The idea is that the pages of the file will be cached in the client's memory, so it is a waste of the server's memory to cache them a second time. With this usage the sticky bit also implies that the filesystem may fail to record the file's modification time onto disk reliably (the idea being that no-one cares for a swap file).

This bit is only available on BSD systems (and those derived from them). Therefore one has to use the `_GNU_SOURCE` feature select macro, or not define any feature test macros, to get the definition (see Section 1.3.4 [Feature Test Macros], page 15).

The actual bit values of the symbols are listed in the table above so you can decode file mode values when debugging your programs. These bit values are correct for most systems, but they are not guaranteed.

Warning: Writing explicit numbers for file permissions is bad practice. Not only is it not portable, it also requires everyone who reads your program to remember what the bits mean. To make your program clean use the symbolic names.

14.9.6 How Your Access to a File is Decided

Recall that the operating system normally decides access permission for a file based on the effective user and group IDs of the process and its supplementary group IDs, together with the file's owner, group and permission bits. These concepts are discussed in detail in Section 30.2 [The Persona of a Process], page 815.

If the effective user ID of the process matches the owner user ID of the file, then permissions for read, write, and execute/search are controlled by the corresponding "user" (or "owner") bits. Likewise, if any of the effective group ID or supplementary group IDs of the process matches the group owner ID of the file, then permissions are controlled by the "group" bits. Otherwise, permissions are controlled by the "other" bits.

Privileged users, like 'root', can access any file regardless of its permission bits. As a special case, for a file to be executable even by a privileged user, at least one of its execute bits must be set.

14.9.7 Assigning File Permissions

The primitive functions for creating files (for example, **open** or **mkdir**) take a *mode* argument, which specifies the file permissions to give the newly created file. This mode is modified by the process's *file creation mask*, or *umask*, before it is used.

The bits that are set in the file creation mask identify permissions that are always to be disabled for newly created files. For example, if you set all the "other" access bits in the mask, then newly created files are not accessible at all to processes in the "other" category, even if the *mode* argument passed to the create function would permit such access. In other words, the file creation mask is the complement of the ordinary access permissions you want to grant.

Programs that create files typically specify a *mode* argument that includes all the permissions that make sense for the particular file. For an ordinary file, this is typically read and write permission for all classes of users. These permissions are then restricted as specified by the individual user's own file creation mask.

To change the permission of an existing file given its name, call **chmod**. This function uses the specified permission bits and ignores the file creation mask.

In normal use, the file creation mask is initialized by the user's login shell (using the **umask** shell command), and inherited by all subprocesses. Application programs normally don't need to worry about the file creation mask. It will automatically do what it is supposed to do.

When your program needs to create a file and bypass the umask for its access permissions, the easiest way to do this is to use **fchmod** after opening the file, rather than changing the umask. In fact, changing the umask is usually done only by shells. They use the **umask** function.

The functions in this section are declared in **sys/stat.h**.

mode_t umask (*mode_t mask*) [Function]

> Preliminary: | MT-Safe | AS-Safe | AC-Safe | See Section 1.2.2.1 [POSIX Safety Concepts], page 2.
>
> The `umask` function sets the file creation mask of the current process to *mask*, and returns the previous value of the file creation mask.
>
> Here is an example showing how to read the mask with `umask` without changing it permanently:
>
> ```
> mode_t
> read_umask (void)
> {
>   mode_t mask = umask (0);
>   umask (mask);
>   return mask;
> }
> ```
>
> However, on GNU/Hurd systems it is better to use `getumask` if you just want to read the mask value, because it is reentrant.

mode_t getumask (*void*) [Function]

> Preliminary: | MT-Safe | AS-Safe | AC-Safe | See Section 1.2.2.1 [POSIX Safety Concepts], page 2.
>
> Return the current value of the file creation mask for the current process. This function is a GNU extension and is only available on GNU/Hurd systems.

int chmod (*const char *filename, mode_t mode*) [Function]

> Preliminary: | MT-Safe | AS-Safe | AC-Safe | See Section 1.2.2.1 [POSIX Safety Concepts], page 2.
>
> The `chmod` function sets the access permission bits for the file named by *filename* to *mode*.
>
> If *filename* is a symbolic link, `chmod` changes the permissions of the file pointed to by the link, not those of the link itself.
>
> This function returns `0` if successful and `-1` if not. In addition to the usual file name errors (see Section 11.2.3 [File Name Errors], page 255), the following `errno` error conditions are defined for this function:
>
> ENOENT   The named file doesn't exist.
>
> EPERM   This process does not have permission to change the access permissions of this file. Only the file's owner (as judged by the effective user ID of the process) or a privileged user can change them.
>
> EROFS   The file resides on a read-only file system.
>
> EFTYPE   *mode* has the `S_ISVTX` bit (the "sticky bit") set, and the named file is not a directory. Some systems do not allow setting the sticky bit on non-directory files, and some do (and only some of those assign a useful meaning to the bit for non-directory files).
>
> You only get `EFTYPE` on systems where the sticky bit has no useful meaning for non-directory files, so it is always safe to just clear the bit in *mode* and call `chmod` again. See Section 14.9.5 [The Mode Bits for Access Permission], page 421, for full details on the sticky bit.

`int fchmod (int filedes, mode_t mode)` [Function]
> Preliminary: | MT-Safe | AS-Safe | AC-Safe | See Section 1.2.2.1 [POSIX Safety Concepts], page 2.

> This is like `chmod`, except that it changes the permissions of the currently open file given by *filedes*.

> The return value from `fchmod` is 0 on success and −1 on failure. The following `errno` error codes are defined for this function:

> `EBADF`   The *filedes* argument is not a valid file descriptor.

> `EINVAL`   The *filedes* argument corresponds to a pipe or socket, or something else that doesn't really have access permissions.

> `EPERM`   This process does not have permission to change the access permissions of this file. Only the file's owner (as judged by the effective user ID of the process) or a privileged user can change them.

> `EROFS`   The file resides on a read-only file system.

14.9.8 Testing Permission to Access a File

In some situations it is desirable to allow programs to access files or devices even if this is not possible with the permissions granted to the user. One possible solution is to set the setuid-bit of the program file. If such a program is started the *effective* user ID of the process is changed to that of the owner of the program file. So to allow write access to files like `/etc/passwd`, which normally can be written only by the super-user, the modifying program will have to be owned by `root` and the setuid-bit must be set.

But besides the files the program is intended to change the user should not be allowed to access any file to which s/he would not have access anyway. The program therefore must explicitly check whether *the user* would have the necessary access to a file, before it reads or writes the file.

To do this, use the function `access`, which checks for access permission based on the process's *real* user ID rather than the effective user ID. (The setuid feature does not alter the real user ID, so it reflects the user who actually ran the program.)

There is another way you could check this access, which is easy to describe, but very hard to use. This is to examine the file mode bits and mimic the system's own access computation. This method is undesirable because many systems have additional access control features; your program cannot portably mimic them, and you would not want to try to keep track of the diverse features that different systems have. Using `access` is simple and automatically does whatever is appropriate for the system you are using.

`access` is *only* appropriate to use in setuid programs. A non-setuid program will always use the effective ID rather than the real ID.

The symbols in this section are declared in `unistd.h`.

`int access (const char *filename, int how)` [Function]
> Preliminary: | MT-Safe | AS-Safe | AC-Safe | See Section 1.2.2.1 [POSIX Safety Concepts], page 2.

The `access` function checks to see whether the file named by *filename* can be accessed in the way specified by the *how* argument. The *how* argument either can be the bitwise OR of the flags `R_OK`, `W_OK`, `X_OK`, or the existence test `F_OK`.

This function uses the *real* user and group IDs of the calling process, rather than the *effective* IDs, to check for access permission. As a result, if you use the function from a `setuid` or `setgid` program (see Section 30.4 [How an Application Can Change Persona], page 816), it gives information relative to the user who actually ran the program.

The return value is `0` if the access is permitted, and `-1` otherwise. (In other words, treated as a predicate function, `access` returns true if the requested access is *denied*.)

In addition to the usual file name errors (see Section 11.2.3 [File Name Errors], page 255), the following `errno` error conditions are defined for this function:

`EACCES`   The access specified by *how* is denied.

`ENOENT`   The file doesn't exist.

`EROFS`   Write permission was requested for a file on a read-only file system.

These macros are defined in the header file `unistd.h` for use as the *how* argument to the `access` function. The values are integer constants.

`int R_OK`   [Macro]
> Flag meaning test for read permission.

`int W_OK`   [Macro]
> Flag meaning test for write permission.

`int X_OK`   [Macro]
> Flag meaning test for execute/search permission.

`int F_OK`   [Macro]
> Flag meaning test for existence of the file.

14.9.9 File Times

Each file has three time stamps associated with it: its access time, its modification time, and its attribute modification time. These correspond to the `st_atime`, `st_mtime`, and `st_ctime` members of the `stat` structure; see Section 14.9 [File Attributes], page 412.

All of these times are represented in calendar time format, as `time_t` objects. This data type is defined in `time.h`. For more information about representation and manipulation of time values, see Section 21.4 [Calendar Time], page 623.

Reading from a file updates its access time attribute, and writing updates its modification time. When a file is created, all three time stamps for that file are set to the current time. In addition, the attribute change time and modification time fields of the directory that contains the new entry are updated.

Adding a new name for a file with the `link` function updates the attribute change time field of the file being linked, and both the attribute change time and modification time fields of the directory containing the new name. These same fields are affected if a file name is deleted with `unlink`, `remove` or `rmdir`. Renaming a file with `rename` affects only the attribute change time and modification time fields of the two parent directories involved, and not the times for the file being renamed.

Changing the attributes of a file (for example, with `chmod`) updates its attribute change time field.

You can also change some of the time stamps of a file explicitly using the `utime` function—all except the attribute change time. You need to include the header file `utime.h` to use this facility.

struct utimbuf   [Data Type]

> The `utimbuf` structure is used with the `utime` function to specify new access and modification times for a file. It contains the following members:
>
> **time_t actime**
>> This is the access time for the file.
>
> **time_t modtime**
>> This is the modification time for the file.

int utime (*const char *filename, const struct utimbuf *times*)   [Function]

> Preliminary: | MT-Safe | AS-Safe | AC-Safe | See Section 1.2.2.1 [POSIX Safety Concepts], page 2.
>
> This function is used to modify the file times associated with the file named *filename*.
>
> If *times* is a null pointer, then the access and modification times of the file are set to the current time. Otherwise, they are set to the values from the `actime` and `modtime` members (respectively) of the `utimbuf` structure pointed to by *times*.
>
> The attribute modification time for the file is set to the current time in either case (since changing the time stamps is itself a modification of the file attributes).
>
> The `utime` function returns 0 if successful and -1 on failure. In addition to the usual file name errors (see Section 11.2.3 [File Name Errors], page 255), the following `errno` error conditions are defined for this function:
>
> **EACCES**
>> There is a permission problem in the case where a null pointer was passed as the *times* argument. In order to update the time stamp on the file, you must either be the owner of the file, have write permission for the file, or be a privileged user.
>
> **ENOENT**   The file doesn't exist.
>
> **EPERM**
>> If the *times* argument is not a null pointer, you must either be the owner of the file or be a privileged user.
>
> **EROFS**   The file lives on a read-only file system.

Each of the three time stamps has a corresponding microsecond part, which extends its resolution. These fields are called `st_atime_usec`, `st_mtime_usec`, and `st_ctime_usec`; each has a value between 0 and 999,999, which indicates the time in microseconds. They correspond to the `tv_usec` field of a `timeval` structure; see Section 21.4.2 [High-Resolution Calendar], page 624.

The `utimes` function is like `utime`, but also lets you specify the fractional part of the file times. The prototype for this function is in the header file `sys/time.h`.

`int utimes` (*const char *filename, const struct timeval tvp*[2])   [Function]
> Preliminary: | MT-Safe | AS-Safe | AC-Safe | See Section 1.2.2.1 [POSIX Safety Concepts], page 2.
>
> This function sets the file access and modification times of the file *filename*. The new file access time is specified by *tvp*[0], and the new modification time by *tvp*[1]. Similar to `utime`, if *tvp* is a null pointer then the access and modification times of the file are set to the current time. This function comes from BSD.
>
> The return values and error conditions are the same as for the `utime` function.

`int lutimes` (*const char *filename, const struct timeval tvp*[2])   [Function]
> Preliminary: | MT-Safe | AS-Safe | AC-Safe | See Section 1.2.2.1 [POSIX Safety Concepts], page 2.
>
> This function is like `utimes`, except that it does not follow symbolic links. If *filename* is the name of a symbolic link, `lutimes` sets the file access and modification times of the symbolic link special file itself (as seen by `lstat`; see Section 14.5 [Symbolic Links], page 406) while `utimes` sets the file access and modification times of the file the symbolic link refers to. This function comes from FreeBSD, and is not available on all platforms (if not available, it will fail with `ENOSYS`).
>
> The return values and error conditions are the same as for the `utime` function.

`int futimes` (*int fd, const struct timeval tvp*[2])   [Function]
> Preliminary: | MT-Safe | AS-Safe | AC-Safe | See Section 1.2.2.1 [POSIX Safety Concepts], page 2.
>
> This function is like `utimes`, except that it takes an open file descriptor as an argument instead of a file name. See Chapter 13 [Low-Level Input/Output], page 333. This function comes from FreeBSD, and is not available on all platforms (if not available, it will fail with `ENOSYS`).
>
> Like `utimes`, `futimes` returns 0 on success and -1 on failure. The following `errno` error conditions are defined for `futimes`:
>
> EACCES   There is a permission problem in the case where a null pointer was passed as the *times* argument. In order to update the time stamp on the file, you must either be the owner of the file, have write permission for the file, or be a privileged user.
>
> EBADF   The *filedes* argument is not a valid file descriptor.
>
> EPERM   If the *times* argument is not a null pointer, you must either be the owner of the file or be a privileged user.
>
> EROFS   The file lives on a read-only file system.

14.9.10 File Size

Normally file sizes are maintained automatically. A file begins with a size of 0 and is automatically extended when data is written past its end. It is also possible to empty a file completely by an `open` or `fopen` call.

However, sometimes it is necessary to *reduce* the size of a file. This can be done with the `truncate` and `ftruncate` functions. They were introduced in BSD Unix. `ftruncate` was later added to POSIX.1.

Some systems allow you to extend a file (creating holes) with these functions. This is useful when using memory-mapped I/O (see Section 13.7 [Memory-mapped I/O], page 350), where files are not automatically extended. However, it is not portable but must be implemented if **mmap** allows mapping of files (i.e., **_POSIX_MAPPED_FILES** is defined).

Using these functions on anything other than a regular file gives *undefined* results. On many systems, such a call will appear to succeed, without actually accomplishing anything.

int truncate (*const char *filename, off_t length*)   [Function]
> Preliminary: | MT-Safe | AS-Safe | AC-Safe | See Section 1.2.2.1 [POSIX Safety Concepts], page 2.
>
> The **truncate** function changes the size of *filename* to *length*. If *length* is shorter than the previous length, data at the end will be lost. The file must be writable by the user to perform this operation.
>
> If *length* is longer, holes will be added to the end. However, some systems do not support this feature and will leave the file unchanged.
>
> When the source file is compiled with **_FILE_OFFSET_BITS == 64** the **truncate** function is in fact **truncate64** and the type **off_t** has 64 bits which makes it possible to handle files up to 2^{63} bytes in length.
>
> The return value is 0 for success, or -1 for an error. In addition to the usual file name errors, the following errors may occur:
>
> EACCES   The file is a directory or not writable.
>
> EINVAL   *length* is negative.
>
> EFBIG   The operation would extend the file beyond the limits of the operating system.
>
> EIO   A hardware I/O error occurred.
>
> EPERM   The file is "append-only" or "immutable".
>
> EINTR   The operation was interrupted by a signal.

int truncate64 (*const char *name, off64_t length*)   [Function]
> Preliminary: | MT-Safe | AS-Safe | AC-Safe | See Section 1.2.2.1 [POSIX Safety Concepts], page 2.
>
> This function is similar to the **truncate** function. The difference is that the *length* argument is 64 bits wide even on 32 bits machines, which allows the handling of files with sizes up to 2^{63} bytes.
>
> When the source file is compiled with **_FILE_OFFSET_BITS == 64** on a 32 bits machine this function is actually available under the name **truncate** and so transparently replaces the 32 bits interface.

int ftruncate (*int fd, off_t length*)   [Function]
> Preliminary: | MT-Safe | AS-Safe | AC-Safe | See Section 1.2.2.1 [POSIX Safety Concepts], page 2.
>
> This is like **truncate**, but it works on a file descriptor *fd* for an opened file instead of a file name to identify the object. The file must be opened for writing to successfully carry out the operation.

The POSIX standard leaves it implementation defined what happens if the specified new *length* of the file is bigger than the original size. The `ftruncate` function might simply leave the file alone and do nothing or it can increase the size to the desired size. In this later case the extended area should be zero-filled. So using `ftruncate` is no reliable way to increase the file size but if it is possible it is probably the fastest way. The function also operates on POSIX shared memory segments if these are implemented by the system.

`ftruncate` is especially useful in combination with `mmap`. Since the mapped region must have a fixed size one cannot enlarge the file by writing something beyond the last mapped page. Instead one has to enlarge the file itself and then remap the file with the new size. The example below shows how this works.

When the source file is compiled with `_FILE_OFFSET_BITS == 64` the `ftruncate` function is in fact `ftruncate64` and the type `off_t` has 64 bits which makes it possible to handle files up to 2^{63} bytes in length.

The return value is 0 for success, or −1 for an error. The following errors may occur:

EBADF   *fd* does not correspond to an open file.

EACCES   *fd* is a directory or not open for writing.

EINVAL   *length* is negative.

EFBIG   The operation would extend the file beyond the limits of the operating system.

EIO   A hardware I/O error occurred.

EPERM   The file is "append-only" or "immutable".

EINTR   The operation was interrupted by a signal.

`int ftruncate64 (int id, off64_t length)`   [Function]
Preliminary: | MT-Safe | AS-Safe | AC-Safe | See Section 1.2.2.1 [POSIX Safety Concepts], page 2.

This function is similar to the `ftruncate` function. The difference is that the *length* argument is 64 bits wide even on 32 bits machines which allows the handling of files with sizes up to 2^{63} bytes.

When the source file is compiled with `_FILE_OFFSET_BITS == 64` on a 32 bits machine this function is actually available under the name `ftruncate` and so transparently replaces the 32 bits interface.

As announced here is a little example of how to use `ftruncate` in combination with `mmap`:

```
int fd;
void *start;
size_t len;

int
add (off_t at, void *block, size_t size)
{
  if (at + size > len)
    {
```

```
        /* Resize the file and remap.  */
        size_t ps = sysconf (_SC_PAGESIZE);
        size_t ns = (at + size + ps - 1) & ~(ps - 1);
        void *np;
        if (ftruncate (fd, ns) < 0)
          return -1;
        np = mmap (NULL, ns, PROT_READ|PROT_WRITE, MAP_SHARED, fd, 0);
        if (np == MAP_FAILED)
          return -1;
        start = np;
        len = ns;
      }
    memcpy ((char *) start + at, block, size);
    return 0;
  }
```

The function **add** writes a block of memory at an arbitrary position in the file. If the current size of the file is too small it is extended. Note that it is extended by a whole number of pages. This is a requirement of **mmap**. The program has to keep track of the real size, and when it has finished a final **ftruncate** call should set the real size of the file.

14.9.11 Storage Allocation

Most file systems support allocating large files in a non-contiguous fashion: the file is split into *fragments* which are allocated sequentially, but the fragments themselves can be scattered across the disk. File systems generally try to avoid such fragmentation because it decreases performance, but if a file gradually increases in size, there might be no other option than to fragment it. In addition, many file systems support *sparse files* with *holes*: regions of null bytes for which no backing storage has been allocated by the file system. When the holes are finally overwritten with data, fragmentation can occur as well.

Explicit allocation of storage for yet-unwritten parts of the file can help the system to avoid fragmentation. Additionally, if storage pre-allocation fails, it is possible to report the out-of-disk error early, often without filling up the entire disk. However, due to deduplication, copy-on-write semantics, and file compression, such pre-allocation may not reliably prevent the out-of-disk-space error from occurring later. Checking for write errors is still required, and writes to memory-mapped regions created with **mmap** can still result in **SIGBUS**.

int posix_fallocate (*int fd*, *off_t offset*, *off_t length*)   [Function]
    Preliminary: | MT-Safe | AS-Safe | AC-Safe | See Section 1.2.2.1 [POSIX Safety Concepts], page 2.

    Allocate backing store for the region of *length* bytes starting at byte *offset* in the file for the descriptor *fd*. The file length is increased to '`length + offset`' if necessary.

    fd must be a regular file opened for writing, or **EBADF** is returned. If there is insufficient disk space to fulfill the allocation request, **ENOSPC** is returned.

    Note: If **fallocate** is not available (because the file system does not support it), **posix_fallocate** is emulated, which has the following drawbacks:

      • It is very inefficient because all file system blocks in the requested range need to be examined (even if they have been allocated before) and potentially rewritten. In contrast, with proper **fallocate** support (see below), the file system can examine the internal file allocation data structures and eliminate holes directly, maybe even using unwritten extents (which are pre-allocated but uninitialized on disk).

- There is a race condition if another thread or process modifies the underlying file in the to-be-allocated area. Non-null bytes could be overwritten with null bytes.

- If *fd* has been opened with the `O_WRONLY` flag, the function will fail with an **errno** value of **EBADF**.

- If *fd* has been opened with the `O_APPEND` flag, the function will fail with an **errno** value of **EBADF**.

- If *length* is zero, `ftruncate` is used to increase the file size as requested, without allocating file system blocks. There is a race condition which means that `ftruncate` can accidentally truncate the file if it has been extended concurrently.

On Linux, if an application does not benefit from emulation or if the emulation is harmful due to its inherent race conditions, the application can use the Linux-specific `fallocate` function, with a zero flag argument. For the `fallocate` function, the GNU C Library does not perform allocation emulation if the file system does not support allocation. Instead, an `EOPNOTSUPP` is returned to the caller.

int **posix_fallocate64** (*int fd*, *off64_t offset*, *off64_t length*)   [Function]
> Preliminary: | MT-Safe | AS-Safe | AC-Safe | See Section 1.2.2.1 [POSIX Safety Concepts], page 2.
>
> This function is a variant of `posix_fallocate64` which accepts 64-bit file offsets on all platforms.

14.10 Making Special Files

The `mknod` function is the primitive for making special files, such as files that correspond to devices. The GNU C Library includes this function for compatibility with BSD.

The prototype for `mknod` is declared in `sys/stat.h`.

int **mknod** (*const char *filename*, *mode_t mode*, *dev_t dev*)   [Function]
> Preliminary: | MT-Safe | AS-Safe | AC-Safe | See Section 1.2.2.1 [POSIX Safety Concepts], page 2.
>
> The `mknod` function makes a special file with name *filename*. The *mode* specifies the mode of the file, and may include the various special file bits, such as `S_IFCHR` (for a character special file) or `S_IFBLK` (for a block special file). See Section 14.9.3 [Testing the Type of a File], page 417.
>
> The *dev* argument specifies which device the special file refers to. Its exact interpretation depends on the kind of special file being created.
>
> The return value is 0 on success and −1 on error. In addition to the usual file name errors (see Section 11.2.3 [File Name Errors], page 255), the following **errno** error conditions are defined for this function:
>
> EPERM   The calling process is not privileged. Only the superuser can create special files.
>
> ENOSPC   The directory or file system that would contain the new file is full and cannot be extended.

EROFS The directory containing the new file can't be modified because it's on a read-only file system.

EEXIST There is already a file named *filename*. If you want to replace this file, you must remove the old file explicitly first.

14.11 Temporary Files

If you need to use a temporary file in your program, you can use the `tmpfile` function to open it. Or you can use the `tmpnam` (better: `tmpnam_r`) function to provide a name for a temporary file and then you can open it in the usual way with `fopen`.

The `tempnam` function is like `tmpnam` but lets you choose what directory temporary files will go in, and something about what their file names will look like. Important for multi-threaded programs is that `tempnam` is reentrant, while `tmpnam` is not since it returns a pointer to a static buffer.

These facilities are declared in the header file `stdio.h`.

FILE * tmpfile (*void*) [Function]
 Preliminary: | MT-Safe | AS-Unsafe heap lock | AC-Unsafe mem fd lock | See Section 1.2.2.1 [POSIX Safety Concepts], page 2.

 This function creates a temporary binary file for update mode, as if by calling `fopen` with mode `"wb+"`. The file is deleted automatically when it is closed or when the program terminates. (On some other ISO C systems the file may fail to be deleted if the program terminates abnormally).

 This function is reentrant.

 When the sources are compiled with `_FILE_OFFSET_BITS == 64` on a 32-bit system this function is in fact `tmpfile64`, i.e., the LFS interface transparently replaces the old interface.

FILE * tmpfile64 (*void*) [Function]
 Preliminary: | MT-Safe | AS-Unsafe heap lock | AC-Unsafe mem fd lock | See Section 1.2.2.1 [POSIX Safety Concepts], page 2.

 This function is similar to `tmpfile`, but the stream it returns a pointer to was opened using `tmpfile64`. Therefore this stream can be used for files larger than 2^{31} bytes on 32-bit machines.

 Please note that the return type is still `FILE *`. There is no special `FILE` type for the LFS interface.

 If the sources are compiled with `_FILE_OFFSET_BITS == 64` on a 32 bits machine this function is available under the name `tmpfile` and so transparently replaces the old interface.

char * tmpnam (*char *result*) [Function]
 Preliminary: | MT-Unsafe race:tmpnam/!result | AS-Unsafe | AC-Safe | See Section 1.2.2.1 [POSIX Safety Concepts], page 2.

 This function constructs and returns a valid file name that does not refer to any existing file. If the *result* argument is a null pointer, the return value is a pointer to an internal static string, which might be modified by subsequent calls and therefore makes this function non-reentrant. Otherwise, the *result* argument should be a pointer to an array of at least `L_tmpnam` characters, and the result is written into that array.

It is possible for `tmpnam` to fail if you call it too many times without removing previously-created files. This is because the limited length of the temporary file names gives room for only a finite number of different names. If `tmpnam` fails it returns a null pointer.

Warning: Between the time the pathname is constructed and the file is created another process might have created a file with the same name using `tmpnam`, leading to a possible security hole. The implementation generates names which can hardly be predicted, but when opening the file you should use the `O_EXCL` flag. Using `tmpfile` or `mkstemp` is a safe way to avoid this problem.

char * tmpnam_r (*char *result*)   [Function]
> Preliminary: | MT-Safe | AS-Safe | AC-Safe | See Section 1.2.2.1 [POSIX Safety Concepts], page 2.
>
> This function is nearly identical to the `tmpnam` function, except that if *result* is a null pointer it returns a null pointer.
>
> This guarantees reentrancy because the non-reentrant situation of `tmpnam` cannot happen here.
>
> **Warning**: This function has the same security problems as `tmpnam`.

int L_tmpnam   [Macro]
> The value of this macro is an integer constant expression that represents the minimum size of a string large enough to hold a file name generated by the `tmpnam` function.

int TMP_MAX   [Macro]
> The macro `TMP_MAX` is a lower bound for how many temporary names you can create with `tmpnam`. You can rely on being able to call `tmpnam` at least this many times before it might fail saying you have made too many temporary file names.
>
> With the GNU C Library, you can create a very large number of temporary file names. If you actually created the files, you would probably run out of disk space before you ran out of names. Some other systems have a fixed, small limit on the number of temporary files. The limit is never less than 25.

char * tempnam (*const char *dir, const char *prefix*)   [Function]
> Preliminary: | MT-Safe env | AS-Unsafe heap | AC-Unsafe mem | See Section 1.2.2.1 [POSIX Safety Concepts], page 2.
>
> This function generates a unique temporary file name. If *prefix* is not a null pointer, up to five characters of this string are used as a prefix for the file name. The return value is a string newly allocated with `malloc`, so you should release its storage with `free` when it is no longer needed.
>
> Because the string is dynamically allocated this function is reentrant.
>
> The directory prefix for the temporary file name is determined by testing each of the following in sequence. The directory must exist and be writable.
>
> - The environment variable `TMPDIR`, if it is defined. For security reasons this only happens if the program is not SUID or SGID enabled.

- The *dir* argument, if it is not a null pointer.
- The value of the `P_tmpdir` macro.
- The directory `/tmp`.

This function is defined for SVID compatibility.

Warning: Between the time the pathname is constructed and the file is created another process might have created a file with the same name using `tempnam`, leading to a possible security hole. The implementation generates names which can hardly be predicted, but when opening the file you should use the `O_EXCL` flag. Using `tmpfile` or `mkstemp` is a safe way to avoid this problem.

char * P_tmpdir   [SVID Macro]

This macro is the name of the default directory for temporary files.

Older Unix systems did not have the functions just described. Instead they used `mktemp` and `mkstemp`. Both of these functions work by modifying a file name template string you pass. The last six characters of this string must be '`XXXXXX`'. These six '`X`'s are replaced with six characters which make the whole string a unique file name. Usually the template string is something like '`/tmp/prefixXXXXXX`', and each program uses a unique *prefix*.

NB: Because `mktemp` and `mkstemp` modify the template string, you *must not* pass string constants to them. String constants are normally in read-only storage, so your program would crash when `mktemp` or `mkstemp` tried to modify the string. These functions are declared in the header file `stdlib.h`.

char * mktemp (*char *template*)   [Function]

Preliminary: | MT-Safe | AS-Safe | AC-Safe | See Section 1.2.2.1 [POSIX Safety Concepts], page 2.

The `mktemp` function generates a unique file name by modifying *template* as described above. If successful, it returns *template* as modified. If `mktemp` cannot find a unique file name, it makes *template* an empty string and returns that. If *template* does not end with '`XXXXXX`', `mktemp` returns a null pointer.

Warning: Between the time the pathname is constructed and the file is created another process might have created a file with the same name using `mktemp`, leading to a possible security hole. The implementation generates names which can hardly be predicted, but when opening the file you should use the `O_EXCL` flag. Using `mkstemp` is a safe way to avoid this problem.

int mkstemp (*char *template*)   [Function]

Preliminary: | MT-Safe | AS-Safe | AC-Safe fd | See Section 1.2.2.1 [POSIX Safety Concepts], page 2.

The `mkstemp` function generates a unique file name just as `mktemp` does, but it also opens the file for you with `open` (see Section 13.1 [Opening and Closing Files], page 333). If successful, it modifies *template* in place and returns a file descriptor for that file open for reading and writing. If `mkstemp` cannot create a uniquely-named file, it returns -1. If *template* does not end with '`XXXXXX`', `mkstemp` returns -1 and does not modify *template*.

The file is opened using mode `0600`. If the file is meant to be used by other users this mode must be changed explicitly.

Unlike `mktemp`, `mkstemp` is actually guaranteed to create a unique file that cannot possibly clash with any other program trying to create a temporary file. This is because it works by calling `open` with the `O_EXCL` flag, which says you want to create a new file and get an error if the file already exists.

char * mkdtemp (*char *template*)   [Function]
> Preliminary: | MT-Safe | AS-Safe | AC-Safe | See Section 1.2.2.1 [POSIX Safety Concepts], page 2.
>
> The `mkdtemp` function creates a directory with a unique name. If it succeeds, it overwrites *template* with the name of the directory, and returns *template*. As with `mktemp` and `mkstemp`, *template* should be a string ending with 'XXXXXX'.
>
> If `mkdtemp` cannot create an uniquely named directory, it returns `NULL` and sets *errno* appropriately. If *template* does not end with 'XXXXXX', `mkdtemp` returns `NULL` and does not modify *template*. *errno* will be set to `EINVAL` in this case.
>
> The directory is created using mode 0700.

The directory created by `mkdtemp` cannot clash with temporary files or directories created by other users. This is because directory creation always works like `open` with `O_EXCL`. See Section 14.8 [Creating Directories], page 411.

The `mkdtemp` function comes from OpenBSD.

15 Pipes and FIFOs

A *pipe* is a mechanism for interprocess communication; data written to the pipe by one process can be read by another process. The data is handled in a first-in, first-out (FIFO) order. The pipe has no name; it is created for one use and both ends must be inherited from the single process which created the pipe.

A *FIFO special file* is similar to a pipe, but instead of being an anonymous, temporary connection, a FIFO has a name or names like any other file. Processes open the FIFO by name in order to communicate through it.

A pipe or FIFO has to be open at both ends simultaneously. If you read from a pipe or FIFO file that doesn't have any processes writing to it (perhaps because they have all closed the file, or exited), the read returns end-of-file. Writing to a pipe or FIFO that doesn't have a reading process is treated as an error condition; it generates a `SIGPIPE` signal, and fails with error code `EPIPE` if the signal is handled or blocked.

Neither pipes nor FIFO special files allow file positioning. Both reading and writing operations happen sequentially; reading from the beginning of the file and writing at the end.

15.1 Creating a Pipe

The primitive for creating a pipe is the `pipe` function. This creates both the reading and writing ends of the pipe. It is not very useful for a single process to use a pipe to talk to itself. In typical use, a process creates a pipe just before it forks one or more child processes (see Section 26.4 [Creating a Process], page 775). The pipe is then used for communication either between the parent or child processes, or between two sibling processes.

The `pipe` function is declared in the header file `unistd.h`.

int pipe (*int filedes*[2]) [Function]

Preliminary: | MT-Safe | AS-Safe | AC-Safe fd | See Section 1.2.2.1 [POSIX Safety Concepts], page 2.

The `pipe` function creates a pipe and puts the file descriptors for the reading and writing ends of the pipe (respectively) into *filedes*[0] and *filedes*[1].

An easy way to remember that the input end comes first is that file descriptor 0 is standard input, and file descriptor 1 is standard output.

If successful, `pipe` returns a value of 0. On failure, -1 is returned. The following `errno` error conditions are defined for this function:

EMFILE   The process has too many files open.

ENFILE   There are too many open files in the entire system. See Section 2.2 [Error Codes], page 23, for more information about `ENFILE`. This error never occurs on GNU/Hurd systems.

Here is an example of a simple program that creates a pipe. This program uses the `fork` function (see Section 26.4 [Creating a Process], page 775) to create a child process. The parent process writes data to the pipe, which is read by the child process.

```
#include <sys/types.h>
#include <unistd.h>
#include <stdio.h>
#include <stdlib.h>

/* Read characters from the pipe and echo them to stdout. */

void
read_from_pipe (int file)
{
  FILE *stream;
  int c;
  stream = fdopen (file, "r");
  while ((c = fgetc (stream)) != EOF)
    putchar (c);
  fclose (stream);
}

/* Write some random text to the pipe. */

void
write_to_pipe (int file)
{
  FILE *stream;
  stream = fdopen (file, "w");
  fprintf (stream, "hello, world!\n");
  fprintf (stream, "goodbye, world!\n");
  fclose (stream);
}

int
main (void)
{
  pid_t pid;
  int mypipe[2];

  /* Create the pipe. */
  if (pipe (mypipe))
    {
      fprintf (stderr, "Pipe failed.\n");
      return EXIT_FAILURE;
    }

  /* Create the child process. */
  pid = fork ();
  if (pid == (pid_t) 0)
    {
      /* This is the child process.
         Close other end first. */
      close (mypipe[1]);
      read_from_pipe (mypipe[0]);
      return EXIT_SUCCESS;
    }
  else if (pid < (pid_t) 0)
    {
      /* The fork failed. */
      fprintf (stderr, "Fork failed.\n");
      return EXIT_FAILURE;
```

```
      }
    else
      {
        /* This is the parent process.
        Close other end first. */
        close (mypipe[0]);
        write_to_pipe (mypipe[1]);
        return EXIT_SUCCESS;
      }
  }
```

15.2 Pipe to a Subprocess

A common use of pipes is to send data to or receive data from a program being run as a subprocess. One way of doing this is by using a combination of **pipe** (to create the pipe), **fork** (to create the subprocess), **dup2** (to force the subprocess to use the pipe as its standard input or output channel), and **exec** (to execute the new program). Or, you can use **popen** and **pclose**.

The advantage of using **popen** and **pclose** is that the interface is much simpler and easier to use. But it doesn't offer as much flexibility as using the low-level functions directly.

FILE * popen (*const char *command, const char *mode*)   [Function]
> Preliminary: | MT-Safe | AS-Unsafe heap corrupt | AC-Unsafe corrupt lock fd mem | See Section 1.2.2.1 [POSIX Safety Concepts], page 2.
>
> The **popen** function is closely related to the **system** function; see Section 26.1 [Running a Command], page 773. It executes the shell command *command* as a subprocess. However, instead of waiting for the command to complete, it creates a pipe to the subprocess and returns a stream that corresponds to that pipe.
>
> If you specify a *mode* argument of "r", you can read from the stream to retrieve data from the standard output channel of the subprocess. The subprocess inherits its standard input channel from the parent process.
>
> Similarly, if you specify a *mode* argument of "w", you can write to the stream to send data to the standard input channel of the subprocess. The subprocess inherits its standard output channel from the parent process.
>
> In the event of an error **popen** returns a null pointer. This might happen if the pipe or stream cannot be created, if the subprocess cannot be forked, or if the program cannot be executed.

int pclose (*FILE *stream*)   [Function]
> Preliminary: | MT-Safe | AS-Unsafe heap plugin corrupt lock | AC-Unsafe corrupt lock fd mem | See Section 1.2.2.1 [POSIX Safety Concepts], page 2.
>
> The **pclose** function is used to close a stream created by **popen**. It waits for the child process to terminate and returns its status value, as for the **system** function.

Here is an example showing how to use **popen** and **pclose** to filter output through another program, in this case the paging program **more**.

```
#include <stdio.h>
#include <stdlib.h>
```

```
void
write_data (FILE * stream)
{
  int i;
  for (i = 0; i < 100; i++)
    fprintf (stream, "%d\n", i);
  if (ferror (stream))
    {
      fprintf (stderr, "Output to stream failed.\n");
      exit (EXIT_FAILURE);
    }
}

int
main (void)
{
  FILE *output;

  output = popen ("more", "w");
  if (!output)
    {
      fprintf (stderr,
               "incorrect parameters or too many files.\n");
      return EXIT_FAILURE;
    }
  write_data (output);
  if (pclose (output) != 0)
    {
      fprintf (stderr,
               "Could not run more or other error.\n");
    }
  return EXIT_SUCCESS;
}
```

15.3 FIFO Special Files

A FIFO special file is similar to a pipe, except that it is created in a different way. Instead of being an anonymous communications channel, a FIFO special file is entered into the file system by calling `mkfifo`.

Once you have created a FIFO special file in this way, any process can open it for reading or writing, in the same way as an ordinary file. However, it has to be open at both ends simultaneously before you can proceed to do any input or output operations on it. Opening a FIFO for reading normally blocks until some other process opens the same FIFO for writing, and vice versa.

The `mkfifo` function is declared in the header file `sys/stat.h`.

int mkfifo (*const char *filename, mode_t mode*)   [Function]
> Preliminary: | MT-Safe | AS-Safe | AC-Safe | See Section 1.2.2.1 [POSIX Safety Concepts], page 2.
>
> The `mkfifo` function makes a FIFO special file with name *filename*. The *mode* argument is used to set the file's permissions; see Section 14.9.7 [Assigning File Permissions], page 423.

The normal, successful return value from `mkfifo` is 0. In the case of an error, `-1` is returned. In addition to the usual file name errors (see Section 11.2.3 [File Name Errors], page 255), the following `errno` error conditions are defined for this function:

`EEXIST`   The named file already exists.

`ENOSPC`   The directory or file system cannot be extended.

`EROFS`   The directory that would contain the file resides on a read-only file system.

15.4 Atomicity of Pipe I/O

Reading or writing pipe data is *atomic* if the size of data written is not greater than `PIPE_BUF`. This means that the data transfer seems to be an instantaneous unit, in that nothing else in the system can observe a state in which it is partially complete. Atomic I/O may not begin right away (it may need to wait for buffer space or for data), but once it does begin it finishes immediately.

Reading or writing a larger amount of data may not be atomic; for example, output data from other processes sharing the descriptor may be interspersed. Also, once `PIPE_BUF` characters have been written, further writes will block until some characters are read.

See Section 32.6 [Limits on File System Capacity], page 874, for information about the `PIPE_BUF` parameter.

16 Sockets

This chapter describes the GNU facilities for interprocess communication using sockets.

A *socket* is a generalized interprocess communication channel. Like a pipe, a socket is represented as a file descriptor. Unlike pipes sockets support communication between unrelated processes, and even between processes running on different machines that communicate over a network. Sockets are the primary means of communicating with other machines; `telnet`, `rlogin`, `ftp`, `talk` and the other familiar network programs use sockets.

Not all operating systems support sockets. In the GNU C Library, the header file `sys/socket.h` exists regardless of the operating system, and the socket functions always exist, but if the system does not really support sockets these functions always fail.

Incomplete: We do not currently document the facilities for broadcast messages or for configuring Internet interfaces. The reentrant functions and some newer functions that are related to IPv6 aren't documented either so far.

16.1 Socket Concepts

When you create a socket, you must specify the style of communication you want to use and the type of protocol that should implement it. The *communication style* of a socket defines the user-level semantics of sending and receiving data on the socket. Choosing a communication style specifies the answers to questions such as these:

- **What are the units of data transmission?** Some communication styles regard the data as a sequence of bytes with no larger structure; others group the bytes into records (which are known in this context as *packets*).

- **Can data be lost during normal operation?** Some communication styles guarantee that all the data sent arrives in the order it was sent (barring system or network crashes); other styles occasionally lose data as a normal part of operation, and may sometimes deliver packets more than once or in the wrong order.

  Designing a program to use unreliable communication styles usually involves taking precautions to detect lost or misordered packets and to retransmit data as needed.

- **Is communication entirely with one partner?** Some communication styles are like a telephone call—you make a *connection* with one remote socket and then exchange data freely. Other styles are like mailing letters—you specify a destination address for each message you send.

You must also choose a *namespace* for naming the socket. A socket name ("address") is meaningful only in the context of a particular namespace. In fact, even the data type to use for a socket name may depend on the namespace. Namespaces are also called "domains", but we avoid that word as it can be confused with other usage of the same term. Each namespace has a symbolic name that starts with 'PF_'. A corresponding symbolic name starting with 'AF_' designates the address format for that namespace.

Finally you must choose the *protocol* to carry out the communication. The protocol determines what low-level mechanism is used to transmit and receive data. Each protocol is valid for a particular namespace and communication style; a namespace is sometimes called a *protocol family* because of this, which is why the namespace names start with 'PF_'.

The rules of a protocol apply to the data passing between two programs, perhaps on different computers; most of these rules are handled by the operating system and you need not know about them. What you do need to know about protocols is this:

- In order to have communication between two sockets, they must specify the *same* protocol.

- Each protocol is meaningful with particular style/namespace combinations and cannot be used with inappropriate combinations. For example, the TCP protocol fits only the byte stream style of communication and the Internet namespace.

- For each combination of style and namespace there is a *default protocol*, which you can request by specifying 0 as the protocol number. And that's what you should normally do—use the default.

Throughout the following description at various places variables/parameters to denote sizes are required. And here the trouble starts. In the first implementations the type of these variables was simply `int`. On most machines at that time an `int` was 32 bits wide, which created a *de facto* standard requiring 32-bit variables. This is important since references to variables of this type are passed to the kernel.

Then the POSIX people came and unified the interface with the words "all size values are of type `size_t`". On 64-bit machines `size_t` is 64 bits wide, so pointers to variables were no longer possible.

The Unix98 specification provides a solution by introducing a type `socklen_t`. This type is used in all of the cases that POSIX changed to use `size_t`. The only requirement of this type is that it be an unsigned type of at least 32 bits. Therefore, implementations which require that references to 32-bit variables be passed can be as happy as implementations which use 64-bit values.

16.2 Communication Styles

The GNU C Library includes support for several different kinds of sockets, each with different characteristics. This section describes the supported socket types. The symbolic constants listed here are defined in `sys/socket.h`.

`int SOCK_STREAM`   [Macro]

> The `SOCK_STREAM` style is like a pipe (see Chapter 15 [Pipes and FIFOs], page 437). It operates over a connection with a particular remote socket and transmits data reliably as a stream of bytes.
>
> Use of this style is covered in detail in Section 16.9 [Using Sockets with Connections], page 468.

`int SOCK_DGRAM`   [Macro]

> The `SOCK_DGRAM` style is used for sending individually-addressed packets unreliably. It is the diametrical opposite of `SOCK_STREAM`.
>
> Each time you write data to a socket of this kind, that data becomes one packet. Since `SOCK_DGRAM` sockets do not have connections, you must specify the recipient address with each packet.
>
> The only guarantee that the system makes about your requests to transmit data is that it will try its best to deliver each packet you send. It may succeed with the sixth

packet after failing with the fourth and fifth packets; the seventh packet may arrive before the sixth, and may arrive a second time after the sixth.

The typical use for `SOCK_DGRAM` is in situations where it is acceptable to simply re-send a packet if no response is seen in a reasonable amount of time.

See Section 16.10 [Datagram Socket Operations], page 480, for detailed information about how to use datagram sockets.

`int SOCK_RAW`   [Macro]

This style provides access to low-level network protocols and interfaces. Ordinary user programs usually have no need to use this style.

16.3 Socket Addresses

The name of a socket is normally called an *address*. The functions and symbols for dealing with socket addresses were named inconsistently, sometimes using the term "name" and sometimes using "address". You can regard these terms as synonymous where sockets are concerned.

A socket newly created with the `socket` function has no address. Other processes can find it for communication only if you give it an address. We call this *binding* the address to the socket, and the way to do it is with the `bind` function.

You need only be concerned with the address of a socket if other processes are to find it and start communicating with it. You can specify an address for other sockets, but this is usually pointless; the first time you send data from a socket, or use it to initiate a connection, the system assigns an address automatically if you have not specified one.

Occasionally a client needs to specify an address because the server discriminates based on address; for example, the rsh and rlogin protocols look at the client's socket address and only bypass password checking if it is less than `IPPORT_RESERVED` (see Section 16.6.3 [Internet Ports], page 460).

The details of socket addresses vary depending on what namespace you are using. See Section 16.5 [The Local Namespace], page 448, or Section 16.6 [The Internet Namespace], page 450, for specific information.

Regardless of the namespace, you use the same functions `bind` and `getsockname` to set and examine a socket's address. These functions use a phony data type, `struct sockaddr *`, to accept the address. In practice, the address lives in a structure of some other data type appropriate to the address format you are using, but you cast its address to `struct sockaddr *` when you pass it to `bind`.

16.3.1 Address Formats

The functions `bind` and `getsockname` use the generic data type `struct sockaddr *` to represent a pointer to a socket address. You can't use this data type effectively to interpret an address or construct one; for that, you must use the proper data type for the socket's namespace.

Thus, the usual practice is to construct an address of the proper namespace-specific type, then cast a pointer to `struct sockaddr *` when you call `bind` or `getsockname`.

The one piece of information that you can get from the **struct sockaddr** data type is the *address format designator*. This tells you which data type to use to understand the address fully.

The symbols in this section are defined in the header file **sys/socket.h**.

struct sockaddr [Data Type]

The **struct sockaddr** type itself has the following members:

short int sa_family

This is the code for the address format of this address. It identifies the format of the data which follows.

char sa_data[14]

This is the actual socket address data, which is format-dependent. Its length also depends on the format, and may well be more than 14. The length 14 of **sa_data** is essentially arbitrary.

Each address format has a symbolic name which starts with 'AF_'. Each of them corresponds to a 'PF_' symbol which designates the corresponding namespace. Here is a list of address format names:

AF_LOCAL This designates the address format that goes with the local namespace. (**PF_LOCAL** is the name of that namespace.) See Section 16.5.2 [Details of Local Namespace], page 448, for information about this address format.

AF_UNIX This is a synonym for **AF_LOCAL**. Although **AF_LOCAL** is mandated by POSIX.1g, **AF_UNIX** is portable to more systems. **AF_UNIX** was the traditional name stemming from BSD, so even most POSIX systems support it. It is also the name of choice in the Unix98 specification. (The same is true for **PF_UNIX** vs. **PF_LOCAL**).

AF_FILE This is another synonym for **AF_LOCAL**, for compatibility. (**PF_FILE** is likewise a synonym for **PF_LOCAL**.)

AF_INET This designates the address format that goes with the Internet namespace. (**PF_INET** is the name of that namespace.) See Section 16.6.1 [Internet Socket Address Formats], page 451.

AF_INET6 This is similar to **AF_INET**, but refers to the IPv6 protocol. (**PF_INET6** is the name of the corresponding namespace.)

AF_UNSPEC

This designates no particular address format. It is used only in rare cases, such as to clear out the default destination address of a "connected" datagram socket. See Section 16.10.1 [Sending Datagrams], page 480.

The corresponding namespace designator symbol **PF_UNSPEC** exists for completeness, but there is no reason to use it in a program.

sys/socket.h defines symbols starting with 'AF_' for many different kinds of networks, most or all of which are not actually implemented. We will document those that really work as we receive information about how to use them.

16.3.2 Setting the Address of a Socket

Use the `bind` function to assign an address to a socket. The prototype for `bind` is in the header file `sys/socket.h`. For examples of use, see Section 16.5.3 [Example of Local-Namespace Sockets], page 449, or see Section 16.6.7 [Internet Socket Example], page 465.

`int bind` (*int socket*, *struct sockaddr *addr, socklen_t length*)   [Function]
> Preliminary: | MT-Safe | AS-Safe | AC-Safe | See Section 1.2.2.1 [POSIX Safety Concepts], page 2.
>
> The `bind` function assigns an address to the socket *socket*. The *addr* and *length* arguments specify the address; the detailed format of the address depends on the namespace. The first part of the address is always the format designator, which specifies a namespace, and says that the address is in the format of that namespace.
>
> The return value is 0 on success and −1 on failure. The following `errno` error conditions are defined for this function:
>
> EBADF   The *socket* argument is not a valid file descriptor.
>
> ENOTSOCK   The descriptor *socket* is not a socket.
>
> EADDRNOTAVAIL
> >   The specified address is not available on this machine.
>
> EADDRINUSE
> >   Some other socket is already using the specified address.
>
> EINVAL   The socket *socket* already has an address.
>
> EACCES   You do not have permission to access the requested address. (In the Internet domain, only the super-user is allowed to specify a port number in the range 0 through `IPPORT_RESERVED` minus one; see Section 16.6.3 [Internet Ports], page 460.)
>
> Additional conditions may be possible depending on the particular namespace of the socket.

16.3.3 Reading the Address of a Socket

Use the function `getsockname` to examine the address of an Internet socket. The prototype for this function is in the header file `sys/socket.h`.

`int getsockname` (*int socket*, *struct sockaddr *addr, socklen_t*   [Function]
   *length-ptr)
> Preliminary: | MT-Safe | AS-Safe | AC-Safe mem/hurd | See Section 1.2.2.1 [POSIX Safety Concepts], page 2.
>
> The `getsockname` function returns information about the address of the socket *socket* in the locations specified by the *addr* and *length-ptr* arguments. Note that the *length-ptr* is a pointer; you should initialize it to be the allocation size of *addr*, and on return it contains the actual size of the address data.
>
> The format of the address data depends on the socket namespace. The length of the information is usually fixed for a given namespace, so normally you can know exactly how much space is needed and can provide that much. The usual practice is

to allocate a place for the value using the proper data type for the socket's namespace, then cast its address to `struct sockaddr *` to pass it to `getsockname`.

The return value is 0 on success and -1 on error. The following `errno` error conditions are defined for this function:

EBADF   The *socket* argument is not a valid file descriptor.

ENOTSOCK   The descriptor *socket* is not a socket.

ENOBUFS   There are not enough internal buffers available for the operation.

You can't read the address of a socket in the file namespace. This is consistent with the rest of the system; in general, there's no way to find a file's name from a descriptor for that file.

16.4 Interface Naming

Each network interface has a name. This usually consists of a few letters that relate to the type of interface, which may be followed by a number if there is more than one interface of that type. Examples might be `lo` (the loopback interface) and `eth0` (the first Ethernet interface).

Although such names are convenient for humans, it would be clumsy to have to use them whenever a program needs to refer to an interface. In such situations an interface is referred to by its *index*, which is an arbitrarily-assigned small positive integer.

The following functions, constants and data types are declared in the header file `net/if.h`.

`size_t IFNAMSIZ`   [Constant]

> This constant defines the maximum buffer size needed to hold an interface name, including its terminating zero byte.

`unsigned int if_nametoindex (const char *ifname)`   [Function]

> Preliminary: | MT-Safe | AS-Unsafe lock | AC-Unsafe lock fd | See Section 1.2.2.1 [POSIX Safety Concepts], page 2.
>
> This function yields the interface index corresponding to a particular name. If no interface exists with the name given, it returns 0.

`char * if_indextoname (unsigned int ifindex, char *ifname)`   [Function]

> Preliminary: | MT-Safe | AS-Unsafe lock | AC-Unsafe lock fd | See Section 1.2.2.1 [POSIX Safety Concepts], page 2.
>
> This function maps an interface index to its corresponding name. The returned name is placed in the buffer pointed to by `ifname`, which must be at least `IFNAMSIZ` bytes in length. If the index was invalid, the function's return value is a null pointer, otherwise it is `ifname`.

`struct if_nameindex`   [Data Type]

> This data type is used to hold the information about a single interface. It has the following members:
>
> `unsigned int if_index;`
>> This is the interface index.

```
char *if_name
```
This is the null-terminated index name.

struct if_nameindex * if_nameindex (*void*)   [Function]
Preliminary: | MT-Safe | AS-Unsafe heap lock/hurd | AC-Unsafe lock/hurd fd mem | See Section 1.2.2.1 [POSIX Safety Concepts], page 2.

This function returns an array of **if_nameindex** structures, one for every interface that is present. The end of the list is indicated by a structure with an interface of 0 and a null name pointer. If an error occurs, this function returns a null pointer.

The returned structure must be freed with **if_freenameindex** after use.

void if_freenameindex (*struct if_nameindex *ptr*)   [Function]
Preliminary: | MT-Safe | AS-Unsafe heap | AC-Unsafe mem | See Section 1.2.2.1 [POSIX Safety Concepts], page 2.

This function frees the structure returned by an earlier call to **if_nameindex**.

16.5 The Local Namespace

This section describes the details of the local namespace, whose symbolic name (required when you create a socket) is **PF_LOCAL**. The local namespace is also known as "Unix domain sockets". Another name is file namespace since socket addresses are normally implemented as file names.

16.5.1 Local Namespace Concepts

In the local namespace socket addresses are file names. You can specify any file name you want as the address of the socket, but you must have write permission on the directory containing it. It's common to put these files in the **/tmp** directory.

One peculiarity of the local namespace is that the name is only used when opening the connection; once open the address is not meaningful and may not exist.

Another peculiarity is that you cannot connect to such a socket from another machine–not even if the other machine shares the file system which contains the name of the socket. You can see the socket in a directory listing, but connecting to it never succeeds. Some programs take advantage of this, such as by asking the client to send its own process ID, and using the process IDs to distinguish between clients. However, we recommend you not use this method in protocols you design, as we might someday permit connections from other machines that mount the same file systems. Instead, send each new client an identifying number if you want it to have one.

After you close a socket in the local namespace, you should delete the file name from the file system. Use **unlink** or **remove** to do this; see Section 14.6 [Deleting Files], page 409.

The local namespace supports just one protocol for any communication style; it is protocol number 0.

16.5.2 Details of Local Namespace

To create a socket in the local namespace, use the constant **PF_LOCAL** as the *namespace* argument to **socket** or **socketpair**. This constant is defined in **sys/socket.h**.

int PF_LOCAL   [Macro]

> This designates the local namespace, in which socket addresses are local names, and its associated family of protocols. PF_LOCAL is the macro used by POSIX.1g.

int PF_UNIX   [Macro]

> This is a synonym for PF_LOCAL, for compatibility's sake.

int PF_FILE   [Macro]

> This is a synonym for PF_LOCAL, for compatibility's sake.

The structure for specifying socket names in the local namespace is defined in the header file sys/un.h:

struct sockaddr_un   [Data Type]

> This structure is used to specify local namespace socket addresses. It has the following members:
>
> short int sun_family
>
> > This identifies the address family or format of the socket address. You should store the value AF_LOCAL to designate the local namespace. See Section 16.3 [Socket Addresses], page 444.
>
> char sun_path[108]
>
> > This is the file name to use.
> >
> > **Incomplete:** Why is 108 a magic number? RMS suggests making this a zero-length array and tweaking the following example to use alloca to allocate an appropriate amount of storage based on the length of the filename.

You should compute the *length* parameter for a socket address in the local namespace as the sum of the size of the sun_family component and the string length (*not* the allocation size!) of the file name string. This can be done using the macro SUN_LEN:

int SUN_LEN (*struct sockaddr_un * ptr*)   [Macro]

> Preliminary: | MT-Safe | AS-Safe | AC-Safe | See Section 1.2.2.1 [POSIX Safety Concepts], page 2.
>
> This macro computes the length of the socket address in the local namespace.

16.5.3 Example of Local-Namespace Sockets

Here is an example showing how to create and name a socket in the local namespace.

```
#include <stddef.h>
#include <stdio.h>
#include <errno.h>
#include <stdlib.h>
#include <string.h>
#include <sys/socket.h>
#include <sys/un.h>

int
make_named_socket (const char *filename)
```

```
{
  struct sockaddr_un name;
  int sock;
  size_t size;

  /* Create the socket. */
  sock = socket (PF_LOCAL, SOCK_DGRAM, 0);
  if (sock < 0)
    {
      perror ("socket");
      exit (EXIT_FAILURE);
    }

  /* Bind a name to the socket. */
  name.sun_family = AF_LOCAL;
  strncpy (name.sun_path, filename, sizeof (name.sun_path));
  name.sun_path[sizeof (name.sun_path) - 1] = '\0';

  /* The size of the address is
     the offset of the start of the filename,
     plus its length (not including the terminating null byte).
     Alternatively you can just do:
     size = SUN_LEN (&name);
  */
  size = (offsetof (struct sockaddr_un, sun_path)
          + strlen (name.sun_path));

  if (bind (sock, (struct sockaddr *) &name, size) < 0)
    {
      perror ("bind");
      exit (EXIT_FAILURE);
    }

  return sock;
}
```

16.6 The Internet Namespace

This section describes the details of the protocols and socket naming conventions used in the Internet namespace.

Originally the Internet namespace used only IP version 4 (IPv4). With the growing number of hosts on the Internet, a new protocol with a larger address space was necessary: IP version 6 (IPv6). IPv6 introduces 128-bit addresses (IPv4 has 32-bit addresses) and other features, and will eventually replace IPv4.

To create a socket in the IPv4 Internet namespace, use the symbolic name `PF_INET` of this namespace as the *namespace* argument to `socket` or `socketpair`. For IPv6 addresses you need the macro `PF_INET6`. These macros are defined in `sys/socket.h`.

int PF_INET   [Macro]
    This designates the IPv4 Internet namespace and associated family of protocols.

int PF_INET6   [Macro]
    This designates the IPv6 Internet namespace and associated family of protocols.

A socket address for the Internet namespace includes the following components:

- The address of the machine you want to connect to. Internet addresses can be specified in several ways; these are discussed in Section 16.6.1 [Internet Socket Address Formats], page 451, Section 16.6.2 [Host Addresses], page 452, and Section 16.6.2.4 [Host Names], page 456.

- A port number for that machine. See Section 16.6.3 [Internet Ports], page 460.

You must ensure that the address and port number are represented in a canonical format called *network byte order*. See Section 16.6.5 [Byte Order Conversion], page 462, for information about this.

16.6.1 Internet Socket Address Formats

In the Internet namespace, for both IPv4 (`AF_INET`) and IPv6 (`AF_INET6`), a socket address consists of a host address and a port on that host. In addition, the protocol you choose serves effectively as a part of the address because local port numbers are meaningful only within a particular protocol.

The data types for representing socket addresses in the Internet namespace are defined in the header file `netinet/in.h`.

`struct sockaddr_in`   [Data Type]

> This is the data type used to represent socket addresses in the Internet namespace. It has the following members:

> `sa_family_t sin_family`
>> This identifies the address family or format of the socket address. You should store the value `AF_INET` in this member. See Section 16.3 [Socket Addresses], page 444.

> `struct in_addr sin_addr`
>> This is the Internet address of the host machine. See Section 16.6.2 [Host Addresses], page 452, and Section 16.6.2.4 [Host Names], page 456, for how to get a value to store here.

> `unsigned short int sin_port`
>> This is the port number. See Section 16.6.3 [Internet Ports], page 460.

When you call `bind` or `getsockname`, you should specify `sizeof (struct sockaddr_in)` as the *length* parameter if you are using an IPv4 Internet namespace socket address.

`struct sockaddr_in6`   [Data Type]

> This is the data type used to represent socket addresses in the IPv6 namespace. It has the following members:

> `sa_family_t sin6_family`
>> This identifies the address family or format of the socket address. You should store the value of `AF_INET6` in this member. See Section 16.3 [Socket Addresses], page 444.

> `struct in6_addr sin6_addr`
>> This is the IPv6 address of the host machine. See Section 16.6.2 [Host Addresses], page 452, and Section 16.6.2.4 [Host Names], page 456, for how to get a value to store here.

`uint32_t sin6_flowinfo`
> This is a currently unimplemented field.

`uint16_t sin6_port`
> This is the port number. See Section 16.6.3 [Internet Ports], page 460.

16.6.2 Host Addresses

Each computer on the Internet has one or more *Internet addresses*, numbers which identify that computer among all those on the Internet. Users typically write IPv4 numeric host addresses as sequences of four numbers, separated by periods, as in '`128.52.46.32`', and IPv6 numeric host addresses as sequences of up to eight numbers separated by colons, as in '`5f03:1200:836f:c100::1`'.

Each computer also has one or more *host names*, which are strings of words separated by periods, as in '`www.gnu.org`'.

Programs that let the user specify a host typically accept both numeric addresses and host names. To open a connection a program needs a numeric address, and so must convert a host name to the numeric address it stands for.

16.6.2.1 Internet Host Addresses

An IPv4 Internet host address is a number containing four bytes of data. Historically these are divided into two parts, a *network number* and a *local network address number* within that network. In the mid-1990s classless addresses were introduced which changed this behavior. Since some functions implicitly expect the old definitions, we first describe the class-based network and will then describe classless addresses. IPv6 uses only classless addresses and therefore the following paragraphs don't apply.

The class-based IPv4 network number consists of the first one, two or three bytes; the rest of the bytes are the local address.

IPv4 network numbers are registered with the Network Information Center (NIC), and are divided into three classes—A, B and C. The local network address numbers of individual machines are registered with the administrator of the particular network.

Class A networks have single-byte numbers in the range 0 to 127. There are only a small number of Class A networks, but they can each support a very large number of hosts. Medium-sized Class B networks have two-byte network numbers, with the first byte in the range 128 to 191. Class C networks are the smallest; they have three-byte network numbers, with the first byte in the range 192-255. Thus, the first 1, 2, or 3 bytes of an Internet address specify a network. The remaining bytes of the Internet address specify the address within that network.

The Class A network 0 is reserved for broadcast to all networks. In addition, the host number 0 within each network is reserved for broadcast to all hosts in that network. These uses are obsolete now but for compatibility reasons you shouldn't use network 0 and host number 0.

The Class A network 127 is reserved for loopback; you can always use the Internet address '`127.0.0.1`' to refer to the host machine.

Since a single machine can be a member of multiple networks, it can have multiple Internet host addresses. However, there is never supposed to be more than one machine with the same host address.

There are four forms of the *standard numbers-and-dots notation* for Internet addresses:

a.b.c.d   This specifies all four bytes of the address individually and is the commonly used representation.

a.b.c   The last part of the address, *c*, is interpreted as a 2-byte quantity. This is useful for specifying host addresses in a Class B network with network address number *a.b*.

a.b   The last part of the address, *b*, is interpreted as a 3-byte quantity. This is useful for specifying host addresses in a Class A network with network address number *a*.

a   If only one part is given, this corresponds directly to the host address number.

Within each part of the address, the usual C conventions for specifying the radix apply. In other words, a leading '0x' or '0X' implies hexadecimal radix; a leading '0' implies octal; and otherwise decimal radix is assumed.

Classless Addresses

IPv4 addresses (and IPv6 addresses also) are now considered classless; the distinction between classes A, B and C can be ignored. Instead an IPv4 host address consists of a 32-bit address and a 32-bit mask. The mask contains set bits for the network part and cleared bits for the host part. The network part is contiguous from the left, with the remaining bits representing the host. As a consequence, the netmask can simply be specified as the number of set bits. Classes A, B and C are just special cases of this general rule. For example, class A addresses have a netmask of '255.0.0.0' or a prefix length of 8.

Classless IPv4 network addresses are written in numbers-and-dots notation with the prefix length appended and a slash as separator. For example the class A network 10 is written as '10.0.0.0/8'.

IPv6 Addresses

IPv6 addresses contain 128 bits (IPv4 has 32 bits) of data. A host address is usually written as eight 16-bit hexadecimal numbers that are separated by colons. Two colons are used to abbreviate strings of consecutive zeros. For example, the IPv6 loopback address '0:0:0:0:0:0:0:1' can just be written as '::1'.

16.6.2.2 Host Address Data Type

IPv4 Internet host addresses are represented in some contexts as integers (type `uint32_t`). In other contexts, the integer is packaged inside a structure of type `struct in_addr`. It would be better if the usage were made consistent, but it is not hard to extract the integer from the structure or put the integer into a structure.

You will find older code that uses `unsigned long int` for IPv4 Internet host addresses instead of `uint32_t` or `struct in_addr`. Historically `unsigned long int` was a 32-bit number but with 64-bit machines this has changed. Using `unsigned long int` might break the code if it is used on machines where this type doesn't have 32 bits. `uint32_t` is specified by Unix98 and guaranteed to have 32 bits.

IPv6 Internet host addresses have 128 bits and are packaged inside a structure of type `struct in6_addr`.

The following basic definitions for Internet addresses are declared in the header file `netinet/in.h`:

`struct in_addr` [Data Type]

This data type is used in certain contexts to contain an IPv4 Internet host address. It has just one field, named `s_addr`, which records the host address number as an `uint32_t`.

`uint32_t INADDR_LOOPBACK` [Macro]

You can use this constant to stand for "the address of this machine," instead of finding its actual address. It is the IPv4 Internet address '`127.0.0.1`', which is usually called '`localhost`'. This special constant saves you the trouble of looking up the address of your own machine. Also, the system usually implements `INADDR_LOOPBACK` specially, avoiding any network traffic for the case of one machine talking to itself.

`uint32_t INADDR_ANY` [Macro]

You can use this constant to stand for "any incoming address" when binding to an address. See Section 16.3.2 [Setting the Address of a Socket], page 446. This is the usual address to give in the `sin_addr` member of `struct sockaddr_in` when you want to accept Internet connections.

`uint32_t INADDR_BROADCAST` [Macro]

This constant is the address you use to send a broadcast message.

`uint32_t INADDR_NONE` [Macro]

This constant is returned by some functions to indicate an error.

`struct in6_addr` [Data Type]

This data type is used to store an IPv6 address. It stores 128 bits of data, which can be accessed (via a union) in a variety of ways.

`struct in6_addr in6addr_loopback` [Constant]

This constant is the IPv6 address '`::1`', the loopback address. See above for a description of what this means. The macro `IN6ADDR_LOOPBACK_INIT` is provided to allow you to initialize your own variables to this value.

`struct in6_addr in6addr_any` [Constant]

This constant is the IPv6 address '`::`', the unspecified address. See above for a description of what this means. The macro `IN6ADDR_ANY_INIT` is provided to allow you to initialize your own variables to this value.

16.6.2.3 Host Address Functions

These additional functions for manipulating Internet addresses are declared in the header file `arpa/inet.h`. They represent Internet addresses in network byte order, and network numbers and local-address-within-network numbers in host byte order. See Section 16.6.5 [Byte Order Conversion], page 462, for an explanation of network and host byte order.

`int inet_aton (const char *name, struct in_addr *addr)` [Function]

Preliminary: | MT-Safe locale | AS-Safe | AC-Safe | See Section 1.2.2.1 [POSIX Safety Concepts], page 2.

This function converts the IPv4 Internet host address *name* from the standard numbers-and-dots notation into binary data and stores it in the `struct in_addr` that *addr* points to. `inet_aton` returns nonzero if the address is valid, zero if not.

uint32_t inet_addr (*const char ***name**)   [Function]

Preliminary: | MT-Safe locale | AS-Safe | AC-Safe | See Section 1.2.2.1 [POSIX Safety Concepts], page 2.

This function converts the IPv4 Internet host address *name* from the standard numbers-and-dots notation into binary data. If the input is not valid, `inet_addr` returns `INADDR_NONE`. This is an obsolete interface to `inet_aton`, described immediately above. It is obsolete because `INADDR_NONE` is a valid address (255.255.255.255), and `inet_aton` provides a cleaner way to indicate error return.

uint32_t inet_network (*const char ***name**)   [Function]

Preliminary: | MT-Safe locale | AS-Safe | AC-Safe | See Section 1.2.2.1 [POSIX Safety Concepts], page 2.

This function extracts the network number from the address *name*, given in the standard numbers-and-dots notation. The returned address is in host order. If the input is not valid, `inet_network` returns −1.

The function works only with traditional IPv4 class A, B and C network types. It doesn't work with classless addresses and shouldn't be used anymore.

char * inet_ntoa (*struct in_addr ***addr**)   [Function]

Preliminary: | MT-Safe locale | AS-Unsafe race | AC-Safe | See Section 1.2.2.1 [POSIX Safety Concepts], page 2.

This function converts the IPv4 Internet host address *addr* to a string in the standard numbers-and-dots notation. The return value is a pointer into a statically-allocated buffer. Subsequent calls will overwrite the same buffer, so you should copy the string if you need to save it.

In multi-threaded programs each thread has its own statically-allocated buffer. But still subsequent calls of `inet_ntoa` in the same thread will overwrite the result of the last call.

Instead of `inet_ntoa` the newer function `inet_ntop` which is described below should be used since it handles both IPv4 and IPv6 addresses.

struct in_addr inet_makeaddr (*uint32_t ***net***, uint32_t ***local**)   [Function]

Preliminary: | MT-Safe | AS-Safe | AC-Safe | See Section 1.2.2.1 [POSIX Safety Concepts], page 2.

This function makes an IPv4 Internet host address by combining the network number *net* with the local-address-within-network number *local*.

uint32_t inet_lnaof (*struct in_addr ***addr**)   [Function]

Preliminary: | MT-Safe | AS-Safe | AC-Safe | See Section 1.2.2.1 [POSIX Safety Concepts], page 2.

This function returns the local-address-within-network part of the Internet host address *addr*.

The function works only with traditional IPv4 class A, B and C network types. It doesn't work with classless addresses and shouldn't be used anymore.

uint32_t inet_netof (*struct in_addr* **addr**)   [Function]
> Preliminary: | MT-Safe | AS-Safe | AC-Safe | See Section 1.2.2.1 [POSIX Safety Concepts], page 2.

> This function returns the network number part of the Internet host address *addr*.

> The function works only with traditional IPv4 class A, B and C network types. It doesn't work with classless addresses and shouldn't be used anymore.

int inet_pton (*int* **af**, *const char* ***cp**, *void* ***buf**)   [Function]
> Preliminary: | MT-Safe locale | AS-Safe | AC-Safe | See Section 1.2.2.1 [POSIX Safety Concepts], page 2.

> This function converts an Internet address (either IPv4 or IPv6) from presentation (textual) to network (binary) format. *af* should be either **AF_INET** or **AF_INET6**, as appropriate for the type of address being converted. *cp* is a pointer to the input string, and *buf* is a pointer to a buffer for the result. It is the caller's responsibility to make sure the buffer is large enough.

const char * inet_ntop (*int* **af**, *const void* ***cp**, *char* ***buf**,   [Function]
        socklen_t **len**)
> Preliminary: | MT-Safe locale | AS-Safe | AC-Safe | See Section 1.2.2.1 [POSIX Safety Concepts], page 2.

> This function converts an Internet address (either IPv4 or IPv6) from network (binary) to presentation (textual) form. *af* should be either **AF_INET** or **AF_INET6**, as appropriate. *cp* is a pointer to the address to be converted. *buf* should be a pointer to a buffer to hold the result, and *len* is the length of this buffer. The return value from the function will be this buffer address.

16.6.2.4 Host Names

Besides the standard numbers-and-dots notation for Internet addresses, you can also refer to a host by a symbolic name. The advantage of a symbolic name is that it is usually easier to remember. For example, the machine with Internet address '158.121.106.19' is also known as 'alpha.gnu.org'; and other machines in the 'gnu.org' domain can refer to it simply as 'alpha'.

Internally, the system uses a database to keep track of the mapping between host names and host numbers. This database is usually either the file /etc/hosts or an equivalent provided by a name server. The functions and other symbols for accessing this database are declared in netdb.h. They are BSD features, defined unconditionally if you include netdb.h.

struct hostent   [Data Type]
> This data type is used to represent an entry in the hosts database. It has the following members:

> char *h_name
>> This is the "official" name of the host.

> char **h_aliases
>> These are alternative names for the host, represented as a null-terminated vector of strings.

`int h_addrtype`

> This is the host address type; in practice, its value is always either `AF_INET` or `AF_INET6`, with the latter being used for IPv6 hosts. In principle other kinds of addresses could be represented in the database as well as Internet addresses; if this were done, you might find a value in this field other than `AF_INET` or `AF_INET6`. See Section 16.3 [Socket Addresses], page 444.

`int h_length`

> This is the length, in bytes, of each address.

`char **h_addr_list`

> This is the vector of addresses for the host. (Recall that the host might be connected to multiple networks and have different addresses on each one.) The vector is terminated by a null pointer.

`char *h_addr`

> This is a synonym for `h_addr_list[0]`; in other words, it is the first host address.

As far as the host database is concerned, each address is just a block of memory `h_length` bytes long. But in other contexts there is an implicit assumption that you can convert IPv4 addresses to a `struct in_addr` or an `uint32_t`. Host addresses in a `struct hostent` structure are always given in network byte order; see Section 16.6.5 [Byte Order Conversion], page 462.

You can use `gethostbyname`, `gethostbyname2` or `gethostbyaddr` to search the hosts database for information about a particular host. The information is returned in a statically-allocated structure; you must copy the information if you need to save it across calls. You can also use `getaddrinfo` and `getnameinfo` to obtain this information.

`struct hostent * gethostbyname (const char *name)`   [Function]

> Preliminary: | MT-Unsafe race:hostbyname env locale | AS-Unsafe dlopen plugin corrupt heap lock | AC-Unsafe lock corrupt mem fd | See Section 1.2.2.1 [POSIX Safety Concepts], page 2.

> The `gethostbyname` function returns information about the host named *name*. If the lookup fails, it returns a null pointer.

`struct hostent * gethostbyname2 (const char *name, int af)`   [Function]

> Preliminary: | MT-Unsafe race:hostbyname2 env locale | AS-Unsafe dlopen plugin corrupt heap lock | AC-Unsafe lock corrupt mem fd | See Section 1.2.2.1 [POSIX Safety Concepts], page 2.

> The `gethostbyname2` function is like `gethostbyname`, but allows the caller to specify the desired address family (e.g. `AF_INET` or `AF_INET6`) of the result.

`struct hostent * gethostbyaddr (const void *addr, socklen_t`   [Function]
`        length, int format)`

> Preliminary: | MT-Unsafe race:hostbyaddr env locale | AS-Unsafe dlopen plugin corrupt heap lock | AC-Unsafe lock corrupt mem fd | See Section 1.2.2.1 [POSIX Safety Concepts], page 2.

The `gethostbyaddr` function returns information about the host with Internet address *addr*. The parameter *addr* is not really a pointer to char - it can be a pointer to an IPv4 or an IPv6 address. The *length* argument is the size (in bytes) of the address at *addr*. *format* specifies the address format; for an IPv4 Internet address, specify a value of `AF_INET`; for an IPv6 Internet address, use `AF_INET6`.

If the lookup fails, `gethostbyaddr` returns a null pointer.

If the name lookup by `gethostbyname` or `gethostbyaddr` fails, you can find out the reason by looking at the value of the variable `h_errno`. (It would be cleaner design for these functions to set `errno`, but use of `h_errno` is compatible with other systems.)

Here are the error codes that you may find in `h_errno`:

`HOST_NOT_FOUND`
> No such host is known in the database.

`TRY_AGAIN`
> This condition happens when the name server could not be contacted. If you try again later, you may succeed then.

`NO_RECOVERY`
> A non-recoverable error occurred.

`NO_ADDRESS`
> The host database contains an entry for the name, but it doesn't have an associated Internet address.

The lookup functions above all have one thing in common: they are not reentrant and therefore unusable in multi-threaded applications. Therefore provides the GNU C Library a new set of functions which can be used in this context.

`int gethostbyname_r` (*const char *restrict* **name**, *struct hostent*   [Function]
     restrict **result_buf**, *char *restrict* **buf**, *size_t* **buflen**, *struct hostent*
     ***restrict* **result**, *int *restrict* **h_errnop**)
> Preliminary: | MT-Safe env locale | AS-Unsafe dlopen plugin corrupt heap lock | AC-Unsafe lock corrupt mem fd | See Section 1.2.2.1 [POSIX Safety Concepts], page 2.

> The `gethostbyname_r` function returns information about the host named *name*. The caller must pass a pointer to an object of type `struct hostent` in the *result_buf* parameter. In addition the function may need extra buffer space and the caller must pass a pointer and the size of the buffer in the *buf* and *buflen* parameters.

> A pointer to the buffer, in which the result is stored, is available in `*result` after the function call successfully returned. The buffer passed as the *buf* parameter can be freed only once the caller has finished with the result hostent struct, or has copied it including all the other memory that it points to. If an error occurs or if no entry is found, the pointer `*result` is a null pointer. Success is signalled by a zero return value. If the function failed the return value is an error number. In addition to the errors defined for `gethostbyname` it can also be `ERANGE`. In this case the call should be repeated with a larger buffer. Additional error information is not stored in the global variable `h_errno` but instead in the object pointed to by *h_errnop*.

Here's a small example:

```
struct hostent *
gethostname (char *host)
{
  struct hostent *hostbuf, *hp;
  size_t hstbuflen;
  char *tmphstbuf;
  int res;
  int herr;

  hostbuf = malloc (sizeof (struct hostent));
  hstbuflen = 1024;
  tmphstbuf = malloc (hstbuflen);

  while ((res = gethostbyname_r (host, hostbuf, tmphstbuf, hstbuflen,
                                 &hp, &herr)) == ERANGE)
    {
      /* Enlarge the buffer.  */
      hstbuflen *= 2;
      tmphstbuf = realloc (tmphstbuf, hstbuflen);
    }

  free (tmphstbuf);
  /*  Check for errors.  */
  if (res || hp == NULL)
    return NULL;
  return hp;
}
```

int gethostbyname2_r (const char *name, int af, struct hostent   [Function]
     *restrict result_buf, char *restrict buf, size_t buflen, struct hostent
     **restrict result, int *restrict h_errnop)

Preliminary: | MT-Safe env locale | AS-Unsafe dlopen plugin corrupt heap lock | AC-Unsafe lock corrupt mem fd | See Section 1.2.2.1 [POSIX Safety Concepts], page 2.

The gethostbyname2_r function is like gethostbyname_r, but allows the caller to specify the desired address family (e.g. AF_INET or AF_INET6) for the result.

int gethostbyaddr_r (const void *addr, socklen_t length, int   [Function]
     format, struct hostent *restrict result_buf, char *restrict buf, size_t
     buflen, struct hostent **restrict result, int *restrict h_errnop)

Preliminary: | MT-Safe env locale | AS-Unsafe dlopen plugin corrupt heap lock | AC-Unsafe lock corrupt mem fd | See Section 1.2.2.1 [POSIX Safety Concepts], page 2.

The gethostbyaddr_r function returns information about the host with Internet address addr. The parameter addr is not really a pointer to char - it can be a pointer to an IPv4 or an IPv6 address. The length argument is the size (in bytes) of the address at addr. format specifies the address format; for an IPv4 Internet address, specify a value of AF_INET; for an IPv6 Internet address, use AF_INET6.

Similar to the gethostbyname_r function, the caller must provide buffers for the result and memory used internally. In case of success the function returns zero. Otherwise the value is an error number where ERANGE has the special meaning that the caller-provided buffer is too small.

You can also scan the entire hosts database one entry at a time using `sethostent`, `gethostent` and `endhostent`. Be careful when using these functions because they are not reentrant.

`void sethostent (`*int stayopen*`)` [Function]

> Preliminary: | MT-Unsafe race:hostent env locale | AS-Unsafe dlopen plugin heap lock | AC-Unsafe corrupt lock fd mem | See Section 1.2.2.1 [POSIX Safety Concepts], page 2.
>
> This function opens the hosts database to begin scanning it. You can then call `gethostent` to read the entries.
>
> If the *stayopen* argument is nonzero, this sets a flag so that subsequent calls to `gethostbyname` or `gethostbyaddr` will not close the database (as they usually would). This makes for more efficiency if you call those functions several times, by avoiding reopening the database for each call.

`struct hostent * gethostent (`*void*`)` [Function]

> Preliminary: | MT-Unsafe race:hostent race:hostentbuf env locale | AS-Unsafe dlopen plugin heap lock | AC-Unsafe corrupt lock fd mem | See Section 1.2.2.1 [POSIX Safety Concepts], page 2.
>
> This function returns the next entry in the hosts database. It returns a null pointer if there are no more entries.

`void endhostent (`*void*`)` [Function]

> Preliminary: | MT-Unsafe race:hostent env locale | AS-Unsafe dlopen plugin heap lock | AC-Unsafe corrupt lock fd mem | See Section 1.2.2.1 [POSIX Safety Concepts], page 2.
>
> This function closes the hosts database.

16.6.3 Internet Ports

A socket address in the Internet namespace consists of a machine's Internet address plus a *port number* which distinguishes the sockets on a given machine (for a given protocol). Port numbers range from 0 to 65,535.

Port numbers less than `IPPORT_RESERVED` are reserved for standard servers, such as `finger` and `telnet`. There is a database that keeps track of these, and you can use the `getservbyname` function to map a service name onto a port number; see Section 16.6.4 [The Services Database], page 461.

If you write a server that is not one of the standard ones defined in the database, you must choose a port number for it. Use a number greater than `IPPORT_USERRESERVED`; such numbers are reserved for servers and won't ever be generated automatically by the system. Avoiding conflicts with servers being run by other users is up to you.

When you use a socket without specifying its address, the system generates a port number for it. This number is between `IPPORT_RESERVED` and `IPPORT_USERRESERVED`.

On the Internet, it is actually legitimate to have two different sockets with the same port number, as long as they never both try to communicate with the same socket address (host address plus port number). You shouldn't duplicate a port number except in special circumstances where a higher-level protocol requires it. Normally, the system won't let you do it; **bind** normally insists on distinct port numbers. To reuse a port number, you must set the socket option **SO_REUSEADDR**. See Section 16.12.2 [Socket-Level Options], page 486.

These macros are defined in the header file **netinet/in.h**.

int IPPORT_RESERVED   [Macro]

Port numbers less than **IPPORT_RESERVED** are reserved for superuser use.

int IPPORT_USERRESERVED   [Macro]

Port numbers greater than or equal to **IPPORT_USERRESERVED** are reserved for explicit use; they will never be allocated automatically.

16.6.4 The Services Database

The database that keeps track of "well-known" services is usually either the file **/etc/services** or an equivalent from a name server. You can use these utilities, declared in **netdb.h**, to access the services database.

struct servent   [Data Type]

This data type holds information about entries from the services database. It has the following members:

char *s_name

This is the "official" name of the service.

char **s_aliases

These are alternate names for the service, represented as an array of strings. A null pointer terminates the array.

int s_port

This is the port number for the service. Port numbers are given in network byte order; see Section 16.6.5 [Byte Order Conversion], page 462.

char *s_proto

This is the name of the protocol to use with this service. See Section 16.6.6 [Protocols Database], page 463.

To get information about a particular service, use the **getservbyname** or **getservbyport** functions. The information is returned in a statically-allocated structure; you must copy the information if you need to save it across calls.

struct servent * getservbyname (*const char *name, const char*   [Function]
        proto)

Preliminary: | MT-Unsafe race:servbyname locale | AS-Unsafe dlopen plugin heap lock | AC-Unsafe corrupt lock fd mem | See Section 1.2.2.1 [POSIX Safety Concepts], page 2.

The **getservbyname** function returns information about the service named *name* using protocol *proto*. If it can't find such a service, it returns a null pointer.

This function is useful for servers as well as for clients; servers use it to determine which port they should listen on (see Section 16.9.2 [Listening for Connections], page 470).

struct servent * getservbyport (*int port, const char *proto*)   [Function]

> Preliminary: | MT-Unsafe race:servbyport locale | AS-Unsafe dlopen plugin heap lock | AC-Unsafe corrupt lock fd mem | See Section 1.2.2.1 [POSIX Safety Concepts], page 2.

> The `getservbyport` function returns information about the service at port *port* using protocol *proto*. If it can't find such a service, it returns a null pointer.

You can also scan the services database using `setservent`, `getservent` and `endservent`. Be careful when using these functions because they are not reentrant.

void setservent (*int stayopen*)   [Function]

> Preliminary: | MT-Unsafe race:servent locale | AS-Unsafe dlopen plugin heap lock | AC-Unsafe corrupt lock fd mem | See Section 1.2.2.1 [POSIX Safety Concepts], page 2.

> This function opens the services database to begin scanning it.

> If the *stayopen* argument is nonzero, this sets a flag so that subsequent calls to `getservbyname` or `getservbyport` will not close the database (as they usually would). This makes for more efficiency if you call those functions several times, by avoiding reopening the database for each call.

struct servent * getservent (*void*)   [Function]

> Preliminary: | MT-Unsafe race:servent race:serventbuf locale | AS-Unsafe dlopen plugin heap lock | AC-Unsafe corrupt lock fd mem | See Section 1.2.2.1 [POSIX Safety Concepts], page 2.

> This function returns the next entry in the services database. If there are no more entries, it returns a null pointer.

void endservent (*void*)   [Function]

> Preliminary: | MT-Unsafe race:servent locale | AS-Unsafe dlopen plugin heap lock | AC-Unsafe corrupt lock fd mem | See Section 1.2.2.1 [POSIX Safety Concepts], page 2.

> This function closes the services database.

16.6.5 Byte Order Conversion

Different kinds of computers use different conventions for the ordering of bytes within a word. Some computers put the most significant byte within a word first (this is called "big-endian" order), and others put it last ("little-endian" order).

So that machines with different byte order conventions can communicate, the Internet protocols specify a canonical byte order convention for data transmitted over the network. This is known as *network byte order*.

When establishing an Internet socket connection, you must make sure that the data in the `sin_port` and `sin_addr` members of the `sockaddr_in` structure are represented in network byte order. If you are encoding integer data in the messages sent through the socket, you should convert this to network byte order too. If you don't do this, your program may fail when running on or talking to other kinds of machines.

If you use `getservbyname` and `gethostbyname` or `inet_addr` to get the port number and host address, the values are already in network byte order, and you can copy them directly into the `sockaddr_in` structure.

Otherwise, you have to convert the values explicitly. Use `htons` and `ntohs` to convert values for the `sin_port` member. Use `htonl` and `ntohl` to convert IPv4 addresses for the `sin_addr` member. (Remember, `struct in_addr` is equivalent to `uint32_t`.) These functions are declared in `netinet/in.h`.

uint16_t htons (*uint16_t hostshort*)   [Function]
 Preliminary: | MT-Safe | AS-Safe | AC-Safe | See Section 1.2.2.1 [POSIX Safety Concepts], page 2.

 This function converts the `uint16_t` integer *hostshort* from host byte order to network byte order.

uint16_t ntohs (*uint16_t netshort*)   [Function]
 Preliminary: | MT-Safe | AS-Safe | AC-Safe | See Section 1.2.2.1 [POSIX Safety Concepts], page 2.

 This function converts the `uint16_t` integer *netshort* from network byte order to host byte order.

uint32_t htonl (*uint32_t hostlong*)   [Function]
 Preliminary: | MT-Safe | AS-Safe | AC-Safe | See Section 1.2.2.1 [POSIX Safety Concepts], page 2.

 This function converts the `uint32_t` integer *hostlong* from host byte order to network byte order.

 This is used for IPv4 Internet addresses.

uint32_t ntohl (*uint32_t netlong*)   [Function]
 Preliminary: | MT-Safe | AS-Safe | AC-Safe | See Section 1.2.2.1 [POSIX Safety Concepts], page 2.

 This function converts the `uint32_t` integer *netlong* from network byte order to host byte order.

 This is used for IPv4 Internet addresses.

16.6.6 Protocols Database

The communications protocol used with a socket controls low-level details of how data are exchanged. For example, the protocol implements things like checksums to detect errors in transmissions, and routing instructions for messages. Normal user programs have little reason to mess with these details directly.

The default communications protocol for the Internet namespace depends on the communication style. For stream communication, the default is TCP ("transmission control protocol"). For datagram communication, the default is UDP ("user datagram protocol"). For reliable datagram communication, the default is RDP ("reliable datagram protocol"). You should nearly always use the default.

Internet protocols are generally specified by a name instead of a number. The network protocols that a host knows about are stored in a database. This is usually either derived from the file /etc/protocols, or it may be an equivalent provided by a name server. You look up the protocol number associated with a named protocol in the database using the getprotobyname function.

Here are detailed descriptions of the utilities for accessing the protocols database. These are declared in netdb.h.

struct protoent   [Data Type]

> This data type is used to represent entries in the network protocols database. It has the following members:

> char *p_name
> > This is the official name of the protocol.

> char **p_aliases
> > These are alternate names for the protocol, specified as an array of strings. The last element of the array is a null pointer.

> int p_proto
> > This is the protocol number (in host byte order); use this member as the *protocol* argument to socket.

You can use getprotobyname and getprotobynumber to search the protocols database for a specific protocol. The information is returned in a statically-allocated structure; you must copy the information if you need to save it across calls.

struct protoent * getprotobyname (*const char *name*)   [Function]
> Preliminary: | MT-Unsafe race:protobyname locale | AS-Unsafe dlopen plugin heap lock | AC-Unsafe corrupt lock fd mem | See Section 1.2.2.1 [POSIX Safety Concepts], page 2.

> The getprotobyname function returns information about the network protocol named *name*. If there is no such protocol, it returns a null pointer.

struct protoent * getprotobynumber (*int protocol*)   [Function]
> Preliminary: | MT-Unsafe race:protobynumber locale | AS-Unsafe dlopen plugin heap lock | AC-Unsafe corrupt lock fd mem | See Section 1.2.2.1 [POSIX Safety Concepts], page 2.

> The getprotobynumber function returns information about the network protocol with number *protocol*. If there is no such protocol, it returns a null pointer.

You can also scan the whole protocols database one protocol at a time by using setprotoent, getprotoent and endprotoent. Be careful when using these functions because they are not reentrant.

void setprotoent (*int stayopen*)   [Function]
> Preliminary: | MT-Unsafe race:protoent locale | AS-Unsafe dlopen plugin heap lock | AC-Unsafe corrupt lock fd mem | See Section 1.2.2.1 [POSIX Safety Concepts], page 2.

> This function opens the protocols database to begin scanning it.

> If the *stayopen* argument is nonzero, this sets a flag so that subsequent calls to getprotobyname or getprotobynumber will not close the database (as they usually

would). This makes for more efficiency if you call those functions several times, by avoiding reopening the database for each call.

struct protoent * getprotoent (*void*)   [Function]

> Preliminary: | MT-Unsafe race:protoent race:protoentbuf locale | AS-Unsafe dlopen plugin heap lock | AC-Unsafe corrupt lock fd mem | See Section 1.2.2.1 [POSIX Safety Concepts], page 2.

> This function returns the next entry in the protocols database. It returns a null pointer if there are no more entries.

void endprotoent (*void*)   [Function]

> Preliminary: | MT-Unsafe race:protoent locale | AS-Unsafe dlopen plugin heap lock | AC-Unsafe corrupt lock fd mem | See Section 1.2.2.1 [POSIX Safety Concepts], page 2.

> This function closes the protocols database.

16.6.7 Internet Socket Example

Here is an example showing how to create and name a socket in the Internet namespace. The newly created socket exists on the machine that the program is running on. Rather than finding and using the machine's Internet address, this example specifies INADDR_ANY as the host address; the system replaces that with the machine's actual address.

```
#include <stdio.h>
#include <stdlib.h>
#include <sys/socket.h>
#include <netinet/in.h>

int
make_socket (uint16_t port)
{
  int sock;
  struct sockaddr_in name;

  /* Create the socket. */
  sock = socket (PF_INET, SOCK_STREAM, 0);
  if (sock < 0)
    {
      perror ("socket");
      exit (EXIT_FAILURE);
    }

  /* Give the socket a name. */
  name.sin_family = AF_INET;
  name.sin_port = htons (port);
  name.sin_addr.s_addr = htonl (INADDR_ANY);
  if (bind (sock, (struct sockaddr *) &name, sizeof (name)) < 0)
    {
      perror ("bind");
      exit (EXIT_FAILURE);
    }

  return sock;
}
```

Here is another example, showing how you can fill in a `sockaddr_in` structure, given a host name string and a port number:

```
#include <stdio.h>
#include <stdlib.h>
#include <sys/socket.h>
#include <netinet/in.h>
#include <netdb.h>

void
init_sockaddr (struct sockaddr_in *name,
               const char *hostname,
               uint16_t port)
{
  struct hostent *hostinfo;

  name->sin_family = AF_INET;
  name->sin_port = htons (port);
  hostinfo = gethostbyname (hostname);
  if (hostinfo == NULL)
    {
      fprintf (stderr, "Unknown host %s.\n", hostname);
      exit (EXIT_FAILURE);
    }
  name->sin_addr = *(struct in_addr *) hostinfo->h_addr;
}
```

16.7 Other Namespaces

Certain other namespaces and associated protocol families are supported but not documented yet because they are not often used. `PF_NS` refers to the Xerox Network Software protocols. `PF_ISO` stands for Open Systems Interconnect. `PF_CCITT` refers to protocols from CCITT. `socket.h` defines these symbols and others naming protocols not actually implemented.

`PF_IMPLINK` is used for communicating between hosts and Internet Message Processors. For information on this and `PF_ROUTE`, an occasionally-used local area routing protocol, see the GNU Hurd Manual (to appear in the future).

16.8 Opening and Closing Sockets

This section describes the actual library functions for opening and closing sockets. The same functions work for all namespaces and connection styles.

16.8.1 Creating a Socket

The primitive for creating a socket is the `socket` function, declared in `sys/socket.h`.

`int socket (int namespace, int style, int protocol)` [Function]
Preliminary: | MT-Safe | AS-Safe | AC-Safe fd | See Section 1.2.2.1 [POSIX Safety Concepts], page 2.

This function creates a socket and specifies communication style *style*, which should be one of the socket styles listed in Section 16.2 [Communication Styles], page 443. The *namespace* argument specifies the namespace; it must be `PF_LOCAL` (see Section 16.5

466

[The Local Namespace], page 448) or `PF_INET` (see Section 16.6 [The Internet Namespace], page 450). *protocol* designates the specific protocol (see Section 16.1 [Socket Concepts], page 442); zero is usually right for *protocol*.

The return value from `socket` is the file descriptor for the new socket, or `-1` in case of error. The following `errno` error conditions are defined for this function:

`EPROTONOSUPPORT`
> The *protocol* or *style* is not supported by the *namespace* specified.

`EMFILE`   The process already has too many file descriptors open.

`ENFILE`   The system already has too many file descriptors open.

`EACCES`   The process does not have the privilege to create a socket of the specified *style* or *protocol*.

`ENOBUFS`   The system ran out of internal buffer space.

The file descriptor returned by the `socket` function supports both read and write operations. However, like pipes, sockets do not support file positioning operations.

For examples of how to call the `socket` function, see Section 16.5.3 [Example of Local-Namespace Sockets], page 449, or Section 16.6.7 [Internet Socket Example], page 465.

16.8.2 Closing a Socket

When you have finished using a socket, you can simply close its file descriptor with `close`; see Section 13.1 [Opening and Closing Files], page 333. If there is still data waiting to be transmitted over the connection, normally `close` tries to complete this transmission. You can control this behavior using the `SO_LINGER` socket option to specify a timeout period; see Section 16.12 [Socket Options], page 485.

You can also shut down only reception or transmission on a connection by calling `shutdown`, which is declared in `sys/socket.h`.

`int shutdown (int socket, int how)`   [Function]
> Preliminary: | MT-Safe | AS-Safe | AC-Safe | See Section 1.2.2.1 [POSIX Safety Concepts], page 2.
>
> The `shutdown` function shuts down the connection of socket *socket*. The argument *how* specifies what action to perform:
>
> 0   Stop receiving data for this socket. If further data arrives, reject it.
>
> 1   Stop trying to transmit data from this socket. Discard any data waiting to be sent. Stop looking for acknowledgement of data already sent; don't retransmit it if it is lost.
>
> 2   Stop both reception and transmission.
>
> The return value is 0 on success and `-1` on failure. The following `errno` error conditions are defined for this function:
>
> `EBADF`   *socket* is not a valid file descriptor.
>
> `ENOTSOCK`   *socket* is not a socket.
>
> `ENOTCONN`   *socket* is not connected.

16.8.3 Socket Pairs

A *socket pair* consists of a pair of connected (but unnamed) sockets. It is very similar to a pipe and is used in much the same way. Socket pairs are created with the `socketpair` function, declared in `sys/socket.h`. A socket pair is much like a pipe; the main difference is that the socket pair is bidirectional, whereas the pipe has one input-only end and one output-only end (see Chapter 15 [Pipes and FIFOs], page 437).

`int socketpair (`*int* `namespace`, *int* `style`, *int* `protocol`, *int*   [Function]
    `filedes`[2])

Preliminary: | MT-Safe | AS-Safe | AC-Safe fd | See Section 1.2.2.1 [POSIX Safety Concepts], page 2.

This function creates a socket pair, returning the file descriptors in `filedes`[0] and `filedes`[1]. The socket pair is a full-duplex communications channel, so that both reading and writing may be performed at either end.

The *namespace*, *style* and *protocol* arguments are interpreted as for the `socket` function. *style* should be one of the communication styles listed in Section 16.2 [Communication Styles], page 443. The *namespace* argument specifies the namespace, which must be `AF_LOCAL` (see Section 16.5 [The Local Namespace], page 448); *protocol* specifies the communications protocol, but zero is the only meaningful value.

If *style* specifies a connectionless communication style, then the two sockets you get are not *connected*, strictly speaking, but each of them knows the other as the default destination address, so they can send packets to each other.

The `socketpair` function returns 0 on success and `-1` on failure. The following `errno` error conditions are defined for this function:

EMFILE   The process has too many file descriptors open.

EAFNOSUPPORT
        The specified namespace is not supported.

EPROTONOSUPPORT
        The specified protocol is not supported.

EOPNOTSUPP
        The specified protocol does not support the creation of socket pairs.

16.9 Using Sockets with Connections

The most common communication styles involve making a connection to a particular other socket, and then exchanging data with that socket over and over. Making a connection is asymmetric; one side (the *client*) acts to request a connection, while the other side (the *server*) makes a socket and waits for the connection request.

- Section 16.9.1 [Making a Connection], page 469, describes what the client program must do to initiate a connection with a server.

- Section 16.9.2 [Listening for Connections], page 470, and Section 16.9.3 [Accepting Connections], page 470, describe what the server program must do to wait for and act upon connection requests from clients.

- Section 16.9.5 [Transferring Data], page 472, describes how data are transferred through the connected socket.

16.9.1 Making a Connection

In making a connection, the client makes a connection while the server waits for and accepts the connection. Here we discuss what the client program must do with the `connect` function, which is declared in `sys/socket.h`.

`int connect` (*int socket, struct sockaddr *addr, socklen_t length*)   [Function]
Preliminary: | MT-Safe | AS-Safe | AC-Safe | See Section 1.2.2.1 [POSIX Safety Concepts], page 2.

The `connect` function initiates a connection from the socket with file descriptor *socket* to the socket whose address is specified by the *addr* and *length* arguments. (This socket is typically on another machine, and it must be already set up as a server.) See Section 16.3 [Socket Addresses], page 444, for information about how these arguments are interpreted.

Normally, `connect` waits until the server responds to the request before it returns. You can set nonblocking mode on the socket *socket* to make `connect` return immediately without waiting for the response. See Section 13.14 [File Status Flags], page 375, for information about nonblocking mode.

The normal return value from `connect` is 0. If an error occurs, `connect` returns −1. The following `errno` error conditions are defined for this function:

EBADF   The socket *socket* is not a valid file descriptor.

ENOTSOCK   File descriptor *socket* is not a socket.

EADDRNOTAVAIL
            The specified address is not available on the remote machine.

EAFNOSUPPORT
            The namespace of the *addr* is not supported by this socket.

EISCONN   The socket *socket* is already connected.

ETIMEDOUT
            The attempt to establish the connection timed out.

ECONNREFUSED
            The server has actively refused to establish the connection.

ENETUNREACH
            The network of the given *addr* isn't reachable from this host.

EADDRINUSE
            The socket address of the given *addr* is already in use.

EINPROGRESS
            The socket *socket* is non-blocking and the connection could not be established immediately. You can determine when the connection is completely established with `select`; see Section 13.8 [Waiting for Input or Output], page 355. Another `connect` call on the same socket, before the connection is completely established, will fail with `EALREADY`.

EALREADY   The socket *socket* is non-blocking and already has a pending connection in progress (see `EINPROGRESS` above).

This function is defined as a cancellation point in multi-threaded programs, so one has to be prepared for this and make sure that allocated resources (like memory, file descriptors, semaphores or whatever) are freed even if the thread is canceled.

16.9.2 Listening for Connections

Now let us consider what the server process must do to accept connections on a socket. First it must use the `listen` function to enable connection requests on the socket, and then accept each incoming connection with a call to `accept` (see Section 16.9.3 [Accepting Connections], page 470). Once connection requests are enabled on a server socket, the `select` function reports when the socket has a connection ready to be accepted (see Section 13.8 [Waiting for Input or Output], page 355).

The `listen` function is not allowed for sockets using connectionless communication styles.

You can write a network server that does not even start running until a connection to it is requested. See Section 16.11.1 [`inetd` Servers], page 484.

In the Internet namespace, there are no special protection mechanisms for controlling access to a port; any process on any machine can make a connection to your server. If you want to restrict access to your server, make it examine the addresses associated with connection requests or implement some other handshaking or identification protocol.

In the local namespace, the ordinary file protection bits control who has access to connect to the socket.

`int listen (int socket, int n)` [Function]
Preliminary: | MT-Safe | AS-Safe | AC-Safe fd | See Section 1.2.2.1 [POSIX Safety Concepts], page 2.

The `listen` function enables the socket *socket* to accept connections, thus making it a server socket.

The argument *n* specifies the length of the queue for pending connections. When the queue fills, new clients attempting to connect fail with `ECONNREFUSED` until the server calls `accept` to accept a connection from the queue.

The `listen` function returns 0 on success and -1 on failure. The following `errno` error conditions are defined for this function:

EBADF   The argument *socket* is not a valid file descriptor.

ENOTSOCK   The argument *socket* is not a socket.

EOPNOTSUPP
          The socket *socket* does not support this operation.

16.9.3 Accepting Connections

When a server receives a connection request, it can complete the connection by accepting the request. Use the function `accept` to do this.

A socket that has been established as a server can accept connection requests from multiple clients. The server's original socket *does not become part of the connection*; instead, `accept` makes a new socket which participates in the connection. `accept` returns the descriptor for this socket. The server's original socket remains available for listening for further connection requests.

The number of pending connection requests on a server socket is finite. If connection requests arrive from clients faster than the server can act upon them, the queue can fill up and additional requests are refused with an `ECONNREFUSED` error. You can specify the maximum length of this queue as an argument to the `listen` function, although the system may also impose its own internal limit on the length of this queue.

int accept (*int socket, struct sockaddr *addr, socklen_t*   [Function]
    length_ptr)

Preliminary: | MT-Safe | AS-Safe | AC-Safe fd | See Section 1.2.2.1 [POSIX Safety Concepts], page 2.

This function is used to accept a connection request on the server socket *socket*.

The `accept` function waits if there are no connections pending, unless the socket *socket* has nonblocking mode set. (You can use `select` to wait for a pending connection, with a nonblocking socket.) See Section 13.14 [File Status Flags], page 375, for information about nonblocking mode.

The *addr* and *length-ptr* arguments are used to return information about the name of the client socket that initiated the connection. See Section 16.3 [Socket Addresses], page 444, for information about the format of the information.

Accepting a connection does not make *socket* part of the connection. Instead, it creates a new socket which becomes connected. The normal return value of `accept` is the file descriptor for the new socket.

After `accept`, the original socket *socket* remains open and unconnected, and continues listening until you close it. You can accept further connections with *socket* by calling `accept` again.

If an error occurs, `accept` returns −1. The following `errno` error conditions are defined for this function:

EBADF   The *socket* argument is not a valid file descriptor.

ENOTSOCK   The descriptor *socket* argument is not a socket.

EOPNOTSUPP
        The descriptor *socket* does not support this operation.

EWOULDBLOCK
        socket has nonblocking mode set, and there are no pending connections immediately available.

This function is defined as a cancellation point in multi-threaded programs, so one has to be prepared for this and make sure that allocated resources (like memory, file descriptors, semaphores or whatever) are freed even if the thread is canceled.

The `accept` function is not allowed for sockets using connectionless communication styles.

16.9.4 Who is Connected to Me?

int getpeername (*int* `socket`, *struct sockaddr* `*addr`, *socklen_t*   [Function]
      `*length-ptr`)

> Preliminary: | MT-Safe | AS-Safe | AC-Safe | See Section 1.2.2.1 [POSIX Safety Concepts], page 2.
>
> The `getpeername` function returns the address of the socket that *socket* is connected to; it stores the address in the memory space specified by *addr* and *length-ptr*. It stores the length of the address in `*length-ptr`.
>
> See Section 16.3 [Socket Addresses], page 444, for information about the format of the address. In some operating systems, `getpeername` works only for sockets in the Internet domain.
>
> The return value is 0 on success and -1 on error. The following `errno` error conditions are defined for this function:
>
> EBADF   The argument *socket* is not a valid file descriptor.
>
> ENOTSOCK   The descriptor *socket* is not a socket.
>
> ENOTCONN   The socket *socket* is not connected.
>
> ENOBUFS   There are not enough internal buffers available.

16.9.5 Transferring Data

Once a socket has been connected to a peer, you can use the ordinary **read** and **write** operations (see Section 13.2 [Input and Output Primitives], page 336) to transfer data. A socket is a two-way communications channel, so read and write operations can be performed at either end.

There are also some I/O modes that are specific to socket operations. In order to specify these modes, you must use the **recv** and **send** functions instead of the more generic **read** and **write** functions. The **recv** and **send** functions take an additional argument which you can use to specify various flags to control special I/O modes. For example, you can specify the `MSG_OOB` flag to read or write out-of-band data, the `MSG_PEEK` flag to peek at input, or the `MSG_DONTROUTE` flag to control inclusion of routing information on output.

16.9.5.1 Sending Data

The **send** function is declared in the header file **sys/socket.h**. If your *flags* argument is zero, you can just as well use **write** instead of **send**; see Section 13.2 [Input and Output Primitives], page 336. If the socket was connected but the connection has broken, you get a `SIGPIPE` signal for any use of **send** or **write** (see Section 24.2.7 [Miscellaneous Signals], page 694).

ssize_t send (*int* `socket`, *const void* `*buffer`, *size_t* `size`, *int*   [Function]
      `flags`)

> Preliminary: | MT-Safe | AS-Safe | AC-Safe | See Section 1.2.2.1 [POSIX Safety Concepts], page 2.
>
> The **send** function is like **write**, but with the additional flags *flags*. The possible values of *flags* are described in Section 16.9.5.3 [Socket Data Options], page 474.

This function returns the number of bytes transmitted, or -1 on failure. If the socket is nonblocking, then **send** (like **write**) can return after sending just part of the data. See Section 13.14 [File Status Flags], page 375, for information about nonblocking mode.

Note, however, that a successful return value merely indicates that the message has been sent without error, not necessarily that it has been received without error.

The following **errno** error conditions are defined for this function:

EBADF   The *socket* argument is not a valid file descriptor.

EINTR   The operation was interrupted by a signal before any data was sent. See Section 24.5 [Primitives Interrupted by Signals], page 711.

ENOTSOCK   The descriptor *socket* is not a socket.

EMSGSIZE   The socket type requires that the message be sent atomically, but the message is too large for this to be possible.

EWOULDBLOCK
           Nonblocking mode has been set on the socket, and the write operation would block. (Normally **send** blocks until the operation can be completed.)

ENOBUFS   There is not enough internal buffer space available.

ENOTCONN   You never connected this socket.

EPIPE   This socket was connected but the connection is now broken. In this case, **send** generates a **SIGPIPE** signal first; if that signal is ignored or blocked, or if its handler returns, then **send** fails with **EPIPE**.

This function is defined as a cancellation point in multi-threaded programs, so one has to be prepared for this and make sure that allocated resources (like memory, file descriptors, semaphores or whatever) are freed even if the thread is canceled.

16.9.5.2 Receiving Data

The **recv** function is declared in the header file **sys/socket.h**. If your *flags* argument is zero, you can just as well use **read** instead of **recv**; see Section 13.2 [Input and Output Primitives], page 336.

ssize_t recv (*int socket, void *buffer, size_t size, int flags*)   [Function]
    Preliminary: | MT-Safe | AS-Safe | AC-Safe | See Section 1.2.2.1 [POSIX Safety Concepts], page 2.

    The **recv** function is like **read**, but with the additional flags *flags*. The possible values of *flags* are described in Section 16.9.5.3 [Socket Data Options], page 474.

    If nonblocking mode is set for *socket*, and no data are available to be read, **recv** fails immediately rather than waiting. See Section 13.14 [File Status Flags], page 375, for information about nonblocking mode.

    This function returns the number of bytes received, or -1 on failure. The following **errno** error conditions are defined for this function:

    EBADF   The *socket* argument is not a valid file descriptor.

ENOTSOCK   The descriptor *socket* is not a socket.

EWOULDBLOCK

> Nonblocking mode has been set on the socket, and the read operation would block. (Normally, `recv` blocks until there is input available to be read.)

EINTR   The operation was interrupted by a signal before any data was read. See Section 24.5 [Primitives Interrupted by Signals], page 711.

ENOTCONN   You never connected this socket.

This function is defined as a cancellation point in multi-threaded programs, so one has to be prepared for this and make sure that allocated resources (like memory, file descriptors, semaphores or whatever) are freed even if the thread is canceled.

16.9.5.3 Socket Data Options

The *flags* argument to `send` and `recv` is a bit mask. You can bitwise-OR the values of the following macros together to obtain a value for this argument. All are defined in the header file `sys/socket.h`.

int MSG_OOB   [Macro]
> Send or receive out-of-band data. See Section 16.9.8 [Out-of-Band Data], page 477.

int MSG_PEEK   [Macro]
> Look at the data but don't remove it from the input queue. This is only meaningful with input functions such as `recv`, not with `send`.

int MSG_DONTROUTE   [Macro]
> Don't include routing information in the message. This is only meaningful with output operations, and is usually only of interest for diagnostic or routing programs. We don't try to explain it here.

16.9.6 Byte Stream Socket Example

Here is an example client program that makes a connection for a byte stream socket in the Internet namespace. It doesn't do anything particularly interesting once it has connected to the server; it just sends a text string to the server and exits.

This program uses `init_sockaddr` to set up the socket address; see Section 16.6.7 [Internet Socket Example], page 465.

```
#include <stdio.h>
#include <errno.h>
#include <stdlib.h>
#include <unistd.h>
#include <sys/types.h>
#include <sys/socket.h>
#include <netinet/in.h>
#include <netdb.h>

#define PORT            5555
#define MESSAGE         "Yow!!! Are we having fun yet?!?"
#define SERVERHOST      "www.gnu.org"
```

```
void
write_to_server (int filedes)
{
  int nbytes;

  nbytes = write (filedes, MESSAGE, strlen (MESSAGE) + 1);
  if (nbytes < 0)
    {
      perror ("write");
      exit (EXIT_FAILURE);
    }
}


int
main (void)
{
  extern void init_sockaddr (struct sockaddr_in *name,
                             const char *hostname,
                             uint16_t port);
  int sock;
  struct sockaddr_in servername;

  /* Create the socket. */
  sock = socket (PF_INET, SOCK_STREAM, 0);
  if (sock < 0)
    {
      perror ("socket (client)");
      exit (EXIT_FAILURE);
    }

  /* Connect to the server. */
  init_sockaddr (&servername, SERVERHOST, PORT);
  if (0 > connect (sock,
                   (struct sockaddr *) &servername,
                   sizeof (servername)))
    {
      perror ("connect (client)");
      exit (EXIT_FAILURE);
    }

  /* Send data to the server. */
  write_to_server (sock);
  close (sock);
  exit (EXIT_SUCCESS);
}
```

16.9.7 Byte Stream Connection Server Example

The server end is much more complicated. Since we want to allow multiple clients to be connected to the server at the same time, it would be incorrect to wait for input from a single client by simply calling **read** or **recv**. Instead, the right thing to do is to use **select** (see Section 13.8 [Waiting for Input or Output], page 355) to wait for input on all of the open sockets. This also allows the server to deal with additional connection requests.

This particular server doesn't do anything interesting once it has gotten a message from a client. It does close the socket for that client when it detects an end-of-file condition (resulting from the client shutting down its end of the connection).

This program uses `make_socket` to set up the socket address; see Section 16.6.7 [Internet Socket Example], page 465.

```c
#include <stdio.h>
#include <errno.h>
#include <stdlib.h>
#include <unistd.h>
#include <sys/types.h>
#include <sys/socket.h>
#include <netinet/in.h>
#include <netdb.h>

#define PORT    5555
#define MAXMSG  512

int
read_from_client (int filedes)
{
  char buffer[MAXMSG];
  int nbytes;

  nbytes = read (filedes, buffer, MAXMSG);
  if (nbytes < 0)
    {
      /* Read error. */
      perror ("read");
      exit (EXIT_FAILURE);
    }
  else if (nbytes == 0)
    /* End-of-file. */
    return -1;
  else
    {
      /* Data read. */
      fprintf (stderr, "Server: got message: `%s'\n", buffer);
      return 0;
    }
}

int
main (void)
{
  extern int make_socket (uint16_t port);
  int sock;
  fd_set active_fd_set, read_fd_set;
  int i;
  struct sockaddr_in clientname;
  size_t size;

  /* Create the socket and set it up to accept connections. */
  sock = make_socket (PORT);
  if (listen (sock, 1) < 0)
    {
      perror ("listen");
```

```
          exit (EXIT_FAILURE);
      }

  /* Initialize the set of active sockets. */
  FD_ZERO (&active_fd_set);
  FD_SET (sock, &active_fd_set);

  while (1)
    {
      /* Block until input arrives on one or more active sockets. */
      read_fd_set = active_fd_set;
      if (select (FD_SETSIZE, &read_fd_set, NULL, NULL, NULL) < 0)
        {
          perror ("select");
          exit (EXIT_FAILURE);
        }

      /* Service all the sockets with input pending. */
      for (i = 0; i < FD_SETSIZE; ++i)
        if (FD_ISSET (i, &read_fd_set))
          {
            if (i == sock)
              {
                /* Connection request on original socket. */
                int new;
                size = sizeof (clientname);
                new = accept (sock,
                              (struct sockaddr *) &clientname,
                              &size);
                if (new < 0)
                  {
                    perror ("accept");
                    exit (EXIT_FAILURE);
                  }
                fprintf (stderr,
                         "Server: connect from host %s, port %hd.\n",
                         inet_ntoa (clientname.sin_addr),
                         ntohs (clientname.sin_port));
                FD_SET (new, &active_fd_set);
              }
            else
              {
                /* Data arriving on an already-connected socket. */
                if (read_from_client (i) < 0)
                  {
                    close (i);
                    FD_CLR (i, &active_fd_set);
                  }
              }
          }
    }
}
```

16.9.8 Out-of-Band Data

Streams with connections permit *out-of-band* data that is delivered with higher priority than ordinary data. Typically the reason for sending out-of-band data is to send notice of an exceptional condition. To send out-of-band data use send, specifying the flag MSG_OOB (see Section 16.9.5.1 [Sending Data], page 472).

Out-of-band data are received with higher priority because the receiving process need not read it in sequence; to read the next available out-of-band data, use recv with the MSG_OOB flag (see Section 16.9.5.2 [Receiving Data], page 473). Ordinary read operations do not read out-of-band data; they read only ordinary data.

When a socket finds that out-of-band data are on their way, it sends a SIGURG signal to the owner process or process group of the socket. You can specify the owner using the F_SETOWN command to the fcntl function; see Section 13.18 [Interrupt-Driven Input], page 387. You must also establish a handler for this signal, as described in Chapter 24 [Signal Handling], page 685, in order to take appropriate action such as reading the out-of-band data.

Alternatively, you can test for pending out-of-band data, or wait until there is out-of-band data, using the select function; it can wait for an exceptional condition on the socket. See Section 13.8 [Waiting for Input or Output], page 355, for more information about select.

Notification of out-of-band data (whether with SIGURG or with select) indicates that out-of-band data are on the way; the data may not actually arrive until later. If you try to read the out-of-band data before it arrives, recv fails with an EWOULDBLOCK error.

Sending out-of-band data automatically places a "mark" in the stream of ordinary data, showing where in the sequence the out-of-band data "would have been". This is useful when the meaning of out-of-band data is "cancel everything sent so far". Here is how you can test, in the receiving process, whether any ordinary data was sent before the mark:

```
success = ioctl (socket, SIOCATMARK, &atmark);
```

The integer variable *atmark* is set to a nonzero value if the socket's read pointer has reached the "mark".

Here's a function to discard any ordinary data preceding the out-of-band mark:

```
int
discard_until_mark (int socket)
{
  while (1)
    {
      /* This is not an arbitrary limit; any size will do.  */
      char buffer[1024];
      int atmark, success;

      /* If we have reached the mark, return.  */
      success = ioctl (socket, SIOCATMARK, &atmark);
      if (success < 0)
        perror ("ioctl");
      if (result)
        return;

      /* Otherwise, read a bunch of ordinary data and discard it.
         This is guaranteed not to read past the mark
         if it starts before the mark.  */
      success = read (socket, buffer, sizeof buffer);
      if (success < 0)
        perror ("read");
    }
```

```
}
```

If you don't want to discard the ordinary data preceding the mark, you may need to read some of it anyway, to make room in internal system buffers for the out-of-band data. If you try to read out-of-band data and get an EWOULDBLOCK error, try reading some ordinary data (saving it so that you can use it when you want it) and see if that makes room. Here is an example:

```
struct buffer
{
  char *buf;
  int size;
  struct buffer *next;
};

/* Read the out-of-band data from SOCKET and return it
     as a `struct bufferfl, which records the address of the data
     and its size.

     It may be necessary to read some ordinary data
     in order to make room for the out-of-band data.
     If so, the ordinary data are saved as a chain of buffers
     found in the `nextfl field of the value.   */

struct buffer *
read_oob (int socket)
{
  struct buffer *tail = 0;
  struct buffer *list = 0;

  while (1)
    {
      /* This is an arbitrary limit.
           Does anyone know how to do this without a limit?   */
#define BUF_SZ 1024
      char *buf = (char *) xmalloc (BUF_SZ);
      int success;
      int atmark;

      /* Try again to read the out-of-band data.   */
      success = recv (socket, buf, BUF_SZ, MSG_OOB);
      if (success >= 0)
        {
          /* We got it, so return it.   */
          struct buffer *link
            = (struct buffer *) xmalloc (sizeof (struct buffer));
          link->buf = buf;
          link->size = success;
          link->next = list;
          return link;
        }

      /* If we fail, see if we are at the mark.   */
      success = ioctl (socket, SIOCATMARK, &atmark);
      if (success < 0)
        perror ("ioctl");
      if (atmark)
        {
          /* At the mark; skipping past more ordinary data cannot help.
```

```
              So just wait a while.  */
          sleep (1);
          continue;
        }

      /* Otherwise, read a bunch of ordinary data and save it.
         This is guaranteed not to read past the mark
         if it starts before the mark.  */
      success = read (socket, buf, BUF_SZ);
      if (success < 0)
        perror ("read");

      /* Save this data in the buffer list.  */
      {
        struct buffer *link
          = (struct buffer *) xmalloc (sizeof (struct buffer));
        link->buf = buf;
        link->size = success;

        /* Add the new link to the end of the list.  */
        if (tail)
          tail->next = link;
        else
          list = link;
        tail = link;
      }
    }
}
```

16.10 Datagram Socket Operations

This section describes how to use communication styles that don't use connections (styles SOCK_DGRAM and SOCK_RDM). Using these styles, you group data into packets and each packet is an independent communication. You specify the destination for each packet individually.

Datagram packets are like letters: you send each one independently with its own destination address, and they may arrive in the wrong order or not at all.

The listen and accept functions are not allowed for sockets using connectionless communication styles.

16.10.1 Sending Datagrams

The normal way of sending data on a datagram socket is by using the sendto function, declared in sys/socket.h.

You can call connect on a datagram socket, but this only specifies a default destination for further data transmission on the socket. When a socket has a default destination you can use send (see Section 16.9.5.1 [Sending Data], page 472) or even write (see Section 13.2 [Input and Output Primitives], page 336) to send a packet there. You can cancel the default destination by calling connect using an address format of AF_UNSPEC in the addr argument. See Section 16.9.1 [Making a Connection], page 469, for more information about the connect function.

ssize_t sendto (*int* `socket`, *const void* `*buffer`, *size_t* `size`, *int*   [Function]
      flags, *struct sockaddr* `*addr`, *socklen_t* `length`)

Preliminary: | MT-Safe | AS-Safe | AC-Safe | See Section 1.2.2.1 [POSIX Safety Concepts], page 2.

The `sendto` function transmits the data in the *buffer* through the socket *socket* to the destination address specified by the *addr* and *length* arguments. The *size* argument specifies the number of bytes to be transmitted.

The *flags* are interpreted the same way as for `send`; see Section 16.9.5.3 [Socket Data Options], page 474.

The return value and error conditions are also the same as for `send`, but you cannot rely on the system to detect errors and report them; the most common error is that the packet is lost or there is no-one at the specified address to receive it, and the operating system on your machine usually does not know this.

It is also possible for one call to `sendto` to report an error owing to a problem related to a previous call.

This function is defined as a cancellation point in multi-threaded programs, so one has to be prepared for this and make sure that allocated resources (like memory, file descriptors, semaphores or whatever) are freed even if the thread is canceled.

16.10.2 Receiving Datagrams

The `recvfrom` function reads a packet from a datagram socket and also tells you where it was sent from. This function is declared in `sys/socket.h`.

ssize_t recvfrom (*int* `socket`, *void* `*buffer`, *size_t* `size`, *int*   [Function]
      flags, *struct sockaddr* `*addr`, *socklen_t* `*length-ptr`)

Preliminary: | MT-Safe | AS-Safe | AC-Safe | See Section 1.2.2.1 [POSIX Safety Concepts], page 2.

The `recvfrom` function reads one packet from the socket *socket* into the buffer *buffer*. The *size* argument specifies the maximum number of bytes to be read.

If the packet is longer than *size* bytes, then you get the first *size* bytes of the packet and the rest of the packet is lost. There's no way to read the rest of the packet. Thus, when you use a packet protocol, you must always know how long a packet to expect.

The *addr* and *length-ptr* arguments are used to return the address where the packet came from. See Section 16.3 [Socket Addresses], page 444. For a socket in the local domain the address information won't be meaningful, since you can't read the address of such a socket (see Section 16.5 [The Local Namespace], page 448). You can specify a null pointer as the *addr* argument if you are not interested in this information.

The *flags* are interpreted the same way as for `recv` (see Section 16.9.5.3 [Socket Data Options], page 474). The return value and error conditions are also the same as for `recv`.

This function is defined as a cancellation point in multi-threaded programs, so one has to be prepared for this and make sure that allocated resources (like memory, file descriptors, semaphores or whatever) are freed even if the thread is canceled.

You can use plain **recv** (see Section 16.9.5.2 [Receiving Data], page 473) instead of
recvfrom if you don't need to find out who sent the packet (either because you know where
it should come from or because you treat all possible senders alike). Even **read** can be used
if you don't want to specify *flags* (see Section 13.2 [Input and Output Primitives], page 336).

16.10.3 Datagram Socket Example

Here is a set of example programs that send messages over a datagram stream in the local
namespace. Both the client and server programs use the **make_named_socket** function that
was presented in Section 16.5.3 [Example of Local-Namespace Sockets], page 449, to create
and name their sockets.

First, here is the server program. It sits in a loop waiting for messages to arrive, bouncing
each message back to the sender. Obviously this isn't a particularly useful program, but it
does show the general ideas involved.

```
#include <stdio.h>
#include <errno.h>
#include <stdlib.h>
#include <sys/socket.h>
#include <sys/un.h>

#define SERVER  "/tmp/serversocket"
#define MAXMSG  512

int
main (void)
{
  int sock;
  char message[MAXMSG];
  struct sockaddr_un name;
  size_t size;
  int nbytes;

  /* Remove the filename first, itfls ok if the call fails */
  unlink (SERVER);

  /* Make the socket, then loop endlessly. */
  sock = make_named_socket (SERVER);
  while (1)
    {
      /* Wait for a datagram. */
      size = sizeof (name);
      nbytes = recvfrom (sock, message, MAXMSG, 0,
                         (struct sockaddr *) & name, &size);
      if (nbytes < 0)
        {
          perror ("recfrom (server)");
          exit (EXIT_FAILURE);
        }

      /* Give a diagnostic message. */
      fprintf (stderr, "Server: got message: %s\n", message);

      /* Bounce the message back to the sender. */
      nbytes = sendto (sock, message, nbytes, 0,
                       (struct sockaddr *) & name, size);
```

```
      if (nbytes < 0)
        {
          perror ("sendto (server)");
          exit (EXIT_FAILURE);
        }
    }
}
```

16.10.4 Example of Reading Datagrams

Here is the client program corresponding to the server above.

It sends a datagram to the server and then waits for a reply. Notice that the socket for
the client (as well as for the server) in this example has to be given a name. This is so
that the server can direct a message back to the client. Since the socket has no associated
connection state, the only way the server can do this is by referencing the name of the
client.

```
#include <stdio.h>
#include <errno.h>
#include <unistd.h>
#include <stdlib.h>
#include <sys/socket.h>
#include <sys/un.h>

#define SERVER  "/tmp/serversocket"
#define CLIENT  "/tmp/mysocket"
#define MAXMSG  512
#define MESSAGE "Yow!!! Are we having fun yet?!?"

int
main (void)
{
  extern int make_named_socket (const char *name);
  int sock;
  char message[MAXMSG];
  struct sockaddr_un name;
  size_t size;
  int nbytes;

  /* Make the socket. */
  sock = make_named_socket (CLIENT);

  /* Initialize the server socket address. */
  name.sun_family = AF_LOCAL;
  strcpy (name.sun_path, SERVER);
  size = strlen (name.sun_path) + sizeof (name.sun_family);

  /* Send the datagram. */
  nbytes = sendto (sock, MESSAGE, strlen (MESSAGE) + 1, 0,
                   (struct sockaddr *) & name, size);
  if (nbytes < 0)
    {
      perror ("sendto (client)");
      exit (EXIT_FAILURE);
    }

  /* Wait for a reply. */
```

```
      nbytes = recvfrom (sock, message, MAXMSG, 0, NULL, 0);
      if (nbytes < 0)
        {
          perror ("recfrom (client)");
          exit (EXIT_FAILURE);
        }

      /* Print a diagnostic message. */
      fprintf (stderr, "Client: got message: %s\n", message);

      /* Clean up. */
      remove (CLIENT);
      close (sock);
    }
```

Keep in mind that datagram socket communications are unreliable. In this example, the client program waits indefinitely if the message never reaches the server or if the server's response never comes back. It's up to the user running the program to kill and restart it if desired. A more automatic solution could be to use **select** (see Section 13.8 [Waiting for Input or Output], page 355) to establish a timeout period for the reply, and in case of timeout either re-send the message or shut down the socket and exit.

16.11 The `inetd` Daemon

We've explained above how to write a server program that does its own listening. Such a server must already be running in order for anyone to connect to it.

Another way to provide a service on an Internet port is to let the daemon program **inetd** do the listening. **inetd** is a program that runs all the time and waits (using **select**) for messages on a specified set of ports. When it receives a message, it accepts the connection (if the socket style calls for connections) and then forks a child process to run the corresponding server program. You specify the ports and their programs in the file `/etc/inetd.conf`.

16.11.1 `inetd` Servers

Writing a server program to be run by **inetd** is very simple. Each time someone requests a connection to the appropriate port, a new server process starts. The connection already exists at this time; the socket is available as the standard input descriptor and as the standard output descriptor (descriptors 0 and 1) in the server process. Thus the server program can begin reading and writing data right away. Often the program needs only the ordinary I/O facilities; in fact, a general-purpose filter program that knows nothing about sockets can work as a byte stream server run by **inetd**.

You can also use **inetd** for servers that use connectionless communication styles. For these servers, **inetd** does not try to accept a connection since no connection is possible. It just starts the server program, which can read the incoming datagram packet from descriptor 0. The server program can handle one request and then exit, or you can choose to write it to keep reading more requests until no more arrive, and then exit. You must specify which of these two techniques the server uses when you configure **inetd**.

16.11.2 Configuring `inetd`

The file `/etc/inetd.conf` tells **inetd** which ports to listen to and what server programs to run for them. Normally each entry in the file is one line, but you can split it onto multiple lines provided all but the first line of the entry start with whitespace. Lines that start with '#' are comments.

Here are two standard entries in `/etc/inetd.conf`:

```
ftp stream tcp nowait root /libexec/ftpd ftpd
talk dgram udp wait root /libexec/talkd talkd
```

An entry has this format:

```
service style protocol wait username program arguments
```

The *service* field says which service this program provides. It should be the name of a service defined in `/etc/services`. `inetd` uses *service* to decide which port to listen on for this entry.

The fields *style* and *protocol* specify the communication style and the protocol to use for the listening socket. The style should be the name of a communication style, converted to lower case and with 'SOCK_' deleted—for example, 'stream' or 'dgram'. *protocol* should be one of the protocols listed in `/etc/protocols`. The typical protocol names are 'tcp' for byte stream connections and 'udp' for unreliable datagrams.

The *wait* field should be either 'wait' or 'nowait'. Use 'wait' if *style* is a connectionless style and the server, once started, handles multiple requests as they come in. Use 'nowait' if `inetd` should start a new process for each message or request that comes in. If *style* uses connections, then *wait* **must** be 'nowait'.

user is the user name that the server should run as. `inetd` runs as root, so it can set the user ID of its children arbitrarily. It's best to avoid using 'root' for *user* if you can; but some servers, such as Telnet and FTP, read a username and password themselves. These servers need to be root initially so they can log in as commanded by the data coming over the network.

program together with *arguments* specifies the command to run to start the server. *program* should be an absolute file name specifying the executable file to run. *arguments* consists of any number of whitespace-separated words, which become the command-line arguments of *program*. The first word in *arguments* is argument zero, which should by convention be the program name itself (sans directories).

If you edit `/etc/inetd.conf`, you can tell `inetd` to reread the file and obey its new contents by sending the `inetd` process the `SIGHUP` signal. You'll have to use `ps` to determine the process ID of the `inetd` process as it is not fixed.

16.12 Socket Options

This section describes how to read or set various options that modify the behavior of sockets and their underlying communications protocols.

When you are manipulating a socket option, you must specify which *level* the option pertains to. This describes whether the option applies to the socket interface, or to a lower-level communications protocol interface.

16.12.1 Socket Option Functions

Here are the functions for examining and modifying socket options. They are declared in `sys/socket.h`.

int getsockopt (*int socket, int* `level`*, int* `optname`*, void *optval,*   [Function]
        *socklen_t *optlen-ptr*)

> Preliminary: | MT-Safe | AS-Safe | AC-Safe | See Section 1.2.2.1 [POSIX Safety Concepts], page 2.
>
> The `getsockopt` function gets information about the value of option *optname* at level *level* for socket *socket*.
>
> The option value is stored in the buffer that *optval* points to. Before the call, you should supply in `*optlen-ptr` the size of this buffer; on return, it contains the number of bytes of information actually stored in the buffer.
>
> Most options interpret the *optval* buffer as a single `int` value.
>
> The actual return value of `getsockopt` is 0 on success and −1 on failure. The following `errno` error conditions are defined:
>
> EBADF   The *socket* argument is not a valid file descriptor.
>
> ENOTSOCK   The descriptor *socket* is not a socket.
>
> ENOPROTOOPT
> > The *optname* doesn't make sense for the given *level*.

int setsockopt (*int socket, int* `level`*, int* `optname`*, const void*   [Function]
        **optval, socklen_t optlen*)

> Preliminary: | MT-Safe | AS-Safe | AC-Safe | See Section 1.2.2.1 [POSIX Safety Concepts], page 2.
>
> This function is used to set the socket option *optname* at level *level* for socket *socket*. The value of the option is passed in the buffer *optval* of size *optlen*.
>
> The return value and error codes for `setsockopt` are the same as for `getsockopt`.

16.12.2 Socket-Level Options

int SOL_SOCKET   [Constant]

> Use this constant as the *level* argument to `getsockopt` or `setsockopt` to manipulate the socket-level options described in this section.

Here is a table of socket-level option names; all are defined in the header file **sys/socket.h**.

SO_DEBUG

> > This option toggles recording of debugging information in the underlying protocol modules. The value has type `int`; a nonzero value means "yes".

SO_REUSEADDR

> > This option controls whether `bind` (see Section 16.3.2 [Setting the Address of a Socket], page 446) should permit reuse of local addresses for this socket. If you enable this option, you can actually have two sockets with the same Internet port number; but the system won't allow you to use the two identically-named sockets in a way that would confuse the Internet. The reason for this option is that some higher-level Internet protocols, including FTP, require you to keep reusing the same port number.
> >
> > The value has type `int`; a nonzero value means "yes".

SO_KEEPALIVE

> This option controls whether the underlying protocol should periodically transmit messages on a connected socket. If the peer fails to respond to these messages, the connection is considered broken. The value has type `int`; a nonzero value means "yes".

SO_DONTROUTE

> This option controls whether outgoing messages bypass the normal message routing facilities. If set, messages are sent directly to the network interface instead. The value has type `int`; a nonzero value means "yes".

SO_LINGER

> This option specifies what should happen when the socket of a type that promises reliable delivery still has untransmitted messages when it is closed; see Section 16.8.2 [Closing a Socket], page 467. The value has type `struct linger`.

> **struct linger** [Data Type]
>
> > This structure type has the following members:
> >
> > > int l_onoff
> > >
> > > > This field is interpreted as a boolean. If nonzero, `close` blocks until the data are transmitted or the timeout period has expired.
> > >
> > > int l_linger
> > >
> > > > This specifies the timeout period, in seconds.

SO_BROADCAST

> This option controls whether datagrams may be broadcast from the socket. The value has type `int`; a nonzero value means "yes".

SO_OOBINLINE

> If this option is set, out-of-band data received on the socket is placed in the normal input queue. This permits it to be read using `read` or `recv` without specifying the `MSG_OOB` flag. See Section 16.9.8 [Out-of-Band Data], page 477. The value has type `int`; a nonzero value means "yes".

SO_SNDBUF

> This option gets or sets the size of the output buffer. The value is a `size_t`, which is the size in bytes.

SO_RCVBUF

> This option gets or sets the size of the input buffer. The value is a `size_t`, which is the size in bytes.

SO_STYLE
SO_TYPE   This option can be used with `getsockopt` only. It is used to get the socket's communication style. `SO_TYPE` is the historical name, and `SO_STYLE` is the preferred name in GNU. The value has type `int` and its value designates a communication style; see Section 16.2 [Communication Styles], page 443.

SO_ERROR

> This option can be used with `getsockopt` only. It is used to reset the error status of the socket. The value is an `int`, which represents the previous error status.

16.13 Networks Database

Many systems come with a database that records a list of networks known to the system developer. This is usually kept either in the file `/etc/networks` or in an equivalent from a name server. This data base is useful for routing programs such as `route`, but it is not useful for programs that simply communicate over the network. We provide functions to access this database, which are declared in `netdb.h`.

`struct netent`   [Data Type]

> This data type is used to represent information about entries in the networks database. It has the following members:
>
> `char *n_name`
>> This is the "official" name of the network.
>
> `char **n_aliases`
>> These are alternative names for the network, represented as a vector of strings. A null pointer terminates the array.
>
> `int n_addrtype`
>> This is the type of the network number; this is always equal to `AF_INET` for Internet networks.
>
> `unsigned long int n_net`
>> This is the network number. Network numbers are returned in host byte order; see Section 16.6.5 [Byte Order Conversion], page 462.

Use the `getnetbyname` or `getnetbyaddr` functions to search the networks database for information about a specific network. The information is returned in a statically-allocated structure; you must copy the information if you need to save it.

`struct netent * getnetbyname` (*const char *name*)   [Function]

> Preliminary: | MT-Unsafe race:netbyname env locale | AS-Unsafe dlopen plugin heap lock | AC-Unsafe corrupt lock fd mem | See Section 1.2.2.1 [POSIX Safety Concepts], page 2.
>
> The `getnetbyname` function returns information about the network named *name*. It returns a null pointer if there is no such network.

`struct netent * getnetbyaddr` (*uint32_t net*, *int type*)   [Function]

> Preliminary: | MT-Unsafe race:netbyaddr locale | AS-Unsafe dlopen plugin heap lock | AC-Unsafe corrupt lock fd mem | See Section 1.2.2.1 [POSIX Safety Concepts], page 2.
>
> The `getnetbyaddr` function returns information about the network of type *type* with number *net*. You should specify a value of `AF_INET` for the *type* argument for Internet networks.
>
> `getnetbyaddr` returns a null pointer if there is no such network.

You can also scan the networks database using `setnetent`, `getnetent` and `endnetent`. Be careful when using these functions because they are not reentrant.

void `setnetent` (*int stayopen*) [Function]
> Preliminary: | MT-Unsafe race:netent env locale | AS-Unsafe dlopen plugin heap lock | AC-Unsafe corrupt lock fd mem | See Section 1.2.2.1 [POSIX Safety Concepts], page 2.
>
> This function opens and rewinds the networks database.
>
> If the *stayopen* argument is nonzero, this sets a flag so that subsequent calls to `getnetbyname` or `getnetbyaddr` will not close the database (as they usually would). This makes for more efficiency if you call those functions several times, by avoiding reopening the database for each call.

struct netent * `getnetent` (*void*) [Function]
> Preliminary: | MT-Unsafe race:netent race:netentbuf env locale | AS-Unsafe dlopen plugin heap lock | AC-Unsafe corrupt lock fd mem | See Section 1.2.2.1 [POSIX Safety Concepts], page 2.
>
> This function returns the next entry in the networks database. It returns a null pointer if there are no more entries.

void `endnetent` (*void*) [Function]
> Preliminary: | MT-Unsafe race:netent env locale | AS-Unsafe dlopen plugin heap lock | AC-Unsafe corrupt lock fd mem | See Section 1.2.2.1 [POSIX Safety Concepts], page 2.
>
> This function closes the networks database.

17 Low-Level Terminal Interface

This chapter describes functions that are specific to terminal devices. You can use these functions to do things like turn off input echoing; set serial line characteristics such as line speed and flow control; and change which characters are used for end-of-file, command-line editing, sending signals, and similar control functions.

Most of the functions in this chapter operate on file descriptors. See Chapter 13 [Low-Level Input/Output], page 333, for more information about what a file descriptor is and how to open a file descriptor for a terminal device.

17.1 Identifying Terminals

The functions described in this chapter only work on files that correspond to terminal devices. You can find out whether a file descriptor is associated with a terminal by using the `isatty` function.

Prototypes for the functions in this section are declared in the header file `unistd.h`.

int isatty (*int filedes*)   [Function]
    Preliminary: | MT-Safe | AS-Safe | AC-Safe | See Section 1.2.2.1 [POSIX Safety Concepts], page 2.

    This function returns 1 if *filedes* is a file descriptor associated with an open terminal device, and 0 otherwise.

If a file descriptor is associated with a terminal, you can get its associated file name using the `ttyname` function. See also the `ctermid` function, described in Section 28.7.1 [Identifying the Controlling Terminal], page 801.

char * ttyname (*int filedes*)   [Function]
    Preliminary: | MT-Unsafe race:ttyname | AS-Unsafe heap lock | AC-Unsafe lock fd mem | See Section 1.2.2.1 [POSIX Safety Concepts], page 2.

    If the file descriptor *filedes* is associated with a terminal device, the `ttyname` function returns a pointer to a statically-allocated, null-terminated string containing the file name of the terminal file. The value is a null pointer if the file descriptor isn't associated with a terminal, or the file name cannot be determined.

int ttyname_r (*int filedes*, *char *buf*, *size_t len*)   [Function]
    Preliminary: | MT-Safe | AS-Unsafe heap | AC-Unsafe mem fd | See Section 1.2.2.1 [POSIX Safety Concepts], page 2.

    The `ttyname_r` function is similar to the `ttyname` function except that it places its result into the user-specified buffer starting at *buf* with length *len*.

    The normal return value from `ttyname_r` is 0. Otherwise an error number is returned to indicate the error. The following `errno` error conditions are defined for this function:

    EBADF   The *filedes* argument is not a valid file descriptor.

    ENOTTY   The *filedes* is not associated with a terminal.

    ERANGE   The buffer length *len* is too small to store the string to be returned.

17.2 I/O Queues

Many of the remaining functions in this section refer to the input and output queues of a terminal device. These queues implement a form of buffering *within the kernel* independent of the buffering implemented by I/O streams (see Chapter 12 [Input/Output on Streams], page 257).

The *terminal input queue* is also sometimes referred to as its *typeahead buffer*. It holds the characters that have been received from the terminal but not yet read by any process.

The size of the input queue is described by the `MAX_INPUT` and `_POSIX_MAX_INPUT` parameters; see Section 32.6 [Limits on File System Capacity], page 874. You are guaranteed a queue size of at least `MAX_INPUT`, but the queue might be larger, and might even dynamically change size. If input flow control is enabled by setting the `IXOFF` input mode bit (see Section 17.4.4 [Input Modes], page 495), the terminal driver transmits STOP and START characters to the terminal when necessary to prevent the queue from overflowing. Otherwise, input may be lost if it comes in too fast from the terminal. In canonical mode, all input stays in the queue until a newline character is received, so the terminal input queue can fill up when you type a very long line. See Section 17.3 [Two Styles of Input: Canonical or Not], page 491.

The *terminal output queue* is like the input queue, but for output; it contains characters that have been written by processes, but not yet transmitted to the terminal. If output flow control is enabled by setting the `IXON` input mode bit (see Section 17.4.4 [Input Modes], page 495), the terminal driver obeys START and STOP characters sent by the terminal to stop and restart transmission of output.

Clearing the terminal input queue means discarding any characters that have been received but not yet read. Similarly, clearing the terminal output queue means discarding any characters that have been written but not yet transmitted.

17.3 Two Styles of Input: Canonical or Not

POSIX systems support two basic modes of input: canonical and noncanonical.

In *canonical input processing* mode, terminal input is processed in lines terminated by newline (`'\n'`), EOF, or EOL characters. No input can be read until an entire line has been typed by the user, and the `read` function (see Section 13.2 [Input and Output Primitives], page 336) returns at most a single line of input, no matter how many bytes are requested.

In canonical input mode, the operating system provides input editing facilities: some characters are interpreted specially to perform editing operations within the current line of text, such as ERASE and KILL. See Section 17.4.9.1 [Characters for Input Editing], page 503.

The constants `_POSIX_MAX_CANON` and `MAX_CANON` parameterize the maximum number of bytes which may appear in a single line of canonical input. See Section 32.6 [Limits on File System Capacity], page 874. You are guaranteed a maximum line length of at least `MAX_CANON` bytes, but the maximum might be larger, and might even dynamically change size.

In *noncanonical input processing* mode, characters are not grouped into lines, and ERASE and KILL processing is not performed. The granularity with which bytes are read in noncanonical input mode is controlled by the MIN and TIME settings. See Section 17.4.10 [Noncanonical Input], page 507.

Most programs use canonical input mode, because this gives the user a way to edit input line by line. The usual reason to use noncanonical mode is when the program accepts single-character commands or provides its own editing facilities.

The choice of canonical or noncanonical input is controlled by the ICANON flag in the c_lflag member of struct termios. See Section 17.4.7 [Local Modes], page 499.

17.4 Terminal Modes

This section describes the various terminal attributes that control how input and output are done. The functions, data structures, and symbolic constants are all declared in the header file termios.h.

Don't confuse terminal attributes with file attributes. A device special file which is associated with a terminal has file attributes as described in Section 14.9 [File Attributes], page 412. These are unrelated to the attributes of the terminal device itself, which are discussed in this section.

17.4.1 Terminal Mode Data Types

The entire collection of attributes of a terminal is stored in a structure of type struct termios. This structure is used with the functions tcgetattr and tcsetattr to read and set the attributes.

struct termios   [Data Type]

A struct termios records all the I/O attributes of a terminal. The structure includes at least the following members:

tcflag_t c_iflag

A bit mask specifying flags for input modes; see Section 17.4.4 [Input Modes], page 495.

tcflag_t c_oflag

A bit mask specifying flags for output modes; see Section 17.4.5 [Output Modes], page 497.

tcflag_t c_cflag

A bit mask specifying flags for control modes; see Section 17.4.6 [Control Modes], page 498.

tcflag_t c_lflag

A bit mask specifying flags for local modes; see Section 17.4.7 [Local Modes], page 499.

cc_t c_cc[NCCS]

An array specifying which characters are associated with various control functions; see Section 17.4.9 [Special Characters], page 503.

The struct termios structure also contains members which encode input and output transmission speeds, but the representation is not specified. See Section 17.4.8 [Line Speed], page 502, for how to examine and store the speed values.

The following sections describe the details of the members of the **struct termios** structure.

tcflag_t   [Data Type]

> This is an unsigned integer type used to represent the various bit masks for terminal flags.

cc_t   [Data Type]

> This is an unsigned integer type used to represent characters associated with various terminal control functions.

int NCCS   [Macro]

> The value of this macro is the number of elements in the **c_cc** array.

17.4.2 Terminal Mode Functions

int tcgetattr (*int filedes, struct termios *termios-p*)   [Function]

> Preliminary: | MT-Safe | AS-Safe | AC-Safe | See Section 1.2.2.1 [POSIX Safety Concepts], page 2.
>
> This function is used to examine the attributes of the terminal device with file descriptor *filedes*. The attributes are returned in the structure that *termios-p* points to.
>
> If successful, **tcgetattr** returns 0. A return value of −1 indicates an error. The following **errno** error conditions are defined for this function:
>
> EBADF   The *filedes* argument is not a valid file descriptor.
>
> ENOTTY   The *filedes* is not associated with a terminal.

int tcsetattr (*int filedes, int when, const struct termios*   [Function]
       termios-p)

> Preliminary: | MT-Safe | AS-Safe | AC-Safe | See Section 1.2.2.1 [POSIX Safety Concepts], page 2.
>
> This function sets the attributes of the terminal device with file descriptor *filedes*. The new attributes are taken from the structure that *termios-p* points to.
>
> The *when* argument specifies how to deal with input and output already queued. It can be one of the following values:
>
> TCSANOW   Make the change immediately.
>
> TCSADRAIN
> > Make the change after waiting until all queued output has been written. You should usually use this option when changing parameters that affect output.
>
> TCSAFLUSH
> > This is like **TCSADRAIN**, but also discards any queued input.
>
> TCSASOFT   This is a flag bit that you can add to any of the above alternatives. Its meaning is to inhibit alteration of the state of the terminal hardware. It

is a BSD extension; it is only supported on BSD systems and GNU/Hurd systems.

Using `TCSASOFT` is exactly the same as setting the `CIGNORE` bit in the `c_cflag` member of the structure *termios-p* points to. See Section 17.4.6 [Control Modes], page 498, for a description of `CIGNORE`.

If this function is called from a background process on its controlling terminal, normally all processes in the process group are sent a `SIGTTOU` signal, in the same way as if the process were trying to write to the terminal. The exception is if the calling process itself is ignoring or blocking `SIGTTOU` signals, in which case the operation is performed and no signal is sent. See Chapter 28 [Job Control], page 786.

If successful, `tcsetattr` returns 0. A return value of −1 indicates an error. The following `errno` error conditions are defined for this function:

`EBADF`   The *filedes* argument is not a valid file descriptor.

`ENOTTY`   The *filedes* is not associated with a terminal.

`EINVAL`   Either the value of the `when` argument is not valid, or there is something wrong with the data in the *termios-p* argument.

Although `tcgetattr` and `tcsetattr` specify the terminal device with a file descriptor, the attributes are those of the terminal device itself and not of the file descriptor. This means that the effects of changing terminal attributes are persistent; if another process opens the terminal file later on, it will see the changed attributes even though it doesn't have anything to do with the open file descriptor you originally specified in changing the attributes.

Similarly, if a single process has multiple or duplicated file descriptors for the same terminal device, changing the terminal attributes affects input and output to all of these file descriptors. This means, for example, that you can't open one file descriptor or stream to read from a terminal in the normal line-buffered, echoed mode; and simultaneously have another file descriptor for the same terminal that you use to read from it in single-character, non-echoed mode. Instead, you have to explicitly switch the terminal back and forth between the two modes.

17.4.3 Setting Terminal Modes Properly

When you set terminal modes, you should call `tcgetattr` first to get the current modes of the particular terminal device, modify only those modes that you are really interested in, and store the result with `tcsetattr`.

It's a bad idea to simply initialize a `struct termios` structure to a chosen set of attributes and pass it directly to `tcsetattr`. Your program may be run years from now, on systems that support members not documented in this manual. The way to avoid setting these members to unreasonable values is to avoid changing them.

What's more, different terminal devices may require different mode settings in order to function properly. So you should avoid blindly copying attributes from one terminal device to another.

When a member contains a collection of independent flags, as the `c_iflag`, `c_oflag` and `c_cflag` members do, even setting the entire member is a bad idea, because particular operating systems have their own flags. Instead, you should start with the current value of the member and alter only the flags whose values matter in your program, leaving any other flags unchanged.

Here is an example of how to set one flag (`ISTRIP`) in the **struct termios** structure while properly preserving all the other data in the structure:

```
int
set_istrip (int desc, int value)
{
  struct termios settings;
  int result;

  result = tcgetattr (desc, &settings);
  if (result < 0)
    {
      perror ("error in tcgetattr");
      return 0;
    }
  settings.c_iflag &= ~ISTRIP;
  if (value)
    settings.c_iflag |= ISTRIP;
  result = tcsetattr (desc, TCSANOW, &settings);
  if (result < 0)
    {
      perror ("error in tcsetattr");
      return 0;
    }
  return 1;
}
```

17.4.4 Input Modes

This section describes the terminal attribute flags that control fairly low-level aspects of input processing: handling of parity errors, break signals, flow control, and RET and LFD characters.

All of these flags are bits in the `c_iflag` member of the **struct termios** structure. The member is an integer, and you change flags using the operators &, | and ^. Don't try to specify the entire value for `c_iflag`—instead, change only specific flags and leave the rest untouched (see Section 17.4.3 [Setting Terminal Modes Properly], page 494).

tcflag_t INPCK   [Macro]

If this bit is set, input parity checking is enabled. If it is not set, no checking at all is done for parity errors on input; the characters are simply passed through to the application.

Parity checking on input processing is independent of whether parity detection and generation on the underlying terminal hardware is enabled; see Section 17.4.6 [Control Modes], page 498. For example, you could clear the `INPCK` input mode flag and set the `PARENB` control mode flag to ignore parity errors on input, but still generate parity on output.

If this bit is set, what happens when a parity error is detected depends on whether the `IGNPAR` or `PARMRK` bits are set. If neither of these bits are set, a byte with a parity error is passed to the application as a `'\0'` character.

`tcflag_t IGNPAR`   [Macro]

If this bit is set, any byte with a framing or parity error is ignored. This is only useful if `INPCK` is also set.

`tcflag_t PARMRK`   [Macro]

If this bit is set, input bytes with parity or framing errors are marked when passed to the program. This bit is meaningful only when `INPCK` is set and `IGNPAR` is not set.

The way erroneous bytes are marked is with two preceding bytes, 377 and 0. Thus, the program actually reads three bytes for one erroneous byte received from the terminal.

If a valid byte has the value 0377, and `ISTRIP` (see below) is not set, the program might confuse it with the prefix that marks a parity error. So a valid byte 0377 is passed to the program as two bytes, 0377 0377, in this case.

`tcflag_t ISTRIP`   [Macro]

If this bit is set, valid input bytes are stripped to seven bits; otherwise, all eight bits are available for programs to read.

`tcflag_t IGNBRK`   [Macro]

If this bit is set, break conditions are ignored.

A *break condition* is defined in the context of asynchronous serial data transmission as a series of zero-value bits longer than a single byte.

`tcflag_t BRKINT`   [Macro]

If this bit is set and `IGNBRK` is not set, a break condition clears the terminal input and output queues and raises a `SIGINT` signal for the foreground process group associated with the terminal.

If neither `BRKINT` nor `IGNBRK` are set, a break condition is passed to the application as a single '\0' character if `PARMRK` is not set, or otherwise as a three-character sequence '\377', '\0', '\0'.

`tcflag_t IGNCR`   [Macro]

If this bit is set, carriage return characters ('\r') are discarded on input. Discarding carriage return may be useful on terminals that send both carriage return and linefeed when you type the RET key.

`tcflag_t ICRNL`   [Macro]

If this bit is set and `IGNCR` is not set, carriage return characters ('\r') received as input are passed to the application as newline characters ('\n').

`tcflag_t INLCR`   [Macro]

If this bit is set, newline characters ('\n') received as input are passed to the application as carriage return characters ('\r').

`tcflag_t IXOFF`   [Macro]

If this bit is set, start/stop control on input is enabled. In other words, the computer sends STOP and START characters as necessary to prevent input from coming in faster than programs are reading it. The idea is that the actual terminal hardware that is generating the input data responds to a STOP character by suspending transmission, and to a START character by resuming transmission. See Section 17.4.9.3 [Special Characters for Flow Control], page 506.

`tcflag_t IXON`   [Macro]

> If this bit is set, start/stop control on output is enabled. In other words, if the computer receives a STOP character, it suspends output until a START character is received. In this case, the STOP and START characters are never passed to the application program. If this bit is not set, then START and STOP can be read as ordinary characters. See Section 17.4.9.3 [Special Characters for Flow Control], page 506.

`tcflag_t IXANY`   [Macro]

> If this bit is set, any input character restarts output when output has been suspended with the STOP character. Otherwise, only the START character restarts output.
>
> This is a BSD extension; it exists only on BSD systems and GNU/Linux and GNU/Hurd systems.

`tcflag_t IMAXBEL`   [Macro]

> If this bit is set, then filling up the terminal input buffer sends a BEL character (code 007) to the terminal to ring the bell.
>
> This is a BSD extension.

17.4.5 Output Modes

This section describes the terminal flags and fields that control how output characters are translated and padded for display. All of these are contained in the `c_oflag` member of the `struct termios` structure.

The `c_oflag` member itself is an integer, and you change the flags and fields using the operators &, |, and ^. Don't try to specify the entire value for `c_oflag`—instead, change only specific flags and leave the rest untouched (see Section 17.4.3 [Setting Terminal Modes Properly], page 494).

`tcflag_t OPOST`   [Macro]

> If this bit is set, output data is processed in some unspecified way so that it is displayed appropriately on the terminal device. This typically includes mapping newline characters (`'\n'`) onto carriage return and linefeed pairs.
>
> If this bit isn't set, the characters are transmitted as-is.

The following three bits are effective only if `OPOST` is set.

`tcflag_t ONLCR`   [Macro]

> If this bit is set, convert the newline character on output into a pair of characters, carriage return followed by linefeed.

`tcflag_t OXTABS`   [Macro]

> If this bit is set, convert tab characters on output into the appropriate number of spaces to emulate a tab stop every eight columns. This bit exists only on BSD systems and GNU/Hurd systems; on GNU/Linux systems it is available as `XTABS`.

`tcflag_t ONOEOT`   [Macro]

> If this bit is set, discard *C-d* characters (code 004) on output. These characters cause many dial-up terminals to disconnect. This bit exists only on BSD systems and GNU/Hurd systems.

17.4.6 Control Modes

This section describes the terminal flags and fields that control parameters usually associated with asynchronous serial data transmission. These flags may not make sense for other kinds of terminal ports (such as a network connection pseudo-terminal). All of these are contained in the `c_cflag` member of the `struct termios` structure.

The `c_cflag` member itself is an integer, and you change the flags and fields using the operators &, |, and ^. Don't try to specify the entire value for `c_cflag`—instead, change only specific flags and leave the rest untouched (see Section 17.4.3 [Setting Terminal Modes Properly], page 494).

`tcflag_t CLOCAL`   [Macro]

> If this bit is set, it indicates that the terminal is connected "locally" and that the modem status lines (such as carrier detect) should be ignored.
>
> On many systems if this bit is not set and you call `open` without the `O_NONBLOCK` flag set, `open` blocks until a modem connection is established.
>
> If this bit is not set and a modem disconnect is detected, a `SIGHUP` signal is sent to the controlling process group for the terminal (if it has one). Normally, this causes the process to exit; see Chapter 24 [Signal Handling], page 685. Reading from the terminal after a disconnect causes an end-of-file condition, and writing causes an `EIO` error to be returned. The terminal device must be closed and reopened to clear the condition.

`tcflag_t HUPCL`   [Macro]

> If this bit is set, a modem disconnect is generated when all processes that have the terminal device open have either closed the file or exited.

`tcflag_t CREAD`   [Macro]

> If this bit is set, input can be read from the terminal. Otherwise, input is discarded when it arrives.

`tcflag_t CSTOPB`   [Macro]

> If this bit is set, two stop bits are used. Otherwise, only one stop bit is used.

`tcflag_t PARENB`   [Macro]

> If this bit is set, generation and detection of a parity bit are enabled. See Section 17.4.4 [Input Modes], page 495, for information on how input parity errors are handled.
>
> If this bit is not set, no parity bit is added to output characters, and input characters are not checked for correct parity.

`tcflag_t PARODD`   [Macro]

> This bit is only useful if `PARENB` is set. If `PARODD` is set, odd parity is used, otherwise even parity is used.

The control mode flags also includes a field for the number of bits per character. You can use the `CSIZE` macro as a mask to extract the value, like this: `settings.c_cflag & CSIZE`.

`tcflag_t CSIZE`   [Macro]

> This is a mask for the number of bits per character.

tcflag_t CS5   [Macro]
> This specifies five bits per byte.

tcflag_t CS6   [Macro]
> This specifies six bits per byte.

tcflag_t CS7   [Macro]
> This specifies seven bits per byte.

tcflag_t CS8   [Macro]
> This specifies eight bits per byte.

The following four bits are BSD extensions; these exist only on BSD systems and GNU/Hurd systems.

tcflag_t CCTS_OFLOW   [Macro]
> If this bit is set, enable flow control of output based on the CTS wire (RS232 protocol).

tcflag_t CRTS_IFLOW   [Macro]
> If this bit is set, enable flow control of input based on the RTS wire (RS232 protocol).

tcflag_t MDMBUF   [Macro]
> If this bit is set, enable carrier-based flow control of output.

tcflag_t CIGNORE   [Macro]
> If this bit is set, it says to ignore the control modes and line speed values entirely. This is only meaningful in a call to `tcsetattr`.
>
> The `c_cflag` member and the line speed values returned by `cfgetispeed` and `cfgetospeed` will be unaffected by the call. CIGNORE is useful if you want to set all the software modes in the other members, but leave the hardware details in `c_cflag` unchanged. (This is how the `TCSASOFT` flag to `tcsettattr` works.)
>
> This bit is never set in the structure filled in by `tcgetattr`.

17.4.7 Local Modes

This section describes the flags for the `c_lflag` member of the `struct termios` structure. These flags generally control higher-level aspects of input processing than the input modes flags described in Section 17.4.4 [Input Modes], page 495, such as echoing, signals, and the choice of canonical or noncanonical input.

The `c_lflag` member itself is an integer, and you change the flags and fields using the operators &, |, and ^. Don't try to specify the entire value for `c_lflag`—instead, change only specific flags and leave the rest untouched (see Section 17.4.3 [Setting Terminal Modes Properly], page 494).

tcflag_t ICANON   [Macro]
> This bit, if set, enables canonical input processing mode. Otherwise, input is processed in noncanonical mode. See Section 17.3 [Two Styles of Input: Canonical or Not], page 491.

tcflag_t ECHO   [Macro]
> If this bit is set, echoing of input characters back to the terminal is enabled.

`tcflag_t ECHOE`   [Macro]

> If this bit is set, echoing indicates erasure of input with the ERASE character by erasing the last character in the current line from the screen. Otherwise, the character erased is re-echoed to show what has happened (suitable for a printing terminal).
>
> This bit only controls the display behavior; the `ICANON` bit by itself controls actual recognition of the ERASE character and erasure of input, without which `ECHOE` is simply irrelevant.

`tcflag_t ECHOPRT`   [Macro]

> This bit, like `ECHOE`, enables display of the ERASE character in a way that is geared to a hardcopy terminal. When you type the ERASE character, a '\' character is printed followed by the first character erased. Typing the ERASE character again just prints the next character erased. Then, the next time you type a normal character, a '/' character is printed before the character echoes.
>
> This is a BSD extension, and exists only in BSD systems and GNU/Linux and GNU/Hurd systems.

`tcflag_t ECHOK`   [Macro]

> This bit enables special display of the KILL character by moving to a new line after echoing the KILL character normally. The behavior of `ECHOKE` (below) is nicer to look at.
>
> If this bit is not set, the KILL character echoes just as it would if it were not the KILL character. Then it is up to the user to remember that the KILL character has erased the preceding input; there is no indication of this on the screen.
>
> This bit only controls the display behavior; the `ICANON` bit by itself controls actual recognition of the KILL character and erasure of input, without which `ECHOK` is simply irrelevant.

`tcflag_t ECHOKE`   [Macro]

> This bit is similar to `ECHOK`. It enables special display of the KILL character by erasing on the screen the entire line that has been killed. This is a BSD extension, and exists only in BSD systems and GNU/Linux and GNU/Hurd systems.

`tcflag_t ECHONL`   [Macro]

> If this bit is set and the `ICANON` bit is also set, then the newline (`'\n'`) character is echoed even if the `ECHO` bit is not set.

`tcflag_t ECHOCTL`   [Macro]

> If this bit is set and the `ECHO` bit is also set, echo control characters with '^' followed by the corresponding text character. Thus, control-A echoes as '^A'. This is usually the preferred mode for interactive input, because echoing a control character back to the terminal could have some undesired effect on the terminal.
>
> This is a BSD extension, and exists only in BSD systems and GNU/Linux and GNU/Hurd systems.

`tcflag_t ISIG`   [Macro]

> This bit controls whether the INTR, QUIT, and SUSP characters are recognized. The functions associated with these characters are performed if and only if this bit is set.

Being in canonical or noncanonical input mode has no effect on the interpretation of these characters.

You should use caution when disabling recognition of these characters. Programs that cannot be interrupted interactively are very user-unfriendly. If you clear this bit, your program should provide some alternate interface that allows the user to interactively send the signals associated with these characters, or to escape from the program.

See Section 17.4.9.2 [Characters that Cause Signals], page 505.

`tcflag_t IEXTEN`   [Macro]

POSIX.1 gives `IEXTEN` implementation-defined meaning, so you cannot rely on this interpretation on all systems.

On BSD systems and GNU/Linux and GNU/Hurd systems, it enables the LNEXT and DISCARD characters. See Section 17.4.9.4 [Other Special Characters], page 507.

`tcflag_t NOFLSH`   [Macro]

Normally, the INTR, QUIT, and SUSP characters cause input and output queues for the terminal to be cleared. If this bit is set, the queues are not cleared.

`tcflag_t TOSTOP`   [Macro]

If this bit is set and the system supports job control, then `SIGTTOU` signals are generated by background processes that attempt to write to the terminal. See Section 28.4 [Access to the Controlling Terminal], page 787.

The following bits are BSD extensions; they exist only on BSD systems and GNU/Hurd systems.

`tcflag_t ALTWERASE`   [Macro]

This bit determines how far the WERASE character should erase. The WERASE character erases back to the beginning of a word; the question is, where do words begin?

If this bit is clear, then the beginning of a word is a nonwhitespace character following a whitespace character. If the bit is set, then the beginning of a word is an alphanumeric character or underscore following a character which is none of those.

See Section 17.4.9.1 [Characters for Input Editing], page 503, for more information about the WERASE character.

`tcflag_t FLUSHO`   [Macro]

This is the bit that toggles when the user types the DISCARD character. While this bit is set, all output is discarded. See Section 17.4.9.4 [Other Special Characters], page 507.

`tcflag_t NOKERNINFO`   [Macro]

Setting this bit disables handling of the STATUS character. See Section 17.4.9.4 [Other Special Characters], page 507.

`tcflag_t PENDIN`   [Macro]

If this bit is set, it indicates that there is a line of input that needs to be reprinted. Typing the REPRINT character sets this bit; the bit remains set until reprinting is finished. See Section 17.4.9.1 [Characters for Input Editing], page 503.

17.4.8 Line Speed

The terminal line speed tells the computer how fast to read and write data on the terminal.

If the terminal is connected to a real serial line, the terminal speed you specify actually controls the line—if it doesn't match the terminal's own idea of the speed, communication does not work. Real serial ports accept only certain standard speeds. Also, particular hardware may not support even all the standard speeds. Specifying a speed of zero hangs up a dialup connection and turns off modem control signals.

If the terminal is not a real serial line (for example, if it is a network connection), then the line speed won't really affect data transmission speed, but some programs will use it to determine the amount of padding needed. It's best to specify a line speed value that matches the actual speed of the actual terminal, but you can safely experiment with different values to vary the amount of padding.

There are actually two line speeds for each terminal, one for input and one for output. You can set them independently, but most often terminals use the same speed for both directions.

The speed values are stored in the **struct termios** structure, but don't try to access them in the **struct termios** structure directly. Instead, you should use the following functions to read and store them:

speed_t cfgetospeed (*const struct termios *termios-p*)   [Function]
> Preliminary: | MT-Safe | AS-Safe | AC-Safe | See Section 1.2.2.1 [POSIX Safety Concepts], page 2.
>
> This function returns the output line speed stored in the structure **termios-p*.

speed_t cfgetispeed (*const struct termios *termios-p*)   [Function]
> Preliminary: | MT-Safe | AS-Safe | AC-Safe | See Section 1.2.2.1 [POSIX Safety Concepts], page 2.
>
> This function returns the input line speed stored in the structure **termios-p*.

int cfsetospeed (*struct termios *termios-p, speed_t speed*)   [Function]
> Preliminary: | MT-Safe | AS-Safe | AC-Safe | See Section 1.2.2.1 [POSIX Safety Concepts], page 2.
>
> This function stores *speed* in **termios-p* as the output speed. The normal return value is 0; a value of −1 indicates an error. If *speed* is not a speed, **cfsetospeed** returns −1.

int cfsetispeed (*struct termios *termios-p, speed_t speed*)   [Function]
> Preliminary: | MT-Safe | AS-Safe | AC-Safe | See Section 1.2.2.1 [POSIX Safety Concepts], page 2.
>
> This function stores *speed* in **termios-p* as the input speed. The normal return value is 0; a value of −1 indicates an error. If *speed* is not a speed, **cfsetospeed** returns −1.

int cfsetspeed (*struct termios *termios-p, speed_t speed*)   [Function]
> Preliminary: | MT-Safe | AS-Safe | AC-Safe | See Section 1.2.2.1 [POSIX Safety Concepts], page 2.

This function stores *speed* in *termios-p* as both the input and output speeds. The normal return value is 0; a value of −1 indicates an error. If *speed* is not a speed, cfsetspeed returns −1. This function is an extension in 4.4 BSD.

speed_t   [Data Type]

The speed_t type is an unsigned integer data type used to represent line speeds.

The functions cfsetospeed and cfsetispeed report errors only for speed values that the system simply cannot handle. If you specify a speed value that is basically acceptable, then those functions will succeed. But they do not check that a particular hardware device can actually support the specified speeds—in fact, they don't know which device you plan to set the speed for. If you use tcsetattr to set the speed of a particular device to a value that it cannot handle, tcsetattr returns −1.

Portability note: In the GNU C Library, the functions above accept speeds measured in bits per second as input, and return speed values measured in bits per second. Other libraries require speeds to be indicated by special codes. For POSIX.1 portability, you must use one of the following symbols to represent the speed; their precise numeric values are system-dependent, but each name has a fixed meaning: B110 stands for 110 bps, B300 for 300 bps, and so on. There is no portable way to represent any speed but these, but these are the only speeds that typical serial lines can support.

```
B0    B50    B75    B110   B134   B150   B200
B300  B600   B1200  B1800  B2400  B4800
B9600 B19200 B38400 B57600 B115200
B230400 B460800
```

BSD defines two additional speed symbols as aliases: EXTA is an alias for B19200 and EXTB is an alias for B38400. These aliases are obsolete.

17.4.9 Special Characters

In canonical input, the terminal driver recognizes a number of special characters which perform various control functions. These include the ERASE character (usually DEL) for editing input, and other editing characters. The INTR character (normally *C-c*) for sending a SIGINT signal, and other signal-raising characters, may be available in either canonical or noncanonical input mode. All these characters are described in this section.

The particular characters used are specified in the c_cc member of the struct termios structure. This member is an array; each element specifies the character for a particular role. Each element has a symbolic constant that stands for the index of that element—for example, VINTR is the index of the element that specifies the INTR character, so storing '=' in *termios*.c_cc[VINTR] specifies '=' as the INTR character.

On some systems, you can disable a particular special character function by specifying the value _POSIX_VDISABLE for that role. This value is unequal to any possible character code. See Section 32.7 [Optional Features in File Support], page 875, for more information about how to tell whether the operating system you are using supports _POSIX_VDISABLE.

17.4.9.1 Characters for Input Editing

These special characters are active only in canonical input mode. See Section 17.3 [Two Styles of Input: Canonical or Not], page 491.

`int VEOF`   [Macro]

> This is the subscript for the EOF character in the special control character array. `termios.c_cc[VEOF]` holds the character itself.

> The EOF character is recognized only in canonical input mode. It acts as a line terminator in the same way as a newline character, but if the EOF character is typed at the beginning of a line it causes **read** to return a byte count of zero, indicating end-of-file. The EOF character itself is discarded.

> Usually, the EOF character is *C-d*.

`int VEOL`   [Macro]

> This is the subscript for the EOL character in the special control character array. `termios.c_cc[VEOL]` holds the character itself.

> The EOL character is recognized only in canonical input mode. It acts as a line terminator, just like a newline character. The EOL character is not discarded; it is read as the last character in the input line.

> You don't need to use the EOL character to make **RET** end a line. Just set the ICRNL flag. In fact, this is the default state of affairs.

`int VEOL2`   [Macro]

> This is the subscript for the EOL2 character in the special control character array. `termios.c_cc[VEOL2]` holds the character itself.

> The EOL2 character works just like the EOL character (see above), but it can be a different character. Thus, you can specify two characters to terminate an input line, by setting EOL to one of them and EOL2 to the other.

> The EOL2 character is a BSD extension; it exists only on BSD systems and GNU/Linux and GNU/Hurd systems.

`int VERASE`   [Macro]

> This is the subscript for the ERASE character in the special control character array. `termios.c_cc[VERASE]` holds the character itself.

> The ERASE character is recognized only in canonical input mode. When the user types the erase character, the previous character typed is discarded. (If the terminal generates multibyte character sequences, this may cause more than one byte of input to be discarded.) This cannot be used to erase past the beginning of the current line of text. The ERASE character itself is discarded.

> Usually, the ERASE character is **DEL**.

`int VWERASE`   [Macro]

> This is the subscript for the WERASE character in the special control character array. `termios.c_cc[VWERASE]` holds the character itself.

> The WERASE character is recognized only in canonical mode. It erases an entire word of prior input, and any whitespace after it; whitespace characters before the word are not erased.

> The definition of a "word" depends on the setting of the **ALTWERASE** mode; see Section 17.4.7 [Local Modes], page 499.

If the **ALTWERASE** mode is not set, a word is defined as a sequence of any characters except space or tab.

If the **ALTWERASE** mode is set, a word is defined as a sequence of characters containing only letters, numbers, and underscores, optionally followed by one character that is not a letter, number, or underscore.

The WERASE character is usually *C-w*.

This is a BSD extension.

int VKILL   [Macro]

This is the subscript for the KILL character in the special control character array. *termios.c_cc[VKILL]* holds the character itself.

The KILL character is recognized only in canonical input mode. When the user types the kill character, the entire contents of the current line of input are discarded. The kill character itself is discarded too.

The KILL character is usually *C-u*.

int VREPRINT   [Macro]

This is the subscript for the REPRINT character in the special control character array. *termios.c_cc[VREPRINT]* holds the character itself.

The REPRINT character is recognized only in canonical mode. It reprints the current input line. If some asynchronous output has come while you are typing, this lets you see the line you are typing clearly again.

The REPRINT character is usually *C-r*.

This is a BSD extension.

17.4.9.2 Characters that Cause Signals

These special characters may be active in either canonical or noncanonical input mode, but only when the **ISIG** flag is set (see Section 17.4.7 [Local Modes], page 499).

int VINTR   [Macro]

This is the subscript for the INTR character in the special control character array. *termios.c_cc[VINTR]* holds the character itself.

The INTR (interrupt) character raises a **SIGINT** signal for all processes in the foreground job associated with the terminal. The INTR character itself is then discarded. See Chapter 24 [Signal Handling], page 685, for more information about signals.

Typically, the INTR character is *C-c*.

int VQUIT   [Macro]

This is the subscript for the QUIT character in the special control character array. *termios.c_cc[VQUIT]* holds the character itself.

The QUIT character raises a **SIGQUIT** signal for all processes in the foreground job associated with the terminal. The QUIT character itself is then discarded. See Chapter 24 [Signal Handling], page 685, for more information about signals.

Typically, the QUIT character is *C-*.

`int VSUSP` [Macro]

> This is the subscript for the SUSP character in the special control character array. `termios.c_cc[VSUSP]` holds the character itself.
>
> The SUSP (suspend) character is recognized only if the implementation supports job control (see Chapter 28 [Job Control], page 786). It causes a `SIGTSTP` signal to be sent to all processes in the foreground job associated with the terminal. The SUSP character itself is then discarded. See Chapter 24 [Signal Handling], page 685, for more information about signals.
>
> Typically, the SUSP character is `C-z`.

Few applications disable the normal interpretation of the SUSP character. If your program does this, it should provide some other mechanism for the user to stop the job. When the user invokes this mechanism, the program should send a `SIGTSTP` signal to the process group of the process, not just to the process itself. See Section 24.6.2 [Signaling Another Process], page 713.

`int VDSUSP` [Macro]

> This is the subscript for the DSUSP character in the special control character array. `termios.c_cc[VDSUSP]` holds the character itself.
>
> The DSUSP (suspend) character is recognized only if the implementation supports job control (see Chapter 28 [Job Control], page 786). It sends a `SIGTSTP` signal, like the SUSP character, but not right away—only when the program tries to read it as input. Not all systems with job control support DSUSP; only BSD-compatible systems do (including GNU/Hurd systems).
>
> See Chapter 24 [Signal Handling], page 685, for more information about signals.
>
> Typically, the DSUSP character is `C-y`.

17.4.9.3 Special Characters for Flow Control

These special characters may be active in either canonical or noncanonical input mode, but their use is controlled by the flags `IXON` and `IXOFF` (see Section 17.4.4 [Input Modes], page 495).

`int VSTART` [Macro]

> This is the subscript for the START character in the special control character array. `termios.c_cc[VSTART]` holds the character itself.
>
> The START character is used to support the `IXON` and `IXOFF` input modes. If `IXON` is set, receiving a START character resumes suspended output; the START character itself is discarded. If `IXANY` is set, receiving any character at all resumes suspended output; the resuming character is not discarded unless it is the START character. If `IXOFF` is set, the system may also transmit START characters to the terminal.
>
> The usual value for the START character is `C-q`. You may not be able to change this value—the hardware may insist on using `C-q` regardless of what you specify.

`int VSTOP` [Macro]

> This is the subscript for the STOP character in the special control character array. `termios.c_cc[VSTOP]` holds the character itself.

The STOP character is used to support the `IXON` and `IXOFF` input modes. If `IXON` is set, receiving a STOP character causes output to be suspended; the STOP character itself is discarded. If `IXOFF` is set, the system may also transmit STOP characters to the terminal, to prevent the input queue from overflowing.

The usual value for the STOP character is *C-s*. You may not be able to change this value—the hardware may insist on using *C-s* regardless of what you specify.

17.4.9.4 Other Special Characters

int VLNEXT [Macro]

This is the subscript for the LNEXT character in the special control character array. *termios.c_cc*[VLNEXT] holds the character itself.

The LNEXT character is recognized only when `IEXTEN` is set, but in both canonical and noncanonical mode. It disables any special significance of the next character the user types. Even if the character would normally perform some editing function or generate a signal, it is read as a plain character. This is the analogue of the *C-q* command in Emacs. "LNEXT" stands for "literal next."

The LNEXT character is usually *C-v*.

This character is available on BSD systems and GNU/Linux and GNU/Hurd systems.

int VDISCARD [Macro]

This is the subscript for the DISCARD character in the special control character array. *termios.c_cc*[VDISCARD] holds the character itself.

The DISCARD character is recognized only when `IEXTEN` is set, but in both canonical and noncanonical mode. Its effect is to toggle the discard-output flag. When this flag is set, all program output is discarded. Setting the flag also discards all output currently in the output buffer. Typing any other character resets the flag.

This character is available on BSD systems and GNU/Linux and GNU/Hurd systems.

int VSTATUS [Macro]

This is the subscript for the STATUS character in the special control character array. *termios.c_cc*[VSTATUS] holds the character itself.

The STATUS character's effect is to print out a status message about how the current process is running.

The STATUS character is recognized only in canonical mode, and only if `NOKERNINFO` is not set.

This character is available only on BSD systems and GNU/Hurd systems.

17.4.10 Noncanonical Input

In noncanonical input mode, the special editing characters such as ERASE and KILL are ignored. The system facilities for the user to edit input are disabled in noncanonical mode, so that all input characters (unless they are special for signal or flow-control purposes) are passed to the application program exactly as typed. It is up to the application program to give the user ways to edit the input, if appropriate.

Noncanonical mode offers special parameters called MIN and TIME for controlling whether and how long to wait for input to be available. You can even use them to avoid ever waiting—to return immediately with whatever input is available, or with no input.

The MIN and TIME are stored in elements of the `c_cc` array, which is a member of the **struct termios** structure. Each element of this array has a particular role, and each element has a symbolic constant that stands for the index of that element. VMIN and VTIME are the names for the indices in the array of the MIN and TIME slots.

`int VMIN` [Macro]

    This is the subscript for the MIN slot in the `c_cc` array. Thus, *termios*.`c_cc[VMIN]` is the value itself.

    The MIN slot is only meaningful in noncanonical input mode; it specifies the minimum number of bytes that must be available in the input queue in order for **read** to return.

`int VTIME` [Macro]

    This is the subscript for the TIME slot in the `c_cc` array. Thus, *termios*.`c_cc[VTIME]` is the value itself.

    The TIME slot is only meaningful in noncanonical input mode; it specifies how long to wait for input before returning, in units of 0.1 seconds.

The MIN and TIME values interact to determine the criterion for when **read** should return; their precise meanings depend on which of them are nonzero. There are four possible cases:

- Both TIME and MIN are nonzero.

  In this case, TIME specifies how long to wait after each input character to see if more input arrives. After the first character received, **read** keeps waiting until either MIN bytes have arrived in all, or TIME elapses with no further input.

  read always blocks until the first character arrives, even if TIME elapses first. **read** can return more than MIN characters if more than MIN happen to be in the queue.

- Both MIN and TIME are zero.

  In this case, **read** always returns immediately with as many characters as are available in the queue, up to the number requested. If no input is immediately available, **read** returns a value of zero.

- MIN is zero but TIME has a nonzero value.

  In this case, **read** waits for time TIME for input to become available; the availability of a single byte is enough to satisfy the read request and cause **read** to return. When it returns, it returns as many characters as are available, up to the number requested. If no input is available before the timer expires, **read** returns a value of zero.

- TIME is zero but MIN has a nonzero value.

  In this case, **read** waits until at least MIN bytes are available in the queue. At that time, **read** returns as many characters as are available, up to the number requested. **read** can return more than MIN characters if more than MIN happen to be in the queue.

What happens if MIN is 50 and you ask to read just 10 bytes? Normally, **read** waits until there are 50 bytes in the buffer (or, more generally, the wait condition described above is satisfied), and then reads 10 of them, leaving the other 40 buffered in the operating system for a subsequent call to read.

Portability note: On some systems, the MIN and TIME slots are actually the same as the EOF and EOL slots. This causes no serious problem because the MIN and TIME slots are used only in noncanonical input and the EOF and EOL slots are used only in canonical input, but it isn't very clean. The GNU C Library allocates separate slots for these uses.

void **cfmakeraw** (*struct termios *termios-p*)   [Function]

> Preliminary: | MT-Safe | AS-Safe | AC-Safe | See Section 1.2.2.1 [POSIX Safety Concepts], page 2.
>
> This function provides an easy way to set up *termios-p* for what has traditionally been called "raw mode" in BSD. This uses noncanonical input, and turns off most processing to give an unmodified channel to the terminal.
>
> It does exactly this:

```
termios-p->c_iflag &= ~(IGNBRK|BRKINT|PARMRK|ISTRIP
                                      |INLCR|IGNCR|ICRNL|IXON);
termios-p->c_oflag &= ~OPOST;
termios-p->c_lflag &= ~(ECHO|ECHONL|ICANON|ISIG|IEXTEN);
termios-p->c_cflag &= ~(CSIZE|PARENB);
termios-p->c_cflag |= CS8;
```

17.5 BSD Terminal Modes

The usual way to get and set terminal modes is with the functions described in Section 17.4 [Terminal Modes], page 492. However, on some systems you can use the BSD-derived functions in this section to do some of the same things. On many systems, these functions do not exist. Even with the GNU C Library, the functions simply fail with errno = ENOSYS with many kernels, including Linux.

The symbols used in this section are declared in sgtty.h.

struct **sgttyb**   [Data Type]

> This structure is an input or output parameter list for gtty and stty.
>
> char **sg_ispeed**
> > Line speed for input
>
> char **sg_ospeed**
> > Line speed for output
>
> char **sg_erase**
> > Erase character
>
> char **sg_kill**
> > Kill character
>
> int **sg_flags**
> > Various flags

int **gtty** (*int filedes, struct sgttyb *attributes*)   [Function]

> Preliminary: | MT-Safe | AS-Safe | AC-Safe | See Section 1.2.2.1 [POSIX Safety Concepts], page 2.

This function gets the attributes of a terminal.

gtty sets *attributes to describe the terminal attributes of the terminal which is open with file descriptor *filedes*.

int stty (int `filedes`, const struct sgttyb *`attributes`)   [Function]
> Preliminary: | MT-Safe | AS-Safe | AC-Safe | See Section 1.2.2.1 [POSIX Safety Concepts], page 2.
>
> This function sets the attributes of a terminal.
>
> stty sets the terminal attributes of the terminal which is open with file descriptor *filedes* to those described by *attributes*.

17.6 Line Control Functions

These functions perform miscellaneous control actions on terminal devices. As regards terminal access, they are treated like doing output: if any of these functions is used by a background process on its controlling terminal, normally all processes in the process group are sent a SIGTTOU signal. The exception is if the calling process itself is ignoring or blocking SIGTTOU signals, in which case the operation is performed and no signal is sent. See Chapter 28 [Job Control], page 786.

int tcsendbreak (int `filedes`, int `duration`)   [Function]
> Preliminary: | MT-Unsafe race:tcattr(filedes)/bsd | AS-Unsafe | AC-Unsafe corrupt/bsd | See Section 1.2.2.1 [POSIX Safety Concepts], page 2.
>
> This function generates a break condition by transmitting a stream of zero bits on the terminal associated with the file descriptor *filedes*. The duration of the break is controlled by the *duration* argument. If zero, the duration is between 0.25 and 0.5 seconds. The meaning of a nonzero value depends on the operating system.
>
> This function does nothing if the terminal is not an asynchronous serial data port.
>
> The return value is normally zero. In the event of an error, a value of −1 is returned. The following errno error conditions are defined for this function:
>
> EBADF   The *filedes* is not a valid file descriptor.
>
> ENOTTY   The *filedes* is not associated with a terminal device.

int tcdrain (int `filedes`)   [Function]
> Preliminary: | MT-Safe | AS-Safe | AC-Safe | See Section 1.2.2.1 [POSIX Safety Concepts], page 2.
>
> The tcdrain function waits until all queued output to the terminal *filedes* has been transmitted.
>
> This function is a cancellation point in multi-threaded programs. This is a problem if the thread allocates some resources (like memory, file descriptors, semaphores or whatever) at the time tcdrain is called. If the thread gets canceled these resources stay allocated until the program ends. To avoid this calls to tcdrain should be protected using cancellation handlers.
>
> The return value is normally zero. In the event of an error, a value of −1 is returned. The following errno error conditions are defined for this function:
>
> EBADF   The *filedes* is not a valid file descriptor.

ENOTTY   The *filedes* is not associated with a terminal device.

EINTR   The operation was interrupted by delivery of a signal. See Section 24.5 [Primitives Interrupted by Signals], page 711.

`int tcflush (int filedes, int queue)`   [Function]
Preliminary: | MT-Safe | AS-Safe | AC-Safe | See Section 1.2.2.1 [POSIX Safety Concepts], page 2.

The `tcflush` function is used to clear the input and/or output queues associated with the terminal file *filedes*. The *queue* argument specifies which queue(s) to clear, and can be one of the following values:

TCIFLUSH

> Clear any input data received, but not yet read.

TCOFLUSH

> Clear any output data written, but not yet transmitted.

TCIOFLUSH

> Clear both queued input and output.

The return value is normally zero. In the event of an error, a value of −1 is returned. The following `errno` error conditions are defined for this function:

EBADF   The *filedes* is not a valid file descriptor.

ENOTTY   The *filedes* is not associated with a terminal device.

EINVAL   A bad value was supplied as the *queue* argument.

It is unfortunate that this function is named `tcflush`, because the term "flush" is normally used for quite another operation—waiting until all output is transmitted— and using it for discarding input or output would be confusing. Unfortunately, the name `tcflush` comes from POSIX and we cannot change it.

`int tcflow (int filedes, int action)`   [Function]
Preliminary: | MT-Unsafe race:tcattr(filedes)/bsd | AS-Unsafe | AC-Safe | See Section 1.2.2.1 [POSIX Safety Concepts], page 2.

The `tcflow` function is used to perform operations relating to XON/XOFF flow control on the terminal file specified by *filedes*.

The *action* argument specifies what operation to perform, and can be one of the following values:

TCOOFF   Suspend transmission of output.

TCOON   Restart transmission of output.

TCIOFF   Transmit a STOP character.

TCION   Transmit a START character.

For more information about the STOP and START characters, see Section 17.4.9 [Special Characters], page 503.

The return value is normally zero. In the event of an error, a value of −1 is returned. The following `errno` error conditions are defined for this function:

EBADF   The *filedes* is not a valid file descriptor.

ENOTTY   The *filedes* is not associated with a terminal device.

EINVAL   A bad value was supplied as the *action* argument.

17.7 Noncanonical Mode Example

Here is an example program that shows how you can set up a terminal device to read single characters in noncanonical input mode, without echo.

```
#include <unistd.h>
#include <stdio.h>
#include <stdlib.h>
#include <termios.h>

/* Use this variable to remember original terminal attributes. */

struct termios saved_attributes;

void
reset_input_mode (void)
{
  tcsetattr (STDIN_FILENO, TCSANOW, &saved_attributes);
}

void
set_input_mode (void)
{
  struct termios tattr;
  char *name;

  /* Make sure stdin is a terminal. */
  if (!isatty (STDIN_FILENO))
    {
      fprintf (stderr, "Not a terminal.\n");
      exit (EXIT_FAILURE);
    }

  /* Save the terminal attributes so we can restore them later. */
  tcgetattr (STDIN_FILENO, &saved_attributes);
  atexit (reset_input_mode);

  /* Set the funny terminal modes. */
  tcgetattr (STDIN_FILENO, &tattr);
  tattr.c_lflag &= ~(ICANON|ECHO); /* Clear ICANON and ECHO. */
  tattr.c_cc[VMIN] = 1;
  tattr.c_cc[VTIME] = 0;
  tcsetattr (STDIN_FILENO, TCSAFLUSH, &tattr);
}

int
main (void)
{
  char c;

  set_input_mode ();

  while (1)
    {
```

```
        read (STDIN_FILENO, &c, 1);
        if (c == '\004')        /* C-d */
          break;
        else
          putchar (c);
    }

  return EXIT_SUCCESS;
}
```

This program is careful to restore the original terminal modes before exiting or terminating with a signal. It uses the `atexit` function (see Section 25.7.3 [Cleanups on Exit], page 770) to make sure this is done by `exit`.

The shell is supposed to take care of resetting the terminal modes when a process is stopped or continued; see Chapter 28 [Job Control], page 786. But some existing shells do not actually do this, so you may wish to establish handlers for job control signals that reset terminal modes. The above example does so.

17.8 Pseudo-Terminals

A *pseudo-terminal* is a special interprocess communication channel that acts like a terminal. One end of the channel is called the *master* side or *master pseudo-terminal device*, the other side is called the *slave* side. Data written to the master side is received by the slave side as if it was the result of a user typing at an ordinary terminal, and data written to the slave side is sent to the master side as if it was written on an ordinary terminal.

Pseudo terminals are the way programs like `xterm` and `emacs` implement their terminal emulation functionality.

17.8.1 Allocating Pseudo-Terminals

This subsection describes functions for allocating a pseudo-terminal, and for making this pseudo-terminal available for actual use. These functions are declared in the header file `stdlib.h`.

`int getpt (`*void*`)`   [Function]

> Preliminary: | MT-Safe | AS-Safe | AC-Safe fd | See Section 1.2.2.1 [POSIX Safety Concepts], page 2.
>
> The `getpt` function returns a new file descriptor for the next available master pseudo-terminal. The normal return value from `getpt` is a non-negative integer file descriptor. In the case of an error, a value of −1 is returned instead. The following `errno` conditions are defined for this function:
>
> ENOENT   There are no free master pseudo-terminals available.
>
> This function is a GNU extension.

`int grantpt (`*int filedes*`)`   [Function]

> Preliminary: | MT-Safe locale | AS-Unsafe dlopen plugin heap lock | AC-Unsafe corrupt lock fd mem | See Section 1.2.2.1 [POSIX Safety Concepts], page 2.
>
> The `grantpt` function changes the ownership and access permission of the slave pseudo-terminal device corresponding to the master pseudo-terminal device associated with the file descriptor *filedes*. The owner is set from the real user ID of the

calling process (see Section 30.2 [The Persona of a Process], page 815), and the group is set to a special group (typically *tty*) or from the real group ID of the calling process. The access permission is set such that the file is both readable and writable by the owner and only writable by the group.

On some systems this function is implemented by invoking a special `setuid` root program (see Section 30.4 [How an Application Can Change Persona], page 816). As a consequence, installing a signal handler for the `SIGCHLD` signal (see Section 24.2.5 [Job Control Signals], page 692) may interfere with a call to `grantpt`.

The normal return value from `grantpt` is 0; a value of −1 is returned in case of failure. The following `errno` error conditions are defined for this function:

EBADF   The *filedes* argument is not a valid file descriptor.

EINVAL   The *filedes* argument is not associated with a master pseudo-terminal device.

EACCES   The slave pseudo-terminal device corresponding to the master associated with *filedes* could not be accessed.

int unlockpt (*int* `filedes`)   [Function]
Preliminary: | MT-Safe | AS-Unsafe heap/bsd | AC-Unsafe mem fd | See Section 1.2.2.1 [POSIX Safety Concepts], page 2.

The `unlockpt` function unlocks the slave pseudo-terminal device corresponding to the master pseudo-terminal device associated with the file descriptor *filedes*. On many systems, the slave can only be opened after unlocking, so portable applications should always call `unlockpt` before trying to open the slave.

The normal return value from `unlockpt` is 0; a value of −1 is returned in case of failure. The following `errno` error conditions are defined for this function:

EBADF   The *filedes* argument is not a valid file descriptor.

EINVAL   The *filedes* argument is not associated with a master pseudo-terminal device.

char * ptsname (*int* `filedes`)   [Function]
Preliminary: | MT-Unsafe race:ptsname | AS-Unsafe heap/bsd | AC-Unsafe mem fd | See Section 1.2.2.1 [POSIX Safety Concepts], page 2.

If the file descriptor *filedes* is associated with a master pseudo-terminal device, the `ptsname` function returns a pointer to a statically-allocated, null-terminated string containing the file name of the associated slave pseudo-terminal file. This string might be overwritten by subsequent calls to `ptsname`.

int ptsname_r (*int* `filedes`, *char* `*buf`, *size_t* `len`)   [Function]
Preliminary: | MT-Safe | AS-Unsafe heap/bsd | AC-Unsafe mem fd | See Section 1.2.2.1 [POSIX Safety Concepts], page 2.

The `ptsname_r` function is similar to the `ptsname` function except that it places its result into the user-specified buffer starting at *buf* with length *len*.

This function is a GNU extension.

Portability Note: On System V derived systems, the file returned by the `ptsname` and `ptsname_r` functions may be STREAMS-based, and therefore require additional processing after opening before it actually behaves as a pseudo terminal.

Typical usage of these functions is illustrated by the following example:

```
int
open_pty_pair (int *amaster, int *aslave)
{
  int master, slave;
  char *name;

  master = getpt ();
  if (master < 0)
    return 0;

  if (grantpt (master) < 0 || unlockpt (master) < 0)
    goto close_master;
  name = ptsname (master);
  if (name == NULL)
    goto close_master;

  slave = open (name, O_RDWR);
  if (slave == -1)
    goto close_master;

  if (isastream (slave))
    {
      if (ioctl (slave, I_PUSH, "ptem") < 0
          || ioctl (slave, I_PUSH, "ldterm") < 0)
        goto close_slave;
    }

  *amaster = master;
  *aslave = slave;
  return 1;

close_slave:
  close (slave);

close_master:
  close (master);
  return 0;
}
```

17.8.2 Opening a Pseudo-Terminal Pair

These functions, derived from BSD, are available in the separate `libutil` library, and declared in `pty.h`.

`int openpty` (*int *amaster, int *aslave, char *name, const struct*   [Function]
      *termios *termp, const struct winsize *winp*)

Preliminary: | MT-Safe locale | AS-Unsafe dlopen plugin heap lock | AC-Unsafe corrupt lock fd mem | See Section 1.2.2.1 [POSIX Safety Concepts], page 2.

This function allocates and opens a pseudo-terminal pair, returning the file descriptor for the master in *amaster*, and the file descriptor for the slave in *aslave*. If the argument *name* is not a null pointer, the file name of the slave pseudo-terminal device is stored in *name. If *termp* is not a null pointer, the terminal attributes of the slave are set to the ones specified in the structure that *termp* points to (see Section 17.4 [Terminal Modes], page 492). Likewise, if *winp* is not a null pointer, the screen size of the slave is set to the values specified in the structure that *winp* points to.

The normal return value from openpty is 0; a value of −1 is returned in case of failure. The following errno conditions are defined for this function:

ENOENT   There are no free pseudo-terminal pairs available.

Warning: Using the openpty function with *name* not set to NULL is **very dangerous** because it provides no protection against overflowing the string *name*. You should use the ttyname function on the file descriptor returned in *slave* to find out the file name of the slave pseudo-terminal device instead.

int forkpty (*int *amaster, char *name, const struct termios*   [Function]
        *termp, const struct winsize *winp*)
Preliminary: | MT-Safe locale | AS-Unsafe dlopen plugin heap lock | AC-Unsafe corrupt lock fd mem | See Section 1.2.2.1 [POSIX Safety Concepts], page 2.

This function is similar to the openpty function, but in addition, forks a new process (see Section 26.4 [Creating a Process], page 775) and makes the newly opened slave pseudo-terminal device the controlling terminal (see Section 28.3 [Controlling Terminal of a Process], page 787) for the child process.

If the operation is successful, there are then both parent and child processes and both see forkpty return, but with different values: it returns a value of 0 in the child process and returns the child's process ID in the parent process.

If the allocation of a pseudo-terminal pair or the process creation failed, forkpty returns a value of −1 in the parent process.

Warning: The forkpty function has the same problems with respect to the *name* argument as openpty.

18 Syslog

This chapter describes facilities for issuing and logging messages of system administration interest. This chapter has nothing to do with programs issuing messages to their own users or keeping private logs (One would typically do that with the facilities described in Chapter 12 [Input/Output on Streams], page 257).

Most systems have a facility called "Syslog" that allows programs to submit messages of interest to system administrators and can be configured to pass these messages on in various ways, such as printing on the console, mailing to a particular person, or recording in a log file for future reference.

A program uses the facilities in this chapter to submit such messages.

18.1 Overview of Syslog

System administrators have to deal with lots of different kinds of messages from a plethora of subsystems within each system, and usually lots of systems as well. For example, an FTP server might report every connection it gets. The kernel might report hardware failures on a disk drive. A DNS server might report usage statistics at regular intervals.

Some of these messages need to be brought to a system administrator's attention immediately. And it may not be just any system administrator – there may be a particular system administrator who deals with a particular kind of message. Other messages just need to be recorded for future reference if there is a problem. Still others may need to have information extracted from them by an automated process that generates monthly reports.

To deal with these messages, most Unix systems have a facility called "Syslog." It is generally based on a daemon called "Syslogd" Syslogd listens for messages on a Unix domain socket named `/dev/log`. Based on classification information in the messages and its configuration file (usually `/etc/syslog.conf`), Syslogd routes them in various ways. Some of the popular routings are:

- Write to the system console
- Mail to a specific user
- Write to a log file
- Pass to another daemon
- Discard

Syslogd can also handle messages from other systems. It listens on the `syslog` UDP port as well as the local socket for messages.

Syslog can handle messages from the kernel itself. But the kernel doesn't write to `/dev/log`; rather, another daemon (sometimes called "Klogd") extracts messages from the kernel and passes them on to Syslog as any other process would (and it properly identifies them as messages from the kernel).

Syslog can even handle messages that the kernel issued before Syslogd or Klogd was running. A Linux kernel, for example, stores startup messages in a kernel message ring and they are normally still there when Klogd later starts up. Assuming Syslogd is running by the time Klogd starts, Klogd then passes everything in the message ring to it.

In order to classify messages for disposition, Syslog requires any process that submits a message to it to provide two pieces of classification information with it:

facility   This identifies who submitted the message. There are a small number of facilities defined. The kernel, the mail subsystem, and an FTP server are examples of recognized facilities. For the complete list, See Section 18.2.2 [syslog, vsyslog], page 520. Keep in mind that these are essentially arbitrary classifications. "Mail subsystem" doesn't have any more meaning than the system administrator gives to it.

priority   This tells how important the content of the message is. Examples of defined priority values are: debug, informational, warning and critical. For the complete list, see Section 18.2.2 [syslog, vsyslog], page 520. Except for the fact that the priorities have a defined order, the meaning of each of these priorities is entirely determined by the system administrator.

A "facility/priority" is a number that indicates both the facility and the priority.

Warning: This terminology is not universal. Some people use "level" to refer to the priority and "priority" to refer to the combination of facility and priority. A Linux kernel has a concept of a message "level," which corresponds both to a Syslog priority and to a Syslog facility/priority (It can be both because the facility code for the kernel is zero, and that makes priority and facility/priority the same value).

The GNU C Library provides functions to submit messages to Syslog. They do it by writing to the `/dev/log` socket. See Section 18.2 [Submitting Syslog Messages], page 518.

The GNU C Library functions only work to submit messages to the Syslog facility on the same system. To submit a message to the Syslog facility on another system, use the socket I/O functions to write a UDP datagram to the `syslog` UDP port on that system. See Chapter 16 [Sockets], page 442.

18.2 Submitting Syslog Messages

The GNU C Library provides functions to submit messages to the Syslog facility:

These functions only work to submit messages to the Syslog facility on the same system. To submit a message to the Syslog facility on another system, use the socket I/O functions to write a UDP datagram to the `syslog` UDP port on that system. See Chapter 16 [Sockets], page 442.

18.2.1 openlog

The symbols referred to in this section are declared in the file `syslog.h`.

void **openlog** (*const char *ident*, *int option*, *int facility*)   [Function]
          Preliminary: | MT-Safe | AS-Unsafe lock | AC-Unsafe lock fd | See Section 1.2.2.1 [POSIX Safety Concepts], page 2.

          `openlog` opens or reopens a connection to Syslog in preparation for submitting messages.

          ident is an arbitrary identification string which future `syslog` invocations will prefix to each message. This is intended to identify the source of the message, and people conventionally set it to the name of the program that will submit the messages.

If *ident* is NULL, or if `openlog` is not called, the default identification string used in Syslog messages will be the program name, taken from argv[0].

Please note that the string pointer *ident* will be retained internally by the Syslog routines. You must not free the memory that *ident* points to. It is also dangerous to pass a reference to an automatic variable since leaving the scope would mean ending the lifetime of the variable. If you want to change the *ident* string, you must call `openlog` again; overwriting the string pointed to by *ident* is not thread-safe.

You can cause the Syslog routines to drop the reference to *ident* and go back to the default string (the program name taken from argv[0]), by calling `closelog`: See Section 18.2.3 [closelog], page 522.

In particular, if you are writing code for a shared library that might get loaded and then unloaded (e.g. a PAM module), and you use `openlog`, you must call `closelog` before any point where your library might get unloaded, as in this example:

```
#include <syslog.h>

void
shared_library_function (void)
{
  openlog ("mylibrary", option, priority);

  syslog (LOG_INFO, "shared library has been invoked");

  closelog ();
}
```

Without the call to `closelog`, future invocations of `syslog` by the program using the shared library may crash, if the library gets unloaded and the memory containing the string `"mylibrary"` becomes unmapped. This is a limitation of the BSD syslog interface.

`openlog` may or may not open the `/dev/log` socket, depending on *option*. If it does, it tries to open it and connect it as a stream socket. If that doesn't work, it tries to open it and connect it as a datagram socket. The socket has the "Close on Exec" attribute, so the kernel will close it if the process performs an exec.

You don't have to use `openlog`. If you call `syslog` without having called `openlog`, `syslog` just opens the connection implicitly and uses defaults for the information in *ident* and *options*.

options is a bit string, with the bits as defined by the following single bit masks:

`LOG_PERROR`

If on, `openlog` sets up the connection so that any `syslog` on this connection writes its message to the calling process' Standard Error stream in addition to submitting it to Syslog. If off, `syslog` does not write the message to Standard Error.

`LOG_CONS`   If on, `openlog` sets up the connection so that a `syslog` on this connection that fails to submit a message to Syslog writes the message instead to system console. If off, `syslog` does not write to the system console (but of course Syslog may write messages it receives to the console).

LOG_PID When on, **openlog** sets up the connection so that a **syslog** on this connection inserts the calling process' Process ID (PID) into the message. When off, **openlog** does not insert the PID.

LOG_NDELAY When on, **openlog** opens and connects the **/dev/log** socket. When off, a future **syslog** call must open and connect the socket.

Portability note: In early systems, the sense of this bit was exactly the opposite.

LOG_ODELAY This bit does nothing. It exists for backward compatibility.

If any other bit in *options* is on, the result is undefined.

facility is the default facility code for this connection. A **syslog** on this connection that specifies default facility causes this facility to be associated with the message. See **syslog** for possible values. A value of zero means the default, which is **LOG_USER**.

If a Syslog connection is already open when you call **openlog**, **openlog** "reopens" the connection. Reopening is like opening except that if you specify zero for the default facility code, the default facility code simply remains unchanged and if you specify LOG_NDELAY and the socket is already open and connected, **openlog** just leaves it that way.

18.2.2 syslog, vsyslog

The symbols referred to in this section are declared in the file **syslog.h**.

void syslog (*int facility_priority, const char *format, ...*)   [Function]
Preliminary: | MT-Safe env locale | AS-Unsafe corrupt heap lock dlopen | AC-Unsafe corrupt lock mem fd | See Section 1.2.2.1 [POSIX Safety Concepts], page 2.

syslog submits a message to the Syslog facility. It does this by writing to the Unix domain socket **/dev/log**.

syslog submits the message with the facility and priority indicated by *facility_priority*. The macro **LOG_MAKEPRI** generates a facility/priority from a facility and a priority, as in the following example:

```
LOG_MAKEPRI(LOG_USER, LOG_WARNING)
```

The possible values for the facility code are (macros):

LOG_USER   A miscellaneous user process

LOG_MAIL   Mail

LOG_DAEMON
            A miscellaneous system daemon

LOG_AUTH   Security (authorization)

LOG_SYSLOG
            Syslog

LOG_LPR   Central printer

LOG_NEWS   Network news (e.g. Usenet)

LOG_UUCP   UUCP

LOG_CRON   Cron and At

LOG_AUTHPRIV

Private security (authorization)

LOG_FTP   Ftp server

LOG_LOCAL0

Locally defined

LOG_LOCAL1

Locally defined

LOG_LOCAL2

Locally defined

LOG_LOCAL3

Locally defined

LOG_LOCAL4

Locally defined

LOG_LOCAL5

Locally defined

LOG_LOCAL6

Locally defined

LOG_LOCAL7

Locally defined

Results are undefined if the facility code is anything else.

NB: syslog recognizes one other facility code: that of the kernel. But you can't specify that facility code with these functions. If you try, it looks the same to syslog as if you are requesting the default facility. But you wouldn't want to anyway, because any program that uses the GNU C Library is not the kernel.

You can use just a priority code as *facility_priority*. In that case, syslog assumes the default facility established when the Syslog connection was opened. See Section 18.2.5 [Syslog Example], page 523.

The possible values for the priority code are (macros):

LOG_EMERG

The message says the system is unusable.

LOG_ALERT

Action on the message must be taken immediately.

LOG_CRIT   The message states a critical condition.

LOG_ERR   The message describes an error.

LOG_WARNING

The message is a warning.

LOG_NOTICE
> The message describes a normal but important event.

LOG_INFO The message is purely informational.

LOG_DEBUG
> The message is only for debugging purposes.

Results are undefined if the priority code is anything else.

If the process does not presently have a Syslog connection open (i.e., it did not call openlog), syslog implicitly opens the connection the same as openlog would, with the following defaults for information that would otherwise be included in an openlog call: The default identification string is the program name. The default default facility is LOG_USER. The default for all the connection options in *options* is as if those bits were off. syslog leaves the Syslog connection open.

If the /dev/log socket is not open and connected, syslog opens and connects it, the same as openlog with the LOG_NDELAY option would.

syslog leaves /dev/log open and connected unless its attempt to send the message failed, in which case syslog closes it (with the hope that a future implicit open will restore the Syslog connection to a usable state).

Example:

```
#include <syslog.h>
syslog (LOG_MAKEPRI(LOG_LOCAL1, LOG_ERROR),
        "Unable to make network connection to %s.  Error=%m", host);
```

void vsyslog (*int facility_priority*, *const char *format*, va_list   [Function]
> *arglist*)
> Preliminary: | MT-Safe env locale | AS-Unsafe corrupt heap lock dlopen | AC-Unsafe corrupt lock mem fd | See Section 1.2.2.1 [POSIX Safety Concepts], page 2.

> This is functionally identical to syslog, with the BSD style variable length argument.

18.2.3 closelog

The symbols referred to in this section are declared in the file syslog.h.

void closelog (*void*)   [Function]
> Preliminary: | MT-Safe | AS-Unsafe lock | AC-Unsafe lock fd | See Section 1.2.2.1 [POSIX Safety Concepts], page 2.

> closelog closes the current Syslog connection, if there is one. This includes closing the /dev/log socket, if it is open. closelog also sets the identification string for Syslog messages back to the default, if openlog was called with a non-NULL argument to *ident*. The default identification string is the program name taken from argv[0].

> If you are writing shared library code that uses openlog to generate custom syslog output, you should use closelog to drop the GNU C Library's internal reference to the *ident* pointer when you are done. Please read the section on openlog for more information: See Section 18.2.1 [openlog], page 518.

closelog does not flush any buffers. You do not have to call closelog before re-opening a Syslog connection with openlog. Syslog connections are automatically closed on exec or exit.

18.2.4 setlogmask

The symbols referred to in this section are declared in the file syslog.h.

int setlogmask (*int mask*)   [Function]

> Preliminary: | MT-Unsafe race:LogMask | AS-Unsafe | AC-Safe | See Section 1.2.2.1 [POSIX Safety Concepts], page 2.
>
> setlogmask sets a mask (the "logmask") that determines which future syslog calls shall be ignored. If a program has not called setlogmask, syslog doesn't ignore any calls. You can use setlogmask to specify that messages of particular priorities shall be ignored in the future.
>
> A setlogmask call overrides any previous setlogmask call.
>
> Note that the logmask exists entirely independently of opening and closing of Syslog connections.
>
> Setting the logmask has a similar effect to, but is not the same as, configuring Syslog. The Syslog configuration may cause Syslog to discard certain messages it receives, but the logmask causes certain messages never to get submitted to Syslog in the first place.
>
> *mask* is a bit string with one bit corresponding to each of the possible message priorities. If the bit is on, syslog handles messages of that priority normally. If it is off, syslog discards messages of that priority. Use the message priority macros described in Section 18.2.2 [syslog, vsyslog], page 520, and the LOG_MASK to construct an appropriate *mask* value, as in this example:
>
>   LOG_MASK(LOG_EMERG) | LOG_MASK(LOG_ERROR)
>
> or
>
>   ~(LOG_MASK(LOG_INFO))
>
> There is also a LOG_UPTO macro, which generates a mask with the bits on for a certain priority and all priorities above it:
>
>   LOG_UPTO(LOG_ERROR)
>
> The unfortunate naming of the macro is due to the fact that internally, higher numbers are used for lower message priorities.

18.2.5 Syslog Example

Here is an example of openlog, syslog, and closelog:

This example sets the logmask so that debug and informational messages get discarded without ever reaching Syslog. So the second syslog in the example does nothing.

```
#include <syslog.h>

setlogmask (LOG_UPTO (LOG_NOTICE));

openlog ("exampleprog", LOG_CONS | LOG_PID | LOG_NDELAY, LOG_LOCAL1);

syslog (LOG_NOTICE, "Program started by User %d", getuid ());
```

```
syslog (LOG_INFO, "A tree falls in a forest");

closelog ();
```

19 Mathematics

This chapter contains information about functions for performing mathematical computations, such as trigonometric functions. Most of these functions have prototypes declared in the header file `math.h`. The complex-valued functions are defined in `complex.h`.

All mathematical functions which take a floating-point argument have three variants, one each for `double`, `float`, and `long double` arguments. The `double` versions are mostly defined in ISO C89. The `float` and `long double` versions are from the numeric extensions to C included in ISO C99.

Which of the three versions of a function should be used depends on the situation. For most calculations, the `float` functions are the fastest. On the other hand, the `long double` functions have the highest precision. `double` is somewhere in between. It is usually wise to pick the narrowest type that can accommodate your data. Not all machines have a distinct `long double` type; it may be the same as `double`.

On some machines, the GNU C Library also provides `_FloatN` and `_FloatNx` types. These types are defined in ISO/IEC TS 18661-3, which extends ISO C and defines floating-point types that are not machine-dependent. When such a type, such as `_Float128`, is supported by the GNU C Library, extra variants for most of the mathematical functions provided for `double`, `float`, and `long double` are also provided for the supported type. Throughout this manual, the `_FloatN` and `_FloatNx` variants of these functions are described along with the `double`, `float`, and `long double` variants and they come from ISO/IEC TS 18661-3, unless explicitly stated otherwise.

Currently, support for `_FloatN` or `_FloatNx` types is only provided for `_Float128` on powerpc64le (PowerPC 64-bits little-endian), x86_64, x86 and ia64.

19.1 Predefined Mathematical Constants

The header `math.h` defines several useful mathematical constants. All values are defined as preprocessor macros starting with `M_`. The values provided are:

`M_E`   The base of natural logarithms.

`M_LOG2E`   The logarithm to base 2 of `M_E`.

`M_LOG10E`   The logarithm to base 10 of `M_E`.

`M_LN2`   The natural logarithm of 2.

`M_LN10`   The natural logarithm of 10.

`M_PI`   Pi, the ratio of a circle's circumference to its diameter.

`M_PI_2`   Pi divided by two.

`M_PI_4`   Pi divided by four.

`M_1_PI`   The reciprocal of pi (1/pi)

`M_2_PI`   Two times the reciprocal of pi.

`M_2_SQRTPI`
        Two times the reciprocal of the square root of pi.

M_SQRT2   The square root of two.

M_SQRT1_2

> The reciprocal of the square root of two (also the square root of 1/2).

These constants come from the Unix98 standard and were also available in 4.4BSD; therefore they are only defined if _XOPEN_SOURCE=500, or a more general feature select macro, is defined. The default set of features includes these constants. See Section 1.3.4 [Feature Test Macros], page 15.

All values are of type double. As an extension, the GNU C Library also defines these constants with type long double. The long double macros have a lowercase '1' appended to their names: M_El, M_PI1, and so forth. These are only available if _GNU_SOURCE is defined.

Likewise, the GNU C Library also defines these constants with the types _FloatN and _FloatNx for the machines that have support for such types enabled (see Chapter 19 [Mathematics], page 525) and if _GNU_SOURCE is defined. When available, the macros names are appended with 'fN' or 'fNx', such as 'f128' for the type _Float128.

Note: Some programs use a constant named PI which has the same value as M_PI. This constant is not standard; it may have appeared in some old AT&T headers, and is mentioned in Stroustrup's book on C++. It infringes on the user's name space, so the GNU C Library does not define it. Fixing programs written to expect it is simple: replace PI with M_PI throughout, or put '-DPI=M_PI' on the compiler command line.

19.2 Trigonometric Functions

These are the familiar sin, cos, and tan functions. The arguments to all of these functions are in units of radians; recall that pi radians equals 180 degrees.

The math library normally defines M_PI to a double approximation of pi. If strict ISO and/or POSIX compliance are requested this constant is not defined, but you can easily define it yourself:

```
#define M_PI 3.14159265358979323846264338327
```

You can also compute the value of pi with the expression acos (-1.0).

double sin (*double x*)	[Function]
float sinf (*float x*)	[Function]
long double sinl (*long double x*)	[Function]
_FloatN sinfN (*_FloatN x*)	[Function]
_FloatNx sinfNx (*_FloatNx x*)	[Function]

> Preliminary: | MT-Safe | AS-Safe | AC-Safe | See Section 1.2.2.1 [POSIX Safety Concepts], page 2.

> These functions return the sine of x, where x is given in radians. The return value is in the range −1 to 1.

double cos (*double x*)	[Function]
float cosf (*float x*)	[Function]
long double cosl (*long double x*)	[Function]
_FloatN cosfN (*_FloatN x*)	[Function]

`_FloatNx cosfNx (_FloatNx x)`   [Function]
> Preliminary: | MT-Safe | AS-Safe | AC-Safe | See Section 1.2.2.1 [POSIX Safety Concepts], page 2.
>
> These functions return the cosine of x, where x is given in radians. The return value is in the range -1 to 1.

`double tan (double x)`   [Function]
`float tanf (float x)`   [Function]
`long double tanl (long double x)`   [Function]
`_FloatN tanfN (_FloatN x)`   [Function]
`_FloatNx tanfNx (_FloatNx x)`   [Function]
> Preliminary: | MT-Safe | AS-Safe | AC-Safe | See Section 1.2.2.1 [POSIX Safety Concepts], page 2.
>
> These functions return the tangent of x, where x is given in radians.
>
> Mathematically, the tangent function has singularities at odd multiples of pi/2. If the argument x is too close to one of these singularities, `tan` will signal overflow.

In many applications where `sin` and `cos` are used, the sine and cosine of the same angle are needed at the same time. It is more efficient to compute them simultaneously, so the library provides a function to do that.

`void sincos (double x, double *sinx, double *cosx)`   [Function]
`void sincosf (float x, float *sinx, float *cosx)`   [Function]
`void sincosl (long double x, long double *sinx, long double *cosx)`   [Function]
`_FloatN sincosfN (_FloatN x, _FloatN *sinx, _FloatN *cosx)`   [Function]
`_FloatNx sincosfNx (_FloatNx x, _FloatNx *sinx, _FloatNx *cosx)` [Function]
> Preliminary: | MT-Safe | AS-Safe | AC-Safe | See Section 1.2.2.1 [POSIX Safety Concepts], page 2.
>
> These functions return the sine of x in `*sinx` and the cosine of x in `*cosx`, where x is given in radians. Both values, `*sinx` and `*cosx`, are in the range of -1 to 1.
>
> All these functions, including the `_FloatN` and `_FloatNx` variants, are GNU extensions. Portable programs should be prepared to cope with their absence.

ISO C99 defines variants of the trig functions which work on complex numbers. The GNU C Library provides these functions, but they are only useful if your compiler supports the new complex types defined by the standard. (As of this writing GCC supports complex numbers, but there are bugs in the implementation.)

`complex double csin (complex double z)`   [Function]
`complex float csinf (complex float z)`   [Function]
`complex long double csinl (complex long double z)`   [Function]
`complex _FloatN csinfN (complex _FloatN z)`   [Function]
`complex _FloatNx csinfNx (complex _FloatNx z)`   [Function]
> Preliminary: | MT-Safe | AS-Safe | AC-Safe | See Section 1.2.2.1 [POSIX Safety Concepts], page 2.
>
> These functions return the complex sine of z. The mathematical definition of the complex sine is

$$\sin(z) = \frac{1}{2i}(e^{zi} - e^{-zi})$$

complex double ccos (*complex double z*)   [Function]
complex float ccosf (*complex float z*)   [Function]
complex long double ccosl (*complex long double z*)   [Function]
complex _FloatN ccosfN (*complex _FloatN z*)   [Function]
complex _FloatNx ccosfNx (*complex _FloatNx z*)   [Function]

> Preliminary: | MT-Safe | AS-Safe | AC-Safe | See Section 1.2.2.1 [POSIX Safety Concepts], page 2.

> These functions return the complex cosine of *z*. The mathematical definition of the complex cosine is

$$\cos(z) = \frac{1}{2}(e^{zi} + e^{-zi})$$

complex double ctan (*complex double z*)   [Function]
complex float ctanf (*complex float z*)   [Function]
complex long double ctanl (*complex long double z*)   [Function]
complex _FloatN ctanfN (*complex _FloatN z*)   [Function]
complex _FloatNx ctanfNx (*complex _FloatNx z*)   [Function]

> Preliminary: | MT-Safe | AS-Safe | AC-Safe | See Section 1.2.2.1 [POSIX Safety Concepts], page 2.

> These functions return the complex tangent of *z*. The mathematical definition of the complex tangent is

$$\tan(z) = -i \cdot \frac{e^{zi} - e^{-zi}}{e^{zi} + e^{-zi}}$$

> The complex tangent has poles at $pi/2 + 2n$, where n is an integer. `ctan` may signal overflow if z is too close to a pole.

19.3 Inverse Trigonometric Functions

These are the usual arcsine, arccosine and arctangent functions, which are the inverses of the sine, cosine and tangent functions respectively.

double asin (*double x*)   [Function]
float asinf (*float x*)   [Function]
long double asinl (*long double x*)   [Function]
_FloatN asinfN (*_FloatN x*)   [Function]
_FloatNx asinfNx (*_FloatNx x*)   [Function]

> Preliminary: | MT-Safe | AS-Safe | AC-Safe | See Section 1.2.2.1 [POSIX Safety Concepts], page 2.

> These functions compute the arcsine of *x*—that is, the value whose sine is *x*. The value is in units of radians. Mathematically, there are infinitely many such values; the one actually returned is the one between -pi/2 and pi/2 (inclusive).

> The arcsine function is defined mathematically only over the domain -1 to 1. If *x* is outside the domain, `asin` signals a domain error.

double acos (*double x*)	[Function]
float acosf (*float x*)	[Function]
long double acosl (*long double x*)	[Function]
_FloatN acosfN (*_FloatN x*)	[Function]
_FloatNx acosfNx (*_FloatNx x*)	[Function]

Preliminary: | MT-Safe | AS-Safe | AC-Safe | See Section 1.2.2.1 [POSIX Safety Concepts], page 2.

These functions compute the arccosine of x—that is, the value whose cosine is x. The value is in units of radians. Mathematically, there are infinitely many such values; the one actually returned is the one between 0 and `pi` (inclusive).

The arccosine function is defined mathematically only over the domain -1 to 1. If x is outside the domain, `acos` signals a domain error.

double atan (*double x*)	[Function]
float atanf (*float x*)	[Function]
long double atanl (*long double x*)	[Function]
_FloatN atanfN (*_FloatN x*)	[Function]
_FloatNx atanfNx (*_FloatNx x*)	[Function]

Preliminary: | MT-Safe | AS-Safe | AC-Safe | See Section 1.2.2.1 [POSIX Safety Concepts], page 2.

These functions compute the arctangent of x—that is, the value whose tangent is x. The value is in units of radians. Mathematically, there are infinitely many such values; the one actually returned is the one between `-pi/2` and `pi/2` (inclusive).

double atan2 (*double y, double x*)	[Function]
float atan2f (*float y, float x*)	[Function]
long double atan2l (*long double y, long double x*)	[Function]
_FloatN atan2fN (*_FloatN y, _FloatN x*)	[Function]
_FloatNx atan2fNx (*_FloatNx y, _FloatNx x*)	[Function]

Preliminary: | MT-Safe | AS-Safe | AC-Safe | See Section 1.2.2.1 [POSIX Safety Concepts], page 2.

This function computes the arctangent of y/x, but the signs of both arguments are used to determine the quadrant of the result, and x is permitted to be zero. The return value is given in radians and is in the range `-pi` to `pi`, inclusive.

If x and y are coordinates of a point in the plane, `atan2` returns the signed angle between the line from the origin to that point and the x-axis. Thus, `atan2` is useful for converting Cartesian coordinates to polar coordinates. (To compute the radial coordinate, use `hypot`; see Section 19.4 [Exponentiation and Logarithms], page 530.)

If both x and y are zero, `atan2` returns zero.

ISO C99 defines complex versions of the inverse trig functions.

complex double casin (*complex double z*)	[Function]
complex float casinf (*complex float z*)	[Function]
complex long double casinl (*complex long double z*)	[Function]
complex _FloatN casinfN (*complex _FloatN z*)	[Function]

complex _FloatNx casinfNx (*complex _FloatNx* **z**)   [Function]
>   Preliminary: | MT-Safe | AS-Safe | AC-Safe | See Section 1.2.2.1 [POSIX Safety Concepts], page 2.
>
>   These functions compute the complex arcsine of *z*—that is, the value whose sine is *z*. The value returned is in radians.
>
>   Unlike the real-valued functions, `casin` is defined for all values of *z*.

complex double cacos (*complex double* **z**)   [Function]
complex float cacosf (*complex float* **z**)   [Function]
complex long double cacosl (*complex long double* **z**)   [Function]
complex _FloatN cacosfN (*complex _FloatN* **z**)   [Function]
complex _FloatNx cacosfNx (*complex _FloatNx* **z**)   [Function]
>   Preliminary: | MT-Safe | AS-Safe | AC-Safe | See Section 1.2.2.1 [POSIX Safety Concepts], page 2.
>
>   These functions compute the complex arccosine of *z*—that is, the value whose cosine is *z*. The value returned is in radians.
>
>   Unlike the real-valued functions, `cacos` is defined for all values of *z*.

complex double catan (*complex double* **z**)   [Function]
complex float catanf (*complex float* **z**)   [Function]
complex long double catanl (*complex long double* **z**)   [Function]
complex _FloatN catanfN (*complex _FloatN* **z**)   [Function]
complex _FloatNx catanfNx (*complex _FloatNx* **z**)   [Function]
>   Preliminary: | MT-Safe | AS-Safe | AC-Safe | See Section 1.2.2.1 [POSIX Safety Concepts], page 2.
>
>   These functions compute the complex arctangent of *z*—that is, the value whose tangent is *z*. The value is in units of radians.

19.4 Exponentiation and Logarithms

double exp (*double* **x**)   [Function]
float expf (*float* **x**)   [Function]
long double expl (*long double* **x**)   [Function]
_FloatN expfN (*_FloatN* **x**)   [Function]
_FloatNx expfNx (*_FloatNx* **x**)   [Function]
>   Preliminary: | MT-Safe | AS-Safe | AC-Safe | See Section 1.2.2.1 [POSIX Safety Concepts], page 2.
>
>   These functions compute e (the base of natural logarithms) raised to the power *x*.
>
>   If the magnitude of the result is too large to be representable, `exp` signals overflow.

double exp2 (*double* **x**)   [Function]
float exp2f (*float* **x**)   [Function]
long double exp2l (*long double* **x**)   [Function]
_FloatN exp2fN (*_FloatN* **x**)   [Function]
_FloatNx exp2fNx (*_FloatNx* **x**)   [Function]
>   Preliminary: | MT-Safe | AS-Safe | AC-Safe | See Section 1.2.2.1 [POSIX Safety Concepts], page 2.

These functions compute 2 raised to the power *x*. Mathematically, `exp2 (x)` is the same as `exp (x * log (2))`.

`double exp10 (`*double x*`)`	[Function]
`float exp10f (`*float x*`)`	[Function]
`long double exp10l (`*long double x*`)`	[Function]
`_FloatN exp10fN (`*_FloatN x*`)`	[Function]
`_FloatNx exp10fNx (`*_FloatNx x*`)`	[Function]
`double pow10 (`*double x*`)`	[Function]
`float pow10f (`*float x*`)`	[Function]
`long double pow10l (`*long double x*`)`	[Function]

> Preliminary: | MT-Safe | AS-Safe | AC-Safe | See Section 1.2.2.1 [POSIX Safety Concepts], page 2.
>
> These functions compute 10 raised to the power *x*. Mathematically, `exp10 (x)` is the same as `exp (x * log (10))`.
>
> The `exp10` functions are from TS 18661-4:2015; the `pow10` names are GNU extensions. The name `exp10` is preferred, since it is analogous to `exp` and `exp2`.

`double log (`*double x*`)`	[Function]
`float logf (`*float x*`)`	[Function]
`long double logl (`*long double x*`)`	[Function]
`_FloatN logfN (`*_FloatN x*`)`	[Function]
`_FloatNx logfNx (`*_FloatNx x*`)`	[Function]

> Preliminary: | MT-Safe | AS-Safe | AC-Safe | See Section 1.2.2.1 [POSIX Safety Concepts], page 2.
>
> These functions compute the natural logarithm of *x*. `exp (log (x))` equals *x*, exactly in mathematics and approximately in C.
>
> If *x* is negative, `log` signals a domain error. If *x* is zero, it returns negative infinity; if *x* is too close to zero, it may signal overflow.

`double log10 (`*double x*`)`	[Function]
`float log10f (`*float x*`)`	[Function]
`long double log10l (`*long double x*`)`	[Function]
`_FloatN log10fN (`*_FloatN x*`)`	[Function]
`_FloatNx log10fNx (`*_FloatNx x*`)`	[Function]

> Preliminary: | MT-Safe | AS-Safe | AC-Safe | See Section 1.2.2.1 [POSIX Safety Concepts], page 2.
>
> These functions return the base-10 logarithm of *x*. `log10 (x)` equals `log (x) / log (10)`.

`double log2 (`*double x*`)`	[Function]
`float log2f (`*float x*`)`	[Function]
`long double log2l (`*long double x*`)`	[Function]
`_FloatN log2fN (`*_FloatN x*`)`	[Function]
`_FloatNx log2fNx (`*_FloatNx x*`)`	[Function]

> Preliminary: | MT-Safe | AS-Safe | AC-Safe | See Section 1.2.2.1 [POSIX Safety Concepts], page 2.

These functions return the base-2 logarithm of *x*. `log2 (`*x*`)` equals `log (`*x*`)` / `log (2)`.

`double logb (`*double x*`)`	[Function]
`float logbf (`*float x*`)`	[Function]
`long double logbl (`*long double x*`)`	[Function]
`_FloatN logbfN (`*_FloatN x*`)`	[Function]
`_FloatNx logbfNx (`*_FloatNx x*`)`	[Function]

Preliminary: | MT-Safe | AS-Safe | AC-Safe | See Section 1.2.2.1 [POSIX Safety Concepts], page 2.

These functions extract the exponent of *x* and return it as a floating-point value. If `FLT_RADIX` is two, `logb` is equal to `floor (log2 (`*x*`))`, except it's probably faster.

If *x* is de-normalized, `logb` returns the exponent *x* would have if it were normalized. If *x* is infinity (positive or negative), `logb` returns ∞. If *x* is zero, `logb` returns ∞. It does not signal.

`int ilogb (`*double x*`)`	[Function]
`int ilogbf (`*float x*`)`	[Function]
`int ilogbl (`*long double x*`)`	[Function]
`int ilogbfN (`*_FloatN x*`)`	[Function]
`int ilogbfNx (`*_FloatNx x*`)`	[Function]
`long int llogb (`*double x*`)`	[Function]
`long int llogbf (`*float x*`)`	[Function]
`long int llogbl (`*long double x*`)`	[Function]
`long int llogbfN (`*_FloatN x*`)`	[Function]
`long int llogbfNx (`*_FloatNx x*`)`	[Function]

Preliminary: | MT-Safe | AS-Safe | AC-Safe | See Section 1.2.2.1 [POSIX Safety Concepts], page 2.

These functions are equivalent to the corresponding `logb` functions except that they return signed integer values. The `ilogb`, `ilogbf`, and `ilogbl` functions are from ISO C99; the `llogb`, `llogbf`, `llogbl` functions are from TS 18661-1:2014; the `ilogbfN`, `ilogbfNx`, `llogbfN`, and `llogbfNx` functions are from TS 18661-3:2015.

Since integers cannot represent infinity and NaN, `ilogb` instead returns an integer that can't be the exponent of a normal floating-point number. `math.h` defines constants so you can check for this.

`int FP_ILOGB0`	[Macro]

`ilogb` returns this value if its argument is 0. The numeric value is either `INT_MIN` or `-INT_MAX`.

This macro is defined in ISO C99.

`long int FP_LLOGB0`	[Macro]

`llogb` returns this value if its argument is 0. The numeric value is either `LONG_MIN` or `-LONG_MAX`.

This macro is defined in TS 18661-1:2014.

int FP_ILOGBNAN [Macro]

> `ilogb` returns this value if its argument is `NaN`. The numeric value is either `INT_MIN` or `INT_MAX`.
>
> This macro is defined in ISO C99.

long int FP_LLOGBNAN [Macro]

> `llogb` returns this value if its argument is `NaN`. The numeric value is either `LONG_MIN` or `LONG_MAX`.
>
> This macro is defined in TS 18661-1:2014.

These values are system specific. They might even be the same. The proper way to test the result of `ilogb` is as follows:

```
i = ilogb (f);
if (i == FP_ILOGB0 || i == FP_ILOGBNAN)
  {
    if (isnan (f))
      {
        /* Handle NaN.  */
      }
    else if (f  == 0.0)
      {
        /* Handle 0.0.  */
      }
    else
      {
        /* Some other value with large exponent,
           perhaps +Inf.  */
      }
  }
```

double pow (*double base, double power*) [Function]
float powf (*float base, float power*) [Function]
long double powl (*long double base, long double power*) [Function]
_FloatN powfN (*_FloatN base, _FloatN power*) [Function]
_FloatNx powfNx (*_FloatNx base, _FloatNx power*) [Function]

> Preliminary: | MT-Safe | AS-Safe | AC-Safe | See Section 1.2.2.1 [POSIX Safety Concepts], page 2.
>
> These are general exponentiation functions, returning *base* raised to *power*.
>
> Mathematically, `pow` would return a complex number when *base* is negative and *power* is not an integral value. `pow` can't do that, so instead it signals a domain error. `pow` may also underflow or overflow the destination type.

double sqrt (*double x*) [Function]
float sqrtf (*float x*) [Function]
long double sqrtl (*long double x*) [Function]
_FloatN sqrtfN (*_FloatN x*) [Function]
_FloatNx sqrtfNx (*_FloatNx x*) [Function]

> Preliminary: | MT-Safe | AS-Safe | AC-Safe | See Section 1.2.2.1 [POSIX Safety Concepts], page 2.
>
> These functions return the nonnegative square root of *x*.

If x is negative, `sqrt` signals a domain error. Mathematically, it should return a complex number.

double cbrt (*double x*)   [Function]
float cbrtf (*float x*)   [Function]
long double cbrtl (*long double x*)   [Function]
_FloatN cbrtfN (*_FloatN x*)   [Function]
_FloatNx cbrtfNx (*_FloatNx x*)   [Function]

> Preliminary: | MT-Safe | AS-Safe | AC-Safe | See Section 1.2.2.1 [POSIX Safety Concepts], page 2.

> These functions return the cube root of x. They cannot fail; every representable real value has a representable real cube root.

double hypot (*double x, double y*)   [Function]
float hypotf (*float x, float y*)   [Function]
long double hypotl (*long double x, long double y*)   [Function]
_FloatN hypotfN (*_FloatN x, _FloatN y*)   [Function]
_FloatNx hypotfNx (*_FloatNx x, _FloatNx y*)   [Function]

> Preliminary: | MT-Safe | AS-Safe | AC-Safe | See Section 1.2.2.1 [POSIX Safety Concepts], page 2.

> These functions return `sqrt (x*x + y*y)`. This is the length of the hypotenuse of a right triangle with sides of length x and y, or the distance of the point (x, y) from the origin. Using this function instead of the direct formula is wise, since the error is much smaller. See also the function `cabs` in Section 20.8.1 [Absolute Value], page 591.

double expm1 (*double x*)   [Function]
float expm1f (*float x*)   [Function]
long double expm1l (*long double x*)   [Function]
_FloatN expm1fN (*_FloatN x*)   [Function]
_FloatNx expm1fNx (*_FloatNx x*)   [Function]

> Preliminary: | MT-Safe | AS-Safe | AC-Safe | See Section 1.2.2.1 [POSIX Safety Concepts], page 2.

> These functions return a value equivalent to `exp (x) - 1`. They are computed in a way that is accurate even if x is near zero—a case where `exp (x) - 1` would be inaccurate owing to subtraction of two numbers that are nearly equal.

double log1p (*double x*)   [Function]
float log1pf (*float x*)   [Function]
long double log1pl (*long double x*)   [Function]
_FloatN log1pfN (*_FloatN x*)   [Function]
_FloatNx log1pfNx (*_FloatNx x*)   [Function]

> Preliminary: | MT-Safe | AS-Safe | AC-Safe | See Section 1.2.2.1 [POSIX Safety Concepts], page 2.

> These functions return a value equivalent to `log (1 + x)`. They are computed in a way that is accurate even if x is near zero.

ISO C99 defines complex variants of some of the exponentiation and logarithm functions.

```
complex double cexp (complex double z)                          [Function]
complex float cexpf (complex float z)                           [Function]
complex long double cexpl (complex long double z)               [Function]
complex _FloatN cexpfN (complex _FloatN z)                      [Function]
complex _FloatNx cexpfNx (complex _FloatNx z)                   [Function]
```
Preliminary: | MT-Safe | AS-Safe | AC-Safe | See Section 1.2.2.1 [POSIX Safety Concepts], page 2.

These functions return e (the base of natural logarithms) raised to the power of z. Mathematically, this corresponds to the value

$$\exp(z) = e^z = e^{\operatorname{Re} z}(\cos(\operatorname{Im} z) + i \sin(\operatorname{Im} z))$$

```
complex double clog (complex double z)                          [Function]
complex float clogf (complex float z)                           [Function]
complex long double clogl (complex long double z)               [Function]
complex _FloatN clogfN (complex _FloatN z)                      [Function]
complex _FloatNx clogfNx (complex _FloatNx z)                   [Function]
```
Preliminary: | MT-Safe | AS-Safe | AC-Safe | See Section 1.2.2.1 [POSIX Safety Concepts], page 2.

These functions return the natural logarithm of z. Mathematically, this corresponds to the value

$$\log(z) = \log|z| + i \arg z$$

clog has a pole at 0, and will signal overflow if z equals or is very close to 0. It is well-defined for all other values of z.

```
complex double clog10 (complex double z)                        [Function]
complex float clog10f (complex float z)                         [Function]
complex long double clog10l (complex long double z)             [Function]
complex _FloatN clog10fN (complex _FloatN z)                    [Function]
complex _FloatNx clog10fNx (complex _FloatNx z)                 [Function]
```
Preliminary: | MT-Safe | AS-Safe | AC-Safe | See Section 1.2.2.1 [POSIX Safety Concepts], page 2.

These functions return the base 10 logarithm of the complex value z. Mathematically, this corresponds to the value

$$\log_{10}(z) = \log_{10}|z| + i \arg z / \log(10)$$

All these functions, including the _FloatN and _FloatNx variants, are GNU extensions.

```
complex double csqrt (complex double z)                         [Function]
complex float csqrtf (complex float z)                          [Function]
complex long double csqrtl (complex long double z)              [Function]
complex _FloatN csqrtfN (_FloatN z)                             [Function]
```

`complex _FloatNx csqrtfNx` (*complex _FloatNx* `z`) [Function]

Preliminary: | MT-Safe | AS-Safe | AC-Safe | See Section 1.2.2.1 [POSIX Safety Concepts], page 2.

These functions return the complex square root of the argument `z`. Unlike the real-valued functions, they are defined for all values of `z`.

`complex double cpow` (*complex double* `base`, *complex double* `power`) [Function]
`complex float cpowf` (*complex float* `base`, *complex float* `power`) [Function]
`complex long double cpowl` (*complex long double* `base`, *complex long double* `power`) [Function]
`complex _FloatN cpowfN` (*complex _FloatN* `base`, *complex _FloatN* `power`) [Function]
`complex _FloatNx cpowfNx` (*complex _FloatNx* `base`, *complex _FloatNx* `power`) [Function]

Preliminary: | MT-Safe | AS-Safe | AC-Safe | See Section 1.2.2.1 [POSIX Safety Concepts], page 2.

These functions return `base` raised to the power of `power`. This is equivalent to `cexp (y * clog (x))`

19.5 Hyperbolic Functions

The functions in this section are related to the exponential functions; see Section 19.4 [Exponentiation and Logarithms], page 530.

`double sinh` (*double* `x`) [Function]
`float sinhf` (*float* `x`) [Function]
`long double sinhl` (*long double* `x`) [Function]
`_FloatN sinhfN` (*_FloatN* `x`) [Function]
`_FloatNx sinhfNx` (*_FloatNx* `x`) [Function]

Preliminary: | MT-Safe | AS-Safe | AC-Safe | See Section 1.2.2.1 [POSIX Safety Concepts], page 2.

These functions return the hyperbolic sine of `x`, defined mathematically as `(exp (x) - exp (-x)) / 2`. They may signal overflow if `x` is too large.

`double cosh` (*double* `x`) [Function]
`float coshf` (*float* `x`) [Function]
`long double coshl` (*long double* `x`) [Function]
`_FloatN coshfN` (*_FloatN* `x`) [Function]
`_FloatNx coshfNx` (*_FloatNx* `x`) [Function]

Preliminary: | MT-Safe | AS-Safe | AC-Safe | See Section 1.2.2.1 [POSIX Safety Concepts], page 2.

These functions return the hyperbolic cosine of `x`, defined mathematically as `(exp (x) + exp (-x)) / 2`. They may signal overflow if `x` is too large.

`double tanh` (*double* `x`) [Function]
`float tanhf` (*float* `x`) [Function]
`long double tanhl` (*long double* `x`) [Function]
`_FloatN tanhfN` (*_FloatN* `x`) [Function]

_FloatNx tanhfNx (_FloatNx x)   [Function]
> Preliminary: | MT-Safe | AS-Safe | AC-Safe | See Section 1.2.2.1 [POSIX Safety
> Concepts], page 2.
>
> These functions return the hyperbolic tangent of x, defined mathematically as
> sinh (x) / cosh (x). They may signal overflow if x is too large.

There are counterparts for the hyperbolic functions which take complex arguments.

complex double csinh (*complex double z*)   [Function]
complex float csinhf (*complex float z*)   [Function]
complex long double csinhl (*complex long double z*)   [Function]
complex _FloatN csinhfN (*complex _FloatN z*)   [Function]
complex _FloatNx csinhfNx (*complex _FloatNx z*)   [Function]
> Preliminary: | MT-Safe | AS-Safe | AC-Safe | See Section 1.2.2.1 [POSIX Safety
> Concepts], page 2.
>
> These functions return the complex hyperbolic sine of z, defined mathematically as
> (exp (z) - exp (-z)) / 2.

complex double ccosh (*complex double z*)   [Function]
complex float ccoshf (*complex float z*)   [Function]
complex long double ccoshl (*complex long double z*)   [Function]
complex _FloatN ccoshfN (*complex _FloatN z*)   [Function]
complex _FloatNx ccoshfNx (*complex _FloatNx z*)   [Function]
> Preliminary: | MT-Safe | AS-Safe | AC-Safe | See Section 1.2.2.1 [POSIX Safety
> Concepts], page 2.
>
> These functions return the complex hyperbolic cosine of z, defined mathematically as
> (exp (z) + exp (-z)) / 2.

complex double ctanh (*complex double z*)   [Function]
complex float ctanhf (*complex float z*)   [Function]
complex long double ctanhl (*complex long double z*)   [Function]
complex _FloatN ctanhfN (*complex _FloatN z*)   [Function]
complex _FloatNx ctanhfNx (*complex _FloatNx z*)   [Function]
> Preliminary: | MT-Safe | AS-Safe | AC-Safe | See Section 1.2.2.1 [POSIX Safety
> Concepts], page 2.
>
> These functions return the complex hyperbolic tangent of z, defined mathematically
> as csinh (z) / ccosh (z).

double asinh (*double x*)   [Function]
float asinhf (*float x*)   [Function]
long double asinhl (*long double x*)   [Function]
_FloatN asinhfN (_FloatN x)   [Function]
_FloatNx asinhfNx (_FloatNx x)   [Function]
> Preliminary: | MT-Safe | AS-Safe | AC-Safe | See Section 1.2.2.1 [POSIX Safety
> Concepts], page 2.
>
> These functions return the inverse hyperbolic sine of x—the value whose hyperbolic
> sine is x.

double acosh (*double x*)   [Function]
float acoshf (*float x*)   [Function]
long double acoshl (*long double x*)   [Function]
_FloatN acoshfN (*_FloatN x*)   [Function]
_FloatNx acoshfNx (*_FloatNx x*)   [Function]
> Preliminary: | MT-Safe | AS-Safe | AC-Safe | See Section 1.2.2.1 [POSIX Safety Concepts], page 2.

> These functions return the inverse hyperbolic cosine of x—the value whose hyperbolic cosine is x. If x is less than 1, `acosh` signals a domain error.

double atanh (*double x*)   [Function]
float atanhf (*float x*)   [Function]
long double atanhl (*long double x*)   [Function]
_FloatN atanhfN (*_FloatN x*)   [Function]
_FloatNx atanhfNx (*_FloatNx x*)   [Function]
> Preliminary: | MT-Safe | AS-Safe | AC-Safe | See Section 1.2.2.1 [POSIX Safety Concepts], page 2.

> These functions return the inverse hyperbolic tangent of x—the value whose hyperbolic tangent is x. If the absolute value of x is greater than 1, `atanh` signals a domain error; if it is equal to 1, `atanh` returns infinity.

complex double casinh (*complex double z*)   [Function]
complex float casinhf (*complex float z*)   [Function]
complex long double casinhl (*complex long double z*)   [Function]
complex _FloatN casinhfN (*complex _FloatN z*)   [Function]
complex _FloatNx casinhfNx (*complex _FloatNx z*)   [Function]
> Preliminary: | MT-Safe | AS-Safe | AC-Safe | See Section 1.2.2.1 [POSIX Safety Concepts], page 2.

> These functions return the inverse complex hyperbolic sine of z—the value whose complex hyperbolic sine is z.

complex double cacosh (*complex double z*)   [Function]
complex float cacoshf (*complex float z*)   [Function]
complex long double cacoshl (*complex long double z*)   [Function]
complex _FloatN cacoshfN (*complex _FloatN z*)   [Function]
complex _FloatNx cacoshfNx (*complex _FloatNx z*)   [Function]
> Preliminary: | MT-Safe | AS-Safe | AC-Safe | See Section 1.2.2.1 [POSIX Safety Concepts], page 2.

> These functions return the inverse complex hyperbolic cosine of z—the value whose complex hyperbolic cosine is z. Unlike the real-valued functions, there are no restrictions on the value of z.

complex double catanh (*complex double z*)   [Function]
complex float catanhf (*complex float z*)   [Function]
complex long double catanhl (*complex long double z*)   [Function]
complex _FloatN catanhfN (*complex _FloatN z*)   [Function]

complex _FloatNx catanhfNx (*complex _FloatNx z*)　　　　　　[Function]
> Preliminary: | MT-Safe | AS-Safe | AC-Safe | See Section 1.2.2.1 [POSIX Safety Concepts], page 2.

> These functions return the inverse complex hyperbolic tangent of *z*—the value whose complex hyperbolic tangent is *z*. Unlike the real-valued functions, there are no restrictions on the value of *z*.

19.6 Special Functions

These are some more exotic mathematical functions which are sometimes useful. Currently they only have real-valued versions.

double erf (*double x*)　　　　　　　　　　　　　　　　　　　[Function]
float erff (*float x*)　　　　　　　　　　　　　　　　　　　　[Function]
long double erfl (*long double x*)　　　　　　　　　　　　　　[Function]
_FloatN erffN (*_FloatN x*)　　　　　　　　　　　　　　　　　[Function]
_FloatNx erffNx (*_FloatNx x*)　　　　　　　　　　　　　　　[Function]
> Preliminary: | MT-Safe | AS-Safe | AC-Safe | See Section 1.2.2.1 [POSIX Safety Concepts], page 2.

> erf returns the error function of *x*. The error function is defined as

$$\operatorname{erf}(x) = \frac{2}{\sqrt{\pi}} \cdot \int_0^x e^{-t^2} \mathrm{d}t$$

double erfc (*double x*)　　　　　　　　　　　　　　　　　　[Function]
float erfcf (*float x*)　　　　　　　　　　　　　　　　　　　[Function]
long double erfcl (*long double x*)　　　　　　　　　　　　　[Function]
_FloatN erfcfN (*_FloatN x*)　　　　　　　　　　　　　　　　[Function]
_FloatNx erfcfNx (*_FloatNx x*)　　　　　　　　　　　　　　　[Function]
> Preliminary: | MT-Safe | AS-Safe | AC-Safe | See Section 1.2.2.1 [POSIX Safety Concepts], page 2.

> erfc returns 1.0 - erf(x), but computed in a fashion that avoids round-off error when *x* is large.

double lgamma (*double x*)　　　　　　　　　　　　　　　　　[Function]
float lgammaf (*float x*)　　　　　　　　　　　　　　　　　　[Function]
long double lgammal (*long double x*)　　　　　　　　　　　　[Function]
_FloatN lgammafN (*_FloatN x*)　　　　　　　　　　　　　　　[Function]
_FloatNx lgammafNx (*_FloatNx x*)　　　　　　　　　　　　　[Function]
> Preliminary: | MT-Unsafe race:signgam | AS-Unsafe | AC-Safe | See Section 1.2.2.1 [POSIX Safety Concepts], page 2.

> lgamma returns the natural logarithm of the absolute value of the gamma function of *x*. The gamma function is defined as

$$\Gamma(x) = \int_0^\infty t^{x-1} e^{-t} \mathrm{d}t$$

The sign of the gamma function is stored in the global variable *signgam*, which is declared in math.h. It is 1 if the intermediate result was positive or zero, or -1 if it was negative.

To compute the real gamma function you can use the `tgamma` function or you can compute the values as follows:

```
lgam = lgamma(x);
gam  = signgam*exp(lgam);
```

The gamma function has singularities at the non-positive integers. `lgamma` will raise the zero divide exception if evaluated at a singularity.

double `lgamma_r` (*double x, int *signp*)	[Function]
float `lgammaf_r` (*float x, int *signp*)	[Function]
long double `lgammal_r` (*long double x, int *signp*)	[Function]
_FloatN `lgammafN_r` (*_FloatN x, int *signp*)	[Function]
_FloatNx `lgammafNx_r` (*_FloatNx x, int *signp*)	[Function]

Preliminary: | MT-Safe | AS-Safe | AC-Safe | See Section 1.2.2.1 [POSIX Safety Concepts], page 2.

`lgamma_r` is just like `lgamma`, but it stores the sign of the intermediate result in the variable pointed to by *signp* instead of in the *signgam* global. This means it is reentrant.

The `lgammafN_r` and `lgammafNx_r` functions are GNU extensions.

double `gamma` (*double x*)	[Function]
float `gammaf` (*float x*)	[Function]
long double `gammal` (*long double x*)	[Function]

Preliminary: | MT-Unsafe race:signgam | AS-Unsafe | AC-Safe | See Section 1.2.2.1 [POSIX Safety Concepts], page 2.

These functions exist for compatibility reasons. They are equivalent to `lgamma` etc. It is better to use `lgamma` since for one the name reflects better the actual computation, and moreover `lgamma` is standardized in ISO C99 while `gamma` is not.

double `tgamma` (*double x*)	[Function]
float `tgammaf` (*float x*)	[Function]
long double `tgammal` (*long double x*)	[Function]
_FloatN `tgammafN` (*_FloatN x*)	[Function]
_FloatNx `tgammafNx` (*_FloatNx x*)	[Function]

Preliminary: | MT-Safe | AS-Safe | AC-Safe | See Section 1.2.2.1 [POSIX Safety Concepts], page 2.

`tgamma` applies the gamma function to *x*. The gamma function is defined as

$$\Gamma(x) = \int_0^\infty t^{x-1} e^{-t} \mathrm{d}t$$

This function was introduced in ISO C99. The _FloatN and _FloatNx variants were introduced in ISO/IEC TS 18661-3.

double `j0` (*double x*)	[Function]
float `j0f` (*float x*)	[Function]
long double `j0l` (*long double x*)	[Function]
_FloatN `j0fN` (*_FloatN x*)	[Function]

_FloatNx j0fNx (_FloatNx x)   [Function]
> Preliminary: | MT-Safe | AS-Safe | AC-Safe | See Section 1.2.2.1 [POSIX Safety
> Concepts], page 2.
>
> j0 returns the Bessel function of the first kind of order 0 of x. It may signal underflow
> if x is too large.
>
> The _FloatN and _FloatNx variants are GNU extensions.

double j1 (double x)   [Function]
float j1f (float x)   [Function]
long double j1l (long double x)   [Function]
_FloatN j1fN (_FloatN x)   [Function]
_FloatNx j1fNx (_FloatNx x)   [Function]
> Preliminary: | MT-Safe | AS-Safe | AC-Safe | See Section 1.2.2.1 [POSIX Safety
> Concepts], page 2.
>
> j1 returns the Bessel function of the first kind of order 1 of x. It may signal underflow
> if x is too large.
>
> The _FloatN and _FloatNx variants are GNU extensions.

double jn (int n, double x)   [Function]
float jnf (int n, float x)   [Function]
long double jnl (int n, long double x)   [Function]
_FloatN jnfN (int n, _FloatN x)   [Function]
_FloatNx jnfNx (int n, _FloatNx x)   [Function]
> Preliminary: | MT-Safe | AS-Safe | AC-Safe | See Section 1.2.2.1 [POSIX Safety
> Concepts], page 2.
>
> jn returns the Bessel function of the first kind of order n of x. It may signal underflow
> if x is too large.
>
> The _FloatN and _FloatNx variants are GNU extensions.

double y0 (double x)   [Function]
float y0f (float x)   [Function]
long double y0l (long double x)   [Function]
_FloatN y0fN (_FloatN x)   [Function]
_FloatNx y0fNx (_FloatNx x)   [Function]
> Preliminary: | MT-Safe | AS-Safe | AC-Safe | See Section 1.2.2.1 [POSIX Safety
> Concepts], page 2.
>
> y0 returns the Bessel function of the second kind of order 0 of x. It may signal
> underflow if x is too large. If x is negative, y0 signals a domain error; if it is zero, y0
> signals overflow and returns $-\infty$.
>
> The _FloatN and _FloatNx variants are GNU extensions.

double y1 (double x)   [Function]
float y1f (float x)   [Function]
long double y1l (long double x)   [Function]
_FloatN y1fN (_FloatN x)   [Function]

`_FloatNx y1fNx` (_*FloatNx x*)   [Function]

> Preliminary: | MT-Safe | AS-Safe | AC-Safe | See Section 1.2.2.1 [POSIX Safety Concepts], page 2.

> y1 returns the Bessel function of the second kind of order 1 of *x*. It may signal underflow if *x* is too large. If *x* is negative, y1 signals a domain error; if it is zero, y1 signals overflow and returns $-\infty$.

> The `_FloatN` and `_FloatNx` variants are GNU extensions.

`double yn` (*int n, double x*)   [Function]
`float ynf` (*int n, float x*)   [Function]
`long double ynl` (*int n, long double x*)   [Function]
`_FloatN ynfN` (*int n, _FloatN x*)   [Function]
`_FloatNx ynfNx` (*int n, _FloatNx x*)   [Function]

> Preliminary: | MT-Safe | AS-Safe | AC-Safe | See Section 1.2.2.1 [POSIX Safety Concepts], page 2.

> yn returns the Bessel function of the second kind of order *n* of *x*. It may signal underflow if *x* is too large. If *x* is negative, yn signals a domain error; if it is zero, yn signals overflow and returns $-\infty$.

> The `_FloatN` and `_FloatNx` variants are GNU extensions.

19.7 Known Maximum Errors in Math Functions

This section lists the known errors of the functions in the math library. Errors are measured in "units of the last place". This is a measure for the relative error. For a number z with the representation $d.d \ldots d \cdot 2^e$ (we assume IEEE floating-point numbers with base 2) the ULP is represented by

$$\frac{|d.d \ldots d - (z/2^e)|}{2^{p-1}}$$

where p is the number of bits in the mantissa of the floating-point number representation. Ideally the error for all functions is always less than 0.5ulps in round-to-nearest mode. Using rounding bits this is also possible and normally implemented for the basic operations. Except for certain functions such as `sqrt`, `fma` and `rint` whose results are fully specified by reference to corresponding IEEE 754 floating-point operations, and conversions between strings and floating point, the GNU C Library does not aim for correctly rounded results for functions in the math library, and does not aim for correctness in whether "inexact" exceptions are raised. Instead, the goals for accuracy of functions without fully specified results are as follows; some functions have bugs meaning they do not meet these goals in all cases. In the future, the GNU C Library may provide some other correctly rounding functions under the names such as `crsin` proposed for an extension to ISO C.

- Each function with a floating-point result behaves as if it computes an infinite-precision result that is within a few ulp (in both real and complex parts, for functions with complex results) of the mathematically correct value of the function (interpreted together with ISO C or POSIX semantics for the function in question) at the exact value passed as the input. Exceptions are raised appropriately for this value and in accordance with

IEEE 754 / ISO C / POSIX semantics, and it is then rounded according to the current rounding direction to the result that is returned to the user. `errno` may also be set (see Section 20.5.4 [Error Reporting by Mathematical Functions], page 586). (The "inexact" exception may be raised, or not raised, even if this is inconsistent with the infinite-precision value.)

- For the IBM `long double` format, as used on PowerPC GNU/Linux, the accuracy goal is weaker for input values not exactly representable in 106 bits of precision; it is as if the input value is some value within 0.5ulp of the value actually passed, where "ulp" is interpreted in terms of a fixed-precision 106-bit mantissa, but not necessarily the exact value actually passed with discontiguous mantissa bits.

- For the IBM `long double` format, functions whose results are fully specified by reference to corresponding IEEE 754 floating-point operations have the same accuracy goals as other functions, but with the error bound being the same as that for division (3ulp). Furthermore, "inexact" and "underflow" exceptions may be raised for all functions for any inputs, even where such exceptions are inconsistent with the returned value, since the underlying floating-point arithmetic has that property.

- Functions behave as if the infinite-precision result computed is zero, infinity or NaN if and only if that is the mathematically correct infinite-precision result. They behave as if the infinite-precision result computed always has the same sign as the mathematically correct result.

- If the mathematical result is more than a few ulp above the overflow threshold for the current rounding direction, the value returned is the appropriate overflow value for the current rounding direction, with the overflow exception raised.

- If the mathematical result has magnitude well below half the least subnormal magnitude, the returned value is either zero or the least subnormal (in each case, with the correct sign), according to the current rounding direction and with the underflow exception raised.

- Where the mathematical result underflows (before rounding) and is not exactly representable as a floating-point value, the function does not behave as if the computed infinite-precision result is an exact value in the subnormal range. This means that the underflow exception is raised other than possibly for cases where the mathematical result is very close to the underflow threshold and the function behaves as if it computes an infinite-precision result that does not underflow. (So there may be spurious underflow exceptions in cases where the underflowing result is exact, but not missing underflow exceptions in cases where it is inexact.)

- The GNU C Library does not aim for functions to satisfy other properties of the underlying mathematical function, such as monotonicity, where not implied by the above goals.

- All the above applies to both real and complex parts, for complex functions.

Therefore many of the functions in the math library have errors. The table lists the maximum error for each function which is exposed by one of the existing tests in the test suite. The table tries to cover as much as possible and list the actual maximum error (or at least a ballpark figure) but this is often not achieved due to the large search space.

The table lists the ULP values for different architectures. Different architectures have different results since their hardware support for floating-point operations varies and also the existing hardware support is different. Only the round-to-nearest rounding mode is covered by this table, and vector versions of functions are not covered. Functions not listed do not have known errors.

Function	AArch64	ARM	Alpha	ColdFire	Generic
acosf	1	1	1	-	-
acos	-	-	-	-	-
acosl	1	-	1	-	-
acosf128	-	-	-	-	-
acoshf	2	2	2	-	-
acosh	2	2	2	-	-
acoshl	2	-	2	-	-
acoshf128	-	-	-	-	-
asinf	1	1	1	-	-
asin	-	-	-	-	-
asinl	1	-	1	-	-
asinf128	-	-	-	-	-
asinhf	1	1	1	-	-
asinh	1	1	1	-	-
asinhl	3	-	3	-	-
asinhf128	-	-	-	-	-
atanf	1	1	1	-	-
atan	1	-	-	-	-
atanl	1	-	1	-	-
atanf128	-	-	-	-	-
atan2f	1	1	1	1	-
atan2	-	-	-	-	-
atan2l	1	-	1	-	-
atan2f128	-	-	-	-	-
atanhf	2	2	2	1	-
atanh	2	2	2	-	-
atanhl	3	-	3	-	-
atanhf128	-	-	-	-	-
cabsf	-	-	-	-	-
cabs	1	1	1	-	-
cabsl	1	-	1	-	-
cabsf128	-	-	-	-	-
cacosf	2 + i 2	2 + i 2	2 + i 2	-	-
cacos	1 + i 2	1 + i 2	1 + i 2	-	-
cacosl	2 + i 2	-	2 + i 2	-	-
cacosf128	-	-	-	-	-
cacoshf	2 + i 2	2 + i 2	2 + i 2	0 + i 1	-
cacosh	2 + i 1	2 + i 1	2 + i 1	-	-
cacoshl	2 + i 2	-	2 + i 2	-	-
cacoshf128	-	-	-	-	-
cargf	1	1	1	-	-
carg	1	-	-	-	-
cargl	2	-	2	-	-
cargf128	-	-	-	-	-
casinf	1 + i 2	1 + i 2	1 + i 2	1 + i 0	-
casin	1 + i 2	1 + i 2	1 + i 2	1 + i 0	-

casinl	2 + i 2	-	2 + i 2	-	-
casinf128	-	-	-	-	-
casinhf	2 + i 1	2 + i 1	2 + i 1	1 + i 6	-
casinh	2 + i 1	2 + i 1	2 + i 1	5 + i 3	-
casinhl	2 + i 2	-	2 + i 2	-	-
casinhf128	-	-	-	-	-
catanf	1 + i 1	1 + i 1	1 + i 1	0 + i 1	-
catan	1 + i 1	1 + i 1	1 + i 1	0 + i 1	-
catanl	1 + i 1	-	1 + i 1	-	-
catanf128	-	-	-	-	-
catanhf	1 + i 1	1 + i 1	1 + i 1	-	-
catanh	1 + i 1	1 + i 1	1 + i 1	4 + i 0	-
catanhl	1 + i 1	-	1 + i 1	-	-
catanhf128	-	-	-	-	-
cbrtf	1	1	1	-	-
cbrt	3	3	3	1	-
cbrtl	1	-	1	-	-
cbrtf128	-	-	-	-	-
ccosf	1 + i 1	1 + i 1	1 + i 1	1 + i 1	-
ccos	1 + i 1	1 + i 1	1 + i 1	1 + i 0	-
ccosl	1 + i 1	-	1 + i 1	-	-
ccosf128	-	-	-	-	-
ccoshf	1 + i 1	1 + i 1	1 + i 1	1 + i 1	-
ccosh	1 + i 1	1 + i 1	1 + i 1	1 + i 0	-
ccoshl	1 + i 1	-	1 + i 1	-	-
ccoshf128	-	-	-	-	-
cexpf	1 + i 2	1 + i 2	1 + i 2	1 + i 1	-
cexp	2 + i 1	2 + i 1	2 + i 1	-	-
cexpl	1 + i 1	-	1 + i 1	-	-
cexpf128	-	-	-	-	-
clogf	3 + i 1	3 + i 1	3 + i 1	1 + i 0	-
clog	3 + i 1	3 + i 0	3 + i 0	-	-
clogl	2 + i 1	-	2 + i 1	-	-
clogf128	-	-	-	-	-
clog10f	4 + i 2	4 + i 2	4 + i 2	1 + i 1	-
clog10	3 + i 2	3 + i 2	3 + i 2	0 + i 1	-
clog10l	2 + i 2	-	2 + i 2	-	-
clog10f128	-	-	-	-	-
cosf	1	1	1	1	-
cos	-	-	-	2	-
cosl	1	-	1	-	-
cosf128	-	-	-	-	-
coshf	1	1	1	-	-
cosh	1	1	1	-	-
coshl	1	-	1	-	-
coshf128	-	-	-	-	-
cpowf	5 + i 2	4 + i 2	4 + i 2	4 + i 2	-

cpow	2 + i 0	2 + i 0	2 + i 0	2 + i 2	-
cpowl	4 + i 1	-	4 + i 1	-	-
cpowf128	-	-	-	-	-
csinf	1 + i 0	1 + i 0	1 + i 0	-	-
csin	1 + i 0	1 + i 0	1 + i 0	-	-
csinl	1 + i 1	-	1 + i 1	-	-
csinf128	-	-	-	-	-
csinhf	1 + i 1	1 + i 1	1 + i 1	1 + i 1	-
csinh	0 + i 1	0 + i 1	0 + i 1	0 + i 1	-
csinhl	1 + i 1	-	1 + i 1	-	-
csinhf128	-	-	-	-	-
csqrtf	2 + i 2	2 + i 2	2 + i 2	1 + i 0	-
csqrt	2 + i 2	2 + i 2	2 + i 2	-	-
csqrtl	2 + i 2	-	2 + i 2	-	-
csqrtf128	-	-	-	-	-
ctanf	1 + i 1	1 + i 1	1 + i 1	-	-
ctan	1 + i 2	1 + i 2	1 + i 2	0 + i 1	-
ctanl	3 + i 3	-	3 + i 3	-	-
ctanf128	-	-	-	-	-
ctanhf	2 + i 1	1 + i 2	1 + i 2	2 + i 1	-
ctanh	2 + i 2	2 + i 2	2 + i 2	1 + i 0	-
ctanhl	3 + i 3	-	3 + i 3	-	-
ctanhf128	-	-	-	-	-
erff	1	1	1	-	-
erf	1	1	1	1	-
erfl	1	-	1	-	-
erff128	-	-	-	-	-
erfcf	2	2	2	-	-
erfc	2	3	3	1	-
erfcl	2	-	2	-	-
erfcf128	-	-	-	-	-
expf	1	1	1	-	-
exp	-	-	-	-	-
expl	1	-	1	-	-
expf128	-	-	-	-	-
exp10f	-	-	-	2	-
exp10	2	2	2	6	-
exp10l	2	-	2	-	-
exp10f128	-	-	-	-	-
exp2f	1	1	1	-	-
exp2	1	1	1	-	-
exp2l	1	-	1	-	-
exp2f128	-	-	-	-	-
expm1f	1	1	1	1	-
expm1	1	1	1	1	-
expm1l	1	-	1	-	-
expm1f128	-	-	-	-	-

fmaf	-	-	-	-	-
fma	-	-	-	-	-
fmal	-	-	-	-	-
fmaf128	-	-	-	-	-
fmodf	-	-	-	-	-
fmod	-	-	-	-	-
fmodl	-	-	-	-	-
fmodf128	-	-	-	-	-
gammaf	4	4	4	-	-
gamma	3	4	4	-	-
gammal	5	-	5	-	-
gammaf128	-	-	-	-	-
hypotf	-	-	-	1	-
hypot	1	1	1	-	-
hypotl	1	-	1	-	-
hypotf128	-	-	-	-	-
j0f	2	2	2	2	-
j0	2	2	2	2	-
j0l	2	-	2	-	-
j0f128	-	-	-	-	-
j1f	2	2	2	2	-
j1	1	1	1	1	-
j1l	4	-	4	-	-
j1f128	-	-	-	-	-
jnf	4	4	4	4	-
jn	4	4	4	4	-
jnl	7	-	7	-	-
jnf128	-	-	-	-	-
lgammaf	4	4	4	2	-
lgamma	3	4	4	1	-
lgammal	5	-	5	-	-
lgammaf128	-	-	-	-	-
logf	1	1	1	-	-
log	-	-	-	-	-
logl	1	-	1	-	-
logf128	-	-	-	-	-
log10f	2	2	2	2	-
log10	2	2	2	1	-
log10l	1	-	1	-	-
log10f128	-	-	-	-	-
log1pf	1	1	1	1	-
log1p	1	1	1	-	-
log1pl	2	-	2	-	-
log1pf128	-	-	-	-	-
log2f	1	1	1	-	-
log2	1	2	2	-	-
log2l	2	-	2	-	-

log2f128	-	-	-	-	-
powf	1	1	1	-	-
pow	-	-	-	-	-
powl	2	-	2	-	-
powf128	-	-	-	-	-
pow10f	-	-	-	-	-
pow10	2	2	2	-	-
pow10l	2	-	2	-	-
pow10f128	-	-	-	-	-
sinf	1	1	1	-	-
sin	-	-	-	-	-
sinl	1	-	1	-	-
sinf128	-	-	-	-	-
sincosf	1	1	1	1	-
sincos	-	-	-	1	-
sincosl	1	-	1	-	-
sincosf128	-	-	-	-	-
sinhf	2	2	2	-	-
sinh	2	2	2	-	-
sinhl	2	-	2	-	-
sinhf128	-	-	-	-	-
sqrtf	-	-	-	-	-
sqrt	-	-	-	-	-
sqrtl	-	-	-	-	-
sqrtf128	-	-	-	-	-
tanf	1	1	1	-	-
tan	-	-	-	1	-
tanl	1	-	1	-	-
tanf128	-	-	-	-	-
tanhf	2	2	2	-	-
tanh	2	2	2	-	-
tanhl	2	-	2	-	-
tanhf128	-	-	-	-	-
tgammaf	4	4	4	1	-
tgamma	5	5	5	1	-
tgammal	4	-	4	-	-
tgammaf128	-	-	-	-	-
y0f	1	1	1	1	-
y0	2	2	2	2	-
y0l	3	-	3	-	-
y0f128	-	-	-	-	-
y1f	2	2	2	2	-
y1	3	3	3	3	-
y1l	2	-	2	-	-
y1f128	-	-	-	-	-
ynf	2	2	2	2	-
yn	3	3	3	3	-

Function	HPPA	IA64	M68k	MIPS 32-bit	MIPS 64-bit
ynl	5	-	5	-	-
ynf128	-	-	-	-	-
acosf	1	-	-	1	1
acos	-	-	-	-	-
acosl	-	-	-	-	1
acosf128	-	-	-	-	-
acoshf	2	-	1	2	2
acosh	2	-	1	2	2
acoshl	-	-	1	-	2
acoshf128	-	-	-	-	-
asinf	1	-	-	1	1
asin	-	-	-	-	-
asinl	-	-	-	-	1
asinf128	-	-	-	-	-
asinhf	1	-	1	1	1
asinh	1	-	1	1	1
asinhl	-	-	1	-	3
asinhf128	-	-	-	-	-
atanf	1	-	-	1	1
atan	-	-	-	-	-
atanl	-	-	-	-	1
atanf128	-	-	-	-	-
atan2f	1	-	1	1	1
atan2	-	-	-	-	-
atan2l	-	-	1	-	1
atan2f128	-	-	-	-	-
atanhf	2	-	-	2	2
atanh	2	-	-	2	2
atanhl	-	-	-	-	3
atanhf128	-	-	-	-	-
cabsf	-	-	-	-	-
cabs	1	-	1	1	1
cabsl	-	-	1	-	1
cabsf128	-	-	-	-	-
cacosf	2 + i 2	2 + i 2	2 + i 1	2 + i 2	2 + i 2
cacos	1 + i 2	1 + i 1	1 + i 1	1 + i 2	1 + i 2
cacosl	-	1 + i 2	1 + i 2	-	2 + i 2
cacosf128	-	-	-	-	-
cacoshf	2 + i 2	2 + i 2	1 + i 2	2 + i 2	2 + i 2
cacosh	2 + i 1	1 + i 1	1 + i 1	2 + i 1	2 + i 1
cacoshl	-	2 + i 1	2 + i 1	-	2 + i 2
cacoshf128	-	-	-	-	-
cargf	1	-	1	1	1
carg	-	-	-	-	-
cargl	-	-	1	-	2

cargf128	-	-	-	-	-
casinf	1 + i 2	1 + i 2	1 + i 1	1 + i 2	1 + i 2
casin	1 + i 2	1 + i 1	1 + i 1	1 + i 2	1 + i 2
casinl	1 + i 0	1 + i 2	1 + i 2	-	2 + i 2
casinf128	-	-	-	-	-
casinhf	2 + i 1	2 + i 1	1 + i 1	2 + i 1	2 + i 1
casinh	5 + i 3	1 + i 1	1 + i 1	2 + i 1	2 + i 1
casinhl	5 + i 3	2 + i 1	2 + i 1	-	2 + i 2
casinhf128	-	-	-	-	-
catanf	1 + i 1	0 + i 1	0 + i 1	1 + i 1	1 + i 1
catan	1 + i 1	0 + i 1	0 + i 1	1 + i 1	1 + i 1
catanl	0 + i 1	0 + i 1	1 + i 1	-	1 + i 1
catanf128	-	-	-	-	-
catanhf	1 + i 1	1 + i 0	1 + i 0	1 + i 1	1 + i 1
catanh	4 + i 1	1 + i 0	1 + i 0	1 + i 1	1 + i 1
catanhl	4 + i 0	1 + i 0	1 + i 1	-	1 + i 1
catanhf128	-	-	-	-	-
cbrtf	1	-	1	1	1
cbrt	3	-	1	3	3
cbrtl	1	-	1	-	1
cbrtf128	-	-	-	-	-
ccosf	1 + i 1	0 + i 1	-	1 + i 1	1 + i 1
ccos	1 + i 1	1 + i 1	-	1 + i 1	1 + i 1
ccosl	1 + i 0	1 + i 1	1 + i 1	-	1 + i 1
ccosf128	-	-	-	-	-
ccoshf	1 + i 1	1 + i 1	-	1 + i 1	1 + i 1
ccosh	1 + i 1	1 + i 1	-	1 + i 1	1 + i 1
ccoshl	1 + i 0	0 + i 1	0 + i 1	-	1 + i 1
ccoshf128	-	-	-	-	-
cexpf	1 + i 2	1 + i 2	-	1 + i 2	1 + i 2
cexp	2 + i 1	2 + i 1	-	2 + i 1	2 + i 1
cexpl	-	1 + i 1	1 + i 1	-	1 + i 1
cexpf128	-	-	-	-	-
clogf	3 + i 1	1 + i 0	2 + i 1	3 + i 1	3 + i 1
clog	3 + i 0	1 + i 1	3 + i 1	3 + i 0	3 + i 0
clogl	-	1 + i 1	3 + i 1	-	2 + i 1
clogf128	-	-	-	-	-
clog10f	4 + i 2	2 + i 1	2 + i 1	4 + i 2	4 + i 2
clog10	3 + i 2	2 + i 1	2 + i 1	3 + i 2	3 + i 2
clog10l	0 + i 1	1 + i 1	3 + i 2	-	2 + i 2
clog10f128	-	-	-	-	-
cosf	1	-	-	1	1
cos	2	1	1	-	-
cosl	2	-	-	-	1
cosf128	-	-	-	-	-
coshf	1	-	-	1	1
cosh	1	-	-	1	1

coshl	-	-	-	-	1
coshf128	-	-	-	-	-
cpowf	4 + i 2	5 + i 2	3 + i 5	4 + i 2	4 + i 2
cpow	2 + i 2	2 + i 0	1 + i 0	2 + i 0	2 + i 0
cpowl	2 + i 2	3 + i 4	3 + i 1	-	4 + i 1
cpowf128	-	-	-	-	-
csinf	1 + i 0	1 + i 1	-	1 + i 0	1 + i 0
csin	1 + i 0	1 + i 0	-	1 + i 0	1 + i 0
csinl	-	1 + i 0	1 + i 0	-	1 + i 1
csinf128	-	-	-	-	-
csinhf	1 + i 1	1 + i 1	-	1 + i 1	1 + i 1
csinh	0 + i 1	1 + i 1	-	0 + i 1	0 + i 1
csinhl	0 + i 1	1 + i 0	1 + i 0	-	1 + i 1
csinhf128	-	-	-	-	-
csqrtf	2 + i 2	1 + i 1	1 + i 1	2 + i 2	2 + i 2
csqrt	2 + i 2	1 + i 1	1 + i 1	2 + i 2	2 + i 2
csqrtl	-	1 + i 1	2 + i 2	-	2 + i 2
csqrtf128	-	-	-	-	-
ctanf	1 + i 1	1 + i 1	1 + i 1	1 + i 1	1 + i 1
ctan	1 + i 2	1 + i 2	1 + i 1	1 + i 2	1 + i 2
ctanl	0 + i 1	2 + i 2	2 + i 2	-	3 + i 3
ctanf128	-	-	-	-	-
ctanhf	1 + i 2	1 + i 1	1 + i 2	1 + i 2	1 + i 2
ctanh	2 + i 2	2 + i 2	1 + i 1	2 + i 2	2 + i 2
ctanhl	1 + i 0	1 + i 2	2 + i 2	-	3 + i 3
ctanhf128	-	-	-	-	-
erff	1	-	1	1	1
erf	1	-	-	1	1
erfl	1	-	1	-	1
erff128	-	-	-	-	-
erfcf	2	-	1	2	2
erfc	3	-	-	3	3
erfcl	1	-	2	-	2
erfcf128	-	-	-	-	-
expf	1	-	-	1	1
exp	-	-	-	-	-
expl	-	-	-	-	1
expf128	-	-	-	-	-
exp10f	2	-	-	-	-
exp10	6	-	-	2	2
exp10l	6	-	-	-	2
exp10f128	-	-	-	-	-
exp2f	1	-	-	1	1
exp2	1	-	1	1	1
exp2l	-	-	-	-	1
exp2f128	-	-	-	-	-
expm1f	1	-	-	1	1

expm1	1	-	-	1	1
expm1l	1	1	-	-	1
expm1f128	-	-	-	-	-
fmaf	-	-	-	-	-
fma	-	-	-	-	-
fmal	-	-	-	-	-
fmaf128	-	-	-	-	-
fmodf	-	-	-	-	-
fmod	-	-	-	-	-
fmodl	-	-	-	-	-
fmodf128	-	-	-	-	-
gammaf	4	-	1	4	4
gamma	4	-	-	4	4
gammal	-	-	2	-	5
gammaf128	-	-	-	-	-
hypotf	1	-	-	-	-
hypot	1	-	1	1	1
hypotl	-	-	1	-	1
hypotf128	-	-	-	-	-
j0f	2	2	2	2	2
j0	2	2	1	2	2
j0l	2	2	2	-	2
j0f128	-	-	-	-	-
j1f	2	2	2	2	2
j1	1	1	-	1	1
j1l	1	1	1	-	4
j1f128	-	-	-	-	-
jnf	5	4	2	4	4
jn	4	4	2	4	4
jnl	4	4	4	-	7
jnf128	-	-	-	-	-
lgammaf	4	-	1	4	4
lgamma	4	-	-	4	4
lgammal	1	-	2	-	5
lgammaf128	-	-	-	-	-
logf	1	-	-	1	1
log	-	-	-	-	-
logl	-	-	-	-	1
logf128	-	-	-	-	-
log10f	2	-	-	2	2
log10	2	-	-	2	2
log10l	1	-	-	-	1
log10f128	-	-	-	-	-
log1pf	1	-	-	1	1
log1p	1	-	-	1	1
log1pl	-	-	-	-	2
log1pf128	-	-	-	-	-

log2f	1	-	-	1	1
log2	2	-	-	2	2
log2l	-	-	-	-	2
log2f128	-	-	-	-	-
powf	1	-	7	1	1
pow	-	-	1	-	-
powl	-	-	9	-	2
powf128	-	-	-	-	-
pow10f	-	-	-	-	-
pow10	2	-	-	2	2
pow10l	-	-	-	-	2
pow10f128	-	-	-	-	-
sinf	1	-	-	1	1
sin	-	1	1	-	-
sinl	-	-	-	-	1
sinf128	-	-	-	-	-
sincosf	1	-	-	1	1
sincos	1	1	-	-	-
sincosl	1	-	-	-	1
sincosf128	-	-	-	-	-
sinhf	2	-	-	2	2
sinh	2	-	-	2	2
sinhl	-	-	-	-	2
sinhf128	-	-	-	-	-
sqrtf	-	-	-	-	-
sqrt	-	-	-	-	-
sqrtl	-	-	-	-	-
sqrtf128	-	-	-	-	-
tanf	1	-	-	1	1
tan	1	-	-	-	-
tanl	1	-	-	-	1
tanf128	-	-	-	-	-
tanhf	2	-	-	2	2
tanh	2	-	-	2	2
tanhl	-	-	-	-	2
tanhf128	-	-	-	-	-
tgammaf	4	-	4	4	4
tgamma	5	-	1	5	5
tgammal	1	1	9	-	4
tgammaf128	-	-	-	-	-
y0f	1	1	1	1	1
y0	2	2	1	2	2
y0l	2	1	1	-	3
y0f128	-	-	-	-	-
y1f	2	2	3	2	2
y1	3	3	1	3	3
y1l	3	2	2	-	2

y1f128	-	-	-	-	-
ynf	2	3	3	2	2
yn	3	3	2	3	3
ynl	3	2	4	-	5
ynf128	-	-	-	-	-

Function	MicroBlaze	Nios II	PowerPC	PowerPC soft-float	S/390
acosf	1	1	1	1	1
acos	-	-	-	-	-
acosl	-	-	1	1	1
acosf128	-	-	1	-	-
acoshf	2	2	2	2	2
acosh	2	2	2	2	2
acoshl	-	-	2	1	2
acoshf128	-	-	2	-	-
asinf	1	1	1	1	1
asin	-	-	-	-	-
asinl	-	-	2	2	1
asinf128	-	-	1	-	-
asinhf	1	1	1	1	1
asinh	1	1	1	1	1
asinhl	-	-	2	2	3
asinhf128	-	-	3	-	-
atanf	1	1	1	1	1
atan	-	-	1	-	-
atanl	-	-	1	1	1
atanf128	-	-	1	-	-
atan2f	1	1	1	1	1
atan2	-	-	-	-	-
atan2l	-	-	2	2	1
atan2f128	-	-	1	-	-
atanhf	2	2	2	2	2
atanh	2	2	2	2	2
atanhl	-	-	2	2	3
atanhf128	-	-	3	-	-
cabsf	-	-	-	-	-
cabs	1	1	1	1	1
cabsl	-	-	1	1	1
cabsf128	-	-	1	-	-
cacosf	2 + i 2	2 + i 2	2 + i 2	2 + i 2	2 + i 2
cacos	1 + i 2	1 + i 2	1 + i 2	1 + i 2	1 + i 2
cacosl	-	-	1 + i 2	2 + i 1	2 + i 2
cacosf128	-	-	2 + i 2	-	-
cacoshf	2 + i 2	2 + i 2	2 + i 2	2 + i 2	2 + i 2
cacosh	2 + i 1	2 + i 1	2 + i 1	2 + i 1	2 + i 1
cacoshl	-	-	2 + i 1	1 + i 2	2 + i 2

cacoshf128	-	-	2 + i 2	-	-
cargf	1	1	1	1	1
carg	-	-	1	-	-
cargl	-	-	2	2	2
cargf128	-	-	2	-	-
casinf	1 + i 2	1 + i 2	1 + i 2	1 + i 2	1 + i 2
casin	1 + i 2	1 + i 2	1 + i 2	1 + i 2	1 + i 2
casinl	-	-	1 + i 2	2 + i 1	2 + i 2
casinf128	-	-	2 + i 2	-	-
casinhf	2 + i 1	2 + i 1	2 + i 1	2 + i 1	2 + i 1
casinh	2 + i 1	2 + i 1	2 + i 1	2 + i 1	2 + i 1
casinhl	-	-	2 + i 1	1 + i 2	2 + i 2
casinhf128	-	-	2 + i 2	-	-
catanf	1 + i 1	1 + i 1	1 + i 1	1 + i 1	1 + i 1
catan	1 + i 1	1 + i 1	1 + i 1	1 + i 1	1 + i 1
catanl	-	-	3 + i 2	3 + i 2	1 + i 1
catanf128	-	-	1 + i 1	-	-
catanhf	1 + i 1	1 + i 1	1 + i 1	1 + i 1	1 + i 1
catanh	1 + i 1	1 + i 1	1 + i 1	1 + i 1	1 + i 1
catanhl	-	-	2 + i 3	2 + i 3	1 + i 1
catanhf128	-	-	1 + i 1	-	-
cbrtf	1	1	1	1	1
cbrt	3	3	3	3	3
cbrtl	-	-	1	1	1
cbrtf128	-	-	1	-	-
ccosf	1 + i 1	1 + i 1	1 + i 1	1 + i 1	1 + i 1
ccos	1 + i 1	1 + i 1	1 + i 1	1 + i 1	1 + i 1
ccosl	-	-	1 + i 2	1 + i 2	1 + i 1
ccosf128	-	-	1 + i 1	-	-
ccoshf	1 + i 1	1 + i 1	1 + i 1	1 + i 1	1 + i 1
ccosh	1 + i 1	1 + i 1	1 + i 1	1 + i 1	1 + i 1
ccoshl	-	-	1 + i 2	1 + i 2	1 + i 1
ccoshf128	-	-	1 + i 1	-	-
cexpf	1 + i 2	1 + i 2	1 + i 2	1 + i 2	1 + i 2
cexp	2 + i 1	2 + i 1	2 + i 1	2 + i 1	2 + i 1
cexpl	-	-	2 + i 2	1 + i 1	1 + i 1
cexpf128	-	-	1 + i 1	-	-
clogf	3 + i 1	3 + i 1	3 + i 1	3 + i 1	3 + i 1
clog	3 + i 0	3 + i 0	3 + i 1	3 + i 0	3 + i 0
clogl	-	-	5 + i 2	2 + i 2	2 + i 1
clogf128	-	-	2 + i 1	-	-
clog10f	4 + i 2	4 + i 2	4 + i 2	4 + i 2	4 + i 2
clog10	3 + i 2	3 + i 2	3 + i 2	3 + i 2	3 + i 2
clog10l	-	-	3 + i 2	3 + i 2	2 + i 2
clog10f128	-	-	2 + i 2	-	-
cosf	1	1	3	1	1
cos	-	-	-	-	-

cosl	-	-	4	4	1
cosf128	-	-	1	-	-
coshf	1	1	1	1	1
cosh	1	1	1	1	1
coshl	-	-	3	3	1
coshf128	-	-	1	-	-
cpowf	4 + i 2	4 + i 2	5 + i 2	4 + i 2	5 + i 2
cpow	2 + i 0	2 + i 0	2 + i 0	2 + i 0	2 + i 0
cpowl	-	-	4 + i 2	4 + i 1	4 + i 1
cpowf128	-	-	4 + i 9	-	-
csinf	1 + i 0	1 + i 0	1 + i 0	1 + i 0	1 + i 0
csin	1 + i 0	1 + i 0	1 + i 0	1 + i 0	1 + i 0
csinl	-	-	2 + i 1	2 + i 1	1 + i 1
csinf128	-	-	1 + i 1	-	-
csinhf	1 + i 1	1 + i 1	1 + i 1	1 + i 1	1 + i 1
csinh	0 + i 1	0 + i 1	0 + i 1	0 + i 1	0 + i 1
csinhl	-	-	1 + i 2	1 + i 2	1 + i 1
csinhf128	-	-	1 + i 1	-	-
csqrtf	2 + i 2	2 + i 2	2 + i 2	2 + i 2	2 + i 2
csqrt	2 + i 2	2 + i 2	2 + i 2	2 + i 2	2 + i 2
csqrtl	-	-	1 + i 1	1 + i 1	2 + i 2
csqrtf128	-	-	2 + i 2	-	-
ctanf	1 + i 1	1 + i 1	1 + i 1	1 + i 1	1 + i 1
ctan	1 + i 2	1 + i 2	1 + i 2	1 + i 2	1 + i 2
ctanl	-	-	3 + i 2	3 + i 2	3 + i 3
ctanf128	-	-	3 + i 3	-	-
ctanhf	1 + i 2	1 + i 2	2 + i 1	1 + i 2	2 + i 1
ctanh	2 + i 2	2 + i 2	2 + i 2	2 + i 2	2 + i 2
ctanhl	-	-	3 + i 3	2 + i 3	3 + i 3
ctanhf128	-	-	3 + i 3	-	-
erff	1	1	1	1	1
erf	1	1	1	1	1
erfl	-	-	1	1	1
erff128	-	-	1	-	-
erfcf	2	2	2	2	2
erfc	3	3	2	3	2
erfcl	-	-	3	3	2
erfcf128	-	-	2	-	-
expf	1	1	1	1	1
exp	-	-	1	-	-
expl	-	-	1	1	1
expf128	-	-	1	-	-
exp10f	-	-	-	-	-
exp10	2	2	2	2	2
exp10l	-	-	1	1	2
exp10f128	-	-	2	-	-
exp2f	1	1	1	1	1

exp2	1	1	1	1	1
exp2l	-	-	2	1	1
exp2f128	-	-	1	-	-
expm1f	1	1	1	1	1
expm1	1	1	1	1	1
expm1l	-	-	1	1	1
expm1f128	-	-	1	-	-
fmaf	-	-	-	-	-
fma	-	-	-	-	-
fmal	-	-	1	1	-
fmaf128	-	-	-	-	-
fmodf	-	-	-	-	-
fmod	-	-	-	-	-
fmodl	-	-	1	1	-
fmodf128	-	-	-	-	-
gammaf	4	4	4	4	4
gamma	4	4	3	4	3
gammal	-	-	3	3	5
gammaf128	-	-	9	-	-
hypotf	-	-	-	-	-
hypot	1	1	1	1	1
hypotl	-	-	1	1	1
hypotf128	-	-	1	-	-
j0f	2	2	2	2	2
j0	2	2	2	2	2
j0l	-	-	2	2	2
j0f128	-	-	2	-	-
j1f	2	2	2	2	2
j1	1	1	1	1	1
j1l	-	-	2	1	4
j1f128	-	-	4	-	-
jnf	4	4	4	4	4
jn	4	4	4	4	4
jnl	-	-	4	4	7
jnf128	-	-	7	-	-
lgammaf	4	4	4	4	4
lgamma	4	4	3	4	3
lgammal	-	-	3	3	5
lgammaf128	-	-	9	-	-
logf	1	1	1	1	1
log	-	-	-	-	-
logl	-	-	1	1	1
logf128	-	-	1	-	-
log10f	2	2	2	2	2
log10	2	2	2	2	2
log10l	-	-	1	1	1
log10f128	-	-	1	-	-

log1pf	1	1	1	1	1
log1p	1	1	1	1	1
log1pl	-	-	2	2	2
log1pf128	-	-	2	-	-
log2f	1	1	1	1	1
log2	2	2	1	2	1
log2l	-	-	1	1	2
log2f128	-	-	2	-	-
powf	1	3	1	1	1
pow	-	-	-	-	-
powl	-	-	1	1	2
powf128	-	-	2	-	-
pow10f	-	-	-	-	-
pow10	2	2	2	2	2
pow10l	-	-	1	1	2
pow10f128	-	-	2	-	-
sinf	1	1	1	1	1
sin	-	-	-	-	-
sinl	-	-	1	1	1
sinf128	-	-	1	-	-
sincosf	1	1	1	1	1
sincos	-	-	-	-	-
sincosl	-	-	1	1	1
sincosf128	-	-	1	-	-
sinhf	2	2	2	2	2
sinh	2	2	2	2	2
sinhl	-	-	3	3	2
sinhf128	-	-	2	-	-
sqrtf	-	-	-	-	-
sqrt	-	-	-	-	-
sqrtl	-	-	1	1	-
sqrtf128	-	-	-	-	-
tanf	1	1	3	1	1
tan	-	-	-	-	-
tanl	-	-	2	2	1
tanf128	-	-	1	-	-
tanhf	2	2	2	2	2
tanh	2	2	2	2	2
tanhl	-	-	1	1	2
tanhf128	-	-	2	-	-
tgammaf	4	5	4	4	4
tgamma	5	5	5	5	5
tgammal	-	-	5	3	4
tgammaf128	-	-	4	-	-
y0f	1	1	1	1	1
y0	2	2	2	2	2
y0l	-	-	1	1	3

y0f128	-	-	3	-	-
y1f	2	2	2	2	2
y1	3	3	3	3	3
y1l	-	-	2	2	2
y1f128	-	-	2	-	-
ynf	2	2	2	2	2
yn	3	3	3	3	3
ynl	-	-	2	2	5
ynf128	-	-	5	-	-

Function	SH	Sparc	Tile	i686	ix86
acosf	-	1	1	-	-
acos	-	-	-	1	1
acosl	-	1	-	1	1
acosf128	-	-	-	1	1
acoshf	-	2	2	-	-
acosh	1	2	2	1	1
acoshl	-	2	-	2	2
acoshf128	-	-	-	2	2
asinf	-	1	1	-	-
asin	-	-	-	1	1
asinl	-	1	-	1	1
asinf128	-	-	-	1	1
asinhf	1	1	1	-	-
asinh	1	1	1	1	1
asinhl	-	3	-	3	3
asinhf128	-	-	-	3	3
atanf	-	1	1	-	-
atan	-	-	-	1	1
atanl	-	1	-	1	1
atanf128	-	-	-	1	1
atan2f	1	1	1	-	-
atan2	-	-	-	1	1
atan2l	-	1	-	1	1
atan2f128	-	-	-	1	1
atanhf	1	2	2	-	-
atanh	-	2	2	1	1
atanhl	-	3	-	3	3
atanhf128	-	-	-	3	3
cabsf	-	-	-	-	-
cabs	-	1	1	1	1
cabsl	-	1	-	1	1
cabsf128	-	-	-	1	1
cacosf	2 + i 2	2 + i 2	2 + i 2	1 + i 1	1 + i 1
cacos	1 + i 1	1 + i 2	1 + i 1	1 + i 1	1 + i 1
cacosl	-	2 + i 2	-	1 + i 2	1 + i 2
cacosf128	-	-	-	2 + i 2	2 + i 2

cacoshf	2 + i 2	2 + i 2	2 + i 2	1 + i 1	1 + i 1
cacosh	1 + i 1	2 + i 1	1 + i 1	1 + i 1	1 + i 1
cacoshl	-	2 + i 2	-	2 + i 1	2 + i 1
cacoshf128	-	-	-	2 + i 2	2 + i 2
cargf	-	1	1	-	-
carg	-	-	-	1	1
cargl	- .	2	-	1	1
cargf128	-	-	-	2	2
casinf	1 + i 2	1 + i 2	1 + i 2	1 + i 1	1 + i 1
casin	1 + i 1	1 + i 2	1 + i 1	1 + i 1	1 + i 1
casinl	-	2 + i 2	-	1 + i 2	1 + i 2
casinf128	-	-	-	2 + i 2	2 + i 2
casinhf	2 + i 1	2 + i 1	2 + i 1	1 + i 1	1 + i 1
casinh	1 + i 1	2 + i 1	1 + i 1	1 + i 1	1 + i 1
casinhl	-	2 + i 2	-	2 + i 1	2 + i 1
casinhf128	-	-	-	2 + i 2	2 + i 2
catanf	1 + i 1	1 + i 1	1 + i 1	0 + i 1	0 + i 1
catan	0 + i 1	1 + i 1	0 + i 1	1 + i 1	1 + i 1
catanl	-	1 + i 1	-	1 + i 1	1 + i 1
catanf128	-	-	-	1 + i 1	1 + i 1
catanhf	1 + i 1	1 + i 1	1 + i 1	1 + i 0	1 + i 0
catanh	1 + i 0	1 + i 1	1 + i 0	1 + i 1	1 + i 1
catanhl	-	1 + i 1	-	1 + i 1	1 + i 1
catanhf128	-	-	-	1 + i 1	1 + i 1
cbrtf	1	1	1	1	1
cbrt	1	3	3	1	1
cbrtl	-	1	-	3	3
cbrtf128	-	-	-	1	1
ccosf	1 + i 1	1 + i 1	1 + i 1	1 + i 1	1 + i 1
ccos	1 + i 1	1 + i 1	1 + i 1	1 + i 1	1 + i 1
ccosl	-	1 + i 1	-	1 + i 1	1 + i 1
ccosf128	-	-	-	1 + i 1	1 + i 1
ccoshf	1 + i 1	1 + i 1	1 + i 1	1 + i 1	1 + i 1
ccosh	1 + i 1	1 + i 1	1 + i 1	1 + i 1	1 + i 1
ccoshl	-	1 + i 1	-	1 + i 1	1 + i 1
ccoshf128	-	-	-	1 + i 1	1 + i 1
cexpf	1 + i 2	1 + i 2	1 + i 2	1 + i 2	1 + i 2
cexp	2 + i 1	2 + i 1	2 + i 1	2 + i 1	2 + i 1
cexpl	-	1 + i 1	-	1 + i 1	1 + i 1
cexpf128	-	-	-	1 + i 1	1 + i 1
clogf	1 + i 1	3 + i 1	3 + i 1	1 + i 0	1 + i 0
clog	1 + i 0	3 + i 0	3 + i 0	2 + i 1	2 + i 1
clogl	-	4 + i 1	-	3 + i 1	3 + i 1
clogf128	-	-	-	2 + i 1	2 + i 1
clog10f	2 + i 1	4 + i 2	4 + i 2	2 + i 0	2 + i 0
clog10	2 + i 1	3 + i 2	3 + i 2	2 + i 1	2 + i 1
clog10l	-	4 + i 2	-	4 + i 2	4 + i 2

clog10f128	-	-	-	2 + i 2	2 + i 2
cosf	1	1	1	-	1
cos	-	-	-	-	-
cosl	-	1	-	1	1
cosf128	-	-	-	1	1
coshf	1	1	1	1	1
cosh	1	1	1	1	1
coshl	-	1	-	2	2
coshf128	-	-	-	1	1
cpowf	4 + i 2	4 + i 2	4 + i 2	5 + i 2	5 + i 2
cpow	2 + i 0	2 + i 0	2 + i 0	2 + i 1	2 + i 0
cpowl	-	4 + i 1	-	3 + i 4	3 + i 4
cpowf128	-	-	-	4 + i 1	4 + i 1
csinf	1 + i 0	1 + i 0	1 + i 0	1 + i 1	1 + i 1
csin	1 + i 0	1 + i 0	1 + i 0	1 + i 1	1 + i 0
csinl	-	1 + i 1	-	1 + i 0	1 + i 0
csinf128	-	-	-	1 + i 1	1 + i 1
csinhf	1 + i 1	1 + i 1	1 + i 1	1 + i 1	0 + i 1
csinh	0 + i 1	0 + i 1	0 + i 1	1 + i 1	0 + i 1
csinhl	-	1 + i 1	-	1 + i 1	1 + i 1
csinhf128	-	-	-	1 + i 1	1 + i 1
csqrtf	1 + i 1	2 + i 2	2 + i 2	0 + i 1	0 + i 1
csqrt	1 + i 1	2 + i 2	2 + i 2	1 + i 1	1 + i 1
csqrtl	-	2 + i 2	-	2 + i 2	2 + i 2
csqrtf128	-	-	-	2 + i 2	2 + i 2
ctanf	1 + i 1	1 + i 1	1 + i 1	1 + i 1	1 + i 1
ctan	1 + i 2	1 + i 2	1 + i 2	1 + i 1	1 + i 1
ctanl	-	3 + i 3	-	2 + i 1	2 + i 1
ctanf128	-	-	-	3 + i 3	3 + i 3
ctanhf	1 + i 2	1 + i 2	1 + i 2	1 + i 1	1 + i 1
ctanh	2 + i 2	2 + i 2	2 + i 2	1 + i 1	1 + i 1
ctanhl	-	3 + i 3	-	1 + i 2	1 + i 2
ctanhf128	-	-	-	3 + i 3	3 + i 3
erff	-	1	1	1	1
erf	1	1	1	1	1
erfl	-	1	-	1	1
erff128	-	-	-	1	1
erfcf	1	2	2	1	1
erfc	1	3	3	1	1
erfcl	-	2	-	3	3
erfcf128	-	-	-	2	2
expf	-	1	1	-	-
exp	-	-	-	1	1
expl	-	1	-	1	1
expf128	-	-	-	1	1
exp10f	-	-	-	-	-
exp10	1	2	2	1	1

exp10l	-	2	-	1	1
exp10f128	-	-	-	2	2
exp2f	-	1	1	-	-
exp2	-	1	1	1	1
exp2l	-	1	-	1	1
exp2f128	-	-	-	1	1
expm1f	1	1	1	-	-
expm1	1	1	1	1	1
expm1l	-	1	-	2	2
expm1f128	-	-	-	1	1
fmaf	-	-	-	-	-
fma	-	-	-	-	-
fmal	-	-	-	-	-
fmaf128	-	-	-	-	-
fmodf	-	-	-	-	-
fmod	-	-	-	-	-
fmodl	-	-	-	-	-
fmodf128	-	-	-	-	-
gammaf	1	4	4	3	2
gamma	1	4	4	3	3
gammal	-	5	-	4	4
gammaf128	-	-	-	-	-
hypotf	-	-	-	-	-
hypot	1	1	1	1	1
hypotl	-	1	-	1	1
hypotf128	-	-	-	1	1
j0f	2	2	2	1	1
j0	2	2	2	2	2
j0l	-	2	-	2	2
j0f128	-	-	-	2	2
j1f	2	2	2	1	1
j1	1	1	1	2	2
j1l	-	4	-	1	1
j1f128	-	-	-	4	4
jnf	4	4	4	3	3
jn	4	4	4	2	2
jnl	-	7	-	4	4
jnf128	-	-	-	7	7
lgammaf	1	4	4	3	2
lgamma	1	4	4	3	3
lgammal	-	5	-	4	4
lgammaf128	-	-	-	5	5
logf	1	1	1	-	-
log	-	-	-	1	1
logl	-	1	-	1	1
logf128	-	-	-	1	1
log10f	2	2	2	-	-

log10	1	2	2	1	1
log10l	-	1	-	1	1
log10f128	-	-	-	1	1
log1pf	1	1	1	-	-
log1p	-	1	1	1	1
log1pl	-	2	-	2	2
log1pf128	-	-	-	2	2
log2f	-	1	1	-	-
log2	-	2	2	1	1
log2l	-	2	-	1	1
log2f128	-	-	-	2	2
powf	1	3	3	-	-
pow	-	-	-	1	1
powl	-	2	-	1	1
powf128	-	-	-	2	2
pow10f	-	-	-	-	-
pow10	1	2	2	1	1
pow10l	-	2	-	1	1
pow10f128	-	-	-	-	-
sinf	1	1	1	-	1
sin	-	-	-	-	-
sinl	-	1	-	1	1
sinf128	-	-	-	1	1
sincosf	1	1	1	-	1
sincos	-	-	-	-	-
sincosl	-	1	-	1	1
sincosf128	-	-	-	1	1
sinhf	-	2	2	-	-
sinh	-	2	2	1	1
sinhl	-	2	-	2	2
sinhf128	-	-	-	2	2
sqrtf	-	-	-	-	-
sqrt	-	-	-	-	-
sqrtl	-	-	-	-	-
sqrtf128	-	-	-	-	-
tanf	-	1	1	1	1
tan	-	-	-	-	-
tanl	-	1	-	2	2
tanf128	-	-	-	1	1
tanhf	-	2	2	-	-
tanh	-	2	2	1	1
tanhl	-	2	-	3	3
tanhf128	-	-	-	2	2
tgammaf	3	5	5	3	3
tgamma	4	5	5	3	3
tgammal	-	4	-	5	5
tgammaf128	-	-	-	4	4

y0f	1	1	1	1	1
y0	2	2	2	1	1
y0l	-	3	-	1	1
y0f128	-	-	-	3	3
y1f	2	2	2	2	2
y1	3	3	3	2	2
y1l	-	2	-	2	2
y1f128	-	-	-	2	2
ynf	2	2	2	3	3
yn	3	3	3	2	2
ynl	-	5	-	4	4
ynf128	-	-	-	5	5

19.8 Pseudo-Random Numbers

This section describes the GNU facilities for generating a series of pseudo-random numbers. The numbers generated are not truly random; typically, they form a sequence that repeats periodically, with a period so large that you can ignore it for ordinary purposes. The random number generator works by remembering a *seed* value which it uses to compute the next random number and also to compute a new seed.

Although the generated numbers look unpredictable within one run of a program, the sequence of numbers is *exactly the same* from one run to the next. This is because the initial seed is always the same. This is convenient when you are debugging a program, but it is unhelpful if you want the program to behave unpredictably. If you want a different pseudo-random series each time your program runs, you must specify a different seed each time. For ordinary purposes, basing the seed on the current time works well. For random numbers in cryptography, see Section 33.5 [Generating Unpredictable Bytes], page 889.

You can obtain repeatable sequences of numbers on a particular machine type by specifying the same initial seed value for the random number generator. There is no standard meaning for a particular seed value; the same seed, used in different C libraries or on different CPU types, will give you different random numbers.

The GNU C Library supports the standard ISO C random number functions plus two other sets derived from BSD and SVID. The BSD and ISO C functions provide identical, somewhat limited functionality. If only a small number of random bits are required, we recommend you use the ISO C interface, **rand** and **srand**. The SVID functions provide a more flexible interface, which allows better random number generator algorithms, provides more random bits (up to 48) per call, and can provide random floating-point numbers. These functions are required by the XPG standard and therefore will be present in all modern Unix systems.

19.8.1 ISO C Random Number Functions

This section describes the random number functions that are part of the ISO C standard.

To use these facilities, you should include the header file **stdlib.h** in your program.

int RAND_MAX   [Macro]

> The value of this macro is an integer constant representing the largest value the **rand** function can return. In the GNU C Library, it is 2147483647, which is the largest signed integer representable in 32 bits. In other libraries, it may be as low as 32767.

int rand (*void*)   [Function]

> Preliminary: | MT-Safe | AS-Unsafe lock | AC-Unsafe lock | See Section 1.2.2.1 [POSIX Safety Concepts], page 2.

> The **rand** function returns the next pseudo-random number in the series. The value ranges from 0 to **RAND_MAX**.

void srand (*unsigned int seed*)   [Function]

> Preliminary: | MT-Safe | AS-Unsafe lock | AC-Unsafe lock | See Section 1.2.2.1 [POSIX Safety Concepts], page 2.

> This function establishes *seed* as the seed for a new series of pseudo-random numbers. If you call **rand** before a seed has been established with **srand**, it uses the value 1 as a default seed.

> To produce a different pseudo-random series each time your program is run, do **srand (time (0))**.

POSIX.1 extended the C standard functions to support reproducible random numbers in multi-threaded programs. However, the extension is badly designed and unsuitable for serious work.

int rand_r (*unsigned int *seed*)   [Function]

> Preliminary: | MT-Safe | AS-Safe | AC-Safe | See Section 1.2.2.1 [POSIX Safety Concepts], page 2.

> This function returns a random number in the range 0 to **RAND_MAX** just as **rand** does. However, all its state is stored in the *seed* argument. This means the RNG's state can only have as many bits as the type **unsigned int** has. This is far too few to provide a good RNG.

> If your program requires a reentrant RNG, we recommend you use the reentrant GNU extensions to the SVID random number generator. The POSIX.1 interface should only be used when the GNU extensions are not available.

19.8.2 BSD Random Number Functions

This section describes a set of random number generation functions that are derived from BSD. There is no advantage to using these functions with the GNU C Library; we support them for BSD compatibility only.

The prototypes for these functions are in **stdlib.h**.

long int random (*void*)   [Function]

> Preliminary: | MT-Safe | AS-Unsafe lock | AC-Unsafe lock | See Section 1.2.2.1 [POSIX Safety Concepts], page 2.

> This function returns the next pseudo-random number in the sequence. The value returned ranges from 0 to 2147483647.

NB: Temporarily this function was defined to return a `int32_t` value to indicate that the return value always contains 32 bits even if `long int` is wider. The standard demands it differently. Users must always be aware of the 32-bit limitation, though.

`void srandom (`*unsigned int* `seed)`   [Function]
  Preliminary: | MT-Safe | AS-Unsafe lock | AC-Unsafe lock | See Section 1.2.2.1 [POSIX Safety Concepts], page 2.

  The `srandom` function sets the state of the random number generator based on the integer *seed*. If you supply a *seed* value of 1, this will cause `random` to reproduce the default set of random numbers.

  To produce a different set of pseudo-random numbers each time your program runs, do `srandom (time (0))`.

`char * initstate (`*unsigned int* `seed,` *char* `*state,` *size_t* `size)`   [Function]
  Preliminary: | MT-Safe | AS-Unsafe lock | AC-Unsafe lock | See Section 1.2.2.1 [POSIX Safety Concepts], page 2.

  The `initstate` function is used to initialize the random number generator state. The argument *state* is an array of *size* bytes, used to hold the state information. It is initialized based on *seed*. The size must be between 8 and 256 bytes, and should be a power of two. The bigger the *state* array, the better.

  The return value is the previous value of the state information array. You can use this value later as an argument to `setstate` to restore that state.

`char * setstate (`*char* `*state)`   [Function]
  Preliminary: | MT-Safe | AS-Unsafe lock | AC-Unsafe lock | See Section 1.2.2.1 [POSIX Safety Concepts], page 2.

  The `setstate` function restores the random number state information *state*. The argument must have been the result of a previous call to *initstate* or *setstate*.

  The return value is the previous value of the state information array. You can use this value later as an argument to `setstate` to restore that state.

  If the function fails the return value is `NULL`.

The four functions described so far in this section all work on a state which is shared by all threads. The state is not directly accessible to the user and can only be modified by these functions. This makes it hard to deal with situations where each thread should have its own pseudo-random number generator.

The GNU C Library contains four additional functions which contain the state as an explicit parameter and therefore make it possible to handle thread-local PRNGs. Besides this there is no difference. In fact, the four functions already discussed are implemented internally using the following interfaces.

The `stdlib.h` header contains a definition of the following type:

`struct random_data`   [Data Type]
  Objects of type `struct random_data` contain the information necessary to represent the state of the PRNG. Although a complete definition of the type is present the type should be treated as opaque.

The functions modifying the state follow exactly the already described functions.

int random_r (*struct random_data *restrict **buf**, int32_t *restrict*   [Function]
    result)

Preliminary: | MT-Safe race:buf | AS-Safe | AC-Unsafe corrupt | See Section 1.2.2.1 [POSIX Safety Concepts], page 2.

The **random_r** function behaves exactly like the **random** function except that it uses and modifies the state in the object pointed to by the first parameter instead of the global state.

int srandom_r (*unsigned int **seed**, struct random_data ***buf***)   [Function]

Preliminary: | MT-Safe race:buf | AS-Safe | AC-Unsafe corrupt | See Section 1.2.2.1 [POSIX Safety Concepts], page 2.

The **srandom_r** function behaves exactly like the **srandom** function except that it uses and modifies the state in the object pointed to by the second parameter instead of the global state.

int initstate_r (*unsigned int **seed**, char *restrict **statebuf**, size_t*   [Function]
    statelen**, struct random_data *restrict **buf)

Preliminary: | MT-Safe race:buf | AS-Safe | AC-Unsafe corrupt | See Section 1.2.2.1 [POSIX Safety Concepts], page 2.

The **initstate_r** function behaves exactly like the **initstate** function except that it uses and modifies the state in the object pointed to by the fourth parameter instead of the global state.

int setstate_r (*char *restrict **statebuf**, struct random_data*   [Function]
    restrict **buf*)

Preliminary: | MT-Safe race:buf | AS-Safe | AC-Unsafe corrupt | See Section 1.2.2.1 [POSIX Safety Concepts], page 2.

The **setstate_r** function behaves exactly like the **setstate** function except that it uses and modifies the state in the object pointed to by the first parameter instead of the global state.

19.8.3 SVID Random Number Function

The C library on SVID systems contains yet another kind of random number generator functions. They use a state of 48 bits of data. The user can choose among a collection of functions which return the random bits in different forms.

Generally there are two kinds of function. The first uses a state of the random number generator which is shared among several functions and by all threads of the process. The second requires the user to handle the state.

All functions have in common that they use the same congruential formula with the same constants. The formula is

```
Y = (a * X + c) mod m
```

where X is the state of the generator at the beginning and Y the state at the end. **a** and **c** are constants determining the way the generator works. By default they are

```
a = 0x5DEECE66D = 25214903917
c = 0xb = 11
```

but they can also be changed by the user. `m` is of course 2^48 since the state consists of a 48-bit array.

The prototypes for these functions are in `stdlib.h`.

double drand48 (*void*) [Function]

    Preliminary: | MT-Unsafe race:drand48 | AS-Unsafe | AC-Unsafe corrupt | See Section 1.2.2.1 [POSIX Safety Concepts], page 2.

    This function returns a `double` value in the range of `0.0` to `1.0` (exclusive). The random bits are determined by the global state of the random number generator in the C library.

    Since the `double` type according to IEEE 754 has a 52-bit mantissa this means 4 bits are not initialized by the random number generator. These are (of course) chosen to be the least significant bits and they are initialized to 0.

double erand48 (*unsigned short int xsubi[3]*) [Function]

    Preliminary: | MT-Unsafe race:drand48 | AS-Unsafe | AC-Unsafe corrupt | See Section 1.2.2.1 [POSIX Safety Concepts], page 2.

    This function returns a `double` value in the range of `0.0` to `1.0` (exclusive), similarly to `drand48`. The argument is an array describing the state of the random number generator.

    This function can be called subsequently since it updates the array to guarantee random numbers. The array should have been initialized before initial use to obtain reproducible results.

long int lrand48 (*void*) [Function]

    Preliminary: | MT-Unsafe race:drand48 | AS-Unsafe | AC-Unsafe corrupt | See Section 1.2.2.1 [POSIX Safety Concepts], page 2.

    The `lrand48` function returns an integer value in the range of 0 to 2^31 (exclusive). Even if the size of the `long int` type can take more than 32 bits, no higher numbers are returned. The random bits are determined by the global state of the random number generator in the C library.

long int nrand48 (*unsigned short int xsubi[3]*) [Function]

    Preliminary: | MT-Unsafe race:drand48 | AS-Unsafe | AC-Unsafe corrupt | See Section 1.2.2.1 [POSIX Safety Concepts], page 2.

    This function is similar to the `lrand48` function in that it returns a number in the range of 0 to 2^31 (exclusive) but the state of the random number generator used to produce the random bits is determined by the array provided as the parameter to the function.

    The numbers in the array are updated afterwards so that subsequent calls to this function yield different results (as is expected of a random number generator). The array should have been initialized before the first call to obtain reproducible results.

long int mrand48 (*void*) [Function]

    Preliminary: | MT-Unsafe race:drand48 | AS-Unsafe | AC-Unsafe corrupt | See Section 1.2.2.1 [POSIX Safety Concepts], page 2.

    The `mrand48` function is similar to `lrand48`. The only difference is that the numbers returned are in the range -2^31 to 2^31 (exclusive).

long int jrand48 (*unsigned short int xsubi*[*3*])   [Function]
>   Preliminary: | MT-Unsafe race:drand48 | AS-Unsafe | AC-Unsafe corrupt | See
>   Section 1.2.2.1 [POSIX Safety Concepts], page 2.

>   The **jrand48** function is similar to **nrand48**. The only difference is that the numbers
>   returned are in the range -2^{31} to 2^{31} (exclusive). For the **xsubi** parameter the
>   same requirements are necessary.

The internal state of the random number generator can be initialized in several ways.
The methods differ in the completeness of the information provided.

void srand48 (*long int seedval*)   [Function]
>   Preliminary: | MT-Unsafe race:drand48 | AS-Unsafe | AC-Unsafe corrupt | See
>   Section 1.2.2.1 [POSIX Safety Concepts], page 2.

>   The **srand48** function sets the most significant 32 bits of the internal state of the
>   random number generator to the least significant 32 bits of the *seedval* parameter.
>   The lower 16 bits are initialized to the value 0x330E. Even if the **long int** type
>   contains more than 32 bits only the lower 32 bits are used.

>   Owing to this limitation, initialization of the state of this function is not very useful.
>   But it makes it easy to use a construct like **srand48 (time (0))**.

>   A side-effect of this function is that the values **a** and **c** from the internal state, which
>   are used in the congruential formula, are reset to the default values given above. This
>   is of importance once the user has called the **lcong48** function (see below).

unsigned short int * seed48 (*unsigned short int seed16v*[*3*])   [Function]
>   Preliminary: | MT-Unsafe race:drand48 | AS-Unsafe | AC-Unsafe corrupt | See
>   Section 1.2.2.1 [POSIX Safety Concepts], page 2.

>   The **seed48** function initializes all 48 bits of the state of the internal random number
>   generator from the contents of the parameter *seed16v*. Here the lower 16 bits of the
>   first element of *seed16v* initialize the least significant 16 bits of the internal state, the
>   lower 16 bits of *seed16v*[1] initialize the mid-order 16 bits of the state and the 16
>   lower bits of *seed16v*[2] initialize the most significant 16 bits of the state.

>   Unlike **srand48** this function lets the user initialize all 48 bits of the state.

>   The value returned by **seed48** is a pointer to an array containing the values of the
>   internal state before the change. This might be useful to restart the random number
>   generator at a certain state. Otherwise the value can simply be ignored.

>   As for **srand48**, the values **a** and **c** from the congruential formula are reset to the
>   default values.

There is one more function to initialize the random number generator which enables
you to specify even more information by allowing you to change the parameters in the
congruential formula.

void lcong48 (*unsigned short int param*[*7*])   [Function]
>   Preliminary: | MT-Unsafe race:drand48 | AS-Unsafe | AC-Unsafe corrupt | See
>   Section 1.2.2.1 [POSIX Safety Concepts], page 2.

The `lcong48` function allows the user to change the complete state of the random number generator. Unlike `srand48` and `seed48`, this function also changes the constants in the congruential formula.

From the seven elements in the array *param* the least significant 16 bits of the entries *param*[0] to *param*[2] determine the initial state, the least significant 16 bits of *param*[3] to *param*[5] determine the 48 bit constant a and *param*[6] determines the 16-bit value c.

All the above functions have in common that they use the global parameters for the congruential formula. In multi-threaded programs it might sometimes be useful to have different parameters in different threads. For this reason all the above functions have a counterpart which works on a description of the random number generator in the user-supplied buffer instead of the global state.

Please note that it is no problem if several threads use the global state if all threads use the functions which take a pointer to an array containing the state. The random numbers are computed following the same loop but if the state in the array is different all threads will obtain an individual random number generator.

The user-supplied buffer must be of type `struct drand48_data`. This type should be regarded as opaque and not manipulated directly.

`int drand48_r (struct drand48_data *buffer, double *result)` [Function]
    Preliminary: | MT-Safe race:buffer | AS-Safe | AC-Unsafe corrupt | See Section 1.2.2.1 [POSIX Safety Concepts], page 2.

    This function is equivalent to the `drand48` function with the difference that it does not modify the global random number generator parameters but instead the parameters in the buffer supplied through the pointer *buffer*. The random number is returned in the variable pointed to by *result*.

    The return value of the function indicates whether the call succeeded. If the value is less than 0 an error occurred and *errno* is set to indicate the problem.

    This function is a GNU extension and should not be used in portable programs.

`int erand48_r (unsigned short int xsubi[3], struct drand48_data` [Function]
        `*buffer, double *result)`
    Preliminary: | MT-Safe race:buffer | AS-Safe | AC-Unsafe corrupt | See Section 1.2.2.1 [POSIX Safety Concepts], page 2.

    The `erand48_r` function works like `erand48`, but in addition it takes an argument *buffer* which describes the random number generator. The state of the random number generator is taken from the `xsubi` array, the parameters for the congruential formula from the global random number generator data. The random number is returned in the variable pointed to by *result*.

    The return value is non-negative if the call succeeded.

    This function is a GNU extension and should not be used in portable programs.

`int lrand48_r (struct drand48_data *buffer, long int *result)` [Function]
    Preliminary: | MT-Safe race:buffer | AS-Safe | AC-Unsafe corrupt | See Section 1.2.2.1 [POSIX Safety Concepts], page 2.

This function is similar to `lrand48`, but in addition it takes a pointer to a buffer describing the state of the random number generator just like `drand48`.

If the return value of the function is non-negative the variable pointed to by *result* contains the result. Otherwise an error occurred.

This function is a GNU extension and should not be used in portable programs.

int **nrand48_r** (*unsigned short int* `xsubi[3]`, *struct drand48_data*   [Function]
    **buffer*, *long int* `*result`)
Preliminary: | MT-Safe race:buffer | AS-Safe | AC-Unsafe corrupt | See Section 1.2.2.1 [POSIX Safety Concepts], page 2.

The `nrand48_r` function works like `nrand48` in that it produces a random number in the range 0 to `2^31`. But instead of using the global parameters for the congruential formula it uses the information from the buffer pointed to by *buffer*. The state is described by the values in *xsubi*.

If the return value is non-negative the variable pointed to by *result* contains the result.

This function is a GNU extension and should not be used in portable programs.

int **mrand48_r** (*struct drand48_data* **buffer*, *long int* `*result`)   [Function]
Preliminary: | MT-Safe race:buffer | AS-Safe | AC-Unsafe corrupt | See Section 1.2.2.1 [POSIX Safety Concepts], page 2.

This function is similar to `mrand48` but like the other reentrant functions it uses the random number generator described by the value in the buffer pointed to by *buffer*.

If the return value is non-negative the variable pointed to by *result* contains the result.

This function is a GNU extension and should not be used in portable programs.

int **jrand48_r** (*unsigned short int* `xsubi[3]`, *struct drand48_data*   [Function]
    **buffer*, *long int* `*result`)
Preliminary: | MT-Safe race:buffer | AS-Safe | AC-Unsafe corrupt | See Section 1.2.2.1 [POSIX Safety Concepts], page 2.

The `jrand48_r` function is similar to `jrand48`. Like the other reentrant functions of this function family it uses the congruential formula parameters from the buffer pointed to by *buffer*.

If the return value is non-negative the variable pointed to by *result* contains the result.

This function is a GNU extension and should not be used in portable programs.

Before any of the above functions are used the buffer of type **struct drand48_data** should be initialized. The easiest way to do this is to fill the whole buffer with null bytes, e.g. by

```
memset (buffer, '\0', sizeof (struct drand48_data));
```

Using any of the reentrant functions of this family now will automatically initialize the random number generator to the default values for the state and the parameters of the congruential formula.

The other possibility is to use any of the functions which explicitly initialize the buffer. Though it might be obvious how to initialize the buffer from looking at the parameter to the function, it is highly recommended to use these functions since the result might not always be what you expect.

int srand48_r (*long int* `seedval`, *struct drand48_data* `*buffer`)   [Function]
Preliminary: | MT-Safe race:buffer | AS-Safe | AC-Unsafe corrupt | See Section 1.2.2.1 [POSIX Safety Concepts], page 2.

The description of the random number generator represented by the information in *buffer* is initialized similarly to what the function `srand48` does. The state is initialized from the parameter *seedval* and the parameters for the congruential formula are initialized to their default values.

If the return value is non-negative the function call succeeded.

This function is a GNU extension and should not be used in portable programs.

int seed48_r (*unsigned short int* `seed16v[3]`, *struct drand48_data* `*buffer`)   [Function]
Preliminary: | MT-Safe race:buffer | AS-Safe | AC-Unsafe corrupt | See Section 1.2.2.1 [POSIX Safety Concepts], page 2.

This function is similar to `srand48_r` but like `seed48` it initializes all 48 bits of the state from the parameter *seed16v*.

If the return value is non-negative the function call succeeded. It does not return a pointer to the previous state of the random number generator like the `seed48` function does. If the user wants to preserve the state for a later re-run s/he can copy the whole buffer pointed to by *buffer*.

This function is a GNU extension and should not be used in portable programs.

int lcong48_r (*unsigned short int* `param[7]`, *struct drand48_data* `*buffer`)   [Function]
Preliminary: | MT-Safe race:buffer | AS-Safe | AC-Unsafe corrupt | See Section 1.2.2.1 [POSIX Safety Concepts], page 2.

This function initializes all aspects of the random number generator described in *buffer* with the data in *param*. Here it is especially true that the function does more than just copying the contents of *param* and *buffer*. More work is required and therefore it is important to use this function rather than initializing the random number generator directly.

If the return value is non-negative the function call succeeded.

This function is a GNU extension and should not be used in portable programs.

19.9 Is Fast Code or Small Code preferred?

If an application uses many floating point functions it is often the case that the cost of the function calls themselves is not negligible. Modern processors can often execute the operations themselves very fast, but the function call disrupts the instruction pipeline.

For this reason the GNU C Library provides optimizations for many of the frequently-used math functions. When GNU CC is used and the user activates the optimizer, several new inline functions and macros are defined. These new functions and macros have the same names as the library functions and so are used instead of the latter. In the case of inline functions the compiler will decide whether it is reasonable to use them, and this decision is usually correct.

This means that no calls to the library functions may be necessary, and can increase the speed of generated code significantly. The drawback is that code size will increase, and the increase is not always negligible.

There are two kinds of inline functions: those that give the same result as the library functions and others that might not set `errno` and might have a reduced precision and/or argument range in comparison with the library functions. The latter inline functions are only available if the flag `-ffast-math` is given to GNU CC.

In cases where the inline functions and macros are not wanted the symbol `__NO_MATH_INLINES` should be defined before any system header is included. This will ensure that only library functions are used. Of course, it can be determined for each file in the project whether giving this option is preferable or not.

Not all hardware implements the entire IEEE 754 standard, and even if it does there may be a substantial performance penalty for using some of its features. For example, enabling traps on some processors forces the FPU to run un-pipelined, which can more than double calculation time.

20 Arithmetic Functions

This chapter contains information about functions for doing basic arithmetic operations, such as splitting a float into its integer and fractional parts or retrieving the imaginary part of a complex value. These functions are declared in the header files `math.h` and `complex.h`.

20.1 Integers

The C language defines several integer data types: integer, short integer, long integer, and character, all in both signed and unsigned varieties. The GNU C compiler extends the language to contain long long integers as well.

The C integer types were intended to allow code to be portable among machines with different inherent data sizes (word sizes), so each type may have different ranges on different machines. The problem with this is that a program often needs to be written for a particular range of integers, and sometimes must be written for a particular size of storage, regardless of what machine the program runs on.

To address this problem, the GNU C Library contains C type definitions you can use to declare integers that meet your exact needs. Because the GNU C Library header files are customized to a specific machine, your program source code doesn't have to be.

These `typedef`s are in `stdint.h`.

If you require that an integer be represented in exactly N bits, use one of the following types, with the obvious mapping to bit size and signedness:

- int8_t
- int16_t
- int32_t
- int64_t
- uint8_t
- uint16_t
- uint32_t
- uint64_t

If your C compiler and target machine do not allow integers of a certain size, the corresponding above type does not exist.

If you don't need a specific storage size, but want the smallest data structure with *at least* N bits, use one of these:

- int_least8_t
- int_least16_t
- int_least32_t
- int_least64_t
- uint_least8_t
- uint_least16_t
- uint_least32_t
- uint_least64_t

If you don't need a specific storage size, but want the data structure that allows the fastest access while having at least N bits (and among data structures with the same access speed, the smallest one), use one of these:

- int_fast8_t
- int_fast16_t
- int_fast32_t
- int_fast64_t
- uint_fast8_t
- uint_fast16_t
- uint_fast32_t
- uint_fast64_t

If you want an integer with the widest range possible on the platform on which it is being used, use one of the following. If you use these, you should write code that takes into account the variable size and range of the integer.

- intmax_t
- uintmax_t

The GNU C Library also provides macros that tell you the maximum and minimum possible values for each integer data type. The macro names follow these examples: `INT32_MAX`, `UINT8_MAX`, `INT_FAST32_MIN`, `INT_LEAST64_MIN`, `UINTMAX_MAX`, `INTMAX_MAX`, `INTMAX_MIN`. Note that there are no macros for unsigned integer minima. These are always zero. Similiarly, there are macros such as `INTMAX_WIDTH` for the width of these types. Those macros for integer type widths come from TS 18661-1:2014.

There are similar macros for use with C's built in integer types which should come with your C compiler. These are described in Section A.5 [Data Type Measurements], page 916.

Don't forget you can use the C `sizeof` function with any of these data types to get the number of bytes of storage each uses.

20.2 Integer Division

This section describes functions for performing integer division. These functions are redundant when GNU CC is used, because in GNU C the '/' operator always rounds towards zero. But in other C implementations, '/' may round differently with negative arguments. `div` and `ldiv` are useful because they specify how to round the quotient: towards zero. The remainder has the same sign as the numerator.

These functions are specified to return a result r such that the value `r.quot*`*denominator* `+ r.rem` equals *numerator*.

To use these facilities, you should include the header file `stdlib.h` in your program.

`div_t`   [Data Type]

This is a structure type used to hold the result returned by the `div` function. It has the following members:

`int quot`   The quotient from the division.

`int rem`   The remainder from the division.

`div_t div` (*int numerator, int denominator*) [Function]
> Preliminary: | MT-Safe | AS-Safe | AC-Safe | See Section 1.2.2.1 [POSIX Safety Concepts], page 2.
>
> The function `div` computes the quotient and remainder from the division of *numerator* by *denominator*, returning the result in a structure of type `div_t`.
>
> If the result cannot be represented (as in a division by zero), the behavior is undefined.
>
> Here is an example, albeit not a very useful one.
>
> ```
> div_t result;
> result = div (20, -6);
> ```
>
> Now `result.quot` is -3 and `result.rem` is 2.

`ldiv_t` [Data Type]
> This is a structure type used to hold the result returned by the `ldiv` function. It has the following members:
>
> `long int quot`
> > The quotient from the division.
>
> `long int rem`
> > The remainder from the division.
>
> (This is identical to `div_t` except that the components are of type `long int` rather than `int`.)

`ldiv_t ldiv` (*long int numerator, long int denominator*) [Function]
> Preliminary: | MT-Safe | AS-Safe | AC-Safe | See Section 1.2.2.1 [POSIX Safety Concepts], page 2.
>
> The `ldiv` function is similar to `div`, except that the arguments are of type `long int` and the result is returned as a structure of type `ldiv_t`.

`lldiv_t` [Data Type]
> This is a structure type used to hold the result returned by the `lldiv` function. It has the following members:
>
> `long long int quot`
> > The quotient from the division.
>
> `long long int rem`
> > The remainder from the division.
>
> (This is identical to `div_t` except that the components are of type `long long int` rather than `int`.)

`lldiv_t lldiv` (*long long int numerator, long long int denominator*) [Function]
> Preliminary: | MT-Safe | AS-Safe | AC-Safe | See Section 1.2.2.1 [POSIX Safety Concepts], page 2.
>
> The `lldiv` function is like the `div` function, but the arguments are of type `long long int` and the result is returned as a structure of type `lldiv_t`.
>
> The `lldiv` function was added in ISO C99.

`imaxdiv_t`   [Data Type]

> This is a structure type used to hold the result returned by the `imaxdiv` function. It has the following members:
>
> `intmax_t quot`
> > The quotient from the division.
>
> `intmax_t rem`
> > The remainder from the division.
>
> (This is identical to `div_t` except that the components are of type `intmax_t` rather than `int`.)
>
> See Section 20.1 [Integers], page 575, for a description of the `intmax_t` type.

`imaxdiv_t imaxdiv` (*intmax_t numerator, intmax_t denominator*)   [Function]

> Preliminary: | MT-Safe | AS-Safe | AC-Safe | See Section 1.2.2.1 [POSIX Safety Concepts], page 2.
>
> The `imaxdiv` function is like the `div` function, but the arguments are of type `intmax_t` and the result is returned as a structure of type `imaxdiv_t`.
>
> See Section 20.1 [Integers], page 575, for a description of the `intmax_t` type.
>
> The `imaxdiv` function was added in ISO C99.

20.3 Floating Point Numbers

Most computer hardware has support for two different kinds of numbers: integers $(\ldots-3, -2, -1, 0, 1, 2, 3\ldots)$ and floating-point numbers. Floating-point numbers have three parts: the *mantissa*, the *exponent*, and the *sign bit*. The real number represented by a floating-point value is given by $(s\ ?\ -1 : 1) \cdot 2^e \cdot M$ where s is the sign bit, e the exponent, and M the mantissa. See Section A.5.3.1 [Floating Point Representation Concepts], page 919, for details. (It is possible to have a different *base* for the exponent, but all modern hardware uses 2.)

Floating-point numbers can represent a finite subset of the real numbers. While this subset is large enough for most purposes, it is important to remember that the only reals that can be represented exactly are rational numbers that have a terminating binary expansion shorter than the width of the mantissa. Even simple fractions such as 1/5 can only be approximated by floating point.

Mathematical operations and functions frequently need to produce values that are not representable. Often these values can be approximated closely enough for practical purposes, but sometimes they can't. Historically there was no way to tell when the results of a calculation were inaccurate. Modern computers implement the IEEE 754 standard for numerical computations, which defines a framework for indicating to the program when the results of calculation are not trustworthy. This framework consists of a set of *exceptions* that indicate why a result could not be represented, and the special values *infinity* and *not a number* (NaN).

20.4 Floating-Point Number Classification Functions

ISO C99 defines macros that let you determine what sort of floating-point number a variable holds.

int fpclassify (*float-type x*)   [Macro]

Preliminary: | MT-Safe | AS-Safe | AC-Safe | See Section 1.2.2.1 [POSIX Safety Concepts], page 2.

This is a generic macro which works on all floating-point types and which returns a value of type `int`. The possible values are:

`FP_NAN`   The floating-point number x is "Not a Number" (see Section 20.5.2 [Infinity and NaN], page 583)

`FP_INFINITE`

The value of x is either plus or minus infinity (see Section 20.5.2 [Infinity and NaN], page 583)

`FP_ZERO`   The value of x is zero. In floating-point formats like IEEE 754, where zero can be signed, this value is also returned if x is negative zero.

`FP_SUBNORMAL`

Numbers whose absolute value is too small to be represented in the normal format are represented in an alternate, *denormalized* format (see Section A.5.3.1 [Floating Point Representation Concepts], page 919). This format is less precise but can represent values closer to zero. `fpclassify` returns this value for values of x in this alternate format.

`FP_NORMAL`

This value is returned for all other values of x. It indicates that there is nothing special about the number.

`fpclassify` is most useful if more than one property of a number must be tested. There are more specific macros which only test one property at a time. Generally these macros execute faster than `fpclassify`, since there is special hardware support for them. You should therefore use the specific macros whenever possible.

int iscanonical (*float-type x*)   [Macro]

Preliminary: | MT-Safe | AS-Safe | AC-Safe | See Section 1.2.2.1 [POSIX Safety Concepts], page 2.

In some floating-point formats, some values have canonical (preferred) and noncanonical encodings (for IEEE interchange binary formats, all encodings are canonical). This macro returns a nonzero value if x has a canonical encoding. It is from TS 18661-1:2014.

Note that some formats have multiple encodings of a value which are all equally canonical; `iscanonical` returns a nonzero value for all such encodings. Also, formats may have encodings that do not correspond to any valid value of the type. In ISO C terms these are *trap representations*; in the GNU C Library, `iscanonical` returns zero for such encodings.

`int isfinite (float-type x)` [Macro]

Preliminary: | MT-Safe | AS-Safe | AC-Safe | See Section 1.2.2.1 [POSIX Safety Concepts], page 2.

This macro returns a nonzero value if x is finite: not plus or minus infinity, and not NaN. It is equivalent to

    (fpclassify (x) != FP_NAN && fpclassify (x) != FP_INFINITE)

`isfinite` is implemented as a macro which accepts any floating-point type.

`int isnormal (float-type x)` [Macro]

Preliminary: | MT-Safe | AS-Safe | AC-Safe | See Section 1.2.2.1 [POSIX Safety Concepts], page 2.

This macro returns a nonzero value if x is finite and normalized. It is equivalent to

    (fpclassify (x) == FP_NORMAL)

`int isnan (float-type x)` [Macro]

Preliminary: | MT-Safe | AS-Safe | AC-Safe | See Section 1.2.2.1 [POSIX Safety Concepts], page 2.

This macro returns a nonzero value if x is NaN. It is equivalent to

    (fpclassify (x) == FP_NAN)

`int issignaling (float-type x)` [Macro]

Preliminary: | MT-Safe | AS-Safe | AC-Safe | See Section 1.2.2.1 [POSIX Safety Concepts], page 2.

This macro returns a nonzero value if x is a signaling NaN (sNaN). It is from TS 18661-1:2014.

`int issubnormal (float-type x)` [Macro]

Preliminary: | MT-Safe | AS-Safe | AC-Safe | See Section 1.2.2.1 [POSIX Safety Concepts], page 2.

This macro returns a nonzero value if x is subnormal. It is from TS 18661-1:2014.

`int iszero (float-type x)` [Macro]

Preliminary: | MT-Safe | AS-Safe | AC-Safe | See Section 1.2.2.1 [POSIX Safety Concepts], page 2.

This macro returns a nonzero value if x is zero. It is from TS 18661-1:2014.

Another set of floating-point classification functions was provided by BSD. The GNU C Library also supports these functions; however, we recommend that you use the ISO C99 macros in new code. Those are standard and will be available more widely. Also, since they are macros, you do not have to worry about the type of their argument.

`int isinf (double x)` [Function]
`int isinff (float x)` [Function]
`int isinfl (long double x)` [Function]

Preliminary: | MT-Safe | AS-Safe | AC-Safe | See Section 1.2.2.1 [POSIX Safety Concepts], page 2.

This function returns -1 if x represents negative infinity, 1 if x represents positive infinity, and 0 otherwise.

int isnan (*double x*)   [Function]

int isnanf (*float x*)   [Function]

int isnanl (*long double x*)   [Function]

> Preliminary: | MT-Safe | AS-Safe | AC-Safe | See Section 1.2.2.1 [POSIX Safety Concepts], page 2.
>
> This function returns a nonzero value if *x* is a "not a number" value, and zero otherwise.
>
> **NB:** The `isnan` macro defined by ISO C99 overrides the BSD function. This is normally not a problem, because the two routines behave identically. However, if you really need to get the BSD function for some reason, you can write
>
> > (isnan) (x)

int finite (*double x*)   [Function]

int finitef (*float x*)   [Function]

int finitel (*long double x*)   [Function]

> Preliminary: | MT-Safe | AS-Safe | AC-Safe | See Section 1.2.2.1 [POSIX Safety Concepts], page 2.
>
> This function returns a nonzero value if *x* is finite or a "not a number" value, and zero otherwise.

Portability Note: The functions listed in this section are BSD extensions.

20.5 Errors in Floating-Point Calculations

20.5.1 FP Exceptions

The IEEE 754 standard defines five *exceptions* that can occur during a calculation. Each corresponds to a particular sort of error, such as overflow.

When exceptions occur (when exceptions are *raised*, in the language of the standard), one of two things can happen. By default the exception is simply noted in the floating-point *status word*, and the program continues as if nothing had happened. The operation produces a default value, which depends on the exception (see the table below). Your program can check the status word to find out which exceptions happened.

Alternatively, you can enable *traps* for exceptions. In that case, when an exception is raised, your program will receive the `SIGFPE` signal. The default action for this signal is to terminate the program. See Chapter 24 [Signal Handling], page 685, for how you can change the effect of the signal.

In the System V math library, the user-defined function `matherr` is called when certain exceptions occur inside math library functions. However, the Unix98 standard deprecates this interface. We support it for historical compatibility, but recommend that you do not use it in new programs. When this interface is used, exceptions may not be raised.

The exceptions defined in IEEE 754 are:

'Invalid Operation'

> > This exception is raised if the given operands are invalid for the operation to be performed. Examples are (see IEEE 754, section 7):
> >
> > 1. Addition or subtraction: $\infty - \infty$. (But $\infty + \infty = \infty$).

2. Multiplication: $0 \cdot \infty$.

3. Division: $0/0$ or ∞/∞.

4. Remainder: x REM y, where y is zero or x is infinite.

5. Square root if the operand is less than zero. More generally, any mathematical function evaluated outside its domain produces this exception.

6. Conversion of a floating-point number to an integer or decimal string, when the number cannot be represented in the target format (due to overflow, infinity, or NaN).

7. Conversion of an unrecognizable input string.

8. Comparison via predicates involving $<$ or $>$, when one or other of the operands is NaN. You can prevent this exception by using the unordered comparison functions instead; see Section 20.8.6 [Floating-Point Comparison Functions], page 602.

If the exception does not trap, the result of the operation is NaN.

'Division by Zero'

This exception is raised when a finite nonzero number is divided by zero. If no trap occurs the result is either $+\infty$ or $-\infty$, depending on the signs of the operands.

'Overflow'

This exception is raised whenever the result cannot be represented as a finite value in the precision format of the destination. If no trap occurs the result depends on the sign of the intermediate result and the current rounding mode (IEEE 754, section 7.3):

1. Round to nearest carries all overflows to ∞ with the sign of the intermediate result.

2. Round toward 0 carries all overflows to the largest representable finite number with the sign of the intermediate result.

3. Round toward $-\infty$ carries positive overflows to the largest representable finite number and negative overflows to $-\infty$.

4. Round toward ∞ carries negative overflows to the most negative representable finite number and positive overflows to ∞.

Whenever the overflow exception is raised, the inexact exception is also raised.

'Underflow'

The underflow exception is raised when an intermediate result is too small to be calculated accurately, or if the operation's result rounded to the destination precision is too small to be normalized.

When no trap is installed for the underflow exception, underflow is signaled (via the underflow flag) only when both tininess and loss of accuracy have been detected. If no trap handler is installed the operation continues with an imprecise small value, or zero if the destination precision cannot hold the small exact result.

'Inexact' This exception is signalled if a rounded result is not exact (such as when calculating the square root of two) or a result overflows without an overflow trap.

20.5.2 Infinity and NaN

IEEE 754 floating point numbers can represent positive or negative infinity, and *NaN* (not a number). These three values arise from calculations whose result is undefined or cannot be represented accurately. You can also deliberately set a floating-point variable to any of them, which is sometimes useful. Some examples of calculations that produce infinity or NaN:

$$\frac{1}{0} = \infty$$

$$\log 0 = -\infty$$

$$\sqrt{-1} = \text{NaN}$$

When a calculation produces any of these values, an exception also occurs; see Section 20.5.1 [FP Exceptions], page 581.

The basic operations and math functions all accept infinity and NaN and produce sensible output. Infinities propagate through calculations as one would expect: for example, $2+\infty = \infty$, $4/\infty = 0$, atan $(\infty) = \pi/2$. NaN, on the other hand, infects any calculation that involves it. Unless the calculation would produce the same result no matter what real value replaced NaN, the result is NaN.

In comparison operations, positive infinity is larger than all values except itself and NaN, and negative infinity is smaller than all values except itself and NaN. NaN is *unordered*: it is not equal to, greater than, or less than anything, *including itself.* x == x is false if the value of x is NaN. You can use this to test whether a value is NaN or not, but the recommended way to test for NaN is with the isnan function (see Section 20.4 [Floating-Point Number Classification Functions], page 579). In addition, <, >, <=, and >= will raise an exception when applied to NaNs.

math.h defines macros that allow you to explicitly set a variable to infinity or NaN.

float INFINITY   [Macro]

> An expression representing positive infinity. It is equal to the value produced by mathematical operations like 1.0 / 0.0. -INFINITY represents negative infinity.

> You can test whether a floating-point value is infinite by comparing it to this macro. However, this is not recommended; you should use the isfinite macro instead. See Section 20.4 [Floating-Point Number Classification Functions], page 579.

> This macro was introduced in the ISO C99 standard.

float NAN   [Macro]

> An expression representing a value which is "not a number". This macro is a GNU extension, available only on machines that support the "not a number" value—that is to say, on all machines that support IEEE floating point.

> You can use '#ifdef NAN' to test whether the machine supports NaN. (Of course, you must arrange for GNU extensions to be visible, such as by defining _GNU_SOURCE, and then you must include math.h.)

`float SNANF`	[Macro]
`double SNAN`	[Macro]
`long double SNANL`	[Macro]
`_FloatN SNANFN`	[Macro]
`_FloatNx SNANFNx`	[Macro]

>   These macros, defined by TS 18661-1:2014 and TS 18661-3:2015, are constant expressions for signaling NaNs.

`int FE_SNANS_ALWAYS_SIGNAL`	[Macro]

>   This macro, defined by TS 18661-1:2014, is defined to `1` in `fenv.h` to indicate that functions and operations with signaling NaN inputs and floating-point results always raise the invalid exception and return a quiet NaN, even in cases (such as `fmax`, `hypot` and `pow`) where a quiet NaN input can produce a non-NaN result. Because some compiler optimizations may not handle signaling NaNs correctly, this macro is only defined if compiler support for signaling NaNs is enabled. That support can be enabled with the GCC option `-fsignaling-nans`.

IEEE 754 also allows for another unusual value: negative zero. This value is produced when you divide a positive number by negative infinity, or when a negative result is smaller than the limits of representation.

20.5.3 Examining the FPU status word

ISO C99 defines functions to query and manipulate the floating-point status word. You can use these functions to check for untrapped exceptions when it's convenient, rather than worrying about them in the middle of a calculation.

These constants represent the various IEEE 754 exceptions. Not all FPUs report all the different exceptions. Each constant is defined if and only if the FPU you are compiling for supports that exception, so you can test for FPU support with '`#ifdef`'. They are defined in `fenv.h`.

`FE_INEXACT`
>   The inexact exception.

`FE_DIVBYZERO`
>   The divide by zero exception.

`FE_UNDERFLOW`
>   The underflow exception.

`FE_OVERFLOW`
>   The overflow exception.

`FE_INVALID`
>   The invalid exception.

The macro `FE_ALL_EXCEPT` is the bitwise OR of all exception macros which are supported by the FP implementation.

These functions allow you to clear exception flags, test for exceptions, and save and restore the set of exceptions flagged.

int feclearexcept (*int excepts*)   [Function]

Preliminary: | MT-Safe | AS-Safe !posix | AC-Safe !posix | See Section 1.2.2.1 [POSIX Safety Concepts], page 2.

This function clears all of the supported exception flags indicated by *excepts*.

The function returns zero in case the operation was successful, a non-zero value otherwise.

int feraiseexcept (*int excepts*)   [Function]

Preliminary: | MT-Safe | AS-Safe | AC-Safe | See Section 1.2.2.1 [POSIX Safety Concepts], page 2.

This function raises the supported exceptions indicated by *excepts*. If more than one exception bit in *excepts* is set the order in which the exceptions are raised is undefined except that overflow (`FE_OVERFLOW`) or underflow (`FE_UNDERFLOW`) are raised before inexact (`FE_INEXACT`). Whether for overflow or underflow the inexact exception is also raised is also implementation dependent.

The function returns zero in case the operation was successful, a non-zero value otherwise.

int fesetexcept (*int excepts*)   [Function]

Preliminary: | MT-Safe | AS-Safe | AC-Safe | See Section 1.2.2.1 [POSIX Safety Concepts], page 2.

This function sets the supported exception flags indicated by *excepts*, like `feraiseexcept`, but without causing enabled traps to be taken. `fesetexcept` is from TS 18661-1:2014.

The function returns zero in case the operation was successful, a non-zero value otherwise.

int fetestexcept (*int excepts*)   [Function]

Preliminary: | MT-Safe | AS-Safe | AC-Safe | See Section 1.2.2.1 [POSIX Safety Concepts], page 2.

Test whether the exception flags indicated by the parameter *except* are currently set. If any of them are, a nonzero value is returned which specifies which exceptions are set. Otherwise the result is zero.

To understand these functions, imagine that the status word is an integer variable named *status*. `feclearexcept` is then equivalent to '`status &= ~excepts`' and `fetestexcept` is equivalent to '`(status & excepts)`'. The actual implementation may be very different, of course.

Exception flags are only cleared when the program explicitly requests it, by calling `feclearexcept`. If you want to check for exceptions from a set of calculations, you should clear all the flags first. Here is a simple example of the way to use `fetestexcept`:

```
{
  double f;
  int raised;
  feclearexcept (FE_ALL_EXCEPT);
  f = compute ();
  raised = fetestexcept (FE_OVERFLOW | FE_INVALID);
  if (raised & FE_OVERFLOW) { /* ... */ }
```

```
        if (raised & FE_INVALID) { /* ... */ }
        /* ... */
    }
```

You cannot explicitly set bits in the status word. You can, however, save the entire status word and restore it later. This is done with the following functions:

int fegetexceptflag (*fexcept_t *flagp*, *int excepts*)   [Function]
>   Preliminary: | MT-Safe | AS-Safe | AC-Safe | See Section 1.2.2.1 [POSIX Safety Concepts], page 2.
>
>   This function stores in the variable pointed to by *flagp* an implementation-defined value representing the current setting of the exception flags indicated by *excepts*.
>
>   The function returns zero in case the operation was successful, a non-zero value otherwise.

int fesetexceptflag (*const fexcept_t *flagp*, *int excepts*)   [Function]
>   Preliminary: | MT-Safe | AS-Safe | AC-Safe | See Section 1.2.2.1 [POSIX Safety Concepts], page 2.
>
>   This function restores the flags for the exceptions indicated by *excepts* to the values stored in the variable pointed to by *flagp*.
>
>   The function returns zero in case the operation was successful, a non-zero value otherwise.

Note that the value stored in `fexcept_t` bears no resemblance to the bit mask returned by `fetestexcept`. The type may not even be an integer. Do not attempt to modify an `fexcept_t` variable.

int fetestexceptflag (*const fexcept_t *flagp*, *int excepts*)   [Function]
>   Preliminary: | MT-Safe | AS-Safe | AC-Safe | See Section 1.2.2.1 [POSIX Safety Concepts], page 2.
>
>   Test whether the exception flags indicated by the parameter *excepts* are set in the variable pointed to by *flagp*. If any of them are, a nonzero value is returned which specifies which exceptions are set. Otherwise the result is zero. `fetestexceptflag` is from TS 18661-1:2014.

20.5.4 Error Reporting by Mathematical Functions

Many of the math functions are defined only over a subset of the real or complex numbers. Even if they are mathematically defined, their result may be larger or smaller than the range representable by their return type without loss of accuracy. These are known as *domain errors*, *overflows*, and *underflows*, respectively. Math functions do several things when one of these errors occurs. In this manual we will refer to the complete response as *signalling* a domain error, overflow, or underflow.

When a math function suffers a domain error, it raises the invalid exception and returns NaN. It also sets *errno* to EDOM; this is for compatibility with old systems that do not support IEEE 754 exception handling. Likewise, when overflow occurs, math functions raise the overflow exception and, in the default rounding mode, return ∞ or $-\infty$ as appropriate (in other rounding modes, the largest finite value of the appropriate sign is returned when appropriate for that rounding mode). They also set *errno* to **ERANGE** if returning ∞ or

$-\infty$; *errno* may or may not be set to `ERANGE` when a finite value is returned on overflow. When underflow occurs, the underflow exception is raised, and zero (appropriately signed) or a subnormal value, as appropriate for the mathematical result of the function and the rounding mode, is returned. *errno* may be set to `ERANGE`, but this is not guaranteed; it is intended that the GNU C Library should set it when the underflow is to an appropriately signed zero, but not necessarily for other underflows.

When a math function has an argument that is a signaling NaN, the GNU C Library does not consider this a domain error, so `errno` is unchanged, but the invalid exception is still raised (except for a few functions that are specified to handle signaling NaNs differently).

Some of the math functions are defined mathematically to result in a complex value over parts of their domains. The most familiar example of this is taking the square root of a negative number. The complex math functions, such as `csqrt`, will return the appropriate complex value in this case. The real-valued functions, such as `sqrt`, will signal a domain error.

Some older hardware does not support infinities. On that hardware, overflows instead return a particular very large number (usually the largest representable number). `math.h` defines macros you can use to test for overflow on both old and new hardware.

double HUGE_VAL	[Macro]
float HUGE_VALF	[Macro]
long double HUGE_VALL	[Macro]
_FloatN HUGE_VAL_FN	[Macro]
_FloatNx HUGE_VAL_FNx	[Macro]

> An expression representing a particular very large number. On machines that use IEEE 754 floating point format, `HUGE_VAL` is infinity. On other machines, it's typically the largest positive number that can be represented.
>
> Mathematical functions return the appropriately typed version of `HUGE_VAL` or $-$`HUGE_VAL` when the result is too large to be represented.

20.6 Rounding Modes

Floating-point calculations are carried out internally with extra precision, and then rounded to fit into the destination type. This ensures that results are as precise as the input data. IEEE 754 defines four possible rounding modes:

Round to nearest.

> This is the default mode. It should be used unless there is a specific need for one of the others. In this mode results are rounded to the nearest representable value. If the result is midway between two representable values, the even representable is chosen. *Even* here means the lowest-order bit is zero. This rounding mode prevents statistical bias and guarantees numeric stability: round-off errors in a lengthy calculation will remain smaller than half of `FLT_EPSILON`.

Round toward plus Infinity.

> All results are rounded to the smallest representable value which is greater than the result.

Round toward minus Infinity.

> All results are rounded to the largest representable value which is less than the result.

Round toward zero.

> All results are rounded to the largest representable value whose magnitude is less than that of the result. In other words, if the result is negative it is rounded up; if it is positive, it is rounded down.

`fenv.h` defines constants which you can use to refer to the various rounding modes. Each one will be defined if and only if the FPU supports the corresponding rounding mode.

`FE_TONEAREST`

> Round to nearest.

`FE_UPWARD`

> Round toward $+\infty$.

`FE_DOWNWARD`

> Round toward $-\infty$.

`FE_TOWARDZERO`

> Round toward zero.

Underflow is an unusual case. Normally, IEEE 754 floating point numbers are always normalized (see Section A.5.3.1 [Floating Point Representation Concepts], page 919). Numbers smaller than 2^r (where r is the minimum exponent, `FLT_MIN_RADIX-1` for *float*) cannot be represented as normalized numbers. Rounding all such numbers to zero or 2^r would cause some algorithms to fail at 0. Therefore, they are left in denormalized form. That produces loss of precision, since some bits of the mantissa are stolen to indicate the decimal point.

If a result is too small to be represented as a denormalized number, it is rounded to zero. However, the sign of the result is preserved; if the calculation was negative, the result is *negative zero*. Negative zero can also result from some operations on infinity, such as $4/-\infty$.

At any time, one of the above four rounding modes is selected. You can find out which one with this function:

int **fegetround** (*void*)   [Function]

> Preliminary: | MT-Safe | AS-Safe | AC-Safe | See Section 1.2.2.1 [POSIX Safety Concepts], page 2.

> Returns the currently selected rounding mode, represented by one of the values of the defined rounding mode macros.

To change the rounding mode, use this function:

int **fesetround** (*int round*)   [Function]

> Preliminary: | MT-Safe | AS-Safe | AC-Safe | See Section 1.2.2.1 [POSIX Safety Concepts], page 2.

> Changes the currently selected rounding mode to *round*. If *round* does not correspond to one of the supported rounding modes nothing is changed. `fesetround` returns zero if it changed the rounding mode, or a nonzero value if the mode is not supported.

You should avoid changing the rounding mode if possible. It can be an expensive operation; also, some hardware requires you to compile your program differently for it to work. The resulting code may run slower. See your compiler documentation for details.

20.7 Floating-Point Control Functions

IEEE 754 floating-point implementations allow the programmer to decide whether traps will occur for each of the exceptions, by setting bits in the *control word*. In C, traps result in the program receiving the SIGFPE signal; see Chapter 24 [Signal Handling], page 685.

NB: IEEE 754 says that trap handlers are given details of the exceptional situation, and can set the result value. C signals do not provide any mechanism to pass this information back and forth. Trapping exceptions in C is therefore not very useful.

It is sometimes necessary to save the state of the floating-point unit while you perform some calculation. The library provides functions which save and restore the exception flags, the set of exceptions that generate traps, and the rounding mode. This information is known as the *floating-point environment*.

The functions to save and restore the floating-point environment all use a variable of type fenv_t to store information. This type is defined in fenv.h. Its size and contents are implementation-defined. You should not attempt to manipulate a variable of this type directly.

To save the state of the FPU, use one of these functions:

int fegetenv (*fenv_t *envp*)   [Function]
> Preliminary: | MT-Safe | AS-Safe | AC-Safe | See Section 1.2.2.1 [POSIX Safety Concepts], page 2.
>
> Store the floating-point environment in the variable pointed to by *envp*.
>
> The function returns zero in case the operation was successful, a non-zero value otherwise.

int feholdexcept (*fenv_t *envp*)   [Function]
> Preliminary: | MT-Safe | AS-Safe | AC-Safe | See Section 1.2.2.1 [POSIX Safety Concepts], page 2.
>
> Store the current floating-point environment in the object pointed to by *envp*. Then clear all exception flags, and set the FPU to trap no exceptions. Not all FPUs support trapping no exceptions; if feholdexcept cannot set this mode, it returns nonzero value. If it succeeds, it returns zero.

The functions which restore the floating-point environment can take these kinds of arguments:

- Pointers to fenv_t objects, which were initialized previously by a call to fegetenv or feholdexcept.

- The special macro FE_DFL_ENV which represents the floating-point environment as it was available at program start.

- Implementation defined macros with names starting with FE_ and having type fenv_t *.

If possible, the GNU C Library defines a macro `FE_NOMASK_ENV` which represents an environment where every exception raised causes a trap to occur. You can test for this macro using `#ifdef`. It is only defined if `_GNU_SOURCE` is defined.

Some platforms might define other predefined environments.

To set the floating-point environment, you can use either of these functions:

`int fesetenv` (*const fenv_t *envp*)   [Function]
> Preliminary: | MT-Safe | AS-Safe | AC-Safe | See Section 1.2.2.1 [POSIX Safety Concepts], page 2.
>
> Set the floating-point environment to that described by *envp*.
>
> The function returns zero in case the operation was successful, a non-zero value otherwise.

`int feupdateenv` (*const fenv_t *envp*)   [Function]
> Preliminary: | MT-Safe | AS-Safe | AC-Safe | See Section 1.2.2.1 [POSIX Safety Concepts], page 2.
>
> Like `fesetenv`, this function sets the floating-point environment to that described by *envp*. However, if any exceptions were flagged in the status word before `feupdateenv` was called, they remain flagged after the call. In other words, after `feupdateenv` is called, the status word is the bitwise OR of the previous status word and the one saved in *envp*.
>
> The function returns zero in case the operation was successful, a non-zero value otherwise.

TS 18661-1:2014 defines additional functions to save and restore floating-point control modes (such as the rounding mode and whether traps are enabled) while leaving other status (such as raised flags) unchanged.

The special macro `FE_DFL_MODE` may be passed to `fesetmode`. It represents the floating-point control modes at program start.

`int fegetmode` (*femode_t *modep*)   [Function]
> Preliminary: | MT-Safe | AS-Safe | AC-Safe | See Section 1.2.2.1 [POSIX Safety Concepts], page 2.
>
> Store the floating-point control modes in the variable pointed to by *modep*.
>
> The function returns zero in case the operation was successful, a non-zero value otherwise.

`int fesetmode` (*const femode_t *modep*)   [Function]
> Preliminary: | MT-Safe | AS-Safe | AC-Safe | See Section 1.2.2.1 [POSIX Safety Concepts], page 2.
>
> Set the floating-point control modes to those described by *modep*.
>
> The function returns zero in case the operation was successful, a non-zero value otherwise.

To control for individual exceptions if raising them causes a trap to occur, you can use the following two functions.

Portability Note: These functions are all GNU extensions.

int feenableexcept (*int excepts*) [Function]

Preliminary: | MT-Safe | AS-Safe | AC-Safe | See Section 1.2.2.1 [POSIX Safety Concepts], page 2.

This function enables traps for each of the exceptions as indicated by the parameter *excepts*. The individual exceptions are described in Section 20.5.3 [Examining the FPU status word], page 584. Only the specified exceptions are enabled, the status of the other exceptions is not changed.

The function returns the previous enabled exceptions in case the operation was successful, -1 otherwise.

int fedisableexcept (*int excepts*) [Function]

Preliminary: | MT-Safe | AS-Safe | AC-Safe | See Section 1.2.2.1 [POSIX Safety Concepts], page 2.

This function disables traps for each of the exceptions as indicated by the parameter *excepts*. The individual exceptions are described in Section 20.5.3 [Examining the FPU status word], page 584. Only the specified exceptions are disabled, the status of the other exceptions is not changed.

The function returns the previous enabled exceptions in case the operation was successful, -1 otherwise.

int fegetexcept (*void*) [Function]

Preliminary: | MT-Safe | AS-Safe | AC-Safe | See Section 1.2.2.1 [POSIX Safety Concepts], page 2.

The function returns a bitmask of all currently enabled exceptions. It returns -1 in case of failure.

20.8 Arithmetic Functions

The C library provides functions to do basic operations on floating-point numbers. These include absolute value, maximum and minimum, normalization, bit twiddling, rounding, and a few others.

20.8.1 Absolute Value

These functions are provided for obtaining the *absolute value* (or *magnitude*) of a number. The absolute value of a real number x is x if x is positive, $-x$ if x is negative. For a complex number z, whose real part is x and whose imaginary part is y, the absolute value is sqrt ($x*x + y*y$).

Prototypes for abs, labs and llabs are in stdlib.h; imaxabs is declared in inttypes.h; the fabs functions are declared in math.h; the cabs functions are declared in complex.h.

int abs (*int number*) [Function]
long int labs (*long int number*) [Function]
long long int llabs (*long long int number*) [Function]
intmax_t imaxabs (*intmax_t number*) [Function]

Preliminary: | MT-Safe | AS-Safe | AC-Safe | See Section 1.2.2.1 [POSIX Safety Concepts], page 2.

These functions return the absolute value of *number*.

Most computers use a two's complement integer representation, in which the absolute value of `INT_MIN` (the smallest possible `int`) cannot be represented; thus, `abs (INT_MIN)` is not defined.

`llabs` and `imaxdiv` are new to ISO C99.

See Section 20.1 [Integers], page 575, for a description of the `intmax_t` type.

`double fabs (`*double* `number)`   [Function]
`float fabsf (`*float* `number)`   [Function]
`long double fabsl (`*long double* `number)`   [Function]
`_FloatN fabsfN (`*_FloatN* `number)`   [Function]
`_FloatNx fabsfNx (`*_FloatNx* `number)`   [Function]

> Preliminary: | MT-Safe | AS-Safe | AC-Safe | See Section 1.2.2.1 [POSIX Safety Concepts], page 2.

> This function returns the absolute value of the floating-point number *number*.

`double cabs (`*complex double* `z)`   [Function]
`float cabsf (`*complex float* `z)`   [Function]
`long double cabsl (`*complex long double* `z)`   [Function]
`_FloatN cabsfN (`*complex _FloatN* `z)`   [Function]
`_FloatNx cabsfNx (`*complex _FloatNx* `z)`   [Function]

> Preliminary: | MT-Safe | AS-Safe | AC-Safe | See Section 1.2.2.1 [POSIX Safety Concepts], page 2.

> These functions return the absolute value of the complex number *z* (see Section 20.9 [Complex Numbers], page 606). The absolute value of a complex number is:

> > `sqrt (creal (z) * creal (z) + cimag (z) * cimag (z))`

This function should always be used instead of the direct formula because it takes special care to avoid losing precision. It may also take advantage of hardware support for this operation. See `hypot` in Section 19.4 [Exponentiation and Logarithms], page 530.

20.8.2 Normalization Functions

The functions described in this section are primarily provided as a way to efficiently perform certain low-level manipulations on floating point numbers that are represented internally using a binary radix; see Section A.5.3.1 [Floating Point Representation Concepts], page 919. These functions are required to have equivalent behavior even if the representation does not use a radix of 2, but of course they are unlikely to be particularly efficient in those cases.

All these functions are declared in `math.h`.

`double frexp (`*double* `value, int *exponent)`   [Function]
`float frexpf (`*float* `value, int *exponent)`   [Function]
`long double frexpl (`*long double* `value, int *exponent)`   [Function]
`_FloatN frexpfN (`*_FloatN* `value, int *exponent)`   [Function]
`_FloatNx frexpfNx (`*_FloatNx* `value, int *exponent)`   [Function]

> Preliminary: | MT-Safe | AS-Safe | AC-Safe | See Section 1.2.2.1 [POSIX Safety Concepts], page 2.

> These functions are used to split the number *value* into a normalized fraction and an exponent.

If the argument *value* is not zero, the return value is *value* times a power of two, and its magnitude is always in the range 1/2 (inclusive) to 1 (exclusive). The corresponding exponent is stored in *exponent*; the return value multiplied by 2 raised to this exponent equals the original number *value*.

For example, `frexp (12.8, &exponent)` returns `0.8` and stores `4` in `exponent`.

If *value* is zero, then the return value is zero and zero is stored in *exponent*.

double `ldexp` (*double value, int exponent*)   [Function]
float `ldexpf` (*float value, int exponent*)   [Function]
long double `ldexpl` (*long double value, int exponent*)   [Function]
_FloatN `ldexpfN` (*_FloatN value, int exponent*)   [Function]
_FloatNx `ldexpfNx` (*_FloatNx value, int exponent*)   [Function]

> Preliminary: | MT-Safe | AS-Safe | AC-Safe | See Section 1.2.2.1 [POSIX Safety Concepts], page 2.
>
> These functions return the result of multiplying the floating-point number *value* by 2 raised to the power *exponent*. (It can be used to reassemble floating-point numbers that were taken apart by `frexp`.)
>
> For example, `ldexp (0.8, 4)` returns `12.8`.

The following functions, which come from BSD, provide facilities equivalent to those of `ldexp` and `frexp`. See also the ISO C function `logb` which originally also appeared in BSD. The _FloatN and _FloatN variants of the following functions come from TS 18661-3:2015.

double `scalb` (*double value, double exponent*)   [Function]
float `scalbf` (*float value, float exponent*)   [Function]
long double `scalbl` (*long double value, long double exponent*)   [Function]

> Preliminary: | MT-Safe | AS-Safe | AC-Safe | See Section 1.2.2.1 [POSIX Safety Concepts], page 2.
>
> The `scalb` function is the BSD name for `ldexp`.

double `scalbn` (*double x, int n*)   [Function]
float `scalbnf` (*float x, int n*)   [Function]
long double `scalbnl` (*long double x, int n*)   [Function]
_FloatN `scalbnfN` (*_FloatN x, int n*)   [Function]
_FloatNx `scalbnfNx` (*_FloatNx x, int n*)   [Function]

> Preliminary: | MT-Safe | AS-Safe | AC-Safe | See Section 1.2.2.1 [POSIX Safety Concepts], page 2.
>
> `scalbn` is identical to `scalb`, except that the exponent *n* is an `int` instead of a floating-point number.

double `scalbln` (*double x, long int n*)   [Function]
float `scalblnf` (*float x, long int n*)   [Function]
long double `scalblnl` (*long double x, long int n*)   [Function]
_FloatN `scalblnfN` (*_FloatN x, long int n*)   [Function]
_FloatNx `scalblnfNx` (*_FloatNx x, long int n*)   [Function]

> Preliminary: | MT-Safe | AS-Safe | AC-Safe | See Section 1.2.2.1 [POSIX Safety Concepts], page 2.

scalbln is identical to scalb, except that the exponent n is a long int instead of a floating-point number.

double significand (*double* x)   [Function]
float significandf (*float* x)   [Function]
long double significandl (*long double* x)   [Function]

    Preliminary: | MT-Safe | AS-Safe | AC-Safe | See Section 1.2.2.1 [POSIX Safety Concepts], page 2.

    significand returns the mantissa of x scaled to the range $[1, 2)$. It is equivalent to scalb (*x*, (double) -ilogb (*x*)).

    This function exists mainly for use in certain standardized tests of IEEE 754 conformance.

20.8.3 Rounding Functions

The functions listed here perform operations such as rounding and truncation of floating-point values. Some of these functions convert floating point numbers to integer values. They are all declared in math.h.

You can also convert floating-point numbers to integers simply by casting them to int. This discards the fractional part, effectively rounding towards zero. However, this only works if the result can actually be represented as an int—for very large numbers, this is impossible. The functions listed here return the result as a double instead to get around this problem.

The fromfp functions use the following macros, from TS 18661-1:2014, to specify the direction of rounding. These correspond to the rounding directions defined in IEEE 754-2008.

FP_INT_UPWARD
        Round toward $+\infty$.

FP_INT_DOWNWARD
        Round toward $-\infty$.

FP_INT_TOWARDZERO
        Round toward zero.

FP_INT_TONEARESTFROMZERO
        Round to nearest, ties round away from zero.

FP_INT_TONEAREST
        Round to nearest, ties round to even.

double ceil (*double* x)   [Function]
float ceilf (*float* x)   [Function]
long double ceill (*long double* x)   [Function]
_FloatN ceilfN (*_FloatN* x)   [Function]
_FloatNx ceilfNx (*_FloatNx* x)   [Function]

    Preliminary: | MT-Safe | AS-Safe | AC-Safe | See Section 1.2.2.1 [POSIX Safety Concepts], page 2.

    These functions round x upwards to the nearest integer, returning that value as a double. Thus, ceil (1.5) is 2.0.

double floor (*double x*)   [Function]
float floorf (*float x*)   [Function]
long double floorl (*long double x*)   [Function]
_FloatN floorfN (*_FloatN x*)   [Function]
_FloatNx floorfNx (*_FloatNx x*)   [Function]
> Preliminary: | MT-Safe | AS-Safe | AC-Safe | See Section 1.2.2.1 [POSIX Safety Concepts], page 2.

> These functions round *x* downwards to the nearest integer, returning that value as a double. Thus, floor (1.5) is 1.0 and floor (-1.5) is -2.0.

double trunc (*double x*)   [Function]
float truncf (*float x*)   [Function]
long double truncl (*long double x*)   [Function]
_FloatN truncfN (*_FloatN x*)   [Function]
_FloatNx truncfNx (*_FloatNx x*)   [Function]
> Preliminary: | MT-Safe | AS-Safe | AC-Safe | See Section 1.2.2.1 [POSIX Safety Concepts], page 2.

> The trunc functions round *x* towards zero to the nearest integer (returned in floating-point format). Thus, trunc (1.5) is 1.0 and trunc (-1.5) is -1.0.

double rint (*double x*)   [Function]
float rintf (*float x*)   [Function]
long double rintl (*long double x*)   [Function]
_FloatN rintfN (*_FloatN x*)   [Function]
_FloatNx rintfNx (*_FloatNx x*)   [Function]
> Preliminary: | MT-Safe | AS-Safe | AC-Safe | See Section 1.2.2.1 [POSIX Safety Concepts], page 2.

> These functions round *x* to an integer value according to the current rounding mode. See Section A.5.3.2 [Floating Point Parameters], page 921, for information about the various rounding modes. The default rounding mode is to round to the nearest integer; some machines support other modes, but round-to-nearest is always used unless you explicitly select another.

> If *x* was not initially an integer, these functions raise the inexact exception.

double nearbyint (*double x*)   [Function]
float nearbyintf (*float x*)   [Function]
long double nearbyintl (*long double x*)   [Function]
_FloatN nearbyintfN (*_FloatN x*)   [Function]
_FloatNx nearbyintfNx (*_FloatNx x*)   [Function]
> Preliminary: | MT-Safe | AS-Safe | AC-Safe | See Section 1.2.2.1 [POSIX Safety Concepts], page 2.

> These functions return the same value as the rint functions, but do not raise the inexact exception if *x* is not an integer.

double round (*double x*)   [Function]
float roundf (*float x*)   [Function]
long double roundl (*long double x*)   [Function]

_FloatN roundfN (_FloatN x)   [Function]
_FloatNx roundfNx (_FloatNx x)   [Function]
> Preliminary: | MT-Safe | AS-Safe | AC-Safe | See Section 1.2.2.1 [POSIX Safety
> Concepts], page 2.
>
> These functions are similar to rint, but they round halfway cases away from zero
> instead of to the nearest integer (or other current rounding mode).

double roundeven (double x)   [Function]
float roundevenf (float x)   [Function]
long double roundevenl (long double x)   [Function]
_FloatN roundevenfN (_FloatN x)   [Function]
_FloatNx roundevenfNx (_FloatNx x)   [Function]
> Preliminary: | MT-Safe | AS-Safe | AC-Safe | See Section 1.2.2.1 [POSIX Safety
> Concepts], page 2.
>
> These functions, from TS 18661-1:2014 and TS 18661-3:2015, are similar to round,
> but they round halfway cases to even instead of away from zero.

long int lrint (double x)   [Function]
long int lrintf (float x)   [Function]
long int lrintl (long double x)   [Function]
long int lrintfN (_FloatN x)   [Function]
long int lrintfNx (_FloatNx x)   [Function]
> Preliminary: | MT-Safe | AS-Safe | AC-Safe | See Section 1.2.2.1 [POSIX Safety
> Concepts], page 2.
>
> These functions are just like rint, but they return a long int instead of a floating-
> point number.

long long int llrint (double x)   [Function]
long long int llrintf (float x)   [Function]
long long int llrintl (long double x)   [Function]
long long int llrintfN (_FloatN x)   [Function]
long long int llrintfNx (_FloatNx x)   [Function]
> Preliminary: | MT-Safe | AS-Safe | AC-Safe | See Section 1.2.2.1 [POSIX Safety
> Concepts], page 2.
>
> These functions are just like rint, but they return a long long int instead of a
> floating-point number.

long int lround (double x)   [Function]
long int lroundf (float x)   [Function]
long int lroundl (long double x)   [Function]
long int lroundfN (_FloatN x)   [Function]
long int lroundfNx (_FloatNx x)   [Function]
> Preliminary: | MT-Safe | AS-Safe | AC-Safe | See Section 1.2.2.1 [POSIX Safety
> Concepts], page 2.
>
> These functions are just like round, but they return a long int instead of a floating-
> point number.

long long int llround (*double x*) [Function]
long long int llroundf (*float x*) [Function]
long long int llroundl (*long double x*) [Function]
long long int llroundfN (*_FloatN x*) [Function]
long long int llroundfNx (*_FloatNx x*) [Function]
> Preliminary: | MT-Safe | AS-Safe | AC-Safe | See Section 1.2.2.1 [POSIX Safety Concepts], page 2.

> These functions are just like **round**, but they return a **long long int** instead of a floating-point number.

intmax_t fromfp (*double x, int round, unsigned int width*) [Function]
intmax_t fromfpf (*float x, int round, unsigned int width*) [Function]
intmax_t fromfpl (*long double x, int round, unsigned int width*) [Function]
intmax_t fromfpfN (*_FloatN x, int round, unsigned int width*) [Function]
intmax_t fromfpfNx (*_FloatNx x, int round, unsigned int width*) [Function]
uintmax_t ufromfp (*double x, int round, unsigned int width*) [Function]
uintmax_t ufromfpf (*float x, int round, unsigned int width*) [Function]
uintmax_t ufromfpl (*long double x, int round, unsigned int width*) [Function]
uintmax_t ufromfpfN (*_FloatN x, int round, unsigned int width*) [Function]
uintmax_t ufromfpfNx (*_FloatNx x, int round, unsigned int width*) [Function]
intmax_t fromfpx (*double x, int round, unsigned int width*) [Function]
intmax_t fromfpxf (*float x, int round, unsigned int width*) [Function]
intmax_t fromfpxl (*long double x, int round, unsigned int width*) [Function]
intmax_t fromfpxfN (*_FloatN x, int round, unsigned int width*) [Function]
intmax_t fromfpxfNx (*_FloatNx x, int round, unsigned int width*) [Function]
uintmax_t ufromfpx (*double x, int round, unsigned int width*) [Function]
uintmax_t ufromfpxf (*float x, int round, unsigned int width*) [Function]
uintmax_t ufromfpxl (*long double x, int round, unsigned int width*) [Function]
uintmax_t ufromfpxfN (*_FloatN x, int round, unsigned int width*) [Function]
uintmax_t ufromfpxfNx (*_FloatNx x, int round, unsigned int width*) [Function]
> Preliminary: | MT-Safe | AS-Safe | AC-Safe | See Section 1.2.2.1 [POSIX Safety Concepts], page 2.

> These functions, from TS 18661-1:2014 and TS 18661-3:2015, convert a floating-point number to an integer according to the rounding direction *round* (one of the **FP_INT_*** macros). If the integer is outside the range of a signed or unsigned (depending on the return type of the function) type of width *width* bits (or outside the range of the return type, if *width* is larger), or if *x* is infinite or NaN, or if *width* is zero, a domain error occurs and an unspecified value is returned. The functions with an 'x' in their names raise the inexact exception when a domain error does not occur and the argument is not an integer; the other functions do not raise the inexact exception.

double modf (*double value, double *integer-part*) [Function]
float modff (*float value, float *integer-part*) [Function]
long double modfl (*long double value, long double [Function]
> *integer-part*)
_FloatN modffN (*_FloatN value, _FloatN *integer-part*) [Function]

`_FloatNx modffNx (`*_FloatNx value, _FloatNx *integer-part*`)` [Function]
> Preliminary: | MT-Safe | AS-Safe | AC-Safe | See Section 1.2.2.1 [POSIX Safety Concepts], page 2.

> These functions break the argument *value* into an integer part and a fractional part (between `-1` and `1`, exclusive). Their sum equals *value*. Each of the parts has the same sign as *value*, and the integer part is always rounded toward zero.

> `modf` stores the integer part in `*integer-part`, and returns the fractional part. For example, `modf (2.5, &intpart)` returns `0.5` and stores `2.0` into `intpart`.

20.8.4 Remainder Functions

The functions in this section compute the remainder on division of two floating-point numbers. Each is a little different; pick the one that suits your problem.

`double fmod (`*double numerator, double denominator*`)` [Function]
`float fmodf (`*float numerator, float denominator*`)` [Function]
`long double fmodl (`*long double numerator, long double denominator*`)` [Function]
`_FloatN fmodfN (`*_FloatN numerator, _FloatN denominator*`)` [Function]
`_FloatNx fmodfNx (`*_FloatNx numerator, _FloatNx denominator*`)` [Function]
> Preliminary: | MT-Safe | AS-Safe | AC-Safe | See Section 1.2.2.1 [POSIX Safety Concepts], page 2.

> These functions compute the remainder from the division of *numerator* by *denominator*. Specifically, the return value is `numerator - n * denominator`, where n is the quotient of *numerator* divided by *denominator*, rounded towards zero to an integer. Thus, `fmod (6.5, 2.3)` returns `1.9`, which is `6.5` minus `4.6`.

> The result has the same sign as the *numerator* and has magnitude less than the magnitude of the *denominator*.

> If *denominator* is zero, `fmod` signals a domain error.

`double remainder (`*double numerator, double denominator*`)` [Function]
`float remainderf (`*float numerator, float denominator*`)` [Function]
`long double remainderl (`*long double numerator, long double denominator*`)` [Function]
`_FloatN remainderfN (`*_FloatN numerator, _FloatN denominator*`)` [Function]
`_FloatNx remainderfNx (`*_FloatNx numerator, _FloatNx denominator*`)` [Function]
> Preliminary: | MT-Safe | AS-Safe | AC-Safe | See Section 1.2.2.1 [POSIX Safety Concepts], page 2.

> These functions are like `fmod` except that they round the internal quotient n to the nearest integer instead of towards zero to an integer. For example, `remainder (6.5, 2.3)` returns `-0.4`, which is `6.5` minus `6.9`.

> The absolute value of the result is less than or equal to half the absolute value of the *denominator*. The difference between `fmod (`*numerator, denominator*`)` and `remainder (`*numerator, denominator*`)` is always either *denominator*, minus *denominator*, or zero.

> If *denominator* is zero, `remainder` signals a domain error.

double drem (*double numerator, double denominator*)   [Function]
float dremf (*float numerator, float denominator*)   [Function]
long double dreml (*long double numerator, long double*   [Function]
    denominator)

> Preliminary: | MT-Safe | AS-Safe | AC-Safe | See Section 1.2.2.1 [POSIX Safety Concepts], page 2.

> This function is another name for remainder.

20.8.5 Setting and modifying single bits of FP values

There are some operations that are too complicated or expensive to perform by hand on floating-point numbers. ISO C99 defines functions to do these operations, which mostly involve changing single bits.

double copysign (*double x, double y*)   [Function]
float copysignf (*float x, float y*)   [Function]
long double copysignl (*long double x, long double y*)   [Function]
_FloatN copysignfN (*_FloatN x, _FloatN y*)   [Function]
_FloatNx copysignfNx (*_FloatNx x, _FloatNx y*)   [Function]

> Preliminary: | MT-Safe | AS-Safe | AC-Safe | See Section 1.2.2.1 [POSIX Safety Concepts], page 2.

> These functions return x but with the sign of y. They work even if x or y are NaN or zero. Both of these can carry a sign (although not all implementations support it) and this is one of the few operations that can tell the difference.

> copysign never raises an exception.

> This function is defined in IEC 559 (and the appendix with recommended functions in IEEE 754/IEEE 854).

int signbit (*float-type x*)   [Function]

> Preliminary: | MT-Safe | AS-Safe | AC-Safe | See Section 1.2.2.1 [POSIX Safety Concepts], page 2.

> signbit is a generic macro which can work on all floating-point types. It returns a nonzero value if the value of x has its sign bit set.

> This is not the same as x < 0.0, because IEEE 754 floating point allows zero to be signed. The comparison -0.0 < 0.0 is false, but signbit (-0.0) will return a nonzero value.

double nextafter (*double x, double y*)   [Function]
float nextafterf (*float x, float y*)   [Function]
long double nextafterl (*long double x, long double y*)   [Function]
_FloatN nextafterfN (*_FloatN x, _FloatN y*)   [Function]
_FloatNx nextafterfNx (*_FloatNx x, _FloatNx y*)   [Function]

> Preliminary: | MT-Safe | AS-Safe | AC-Safe | See Section 1.2.2.1 [POSIX Safety Concepts], page 2.

> The nextafter function returns the next representable neighbor of x in the direction towards y. The size of the step between x and the result depends on the type of the result. If $x = y$ the function simply returns y. If either value is NaN, NaN is returned.

Otherwise a value corresponding to the value of the least significant bit in the mantissa is added or subtracted, depending on the direction. `nextafter` will signal overflow or underflow if the result goes outside of the range of normalized numbers.

This function is defined in IEC 559 (and the appendix with recommended functions in IEEE 754/IEEE 854).

double nexttoward (*double x, long double y*)	[Function]
float nexttowardf (*float x, long double y*)	[Function]
long double nexttowardl (*long double x, long double y*)	[Function]

Preliminary: | MT-Safe | AS-Safe | AC-Safe | See Section 1.2.2.1 [POSIX Safety Concepts], page 2.

These functions are identical to the corresponding versions of `nextafter` except that their second argument is a `long double`.

double nextup (*double x*)	[Function]
float nextupf (*float x*)	[Function]
long double nextupl (*long double x*)	[Function]
_FloatN nextupfN (*_FloatN x*)	[Function]
_FloatNx nextupfNx (*_FloatNx x*)	[Function]

Preliminary: | MT-Safe | AS-Safe | AC-Safe | See Section 1.2.2.1 [POSIX Safety Concepts], page 2.

The **nextup** function returns the next representable neighbor of x in the direction of positive infinity. If x is the smallest negative subnormal number in the type of x the function returns -0. If $x = 0$ the function returns the smallest positive subnormal number in the type of x. If x is NaN, NaN is returned. If x is $+\infty$, $+\infty$ is returned. **nextup** is from TS 18661-1:2014 and TS 18661-3:2015. **nextup** never raises an exception except for signaling NaNs.

double nextdown (*double x*)	[Function]
float nextdownf (*float x*)	[Function]
long double nextdownl (*long double x*)	[Function]
_FloatN nextdownfN (*_FloatN x*)	[Function]
_FloatNx nextdownfNx (*_FloatNx x*)	[Function]

Preliminary: | MT-Safe | AS-Safe | AC-Safe | See Section 1.2.2.1 [POSIX Safety Concepts], page 2.

The **nextdown** function returns the next representable neighbor of x in the direction of negative infinity. If x is the smallest positive subnormal number in the type of x the function returns +0. If $x = 0$ the function returns the smallest negative subnormal number in the type of x. If x is NaN, NaN is returned. If x is $-\infty$, $-\infty$ is returned. **nextdown** is from TS 18661-1:2014 and TS 18661-3:2015. **nextdown** never raises an exception except for signaling NaNs.

double nan (*const char *tagp*)	[Function]
float nanf (*const char *tagp*)	[Function]
long double nanl (*const char *tagp*)	[Function]
_FloatN nanfN (*const char *tagp*)	[Function]

`_FloatNx nanfNx` (*const char *tagp*) [Function]
Preliminary: | MT-Safe locale | AS-Safe | AC-Safe | See Section 1.2.2.1 [POSIX Safety Concepts], page 2.

The `nan` function returns a representation of NaN, provided that NaN is supported by the target platform. `nan ("n-char-sequence")` is equivalent to `strtod ("NAN(n-char-sequence)")`.

The argument *tagp* is used in an unspecified manner. On IEEE 754 systems, there are many representations of NaN, and *tagp* selects one. On other systems it may do nothing.

`int canonicalize` (*double *cx, const double *x*) [Function]
`int canonicalizef` (*float *cx, const float *x*) [Function]
`int canonicalizel` (*long double *cx, const long double *x*) [Function]
`int canonicalizefN` (*_FloatN *cx, const _FloatN *x*) [Function]
`int canonicalizefNx` (*_FloatNx *cx, const _FloatNx *x*) [Function]
Preliminary: | MT-Safe | AS-Safe | AC-Safe | See Section 1.2.2.1 [POSIX Safety Concepts], page 2.

In some floating-point formats, some values have canonical (preferred) and noncanonical encodings (for IEEE interchange binary formats, all encodings are canonical). These functions, defined by TS 18661-1:2014 and TS 18661-3:2015, attempt to produce a canonical version of the floating-point value pointed to by *x*; if that value is a signaling NaN, they raise the invalid exception and produce a quiet NaN. If a canonical value is produced, it is stored in the object pointed to by *cx*, and these functions return zero. Otherwise (if a canonical value could not be produced because the object pointed to by *x* is not a valid representation of any floating-point value), the object pointed to by *cx* is unchanged and a nonzero value is returned.

Note that some formats have multiple encodings of a value which are all equally canonical; when such an encoding is used as an input to this function, any such encoding of the same value (or of the corresponding quiet NaN, if that value is a signaling NaN) may be produced as output.

`double getpayload` (*const double *x*) [Function]
`float getpayloadf` (*const float *x*) [Function]
`long double getpayloadl` (*const long double *x*) [Function]
`_FloatN getpayloadfN` (*const _FloatN *x*) [Function]
`_FloatNx getpayloadfNx` (*const _FloatNx *x*) [Function]
Preliminary: | MT-Safe | AS-Safe | AC-Safe | See Section 1.2.2.1 [POSIX Safety Concepts], page 2.

IEEE 754 defines the *payload* of a NaN to be an integer value encoded in the representation of the NaN. Payloads are typically propagated from NaN inputs to the result of a floating-point operation. These functions, defined by TS 18661-1:2014 and TS 18661-3:2015, return the payload of the NaN pointed to by *x* (returned as a positive integer, or positive zero, represented as a floating-point number); if *x* is not a NaN, they return an unspecified value. They raise no floating-point exceptions even for signaling NaNs.

int setpayload (*double *x, double* `payload`)   [Function]
int setpayloadf (*float *x, float* `payload`)   [Function]
int setpayloadl (*long double *x, long double* `payload`)   [Function]
int setpayloadfN (*_FloatN *x, _FloatN* `payload`)   [Function]
int setpayloadfNx (*_FloatNx *x, _FloatNx* `payload`)   [Function]
>   Preliminary: | MT-Safe | AS-Safe | AC-Safe | See Section 1.2.2.1 [POSIX Safety
>   Concepts], page 2.

>   These functions, defined by TS 18661-1:2014 and TS 18661-3:2015, set the object
>   pointed to by x to a quiet NaN with payload *payload* and a zero sign bit and return
>   zero. If *payload* is not a positive-signed integer that is a valid payload for a quiet
>   NaN of the given type, the object pointed to by x is set to positive zero and a nonzero
>   value is returned. They raise no floating-point exceptions.

int setpayloadsig (*double *x, double* `payload`)   [Function]
int setpayloadsigf (*float *x, float* `payload`)   [Function]
int setpayloadsigl (*long double *x, long double* `payload`)   [Function]
int setpayloadsigfN (*_FloatN *x, _FloatN* `payload`)   [Function]
int setpayloadsigfNx (*_FloatNx *x, _FloatNx* `payload`)   [Function]
>   Preliminary: | MT-Safe | AS-Safe | AC-Safe | See Section 1.2.2.1 [POSIX Safety
>   Concepts], page 2.

>   These functions, defined by TS 18661-1:2014 and TS 18661-3:2015, set the object
>   pointed to by x to a signaling NaN with payload *payload* and a zero sign bit and
>   return zero. If *payload* is not a positive-signed integer that is a valid payload for a
>   signaling NaN of the given type, the object pointed to by x is set to positive zero and
>   a nonzero value is returned. They raise no floating-point exceptions.

20.8.6 Floating-Point Comparison Functions

The standard C comparison operators provoke exceptions when one or other of the operands
is NaN. For example,

```
int v = a < 1.0;
```

will raise an exception if *a* is NaN. (This does *not* happen with == and !=; those merely
return false and true, respectively, when NaN is examined.) Frequently this exception is
undesirable. ISO C99 therefore defines comparison functions that do not raise exceptions
when NaN is examined. All of the functions are implemented as macros which allow their
arguments to be of any floating-point type. The macros are guaranteed to evaluate their
arguments only once. TS 18661-1:2014 adds such a macro for an equality comparison that
does raise an exception for a NaN argument; it also adds functions that provide a total
ordering on all floating-point values, including NaNs, without raising any exceptions even
for signaling NaNs.

int isgreater (*real-floating x, real-floating y*)   [Macro]
>   Preliminary: | MT-Safe | AS-Safe | AC-Safe | See Section 1.2.2.1 [POSIX Safety
>   Concepts], page 2.

>   This macro determines whether the argument x is greater than y. It is equivalent to
>   (x) > (y), but no exception is raised if x or y are NaN.

int isgreaterequal (*real-floating* **x**, *real-floating* **y**)   [Macro]
Preliminary: | MT-Safe | AS-Safe | AC-Safe | See Section 1.2.2.1 [POSIX Safety Concepts], page 2.

This macro determines whether the argument *x* is greater than or equal to *y*. It is equivalent to `(x) >= (y)`, but no exception is raised if *x* or *y* are NaN.

int isless (*real-floating* **x**, *real-floating* **y**)   [Macro]
Preliminary: | MT-Safe | AS-Safe | AC-Safe | See Section 1.2.2.1 [POSIX Safety Concepts], page 2.

This macro determines whether the argument *x* is less than *y*. It is equivalent to `(x) < (y)`, but no exception is raised if *x* or *y* are NaN.

int islessequal (*real-floating* **x**, *real-floating* **y**)   [Macro]
Preliminary: | MT-Safe | AS-Safe | AC-Safe | See Section 1.2.2.1 [POSIX Safety Concepts], page 2.

This macro determines whether the argument *x* is less than or equal to *y*. It is equivalent to `(x) <= (y)`, but no exception is raised if *x* or *y* are NaN.

int islessgreater (*real-floating* **x**, *real-floating* **y**)   [Macro]
Preliminary: | MT-Safe | AS-Safe | AC-Safe | See Section 1.2.2.1 [POSIX Safety Concepts], page 2.

This macro determines whether the argument *x* is less or greater than *y*. It is equivalent to `(x) < (y) || (x) > (y)` (although it only evaluates *x* and *y* once), but no exception is raised if *x* or *y* are NaN.

This macro is not equivalent to `x != y`, because that expression is true if *x* or *y* are NaN.

int isunordered (*real-floating* **x**, *real-floating* **y**)   [Macro]
Preliminary: | MT-Safe | AS-Safe | AC-Safe | See Section 1.2.2.1 [POSIX Safety Concepts], page 2.

This macro determines whether its arguments are unordered. In other words, it is true if *x* or *y* are NaN, and false otherwise.

int iseqsig (*real-floating* **x**, *real-floating* **y**)   [Macro]
Preliminary: | MT-Safe | AS-Safe | AC-Safe | See Section 1.2.2.1 [POSIX Safety Concepts], page 2.

This macro determines whether its arguments are equal. It is equivalent to `(x) == (y)`, but it raises the invalid exception and sets `errno` to `EDOM` if either argument is a NaN.

int totalorder (*double* **x**, *double* **y**)   [Function]
int totalorderf (*float* **x**, *float* **y**)   [Function]
int totalorderl (*long double* **x**, *long double* **y**)   [Function]
int totalorderfN (*_FloatN* **x**, *_FloatN* **y**)   [Function]
int totalorderfNx (*_FloatNx* **x**, *_FloatNx* **y**)   [Function]
Preliminary: | MT-Safe | AS-Safe | AC-Safe | See Section 1.2.2.1 [POSIX Safety Concepts], page 2.

These functions determine whether the total order relationship, defined in IEEE 754-2008, is true for x and y, returning nonzero if it is true and zero if it is false. No exceptions are raised even for signaling NaNs. The relationship is true if they are the same floating-point value (including sign for zero and NaNs, and payload for NaNs), or if x comes before y in the following order: negative quiet NaNs, in order of decreasing payload; negative signaling NaNs, in order of decreasing payload; negative infinity; finite numbers, in ascending order, with negative zero before positive zero; positive infinity; positive signaling NaNs, in order of increasing payload; positive quiet NaNs, in order of increasing payload.

int totalordermag (*double x, double y*)	[Function]
int totalordermagf (*float x, float y*)	[Function]
int totalordermagl (*long double x, long double y*)	[Function]
int totalordermagfN (*_FloatN x, _FloatN y*)	[Function]
int totalordermagfNx (*_FloatNx x, _FloatNx y*)	[Function]

Preliminary: | MT-Safe | AS-Safe | AC-Safe | See Section 1.2.2.1 [POSIX Safety Concepts], page 2.

These functions determine whether the total order relationship, defined in IEEE 754-2008, is true for the absolute values of x and y, returning nonzero if it is true and zero if it is false. No exceptions are raised even for signaling NaNs.

Not all machines provide hardware support for these operations. On machines that don't, the macros can be very slow. Therefore, you should not use these functions when NaN is not a concern.

NB: There are no macros isequal or isunequal. They are unnecessary, because the == and != operators do *not* throw an exception if one or both of the operands are NaN.

20.8.7 Miscellaneous FP arithmetic functions

The functions in this section perform miscellaneous but common operations that are awkward to express with C operators. On some processors these functions can use special machine instructions to perform these operations faster than the equivalent C code.

double fmin (*double x, double y*)	[Function]
float fminf (*float x, float y*)	[Function]
long double fminl (*long double x, long double y*)	[Function]
_FloatN fminfN (*_FloatN x, _FloatN y*)	[Function]
_FloatNx fminfNx (*_FloatNx x, _FloatNx y*)	[Function]

Preliminary: | MT-Safe | AS-Safe | AC-Safe | See Section 1.2.2.1 [POSIX Safety Concepts], page 2.

The fmin function returns the lesser of the two values x and y. It is similar to the expression

```
((x) < (y) ? (x) : (y))
```

except that x and y are only evaluated once.

If an argument is NaN, the other argument is returned. If both arguments are NaN, NaN is returned.

double **fmax** (*double x, double y*)   [Function]

float **fmaxf** (*float x, float y*)   [Function]

long double **fmaxl** (*long double x, long double y*)   [Function]

_FloatN **fmaxfN** (*_FloatN x, _FloatN y*)   [Function]

_FloatNx **fmaxfNx** (*_FloatNx x, _FloatNx y*)   [Function]

> Preliminary: | MT-Safe | AS-Safe | AC-Safe | See Section 1.2.2.1 [POSIX Safety Concepts], page 2.
>
> The **fmax** function returns the greater of the two values *x* and *y*.
>
> If an argument is NaN, the other argument is returned. If both arguments are NaN, NaN is returned.

double **fminmag** (*double x, double y*)   [Function]

float **fminmagf** (*float x, float y*)   [Function]

long double **fminmagl** (*long double x, long double y*)   [Function]

_FloatN **fminmagfN** (*_FloatN x, _FloatN y*)   [Function]

_FloatNx **fminmagfNx** (*_FloatNx x, _FloatNx y*)   [Function]

> Preliminary: | MT-Safe | AS-Safe | AC-Safe | See Section 1.2.2.1 [POSIX Safety Concepts], page 2.
>
> These functions, from TS 18661-1:2014 and TS 18661-3:2015, return whichever of the two values *x* and *y* has the smaller absolute value. If both have the same absolute value, or either is NaN, they behave the same as the **fmin** functions.

double **fmaxmag** (*double x, double y*)   [Function]

float **fmaxmagf** (*float x, float y*)   [Function]

long double **fmaxmagl** (*long double x, long double y*)   [Function]

_FloatN **fmaxmagfN** (*_FloatN x, _FloatN y*)   [Function]

_FloatNx **fmaxmagfNx** (*_FloatNx x, _FloatNx y*)   [Function]

> Preliminary: | MT-Safe | AS-Safe | AC-Safe | See Section 1.2.2.1 [POSIX Safety Concepts], page 2.
>
> These functions, from TS 18661-1:2014, return whichever of the two values *x* and *y* has the greater absolute value. If both have the same absolute value, or either is NaN, they behave the same as the **fmax** functions.

double **fdim** (*double x, double y*)   [Function]

float **fdimf** (*float x, float y*)   [Function]

long double **fdiml** (*long double x, long double y*)   [Function]

_FloatN **fdimfN** (*_FloatN x, _FloatN y*)   [Function]

_FloatNx **fdimfNx** (*_FloatNx x, _FloatNx y*)   [Function]

> Preliminary: | MT-Safe | AS-Safe | AC-Safe | See Section 1.2.2.1 [POSIX Safety Concepts], page 2.
>
> The **fdim** function returns the positive difference between *x* and *y*. The positive difference is $x - y$ if *x* is greater than *y*, and 0 otherwise.
>
> If *x*, *y*, or both are NaN, NaN is returned.

double **fma** (*double x, double y, double z*)   [Function]

float **fmaf** (*float x, float y, float z*)   [Function]

long double **fmal** (*long double x, long double y, long double z*)   [Function]

_FloatN fmafN (_FloatN x, _FloatN y, _FloatN z)   [Function]
_FloatNx fmafNx (_FloatNx x, _FloatNx y, _FloatNx z)   [Function]
  Preliminary: | MT-Safe | AS-Safe | AC-Safe | See Section 1.2.2.1 [POSIX Safety Concepts], page 2.

  The `fma` function performs floating-point multiply-add. This is the operation $(x \cdot y) + z$, but the intermediate result is not rounded to the destination type. This can sometimes improve the precision of a calculation.

  This function was introduced because some processors have a special instruction to perform multiply-add. The C compiler cannot use it directly, because the expression 'x*y + z' is defined to round the intermediate result. `fma` lets you choose when you want to round only once.

  On processors which do not implement multiply-add in hardware, `fma` can be very slow since it must avoid intermediate rounding. `math.h` defines the symbols FP_FAST_FMA, FP_FAST_FMAF, and FP_FAST_FMAL when the corresponding version of `fma` is no slower than the expression 'x*y + z'. In the GNU C Library, this always means the operation is implemented in hardware.

20.9 Complex Numbers

ISO C99 introduces support for complex numbers in C. This is done with a new type qualifier, `complex`. It is a keyword if and only if `complex.h` has been included. There are three complex types, corresponding to the three real types: `float complex`, `double complex`, and `long double complex`.

  Likewise, on machines that have support for _FloatN or _FloatNx enabled, the complex types _FloatN complex and _FloatNx complex are also available if `complex.h` has been included; see Chapter 19 [Mathematics], page 525.

  To construct complex numbers you need a way to indicate the imaginary part of a number. There is no standard notation for an imaginary floating point constant. Instead, `complex.h` defines two macros that can be used to create complex numbers.

const float complex _Complex_I   [Macro]
  This macro is a representation of the complex number "$0 + 1i$". Multiplying a real floating-point value by _Complex_I gives a complex number whose value is purely imaginary. You can use this to construct complex constants:

    $3.0 + 4.0i$ = 3.0 + 4.0 * _Complex_I

  Note that _Complex_I * _Complex_I has the value −1, but the type of that value is `complex`.

_Complex_I is a bit of a mouthful. `complex.h` also defines a shorter name for the same constant.

const float complex I   [Macro]
  This macro has exactly the same value as _Complex_I. Most of the time it is preferable. However, it causes problems if you want to use the identifier I for something else. You can safely write

    ```
#include <complex.h>
#undef I
```

if you need I for your own purposes. (In that case we recommend you also define some other short name for _Complex_I, such as J.)

20.10 Projections, Conjugates, and Decomposing of Complex Numbers

ISO C99 also defines functions that perform basic operations on complex numbers, such as decomposition and conjugation. The prototypes for all these functions are in complex.h. All functions are available in three variants, one for each of the three complex types.

double creal (*complex double z*)   [Function]
float crealf (*complex float z*)   [Function]
long double creall (*complex long double z*)   [Function]
_FloatN crealfN (*complex _FloatN z*)   [Function]
_FloatNx crealfNx (*complex _FloatNx z*)   [Function]
> Preliminary: | MT-Safe | AS-Safe | AC-Safe | See Section 1.2.2.1 [POSIX Safety Concepts], page 2.
>
> These functions return the real part of the complex number *z*.

double cimag (*complex double z*)   [Function]
float cimagf (*complex float z*)   [Function]
long double cimagl (*complex long double z*)   [Function]
_FloatN cimagfN (*complex _FloatN z*)   [Function]
_FloatNx cimagfNx (*complex _FloatNx z*)   [Function]
> Preliminary: | MT-Safe | AS-Safe | AC-Safe | See Section 1.2.2.1 [POSIX Safety Concepts], page 2.
>
> These functions return the imaginary part of the complex number *z*.

complex double conj (*complex double z*)   [Function]
complex float conjf (*complex float z*)   [Function]
complex long double conjl (*complex long double z*)   [Function]
complex _FloatN conjfN (*complex _FloatN z*)   [Function]
complex _FloatNx conjfNx (*complex _FloatNx z*)   [Function]
> Preliminary: | MT-Safe | AS-Safe | AC-Safe | See Section 1.2.2.1 [POSIX Safety Concepts], page 2.
>
> These functions return the conjugate value of the complex number *z*. The conjugate of a complex number has the same real part and a negated imaginary part. In other words, 'conj(a + bi) = a + -bi'.

double carg (*complex double z*)   [Function]
float cargf (*complex float z*)   [Function]
long double cargl (*complex long double z*)   [Function]
_FloatN cargfN (*complex _FloatN z*)   [Function]
_FloatNx cargfNx (*complex _FloatNx z*)   [Function]
> Preliminary: | MT-Safe | AS-Safe | AC-Safe | See Section 1.2.2.1 [POSIX Safety Concepts], page 2.
>
> These functions return the argument of the complex number *z*. The argument of a complex number is the angle in the complex plane between the positive real axis and

a line passing through zero and the number. This angle is measured in the usual fashion and ranges from $-\pi$ to π.

`carg` has a branch cut along the negative real axis.

complex double **cproj** (*complex double z*)   [Function]
complex float **cprojf** (*complex float z*)   [Function]
complex long double **cprojl** (*complex long double z*)   [Function]
complex _FloatN **cprojfN** (*complex _FloatN z*)   [Function]
complex _FloatNx **cprojfNx** (*complex _FloatNx z*)   [Function]

> Preliminary: | MT-Safe | AS-Safe | AC-Safe | See Section 1.2.2.1 [POSIX Safety Concepts], page 2.

> These functions return the projection of the complex value *z* onto the Riemann sphere. Values with an infinite imaginary part are projected to positive infinity on the real axis, even if the real part is NaN. If the real part is infinite, the result is equivalent to
>
> > `INFINITY + I * copysign (0.0, cimag (z))`

20.11 Parsing of Numbers

This section describes functions for "reading" integer and floating-point numbers from a string. It may be more convenient in some cases to use **sscanf** or one of the related functions; see Section 12.14 [Formatted Input], page 301. But often you can make a program more robust by finding the tokens in the string by hand, then converting the numbers one by one.

20.11.1 Parsing of Integers

The 'str' functions are declared in **stdlib.h** and those beginning with 'wcs' are declared in **wchar.h**. One might wonder about the use of **restrict** in the prototypes of the functions in this section. It is seemingly useless but the ISO C standard uses it (for the functions defined there) so we have to do it as well.

long int **strtol** (*const char *restrict string, char **restrict*   [Function]
     tailptr, int base)

> Preliminary: | MT-Safe locale | AS-Safe | AC-Safe | See Section 1.2.2.1 [POSIX Safety Concepts], page 2.

> The **strtol** ("string-to-long") function converts the initial part of *string* to a signed integer, which is returned as a value of type **long int**.

> This function attempts to decompose *string* as follows:

> - A (possibly empty) sequence of whitespace characters. Which characters are whitespace is determined by the **isspace** function (see Section 4.1 [Classification of Characters], page 81). These are discarded.

> - An optional plus or minus sign ('+' or '-').

> - A nonempty sequence of digits in the radix specified by *base*.

>   If *base* is zero, decimal radix is assumed unless the series of digits begins with '0' (specifying octal radix), or '0x' or '0X' (specifying hexadecimal radix); in other words, the same syntax used for integer constants in C.

Otherwise *base* must have a value between 2 and 36. If *base* is 16, the digits may optionally be preceded by '0x' or '0X'. If base has no legal value the value returned is 0l and the global variable `errno` is set to `EINVAL`.

- Any remaining characters in the string. If *tailptr* is not a null pointer, `strtol` stores a pointer to this tail in `*tailptr`.

If the string is empty, contains only whitespace, or does not contain an initial substring that has the expected syntax for an integer in the specified *base*, no conversion is performed. In this case, `strtol` returns a value of zero and the value stored in `*tailptr` is the value of *string*.

In a locale other than the standard "C" locale, this function may recognize additional implementation-dependent syntax.

If the string has valid syntax for an integer but the value is not representable because of overflow, `strtol` returns either `LONG_MAX` or `LONG_MIN` (see Section A.5.2 [Range of an Integer Type], page 918), as appropriate for the sign of the value. It also sets `errno` to `ERANGE` to indicate there was overflow.

You should not check for errors by examining the return value of `strtol`, because the string might be a valid representation of 0l, `LONG_MAX`, or `LONG_MIN`. Instead, check whether *tailptr* points to what you expect after the number (e.g. '\0' if the string should end after the number). You also need to clear *errno* before the call and check it afterward, in case there was overflow.

There is an example at the end of this section.

`long int` **wcstol** (*const wchar_t *restrict* **string**, *wchar_t **restrict*   [Function]
     tailptr, *int* **base**)
Preliminary: | MT-Safe locale | AS-Safe | AC-Safe | See Section 1.2.2.1 [POSIX Safety Concepts], page 2.

The `wcstol` function is equivalent to the `strtol` function in nearly all aspects but handles wide character strings.

The `wcstol` function was introduced in Amendment 1 of ISO C90.

`unsigned long int` **strtoul** (*const char *retrict* **string**, *char*   [Function]
     ***restrict* **tailptr**, *int* **base**)
Preliminary: | MT-Safe locale | AS-Safe | AC-Safe | See Section 1.2.2.1 [POSIX Safety Concepts], page 2.

The `strtoul` ("string-to-unsigned-long") function is like `strtol` except it converts to an `unsigned long int` value. The syntax is the same as described above for `strtol`. The value returned on overflow is `ULONG_MAX` (see Section A.5.2 [Range of an Integer Type], page 918).

If *string* depicts a negative number, `strtoul` acts the same as *strtol* but casts the result to an unsigned integer. That means for example that `strtoul` on "-1" returns `ULONG_MAX` and an input more negative than `LONG_MIN` returns (`ULONG_MAX` + 1) / 2.

`strtoul` sets *errno* to `EINVAL` if *base* is out of range, or `ERANGE` on overflow.

unsigned long int wcstoul (*const wchar_t *restrict* **string**,   [Function]
    *wchar_t **restrict* **tailptr**, *int* **base**)
> Preliminary: | MT-Safe locale | AS-Safe | AC-Safe | See Section 1.2.2.1 [POSIX Safety Concepts], page 2.

> The `wcstoul` function is equivalent to the `strtoul` function in nearly all aspects but handles wide character strings.

> The `wcstoul` function was introduced in Amendment 1 of ISO C90.

long long int strtoll (*const char *restrict* **string**, *char **restrict*   [Function]
    tailptr, *int* **base**)
> Preliminary: | MT-Safe locale | AS-Safe | AC-Safe | See Section 1.2.2.1 [POSIX Safety Concepts], page 2.

> The `strtoll` function is like `strtol` except that it returns a `long long int` value, and accepts numbers with a correspondingly larger range.

> If the string has valid syntax for an integer but the value is not representable because of overflow, `strtoll` returns either `LLONG_MAX` or `LLONG_MIN` (see Section A.5.2 [Range of an Integer Type], page 918), as appropriate for the sign of the value. It also sets `errno` to `ERANGE` to indicate there was overflow.

> The `strtoll` function was introduced in ISO C99.

long long int wcstoll (*const wchar_t *restrict* **string**, *wchar_t*   [Function]
    restrict* **tailptr, *int* **base**)
> Preliminary: | MT-Safe locale | AS-Safe | AC-Safe | See Section 1.2.2.1 [POSIX Safety Concepts], page 2.

> The `wcstoll` function is equivalent to the `strtoll` function in nearly all aspects but handles wide character strings.

> The `wcstoll` function was introduced in Amendment 1 of ISO C90.

long long int strtoq (*const char *restrict* **string**, *char **restrict*   [Function]
    tailptr, *int* **base**)
> Preliminary: | MT-Safe locale | AS-Safe | AC-Safe | See Section 1.2.2.1 [POSIX Safety Concepts], page 2.

> `strtoq` ("string-to-quad-word") is the BSD name for `strtoll`.

long long int wcstoq (*const wchar_t *restrict* **string**, *wchar_t*   [Function]
    restrict* **tailptr, *int* **base**)
> Preliminary: | MT-Safe locale | AS-Safe | AC-Safe | See Section 1.2.2.1 [POSIX Safety Concepts], page 2.

> The `wcstoq` function is equivalent to the `strtoq` function in nearly all aspects but handles wide character strings.

> The `wcstoq` function is a GNU extension.

unsigned long long int strtoull (*const char *restrict* **string**,   [Function]
    *char **restrict* **tailptr**, *int* **base**)
> Preliminary: | MT-Safe locale | AS-Safe | AC-Safe | See Section 1.2.2.1 [POSIX Safety Concepts], page 2.

The `strtoull` function is related to `strtoll` the same way `strtoul` is related to `strtol`.

The `strtoull` function was introduced in ISO C99.

unsigned long long int wcstoull (*const wchar_t *restrict*   [Function]
    *string, wchar_t **restrict* `tailptr`, *int* `base`)
Preliminary: | MT-Safe locale | AS-Safe | AC-Safe | See Section 1.2.2.1 [POSIX Safety Concepts], page 2.

The `wcstoull` function is equivalent to the `strtoull` function in nearly all aspects but handles wide character strings.

The `wcstoull` function was introduced in Amendment 1 of ISO C90.

unsigned long long int strtouq (*const char *restrict* `string`,   [Function]
    *char **restrict* `tailptr`, *int* `base`)
Preliminary: | MT-Safe locale | AS-Safe | AC-Safe | See Section 1.2.2.1 [POSIX Safety Concepts], page 2.

`strtouq` is the BSD name for `strtoull`.

unsigned long long int wcstouq (*const wchar_t *restrict* `string`,   [Function]
    *wchar_t **restrict* `tailptr`, *int* `base`)
Preliminary: | MT-Safe locale | AS-Safe | AC-Safe | See Section 1.2.2.1 [POSIX Safety Concepts], page 2.

The `wcstouq` function is equivalent to the `strtouq` function in nearly all aspects but handles wide character strings.

The `wcstouq` function is a GNU extension.

intmax_t strtoimax (*const char *restrict* `string`, *char **restrict*   [Function]
    `tailptr`, *int* `base`)
Preliminary: | MT-Safe locale | AS-Safe | AC-Safe | See Section 1.2.2.1 [POSIX Safety Concepts], page 2.

The `strtoimax` function is like `strtol` except that it returns a `intmax_t` value, and accepts numbers of a corresponding range.

If the string has valid syntax for an integer but the value is not representable because of overflow, `strtoimax` returns either `INTMAX_MAX` or `INTMAX_MIN` (see Section 20.1 [Integers], page 575), as appropriate for the sign of the value. It also sets `errno` to `ERANGE` to indicate there was overflow.

See Section 20.1 [Integers], page 575, for a description of the `intmax_t` type. The `strtoimax` function was introduced in ISO C99.

intmax_t wcstoimax (*const wchar_t *restrict* `string`, *wchar_t*   [Function]
    ***restrict* `tailptr`, *int* `base`)
Preliminary: | MT-Safe locale | AS-Safe | AC-Safe | See Section 1.2.2.1 [POSIX Safety Concepts], page 2.

The `wcstoimax` function is equivalent to the `strtoimax` function in nearly all aspects but handles wide character strings.

The `wcstoimax` function was introduced in ISO C99.

uintmax_t **strtoumax** (*const char *restrict* **string**, *char **restrict*   [Function]
        tailptr, *int* **base**)
> Preliminary: | MT-Safe locale | AS-Safe | AC-Safe | See Section 1.2.2.1 [POSIX Safety Concepts], page 2.

> The strtoumax function is related to strtoimax the same way that strtoul is related to strtol.

> See Section 20.1 [Integers], page 575, for a description of the intmax_t type. The strtoumax function was introduced in ISO C99.

uintmax_t **wcstoumax** (*const wchar_t *restrict* **string**, *wchar_t*   [Function]
        ***restrict* **tailptr**, *int* **base**)
> Preliminary: | MT-Safe locale | AS-Safe | AC-Safe | See Section 1.2.2.1 [POSIX Safety Concepts], page 2.

> The wcstoumax function is equivalent to the strtoumax function in nearly all aspects but handles wide character strings.

> The wcstoumax function was introduced in ISO C99.

long int **atol** (*const char *****string**)   [Function]
> Preliminary: | MT-Safe locale | AS-Safe | AC-Safe | See Section 1.2.2.1 [POSIX Safety Concepts], page 2.

> This function is similar to the strtol function with a *base* argument of 10, except that it need not detect overflow errors. The atol function is provided mostly for compatibility with existing code; using strtol is more robust.

int **atoi** (*const char *****string**)   [Function]
> Preliminary: | MT-Safe locale | AS-Safe | AC-Safe | See Section 1.2.2.1 [POSIX Safety Concepts], page 2.

> This function is like atol, except that it returns an int. The atoi function is also considered obsolete; use strtol instead.

long long int **atoll** (*const char *****string**)   [Function]
> Preliminary: | MT-Safe locale | AS-Safe | AC-Safe | See Section 1.2.2.1 [POSIX Safety Concepts], page 2.

> This function is similar to atol, except it returns a long long int.

> The atoll function was introduced in ISO C99. It too is obsolete (despite having just been added); use strtoll instead.

All the functions mentioned in this section so far do not handle alternative representations of characters as described in the locale data. Some locales specify thousands separator and the way they have to be used which can help to make large numbers more readable. To read such numbers one has to use the scanf functions with the '´' flag.

Here is a function which parses a string as a sequence of integers and returns the sum of them:

```
int
sum_ints_from_string (char *string)
{
  int sum = 0;
```

```
while (1) {
  char *tail;
  int next;

  /* Skip whitespace by hand, to detect the end.  */
  while (isspace (*string)) string++;
  if (*string == 0)
    break;

  /* There is more nonwhitespace,  */
  /* so it ought to be another number.  */
  errno = 0;
  /* Parse it.  */
  next = strtol (string, &tail, 0);
  /* Add it in, if not overflow.  */
  if (errno)
    printf ("Overflow\n");
  else
    sum += next;
  /* Advance past it.  */
  string = tail;
}

return sum;
}
```

20.11.2 Parsing of Floats

The 'str' functions are declared in **stdlib.h** and those beginning with 'wcs' are declared in **wchar.h**. One might wonder about the use of **restrict** in the prototypes of the functions in this section. It is seemingly useless but the ISO C standard uses it (for the functions defined there) so we have to do it as well.

double strtod (*const char *restrict* **string**, *char **restrict*   [Function]
        tailptr)

Preliminary: | MT-Safe locale | AS-Safe | AC-Safe | See Section 1.2.2.1 [POSIX Safety Concepts], page 2.

The **strtod** ("string-to-double") function converts the initial part of *string* to a floating-point number, which is returned as a value of type **double**.

This function attempts to decompose *string* as follows:

- A (possibly empty) sequence of whitespace characters. Which characters are whitespace is determined by the **isspace** function (see Section 4.1 [Classification of Characters], page 81). These are discarded.

- An optional plus or minus sign ('+' or '-').

- A floating point number in decimal or hexadecimal format. The decimal format is:

    - A nonempty sequence of digits optionally containing a decimal-point character—normally '.', but it depends on the locale (see Section 7.7.1.1 [Generic Numeric Formatting Parameters], page 182).

    - An optional exponent part, consisting of a character 'e' or 'E', an optional sign, and a sequence of digits.

The hexadecimal format is as follows:

> - A 0x or 0X followed by a nonempty sequence of hexadecimal digits optionally containing a decimal-point character—normally '.', but it depends on the locale (see Section 7.7.1.1 [Generic Numeric Formatting Parameters], page 182).

> - An optional binary-exponent part, consisting of a character 'p' or 'P', an optional sign, and a sequence of digits.

- Any remaining characters in the string. If *tailptr* is not a null pointer, a pointer to this tail of the string is stored in *`*tailptr`*.

If the string is empty, contains only whitespace, or does not contain an initial substring that has the expected syntax for a floating-point number, no conversion is performed. In this case, `strtod` returns a value of zero and the value returned in *`*tailptr`* is the value of *string*.

In a locale other than the standard `"C"` or `"POSIX"` locales, this function may recognize additional locale-dependent syntax.

If the string has valid syntax for a floating-point number but the value is outside the range of a `double`, `strtod` will signal overflow or underflow as described in Section 20.5.4 [Error Reporting by Mathematical Functions], page 586.

`strtod` recognizes four special input strings. The strings `"inf"` and `"infinity"` are converted to ∞, or to the largest representable value if the floating-point format doesn't support infinities. You can prepend a `"+"` or `"-"` to specify the sign. Case is ignored when scanning these strings.

The strings `"nan"` and `"nan(chars...)"` are converted to NaN. Again, case is ignored. If *chars...* are provided, they are used in some unspecified fashion to select a particular representation of NaN (there can be several).

Since zero is a valid result as well as the value returned on error, you should check for errors in the same way as for `strtol`, by examining *errno* and *tailptr*.

---

float strtof (*const char *string*, *char **tailptr*)   [Function]
long double strtold (*const char *string*, *char **tailptr*)   [Function]

> Preliminary: | MT-Safe locale | AS-Safe | AC-Safe | See Section 1.2.2.1 [POSIX Safety Concepts], page 2.

> These functions are analogous to `strtod`, but return `float` and `long double` values respectively. They report errors in the same way as `strtod`. `strtof` can be substantially faster than `strtod`, but has less precision; conversely, `strtold` can be much slower but has more precision (on systems where `long double` is a separate type).

> These functions have been GNU extensions and are new to ISO C99.

_FloatN strtofN (*const char *string*, *char **tailptr*)   [Function]
_FloatNx strtofNx (*const char *string*, *char **tailptr*)   [Function]

> Preliminary: | MT-Safe locale | AS-Safe | AC-Safe | See Section 1.2.2.1 [POSIX Safety Concepts], page 2.

> These functions are like `strtod`, except for the return type.

> They were introduced in ISO/IEC TS 18661-3 and are available on machines that support the related types; see Chapter 19 [Mathematics], page 525.

double **wcstod** (*const wchar_t *restrict* **string**, *wchar_t **restrict*   [Function]
    tailptr)
float **wcstof** (*const wchar_t *string*, *wchar_t **tailptr*)   [Function]
long double **wcstold** (*const wchar_t *string*, *wchar_t **tailptr*)   [Function]
_FloatN **wcstof*N*** (*const wchar_t *string*, *wchar_t **tailptr*)   [Function]
_FloatNx **wcstof*N*x** (*const wchar_t *string*, *wchar_t **tailptr*)   [Function]
      Preliminary: | MT-Safe locale | AS-Safe | AC-Safe | See Section 1.2.2.1 [POSIX
      Safety Concepts], page 2.

      The `wcstod`, `wcstof`, `wcstol`, `wcstof`*N*, and `wcstof`*N*`x` functions are equivalent in
      nearly all aspects to the `strtod`, `strtof`, `strtold`, `strtof`*N*, and `strtof`*N*`x` functions,
      but they handle wide character strings.

      The `wcstod` function was introduced in Amendment 1 of ISO C90. The `wcstof` and
      `wcstold` functions were introduced in ISO C99.

      The `wcstof`*N* and `wcstof`*N*`x` functions are not in any standard, but are added to
      provide completeness for the non-deprecated interface of wide character string to
      floating-point conversion functions. They are only available on machines that support
      the related types; see Chapter 19 [Mathematics], page 525.

double **atof** (*const char *string*)   [Function]
      Preliminary: | MT-Safe locale | AS-Safe | AC-Safe | See Section 1.2.2.1 [POSIX
      Safety Concepts], page 2.

      This function is similar to the `strtod` function, except that it need not detect overflow
      and underflow errors. The `atof` function is provided mostly for compatibility with
      existing code; using `strtod` is more robust.

    The GNU C Library also provides '`_l`' versions of these functions, which take an additional argument, the locale to use in conversion.

    See also Section 20.11.1 [Parsing of Integers], page 608.

20.12 Printing of Floats

The '`strfrom`' functions are declared in `stdlib.h`.

int **strfromd** (*char *restrict* **string**, *size_t* **size**, *const char*   [Function]
    restrict* **format, *double* **value**)
int **strfromf** (*char *restrict* **string**, *size_t* **size**, *const char*   [Function]
    restrict* **format, *float* **value**)
int **strfroml** (*char *restrict* **string**, *size_t* **size**, *const char*   [Function]
    restrict* **format, *long double* **value**)
      Preliminary: | MT-Safe locale | AS-Unsafe heap | AC-Unsafe mem | See
      Section 1.2.2.1 [POSIX Safety Concepts], page 2.

      The functions `strfromd` ("string-from-double"), `strfromf` ("string-from-float"), and
      `strfroml` ("string-from-long-double") convert the floating-point number *value* to a
      string of characters and stores them into the area pointed to by *string*. The conversion
      writes at most *size* characters and respects the format specified by *format*.

      The format string must start with the character '%'. An optional precision follows,
      which starts with a period, '.', and may be followed by a decimal integer, representing

the precision. If a decimal integer is not specified after the period, the precision is taken to be zero. The character '*' is not allowed. Finally, the format string ends with one of the following conversion specifiers: 'a', 'A', 'e', 'E', 'f', 'F', 'g' or 'G' (see Section 12.12.3 [Table of Output Conversions], page 281). Invalid format strings result in undefined behavior.

These functions return the number of characters that would have been written to *string* had *size* been sufficiently large, not counting the terminating null character. Thus, the null-terminated output has been completely written if and only if the returned value is less than *size*.

These functions were introduced by ISO/IEC TS 18661-1.

int **strfromfN** (*char *restrict* **string**, *size_t* **size**, *const char* [Function]
　　　*restrict **format**, *_FloatN* **value**)
int **strfromfNx** (*char *restrict* **string**, *size_t* **size**, *const char* [Function]
　　　*restrict **format**, *_FloatNx* **value**)
　　　Preliminary: | MT-Safe locale | AS-Unsafe heap | AC-Unsafe mem | See Section 1.2.2.1 [POSIX Safety Concepts], page 2.

　　　These functions are like **strfromd**, except for the type of **value**.

　　　They were introduced in ISO/IEC TS 18661-3 and are available on machines that support the related types; see Chapter 19 [Mathematics], page 525.

20.13 Old-fashioned System V number-to-string functions

The old System V C library provided three functions to convert numbers to strings, with unusual and hard-to-use semantics. The GNU C Library also provides these functions and some natural extensions.

These functions are only available in the GNU C Library and on systems descended from AT&T Unix. Therefore, unless these functions do precisely what you need, it is better to use **sprintf**, which is standard.

All these functions are defined in **stdlib.h**.

char * **ecvt** (*double* **value**, *int* **ndigit**, *int *decpt*, *int *neg*) [Function]
　　　Preliminary: | MT-Unsafe race:ecvt | AS-Unsafe | AC-Safe | See Section 1.2.2.1 [POSIX Safety Concepts], page 2.

　　　The function **ecvt** converts the floating-point number *value* to a string with at most *ndigit* decimal digits. The returned string contains no decimal point or sign. The first digit of the string is non-zero (unless *value* is actually zero) and the last digit is rounded to nearest. *decpt* is set to the index in the string of the first digit after the decimal point. *neg* is set to a nonzero value if *value* is negative, zero otherwise.

　　　If *ndigit* decimal digits would exceed the precision of a **double** it is reduced to a system-specific value.

　　　The returned string is statically allocated and overwritten by each call to **ecvt**.

　　　If *value* is zero, it is implementation defined whether *decpt* is 0 or 1.

　　　For example: **ecvt (12.3, 5, &d, &n)** returns "12300" and sets *d* to 2 and *n* to 0.

char * **fcvt** (*double* value, *int* ndigit, *int* *decpt, *int* *neg*)   [Function]
Preliminary: | MT-Unsafe race:fcvt | AS-Unsafe heap | AC-Unsafe mem | See
Section 1.2.2.1 [POSIX Safety Concepts], page 2.

The function **fcvt** is like **ecvt**, but *ndigit* specifies the number of digits after the
decimal point. If *ndigit* is less than zero, *value* is rounded to the *ndigit* + 1'th place
to the left of the decimal point. For example, if *ndigit* is -1, *value* will be rounded to
the nearest 10. If *ndigit* is negative and larger than the number of digits to the left
of the decimal point in *value*, *value* will be rounded to one significant digit.

If *ndigit* decimal digits would exceed the precision of a **double** it is reduced to a
system-specific value.

The returned string is statically allocated and overwritten by each call to **fcvt**.

char * **gcvt** (*double* value, *int* ndigit, *char* *buf*)   [Function]
Preliminary: | MT-Safe | AS-Safe | AC-Safe | See Section 1.2.2.1 [POSIX Safety
Concepts], page 2.

gcvt is functionally equivalent to 'sprintf(buf, "%*g", ndigit, value'. It is provided only for compatibility's sake. It returns *buf*.

If *ndigit* decimal digits would exceed the precision of a **double** it is reduced to a
system-specific value.

As extensions, the GNU C Library provides versions of these three functions that take
long double arguments.

char * **qecvt** (*long double* value, *int* ndigit, *int* *decpt, *int* *neg*)   [Function]
Preliminary: | MT-Unsafe race:qecvt | AS-Unsafe | AC-Safe | See Section 1.2.2.1
[POSIX Safety Concepts], page 2.

This function is equivalent to **ecvt** except that it takes a **long double** for the first
parameter and that *ndigit* is restricted by the precision of a **long double**.

char * **qfcvt** (*long double* value, *int* ndigit, *int* *decpt, *int* *neg*)   [Function]
Preliminary: | MT-Unsafe race:qfcvt | AS-Unsafe heap | AC-Unsafe mem | See
Section 1.2.2.1 [POSIX Safety Concepts], page 2.

This function is equivalent to **fcvt** except that it takes a **long double** for the first
parameter and that *ndigit* is restricted by the precision of a **long double**.

char * **qgcvt** (*long double* value, *int* ndigit, *char* *buf*)   [Function]
Preliminary: | MT-Safe | AS-Safe | AC-Safe | See Section 1.2.2.1 [POSIX Safety
Concepts], page 2.

This function is equivalent to **gcvt** except that it takes a **long double** for the first
parameter and that *ndigit* is restricted by the precision of a **long double**.

The **ecvt** and **fcvt** functions, and their **long double** equivalents, all return a string
located in a static buffer which is overwritten by the next call to the function. The GNU
C Library provides another set of extended functions which write the converted string into
a user-supplied buffer. These have the conventional **_r** suffix.

gcvt_r is not necessary, because **gcvt** already uses a user-supplied buffer.

int ecvt_r (*double* value, *int* ndigit, *int* *decpt, *int* *neg, *char*   [Function]
    *buf, *size_t* len)

> Preliminary: | MT-Safe | AS-Safe | AC-Safe | See Section 1.2.2.1 [POSIX Safety Concepts], page 2.
>
> The ecvt_r function is the same as ecvt, except that it places its result into the user-specified buffer pointed to by *buf*, with length *len*. The return value is −1 in case of an error and zero otherwise.
>
> This function is a GNU extension.

int fcvt_r (*double* value, *int* ndigit, *int* *decpt, *int* *neg, *char*   [Function]
    *buf, *size_t* len)

> Preliminary: | MT-Safe | AS-Safe | AC-Safe | See Section 1.2.2.1 [POSIX Safety Concepts], page 2.
>
> The fcvt_r function is the same as fcvt, except that it places its result into the user-specified buffer pointed to by *buf*, with length *len*. The return value is −1 in case of an error and zero otherwise.
>
> This function is a GNU extension.

int qecvt_r (*long double* value, *int* ndigit, *int* *decpt, *int* *neg,   [Function]
    char *buf, *size_t* len)

> Preliminary: | MT-Safe | AS-Safe | AC-Safe | See Section 1.2.2.1 [POSIX Safety Concepts], page 2.
>
> The qecvt_r function is the same as qecvt, except that it places its result into the user-specified buffer pointed to by *buf*, with length *len*. The return value is −1 in case of an error and zero otherwise.
>
> This function is a GNU extension.

int qfcvt_r (*long double* value, *int* ndigit, *int* *decpt, *int* *neg,   [Function]
    char *buf, *size_t* len)

> Preliminary: | MT-Safe | AS-Safe | AC-Safe | See Section 1.2.2.1 [POSIX Safety Concepts], page 2.
>
> The qfcvt_r function is the same as qfcvt, except that it places its result into the user-specified buffer pointed to by *buf*, with length *len*. The return value is −1 in case of an error and zero otherwise.
>
> This function is a GNU extension.

21 Date and Time

This chapter describes functions for manipulating dates and times, including functions for determining what time it is and conversion between different time representations.

21.1 Time Basics

Discussing time in a technical manual can be difficult because the word "time" in English refers to lots of different things. In this manual, we use a rigorous terminology to avoid confusion, and the only thing we use the simple word "time" for is to talk about the abstract concept.

A *calendar time* is a point in the time continuum, for example November 4, 1990, at 18:02.5 UTC. Sometimes this is called "absolute time".

We don't speak of a "date", because that is inherent in a calendar time.

An *interval* is a contiguous part of the time continuum between two calendar times, for example the hour between 9:00 and 10:00 on July 4, 1980.

An *elapsed time* is the length of an interval, for example, 35 minutes. People sometimes sloppily use the word "interval" to refer to the elapsed time of some interval.

An *amount of time* is a sum of elapsed times, which need not be of any specific intervals. For example, the amount of time it takes to read a book might be 9 hours, independently of when and in how many sittings it is read.

A *period* is the elapsed time of an interval between two events, especially when they are part of a sequence of regularly repeating events.

CPU time is like calendar time, except that it is based on the subset of the time continuum when a particular process is actively using a CPU. CPU time is, therefore, relative to a process.

Processor time is an amount of time that a CPU is in use. In fact, it's a basic system resource, since there's a limit to how much can exist in any given interval (that limit is the elapsed time of the interval times the number of CPUs in the processor). People often call this CPU time, but we reserve the latter term in this manual for the definition above.

21.2 Elapsed Time

One way to represent an elapsed time is with a simple arithmetic data type, as with the following function to compute the elapsed time between two calendar times. This function is declared in `time.h`.

`double difftime (`*time_t time1*`, `*time_t time0*`)` [Function]
> Preliminary: | MT-Safe | AS-Safe | AC-Safe | See Section 1.2.2.1 [POSIX Safety Concepts], page 2.
>
> The `difftime` function returns the number of seconds of elapsed time between calendar time *time1* and calendar time *time0*, as a value of type `double`. The difference ignores leap seconds unless leap second support is enabled.
>
> In the GNU C Library, you can simply subtract `time_t` values. But on other systems, the `time_t` data type might use some other encoding where subtraction doesn't work directly.

The GNU C Library provides two data types specifically for representing an elapsed time. They are used by various GNU C Library functions, and you can use them for your own purposes too. They're exactly the same except that one has a resolution in microseconds, and the other, newer one, is in nanoseconds.

struct timeval   [Data Type]

The struct timeval structure represents an elapsed time. It is declared in sys/time.h and has the following members:

time_t tv_sec

This represents the number of whole seconds of elapsed time.

long int tv_usec

This is the rest of the elapsed time (a fraction of a second), represented as the number of microseconds. It is always less than one million.

struct timespec   [Data Type]

The struct timespec structure represents an elapsed time. It is declared in time.h and has the following members:

time_t tv_sec

This represents the number of whole seconds of elapsed time.

long int tv_nsec

This is the rest of the elapsed time (a fraction of a second), represented as the number of nanoseconds. It is always less than one billion.

It is often necessary to subtract two values of type struct timeval or struct timespec. Here is the best way to do this. It works even on some peculiar operating systems where the tv_sec member has an unsigned type.

```
/* Subtract the `struct timevalfl values X and Y,
   storing the result in RESULT.
   Return 1 if the difference is negative, otherwise 0. */

int
timeval_subtract (struct timeval *result, struct timeval *x, struct timeval *y)
{
  /* Perform the carry for the later subtraction by updating y. */
  if (x->tv_usec < y->tv_usec) {
    int nsec = (y->tv_usec - x->tv_usec) / 1000000 + 1;
    y->tv_usec -= 1000000 * nsec;
    y->tv_sec += nsec;
  }
  if (x->tv_usec - y->tv_usec > 1000000) {
    int nsec = (x->tv_usec - y->tv_usec) / 1000000;
    y->tv_usec += 1000000 * nsec;
    y->tv_sec -= nsec;
  }

  /* Compute the time remaining to wait.
     tv_usec is certainly positive. */
  result->tv_sec = x->tv_sec - y->tv_sec;
  result->tv_usec = x->tv_usec - y->tv_usec;
```

```
    /* Return 1 if result is negative. */
    return x->tv_sec < y->tv_sec;
}
```

Common functions that use `struct timeval` are `gettimeofday` and `settimeofday`.

There are no GNU C Library functions specifically oriented toward dealing with elapsed times, but the calendar time, processor time, and alarm and sleeping functions have a lot to do with them.

21.3 Processor And CPU Time

If you're trying to optimize your program or measure its efficiency, it's very useful to know how much processor time it uses. For that, calendar time and elapsed times are useless because a process may spend time waiting for I/O or for other processes to use the CPU. However, you can get the information with the functions in this section.

CPU time (see Section 21.1 [Time Basics], page 619) is represented by the data type `clock_t`, which is a number of *clock ticks*. It gives the total amount of time a process has actively used a CPU since some arbitrary event. On GNU systems, that event is the creation of the process. While arbitrary in general, the event is always the same event for any particular process, so you can always measure how much time on the CPU a particular computation takes by examining the process' CPU time before and after the computation.

On GNU/Linux and GNU/Hurd systems, `clock_t` is equivalent to `long int` and `CLOCKS_PER_SEC` is an integer value. But in other systems, both `clock_t` and the macro `CLOCKS_PER_SEC` can be either integer or floating-point types. Casting CPU time values to `double`, as in the example above, makes sure that operations such as arithmetic and printing work properly and consistently no matter what the underlying representation is.

Note that the clock can wrap around. On a 32bit system with `CLOCKS_PER_SEC` set to one million this function will return the same value approximately every 72 minutes.

For additional functions to examine a process' use of processor time, and to control it, see Chapter 22 [Resource Usage And Limitation], page 654.

21.3.1 CPU Time Inquiry

To get a process' CPU time, you can use the `clock` function. This facility is declared in the header file `time.h`.

In typical usage, you call the `clock` function at the beginning and end of the interval you want to time, subtract the values, and then divide by `CLOCKS_PER_SEC` (the number of clock ticks per second) to get processor time, like this:

```
#include <time.h>

clock_t start, end;
double cpu_time_used;

start = clock();
... /* Do the work. */
end = clock();
cpu_time_used = ((double) (end - start)) / CLOCKS_PER_SEC;
```

Do not use a single CPU time as an amount of time; it doesn't work that way. Either do a subtraction as shown above or query processor time directly. See Section 21.3.2 [Processor Time Inquiry], page 622.

Different computers and operating systems vary wildly in how they keep track of CPU time. It's common for the internal processor clock to have a resolution somewhere between a hundredth and millionth of a second.

int CLOCKS_PER_SEC   [Macro]
> The value of this macro is the number of clock ticks per second measured by the `clock` function. POSIX requires that this value be one million independent of the actual resolution.

clock_t   [Data Type]
> This is the type of the value returned by the `clock` function. Values of type `clock_t` are numbers of clock ticks.

clock_t clock (*void*)   [Function]
> Preliminary: | MT-Safe | AS-Safe | AC-Safe | See Section 1.2.2.1 [POSIX Safety Concepts], page 2.
>
> This function returns the calling process' current CPU time. If the CPU time is not available or cannot be represented, `clock` returns the value `(clock_t)(-1)`.

21.3.2 Processor Time Inquiry

The `times` function returns information about a process' consumption of processor time in a `struct tms` object, in addition to the process' CPU time. See Section 21.1 [Time Basics], page 619. You should include the header file `sys/times.h` to use this facility.

struct tms   [Data Type]
> The `tms` structure is used to return information about process times. It contains at least the following members:
>
> **clock_t tms_utime**
>> This is the total processor time the calling process has used in executing the instructions of its program.
>
> **clock_t tms_stime**
>> This is the processor time the system has used on behalf of the calling process.
>
> **clock_t tms_cutime**
>> This is the sum of the `tms_utime` values and the `tms_cutime` values of all terminated child processes of the calling process, whose status has been reported to the parent process by `wait` or `waitpid`; see Section 26.6 [Process Completion], page 779. In other words, it represents the total processor time used in executing the instructions of all the terminated child processes of the calling process, excluding child processes which have not yet been reported by `wait` or `waitpid`.

clock_t tms_cstime

> This is similar to **tms_cutime**, but represents the total processor time the system has used on behalf of all the terminated child processes of the calling process.

All of the times are given in numbers of clock ticks. Unlike CPU time, these are the actual amounts of time; not relative to any event. See Section 26.4 [Creating a Process], page 775.

int CLK_TCK [Macro]

> This is an obsolete name for the number of clock ticks per second. Use **sysconf** (**_SC_CLK_TCK**) instead.

clock_t times (*struct tms *buffer*) [Function]

> Preliminary: | MT-Safe | AS-Safe | AC-Safe | See Section 1.2.2.1 [POSIX Safety Concepts], page 2.

> The **times** function stores the processor time information for the calling process in *buffer*.

> The return value is the number of clock ticks since an arbitrary point in the past, e.g. since system start-up. **times** returns (**clock_t**)(**-1**) to indicate failure.

Portability Note: The **clock** function described in Section 21.3.1 [CPU Time Inquiry], page 621, is specified by the ISO C standard. The **times** function is a feature of POSIX.1. On GNU systems, the CPU time is defined to be equivalent to the sum of the **tms_utime** and **tms_stime** fields returned by **times**.

21.4 Calendar Time

This section describes facilities for keeping track of calendar time. See Section 21.1 [Time Basics], page 619.

The GNU C Library represents calendar time three ways:

- *Simple time* (the **time_t** data type) is a compact representation, typically giving the number of seconds of elapsed time since some implementation-specific base time.

- There is also a "high-resolution time" representation. Like simple time, this represents a calendar time as an elapsed time since a base time, but instead of measuring in whole seconds, it uses a **struct timeval** data type, which includes fractions of a second. Use this time representation instead of simple time when you need greater precision.

- *Local time* or *broken-down time* (the **struct tm** data type) represents a calendar time as a set of components specifying the year, month, and so on in the Gregorian calendar, for a specific time zone. This calendar time representation is usually used only to communicate with people.

21.4.1 Simple Calendar Time

This section describes the **time_t** data type for representing calendar time as simple time, and the functions which operate on simple time objects. These facilities are declared in the header file **time.h**.

`time_t`   [Data Type]

> This is the data type used to represent simple time. Sometimes, it also represents an elapsed time. When interpreted as a calendar time value, it represents the number of seconds elapsed since 00:00:00 on January 1, 1970, Coordinated Universal Time. (This calendar time is sometimes referred to as the *epoch*.) POSIX requires that this count not include leap seconds, but on some systems this count includes leap seconds if you set `TZ` to certain values (see Section 21.4.7 [Specifying the Time Zone with `TZ`], page 646).
>
> Note that a simple time has no concept of local time zone. Calendar Time T is the same instant in time regardless of where on the globe the computer is.
>
> In the GNU C Library, `time_t` is equivalent to `long int`. In other systems, `time_t` might be either an integer or floating-point type.

The function `difftime` tells you the elapsed time between two simple calendar times, which is not always as easy to compute as just subtracting. See Section 21.2 [Elapsed Time], page 619.

`time_t time (time_t *result)`   [Function]

> Preliminary: | MT-Safe | AS-Safe | AC-Safe | See Section 1.2.2.1 [POSIX Safety Concepts], page 2.
>
> The `time` function returns the current calendar time as a value of type `time_t`. If the argument *result* is not a null pointer, the calendar time value is also stored in *result*. If the current calendar time is not available, the value `(time_t)(-1)` is returned.

`int stime (const time_t *newtime)`   [Function]

> Preliminary: | MT-Safe | AS-Safe | AC-Safe | See Section 1.2.2.1 [POSIX Safety Concepts], page 2.
>
> `stime` sets the system clock, i.e., it tells the system that the current calendar time is *newtime*, where `newtime` is interpreted as described in the above definition of `time_t`.
>
> `settimeofday` is a newer function which sets the system clock to better than one second precision. `settimeofday` is generally a better choice than `stime`. See Section 21.4.2 [High-Resolution Calendar], page 624.
>
> Only the superuser can set the system clock.
>
> If the function succeeds, the return value is zero. Otherwise, it is `-1` and `errno` is set accordingly:
>
> `EPERM`   The process is not superuser.

21.4.2 High-Resolution Calendar

The `time_t` data type used to represent simple times has a resolution of only one second. Some applications need more precision.

So, the GNU C Library also contains functions which are capable of representing calendar times to a higher resolution than one second. The functions and the associated data types described in this section are declared in `sys/time.h`.

struct timezone   [Data Type]

> The **struct timezone** structure is used to hold minimal information about the local
> time zone. It has the following members:
>
> **int tz_minuteswest**
>> This is the number of minutes west of UTC.
>
> **int tz_dsttime**
>> If nonzero, Daylight Saving Time applies during some part of the year.
>
> The **struct timezone** type is obsolete and should never be used. Instead, use the fa-
> cilities described in Section 21.4.8 [Functions and Variables for Time Zones], page 648.

int gettimeofday (*struct timeval *tp, struct timezone *tzp*)   [Function]

> Preliminary: | MT-Safe | AS-Safe | AC-Safe | See Section 1.2.2.1 [POSIX Safety
> Concepts], page 2.
>
> The **gettimeofday** function returns the current calendar time as the elapsed time
> since the epoch in the **struct timeval** structure indicated by *tp*. (see Section 21.2
> [Elapsed Time], page 619, for a description of **struct timeval**). Information about
> the time zone is returned in the structure pointed to by *tzp*. If the *tzp* argument is
> a null pointer, time zone information is ignored.
>
> The return value is 0 on success and −1 on failure. The following **errno** error condition
> is defined for this function:
>
> **ENOSYS**   The operating system does not support getting time zone information,
> and *tzp* is not a null pointer. GNU systems do not support using
> **struct timezone** to represent time zone information; that is an obsolete
> feature of 4.3 BSD. Instead, use the facilities described in Section 21.4.8
> [Functions and Variables for Time Zones], page 648.

int settimeofday (*const struct timeval *tp, const struct timezone*   [Function]
>   **tzp*)
> Preliminary: | MT-Safe | AS-Safe | AC-Safe | See Section 1.2.2.1 [POSIX Safety
> Concepts], page 2.
>
> The **settimeofday** function sets the current calendar time in the system clock ac-
> cording to the arguments. As for **gettimeofday**, the calendar time is represented
> as the elapsed time since the epoch. As for **gettimeofday**, time zone information is
> ignored if *tzp* is a null pointer.
>
> You must be a privileged user in order to use **settimeofday**.
>
> Some kernels automatically set the system clock from some source such as a hardware
> clock when they start up. Others, including Linux, place the system clock in an
> "invalid" state (in which attempts to read the clock fail). A call of **stime** removes
> the system clock from an invalid state, and system startup scripts typically run a
> program that calls **stime**.
>
> **settimeofday** causes a sudden jump forwards or backwards, which can cause a variety
> of problems in a system. Use **adjtime** (below) to make a smooth transition from one
> time to another by temporarily speeding up or slowing down the clock.
>
> With a Linux kernel, **adjtimex** does the same thing and can also make permanent
> changes to the speed of the system clock so it doesn't need to be corrected as often.

The return value is 0 on success and −1 on failure. The following `errno` error conditions are defined for this function:

EPERM   This process cannot set the clock because it is not privileged.

ENOSYS   The operating system does not support setting time zone information, and *tzp* is not a null pointer.

int adjtime (*const struct timeval *delta, struct timeval *olddelta*)   [Function]
> Preliminary: | MT-Safe | AS-Safe | AC-Safe | See Section 1.2.2.1 [POSIX Safety Concepts], page 2.
>
> This function speeds up or slows down the system clock in order to make a gradual adjustment. This ensures that the calendar time reported by the system clock is always monotonically increasing, which might not happen if you simply set the clock.
>
> The *delta* argument specifies a relative adjustment to be made to the clock time. If negative, the system clock is slowed down for a while until it has lost this much elapsed time. If positive, the system clock is speeded up for a while.
>
> If the *olddelta* argument is not a null pointer, the `adjtime` function returns information about any previous time adjustment that has not yet completed.
>
> This function is typically used to synchronize the clocks of computers in a local network. You must be a privileged user to use it.
>
> With a Linux kernel, you can use the `adjtimex` function to permanently change the clock speed.
>
> The return value is 0 on success and −1 on failure. The following `errno` error condition is defined for this function:
>
> EPERM   You do not have privilege to set the time.

Portability Note: The `gettimeofday`, `settimeofday`, and `adjtime` functions are derived from BSD.

Symbols for the following function are declared in `sys/timex.h`.

int adjtimex (*struct timex *timex*)   [Function]
> Preliminary: | MT-Safe | AS-Safe | AC-Safe | See Section 1.2.2.1 [POSIX Safety Concepts], page 2.
>
> `adjtimex` is functionally identical to `ntp_adjtime`. See Section 21.4.4 [High Accuracy Clock], page 629.
>
> This function is present only with a Linux kernel.

21.4.3 Broken-down Time

Calendar time is represented by the usual GNU C Library functions as an elapsed time since a fixed base calendar time. This is convenient for computation, but has no relation to the way people normally think of calendar time. By contrast, *broken-down time* is a binary representation of calendar time separated into year, month, day, and so on. Broken-down time values are not useful for calculations, but they are useful for printing human readable time information.

A broken-down time value is always relative to a choice of time zone, and it also indicates which time zone that is.

The symbols in this section are declared in the header file `time.h`.

struct tm   [Data Type]

> This is the data type used to represent a broken-down time. The structure contains at least the following members, which can appear in any order.

> int tm_sec
>> This is the number of full seconds since the top of the minute (normally in the range 0 through 59, but the actual upper limit is 60, to allow for leap seconds if leap second support is available).

> int tm_min
>> This is the number of full minutes since the top of the hour (in the range 0 through 59).

> int tm_hour
>> This is the number of full hours past midnight (in the range 0 through 23).

> int tm_mday
>> This is the ordinal day of the month (in the range 1 through 31). Watch out for this one! As the only ordinal number in the structure, it is inconsistent with the rest of the structure.

> int tm_mon
>> This is the number of full calendar months since the beginning of the year (in the range 0 through 11). Watch out for this one! People usually use ordinal numbers for month-of-year (where January = 1).

> int tm_year
>> This is the number of full calendar years since 1900.

> int tm_wday
>> This is the number of full days since Sunday (in the range 0 through 6).

> int tm_yday
>> This is the number of full days since the beginning of the year (in the range 0 through 365).

> int tm_isdst
>> This is a flag that indicates whether Daylight Saving Time is (or was, or will be) in effect at the time described. The value is positive if Daylight Saving Time is in effect, zero if it is not, and negative if the information is not available.

> long int tm_gmtoff
>> This field describes the time zone that was used to compute this broken-down time value, including any adjustment for daylight saving; it is the number of seconds that you must add to UTC to get local time. You can also think of this as the number of seconds east of UTC. For example, for U.S. Eastern Standard Time, the value is -5*60*60. The tm_gmtoff field is derived from BSD and is a GNU library extension; it is not visible in a strict ISO C environment.

`const char *tm_zone`
> This field is the name for the time zone that was used to compute this broken-down time value. Like `tm_gmtoff`, this field is a BSD and GNU extension, and is not visible in a strict ISO C environment.

`struct tm * localtime (const time_t *time)`   [Function]
> Preliminary: | MT-Unsafe race:tmbuf env locale | AS-Unsafe heap lock | AC-Unsafe lock mem fd | See Section 1.2.2.1 [POSIX Safety Concepts], page 2.
>
> The `localtime` function converts the simple time pointed to by *time* to broken-down time representation, expressed relative to the user's specified time zone.
>
> The return value is a pointer to a static broken-down time structure, which might be overwritten by subsequent calls to `ctime`, `gmtime`, or `localtime`. (But no other library function overwrites the contents of this object.)
>
> The return value is the null pointer if *time* cannot be represented as a broken-down time; typically this is because the year cannot fit into an `int`.
>
> Calling `localtime` also sets the current time zone as if `tzset` were called. See Section 21.4.8 [Functions and Variables for Time Zones], page 648.

Using the `localtime` function is a big problem in multi-threaded programs. The result is returned in a static buffer and this is used in all threads. POSIX.1c introduced a variant of this function.

`struct tm * localtime_r (const time_t *time, struct tm *resultp)`   [Function]
> Preliminary: | MT-Safe env locale | AS-Unsafe heap lock | AC-Unsafe lock mem fd | See Section 1.2.2.1 [POSIX Safety Concepts], page 2.
>
> The `localtime_r` function works just like the `localtime` function. It takes a pointer to a variable containing a simple time and converts it to the broken-down time format.
>
> But the result is not placed in a static buffer. Instead it is placed in the object of type `struct tm` to which the parameter *resultp* points.
>
> If the conversion is successful the function returns a pointer to the object the result was written into, i.e., it returns *resultp*.

`struct tm * gmtime (const time_t *time)`   [Function]
> Preliminary: | MT-Unsafe race:tmbuf env locale | AS-Unsafe heap lock | AC-Unsafe lock mem fd | See Section 1.2.2.1 [POSIX Safety Concepts], page 2.
>
> This function is similar to `localtime`, except that the broken-down time is expressed as Coordinated Universal Time (UTC) (formerly called Greenwich Mean Time (GMT)) rather than relative to a local time zone.

As for the `localtime` function we have the problem that the result is placed in a static variable. POSIX.1c also provides a replacement for `gmtime`.

`struct tm * gmtime_r (const time_t *time, struct tm *resultp)`   [Function]
> Preliminary: | MT-Safe env locale | AS-Unsafe heap lock | AC-Unsafe lock mem fd | See Section 1.2.2.1 [POSIX Safety Concepts], page 2.
>
> This function is similar to `localtime_r`, except that it converts just like `gmtime` the given time as Coordinated Universal Time.

If the conversion is successful the function returns a pointer to the object the result was written into, i.e., it returns *resultp*.

time_t mktime (*struct tm *brokentime*) [Function]
> Preliminary: | MT-Safe env locale | AS-Unsafe heap lock | AC-Unsafe lock mem fd
> | See Section 1.2.2.1 [POSIX Safety Concepts], page 2.
>
> The `mktime` function converts a broken-down time structure to a simple time representation. It also normalizes the contents of the broken-down time structure, and fills in some components based on the values of the others.
>
> The `mktime` function ignores the specified contents of the `tm_wday`, `tm_yday`, `tm_gmtoff`, and `tm_zone` members of the broken-down time structure. It uses the values of the other components to determine the calendar time; it's permissible for these components to have unnormalized values outside their normal ranges. The last thing that `mktime` does is adjust the components of the *brokentime* structure, including the members that were initially ignored.
>
> If the specified broken-down time cannot be represented as a simple time, `mktime` returns a value of `(time_t)(-1)` and does not modify the contents of *brokentime*.
>
> Calling `mktime` also sets the current time zone as if `tzset` were called; `mktime` uses this information instead of *brokentime*'s initial `tm_gmtoff` and `tm_zone` members. See Section 21.4.8 [Functions and Variables for Time Zones], page 648.

time_t timelocal (*struct tm *brokentime*) [Function]
> Preliminary: | MT-Safe env locale | AS-Unsafe heap lock | AC-Unsafe lock mem fd
> | See Section 1.2.2.1 [POSIX Safety Concepts], page 2.
>
> `timelocal` is functionally identical to `mktime`, but more mnemonically named. Note that it is the inverse of the `localtime` function.
>
> **Portability note:** `mktime` is essentially universally available. `timelocal` is rather rare.

time_t timegm (*struct tm *brokentime*) [Function]
> Preliminary: | MT-Safe env locale | AS-Unsafe heap lock | AC-Unsafe lock mem fd
> | See Section 1.2.2.1 [POSIX Safety Concepts], page 2.
>
> `timegm` is functionally identical to `mktime` except it always takes the input values to be Coordinated Universal Time (UTC) regardless of any local time zone setting.
>
> Note that `timegm` is the inverse of `gmtime`.
>
> **Portability note:** `mktime` is essentially universally available. `timegm` is rather rare. For the most portable conversion from a UTC broken-down time to a simple time, set the `TZ` environment variable to UTC, call `mktime`, then set `TZ` back.

21.4.4 High Accuracy Clock

The `ntp_gettime` and `ntp_adjtime` functions provide an interface to monitor and manipulate the system clock to maintain high accuracy time. For example, you can fine tune the speed of the clock or synchronize it with another time source.

A typical use of these functions is by a server implementing the Network Time Protocol to synchronize the clocks of multiple systems and high precision clocks.

These functions are declared in `sys/timex.h`.

struct ntptimeval   [Data Type]

This structure is used for information about the system clock. It contains the following members:

struct timeval time

This is the current calendar time, expressed as the elapsed time since the epoch. The **struct timeval** data type is described in Section 21.2 [Elapsed Time], page 619.

long int maxerror

This is the maximum error, measured in microseconds. Unless updated via **ntp_adjtime** periodically, this value will reach some platform-specific maximum value.

long int esterror

This is the estimated error, measured in microseconds. This value can be set by **ntp_adjtime** to indicate the estimated offset of the system clock from the true calendar time.

int ntp_gettime (*struct ntptimeval *tptr*)   [Function]

Preliminary: | MT-Safe | AS-Safe | AC-Safe | See Section 1.2.2.1 [POSIX Safety Concepts], page 2.

The **ntp_gettime** function sets the structure pointed to by *tptr* to current values. The elements of the structure afterwards contain the values the timer implementation in the kernel assumes. They might or might not be correct. If they are not, an **ntp_adjtime** call is necessary.

The return value is 0 on success and other values on failure. The following **errno** error conditions are defined for this function:

TIME_ERROR

The precision clock model is not properly set up at the moment, thus the clock must be considered unsynchronized, and the values should be treated with care.

struct timex   [Data Type]

This structure is used to control and monitor the system clock. It contains the following members:

unsigned int modes

This variable controls whether and which values are set. Several symbolic constants have to be combined with *binary or* to specify the effective mode. These constants start with **MOD_**.

long int offset

This value indicates the current offset of the system clock from the true calendar time. The value is given in microseconds. If bit **MOD_OFFSET** is set in **modes**, the offset (and possibly other dependent values) can be set. The offset's absolute value must not exceed **MAXPHASE**.

long int frequency

This value indicates the difference in frequency between the true calendar time and the system clock. The value is expressed as scaled PPM (parts per million, 0.0001%). The scaling is `1 << SHIFT_USEC`. The value can be set with bit `MOD_FREQUENCY`, but the absolute value must not exceed `MAXFREQ`.

`long int maxerror`

This is the maximum error, measured in microseconds. A new value can be set using bit `MOD_MAXERROR`. Unless updated via `ntp_adjtime` periodically, this value will increase steadily and reach some platform-specific maximum value.

`long int esterror`

This is the estimated error, measured in microseconds. This value can be set using bit `MOD_ESTERROR`.

`int status`

This variable reflects the various states of the clock machinery. There are symbolic constants for the significant bits, starting with `STA_`. Some of these flags can be updated using the `MOD_STATUS` bit.

`long int constant`

This value represents the bandwidth or stiffness of the PLL (phase locked loop) implemented in the kernel. The value can be changed using bit `MOD_TIMECONST`.

`long int precision`

This value represents the accuracy or the maximum error when reading the system clock. The value is expressed in microseconds.

`long int tolerance`

This value represents the maximum frequency error of the system clock in scaled PPM. This value is used to increase the **maxerror** every second.

`struct timeval time`

The current calendar time.

`long int tick`

The elapsed time between clock ticks in microseconds. A clock tick is a periodic timer interrupt on which the system clock is based.

`long int ppsfreq`

This is the first of a few optional variables that are present only if the system clock can use a PPS (pulse per second) signal to discipline the system clock. The value is expressed in scaled PPM and it denotes the difference in frequency between the system clock and the PPS signal.

`long int jitter`

This value expresses a median filtered average of the PPS signal's dispersion in microseconds.

`int shift` This value is a binary exponent for the duration of the PPS calibration interval, ranging from `PPS_SHIFT` to `PPS_SHIFTMAX`.

`long int stabil`

This value represents the median filtered dispersion of the PPS frequency in scaled PPM.

long int jitcnt

> This counter represents the number of pulses where the jitter exceeded the allowed maximum MAXTIME.

long int calcnt

> This counter reflects the number of successful calibration intervals.

long int errcnt

> This counter represents the number of calibration errors (caused by large offsets or jitter).

long int stbcnt

> This counter denotes the number of calibrations where the stability exceeded the threshold.

int ntp_adjtime (struct timex *tptr)   [Function]
Preliminary: | MT-Safe | AS-Safe | AC-Safe | See Section 1.2.2.1 [POSIX Safety Concepts], page 2.

The ntp_adjtime function sets the structure specified by tptr to current values.

In addition, ntp_adjtime updates some settings to match what you pass to it in *tptr. Use the modes element of *tptr to select what settings to update. You can set offset, freq, maxerror, esterror, status, constant, and tick.

modes = zero means set nothing.

Only the superuser can update settings.

The return value is 0 on success and other values on failure. The following errno error conditions are defined for this function:

TIME_ERROR

> The high accuracy clock model is not properly set up at the moment, thus the clock must be considered unsynchronized, and the values should be treated with care. Another reason could be that the specified new values are not allowed.

EPERM   The process specified a settings update, but is not superuser.

For more details see RFC1305 (Network Time Protocol, Version 3) and related documents.

Portability note: Early versions of the GNU C Library did not have this function but did have the synonymous adjtimex.

21.4.5 Formatting Calendar Time

The functions described in this section format calendar time values as strings. These functions are declared in the header file time.h.

char * asctime (const struct tm *brokentime)   [Function]
Preliminary: | MT-Unsafe race:asctime locale | AS-Unsafe | AC-Safe | See Section 1.2.2.1 [POSIX Safety Concepts], page 2.

The asctime function converts the broken-down time value that brokentime points to into a string in a standard format:

```
"Tue May 21 13:46:22 1991\n"
```

The abbreviations for the days of week are: 'Sun', 'Mon', 'Tue', 'Wed', 'Thu', 'Fri', and 'Sat'.

The abbreviations for the months are: 'Jan', 'Feb', 'Mar', 'Apr', 'May', 'Jun', 'Jul', 'Aug', 'Sep', 'Oct', 'Nov', and 'Dec'.

The return value points to a statically allocated string, which might be overwritten by subsequent calls to `asctime` or `ctime`. (But no other library function overwrites the contents of this string.)

char * asctime_r (*const struct tm *brokentime, char *buffer*)   [Function]
Preliminary: | MT-Safe locale | AS-Safe | AC-Safe | See Section 1.2.2.1 [POSIX Safety Concepts], page 2.

This function is similar to `asctime` but instead of placing the result in a static buffer it writes the string in the buffer pointed to by the parameter *buffer*. This buffer should have room for at least 26 bytes, including the terminating null.

If no error occurred the function returns a pointer to the string the result was written into, i.e., it returns *buffer*. Otherwise it returns `NULL`.

char * ctime (*const time_t *time*)   [Function]
Preliminary: | MT-Unsafe race:tmbuf race:asctime env locale | AS-Unsafe heap lock | AC-Unsafe lock mem fd | See Section 1.2.2.1 [POSIX Safety Concepts], page 2.

The `ctime` function is similar to `asctime`, except that you specify the calendar time argument as a `time_t` simple time value rather than in broken-down local time format. It is equivalent to

```
asctime (localtime (time))
```

Calling `ctime` also sets the current time zone as if `tzset` were called. See Section 21.4.8 [Functions and Variables for Time Zones], page 648.

char * ctime_r (*const time_t *time, char *buffer*)   [Function]
Preliminary: | MT-Safe env locale | AS-Unsafe heap lock | AC-Unsafe lock mem fd | See Section 1.2.2.1 [POSIX Safety Concepts], page 2.

This function is similar to `ctime`, but places the result in the string pointed to by *buffer*. It is equivalent to (written using gcc extensions, see Section "Statement Exprs" in *Porting and Using gcc*):

```
({ struct tm tm; asctime_r (localtime_r (time, &tm), buf); })
```

If no error occurred the function returns a pointer to the string the result was written into, i.e., it returns *buffer*. Otherwise it returns `NULL`.

size_t strftime (*char *s, size_t size, const char *template, const   [Function]
      struct tm *brokentime*)
Preliminary: | MT-Safe env locale | AS-Unsafe corrupt heap lock dlopen | AC-Unsafe corrupt lock mem fd | See Section 1.2.2.1 [POSIX Safety Concepts], page 2.

This function is similar to the `sprintf` function (see Section 12.14 [Formatted Input], page 301), but the conversion specifications that can appear in the format template *template* are specialized for printing components of the date and time *brokentime* according to the locale currently specified for time conversion (see Chapter 7 [Locales and Internationalization], page 176) and the current time zone (see Section 21.4.8 [Functions and Variables for Time Zones], page 648).

Ordinary characters appearing in the *template* are copied to the output string *s*; this can include multibyte character sequences. Conversion specifiers are introduced by a '%' character, followed by an optional flag which can be one of the following. These flags are all GNU extensions. The first three affect only the output of numbers:

_   The number is padded with spaces.

-         The number is not padded at all.

0   The number is padded with zeros even if the format specifies padding with spaces.

^   The output uses uppercase characters, but only if this is possible (see Section 4.2 [Case Conversion], page 83).

The default action is to pad the number with zeros to keep it a constant width. Numbers that do not have a range indicated below are never padded, since there is no natural width for them.

Following the flag an optional specification of the width is possible. This is specified in decimal notation. If the natural size of the output of the field has less than the specified number of characters, the result is written right adjusted and space padded to the given size.

An optional modifier can follow the optional flag and width specification. The modifiers, which were first standardized by POSIX.2-1992 and by ISO C99, are:

E   Use the locale's alternate representation for date and time. This modifier applies to the %c, %C, %x, %X, %y and %Y format specifiers. In a Japanese locale, for example, %Ex might yield a date format based on the Japanese Emperors' reigns.

O   Use the locale's alternate numeric symbols for numbers. This modifier applies only to numeric format specifiers.

If the format supports the modifier but no alternate representation is available, it is ignored.

The conversion specifier ends with a format specifier taken from the following list. The whole '%' sequence is replaced in the output string as follows:

%a   The abbreviated weekday name according to the current locale.

%A   The full weekday name according to the current locale.

%b   The abbreviated month name according to the current locale.

%B   The full month name according to the current locale.

            Using %B together with %d produces grammatically incorrect results for some locales.

%c   The preferred calendar time representation for the current locale.

%C	The century of the year. This is equivalent to the greatest integer not greater than the year divided by 100. This format was first standardized by POSIX.2-1992 and by ISO C99.
%d	The day of the month as a decimal number (range 01 through 31).
%D	The date using the format %m/%d/%y. This format was first standardized by POSIX.2-1992 and by ISO C99.
%e	The day of the month like with %d, but padded with spaces (range 1 through 31). This format was first standardized by POSIX.2-1992 and by ISO C99.
%F	The date using the format %Y-%m-%d. This is the form specified in the ISO 8601 standard and is the preferred form for all uses. This format was first standardized by ISO C99 and by POSIX.1-2001.
%g	The year corresponding to the ISO week number, but without the century (range 00 through 99). This has the same format and value as %y, except that if the ISO week number (see %V) belongs to the previous or next year, that year is used instead. This format was first standardized by ISO C99 and by POSIX.1-2001.
%G	The year corresponding to the ISO week number. This has the same format and value as %Y, except that if the ISO week number (see %V) belongs to the previous or next year, that year is used instead. This format was first standardized by ISO C99 and by POSIX.1-2001 but was previously available as a GNU extension.
%h	The abbreviated month name according to the current locale. The action is the same as for %b. This format was first standardized by POSIX.2-1992 and by ISO C99.
%H	The hour as a decimal number, using a 24-hour clock (range 00 through 23).
%I	The hour as a decimal number, using a 12-hour clock (range 01 through 12).
%j	The day of the year as a decimal number (range 001 through 366).
%k	The hour as a decimal number, using a 24-hour clock like %H, but padded with spaces (range 0 through 23). This format is a GNU extension.
%l	The hour as a decimal number, using a 12-hour clock like %I, but padded with spaces (range 1 through 12). This format is a GNU extension.
%m	The month as a decimal number (range 01 through 12).
%M	The minute as a decimal number (range 00 through 59).

%n A single '\n' (newline) character.

    This format was first standardized by POSIX.2-1992 and by ISO C99.

%p Either 'AM' or 'PM', according to the given time value; or the corresponding strings for the current locale. Noon is treated as 'PM' and midnight as 'AM'. In most locales 'AM'/'PM' format is not supported, in such cases "%p" yields an empty string.

%P Either 'am' or 'pm', according to the given time value; or the corresponding strings for the current locale, printed in lowercase characters. Noon is treated as 'pm' and midnight as 'am'. In most locales 'AM'/'PM' format is not supported, in such cases "%P" yields an empty string.

    This format is a GNU extension.

%r The complete calendar time using the AM/PM format of the current locale.

    This format was first standardized by POSIX.2-1992 and by ISO C99. In the POSIX locale, this format is equivalent to %I:%M:%S %p.

%R The hour and minute in decimal numbers using the format %H:%M.

    This format was first standardized by ISO C99 and by POSIX.1-2001 but was previously available as a GNU extension.

%s The number of seconds since the epoch, i.e., since 1970-01-01 00:00:00 UTC. Leap seconds are not counted unless leap second support is available.

    This format is a GNU extension.

%S The seconds as a decimal number (range 00 through 60).

%t A single '\t' (tabulator) character.

    This format was first standardized by POSIX.2-1992 and by ISO C99.

%T The time of day using decimal numbers using the format %H:%M:%S.

    This format was first standardized by POSIX.2-1992 and by ISO C99.

%u The day of the week as a decimal number (range 1 through 7), Monday being 1.

    This format was first standardized by POSIX.2-1992 and by ISO C99.

%U The week number of the current year as a decimal number (range 00 through 53), starting with the first Sunday as the first day of the first week. Days preceding the first Sunday in the year are considered to be in week 00.

%V The ISO 8601:1988 week number as a decimal number (range 01 through 53). ISO weeks start with Monday and end with Sunday. Week 01 of a year is the first week which has the majority of its days in that year; this is equivalent to the week containing the year's first Thursday, and it is also equivalent to the week containing January 4. Week 01 of a year can contain days from the previous year. The week before week 01 of a year is the last week (52 or 53) of the previous year even if it contains days from the new year.

This format was first standardized by POSIX.2-1992 and by ISO C99.

%w   The day of the week as a decimal number (range 0 through 6), Sunday being 0.

%W   The week number of the current year as a decimal number (range 00 through 53), starting with the first Monday as the first day of the first week. All days preceding the first Monday in the year are considered to be in week 00.

%x   The preferred date representation for the current locale.

%X   The preferred time of day representation for the current locale.

%y   The year without a century as a decimal number (range 00 through 99). This is equivalent to the year modulo 100.

%Y   The year as a decimal number, using the Gregorian calendar. Years before the year 1 are numbered 0, -1, and so on.

%z   RFC 822/ISO 8601:1988 style numeric time zone (e.g., -0600 or +0100), or nothing if no time zone is determinable.

This format was first standardized by ISO C99 and by POSIX.1-2001 but was previously available as a GNU extension.

In the POSIX locale, a full RFC 822 timestamp is generated by the format '"%a, %d %b %Y %H:%M:%S %z"' (or the equivalent '"%a, %d %b %Y %T %z"').

%Z   The time zone abbreviation (empty if the time zone can't be determined).

%%   A literal '%' character.

The *size* parameter can be used to specify the maximum number of characters to be stored in the array *s*, including the terminating null character. If the formatted time requires more than *size* characters, **strftime** returns zero and the contents of the array *s* are undefined. Otherwise the return value indicates the number of characters placed in the array *s*, not including the terminating null character.

Warning: This convention for the return value which is prescribed in ISO C can lead to problems in some situations. For certain format strings and certain locales the output really can be the empty string and this cannot be discovered by testing the return value only. E.g., in most locales the AM/PM time format is not supported (most of the world uses the 24 hour time representation). In such locales "%p" will return the empty string, i.e., the return value is zero. To detect situations like this something similar to the following code should be used:

```
buf[0] = '\1';
len = strftime (buf, bufsize, format, tp);
if (len == 0 && buf[0] != '\0')
  {
    /* Something went wrong in the strftime call. */
    ...
  }
```

If *s* is a null pointer, `strftime` does not actually write anything, but instead returns the number of characters it would have written.

Calling `strftime` also sets the current time zone as if `tzset` were called; `strftime` uses this information instead of *brokentime*'s `tm_gmtoff` and `tm_zone` members. See Section 21.4.8 [Functions and Variables for Time Zones], page 648.

For an example of `strftime`, see Section 21.4.9 [Time Functions Example], page 649.

size_t wcsftime (*wchar_t *s, size_t `size`, const wchar_t*   [Function]
     *`*template`, const struct tm *`*brokentime`*)
    Preliminary: | MT-Safe env locale | AS-Unsafe corrupt heap lock dlopen | AC-Unsafe corrupt lock mem fd | See Section 1.2.2.1 [POSIX Safety Concepts], page 2.

The `wcsftime` function is equivalent to the `strftime` function with the difference that it operates on wide character strings. The buffer where the result is stored, pointed to by *s*, must be an array of wide characters. The parameter *size* which specifies the size of the output buffer gives the number of wide characters, not the number of bytes.

Also the format string *template* is a wide character string. Since all characters needed to specify the format string are in the basic character set it is portably possible to write format strings in the C source code using the `L"..."` notation. The parameter *brokentime* has the same meaning as in the `strftime` call.

The `wcsftime` function supports the same flags, modifiers, and format specifiers as the `strftime` function.

The return value of `wcsftime` is the number of wide characters stored in `s`. When more characters would have to be written than can be placed in the buffer *s* the return value is zero, with the same problems indicated in the `strftime` documentation.

21.4.6 Convert textual time and date information back

The ISO C standard does not specify any functions which can convert the output of the `strftime` function back into a binary format. This led to a variety of more-or-less successful implementations with different interfaces over the years. Then the Unix standard was extended by the addition of two functions: `strptime` and `getdate`. Both have strange interfaces but at least they are widely available.

21.4.6.1 Interpret string according to given format

The first function is rather low-level. It is nevertheless frequently used in software since it is better known. Its interface and implementation are heavily influenced by the `getdate` function, which is defined and implemented in terms of calls to `strptime`.

char * strptime (*const char *s, const char *fmt, struct tm *tp*)   [Function]
    Preliminary: | MT-Safe env locale | AS-Unsafe heap lock | AC-Unsafe lock mem fd | See Section 1.2.2.1 [POSIX Safety Concepts], page 2.

The `strptime` function parses the input string *s* according to the format string *fmt* and stores its results in the structure *tp*.

The input string could be generated by a `strftime` call or obtained any other way. It does not need to be in a human-recognizable format; e.g. a date passed as `"02:1999:9"` is acceptable, even though it is ambiguous without context. As long as the format string *fmt* matches the input string the function will succeed.

The user has to make sure, though, that the input can be parsed in a unambiguous way. The string `"1999112"` can be parsed using the format `"%Y%m%d"` as 1999-1-12, 1999-11-2, or even 19991-1-2. It is necessary to add appropriate separators to reliably get results.

The format string consists of the same components as the format string of the `strftime` function. The only difference is that the flags `_`, `-`, `0`, and `^` are not allowed. Several of the distinct formats of `strftime` do the same work in `strptime` since differences like case of the input do not matter. For reasons of symmetry all formats are supported, though.

The modifiers `E` and `O` are also allowed everywhere the `strftime` function allows them.

The formats are:

`%a`

`%A`
: The weekday name according to the current locale, in abbreviated form or the full name.

`%b`

`%B`

`%h`
: The month name according to the current locale, in abbreviated form or the full name.

`%c`
: The date and time representation for the current locale.

`%Ec`
: Like `%c` but the locale's alternative date and time format is used.

`%C`
: The century of the year.

  It makes sense to use this format only if the format string also contains the `%y` format.

`%EC`
: The locale's representation of the period.

  Unlike `%C` it sometimes makes sense to use this format since some cultures represent years relative to the beginning of eras instead of using the Gregorian years.

`%d`

`%e`
: The day of the month as a decimal number (range 1 through 31). Leading zeroes are permitted but not required.

`%Od`

`%Oe`
: Same as `%d` but using the locale's alternative numeric symbols.

  Leading zeroes are permitted but not required.

`%D`
: Equivalent to `%m/%d/%y`.

`%F`
: Equivalent to `%Y-%m-%d`, which is the ISO 8601 date format.

  This is a GNU extension following an ISO C99 extension to `strftime`.

`%g`
: The year corresponding to the ISO week number, but without the century (range 00 through 99).

  Note: Currently, this is not fully implemented. The format is recognized, input is consumed but no field in *tm* is set.

  This format is a GNU extension following a GNU extension of `strftime`.

%G	The year corresponding to the ISO week number.
	Note: Currently, this is not fully implemented. The format is recognized, input is consumed but no field in *tm* is set.
	This format is a GNU extension following a GNU extension of `strftime`.
%H	
%k	The hour as a decimal number, using a 24-hour clock (range 00 through 23).
	%k is a GNU extension following a GNU extension of `strftime`.
%OH	Same as %H but using the locale's alternative numeric symbols.
%I	
%l	The hour as a decimal number, using a 12-hour clock (range 01 through 12).
	%l is a GNU extension following a GNU extension of `strftime`.
%OI	Same as %I but using the locale's alternative numeric symbols.
%j	The day of the year as a decimal number (range 1 through 366).
	Leading zeroes are permitted but not required.
%m	The month as a decimal number (range 1 through 12).
	Leading zeroes are permitted but not required.
%Om	Same as %m but using the locale's alternative numeric symbols.
%M	The minute as a decimal number (range 0 through 59).
	Leading zeroes are permitted but not required.
%OM	Same as %M but using the locale's alternative numeric symbols.
%n	
%t	Matches any white space.
%p	
%P	The locale-dependent equivalent to 'AM' or 'PM'.
	This format is not useful unless %I or %l is also used. Another complication is that the locale might not define these values at all and therefore the conversion fails.
	%P is a GNU extension following a GNU extension to `strftime`.
%r	The complete time using the AM/PM format of the current locale.
	A complication is that the locale might not define this format at all and therefore the conversion fails.
%R	The hour and minute in decimal numbers using the format %H:%M.
	%R is a GNU extension following a GNU extension to `strftime`.
%s	The number of seconds since the epoch, i.e., since 1970-01-01 00:00:00 UTC. Leap seconds are not counted unless leap second support is available.
	%s is a GNU extension following a GNU extension to `strftime`.

%S	The seconds as a decimal number (range 0 through 60).
	Leading zeroes are permitted but not required.
	NB: The Unix specification says the upper bound on this value is 61, a result of a decision to allow double leap seconds. You will not see the value 61 because no minute has more than one leap second, but the myth persists.
%OS	Same as %S but using the locale's alternative numeric symbols.
%T	Equivalent to the use of %H:%M:%S in this place.
%u	The day of the week as a decimal number (range 1 through 7), Monday being 1.
	Leading zeroes are permitted but not required.
	Note: Currently, this is not fully implemented. The format is recognized, input is consumed but no field in *tm* is set.
%U	The week number of the current year as a decimal number (range 0 through 53).
	Leading zeroes are permitted but not required.
%OU	Same as %U but using the locale's alternative numeric symbols.
%V	The ISO 8601:1988 week number as a decimal number (range 1 through 53).
	Leading zeroes are permitted but not required.
	Note: Currently, this is not fully implemented. The format is recognized, input is consumed but no field in *tm* is set.
%w	The day of the week as a decimal number (range 0 through 6), Sunday being 0.
	Leading zeroes are permitted but not required.
	Note: Currently, this is not fully implemented. The format is recognized, input is consumed but no field in *tm* is set.
%Ow	Same as %w but using the locale's alternative numeric symbols.
%W	The week number of the current year as a decimal number (range 0 through 53).
	Leading zeroes are permitted but not required.
	Note: Currently, this is not fully implemented. The format is recognized, input is consumed but no field in *tm* is set.
%OW	Same as %W but using the locale's alternative numeric symbols.
%x	The date using the locale's date format.
%Ex	Like %x but the locale's alternative data representation is used.
%X	The time using the locale's time format.
%EX	Like %X but the locale's alternative time representation is used.

%y   The year without a century as a decimal number (range 0 through 99). Leading zeroes are permitted but not required.

            Note that it is questionable to use this format without the %C format. The strptime function does regard input values in the range 68 to 99 as the years 1969 to 1999 and the values 0 to 68 as the years 2000 to 2068. But maybe this heuristic fails for some input data.

            Therefore it is best to avoid %y completely and use %Y instead.

%Ey   The offset from %EC in the locale's alternative representation.

%Oy   The offset of the year (from %C) using the locale's alternative numeric symbols.

%Y   The year as a decimal number, using the Gregorian calendar.

%EY   The full alternative year representation.

%z   The offset from GMT in ISO 8601/RFC822 format.

%Z   The timezone name.

            Note: Currently, this is not fully implemented. The format is recognized, input is consumed but no field in *tm* is set.

%%   A literal '%' character.

All other characters in the format string must have a matching character in the input string. Exceptions are white spaces in the input string which can match zero or more whitespace characters in the format string.

Portability Note: The XPG standard advises applications to use at least one whitespace character (as specified by isspace) or other non-alphanumeric characters between any two conversion specifications. The GNU C Library does not have this limitation but other libraries might have trouble parsing formats like "%d%m%Y%H%M%S".

The strptime function processes the input string from right to left. Each of the three possible input elements (white space, literal, or format) are handled one after the other. If the input cannot be matched to the format string the function stops. The remainder of the format and input strings are not processed.

The function returns a pointer to the first character it was unable to process. If the input string contains more characters than required by the format string the return value points right after the last consumed input character. If the whole input string is consumed the return value points to the NULL byte at the end of the string. If an error occurs, i.e., strptime fails to match all of the format string, the function returns NULL.

The specification of the function in the XPG standard is rather vague, leaving out a few important pieces of information. Most importantly, it does not specify what happens to those elements of *tm* which are not directly initialized by the different formats. The implementations on different Unix systems vary here.

The GNU C Library implementation does not touch those fields which are not directly initialized. Exceptions are the tm_wday and tm_yday elements, which are recomputed if any of the year, month, or date elements changed. This has two implications:

- Before calling the `strptime` function for a new input string, you should prepare the *tm* structure you pass. Normally this will mean initializing all values to zero. Alternatively, you can set all fields to values like `INT_MAX`, allowing you to determine which elements were set by the function call. Zero does not work here since it is a valid value for many of the fields.

  Careful initialization is necessary if you want to find out whether a certain field in *tm* was initialized by the function call.

- You can construct a `struct tm` value with several consecutive `strptime` calls. A useful application of this is e.g. the parsing of two separate strings, one containing date information and the other time information. By parsing one after the other without clearing the structure in-between, you can construct a complete broken-down time.

The following example shows a function which parses a string which contains the date information in either US style or ISO 8601 form:

```
const char *
parse_date (const char *input, struct tm *tm)
{
  const char *cp;

  /* First clear the result structure.  */
  memset (tm, '\0', sizeof (*tm));

  /* Try the ISO format first.  */
  cp = strptime (input, "%F", tm);
  if (cp == NULL)
    {
      /* Does not match.  Try the US form.  */
      cp = strptime (input, "%D", tm);
    }

  return cp;
}
```

21.4.6.2 A More User-friendly Way to Parse Times and Dates

The Unix standard defines another function for parsing date strings. The interface is weird, but if the function happens to suit your application it is just fine. It is problematic to use this function in multi-threaded programs or libraries, since it returns a pointer to a static variable, and uses a global variable and global state (an environment variable).

`getdate_err`   [Variable]

This variable of type `int` contains the error code of the last unsuccessful call to `getdate`. Defined values are:

1   The environment variable `DATEMSK` is not defined or null.

2   The template file denoted by the `DATEMSK` environment variable cannot be opened.

3   Information about the template file cannot retrieved.

4   The template file is not a regular file.

5   An I/O error occurred while reading the template file.

6   Not enough memory available to execute the function.

7   The template file contains no matching template.

8   The input date is invalid, but would match a template otherwise. This includes dates like February 31st, and dates which cannot be represented in a `time_t` variable.

`struct tm * getdate (const char *string)`   [Function]
Preliminary: | MT-Unsafe race:getdate env locale | AS-Unsafe heap lock | AC-Unsafe lock mem fd | See Section 1.2.2.1 [POSIX Safety Concepts], page 2.

The interface to `getdate` is the simplest possible for a function to parse a string and return the value. *string* is the input string and the result is returned in a statically-allocated variable.

The details about how the string is processed are hidden from the user. In fact, they can be outside the control of the program. Which formats are recognized is controlled by the file named by the environment variable `DATEMSK`. This file should contain lines of valid format strings which could be passed to `strptime`.

The `getdate` function reads these format strings one after the other and tries to match the input string. The first line which completely matches the input string is used.

Elements not initialized through the format string retain the values present at the time of the `getdate` function call.

The formats recognized by `getdate` are the same as for `strptime`. See above for an explanation. There are only a few extensions to the `strptime` behavior:

- If the `%Z` format is given the broken-down time is based on the current time of the timezone matched, not of the current timezone of the runtime environment.

  Note: This is not implemented (currently). The problem is that timezone names are not unique. If a fixed timezone is assumed for a given string (say `EST` meaning US East Coast time), then uses for countries other than the USA will fail. So far we have found no good solution to this.

- If only the weekday is specified the selected day depends on the current date. If the current weekday is greater than or equal to the `tm_wday` value the current week's day is chosen, otherwise the day next week is chosen.

- A similar heuristic is used when only the month is given and not the year. If the month is greater than or equal to the current month, then the current year is used. Otherwise it wraps to next year. The first day of the month is assumed if one is not explicitly specified.

- The current hour, minute, and second are used if the appropriate value is not set through the format.

- If no date is given tomorrow's date is used if the time is smaller than the current time. Otherwise today's date is taken.

It should be noted that the format in the template file need not only contain format elements. The following is a list of possible format strings (taken from the Unix standard):

%m

```
%A %B %d, %Y %H:%M:%S
%A
%B
%m/%d/%y %I %p
%d,%m,%Y %H:%M
at %A the %dst of %B in %Y
run job at %I %p,%B %dnd
%A den %d. %B %Y %H.%M Uhr
```

As you can see, the template list can contain very specific strings like `run job at %I %p,%B %dnd`. Using the above list of templates and assuming the current time is Mon Sep 22 12:19:47 EDT 1986, we can obtain the following results for the given input.

Input	Match	Result
Mon	%a	Mon Sep 22 12:19:47 EDT 1986
Sun	%a	Sun Sep 28 12:19:47 EDT 1986
Fri	%a	Fri Sep 26 12:19:47 EDT 1986
September	%B	Mon Sep 1 12:19:47 EDT 1986
January	%B	Thu Jan 1 12:19:47 EST 1987
December	%B	Mon Dec 1 12:19:47 EST 1986
Sep Mon	%b %a	Mon Sep 1 12:19:47 EDT 1986
Jan Fri	%b %a	Fri Jan 2 12:19:47 EST 1987
Dec Mon	%b %a	Mon Dec 1 12:19:47 EST 1986
Jan Wed 1989	%b %a %Y	Wed Jan 4 12:19:47 EST 1989
Fri 9	%a %H	Fri Sep 26 09:00:00 EDT 1986
Feb 10:30	%b %H:%S	Sun Feb 1 10:00:30 EST 1987
10:30	%H:%M	Tue Sep 23 10:30:00 EDT 1986
13:30	%H:%M	Mon Sep 22 13:30:00 EDT 1986

The return value of the function is a pointer to a static variable of type `struct tm`, or a null pointer if an error occurred. The result is only valid until the next `getdate` call, making this function unusable in multi-threaded applications.

The `errno` variable is *not* changed. Error conditions are stored in the global variable `getdate_err`. See the description above for a list of the possible error values.

Warning: The `getdate` function should *never* be used in SUID-programs. The reason is obvious: using the `DATEMSK` environment variable you can get the function to open any arbitrary file and chances are high that with some bogus input (such as a binary file) the program will crash.

`int getdate_r` (*const char *string, struct tm *tp*)   [Function]
Preliminary: | MT-Safe env locale | AS-Unsafe heap lock | AC-Unsafe lock mem fd | See Section 1.2.2.1 [POSIX Safety Concepts], page 2.

The `getdate_r` function is the reentrant counterpart of `getdate`. It does not use the global variable `getdate_err` to signal an error, but instead returns an error code. The same error codes as described in the `getdate_err` documentation above are used, with 0 meaning success.

Moreover, `getdate_r` stores the broken-down time in the variable of type `struct tm` pointed to by the second argument, rather than in a static variable.

This function is not defined in the Unix standard. Nevertheless it is available on some other Unix systems as well.

The warning against using `getdate` in SUID-programs applies to `getdate_r` as well.

21.4.7 Specifying the Time Zone with TZ

In POSIX systems, a user can specify the time zone by means of the `TZ` environment variable. For information about how to set environment variables, see Section 25.4 [Environment Variables], page 762. The functions for accessing the time zone are declared in `time.h`.

You should not normally need to set `TZ`. If the system is configured properly, the default time zone will be correct. You might set `TZ` if you are using a computer over a network from a different time zone, and would like times reported to you in the time zone local to you, rather than what is local to the computer.

In POSIX.1 systems the value of the `TZ` variable can be in one of three formats. With the GNU C Library, the most common format is the last one, which can specify a selection from a large database of time zone information for many regions of the world. The first two formats are used to describe the time zone information directly, which is both more cumbersome and less precise. But the POSIX.1 standard only specifies the details of the first two formats, so it is good to be familiar with them in case you come across a POSIX.1 system that doesn't support a time zone information database.

The first format is used when there is no Daylight Saving Time (or summer time) in the local time zone:

> *std offset*

The *std* string specifies the name of the time zone. It must be three or more characters long and must not contain a leading colon, embedded digits, commas, nor plus and minus signs. There is no space character separating the time zone name from the *offset*, so these restrictions are necessary to parse the specification correctly.

The *offset* specifies the time value you must add to the local time to get a Coordinated Universal Time value. It has syntax like [+|-]*hh*[:*mm*[:*ss*]]. This is positive if the local time zone is west of the Prime Meridian and negative if it is east. The hour must be between 0 and 24, and the minute and seconds between 0 and 59.

For example, here is how we would specify Eastern Standard Time, but without any Daylight Saving Time alternative:

> `EST+5`

The second format is used when there is Daylight Saving Time:

> *std offset dst* [*offset*],*start*[/*time*],*end*[/*time*]

The initial *std* and *offset* specify the standard time zone, as described above. The *dst* string and *offset* specify the name and offset for the corresponding Daylight Saving Time zone; if the *offset* is omitted, it defaults to one hour ahead of standard time.

The remainder of the specification describes when Daylight Saving Time is in effect. The *start* field is when Daylight Saving Time goes into effect and the *end* field is when the change is made back to standard time. The following formats are recognized for these fields:

J*n*   This specifies the Julian day, with *n* between 1 and 365. February 29 is never counted, even in leap years.

n   This specifies the Julian day, with *n* between 0 and 365. February 29 is counted in leap years.

`Mm.w.d`   This specifies day *d* of week *w* of month *m*. The day *d* must be between 0 (Sunday) and **6**. The week *w* must be between **1** and **5**; week **1** is the first week in which day *d* occurs, and week **5** specifies the *last d* day in the month. The month *m* should be between **1** and **12**.

The *time* fields specify when, in the local time currently in effect, the change to the other time occurs. If omitted, the default is `02:00:00`. The hours part of the time fields can range from −167 through 167; this is an extension to POSIX.1, which allows only the range 0 through 24.

Here are some example `TZ` values, including the appropriate Daylight Saving Time and its dates of applicability. In North American Eastern Standard Time (EST) and Eastern Daylight Time (EDT), the normal offset from UTC is 5 hours; since this is west of the prime meridian, the sign is positive. Summer time begins on March's second Sunday at 2:00am, and ends on November's first Sunday at 2:00am.

```
EST+5EDT,M3.2.0/2,M11.1.0/2
```

Israel Standard Time (IST) and Israel Daylight Time (IDT) are 2 hours ahead of the prime meridian in winter, springing forward an hour on March's fourth Thursday at 26:00 (i.e., 02:00 on the first Friday on or after March 23), and falling back on October's last Sunday at 02:00.

```
IST-2IDT,M3.4.4/26,M10.5.0
```

Western Argentina Summer Time (WARST) is 3 hours behind the prime meridian all year. There is a dummy fall-back transition on December 31 at 25:00 daylight saving time (i.e., 24:00 standard time, equivalent to January 1 at 00:00 standard time), and a simultaneous spring-forward transition on January 1 at 00:00 standard time, so daylight saving time is in effect all year and the initial `WART` is a placeholder.

```
WART4WARST,J1/0,J365/25
```

Western Greenland Time (WGT) and Western Greenland Summer Time (WGST) are 3 hours behind UTC in the winter. Its clocks follow the European Union rules of springing forward by one hour on March's last Sunday at 01:00 UTC (−02:00 local time) and falling back on October's last Sunday at 01:00 UTC (−01:00 local time).

```
WGT3WGST,M3.5.0/-2,M10.5.0/-1
```

The schedule of Daylight Saving Time in any particular jurisdiction has changed over the years. To be strictly correct, the conversion of dates and times in the past should be based on the schedule that was in effect then. However, this format has no facilities to let you specify how the schedule has changed from year to year. The most you can do is specify one particular schedule—usually the present day schedule—and this is used to convert any date, no matter when. For precise time zone specifications, it is best to use the time zone information database (see below).

The third format looks like this:

```
:characters
```

Each operating system interprets this format differently; in the GNU C Library, *characters* is the name of a file which describes the time zone.

If the `TZ` environment variable does not have a value, the operation chooses a time zone by default. In the GNU C Library, the default time zone is like the specification '`TZ=:/etc/localtime`' (or '`TZ=:/usr/local/etc/localtime`', depending on how the GNU

C Library was configured; see Appendix C [Installing the GNU C Library], page 1043). Other C libraries use their own rule for choosing the default time zone, so there is little we can say about them.

If *characters* begins with a slash, it is an absolute file name; otherwise the library looks for the file `/usr/share/zoneinfo/characters`. The `zoneinfo` directory contains data files describing local time zones in many different parts of the world. The names represent major cities, with subdirectories for geographical areas; for example, `America/New_York`, `Europe/London`, `Asia/Hong_Kong`. These data files are installed by the system administrator, who also sets `/etc/localtime` to point to the data file for the local time zone. The files typically come from the Time Zone Database (`http://www.iana.org/time-zones`) of time zone and daylight saving time information for most regions of the world, which is maintained by a community of volunteers and put in the public domain.

21.4.8 Functions and Variables for Time Zones

`char * tzname [2]`   [Variable]

>   The array `tzname` contains two strings, which are the standard names of the pair of time zones (standard and Daylight Saving) that the user has selected. `tzname[0]` is the name of the standard time zone (for example, `"EST"`), and `tzname[1]` is the name for the time zone when Daylight Saving Time is in use (for example, `"EDT"`). These correspond to the *std* and *dst* strings (respectively) from the `TZ` environment variable. If Daylight Saving Time is never used, `tzname[1]` is the empty string.

>   The `tzname` array is initialized from the `TZ` environment variable whenever `tzset`, `ctime`, `strftime`, `mktime`, or `localtime` is called. If multiple abbreviations have been used (e.g. `"EWT"` and `"EDT"` for U.S. Eastern War Time and Eastern Daylight Time), the array contains the most recent abbreviation.

>   The `tzname` array is required for POSIX.1 compatibility, but in GNU programs it is better to use the `tm_zone` member of the broken-down time structure, since `tm_zone` reports the correct abbreviation even when it is not the latest one.

>   Though the strings are declared as `char *` the user must refrain from modifying these strings. Modifying the strings will almost certainly lead to trouble.

`void tzset (void)`   [Function]

>   Preliminary: | MT-Safe env locale | AS-Unsafe heap lock | AC-Unsafe lock mem fd | See Section 1.2.2.1 [POSIX Safety Concepts], page 2.

>   The `tzset` function initializes the `tzname` variable from the value of the `TZ` environment variable. It is not usually necessary for your program to call this function, because it is called automatically when you use the other time conversion functions that depend on the time zone.

The following variables are defined for compatibility with System V Unix. Like `tzname`, these variables are set by calling `tzset` or the other time conversion functions.

`long int timezone`   [Variable]

>   This contains the difference between UTC and the latest local standard time, in seconds west of UTC. For example, in the U.S. Eastern time zone, the value is `5*60*60`. Unlike the `tm_gmtoff` member of the broken-down time structure, this value is not

adjusted for daylight saving, and its sign is reversed. In GNU programs it is better to use `tm_gmtoff`, since it contains the correct offset even when it is not the latest one.

`int daylight` [Variable]

This variable has a nonzero value if Daylight Saving Time rules apply. A nonzero value does not necessarily mean that Daylight Saving Time is now in effect; it means only that Daylight Saving Time is sometimes in effect.

21.4.9 Time Functions Example

Here is an example program showing the use of some of the calendar time functions.

```
#include <time.h>
#include <stdio.h>

#define SIZE 256

int
main (void)
{
  char buffer[SIZE];
  time_t curtime;
  struct tm *loctime;

  /* Get the current time. */
  curtime = time (NULL);

  /* Convert it to local time representation. */
  loctime = localtime (&curtime);

  /* Print out the date and time in the standard format. */
  fputs (asctime (loctime), stdout);

  /* Print it out in a nice format. */
  strftime (buffer, SIZE, "Today is %A, %B %d.\n", loctime);
  fputs (buffer, stdout);
  strftime (buffer, SIZE, "The time is %I:%M %p.\n", loctime);
  fputs (buffer, stdout);

  return 0;
}
```

It produces output like this:

```
Wed Jul 31 13:02:36 1991
Today is Wednesday, July 31.
The time is 01:02 PM.
```

21.5 Setting an Alarm

The `alarm` and `setitimer` functions provide a mechanism for a process to interrupt itself in the future. They do this by setting a timer; when the timer expires, the process receives a signal.

Each process has three independent interval timers available:

- A real-time timer that counts elapsed time. This timer sends a `SIGALRM` signal to the process when it expires.

- A virtual timer that counts processor time used by the process. This timer sends a `SIGVTALRM` signal to the process when it expires.

- A profiling timer that counts both processor time used by the process, and processor time spent in system calls on behalf of the process. This timer sends a `SIGPROF` signal to the process when it expires.

  This timer is useful for profiling in interpreters. The interval timer mechanism does not have the fine granularity necessary for profiling native code.

You can only have one timer of each kind set at any given time. If you set a timer that has not yet expired, that timer is simply reset to the new value.

You should establish a handler for the appropriate alarm signal using `signal` or `sigaction` before issuing a call to `setitimer` or `alarm`. Otherwise, an unusual chain of events could cause the timer to expire before your program establishes the handler. In this case it would be terminated, since termination is the default action for the alarm signals. See Chapter 24 [Signal Handling], page 685.

To be able to use the alarm function to interrupt a system call which might block otherwise indefinitely it is important to *not* set the `SA_RESTART` flag when registering the signal handler using `sigaction`. When not using `sigaction` things get even uglier: the `signal` function has fixed semantics with respect to restarts. The BSD semantics for this function is to set the flag. Therefore, if `sigaction` for whatever reason cannot be used, it is necessary to use `sysv_signal` and not `signal`.

The `setitimer` function is the primary means for setting an alarm. This facility is declared in the header file `sys/time.h`. The `alarm` function, declared in `unistd.h`, provides a somewhat simpler interface for setting the real-time timer.

`struct itimerval`   [Data Type]

This structure is used to specify when a timer should expire. It contains the following members:

`struct timeval it_interval`

This is the period between successive timer interrupts. If zero, the alarm will only be sent once.

`struct timeval it_value`

This is the period between now and the first timer interrupt. If zero, the alarm is disabled.

The `struct timeval` data type is described in Section 21.2 [Elapsed Time], page 619.

`int setitimer (int which, const struct itimerval *new, struct`   [Function]
`        itimerval *old)`

Preliminary: | MT-Safe timer | AS-Safe | AC-Safe | See Section 1.2.2.1 [POSIX Safety Concepts], page 2.

The `setitimer` function sets the timer specified by *which* according to *new*. The *which* argument can have a value of `ITIMER_REAL`, `ITIMER_VIRTUAL`, or `ITIMER_PROF`.

If *old* is not a null pointer, `setitimer` returns information about any previous unexpired timer of the same kind in the structure it points to.

The return value is 0 on success and -1 on failure. The following **errno** error conditions are defined for this function:

EINVAL   The timer period is too large.

int getitimer (*int which, struct itimerval *old*)   [Function]
> Preliminary: | MT-Safe | AS-Safe | AC-Safe | See Section 1.2.2.1 [POSIX Safety Concepts], page 2.
>
> The **getitimer** function stores information about the timer specified by *which* in the structure pointed at by *old*.
>
> The return value and error conditions are the same as for **setitimer**.

ITIMER_REAL
> This constant can be used as the *which* argument to the **setitimer** and **getitimer** functions to specify the real-time timer.

ITIMER_VIRTUAL
> This constant can be used as the *which* argument to the **setitimer** and **getitimer** functions to specify the virtual timer.

ITIMER_PROF
> This constant can be used as the *which* argument to the **setitimer** and **getitimer** functions to specify the profiling timer.

unsigned int alarm (*unsigned int seconds*)   [Function]
> Preliminary: | MT-Safe timer | AS-Safe | AC-Safe | See Section 1.2.2.1 [POSIX Safety Concepts], page 2.
>
> The **alarm** function sets the real-time timer to expire in *seconds* seconds. If you want to cancel any existing alarm, you can do this by calling **alarm** with a *seconds* argument of zero.
>
> The return value indicates how many seconds remain before the previous alarm would have been sent. If there was no previous alarm, **alarm** returns zero.

The **alarm** function could be defined in terms of **setitimer** like this:

```
unsigned int
alarm (unsigned int seconds)
{
  struct itimerval old, new;
  new.it_interval.tv_usec = 0;
  new.it_interval.tv_sec = 0;
  new.it_value.tv_usec = 0;
  new.it_value.tv_sec = (long int) seconds;
  if (setitimer (ITIMER_REAL, &new, &old) < 0)
    return 0;
  else
    return old.it_value.tv_sec;
}
```

There is an example showing the use of the **alarm** function in Section 24.4.1 [Signal Handlers that Return], page 702.

If you simply want your process to wait for a given number of seconds, you should use the **sleep** function. See Section 21.6 [Sleeping], page 652.

You shouldn't count on the signal arriving precisely when the timer expires. In a multi-processing environment there is typically some amount of delay involved.

Portability Note: The `setitimer` and `getitimer` functions are derived from BSD Unix, while the `alarm` function is specified by the POSIX.1 standard. `setitimer` is more powerful than `alarm`, but `alarm` is more widely used.

21.6 Sleeping

The function `sleep` gives a simple way to make the program wait for a short interval. If your program doesn't use signals (except to terminate), then you can expect `sleep` to wait reliably throughout the specified interval. Otherwise, `sleep` can return sooner if a signal arrives; if you want to wait for a given interval regardless of signals, use `select` (see Section 13.8 [Waiting for Input or Output], page 355) and don't specify any descriptors to wait for.

`unsigned int sleep (`*unsigned int seconds*`)` [Function]

> Preliminary: | MT-Unsafe sig:SIGCHLD/linux | AS-Unsafe | AC-Unsafe | See Section 1.2.2.1 [POSIX Safety Concepts], page 2.

> The `sleep` function waits for *seconds* seconds or until a signal is delivered, whichever happens first.

> If `sleep` returns because the requested interval is over, it returns a value of zero. If it returns because of delivery of a signal, its return value is the remaining time in the sleep interval.

> The `sleep` function is declared in `unistd.h`.

Resist the temptation to implement a sleep for a fixed amount of time by using the return value of `sleep`, when nonzero, to call `sleep` again. This will work with a certain amount of accuracy as long as signals arrive infrequently. But each signal can cause the eventual wakeup time to be off by an additional second or so. Suppose a few signals happen to arrive in rapid succession by bad luck—there is no limit on how much this could shorten or lengthen the wait.

Instead, compute the calendar time at which the program should stop waiting, and keep trying to wait until that calendar time. This won't be off by more than a second. With just a little more work, you can use `select` and make the waiting period quite accurate. (Of course, heavy system load can cause additional unavoidable delays—unless the machine is dedicated to one application, there is no way you can avoid this.)

On some systems, `sleep` can do strange things if your program uses `SIGALRM` explicitly. Even if `SIGALRM` signals are being ignored or blocked when `sleep` is called, `sleep` might return prematurely on delivery of a `SIGALRM` signal. If you have established a handler for `SIGALRM` signals and a `SIGALRM` signal is delivered while the process is sleeping, the action taken might be just to cause `sleep` to return instead of invoking your handler. And, if `sleep` is interrupted by delivery of a signal whose handler requests an alarm or alters the handling of `SIGALRM`, this handler and `sleep` will interfere.

On GNU systems, it is safe to use `sleep` and `SIGALRM` in the same program, because `sleep` does not work by means of `SIGALRM`.

int nanosleep (*const struct timespec* ***requested_time**, *struct* [Function]
    timespec ***remaining**)
    Preliminary: | MT-Safe | AS-Safe | AC-Safe | See Section 1.2.2.1 [POSIX Safety
    Concepts], page 2.

If resolution to seconds is not enough the **nanosleep** function can be used. As the
name suggests the sleep interval can be specified in nanoseconds. The actual elapsed
time of the sleep interval might be longer since the system rounds the elapsed time
you request up to the next integer multiple of the actual resolution the system can
deliver.

***requested_time** is the elapsed time of the interval you want to sleep.

The function returns as ***remaining** the elapsed time left in the interval for which
you requested to sleep. If the interval completed without getting interrupted by a
signal, this is zero.

struct timespec is described in See Section 21.2 [Elapsed Time], page 619.

If the function returns because the interval is over the return value is zero. If the
function returns −1 the global variable *errno* is set to the following values:

EINTR   The call was interrupted because a signal was delivered to the thread. If
    the *remaining* parameter is not the null pointer the structure pointed to
    by *remaining* is updated to contain the remaining elapsed time.

EINVAL   The nanosecond value in the *requested_time* parameter contains an illegal
    value. Either the value is negative or greater than or equal to 1000 million.

This function is a cancellation point in multi-threaded programs. This is a problem
if the thread allocates some resources (like memory, file descriptors, semaphores or
whatever) at the time **nanosleep** is called. If the thread gets canceled these resources
stay allocated until the program ends. To avoid this calls to **nanosleep** should be
protected using cancellation handlers.

The **nanosleep** function is declared in **time.h**.

22 Resource Usage And Limitation

This chapter describes functions for examining how much of various kinds of resources (CPU time, memory, etc.) a process has used and getting and setting limits on future usage.

22.1 Resource Usage

The function `getrusage` and the data type `struct rusage` are used to examine the resource usage of a process. They are declared in `sys/resource.h`.

`int getrusage (`*int* `processes,` *struct rusage* `*rusage)` [Function]
> Preliminary: | MT-Safe | AS-Safe | AC-Safe | See Section 1.2.2.1 [POSIX Safety Concepts], page 2.
>
> This function reports resource usage totals for processes specified by *processes*, storing the information in **rusage*.
>
> In most systems, *processes* has only two valid values:
>
> `RUSAGE_SELF`
> > Just the current process.
>
> `RUSAGE_CHILDREN`
> > All child processes (direct and indirect) that have already terminated.
>
> The return value of `getrusage` is zero for success, and `-1` for failure.
>
> `EINVAL`   The argument *processes* is not valid.

One way of getting resource usage for a particular child process is with the function `wait4`, which returns totals for a child when it terminates. See Section 26.8 [BSD Process Wait Function], page 782.

`struct rusage` [Data Type]
> This data type stores various resource usage statistics. It has the following members, and possibly others:
>
> `struct timeval ru_utime`
> > Time spent executing user instructions.
>
> `struct timeval ru_stime`
> > Time spent in operating system code on behalf of *processes*.
>
> `long int ru_maxrss`
> > The maximum resident set size used, in kilobytes. That is, the maximum number of kilobytes of physical memory that *processes* used simultaneously.
>
> `long int ru_ixrss`
> > An integral value expressed in kilobytes times ticks of execution, which indicates the amount of memory used by text that was shared with other processes.
>
> `long int ru_idrss`
> > An integral value expressed the same way, which is the amount of unshared memory used for data.

`long int ru_isrss`

> An integral value expressed the same way, which is the amount of unshared memory used for stack space.

`long int ru_minflt`

> The number of page faults which were serviced without requiring any I/O.

`long int ru_majflt`

> The number of page faults which were serviced by doing I/O.

`long int ru_nswap`

> The number of times *processes* was swapped entirely out of main memory.

`long int ru_inblock`

> The number of times the file system had to read from the disk on behalf of *processes*.

`long int ru_oublock`

> The number of times the file system had to write to the disk on behalf of *processes*.

`long int ru_msgsnd`

> Number of IPC messages sent.

`long int ru_msgrcv`

> Number of IPC messages received.

`long int ru_nsignals`

> Number of signals received.

`long int ru_nvcsw`

> The number of times *processes* voluntarily invoked a context switch (usually to wait for some service).

`long int ru_nivcsw`

> The number of times an involuntary context switch took place (because a time slice expired, or another process of higher priority was scheduled).

vtimes is a historical function that does some of what **getrusage** does. **getrusage** is a better choice.

vtimes and its **vtimes** data structure are declared in **sys/vtimes.h**.

`int vtimes (`*struct vtimes* `*`***current***`,` *struct vtimes* `*`***child***`)`   [Function]

> Preliminary: | MT-Safe | AS-Safe | AC-Safe | See Section 1.2.2.1 [POSIX Safety Concepts], page 2.
>
> **vtimes** reports resource usage totals for a process.
>
> If *current* is non-null, **vtimes** stores resource usage totals for the invoking process alone in the structure to which it points. If *child* is non-null, **vtimes** stores resource usage totals for all past children (which have terminated) of the invoking process in the structure to which it points.

`struct vtimes`   [Data Type]

> This data type contains information about the resource usage of a process. Each member corresponds to a member of the `struct rusage` data type described above.

> `vm_utime`   User CPU time. Analogous to `ru_utime` in `struct rusage`

> `vm_stime`   System CPU time. Analogous to `ru_stime` in `struct rusage`

> `vm_idsrss`

>> Data and stack memory. The sum of the values that would be reported as `ru_idrss` and `ru_isrss` in `struct rusage`

> `vm_ixrss`   Shared memory. Analogous to `ru_ixrss` in `struct rusage`

> `vm_maxrss`

>> Maximent resident set size. Analogous to `ru_maxrss` in `struct rusage`

> `vm_majflt`

>> Major page faults. Analogous to `ru_majflt` in `struct rusage`

> `vm_minflt`

>> Minor page faults. Analogous to `ru_minflt` in `struct rusage`

> `vm_nswap`   Swap count. Analogous to `ru_nswap` in `struct rusage`

> `vm_inblk`   Disk reads. Analogous to `ru_inblk` in `struct rusage`

> `vm_oublk`   Disk writes. Analogous to `ru_oublk` in `struct rusage`

The return value is zero if the function succeeds; `-1` otherwise.

An additional historical function for examining resource usage, `vtimes`, is supported but not documented here. It is declared in `sys/vtimes.h`.

22.2 Limiting Resource Usage

You can specify limits for the resource usage of a process. When the process tries to exceed a limit, it may get a signal, or the system call by which it tried to do so may fail, depending on the resource. Each process initially inherits its limit values from its parent, but it can subsequently change them.

There are two per-process limits associated with a resource:

current limit

> The current limit is the value the system will not allow usage to exceed. It is also called the "soft limit" because the process being limited can generally raise the current limit at will.

maximum limit

> The maximum limit is the maximum value to which a process is allowed to set its current limit. It is also called the "hard limit" because there is no way for a process to get around it. A process may lower its own maximum limit, but only the superuser may increase a maximum limit.

The symbols for use with `getrlimit`, `setrlimit`, `getrlimit64`, and `setrlimit64` are defined in `sys/resource.h`.

int getrlimit (*int resource, struct rlimit *rlp*)   [Function]
    Preliminary: | MT-Safe | AS-Safe | AC-Safe | See Section 1.2.2.1 [POSIX Safety Concepts], page 2.

    Read the current and maximum limits for the resource *resource* and store them in **rlp*.

    The return value is 0 on success and -1 on failure. The only possible `errno` error condition is `EFAULT`.

    When the sources are compiled with `_FILE_OFFSET_BITS == 64` on a 32-bit system this function is in fact `getrlimit64`. Thus, the LFS interface transparently replaces the old interface.

int getrlimit64 (*int resource, struct rlimit64 *rlp*)   [Function]
    Preliminary: | MT-Safe | AS-Safe | AC-Safe | See Section 1.2.2.1 [POSIX Safety Concepts], page 2.

    This function is similar to `getrlimit` but its second parameter is a pointer to a variable of type `struct rlimit64`, which allows it to read values which wouldn't fit in the member of a `struct rlimit`.

    If the sources are compiled with `_FILE_OFFSET_BITS == 64` on a 32-bit machine, this function is available under the name `getrlimit` and so transparently replaces the old interface.

int setrlimit (*int resource, const struct rlimit *rlp*)   [Function]
    Preliminary: | MT-Safe | AS-Safe | AC-Safe | See Section 1.2.2.1 [POSIX Safety Concepts], page 2.

    Store the current and maximum limits for the resource *resource* in **rlp*.

    The return value is 0 on success and -1 on failure. The following `errno` error condition is possible:

    EPERM

        • The process tried to raise a current limit beyond the maximum limit.

        • The process tried to raise a maximum limit, but is not superuser.

    When the sources are compiled with `_FILE_OFFSET_BITS == 64` on a 32-bit system this function is in fact `setrlimit64`. Thus, the LFS interface transparently replaces the old interface.

int setrlimit64 (*int resource, const struct rlimit64 *rlp*)   [Function]
    Preliminary: | MT-Safe | AS-Safe | AC-Safe | See Section 1.2.2.1 [POSIX Safety Concepts], page 2.

    This function is similar to `setrlimit` but its second parameter is a pointer to a variable of type `struct rlimit64` which allows it to set values which wouldn't fit in the member of a `struct rlimit`.

    If the sources are compiled with `_FILE_OFFSET_BITS == 64` on a 32-bit machine this function is available under the name `setrlimit` and so transparently replaces the old interface.

`struct rlimit`   [Data Type]

> This structure is used with `getrlimit` to receive limit values, and with `setrlimit` to specify limit values for a particular process and resource. It has two fields:
>
> `rlim_t rlim_cur`
> > The current limit
>
> `rlim_t rlim_max`
> > The maximum limit.
>
> For `getrlimit`, the structure is an output; it receives the current values. For `setrlimit`, it specifies the new values.

For the LFS functions a similar type is defined in `sys/resource.h`.

`struct rlimit64`   [Data Type]

> This structure is analogous to the `rlimit` structure above, but its components have wider ranges. It has two fields:
>
> `rlim64_t rlim_cur`
> > This is analogous to `rlimit.rlim_cur`, but with a different type.
>
> `rlim64_t rlim_max`
> > This is analogous to `rlimit.rlim_max`, but with a different type.

Here is a list of resources for which you can specify a limit. Memory and file sizes are measured in bytes.

`RLIMIT_CPU`
> The maximum amount of CPU time the process can use. If it runs for longer than this, it gets a signal: `SIGXCPU`. The value is measured in seconds. See Section 24.2.6 [Operation Error Signals], page 693.

`RLIMIT_FSIZE`
> The maximum size of file the process can create. Trying to write a larger file causes a signal: `SIGXFSZ`. See Section 24.2.6 [Operation Error Signals], page 693.

`RLIMIT_DATA`
> The maximum size of data memory for the process. If the process tries to allocate data memory beyond this amount, the allocation function fails.

`RLIMIT_STACK`
> The maximum stack size for the process. If the process tries to extend its stack past this size, it gets a `SIGSEGV` signal. See Section 24.2.1 [Program Error Signals], page 687.

`RLIMIT_CORE`
> The maximum size core file that this process can create. If the process terminates and would dump a core file larger than this, then no core file is created. So setting this limit to zero prevents core files from ever being created.

`RLIMIT_RSS`
> The maximum amount of physical memory that this process should get. This parameter is a guide for the system's scheduler and memory allocator; the system may give the process more memory when there is a surplus.

RLIMIT_MEMLOCK

> The maximum amount of memory that can be locked into physical memory (so it will never be paged out).

RLIMIT_NPROC

> The maximum number of processes that can be created with the same user ID. If you have reached the limit for your user ID, `fork` will fail with `EAGAIN`. See Section 26.4 [Creating a Process], page 775.

RLIMIT_NOFILE
RLIMIT_OFILE

> The maximum number of files that the process can open. If it tries to open more files than this, its open attempt fails with `errno EMFILE`. See Section 2.2 [Error Codes], page 23. Not all systems support this limit; GNU does, and 4.4 BSD does.

RLIMIT_AS

> The maximum size of total memory that this process should get. If the process tries to allocate more memory beyond this amount with, for example, `brk`, `malloc`, `mmap` or `sbrk`, the allocation function fails.

RLIM_NLIMITS

> The number of different resource limits. Any valid *resource* operand must be less than `RLIM_NLIMITS`.

`rlim_t RLIM_INFINITY`   [Constant]

> This constant stands for a value of "infinity" when supplied as the limit value in `setrlimit`.

The following are historical functions to do some of what the functions above do. The functions above are better choices.

`ulimit` and the command symbols are declared in `ulimit.h`.

`long int ulimit` (*int cmd, . . .*)   [Function]

> Preliminary: | MT-Safe | AS-Safe | AC-Safe | See Section 1.2.2.1 [POSIX Safety Concepts], page 2.
>
> `ulimit` gets the current limit or sets the current and maximum limit for a particular resource for the calling process according to the command *cmd*.
>
> If you are getting a limit, the command argument is the only argument. If you are setting a limit, there is a second argument: `long int` *limit* which is the value to which you are setting the limit.
>
> The *cmd* values and the operations they specify are:
>
> GETFSIZE   Get the current limit on the size of a file, in units of 512 bytes.
>
> SETFSIZE   Set the current and maximum limit on the size of a file to *limit* * 512 bytes.
>
> There are also some other *cmd* values that may do things on some systems, but they are not supported.
>
> Only the superuser may increase a maximum limit.

When you successfully get a limit, the return value of `ulimit` is that limit, which is never negative. When you successfully set a limit, the return value is zero. When the function fails, the return value is −1 and `errno` is set according to the reason:

EPERM   A process tried to increase a maximum limit, but is not superuser.

`vlimit` and its resource symbols are declared in `sys/vlimit.h`.

int vlimit (*int resource*, *int limit*)   [Function]
Preliminary: | MT-Unsafe race:setrlimit | AS-Unsafe | AC-Safe | See Section 1.2.2.1 [POSIX Safety Concepts], page 2.

`vlimit` sets the current limit for a resource for a process.

resource identifies the resource:

LIM_CPU   Maximum CPU time. Same as `RLIMIT_CPU` for `setrlimit`.

LIM_FSIZE
          Maximum file size. Same as `RLIMIT_FSIZE` for `setrlimit`.

LIM_DATA   Maximum data memory. Same as `RLIMIT_DATA` for `setrlimit`.

LIM_STACK
          Maximum stack size. Same as `RLIMIT_STACK` for `setrlimit`.

LIM_CORE   Maximum core file size. Same as `RLIMIT_COR` for `setrlimit`.

LIM_MAXRSS
          Maximum physical memory. Same as `RLIMIT_RSS` for `setrlimit`.

The return value is zero for success, and −1 with `errno` set accordingly for failure:

EPERM   The process tried to set its current limit beyond its maximum limit.

22.3 Process CPU Priority And Scheduling

When multiple processes simultaneously require CPU time, the system's scheduling policy and process CPU priorities determine which processes get it. This section describes how that determination is made and GNU C Library functions to control it.

It is common to refer to CPU scheduling simply as scheduling and a process' CPU priority simply as the process' priority, with the CPU resource being implied. Bear in mind, though, that CPU time is not the only resource a process uses or that processes contend for. In some cases, it is not even particularly important. Giving a process a high "priority" may have very little effect on how fast a process runs with respect to other processes. The priorities discussed in this section apply only to CPU time.

CPU scheduling is a complex issue and different systems do it in wildly different ways. New ideas continually develop and find their way into the intricacies of the various systems' scheduling algorithms. This section discusses the general concepts, some specifics of systems that commonly use the GNU C Library, and some standards.

For simplicity, we talk about CPU contention as if there is only one CPU in the system. But all the same principles apply when a processor has multiple CPUs, and knowing that the number of processes that can run at any one time is equal to the number of CPUs, you can easily extrapolate the information.

The functions described in this section are all defined by the POSIX.1 and POSIX.1b standards (the `sched...` functions are POSIX.1b). However, POSIX does not define any semantics for the values that these functions get and set. In this chapter, the semantics are based on the Linux kernel's implementation of the POSIX standard. As you will see, the Linux implementation is quite the inverse of what the authors of the POSIX syntax had in mind.

22.3.1 Absolute Priority

Every process has an absolute priority, and it is represented by a number. The higher the number, the higher the absolute priority.

On systems of the past, and most systems today, all processes have absolute priority 0 and this section is irrelevant. In that case, See Section 22.3.4 [Traditional Scheduling], page 666. Absolute priorities were invented to accommodate realtime systems, in which it is vital that certain processes be able to respond to external events happening in real time, which means they cannot wait around while some other process that *wants to*, but doesn't *need to* run occupies the CPU.

When two processes are in contention to use the CPU at any instant, the one with the higher absolute priority always gets it. This is true even if the process with the lower priority is already using the CPU (i.e., the scheduling is preemptive). Of course, we're only talking about processes that are running or "ready to run," which means they are ready to execute instructions right now. When a process blocks to wait for something like I/O, its absolute priority is irrelevant.

NB: The term "runnable" is a synonym for "ready to run."

When two processes are running or ready to run and both have the same absolute priority, it's more interesting. In that case, who gets the CPU is determined by the scheduling policy. If the processes have absolute priority 0, the traditional scheduling policy described in Section 22.3.4 [Traditional Scheduling], page 666, applies. Otherwise, the policies described in Section 22.3.2 [Realtime Scheduling], page 662, apply.

You normally give an absolute priority above 0 only to a process that can be trusted not to hog the CPU. Such processes are designed to block (or terminate) after relatively short CPU runs.

A process begins life with the same absolute priority as its parent process. Functions described in Section 22.3.3 [Basic Scheduling Functions], page 663, can change it.

Only a privileged process can change a process' absolute priority to something other than 0. Only a privileged process or the target process' owner can change its absolute priority at all.

POSIX requires absolute priority values used with the realtime scheduling policies to be consecutive with a range of at least 32. On Linux, they are 1 through 99. The functions `sched_get_priority_max` and `sched_set_priority_min` portably tell you what the range is on a particular system.

22.3.1.1 Using Absolute Priority

One thing you must keep in mind when designing real time applications is that having higher absolute priority than any other process doesn't guarantee the process can run continuously. Two things that can wreck a good CPU run are interrupts and page faults.

Interrupt handlers live in that limbo between processes. The CPU is executing instructions, but they aren't part of any process. An interrupt will stop even the highest priority process. So you must allow for slight delays and make sure that no device in the system has an interrupt handler that could cause too long a delay between instructions for your process.

Similarly, a page fault causes what looks like a straightforward sequence of instructions to take a long time. The fact that other processes get to run while the page faults in is of no consequence, because as soon as the I/O is complete, the higher priority process will kick them out and run again, but the wait for the I/O itself could be a problem. To neutralize this threat, use `mlock` or `mlockall`.

There are a few ramifications of the absoluteness of this priority on a single-CPU system that you need to keep in mind when you choose to set a priority and also when you're working on a program that runs with high absolute priority. Consider a process that has higher absolute priority than any other process in the system and due to a bug in its program, it gets into an infinite loop. It will never cede the CPU. You can't run a command to kill it because your command would need to get the CPU in order to run. The errant program is in complete control. It controls the vertical, it controls the horizontal.

There are two ways to avoid this: 1) keep a shell running somewhere with a higher absolute priority or 2) keep a controlling terminal attached to the high priority process group. All the priority in the world won't stop an interrupt handler from running and delivering a signal to the process if you hit Control-C.

Some systems use absolute priority as a means of allocating a fixed percentage of CPU time to a process. To do this, a super high priority privileged process constantly monitors the process' CPU usage and raises its absolute priority when the process isn't getting its entitled share and lowers it when the process is exceeding it.

NB: The absolute priority is sometimes called the "static priority." We don't use that term in this manual because it misses the most important feature of the absolute priority: its absoluteness.

22.3.2 Realtime Scheduling

Whenever two processes with the same absolute priority are ready to run, the kernel has a decision to make, because only one can run at a time. If the processes have absolute priority 0, the kernel makes this decision as described in Section 22.3.4 [Traditional Scheduling], page 666. Otherwise, the decision is as described in this section.

If two processes are ready to run but have different absolute priorities, the decision is much simpler, and is described in Section 22.3.1 [Absolute Priority], page 661.

Each process has a scheduling policy. For processes with absolute priority other than zero, there are two available:

1. First Come First Served

2. Round Robin

The most sensible case is where all the processes with a certain absolute priority have the same scheduling policy. We'll discuss that first.

In Round Robin, processes share the CPU, each one running for a small quantum of time ("time slice") and then yielding to another in a circular fashion. Of course, only processes that are ready to run and have the same absolute priority are in this circle.

In First Come First Served, the process that has been waiting the longest to run gets the CPU, and it keeps it until it voluntarily relinquishes the CPU, runs out of things to do (blocks), or gets preempted by a higher priority process.

First Come First Served, along with maximal absolute priority and careful control of interrupts and page faults, is the one to use when a process absolutely, positively has to run at full CPU speed or not at all.

Judicious use of `sched_yield` function invocations by processes with First Come First Served scheduling policy forms a good compromise between Round Robin and First Come First Served.

To understand how scheduling works when processes of different scheduling policies occupy the same absolute priority, you have to know the nitty gritty details of how processes enter and exit the ready to run list.

In both cases, the ready to run list is organized as a true queue, where a process gets pushed onto the tail when it becomes ready to run and is popped off the head when the scheduler decides to run it. Note that ready to run and running are two mutually exclusive states. When the scheduler runs a process, that process is no longer ready to run and no longer in the ready to run list. When the process stops running, it may go back to being ready to run again.

The only difference between a process that is assigned the Round Robin scheduling policy and a process that is assigned First Come First Serve is that in the former case, the process is automatically booted off the CPU after a certain amount of time. When that happens, the process goes back to being ready to run, which means it enters the queue at the tail. The time quantum we're talking about is small. Really small. This is not your father's timesharing. For example, with the Linux kernel, the round robin time slice is a thousand times shorter than its typical time slice for traditional scheduling.

A process begins life with the same scheduling policy as its parent process. Functions described in Section 22.3.3 [Basic Scheduling Functions], page 663, can change it.

Only a privileged process can set the scheduling policy of a process that has absolute priority higher than 0.

22.3.3 Basic Scheduling Functions

This section describes functions in the GNU C Library for setting the absolute priority and scheduling policy of a process.

Portability Note: On systems that have the functions in this section, the macro _POSIX_PRIORITY_SCHEDULING is defined in `<unistd.h>`.

For the case that the scheduling policy is traditional scheduling, more functions to fine tune the scheduling are in Section 22.3.4 [Traditional Scheduling], page 666.

Don't try to make too much out of the naming and structure of these functions. They don't match the concepts described in this manual because the functions are as defined by POSIX.1b, but the implementation on systems that use the GNU C Library is the inverse of what the POSIX structure contemplates. The POSIX scheme assumes that the primary scheduling parameter is the scheduling policy and that the priority value, if any, is a parameter of the scheduling policy. In the implementation, though, the priority value is king and the scheduling policy, if anything, only fine tunes the effect of that priority.

The symbols in this section are declared by including file `sched.h`.

`struct sched_param`   [Data Type]

> This structure describes an absolute priority.

> > `int sched_priority`
> >
> > > absolute priority value

`int sched_setscheduler` (*pid_t* `pid`, *int* `policy`, *const struct*   [Function]
      sched_param `*param`)

> Preliminary: | MT-Safe | AS-Safe | AC-Safe | See Section 1.2.2.1 [POSIX Safety Concepts], page 2.

> This function sets both the absolute priority and the scheduling policy for a process.

> It assigns the absolute priority value given by *param* and the scheduling policy *policy* to the process with Process ID *pid*, or the calling process if *pid* is zero. If *policy* is negative, `sched_setscheduler` keeps the existing scheduling policy.

> The following macros represent the valid values for *policy*:

`SCHED_OTHER`

> > Traditional Scheduling

`SCHED_FIFO`

> > First In First Out

`SCHED_RR`   Round Robin

On success, the return value is 0. Otherwise, it is −1 and `ERRNO` is set accordingly. The `errno` values specific to this function are:

`EPERM`

> > - The calling process does not have `CAP_SYS_NICE` permission and *policy* is not `SCHED_OTHER` (or it's negative and the existing policy is not `SCHED_OTHER`.
> > - The calling process does not have `CAP_SYS_NICE` permission and its owner is not the target process' owner. I.e., the effective uid of the calling process is neither the effective nor the real uid of process *pid*.

`ESRCH`   There is no process with pid *pid* and *pid* is not zero.

`EINVAL`

> > - *policy* does not identify an existing scheduling policy.
> > - The absolute priority value identified by *param* is outside the valid range for the scheduling policy *policy* (or the existing scheduling policy if *policy* is negative) or *param* is null. `sched_get_priority_max` and `sched_get_priority_min` tell you what the valid range is.
> > - *pid* is negative.

`int sched_getscheduler` (*pid_t* `pid`)   [Function]

> Preliminary: | MT-Safe | AS-Safe | AC-Safe | See Section 1.2.2.1 [POSIX Safety Concepts], page 2.

> This function returns the scheduling policy assigned to the process with Process ID (pid) *pid*, or the calling process if *pid* is zero.

The return value is the scheduling policy. See `sched_setscheduler` for the possible values.

If the function fails, the return value is instead `-1` and `errno` is set accordingly.

The `errno` values specific to this function are:

ESRCH   There is no process with pid *pid* and it is not zero.

EINVAL   *pid* is negative.

Note that this function is not an exact mate to `sched_setscheduler` because while that function sets the scheduling policy and the absolute priority, this function gets only the scheduling policy. To get the absolute priority, use `sched_getparam`.

int sched_setparam (*pid_t* `pid`, *const struct sched_param* `*param`)   [Function]
Preliminary: | MT-Safe | AS-Safe | AC-Safe | See Section 1.2.2.1 [POSIX Safety Concepts], page 2.

This function sets a process' absolute priority.

It is functionally identical to `sched_setscheduler` with *policy* = `-1`.

int sched_getparam (*pid_t* `pid`, *struct sched_param* `*param`)   [Function]
Preliminary: | MT-Safe | AS-Safe | AC-Safe | See Section 1.2.2.1 [POSIX Safety Concepts], page 2.

This function returns a process' absolute priority.

pid is the Process ID (pid) of the process whose absolute priority you want to know.

param is a pointer to a structure in which the function stores the absolute priority of the process.

On success, the return value is `0`. Otherwise, it is `-1` and `errno` is set accordingly. The `errno` values specific to this function are:

ESRCH   There is no process with pid *pid* and it is not zero.

EINVAL   *pid* is negative.

int sched_get_priority_min (*int* `policy`)   [Function]
Preliminary: | MT-Safe | AS-Safe | AC-Safe | See Section 1.2.2.1 [POSIX Safety Concepts], page 2.

This function returns the lowest absolute priority value that is allowable for a process with scheduling policy *policy*.

On Linux, it is 0 for SCHED_OTHER and 1 for everything else.

On success, the return value is 0. Otherwise, it is `-1` and `ERRNO` is set accordingly. The `errno` values specific to this function are:

EINVAL   *policy* does not identify an existing scheduling policy.

int sched_get_priority_max (*int* `policy`)   [Function]
Preliminary: | MT-Safe | AS-Safe | AC-Safe | See Section 1.2.2.1 [POSIX Safety Concepts], page 2.

This function returns the highest absolute priority value that is allowable for a process that with scheduling policy *policy*.

On Linux, it is 0 for SCHED_OTHER and 99 for everything else.

On success, the return value is 0. Otherwise, it is −1 and ERRNO is set accordingly. The errno values specific to this function are:

EINVAL   *policy* does not identify an existing scheduling policy.

int sched_rr_get_interval (*pid_t pid*, *struct timespec*   [Function]
       *interval)
Preliminary: | MT-Safe | AS-Safe | AC-Safe | See Section 1.2.2.1 [POSIX Safety Concepts], page 2.

This function returns the length of the quantum (time slice) used with the Round Robin scheduling policy, if it is used, for the process with Process ID *pid*.

It returns the length of time as *interval*.

With a Linux kernel, the round robin time slice is always 150 microseconds, and *pid* need not even be a real pid.

The return value is 0 on success and in the pathological case that it fails, the return value is −1 and errno is set accordingly. There is nothing specific that can go wrong with this function, so there are no specific errno values.

int sched_yield (*void*)   [Function]
Preliminary: | MT-Safe | AS-Safe | AC-Safe | See Section 1.2.2.1 [POSIX Safety Concepts], page 2.

This function voluntarily gives up the process' claim on the CPU.

Technically, sched_yield causes the calling process to be made immediately ready to run (as opposed to running, which is what it was before). This means that if it has absolute priority higher than 0, it gets pushed onto the tail of the queue of processes that share its absolute priority and are ready to run, and it will run again when its turn next arrives. If its absolute priority is 0, it is more complicated, but still has the effect of yielding the CPU to other processes.

If there are no other processes that share the calling process' absolute priority, this function doesn't have any effect.

To the extent that the containing program is oblivious to what other processes in the system are doing and how fast it executes, this function appears as a no-op.

The return value is 0 on success and in the pathological case that it fails, the return value is −1 and errno is set accordingly. There is nothing specific that can go wrong with this function, so there are no specific errno values.

22.3.4 Traditional Scheduling

This section is about the scheduling among processes whose absolute priority is 0. When the system hands out the scraps of CPU time that are left over after the processes with higher absolute priority have taken all they want, the scheduling described herein determines who among the great unwashed processes gets them.

22.3.4.1 Introduction To Traditional Scheduling

Long before there was absolute priority (See Section 22.3.1 [Absolute Priority], page 661), Unix systems were scheduling the CPU using this system. When POSIX came in like the Romans and imposed absolute priorities to accommodate the needs of realtime processing, it left the indigenous Absolute Priority Zero processes to govern themselves by their own familiar scheduling policy.

Indeed, absolute priorities higher than zero are not available on many systems today and are not typically used when they are, being intended mainly for computers that do realtime processing. So this section describes the only scheduling many programmers need to be concerned about.

But just to be clear about the scope of this scheduling: Any time a process with an absolute priority of 0 and a process with an absolute priority higher than 0 are ready to run at the same time, the one with absolute priority 0 does not run. If it's already running when the higher priority ready-to-run process comes into existence, it stops immediately.

In addition to its absolute priority of zero, every process has another priority, which we will refer to as "dynamic priority" because it changes over time. The dynamic priority is meaningless for processes with an absolute priority higher than zero.

The dynamic priority sometimes determines who gets the next turn on the CPU. Sometimes it determines how long turns last. Sometimes it determines whether a process can kick another off the CPU.

In Linux, the value is a combination of these things, but mostly it just determines the length of the time slice. The higher a process' dynamic priority, the longer a shot it gets on the CPU when it gets one. If it doesn't use up its time slice before giving up the CPU to do something like wait for I/O, it is favored for getting the CPU back when it's ready for it, to finish out its time slice. Other than that, selection of processes for new time slices is basically round robin. But the scheduler does throw a bone to the low priority processes: A process' dynamic priority rises every time it is snubbed in the scheduling process. In Linux, even the fat kid gets to play.

The fluctuation of a process' dynamic priority is regulated by another value: The "nice" value. The nice value is an integer, usually in the range -20 to 20, and represents an upper limit on a process' dynamic priority. The higher the nice number, the lower that limit.

On a typical Linux system, for example, a process with a nice value of 20 can get only 10 milliseconds on the CPU at a time, whereas a process with a nice value of -20 can achieve a high enough priority to get 400 milliseconds.

The idea of the nice value is deferential courtesy. In the beginning, in the Unix garden of Eden, all processes shared equally in the bounty of the computer system. But not all processes really need the same share of CPU time, so the nice value gave a courteous process the ability to refuse its equal share of CPU time that others might prosper. Hence, the higher a process' nice value, the nicer the process is. (Then a snake came along and offered some process a negative nice value and the system became the crass resource allocation system we know today.)

Dynamic priorities tend upward and downward with an objective of smoothing out allocation of CPU time and giving quick response time to infrequent requests. But they never exceed their nice limits, so on a heavily loaded CPU, the nice value effectively determines how fast a process runs.

In keeping with the socialistic heritage of Unix process priority, a process begins life with the same nice value as its parent process and can raise it at will. A process can also raise the nice value of any other process owned by the same user (or effective user). But only a privileged process can lower its nice value. A privileged process can also raise or lower another process' nice value.

GNU C Library functions for getting and setting nice values are described in See Section 22.3.4.2 [Functions For Traditional Scheduling], page 668.

22.3.4.2 Functions For Traditional Scheduling

This section describes how you can read and set the nice value of a process. All these symbols are declared in `sys/resource.h`.

The function and macro names are defined by POSIX, and refer to "priority," but the functions actually have to do with nice values, as the terms are used both in the manual and POSIX.

The range of valid nice values depends on the kernel, but typically it runs from -20 to 20. A lower nice value corresponds to higher priority for the process. These constants describe the range of priority values:

PRIO_MIN   The lowest valid nice value.

PRIO_MAX   The highest valid nice value.

int getpriority (*int class*, *int id*)   [Function]
> Preliminary: | MT-Safe | AS-Safe | AC-Safe | See Section 1.2.2.1 [POSIX Safety Concepts], page 2.
>
> Return the nice value of a set of processes; *class* and *id* specify which ones (see below). If the processes specified do not all have the same nice value, this returns the lowest value that any of them has.
>
> On success, the return value is 0. Otherwise, it is -1 and `errno` is set accordingly. The `errno` values specific to this function are:
>
> ESRCH   The combination of *class* and *id* does not match any existing process.
>
> EINVAL   The value of *class* is not valid.
>
> If the return value is -1, it could indicate failure, or it could be the nice value. The only way to make certain is to set `errno = 0` before calling `getpriority`, then use `errno != 0` afterward as the criterion for failure.

int setpriority (*int class*, *int id*, *int niceval*)   [Function]
> Preliminary: | MT-Safe | AS-Safe | AC-Safe | See Section 1.2.2.1 [POSIX Safety Concepts], page 2.
>
> Set the nice value of a set of processes to *niceval*; *class* and *id* specify which ones (see below).
>
> The return value is 0 on success, and -1 on failure. The following `errno` error condition are possible for this function:
>
> ESRCH   The combination of *class* and *id* does not match any existing process.
>
> EINVAL   The value of *class* is not valid.

EPERM The call would set the nice value of a process which is owned by a different user than the calling process (i.e., the target process' real or effective uid does not match the calling process' effective uid) and the calling process does not have `CAP_SYS_NICE` permission.

EACCES The call would lower the process' nice value and the process does not have `CAP_SYS_NICE` permission.

The arguments *class* and *id* together specify a set of processes in which you are interested. These are the possible values of *class*:

PRIO_PROCESS

 One particular process. The argument *id* is a process ID (pid).

PRIO_PGRP

 All the processes in a particular process group. The argument *id* is a process group ID (pgid).

PRIO_USER

 All the processes owned by a particular user (i.e., whose real uid indicates the user). The argument *id* is a user ID (uid).

If the argument *id* is 0, it stands for the calling process, its process group, or its owner (real uid), according to *class*.

int nice (*int increment*)   [Function]

 Preliminary: | MT-Unsafe race:setpriority | AS-Unsafe | AC-Safe | See Section 1.2.2.1 [POSIX Safety Concepts], page 2.

 Increment the nice value of the calling process by *increment*. The return value is the new nice value on success, and -1 on failure. In the case of failure, `errno` will be set to the same values as for `setpriority`.

 Here is an equivalent definition of `nice`:

```
int
nice (int increment)
{
  int result, old = getpriority (PRIO_PROCESS, 0);
  result = setpriority (PRIO_PROCESS, 0, old + increment);
  if (result != -1)
      return old + increment;
  else
      return -1;
}
```

22.3.5 Limiting execution to certain CPUs

On a multi-processor system the operating system usually distributes the different processes which are runnable on all available CPUs in a way which allows the system to work most efficiently. Which processes and threads run can be to some extend be control with the scheduling functionality described in the last sections. But which CPU finally executes which process or thread is not covered.

There are a number of reasons why a program might want to have control over this aspect of the system as well:

- One thread or process is responsible for absolutely critical work which under no circumstances must be interrupted or hindered from making progress by other processes or threads using CPU resources. In this case the special process would be confined to a CPU which no other process or thread is allowed to use.

- The access to certain resources (RAM, I/O ports) has different costs from different CPUs. This is the case in NUMA (Non-Uniform Memory Architecture) machines. Preferably memory should be accessed locally but this requirement is usually not visible to the scheduler. Therefore forcing a process or thread to the CPUs which have local access to the most-used memory helps to significantly boost the performance.

- In controlled runtimes resource allocation and book-keeping work (for instance garbage collection) is performance local to processors. This can help to reduce locking costs if the resources do not have to be protected from concurrent accesses from different processors.

The POSIX standard up to this date is of not much help to solve this problem. The Linux kernel provides a set of interfaces to allow specifying *affinity sets* for a process. The scheduler will schedule the thread or process on CPUs specified by the affinity masks. The interfaces which the GNU C Library define follow to some extent the Linux kernel interface.

`cpu_set_t`   [Data Type]

This data set is a bitset where each bit represents a CPU. How the system's CPUs are mapped to bits in the bitset is system dependent. The data type has a fixed size; in the unlikely case that the number of bits are not sufficient to describe the CPUs of the system a different interface has to be used.

This type is a GNU extension and is defined in `sched.h`.

To manipulate the bitset, to set and reset bits, a number of macros are defined. Some of the macros take a CPU number as a parameter. Here it is important to never exceed the size of the bitset. The following macro specifies the number of bits in the `cpu_set_t` bitset.

`int CPU_SETSIZE`   [Macro]

The value of this macro is the maximum number of CPUs which can be handled with a `cpu_set_t` object.

The type `cpu_set_t` should be considered opaque; all manipulation should happen via the next four macros.

`void CPU_ZERO (`*cpu_set_t *set*`)`   [Macro]

Preliminary: | MT-Safe | AS-Safe | AC-Safe | See Section 1.2.2.1 [POSIX Safety Concepts], page 2.

This macro initializes the CPU set *set* to be the empty set.

This macro is a GNU extension and is defined in `sched.h`.

`void CPU_SET (`*int cpu, cpu_set_t *set*`)`   [Macro]

Preliminary: | MT-Safe | AS-Safe | AC-Safe | See Section 1.2.2.1 [POSIX Safety Concepts], page 2.

This macro adds *cpu* to the CPU set *set*.

The *cpu* parameter must not have side effects since it is evaluated more than once.

This macro is a GNU extension and is defined in `sched.h`.

void CPU_CLR (*int cpu, cpu_set_t *set*)   [Macro]
> Preliminary: | MT-Safe | AS-Safe | AC-Safe | See Section 1.2.2.1 [POSIX Safety Concepts], page 2.
>
> This macro removes *cpu* from the CPU set *set*.
>
> The *cpu* parameter must not have side effects since it is evaluated more than once.
>
> This macro is a GNU extension and is defined in **sched.h**.

int CPU_ISSET (*int cpu, const cpu_set_t *set*)   [Macro]
> Preliminary: | MT-Safe | AS-Safe | AC-Safe | See Section 1.2.2.1 [POSIX Safety Concepts], page 2.
>
> This macro returns a nonzero value (true) if *cpu* is a member of the CPU set *set*, and zero (false) otherwise.
>
> The *cpu* parameter must not have side effects since it is evaluated more than once.
>
> This macro is a GNU extension and is defined in **sched.h**.

CPU bitsets can be constructed from scratch or the currently installed affinity mask can be retrieved from the system.

int sched_getaffinity (*pid_t pid, size_t cpusetsize, cpu_set_t*   [Function]
> *cpuset*)
> Preliminary: | MT-Safe | AS-Safe | AC-Safe | See Section 1.2.2.1 [POSIX Safety Concepts], page 2.
>
> This function stores the CPU affinity mask for the process or thread with the ID *pid* in the *cpusetsize* bytes long bitmap pointed to by *cpuset*. If successful, the function always initializes all bits in the **cpu_set_t** object and returns zero.
>
> If *pid* does not correspond to a process or thread on the system the or the function fails for some other reason, it returns **-1** and **errno** is set to represent the error condition.
>
> **ESRCH**   No process or thread with the given ID found.
>
> **EFAULT**   The pointer *cpuset* does not point to a valid object.
>
> This function is a GNU extension and is declared in **sched.h**.

Note that it is not portably possible to use this information to retrieve the information for different POSIX threads. A separate interface must be provided for that.

int sched_setaffinity (*pid_t pid, size_t cpusetsize, const*   [Function]
> *cpu_set_t *cpuset*)
> Preliminary: | MT-Safe | AS-Safe | AC-Safe | See Section 1.2.2.1 [POSIX Safety Concepts], page 2.
>
> This function installs the *cpusetsize* bytes long affinity mask pointed to by *cpuset* for the process or thread with the ID *pid*. If successful the function returns zero and the scheduler will in the future take the affinity information into account.
>
> If the function fails it will return **-1** and **errno** is set to the error code:
>
> **ESRCH**   No process or thread with the given ID found.

EFAULT   The pointer *cpuset* does not point to a valid object.

EINVAL   The bitset is not valid. This might mean that the affinity set might not leave a processor for the process or thread to run on.

This function is a GNU extension and is declared in `sched.h`.

22.4 Querying memory available resources

The amount of memory available in the system and the way it is organized determines oftentimes the way programs can and have to work. For functions like `mmap` it is necessary to know about the size of individual memory pages and knowing how much memory is available enables a program to select appropriate sizes for, say, caches. Before we get into these details a few words about memory subsystems in traditional Unix systems will be given.

22.4.1 Overview about traditional Unix memory handling

Unix systems normally provide processes virtual address spaces. This means that the addresses of the memory regions do not have to correspond directly to the addresses of the actual physical memory which stores the data. An extra level of indirection is introduced which translates virtual addresses into physical addresses. This is normally done by the hardware of the processor.

Using a virtual address space has several advantages. The most important is process isolation. The different processes running on the system cannot interfere directly with each other. No process can write into the address space of another process (except when shared memory is used but then it is wanted and controlled).

Another advantage of virtual memory is that the address space the processes see can actually be larger than the physical memory available. The physical memory can be extended by storage on an external media where the content of currently unused memory regions is stored. The address translation can then intercept accesses to these memory regions and make memory content available again by loading the data back into memory. This concept makes it necessary that programs which have to use lots of memory know the difference between available virtual address space and available physical memory. If the working set of virtual memory of all the processes is larger than the available physical memory the system will slow down dramatically due to constant swapping of memory content from the memory to the storage media and back. This is called "thrashing".

A final aspect of virtual memory which is important and follows from what is said in the last paragraph is the granularity of the virtual address space handling. When we said that the virtual address handling stores memory content externally it cannot do this on a byte-by-byte basis. The administrative overhead does not allow this (leaving alone the processor hardware). Instead several thousand bytes are handled together and form a *page*. The size of each page is always a power of two bytes. The smallest page size in use today is 4096, with 8192, 16384, and 65536 being other popular sizes.

22.4.2 How to get information about the memory subsystem?

The page size of the virtual memory the process sees is essential to know in several situations. Some programming interfaces (e.g., `mmap`, see Section 13.7 [Memory-mapped I/O], page 350) require the user to provide information adjusted to the page size. In the case of `mmap` it is necessary to provide a length argument which is a multiple of the page size. Another place where the knowledge about the page size is useful is in memory allocation. If one allocates pieces of memory in larger chunks which are then subdivided by the application code it is useful to adjust the size of the larger blocks to the page size. If the total memory requirement for the block is close (but not larger) to a multiple of the page size the kernel's memory handling can work more effectively since it only has to allocate memory pages which are fully used. (To do this optimization it is necessary to know a bit about the memory allocator which will require a bit of memory itself for each block and this overhead must not push the total size over the page size multiple.)

The page size traditionally was a compile time constant. But recent development of processors changed this. Processors now support different page sizes and they can possibly even vary among different processes on the same system. Therefore the system should be queried at runtime about the current page size and no assumptions (except about it being a power of two) should be made.

The correct interface to query about the page size is `sysconf` (see Section 32.4.1 [Definition of `sysconf`], page 865) with the parameter `_SC_PAGESIZE`. There is a much older interface available, too.

`int getpagesize (void)` [Function]

> Preliminary: | MT-Safe | AS-Safe | AC-Safe | See Section 1.2.2.1 [POSIX Safety Concepts], page 2.

> The `getpagesize` function returns the page size of the process. This value is fixed for the runtime of the process but can vary in different runs of the application.

> The function is declared in `unistd.h`.

Widely available on System V derived systems is a method to get information about the physical memory the system has. The call

```
sysconf (_SC_PHYS_PAGES)
```

returns the total number of pages of physical memory the system has. This does not mean all this memory is available. This information can be found using

```
sysconf (_SC_AVPHYS_PAGES)
```

These two values help to optimize applications. The value returned for `_SC_AVPHYS_PAGES` is the amount of memory the application can use without hindering any other process (given that no other process increases its memory usage). The value returned for `_SC_PHYS_PAGES` is more or less a hard limit for the working set. If all applications together constantly use more than that amount of memory the system is in trouble.

The GNU C Library provides in addition to these already described way to get this information two functions. They are declared in the file `sys/sysinfo.h`. Programmers should prefer to use the `sysconf` method described above.

`long int get_phys_pages (void)` [Function]

> Preliminary: | MT-Safe | AS-Unsafe heap lock | AC-Unsafe lock fd mem | See Section 1.2.2.1 [POSIX Safety Concepts], page 2.

> The `get_phys_pages` function returns the total number of pages of physical memory the system has. To get the amount of memory this number has to be multiplied by the page size.

This function is a GNU extension.

long int get_avphys_pages (*void*)   [Function]
> Preliminary: | MT-Safe | AS-Unsafe heap lock | AC-Unsafe lock fd mem | See Section 1.2.2.1 [POSIX Safety Concepts], page 2.

> The `get_avphys_pages` function returns the number of available pages of physical memory the system has. To get the amount of memory this number has to be multiplied by the page size.

> This function is a GNU extension.

22.5 Learn about the processors available

The use of threads or processes with shared memory allows an application to take advantage of all the processing power a system can provide. If the task can be parallelized the optimal way to write an application is to have at any time as many processes running as there are processors. To determine the number of processors available to the system one can run

>   sysconf (_SC_NPROCESSORS_CONF)

which returns the number of processors the operating system configured. But it might be possible for the operating system to disable individual processors and so the call

>   sysconf (_SC_NPROCESSORS_ONLN)

returns the number of processors which are currently online (i.e., available).

For these two pieces of information the GNU C Library also provides functions to get the information directly. The functions are declared in `sys/sysinfo.h`.

int get_nprocs_conf (*void*)   [Function]
> Preliminary: | MT-Safe | AS-Unsafe heap lock | AC-Unsafe lock fd mem | See Section 1.2.2.1 [POSIX Safety Concepts], page 2.

> The `get_nprocs_conf` function returns the number of processors the operating system configured.

> This function is a GNU extension.

int get_nprocs (*void*)   [Function]
> Preliminary: | MT-Safe | AS-Safe | AC-Safe fd | See Section 1.2.2.1 [POSIX Safety Concepts], page 2.

> The `get_nprocs` function returns the number of available processors.

> This function is a GNU extension.

Before starting more threads it should be checked whether the processors are not already overused. Unix systems calculate something called the *load average*. This is a number indicating how many processes were running. This number is an average over different periods of time (normally 1, 5, and 15 minutes).

int getloadavg (*double* `loadavg[]`, *int* `nelem`)   [Function]
> Preliminary: | MT-Safe | AS-Safe | AC-Safe fd | See Section 1.2.2.1 [POSIX Safety Concepts], page 2.

> This function gets the 1, 5 and 15 minute load averages of the system. The values are placed in *loadavg*. `getloadavg` will place at most *nelem* elements into the array but

never more than three elements. The return value is the number of elements written to *loadavg*, or -1 on error.

This function is declared in `stdlib.h`.

23 Non-Local Exits

Sometimes when your program detects an unusual situation inside a deeply nested set of function calls, you would like to be able to immediately return to an outer level of control. This section describes how you can do such *non-local exits* using the `setjmp` and `longjmp` functions.

23.1 Introduction to Non-Local Exits

As an example of a situation where a non-local exit can be useful, suppose you have an interactive program that has a "main loop" that prompts for and executes commands. Suppose the "read" command reads input from a file, doing some lexical analysis and parsing of the input while processing it. If a low-level input error is detected, it would be useful to be able to return immediately to the "main loop" instead of having to make each of the lexical analysis, parsing, and processing phases all have to explicitly deal with error situations initially detected by nested calls.

(On the other hand, if each of these phases has to do a substantial amount of cleanup when it exits—such as closing files, deallocating buffers or other data structures, and the like—then it can be more appropriate to do a normal return and have each phase do its own cleanup, because a non-local exit would bypass the intervening phases and their associated cleanup code entirely. Alternatively, you could use a non-local exit but do the cleanup explicitly either before or after returning to the "main loop".)

In some ways, a non-local exit is similar to using the 'return' statement to return from a function. But while 'return' abandons only a single function call, transferring control back to the point at which it was called, a non-local exit can potentially abandon many levels of nested function calls.

You identify return points for non-local exits by calling the function `setjmp`. This function saves information about the execution environment in which the call to `setjmp` appears in an object of type `jmp_buf`. Execution of the program continues normally after the call to `setjmp`, but if an exit is later made to this return point by calling `longjmp` with the corresponding `jmp_buf` object, control is transferred back to the point where `setjmp` was called. The return value from `setjmp` is used to distinguish between an ordinary return and a return made by a call to `longjmp`, so calls to `setjmp` usually appear in an 'if' statement.

Here is how the example program described above might be set up:

```
#include <setjmp.h>
#include <stdlib.h>
#include <stdio.h>

jmp_buf main_loop;

void
abort_to_main_loop (int status)
{
  longjmp (main_loop, status);
}

int
main (void)
```

```
{
  while (1)
    if (setjmp (main_loop))
      puts ("Back at main loop....");
    else
      do_command ();
}


void
do_command (void)
{
  char buffer[128];
  if (fgets (buffer, 128, stdin) == NULL)
    abort_to_main_loop (-1);
  else
    exit (EXIT_SUCCESS);
}
```

The function `abort_to_main_loop` causes an immediate transfer of control back to the main loop of the program, no matter where it is called from.

The flow of control inside the `main` function may appear a little mysterious at first, but it is actually a common idiom with `setjmp`. A normal call to `setjmp` returns zero, so the "else" clause of the conditional is executed. If `abort_to_main_loop` is called somewhere within the execution of `do_command`, then it actually appears as if the *same* call to `setjmp` in `main` were returning a second time with a value of -1.

So, the general pattern for using `setjmp` looks something like:

```
if (setjmp (buffer))
  /* Code to clean up after premature return. */
  ...
else
  /* Code to be executed normally after setting up the return point. */
  ...
```

23.2 Details of Non-Local Exits

Here are the details on the functions and data structures used for performing non-local exits. These facilities are declared in `setjmp.h`.

`jmp_buf`   [Data Type]

Objects of type `jmp_buf` hold the state information to be restored by a non-local exit. The contents of a `jmp_buf` identify a specific place to return to.

`int setjmp (jmp_buf state)`   [Macro]

Preliminary: | MT-Safe | AS-Safe | AC-Safe | See Section 1.2.2.1 [POSIX Safety Concepts], page 2.

When called normally, `setjmp` stores information about the execution state of the program in *state* and returns zero. If `longjmp` is later used to perform a non-local exit to this *state*, `setjmp` returns a nonzero value.

`void longjmp (jmp_buf state, int value)`   [Function]

Preliminary: | MT-Safe | AS-Unsafe plugin corrupt lock/hurd | AC-Unsafe corrupt lock/hurd | See Section 1.2.2.1 [POSIX Safety Concepts], page 2.

This function restores current execution to the state saved in *state*, and continues execution from the call to `setjmp` that established that return point. Returning from `setjmp` by means of `longjmp` returns the *value* argument that was passed to `longjmp`, rather than 0. (But if *value* is given as 0, `setjmp` returns 1).

There are a lot of obscure but important restrictions on the use of `setjmp` and `longjmp`. Most of these restrictions are present because non-local exits require a fair amount of magic on the part of the C compiler and can interact with other parts of the language in strange ways.

The `setjmp` function is actually a macro without an actual function definition, so you shouldn't try to '#undef' it or take its address. In addition, calls to `setjmp` are safe in only the following contexts:

- As the test expression of a selection or iteration statement (such as 'if', 'switch', or 'while').

- As one operand of an equality or comparison operator that appears as the test expression of a selection or iteration statement. The other operand must be an integer constant expression.

- As the operand of a unary '!' operator, that appears as the test expression of a selection or iteration statement.

- By itself as an expression statement.

Return points are valid only during the dynamic extent of the function that called `setjmp` to establish them. If you `longjmp` to a return point that was established in a function that has already returned, unpredictable and disastrous things are likely to happen.

You should use a nonzero *value* argument to `longjmp`. While `longjmp` refuses to pass back a zero argument as the return value from `setjmp`, this is intended as a safety net against accidental misuse and is not really good programming style.

When you perform a non-local exit, accessible objects generally retain whatever values they had at the time `longjmp` was called. The exception is that the values of automatic variables local to the function containing the `setjmp` call that have been changed since the call to `setjmp` are indeterminate, unless you have declared them `volatile`.

23.3 Non-Local Exits and Signals

In BSD Unix systems, `setjmp` and `longjmp` also save and restore the set of blocked signals; see Section 24.7 [Blocking Signals], page 716. However, the POSIX.1 standard requires `setjmp` and `longjmp` not to change the set of blocked signals, and provides an additional pair of functions (`sigsetjmp` and `siglongjmp`) to get the BSD behavior.

The behavior of `setjmp` and `longjmp` in the GNU C Library is controlled by feature test macros; see Section 1.3.4 [Feature Test Macros], page 15. The default in the GNU C Library is the POSIX.1 behavior rather than the BSD behavior.

The facilities in this section are declared in the header file `setjmp.h`.

`sigjmp_buf`   [Data Type]

This is similar to `jmp_buf`, except that it can also store state information about the set of blocked signals.

int **sigsetjmp** (*sigjmp_buf* `state`, *int* `savesigs`)   [Function]
> Preliminary: | MT-Safe | AS-Unsafe lock/hurd | AC-Unsafe lock/hurd | See
> Section 1.2.2.1 [POSIX Safety Concepts], page 2.
>
> This is similar to `setjmp`. If *savesigs* is nonzero, the set of blocked signals is saved in
> *state* and will be restored if a `siglongjmp` is later performed with this *state*.

void **siglongjmp** (*sigjmp_buf* `state`, *int* `value`)   [Function]
> Preliminary: | MT-Safe | AS-Unsafe plugin corrupt lock/hurd | AC-Unsafe corrupt
> lock/hurd | See Section 1.2.2.1 [POSIX Safety Concepts], page 2.
>
> This is similar to `longjmp` except for the type of its *state* argument. If the `sigsetjmp`
> call that set this *state* used a nonzero *savesigs* flag, `siglongjmp` also restores the set
> of blocked signals.

23.4 Complete Context Control

The Unix standard provides one more set of functions to control the execution path and these
functions are more powerful than those discussed in this chapter so far. These functions
were part of the original System V API and by this route were added to the Unix API.
Besides on branded Unix implementations these interfaces are not widely available. Not all
platforms and/or architectures the GNU C Library is available on provide this interface.
Use `configure` to detect the availability.

Similar to the `jmp_buf` and `sigjmp_buf` types used for the variables to contain the state
of the `longjmp` functions the interfaces of interest here have an appropriate type as well.
Objects of this type are normally much larger since more information is contained. The
type is also used in a few more places as we will see. The types and functions described in
this section are all defined and declared respectively in the `ucontext.h` header file.

ucontext_t   [Data Type]
> The `ucontext_t` type is defined as a structure with at least the following elements:
>
> `ucontext_t *uc_link`
>> This is a pointer to the next context structure which is used if the context
>> described in the current structure returns.
>
> `sigset_t uc_sigmask`
>> Set of signals which are blocked when this context is used.
>
> `stack_t uc_stack`
>> Stack used for this context. The value need not be (and normally is
>> not) the stack pointer. See Section 24.9 [Using a Separate Signal Stack],
>> page 725.
>
> `mcontext_t uc_mcontext`
>> This element contains the actual state of the process. The `mcontext_t`
>> type is also defined in this header but the definition should be treated
>> as opaque. Any use of knowledge of the type makes applications less
>> portable.

Objects of this type have to be created by the user. The initialization and modification
happens through one of the following functions:

`int getcontext` (*ucontext_t *ucp*)   [Function]

> Preliminary: | MT-Safe race:ucp | AS-Safe | AC-Safe | See Section 1.2.2.1 [POSIX Safety Concepts], page 2.
>
> The `getcontext` function initializes the variable pointed to by *ucp* with the context of the calling thread. The context contains the content of the registers, the signal mask, and the current stack. Executing the contents would start at the point where the `getcontext` call just returned.
>
> The function returns 0 if successful. Otherwise it returns −1 and sets *errno* accordingly.

The `getcontext` function is similar to `setjmp` but it does not provide an indication of whether `getcontext` is returning for the first time or whether an initialized context has just been restored. If this is necessary the user has to determine this herself. This must be done carefully since the context contains registers which might contain register variables. This is a good situation to define variables with `volatile`.

Once the context variable is initialized it can be used as is or it can be modified using the `makecontext` function. The latter is normally done when implementing co-routines or similar constructs.

`void makecontext` (*ucontext_t *ucp*, *void (*func) (void)*, *int argc*,   [Function]
    ...)

> Preliminary: | MT-Safe race:ucp | AS-Safe | AC-Safe | See Section 1.2.2.1 [POSIX Safety Concepts], page 2.
>
> The *ucp* parameter passed to `makecontext` shall be initialized by a call to `getcontext`. The context will be modified in a way such that if the context is resumed it will start by calling the function `func` which gets *argc* integer arguments passed. The integer arguments which are to be passed should follow the *argc* parameter in the call to `makecontext`.
>
> Before the call to this function the `uc_stack` and `uc_link` element of the *ucp* structure should be initialized. The `uc_stack` element describes the stack which is used for this context. No two contexts which are used at the same time should use the same memory region for a stack.
>
> The `uc_link` element of the object pointed to by *ucp* should be a pointer to the context to be executed when the function *func* returns or it should be a null pointer. See `setcontext` for more information about the exact use.

While allocating the memory for the stack one has to be careful. Most modern processors keep track of whether a certain memory region is allowed to contain code which is executed or not. Data segments and heap memory are normally not tagged to allow this. The result is that programs would fail. Examples for such code include the calling sequences the GNU C compiler generates for calls to nested functions. Safe ways to allocate stacks correctly include using memory on the original thread's stack or explicitly allocating memory tagged for execution using (see Section 13.7 [Memory-mapped I/O], page 350).

Compatibility note: The current Unix standard is very imprecise about the way the stack is allocated. All implementations seem to agree that the `uc_stack` element must be used but the values stored in the elements of the `stack_t` value are unclear. The GNU C Library and most other Unix implementations require the `ss_sp` value of the `uc_stack` element to point to the base of the memory region allocated for the stack and the size of the memory region is stored in `ss_size`. There are implementations out there which require `ss_sp` to be set to the value the stack pointer will have (which can, depending on the direction the stack grows, be different). This difference makes the `makecontext` function hard to use and it requires detection of the platform at compile time.

`int setcontext (const ucontext_t *ucp)`   [Function]

> Preliminary: | MT-Safe race:ucp | AS-Unsafe corrupt | AC-Unsafe corrupt | See Section 1.2.2.1 [POSIX Safety Concepts], page 2.
>
> The `setcontext` function restores the context described by *ucp*. The context is not modified and can be reused as often as wanted.
>
> If the context was created by `getcontext` execution resumes with the registers filled with the same values and the same stack as if the `getcontext` call just returned.
>
> If the context was modified with a call to `makecontext` execution continues with the function passed to `makecontext` which gets the specified parameters passed. If this function returns execution is resumed in the context which was referenced by the `uc_link` element of the context structure passed to `makecontext` at the time of the call. If `uc_link` was a null pointer the application terminates normally with an exit status value of `EXIT_SUCCESS` (see Section 25.7 [Program Termination], page 768).
>
> If the context was created by a call to a signal handler or from any other source then the behaviour of `setcontext` is unspecified.
>
> Since the context contains information about the stack no two threads should use the same context at the same time. The result in most cases would be disastrous.
>
> The `setcontext` function does not return unless an error occurred in which case it returns `-1`.

The `setcontext` function simply replaces the current context with the one described by the *ucp* parameter. This is often useful but there are situations where the current context has to be preserved.

`int swapcontext (ucontext_t *restrict oucp, const ucontext_t`   [Function]
        `*restrict ucp)`

> Preliminary: | MT-Safe race:oucp race:ucp | AS-Unsafe corrupt | AC-Unsafe corrupt | See Section 1.2.2.1 [POSIX Safety Concepts], page 2.
>
> The `swapcontext` function is similar to `setcontext` but instead of just replacing the current context the latter is first saved in the object pointed to by *oucp* as if this was a call to `getcontext`. The saved context would resume after the call to `swapcontext`.
>
> Once the current context is saved the context described in *ucp* is installed and execution continues as described in this context.
>
> If `swapcontext` succeeds the function does not return unless the context *oucp* is used without prior modification by `makecontext`. The return value in this case is `0`. If the function fails it returns `-1` and sets *errno* accordingly.

Example for SVID Context Handling

The easiest way to use the context handling functions is as a replacement for `setjmp` and `longjmp`. The context contains on most platforms more information which may lead to fewer surprises but this also means using these functions is more expensive (besides being less portable).

```
int
random_search (int n, int (*fp) (int, ucontext_t *))
{
  volatile int cnt = 0;
  ucontext_t uc;

  /* Safe current context.  */
  if (getcontext (&uc) < 0)
    return -1;

  /* If we have not tried n times try again.  */
  if (cnt++ < n)
    /* Call the function with a new random number
       and the context.  */
    if (fp (rand (), &uc) != 0)
      /* We found what we were looking for.  */
      return 1;

  /* Not found.  */
  return 0;
}
```

Using contexts in such a way enables emulating exception handling. The search functions passed in the *fp* parameter could be very large, nested, and complex which would make it complicated (or at least would require a lot of code) to leave the function with an error value which has to be passed down to the caller. By using the context it is possible to leave the search function in one step and allow restarting the search which also has the nice side effect that it can be significantly faster.

Something which is harder to implement with `setjmp` and `longjmp` is to switch temporarily to a different execution path and then resume where execution was stopped.

```
#include <signal.h>
#include <stdio.h>
#include <stdlib.h>
#include <ucontext.h>
#include <sys/time.h>

/* Set by the signal handler. */
static volatile int expired;

/* The contexts. */
static ucontext_t uc[3];

/* We do only a certain number of switches. */
static int switches;


/* This is the function doing the work.  It is just a
   skeleton, real code has to be filled in. */
static void
```

```
f (int n)
{
  int m = 0;
  while (1)
    {
      /* This is where the work would be done. */
      if (++m % 100 == 0)
        {
          putchar ('.');
          fflush (stdout);
        }

      /* Regularly the expire variable must be checked. */
      if (expired)
        {
          /* We do not want the program to run forever. */
          if (++switches == 20)
            return;

          printf ("\nswitching from %d to %d\n", n, 3 - n);
          expired = 0;
          /* Switch to the other context, saving the current one. */
          swapcontext (&uc[n], &uc[3 - n]);
        }
    }
}

/* This is the signal handler which simply set the variable. */
void
handler (int signal)
{
  expired = 1;
}


int
main (void)
{
  struct sigaction sa;
  struct itimerval it;
  char st1[8192];
  char st2[8192];

  /* Initialize the data structures for the interval timer. */
  sa.sa_flags = SA_RESTART;
  sigfillset (&sa.sa_mask);
  sa.sa_handler = handler;
  it.it_interval.tv_sec = 0;
  it.it_interval.tv_usec = 1;
  it.it_value = it.it_interval;

  /* Install the timer and get the context we can manipulate. */
  if (sigaction (SIGPROF, &sa, NULL) < 0
      || setitimer (ITIMER_PROF, &it, NULL) < 0
      || getcontext (&uc[1]) == -1
      || getcontext (&uc[2]) == -1)
    abort ();
```

```
/* Create a context with a separate stack which causes the
   function f to be call with the parameter 1.
   Note that the uc_link points to the main context
   which will cause the program to terminate once the function
   return. */
uc[1].uc_link = &uc[0];
uc[1].uc_stack.ss_sp = st1;
uc[1].uc_stack.ss_size = sizeof st1;
makecontext (&uc[1], (void (*) (void)) f, 1, 1);

/* Similarly, but 2 is passed as the parameter to f. */
uc[2].uc_link = &uc[0];
uc[2].uc_stack.ss_sp = st2;
uc[2].uc_stack.ss_size = sizeof st2;
makecontext (&uc[2], (void (*) (void)) f, 1, 2);

/* Start running. */
swapcontext (&uc[0], &uc[1]);
putchar ('\n');

return 0;
}
```

This an example how the context functions can be used to implement co-routines or cooperative multi-threading. All that has to be done is to call every once in a while `swapcontext` to continue running a different context. It is not recommended to do the context switching from the signal handler directly since leaving the signal handler via `setcontext` if the signal was delivered during code that was not asynchronous signal safe could lead to problems. Setting a variable in the signal handler and checking it in the body of the functions which are executed is a safer approach. Since `swapcontext` is saving the current context it is possible to have multiple different scheduling points in the code. Execution will always resume where it was left.

24 Signal Handling

A *signal* is a software interrupt delivered to a process. The operating system uses signals to report exceptional situations to an executing program. Some signals report errors such as references to invalid memory addresses; others report asynchronous events, such as disconnection of a phone line.

The GNU C Library defines a variety of signal types, each for a particular kind of event. Some kinds of events make it inadvisable or impossible for the program to proceed as usual, and the corresponding signals normally abort the program. Other kinds of signals that report harmless events are ignored by default.

If you anticipate an event that causes signals, you can define a handler function and tell the operating system to run it when that particular type of signal arrives.

Finally, one process can send a signal to another process; this allows a parent process to abort a child, or two related processes to communicate and synchronize.

24.1 Basic Concepts of Signals

This section explains basic concepts of how signals are generated, what happens after a signal is delivered, and how programs can handle signals.

24.1.1 Some Kinds of Signals

A signal reports the occurrence of an exceptional event. These are some of the events that can cause (or *generate*, or *raise*) a signal:

- A program error such as dividing by zero or issuing an address outside the valid range.

- A user request to interrupt or terminate the program. Most environments are set up to let a user suspend the program by typing *C-z*, or terminate it with *C-c*. Whatever key sequence is used, the operating system sends the proper signal to interrupt the process.

- The termination of a child process.

- Expiration of a timer or alarm.

- A call to `kill` or `raise` by the same process.

- A call to `kill` from another process. Signals are a limited but useful form of interprocess communication.

- An attempt to perform an I/O operation that cannot be done. Examples are reading from a pipe that has no writer (see Chapter 15 [Pipes and FIFOs], page 437), and reading or writing to a terminal in certain situations (see Chapter 28 [Job Control], page 786).

Each of these kinds of events (excepting explicit calls to `kill` and `raise`) generates its own particular kind of signal. The various kinds of signals are listed and described in detail in Section 24.2 [Standard Signals], page 687.

24.1.2 Concepts of Signal Generation

In general, the events that generate signals fall into three major categories: errors, external events, and explicit requests.

An error means that a program has done something invalid and cannot continue execution. But not all kinds of errors generate signals—in fact, most do not. For example, opening a nonexistent file is an error, but it does not raise a signal; instead, `open` returns `-1`. In general, errors that are necessarily associated with certain library functions are reported by returning a value that indicates an error. The errors which raise signals are those which can happen anywhere in the program, not just in library calls. These include division by zero and invalid memory addresses.

An external event generally has to do with I/O or other processes. These include the arrival of input, the expiration of a timer, and the termination of a child process.

An explicit request means the use of a library function such as `kill` whose purpose is specifically to generate a signal.

Signals may be generated *synchronously* or *asynchronously*. A synchronous signal pertains to a specific action in the program, and is delivered (unless blocked) during that action. Most errors generate signals synchronously, and so do explicit requests by a process to generate a signal for that same process. On some machines, certain kinds of hardware errors (usually floating-point exceptions) are not reported completely synchronously, but may arrive a few instructions later.

Asynchronous signals are generated by events outside the control of the process that receives them. These signals arrive at unpredictable times during execution. External events generate signals asynchronously, and so do explicit requests that apply to some other process.

A given type of signal is either typically synchronous or typically asynchronous. For example, signals for errors are typically synchronous because errors generate signals synchronously. But any type of signal can be generated synchronously or asynchronously with an explicit request.

24.1.3 How Signals Are Delivered

When a signal is generated, it becomes *pending*. Normally it remains pending for just a short period of time and then is *delivered* to the process that was signaled. However, if that kind of signal is currently *blocked*, it may remain pending indefinitely—until signals of that kind are *unblocked*. Once unblocked, it will be delivered immediately. See Section 24.7 [Blocking Signals], page 716.

When the signal is delivered, whether right away or after a long delay, the *specified action* for that signal is taken. For certain signals, such as `SIGKILL` and `SIGSTOP`, the action is fixed, but for most signals, the program has a choice: ignore the signal, specify a *handler function*, or accept the *default action* for that kind of signal. The program specifies its choice using functions such as `signal` or `sigaction` (see Section 24.3 [Specifying Signal Actions], page 695). We sometimes say that a handler *catches* the signal. While the handler is running, that particular signal is normally blocked.

If the specified action for a kind of signal is to ignore it, then any such signal which is generated is discarded immediately. This happens even if the signal is also blocked at the time. A signal discarded in this way will never be delivered, not even if the program subsequently specifies a different action for that kind of signal and then unblocks it.

If a signal arrives which the program has neither handled nor ignored, its *default action* takes place. Each kind of signal has its own default action, documented below (see

Section 24.2 [Standard Signals], page 687). For most kinds of signals, the default action is to terminate the process. For certain kinds of signals that represent "harmless" events, the default action is to do nothing.

When a signal terminates a process, its parent process can determine the cause of termination by examining the termination status code reported by the `wait` or `waitpid` functions. (This is discussed in more detail in Section 26.6 [Process Completion], page 779.) The information it can get includes the fact that termination was due to a signal and the kind of signal involved. If a program you run from a shell is terminated by a signal, the shell typically prints some kind of error message.

The signals that normally represent program errors have a special property: when one of these signals terminates the process, it also writes a *core dump file* which records the state of the process at the time of termination. You can examine the core dump with a debugger to investigate what caused the error.

If you raise a "program error" signal by explicit request, and this terminates the process, it makes a core dump file just as if the signal had been due directly to an error.

24.2 Standard Signals

This section lists the names for various standard kinds of signals and describes what kind of event they mean. Each signal name is a macro which stands for a positive integer—the *signal number* for that kind of signal. Your programs should never make assumptions about the numeric code for a particular kind of signal, but rather refer to them always by the names defined here. This is because the number for a given kind of signal can vary from system to system, but the meanings of the names are standardized and fairly uniform.

The signal names are defined in the header file `signal.h`.

`int NSIG`   [Macro]

> The value of this symbolic constant is the total number of signals defined. Since the signal numbers are allocated consecutively, `NSIG` is also one greater than the largest defined signal number.

24.2.1 Program Error Signals

The following signals are generated when a serious program error is detected by the operating system or the computer itself. In general, all of these signals are indications that your program is seriously broken in some way, and there's usually no way to continue the computation which encountered the error.

Some programs handle program error signals in order to tidy up before terminating; for example, programs that turn off echoing of terminal input should handle program error signals in order to turn echoing back on. The handler should end by specifying the default action for the signal that happened and then reraising it; this will cause the program to terminate with that signal, as if it had not had a handler. (See Section 24.4.2 [Handlers That Terminate the Process], page 703.)

Termination is the sensible ultimate outcome from a program error in most programs. However, programming systems such as Lisp that can load compiled user programs might need to keep executing even if a user program incurs an error. These programs have handlers which use `longjmp` to return control to the command level.

The default action for all of these signals is to cause the process to terminate. If you block or ignore these signals or establish handlers for them that return normally, your program will probably break horribly when such signals happen, unless they are generated by `raise` or `kill` instead of a real error.

When one of these program error signals terminates a process, it also writes a *core dump file* which records the state of the process at the time of termination. The core dump file is named `core` and is written in whichever directory is current in the process at the time. (On GNU/Hurd systems, you can specify the file name for core dumps with the environment variable `COREFILE`.) The purpose of core dump files is so that you can examine them with a debugger to investigate what caused the error.

`int SIGFPE`   [Macro]

> The `SIGFPE` signal reports a fatal arithmetic error. Although the name is derived from "floating-point exception", this signal actually covers all arithmetic errors, including division by zero and overflow. If a program stores integer data in a location which is then used in a floating-point operation, this often causes an "invalid operation" exception, because the processor cannot recognize the data as a floating-point number.

> Actual floating-point exceptions are a complicated subject because there are many types of exceptions with subtly different meanings, and the `SIGFPE` signal doesn't distinguish between them. The *IEEE Standard for Binary Floating-Point Arithmetic (ANSI/IEEE Std 754-1985 and ANSI/IEEE Std 854-1987)* defines various floating-point exceptions and requires conforming computer systems to report their occurrences. However, this standard does not specify how the exceptions are reported, or what kinds of handling and control the operating system can offer to the programmer.

BSD systems provide the `SIGFPE` handler with an extra argument that distinguishes various causes of the exception. In order to access this argument, you must define the handler to accept two arguments, which means you must cast it to a one-argument function type in order to establish the handler. The GNU C Library does provide this extra argument, but the value is meaningful only on operating systems that provide the information (BSD systems and GNU systems).

`FPE_INTOVF_TRAP`

> Integer overflow (impossible in a C program unless you enable overflow trapping in a hardware-specific fashion).

`FPE_INTDIV_TRAP`

> Integer division by zero.

`FPE_SUBRNG_TRAP`

> Subscript-range (something that C programs never check for).

`FPE_FLTOVF_TRAP`

> Floating overflow trap.

`FPE_FLTDIV_TRAP`

> Floating/decimal division by zero.

FPE_FLTUND_TRAP

> Floating underflow trap. (Trapping on floating underflow is not normally enabled.)

FPE_DECOVF_TRAP

> Decimal overflow trap. (Only a few machines have decimal arithmetic and C never uses it.)

int SIGILL   [Macro]

> The name of this signal is derived from "illegal instruction"; it usually means your program is trying to execute garbage or a privileged instruction. Since the C compiler generates only valid instructions, SIGILL typically indicates that the executable file is corrupted, or that you are trying to execute data. Some common ways of getting into the latter situation are by passing an invalid object where a pointer to a function was expected, or by writing past the end of an automatic array (or similar problems with pointers to automatic variables) and corrupting other data on the stack such as the return address of a stack frame.
>
> SIGILL can also be generated when the stack overflows, or when the system has trouble running the handler for a signal.

int SIGSEGV   [Macro]

> This signal is generated when a program tries to read or write outside the memory that is allocated for it, or to write memory that can only be read. (Actually, the signals only occur when the program goes far enough outside to be detected by the system's memory protection mechanism.) The name is an abbreviation for "segmentation violation".
>
> Common ways of getting a SIGSEGV condition include dereferencing a null or uninitialized pointer, or when you use a pointer to step through an array, but fail to check for the end of the array. It varies among systems whether dereferencing a null pointer generates SIGSEGV or SIGBUS.

int SIGBUS   [Macro]

> This signal is generated when an invalid pointer is dereferenced. Like SIGSEGV, this signal is typically the result of dereferencing an uninitialized pointer. The difference between the two is that SIGSEGV indicates an invalid access to valid memory, while SIGBUS indicates an access to an invalid address. In particular, SIGBUS signals often result from dereferencing a misaligned pointer, such as referring to a four-word integer at an address not divisible by four. (Each kind of computer has its own requirements for address alignment.)
>
> The name of this signal is an abbreviation for "bus error".

int SIGABRT   [Macro]

> This signal indicates an error detected by the program itself and reported by calling abort. See Section 25.7.4 [Aborting a Program], page 771.

int SIGIOT   [Macro]

> Generated by the PDP-11 "iot" instruction. On most machines, this is just another name for SIGABRT.

`int SIGTRAP`   [Macro]

> Generated by the machine's breakpoint instruction, and possibly other trap instructions. This signal is used by debuggers. Your program will probably only see `SIGTRAP` if it is somehow executing bad instructions.

`int SIGEMT`   [Macro]

> Emulator trap; this results from certain unimplemented instructions which might be emulated in software, or the operating system's failure to properly emulate them.

`int SIGSYS`   [Macro]

> Bad system call; that is to say, the instruction to trap to the operating system was executed, but the code number for the system call to perform was invalid.

24.2.2 Termination Signals

These signals are all used to tell a process to terminate, in one way or another. They have different names because they're used for slightly different purposes, and programs might want to handle them differently.

The reason for handling these signals is usually so your program can tidy up as appropriate before actually terminating. For example, you might want to save state information, delete temporary files, or restore the previous terminal modes. Such a handler should end by specifying the default action for the signal that happened and then reraising it; this will cause the program to terminate with that signal, as if it had not had a handler. (See Section 24.4.2 [Handlers That Terminate the Process], page 703.)

The (obvious) default action for all of these signals is to cause the process to terminate.

`int SIGTERM`   [Macro]

> The `SIGTERM` signal is a generic signal used to cause program termination. Unlike `SIGKILL`, this signal can be blocked, handled, and ignored. It is the normal way to politely ask a program to terminate.
>
> The shell command `kill` generates `SIGTERM` by default.

`int SIGINT`   [Macro]

> The `SIGINT` ("program interrupt") signal is sent when the user types the INTR character (normally `C-c`). See Section 17.4.9 [Special Characters], page 503, for information about terminal driver support for `C-c`.

`int SIGQUIT`   [Macro]

> The `SIGQUIT` signal is similar to `SIGINT`, except that it's controlled by a different key—the QUIT character, usually `C-\`—and produces a core dump when it terminates the process, just like a program error signal. You can think of this as a program error condition "detected" by the user.
>
> See Section 24.2.1 [Program Error Signals], page 687, for information about core dumps. See Section 17.4.9 [Special Characters], page 503, for information about terminal driver support.
>
> Certain kinds of cleanups are best omitted in handling `SIGQUIT`. For example, if the program creates temporary files, it should handle the other termination requests by deleting the temporary files. But it is better for `SIGQUIT` not to delete them, so that the user can examine them in conjunction with the core dump.

`int SIGKILL` [Macro]

> The `SIGKILL` signal is used to cause immediate program termination. It cannot be handled or ignored, and is therefore always fatal. It is also not possible to block this signal.
>
> This signal is usually generated only by explicit request. Since it cannot be handled, you should generate it only as a last resort, after first trying a less drastic method such as `C-c` or `SIGTERM`. If a process does not respond to any other termination signals, sending it a `SIGKILL` signal will almost always cause it to go away.
>
> In fact, if `SIGKILL` fails to terminate a process, that by itself constitutes an operating system bug which you should report.
>
> The system will generate `SIGKILL` for a process itself under some unusual conditions where the program cannot possibly continue to run (even to run a signal handler).

`int SIGHUP` [Macro]

> The `SIGHUP` ("hang-up") signal is used to report that the user's terminal is disconnected, perhaps because a network or telephone connection was broken. For more information about this, see Section 17.4.6 [Control Modes], page 498.
>
> This signal is also used to report the termination of the controlling process on a terminal to jobs associated with that session; this termination effectively disconnects all processes in the session from the controlling terminal. For more information, see Section 25.7.5 [Termination Internals], page 771.

24.2.3 Alarm Signals

These signals are used to indicate the expiration of timers. See Section 21.5 [Setting an Alarm], page 649, for information about functions that cause these signals to be sent.

The default behavior for these signals is to cause program termination. This default is rarely useful, but no other default would be useful; most of the ways of using these signals would require handler functions in any case.

`int SIGALRM` [Macro]

> This signal typically indicates expiration of a timer that measures real or clock time. It is used by the `alarm` function, for example.

`int SIGVTALRM` [Macro]

> This signal typically indicates expiration of a timer that measures CPU time used by the current process. The name is an abbreviation for "virtual time alarm".

`int SIGPROF` [Macro]

> This signal typically indicates expiration of a timer that measures both CPU time used by the current process, and CPU time expended on behalf of the process by the system. Such a timer is used to implement code profiling facilities, hence the name of this signal.

24.2.4 Asynchronous I/O Signals

The signals listed in this section are used in conjunction with asynchronous I/O facilities. You have to take explicit action by calling `fcntl` to enable a particular file descriptor to generate these signals (see Section 13.18 [Interrupt-Driven Input], page 387). The default action for these signals is to ignore them.

`int SIGIO` [Macro]

This signal is sent when a file descriptor is ready to perform input or output.

On most operating systems, terminals and sockets are the only kinds of files that can generate `SIGIO`; other kinds, including ordinary files, never generate `SIGIO` even if you ask them to.

On GNU systems `SIGIO` will always be generated properly if you successfully set asynchronous mode with `fcntl`.

`int SIGURG` [Macro]

This signal is sent when "urgent" or out-of-band data arrives on a socket. See Section 16.9.8 [Out-of-Band Data], page 477.

`int SIGPOLL` [Macro]

This is a System V signal name, more or less similar to `SIGIO`. It is defined only for compatibility.

24.2.5 Job Control Signals

These signals are used to support job control. If your system doesn't support job control, then these macros are defined but the signals themselves can't be raised or handled.

You should generally leave these signals alone unless you really understand how job control works. See Chapter 28 [Job Control], page 786.

`int SIGCHLD` [Macro]

This signal is sent to a parent process whenever one of its child processes terminates or stops.

The default action for this signal is to ignore it. If you establish a handler for this signal while there are child processes that have terminated but not reported their status via `wait` or `waitpid` (see Section 26.6 [Process Completion], page 779), whether your new handler applies to those processes or not depends on the particular operating system.

`int SIGCLD` [Macro]

This is an obsolete name for `SIGCHLD`.

`int SIGCONT` [Macro]

You can send a `SIGCONT` signal to a process to make it continue. This signal is special—it always makes the process continue if it is stopped, before the signal is delivered. The default behavior is to do nothing else. You cannot block this signal. You can set a handler, but `SIGCONT` always makes the process continue regardless.

Most programs have no reason to handle `SIGCONT`; they simply resume execution without realizing they were ever stopped. You can use a handler for `SIGCONT` to make a program do something special when it is stopped and continued—for example, to reprint a prompt when it is suspended while waiting for input.

`int SIGSTOP` [Macro]

The `SIGSTOP` signal stops the process. It cannot be handled, ignored, or blocked.

int `SIGTSTP`   [Macro]

> The `SIGTSTP` signal is an interactive stop signal. Unlike `SIGSTOP`, this signal can be handled and ignored.
>
> Your program should handle this signal if you have a special need to leave files or system tables in a secure state when a process is stopped. For example, programs that turn off echoing should handle `SIGTSTP` so they can turn echoing back on before stopping.
>
> This signal is generated when the user types the SUSP character (normally *C-z*). For more information about terminal driver support, see Section 17.4.9 [Special Characters], page 503.

int `SIGTTIN`   [Macro]

> A process cannot read from the user's terminal while it is running as a background job. When any process in a background job tries to read from the terminal, all of the processes in the job are sent a `SIGTTIN` signal. The default action for this signal is to stop the process. For more information about how this interacts with the terminal driver, see Section 28.4 [Access to the Controlling Terminal], page 787.

int `SIGTTOU`   [Macro]

> This is similar to `SIGTTIN`, but is generated when a process in a background job attempts to write to the terminal or set its modes. Again, the default action is to stop the process. `SIGTTOU` is only generated for an attempt to write to the terminal if the `TOSTOP` output mode is set; see Section 17.4.5 [Output Modes], page 497.

While a process is stopped, no more signals can be delivered to it until it is continued, except `SIGKILL` signals and (obviously) `SIGCONT` signals. The signals are marked as pending, but not delivered until the process is continued. The `SIGKILL` signal always causes termination of the process and can't be blocked, handled or ignored. You can ignore `SIGCONT`, but it always causes the process to be continued anyway if it is stopped. Sending a `SIGCONT` signal to a process causes any pending stop signals for that process to be discarded. Likewise, any pending `SIGCONT` signals for a process are discarded when it receives a stop signal.

When a process in an orphaned process group (see Section 28.5 [Orphaned Process Groups], page 788) receives a `SIGTSTP`, `SIGTTIN`, or `SIGTTOU` signal and does not handle it, the process does not stop. Stopping the process would probably not be very useful, since there is no shell program that will notice it stop and allow the user to continue it. What happens instead depends on the operating system you are using. Some systems may do nothing; others may deliver another signal instead, such as `SIGKILL` or `SIGHUP`. On GNU/Hurd systems, the process dies with `SIGKILL`; this avoids the problem of many stopped, orphaned processes lying around the system.

24.2.6 Operation Error Signals

These signals are used to report various errors generated by an operation done by the program. They do not necessarily indicate a programming error in the program, but an error that prevents an operating system call from completing. The default action for all of them is to cause the process to terminate.

`int` `SIGPIPE`   [Macro]

> Broken pipe. If you use pipes or FIFOs, you have to design your application so that one process opens the pipe for reading before another starts writing. If the reading process never starts, or terminates unexpectedly, writing to the pipe or FIFO raises a `SIGPIPE` signal. If `SIGPIPE` is blocked, handled or ignored, the offending call fails with `EPIPE` instead.

> Pipes and FIFO special files are discussed in more detail in Chapter 15 [Pipes and FIFOs], page 437.

> Another cause of `SIGPIPE` is when you try to output to a socket that isn't connected. See Section 16.9.5.1 [Sending Data], page 472.

`int` `SIGLOST`   [Macro]

> Resource lost. This signal is generated when you have an advisory lock on an NFS file, and the NFS server reboots and forgets about your lock.

> On GNU/Hurd systems, `SIGLOST` is generated when any server program dies unexpectedly. It is usually fine to ignore the signal; whatever call was made to the server that died just returns an error.

`int` `SIGXCPU`   [Macro]

> CPU time limit exceeded. This signal is generated when the process exceeds its soft resource limit on CPU time. See Section 22.2 [Limiting Resource Usage], page 656.

`int` `SIGXFSZ`   [Macro]

> File size limit exceeded. This signal is generated when the process attempts to extend a file so it exceeds the process's soft resource limit on file size. See Section 22.2 [Limiting Resource Usage], page 656.

24.2.7 Miscellaneous Signals

These signals are used for various other purposes. In general, they will not affect your program unless it explicitly uses them for something.

`int` `SIGUSR1`   [Macro]
`int` `SIGUSR2`   [Macro]

> The `SIGUSR1` and `SIGUSR2` signals are set aside for you to use any way you want. They're useful for simple interprocess communication, if you write a signal handler for them in the program that receives the signal.

> There is an example showing the use of `SIGUSR1` and `SIGUSR2` in Section 24.6.2 [Signaling Another Process], page 713.

> The default action is to terminate the process.

`int` `SIGWINCH`   [Macro]

> Window size change. This is generated on some systems (including GNU) when the terminal driver's record of the number of rows and columns on the screen is changed. The default action is to ignore it.

> If a program does full-screen display, it should handle `SIGWINCH`. When the signal arrives, it should fetch the new screen size and reformat its display accordingly.

`int SIGINFO`   [Macro]

Information request. On 4.4 BSD and GNU/Hurd systems, this signal is sent to all the processes in the foreground process group of the controlling terminal when the user types the STATUS character in canonical mode; see Section 17.4.9.2 [Characters that Cause Signals], page 505.

If the process is the leader of the process group, the default action is to print some status information about the system and what the process is doing. Otherwise the default is to do nothing.

24.2.8 Signal Messages

We mentioned above that the shell prints a message describing the signal that terminated a child process. The clean way to print a message describing a signal is to use the functions `strsignal` and `psignal`. These functions use a signal number to specify which kind of signal to describe. The signal number may come from the termination status of a child process (see Section 26.6 [Process Completion], page 779) or it may come from a signal handler in the same process.

`char * strsignal (int signum)`   [Function]

Preliminary: | MT-Unsafe race:strsignal locale | AS-Unsafe init i18n corrupt heap | AC-Unsafe init corrupt mem | See Section 1.2.2.1 [POSIX Safety Concepts], page 2.

This function returns a pointer to a statically-allocated string containing a message describing the signal *signum*. You should not modify the contents of this string; and, since it can be rewritten on subsequent calls, you should save a copy of it if you need to reference it later.

This function is a GNU extension, declared in the header file `string.h`.

`void psignal (int signum, const char *message)`   [Function]

Preliminary: | MT-Safe locale | AS-Unsafe corrupt i18n heap | AC-Unsafe lock corrupt mem | See Section 1.2.2.1 [POSIX Safety Concepts], page 2.

This function prints a message describing the signal *signum* to the standard error output stream `stderr`; see Section 12.2 [Standard Streams], page 257.

If you call `psignal` with a *message* that is either a null pointer or an empty string, `psignal` just prints the message corresponding to *signum*, adding a trailing newline.

If you supply a non-null *message* argument, then `psignal` prefixes its output with this string. It adds a colon and a space character to separate the *message* from the string corresponding to *signum*.

This function is a BSD feature, declared in the header file `signal.h`.

There is also an array `sys_siglist` which contains the messages for the various signal codes. This array exists on BSD systems, unlike `strsignal`.

24.3 Specifying Signal Actions

The simplest way to change the action for a signal is to use the `signal` function. You can specify a built-in action (such as to ignore the signal), or you can *establish a handler*.

The GNU C Library also implements the more versatile `sigaction` facility. This section describes both facilities and gives suggestions on which to use when.

24.3.1 Basic Signal Handling

The `signal` function provides a simple interface for establishing an action for a particular signal. The function and associated macros are declared in the header file `signal.h`.

`sighandler_t`   [Data Type]

> This is the type of signal handler functions. Signal handlers take one integer argument specifying the signal number, and have return type `void`. So, you should define handler functions like this:
>
> ```
>     void handler (int signum) { ... }
> ```
>
> The name `sighandler_t` for this data type is a GNU extension.

`sighandler_t signal (`*int signum*`, `*sighandler_t action*`)`   [Function]

> Preliminary: | MT-Safe sigintr | AS-Safe | AC-Safe | See Section 1.2.2.1 [POSIX Safety Concepts], page 2.
>
> The `signal` function establishes *action* as the action for the signal *signum*.
>
> The first argument, *signum*, identifies the signal whose behavior you want to control, and should be a signal number. The proper way to specify a signal number is with one of the symbolic signal names (see Section 24.2 [Standard Signals], page 687)—don't use an explicit number, because the numerical code for a given kind of signal may vary from operating system to operating system.
>
> The second argument, *action*, specifies the action to use for the signal *signum*. This can be one of the following:
>
> `SIG_DFL` `SIG_DFL` specifies the default action for the particular signal. The default actions for various kinds of signals are stated in Section 24.2 [Standard Signals], page 687.
>
> `SIG_IGN` `SIG_IGN` specifies that the signal should be ignored.
>
> > Your program generally should not ignore signals that represent serious events or that are normally used to request termination. You cannot ignore the `SIGKILL` or `SIGSTOP` signals at all. You can ignore program error signals like `SIGSEGV`, but ignoring the error won't enable the program to continue executing meaningfully. Ignoring user requests such as `SIGINT`, `SIGQUIT`, and `SIGTSTP` is unfriendly.
> >
> > When you do not wish signals to be delivered during a certain part of the program, the thing to do is to block them, not ignore them. See Section 24.7 [Blocking Signals], page 716.
>
> *handler*   Supply the address of a handler function in your program, to specify running this handler as the way to deliver the signal.
>
> > For more information about defining signal handler functions, see Section 24.4 [Defining Signal Handlers], page 702.

If you set the action for a signal to `SIG_IGN`, or if you set it to `SIG_DFL` and the default action is to ignore that signal, then any pending signals of that type are discarded (even if they are blocked). Discarding the pending signals means that they will never be delivered, not even if you subsequently specify another action and unblock this kind of signal.

The **signal** function returns the action that was previously in effect for the specified *signum*. You can save this value and restore it later by calling **signal** again.

If **signal** can't honor the request, it returns **SIG_ERR** instead. The following **errno** error conditions are defined for this function:

EINVAL   You specified an invalid *signum*; or you tried to ignore or provide a handler for **SIGKILL** or **SIGSTOP**.

Compatibility Note: A problem encountered when working with the **signal** function is that it has different semantics on BSD and SVID systems. The difference is that on SVID systems the signal handler is deinstalled after signal delivery. On BSD systems the handler must be explicitly deinstalled. In the GNU C Library we use the BSD version by default. To use the SVID version you can either use the function **sysv_signal** (see below) or use the **_XOPEN_SOURCE** feature select macro (see Section 1.3.4 [Feature Test Macros], page 15). In general, use of these functions should be avoided because of compatibility problems. It is better to use **sigaction** if it is available since the results are much more reliable.

Here is a simple example of setting up a handler to delete temporary files when certain fatal signals happen:

```
#include <signal.h>

void
termination_handler (int signum)
{
  struct temp_file *p;

  for (p = temp_file_list; p; p = p->next)
    unlink (p->name);
}

int
main (void)
{
  ...
  if (signal (SIGINT, termination_handler) == SIG_IGN)
    signal (SIGINT, SIG_IGN);
  if (signal (SIGHUP, termination_handler) == SIG_IGN)
    signal (SIGHUP, SIG_IGN);
  if (signal (SIGTERM, termination_handler) == SIG_IGN)
    signal (SIGTERM, SIG_IGN);
  ...
}
```

Note that if a given signal was previously set to be ignored, this code avoids altering that setting. This is because non-job-control shells often ignore certain signals when starting children, and it is important for the children to respect this.

We do not handle **SIGQUIT** or the program error signals in this example because these are designed to provide information for debugging (a core dump), and the temporary files may give useful information.

sighandler_t sysv_signal (*int* **signum**, *sighandler_t* **action**)   [Function]
    Preliminary: | MT-Safe | AS-Safe | AC-Safe | See Section 1.2.2.1 [POSIX Safety Concepts], page 2.

The `sysv_signal` implements the behavior of the standard `signal` function as found on SVID systems. The difference to BSD systems is that the handler is deinstalled after a delivery of a signal.

Compatibility Note: As said above for `signal`, this function should be avoided when possible. `sigaction` is the preferred method.

`sighandler_t ssignal` (*int signum, sighandler_t action*)   [Function]
> Preliminary: | MT-Safe sigintr | AS-Safe | AC-Safe | See Section 1.2.2.1 [POSIX Safety Concepts], page 2.

> The `ssignal` function does the same thing as `signal`; it is provided only for compatibility with SVID.

`sighandler_t SIG_ERR`   [Macro]
> The value of this macro is used as the return value from `signal` to indicate an error.

24.3.2 Advanced Signal Handling

The `sigaction` function has the same basic effect as `signal`: to specify how a signal should be handled by the process. However, `sigaction` offers more control, at the expense of more complexity. In particular, `sigaction` allows you to specify additional flags to control when the signal is generated and how the handler is invoked.

The `sigaction` function is declared in `signal.h`.

`struct sigaction`   [Data Type]
> Structures of type `struct sigaction` are used in the `sigaction` function to specify all the information about how to handle a particular signal. This structure contains at least the following members:

> `sighandler_t sa_handler`
>> This is used in the same way as the *action* argument to the `signal` function. The value can be `SIG_DFL`, `SIG_IGN`, or a function pointer. See Section 24.3.1 [Basic Signal Handling], page 696.

> `sigset_t sa_mask`
>> This specifies a set of signals to be blocked while the handler runs. Blocking is explained in Section 24.7.5 [Blocking Signals for a Handler], page 720. Note that the signal that was delivered is automatically blocked by default before its handler is started; this is true regardless of the value in `sa_mask`. If you want that signal not to be blocked within its handler, you must write code in the handler to unblock it.

> `int sa_flags`
>> This specifies various flags which can affect the behavior of the signal. These are described in more detail in Section 24.3.5 [Flags for `sigaction`], page 700.

`int sigaction` (*int signum, const struct sigaction *restrict action,*   [Function]
> *struct sigaction *restrict old-action*)
> Preliminary: | MT-Safe | AS-Safe | AC-Safe | See Section 1.2.2.1 [POSIX Safety Concepts], page 2.

The *action* argument is used to set up a new action for the signal *signum*, while the *old-action* argument is used to return information about the action previously associated with this signal. (In other words, *old-action* has the same purpose as the **signal** function's return value—you can check to see what the old action in effect for the signal was, and restore it later if you want.)

Either *action* or *old-action* can be a null pointer. If *old-action* is a null pointer, this simply suppresses the return of information about the old action. If *action* is a null pointer, the action associated with the signal *signum* is unchanged; this allows you to inquire about how a signal is being handled without changing that handling.

The return value from **sigaction** is zero if it succeeds, and **-1** on failure. The following **errno** error conditions are defined for this function:

EINVAL   The *signum* argument is not valid, or you are trying to trap or ignore SIGKILL or SIGSTOP.

24.3.3 Interaction of `signal` and `sigaction`

It's possible to use both the **signal** and **sigaction** functions within a single program, but you have to be careful because they can interact in slightly strange ways.

The **sigaction** function specifies more information than the **signal** function, so the return value from **signal** cannot express the full range of **sigaction** possibilities. Therefore, if you use **signal** to save and later reestablish an action, it may not be able to reestablish properly a handler that was established with **sigaction**.

To avoid having problems as a result, always use **sigaction** to save and restore a handler if your program uses **sigaction** at all. Since **sigaction** is more general, it can properly save and reestablish any action, regardless of whether it was established originally with **signal** or **sigaction**.

On some systems if you establish an action with **signal** and then examine it with **sigaction**, the handler address that you get may not be the same as what you specified with **signal**. It may not even be suitable for use as an action argument with **signal**. But you can rely on using it as an argument to **sigaction**. This problem never happens on GNU systems.

So, you're better off using one or the other of the mechanisms consistently within a single program.

Portability Note: The basic **signal** function is a feature of ISO C, while **sigaction** is part of the POSIX.1 standard. If you are concerned about portability to non-POSIX systems, then you should use the **signal** function instead.

24.3.4 `sigaction` Function Example

In Section 24.3.1 [Basic Signal Handling], page 696, we gave an example of establishing a simple handler for termination signals using **signal**. Here is an equivalent example using **sigaction**:

```
#include <signal.h>

void
termination_handler (int signum)
{
```

```
      struct temp_file *p;

    for (p = temp_file_list; p; p = p->next)
      unlink (p->name);
  }

  int
  main (void)
  {
    ...
    struct sigaction new_action, old_action;

    /* Set up the structure to specify the new action. */
    new_action.sa_handler = termination_handler;
    sigemptyset (&new_action.sa_mask);
    new_action.sa_flags = 0;

    sigaction (SIGINT, NULL, &old_action);
    if (old_action.sa_handler != SIG_IGN)
      sigaction (SIGINT, &new_action, NULL);
    sigaction (SIGHUP, NULL, &old_action);
    if (old_action.sa_handler != SIG_IGN)
      sigaction (SIGHUP, &new_action, NULL);
    sigaction (SIGTERM, NULL, &old_action);
    if (old_action.sa_handler != SIG_IGN)
      sigaction (SIGTERM, &new_action, NULL);
    ...
  }
```

The program just loads the `new_action` structure with the desired parameters and passes it in the `sigaction` call. The usage of `sigemptyset` is described later; see Section 24.7 [Blocking Signals], page 716.

As in the example using `signal`, we avoid handling signals previously set to be ignored. Here we can avoid altering the signal handler even momentarily, by using the feature of `sigaction` that lets us examine the current action without specifying a new one.

Here is another example. It retrieves information about the current action for `SIGINT` without changing that action.

```
      struct sigaction query_action;

  if (sigaction (SIGINT, NULL, &query_action) < 0)
    /* sigaction returns -1 in case of error. */
  else if (query_action.sa_handler == SIG_DFL)
    /* SIGINT is handled in the default, fatal manner. */
  else if (query_action.sa_handler == SIG_IGN)
    /* SIGINT is ignored. */
  else
    /* A programmer-defined signal handler is in effect. */
```

24.3.5 Flags for `sigaction`

The `sa_flags` member of the `sigaction` structure is a catch-all for special features. Most of the time, `SA_RESTART` is a good value to use for this field.

The value of `sa_flags` is interpreted as a bit mask. Thus, you should choose the flags you want to set, OR those flags together, and store the result in the `sa_flags` member of your `sigaction` structure.

Each signal number has its own set of flags. Each call to **sigaction** affects one particular signal number, and the flags that you specify apply only to that particular signal.

In the GNU C Library, establishing a handler with **signal** sets all the flags to zero except for **SA_RESTART**, whose value depends on the settings you have made with **siginterrupt**. See Section 24.5 [Primitives Interrupted by Signals], page 711, to see what this is about.

These macros are defined in the header file **signal.h**.

int **SA_NOCLDSTOP** [Macro]

> This flag is meaningful only for the **SIGCHLD** signal. When the flag is set, the system delivers the signal for a terminated child process but not for one that is stopped. By default, **SIGCHLD** is delivered for both terminated children and stopped children.
>
> Setting this flag for a signal other than **SIGCHLD** has no effect.

int **SA_ONSTACK** [Macro]

> If this flag is set for a particular signal number, the system uses the signal stack when delivering that kind of signal. See Section 24.9 [Using a Separate Signal Stack], page 725. If a signal with this flag arrives and you have not set a signal stack, the system terminates the program with **SIGILL**.

int **SA_RESTART** [Macro]

> This flag controls what happens when a signal is delivered during certain primitives (such as **open**, **read** or **write**), and the signal handler returns normally. There are two alternatives: the library function can resume, or it can return failure with error code **EINTR**.
>
> The choice is controlled by the **SA_RESTART** flag for the particular kind of signal that was delivered. If the flag is set, returning from a handler resumes the library function. If the flag is clear, returning from a handler makes the function fail. See Section 24.5 [Primitives Interrupted by Signals], page 711.

24.3.6 Initial Signal Actions

When a new process is created (see Section 26.4 [Creating a Process], page 775), it inherits handling of signals from its parent process. However, when you load a new process image using the **exec** function (see Section 26.5 [Executing a File], page 776), any signals that you've defined your own handlers for revert to their **SIG_DFL** handling. (If you think about it a little, this makes sense; the handler functions from the old program are specific to that program, and aren't even present in the address space of the new program image.) Of course, the new program can establish its own handlers.

When a program is run by a shell, the shell normally sets the initial actions for the child process to **SIG_DFL** or **SIG_IGN**, as appropriate. It's a good idea to check to make sure that the shell has not set up an initial action of **SIG_IGN** before you establish your own signal handlers.

Here is an example of how to establish a handler for **SIGHUP**, but not if **SIGHUP** is currently ignored:

```
      ...
      struct sigaction temp;

      sigaction (SIGHUP, NULL, &temp);

      if (temp.sa_handler != SIG_IGN)
        {
          temp.sa_handler = handle_sighup;
          sigemptyset (&temp.sa_mask);
          sigaction (SIGHUP, &temp, NULL);
        }
```

24.4 Defining Signal Handlers

This section describes how to write a signal handler function that can be established with the `signal` or `sigaction` functions.

A signal handler is just a function that you compile together with the rest of the program. Instead of directly invoking the function, you use `signal` or `sigaction` to tell the operating system to call it when a signal arrives. This is known as *establishing* the handler. See Section 24.3 [Specifying Signal Actions], page 695.

There are two basic strategies you can use in signal handler functions:

- You can have the handler function note that the signal arrived by tweaking some global data structures, and then return normally.

- You can have the handler function terminate the program or transfer control to a point where it can recover from the situation that caused the signal.

You need to take special care in writing handler functions because they can be called asynchronously. That is, a handler might be called at any point in the program, unpredictably. If two signals arrive during a very short interval, one handler can run within another. This section describes what your handler should do, and what you should avoid.

24.4.1 Signal Handlers that Return

Handlers which return normally are usually used for signals such as `SIGALRM` and the I/O and interprocess communication signals. But a handler for `SIGINT` might also return normally after setting a flag that tells the program to exit at a convenient time.

It is not safe to return normally from the handler for a program error signal, because the behavior of the program when the handler function returns is not defined after a program error. See Section 24.2.1 [Program Error Signals], page 687.

Handlers that return normally must modify some global variable in order to have any effect. Typically, the variable is one that is examined periodically by the program during normal operation. Its data type should be `sig_atomic_t` for reasons described in Section 24.4.7 [Atomic Data Access and Signal Handling], page 709.

Here is a simple example of such a program. It executes the body of the loop until it has noticed that a `SIGALRM` signal has arrived. This technique is useful because it allows the iteration in progress when the signal arrives to complete before the loop exits.

```
      #include <signal.h>
      #include <stdio.h>
      #include <stdlib.h>
```

```
/* This flag controls termination of the main loop. */
volatile sig_atomic_t keep_going = 1;

/* The signal handler just clears the flag and re-enables itself. */
void
catch_alarm (int sig)
{
  keep_going = 0;
  signal (sig, catch_alarm);
}

void
do_stuff (void)
{
  puts ("Doing stuff while waiting for alarm....");
}

int
main (void)
{
  /* Establish a handler for SIGALRM signals. */
  signal (SIGALRM, catch_alarm);

  /* Set an alarm to go off in a little while. */
  alarm (2);

  /* Check the flag once in a while to see when to quit. */
  while (keep_going)
    do_stuff ();

  return EXIT_SUCCESS;
}
```

24.4.2 Handlers That Terminate the Process

Handler functions that terminate the program are typically used to cause orderly cleanup or recovery from program error signals and interactive interrupts.

The cleanest way for a handler to terminate the process is to raise the same signal that ran the handler in the first place. Here is how to do this:

```
volatile sig_atomic_t fatal_error_in_progress = 0;

void
fatal_error_signal (int sig)
{
  /* Since this handler is established for more than one kind of signal,
       it might still get invoked recursively by delivery of some other kind
       of signal.  Use a static variable to keep track of that. */
  if (fatal_error_in_progress)
    raise (sig);
  fatal_error_in_progress = 1;

  /* Now do the clean up actions:
       - reset terminal modes
       - kill child processes
       - remove lock files */
  ...
```

```
    /* Now reraise the signal.  We reactivate the signalfls
       default handling, which is to terminate the process.
       We could just call exit or abort,
       but reraising the signal sets the return status
       from the process correctly. */
  signal (sig, SIG_DFL);
  raise (sig);
}
```

24.4.3 Nonlocal Control Transfer in Handlers

You can do a nonlocal transfer of control out of a signal handler using the `setjmp` and `longjmp` facilities (see Chapter 23 [Non-Local Exits], page 676).

When the handler does a nonlocal control transfer, the part of the program that was running will not continue. If this part of the program was in the middle of updating an important data structure, the data structure will remain inconsistent. Since the program does not terminate, the inconsistency is likely to be noticed later on.

There are two ways to avoid this problem. One is to block the signal for the parts of the program that update important data structures. Blocking the signal delays its delivery until it is unblocked, once the critical updating is finished. See Section 24.7 [Blocking Signals], page 716.

The other way is to re-initialize the crucial data structures in the signal handler, or to make their values consistent.

Here is a rather schematic example showing the reinitialization of one global variable.

```
#include <signal.h>
#include <setjmp.h>

jmp_buf return_to_top_level;

volatile sig_atomic_t waiting_for_input;

void
handle_sigint (int signum)
{
  /* We may have been waiting for input when the signal arrived,
     but we are no longer waiting once we transfer control. */
  waiting_for_input = 0;
  longjmp (return_to_top_level, 1);
}

int
main (void)
{
  ...
  signal (SIGINT, sigint_handler);
  ...
  while (1) {
    prepare_for_command ();
    if (setjmp (return_to_top_level) == 0)
      read_and_execute_command ();
  }
}
```

```
/* Imagine this is a subroutine used by various commands. */
char *
read_data ()
{
  if (input_from_terminal) {
    waiting_for_input = 1;
    ...
    waiting_for_input = 0;
  } else {
    ...
  }
}
```

24.4.4 Signals Arriving While a Handler Runs

What happens if another signal arrives while your signal handler function is running?

When the handler for a particular signal is invoked, that signal is automatically blocked until the handler returns. That means that if two signals of the same kind arrive close together, the second one will be held until the first has been handled. (The handler can explicitly unblock the signal using `sigprocmask`, if you want to allow more signals of this type to arrive; see Section 24.7.3 [Process Signal Mask], page 718.)

However, your handler can still be interrupted by delivery of another kind of signal. To avoid this, you can use the `sa_mask` member of the action structure passed to `sigaction` to explicitly specify which signals should be blocked while the signal handler runs. These signals are in addition to the signal for which the handler was invoked, and any other signals that are normally blocked by the process. See Section 24.7.5 [Blocking Signals for a Handler], page 720.

When the handler returns, the set of blocked signals is restored to the value it had before the handler ran. So using `sigprocmask` inside the handler only affects what signals can arrive during the execution of the handler itself, not what signals can arrive once the handler returns.

Portability Note: Always use `sigaction` to establish a handler for a signal that you expect to receive asynchronously, if you want your program to work properly on System V Unix. On this system, the handling of a signal whose handler was established with `signal` automatically sets the signal's action back to `SIG_DFL`, and the handler must re-establish itself each time it runs. This practice, while inconvenient, does work when signals cannot arrive in succession. However, if another signal can arrive right away, it may arrive before the handler can re-establish itself. Then the second signal would receive the default handling, which could terminate the process.

24.4.5 Signals Close Together Merge into One

If multiple signals of the same type are delivered to your process before your signal handler has a chance to be invoked at all, the handler may only be invoked once, as if only a single signal had arrived. In effect, the signals merge into one. This situation can arise when the signal is blocked, or in a multiprocessing environment where the system is busy running some other processes while the signals are delivered. This means, for example, that you cannot reliably use a signal handler to count signals. The only distinction you can reliably make is whether at least one signal has arrived since a given time in the past.

Here is an example of a handler for `SIGCHLD` that compensates for the fact that the number of signals received may not equal the number of child processes that generate them. It assumes that the program keeps track of all the child processes with a chain of structures as follows:

```
struct process
{
  struct process *next;
  /* The process ID of this child.  */
  int pid;
  /* The descriptor of the pipe or pseudo terminal
     on which output comes from this child.  */
  int input_descriptor;
  /* Nonzero if this process has stopped or terminated.  */
  sig_atomic_t have_status;
  /* The status of this child; 0 if running,
     otherwise a status value from waitpid.  */
  int status;
};
```

```
struct process *process_list;
```

This example also uses a flag to indicate whether signals have arrived since some time in the past—whenever the program last cleared it to zero.

```
/* Nonzero means some childfls status has changed
     so look at process_list for the details.  */
int process_status_change;
```

Here is the handler itself:

```
void
sigchld_handler (int signo)
{
  int old_errno = errno;

  while (1) {
    register int pid;
    int w;
    struct process *p;

    /* Keep asking for a status until we get a definitive result.  */
    do
      {
        errno = 0;
        pid = waitpid (WAIT_ANY, &w, WNOHANG | WUNTRACED);
      }
    while (pid <= 0 && errno == EINTR);

    if (pid <= 0) {
      /* A real failure means there are no more
         stopped or terminated child processes, so return.  */
      errno = old_errno;
      return;
    }

    /* Find the process that signaled us, and record its status.  */

    for (p = process_list; p; p = p->next)
      if (p->pid == pid) {
        p->status = w;
```

```
            /* Indicate that the status field
               has data to look at.  We do this only after storing it.  */
            p->have_status = 1;

            /* If process has terminated, stop waiting for its output.  */
            if (WIFSIGNALED (w) || WIFEXITED (w))
              if (p->input_descriptor)
                FD_CLR (p->input_descriptor, &input_wait_mask);

            /* The program should check this flag from time to time
               to see if there is any news in process_list.  */
            ++process_status_change;
          }

        /* Loop around to handle all the processes
           that have something to tell us.  */
      }
    }
```

Here is the proper way to check the flag `process_status_change`:

```
if (process_status_change) {
  struct process *p;
  process_status_change = 0;
  for (p = process_list; p; p = p->next)
    if (p->have_status) {
      ... Examine p->status ...
    }
}
```

It is vital to clear the flag before examining the list; otherwise, if a signal were delivered just before the clearing of the flag, and after the appropriate element of the process list had been checked, the status change would go unnoticed until the next signal arrived to set the flag again. You could, of course, avoid this problem by blocking the signal while scanning the list, but it is much more elegant to guarantee correctness by doing things in the right order.

The loop which checks process status avoids examining `p->status` until it sees that status has been validly stored. This is to make sure that the status cannot change in the middle of accessing it. Once `p->have_status` is set, it means that the child process is stopped or terminated, and in either case, it cannot stop or terminate again until the program has taken notice. See Section 24.4.7.3 [Atomic Usage Patterns], page 711, for more information about coping with interruptions during accesses of a variable.

Here is another way you can test whether the handler has run since the last time you checked. This technique uses a counter which is never changed outside the handler. Instead of clearing the count, the program remembers the previous value and sees whether it has changed since the previous check. The advantage of this method is that different parts of the program can check independently, each part checking whether there has been a signal since that part last checked.

```
sig_atomic_t process_status_change;

sig_atomic_t last_process_status_change;

...
{
  sig_atomic_t prev = last_process_status_change;
```

```
    last_process_status_change = process_status_change;
    if (last_process_status_change != prev) {
      struct process *p;
      for (p = process_list; p; p = p->next)
        if (p->have_status) {
          ... Examine p->status ...
        }
    }
  }
```

24.4.6 Signal Handling and Nonreentrant Functions

Handler functions usually don't do very much. The best practice is to write a handler that does nothing but set an external variable that the program checks regularly, and leave all serious work to the program. This is best because the handler can be called asynchronously, at unpredictable times—perhaps in the middle of a primitive function, or even between the beginning and the end of a C operator that requires multiple instructions. The data structures being manipulated might therefore be in an inconsistent state when the handler function is invoked. Even copying one `int` variable into another can take two instructions on most machines.

This means you have to be very careful about what you do in a signal handler.

- If your handler needs to access any global variables from your program, declare those variables `volatile`. This tells the compiler that the value of the variable might change asynchronously, and inhibits certain optimizations that would be invalidated by such modifications.

- If you call a function in the handler, make sure it is *reentrant* with respect to signals, or else make sure that the signal cannot interrupt a call to a related function.

A function can be non-reentrant if it uses memory that is not on the stack.

- If a function uses a static variable or a global variable, or a dynamically-allocated object that it finds for itself, then it is non-reentrant and any two calls to the function can interfere.

  For example, suppose that the signal handler uses `gethostbyname`. This function returns its value in a static object, reusing the same object each time. If the signal happens to arrive during a call to `gethostbyname`, or even after one (while the program is still using the value), it will clobber the value that the program asked for.

  However, if the program does not use `gethostbyname` or any other function that returns information in the same object, or if it always blocks signals around each use, then you are safe.

  There are a large number of library functions that return values in a fixed object, always reusing the same object in this fashion, and all of them cause the same problem. Function descriptions in this manual always mention this behavior.

- If a function uses and modifies an object that you supply, then it is potentially non-reentrant; two calls can interfere if they use the same object.

  This case arises when you do I/O using streams. Suppose that the signal handler prints a message with `fprintf`. Suppose that the program was in the middle of an `fprintf` call using the same stream when the signal was delivered. Both the signal handler's message and the program's data could be corrupted, because both calls operate on the same data structure—the stream itself.

However, if you know that the stream that the handler uses cannot possibly be used by the program at a time when signals can arrive, then you are safe. It is no problem if the program uses some other stream.

- On most systems, `malloc` and `free` are not reentrant, because they use a static data structure which records what memory blocks are free. As a result, no library functions that allocate or free memory are reentrant. This includes functions that allocate space to store a result.

  The best way to avoid the need to allocate memory in a handler is to allocate in advance space for signal handlers to use.

  The best way to avoid freeing memory in a handler is to flag or record the objects to be freed, and have the program check from time to time whether anything is waiting to be freed. But this must be done with care, because placing an object on a chain is not atomic, and if it is interrupted by another signal handler that does the same thing, you could "lose" one of the objects.

- Any function that modifies `errno` is non-reentrant, but you can correct for this: in the handler, save the original value of `errno` and restore it before returning normally. This prevents errors that occur within the signal handler from being confused with errors from system calls at the point the program is interrupted to run the handler.

  This technique is generally applicable; if you want to call in a handler a function that modifies a particular object in memory, you can make this safe by saving and restoring that object.

- Merely reading from a memory object is safe provided that you can deal with any of the values that might appear in the object at a time when the signal can be delivered. Keep in mind that assignment to some data types requires more than one instruction, which means that the handler could run "in the middle of" an assignment to the variable if its type is not atomic. See Section 24.4.7 [Atomic Data Access and Signal Handling], page 709.

- Merely writing into a memory object is safe as long as a sudden change in the value, at any time when the handler might run, will not disturb anything.

24.4.7 Atomic Data Access and Signal Handling

Whether the data in your application concerns atoms, or mere text, you have to be careful about the fact that access to a single datum is not necessarily *atomic*. This means that it can take more than one instruction to read or write a single object. In such cases, a signal handler might be invoked in the middle of reading or writing the object.

There are three ways you can cope with this problem. You can use data types that are always accessed atomically; you can carefully arrange that nothing untoward happens if an access is interrupted, or you can block all signals around any access that had better not be interrupted (see Section 24.7 [Blocking Signals], page 716).

24.4.7.1 Problems with Non-Atomic Access

Here is an example which shows what can happen if a signal handler runs in the middle of modifying a variable. (Interrupting the reading of a variable can also lead to paradoxical results, but here we only show writing.)

```
#include <signal.h>
#include <stdio.h>

volatile struct two_words { int a, b; } memory;

void
handler(int signum)
{
    printf ("%d,%d\n", memory.a, memory.b);
    alarm (1);
}

int
main (void)
{
    static struct two_words zeros = { 0, 0 }, ones = { 1, 1 };
    signal (SIGALRM, handler);
    memory = zeros;
    alarm (1);
    while (1)
      {
        memory = zeros;
        memory = ones;
      }
}
```

This program fills **memory** with zeros, ones, zeros, ones, alternating forever; meanwhile, once per second, the alarm signal handler prints the current contents. (Calling `printf` in the handler is safe in this program because it is certainly not being called outside the handler when the signal happens.)

Clearly, this program can print a pair of zeros or a pair of ones. But that's not all it can do! On most machines, it takes several instructions to store a new value in **memory**, and the value is stored one word at a time. If the signal is delivered in between these instructions, the handler might find that **memory.a** is zero and **memory.b** is one (or vice versa).

On some machines it may be possible to store a new value in **memory** with just one instruction that cannot be interrupted. On these machines, the handler will always print two zeros or two ones.

24.4.7.2 Atomic Types

To avoid uncertainty about interrupting access to a variable, you can use a particular data type for which access is always atomic: `sig_atomic_t`. Reading and writing this data type is guaranteed to happen in a single instruction, so there's no way for a handler to run "in the middle" of an access.

The type `sig_atomic_t` is always an integer data type, but which one it is, and how many bits it contains, may vary from machine to machine.

`sig_atomic_t`   [Data Type]
> This is an integer data type. Objects of this type are always accessed atomically.

In practice, you can assume that `int` is atomic. You can also assume that pointer types are atomic; that is very convenient. Both of these assumptions are true on all of the machines that the GNU C Library supports and on all POSIX systems we know of.

24.4.7.3 Atomic Usage Patterns

Certain patterns of access avoid any problem even if an access is interrupted. For example, a flag which is set by the handler, and tested and cleared by the main program from time to time, is always safe even if access actually requires two instructions. To show that this is so, we must consider each access that could be interrupted, and show that there is no problem if it is interrupted.

An interrupt in the middle of testing the flag is safe because either it's recognized to be nonzero, in which case the precise value doesn't matter, or it will be seen to be nonzero the next time it's tested.

An interrupt in the middle of clearing the flag is no problem because either the value ends up zero, which is what happens if a signal comes in just before the flag is cleared, or the value ends up nonzero, and subsequent events occur as if the signal had come in just after the flag was cleared. As long as the code handles both of these cases properly, it can also handle a signal in the middle of clearing the flag. (This is an example of the sort of reasoning you need to do to figure out whether non-atomic usage is safe.)

Sometimes you can ensure uninterrupted access to one object by protecting its use with another object, perhaps one whose type guarantees atomicity. See Section 24.4.5 [Signals Close Together Merge into One], page 705, for an example.

24.5 Primitives Interrupted by Signals

A signal can arrive and be handled while an I/O primitive such as `open` or `read` is waiting for an I/O device. If the signal handler returns, the system faces the question: what should happen next?

POSIX specifies one approach: make the primitive fail right away. The error code for this kind of failure is `EINTR`. This is flexible, but usually inconvenient. Typically, POSIX applications that use signal handlers must check for `EINTR` after each library function that can return it, in order to try the call again. Often programmers forget to check, which is a common source of error.

The GNU C Library provides a convenient way to retry a call after a temporary failure, with the macro `TEMP_FAILURE_RETRY`:

`TEMP_FAILURE_RETRY (expression)`   [Macro]

    This macro evaluates *expression* once, and examines its value as type `long int`. If the value equals −1, that indicates a failure and `errno` should be set to show what kind of failure. If it fails and reports error code `EINTR`, `TEMP_FAILURE_RETRY` evaluates it again, and over and over until the result is not a temporary failure.

    The value returned by `TEMP_FAILURE_RETRY` is whatever value *expression* produced.

BSD avoids `EINTR` entirely and provides a more convenient approach: to restart the interrupted primitive, instead of making it fail. If you choose this approach, you need not be concerned with `EINTR`.

You can choose either approach with the GNU C Library. If you use `sigaction` to establish a signal handler, you can specify how that handler should behave. If you specify the `SA_RESTART` flag, return from that handler will resume a primitive; otherwise, return from that handler will cause `EINTR`. See Section 24.3.5 [Flags for `sigaction`], page 700.

Another way to specify the choice is with the `siginterrupt` function. See Section 24.10 [BSD Signal Handling], page 727.

When you don't specify with `sigaction` or `siginterrupt` what a particular handler should do, it uses a default choice. The default choice in the GNU C Library is to make primitives fail with `EINTR`.

The description of each primitive affected by this issue lists `EINTR` among the error codes it can return.

There is one situation where resumption never happens no matter which choice you make: when a data-transfer function such as `read` or `write` is interrupted by a signal after transferring part of the data. In this case, the function returns the number of bytes already transferred, indicating partial success.

This might at first appear to cause unreliable behavior on record-oriented devices (including datagram sockets; see Section 16.10 [Datagram Socket Operations], page 480), where splitting one `read` or `write` into two would read or write two records. Actually, there is no problem, because interruption after a partial transfer cannot happen on such devices; they always transfer an entire record in one burst, with no waiting once data transfer has started.

24.6 Generating Signals

Besides signals that are generated as a result of a hardware trap or interrupt, your program can explicitly send signals to itself or to another process.

24.6.1 Signaling Yourself

A process can send itself a signal with the `raise` function. This function is declared in `signal.h`.

int raise (*int signum*)   [Function]
> Preliminary: | MT-Safe | AS-Safe | AC-Safe | See Section 1.2.2.1 [POSIX Safety Concepts], page 2.
>
> The `raise` function sends the signal *signum* to the calling process. It returns zero if successful and a nonzero value if it fails. About the only reason for failure would be if the value of *signum* is invalid.

int gsignal (*int signum*)   [Function]
> Preliminary: | MT-Safe | AS-Safe | AC-Safe | See Section 1.2.2.1 [POSIX Safety Concepts], page 2.
>
> The `gsignal` function does the same thing as `raise`; it is provided only for compatibility with SVID.

One convenient use for `raise` is to reproduce the default behavior of a signal that you have trapped. For instance, suppose a user of your program types the SUSP character (usually *C-z*; see Section 17.4.9 [Special Characters], page 503) to send it an interactive stop signal (SIGTSTP), and you want to clean up some internal data buffers before stopping. You might set this up like this:

```
#include <signal.h>

/* When a stop signal arrives, set the action back to the default
   and then resend the signal after doing cleanup actions. */

void
tstp_handler (int sig)
{
  signal (SIGTSTP, SIG_DFL);
  /* Do cleanup actions here. */
  ...
  raise (SIGTSTP);
}

/* When the process is continued again, restore the signal handler. */

void
cont_handler (int sig)
{
  signal (SIGCONT, cont_handler);
  signal (SIGTSTP, tstp_handler);
}

/* Enable both handlers during program initialization. */

int
main (void)
{
  signal (SIGCONT, cont_handler);
  signal (SIGTSTP, tstp_handler);
  ...
}
```

Portability note: raise was invented by the ISO C committee. Older systems may not support it, so using kill may be more portable. See Section 24.6.2 [Signaling Another Process], page 713.

24.6.2 Signaling Another Process

The kill function can be used to send a signal to another process. In spite of its name, it can be used for a lot of things other than causing a process to terminate. Some examples of situations where you might want to send signals between processes are:

- A parent process starts a child to perform a task—perhaps having the child running an infinite loop—and then terminates the child when the task is no longer needed.

- A process executes as part of a group, and needs to terminate or notify the other processes in the group when an error or other event occurs.

- Two processes need to synchronize while working together.

This section assumes that you know a little bit about how processes work. For more information on this subject, see Chapter 26 [Processes], page 773.

The kill function is declared in **signal.h**.

`int kill (pid_t pid, int signum)`   [Function]
> Preliminary: | MT-Safe | AS-Safe | AC-Safe | See Section 1.2.2.1 [POSIX Safety Concepts], page 2.
>
> The `kill` function sends the signal *signum* to the process or process group specified by *pid*. Besides the signals listed in Section 24.2 [Standard Signals], page 687, *signum* can also have a value of zero to check the validity of the *pid*.
>
> The *pid* specifies the process or process group to receive the signal:
>
> *pid* > 0   The process whose identifier is *pid*.
>
> *pid* == 0   All processes in the same process group as the sender.
>
> *pid* < -1   The process group whose identifier is −*pid*.
>
> *pid* == -1 If the process is privileged, send the signal to all processes except for some special system processes. Otherwise, send the signal to all processes with the same effective user ID.
>
> A process can send a signal to itself with a call like `kill (getpid(), signum)`. If `kill` is used by a process to send a signal to itself, and the signal is not blocked, then `kill` delivers at least one signal (which might be some other pending unblocked signal instead of the signal *signum*) to that process before it returns.
>
> The return value from `kill` is zero if the signal can be sent successfully. Otherwise, no signal is sent, and a value of −1 is returned. If *pid* specifies sending a signal to several processes, `kill` succeeds if it can send the signal to at least one of them. There's no way you can tell which of the processes got the signal or whether all of them did.
>
> The following `errno` error conditions are defined for this function:
>
> EINVAL   The *signum* argument is an invalid or unsupported number.
>
> EPERM   You do not have the privilege to send a signal to the process or any of the processes in the process group named by *pid*.
>
> ESRCH   The *pid* argument does not refer to an existing process or group.

`int killpg (int pgid, int signum)`   [Function]
> Preliminary: | MT-Safe | AS-Safe | AC-Safe | See Section 1.2.2.1 [POSIX Safety Concepts], page 2.
>
> This is similar to `kill`, but sends signal *signum* to the process group *pgid*. This function is provided for compatibility with BSD; using `kill` to do this is more portable.

As a simple example of `kill`, the call `kill (getpid (), sig)` has the same effect as `raise (sig)`.

24.6.3 Permission for using `kill`

There are restrictions that prevent you from using `kill` to send signals to any random process. These are intended to prevent antisocial behavior such as arbitrarily killing off processes belonging to another user. In typical use, `kill` is used to pass signals between parent, child, and sibling processes, and in these situations you normally do have permission to send signals. The only common exception is when you run a setuid program in a child process; if the program changes its real UID as well as its effective UID, you may not have permission to send a signal. The **su** program does this.

Whether a process has permission to send a signal to another process is determined by the user IDs of the two processes. This concept is discussed in detail in Section 30.2 [The Persona of a Process], page 815.

Generally, for a process to be able to send a signal to another process, either the sending process must belong to a privileged user (like 'root'), or the real or effective user ID of the sending process must match the real or effective user ID of the receiving process. If the receiving process has changed its effective user ID from the set-user-ID mode bit on its process image file, then the owner of the process image file is used in place of its current effective user ID. In some implementations, a parent process might be able to send signals to a child process even if the user ID's don't match, and other implementations might enforce other restrictions.

The **SIGCONT** signal is a special case. It can be sent if the sender is part of the same session as the receiver, regardless of user IDs.

24.6.4 Using `kill` for Communication

Here is a longer example showing how signals can be used for interprocess communication. This is what the **SIGUSR1** and **SIGUSR2** signals are provided for. Since these signals are fatal by default, the process that is supposed to receive them must trap them through **signal** or **sigaction**.

In this example, a parent process forks a child process and then waits for the child to complete its initialization. The child process tells the parent when it is ready by sending it a **SIGUSR1** signal, using the **kill** function.

```
#include <signal.h>
#include <stdio.h>
#include <sys/types.h>
#include <unistd.h>

/* When a SIGUSR1 signal arrives, set this variable. */
volatile sig_atomic_t usr_interrupt = 0;

void
synch_signal (int sig)
{
  usr_interrupt = 1;
}

/* The child process executes this function. */
void
child_function (void)
{
  /* Perform initialization. */
  printf ("I'm here!!!  My pid is %d.\n", (int) getpid ());

  /* Let parent know youflre done. */
  kill (getppid (), SIGUSR1);

  /* Continue with execution. */
  puts ("Bye, now....");
```

```
      exit (0);
    }

    int
    main (void)
    {
      struct sigaction usr_action;
      sigset_t block_mask;
      pid_t child_id;

      /* Establish the signal handler. */
      sigfillset (&block_mask);
      usr_action.sa_handler = synch_signal;
      usr_action.sa_mask = block_mask;
      usr_action.sa_flags = 0;
      sigaction (SIGUSR1, &usr_action, NULL);

      /* Create the child process. */
      child_id = fork ();
      if (child_id == 0)
        child_function ();              /* Does not return. */

      /* Busy wait for the child to send a signal. */
      while (!usr_interrupt)
        ;

      /* Now continue execution. */
      puts ("That's all, folks!");

      return 0;
    }
```

This example uses a busy wait, which is bad, because it wastes CPU cycles that other programs could otherwise use. It is better to ask the system to wait until the signal arrives. See the example in Section 24.8 [Waiting for a Signal], page 723.

24.7 Blocking Signals

Blocking a signal means telling the operating system to hold it and deliver it later. Generally, a program does not block signals indefinitely—it might as well ignore them by setting their actions to SIG_IGN. But it is useful to block signals briefly, to prevent them from interrupting sensitive operations. For instance:

- You can use the sigprocmask function to block signals while you modify global variables that are also modified by the handlers for these signals.

- You can set sa_mask in your sigaction call to block certain signals while a particular signal handler runs. This way, the signal handler can run without being interrupted itself by signals.

24.7.1 Why Blocking Signals is Useful

Temporary blocking of signals with sigprocmask gives you a way to prevent interrupts during critical parts of your code. If signals arrive in that part of the program, they are delivered later, after you unblock them.

One example where this is useful is for sharing data between a signal handler and the rest of the program. If the type of the data is not sig_atomic_t (see Section 24.4.7 [Atomic

Data Access and Signal Handling], page 709), then the signal handler could run when the rest of the program has only half finished reading or writing the data. This would lead to confusing consequences.

To make the program reliable, you can prevent the signal handler from running while the rest of the program is examining or modifying that data—by blocking the appropriate signal around the parts of the program that touch the data.

Blocking signals is also necessary when you want to perform a certain action only if a signal has not arrived. Suppose that the handler for the signal sets a flag of type `sig_atomic_t`; you would like to test the flag and perform the action if the flag is not set. This is unreliable. Suppose the signal is delivered immediately after you test the flag, but before the consequent action: then the program will perform the action even though the signal has arrived.

The only way to test reliably for whether a signal has yet arrived is to test while the signal is blocked.

24.7.2 Signal Sets

All of the signal blocking functions use a data structure called a *signal set* to specify what signals are affected. Thus, every activity involves two stages: creating the signal set, and then passing it as an argument to a library function.

These facilities are declared in the header file `signal.h`.

`sigset_t` [Data Type]

> The `sigset_t` data type is used to represent a signal set. Internally, it may be implemented as either an integer or structure type.
>
> For portability, use only the functions described in this section to initialize, change, and retrieve information from `sigset_t` objects—don't try to manipulate them directly.

There are two ways to initialize a signal set. You can initially specify it to be empty with `sigemptyset` and then add specified signals individually. Or you can specify it to be full with `sigfillset` and then delete specified signals individually.

You must always initialize the signal set with one of these two functions before using it in any other way. Don't try to set all the signals explicitly because the `sigset_t` object might include some other information (like a version field) that needs to be initialized as well. (In addition, it's not wise to put into your program an assumption that the system has no signals aside from the ones you know about.)

`int sigemptyset (sigset_t *set)` [Function]

> Preliminary: | MT-Safe | AS-Safe | AC-Safe | See Section 1.2.2.1 [POSIX Safety Concepts], page 2.
>
> This function initializes the signal set *set* to exclude all of the defined signals. It always returns 0.

`int sigfillset (sigset_t *set)` [Function]

> Preliminary: | MT-Safe | AS-Safe | AC-Safe | See Section 1.2.2.1 [POSIX Safety Concepts], page 2.

This function initializes the signal set *set* to include all of the defined signals. Again, the return value is 0.

int sigaddset (*sigset_t *set, int signum*)   [Function]
Preliminary: | MT-Safe | AS-Safe | AC-Safe | See Section 1.2.2.1 [POSIX Safety Concepts], page 2.

This function adds the signal *signum* to the signal set *set*. All `sigaddset` does is modify *set*; it does not block or unblock any signals.

The return value is 0 on success and -1 on failure. The following `errno` error condition is defined for this function:

EINVAL   The *signum* argument doesn't specify a valid signal.

int sigdelset (*sigset_t *set, int signum*)   [Function]
Preliminary: | MT-Safe | AS-Safe | AC-Safe | See Section 1.2.2.1 [POSIX Safety Concepts], page 2.

This function removes the signal *signum* from the signal set *set*. All `sigdelset` does is modify *set*; it does not block or unblock any signals. The return value and error conditions are the same as for `sigaddset`.

Finally, there is a function to test what signals are in a signal set:

int sigismember (*const sigset_t *set, int signum*)   [Function]
Preliminary: | MT-Safe | AS-Safe | AC-Safe | See Section 1.2.2.1 [POSIX Safety Concepts], page 2.

The `sigismember` function tests whether the signal *signum* is a member of the signal set *set*. It returns 1 if the signal is in the set, 0 if not, and -1 if there is an error.

The following `errno` error condition is defined for this function:

EINVAL   The *signum* argument doesn't specify a valid signal.

24.7.3 Process Signal Mask

The collection of signals that are currently blocked is called the *signal mask*. Each process has its own signal mask. When you create a new process (see Section 26.4 [Creating a Process], page 775), it inherits its parent's mask. You can block or unblock signals with total flexibility by modifying the signal mask.

The prototype for the `sigprocmask` function is in `signal.h`.

Note that you must not use `sigprocmask` in multi-threaded processes, because each thread has its own signal mask and there is no single process signal mask. According to POSIX, the behavior of `sigprocmask` in a multi-threaded process is "unspecified". Instead, use `pthread_sigmask`.

int sigprocmask (*int how, const sigset_t *restrict set, sigset_t*   [Function]
        **restrict oldset*)
Preliminary: | MT-Unsafe race:sigprocmask/bsd(SIG_UNBLOCK) | AS-Unsafe lock/hurd | AC-Unsafe lock/hurd | See Section 1.2.2.1 [POSIX Safety Concepts], page 2.

The `sigprocmask` function is used to examine or change the calling process's signal mask. The *how* argument determines how the signal mask is changed, and must be one of the following values:

`SIG_BLOCK`

> Block the signals in `set`—add them to the existing mask. In other words, the new mask is the union of the existing mask and *set*.

`SIG_UNBLOCK`

> Unblock the signals in *set*—remove them from the existing mask.

`SIG_SETMASK`

> Use *set* for the mask; ignore the previous value of the mask.

The last argument, *oldset*, is used to return information about the old process signal mask. If you just want to change the mask without looking at it, pass a null pointer as the *oldset* argument. Similarly, if you want to know what's in the mask without changing it, pass a null pointer for *set* (in this case the *how* argument is not significant). The *oldset* argument is often used to remember the previous signal mask in order to restore it later. (Since the signal mask is inherited over **fork** and **exec** calls, you can't predict what its contents are when your program starts running.)

If invoking `sigprocmask` causes any pending signals to be unblocked, at least one of those signals is delivered to the process before `sigprocmask` returns. The order in which pending signals are delivered is not specified, but you can control the order explicitly by making multiple `sigprocmask` calls to unblock various signals one at a time.

The `sigprocmask` function returns 0 if successful, and -1 to indicate an error. The following **errno** error conditions are defined for this function:

`EINVAL`   The *how* argument is invalid.

You can't block the `SIGKILL` and `SIGSTOP` signals, but if the signal set includes these, `sigprocmask` just ignores them instead of returning an error status.

Remember, too, that blocking program error signals such as `SIGFPE` leads to undesirable results for signals generated by an actual program error (as opposed to signals sent with **raise** or **kill**). This is because your program may be too broken to be able to continue executing to a point where the signal is unblocked again. See Section 24.2.1 [Program Error Signals], page 687.

24.7.4 Blocking to Test for Delivery of a Signal

Now for a simple example. Suppose you establish a handler for `SIGALRM` signals that sets a flag whenever a signal arrives, and your main program checks this flag from time to time and then resets it. You can prevent additional `SIGALRM` signals from arriving in the meantime by wrapping the critical part of the code with calls to `sigprocmask`, like this:

```
/* This variable is set by the SIGALRM signal handler. */
volatile sig_atomic_t flag = 0;

int
main (void)
{
```

```
sigset_t block_alarm;

. . .

/* Initialize the signal mask. */
sigemptyset (&block_alarm);
sigaddset (&block_alarm, SIGALRM);

while (1)
  {
    /* Check if a signal has arrived; if so, reset the flag. */
    sigprocmask (SIG_BLOCK, &block_alarm, NULL);
    if (flag)
      {
        actions-if-not-arrived
        flag = 0;
      }
    sigprocmask (SIG_UNBLOCK, &block_alarm, NULL);

    . . .
  }
}
```

24.7.5 Blocking Signals for a Handler

When a signal handler is invoked, you usually want it to be able to finish without being interrupted by another signal. From the moment the handler starts until the moment it finishes, you must block signals that might confuse it or corrupt its data.

When a handler function is invoked on a signal, that signal is automatically blocked (in addition to any other signals that are already in the process's signal mask) during the time the handler is running. If you set up a handler for SIGTSTP, for instance, then the arrival of that signal forces further SIGTSTP signals to wait during the execution of the handler.

However, by default, other kinds of signals are not blocked; they can arrive during handler execution.

The reliable way to block other kinds of signals during the execution of the handler is to use the **sa_mask** member of the **sigaction** structure.

Here is an example:

```
#include <signal.h>
#include <stddef.h>

void catch_stop ();

void
install_handler (void)
{
  struct sigaction setup_action;
  sigset_t block_mask;

  sigemptyset (&block_mask);
  /* Block other terminal-generated signals while handler runs. */
  sigaddset (&block_mask, SIGINT);
  sigaddset (&block_mask, SIGQUIT);
  setup_action.sa_handler = catch_stop;
  setup_action.sa_mask = block_mask;
```

```
        setup_action.sa_flags = 0;
        sigaction (SIGTSTP, &setup_action, NULL);
}
```

This is more reliable than blocking the other signals explicitly in the code for the handler. If you block signals explicitly in the handler, you can't avoid at least a short interval at the beginning of the handler where they are not yet blocked.

You cannot remove signals from the process's current mask using this mechanism. However, you can make calls to `sigprocmask` within your handler to block or unblock signals as you wish.

In any case, when the handler returns, the system restores the mask that was in place before the handler was entered. If any signals that become unblocked by this restoration are pending, the process will receive those signals immediately, before returning to the code that was interrupted.

24.7.6 Checking for Pending Signals

You can find out which signals are pending at any time by calling `sigpending`. This function is declared in `signal.h`.

int sigpending (*sigset_t *set*)   [Function]
> Preliminary: | MT-Safe | AS-Unsafe lock/hurd | AC-Unsafe lock/hurd | See Section 1.2.2.1 [POSIX Safety Concepts], page 2.
>
> The `sigpending` function stores information about pending signals in *set*. If there is a pending signal that is blocked from delivery, then that signal is a member of the returned set. (You can test whether a particular signal is a member of this set using `sigismember`; see Section 24.7.2 [Signal Sets], page 717.)
>
> The return value is 0 if successful, and -1 on failure.

Testing whether a signal is pending is not often useful. Testing when that signal is not blocked is almost certainly bad design.

Here is an example.

```
#include <signal.h>
#include <stddef.h>

sigset_t base_mask, waiting_mask;

sigemptyset (&base_mask);
sigaddset (&base_mask, SIGINT);
sigaddset (&base_mask, SIGTSTP);

/* Block user interrupts while doing other processing. */
sigprocmask (SIG_SETMASK, &base_mask, NULL);
...

/* After a while, check to see whether any signals are pending. */
sigpending (&waiting_mask);
if (sigismember (&waiting_mask, SIGINT)) {
  /* User has tried to kill the process. */
}
else if (sigismember (&waiting_mask, SIGTSTP)) {
  /* User has tried to stop the process. */
```

```
}
```

Remember that if there is a particular signal pending for your process, additional signals of that same type that arrive in the meantime might be discarded. For example, if a `SIGINT` signal is pending when another `SIGINT` signal arrives, your program will probably only see one of them when you unblock this signal.

Portability Note: The `sigpending` function is new in POSIX.1. Older systems have no equivalent facility.

24.7.7 Remembering a Signal to Act On Later

Instead of blocking a signal using the library facilities, you can get almost the same results by making the handler set a flag to be tested later, when you "unblock". Here is an example:

```
/* If this flag is nonzero, donflt handle the signal right away. */
volatile sig_atomic_t signal_pending;

/* This is nonzero if a signal arrived and was not handled. */
volatile sig_atomic_t defer_signal;

void
handler (int signum)
{
  if (defer_signal)
    signal_pending = signum;
  else
    ... /* ``Reallyflfl handle the signal. */
}


...

void
update_mumble (int frob)
{
  /* Prevent signals from having immediate effect. */
  defer_signal++;
  /* Now update mumble, without worrying about interruption. */
  mumble.a = 1;
  mumble.b = hack ();
  mumble.c = frob;
  /* We have updated mumble.  Handle any signal that came in. */
  defer_signal--;
  if (defer_signal == 0 && signal_pending != 0)
    raise (signal_pending);
}
```

Note how the particular signal that arrives is stored in `signal_pending`. That way, we can handle several types of inconvenient signals with the same mechanism.

We increment and decrement `defer_signal` so that nested critical sections will work properly; thus, if `update_mumble` were called with `signal_pending` already nonzero, signals would be deferred not only within `update_mumble`, but also within the caller. This is also why we do not check `signal_pending` if `defer_signal` is still nonzero.

The incrementing and decrementing of `defer_signal` each require more than one instruction; it is possible for a signal to happen in the middle. But that does not cause any problem. If the signal happens early enough to see the value from before the increment or decrement, that is equivalent to a signal which came before the beginning of the increment or decrement, which is a case that works properly.

It is absolutely vital to decrement `defer_signal` before testing `signal_pending`, because this avoids a subtle bug. If we did these things in the other order, like this,

```
if (defer_signal == 1 && signal_pending != 0)
  raise (signal_pending);
defer_signal--;
```

then a signal arriving in between the `if` statement and the decrement would be effectively "lost" for an indefinite amount of time. The handler would merely set `defer_signal`, but the program having already tested this variable, it would not test the variable again.

Bugs like these are called *timing errors*. They are especially bad because they happen only rarely and are nearly impossible to reproduce. You can't expect to find them with a debugger as you would find a reproducible bug. So it is worth being especially careful to avoid them.

(You would not be tempted to write the code in this order, given the use of `defer_signal` as a counter which must be tested along with `signal_pending`. After all, testing for zero is cleaner than testing for one. But if you did not use `defer_signal` as a counter, and gave it values of zero and one only, then either order might seem equally simple. This is a further advantage of using a counter for `defer_signal`: it will reduce the chance you will write the code in the wrong order and create a subtle bug.)

24.8 Waiting for a Signal

If your program is driven by external events, or uses signals for synchronization, then when it has nothing to do it should probably wait until a signal arrives.

24.8.1 Using pause

The simple way to wait until a signal arrives is to call **pause**. Please read about its disadvantages, in the following section, before you use it.

`int pause (void)` [Function]

Preliminary: | MT-Unsafe race:sigprocmask/!bsd!linux | AS-Unsafe lock/hurd | AC-Unsafe lock/hurd | See Section 1.2.2.1 [POSIX Safety Concepts], page 2.

The **pause** function suspends program execution until a signal arrives whose action is either to execute a handler function, or to terminate the process.

If the signal causes a handler function to be executed, then **pause** returns. This is considered an unsuccessful return (since "successful" behavior would be to suspend the program forever), so the return value is -1. Even if you specify that other primitives should resume when a system handler returns (see Section 24.5 [Primitives Interrupted by Signals], page 711), this has no effect on **pause**; it always fails when a signal is handled.

The following **errno** error conditions are defined for this function:

EINTR   The function was interrupted by delivery of a signal.

If the signal causes program termination, **pause** doesn't return (obviously).

This function is a cancellation point in multithreaded programs. This is a problem if the thread allocates some resources (like memory, file descriptors, semaphores or whatever) at the time `pause` is called. If the thread gets cancelled these resources stay allocated until the program ends. To avoid this calls to `pause` should be protected using cancellation handlers.

The `pause` function is declared in `unistd.h`.

24.8.2 Problems with `pause`

The simplicity of `pause` can conceal serious timing errors that can make a program hang mysteriously.

It is safe to use `pause` if the real work of your program is done by the signal handlers themselves, and the "main program" does nothing but call `pause`. Each time a signal is delivered, the handler will do the next batch of work that is to be done, and then return, so that the main loop of the program can call `pause` again.

You can't safely use `pause` to wait until one more signal arrives, and then resume real work. Even if you arrange for the signal handler to cooperate by setting a flag, you still can't use `pause` reliably. Here is an example of this problem:

```
/* usr_interrupt is set by the signal handler.  */
if (!usr_interrupt)
  pause ();

/* Do work once the signal arrives.  */
...
```

This has a bug: the signal could arrive after the variable `usr_interrupt` is checked, but before the call to `pause`. If no further signals arrive, the process would never wake up again.

You can put an upper limit on the excess waiting by using `sleep` in a loop, instead of using `pause`. (See Section 21.6 [Sleeping], page 652, for more about `sleep`.) Here is what this looks like:

```
/* usr_interrupt is set by the signal handler.
while (!usr_interrupt)
  sleep (1);

/* Do work once the signal arrives.  */
...
```

For some purposes, that is good enough. But with a little more complexity, you can wait reliably until a particular signal handler is run, using `sigsuspend`.

24.8.3 Using `sigsuspend`

The clean and reliable way to wait for a signal to arrive is to block it and then use `sigsuspend`. By using `sigsuspend` in a loop, you can wait for certain kinds of signals, while letting other kinds of signals be handled by their handlers.

`int sigsuspend (const sigset_t *set)`   [Function]

> Preliminary: | MT-Unsafe race:sigprocmask/!bsd!linux | AS-Unsafe lock/hurd | AC-Unsafe lock/hurd | See Section 1.2.2.1 [POSIX Safety Concepts], page 2.
>
> This function replaces the process's signal mask with *set* and then suspends the process until a signal is delivered whose action is either to terminate the process or invoke a signal handling function. In other words, the program is effectively suspended until one of the signals that is not a member of *set* arrives.

If the process is woken up by delivery of a signal that invokes a handler function, and the handler function returns, then `sigsuspend` also returns.

The mask remains *set* only as long as `sigsuspend` is waiting. The function `sigsuspend` always restores the previous signal mask when it returns.

The return value and error conditions are the same as for `pause`.

With `sigsuspend`, you can replace the `pause` or `sleep` loop in the previous section with something completely reliable:

```
sigset_t mask, oldmask;

...

/* Set up the mask of signals to temporarily block. */
sigemptyset (&mask);
sigaddset (&mask, SIGUSR1);

...

/* Wait for a signal to arrive. */
sigprocmask (SIG_BLOCK, &mask, &oldmask);
while (!usr_interrupt)
  sigsuspend (&oldmask);
sigprocmask (SIG_UNBLOCK, &mask, NULL);
```

This last piece of code is a little tricky. The key point to remember here is that when `sigsuspend` returns, it resets the process's signal mask to the original value, the value from before the call to `sigsuspend`—in this case, the `SIGUSR1` signal is once again blocked. The second call to `sigprocmask` is necessary to explicitly unblock this signal.

One other point: you may be wondering why the `while` loop is necessary at all, since the program is apparently only waiting for one `SIGUSR1` signal. The answer is that the mask passed to `sigsuspend` permits the process to be woken up by the delivery of other kinds of signals, as well—for example, job control signals. If the process is woken up by a signal that doesn't set `usr_interrupt`, it just suspends itself again until the "right" kind of signal eventually arrives.

This technique takes a few more lines of preparation, but that is needed just once for each kind of wait criterion you want to use. The code that actually waits is just four lines.

24.9 Using a Separate Signal Stack

A signal stack is a special area of memory to be used as the execution stack during signal handlers. It should be fairly large, to avoid any danger that it will overflow in turn; the macro `SIGSTKSZ` is defined to a canonical size for signal stacks. You can use `malloc` to allocate the space for the stack. Then call `sigaltstack` or `sigstack` to tell the system to use that space for the signal stack.

You don't need to write signal handlers differently in order to use a signal stack. Switching from one stack to the other happens automatically. (Some non-GNU debuggers on some machines may get confused if you examine a stack trace while a handler that uses the signal stack is running.)

There are two interfaces for telling the system to use a separate signal stack. `sigstack` is the older interface, which comes from 4.2 BSD. `sigaltstack` is the newer interface, and comes from 4.4 BSD. The `sigaltstack` interface has the advantage that it does not require your program to know which direction the stack grows, which depends on the specific machine and operating system.

`stack_t`   [Data Type]

> This structure describes a signal stack. It contains the following members:

> `void *ss_sp`
>> This points to the base of the signal stack.

> `size_t ss_size`
>> This is the size (in bytes) of the signal stack which '`ss_sp`' points to. You should set this to however much space you allocated for the stack.

>> There are two macros defined in `signal.h` that you should use in calculating this size:

>> SIGSTKSZ   This is the canonical size for a signal stack. It is judged to be sufficient for normal uses.

>> MINSIGSTKSZ

>>> This is the amount of signal stack space the operating system needs just to implement signal delivery. The size of a signal stack **must** be greater than this.

>>> For most cases, just using SIGSTKSZ for `ss_size` is sufficient. But if you know how much stack space your program's signal handlers will need, you may want to use a different size. In this case, you should allocate MINSIGSTKSZ additional bytes for the signal stack and increase `ss_size` accordingly.

> `int ss_flags`
>> This field contains the bitwise OR of these flags:

>> SS_DISABLE

>>> This tells the system that it should not use the signal stack.

>> SS_ONSTACK

>>> This is set by the system, and indicates that the signal stack is currently in use. If this bit is not set, then signals will be delivered on the normal user stack.

`int sigaltstack (const stack_t *restrict stack, stack_t *restrict`   [Function]
    `oldstack)`

> Preliminary: | MT-Safe | AS-Unsafe lock/hurd | AC-Unsafe lock/hurd | See Section 1.2.2.1 [POSIX Safety Concepts], page 2.

> The `sigaltstack` function specifies an alternate stack for use during signal handling. When a signal is received by the process and its action indicates that the signal stack is used, the system arranges a switch to the currently installed signal stack while the handler for that signal is executed.

> If *oldstack* is not a null pointer, information about the currently installed signal stack is returned in the location it points to. If *stack* is not a null pointer, then this is installed as the new stack for use by signal handlers.

The return value is 0 on success and -1 on failure. If `sigaltstack` fails, it sets `errno` to one of these values:

EINVAL   You tried to disable a stack that was in fact currently in use.

ENOMEM   The size of the alternate stack was too small. It must be greater than `MINSIGSTKSZ`.

Here is the older `sigstack` interface. You should use `sigaltstack` instead on systems that have it.

`struct sigstack`   [Data Type]

This structure describes a signal stack. It contains the following members:

`void *ss_sp`
> This is the stack pointer. If the stack grows downwards on your machine, this should point to the top of the area you allocated. If the stack grows upwards, it should point to the bottom.

`int ss_onstack`
> This field is true if the process is currently using this stack.

`int sigstack (struct sigstack *stack, struct sigstack *oldstack)`   [Function]
Preliminary: | MT-Safe | AS-Unsafe lock/hurd | AC-Unsafe lock/hurd | See Section 1.2.2.1 [POSIX Safety Concepts], page 2.

The `sigstack` function specifies an alternate stack for use during signal handling. When a signal is received by the process and its action indicates that the signal stack is used, the system arranges a switch to the currently installed signal stack while the handler for that signal is executed.

If *oldstack* is not a null pointer, information about the currently installed signal stack is returned in the location it points to. If *stack* is not a null pointer, then this is installed as the new stack for use by signal handlers.

The return value is 0 on success and -1 on failure.

24.10 BSD Signal Handling

This section describes alternative signal handling functions derived from BSD Unix. These facilities were an advance, in their time; today, they are mostly obsolete, and supported mainly for compatibility with BSD Unix.

There are many similarities between the BSD and POSIX signal handling facilities, because the POSIX facilities were inspired by the BSD facilities. Besides having different names for all the functions to avoid conflicts, the main difference between the two is that BSD Unix represents signal masks as an `int` bit mask, rather than as a `sigset_t` object.

The BSD facilities are declared in `signal.h`.

`int siginterrupt (int signum, int failflag)`   [Function]
Preliminary: | MT-Unsafe const:sigintr | AS-Unsafe | AC-Unsafe corrupt | See Section 1.2.2.1 [POSIX Safety Concepts], page 2.

This function specifies which approach to use when certain primitives are interrupted by handling signal *signum*. If *failflag* is false, signal *signum* restarts primitives. If *failflag* is true, handling *signum* causes these primitives to fail with error code `EINTR`. See Section 24.5 [Primitives Interrupted by Signals], page 711.

int sigmask (*int signum*)   [Macro]
> Preliminary: | MT-Safe | AS-Safe | AC-Safe | See Section 1.2.2.1 [POSIX Safety Concepts], page 2.
>
> This macro returns a signal mask that has the bit for signal *signum* set. You can bitwise-OR the results of several calls to `sigmask` together to specify more than one signal. For example,
>
> ```
> (sigmask (SIGTSTP) | sigmask (SIGSTOP)
>   | sigmask (SIGTTIN) | sigmask (SIGTTOU))
> ```
>
> specifies a mask that includes all the job-control stop signals.

int sigblock (*int mask*)   [Function]
> Preliminary: | MT-Safe | AS-Unsafe lock/hurd | AC-Unsafe lock/hurd | See Section 1.2.2.1 [POSIX Safety Concepts], page 2.
>
> This function is equivalent to `sigprocmask` (see Section 24.7.3 [Process Signal Mask], page 718) with a *how* argument of `SIG_BLOCK`: it adds the signals specified by *mask* to the calling process's set of blocked signals. The return value is the previous set of blocked signals.

int sigsetmask (*int mask*)   [Function]
> Preliminary: | MT-Safe | AS-Unsafe lock/hurd | AC-Unsafe lock/hurd | See Section 1.2.2.1 [POSIX Safety Concepts], page 2.
>
> This function is equivalent to `sigprocmask` (see Section 24.7.3 [Process Signal Mask], page 718) with a *how* argument of `SIG_SETMASK`: it sets the calling process's signal mask to *mask*. The return value is the previous set of blocked signals.

int sigpause (*int mask*)   [Function]
> Preliminary: | MT-Unsafe race:sigprocmask/!bsd!linux | AS-Unsafe lock/hurd | AC-Unsafe lock/hurd | See Section 1.2.2.1 [POSIX Safety Concepts], page 2.
>
> This function is the equivalent of `sigsuspend` (see Section 24.8 [Waiting for a Signal], page 723): it sets the calling process's signal mask to *mask*, and waits for a signal to arrive. On return the previous set of blocked signals is restored.

25 The Basic Program/System Interface

Processes are the primitive units for allocation of system resources. Each process has its own address space and (usually) one thread of control. A process executes a program; you can have multiple processes executing the same program, but each process has its own copy of the program within its own address space and executes it independently of the other copies. Though it may have multiple threads of control within the same program and a program may be composed of multiple logically separate modules, a process always executes exactly one program.

Note that we are using a specific definition of "program" for the purposes of this manual, which corresponds to a common definition in the context of Unix systems. In popular usage, "program" enjoys a much broader definition; it can refer for example to a system's kernel, an editor macro, a complex package of software, or a discrete section of code executing within a process.

Writing the program is what this manual is all about. This chapter explains the most basic interface between your program and the system that runs, or calls, it. This includes passing of parameters (arguments and environment) from the system, requesting basic services from the system, and telling the system the program is done.

A program starts another program with the **exec** family of system calls. This chapter looks at program startup from the execee's point of view. To see the event from the execor's point of view, see Section 26.5 [Executing a File], page 776.

25.1 Program Arguments

The system starts a C program by calling the function **main**. It is up to you to write a function named **main**—otherwise, you won't even be able to link your program without errors.

In ISO C you can define **main** either to take no arguments, or to take two arguments that represent the command line arguments to the program, like this:

```
int main (int argc, char *argv[])
```

The command line arguments are the whitespace-separated tokens given in the shell command used to invoke the program; thus, in 'cat foo bar', the arguments are 'foo' and 'bar'. The only way a program can look at its command line arguments is via the arguments of **main**. If **main** doesn't take arguments, then you cannot get at the command line.

The value of the *argc* argument is the number of command line arguments. The *argv* argument is a vector of C strings; its elements are the individual command line argument strings. The file name of the program being run is also included in the vector as the first element; the value of *argc* counts this element. A null pointer always follows the last element: *argv*[*argc*] is this null pointer.

For the command 'cat foo bar', *argc* is 3 and *argv* has three elements, "cat", "foo" and "bar".

In Unix systems you can define **main** a third way, using three arguments:

```
int main (int argc, char *argv[], char *envp[])
```

The first two arguments are just the same. The third argument *envp* gives the program's environment; it is the same as the value of **environ**. See Section 25.4 [Environment Variables], page 762. POSIX.1 does not allow this three-argument form, so to be portable it is best to write `main` to take two arguments, and use the value of `environ`.

25.1.1 Program Argument Syntax Conventions

POSIX recommends these conventions for command line arguments. `getopt` (see Section 25.2 [Parsing program options using `getopt`], page 731) and `argp_parse` (see Section 25.3 [Parsing Program Options with Argp], page 738) make it easy to implement them.

- Arguments are options if they begin with a hyphen delimiter ('-').

- Multiple options may follow a hyphen delimiter in a single token if the options do not take arguments. Thus, '-abc' is equivalent to '-a -b -c'.

- Option names are single alphanumeric characters (as for `isalnum`; see Section 4.1 [Classification of Characters], page 81).

- Certain options require an argument. For example, the '-o' command of the `ld` command requires an argument—an output file name.

- An option and its argument may or may not appear as separate tokens. (In other words, the whitespace separating them is optional.) Thus, '-o foo' and '-ofoo' are equivalent.

- Options typically precede other non-option arguments.

  The implementations of `getopt` and `argp_parse` in the GNU C Library normally make it appear as if all the option arguments were specified before all the non-option arguments for the purposes of parsing, even if the user of your program intermixed option and non-option arguments. They do this by reordering the elements of the *argv* array. This behavior is nonstandard; if you want to suppress it, define the `_POSIX_OPTION_ORDER` environment variable. See Section 25.4.2 [Standard Environment Variables], page 765.

- The argument '--' terminates all options; any following arguments are treated as non-option arguments, even if they begin with a hyphen.

- A token consisting of a single hyphen character is interpreted as an ordinary non-option argument. By convention, it is used to specify input from or output to the standard input and output streams.

- Options may be supplied in any order, or appear multiple times. The interpretation is left up to the particular application program.

GNU adds *long options* to these conventions. Long options consist of '--' followed by a name made of alphanumeric characters and dashes. Option names are typically one to three words long, with hyphens to separate words. Users can abbreviate the option names as long as the abbreviations are unique.

To specify an argument for a long option, write '--*name*=*value*'. This syntax enables a long option to accept an argument that is itself optional.

Eventually, GNU systems will provide completion for long option names in the shell.

25.1.2 Parsing Program Arguments

If the syntax for the command line arguments to your program is simple enough, you can simply pick the arguments off from *argv* by hand. But unless your program takes a fixed number of arguments, or all of the arguments are interpreted in the same way (as file names, for example), you are usually better off using `getopt` (see Section 25.2 [Parsing program options using `getopt`], page 731) or `argp_parse` (see Section 25.3 [Parsing Program Options with Argp], page 738) to do the parsing.

`getopt` is more standard (the short-option only version of it is a part of the POSIX standard), but using `argp_parse` is often easier, both for very simple and very complex option structures, because it does more of the dirty work for you.

25.2 Parsing program options using getopt

The `getopt` and `getopt_long` functions automate some of the chore involved in parsing typical unix command line options.

25.2.1 Using the getopt function

Here are the details about how to call the `getopt` function. To use this facility, your program must include the header file `unistd.h`.

`int opterr`   [Variable]

If the value of this variable is nonzero, then `getopt` prints an error message to the standard error stream if it encounters an unknown option character or an option with a missing required argument. This is the default behavior. If you set this variable to zero, `getopt` does not print any messages, but it still returns the character ? to indicate an error.

`int optopt`   [Variable]

When `getopt` encounters an unknown option character or an option with a missing required argument, it stores that option character in this variable. You can use this for providing your own diagnostic messages.

`int optind`   [Variable]

This variable is set by `getopt` to the index of the next element of the *argv* array to be processed. Once `getopt` has found all of the option arguments, you can use this variable to determine where the remaining non-option arguments begin. The initial value of this variable is 1.

`char * optarg`   [Variable]

This variable is set by `getopt` to point at the value of the option argument, for those options that accept arguments.

`int getopt (int argc, char *const *argv, const char *options)`   [Function]

Preliminary: | MT-Unsafe race:getopt env | AS-Unsafe heap i18n lock corrupt | AC-Unsafe mem lock corrupt | See Section 1.2.2.1 [POSIX Safety Concepts], page 2.

The `getopt` function gets the next option argument from the argument list specified by the *argv* and *argc* arguments. Normally these values come directly from the arguments received by `main`.

The *options* argument is a string that specifies the option characters that are valid for this program. An option character in this string can be followed by a colon (':')

to indicate that it takes a required argument. If an option character is followed by two colons (':::'), its argument is optional; this is a GNU extension.

getopt has three ways to deal with options that follow non-options *argv* elements. The special argument '--' forces in all cases the end of option scanning.

- The default is to permute the contents of *argv* while scanning it so that eventually all the non-options are at the end. This allows options to be given in any order, even with programs that were not written to expect this.

- If the *options* argument string begins with a hyphen ('-'), this is treated specially. It permits arguments that are not options to be returned as if they were associated with option character '\1'.

- POSIX demands the following behavior: the first non-option stops option processing. This mode is selected by either setting the environment variable **POSIXLY_CORRECT** or beginning the *options* argument string with a plus sign ('+').

The **getopt** function returns the option character for the next command line option. When no more option arguments are available, it returns -1. There may still be more non-option arguments; you must compare the external variable **optind** against the *argc* parameter to check this.

If the option has an argument, **getopt** returns the argument by storing it in the variable *optarg*. You don't ordinarily need to copy the **optarg** string, since it is a pointer into the original *argv* array, not into a static area that might be overwritten.

If **getopt** finds an option character in *argv* that was not included in *options*, or a missing option argument, it returns '?' and sets the external variable **optopt** to the actual option character. If the first character of *options* is a colon (':'), then **getopt** returns ':' instead of '?' to indicate a missing option argument. In addition, if the external variable **opterr** is nonzero (which is the default), **getopt** prints an error message.

25.2.2 Example of Parsing Arguments with getopt

Here is an example showing how **getopt** is typically used. The key points to notice are:

- Normally, **getopt** is called in a loop. When **getopt** returns -1, indicating no more options are present, the loop terminates.

- A **switch** statement is used to dispatch on the return value from **getopt**. In typical use, each case just sets a variable that is used later in the program.

- A second loop is used to process the remaining non-option arguments.

```c
#include <ctype.h>
#include <stdio.h>
#include <stdlib.h>
#include <unistd.h>

int
main (int argc, char **argv)
{
  int aflag = 0;
  int bflag = 0;
  char *cvalue = NULL;
  int index;
  int c;

  opterr = 0;

  while ((c = getopt (argc, argv, "abc:")) != -1)
    switch (c)
      {
      case 'a':
        aflag = 1;
        break;
      case 'b':
        bflag = 1;
        break;
      case 'c':
        cvalue = optarg;
        break;
      case '?':
        if (optopt == 'c')
          fprintf (stderr, "Option -%c requires an argument.\n", optopt);
        else if (isprint (optopt))
          fprintf (stderr, "Unknown option `-%c'.\n", optopt);
        else
          fprintf (stderr,
                   "Unknown option character `\\x%x'.\n",
                   optopt);
        return 1;
      default:
        abort ();
      }

  printf ("aflag = %d, bflag = %d, cvalue = %s\n",
          aflag, bflag, cvalue);

  for (index = optind; index < argc; index++)
    printf ("Non-option argument %s\n", argv[index]);
  return 0;
}
```

Here are some examples showing what this program prints with different combinations of arguments:

```
% testopt
aflag = 0, bflag = 0, cvalue = (null)

% testopt -a -b
aflag = 1, bflag = 1, cvalue = (null)
```

```
% testopt -ab
aflag = 1, bflag = 1, cvalue = (null)

% testopt -c foo
aflag = 0, bflag = 0, cvalue = foo

% testopt -cfoo
aflag = 0, bflag = 0, cvalue = foo

% testopt arg1
aflag = 0, bflag = 0, cvalue = (null)
Non-option argument arg1

% testopt -a arg1
aflag = 1, bflag = 0, cvalue = (null)
Non-option argument arg1

% testopt -c foo arg1
aflag = 0, bflag = 0, cvalue = foo
Non-option argument arg1

% testopt -a -- -b
aflag = 1, bflag = 0, cvalue = (null)
Non-option argument -b

% testopt -a -
aflag = 1, bflag = 0, cvalue = (null)
Non-option argument -
```

25.2.3 Parsing Long Options with getopt_long

To accept GNU-style long options as well as single-character options, use `getopt_long` instead of `getopt`. This function is declared in `getopt.h`, not `unistd.h`. You should make every program accept long options if it uses any options, for this takes little extra work and helps beginners remember how to use the program.

struct option   [Data Type]

This structure describes a single long option name for the sake of `getopt_long`. The argument *longopts* must be an array of these structures, one for each long option. Terminate the array with an element containing all zeros.

The **struct option** structure has these fields:

const char *name

This field is the name of the option. It is a string.

int has_arg

This field says whether the option takes an argument. It is an integer, and there are three legitimate values: `no_argument`, `required_argument` and `optional_argument`.

int *flag
int val   These fields control how to report or act on the option when it occurs.

If `flag` is a null pointer, then the `val` is a value which identifies this option. Often these values are chosen to uniquely identify particular long options.

If `flag` is not a null pointer, it should be the address of an `int` variable which is the flag for this option. The value in `val` is the value to store in the flag to indicate that the option was seen.

int getopt_long (int *argc*, char *const *argv*, const char   [Function]
      shortopts, const struct option *longopts*, int *indexptr*)

Preliminary: | MT-Unsafe race:getopt env | AS-Unsafe heap i18n lock corrupt |
AC-Unsafe mem lock corrupt | See Section 1.2.2.1 [POSIX Safety Concepts], page 2.

Decode options from the vector *argv* (whose length is *argc*). The argument *shortopts* describes the short options to accept, just as it does in `getopt`. The argument *longopts* describes the long options to accept (see above).

When `getopt_long` encounters a short option, it does the same thing that `getopt` would do: it returns the character code for the option, and stores the option's argument (if it has one) in `optarg`.

When `getopt_long` encounters a long option, it takes actions based on the `flag` and `val` fields of the definition of that option.

If `flag` is a null pointer, then `getopt_long` returns the contents of `val` to indicate which option it found. You should arrange distinct values in the `val` field for options with different meanings, so you can decode these values after `getopt_long` returns. If the long option is equivalent to a short option, you can use the short option's character code in `val`.

If `flag` is not a null pointer, that means this option should just set a flag in the program. The flag is a variable of type `int` that you define. Put the address of the flag in the `flag` field. Put in the `val` field the value you would like this option to store in the flag. In this case, `getopt_long` returns 0.

For any long option, `getopt_long` tells you the index in the array *longopts* of the options definition, by storing it into **indexptr*. You can get the name of the option with *longopts[*indexptr]*`.name`. So you can distinguish among long options either by the values in their `val` fields or by their indices. You can also distinguish in this way among long options that set flags.

When a long option has an argument, `getopt_long` puts the argument value in the variable `optarg` before returning. When the option has no argument, the value in `optarg` is a null pointer. This is how you can tell whether an optional argument was supplied.

When `getopt_long` has no more options to handle, it returns -1, and leaves in the variable `optind` the index in *argv* of the next remaining argument.

Since long option names were used before `getopt_long` was invented there are program interfaces which require programs to recognize options like '-option value' instead of '--option value'. To enable these programs to use the GNU getopt functionality there is one more function available.

int getopt_long_only (int *argc*, char *const *argv*, const char   [Function]
      shortopts, const struct option *longopts*, int *indexptr*)

Preliminary: | MT-Unsafe race:getopt env | AS-Unsafe heap i18n lock corrupt |
AC-Unsafe mem lock corrupt | See Section 1.2.2.1 [POSIX Safety Concepts], page 2.

The `getopt_long_only` function is equivalent to the `getopt_long` function but it allows the user of the application to pass long options with only '-' instead of '--'. The '--' prefix is still recognized but instead of looking through the short options if a '-' is seen it is first tried whether this parameter names a long option. If not, it is parsed as a short option.

Assuming `getopt_long_only` is used starting an application with

        app -foo

the `getopt_long_only` will first look for a long option named 'foo'. If this is not found, the short options 'f', 'o', and again 'o' are recognized.

25.2.4 Example of Parsing Long Options with `getopt_long`

```
#include <stdio.h>
#include <stdlib.h>
#include <getopt.h>

/* Flag set by '--verbose'. */
static int verbose_flag;

int
main (int argc, char **argv)
{
  int c;

  while (1)
    {
      static struct option long_options[] =
        {
          /* These options set a flag. */
          {"verbose", no_argument,       &verbose_flag, 1},
          {"brief",   no_argument,       &verbose_flag, 0},
          /* These options donflt set a flag.
          We distinguish them by their indices. */
          {"add",     no_argument,       0, 'a'},
          {"append",  no_argument,       0, 'b'},
          {"delete",  required_argument, 0, 'd'},
          {"create",  required_argument, 0, 'c'},
          {"file",    required_argument, 0, 'f'},
          {0, 0, 0, 0}
        };
      /* getopt_long stores the option index here. */
      int option_index = 0;

      c = getopt_long (argc, argv, "abc:d:f:",
                       long_options, &option_index);

      /* Detect the end of the options. */
      if (c == -1)
        break;

      switch (c)
        {
        case 0:
          /* If this option set a flag, do nothing else now. */
          if (long_options[option_index].flag != 0)
```

```
          break;
        printf ("option %s", long_options[option_index].name);
        if (optarg)
          printf (" with arg %s", optarg);
        printf ("\n");
        break;

      case 'a':
        puts ("option -a\n");
        break;

      case 'b':
        puts ("option -b\n");
        break;

      case 'c':
        printf ("option -c with value `%s'\n", optarg);
        break;

      case 'd':
        printf ("option -d with value `%s'\n", optarg);
        break;

      case 'f':
        printf ("option -f with value `%s'\n", optarg);
        break;

      case '?':
        /* getopt_long already printed an error message. */
        break;

      default:
        abort ();
      }
  }

/* Instead of reporting '--verbose'
   and '--brief' as they are encountered,
   we report the final status resulting from them. */
if (verbose_flag)
  puts ("verbose flag is set");

/* Print any remaining command line arguments (not options). */
if (optind < argc)
  {
    printf ("non-option ARGV-elements: ");
    while (optind < argc)
      printf ("%s ", argv[optind++]);
    putchar ('\n');
  }

exit (0);
}
```

25.3 Parsing Program Options with Argp

Argp is an interface for parsing unix-style argument vectors. See Section 25.1 [Program Arguments], page 729.

Argp provides features unavailable in the more commonly used `getopt` interface. These features include automatically producing output in response to the '`--help`' and '`--version`' options, as described in the GNU coding standards. Using argp makes it less likely that programmers will neglect to implement these additional options or keep them up to date.

Argp also provides the ability to merge several independently defined option parsers into one, mediating conflicts between them and making the result appear seamless. A library can export an argp option parser that user programs might employ in conjunction with their own option parsers, resulting in less work for the user programs. Some programs may use only argument parsers exported by libraries, thereby achieving consistent and efficient option-parsing for abstractions implemented by the libraries.

The header file `<argp.h>` should be included to use argp.

25.3.1 The `argp_parse` Function

The main interface to argp is the `argp_parse` function. In many cases, calling `argp_parse` is the only argument-parsing code needed in `main`. See Section 25.1 [Program Arguments], page 729.

error_t **argp_parse** (*const struct argp* *argp*, *int* **argc**, *char*　　　　　 [Function]
　　　argv, *unsigned* **flags**, *int* *arg_index*, *void* *input*)
　　　Preliminary: | MT-Unsafe race:argpbuf locale env | AS-Unsafe heap i18n lock corrupt
　　　| AC-Unsafe mem lock corrupt | See Section 1.2.2.1 [POSIX Safety Concepts], page 2.

　　　The `argp_parse` function parses the arguments in *argv*, of length *argc*, using the argp
　　　parser *argp*. See Section 25.3.3 [Specifying Argp Parsers], page 739. Passing a null
　　　pointer for *argp* is the same as using a `struct argp` containing all zeros.

　　　flags is a set of flag bits that modify the parsing behavior. See Section 25.3.7 [Flags
　　　for `argp_parse`], page 748. *input* is passed through to the argp parser *argp*, and has
　　　meaning defined by *argp*. A typical usage is to pass a pointer to a structure which is
　　　used for specifying parameters to the parser and passing back the results.

　　　Unless the `ARGP_NO_EXIT` or `ARGP_NO_HELP` flags are included in *flags*, calling `argp_`
　　　`parse` may result in the program exiting. This behavior is true if an error is detected,
　　　or when an unknown option is encountered. See Section 25.7 [Program Termination],
　　　page 768.

　　　If *arg_index* is non-null, the index of the first unparsed option in *argv* is returned as
　　　a value.

　　　The return value is zero for successful parsing, or an error code (see Section 2.2 [Error
　　　Codes], page 23) if an error is detected. Different argp parsers may return arbitrary
　　　error codes, but the standard error codes are: `ENOMEM` if a memory allocation error
　　　occurred, or `EINVAL` if an unknown option or option argument is encountered.

25.3.2 Argp Global Variables

These variables make it easy for user programs to implement the '--version' option and provide a bug-reporting address in the '--help' output. These are implemented in argp by default.

const char * argp_program_version [Variable]

> If defined or set by the user program to a non-zero value, then a '--version' option is added when parsing with **argp_parse**, which will print the '--version' string followed by a newline and exit. The exception to this is if the **ARGP_NO_EXIT** flag is used.

const char * argp_program_bug_address [Variable]

> If defined or set by the user program to a non-zero value, **argp_program_bug_address** should point to a string that will be printed at the end of the standard output for the '--help' option, embedded in a sentence that says 'Report bugs to *address*.'.

argp_program_version_hook [Variable]

> If defined or set by the user program to a non-zero value, a '--version' option is added when parsing with **arg_parse**, which prints the program version and exits with a status of zero. This is not the case if the **ARGP_NO_HELP** flag is used. If the **ARGP_NO_EXIT** flag is set, the exit behavior of the program is suppressed or modified, as when the argp parser is going to be used by other programs.
>
> It should point to a function with this type of signature:
>
> > void *print-version* (FILE **stream*, struct argp_state **state*)
>
> See Section 25.3.5.2 [Argp Parsing State], page 745, for an explanation of *state*.
>
> This variable takes precedence over **argp_program_version**, and is useful if a program has version information not easily expressed in a simple string.

error_t argp_err_exit_status [Variable]

> This is the exit status used when argp exits due to a parsing error. If not defined or set by the user program, this defaults to: **EX_USAGE** from **<sysexits.h>**.

25.3.3 Specifying Argp Parsers

The first argument to the **argp_parse** function is a pointer to a **struct argp**, which is known as an *argp parser*:

struct argp [Data Type]

> This structure specifies how to parse a given set of options and arguments, perhaps in conjunction with other argp parsers. It has the following fields:
>
> **const struct argp_option *options**
>
> > A pointer to a vector of **argp_option** structures specifying which options this argp parser understands; it may be zero if there are no options at all. See Section 25.3.4 [Specifying Options in an Argp Parser], page 740.
>
> **argp_parser_t parser**
>
> > A pointer to a function that defines actions for this parser; it is called for each option parsed, and at other well-defined points in the parsing

process. A value of zero is the same as a pointer to a function that always returns `ARGP_ERR_UNKNOWN`. See Section 25.3.5 [Argp Parser Functions], page 742.

const char *args_doc

> If non-zero, a string describing what non-option arguments are called by this parser. This is only used to print the 'Usage:' message. If it contains newlines, the strings separated by them are considered alternative usage patterns and printed on separate lines. Lines after the first are prefixed by ' or: ' instead of 'Usage:'.

const char *doc

> If non-zero, a string containing extra text to be printed before and after the options in a long help message, with the two sections separated by a vertical tab ('\v', '\013') character. By convention, the documentation before the options is just a short string explaining what the program does. Documentation printed after the options describe behavior in more detail.

const struct argp_child *children

> A pointer to a vector of `argp_child` structures. This pointer specifies which additional argp parsers should be combined with this one. See Section 25.3.6 [Combining Multiple Argp Parsers], page 748.

char *(*help_filter)(int *key*, const char *text*, void *input*)

> If non-zero, a pointer to a function that filters the output of help messages. See Section 25.3.8 [Customizing Argp Help Output], page 749.

const char *argp_domain

> If non-zero, the strings used in the argp library are translated using the domain described by this string. If zero, the current default domain is used.

Of the above group, `options`, `parser`, `args_doc`, and the `doc` fields are usually all that are needed. If an argp parser is defined as an initialized C variable, only the fields used need be specified in the initializer. The rest will default to zero due to the way C structure initialization works. This design is exploited in most argp structures; the most-used fields are grouped near the beginning, the unused fields left unspecified.

25.3.4 Specifying Options in an Argp Parser

The `options` field in a `struct argp` points to a vector of `struct argp_option` structures, each of which specifies an option that the argp parser supports. Multiple entries may be used for a single option provided it has multiple names. This should be terminated by an entry with zero in all fields. Note that when using an initialized C array for options, writing { 0 } is enough to achieve this.

struct argp_option   [Data Type]

> This structure specifies a single option that an argp parser understands, as well as how to parse and document that option. It has the following fields:

const char *name

> The long name for this option, corresponding to the long option '--*name*'; this field may be zero if this option *only* has a short name. To specify

multiple names for an option, additional entries may follow this one, with the `OPTION_ALIAS` flag set. See Section 25.3.4.1 [Flags for Argp Options], page 741.

int key
: The integer key provided by the current option to the option parser. If *key* has a value that is a printable ASCII character (i.e., `isascii (`*key*`)` is true), it *also* specifies a short option '`-`*char*', where *char* is the ASCII character with the code *key*.

const char *arg
: If non-zero, this is the name of an argument associated with this option, which must be provided (e.g., with the '`--`*name*`=`*value*' or '`-`*char value*' syntaxes), unless the `OPTION_ARG_OPTIONAL` flag (see Section 25.3.4.1 [Flags for Argp Options], page 741) is set, in which case it *may* be provided.

int flags
: Flags associated with this option, some of which are referred to above. See Section 25.3.4.1 [Flags for Argp Options], page 741.

const char *doc
: A documentation string for this option, for printing in help messages.

  If both the **name** and **key** fields are zero, this string will be printed tabbed left from the normal option column, making it useful as a group header. This will be the first thing printed in its group. In this usage, it's conventional to end the string with a ':' character.

int group
: Group identity for this option.

  In a long help message, options are sorted alphabetically within each group, and the groups presented in the order 0, 1, 2, ..., n, $-m$, ..., -2, -1.

  Every entry in an options array with this field 0 will inherit the group number of the previous entry, or zero if it's the first one. If it's a group header with **name** and **key** fields both zero, the previous entry + 1 is the default. Automagic options such as '`--help`' are put into group -1.

  Note that because of C structure initialization rules, this field often need not be specified, because 0 is the correct value.

25.3.4.1 Flags for Argp Options

The following flags may be or'd together in the **flags** field of a **struct argp_option**. These flags control various aspects of how that option is parsed or displayed in help messages:

OPTION_ARG_OPTIONAL
: The argument associated with this option is optional.

OPTION_HIDDEN
: This option isn't displayed in any help messages.

OPTION_ALIAS
: This option is an alias for the closest previous non-alias option. This means that it will be displayed in the same help entry, and will inherit fields other than **name** and **key** from the option being aliased.

OPTION_DOC

> This option isn't actually an option and should be ignored by the actual option parser. It is an arbitrary section of documentation that should be displayed in much the same manner as the options. This is known as a *documentation option*.
>
> If this flag is set, then the option **name** field is displayed unmodified (e.g., no '--' prefix is added) at the left-margin where a *short* option would normally be displayed, and this documentation string is left in its usual place. For purposes of sorting, any leading whitespace and punctuation is ignored, unless the first non-whitespace character is '-'. This entry is displayed after all options, after OPTION_DOC entries with a leading '-', in the same group.

OPTION_NO_USAGE

> This option shouldn't be included in 'long' usage messages, but should still be included in other help messages. This is intended for options that are completely documented in an argp's **args_doc** field. See Section 25.3.3 [Specifying Argp Parsers], page 739. Including this option in the generic usage list would be redundant, and should be avoided.
>
> For instance, if **args_doc** is "FOO BAR\n-x BLAH", and the '-x' option's purpose is to distinguish these two cases, '-x' should probably be marked OPTION_NO_ USAGE.

25.3.5 Argp Parser Functions

The function pointed to by the **parser** field in a **struct argp** (see Section 25.3.3 [Specifying Argp Parsers], page 739) defines what actions take place in response to each option or argument parsed. It is also used as a hook, allowing a parser to perform tasks at certain other points during parsing.

Argp parser functions have the following type signature:

```
error_t parser (int key, char *arg, struct argp_state *state)
```

where the arguments are as follows:

key
> For each option that is parsed, *parser* is called with a value of *key* from that option's **key** field in the option vector. See Section 25.3.4 [Specifying Options in an Argp Parser], page 740. *parser* is also called at other times with special reserved keys, such as ARGP_KEY_ARG for non-option arguments. See Section 25.3.5.1 [Special Keys for Argp Parser Functions], page 743.

arg
> If *key* is an option, *arg* is its given value. This defaults to zero if no value is specified. Only options that have a non-zero **arg** field can ever have a value. These must *always* have a value unless the OPTION_ARG_OPTIONAL flag is specified. If the input being parsed specifies a value for an option that doesn't allow one, an error results before *parser* ever gets called.
>
> If *key* is ARGP_KEY_ARG, *arg* is a non-option argument. Other special keys always have a zero *arg*.

state
> *state* points to a **struct argp_state**, containing useful information about the current parsing state for use by *parser*. See Section 25.3.5.2 [Argp Parsing State], page 745.

When *parser* is called, it should perform whatever action is appropriate for *key*, and return 0 for success, `ARGP_ERR_UNKNOWN` if the value of *key* is not handled by this parser function, or a unix error code if a real error occurred. See Section 2.2 [Error Codes], page 23.

`int ARGP_ERR_UNKNOWN`   [Macro]

> Argp parser functions should return `ARGP_ERR_UNKNOWN` for any *key* value they do not recognize, or for non-option arguments (*key* == `ARGP_KEY_ARG`) that they are not equipped to handle.

A typical parser function uses a switch statement on *key*:

```
error_t
parse_opt (int key, char *arg, struct argp_state *state)
{
  switch (key)
    {
    case option_key:
      action
      break;
    ...
    default:
      return ARGP_ERR_UNKNOWN;
    }
  return 0;
}
```

25.3.5.1 Special Keys for Argp Parser Functions

In addition to key values corresponding to user options, the *key* argument to argp parser functions may have a number of other special values. In the following example *arg* and *state* refer to parser function arguments. See Section 25.3.5 [Argp Parser Functions], page 742.

`ARGP_KEY_ARG`

> This is not an option at all, but rather a command line argument, whose value is pointed to by *arg*.

> When there are multiple parser functions in play due to argp parsers being combined, it's impossible to know which one will handle a specific argument. Each is called until one returns 0 or an error other than `ARGP_ERR_UNKNOWN`; if an argument is not handled, `argp_parse` immediately returns success, without parsing any more arguments.

> Once a parser function returns success for this key, that fact is recorded, and the `ARGP_KEY_NO_ARGS` case won't be used. *However*, if while processing the argument a parser function decrements the **next** field of its *state* argument, the option won't be considered processed; this is to allow you to actually modify the argument, perhaps into an option, and have it processed again.

`ARGP_KEY_ARGS`

> If a parser function returns `ARGP_ERR_UNKNOWN` for `ARGP_KEY_ARG`, it is immediately called again with the key `ARGP_KEY_ARGS`, which has a similar meaning, but is slightly more convenient for consuming all remaining arguments. *arg* is 0, and the tail of the argument vector may be found at **state->argv + state->next**. If success is returned for this key, and **state->next** is unchanged, all remaining arguments are considered to have been consumed. Otherwise, the

amount by which *state->next* has been adjusted indicates how many were used. Here's an example that uses both, for different args:

```
    ...
case ARGP_KEY_ARG:
  if (state->arg_num == 0)
    /* First argument */
    first_arg = arg;
  else
    /* Let the next case parse it.  */
    return ARGP_KEY_UNKNOWN;
  break;
case ARGP_KEY_ARGS:
  remaining_args = state->argv + state->next;
  num_remaining_args = state->argc - state->next;
  break;
```

ARGP_KEY_END

> This indicates that there are no more command line arguments. Parser functions are called in a different order, children first. This allows each parser to clean up its state for the parent.

ARGP_KEY_NO_ARGS

> Because it's common to do some special processing if there aren't any non-option args, parser functions are called with this key if they didn't successfully process any non-option arguments. This is called just before ARGP_KEY_END, where more general validity checks on previously parsed arguments take place.

ARGP_KEY_INIT

> This is passed in before any parsing is done. Afterwards, the values of each element of the **child_input** field of *state*, if any, are copied to each child's state to be the initial value of the **input** when *their* parsers are called.

ARGP_KEY_SUCCESS

> Passed in when parsing has successfully been completed, even if arguments remain.

ARGP_KEY_ERROR

> Passed in if an error has occurred and parsing is terminated. In this case a call with a key of ARGP_KEY_SUCCESS is never made.

ARGP_KEY_FINI

> The final key ever seen by any parser, even after ARGP_KEY_SUCCESS and ARGP_KEY_ERROR. Any resources allocated by ARGP_KEY_INIT may be freed here. At times, certain resources allocated are to be returned to the caller after a successful parse. In that case, those particular resources can be freed in the ARGP_KEY_ERROR case.

In all cases, ARGP_KEY_INIT is the first key seen by parser functions, and ARGP_KEY_FINI the last, unless an error was returned by the parser for ARGP_KEY_INIT. Other keys can occur in one the following orders. *opt* refers to an arbitrary option key:

opt... ARGP_KEY_NO_ARGS ARGP_KEY_END ARGP_KEY_SUCCESS

> The arguments being parsed did not contain any non-option arguments.

(*opt* | ARGP_KEY_ARG)... ARGP_KEY_END ARGP_KEY_SUCCESS
> All non-option arguments were successfully handled by a parser function. There may be multiple parser functions if multiple argp parsers were combined.

(*opt* | ARGP_KEY_ARG)... ARGP_KEY_SUCCESS
> Some non-option argument went unrecognized.
>
> This occurs when every parser function returns ARGP_KEY_UNKNOWN for an argument, in which case parsing stops at that argument if *arg_index* is a null pointer. Otherwise an error occurs.

In all cases, if a non-null value for *arg_index* gets passed to **argp_parse**, the index of the first unparsed command-line argument is passed back in that value.

If an error occurs and is either detected by argp or because a parser function returned an error value, each parser is called with ARGP_KEY_ERROR. No further calls are made, except the final call with ARGP_KEY_FINI.

25.3.5.2 Argp Parsing State

The third argument to argp parser functions (see Section 25.3.5 [Argp Parser Functions], page 742) is a pointer to a **struct argp_state**, which contains information about the state of the option parsing.

struct argp_state   [Data Type]
> This structure has the following fields, which may be modified as noted:
>
> **const struct argp *const root_argp**
>> The top level argp parser being parsed. Note that this is often *not* the same **struct argp** passed into **argp_parse** by the invoking program. See Section 25.3 [Parsing Program Options with Argp], page 738. It is an internal argp parser that contains options implemented by **argp_parse** itself, such as '--help'.
>
> **int argc**
> **char **argv**
>> The argument vector being parsed. This may be modified.
>
> **int next**   The index in **argv** of the next argument to be parsed. This may be modified.
>>
>> One way to consume all remaining arguments in the input is to set *state->next = state->argc*, perhaps after recording the value of the **next** field to find the consumed arguments. The current option can be re-parsed immediately by decrementing this field, then modifying *state->argv[state->next]* to reflect the option that should be reexamined.
>
> **unsigned flags**
>> The flags supplied to **argp_parse**. These may be modified, although some flags may only take effect when **argp_parse** is first invoked. See Section 25.3.7 [Flags for **argp_parse**], page 748.

unsigned arg_num

> While calling a parsing function with the *key* argument ARGP_KEY_ARG, this represents the number of the current arg, starting at 0. It is incremented after each ARGP_KEY_ARG call returns. At all other times, this is the number of ARGP_KEY_ARG arguments that have been processed.

int quoted

> If non-zero, the index in argv of the first argument following a special '--' argument. This prevents anything that follows from being interpreted as an option. It is only set after argument parsing has proceeded past this point.

void *input

> An arbitrary pointer passed in from the caller of argp_parse, in the *input* argument.

void **child_inputs

> These are values that will be passed to child parsers. This vector will be the same length as the number of children in the current parser. Each child parser will be given the value of *state*->child_inputs[i] as *its* *state*->input field, where *i* is the index of the child in the this parser's children field. See Section 25.3.6 [Combining Multiple Argp Parsers], page 748.

void *hook

> For the parser function's use. Initialized to 0, but otherwise ignored by argp.

char *name

> The name used when printing messages. This is initialized to argv[0], or program_invocation_name if argv[0] is unavailable.

FILE *err_stream
FILE *out_stream

> The stdio streams used when argp prints. Error messages are printed to err_stream, all other output, such as '--help' output) to out_stream. These are initialized to stderr and stdout respectively. See Section 12.2 [Standard Streams], page 257.

void *pstate

> Private, for use by the argp implementation.

25.3.5.3 Functions For Use in Argp Parsers

Argp provides a number of functions available to the user of argp (see Section 25.3.5 [Argp Parser Functions], page 742), mostly for producing error messages. These take as their first argument the *state* argument to the parser function. See Section 25.3.5.2 [Argp Parsing State], page 745.

void **argp_usage** (*const struct argp_state *state*)   [Function]
> Preliminary: | MT-Unsafe race:argpbuf env locale | AS-Unsafe heap i18n corrupt | AC-Unsafe mem corrupt lock | See Section 1.2.2.1 [POSIX Safety Concepts], page 2.

Outputs the standard usage message for the argp parser referred to by *state* to `state->err_stream` and terminates the program with `exit (argp_err_exit_status)`. See Section 25.3.2 [Argp Global Variables], page 739.

void **argp_error** (*const struct argp_state *state, const char *fmt,* [Function]
     ...)

Preliminary: | MT-Unsafe race:argpbuf env locale | AS-Unsafe heap i18n corrupt | AC-Unsafe mem corrupt lock | See Section 1.2.2.1 [POSIX Safety Concepts], page 2.

Prints the printf format string *fmt* and following args, preceded by the program name and ':', and followed by a 'Try ... --help' message, and terminates the program with an exit status of `argp_err_exit_status`. See Section 25.3.2 [Argp Global Variables], page 739.

void **argp_failure** (*const struct argp_state *state, int* `status`, *int* [Function]
     *errnum, const char *fmt, ...*)

Preliminary: | MT-Safe | AS-Unsafe corrupt heap | AC-Unsafe lock corrupt mem | See Section 1.2.2.1 [POSIX Safety Concepts], page 2.

Similar to the standard GNU error-reporting function `error`, this prints the program name and ':', the printf format string *fmt*, and the appropriate following args. If it is non-zero, the standard unix error text for *errnum* is printed. If *status* is non-zero, it terminates the program with that value as its exit status.

The difference between `argp_failure` and `argp_error` is that `argp_error` is for *parsing errors*, whereas `argp_failure` is for other problems that occur during parsing but don't reflect a syntactic problem with the input, such as illegal values for options, bad phase of the moon, etc.

void **argp_state_help** (*const struct argp_state *state, FILE* [Function]
     **stream, unsigned* `flags`)

Preliminary: | MT-Unsafe race:argpbuf env locale | AS-Unsafe heap i18n corrupt | AC-Unsafe mem corrupt lock | See Section 1.2.2.1 [POSIX Safety Concepts], page 2.

Outputs a help message for the argp parser referred to by *state*, to *stream*. The *flags* argument determines what sort of help message is produced. See Section 25.3.10 [Flags for the `argp_help` Function], page 750.

Error output is sent to `state->err_stream`, and the program name printed is `state->name`.

The output or program termination behavior of these functions may be suppressed if the `ARGP_NO_EXIT` or `ARGP_NO_ERRS` flags are passed to `argp_parse`. See Section 25.3.7 [Flags for `argp_parse`], page 748.

This behavior is useful if an argp parser is exported for use by other programs (e.g., by a library), and may be used in a context where it is not desirable to terminate the program in response to parsing errors. In argp parsers intended for such general use, and for the case where the program *doesn't* terminate, calls to any of these functions should be followed by code that returns the appropriate error code:

```
if (bad argument syntax)
  {
    argp_usage (state);
```

```
        return EINVAL;
    }
```

If a parser function will *only* be used when `ARGP_NO_EXIT` is not set, the return may be omitted.

25.3.6 Combining Multiple Argp Parsers

The `children` field in a `struct argp` enables other argp parsers to be combined with the referencing one for the parsing of a single set of arguments. This field should point to a vector of `struct argp_child`, which is terminated by an entry having a value of zero in the `argp` field.

Where conflicts between combined parsers arise, as when two specify an option with the same name, the parser conflicts are resolved in favor of the parent argp parser(s), or the earlier of the argp parsers in the list of children.

`struct argp_child`   [Data Type]

> An entry in the list of subsidiary argp parsers pointed to by the `children` field in a `struct argp`. The fields are as follows:

> `const struct argp *argp`
> > The child argp parser, or zero to end of the list.

> `int flags`   Flags for this child.

> `const char *header`
> > If non-zero, this is an optional header to be printed within help output before the child options. As a side-effect, a non-zero value forces the child options to be grouped together. To achieve this effect without actually printing a header string, use a value of `""`. As with header strings specified in an option entry, the conventional value of the last character is ':'. See Section 25.3.4 [Specifying Options in an Argp Parser], page 740.

> `int group`   This is where the child options are grouped relative to the other 'consolidated' options in the parent argp parser. The values are the same as the `group` field in `struct argp_option`. See Section 25.3.4 [Specifying Options in an Argp Parser], page 740. All child-groupings follow parent options at a particular group level. If both this field and `header` are zero, then the child's options aren't grouped together, they are merged with parent options at the parent option group level.

25.3.7 Flags for `argp_parse`

The default behavior of `argp_parse` is designed to be convenient for the most common case of parsing program command line argument. To modify these defaults, the following flags may be or'd together in the *flags* argument to `argp_parse`:

`ARGP_PARSE_ARGV0`
> > Don't ignore the first element of the *argv* argument to `argp_parse`. Unless `ARGP_NO_ERRS` is set, the first element of the argument vector is skipped for option parsing purposes, as it corresponds to the program name in a command line.

ARGP_NO_ERRS

> Don't print error messages for unknown options to `stderr`; unless this flag is set, `ARGP_PARSE_ARGV0` is ignored, as `argv[0]` is used as the program name in the error messages. This flag implies `ARGP_NO_EXIT`. This is based on the assumption that silent exiting upon errors is bad behavior.

ARGP_NO_ARGS

> Don't parse any non-option args. Normally these are parsed by calling the parse functions with a key of `ARGP_KEY_ARG`, the actual argument being the value. This flag needn't normally be set, as the default behavior is to stop parsing as soon as an argument fails to be parsed. See Section 25.3.5 [Argp Parser Functions], page 742.

ARGP_IN_ORDER

> Parse options and arguments in the same order they occur on the command line. Normally they're rearranged so that all options come first.

ARGP_NO_HELP

> Don't provide the standard long option '`--help`', which ordinarily causes usage and option help information to be output to `stdout` and `exit (0)`.

ARGP_NO_EXIT

> Don't exit on errors, although they may still result in error messages.

ARGP_LONG_ONLY

> Use the GNU getopt 'long-only' rules for parsing arguments. This allows long-options to be recognized with only a single '`-`' (i.e., '`-help`'). This results in a less useful interface, and its use is discouraged as it conflicts with the way most GNU programs work as well as the GNU coding standards.

ARGP_SILENT

> Turns off any message-printing/exiting options, specifically `ARGP_NO_EXIT`, `ARGP_NO_ERRS`, and `ARGP_NO_HELP`.

25.3.8 Customizing Argp Help Output

The `help_filter` field in a `struct argp` is a pointer to a function that filters the text of help messages before displaying them. They have a function signature like:

```
char *help-filter (int key, const char *text, void *input)
```

Where *key* is either a key from an option, in which case *text* is that option's help text. See Section 25.3.4 [Specifying Options in an Argp Parser], page 740. Alternately, one of the special keys with names beginning with '`ARGP_KEY_HELP_`' might be used, describing which other help text *text* will contain. See Section 25.3.8.1 [Special Keys for Argp Help Filter Functions], page 750.

The function should return either *text* if it remains as-is, or a replacement string allocated using `malloc`. This will be either be freed by argp or zero, which prints nothing. The value of *text* is supplied *after* any translation has been done, so if any of the replacement text needs translation, it will be done by the filter function. *input* is either the input supplied to `argp_parse` or it is zero, if `argp_help` was called directly by the user.

25.3.8.1 Special Keys for Argp Help Filter Functions

The following special values may be passed to an argp help filter function as the first argument in addition to key values for user options. They specify which help text the *text* argument contains:

`ARGP_KEY_HELP_PRE_DOC`
>   The help text preceding options.

`ARGP_KEY_HELP_POST_DOC`
>   The help text following options.

`ARGP_KEY_HELP_HEADER`
>   The option header string.

`ARGP_KEY_HELP_EXTRA`
>   This is used after all other documentation; *text* is zero for this key.

`ARGP_KEY_HELP_DUP_ARGS_NOTE`
>   The explanatory note printed when duplicate option arguments have been suppressed.

`ARGP_KEY_HELP_ARGS_DOC`
>   The argument doc string; formally the `args_doc` field from the argp parser. See Section 25.3.3 [Specifying Argp Parsers], page 739.

25.3.9 The `argp_help` Function

Normally programs using argp need not be written with particular printing argument-usage-type help messages in mind as the standard '`--help`' option is handled automatically by argp. Typical error cases can be handled using `argp_usage` and `argp_error`. See Section 25.3.5.3 [Functions For Use in Argp Parsers], page 746. However, if it's desirable to print a help message in some context other than parsing the program options, argp offers the `argp_help` interface.

`void` **`argp_help`** (*const struct argp* ***`argp`**, *FILE* ***`stream`**, *unsigned*   [Function]
    ***`flags`**, char* ***`name`**)
>   Preliminary: | MT-Unsafe race:argpbuf env locale | AS-Unsafe heap i18n corrupt | AC-Unsafe mem corrupt lock | See Section 1.2.2.1 [POSIX Safety Concepts], page 2.
>
>   This outputs a help message for the argp parser *argp* to *stream*. The type of messages printed will be determined by *flags*.
>
>   Any options such as '`--help`' that are implemented automatically by argp itself will *not* be present in the help output; for this reason it is best to use `argp_state_help` if calling from within an argp parser function. See Section 25.3.5.3 [Functions For Use in Argp Parsers], page 746.

25.3.10 Flags for the `argp_help` Function

When calling `argp_help` (see Section 25.3.9 [The `argp_help` Function], page 750) or `argp_state_help` (see Section 25.3.5.3 [Functions For Use in Argp Parsers], page 746) the exact output is determined by the *flags* argument. This should consist of any of the following flags, or'd together:

ARGP_HELP_USAGE

      A unix 'Usage:' message that explicitly lists all options.

ARGP_HELP_SHORT_USAGE

      A unix 'Usage:' message that displays an appropriate placeholder to indicate where the options go; useful for showing the non-option argument syntax.

ARGP_HELP_SEE

      A 'Try ... for more help' message; '...' contains the program name and '--help'.

ARGP_HELP_LONG

      A verbose option help message that gives each option available along with its documentation string.

ARGP_HELP_PRE_DOC

      The part of the argp parser doc string preceding the verbose option help.

ARGP_HELP_POST_DOC

      The part of the argp parser doc string that following the verbose option help.

ARGP_HELP_DOC

      (ARGP_HELP_PRE_DOC | ARGP_HELP_POST_DOC)

ARGP_HELP_BUG_ADDR

      A message that prints where to report bugs for this program, if the argp_program_bug_address variable contains this information.

ARGP_HELP_LONG_ONLY

      This will modify any output to reflect the ARGP_LONG_ONLY mode.

The following flags are only understood when used with argp_state_help. They control whether the function returns after printing its output, or terminates the program:

ARGP_HELP_EXIT_ERR

      This will terminate the program with exit (argp_err_exit_status).

ARGP_HELP_EXIT_OK

      This will terminate the program with exit (0).

The following flags are combinations of the basic flags for printing standard messages:

ARGP_HELP_STD_ERR

      Assuming that an error message for a parsing error has printed, this prints a message on how to get help, and terminates the program with an error.

ARGP_HELP_STD_USAGE

      This prints a standard usage message and terminates the program with an error. This is used when no other specific error messages are appropriate or available.

ARGP_HELP_STD_HELP

      This prints the standard response for a '--help' option, and terminates the program successfully.

25.3.11 Argp Examples

These example programs demonstrate the basic usage of argp.

25.3.11.1 A Minimal Program Using Argp

This is perhaps the smallest program possible that uses argp. It won't do much except give an error message and exit when there are any arguments, and prints a rather pointless message for '--help'.

```
/* This is (probably) the smallest possible program that
   uses argp. It wonflt do much except give an error
   messages and exit when there are any arguments, and print
   a (rather pointless) messages for –help. */

#include <stdlib.h>
#include <argp.h>

int
main (int argc, char **argv)
{
  argp_parse (0, argc, argv, 0, 0, 0);
  exit (0);
}
```

25.3.11.2 A Program Using Argp with Only Default Options

This program doesn't use any options or arguments, it uses argp to be compliant with the GNU standard command line format.

In addition to giving no arguments and implementing a '--help' option, this example has a '--version' option, which will put the given documentation string and bug address in the '--help' output, as per GNU standards.

The variable `argp` contains the argument parser specification. Adding fields to this structure is the way most parameters are passed to `argp_parse`. The first three fields are normally used, but they are not in this small program. There are also two global variables that argp can use defined here, `argp_program_version` and `argp_program_bug_address`. They are considered global variables because they will almost always be constant for a given program, even if they use different argument parsers for various tasks.

```
/* This program doesnflt use any options or arguments, but uses
   argp to be compliant with the GNU standard command line
   format.

   In addition to making sure no arguments are given, and
   implementing a –help option, this example will have a
   –version option, and will put the given documentation string
   and bug address in the –help output, as per GNU standards.

   The variable ARGP contains the argument parser specification;
   adding fields to this structure is the way most parameters are
   passed to argp_parse (the first three fields are usually used,
   but not in this small program).  There are also two global
   variables that argp knows about defined here,
   ARGP_PROGRAM_VERSION and ARGP_PROGRAM_BUG_ADDRESS (they are
   global variables because they will almost always be constant
   for a given program, even if it uses different argument
   parsers for various tasks). */

#include <stdlib.h>
```

```
#include <argp.h>

const char *argp_program_version =
  "argp-ex2 1.0";
const char *argp_program_bug_address =
  "<bug-gnu-utils@gnu.org>";

/* Program documentation. */
static char doc[] =
  "Argp example #2 -- a pretty minimal program using argp";

/* Our argument parser.  The options, parser, and
   args_doc fields are zero because we have neither options or
   arguments; doc and argp_program_bug_address will be
   used in the output for '--help', and the '--version'
   option will print out argp_program_version. */
static struct argp argp = { 0, 0, 0, doc };

int
main (int argc, char **argv)
{
  argp_parse (&argp, argc, argv, 0, 0, 0);
  exit (0);
}
```

25.3.11.3 A Program Using Argp with User Options

This program uses the same features as example 2, adding user options and arguments.

We now use the first four fields in **argp** (see Section 25.3.3 [Specifying Argp Parsers], page 739) and specify **parse_opt** as the parser function. See Section 25.3.5 [Argp Parser Functions], page 742.

Note that in this example, **main** uses a structure to communicate with the **parse_opt** function, a pointer to which it passes in the **input** argument to **argp_parse**. See Section 25.3 [Parsing Program Options with Argp], page 738. It is retrieved by **parse_opt** through the **input** field in its **state** argument. See Section 25.3.5.2 [Argp Parsing State], page 745. Of course, it's also possible to use global variables instead, but using a structure like this is somewhat more flexible and clean.

```
/* This program uses the same features as example 2, and uses options and
   arguments.

   We now use the first four fields in ARGP, so herefls a description of them:
     OPTIONS  – A pointer to a vector of struct argp_option (see below)
     PARSER   – A function to parse a single option, called by argp
     ARGS_DOC – A string describing how the non-option arguments should look
     DOC      – A descriptive string about this program; if it contains a
                vertical tab character (\v), the part after it will be
                printed *following* the options

   The function PARSER takes the following arguments:
     KEY – An integer specifying which option this is (taken
           from the KEY field in each struct argp_option), or
           a special key specifying something else; the only
           special keys we use here are ARGP_KEY_ARG, meaning
           a non-option argument, and ARGP_KEY_END, meaning
           that all arguments have been parsed
```

ARG – For an option KEY, the string value of its
          argument, or NULL if it has none
STATE– A pointer to a struct argp_state, containing
          various useful information about the parsing state; used here
          are the INPUT field, which reflects the INPUT argument to
          argp_parse, and the ARG_NUM field, which is the number of the
          current non-option argument being parsed
It should return either 0, meaning success, ARGP_ERR_UNKNOWN, meaning the
given KEY wasnflt recognized, or an errno value indicating some other
error.

Note that in this example, main uses a structure to communicate with the
parse_opt function, a pointer to which it passes in the INPUT argument to
argp_parse. Of course, itfls also possible to use global variables
instead, but this is somewhat more flexible.

The OPTIONS field contains a pointer to a vector of struct argp_optionfls;
that structure has the following fields (if you assign your option
structures using array initialization like this example, unspecified
fields will be defaulted to 0, and need not be specified):
NAME   – The name of this optionfls long option (may be zero)
KEY   – The KEY to pass to the PARSER function when parsing this option,
          and the name of this optionfls short option, if it is a
          printable ascii character
ARG   – The name of this optionfls argument, if any
FLAGS – Flags describing this option; some of them are:
          OPTION_ARG_OPTIONAL – The argument to this option is optional
          OPTION_ALIAS   – This option is an alias for the
                                  previous option
          OPTION_HIDDEN   – Donflt show this option in –help output
DOC   – A documentation string for this option, shown in –help output

An options vector should be terminated by an option with all fields zero. */

```
#include <stdlib.h>
#include <argp.h>

const char *argp_program_version =
  "argp-ex3 1.0";
const char *argp_program_bug_address =
  "<bug-gnu-utils@gnu.org>";

/* Program documentation. */
static char doc[] =
  "Argp example #3 -- a program with options and arguments using argp";

/* A description of the arguments we accept. */
static char args_doc[] = "ARG1 ARG2";

/* The options we understand. */
static struct argp_option options[] = {
  {"verbose",  'v', 0,      0,  "Produce verbose output" },
  {"quiet",    'q', 0,      0,  "Don't produce any output" },
  {"silent",   's', 0,      OPTION_ALIAS },
  {"output",   'o', "FILE", 0,
   "Output to FILE instead of standard output" },
  { 0 }
};
```

```
/* Used by main to communicate with parse_opt. */
struct arguments
{
  char *args[2];              /* arg1 & arg2 */
  int silent, verbose;
  char *output_file;
};

/* Parse a single option. */
static error_t
parse_opt (int key, char *arg, struct argp_state *state)
{
  /* Get the input argument from argp_parse, which we
     know is a pointer to our arguments structure. */
  struct arguments *arguments = state->input;

  switch (key)
    {
    case 'q': case 's':
      arguments->silent = 1;
      break;
    case 'v':
      arguments->verbose = 1;
      break;
    case 'o':
      arguments->output_file = arg;
      break;

    case ARGP_KEY_ARG:
      if (state->arg_num >= 2)
        /* Too many arguments. */
        argp_usage (state);

      arguments->args[state->arg_num] = arg;

      break;

    case ARGP_KEY_END:
      if (state->arg_num < 2)
        /* Not enough arguments. */
        argp_usage (state);
      break;

    default:
      return ARGP_ERR_UNKNOWN;
    }
  return 0;
}

/* Our argp parser. */
static struct argp argp = { options, parse_opt, args_doc, doc };

int
main (int argc, char **argv)
{
  struct arguments arguments;
```

```
/* Default values. */
arguments.silent = 0;
arguments.verbose = 0;
arguments.output_file = "-";

/* Parse our arguments; every option seen by parse_opt will
   be reflected in arguments. */
argp_parse (&argp, argc, argv, 0, 0, &arguments);

printf ("ARG1 = %s\nARG2 = %s\nOUTPUT_FILE = %s\n"
        "VERBOSE = %s\nSILENT = %s\n",
        arguments.args[0], arguments.args[1],
        arguments.output_file,
        arguments.verbose ? "yes" : "no",
        arguments.silent ? "yes" : "no");

exit (0);
}
```

25.3.11.4 A Program Using Multiple Combined Argp Parsers

This program uses the same features as example 3, but has more options, and presents more structure in the '--help' output. It also illustrates how you can 'steal' the remainder of the input arguments past a certain point for programs that accept a list of items. It also illustrates the *key* value `ARGP_KEY_NO_ARGS`, which is only given if no non-option arguments were supplied to the program. See Section 25.3.5.1 [Special Keys for Argp Parser Functions], page 743.

For structuring help output, two features are used: *headers* and a two part option string. The *headers* are entries in the options vector. See Section 25.3.4 [Specifying Options in an Argp Parser], page 740. The first four fields are zero. The two part documentation string are in the variable `doc`, which allows documentation both before and after the options. See Section 25.3.3 [Specifying Argp Parsers], page 739, the two parts of `doc` are separated by a vertical-tab character ('\v', or '\013'). By convention, the documentation before the options is a short string stating what the program does, and after any options it is longer, describing the behavior in more detail. All documentation strings are automatically filled for output, although newlines may be included to force a line break at a particular point. In addition, documentation strings are passed to the `gettext` function, for possible translation into the current locale.

```
/* This program uses the same features as example 3, but has more
   options, and somewhat more structure in the -help output.  It
   also shows how you can `stealfl the remainder of the input
   arguments past a certain point, for programs that accept a
   list of items.  It also shows the special argp KEY value
   ARGP_KEY_NO_ARGS, which is only given if no non-option
   arguments were supplied to the program.

   For structuring the help output, two features are used,
   *headers* which are entries in the options vector with the
   first four fields being zero, and a two part documentation
   string (in the variable DOC), which allows documentation both
   before and after the options; the two parts of DOC are
   separated by a vertical-tab character (fl\vfl, or fl\013fl).  By
   convention, the documentation before the options is just a
```

short string saying what the program does, and that afterwards
is longer, describing the behavior in more detail. All
documentation strings are automatically filled for output,
although newlines may be included to force a line break at a
particular point. All documentation strings are also passed to
the `gettextfl function, for possible translation into the
current locale. */

```
#include <stdlib.h>
#include <error.h>
#include <argp.h>

const char *argp_program_version =
  "argp-ex4 1.0";
const char *argp_program_bug_address =
  "<bug-gnu-utils@prep.ai.mit.edu>";

/* Program documentation. */
static char doc[] =
  "Argp example #4 -- a program with somewhat more complicated\
options\
\vThis part of the documentation comes *after* the options;\
 note that the text is automatically filled, but it's possible\
 to force a line-break, e.g.\n<-- here.";

/* A description of the arguments we accept. */
static char args_doc[] = "ARG1 [STRING...]";

/* Keys for options without short-options. */
#define OPT_ABORT  1              /* -abort */

/* The options we understand. */
static struct argp_option options[] = {
  {"verbose",  'v', 0,       0, "Produce verbose output" },
  {"quiet",    'q', 0,       0, "Don't produce any output" },
  {"silent",   's', 0,       OPTION_ALIAS },
  {"output",   'o', "FILE",  0,
   "Output to FILE instead of standard output" },

  {0,0,0,0, "The following options should be grouped together:" },
  {"repeat",   'r', "COUNT", OPTION_ARG_OPTIONAL,
   "Repeat the output COUNT (default 10) times"},
  {"abort",    OPT_ABORT, 0, 0, "Abort before showing any output"},

  { 0 }
};

/* Used by main to communicate with parse_opt. */
struct arguments
{
  char *arg1;                /* arg1 */
  char **strings;            /* [string...] */
  int silent, verbose, abort; /* '-s', '-v', '--abort' */
  char *output_file;         /* file arg to '--output' */
  int repeat_count;          /* count arg to '--repeat' */
};

/* Parse a single option. */
```

```
static error_t
parse_opt (int key, char *arg, struct argp_state *state)
{
  /* Get the input argument from argp_parse, which we
     know is a pointer to our arguments structure. */
  struct arguments *arguments = state->input;

  switch (key)
    {
    case 'q': case 's':
      arguments->silent = 1;
      break;
    case 'v':
      arguments->verbose = 1;
      break;
    case 'o':
      arguments->output_file = arg;
      break;
    case 'r':
      arguments->repeat_count = arg ? atoi (arg) : 10;
      break;
    case OPT_ABORT:
      arguments->abort = 1;
      break;

    case ARGP_KEY_NO_ARGS:
      argp_usage (state);

    case ARGP_KEY_ARG:
      /* Here we know that state->arg_num == 0, since we
         force argument parsing to end before any more arguments can
         get here. */
      arguments->arg1 = arg;

      /* Now we consume all the rest of the arguments.
         state->next is the index in state->argv of the
         next argument to be parsed, which is the first string
         weflre interested in, so we can just use
         &state->argv[state->next] as the value for
         arguments->strings.

         In addition, by setting state->next to the end
         of the arguments, we can force argp to stop parsing here and
         return. */
      arguments->strings = &state->argv[state->next];
      state->next = state->argc;

      break;

    default:
      return ARGP_ERR_UNKNOWN;
    }
  return 0;
}

/* Our argp parser. */
static struct argp argp = { options, parse_opt, args_doc, doc };
```

```
int
main (int argc, char **argv)
{
  int i, j;
  struct arguments arguments;

  /* Default values. */
  arguments.silent = 0;
  arguments.verbose = 0;
  arguments.output_file = "-";
  arguments.repeat_count = 1;
  arguments.abort = 0;

  /* Parse our arguments; every option seen by parse_opt will be
     reflected in arguments. */
  argp_parse (&argp, argc, argv, 0, 0, &arguments);

  if (arguments.abort)
    error (10, 0, "ABORTED");

  for (i = 0; i < arguments.repeat_count; i++)
    {
      printf ("ARG1 = %s\n", arguments.arg1);
      printf ("STRINGS = ");
      for (j = 0; arguments.strings[j]; j++)
        printf (j == 0 ? "%s" : ", %s", arguments.strings[j]);
      printf ("\n");
      printf ("OUTPUT_FILE = %s\nVERBOSE = %s\nSILENT = %s\n",
              arguments.output_file,
              arguments.verbose ? "yes" : "no",
              arguments.silent ? "yes" : "no");
    }

  exit (0);
}
```

25.3.12 Argp User Customization

The formatting of argp '--help' output may be controlled to some extent by a program's users, by setting the ARGP_HELP_FMT environment variable to a comma-separated list of tokens. Whitespace is ignored:

'dup-args'
'no-dup-args'

> These turn *duplicate-argument-mode* on or off. In duplicate argument mode, if an option that accepts an argument has multiple names, the argument is shown for each name. Otherwise, it is only shown for the first long option. A note is subsequently printed so the user knows that it applies to other names as well. The default is 'no-dup-args', which is less consistent, but prettier.

'dup-args-note'
'no-dup-args-note'

> These will enable or disable the note informing the user of suppressed option argument duplication. The default is 'dup-args-note'.

'short-opt-col=n'

> This prints the first short option in column *n*. The default is 2.

'long-opt-col=*n*'

> This prints the first long option in column *n*. The default is 6.

'doc-opt-col=*n*'

> This prints 'documentation options' (see Section 25.3.4.1 [Flags for Argp Options], page 741) in column *n*. The default is 2.

'opt-doc-col=*n*'

> This prints the documentation for options starting in column *n*. The default is 29.

'header-col=*n*'

> This will indent the group headers that document groups of options to column *n*. The default is 1.

'usage-indent=*n*'

> This will indent continuation lines in 'Usage:' messages to column *n*. The default is 12.

'rmargin=*n*'

> This will word wrap help output at or before column *n*. The default is 79.

25.3.12.1 Parsing of Suboptions

Having a single level of options is sometimes not enough. There might be too many options which have to be available or a set of options is closely related.

For this case some programs use suboptions. One of the most prominent programs is certainly mount(8). The -o option take one argument which itself is a comma separated list of options. To ease the programming of code like this the function getsubopt is available.

int getsubopt (*char **optionp, char *const *tokens, char*   [Function]
     ***valuep*)

> Preliminary: | MT-Safe | AS-Safe | AC-Safe | See Section 1.2.2.1 [POSIX Safety Concepts], page 2.
>
> The *optionp* parameter must be a pointer to a variable containing the address of the string to process. When the function returns, the reference is updated to point to the next suboption or to the terminating '\0' character if there are no more suboptions available.
>
> The *tokens* parameter references an array of strings containing the known suboptions. All strings must be '\0' terminated and to mark the end a null pointer must be stored. When getsubopt finds a possible legal suboption it compares it with all strings available in the *tokens* array and returns the index in the string as the indicator.
>
> In case the suboption has an associated value introduced by a '=' character, a pointer to the value is returned in *valuep*. The string is '\0' terminated. If no argument is available *valuep* is set to the null pointer. By doing this the caller can check whether a necessary value is given or whether no unexpected value is present.
>
> In case the next suboption in the string is not mentioned in the *tokens* array the starting address of the suboption including a possible value is returned in *valuep* and the return value of the function is '-1'.

25.3.13 Parsing of Suboptions Example

The code which might appear in the mount(8) program is a perfect example of the use of
getsubopt:

```
#include <stdio.h>
#include <stdlib.h>
#include <unistd.h>

int do_all;
const char *type;
int read_size;
int write_size;
int read_only;

enum
{
  RO_OPTION = 0,
  RW_OPTION,
  READ_SIZE_OPTION,
  WRITE_SIZE_OPTION,
  THE_END
};

const char *mount_opts[] =
{
  [RO_OPTION] = "ro",
  [RW_OPTION] = "rw",
  [READ_SIZE_OPTION] = "rsize",
  [WRITE_SIZE_OPTION] = "wsize",
  [THE_END] = NULL
};

int
main (int argc, char **argv)
{
  char *subopts, *value;
  int opt;

  while ((opt = getopt (argc, argv, "at:o:")) != -1)
    switch (opt)
      {
      case 'a':
        do_all = 1;
        break;
      case 't':
        type = optarg;
        break;
      case 'o':
        subopts = optarg;
        while (*subopts != '\0')
          switch (getsubopt (&subopts, mount_opts, &value))
            {
            case RO_OPTION:
              read_only = 1;
              break;
            case RW_OPTION:
              read_only = 0;
```

```
            break;
          case READ_SIZE_OPTION:
            if (value == NULL)
              abort ();
            read_size = atoi (value);
            break;
          case WRITE_SIZE_OPTION:
            if (value == NULL)
              abort ();
            write_size = atoi (value);
            break;
          default:
            /* Unknown suboption. */
            printf ("Unknown suboption `%s'\n", value);
            break;
          }
        break;
      default:
        abort ();
      }

    /* Do the real work. */

    return 0;
  }
```

25.4 Environment Variables

When a program is executed, it receives information about the context in which it was invoked in two ways. The first mechanism uses the *argv* and *argc* arguments to its **main** function, and is discussed in Section 25.1 [Program Arguments], page 729. The second mechanism uses *environment variables* and is discussed in this section.

The *argv* mechanism is typically used to pass command-line arguments specific to the particular program being invoked. The environment, on the other hand, keeps track of information that is shared by many programs, changes infrequently, and that is less frequently used.

The environment variables discussed in this section are the same environment variables that you set using assignments and the **export** command in the shell. Programs executed from the shell inherit all of the environment variables from the shell.

Standard environment variables are used for information about the user's home directory, terminal type, current locale, and so on; you can define additional variables for other purposes. The set of all environment variables that have values is collectively known as the *environment*.

Names of environment variables are case-sensitive and must not contain the character '='. System-defined environment variables are invariably uppercase.

The values of environment variables can be anything that can be represented as a string. A value must not contain an embedded null character, since this is assumed to terminate the string.

25.4.1 Environment Access

The value of an environment variable can be accessed with the `getenv` function. This is declared in the header file `stdlib.h`.

Libraries should use `secure_getenv` instead of `getenv`, so that they do not accidentally use untrusted environment variables. Modifications of environment variables are not allowed in multi-threaded programs. The `getenv` and `secure_getenv` functions can be safely used in multi-threaded programs.

char * getenv (*const char *name*)   [Function]
> Preliminary: | MT-Safe env | AS-Safe | AC-Safe | See Section 1.2.2.1 [POSIX Safety Concepts], page 2.
>
> This function returns a string that is the value of the environment variable *name*. You must not modify this string. In some non-Unix systems not using the GNU C Library, it might be overwritten by subsequent calls to `getenv` (but not by any other library function). If the environment variable *name* is not defined, the value is a null pointer.

char * secure_getenv (*const char *name*)   [Function]
> Preliminary: | MT-Safe env | AS-Safe | AC-Safe | See Section 1.2.2.1 [POSIX Safety Concepts], page 2.
>
> This function is similar to `getenv`, but it returns a null pointer if the environment is untrusted. This happens when the program file has SUID or SGID bits set. General-purpose libraries should always prefer this function over `getenv` to avoid vulnerabilities if the library is referenced from a SUID/SGID program.
>
> This function is a GNU extension.

int putenv (*char *string*)   [Function]
> Preliminary: | MT-Unsafe const:env | AS-Unsafe heap lock | AC-Unsafe corrupt lock mem | See Section 1.2.2.1 [POSIX Safety Concepts], page 2.
>
> The `putenv` function adds or removes definitions from the environment. If the *string* is of the form '`name=value`', the definition is added to the environment. Otherwise, the *string* is interpreted as the name of an environment variable, and any definition for this variable in the environment is removed.
>
> If the function is successful it returns 0. Otherwise the return value is nonzero and `errno` is set to indicate the error.
>
> The difference to the `setenv` function is that the exact string given as the parameter *string* is put into the environment. If the user should change the string after the `putenv` call this will reflect automatically in the environment. This also requires that *string* not be an automatic variable whose scope is left before the variable is removed from the environment. The same applies of course to dynamically allocated variables which are freed later.
>
> This function is part of the extended Unix interface. You should define *_XOPEN_SOURCE* before including any header.

int setenv (*const char *name, const char *value, int replace*)   [Function]
> Preliminary: | MT-Unsafe const:env | AS-Unsafe heap lock | AC-Unsafe corrupt lock mem | See Section 1.2.2.1 [POSIX Safety Concepts], page 2.

The `setenv` function can be used to add a new definition to the environment. The entry with the name *name* is replaced by the value '*name=value*'. Please note that this is also true if *value* is the empty string. To do this a new string is created and the strings *name* and *value* are copied. A null pointer for the *value* parameter is illegal. If the environment already contains an entry with key *name* the *replace* parameter controls the action. If replace is zero, nothing happens. Otherwise the old entry is replaced by the new one.

Please note that you cannot remove an entry completely using this function.

If the function is successful it returns 0. Otherwise the environment is unchanged and the return value is -1 and `errno` is set.

This function was originally part of the BSD library but is now part of the Unix standard.

`int unsetenv` (*const char *name*)   [Function]
    Preliminary: | MT-Unsafe const:env | AS-Unsafe lock | AC-Unsafe lock | See Section 1.2.2.1 [POSIX Safety Concepts], page 2.

    Using this function one can remove an entry completely from the environment. If the environment contains an entry with the key *name* this whole entry is removed. A call to this function is equivalent to a call to `putenv` when the *value* part of the string is empty.

    The function returns -1 if *name* is a null pointer, points to an empty string, or points to a string containing a = character. It returns 0 if the call succeeded.

    This function was originally part of the BSD library but is now part of the Unix standard. The BSD version had no return value, though.

There is one more function to modify the whole environment. This function is said to be used in the POSIX.9 (POSIX bindings for Fortran 77) and so one should expect it did made it into POSIX.1. But this never happened. But we still provide this function as a GNU extension to enable writing standard compliant Fortran environments.

`int clearenv` (*void*)   [Function]
    Preliminary: | MT-Unsafe const:env | AS-Unsafe heap lock | AC-Unsafe lock mem | See Section 1.2.2.1 [POSIX Safety Concepts], page 2.

    The `clearenv` function removes all entries from the environment. Using `putenv` and `setenv` new entries can be added again later.

    If the function is successful it returns 0. Otherwise the return value is nonzero.

You can deal directly with the underlying representation of environment objects to add more variables to the environment (for example, to communicate with another program you are about to execute; see Section 26.5 [Executing a File], page 776).

`char ** environ`   [Variable]
    The environment is represented as an array of strings. Each string is of the format '*name=value*'. The order in which strings appear in the environment is not significant, but the same *name* must not appear more than once. The last element of the array is a null pointer.

    This variable is declared in the header file `unistd.h`.

    If you just want to get the value of an environment variable, use `getenv`.

Unix systems, and GNU systems, pass the initial value of `environ` as the third argument to `main`. See Section 25.1 [Program Arguments], page 729.

25.4.2 Standard Environment Variables

These environment variables have standard meanings. This doesn't mean that they are always present in the environment; but if these variables *are* present, they have these meanings. You shouldn't try to use these environment variable names for some other purpose.

`HOME`

> This is a string representing the user's *home directory*, or initial default working directory.
>
> The user can set `HOME` to any value. If you need to make sure to obtain the proper home directory for a particular user, you should not use `HOME`; instead, look up the user's name in the user database (see Section 30.13 [User Database], page 834).
>
> For most purposes, it is better to use `HOME`, precisely because this lets the user specify the value.

`LOGNAME`

> This is the name that the user used to log in. Since the value in the environment can be tweaked arbitrarily, this is not a reliable way to identify the user who is running a program; a function like `getlogin` (see Section 30.11 [Identifying Who Logged In], page 825) is better for that purpose.
>
> For most purposes, it is better to use `LOGNAME`, precisely because this lets the user specify the value.

`PATH`

> A *path* is a sequence of directory names which is used for searching for a file. The variable `PATH` holds a path used for searching for programs to be run.
>
> The `execlp` and `execvp` functions (see Section 26.5 [Executing a File], page 776) use this environment variable, as do many shells and other utilities which are implemented in terms of those functions.
>
> The syntax of a path is a sequence of directory names separated by colons. An empty string instead of a directory name stands for the current directory (see Section 14.1 [Working Directory], page 390).
>
> A typical value for this environment variable might be a string like:
>
> > `:/bin:/etc:/usr/bin:/usr/new/X11:/usr/new:/usr/local/bin`
>
> This means that if the user tries to execute a program named `foo`, the system will look for files named `foo`, `/bin/foo`, `/etc/foo`, and so on. The first of these files that exists is the one that is executed.

`TERM`

> This specifies the kind of terminal that is receiving program output. Some programs can make use of this information to take advantage of special escape sequences or terminal modes supported by particular kinds of terminals. Many

programs which use the termcap library (see Section "Finding a Terminal Description" in *The Termcap Library Manual*) use the `TERM` environment variable, for example.

TZ

This specifies the time zone. See Section 21.4.7 [Specifying the Time Zone with `TZ`], page 646, for information about the format of this string and how it is used.

LANG

This specifies the default locale to use for attribute categories where neither `LC_ALL` nor the specific environment variable for that category is set. See Chapter 7 [Locales and Internationalization], page 176, for more information about locales.

LC_ALL

If this environment variable is set it overrides the selection for all the locales done using the other `LC_*` environment variables. The value of the other `LC_*` environment variables is simply ignored in this case.

LC_COLLATE

This specifies what locale to use for string sorting.

LC_CTYPE

This specifies what locale to use for character sets and character classification.

LC_MESSAGES

This specifies what locale to use for printing messages and to parse responses.

LC_MONETARY

This specifies what locale to use for formatting monetary values.

LC_NUMERIC

This specifies what locale to use for formatting numbers.

LC_TIME

This specifies what locale to use for formatting date/time values.

NLSPATH

This specifies the directories in which the `catopen` function looks for message translation catalogs.

_POSIX_OPTION_ORDER

If this environment variable is defined, it suppresses the usual reordering of command line arguments by `getopt` and `argp_parse`. See Section 25.1.1 [Program Argument Syntax Conventions], page 730.

25.5 Auxiliary Vector

When a program is executed, it receives information from the operating system about the environment in which it is operating. The form of this information is a table of key-value pairs, where the keys are from the set of 'AT_' values in `elf.h`. Some of the data is provided by the kernel for libc consumption, and may be obtained by ordinary interfaces, such as `sysconf`. However, on a platform-by-platform basis there may be information that is not available any other way.

25.5.1 Definition of getauxval

unsigned long int getauxval (*unsigned long int type*)   [Function]
> Preliminary: | MT-Safe | AS-Safe | AC-Safe | See Section 1.2.2.1 [POSIX Safety
> Concepts], page 2.
>
> This function is used to inquire about the entries in the auxiliary vector. The *type*
> argument should be one of the 'AT_' symbols defined in elf.h. If a matching entry
> is found, the value is returned; if the entry is not found, zero is returned and errno
> is set to ENOENT.

For some platforms, the key AT_HWCAP is the easiest way to inquire about any instruction
set extensions available at runtime. In this case, there will (of necessity) be a platform-
specific set of 'HWCAP_' values masked together that describe the capabilities of the cpu on
which the program is being executed.

25.6 System Calls

A system call is a request for service that a program makes of the kernel. The service
is generally something that only the kernel has the privilege to do, such as doing I/O.
Programmers don't normally need to be concerned with system calls because there are
functions in the GNU C Library to do virtually everything that system calls do. These
functions work by making system calls themselves. For example, there is a system call that
changes the permissions of a file, but you don't need to know about it because you can just
use the GNU C Library's chmod function.

System calls are sometimes called kernel calls.

However, there are times when you want to make a system call explicitly, and for that,
the GNU C Library provides the syscall function. syscall is harder to use and less
portable than functions like chmod, but easier and more portable than coding the system
call in assembler instructions.

syscall is most useful when you are working with a system call which is special to your
system or is newer than the GNU C Library you are using. syscall is implemented in an
entirely generic way; the function does not know anything about what a particular system
call does or even if it is valid.

The description of syscall in this section assumes a certain protocol for system calls
on the various platforms on which the GNU C Library runs. That protocol is not defined
by any strong authority, but we won't describe it here either because anyone who is coding
syscall probably won't accept anything less than kernel and C library source code as a
specification of the interface between them anyway.

syscall is declared in unistd.h.

long int syscall (*long int sysno, ...*)   [Function]
> Preliminary: | MT-Safe | AS-Safe | AC-Safe | See Section 1.2.2.1 [POSIX Safety
> Concepts], page 2.
>
> syscall performs a generic system call.
>
> *sysno* is the system call number. Each kind of system call is identified by a number.
> Macros for all the possible system call numbers are defined in sys/syscall.h

The remaining arguments are the arguments for the system call, in order, and their meanings depend on the kind of system call. Each kind of system call has a definite number of arguments, from zero to five. If you code more arguments than the system call takes, the extra ones to the right are ignored.

The return value is the return value from the system call, unless the system call failed. In that case, `syscall` returns -1 and sets `errno` to an error code that the system call returned. Note that system calls do not return -1 when they succeed.

If you specify an invalid *sysno*, `syscall` returns -1 with `errno` = ENOSYS.

Example:

```
#include <unistd.h>
#include <sys/syscall.h>
#include <errno.h>

...

int rc;

rc = syscall(SYS_chmod, "/etc/passwd", 0444);

if (rc == -1)
   fprintf(stderr, "chmod failed, errno = %d\n", errno);
```

This, if all the compatibility stars are aligned, is equivalent to the following preferable code:

```
#include <sys/types.h>
#include <sys/stat.h>
#include <errno.h>

...

int rc;

rc = chmod("/etc/passwd", 0444);
if (rc == -1)
   fprintf(stderr, "chmod failed, errno = %d\n", errno);
```

25.7 Program Termination

The usual way for a program to terminate is simply for its `main` function to return. The *exit status value* returned from the `main` function is used to report information back to the process's parent process or shell.

A program can also terminate normally by calling the `exit` function.

In addition, programs can be terminated by signals; this is discussed in more detail in Chapter 24 [Signal Handling], page 685. The `abort` function causes a signal that kills the program.

25.7.1 Normal Termination

A process terminates normally when its program signals it is done by calling `exit`. Returning from `main` is equivalent to calling `exit`, and the value that `main` returns is used as the argument to `exit`.

`void exit (int status)`   [Function]

    Preliminary: | MT-Unsafe race:exit | AS-Unsafe corrupt | AC-Unsafe corrupt lock | See Section 1.2.2.1 [POSIX Safety Concepts], page 2.

    The `exit` function tells the system that the program is done, which causes it to terminate the process.

    status is the program's exit status, which becomes part of the process' termination status. This function does not return.

Normal termination causes the following actions:

1. Functions that were registered with the `atexit` or `on_exit` functions are called in the reverse order of their registration. This mechanism allows your application to specify its own "cleanup" actions to be performed at program termination. Typically, this is used to do things like saving program state information in a file, or unlocking locks in shared data bases.

2. All open streams are closed, writing out any buffered output data. See Section 12.4 [Closing Streams], page 262. In addition, temporary files opened with the `tmpfile` function are removed; see Section 14.11 [Temporary Files], page 433.

3. `_exit` is called, terminating the program. See Section 25.7.5 [Termination Internals], page 771.

25.7.2 Exit Status

When a program exits, it can return to the parent process a small amount of information about the cause of termination, using the *exit status*. This is a value between 0 and 255 that the exiting process passes as an argument to `exit`.

Normally you should use the exit status to report very broad information about success or failure. You can't provide a lot of detail about the reasons for the failure, and most parent processes would not want much detail anyway.

There are conventions for what sorts of status values certain programs should return. The most common convention is simply 0 for success and 1 for failure. Programs that perform comparison use a different convention: they use status 1 to indicate a mismatch, and status 2 to indicate an inability to compare. Your program should follow an existing convention if an existing convention makes sense for it.

A general convention reserves status values 128 and up for special purposes. In particular, the value 128 is used to indicate failure to execute another program in a subprocess. This convention is not universally obeyed, but it is a good idea to follow it in your programs.

Warning: Don't try to use the number of errors as the exit status. This is actually not very useful; a parent process would generally not care how many errors occurred. Worse than that, it does not work, because the status value is truncated to eight bits. Thus, if the program tried to report 256 errors, the parent would receive a report of 0 errors—that is, success.

For the same reason, it does not work to use the value of `errno` as the exit status—these can exceed 255.

Portability note: Some non-POSIX systems use different conventions for exit status values. For greater portability, you can use the macros `EXIT_SUCCESS` and `EXIT_FAILURE` for the conventional status value for success and failure, respectively. They are declared in the file `stdlib.h`.

`int EXIT_SUCCESS`   [Macro]

This macro can be used with the `exit` function to indicate successful program completion.

On POSIX systems, the value of this macro is 0. On other systems, the value might be some other (possibly non-constant) integer expression.

`int EXIT_FAILURE`   [Macro]

This macro can be used with the `exit` function to indicate unsuccessful program completion in a general sense.

On POSIX systems, the value of this macro is 1. On other systems, the value might be some other (possibly non-constant) integer expression. Other nonzero status values also indicate failures. Certain programs use different nonzero status values to indicate particular kinds of "non-success". For example, `diff` uses status value 1 to mean that the files are different, and 2 or more to mean that there was difficulty in opening the files.

Don't confuse a program's exit status with a process' termination status. There are lots of ways a process can terminate besides having its program finish. In the event that the process termination *is* caused by program termination (i.e., `exit`), though, the program's exit status becomes part of the process' termination status.

25.7.3 Cleanups on Exit

Your program can arrange to run its own cleanup functions if normal termination happens. If you are writing a library for use in various application programs, then it is unreliable to insist that all applications call the library's cleanup functions explicitly before exiting. It is much more robust to make the cleanup invisible to the application, by setting up a cleanup function in the library itself using `atexit` or `on_exit`.

`int atexit (void (*function) (void))`   [Function]

Preliminary: | MT-Safe | AS-Unsafe heap lock | AC-Unsafe lock mem | See Section 1.2.2.1 [POSIX Safety Concepts], page 2.

The `atexit` function registers the function *function* to be called at normal program termination. The *function* is called with no arguments.

The return value from `atexit` is zero on success and nonzero if the function cannot be registered.

`int on_exit (void (*function)(int status, void *arg), void *arg)`   [Function]

Preliminary: | MT-Safe | AS-Unsafe heap lock | AC-Unsafe lock mem | See Section 1.2.2.1 [POSIX Safety Concepts], page 2.

This function is a somewhat more powerful variant of `atexit`. It accepts two arguments, a function *function* and an arbitrary pointer *arg*. At normal program termination, the *function* is called with two arguments: the *status* value passed to `exit`, and the *arg*.

This function is included in the GNU C Library only for compatibility for SunOS, and may not be supported by other implementations.

Here's a trivial program that illustrates the use of `exit` and `atexit`:

```
#include <stdio.h>
#include <stdlib.h>

void
bye (void)
{
  puts ("Goodbye, cruel world....");
}

int
main (void)
{
  atexit (bye);
  exit (EXIT_SUCCESS);
}
```

When this program is executed, it just prints the message and exits.

25.7.4 Aborting a Program

You can abort your program using the `abort` function. The prototype for this function is in `stdlib.h`.

void abort (*void*)   [Function]
Preliminary: | MT-Safe | AS-Unsafe corrupt | AC-Unsafe lock corrupt | See Section 1.2.2.1 [POSIX Safety Concepts], page 2.

The `abort` function causes abnormal program termination. This does not execute cleanup functions registered with `atexit` or `on_exit`.

This function actually terminates the process by raising a `SIGABRT` signal, and your program can include a handler to intercept this signal; see Chapter 24 [Signal Handling], page 685.

Future Change Warning: Proposed Federal censorship regulations may prohibit us from giving you information about the possibility of calling this function. We would be required to say that this is not an acceptable way of terminating a program.

25.7.5 Termination Internals

The `_exit` function is the primitive used for process termination by `exit`. It is declared in the header file `unistd.h`.

`void _exit (int status)` [Function]

> Preliminary: | MT-Safe | AS-Safe | AC-Safe | See Section 1.2.2.1 [POSIX Safety Concepts], page 2.

> The `_exit` function is the primitive for causing a process to terminate with status *status*. Calling this function does not execute cleanup functions registered with `atexit` or `on_exit`.

`void _Exit (int status)` [Function]

> Preliminary: | MT-Safe | AS-Safe | AC-Safe | See Section 1.2.2.1 [POSIX Safety Concepts], page 2.

> The `_Exit` function is the ISO C equivalent to `_exit`. The ISO C committee members were not sure whether the definitions of `_exit` and `_Exit` were compatible so they have not used the POSIX name.

> This function was introduced in ISO C99 and is declared in `stdlib.h`.

When a process terminates for any reason—either because the program terminates, or as a result of a signal—the following things happen:

- All open file descriptors in the process are closed. See Chapter 13 [Low-Level Input/Output], page 333. Note that streams are not flushed automatically when the process terminates; see Chapter 12 [Input/Output on Streams], page 257.

- A process exit status is saved to be reported back to the parent process via `wait` or `waitpid`; see Section 26.6 [Process Completion], page 779. If the program exited, this status includes as its low-order 8 bits the program exit status.

- Any child processes of the process being terminated are assigned a new parent process. (On most systems, including GNU, this is the `init` process, with process ID 1.)

- A `SIGCHLD` signal is sent to the parent process.

- If the process is a session leader that has a controlling terminal, then a `SIGHUP` signal is sent to each process in the foreground job, and the controlling terminal is disassociated from that session. See Chapter 28 [Job Control], page 786.

- If termination of a process causes a process group to become orphaned, and any member of that process group is stopped, then a `SIGHUP` signal and a `SIGCONT` signal are sent to each process in the group. See Chapter 28 [Job Control], page 786.

26 Processes

Processes are the primitive units for allocation of system resources. Each process has its own address space and (usually) one thread of control. A process executes a program; you can have multiple processes executing the same program, but each process has its own copy of the program within its own address space and executes it independently of the other copies.

Processes are organized hierarchically. Each process has a *parent process* which explicitly arranged to create it. The processes created by a given parent are called its *child processes*. A child inherits many of its attributes from the parent process.

This chapter describes how a program can create, terminate, and control child processes. Actually, there are three distinct operations involved: creating a new child process, causing the new process to execute a program, and coordinating the completion of the child process with the original program.

The `system` function provides a simple, portable mechanism for running another program; it does all three steps automatically. If you need more control over the details of how this is done, you can use the primitive functions to do each step individually instead.

26.1 Running a Command

The easy way to run another program is to use the `system` function. This function does all the work of running a subprogram, but it doesn't give you much control over the details: you have to wait until the subprogram terminates before you can do anything else.

`int system` (*const char *command*) [Function]

> Preliminary: | MT-Safe | AS-Unsafe plugin heap lock | AC-Unsafe lock mem | See Section 1.2.2.1 [POSIX Safety Concepts], page 2.
>
> This function executes *command* as a shell command. In the GNU C Library, it always uses the default shell `sh` to run the command. In particular, it searches the directories in `PATH` to find programs to execute. The return value is `-1` if it wasn't possible to create the shell process, and otherwise is the status of the shell process. See Section 26.6 [Process Completion], page 779, for details on how this status code can be interpreted.
>
> If the *command* argument is a null pointer, a return value of zero indicates that no command processor is available.
>
> This function is a cancellation point in multi-threaded programs. This is a problem if the thread allocates some resources (like memory, file descriptors, semaphores or whatever) at the time `system` is called. If the thread gets canceled these resources stay allocated until the program ends. To avoid this calls to `system` should be protected using cancellation handlers.
>
> The `system` function is declared in the header file `stdlib.h`.

Portability Note: Some C implementations may not have any notion of a command processor that can execute other programs. You can determine whether a command processor exists by executing `system (NULL)`; if the return value is nonzero, a command processor is available.

The `popen` and `pclose` functions (see Section 15.2 [Pipe to a Subprocess], page 439) are closely related to the `system` function. They allow the parent process to communicate with the standard input and output channels of the command being executed.

26.2 Process Creation Concepts

This section gives an overview of processes and of the steps involved in creating a process and making it run another program.

Each process is named by a *process ID* number. A unique process ID is allocated to each process when it is created. The *lifetime* of a process ends when its termination is reported to its parent process; at that time, all of the process resources, including its process ID, are freed.

Processes are created with the `fork` system call (so the operation of creating a new process is sometimes called *forking* a process). The *child process* created by `fork` is a copy of the original *parent process*, except that it has its own process ID.

After forking a child process, both the parent and child processes continue to execute normally. If you want your program to wait for a child process to finish executing before continuing, you must do this explicitly after the fork operation, by calling `wait` or `waitpid` (see Section 26.6 [Process Completion], page 779). These functions give you limited information about why the child terminated—for example, its exit status code.

A newly forked child process continues to execute the same program as its parent process, at the point where the `fork` call returns. You can use the return value from `fork` to tell whether the program is running in the parent process or the child.

Having several processes run the same program is only occasionally useful. But the child can execute another program using one of the `exec` functions; see Section 26.5 [Executing a File], page 776. The program that the process is executing is called its *process image*. Starting execution of a new program causes the process to forget all about its previous process image; when the new program exits, the process exits too, instead of returning to the previous process image.

26.3 Process Identification

The `pid_t` data type represents process IDs. You can get the process ID of a process by calling `getpid`. The function `getppid` returns the process ID of the parent of the current process (this is also known as the *parent process ID*). Your program should include the header files `unistd.h` and `sys/types.h` to use these functions.

`pid_t`   [Data Type]
>   The `pid_t` data type is a signed integer type which is capable of representing a process ID. In the GNU C Library, this is an `int`.

`pid_t getpid` (*void*)   [Function]
>   Preliminary: | MT-Safe | AS-Safe | AC-Safe | See Section 1.2.2.1 [POSIX Safety Concepts], page 2.
>
>   The `getpid` function returns the process ID of the current process.

pid_t getppid (*void*) [Function]

> Preliminary: | MT-Safe | AS-Safe | AC-Safe | See Section 1.2.2.1 [POSIX Safety Concepts], page 2.
>
> The `getppid` function returns the process ID of the parent of the current process.

26.4 Creating a Process

The `fork` function is the primitive for creating a process. It is declared in the header file `unistd.h`.

pid_t fork (*void*) [Function]

> Preliminary: | MT-Safe | AS-Unsafe plugin | AC-Unsafe lock | See Section 1.2.2.1 [POSIX Safety Concepts], page 2.
>
> The `fork` function creates a new process.
>
> If the operation is successful, there are then both parent and child processes and both see `fork` return, but with different values: it returns a value of 0 in the child process and returns the child's process ID in the parent process.
>
> If process creation failed, `fork` returns a value of -1 in the parent process. The following `errno` error conditions are defined for `fork`:
>
> EAGAIN   There aren't enough system resources to create another process, or the user already has too many processes running. This means exceeding the `RLIMIT_NPROC` resource limit, which can usually be increased; see Section 22.2 [Limiting Resource Usage], page 656.
>
> ENOMEM   The process requires more space than the system can supply.

The specific attributes of the child process that differ from the parent process are:

- The child process has its own unique process ID.

- The parent process ID of the child process is the process ID of its parent process.

- The child process gets its own copies of the parent process's open file descriptors. Subsequently changing attributes of the file descriptors in the parent process won't affect the file descriptors in the child, and vice versa. See Section 13.11 [Control Operations on Files], page 371. However, the file position associated with each descriptor is shared by both processes; see Section 11.1.2 [File Position], page 253.

- The elapsed processor times for the child process are set to zero; see Section 21.3.2 [Processor Time Inquiry], page 622.

- The child doesn't inherit file locks set by the parent process. See Section 13.11 [Control Operations on Files], page 371.

- The child doesn't inherit alarms set by the parent process. See Section 21.5 [Setting an Alarm], page 649.

- The set of pending signals (see Section 24.1.3 [How Signals Are Delivered], page 686) for the child process is cleared. (The child process inherits its mask of blocked signals and signal actions from the parent process.)

`pid_t vfork (void)` [Function]

> Preliminary: | MT-Safe | AS-Unsafe plugin | AC-Unsafe lock | See Section 1.2.2.1 [POSIX Safety Concepts], page 2.
>
> The `vfork` function is similar to `fork` but on some systems it is more efficient; however, there are restrictions you must follow to use it safely.
>
> While `fork` makes a complete copy of the calling process's address space and allows both the parent and child to execute independently, `vfork` does not make this copy. Instead, the child process created with `vfork` shares its parent's address space until it calls `_exit` or one of the `exec` functions. In the meantime, the parent process suspends execution.
>
> You must be very careful not to allow the child process created with `vfork` to modify any global data or even local variables shared with the parent. Furthermore, the child process cannot return from (or do a long jump out of) the function that called `vfork`! This would leave the parent process's control information very confused. If in doubt, use `fork` instead.
>
> Some operating systems don't really implement `vfork`. The GNU C Library permits you to use `vfork` on all systems, but actually executes `fork` if `vfork` isn't available. If you follow the proper precautions for using `vfork`, your program will still work even if the system uses `fork` instead.

26.5 Executing a File

This section describes the `exec` family of functions, for executing a file as a process image. You can use these functions to make a child process execute a new program after it has been forked.

To see the effects of `exec` from the point of view of the called program, see Chapter 25 [The Basic Program/System Interface], page 729.

The functions in this family differ in how you specify the arguments, but otherwise they all do the same thing. They are declared in the header file `unistd.h`.

`int execv (const char *filename, char *const argv[])` [Function]

> Preliminary: | MT-Safe | AS-Safe | AC-Safe | See Section 1.2.2.1 [POSIX Safety Concepts], page 2.
>
> The `execv` function executes the file named by *filename* as a new process image.
>
> The *argv* argument is an array of null-terminated strings that is used to provide a value for the `argv` argument to the `main` function of the program to be executed. The last element of this array must be a null pointer. By convention, the first element of this array is the file name of the program sans directory names. See Section 25.1 [Program Arguments], page 729, for full details on how programs can access these arguments.
>
> The environment for the new process image is taken from the `environ` variable of the current process image; see Section 25.4 [Environment Variables], page 762, for information about environments.

`int execl (const char *filename, const char *arg0, ...)` [Function]

> Preliminary: | MT-Safe | AS-Unsafe heap | AC-Unsafe mem | See Section 1.2.2.1 [POSIX Safety Concepts], page 2.

This is similar to `execv`, but the *argv* strings are specified individually instead of as an array. A null pointer must be passed as the last such argument.

int execve (*const char *filename, char *const* `argv[]`, *char *const*   [Function]
    env[])

Preliminary: | MT-Safe | AS-Safe | AC-Safe | See Section 1.2.2.1 [POSIX Safety Concepts], page 2.

This is similar to `execv`, but permits you to specify the environment for the new program explicitly as the *env* argument. This should be an array of strings in the same format as for the `environ` variable; see Section 25.4.1 [Environment Access], page 763.

int execle (*const char *filename, const char *arg0, . . . , char*   [Function]
    *const env[])

Preliminary: | MT-Safe | AS-Unsafe heap | AC-Unsafe mem | See Section 1.2.2.1 [POSIX Safety Concepts], page 2.

This is similar to `execl`, but permits you to specify the environment for the new program explicitly. The environment argument is passed following the null pointer that marks the last *argv* argument, and should be an array of strings in the same format as for the `environ` variable.

int execvp (*const char *filename, char *const* `argv[]`)   [Function]

Preliminary: | MT-Safe env | AS-Unsafe heap | AC-Unsafe mem | See Section 1.2.2.1 [POSIX Safety Concepts], page 2.

The `execvp` function is similar to `execv`, except that it searches the directories listed in the `PATH` environment variable (see Section 25.4.2 [Standard Environment Variables], page 765) to find the full file name of a file from *filename* if *filename* does not contain a slash.

This function is useful for executing system utility programs, because it looks for them in the places that the user has chosen. Shells use it to run the commands that users type.

int execlp (*const char *filename, const char *arg0, . . .*)   [Function]

Preliminary: | MT-Safe env | AS-Unsafe heap | AC-Unsafe mem | See Section 1.2.2.1 [POSIX Safety Concepts], page 2.

This function is like `execl`, except that it performs the same file name searching as the `execvp` function.

The size of the argument list and environment list taken together must not be greater than `ARG_MAX` bytes. See Section 32.1 [General Capacity Limits], page 862. On GNU/Hurd systems, the size (which compares against `ARG_MAX`) includes, for each string, the number of characters in the string, plus the size of a `char *`, plus one, rounded up to a multiple of the size of a `char *`. Other systems may have somewhat different rules for counting.

These functions normally don't return, since execution of a new program causes the currently executing program to go away completely. A value of −1 is returned in the event of a failure. In addition to the usual file name errors (see Section 11.2.3 [File Name Errors], page 255), the following **errno** error conditions are defined for these functions:

E2BIG   The combined size of the new program's argument list and environment list is larger than **ARG_MAX** bytes. GNU/Hurd systems have no specific limit on the argument list size, so this error code cannot result, but you may get **ENOMEM** instead if the arguments are too big for available memory.

ENOEXEC   The specified file can't be executed because it isn't in the right format.

ENOMEM   Executing the specified file requires more storage than is available.

If execution of the new file succeeds, it updates the access time field of the file as if the file had been read. See Section 14.9.9 [File Times], page 426, for more details about access times of files.

The point at which the file is closed again is not specified, but is at some point before the process exits or before another process image is executed.

Executing a new process image completely changes the contents of memory, copying only the argument and environment strings to new locations. But many other attributes of the process are unchanged:

- The process ID and the parent process ID. See Section 26.2 [Process Creation Concepts], page 774.

- Session and process group membership. See Section 28.1 [Concepts of Job Control], page 786.

- Real user ID and group ID, and supplementary group IDs. See Section 30.2 [The Persona of a Process], page 815.

- Pending alarms. See Section 21.5 [Setting an Alarm], page 649.

- Current working directory and root directory. See Section 14.1 [Working Directory], page 390. On GNU/Hurd systems, the root directory is not copied when executing a setuid program; instead the system default root directory is used for the new program.

- File mode creation mask. See Section 14.9.7 [Assigning File Permissions], page 423.

- Process signal mask; see Section 24.7.3 [Process Signal Mask], page 718.

- Pending signals; see Section 24.7 [Blocking Signals], page 716.

- Elapsed processor time associated with the process; see Section 21.3.2 [Processor Time Inquiry], page 622.

If the set-user-ID and set-group-ID mode bits of the process image file are set, this affects the effective user ID and effective group ID (respectively) of the process. These concepts are discussed in detail in Section 30.2 [The Persona of a Process], page 815.

Signals that are set to be ignored in the existing process image are also set to be ignored in the new process image. All other signals are set to the default action in the new process image. For more information about signals, see Chapter 24 [Signal Handling], page 685.

File descriptors open in the existing process image remain open in the new process image, unless they have the **FD_CLOEXEC** (close-on-exec) flag set. The files that remain open inherit all attributes of the open file descriptors from the existing process image, including file locks. File descriptors are discussed in Chapter 13 [Low-Level Input/Output], page 333.

Streams, by contrast, cannot survive through `exec` functions, because they are located in the memory of the process itself. The new process image has no streams except those it creates afresh. Each of the streams in the pre-`exec` process image has a descriptor inside it, and these descriptors do survive through `exec` (provided that they do not have `FD_CLOEXEC` set). The new process image can reconnect these to new streams using `fdopen` (see Section 13.4 [Descriptors and Streams], page 346).

26.6 Process Completion

The functions described in this section are used to wait for a child process to terminate or stop, and determine its status. These functions are declared in the header file `sys/wait.h`.

`pid_t waitpid (pid_t pid, int *status-ptr, int options)` [Function]

Preliminary: | MT-Safe | AS-Safe | AC-Safe | See Section 1.2.2.1 [POSIX Safety Concepts], page 2.

The `waitpid` function is used to request status information from a child process whose process ID is *pid*. Normally, the calling process is suspended until the child process makes status information available by terminating.

Other values for the *pid* argument have special interpretations. A value of `-1` or `WAIT_ANY` requests status information for any child process; a value of 0 or `WAIT_MYPGRP` requests information for any child process in the same process group as the calling process; and any other negative value − *pgid* requests information for any child process whose process group ID is *pgid*.

If status information for a child process is available immediately, this function returns immediately without waiting. If more than one eligible child process has status information available, one of them is chosen randomly, and its status is returned immediately. To get the status from the other eligible child processes, you need to call `waitpid` again.

The *options* argument is a bit mask. Its value should be the bitwise OR (that is, the '|' operator) of zero or more of the `WNOHANG` and `WUNTRACED` flags. You can use the `WNOHANG` flag to indicate that the parent process shouldn't wait; and the `WUNTRACED` flag to request status information from stopped processes as well as processes that have terminated.

The status information from the child process is stored in the object that *status-ptr* points to, unless *status-ptr* is a null pointer.

This function is a cancellation point in multi-threaded programs. This is a problem if the thread allocates some resources (like memory, file descriptors, semaphores or whatever) at the time `waitpid` is called. If the thread gets canceled these resources stay allocated until the program ends. To avoid this calls to `waitpid` should be protected using cancellation handlers.

The return value is normally the process ID of the child process whose status is reported. If there are child processes but none of them is waiting to be noticed, `waitpid` will block until one is. However, if the `WNOHANG` option was specified, `waitpid` will return zero instead of blocking.

If a specific PID to wait for was given to `waitpid`, it will ignore all other children (if any). Therefore if there are children waiting to be noticed but the child whose PID was specified is not one of them, `waitpid` will block or return zero as described above.

A value of `-1` is returned in case of error. The following `errno` error conditions are defined for this function:

EINTR   The function was interrupted by delivery of a signal to the calling process. See Section 24.5 [Primitives Interrupted by Signals], page 711.

ECHILD   There are no child processes to wait for, or the specified *pid* is not a child of the calling process.

EINVAL   An invalid value was provided for the *options* argument.

These symbolic constants are defined as values for the *pid* argument to the `waitpid` function.

WAIT_ANY

This constant macro (whose value is `-1`) specifies that `waitpid` should return status information about any child process.

WAIT_MYPGRP

This constant (with value 0) specifies that `waitpid` should return status information about any child process in the same process group as the calling process.

These symbolic constants are defined as flags for the *options* argument to the `waitpid` function. You can bitwise-OR the flags together to obtain a value to use as the argument.

WNOHANG

This flag specifies that `waitpid` should return immediately instead of waiting, if there is no child process ready to be noticed.

WUNTRACED

This flag specifies that `waitpid` should report the status of any child processes that have been stopped as well as those that have terminated.

`pid_t wait (int *status-ptr)`   [Function]
Preliminary: | MT-Safe | AS-Safe | AC-Safe | See Section 1.2.2.1 [POSIX Safety Concepts], page 2.

This is a simplified version of `waitpid`, and is used to wait until any one child process terminates. The call:

        wait (&status)

is exactly equivalent to:

        waitpid (-1, &status, 0)

This function is a cancellation point in multi-threaded programs. This is a problem if the thread allocates some resources (like memory, file descriptors, semaphores or whatever) at the time `wait` is called. If the thread gets canceled these resources stay allocated until the program ends. To avoid this calls to `wait` should be protected using cancellation handlers.

`pid_t wait4` (*pid_t pid*, *int *status-ptr*, *int options*, *struct rusage*   [Function]
     **usage*)

> Preliminary: | MT-Safe | AS-Safe | AC-Safe | See Section 1.2.2.1 [POSIX Safety Concepts], page 2.
>
> If *usage* is a null pointer, `wait4` is equivalent to `waitpid` (*pid, status-ptr, options*).
>
> If *usage* is not null, `wait4` stores usage figures for the child process in **rusage* (but only if the child has terminated, not if it has stopped). See Section 22.1 [Resource Usage], page 654.
>
> This function is a BSD extension.

Here's an example of how to use `waitpid` to get the status from all child processes that have terminated, without ever waiting. This function is designed to be a handler for `SIGCHLD`, the signal that indicates that at least one child process has terminated.

```
void
sigchld_handler (int signum)
{
  int pid, status, serrno;
  serrno = errno;
  while (1)
    {
      pid = waitpid (WAIT_ANY, &status, WNOHANG);
      if (pid < 0)
        {
          perror ("waitpid");
          break;
        }
      if (pid == 0)
        break;
      notice_termination (pid, status);
    }
  errno = serrno;
}
```

26.7 Process Completion Status

If the exit status value (see Section 25.7 [Program Termination], page 768) of the child process is zero, then the status value reported by `waitpid` or `wait` is also zero. You can test for other kinds of information encoded in the returned status value using the following macros. These macros are defined in the header file `sys/wait.h`.

`int WIFEXITED` (*int status*)   [Macro]

> Preliminary: | MT-Safe | AS-Safe | AC-Safe | See Section 1.2.2.1 [POSIX Safety Concepts], page 2.
>
> This macro returns a nonzero value if the child process terminated normally with `exit` or `_exit`.

`int WEXITSTATUS` (*int status*)   [Macro]

> Preliminary: | MT-Safe | AS-Safe | AC-Safe | See Section 1.2.2.1 [POSIX Safety Concepts], page 2.
>
> If `WIFEXITED` is true of *status*, this macro returns the low-order 8 bits of the exit status value from the child process. See Section 25.7.2 [Exit Status], page 769.

`int WIFSIGNALED (int status)`   [Macro]
> Preliminary: | MT-Safe | AS-Safe | AC-Safe | See Section 1.2.2.1 [POSIX Safety
> Concepts], page 2.

> This macro returns a nonzero value if the child process terminated because it received
> a signal that was not handled. See Chapter 24 [Signal Handling], page 685.

`int WTERMSIG (int status)`   [Macro]
> Preliminary: | MT-Safe | AS-Safe | AC-Safe | See Section 1.2.2.1 [POSIX Safety
> Concepts], page 2.

> If `WIFSIGNALED` is true of *status*, this macro returns the signal number of the signal
> that terminated the child process.

`int WCOREDUMP (int status)`   [Macro]
> Preliminary: | MT-Safe | AS-Safe | AC-Safe | See Section 1.2.2.1 [POSIX Safety
> Concepts], page 2.

> This macro returns a nonzero value if the child process terminated and produced a
> core dump.

`int WIFSTOPPED (int status)`   [Macro]
> Preliminary: | MT-Safe | AS-Safe | AC-Safe | See Section 1.2.2.1 [POSIX Safety
> Concepts], page 2.

> This macro returns a nonzero value if the child process is stopped.

`int WSTOPSIG (int status)`   [Macro]
> Preliminary: | MT-Safe | AS-Safe | AC-Safe | See Section 1.2.2.1 [POSIX Safety
> Concepts], page 2.

> If `WIFSTOPPED` is true of *status*, this macro returns the signal number of the signal
> that caused the child process to stop.

26.8 BSD Process Wait Function

The GNU C Library also provides the `wait3` function for compatibility with BSD. This
function is declared in `sys/wait.h`. It is the predecessor to `wait4`, which is more flexible.
`wait3` is now obsolete.

`pid_t wait3 (int *status-ptr, int options, struct rusage *usage)`   [Function]
> Preliminary: | MT-Safe | AS-Safe | AC-Safe | See Section 1.2.2.1 [POSIX Safety
> Concepts], page 2.

> If *usage* is a null pointer, `wait3` is equivalent to `waitpid (-1, status-ptr,
> options)`.

> If *usage* is not null, `wait3` stores usage figures for the child process in *`*rusage`* (but
> only if the child has terminated, not if it has stopped). See Section 22.1 [Resource
> Usage], page 654.

26.9 Process Creation Example

Here is an example program showing how you might write a function similar to the built-in
`system`. It executes its *command* argument using the equivalent of 'sh -c *command*'.

```
#include <stddef.h>
#include <stdlib.h>
#include <unistd.h>
#include <sys/types.h>
#include <sys/wait.h>

/* Execute the command using this shell program.  */
#define SHELL "/bin/sh"

int
my_system (const char *command)
{
  int status;
  pid_t pid;

  pid = fork ();
  if (pid == 0)
    {
      /* This is the child process.  Execute the shell command. */
      execl (SHELL, SHELL, "-c", command, NULL);
      _exit (EXIT_FAILURE);
    }
  else if (pid < 0)
    /* The fork failed.  Report failure.  */
    status = -1;
  else
    /* This is the parent process.  Wait for the child to complete.  */
    if (waitpid (pid, &status, 0) != pid)
      status = -1;
  return status;
}
```

There are a couple of things you should pay attention to in this example.

Remember that the first `argv` argument supplied to the program represents the name of
the program being executed. That is why, in the call to `execl`, SHELL is supplied once to
name the program to execute and a second time to supply a value for `argv[0]`.

The `execl` call in the child process doesn't return if it is successful. If it fails, you must
do something to make the child process terminate. Just returning a bad status code with
`return` would leave two processes running the original program. Instead, the right behavior
is for the child process to report failure to its parent process.

Call `_exit` to accomplish this. The reason for using `_exit` instead of `exit` is to avoid
flushing fully buffered streams such as `stdout`. The buffers of these streams probably
contain data that was copied from the parent process by the `fork`, data that will be output
eventually by the parent process. Calling `exit` in the child would output the data twice.
See Section 25.7.5 [Termination Internals], page 771.

27 Inter-Process Communication

This chapter describes the GNU C Library inter-process communication primitives.

27.1 Semaphores

The GNU C Library implements the semaphore APIs as defined in POSIX and System V. Semaphores can be used by multiple processes to coordinate shared resources. The following is a complete list of the semaphore functions provided by the GNU C Library.

27.1.1 System V Semaphores

int semctl (*int* `semid`, *int* `semnum`, *int* `cmd`);   [Function]
> Preliminary: | MT-Safe | AS-Safe | AC-Unsafe corrupt/linux | See Section 1.2.2.1 [POSIX Safety Concepts], page 2.

int semget (*key_t* `key`, *int* `nsems`, *int* `semflg`);   [Function]
> Preliminary: | MT-Safe | AS-Safe | AC-Safe | See Section 1.2.2.1 [POSIX Safety Concepts], page 2.

int semop (*int* `semid`, *struct sembuf* `*sops`, *size_t* `nsops`);   [Function]
> Preliminary: | MT-Safe | AS-Safe | AC-Safe | See Section 1.2.2.1 [POSIX Safety Concepts], page 2.

int semtimedop (*int* `semid`, *struct sembuf* `*sops`, *size_t* `nsops`, *const*   [Function]
>   *struct timespec* `*timeout`);
> Preliminary: | MT-Safe | AS-Safe | AC-Safe | See Section 1.2.2.1 [POSIX Safety Concepts], page 2.

27.1.2 POSIX Semaphores

int sem_init (*sem_t* `*sem`, *int* `pshared`, *unsigned int* `value`);   [Function]
> Preliminary: | MT-Safe | AS-Safe | AC-Unsafe corrupt | See Section 1.2.2.1 [POSIX Safety Concepts], page 2.

int sem_destroy (*sem_t* `*sem`);   [Function]
> Preliminary: | MT-Safe | AS-Safe | AC-Safe | See Section 1.2.2.1 [POSIX Safety Concepts], page 2.

sem_t *sem_open (*const char* `*name`, *int* `oflag`, ...);   [Function]
> Preliminary: | MT-Safe | AS-Unsafe init | AC-Unsafe init | See Section 1.2.2.1 [POSIX Safety Concepts], page 2.

int sem_close (*sem_t* `*sem`);   [Function]
> Preliminary: | MT-Safe | AS-Unsafe lock | AC-Unsafe lock | See Section 1.2.2.1 [POSIX Safety Concepts], page 2.

int sem_unlink (*const char* `*name`);   [Function]
> Preliminary: | MT-Safe | AS-Unsafe init | AC-Unsafe corrupt | See Section 1.2.2.1 [POSIX Safety Concepts], page 2.

`int sem_wait (`*`sem_t *sem`*`);` [Function]
> Preliminary: | MT-Safe | AS-Safe | AC-Unsafe corrupt | See Section 1.2.2.1 [POSIX Safety Concepts], page 2.

`int sem_timedwait (`*`sem_t *sem, const struct timespec *abstime`*`);` [Function]
> Preliminary: | MT-Safe | AS-Safe | AC-Unsafe corrupt | See Section 1.2.2.1 [POSIX Safety Concepts], page 2.

`int sem_trywait (`*`sem_t *sem`*`);` [Function]
> Preliminary: | MT-Safe | AS-Safe | AC-Safe | See Section 1.2.2.1 [POSIX Safety Concepts], page 2.

`int sem_post (`*`sem_t *sem`*`);` [Function]
> Preliminary: | MT-Safe | AS-Safe | AC-Safe | See Section 1.2.2.1 [POSIX Safety Concepts], page 2.

`int sem_getvalue (`*`sem_t *sem, int *sval`*`);` [Function]
> Preliminary: | MT-Safe | AS-Safe | AC-Safe | See Section 1.2.2.1 [POSIX Safety Concepts], page 2.

28 Job Control

Job control refers to the protocol for allowing a user to move between multiple *process groups* (or *jobs*) within a single *login session*. The job control facilities are set up so that appropriate behavior for most programs happens automatically and they need not do anything special about job control. So you can probably ignore the material in this chapter unless you are writing a shell or login program.

You need to be familiar with concepts relating to process creation (see Section 26.2 [Process Creation Concepts], page 774) and signal handling (see Chapter 24 [Signal Handling], page 685) in order to understand this material presented in this chapter.

28.1 Concepts of Job Control

The fundamental purpose of an interactive shell is to read commands from the user's terminal and create processes to execute the programs specified by those commands. It can do this using the `fork` (see Section 26.4 [Creating a Process], page 775) and `exec` (see Section 26.5 [Executing a File], page 776) functions.

A single command may run just one process—but often one command uses several processes. If you use the '|' operator in a shell command, you explicitly request several programs in their own processes. But even if you run just one program, it can use multiple processes internally. For example, a single compilation command such as 'cc -c foo.c' typically uses four processes (though normally only two at any given time). If you run `make`, its job is to run other programs in separate processes.

The processes belonging to a single command are called a *process group* or *job*. This is so that you can operate on all of them at once. For example, typing *C-c* sends the signal `SIGINT` to terminate all the processes in the foreground process group.

A *session* is a larger group of processes. Normally all the processes that stem from a single login belong to the same session.

Every process belongs to a process group. When a process is created, it becomes a member of the same process group and session as its parent process. You can put it in another process group using the `setpgid` function, provided the process group belongs to the same session.

The only way to put a process in a different session is to make it the initial process of a new session, or a *session leader*, using the `setsid` function. This also puts the session leader into a new process group, and you can't move it out of that process group again.

Usually, new sessions are created by the system login program, and the session leader is the process running the user's login shell.

A shell that supports job control must arrange to control which job can use the terminal at any time. Otherwise there might be multiple jobs trying to read from the terminal at once, and confusion about which process should receive the input typed by the user. To prevent this, the shell must cooperate with the terminal driver using the protocol described in this chapter.

The shell can give unlimited access to the controlling terminal to only one process group at a time. This is called the *foreground job* on that controlling terminal. Other process groups managed by the shell that are executing without such access to the terminal are called *background jobs*.

If a background job needs to read from its controlling terminal, it is *stopped* by the terminal driver; if the `TOSTOP` mode is set, likewise for writing. The user can stop a foreground job by typing the SUSP character (see Section 17.4.9 [Special Characters], page 503) and a program can stop any job by sending it a `SIGSTOP` signal. It's the responsibility of the shell to notice when jobs stop, to notify the user about them, and to provide mechanisms for allowing the user to interactively continue stopped jobs and switch jobs between foreground and background.

See Section 28.4 [Access to the Controlling Terminal], page 787, for more information about I/O to the controlling terminal.

28.2 Job Control is Optional

Not all operating systems support job control. GNU systems do support job control, but if you are using the GNU C Library on some other system, that system may not support job control itself.

You can use the `_POSIX_JOB_CONTROL` macro to test at compile-time whether the system supports job control. See Section 32.2 [Overall System Options], page 863.

If job control is not supported, then there can be only one process group per session, which behaves as if it were always in the foreground. The functions for creating additional process groups simply fail with the error code `ENOSYS`.

The macros naming the various job control signals (see Section 24.2.5 [Job Control Signals], page 692) are defined even if job control is not supported. However, the system never generates these signals, and attempts to send a job control signal or examine or specify their actions report errors or do nothing.

28.3 Controlling Terminal of a Process

One of the attributes of a process is its controlling terminal. Child processes created with `fork` inherit the controlling terminal from their parent process. In this way, all the processes in a session inherit the controlling terminal from the session leader. A session leader that has control of a terminal is called the *controlling process* of that terminal.

You generally do not need to worry about the exact mechanism used to allocate a controlling terminal to a session, since it is done for you by the system when you log in.

An individual process disconnects from its controlling terminal when it calls `setsid` to become the leader of a new session. See Section 28.7.2 [Process Group Functions], page 801.

28.4 Access to the Controlling Terminal

Processes in the foreground job of a controlling terminal have unrestricted access to that terminal; background processes do not. This section describes in more detail what happens when a process in a background job tries to access its controlling terminal.

When a process in a background job tries to read from its controlling terminal, the process group is usually sent a `SIGTTIN` signal. This normally causes all of the processes in that group to stop (unless they handle the signal and don't stop themselves). However, if the reading process is ignoring or blocking this signal, then **read** fails with an **EIO** error instead.

Similarly, when a process in a background job tries to write to its controlling terminal, the default behavior is to send a **SIGTTOU** signal to the process group. However, the behavior is modified by the **TOSTOP** bit of the local modes flags (see Section 17.4.7 [Local Modes], page 499). If this bit is not set (which is the default), then writing to the controlling terminal is always permitted without sending a signal. Writing is also permitted if the **SIGTTOU** signal is being ignored or blocked by the writing process.

Most other terminal operations that a program can do are treated as reading or as writing. (The description of each operation should say which.)

For more information about the primitive **read** and **write** functions, see Section 13.2 [Input and Output Primitives], page 336.

28.5 Orphaned Process Groups

When a controlling process terminates, its terminal becomes free and a new session can be established on it. (In fact, another user could log in on the terminal.) This could cause a problem if any processes from the old session are still trying to use that terminal.

To prevent problems, process groups that continue running even after the session leader has terminated are marked as *orphaned process groups*.

When a process group becomes an orphan, its processes are sent a **SIGHUP** signal. Ordinarily, this causes the processes to terminate. However, if a program ignores this signal or establishes a handler for it (see Chapter 24 [Signal Handling], page 685), it can continue running as in the orphan process group even after its controlling process terminates; but it still cannot access the terminal any more.

28.6 Implementing a Job Control Shell

This section describes what a shell must do to implement job control, by presenting an extensive sample program to illustrate the concepts involved.

- Section 28.6.1 [Data Structures for the Shell], page 789, introduces the example and presents its primary data structures.

- Section 28.6.2 [Initializing the Shell], page 790, discusses actions which the shell must perform to prepare for job control.

- Section 28.6.3 [Launching Jobs], page 791, includes information about how to create jobs to execute commands.

- Section 28.6.4 [Foreground and Background], page 795, discusses what the shell should do differently when launching a job in the foreground as opposed to a background job.

- Section 28.6.5 [Stopped and Terminated Jobs], page 796, discusses reporting of job status back to the shell.

- Section 28.6.6 [Continuing Stopped Jobs], page 799, tells you how to continue jobs that have been stopped.

- Section 28.6.7 [The Missing Pieces], page 800, discusses other parts of the shell.

28.6.1 Data Structures for the Shell

All of the program examples included in this chapter are part of a simple shell program. This section presents data structures and utility functions which are used throughout the example.

The sample shell deals mainly with two data structures. The `job` type contains information about a job, which is a set of subprocesses linked together with pipes. The `process` type holds information about a single subprocess. Here are the relevant data structure declarations:

```
/* A process is a single process.  */
typedef struct process
{
  struct process *next;       /* next process in pipeline */
  char **argv;                /* for exec */
  pid_t pid;                  /* process ID */
  char completed;             /* true if process has completed */
  char stopped;               /* true if process has stopped */
  int status;                 /* reported status value */
} process;

/* A job is a pipeline of processes.  */
typedef struct job
{
  struct job *next;           /* next active job */
  char *command;              /* command line, used for messages */
  process *first_process;     /* list of processes in this job */
  pid_t pgid;                 /* process group ID */
  char notified;              /* true if user told about stopped job */
  struct termios tmodes;      /* saved terminal modes */
  int stdin, stdout, stderr;  /* standard i/o channels */
} job;

/* The active jobs are linked into a list.  This is its head.  */
job *first_job = NULL;
```

Here are some utility functions that are used for operating on `job` objects.

```
/* Find the active job with the indicated pgid.  */
job *
find_job (pid_t pgid)
{
  job *j;

  for (j = first_job; j; j = j->next)
    if (j->pgid == pgid)
      return j;
  return NULL;
}
```

```
/* Return true if all processes in the job have stopped or completed.  */
int
job_is_stopped (job *j)
{
  process *p;

  for (p = j->first_process; p; p = p->next)
    if (!p->completed && !p->stopped)
      return 0;
  return 1;
}

/* Return true if all processes in the job have completed.  */
int
job_is_completed (job *j)
{
  process *p;

  for (p = j->first_process; p; p = p->next)
    if (!p->completed)
      return 0;
  return 1;
}
```

28.6.2 Initializing the Shell

When a shell program that normally performs job control is started, it has to be careful in case it has been invoked from another shell that is already doing its own job control.

A subshell that runs interactively has to ensure that it has been placed in the foreground by its parent shell before it can enable job control itself. It does this by getting its initial process group ID with the getpgrp function, and comparing it to the process group ID of the current foreground job associated with its controlling terminal (which can be retrieved using the tcgetpgrp function).

If the subshell is not running as a foreground job, it must stop itself by sending a SIGTTIN signal to its own process group. It may not arbitrarily put itself into the foreground; it must wait for the user to tell the parent shell to do this. If the subshell is continued again, it should repeat the check and stop itself again if it is still not in the foreground.

Once the subshell has been placed into the foreground by its parent shell, it can enable its own job control. It does this by calling setpgid to put itself into its own process group, and then calling tcsetpgrp to place this process group into the foreground.

When a shell enables job control, it should set itself to ignore all the job control stop signals so that it doesn't accidentally stop itself. You can do this by setting the action for all the stop signals to SIG_IGN.

A subshell that runs non-interactively cannot and should not support job control. It must leave all processes it creates in the same process group as the shell itself; this allows the non-interactive shell and its child processes to be treated as a single job by the parent shell. This is easy to do—just don't use any of the job control primitives—but you must remember to make the shell do it.

Here is the initialization code for the sample shell that shows how to do all of this.

```
/* Keep track of attributes of the shell.  */
```

```
#include <sys/types.h>
#include <termios.h>
#include <unistd.h>

pid_t shell_pgid;
struct termios shell_tmodes;
int shell_terminal;
int shell_is_interactive;


/* Make sure the shell is running interactively as the foreground job
   before proceeding. */

void
init_shell ()
{

  /* See if we are running interactively.  */
  shell_terminal = STDIN_FILENO;
  shell_is_interactive = isatty (shell_terminal);

  if (shell_is_interactive)
    {
      /* Loop until we are in the foreground.  */
      while (tcgetpgrp (shell_terminal) != (shell_pgid = getpgrp ()))
        kill (- shell_pgid, SIGTTIN);

      /* Ignore interactive and job-control signals.  */
      signal (SIGINT, SIG_IGN);
      signal (SIGQUIT, SIG_IGN);
      signal (SIGTSTP, SIG_IGN);
      signal (SIGTTIN, SIG_IGN);
      signal (SIGTTOU, SIG_IGN);
      signal (SIGCHLD, SIG_IGN);

      /* Put ourselves in our own process group.  */
      shell_pgid = getpid ();
      if (setpgid (shell_pgid, shell_pgid) < 0)
        {
          perror ("Couldn't put the shell in its own process group");
          exit (1);
        }

      /* Grab control of the terminal.  */
      tcsetpgrp (shell_terminal, shell_pgid);

      /* Save default terminal attributes for shell.  */
      tcgetattr (shell_terminal, &shell_tmodes);
    }
}
```

28.6.3 Launching Jobs

Once the shell has taken responsibility for performing job control on its controlling terminal, it can launch jobs in response to commands typed by the user.

To create the processes in a process group, you use the same **fork** and **exec** functions described in Section 26.2 [Process Creation Concepts], page 774. Since there are multiple child processes involved, though, things are a little more complicated and you must be careful to do things in the right order. Otherwise, nasty race conditions can result.

You have two choices for how to structure the tree of parent-child relationships among the processes. You can either make all the processes in the process group be children of the shell process, or you can make one process in group be the ancestor of all the other processes in that group. The sample shell program presented in this chapter uses the first approach because it makes bookkeeping somewhat simpler.

As each process is forked, it should put itself in the new process group by calling `setpgid`; see Section 28.7.2 [Process Group Functions], page 801. The first process in the new group becomes its *process group leader*, and its process ID becomes the *process group ID* for the group.

The shell should also call `setpgid` to put each of its child processes into the new process group. This is because there is a potential timing problem: each child process must be put in the process group before it begins executing a new program, and the shell depends on having all the child processes in the group before it continues executing. If both the child processes and the shell call `setpgid`, this ensures that the right things happen no matter which process gets to it first.

If the job is being launched as a foreground job, the new process group also needs to be put into the foreground on the controlling terminal using `tcsetpgrp`. Again, this should be done by the shell as well as by each of its child processes, to avoid race conditions.

The next thing each child process should do is to reset its signal actions.

During initialization, the shell process set itself to ignore job control signals; see Section 28.6.2 [Initializing the Shell], page 790. As a result, any child processes it creates also ignore these signals by inheritance. This is definitely undesirable, so each child process should explicitly set the actions for these signals back to `SIG_DFL` just after it is forked.

Since shells follow this convention, applications can assume that they inherit the correct handling of these signals from the parent process. But every application has a responsibility not to mess up the handling of stop signals. Applications that disable the normal interpretation of the SUSP character should provide some other mechanism for the user to stop the job. When the user invokes this mechanism, the program should send a `SIGTSTP` signal to the process group of the process, not just to the process itself. See Section 24.6.2 [Signaling Another Process], page 713.

Finally, each child process should call `exec` in the normal way. This is also the point at which redirection of the standard input and output channels should be handled. See Section 13.12 [Duplicating Descriptors], page 373, for an explanation of how to do this.

Here is the function from the sample shell program' that is responsible for launching a program. The function is executed by each child process immediately after it has been forked by the shell, and never returns.

```
void
launch_process (process *p, pid_t pgid,
                int infile, int outfile, int errfile,
                int foreground)
{
  pid_t pid;

  if (shell_is_interactive)
```

```
  {
    /* Put the process into the process group and give the process group
       the terminal, if appropriate.
       This has to be done both by the shell and in the individual
       child processes because of potential race conditions.   */
    pid = getpid ();
    if (pgid == 0) pgid = pid;
    setpgid (pid, pgid);
    if (foreground)
      tcsetpgrp (shell_terminal, pgid);

    /* Set the handling for job control signals back to the default.   */
    signal (SIGINT, SIG_DFL);
    signal (SIGQUIT, SIG_DFL);
    signal (SIGTSTP, SIG_DFL);
    signal (SIGTTIN, SIG_DFL);
    signal (SIGTTOU, SIG_DFL);
    signal (SIGCHLD, SIG_DFL);
  }

/* Set the standard input/output channels of the new process.   */
if (infile != STDIN_FILENO)
  {
    dup2 (infile, STDIN_FILENO);
    close (infile);
  }
if (outfile != STDOUT_FILENO)
  {
    dup2 (outfile, STDOUT_FILENO);
    close (outfile);
  }
if (errfile != STDERR_FILENO)
  {
    dup2 (errfile, STDERR_FILENO);
    close (errfile);
  }

/* Exec the new process.  Make sure we exit.  */
execvp (p->argv[0], p->argv);
perror ("execvp");
exit (1);
}
```

If the shell is not running interactively, this function does not do anything with process groups or signals. Remember that a shell not performing job control must keep all of its subprocesses in the same process group as the shell itself.

Next, here is the function that actually launches a complete job. After creating the child processes, this function calls some other functions to put the newly created job into the foreground or background; these are discussed in Section 28.6.4 [Foreground and Background], page 795.

```
void
launch_job (job *j, int foreground)
{
  process *p;
  pid_t pid;
  int mypipe[2], infile, outfile;
```

```
  infile = j->stdin;
  for (p = j->first_process; p; p = p->next)
    {
      /* Set up pipes, if necessary.  */
      if (p->next)
        {
          if (pipe (mypipe) < 0)
            {
              perror ("pipe");
              exit (1);
            }
          outfile = mypipe[1];
        }
      else
        outfile = j->stdout;

      /* Fork the child processes.  */
      pid = fork ();
      if (pid == 0)
        /* This is the child process.  */
        launch_process (p, j->pgid, infile,
                        outfile, j->stderr, foreground);
      else if (pid < 0)
        {
          /* The fork failed.  */
          perror ("fork");
          exit (1);
        }
      else
        {
          /* This is the parent process.  */
          p->pid = pid;
          if (shell_is_interactive)
            {
              if (!j->pgid)
                j->pgid = pid;
              setpgid (pid, j->pgid);
            }
        }

      /* Clean up after pipes.  */
      if (infile != j->stdin)
        close (infile);
      if (outfile != j->stdout)
        close (outfile);
      infile = mypipe[0];
    }

  format_job_info (j, "launched");

  if (!shell_is_interactive)
    wait_for_job (j);
  else if (foreground)
    put_job_in_foreground (j, 0);
  else
    put_job_in_background (j, 0);
}
```

28.6.4 Foreground and Background

Now let's consider what actions must be taken by the shell when it launches a job into the foreground, and how this differs from what must be done when a background job is launched.

When a foreground job is launched, the shell must first give it access to the controlling terminal by calling `tcsetpgrp`. Then, the shell should wait for processes in that process group to terminate or stop. This is discussed in more detail in Section 28.6.5 [Stopped and Terminated Jobs], page 796.

When all of the processes in the group have either completed or stopped, the shell should regain control of the terminal for its own process group by calling `tcsetpgrp` again. Since stop signals caused by I/O from a background process or a SUSP character typed by the user are sent to the process group, normally all the processes in the job stop together.

The foreground job may have left the terminal in a strange state, so the shell should restore its own saved terminal modes before continuing. In case the job is merely stopped, the shell should first save the current terminal modes so that it can restore them later if the job is continued. The functions for dealing with terminal modes are `tcgetattr` and `tcsetattr`; these are described in Section 17.4 [Terminal Modes], page 492.

Here is the sample shell's function for doing all of this.

```
/* Put job j in the foreground.  If cont is nonzero,
   restore the saved terminal modes and send the process group a
   SIGCONT signal to wake it up before we block.  */

void
put_job_in_foreground (job *j, int cont)
{
  /* Put the job into the foreground.  */
  tcsetpgrp (shell_terminal, j->pgid);

  /* Send the job a continue signal, if necessary.  */
  if (cont)
    {
      tcsetattr (shell_terminal, TCSADRAIN, &j->tmodes);
      if (kill (- j->pgid, SIGCONT) < 0)
        perror ("kill (SIGCONT)");
    }

  /* Wait for it to report.  */
  wait_for_job (j);

  /* Put the shell back in the foreground.  */
  tcsetpgrp (shell_terminal, shell_pgid);

  /* Restore the shellfls terminal modes.  */
  tcgetattr (shell_terminal, &j->tmodes);
  tcsetattr (shell_terminal, TCSADRAIN, &shell_tmodes);
}
```

If the process group is launched as a background job, the shell should remain in the foreground itself and continue to read commands from the terminal.

In the sample shell, there is not much that needs to be done to put a job into the background. Here is the function it uses:

```
/* Put a job in the background.  If the cont argument is true, send
```

```
                    the process group a SIGCONT signal to wake it up.  */

        void
        put_job_in_background (job *j, int cont)
        {
          /* Send the job a continue signal, if necessary.  */
          if (cont)
            if (kill (-j->pgid, SIGCONT) < 0)
              perror ("kill (SIGCONT)");
        }
```

28.6.5 Stopped and Terminated Jobs

When a foreground process is launched, the shell must block until all of the processes in that job have either terminated or stopped. It can do this by calling the `waitpid` function; see Section 26.6 [Process Completion], page 779. Use the `WUNTRACED` option so that status is reported for processes that stop as well as processes that terminate.

The shell must also check on the status of background jobs so that it can report terminated and stopped jobs to the user; this can be done by calling `waitpid` with the `WNOHANG` option. A good place to put a such a check for terminated and stopped jobs is just before prompting for a new command.

The shell can also receive asynchronous notification that there is status information available for a child process by establishing a handler for `SIGCHLD` signals. See Chapter 24 [Signal Handling], page 685.

In the sample shell program, the `SIGCHLD` signal is normally ignored. This is to avoid reentrancy problems involving the global data structures the shell manipulates. But at specific times when the shell is not using these data structures—such as when it is waiting for input on the terminal—it makes sense to enable a handler for `SIGCHLD`. The same function that is used to do the synchronous status checks (`do_job_notification`, in this case) can also be called from within this handler.

Here are the parts of the sample shell program that deal with checking the status of jobs and reporting the information to the user.

```
        /* Store the status of the process pid that was returned by waitpid.
           Return 0 if all went well, nonzero otherwise.  */

        int
        mark_process_status (pid_t pid, int status)
        {
          job *j;
          process *p;
```

```
      if (pid > 0)
        {
          /* Update the record for the process.  */
          for (j = first_job; j; j = j->next)
            for (p = j->first_process; p; p = p->next)
              if (p->pid == pid)
                {
                  p->status = status;
                  if (WIFSTOPPED (status))
                    p->stopped = 1;
                  else
                    {
                      p->completed = 1;
                      if (WIFSIGNALED (status))
                        fprintf (stderr, "%d: Terminated by signal %d.\n",
                                 (int) pid, WTERMSIG (p->status));
                    }
                  return 0;
                }
          fprintf (stderr, "No child process %d.\n", pid);
          return -1;
        }
      else if (pid == 0 || errno == ECHILD)
        /* No processes ready to report.  */
        return -1;
      else {
        /* Other weird errors.  */
        perror ("waitpid");
        return -1;
      }
}

/* Check for processes that have status information available,
   without blocking.  */

void
update_status (void)
{
  int status;
  pid_t pid;

  do
    pid = waitpid (WAIT_ANY, &status, WUNTRACED|WNOHANG);
  while (!mark_process_status (pid, status));
}
```

```
/* Check for processes that have status information available,
     blocking until all processes in the given job have reported.  */

void
wait_for_job (job *j)
{
  int status;
  pid_t pid;

  do
    pid = waitpid (WAIT_ANY, &status, WUNTRACED);
  while (!mark_process_status (pid, status)
         && !job_is_stopped (j)
         && !job_is_completed (j));
}

/* Format information about job status for the user to look at.  */

void
format_job_info (job *j, const char *status)
{
  fprintf (stderr, "%ld (%s): %s\n", (long)j->pgid, status, j->command);
}
```

```
/* Notify the user about stopped or terminated jobs.
   Delete terminated jobs from the active job list.  */

void
do_job_notification (void)
{
  job *j, *jlast, *jnext;
  process *p;

  /* Update status information for child processes.  */
  update_status ();

  jlast = NULL;
  for (j = first_job; j; j = jnext)
    {
      jnext = j->next;

      /* If all processes have completed, tell the user the job has
         completed and delete it from the list of active jobs.  */
      if (job_is_completed (j)) {
        format_job_info (j, "completed");
        if (jlast)
          jlast->next = jnext;
        else
          first_job = jnext;
        free_job (j);
      }

      /* Notify the user about stopped jobs,
         marking them so that we wonflt do this more than once.  */
      else if (job_is_stopped (j) && !j->notified) {
        format_job_info (j, "stopped");
        j->notified = 1;
        jlast = j;
      }

      /* Donflt say anything about jobs that are still running.  */
      else
        jlast = j;
    }
}
```

28.6.6 Continuing Stopped Jobs

The shell can continue a stopped job by sending a SIGCONT signal to its process group. If the job is being continued in the foreground, the shell should first invoke tcsetpgrp to give the job access to the terminal, and restore the saved terminal settings. After continuing a job in the foreground, the shell should wait for the job to stop or complete, as if the job had just been launched in the foreground.

The sample shell program handles both newly created and continued jobs with the same pair of functions, put_job_in_foreground and put_job_in_background. The definitions of these functions were given in Section 28.6.4 [Foreground and Background], page 795. When continuing a stopped job, a nonzero value is passed as the *cont* argument to ensure that the SIGCONT signal is sent and the terminal modes reset, as appropriate.

This leaves only a function for updating the shell's internal bookkeeping about the job being continued:

```
/* Mark a stopped job J as being running again.  */

void
mark_job_as_running (job *j)
{
  Process *p;

  for (p = j->first_process; p; p = p->next)
    p->stopped = 0;
  j->notified = 0;
}

/* Continue the job J.  */

void
continue_job (job *j, int foreground)
{
  mark_job_as_running (j);
  if (foreground)
    put_job_in_foreground (j, 1);
  else
    put_job_in_background (j, 1);
}
```

28.6.7 The Missing Pieces

The code extracts for the sample shell included in this chapter are only a part of the entire shell program. In particular, nothing at all has been said about how `job` and `program` data structures are allocated and initialized.

Most real shells provide a complex user interface that has support for a command language; variables; abbreviations, substitutions, and pattern matching on file names; and the like. All of this is far too complicated to explain here! Instead, we have concentrated on showing how to implement the core process creation and job control functions that can be called from such a shell.

Here is a table summarizing the major entry points we have presented:

`void init_shell (void)`

> Initialize the shell's internal state. See Section 28.6.2 [Initializing the Shell], page 790.

`void launch_job (job *j, int foreground)`

> Launch the job *j* as either a foreground or background job. See Section 28.6.3 [Launching Jobs], page 791.

`void do_job_notification (void)`

> Check for and report any jobs that have terminated or stopped. Can be called synchronously or within a handler for `SIGCHLD` signals. See Section 28.6.5 [Stopped and Terminated Jobs], page 796.

`void continue_job (job *j, int foreground)`

> Continue the job *j*. See Section 28.6.6 [Continuing Stopped Jobs], page 799.

Of course, a real shell would also want to provide other functions for managing jobs. For example, it would be useful to have commands to list all active jobs or to send a signal (such as SIGKILL) to a job.

28.7 Functions for Job Control

This section contains detailed descriptions of the functions relating to job control.

28.7.1 Identifying the Controlling Terminal

You can use the ctermid function to get a file name that you can use to open the controlling terminal. In the GNU C Library, it returns the same string all the time: "/dev/tty". That is a special "magic" file name that refers to the controlling terminal of the current process (if it has one). To find the name of the specific terminal device, use ttyname; see Section 17.1 [Identifying Terminals], page 490.

The function ctermid is declared in the header file stdio.h.

char * ctermid (*char *string*)   [Function]
> Preliminary: | MT-Safe !posix/!string | AS-Safe | AC-Safe | See Section 1.2.2.1 [POSIX Safety Concepts], page 2.
>
> The ctermid function returns a string containing the file name of the controlling terminal for the current process. If *string* is not a null pointer, it should be an array that can hold at least L_ctermid characters; the string is returned in this array. Otherwise, a pointer to a string in a static area is returned, which might get overwritten on subsequent calls to this function.
>
> An empty string is returned if the file name cannot be determined for any reason. Even if a file name is returned, access to the file it represents is not guaranteed.

int L_ctermid   [Macro]
> The value of this macro is an integer constant expression that represents the size of a string large enough to hold the file name returned by ctermid.

See also the isatty and ttyname functions, in Section 17.1 [Identifying Terminals], page 490.

28.7.2 Process Group Functions

Here are descriptions of the functions for manipulating process groups. Your program should include the header files sys/types.h and unistd.h to use these functions.

pid_t setsid (*void*)   [Function]
> Preliminary: | MT-Safe | AS-Safe | AC-Safe | See Section 1.2.2.1 [POSIX Safety Concepts], page 2.
>
> The setsid function creates a new session. The calling process becomes the session leader, and is put in a new process group whose process group ID is the same as the process ID of that process. There are initially no other processes in the new process group, and no other process groups in the new session.
>
> This function also makes the calling process have no controlling terminal.

The **setsid** function returns the new process group ID of the calling process if successful. A return value of -1 indicates an error. The following **errno** error conditions are defined for this function:

EPERM   The calling process is already a process group leader, or there is already another process group around that has the same process group ID.

pid_t getsid (*pid_t pid*)   [Function]
Preliminary: | MT-Safe | AS-Safe | AC-Safe | See Section 1.2.2.1 [POSIX Safety Concepts], page 2.

The **getsid** function returns the process group ID of the session leader of the specified process. If a *pid* is 0, the process group ID of the session leader of the current process is returned.

In case of error -1 is returned and **errno** is set. The following **errno** error conditions are defined for this function:

ESRCH   There is no process with the given process ID *pid*.

EPERM   The calling process and the process specified by *pid* are in different sessions, and the implementation doesn't allow to access the process group ID of the session leader of the process with ID *pid* from the calling process.

pid_t getpgrp (*void*)   [Function]
Preliminary: | MT-Safe | AS-Safe | AC-Safe | See Section 1.2.2.1 [POSIX Safety Concepts], page 2.

The **getpgrp** function returns the process group ID of the calling process.

int getpgid (*pid_t pid*)   [Function]
Preliminary: | MT-Safe | AS-Safe | AC-Safe | See Section 1.2.2.1 [POSIX Safety Concepts], page 2.

The **getpgid** function returns the process group ID of the process *pid*. You can supply a value of 0 for the *pid* argument to get information about the calling process.

In case of error -1 is returned and **errno** is set. The following **errno** error conditions are defined for this function:

ESRCH   There is no process with the given process ID *pid*. The calling process and the process specified by *pid* are in different sessions, and the implementation doesn't allow to access the process group ID of the process with ID *pid* from the calling process.

int setpgid (*pid_t pid*, *pid_t pgid*)   [Function]
Preliminary: | MT-Safe | AS-Safe | AC-Safe | See Section 1.2.2.1 [POSIX Safety Concepts], page 2.

The **setpgid** function puts the process *pid* into the process group *pgid*. As a special case, either *pid* or *pgid* can be zero to indicate the process ID of the calling process.

This function fails on a system that does not support job control. See Section 28.2 [Job Control is Optional], page 787, for more information.

If the operation is successful, **setpgid** returns zero. Otherwise it returns **-1**. The following **errno** error conditions are defined for this function:

EACCES   The child process named by *pid* has executed an **exec** function since it was forked.

EINVAL   The value of the *pgid* is not valid.

ENOSYS   The system doesn't support job control.

EPERM   The process indicated by the *pid* argument is a session leader, or is not in the same session as the calling process, or the value of the *pgid* argument doesn't match a process group ID in the same session as the calling process.

ESRCH   The process indicated by the *pid* argument is not the calling process or a child of the calling process.

int setpgrp (*pid_t pid, pid_t pgid*)   [Function]
Preliminary: | MT-Safe | AS-Safe | AC-Safe | See Section 1.2.2.1 [POSIX Safety Concepts], page 2.

This is the BSD Unix name for **setpgid**. Both functions do exactly the same thing.

28.7.3 Functions for Controlling Terminal Access

These are the functions for reading or setting the foreground process group of a terminal. You should include the header files **sys/types.h** and **unistd.h** in your application to use these functions.

Although these functions take a file descriptor argument to specify the terminal device, the foreground job is associated with the terminal file itself and not a particular open file descriptor.

pid_t tcgetpgrp (*int filedes*)   [Function]
Preliminary: | MT-Safe | AS-Safe | AC-Safe | See Section 1.2.2.1 [POSIX Safety Concepts], page 2.

This function returns the process group ID of the foreground process group associated with the terminal open on descriptor *filedes*.

If there is no foreground process group, the return value is a number greater than 1 that does not match the process group ID of any existing process group. This can happen if all of the processes in the job that was formerly the foreground job have terminated, and no other job has yet been moved into the foreground.

In case of an error, a value of **-1** is returned. The following **errno** error conditions are defined for this function:

EBADF   The *filedes* argument is not a valid file descriptor.

ENOSYS   The system doesn't support job control.

ENOTTY   The terminal file associated with the *filedes* argument isn't the controlling terminal of the calling process.

int tcsetpgrp (*int filedes*, *pid_t pgid*)   [Function]
Preliminary: | MT-Safe | AS-Safe | AC-Safe | See Section 1.2.2.1 [POSIX Safety
Concepts], page 2.

This function is used to set a terminal's foreground process group ID. The argument
filedes is a descriptor which specifies the terminal; *pgid* specifies the process group.
The calling process must be a member of the same session as *pgid* and must have the
same controlling terminal.

For terminal access purposes, this function is treated as output. If it is called from a
background process on its controlling terminal, normally all processes in the process
group are sent a `SIGTTOU` signal. The exception is if the calling process itself is
ignoring or blocking `SIGTTOU` signals, in which case the operation is performed and
no signal is sent.

If successful, `tcsetpgrp` returns 0. A return value of `-1` indicates an error. The
following `errno` error conditions are defined for this function:

`EBADF`   The *filedes* argument is not a valid file descriptor.

`EINVAL`   The *pgid* argument is not valid.

`ENOSYS`   The system doesn't support job control.

`ENOTTY`   The *filedes* isn't the controlling terminal of the calling process.

`EPERM`   The *pgid* isn't a process group in the same session as the calling process.

pid_t tcgetsid (*int fildes*)   [Function]
Preliminary: | MT-Safe | AS-Safe | AC-Safe | See Section 1.2.2.1 [POSIX Safety
Concepts], page 2.

This function is used to obtain the process group ID of the session for which the
terminal specified by *fildes* is the controlling terminal. If the call is successful the
group ID is returned. Otherwise the return value is `(pid_t) -1` and the global variable
errno is set to the following value:

`EBADF`   The *filedes* argument is not a valid file descriptor.

`ENOTTY`   The calling process does not have a controlling terminal, or the file is not
             the controlling terminal.

29 System Databases and Name Service Switch

Various functions in the C Library need to be configured to work correctly in the local environment. Traditionally, this was done by using files (e.g., /etc/passwd), but other nameservices (like the Network Information Service (NIS) and the Domain Name Service (DNS)) became popular, and were hacked into the C library, usually with a fixed search order.

The GNU C Library contains a cleaner solution to this problem. It is designed after a method used by Sun Microsystems in the C library of Solaris 2. The GNU C Library follows their name and calls this scheme *Name Service Switch* (NSS).

Though the interface might be similar to Sun's version there is no common code. We never saw any source code of Sun's implementation and so the internal interface is incompatible. This also manifests in the file names we use as we will see later.

29.1 NSS Basics

The basic idea is to put the implementation of the different services offered to access the databases in separate modules. This has some advantages:

1. Contributors can add new services without adding them to the GNU C Library.

2. The modules can be updated separately.

3. The C library image is smaller.

To fulfill the first goal above, the ABI of the modules will be described below. For getting the implementation of a new service right it is important to understand how the functions in the modules get called. They are in no way designed to be used by the programmer directly. Instead the programmer should only use the documented and standardized functions to access the databases.

The databases available in the NSS are

aliases   Mail aliases

ethers   Ethernet numbers,

group   Groups of users, see Section 30.14 [Group Database], page 838.

hosts   Host names and numbers, see Section 16.6.2.4 [Host Names], page 456.

netgroup   Network wide list of host and users, see Section 30.16 [Netgroup Database], page 842.

networks   Network names and numbers, see Section 16.13 [Networks Database], page 488.

protocols
            Network protocols, see Section 16.6.6 [Protocols Database], page 463.

passwd   User passwords, see Section 30.13 [User Database], page 834.

rpc   Remote procedure call names and numbers,

services   Network services, see Section 16.6.4 [The Services Database], page 461.

shadow   Shadow user passwords,

There will be some more added later (automount, bootparams, netmasks, and publickey).

29.2 The NSS Configuration File

Somehow the NSS code must be told about the wishes of the user. For this reason there is the file /etc/nsswitch.conf. For each database, this file contains a specification of how the lookup process should work. The file could look like this:

```
# /etc/nsswitch.conf
#
# Name Service Switch configuration file.
#

passwd:     db files nis
shadow:     files
group:      db files nis

hosts:      files nisplus nis dns
networks:   nisplus [NOTFOUND=return] files

ethers:     nisplus [NOTFOUND=return] db files
protocols:  nisplus [NOTFOUND=return] db files
rpc:        nisplus [NOTFOUND=return] db files
services:   nisplus [NOTFOUND=return] db files
```

The first column is the database as you can guess from the table above. The rest of the line specifies how the lookup process works. Please note that you specify the way it works for each database individually. This cannot be done with the old way of a monolithic implementation.

The configuration specification for each database can contain two different items:

- the service specification like `files`, `db`, or `nis`.

- the reaction on lookup result like `[NOTFOUND=return]`.

29.2.1 Services in the NSS configuration File

The above example file mentions five different services: `files`, `db`, `dns`, `nis`, and `nisplus`. This does not mean these services are available on all sites and neither does it mean these are all the services which will ever be available.

In fact, these names are simply strings which the NSS code uses to find the implicitly addressed functions. The internal interface will be described later. Visible to the user are the modules which implement an individual service.

Assume the service *name* shall be used for a lookup. The code for this service is implemented in a module called `libnss_name`. On a system supporting shared libraries this is in fact a shared library with the name (for example) `libnss_name.so.2`. The number at the end is the currently used version of the interface which will not change frequently. Normally the user should not have to be cognizant of these files since they should be placed in a directory where they are found automatically. Only the names of all available services are important.

29.2.2 Actions in the NSS configuration

The second item in the specification gives the user much finer control on the lookup process. Action items are placed between two service names and are written within brackets. The general form is

> [(!? *status* = *action*)+]

where

> *status* ⇒ success | notfound | unavail | tryagain
> *action* ⇒ return | continue

The case of the keywords is insignificant. The *status* values are the results of a call to a lookup function of a specific service. They mean:

'success'   No error occurred and the wanted entry is returned. The default action for this is return.

'notfound'

The lookup process works ok but the needed value was not found. The default action is continue.

'unavail'   The service is permanently unavailable. This can either mean the needed file is not available, or, for DNS, the server is not available or does not allow queries. The default action is continue.

'tryagain'

The service is temporarily unavailable. This could mean a file is locked or a server currently cannot accept more connections. The default action is continue.

The *action* values mean:

'return'

If the status matches, stop the lookup process at this service specification. If an entry is available, provide it to the application. If an error occurred, report it to the application. In case of a prior 'merge' action, the data is combined with previous lookup results, as explained below.

'continue'

If the status matches, proceed with the lookup process at the next entry, discarding the result of the current lookup (and any merged data). An exception is the 'initgroups' database and the 'success' status, where 'continue' acts like merge below.

'merge'

Proceed with the lookup process, retaining the current lookup result. This action is useful only with the 'success' status. If a subsequent service lookup succeeds and has a matching 'return' specification, the results are merged, the lookup process ends, and the merged results are returned to the application. If the following service has a matching 'merge' action, the lookup process continues, retaining the combined data from this and any previous lookups.

After a merge action, errors from subsequent lookups are ignored, and the data gathered so far will be returned.

The 'merge' only applies to the 'success' status. It is currently implemented for the 'group' database and its group members field, 'gr_mem'. If specified for other databases, it causes the lookup to fail (if the *status* matches).

When processing 'merge' for 'group' membership, the group GID and name must be identical for both entries. If only one or the other is a match, the behavior is undefined.

If we have a line like

```
ethers: nisplus [NOTFOUND=return] db files
```

this is equivalent to

```
ethers: nisplus [SUCCESS=return NOTFOUND=return UNAVAIL=continue
                 TRYAGAIN=continue]
        db       [SUCCESS=return NOTFOUND=continue UNAVAIL=continue
                 TRYAGAIN=continue]
        files
```

(except that it would have to be written on one line). The default value for the actions are normally what you want, and only need to be changed in exceptional cases.

If the optional ! is placed before the *status* this means the following action is used for all statuses but *status* itself. I.e., ! is negation as in the C language (and others).

Before we explain the exception which makes this action item necessary one more remark: obviously it makes no sense to add another action item after the **files** service. Since there is no other service following the action *always* is **return**.

Now, why is this [NOTFOUND=return] action useful? To understand this we should know that the **nisplus** service is often complete; i.e., if an entry is not available in the NIS+ tables it is not available anywhere else. This is what is expressed by this action item: it is useless to examine further services since they will not give us a result.

The situation would be different if the NIS+ service is not available because the machine is booting. In this case the return value of the lookup function is not **notfound** but instead **unavail**. And as you can see in the complete form above: in this situation the **db** and **files** services are used. Neat, isn't it? The system administrator need not pay special care for the time the system is not completely ready to work (while booting or shutdown or network problems).

29.2.3 Notes on the NSS Configuration File

Finally a few more hints. The NSS implementation is not completely helpless if /etc/nsswitch.conf does not exist. For all supported databases there is a default value so it should normally be possible to get the system running even if the file is corrupted or missing.

For the **hosts** and **networks** databases the default value is **dns [!UNAVAIL=return] files**. I.e., the system is prepared for the DNS service not to be available but if it is available the answer it returns is definitive.

The **passwd**, **group**, and **shadow** databases are traditionally handled in a special way. The appropriate files in the /etc directory are read but if an entry with a name starting with a + character is found NIS is used. This kind of lookup remains possible by using the special lookup service **compat** and the default value for the three databases above is **compat [NOTFOUND=return] files**.

For all other databases the default value is nis [NOTFOUND=return] files. This solution gives the best chance to be correct since NIS and file based lookups are used.

A second point is that the user should try to optimize the lookup process. The different service have different response times. A simple file look up on a local file could be fast, but if the file is long and the needed entry is near the end of the file this may take quite some time. In this case it might be better to use the db service which allows fast local access to large data sets.

Often the situation is that some global information like NIS must be used. So it is unavoidable to use service entries like nis etc. But one should avoid slow services like this if possible.

29.3 NSS Module Internals

Now it is time to describe what the modules look like. The functions contained in a module are identified by their names. I.e., there is no jump table or the like. How this is done is of no interest here; those interested in this topic should read about Dynamic Linking.

29.3.1 The Naming Scheme of the NSS Modules

The name of each function consists of various parts:

_nss_service_function

service of course corresponds to the name of the module this function is found in.[1] The function part is derived from the interface function in the C library itself. If the user calls the function gethostbyname and the service used is files the function

_nss_files_gethostbyname_r

in the module

libnss_files.so.2

is used. You see, what is explained above in not the whole truth. In fact the NSS modules only contain reentrant versions of the lookup functions. I.e., if the user would call the gethostbyname_r function this also would end in the above function. For all user interface functions the C library maps this call to a call to the reentrant function. For reentrant functions this is trivial since the interface is (nearly) the same. For the non-reentrant version the library keeps internal buffers which are used to replace the user supplied buffer.

I.e., the reentrant functions *can* have counterparts. No service module is forced to have functions for all databases and all kinds to access them. If a function is not available it is simply treated as if the function would return unavail (see Section 29.2.2 [Actions in the NSS configuration], page 807).

The file name libnss_files.so.2 would be on a Solaris 2 system nss_files.so.2. This is the difference mentioned above. Sun's NSS modules are usable as modules which get indirectly loaded only.

The NSS modules in the GNU C Library are prepared to be used as normal libraries themselves. This is *not* true at the moment, though. However, the organization of the

---

[1] Now you might ask why this information is duplicated. The answer is that we want to make it possible to link directly with these shared objects.

name space in the modules does not make it impossible like it is for Solaris. Now you can see why the modules are still libraries.[2]

29.3.2 The Interface of the Function in NSS Modules

Now we know about the functions contained in the modules. It is now time to describe the types. When we mentioned the reentrant versions of the functions above, this means there are some additional arguments (compared with the standard, non-reentrant versions). The prototypes for the non-reentrant and reentrant versions of our function above are:

```
struct hostent *gethostbyname (const char *name)

int gethostbyname_r (const char *name, struct hostent *result_buf,
                     char *buf, size_t buflen, struct hostent **result,
                     int *h_errnop)
```

The actual prototype of the function in the NSS modules in this case is

```
enum nss_status _nss_files_gethostbyname_r (const char *name,
                                            struct hostent *result_buf,
                                            char *buf, size_t buflen,
                                            int *errnop, int *h_errnop)
```

I.e., the interface function is in fact the reentrant function with the change of the return value, the omission of the *result* parameter, and the addition of the *errnop* parameter. While the user-level function returns a pointer to the result the reentrant function return an **enum nss_status** value:

NSS_STATUS_TRYAGAIN
> numeric value −2

NSS_STATUS_UNAVAIL
> numeric value −1

NSS_STATUS_NOTFOUND
> numeric value 0

NSS_STATUS_SUCCESS
> numeric value 1

Now you see where the action items of the /etc/nsswitch.conf file are used.

If you study the source code you will find there is a fifth value: NSS_STATUS_RETURN. This is an internal use only value, used by a few functions in places where none of the above value can be used. If necessary the source code should be examined to learn about the details.

In case the interface function has to return an error it is important that the correct error code is stored in *errnop*. Some return status values have only one associated error code, others have more.

NSS_STATUS_TRYAGAIN	EAGAIN	One of the functions used ran temporarily out of resources or a service is currently not available.

---

[2] There is a second explanation: we were too lazy to change the Makefiles to allow the generation of shared objects not starting with **lib** but don't tell this to anybody.

	ERANGE	The provided buffer is not large enough. The function should be called again with a larger buffer.
NSS_STATUS_UNAVAIL	ENOENT	A necessary input file cannot be found.
NSS_STATUS_NOTFOUND	ENOENT	The requested entry is not available.
NSS_STATUS_NOTFOUND	SUCCESS	There are no entries. Use this to avoid returning errors for inactive services which may be enabled at a later time. This is not the same as the service being temporarily unavailable.

These are proposed values. There can be other error codes and the described error codes can have different meaning. **With one exception:** when returning NSS_STATUS_TRYAGAIN the error code **ERANGE** *must* mean that the user provided buffer is too small. Everything else is non-critical.

In statically linked programs, the main application and NSS modules do not share the same thread-local variable **errno**, which is the reason why there is an explicit *errnop* function argument.

The above function has something special which is missing for almost all the other module functions. There is an argument *h_errnop*. This points to a variable which will be filled with the error code in case the execution of the function fails for some reason. (In statically linked programs, the thread-local variable **h_errno** is not shared with the main application.)

The **get**XXX**by**YYY functions are the most important functions in the NSS modules. But there are others which implement the other ways to access system databases (say for the password database, there are **setpwent**, **getpwent**, and **endpwent**). These will be described in more detail later. Here we give a general way to determine the signature of the module function:

- the return value is **enum nss_status**;
- the name (see Section 29.3.1 [The Naming Scheme of the NSS Modules], page 809);
- the first arguments are identical to the arguments of the non-reentrant function;
- the next four arguments are:

STRUCT_TYPE *result_buf

> pointer to buffer where the result is stored. **STRUCT_TYPE** is normally a struct which corresponds to the database.

char *buffer

> pointer to a buffer where the function can store additional data for the result etc.

size_t buflen

> length of the buffer pointed to by *buffer*.

int *errnop

> the low-level error code to return to the application. If the return value is not **NSS_STATUS_SUCCESS**, *errnop* needs to be set to a non-zero value.

An NSS module should never set *errnop* to zero. The value ERANGE is special, as described above.

- possibly a last argument *h_errnop*, for the host name and network name lookup functions. If the return value is not NSS_STATUS_SUCCESS, *h_errnop* needs to be set to a non-zero value. A generic error code is NETDB_INTERNAL, which instructs the caller to examine *errnop* for further details. (This includes the ERANGE special case.)

This table is correct for all functions but the set...ent and end...ent functions.

29.4 Extending NSS

One of the advantages of NSS mentioned above is that it can be extended quite easily. There are two ways in which the extension can happen: adding another database or adding another service. The former is normally done only by the C library developers. It is here only important to remember that adding another database is independent from adding another service because a service need not support all databases or lookup functions.

A designer/implementer of a new service is therefore free to choose the databases s/he is interested in and leave the rest for later (or completely aside).

29.4.1 Adding another Service to NSS

The sources for a new service need not (and should not) be part of the GNU C Library itself. The developer retains complete control over the sources and its development. The links between the C library and the new service module consists solely of the interface functions.

Each module is designed following a specific interface specification. For now the version is 2 (the interface in version 1 was not adequate) and this manifests in the version number of the shared library object of the NSS modules: they have the extension .2. If the interface changes again in an incompatible way, this number will be increased. Modules using the old interface will still be usable.

Developers of a new service will have to make sure that their module is created using the correct interface number. This means the file itself must have the correct name and on ELF systems the *soname* (Shared Object Name) must also have this number. Building a module from a bunch of object files on an ELF system using GNU CC could be done like this:

```
gcc -shared -o libnss_NAME.so.2 -Wl,-soname,libnss_NAME.so.2 OBJECTS
```

Section "Link Options" in *GNU CC*, to learn more about this command line.

To use the new module the library must be able to find it. This can be achieved by using options for the dynamic linker so that it will search the directory where the binary is placed. For an ELF system this could be done by adding the wanted directory to the value of LD_LIBRARY_PATH.

But this is not always possible since some programs (those which run under IDs which do not belong to the user) ignore this variable. Therefore the stable version of the module should be placed into a directory which is searched by the dynamic linker. Normally this should be the directory $prefix/lib, where $prefix corresponds to the value given to configure using the --prefix option. But be careful: this should only be done if it is clear the module does not cause any harm. System administrators should be careful.

29.4.2 Internals of the NSS Module Functions

Until now we only provided the syntactic interface for the functions in the NSS module. In fact there is not much more we can say since the implementation obviously is different for each function. But a few general rules must be followed by all functions.

In fact there are four kinds of different functions which may appear in the interface. All derive from the traditional ones for system databases. *db* in the following table is normally an abbreviation for the database (e.g., it is `pw` for the password database).

enum nss_status **_nss_*database*_setdbent** (void)

> This function prepares the service for following operations. For a simple file based lookup this means files could be opened, for other services this function simply is a noop.
>
> One special case for this function is that it takes an additional argument for some *databases* (i.e., the interface is `int setdbent (int)`). Section 16.6.2.4 [Host Names], page 456, which describes the `sethostent` function.
>
> The return value should be *NSS_STATUS_SUCCESS* or according to the table above in case of an error (see Section 29.3.2 [The Interface of the Function in NSS Modules], page 810).

enum nss_status **_nss_*database*_enddbent** (void)

> This function simply closes all files which are still open or removes buffer caches. If there are no files or buffers to remove this is again a simple noop.
>
> There normally is no return value other than *NSS_STATUS_SUCCESS*.

enum nss_status **_nss_*database*_getdbent_r** (*STRUCTURE* *result, char *buffer, size_t buflen, int *errnop)

> Since this function will be called several times in a row to retrieve one entry after the other it must keep some kind of state. But this also means the functions are not really reentrant. They are reentrant only in that simultaneous calls to this function will not try to write the retrieved data in the same place (as it would be the case for the non-reentrant functions); instead, it writes to the structure pointed to by the *result* parameter. But the calls share a common state and in the case of a file access this means they return neighboring entries in the file.
>
> The buffer of length *buflen* pointed to by *buffer* can be used for storing some additional data for the result. It is *not* guaranteed that the same buffer will be passed for the next call of this function. Therefore one must not misuse this buffer to save some state information from one call to another.
>
> Before the function returns with a failure code, the implementation should store the value of the local *errno* variable in the variable pointed to be *errnop*. This is important to guarantee the module working in statically linked programs. The stored value must not be zero.
>
> As explained above this function could also have an additional last argument. This depends on the database used; it happens only for `host` and `networks`.
>
> The function shall return `NSS_STATUS_SUCCESS` as long as there are more entries. When the last entry was read it should return `NSS_STATUS_NOTFOUND`. When the buffer given as an argument is too small for the data to be returned

NSS_STATUS_TRYAGAIN should be returned. When the service was not formerly initialized by a call to _nss_*DATABASE*_setdbent all return values allowed for this function can also be returned here.

enum nss_status _nss_*DATABASE*_getdbby*XX*_r (*PARAMS*, *STRUCTURE* *result, char *buffer, size_t buflen, int *errnop)

This function shall return the entry from the database which is addressed by the *PARAMS*. The type and number of these arguments vary. It must be individually determined by looking to the user-level interface functions. All arguments given to the non-reentrant version are here described by *PARAMS*.

The result must be stored in the structure pointed to by *result*. If there are additional data to return (say strings, where the *result* structure only contains pointers) the function must use the *buffer* of length *buflen*. There must not be any references to non-constant global data.

The implementation of this function should honor the *stayopen* flag set by the set*DB*ent function whenever this makes sense.

Before the function returns, the implementation should store the value of the local *errno* variable in the variable pointed to by *errnop*. This is important to guarantee the module works in statically linked programs.

Again, this function takes an additional last argument for the host and networks database.

The return value should as always follow the rules given above (see Section 29.3.2 [The Interface of the Function in NSS Modules], page 810).

30 Users and Groups

Every user who can log in on the system is identified by a unique number called the *user ID*. Each process has an effective user ID which says which user's access permissions it has.

Users are classified into *groups* for access control purposes. Each process has one or more *group ID values* which say which groups the process can use for access to files.

The effective user and group IDs of a process collectively form its *persona*. This determines which files the process can access. Normally, a process inherits its persona from the parent process, but under special circumstances a process can change its persona and thus change its access permissions.

Each file in the system also has a user ID and a group ID. Access control works by comparing the user and group IDs of the file with those of the running process.

The system keeps a database of all the registered users, and another database of all the defined groups. There are library functions you can use to examine these databases.

30.1 User and Group IDs

Each user account on a computer system is identified by a *user name* (or *login name*) and *user ID*. Normally, each user name has a unique user ID, but it is possible for several login names to have the same user ID. The user names and corresponding user IDs are stored in a data base which you can access as described in Section 30.13 [User Database], page 834.

Users are classified in *groups*. Each user name belongs to one *default group* and may also belong to any number of *supplementary groups*. Users who are members of the same group can share resources (such as files) that are not accessible to users who are not a member of that group. Each group has a *group name* and *group ID*. See Section 30.14 [Group Database], page 838, for how to find information about a group ID or group name.

30.2 The Persona of a Process

At any time, each process has an *effective user ID*, a *effective group ID*, and a set of *supplementary group IDs*. These IDs determine the privileges of the process. They are collectively called the *persona* of the process, because they determine "who it is" for purposes of access control.

Your login shell starts out with a persona which consists of your user ID, your default group ID, and your supplementary group IDs (if you are in more than one group). In normal circumstances, all your other processes inherit these values.

A process also has a *real user ID* which identifies the user who created the process, and a *real group ID* which identifies that user's default group. These values do not play a role in access control, so we do not consider them part of the persona. But they are also important.

Both the real and effective user ID can be changed during the lifetime of a process. See Section 30.3 [Why Change the Persona of a Process?], page 816.

For details on how a process's effective user ID and group IDs affect its permission to access files, see Section 14.9.6 [How Your Access to a File is Decided], page 423.

The effective user ID of a process also controls permissions for sending signals using the `kill` function. See Section 24.6.2 [Signaling Another Process], page 713.

Finally, there are many operations which can only be performed by a process whose effective user ID is zero. A process with this user ID is a *privileged process*. Commonly the user name `root` is associated with user ID 0, but there may be other user names with this ID.

30.3 Why Change the Persona of a Process?

The most obvious situation where it is necessary for a process to change its user and/or group IDs is the `login` program. When `login` starts running, its user ID is `root`. Its job is to start a shell whose user and group IDs are those of the user who is logging in. (To accomplish this fully, `login` must set the real user and group IDs as well as its persona. But this is a special case.)

The more common case of changing persona is when an ordinary user program needs access to a resource that wouldn't ordinarily be accessible to the user actually running it.

For example, you may have a file that is controlled by your program but that shouldn't be read or modified directly by other users, either because it implements some kind of locking protocol, or because you want to preserve the integrity or privacy of the information it contains. This kind of restricted access can be implemented by having the program change its effective user or group ID to match that of the resource.

Thus, imagine a game program that saves scores in a file. The game program itself needs to be able to update this file no matter who is running it, but if users can write the file without going through the game, they can give themselves any scores they like. Some people consider this undesirable, or even reprehensible. It can be prevented by creating a new user ID and login name (say, `games`) to own the scores file, and make the file writable only by this user. Then, when the game program wants to update this file, it can change its effective user ID to be that for `games`. In effect, the program must adopt the persona of `games` so it can write to the scores file.

30.4 How an Application Can Change Persona

The ability to change the persona of a process can be a source of unintentional privacy violations, or even intentional abuse. Because of the potential for problems, changing persona is restricted to special circumstances.

You can't arbitrarily set your user ID or group ID to anything you want; only privileged processes can do that. Instead, the normal way for a program to change its persona is that it has been set up in advance to change to a particular user or group. This is the function of the setuid and setgid bits of a file's access mode. See Section 14.9.5 [The Mode Bits for Access Permission], page 421.

When the setuid bit of an executable file is on, executing that file gives the process a third user ID: the *file user ID*. This ID is set to the owner ID of the file. The system then changes the effective user ID to the file user ID. The real user ID remains as it was. Likewise, if the setgid bit is on, the process is given a *file group ID* equal to the group ID of the file, and its effective group ID is changed to the file group ID.

If a process has a file ID (user or group), then it can at any time change its effective ID to its real ID and back to its file ID. Programs use this feature to relinquish their special privileges except when they actually need them. This makes it less likely that they can be tricked into doing something inappropriate with their privileges.

Portability Note: Older systems do not have file IDs. To determine if a system has this feature, you can test the compiler define `_POSIX_SAVED_IDS`. (In the POSIX standard, file IDs are known as saved IDs.)

See Section 14.9 [File Attributes], page 412, for a more general discussion of file modes and accessibility.

30.5 Reading the Persona of a Process

Here are detailed descriptions of the functions for reading the user and group IDs of a process, both real and effective. To use these facilities, you must include the header files `sys/types.h` and `unistd.h`.

`uid_t`   [Data Type]

>   This is an integer data type used to represent user IDs. In the GNU C Library, this is an alias for `unsigned int`.

`gid_t`   [Data Type]

>   This is an integer data type used to represent group IDs. In the GNU C Library, this is an alias for `unsigned int`.

`uid_t getuid (void)`   [Function]

>   Preliminary: | MT-Safe | AS-Safe | AC-Safe | See Section 1.2.2.1 [POSIX Safety Concepts], page 2.
>
>   The `getuid` function returns the real user ID of the process.

`gid_t getgid (void)`   [Function]

>   Preliminary: | MT-Safe | AS-Safe | AC-Safe | See Section 1.2.2.1 [POSIX Safety Concepts], page 2.
>
>   The `getgid` function returns the real group ID of the process.

`uid_t geteuid (void)`   [Function]

>   Preliminary: | MT-Safe | AS-Safe | AC-Safe | See Section 1.2.2.1 [POSIX Safety Concepts], page 2.
>
>   The `geteuid` function returns the effective user ID of the process.

`gid_t getegid (void)`   [Function]

>   Preliminary: | MT-Safe | AS-Safe | AC-Safe | See Section 1.2.2.1 [POSIX Safety Concepts], page 2.
>
>   The `getegid` function returns the effective group ID of the process.

`int getgroups (int count, gid_t *groups)`   [Function]

>   Preliminary: | MT-Safe | AS-Safe | AC-Safe | See Section 1.2.2.1 [POSIX Safety Concepts], page 2.
>
>   The `getgroups` function is used to inquire about the supplementary group IDs of the process. Up to *count* of these group IDs are stored in the array *groups*; the return value from the function is the number of group IDs actually stored. If *count* is smaller than the total number of supplementary group IDs, then `getgroups` returns a value of -1 and `errno` is set to `EINVAL`.

If *count* is zero, then `getgroups` just returns the total number of supplementary group IDs. On systems that do not support supplementary groups, this will always be zero.

Here's how to use `getgroups` to read all the supplementary group IDs:

```
gid_t *
read_all_groups (void)
{
  int ngroups = getgroups (0, NULL);
  gid_t *groups
    = (gid_t *) xmalloc (ngroups * sizeof (gid_t));
  int val = getgroups (ngroups, groups);
  if (val < 0)
    {
      free (groups);
      return NULL;
    }
  return groups;
}
```

30.6 Setting the User ID

This section describes the functions for altering the user ID (real and/or effective) of a process. To use these facilities, you must include the header files `sys/types.h` and `unistd.h`.

`int seteuid (uid_t neweuid)`   [Function]

Preliminary: | MT-Safe | AS-Unsafe lock | AC-Unsafe lock | See Section 1.2.2.1 [POSIX Safety Concepts], page 2.

This function sets the effective user ID of a process to *neweuid*, provided that the process is allowed to change its effective user ID. A privileged process (effective user ID zero) can change its effective user ID to any legal value. An unprivileged process with a file user ID can change its effective user ID to its real user ID or to its file user ID. Otherwise, a process may not change its effective user ID at all.

The `seteuid` function returns a value of 0 to indicate successful completion, and a value of -1 to indicate an error. The following `errno` error conditions are defined for this function:

EINVAL   The value of the *neweuid* argument is invalid.

EPERM   The process may not change to the specified ID.

Older systems (those without the `_POSIX_SAVED_IDS` feature) do not have this function.

`int setuid (uid_t newuid)`   [Function]

Preliminary: | MT-Safe | AS-Unsafe lock | AC-Unsafe lock | See Section 1.2.2.1 [POSIX Safety Concepts], page 2.

If the calling process is privileged, this function sets both the real and effective user IDs of the process to *newuid*. It also deletes the file user ID of the process, if any. *newuid* may be any legal value. (Once this has been done, there is no way to recover the old effective user ID.)

If the process is not privileged, and the system supports the `_POSIX_SAVED_IDS` feature, then this function behaves like `seteuid`.

The return values and error conditions are the same as for `seteuid`.

`int setreuid (uid_t ruid, uid_t euid)`   [Function]
Preliminary: | MT-Safe | AS-Unsafe lock | AC-Unsafe lock | See Section 1.2.2.1
[POSIX Safety Concepts], page 2.

This function sets the real user ID of the process to *ruid* and the effective user ID to
euid. If *ruid* is `-1`, it means not to change the real user ID; likewise if *euid* is `-1`, it
means not to change the effective user ID.

The `setreuid` function exists for compatibility with 4.3 BSD Unix, which does not
support file IDs. You can use this function to swap the effective and real user IDs of
the process. (Privileged processes are not limited to this particular usage.) If file IDs
are supported, you should use that feature instead of this function. See Section 30.8
[Enabling and Disabling Setuid Access], page 821.

The return value is `0` on success and `-1` on failure. The following `errno` error conditions are defined for this function:

`EPERM`   The process does not have the appropriate privileges; you do not have
            permission to change to the specified ID.

30.7 Setting the Group IDs

This section describes the functions for altering the group IDs (real and effective) of a process. To use these facilities, you must include the header files `sys/types.h` and `unistd.h`.

`int setegid (gid_t newgid)`   [Function]
Preliminary: | MT-Safe | AS-Unsafe lock | AC-Unsafe lock | See Section 1.2.2.1
[POSIX Safety Concepts], page 2.

This function sets the effective group ID of the process to *newgid*, provided that the
process is allowed to change its group ID. Just as with `seteuid`, if the process is
privileged it may change its effective group ID to any value; if it isn't, but it has a
file group ID, then it may change to its real group ID or file group ID; otherwise it
may not change its effective group ID.

Note that a process is only privileged if its effective *user* ID is zero. The effective
group ID only affects access permissions.

The return values and error conditions for `setegid` are the same as those for `seteuid`.

This function is only present if `_POSIX_SAVED_IDS` is defined.

`int setgid (gid_t newgid)`   [Function]
Preliminary: | MT-Safe | AS-Unsafe lock | AC-Unsafe lock | See Section 1.2.2.1
[POSIX Safety Concepts], page 2.

This function sets both the real and effective group ID of the process to *newgid*,
provided that the process is privileged. It also deletes the file group ID, if any.

If the process is not privileged, then `setgid` behaves like `setegid`.

The return values and error conditions for `setgid` are the same as those for `seteuid`.

`int setregid (gid_t rgid, gid_t egid)` [Function]
> Preliminary: | MT-Safe | AS-Unsafe lock | AC-Unsafe lock | See Section 1.2.2.1 [POSIX Safety Concepts], page 2.
>
> This function sets the real group ID of the process to *rgid* and the effective group ID to *egid*. If *rgid* is `-1`, it means not to change the real group ID; likewise if *egid* is `-1`, it means not to change the effective group ID.
>
> The `setregid` function is provided for compatibility with 4.3 BSD Unix, which does not support file IDs. You can use this function to swap the effective and real group IDs of the process. (Privileged processes are not limited to this usage.) If file IDs are supported, you should use that feature instead of using this function. See Section 30.8 [Enabling and Disabling Setuid Access], page 821.
>
> The return values and error conditions for `setregid` are the same as those for `setreuid`.

`setuid` and `setgid` behave differently depending on whether the effective user ID at the time is zero. If it is not zero, they behave like `seteuid` and `setegid`. If it is, they change both effective and real IDs and delete the file ID. To avoid confusion, we recommend you always use `seteuid` and `setegid` except when you know the effective user ID is zero and your intent is to change the persona permanently. This case is rare—most of the programs that need it, such as `login` and `su`, have already been written.

Note that if your program is setuid to some user other than `root`, there is no way to drop privileges permanently.

The system also lets privileged processes change their supplementary group IDs. To use `setgroups` or `initgroups`, your programs should include the header file `grp.h`.

`int setgroups (size_t count, const gid_t *groups)` [Function]
> Preliminary: | MT-Safe | AS-Unsafe lock | AC-Unsafe lock | See Section 1.2.2.1 [POSIX Safety Concepts], page 2.
>
> This function sets the process's supplementary group IDs. It can only be called from privileged processes. The *count* argument specifies the number of group IDs in the array *groups*.
>
> This function returns 0 if successful and `-1` on error. The following `errno` error conditions are defined for this function:
>
> EPERM   The calling process is not privileged.

`int initgroups (const char *user, gid_t group)` [Function]
> Preliminary: | MT-Safe locale | AS-Unsafe dlopen plugin heap lock | AC-Unsafe corrupt mem fd lock | See Section 1.2.2.1 [POSIX Safety Concepts], page 2.
>
> The `initgroups` function sets the process's supplementary group IDs to be the normal default for the user name *user*. The group *group* is automatically included.
>
> This function works by scanning the group database for all the groups *user* belongs to. It then calls `setgroups` with the list it has constructed.
>
> The return values and error conditions are the same as for `setgroups`.

If you are interested in the groups a particular user belongs to, but do not want to change the process's supplementary group IDs, you can use `getgrouplist`. To use `getgrouplist`, your programs should include the header file `grp.h`.

```
int getgrouplist (const char *user, gid_t group, gid_t *groups,          [Function]
        int *ngroups)
```
Preliminary: | MT-Safe locale | AS-Unsafe dlopen plugin heap lock | AC-Unsafe
corrupt mem fd lock | See Section 1.2.2.1 [POSIX Safety Concepts], page 2.

The `getgrouplist` function scans the group database for all the groups *user* belongs
to. Up to *ngroups group IDs corresponding to these groups are stored in the array
groups; the return value from the function is the number of group IDs actually stored.
If *ngroups is smaller than the total number of groups found, then `getgrouplist`
returns a value of −1 and stores the actual number of groups in *ngroups. The group
group is automatically included in the list of groups returned by `getgrouplist`.

Here's how to use `getgrouplist` to read all supplementary groups for *user*:

```
gid_t *
supplementary_groups (char *user)
{
  int ngroups = 16;
  gid_t *groups
    = (gid_t *) xmalloc (ngroups * sizeof (gid_t));
  struct passwd *pw = getpwnam (user);

  if (pw == NULL)
    return NULL;

  if (getgrouplist (pw->pw_name, pw->pw_gid, groups, &ngroups) < 0)
    {
      groups = xrealloc (ngroups * sizeof (gid_t));
      getgrouplist (pw->pw_name, pw->pw_gid, groups, &ngroups);
    }
  return groups;
}
```

30.8 Enabling and Disabling Setuid Access

A typical setuid program does not need its special access all of the time. It's a good idea
to turn off this access when it isn't needed, so it can't possibly give unintended access.

If the system supports the `_POSIX_SAVED_IDS` feature, you can accomplish this with
`seteuid`. When the game program starts, its real user ID is `jdoe`, its effective user ID is
`games`, and its saved user ID is also `games`. The program should record both user ID values
once at the beginning, like this:

```
user_user_id = getuid ();
game_user_id = geteuid ();
```

Then it can turn off game file access with

```
seteuid (user_user_id);
```

and turn it on with

```
seteuid (game_user_id);
```

Throughout this process, the real user ID remains `jdoe` and the file user ID remains `games`,
so the program can always set its effective user ID to either one.

On other systems that don't support file user IDs, you can turn setuid access on and off
by using `setreuid` to swap the real and effective user IDs of the process, as follows:

```
setreuid (geteuid (), getuid ());
```

This special case is always allowed—it cannot fail.

Why does this have the effect of toggling the setuid access? Suppose a game program has just started, and its real user ID is jdoe while its effective user ID is games. In this state, the game can write the scores file. If it swaps the two uids, the real becomes games and the effective becomes jdoe; now the program has only jdoe access. Another swap brings games back to the effective user ID and restores access to the scores file.

In order to handle both kinds of systems, test for the saved user ID feature with a preprocessor conditional, like this:

```
#ifdef _POSIX_SAVED_IDS
  seteuid (user_user_id);
#else
  setreuid (geteuid (), getuid ());
#endif
```

30.9 Setuid Program Example

Here's an example showing how to set up a program that changes its effective user ID.

This is part of a game program called caber-toss that manipulates a file scores that should be writable only by the game program itself. The program assumes that its executable file will be installed with the setuid bit set and owned by the same user as the scores file. Typically, a system administrator will set up an account like games for this purpose.

The executable file is given mode 4755, so that doing an 'ls -l' on it produces output like:

```
-rwsr-xr-x   1 games    184422 Jul 30 15:17 caber-toss
```

The setuid bit shows up in the file modes as the 's'.

The scores file is given mode 644, and doing an 'ls -l' on it shows:

```
-rw-r--r--  1 games          0 Jul 31 15:33 scores
```

Here are the parts of the program that show how to set up the changed user ID. This program is conditionalized so that it makes use of the file IDs feature if it is supported, and otherwise uses setreuid to swap the effective and real user IDs.

```
#include <stdio.h>
#include <sys/types.h>
#include <unistd.h>
#include <stdlib.h>


/* Remember the effective and real UIDs. */

static uid_t euid, ruid;


/* Restore the effective UID to its original value. */

void
do_setuid (void)
{
  int status;

#ifdef _POSIX_SAVED_IDS
```

```
      status = seteuid (euid);
#else
      status = setreuid (ruid, euid);
#endif
    if (status < 0) {
      fprintf (stderr, "Couldn't set uid.\n");
      exit (status);
      }
  }


/* Set the effective UID to the real UID. */

void
undo_setuid (void)
{
  int status;

#ifdef _POSIX_SAVED_IDS
  status = seteuid (ruid);
#else
  status = setreuid (euid, ruid);
#endif
    if (status < 0) {
      fprintf (stderr, "Couldn't set uid.\n");
      exit (status);
      }
  }

/* Main program. */

int
main (void)
{
  /* Remember the real and effective user IDs.  */
  ruid = getuid ();
  euid = geteuid ();
  undo_setuid ();

  /* Do the game and record the score.  */
  ...
  }
```

Notice how the first thing the `main` function does is to set the effective user ID back to the real user ID. This is so that any other file accesses that are performed while the user is playing the game use the real user ID for determining permissions. Only when the program needs to open the scores file does it switch back to the file user ID, like this:

```
/* Record the score. */

int
record_score (int score)
{
  FILE *stream;
  char *myname;

  /* Open the scores file. */
  do_setuid ();
  stream = fopen (SCORES_FILE, "a");
```

```
  undo_setuid ();

  /* Write the score to the file. */
  if (stream)
    {
      myname = cuserid (NULL);
      if (score < 0)
        fprintf (stream, "%10s: Couldn't lift the caber.\n", myname);
      else
        fprintf (stream, "%10s: %d feet.\n", myname, score);
      fclose (stream);
      return 0;
    }
  else
    return -1;
}
```

30.10 Tips for Writing Setuid Programs

It is easy for setuid programs to give the user access that isn't intended—in fact, if you want to avoid this, you need to be careful. Here are some guidelines for preventing unintended access and minimizing its consequences when it does occur:

- Don't have **setuid** programs with privileged user IDs such as **root** unless it is absolutely necessary. If the resource is specific to your particular program, it's better to define a new, nonprivileged user ID or group ID just to manage that resource. It's better if you can write your program to use a special group than a special user.

- Be cautious about using the **exec** functions in combination with changing the effective user ID. Don't let users of your program execute arbitrary programs under a changed user ID. Executing a shell is especially bad news. Less obviously, the **execlp** and **execvp** functions are a potential risk (since the program they execute depends on the user's **PATH** environment variable).

  If you must **exec** another program under a changed ID, specify an absolute file name (see Section 11.2.2 [File Name Resolution], page 255) for the executable, and make sure that the protections on that executable and *all* containing directories are such that ordinary users cannot replace it with some other program.

  You should also check the arguments passed to the program to make sure they do not have unexpected effects. Likewise, you should examine the environment variables. Decide which arguments and variables are safe, and reject all others.

  You should never use **system** in a privileged program, because it invokes a shell.

- Only use the user ID controlling the resource in the part of the program that actually uses that resource. When you're finished with it, restore the effective user ID back to the actual user's user ID. See Section 30.8 [Enabling and Disabling Setuid Access], page 821.

- If the **setuid** part of your program needs to access other files besides the controlled resource, it should verify that the real user would ordinarily have permission to access those files. You can use the **access** function (see Section 14.9.6 [How Your Access to a File is Decided], page 423) to check this; it uses the real user and group IDs, rather than the effective IDs.

30.11 Identifying Who Logged In

You can use the functions listed in this section to determine the login name of the user who is running a process, and the name of the user who logged in the current session. See also the function `getuid` and friends (see Section 30.5 [Reading the Persona of a Process], page 817). How this information is collected by the system and how to control/add/remove information from the background storage is described in Section 30.12 [The User Accounting Database], page 826.

The `getlogin` function is declared in `unistd.h`, while `cuserid` and `L_cuserid` are declared in `stdio.h`.

---

char * getlogin (*void*)   [Function]

> Preliminary: | MT-Unsafe race:getlogin race:utent sig:ALRM timer locale | AS-Unsafe dlopen plugin heap lock | AC-Unsafe corrupt lock fd mem | See Section 1.2.2.1 [POSIX Safety Concepts], page 2.
>
> The `getlogin` function returns a pointer to a string containing the name of the user logged in on the controlling terminal of the process, or a null pointer if this information cannot be determined. The string is statically allocated and might be overwritten on subsequent calls to this function or to `cuserid`.

---

char * cuserid (*char *string*)   [Function]

> Preliminary: | MT-Unsafe race:cuserid/!string locale | AS-Unsafe dlopen plugin heap lock | AC-Unsafe corrupt lock fd mem | See Section 1.2.2.1 [POSIX Safety Concepts], page 2.
>
> The `cuserid` function returns a pointer to a string containing a user name associated with the effective ID of the process. If *string* is not a null pointer, it should be an array that can hold at least `L_cuserid` characters; the string is returned in this array. Otherwise, a pointer to a string in a static area is returned. This string is statically allocated and might be overwritten on subsequent calls to this function or to `getlogin`.
>
> The use of this function is deprecated since it is marked to be withdrawn in XPG4.2 and has already been removed from newer revisions of POSIX.1.

---

int L_cuserid   [Macro]

> An integer constant that indicates how long an array you might need to store a user name.

These functions let your program identify positively the user who is running or the user who logged in this session. (These can differ when setuid programs are involved; see Section 30.2 [The Persona of a Process], page 815.) The user cannot do anything to fool these functions.

For most purposes, it is more useful to use the environment variable `LOGNAME` to find out who the user is. This is more flexible precisely because the user can set `LOGNAME` arbitrarily. See Section 25.4.2 [Standard Environment Variables], page 765.

30.12 The User Accounting Database

Most Unix-like operating systems keep track of logged in users by maintaining a user accounting database. This user accounting database stores for each terminal, who has logged on, at what time, the process ID of the user's login shell, etc., etc., but also stores information about the run level of the system, the time of the last system reboot, and possibly more.

The user accounting database typically lives in /etc/utmp, /var/adm/utmp or /var/run/utmp. However, these files should **never** be accessed directly. For reading information from and writing information to the user accounting database, the functions described in this section should be used.

30.12.1 Manipulating the User Accounting Database

These functions and the corresponding data structures are declared in the header file utmp.h.

struct exit_status   [Data Type]
> The exit_status data structure is used to hold information about the exit status of processes marked as DEAD_PROCESS in the user accounting database.
>
> short int e_termination
>> The exit status of the process.
>
> short int e_exit
>> The exit status of the process.

struct utmp   [Data Type]
> The utmp data structure is used to hold information about entries in the user accounting database. On GNU systems it has the following members:
>
> short int ut_type
>> Specifies the type of login; one of EMPTY, RUN_LVL, BOOT_TIME, OLD_TIME, NEW_TIME, INIT_PROCESS, LOGIN_PROCESS, USER_PROCESS, DEAD_PROCESS or ACCOUNTING.
>
> pid_t ut_pid
>> The process ID number of the login process.
>
> char ut_line[]
>> The device name of the tty (without /dev/).
>
> char ut_id[]
>> The inittab ID of the process.
>
> char ut_user[]
>> The user's login name.
>
> char ut_host[]
>> The name of the host from which the user logged in.
>
> struct exit_status ut_exit
>> The exit status of a process marked as DEAD_PROCESS.

long ut_session
> The Session ID, used for windowing.

struct timeval ut_tv
> Time the entry was made. For entries of type OLD_TIME this is the time when the system clock changed, and for entries of type NEW_TIME this is the time the system clock was set to.

int32_t ut_addr_v6[4]
> The Internet address of a remote host.

The ut_type, ut_pid, ut_id, ut_tv, and ut_host fields are not available on all systems. Portable applications therefore should be prepared for these situations. To help do this the utmp.h header provides macros _HAVE_UT_TYPE, _HAVE_UT_PID, _HAVE_UT_ID, _HAVE_UT_TV, and _HAVE_UT_HOST if the respective field is available. The programmer can handle the situations by using #ifdef in the program code.

The following macros are defined for use as values for the ut_type member of the utmp structure. The values are integer constants.

EMPTY
> This macro is used to indicate that the entry contains no valid user accounting information.

RUN_LVL
> This macro is used to identify the system's runlevel.

BOOT_TIME
> This macro is used to identify the time of system boot.

OLD_TIME
> This macro is used to identify the time when the system clock changed.

NEW_TIME
> This macro is used to identify the time after the system clock changed.

INIT_PROCESS
> This macro is used to identify a process spawned by the init process.

LOGIN_PROCESS
> This macro is used to identify the session leader of a logged in user.

USER_PROCESS
> This macro is used to identify a user process.

DEAD_PROCESS
> This macro is used to identify a terminated process.

ACCOUNTING
> ???

The size of the ut_line, ut_id, ut_user and ut_host arrays can be found using the sizeof operator.

Many older systems have, instead of an ut_tv member, an ut_time member, usually of type time_t, for representing the time associated with the entry. Therefore, for backwards compatibility only, utmp.h defines ut_time as an alias for ut_tv.tv_sec.

void setutent (*void*) [Function]
> Preliminary: | MT-Unsafe race:utent | AS-Unsafe lock | AC-Unsafe lock fd | See Section 1.2.2.1 [POSIX Safety Concepts], page 2.

This function opens the user accounting database to begin scanning it. You can then call `getutent`, `getutid` or `getutline` to read entries and `pututline` to write entries.

If the database is already open, it resets the input to the beginning of the database.

struct utmp * getutent (*void*)   [Function]
Preliminary: | MT-Unsafe init race:utent race:utentbuf sig:ALRM timer | AS-Unsafe heap lock | AC-Unsafe lock fd mem | See Section 1.2.2.1 [POSIX Safety Concepts], page 2.

The `getutent` function reads the next entry from the user accounting database. It returns a pointer to the entry, which is statically allocated and may be overwritten by subsequent calls to `getutent`. You must copy the contents of the structure if you wish to save the information or you can use the `getutent_r` function which stores the data in a user-provided buffer.

A null pointer is returned in case no further entry is available.

void endutent (*void*)   [Function]
Preliminary: | MT-Unsafe race:utent | AS-Unsafe lock | AC-Unsafe lock fd | See Section 1.2.2.1 [POSIX Safety Concepts], page 2.

This function closes the user accounting database.

struct utmp * getutid (*const struct utmp *id*)   [Function]
Preliminary: | MT-Unsafe init race:utent sig:ALRM timer | AS-Unsafe lock heap | AC-Unsafe lock mem fd | See Section 1.2.2.1 [POSIX Safety Concepts], page 2.

This function searches forward from the current point in the database for an entry that matches *id*. If the `ut_type` member of the *id* structure is one of `RUN_LVL`, `BOOT_TIME`, `OLD_TIME` or `NEW_TIME` the entries match if the `ut_type` members are identical. If the `ut_type` member of the *id* structure is `INIT_PROCESS`, `LOGIN_PROCESS`, `USER_PROCESS` or `DEAD_PROCESS`, the entries match if the `ut_type` member of the entry read from the database is one of these four, and the `ut_id` members match. However if the `ut_id` member of either the *id* structure or the entry read from the database is empty it checks if the `ut_line` members match instead. If a matching entry is found, `getutid` returns a pointer to the entry, which is statically allocated, and may be overwritten by a subsequent call to `getutent`, `getutid` or `getutline`. You must copy the contents of the structure if you wish to save the information.

A null pointer is returned in case the end of the database is reached without a match.

The `getutid` function may cache the last read entry. Therefore, if you are using `getutid` to search for multiple occurrences, it is necessary to zero out the static data after each call. Otherwise `getutid` could just return a pointer to the same entry over and over again.

struct utmp * getutline (*const struct utmp *line*)   [Function]
Preliminary: | MT-Unsafe init race:utent sig:ALRM timer | AS-Unsafe heap lock | AC-Unsafe lock fd mem | See Section 1.2.2.1 [POSIX Safety Concepts], page 2.

This function searches forward from the current point in the database until it finds an entry whose `ut_type` value is `LOGIN_PROCESS` or `USER_PROCESS`, and whose `ut_line` member matches the `ut_line` member of the *line* structure. If it finds such an entry, it returns a pointer to the entry which is statically allocated, and may be overwritten by a subsequent call to `getutent`, `getutid` or `getutline`. You must copy the contents of the structure if you wish to save the information.

A null pointer is returned in case the end of the database is reached without a match.

The `getutline` function may cache the last read entry. Therefore if you are using `getutline` to search for multiple occurrences, it is necessary to zero out the static data after each call. Otherwise `getutline` could just return a pointer to the same entry over and over again.

`struct utmp * pututline (const struct utmp *utmp)`   [Function]
> Preliminary: | MT-Unsafe race:utent sig:ALRM timer | AS-Unsafe lock | AC-Unsafe lock fd | See Section 1.2.2.1 [POSIX Safety Concepts], page 2.
>
> The `pututline` function inserts the entry `*utmp` at the appropriate place in the user accounting database. If it finds that it is not already at the correct place in the database, it uses `getutid` to search for the position to insert the entry, however this will not modify the static structure returned by `getutent`, `getutid` and `getutline`. If this search fails, the entry is appended to the database.
>
> The `pututline` function returns a pointer to a copy of the entry inserted in the user accounting database, or a null pointer if the entry could not be added. The following `errno` error conditions are defined for this function:
>
> EPERM   The process does not have the appropriate privileges; you cannot modify the user accounting database.

All the `get*` functions mentioned before store the information they return in a static buffer. This can be a problem in multi-threaded programs since the data returned for the request is overwritten by the return value data in another thread. Therefore the GNU C Library provides as extensions three more functions which return the data in a user-provided buffer.

`int getutent_r (struct utmp *buffer, struct utmp **result)`   [Function]
> Preliminary: | MT-Unsafe race:utent sig:ALRM timer | AS-Unsafe lock | AC-Unsafe lock fd | See Section 1.2.2.1 [POSIX Safety Concepts], page 2.
>
> The `getutent_r` is equivalent to the `getutent` function. It returns the next entry from the database. But instead of storing the information in a static buffer it stores it in the buffer pointed to by the parameter *buffer*.
>
> If the call was successful, the function returns 0 and the pointer variable pointed to by the parameter *result* contains a pointer to the buffer which contains the result (this is most probably the same value as *buffer*). If something went wrong during the execution of `getutent_r` the function returns -1.
>
> This function is a GNU extension.

`int getutid_r (const struct utmp *id, struct utmp *buffer, struct`   [Function]
        `utmp **result)`
> Preliminary: | MT-Unsafe race:utent sig:ALRM timer | AS-Unsafe lock | AC-Unsafe lock fd | See Section 1.2.2.1 [POSIX Safety Concepts], page 2.

This function retrieves just like `getutid` the next entry matching the information stored in *id*. But the result is stored in the buffer pointed to by the parameter *buffer*.

If successful the function returns 0 and the pointer variable pointed to by the parameter *result* contains a pointer to the buffer with the result (probably the same as *result*. If not successful the function return -1.

This function is a GNU extension.

int **getutline_r** (*const struct utmp *line, struct utmp *buffer,*   [Function]
    struct utmp **result)

Preliminary: | MT-Unsafe race:utent sig:ALRM timer | AS-Unsafe lock | AC-Unsafe lock fd | See Section 1.2.2.1 [POSIX Safety Concepts], page 2.

This function retrieves just like `getutline` the next entry matching the information stored in *line*. But the result is stored in the buffer pointed to by the parameter *buffer*.

If successful the function returns 0 and the pointer variable pointed to by the parameter *result* contains a pointer to the buffer with the result (probably the same as *result*. If not successful the function return -1.

This function is a GNU extension.

In addition to the user accounting database, most systems keep a number of similar databases. For example most systems keep a log file with all previous logins (usually in `/etc/wtmp` or `/var/log/wtmp`).

For specifying which database to examine, the following function should be used.

int **utmpname** (*const char *file*)   [Function]

Preliminary: | MT-Unsafe race:utent | AS-Unsafe lock heap | AC-Unsafe lock mem | See Section 1.2.2.1 [POSIX Safety Concepts], page 2.

The `utmpname` function changes the name of the database to be examined to *file*, and closes any previously opened database. By default `getutent`, `getutid`, `getutline` and `pututline` read from and write to the user accounting database.

The following macros are defined for use as the *file* argument:

char * **_PATH_UTMP**   [Macro]
    This macro is used to specify the user accounting database.

char * **_PATH_WTMP**   [Macro]
    This macro is used to specify the user accounting log file.

The `utmpname` function returns a value of 0 if the new name was successfully stored, and a value of -1 to indicate an error. Note that `utmpname` does not try to open the database, and that therefore the return value does not say anything about whether the database can be successfully opened.

Specially for maintaining log-like databases the GNU C Library provides the following function:

void updwtmp (*const char *wtmp_file, const struct utmp *utmp*)   [Function]
    Preliminary: | MT-Unsafe sig:ALRM timer | AS-Unsafe | AC-Unsafe fd | See
    Section 1.2.2.1 [POSIX Safety Concepts], page 2.

    The **updwtmp** function appends the entry **utmp* to the database specified by
    wtmp_file.   For possible values for the *wtmp_file* argument see the **utmpname**
    function.

Portability Note: Although many operating systems provide a subset of these functions,
they are not standardized. There are often subtle differences in the return types, and there
are considerable differences between the various definitions of **struct utmp**. When programming for the GNU C Library, it is probably best to stick with the functions described
in this section. If however, you want your program to be portable, consider using the
XPG functions described in Section 30.12.2 [XPG User Accounting Database Functions],
page 831, or take a look at the BSD compatible functions in Section 30.12.3 [Logging In
and Out], page 833.

30.12.2 XPG User Accounting Database Functions

These functions, described in the X/Open Portability Guide, are declared in the header file
utmpx.h.

struct utmpx   [Data Type]
    The **utmpx** data structure contains at least the following members:

    short int ut_type
            Specifies the type of login; one of **EMPTY**, **RUN_LVL**, **BOOT_TIME**,
            OLD_TIME, **NEW_TIME**, **INIT_PROCESS**, **LOGIN_PROCESS**, **USER_PROCESS** or
            DEAD_PROCESS.

    pid_t ut_pid
            The process ID number of the login process.

    char ut_line[]
            The device name of the tty (without **/dev/**).

    char ut_id[]
            The inittab ID of the process.

    char ut_user[]
            The user's login name.

    struct timeval ut_tv
            Time the entry was made. For entries of type **OLD_TIME** this is the time
            when the system clock changed, and for entries of type **NEW_TIME** this is
            the time the system clock was set to.

    In the GNU C Library, **struct utmpx** is identical to **struct utmp** except for the fact
    that including **utmpx.h** does not make visible the declaration of **struct exit_status**.

    The following macros are defined for use as values for the **ut_type** member of the **utmpx**
structure. The values are integer constants and are, in the GNU C Library, identical to the
definitions in **utmp.h**.

EMPTY   This macro is used to indicate that the entry contains no valid user accounting
            information.

RUN_LVL   This macro is used to identify the system's runlevel.

BOOT_TIME
        This macro is used to identify the time of system boot.

OLD_TIME   This macro is used to identify the time when the system clock changed.

NEW_TIME   This macro is used to identify the time after the system clock changed.

INIT_PROCESS
        This macro is used to identify a process spawned by the init process.

LOGIN_PROCESS
        This macro is used to identify the session leader of a logged in user.

USER_PROCESS
        This macro is used to identify a user process.

DEAD_PROCESS
        This macro is used to identify a terminated process.

The size of the `ut_line`, `ut_id` and `ut_user` arrays can be found using the `sizeof` operator.

`void setutxent (`*void*`)`   [Function]
    Preliminary: | MT-Unsafe race:utent | AS-Unsafe lock | AC-Unsafe lock fd | See Section 1.2.2.1 [POSIX Safety Concepts], page 2.

    This function is similar to `setutent`. In the GNU C Library it is simply an alias for `setutent`.

`struct utmpx * getutxent (`*void*`)`   [Function]
    Preliminary: | MT-Unsafe init race:utent sig:ALRM timer | AS-Unsafe heap lock | AC-Unsafe lock fd mem | See Section 1.2.2.1 [POSIX Safety Concepts], page 2.

    The `getutxent` function is similar to `getutent`, but returns a pointer to a `struct utmpx` instead of `struct utmp`. In the GNU C Library it simply is an alias for `getutent`.

`void endutxent (`*void*`)`   [Function]
    Preliminary: | MT-Unsafe race:utent | AS-Unsafe lock | AC-Unsafe lock | See Section 1.2.2.1 [POSIX Safety Concepts], page 2.

    This function is similar to `endutent`. In the GNU C Library it is simply an alias for `endutent`.

`struct utmpx * getutxid (`*const struct utmpx *id*`)`   [Function]
    Preliminary: | MT-Unsafe init race:utent sig:ALRM timer | AS-Unsafe lock heap | AC-Unsafe lock mem fd | See Section 1.2.2.1 [POSIX Safety Concepts], page 2.

    This function is similar to `getutid`, but uses `struct utmpx` instead of `struct utmp`. In the GNU C Library it is simply an alias for `getutid`.

`struct utmpx * getutxline (`*const struct utmpx *line*`)`   [Function]
    Preliminary: | MT-Unsafe init race:utent sig:ALRM timer | AS-Unsafe heap lock | AC-Unsafe lock fd mem | See Section 1.2.2.1 [POSIX Safety Concepts], page 2.

    This function is similar to `getutid`, but uses `struct utmpx` instead of `struct utmp`. In the GNU C Library it is simply an alias for `getutline`.

struct utmpx * pututxline (*const struct utmpx *utmp*) [Function]
Preliminary: | MT-Unsafe race:utent sig:ALRM timer | AS-Unsafe lock | AC-Unsafe lock fd | See Section 1.2.2.1 [POSIX Safety Concepts], page 2.

The `pututxline` function is functionally identical to `pututline`, but uses `struct utmpx` instead of `struct utmp`. In the GNU C Library, `pututxline` is simply an alias for `pututline`.

int utmpxname (*const char *file*) [Function]
Preliminary: | MT-Unsafe race:utent | AS-Unsafe lock heap | AC-Unsafe lock mem | See Section 1.2.2.1 [POSIX Safety Concepts], page 2.

The `utmpxname` function is functionally identical to `utmpname`. In the GNU C Library, `utmpxname` is simply an alias for `utmpname`.

You can translate between a traditional `struct utmp` and an XPG `struct utmpx` with the following functions. In the GNU C Library, these functions are merely copies, since the two structures are identical.

int getutmp (*const struct utmpx *utmpx, struct utmp *utmp*) [Function]
Preliminary: | MT-Safe | AS-Safe | AC-Safe | See Section 1.2.2.1 [POSIX Safety Concepts], page 2.

`getutmp` copies the information, insofar as the structures are compatible, from *utmpx* to *utmp*.

int getutmpx (*const struct utmp *utmp, struct utmpx *utmpx*) [Function]
Preliminary: | MT-Safe | AS-Safe | AC-Safe | See Section 1.2.2.1 [POSIX Safety Concepts], page 2.

`getutmpx` copies the information, insofar as the structures are compatible, from *utmp* to *utmpx*.

30.12.3 Logging In and Out

These functions, derived from BSD, are available in the separate `libutil` library, and declared in `utmp.h`.

Note that the `ut_user` member of `struct utmp` is called `ut_name` in BSD. Therefore, `ut_name` is defined as an alias for `ut_user` in `utmp.h`.

int login_tty (*int filedes*) [Function]
Preliminary: | MT-Unsafe race:ttyname | AS-Unsafe heap lock | AC-Unsafe lock fd mem | See Section 1.2.2.1 [POSIX Safety Concepts], page 2.

This function makes *filedes* the controlling terminal of the current process, redirects standard input, standard output and standard error output to this terminal, and closes *filedes*.

This function returns 0 on successful completion, and -1 on error.

void login (*const struct utmp *entry*) [Function]
Preliminary: | MT-Unsafe race:utent sig:ALRM timer | AS-Unsafe lock heap | AC-Unsafe lock corrupt fd mem | See Section 1.2.2.1 [POSIX Safety Concepts], page 2.

The `login` functions inserts an entry into the user accounting database. The `ut_line` member is set to the name of the terminal on standard input. If standard input is not a terminal `login` uses standard output or standard error output to determine the name of the terminal. If `struct utmp` has a `ut_type` member, `login` sets it to `USER_PROCESS`, and if there is an `ut_pid` member, it will be set to the process ID of the current process. The remaining entries are copied from *entry*.

A copy of the entry is written to the user accounting log file.

int logout (*const char *ut_line*)   [Function]
> Preliminary: | MT-Unsafe race:utent sig:ALRM timer | AS-Unsafe lock heap | AC-Unsafe lock fd mem | See Section 1.2.2.1 [POSIX Safety Concepts], page 2.
>
> This function modifies the user accounting database to indicate that the user on *ut_line* has logged out.
>
> The `logout` function returns 1 if the entry was successfully written to the database, or 0 on error.

void logwtmp (*const char *ut_line, const char *ut_name, const*   [Function]
> *char *ut_host*)
> Preliminary: | MT-Unsafe sig:ALRM timer | AS-Unsafe | AC-Unsafe fd | See Section 1.2.2.1 [POSIX Safety Concepts], page 2.
>
> The `logwtmp` function appends an entry to the user accounting log file, for the current time and the information provided in the *ut_line*, *ut_name* and *ut_host* arguments.

Portability Note: The BSD `struct utmp` only has the `ut_line`, `ut_name`, `ut_host` and `ut_time` members. Older systems do not even have the `ut_host` member.

30.13 User Database

This section describes how to search and scan the database of registered users. The database itself is kept in the file `/etc/passwd` on most systems, but on some systems a special network server gives access to it.

30.13.1 The Data Structure that Describes a User

The functions and data structures for accessing the system user database are declared in the header file `pwd.h`.

struct passwd   [Data Type]
> The `passwd` data structure is used to hold information about entries in the system user data base. It has at least the following members:
>
> char *pw_name
>> The user's login name.
>
> char *pw_passwd.
>> The encrypted password string.
>
> uid_t pw_uid
>> The user ID number.

`gid_t pw_gid`
> The user's default group ID number.

`char *pw_gecos`
> A string typically containing the user's real name, and possibly other information such as a phone number.

`char *pw_dir`
> The user's home directory, or initial working directory. This might be a null pointer, in which case the interpretation is system-dependent.

`char *pw_shell`
> The user's default shell, or the initial program run when the user logs in. This might be a null pointer, indicating that the system default should be used.

30.13.2 Looking Up One User

You can search the system user database for information about a specific user using `getpwuid` or `getpwnam`. These functions are declared in `pwd.h`.

struct passwd * getpwuid (*uid_t* **uid**)   [Function]
> Preliminary: | MT-Unsafe race:pwuid locale | AS-Unsafe dlopen plugin heap lock | AC-Unsafe corrupt lock fd mem | See Section 1.2.2.1 [POSIX Safety Concepts], page 2.

> This function returns a pointer to a statically-allocated structure containing information about the user whose user ID is *uid*. This structure may be overwritten on subsequent calls to `getpwuid`.

> A null pointer value indicates there is no user in the data base with user ID *uid*.

int getpwuid_r (*uid_t* **uid**, *struct passwd* ***result_buf**, *char*   [Function]
> ***buffer**, *size_t* **buflen**, *struct passwd* ****result**)
> Preliminary: | MT-Safe locale | AS-Unsafe dlopen plugin heap lock | AC-Unsafe corrupt lock fd mem | See Section 1.2.2.1 [POSIX Safety Concepts], page 2.

> This function is similar to `getpwuid` in that it returns information about the user whose user ID is *uid*. However, it fills the user supplied structure pointed to by *result_buf* with the information instead of using a static buffer. The first *buflen* bytes of the additional buffer pointed to by *buffer* are used to contain additional information, normally strings which are pointed to by the elements of the result structure.

> If a user with ID *uid* is found, the pointer returned in *result* points to the record which contains the wanted data (i.e., *result* contains the value *result_buf*). If no user is found or if an error occurred, the pointer returned in *result* is a null pointer. The function returns zero or an error code. If the buffer *buffer* is too small to contain all the needed information, the error code **ERANGE** is returned and *errno* is set to **ERANGE**.

struct passwd * getpwnam (*const char* ***name**)   [Function]
> Preliminary: | MT-Unsafe race:pwnam locale | AS-Unsafe dlopen plugin heap lock | AC-Unsafe corrupt lock fd mem | See Section 1.2.2.1 [POSIX Safety Concepts], page 2.

This function returns a pointer to a statically-allocated structure containing information about the user whose user name is *name*. This structure may be overwritten on subsequent calls to `getpwnam`.

A null pointer return indicates there is no user named *name*.

int getpwnam_r (*const char *name, struct passwd *result_buf,*   [Function]
      char *buffer, size_t buflen, struct passwd **result)

Preliminary: | MT-Safe locale | AS-Unsafe dlopen plugin heap lock | AC-Unsafe corrupt lock fd mem | See Section 1.2.2.1 [POSIX Safety Concepts], page 2.

This function is similar to `getpwnam` in that it returns information about the user whose user name is *name*. However, like `getpwuid_r`, it fills the user supplied buffers in *result_buf* and *buffer* with the information instead of using a static buffer.

The return values are the same as for `getpwuid_r`.

30.13.3 Scanning the List of All Users

This section explains how a program can read the list of all users in the system, one user at a time. The functions described here are declared in `pwd.h`.

You can use the `fgetpwent` function to read user entries from a particular file.

struct passwd * fgetpwent (*FILE *stream*)   [Function]

Preliminary: | MT-Unsafe race:fpwent | AS-Unsafe corrupt lock | AC-Unsafe corrupt lock | See Section 1.2.2.1 [POSIX Safety Concepts], page 2.

This function reads the next user entry from *stream* and returns a pointer to the entry. The structure is statically allocated and is rewritten on subsequent calls to `fgetpwent`. You must copy the contents of the structure if you wish to save the information.

The stream must correspond to a file in the same format as the standard password database file.

int fgetpwent_r (*FILE *stream, struct passwd *result_buf, char*   [Function]
      *buffer, size_t buflen, struct passwd **result)

Preliminary: | MT-Safe | AS-Unsafe corrupt | AC-Unsafe corrupt lock | See Section 1.2.2.1 [POSIX Safety Concepts], page 2.

This function is similar to `fgetpwent` in that it reads the next user entry from *stream*. But the result is returned in the structure pointed to by *result_buf*. The first *buflen* bytes of the additional buffer pointed to by *buffer* are used to contain additional information, normally strings which are pointed to by the elements of the result structure.

The stream must correspond to a file in the same format as the standard password database file.

If the function returns zero *result* points to the structure with the wanted data (normally this is in *result_buf*). If errors occurred the return value is nonzero and *result* contains a null pointer.

The way to scan all the entries in the user database is with `setpwent`, `getpwent`, and `endpwent`.

void setpwent (*void*) [Function]

> Preliminary: | MT-Unsafe race:pwent locale | AS-Unsafe dlopen plugin heap lock | AC-Unsafe corrupt lock fd mem | See Section 1.2.2.1 [POSIX Safety Concepts], page 2.

> This function initializes a stream which `getpwent` and `getpwent_r` use to read the user database.

struct passwd * getpwent (*void*) [Function]

> Preliminary: | MT-Unsafe race:pwent race:pwentbuf locale | AS-Unsafe dlopen plugin heap lock | AC-Unsafe corrupt lock fd mem | See Section 1.2.2.1 [POSIX Safety Concepts], page 2.

> The `getpwent` function reads the next entry from the stream initialized by `setpwent`. It returns a pointer to the entry. The structure is statically allocated and is rewritten on subsequent calls to `getpwent`. You must copy the contents of the structure if you wish to save the information.

> A null pointer is returned when no more entries are available.

int getpwent_r (*struct passwd *result_buf, char *buffer, size_t* [Function]
    *buflen, struct passwd **result*)

> Preliminary: | MT-Unsafe race:pwent locale | AS-Unsafe dlopen plugin heap lock | AC-Unsafe corrupt lock fd mem | See Section 1.2.2.1 [POSIX Safety Concepts], page 2.

> This function is similar to `getpwent` in that it returns the next entry from the stream initialized by `setpwent`. Like `fgetpwent_r`, it uses the user-supplied buffers in *result_buf* and *buffer* to return the information requested.

> The return values are the same as for `fgetpwent_r`.

void endpwent (*void*) [Function]

> Preliminary: | MT-Unsafe race:pwent locale | AS-Unsafe dlopen plugin heap lock | AC-Unsafe corrupt lock fd mem | See Section 1.2.2.1 [POSIX Safety Concepts], page 2.

> This function closes the internal stream used by `getpwent` or `getpwent_r`.

30.13.4 Writing a User Entry

int putpwent (*const struct passwd *p, FILE *stream*) [Function]

> Preliminary: | MT-Safe locale | AS-Unsafe corrupt | AC-Unsafe lock corrupt | See Section 1.2.2.1 [POSIX Safety Concepts], page 2.

> This function writes the user entry *p to the stream *stream*, in the format used for the standard user database file. The return value is zero on success and nonzero on failure.

> This function exists for compatibility with SVID. We recommend that you avoid using it, because it makes sense only on the assumption that the **struct passwd** structure has no members except the standard ones; on a system which merges the traditional Unix data base with other extended information about users, adding an entry using this function would inevitably leave out much of the important information.

The group and user ID fields are left empty if the group or user name starts with a -
or +.

The function `putpwent` is declared in `pwd.h`.

30.14 Group Database

This section describes how to search and scan the database of registered groups. The
database itself is kept in the file `/etc/group` on most systems, but on some systems a
special network service provides access to it.

30.14.1 The Data Structure for a Group

The functions and data structures for accessing the system group database are declared in
the header file `grp.h`.

struct group   [Data Type]

>   The `group` structure is used to hold information about an entry in the system group
>   database. It has at least the following members:

>   `char *gr_name`
>   >   The name of the group.

>   `gid_t gr_gid`
>   >   The group ID of the group.

>   `char **gr_mem`
>   >   A vector of pointers to the names of users in the group. Each user name
>   >   is a null-terminated string, and the vector itself is terminated by a null
>   >   pointer.

30.14.2 Looking Up One Group

You can search the group database for information about a specific group using `getgrgid`
or `getgrnam`. These functions are declared in `grp.h`.

struct group * getgrgid (*gid_t gid*)   [Function]

>   Preliminary: | MT-Unsafe race:grgid locale | AS-Unsafe dlopen plugin heap lock
> | AC-Unsafe corrupt lock fd mem | See Section 1.2.2.1 [POSIX Safety Concepts],
>   page 2.

>   This function returns a pointer to a statically-allocated structure containing informa-
>   tion about the group whose group ID is *gid*. This structure may be overwritten by
>   subsequent calls to `getgrgid`.

>   A null pointer indicates there is no group with ID *gid*.

int getgrgid_r (*gid_t gid*, *struct group *result_buf*, *char   [Function]
    buffer*, *size_t buflen*, *struct group **result*)

>   Preliminary: | MT-Safe locale | AS-Unsafe dlopen plugin heap lock | AC-Unsafe
>   corrupt lock fd mem | See Section 1.2.2.1 [POSIX Safety Concepts], page 2.

>   This function is similar to `getgrgid` in that it returns information about the group
>   whose group ID is *gid*. However, it fills the user supplied structure pointed to by
>   *result_buf* with the information instead of using a static buffer. The first *buflen*

bytes of the additional buffer pointed to by *buffer* are used to contain additional information, normally strings which are pointed to by the elements of the result structure.

If a group with ID *gid* is found, the pointer returned in *result* points to the record which contains the wanted data (i.e., *result* contains the value *result_buf*). If no group is found or if an error occurred, the pointer returned in *result* is a null pointer. The function returns zero or an error code. If the buffer *buffer* is too small to contain all the needed information, the error code ERANGE is returned and *errno* is set to ERANGE.

struct group * getgrnam (*const char *name*)   [Function]
> Preliminary: | MT-Unsafe race:grnam locale | AS-Unsafe dlopen plugin heap lock | AC-Unsafe corrupt lock fd mem | See Section 1.2.2.1 [POSIX Safety Concepts], page 2.
>
> This function returns a pointer to a statically-allocated structure containing information about the group whose group name is *name*. This structure may be overwritten by subsequent calls to getgrnam.
>
> A null pointer indicates there is no group named *name*.

int getgrnam_r (*const char *name, struct group *result_buf, char*   [Function]
> **buffer, size_t buflen, struct group **result*)
> Preliminary: | MT-Safe locale | AS-Unsafe dlopen plugin heap lock | AC-Unsafe corrupt lock fd mem | See Section 1.2.2.1 [POSIX Safety Concepts], page 2.
>
> This function is similar to getgrnam in that it returns information about the group whose group name is *name*. Like getgrgid_r, it uses the user supplied buffers in *result_buf* and *buffer*, not a static buffer.
>
> The return values are the same as for getgrgid_r.

30.14.3 Scanning the List of All Groups

This section explains how a program can read the list of all groups in the system, one group at a time. The functions described here are declared in grp.h.

You can use the fgetgrent function to read group entries from a particular file.

struct group * fgetgrent (*FILE *stream*)   [Function]
> Preliminary: | MT-Unsafe race:fgrent | AS-Unsafe corrupt lock | AC-Unsafe corrupt lock | See Section 1.2.2.1 [POSIX Safety Concepts], page 2.
>
> The fgetgrent function reads the next entry from *stream*. It returns a pointer to the entry. The structure is statically allocated and is overwritten on subsequent calls to fgetgrent. You must copy the contents of the structure if you wish to save the information.
>
> The stream must correspond to a file in the same format as the standard group database file.

int fgetgrent_r (*FILE *stream, struct group *result_buf, char*   [Function]
> **buffer, size_t buflen, struct group **result*)
> Preliminary: | MT-Safe | AS-Unsafe corrupt | AC-Unsafe corrupt lock | See Section 1.2.2.1 [POSIX Safety Concepts], page 2.

This function is similar to `fgetgrent` in that it reads the next user entry from *stream*. But the result is returned in the structure pointed to by *result_buf*. The first *buflen* bytes of the additional buffer pointed to by *buffer* are used to contain additional information, normally strings which are pointed to by the elements of the result structure.

This stream must correspond to a file in the same format as the standard group database file.

If the function returns zero *result* points to the structure with the wanted data (normally this is in *result_buf*). If errors occurred the return value is non-zero and *result* contains a null pointer.

The way to scan all the entries in the group database is with `setgrent`, `getgrent`, and `endgrent`.

void setgrent (*void*)   [Function]
> Preliminary: | MT-Unsafe race:grent locale | AS-Unsafe dlopen plugin heap lock | AC-Unsafe corrupt lock fd mem | See Section 1.2.2.1 [POSIX Safety Concepts], page 2.
>
> This function initializes a stream for reading from the group data base. You use this stream by calling `getgrent` or `getgrent_r`.

struct group * getgrent (*void*)   [Function]
> Preliminary: | MT-Unsafe race:grent race:grentbuf locale | AS-Unsafe dlopen plugin heap lock | AC-Unsafe corrupt lock fd mem | See Section 1.2.2.1 [POSIX Safety Concepts], page 2.
>
> The `getgrent` function reads the next entry from the stream initialized by `setgrent`. It returns a pointer to the entry. The structure is statically allocated and is overwritten on subsequent calls to `getgrent`. You must copy the contents of the structure if you wish to save the information.

int getgrent_r (*struct group *result_buf, char *buffer, size_t*   [Function]
>   *buflen, struct group **result*)
> Preliminary: | MT-Unsafe race:grent locale | AS-Unsafe dlopen plugin heap lock | AC-Unsafe corrupt lock fd mem | See Section 1.2.2.1 [POSIX Safety Concepts], page 2.
>
> This function is similar to `getgrent` in that it returns the next entry from the stream initialized by `setgrent`. Like `fgetgrent_r`, it places the result in user-supplied buffers pointed to by *result_buf* and *buffer*.
>
> If the function returns zero *result* contains a pointer to the data (normally equal to *result_buf*). If errors occurred the return value is non-zero and *result* contains a null pointer.

void endgrent (*void*)   [Function]
> Preliminary: | MT-Unsafe race:grent locale | AS-Unsafe dlopen plugin heap lock | AC-Unsafe corrupt lock fd mem | See Section 1.2.2.1 [POSIX Safety Concepts], page 2.
>
> This function closes the internal stream used by `getgrent` or `getgrent_r`.

30.15 User and Group Database Example

Here is an example program showing the use of the system database inquiry functions. The program prints some information about the user running the program.

```
#include <grp.h>
#include <pwd.h>
#include <sys/types.h>
#include <unistd.h>
#include <stdlib.h>

int
main (void)
{
  uid_t me;
  struct passwd *my_passwd;
  struct group *my_group;
  char **members;

  /* Get information about the user ID. */
  me = getuid ();
  my_passwd = getpwuid (me);
  if (!my_passwd)
    {
      printf ("Couldn't find out about user %d.\n", (int) me);
      exit (EXIT_FAILURE);
    }

  /* Print the information. */
  printf ("I am %s.\n", my_passwd->pw_gecos);
  printf ("My login name is %s.\n", my_passwd->pw_name);
  printf ("My uid is %d.\n", (int) (my_passwd->pw_uid));
  printf ("My home directory is %s.\n", my_passwd->pw_dir);
  printf ("My default shell is %s.\n", my_passwd->pw_shell);

  /* Get information about the default group ID. */
  my_group = getgrgid (my_passwd->pw_gid);
  if (!my_group)
    {
      printf ("Couldn't find out about group %d.\n",
              (int) my_passwd->pw_gid);
      exit (EXIT_FAILURE);
    }

  /* Print the information. */
  printf ("My default group is %s (%d).\n",
          my_group->gr_name, (int) (my_passwd->pw_gid));
  printf ("The members of this group are:\n");
  members = my_group->gr_mem;
  while (*members)
    {
      printf ("  %s\n", *(members));
      members++;
    }

  return EXIT_SUCCESS;
}
```

Here is some output from this program:

```
I am Throckmorton Snurd.
My login name is snurd.
My uid is 31093.
My home directory is /home/fsg/snurd.
My default shell is /bin/sh.
My default group is guest (12).
The members of this group are:
  friedman
  tami
```

30.16 Netgroup Database

30.16.1 Netgroup Data

Sometimes it is useful to group users according to other criteria (see Section 30.14 [Group Database], page 838). E.g., it is useful to associate a certain group of users with a certain machine. On the other hand grouping of host names is not supported so far.

In Sun Microsystems' SunOS appeared a new kind of database, the netgroup database. It allows grouping hosts, users, and domains freely, giving them individual names. To be more concrete, a netgroup is a list of triples consisting of a host name, a user name, and a domain name where any of the entries can be a wildcard entry matching all inputs. A last possibility is that names of other netgroups can also be given in the list specifying a netgroup. So one can construct arbitrary hierarchies without loops.

Sun's implementation allows netgroups only for the **nis** or **nisplus** service, see Section 29.2.1 [Services in the NSS configuration File], page 806. The implementation in the GNU C Library has no such restriction. An entry in either of the input services must have the following form:

> *groupname* (*groupname* | (*hostname*,*username*,*domainname*))+

Any of the fields in the triple can be empty which means anything matches. While describing the functions we will see that the opposite case is useful as well. I.e., there may be entries which will not match any input. For entries like this, a name consisting of the single character - shall be used.

30.16.2 Looking up one Netgroup

The lookup functions for netgroups are a bit different than all other system database handling functions. Since a single netgroup can contain many entries a two-step process is needed. First a single netgroup is selected and then one can iterate over all entries in this netgroup. These functions are declared in **netdb.h**.

int setnetgrent (*const char *netgroup*) [Function]

> Preliminary: | MT-Unsafe race:netgrent locale | AS-Unsafe dlopen plugin heap lock | AC-Unsafe corrupt lock fd mem | See Section 1.2.2.1 [POSIX Safety Concepts], page 2.
>
> A call to this function initializes the internal state of the library to allow following calls of **getnetgrent** to iterate over all entries in the netgroup with name *netgroup*.
>
> When the call is successful (i.e., when a netgroup with this name exists) the return value is **1**. When the return value is **0** no netgroup of this name is known or some other error occurred.

It is important to remember that there is only one single state for iterating the netgroups. Even if the programmer uses the `getnetgrent_r` function the result is not really reentrant since always only one single netgroup at a time can be processed. If the program needs to process more than one netgroup simultaneously she must protect this by using external locking. This problem was introduced in the original netgroups implementation in SunOS and since we must stay compatible it is not possible to change this.

Some other functions also use the netgroups state. Currently these are the `innetgr` function and parts of the implementation of the `compat` service part of the NSS implementation.

---

int **getnetgrent** (*char **hostp, char **userp, char **domainp*)   [Function]

> Preliminary: | MT-Unsafe race:netgrent race:netgrentbuf locale | AS-Unsafe dlopen plugin heap lock | AC-Unsafe corrupt lock fd mem | See Section 1.2.2.1 [POSIX Safety Concepts], page 2.
>
> This function returns the next unprocessed entry of the currently selected netgroup. The string pointers, in which addresses are passed in the arguments *hostp*, *userp*, and *domainp*, will contain after a successful call pointers to appropriate strings. If the string in the next entry is empty the pointer has the value `NULL`. The returned string pointers are only valid if none of the netgroup related functions are called.
>
> The return value is `1` if the next entry was successfully read. A value of `0` means no further entries exist or internal errors occurred.

---

int **getnetgrent_r** (*char **hostp, char **userp, char **domainp*,   [Function]
    char *buffer, size_t buflen)

> Preliminary: | MT-Unsafe race:netgrent locale | AS-Unsafe dlopen plugin heap lock | AC-Unsafe corrupt lock fd mem | See Section 1.2.2.1 [POSIX Safety Concepts], page 2.
>
> This function is similar to `getnetgrent` with only one exception: the strings the three string pointers *hostp*, *userp*, and *domainp* point to, are placed in the buffer of *buflen* bytes starting at *buffer*. This means the returned values are valid even after other netgroup related functions are called.
>
> The return value is `1` if the next entry was successfully read and the buffer contains enough room to place the strings in it. `0` is returned in case no more entries are found, the buffer is too small, or internal errors occurred.
>
> This function is a GNU extension. The original implementation in the SunOS libc does not provide this function.

---

void **endnetgrent** (*void*)   [Function]

> Preliminary: | MT-Unsafe race:netgrent | AS-Unsafe dlopen plugin heap lock | AC-Unsafe corrupt lock fd mem | See Section 1.2.2.1 [POSIX Safety Concepts], page 2.
>
> This function frees all buffers which were allocated to process the last selected netgroup. As a result all string pointers returned by calls to `getnetgrent` are invalid afterwards.

30.16.3 Testing for Netgroup Membership

It is often not necessary to scan the whole netgroup since often the only interesting question is whether a given entry is part of the selected netgroup.

`int innetgr` (*const char *netgroup, const char *host, const char*   [Function]
      *user, const char *domain)

> Preliminary: | MT-Unsafe race:netgrent locale | AS-Unsafe dlopen plugin heap lock
> | AC-Unsafe corrupt lock fd mem | See Section 1.2.2.1 [POSIX Safety Concepts],
> page 2.
>
> This function tests whether the triple specified by the parameters *host*, *user*, and
> *domain* is part of the netgroup *netgroup*. Using this function has the advantage that
>
> 1. no other netgroup function can use the global netgroup state since internal locking
>   is used and
>
> 2. the function is implemented more efficiently than successive calls to the other
>   `set/get/endnetgrent` functions.
>
> Any of the pointers *host*, *user*, or *domain* can be `NULL` which means any value is
> accepted in this position. This is also true for the name – which should not match
> any other string otherwise.
>
> The return value is `1` if an entry matching the given triple is found in the netgroup.
> The return value is `0` if the netgroup itself is not found, the netgroup does not contain
> the triple or internal errors occurred.

31 System Management

This chapter describes facilities for controlling the system that underlies a process (including the operating system and hardware) and for getting information about it. Anyone can generally use the informational facilities, but usually only a properly privileged process can make changes.

To get information on parameters of the system that are built into the system, such as the maximum length of a filename, Chapter 32 [System Configuration Parameters], page 862.

31.1 Host Identification

This section explains how to identify the particular system on which your program is running. First, let's review the various ways computer systems are named, which is a little complicated because of the history of the development of the Internet.

Every Unix system (also known as a host) has a host name, whether it's connected to a network or not. In its simplest form, as used before computer networks were an issue, it's just a word like 'chicken'.

But any system attached to the Internet or any network like it conforms to a more rigorous naming convention as part of the Domain Name System (DNS). In the DNS, every host name is composed of two parts:

1. hostname
2. domain name

You will note that "hostname" looks a lot like "host name", but is not the same thing, and that people often incorrectly refer to entire host names as "domain names."

In the DNS, the full host name is properly called the FQDN (Fully Qualified Domain Name) and consists of the hostname, then a period, then the domain name. The domain name itself usually has multiple components separated by periods. So for example, a system's hostname may be 'chicken' and its domain name might be 'ai.mit.edu', so its FQDN (which is its host name) is 'chicken.ai.mit.edu'.

Adding to the confusion, though, is that the DNS is not the only name space in which a computer needs to be known. Another name space is the NIS (aka YP) name space. For NIS purposes, there is another domain name, which is called the NIS domain name or the YP domain name. It need not have anything to do with the DNS domain name.

Confusing things even more is the fact that in the DNS, it is possible for multiple FQDNs to refer to the same system. However, there is always exactly one of them that is the true host name, and it is called the canonical FQDN.

In some contexts, the host name is called a "node name."

For more information on DNS host naming, see Section 16.6.2.4 [Host Names], page 456.

Prototypes for these functions appear in `unistd.h`.

The programs `hostname`, `hostid`, and `domainname` work by calling these functions.

`int gethostname (char *name, size_t size)` [Function]
> Preliminary: | MT-Safe | AS-Safe | AC-Safe | See Section 1.2.2.1 [POSIX Safety Concepts], page 2.

This function returns the host name of the system on which it is called, in the array *name*. The *size* argument specifies the size of this array, in bytes. Note that this is *not* the DNS hostname. If the system participates in the DNS, this is the FQDN (see above).

The return value is 0 on success and -1 on failure. In the GNU C Library, `gethostname` fails if *size* is not large enough; then you can try again with a larger array. The following `errno` error condition is defined for this function:

ENAMETOOLONG
> The *size* argument is less than the size of the host name plus one.

On some systems, there is a symbol for the maximum possible host name length: MAXHOSTNAMELEN. It is defined in `sys/param.h`. But you can't count on this to exist, so it is cleaner to handle failure and try again.

`gethostname` stores the beginning of the host name in *name* even if the host name won't entirely fit. For some purposes, a truncated host name is good enough. If it is, you can ignore the error code.

int sethostname (*const char* *name, *size_t* length)   [Function]
> Preliminary: | MT-Safe | AS-Safe | AC-Safe | See Section 1.2.2.1 [POSIX Safety Concepts], page 2.
>
> The `sethostname` function sets the host name of the system that calls it to *name*, a string with length *length*. Only privileged processes are permitted to do this.
>
> Usually `sethostname` gets called just once, at system boot time. Often, the program that calls it sets it to the value it finds in the file `/etc/hostname`.
>
> Be sure to set the host name to the full host name, not just the DNS hostname (see above).
>
> The return value is 0 on success and -1 on failure. The following `errno` error condition is defined for this function:
>
> EPERM   This process cannot set the host name because it is not privileged.

int getdomainnname (*char* *name, *size_t* length)   [Function]
> Preliminary: | MT-Safe | AS-Safe | AC-Safe | See Section 1.2.2.1 [POSIX Safety Concepts], page 2.
>
> `getdomainname` returns the NIS (aka YP) domain name of the system on which it is called. Note that this is not the more popular DNS domain name. Get that with `gethostname`.
>
> The specifics of this function are analogous to `gethostname`, above.

int setdomainname (*const char* *name, *size_t* length)   [Function]
> Preliminary: | MT-Safe | AS-Safe | AC-Safe | See Section 1.2.2.1 [POSIX Safety Concepts], page 2.
>
> `setdomainname` sets the NIS (aka YP) domain name of the system on which it is called. Note that this is not the more popular DNS domain name. Set that with `sethostname`.
>
> The specifics of this function are analogous to `sethostname`, above.

long int gethostid (*void*) [Function]

> Preliminary: | MT-Safe hostid env locale | AS-Unsafe dlopen plugin corrupt heap lock | AC-Unsafe lock corrupt mem fd | See Section 1.2.2.1 [POSIX Safety Concepts], page 2.

> This function returns the "host ID" of the machine the program is running on. By convention, this is usually the primary Internet IP address of that machine, converted to a **long int**. However, on some systems it is a meaningless but unique number which is hard-coded for each machine.

> This is not widely used. It arose in BSD 4.2, but was dropped in BSD 4.4. It is not required by POSIX.

> The proper way to query the IP address is to use **gethostbyname** on the results of **gethostname**. For more information on IP addresses, See Section 16.6.2 [Host Addresses], page 452.

int sethostid (*long int id*) [Function]

> Preliminary: | MT-Unsafe const:hostid | AS-Unsafe | AC-Unsafe corrupt fd | See Section 1.2.2.1 [POSIX Safety Concepts], page 2.

> The **sethostid** function sets the "host ID" of the host machine to *id*. Only privileged processes are permitted to do this. Usually it happens just once, at system boot time.

> The proper way to establish the primary IP address of a system is to configure the IP address resolver to associate that IP address with the system's host name as returned by **gethostname**. For example, put a record for the system in **/etc/hosts**.

> See **gethostid** above for more information on host ids.

> The return value is **0** on success and **-1** on failure. The following **errno** error conditions are defined for this function:

> EPERM This process cannot set the host name because it is not privileged.

> ENOSYS The operating system does not support setting the host ID. On some systems, the host ID is a meaningless but unique number hard-coded for each machine.

31.2 Platform Type Identification

You can use the **uname** function to find out some information about the type of computer your program is running on. This function and the associated data type are declared in the header file **sys/utsname.h**.

As a bonus, **uname** also gives some information identifying the particular system your program is running on. This is the same information which you can get with functions targeted to this purpose described in Section 31.1 [Host Identification], page 845.

struct utsname [Data Type]

> The **utsname** structure is used to hold information returned by the **uname** function. It has the following members:

> **char sysname[]**

> > This is the name of the operating system in use.

char release[]

> This is the current release level of the operating system implementation.

char version[]

> This is the current version level within the release of the operating system.

char machine[]

> This is a description of the type of hardware that is in use.
>
> Some systems provide a mechanism to interrogate the kernel directly for this information. On systems without such a mechanism, the GNU C Library fills in this field based on the configuration name that was specified when building and installing the library.
>
> GNU uses a three-part name to describe a system configuration; the three parts are *cpu*, *manufacturer* and *system-type*, and they are separated with dashes. Any possible combination of three names is potentially meaningful, but most such combinations are meaningless in practice and even the meaningful ones are not necessarily supported by any particular GNU program.
>
> Since the value in **machine** is supposed to describe just the hardware, it consists of the first two parts of the configuration name: '*cpu-manufacturer*'. For example, it might be one of these:
>
> "sparc-sun", "i386-*anything*", "m68k-hp", "m68k-sony", "m68k-sun", "mips-dec"

char nodename[]

> This is the host name of this particular computer. In the GNU C Library, the value is the same as that returned by **gethostname**; see Section 31.1 [Host Identification], page 845.
>
> **gethostname** is implemented with a call to **uname**.

char domainname[]

> This is the NIS or YP domain name. It is the same value returned by **getdomainname**; see Section 31.1 [Host Identification], page 845. This element is a relatively recent invention and use of it is not as portable as use of the rest of the structure.

int **uname** (*struct utsname *info*)   [Function]
> Preliminary: | MT-Safe | AS-Safe | AC-Safe | See Section 1.2.2.1 [POSIX Safety Concepts], page 2.

The **uname** function fills in the structure pointed to by *info* with information about the operating system and host machine. A non-negative return value indicates that the data was successfully stored.

-1 as the return value indicates an error. The only error possible is **EFAULT**, which we normally don't mention as it is always a possibility.

31.3 Controlling and Querying Mounts

All files are in filesystems, and before you can access any file, its filesystem must be mounted. Because of Unix's concept of *Everything is a file*, mounting of filesystems is central to doing almost anything. This section explains how to find out what filesystems are currently mounted and what filesystems are available for mounting, and how to change what is mounted.

The classic filesystem is the contents of a disk drive. The concept is considerably more abstract, though, and lots of things other than disk drives can be mounted.

Some block devices don't correspond to traditional devices like disk drives. For example, a loop device is a block device whose driver uses a regular file in another filesystem as its medium. So if that regular file contains appropriate data for a filesystem, you can by mounting the loop device essentially mount a regular file.

Some filesystems aren't based on a device of any kind. The "proc" filesystem, for example, contains files whose data is made up by the filesystem driver on the fly whenever you ask for it. And when you write to it, the data you write causes changes in the system. No data gets stored.

31.3.1 Mount Information

For some programs it is desirable and necessary to access information about whether a certain filesystem is mounted and, if it is, where, or simply to get lists of all the available filesystems. The GNU C Library provides some functions to retrieve this information portably.

Traditionally Unix systems have a file named /etc/fstab which describes all possibly mounted filesystems. The mount program uses this file to mount at startup time of the system all the necessary filesystems. The information about all the filesystems actually mounted is normally kept in a file named either /var/run/mtab or /etc/mtab. Both files share the same syntax and it is crucial that this syntax is followed all the time. Therefore it is best to never directly write to the files. The functions described in this section can do this and they also provide the functionality to convert the external textual representation to the internal representation.

Note that the fstab and mtab files are maintained on a system by *convention*. It is possible for the files not to exist or not to be consistent with what is really mounted or available to mount, if the system's administration policy allows it. But programs that mount and unmount filesystems typically maintain and use these files as described herein.

The filenames given above should never be used directly. The portable way to handle these files is to use the macros _PATH_FSTAB, defined in fstab.h, or _PATH_MNTTAB, defined in mntent.h and paths.h, for fstab; and the macro _PATH_MOUNTED, also defined in mntent.h and paths.h, for mtab. There are also two alternate macro names FSTAB, MNTTAB, and MOUNTED defined but these names are deprecated and kept only for backward compatibility. The names _PATH_MNTTAB and _PATH_MOUNTED should always be used.

31.3.1.1 The fstab file

The internal representation for entries of the file is struct fstab, defined in fstab.h.

struct fstab   [Data Type]

> This structure is used with the getfsent, getfsspec, and getfsfile functions.

> char *fs_spec

> > This element describes the device from which the filesystem is mounted. Normally this is the name of a special device, such as a hard disk partition,

but it could also be a more or less generic string. For *NFS* it would be a hostname and directory name combination.

Even though the element is not declared `const` it shouldn't be modified. The missing `const` has historic reasons, since this function predates ISO C. The same is true for the other string elements of this structure.

`char *fs_file`

> This describes the mount point on the local system. I.e., accessing any file in this filesystem has implicitly or explicitly this string as a prefix.

`char *fs_vfstype`

> This is the type of the filesystem. Depending on what the underlying kernel understands it can be any string.

`char *fs_mntops`

> This is a string containing options passed to the kernel with the `mount` call. Again, this can be almost anything. There can be more than one option, separated from the others by a comma. Each option consists of a name and an optional value part, introduced by an = character.

> If the value of this element must be processed it should ideally be done using the `getsubopt` function; see Section 25.3.12.1 [Parsing of Suboptions], page 760.

`const char *fs_type`

> This name is poorly chosen. This element points to a string (possibly in the `fs_mntops` string) which describes the modes with which the filesystem is mounted. `fstab` defines five macros to describe the possible values:

> `FSTAB_RW`   The filesystem gets mounted with read and write enabled.

> `FSTAB_RQ`   The filesystem gets mounted with read and write enabled. Write access is restricted by quotas.

> `FSTAB_RO`   The filesystem gets mounted read-only.

> `FSTAB_SW`   This is not a real filesystem, it is a swap device.

> `FSTAB_XX`   This entry from the `fstab` file is totally ignored.

> Testing for equality with these values must happen using `strcmp` since these are all strings. Comparing the pointer will probably always fail.

`int fs_freq`

> This element describes the dump frequency in days.

`int fs_passno`

> This element describes the pass number on parallel dumps. It is closely related to the `dump` utility used on Unix systems.

To read the entire content of the of the `fstab` file the GNU C Library contains a set of three functions which are designed in the usual way.

`int setfsent` (*void*)   [Function]

> Preliminary: | MT-Unsafe race:fsent | AS-Unsafe heap corrupt lock | AC-Unsafe corrupt lock mem fd | See Section 1.2.2.1 [POSIX Safety Concepts], page 2.

This function makes sure that the internal read pointer for the `fstab` file is at the beginning of the file. This is done by either opening the file or resetting the read pointer.

Since the file handle is internal to the libc this function is not thread-safe.

This function returns a non-zero value if the operation was successful and the `getfs*` functions can be used to read the entries of the file.

void endfsent (*void*)   [Function]
Preliminary: | MT-Unsafe race:fsent | AS-Unsafe heap corrupt lock | AC-Unsafe corrupt lock mem fd | See Section 1.2.2.1 [POSIX Safety Concepts], page 2.

This function makes sure that all resources acquired by a prior call to `setfsent` (explicitly or implicitly by calling `getfsent`) are freed.

struct fstab * getfsent (*void*)   [Function]
Preliminary: | MT-Unsafe race:fsent locale | AS-Unsafe corrupt heap lock | AC-Unsafe corrupt lock mem | See Section 1.2.2.1 [POSIX Safety Concepts], page 2.

This function returns the next entry of the `fstab` file. If this is the first call to any of the functions handling `fstab` since program start or the last call of `endfsent`, the file will be opened.

The function returns a pointer to a variable of type `struct fstab`. This variable is shared by all threads and therefore this function is not thread-safe. If an error occurred `getfsent` returns a `NULL` pointer.

struct fstab * getfsspec (*const char *name*)   [Function]
Preliminary: | MT-Unsafe race:fsent locale | AS-Unsafe corrupt heap lock | AC-Unsafe corrupt lock mem | See Section 1.2.2.1 [POSIX Safety Concepts], page 2.

This function returns the next entry of the `fstab` file which has a string equal to *name* pointed to by the `fs_spec` element. Since there is normally exactly one entry for each special device it makes no sense to call this function more than once for the same argument. If this is the first call to any of the functions handling `fstab` since program start or the last call of `endfsent`, the file will be opened.

The function returns a pointer to a variable of type `struct fstab`. This variable is shared by all threads and therefore this function is not thread-safe. If an error occurred `getfsent` returns a `NULL` pointer.

struct fstab * getfsfile (*const char *name*)   [Function]
Preliminary: | MT-Unsafe race:fsent locale | AS-Unsafe corrupt heap lock | AC-Unsafe corrupt lock mem | See Section 1.2.2.1 [POSIX Safety Concepts], page 2.

This function returns the next entry of the `fstab` file which has a string equal to *name* pointed to by the `fs_file` element. Since there is normally exactly one entry for each mount point it makes no sense to call this function more than once for the same argument. If this is the first call to any of the functions handling `fstab` since program start or the last call of `endfsent`, the file will be opened.

The function returns a pointer to a variable of type `struct fstab`. This variable is shared by all threads and therefore this function is not thread-safe. If an error occurred `getfsent` returns a `NULL` pointer.

31.3.1.2 The `mtab` file

The following functions and data structure access the `mtab` file.

`struct mntent`   [Data Type]

> This structure is used with the `getmntent`, `getmntent_r`, `addmntent`, and `hasmntopt` functions.

> `char *mnt_fsname`
>> This element contains a pointer to a string describing the name of the special device from which the filesystem is mounted. It corresponds to the `fs_spec` element in `struct fstab`.

> `char *mnt_dir`
>> This element points to a string describing the mount point of the filesystem. It corresponds to the `fs_file` element in `struct fstab`.

> `char *mnt_type`
>> `mnt_type` describes the filesystem type and is therefore equivalent to `fs_vfstype` in `struct fstab`. `mntent.h` defines a few symbolic names for some of the values this string can have. But since the kernel can support arbitrary filesystems it does not make much sense to give them symbolic names. If one knows the symbol name one also knows the filesystem name. Nevertheless here follows the list of the symbols provided in `mntent.h`.

>> `MNTTYPE_IGNORE`
>>> This symbol expands to `"ignore"`. The value is sometimes used in `fstab` files to make sure entries are not used without removing them.

>> `MNTTYPE_NFS`
>>> Expands to `"nfs"`. Using this macro sometimes could make sense since it names the default NFS implementation, in case both version 2 and 3 are supported.

>> `MNTTYPE_SWAP`
>>> This symbol expands to `"swap"`. It names the special `fstab` entry which names one of the possibly multiple swap partitions.

> `char *mnt_opts`
>> The element contains a string describing the options used while mounting the filesystem. As for the equivalent element `fs_mntops` of `struct fstab` it is best to use the function `getsubopt` (see Section 25.3.12.1 [Parsing of Suboptions], page 760) to access the parts of this string.

>> The `mntent.h` file defines a number of macros with string values which correspond to some of the options understood by the kernel. There might be many more options which are possible so it doesn't make much sense to rely on these macros but to be consistent here is the list:

MNTOPT_DEFAULTS

> Expands to "defaults". This option should be used alone since it indicates all values for the customizable values are chosen to be the default.

MNTOPT_RO

> Expands to "ro". See the FSTAB_RO value, it means the filesystem is mounted read-only.

MNTOPT_RW

> Expands to "rw". See the FSTAB_RW value, it means the filesystem is mounted with read and write permissions.

MNTOPT_SUID

> Expands to "suid". This means that the SUID bit (see Section 30.4 [How an Application Can Change Persona], page 816) is respected when a program from the filesystem is started.

MNTOPT_NOSUID

> Expands to "nosuid". This is the opposite of MNTOPT_SUID, the SUID bit for all files from the filesystem is ignored.

MNTOPT_NOAUTO

> Expands to "noauto". At startup time the mount program will ignore this entry if it is started with the -a option to mount all filesystems mentioned in the fstab file.

> As for the FSTAB_* entries introduced above it is important to use strcmp to check for equality.

mnt_freq This elements corresponds to fs_freq and also specifies the frequency in days in which dumps are made.

mnt_passno

> This element is equivalent to fs_passno with the same meaning which is uninteresting for all programs beside dump.

For accessing the mtab file there is again a set of three functions to access all entries in a row. Unlike the functions to handle fstab these functions do not access a fixed file and there is even a thread safe variant of the get function. Besides this the GNU C Library contains functions to alter the file and test for specific options.

FILE * setmntent (const char *file, const char *mode)   [Function]
> Preliminary: | MT-Safe | AS-Unsafe heap lock | AC-Unsafe mem fd lock | See Section 1.2.2.1 [POSIX Safety Concepts], page 2.

> The setmntent function prepares the file named FILE which must be in the format of a fstab and mtab file for the upcoming processing through the other functions of the family. The mode parameter can be chosen in the way the opentype parameter for fopen (see Section 12.3 [Opening Streams], page 258) can be chosen. If the file is opened for writing the file is also allowed to be empty.

> If the file was successfully opened setmntent returns a file handle for future use. Otherwise the return value is NULL and errno is set accordingly.

int endmntent (*FILE *stream*)   [Function]
>   Preliminary: | MT-Safe | AS-Unsafe heap lock | AC-Unsafe lock mem fd | See
>   Section 1.2.2.1 [POSIX Safety Concepts], page 2.
>
>   This function takes for the *stream* parameter a file handle which previously was
>   returned from the `setmntent` call. `endmntent` closes the stream and frees all resources.
>
>   The return value is 1 unless an error occurred in which case it is 0.

struct mntent * getmntent (*FILE *stream*)   [Function]
>   Preliminary: | MT-Unsafe race:mntentbuf locale | AS-Unsafe corrupt heap init |
>   AC-Unsafe init corrupt lock mem | See Section 1.2.2.1 [POSIX Safety Concepts],
>   page 2.
>
>   The `getmntent` function takes as the parameter a file handle previously returned by
>   a successful call to `setmntent`. It returns a pointer to a static variable of type `struct`
>   `mntent` which is filled with the information from the next entry from the file currently
>   read.
>
>   The file format used prescribes the use of spaces or tab characters to separate the
>   fields. This makes it harder to use names containing one of these characters (e.g.,
>   mount points using spaces). Therefore these characters are encoded in the files and
>   the `getmntent` function takes care of the decoding while reading the entries back in.
>   `'\040'` is used to encode a space character, `'\011'` to encode a tab character, `'\012'`
>   to encode a newline character, and `'\\'` to encode a backslash.
>
>   If there was an error or the end of the file is reached the return value is `NULL`.
>
>   This function is not thread-safe since all calls to this function return a pointer to
>   the same static variable. `getmntent_r` should be used in situations where multiple
>   threads access the file.

struct mntent * getmntent_r (*FILE *stream*, *struct mntent*   [Function]
>   **result*, *char *buffer*, *int bufsize*)
>   Preliminary: | MT-Safe locale | AS-Unsafe corrupt heap | AC-Unsafe corrupt lock
>   mem | See Section 1.2.2.1 [POSIX Safety Concepts], page 2.
>
>   The `getmntent_r` function is the reentrant variant of `getmntent`. It also returns the
>   next entry from the file and returns a pointer. The actual variable the values are
>   stored in is not static, though. Instead the function stores the values in the variable
>   pointed to by the *result* parameter. Additional information (e.g., the strings pointed
>   to by the elements of the result) are kept in the buffer of size *bufsize* pointed to by
>   *buffer*.
>
>   Escaped characters (space, tab, backslash) are converted back in the same way as it
>   happens for `getmentent`.
>
>   The function returns a `NULL` pointer in error cases. Errors could be:
>
>   • error while reading the file,
>
>   • end of file reached,
>
>   • *bufsize* is too small for reading a complete new entry.

int addmntent (*FILE *stream*, *const struct mntent *mnt*)   [Function]
>   Preliminary: | MT-Safe race:stream locale | AS-Unsafe corrupt | AC-Unsafe corrupt
> | See Section 1.2.2.1 [POSIX Safety Concepts], page 2.

The `addmntent` function allows adding a new entry to the file previously opened with `setmntent`. The new entries are always appended. I.e., even if the position of the file descriptor is not at the end of the file this function does not overwrite an existing entry following the current position.

The implication of this is that to remove an entry from a file one has to create a new file while leaving out the entry to be removed and after closing the file remove the old one and rename the new file to the chosen name.

This function takes care of spaces and tab characters in the names to be written to the file. It converts them and the backslash character into the format described in the `getmntent` description above.

This function returns 0 in case the operation was successful. Otherwise the return value is 1 and `errno` is set appropriately.

`char * hasmntopt` (*const struct mntent *mnt, const char *opt*)　　　[Function]
Preliminary: | MT-Safe | AS-Safe | AC-Safe | See Section 1.2.2.1 [POSIX Safety Concepts], page 2.

This function can be used to check whether the string pointed to by the `mnt_opts` element of the variable pointed to by *mnt* contains the option *opt*. If this is true a pointer to the beginning of the option in the `mnt_opts` element is returned. If no such option exists the function returns `NULL`.

This function is useful to test whether a specific option is present but when all options have to be processed one is better off with using the `getsubopt` function to iterate over all options in the string.

31.3.1.3 Other (Non-libc) Sources of Mount Information

On a system with a Linux kernel and the `proc` filesystem, you can get information on currently mounted filesystems from the file `mounts` in the `proc` filesystem. Its format is similar to that of the `mtab` file, but represents what is truly mounted without relying on facilities outside the kernel to keep `mtab` up to date.

31.3.2 Mount, Unmount, Remount

This section describes the functions for mounting, unmounting, and remounting filesystems.

Only the superuser can mount, unmount, or remount a filesystem.

These functions do not access the `fstab` and `mtab` files. You should maintain and use these separately. See Section 31.3.1 [Mount Information], page 849.

The symbols in this section are declared in `sys/mount.h`.

`int mount` (*const char *special_file, const char *dir, const char* 　　　[Function]
　　　*fstype, unsigned long int options, const void *data*)
Preliminary: | MT-Safe | AS-Safe | AC-Safe | See Section 1.2.2.1 [POSIX Safety Concepts], page 2.

`mount` mounts or remounts a filesystem. The two operations are quite different and are merged rather unnaturally into this one function. The `MS_REMOUNT` option, explained below, determines whether `mount` mounts or remounts.

For a mount, the filesystem on the block device represented by the device special file named *special_file* gets mounted over the mount point *dir*. This means that the directory *dir* (along with any files in it) is no longer visible; in its place (and still with the name *dir*) is the root directory of the filesystem on the device.

As an exception, if the filesystem type (see below) is one which is not based on a device (e.g. "proc"), `mount` instantiates a filesystem and mounts it over *dir* and ignores *special_file*.

For a remount, *dir* specifies the mount point where the filesystem to be remounted is (and remains) mounted and *special_file* is ignored. Remounting a filesystem means changing the options that control operations on the filesystem while it is mounted. It does not mean unmounting and mounting again.

For a mount, you must identify the type of the filesystem with *fstype*. This type tells the kernel how to access the filesystem and can be thought of as the name of a filesystem driver. The acceptable values are system dependent. On a system with a Linux kernel and the `proc` filesystem, the list of possible values is in the file `filesystems` in the `proc` filesystem (e.g. type `cat /proc/filesystems` to see the list). With a Linux kernel, the types of filesystems that `mount` can mount, and their type names, depends on what filesystem drivers are configured into the kernel or loaded as loadable kernel modules. An example of a common value for *fstype* is `ext2`.

For a remount, `mount` ignores *fstype*.

options specifies a variety of options that apply until the filesystem is unmounted or remounted. The precise meaning of an option depends on the filesystem and with some filesystems, an option may have no effect at all. Furthermore, for some filesystems, some of these options (but never `MS_RDONLY`) can be overridden for individual file accesses via `ioctl`.

options is a bit string with bit fields defined using the following mask and masked value macros:

MS_MGC_MASK

> This multibit field contains a magic number. If it does not have the value `MS_MGC_VAL`, `mount` assumes all the following bits are zero and the *data* argument is a null string, regardless of their actual values.

MS_REMOUNT

> This bit on means to remount the filesystem. Off means to mount it.

MS_RDONLY

> This bit on specifies that no writing to the filesystem shall be allowed while it is mounted. This cannot be overridden by `ioctl`. This option is available on nearly all filesystems.

MS_NOSUID

> This bit on specifies that Setuid and Setgid permissions on files in the filesystem shall be ignored while it is mounted.

MS_NOEXEC

> This bit on specifies that no files in the filesystem shall be executed while the filesystem is mounted.

MS_NODEV This bit on specifies that no device special files in the filesystem shall be accessible while the filesystem is mounted.

MS_SYNCHRONOUS

 This bit on specifies that all writes to the filesystem while it is mounted shall be synchronous; i.e., data shall be synced before each write completes rather than held in the buffer cache.

MS_MANDLOCK

 This bit on specifies that mandatory locks on files shall be permitted while the filesystem is mounted.

MS_NOATIME

 This bit on specifies that access times of files shall not be updated when the files are accessed while the filesystem is mounted.

MS_NODIRATIME

 This bit on specifies that access times of directories shall not be updated when the directories are accessed while the filesystem in mounted.

Any bits not covered by the above masks should be set off; otherwise, results are undefined.

The meaning of *data* depends on the filesystem type and is controlled entirely by the filesystem driver in the kernel.

Example:

```
#include <sys/mount.h>

mount("/dev/hdb", "/cdrom", MS_MGC_VAL | MS_RDONLY | MS_NOSUID, "");

mount("/dev/hda2", "/mnt", MS_MGC_VAL | MS_REMOUNT, "");
```

Appropriate arguments for **mount** are conventionally recorded in the **fstab** table. See Section 31.3.1 [Mount Information], page 849.

The return value is zero if the mount or remount is successful. Otherwise, it is -1 and **errno** is set appropriately. The values of **errno** are filesystem dependent, but here is a general list:

EPERM The process is not superuser.

ENODEV The file system type *fstype* is not known to the kernel.

ENOTBLK The file *dev* is not a block device special file.

EBUSY

- The device is already mounted.
- The mount point is busy. (E.g. it is some process' working directory or has a filesystem mounted on it already).
- The request is to remount read-only, but there are files open for writing.

EINVAL

- A remount was attempted, but there is no filesystem mounted over the specified mount point.

- The supposed filesystem has an invalid superblock.

EACCES

- The filesystem is inherently read-only (possibly due to a switch on the device) and the process attempted to mount it read/write (by setting the `MS_RDONLY` bit off).
- *special_file* or *dir* is not accessible due to file permissions.
- *special_file* is not accessible because it is in a filesystem that is mounted with the `MS_NODEV` option.

EM_FILE   The table of dummy devices is full. `mount` needs to create a dummy device (aka "unnamed" device) if the filesystem being mounted is not one that uses a device.

`int` `umount2` (*const char *file, int flags*)   [Function]
Preliminary: | MT-Safe | AS-Safe | AC-Safe | See Section 1.2.2.1 [POSIX Safety Concepts], page 2.

`umount2` unmounts a filesystem.

You can identify the filesystem to unmount either by the device special file that contains the filesystem or by the mount point. The effect is the same. Specify either as the string *file*.

flags contains the one-bit field identified by the following mask macro:

MNT_FORCE

This bit on means to force the unmounting even if the filesystem is busy, by making it unbusy first. If the bit is off and the filesystem is busy, `umount2` fails with `errno` = EBUSY. Depending on the filesystem, this may override all, some, or no busy conditions.

All other bits in *flags* should be set to zero; otherwise, the result is undefined.

Example:

```
#include <sys/mount.h>

umount2("/mnt", MNT_FORCE);

umount2("/dev/hdd1", 0);
```

After the filesystem is unmounted, the directory that was the mount point is visible, as are any files in it.

As part of unmounting, `umount2` syncs the filesystem.

If the unmounting is successful, the return value is zero. Otherwise, it is `-1` and `errno` is set accordingly:

EPERM   The process is not superuser.

EBUSY   The filesystem cannot be unmounted because it is busy. E.g. it contains a directory that is some process's working directory or a file that some process has open. With some filesystems in some cases, you can avoid this failure with the `MNT_FORCE` option.

> EINVAL   *file* validly refers to a file, but that file is neither a mount point nor a device special file of a currently mounted filesystem.

This function is not available on all systems.

int umount (*const char *file*)   [Function]
> Preliminary: | MT-Safe | AS-Safe | AC-Safe | See Section 1.2.2.1 [POSIX Safety Concepts], page 2.
>
> umount does the same thing as umount2 with *flags* set to zeroes. It is more widely available than umount2 but since it lacks the possibility to forcefully unmount a filesystem is deprecated when umount2 is also available.

31.4 System Parameters

This section describes the sysctl function, which gets and sets a variety of system parameters.

The symbols used in this section are declared in the file sys/sysctl.h.

int sysctl (*int *names, int nlen, void *oldval, size_t *oldlenp,*   [Function]
        void *newval, size_t newlen)
> Preliminary: | MT-Safe | AS-Safe | AC-Safe | See Section 1.2.2.1 [POSIX Safety Concepts], page 2.
>
> sysctl gets or sets a specified system parameter. There are so many of these parameters that it is not practical to list them all here, but here are some examples:
>
> - network domain name
> - paging parameters
> - network Address Resolution Protocol timeout time
> - maximum number of files that may be open
> - root filesystem device
> - when kernel was built
>
> The set of available parameters depends on the kernel configuration and can change while the system is running, particularly when you load and unload loadable kernel modules.
>
> The system parameters with which sysctl is concerned are arranged in a hierarchical structure like a hierarchical filesystem. To identify a particular parameter, you specify a path through the structure in a way analogous to specifying the pathname of a file. Each component of the path is specified by an integer and each of these integers has a macro defined for it by sys/sysctl.h. *names* is the path, in the form of an array of integers. Each component of the path is one element of the array, in order. *nlen* is the number of components in the path.
>
> For example, the first component of the path for all the paging parameters is the value CTL_VM. For the free page thresholds, the second component of the path is VM_FREEPG. So to get the free page threshold values, make *names* an array containing the two elements CTL_VM and VM_FREEPG and make *nlen* = 2.
>
> The format of the value of a parameter depends on the parameter. Sometimes it is an integer; sometimes it is an ASCII string; sometimes it is an elaborate structure. In

the case of the free page thresholds used in the example above, the parameter value is a structure containing several integers.

In any case, you identify a place to return the parameter's value with *oldval* and specify the amount of storage available at that location as **oldlenp*. **oldlenp* does double duty because it is also the output location that contains the actual length of the returned value.

If you don't want the parameter value returned, specify a null pointer for *oldval*.

To set the parameter, specify the address and length of the new value as *newval* and *newlen*. If you don't want to set the parameter, specify a null pointer as *newval*.

If you get and set a parameter in the same `sysctl` call, the value returned is the value of the parameter before it was set.

Each system parameter has a set of permissions similar to the permissions for a file (including the permissions on directories in its path) that determine whether you may get or set it. For the purposes of these permissions, every parameter is considered to be owned by the superuser and Group 0 so processes with that effective uid or gid may have more access to system parameters. Unlike with files, the superuser does not invariably have full permission to all system parameters, because some of them are designed not to be changed ever.

`sysctl` returns a zero return value if it succeeds. Otherwise, it returns `-1` and sets `errno` appropriately. Besides the failures that apply to all system calls, the following are the `errno` codes for all possible failures:

EPERM
: The process is not permitted to access one of the components of the path of the system parameter or is not permitted to access the system parameter itself in the way (read or write) that it requested.

ENOTDIR
: There is no system parameter corresponding to *name*.

EFAULT
: *oldval* is not null, which means the process wanted to read the parameter, but **oldlenp* is zero, so there is no place to return it.

EINVAL

- The process attempted to set a system parameter to a value that is not valid for that parameter.
- The space provided for the return of the system parameter is not the right size for that parameter.

ENOMEM
: This value may be returned instead of the more correct `EINVAL` in some cases where the space provided for the return of the system parameter is too small.

If you have a Linux kernel with the `proc` filesystem, you can get and set most of the same parameters by reading and writing to files in the `sys` directory of the `proc` filesystem. In the `sys` directory, the directory structure represents the hierarchical structure of the parameters. E.g. you can display the free page thresholds with

```
cat /proc/sys/vm/freepages
```

Some more traditional and more widely available, though less general, GNU C Library functions for getting and setting some of the same system parameters are:

- `getdomainname`, `setdomainname`

- `gethostname`, `sethostname` (See Section 31.1 [Host Identification], page 845.)
- `uname` (See Section 31.2 [Platform Type Identification], page 847.)

32 System Configuration Parameters

The functions and macros listed in this chapter give information about configuration parameters of the operating system—for example, capacity limits, presence of optional POSIX features, and the default path for executable files (see Section 32.12 [String-Valued Parameters], page 880).

32.1 General Capacity Limits

The POSIX.1 and POSIX.2 standards specify a number of parameters that describe capacity limitations of the system. These limits can be fixed constants for a given operating system, or they can vary from machine to machine. For example, some limit values may be configurable by the system administrator, either at run time or by rebuilding the kernel, and this should not require recompiling application programs.

Each of the following limit parameters has a macro that is defined in `limits.h` only if the system has a fixed, uniform limit for the parameter in question. If the system allows different file systems or files to have different limits, then the macro is undefined; use `sysconf` to find out the limit that applies at a particular time on a particular machine. See Section 32.4 [Using `sysconf`], page 865.

Each of these parameters also has another macro, with a name starting with '`_POSIX`', which gives the lowest value that the limit is allowed to have on *any* POSIX system. See Section 32.5 [Minimum Values for General Capacity Limits], page 873.

int ARG_MAX   [Macro]
    If defined, the unvarying maximum combined length of the *argv* and *environ* arguments that can be passed to the `exec` functions.

int CHILD_MAX   [Macro]
    If defined, the unvarying maximum number of processes that can exist with the same real user ID at any one time. In BSD and GNU, this is controlled by the `RLIMIT_NPROC` resource limit; see Section 22.2 [Limiting Resource Usage], page 656.

int OPEN_MAX   [Macro]
    If defined, the unvarying maximum number of files that a single process can have open simultaneously. In BSD and GNU, this is controlled by the `RLIMIT_NOFILE` resource limit; see Section 22.2 [Limiting Resource Usage], page 656.

int STREAM_MAX   [Macro]
    If defined, the unvarying maximum number of streams that a single process can have open simultaneously. See Section 12.3 [Opening Streams], page 258.

int TZNAME_MAX   [Macro]
    If defined, the unvarying maximum length of a time zone name. See Section 21.4.8 [Functions and Variables for Time Zones], page 648.

These limit macros are always defined in `limits.h`.

int NGROUPS_MAX [Macro]

> The maximum number of supplementary group IDs that one process can have.
>
> The value of this macro is actually a lower bound for the maximum. That is, you can count on being able to have that many supplementary group IDs, but a particular machine might let you have even more. You can use `sysconf` to see whether a particular machine will let you have more (see Section 32.4 [Using `sysconf`], page 865).

ssize_t SSIZE_MAX [Macro]

> The largest value that can fit in an object of type `ssize_t`. Effectively, this is the limit on the number of bytes that can be read or written in a single operation.
>
> This macro is defined in all POSIX systems because this limit is never configurable.

int RE_DUP_MAX [Macro]

> The largest number of repetitions you are guaranteed is allowed in the construct '\{*min,max*\}' in a regular expression.
>
> The value of this macro is actually a lower bound for the maximum. That is, you can count on being able to have that many repetitions, but a particular machine might let you have even more. You can use `sysconf` to see whether a particular machine will let you have more (see Section 32.4 [Using `sysconf`], page 865). And even the value that `sysconf` tells you is just a lower bound—larger values might work.
>
> This macro is defined in all POSIX.2 systems, because POSIX.2 says it should always be defined even if there is no specific imposed limit.

32.2 Overall System Options

POSIX defines certain system-specific options that not all POSIX systems support. Since these options are provided in the kernel, not in the library, simply using the GNU C Library does not guarantee any of these features are supported; it depends on the system you are using.

You can test for the availability of a given option using the macros in this section, together with the function `sysconf`. The macros are defined only if you include `unistd.h`.

For the following macros, if the macro is defined in `unistd.h`, then the option is supported. Otherwise, the option may or may not be supported; use `sysconf` to find out. See Section 32.4 [Using `sysconf`], page 865.

int _POSIX_JOB_CONTROL [Macro]

> If this symbol is defined, it indicates that the system supports job control. Otherwise, the implementation behaves as if all processes within a session belong to a single process group. See Chapter 28 [Job Control], page 786.

int _POSIX_SAVED_IDS [Macro]

> If this symbol is defined, it indicates that the system remembers the effective user and group IDs of a process before it executes an executable file with the set-user-ID or set-group-ID bits set, and that explicitly changing the effective user or group IDs back to these values is permitted. If this option is not defined, then if a nonprivileged process changes its effective user or group ID to the real user or group ID of the process, it can't change it back again. See Section 30.8 [Enabling and Disabling Setuid Access], page 821.

For the following macros, if the macro is defined in `unistd.h`, then its value indicates whether the option is supported. A value of -1 means no, and any other value means yes. If the macro is not defined, then the option may or may not be supported; use `sysconf` to find out. See Section 32.4 [Using `sysconf`], page 865.

int `_POSIX2_C_DEV`   [Macro]

If this symbol is defined, it indicates that the system has the POSIX.2 C compiler command, `c89`. The GNU C Library always defines this as `1`, on the assumption that you would not have installed it if you didn't have a C compiler.

int `_POSIX2_FORT_DEV`   [Macro]

If this symbol is defined, it indicates that the system has the POSIX.2 Fortran compiler command, `fort77`. The GNU C Library never defines this, because we don't know what the system has.

int `_POSIX2_FORT_RUN`   [Macro]

If this symbol is defined, it indicates that the system has the POSIX.2 `asa` command to interpret Fortran carriage control. The GNU C Library never defines this, because we don't know what the system has.

int `_POSIX2_LOCALEDEF`   [Macro]

If this symbol is defined, it indicates that the system has the POSIX.2 `localedef` command. The GNU C Library never defines this, because we don't know what the system has.

int `_POSIX2_SW_DEV`   [Macro]

If this symbol is defined, it indicates that the system has the POSIX.2 commands `ar`, `make`, and `strip`. The GNU C Library always defines this as `1`, on the assumption that you had to have `ar` and `make` to install the library, and it's unlikely that `strip` would be absent when those are present.

32.3 Which Version of POSIX is Supported

long int `_POSIX_VERSION`   [Macro]

This constant represents the version of the POSIX.1 standard to which the implementation conforms. For an implementation conforming to the 1995 POSIX.1 standard, the value is the integer `199506L`.

`_POSIX_VERSION` is always defined (in `unistd.h`) in any POSIX system.

Usage Note: Don't try to test whether the system supports POSIX by including `unistd.h` and then checking whether `_POSIX_VERSION` is defined. On a non-POSIX system, this will probably fail because there is no `unistd.h`. We do not know of *any* way you can reliably test at compilation time whether your target system supports POSIX or whether `unistd.h` exists.

long int `_POSIX2_C_VERSION`   [Macro]

This constant represents the version of the POSIX.2 standard which the library and system kernel support. We don't know what value this will be for the first version of the POSIX.2 standard, because the value is based on the year and month in which the standard is officially adopted.

The value of this symbol says nothing about the utilities installed on the system.

Usage Note: You can use this macro to tell whether a POSIX.1 system library supports POSIX.2 as well. Any POSIX.1 system contains unistd.h, so include that file and then test defined (_POSIX2_C_VERSION).

32.4 Using sysconf

When your system has configurable system limits, you can use the sysconf function to find out the value that applies to any particular machine. The function and the associated *parameter* constants are declared in the header file unistd.h.

32.4.1 Definition of sysconf

long int sysconf (*int parameter*)   [Function]

Preliminary: | MT-Safe env | AS-Unsafe lock heap | AC-Unsafe lock mem fd | See Section 1.2.2.1 [POSIX Safety Concepts], page 2.

This function is used to inquire about runtime system parameters. The *parameter* argument should be one of the '_SC_' symbols listed below.

The normal return value from sysconf is the value you requested. A value of -1 is returned both if the implementation does not impose a limit, and in case of an error.

The following errno error conditions are defined for this function:

EINVAL   The value of the *parameter* is invalid.

32.4.2 Constants for sysconf Parameters

Here are the symbolic constants for use as the *parameter* argument to sysconf. The values are all integer constants (more specifically, enumeration type values).

_SC_ARG_MAX

Inquire about the parameter corresponding to ARG_MAX.

_SC_CHILD_MAX

Inquire about the parameter corresponding to CHILD_MAX.

_SC_OPEN_MAX

Inquire about the parameter corresponding to OPEN_MAX.

_SC_STREAM_MAX

Inquire about the parameter corresponding to STREAM_MAX.

_SC_TZNAME_MAX

Inquire about the parameter corresponding to TZNAME_MAX.

_SC_NGROUPS_MAX

Inquire about the parameter corresponding to NGROUPS_MAX.

_SC_JOB_CONTROL

Inquire about the parameter corresponding to _POSIX_JOB_CONTROL.

_SC_SAVED_IDS

Inquire about the parameter corresponding to _POSIX_SAVED_IDS.

_SC_VERSION

> Inquire about the parameter corresponding to _POSIX_VERSION.

_SC_CLK_TCK

> Inquire about the number of clock ticks per second; see Section 21.3.1 [CPU Time Inquiry], page 621. The corresponding parameter CLK_TCK is obsolete.

_SC_CHARCLASS_NAME_MAX

> Inquire about the parameter corresponding to maximal length allowed for a character class name in an extended locale specification. These extensions are not yet standardized and so this option is not standardized as well.

_SC_REALTIME_SIGNALS

> Inquire about the parameter corresponding to _POSIX_REALTIME_SIGNALS.

_SC_PRIORITY_SCHEDULING

> Inquire about the parameter corresponding to _POSIX_PRIORITY_SCHEDULING.

_SC_TIMERS

> Inquire about the parameter corresponding to _POSIX_TIMERS.

_SC_ASYNCHRONOUS_IO

> Inquire about the parameter corresponding to _POSIX_ASYNCHRONOUS_IO.

_SC_PRIORITIZED_IO

> Inquire about the parameter corresponding to _POSIX_PRIORITIZED_IO.

_SC_SYNCHRONIZED_IO

> Inquire about the parameter corresponding to _POSIX_SYNCHRONIZED_IO.

_SC_FSYNC

> Inquire about the parameter corresponding to _POSIX_FSYNC.

_SC_MAPPED_FILES

> Inquire about the parameter corresponding to _POSIX_MAPPED_FILES.

_SC_MEMLOCK

> Inquire about the parameter corresponding to _POSIX_MEMLOCK.

_SC_MEMLOCK_RANGE

> Inquire about the parameter corresponding to _POSIX_MEMLOCK_RANGE.

_SC_MEMORY_PROTECTION

> Inquire about the parameter corresponding to _POSIX_MEMORY_PROTECTION.

_SC_MESSAGE_PASSING

> Inquire about the parameter corresponding to _POSIX_MESSAGE_PASSING.

_SC_SEMAPHORES

> Inquire about the parameter corresponding to _POSIX_SEMAPHORES.

_SC_SHARED_MEMORY_OBJECTS

> Inquire about the parameter corresponding to
> _POSIX_SHARED_MEMORY_OBJECTS.

_SC_AIO_LISTIO_MAX

> Inquire about the parameter corresponding to _POSIX_AIO_LISTIO_MAX.

_SC_AIO_MAX

        Inquire about the parameter corresponding to _POSIX_AIO_MAX.

_SC_AIO_PRIO_DELTA_MAX

        Inquire about the value by which a process can decrease its asynchronous I/O priority level from its own scheduling priority. This corresponds to the run-time invariant value AIO_PRIO_DELTA_MAX.

_SC_DELAYTIMER_MAX

        Inquire about the parameter corresponding to _POSIX_DELAYTIMER_MAX.

_SC_MQ_OPEN_MAX

        Inquire about the parameter corresponding to _POSIX_MQ_OPEN_MAX.

_SC_MQ_PRIO_MAX

        Inquire about the parameter corresponding to _POSIX_MQ_PRIO_MAX.

_SC_RTSIG_MAX

        Inquire about the parameter corresponding to _POSIX_RTSIG_MAX.

_SC_SEM_NSEMS_MAX

        Inquire about the parameter corresponding to _POSIX_SEM_NSEMS_MAX.

_SC_SEM_VALUE_MAX

        Inquire about the parameter corresponding to _POSIX_SEM_VALUE_MAX.

_SC_SIGQUEUE_MAX

        Inquire about the parameter corresponding to _POSIX_SIGQUEUE_MAX.

_SC_TIMER_MAX

        Inquire about the parameter corresponding to _POSIX_TIMER_MAX.

_SC_PII   Inquire about the parameter corresponding to _POSIX_PII.

_SC_PII_XTI

        Inquire about the parameter corresponding to _POSIX_PII_XTI.

_SC_PII_SOCKET

        Inquire about the parameter corresponding to _POSIX_PII_SOCKET.

_SC_PII_INTERNET

        Inquire about the parameter corresponding to _POSIX_PII_INTERNET.

_SC_PII_OSI

        Inquire about the parameter corresponding to _POSIX_PII_OSI.

_SC_SELECT

        Inquire about the parameter corresponding to _POSIX_SELECT.

_SC_UIO_MAXIOV

        Inquire about the parameter corresponding to _POSIX_UIO_MAXIOV.

_SC_PII_INTERNET_STREAM

        Inquire about the parameter corresponding to _POSIX_PII_INTERNET_STREAM.

_SC_PII_INTERNET_DGRAM

        Inquire about the parameter corresponding to _POSIX_PII_INTERNET_DGRAM.

`_SC_PII_OSI_COTS`

        Inquire about the parameter corresponding to `_POSIX_PII_OSI_COTS`.

`_SC_PII_OSI_CLTS`

        Inquire about the parameter corresponding to `_POSIX_PII_OSI_CLTS`.

`_SC_PII_OSI_M`

        Inquire about the parameter corresponding to `_POSIX_PII_OSI_M`.

`_SC_T_IOV_MAX`

        Inquire about the value associated with the `T_IOV_MAX` variable.

`_SC_THREADS`

        Inquire about the parameter corresponding to `_POSIX_THREADS`.

`_SC_THREAD_SAFE_FUNCTIONS`

        Inquire about the parameter corresponding to
`_POSIX_THREAD_SAFE_FUNCTIONS`.

`_SC_GETGR_R_SIZE_MAX`

        Inquire about the parameter corresponding to `_POSIX_GETGR_R_SIZE_MAX`.

`_SC_GETPW_R_SIZE_MAX`

        Inquire about the parameter corresponding to `_POSIX_GETPW_R_SIZE_MAX`.

`_SC_LOGIN_NAME_MAX`

        Inquire about the parameter corresponding to `_POSIX_LOGIN_NAME_MAX`.

`_SC_TTY_NAME_MAX`

        Inquire about the parameter corresponding to `_POSIX_TTY_NAME_MAX`.

`_SC_THREAD_DESTRUCTOR_ITERATIONS`

        Inquire about the parameter corresponding to `_POSIX_THREAD_DESTRUCTOR_`
`ITERATIONS`.

`_SC_THREAD_KEYS_MAX`

        Inquire about the parameter corresponding to `_POSIX_THREAD_KEYS_MAX`.

`_SC_THREAD_STACK_MIN`

        Inquire about the parameter corresponding to `_POSIX_THREAD_STACK_MIN`.

`_SC_THREAD_THREADS_MAX`

        Inquire about the parameter corresponding to `_POSIX_THREAD_THREADS_MAX`.

`_SC_THREAD_ATTR_STACKADDR`

        Inquire about the parameter corresponding to
a `_POSIX_THREAD_ATTR_STACKADDR`.

`_SC_THREAD_ATTR_STACKSIZE`

        Inquire about the parameter corresponding to
`_POSIX_THREAD_ATTR_STACKSIZE`.

`_SC_THREAD_PRIORITY_SCHEDULING`

        Inquire about the parameter corresponding to `_POSIX_THREAD_PRIORITY_`
`SCHEDULING`.

_SC_THREAD_PRIO_INHERIT

>Inquire about the parameter corresponding to _POSIX_THREAD_PRIO_INHERIT.

_SC_THREAD_PRIO_PROTECT

>Inquire about the parameter corresponding to _POSIX_THREAD_PRIO_PROTECT.

_SC_THREAD_PROCESS_SHARED

>Inquire about the parameter corresponding to _POSIX_THREAD_PROCESS_ SHARED.

_SC_2_C_DEV

>Inquire about whether the system has the POSIX.2 C compiler command, c89.

_SC_2_FORT_DEV

>Inquire about whether the system has the POSIX.2 Fortran compiler command, fort77.

_SC_2_FORT_RUN

>Inquire about whether the system has the POSIX.2 asa command to interpret Fortran carriage control.

_SC_2_LOCALEDEF

>Inquire about whether the system has the POSIX.2 localedef command.

_SC_2_SW_DEV

>Inquire about whether the system has the POSIX.2 commands ar, make, and strip.

_SC_BC_BASE_MAX

>Inquire about the maximum value of obase in the bc utility.

_SC_BC_DIM_MAX

>Inquire about the maximum size of an array in the bc utility.

_SC_BC_SCALE_MAX

>Inquire about the maximum value of scale in the bc utility.

_SC_BC_STRING_MAX

>Inquire about the maximum size of a string constant in the bc utility.

_SC_COLL_WEIGHTS_MAX

>Inquire about the maximum number of weights that can necessarily be used in defining the collating sequence for a locale.

_SC_EXPR_NEST_MAX

>Inquire about the maximum number of expressions nested within parentheses when using the expr utility.

_SC_LINE_MAX

>Inquire about the maximum size of a text line that the POSIX.2 text utilities can handle.

_SC_EQUIV_CLASS_MAX

>Inquire about the maximum number of weights that can be assigned to an entry of the LC_COLLATE category 'order' keyword in a locale definition. The GNU C Library does not presently support locale definitions.

`_SC_VERSION`

> Inquire about the version number of POSIX.1 that the library and kernel support.

`_SC_2_VERSION`

> Inquire about the version number of POSIX.2 that the system utilities support.

`_SC_PAGESIZE`

> Inquire about the virtual memory page size of the machine. `getpagesize` returns the same value (see Section 22.4.2 [How to get information about the memory subsystem?], page 672).

`_SC_NPROCESSORS_CONF`

> Inquire about the number of configured processors.

`_SC_NPROCESSORS_ONLN`

> Inquire about the number of processors online.

`_SC_PHYS_PAGES`

> Inquire about the number of physical pages in the system.

`_SC_AVPHYS_PAGES`

> Inquire about the number of available physical pages in the system.

`_SC_ATEXIT_MAX`

> Inquire about the number of functions which can be registered as termination functions for `atexit`; see Section 25.7.3 [Cleanups on Exit], page 770.

`_SC_XOPEN_VERSION`

> Inquire about the parameter corresponding to `_XOPEN_VERSION`.

`_SC_XOPEN_XCU_VERSION`

> Inquire about the parameter corresponding to `_XOPEN_XCU_VERSION`.

`_SC_XOPEN_UNIX`

> Inquire about the parameter corresponding to `_XOPEN_UNIX`.

`_SC_XOPEN_REALTIME`

> Inquire about the parameter corresponding to `_XOPEN_REALTIME`.

`_SC_XOPEN_REALTIME_THREADS`

> Inquire about the parameter corresponding to `_XOPEN_REALTIME_THREADS`.

`_SC_XOPEN_LEGACY`

> Inquire about the parameter corresponding to `_XOPEN_LEGACY`.

`_SC_XOPEN_CRYPT`

> Inquire about the parameter corresponding to `_XOPEN_CRYPT`.

`_SC_XOPEN_ENH_I18N`

> Inquire about the parameter corresponding to `_XOPEN_ENH_I18N`.

`_SC_XOPEN_SHM`

> Inquire about the parameter corresponding to `_XOPEN_SHM`.

`_SC_XOPEN_XPG2`

> Inquire about the parameter corresponding to `_XOPEN_XPG2`.

_SC_XOPEN_XPG3

> Inquire about the parameter corresponding to _XOPEN_XPG3.

_SC_XOPEN_XPG4

> Inquire about the parameter corresponding to _XOPEN_XPG4.

_SC_CHAR_BIT

> Inquire about the number of bits in a variable of type `char`.

_SC_CHAR_MAX

> Inquire about the maximum value which can be stored in a variable of type `char`.

_SC_CHAR_MIN

> Inquire about the minimum value which can be stored in a variable of type `char`.

_SC_INT_MAX

> Inquire about the maximum value which can be stored in a variable of type `int`.

_SC_INT_MIN

> Inquire about the minimum value which can be stored in a variable of type `int`.

_SC_LONG_BIT

> Inquire about the number of bits in a variable of type `long int`.

_SC_WORD_BIT

> Inquire about the number of bits in a variable of a register word.

_SC_MB_LEN_MAX

> Inquire about the maximum length of a multi-byte representation of a wide character value.

_SC_NZERO

> Inquire about the value used to internally represent the zero priority level for the process execution.

SC_SSIZE_MAX

> Inquire about the maximum value which can be stored in a variable of type `ssize_t`.

_SC_SCHAR_MAX

> Inquire about the maximum value which can be stored in a variable of type `signed char`.

_SC_SCHAR_MIN

> Inquire about the minimum value which can be stored in a variable of type `signed char`.

_SC_SHRT_MAX

> Inquire about the maximum value which can be stored in a variable of type `short int`.

_SC_SHRT_MIN

> Inquire about the minimum value which can be stored in a variable of type `short int`.

_SC_UCHAR_MAX

> Inquire about the maximum value which can be stored in a variable of type `unsigned char`.

_SC_UINT_MAX

> Inquire about the maximum value which can be stored in a variable of type `unsigned int`.

_SC_ULONG_MAX

> Inquire about the maximum value which can be stored in a variable of type `unsigned long int`.

_SC_USHRT_MAX

> Inquire about the maximum value which can be stored in a variable of type `unsigned short int`.

_SC_NL_ARGMAX

> Inquire about the parameter corresponding to `NL_ARGMAX`.

_SC_NL_LANGMAX

> Inquire about the parameter corresponding to `NL_LANGMAX`.

_SC_NL_MSGMAX

> Inquire about the parameter corresponding to `NL_MSGMAX`.

_SC_NL_NMAX

> Inquire about the parameter corresponding to `NL_NMAX`.

_SC_NL_SETMAX

> Inquire about the parameter corresponding to `NL_SETMAX`.

_SC_NL_TEXTMAX

> Inquire about the parameter corresponding to `NL_TEXTMAX`.

32.4.3 Examples of `sysconf`

We recommend that you first test for a macro definition for the parameter you are interested in, and call **sysconf** only if the macro is not defined. For example, here is how to test whether job control is supported:

```
int
have_job_control (void)
{
#ifdef _POSIX_JOB_CONTROL
  return 1;
#else
  int value = sysconf (_SC_JOB_CONTROL);
  if (value < 0)
    /* If the system is that badly wedged,
       therefls no use trying to go on.  */
    fatal (strerror (errno));
  return value;
#endif
}
```

Here is how to get the value of a numeric limit:

```
int
get_child_max ()
{
#ifdef CHILD_MAX
  return CHILD_MAX;
#else
  int value = sysconf (_SC_CHILD_MAX);
  if (value < 0)
    fatal (strerror (errno));
  return value;
#endif
}
```

32.5 Minimum Values for General Capacity Limits

Here are the names for the POSIX minimum upper bounds for the system limit parameters. The significance of these values is that you can safely push to these limits without checking whether the particular system you are using can go that far.

_POSIX_AIO_LISTIO_MAX

> The most restrictive limit permitted by POSIX for the maximum number of I/O operations that can be specified in a list I/O call. The value of this constant is 2; thus you can add up to two new entries of the list of outstanding operations.

_POSIX_AIO_MAX

> The most restrictive limit permitted by POSIX for the maximum number of outstanding asynchronous I/O operations. The value of this constant is 1. So you cannot expect that you can issue more than one operation and immediately continue with the normal work, receiving the notifications asynchronously.

_POSIX_ARG_MAX

> The value of this macro is the most restrictive limit permitted by POSIX for the maximum combined length of the *argv* and *environ* arguments that can be passed to the **exec** functions. Its value is 4096.

_POSIX_CHILD_MAX

> The value of this macro is the most restrictive limit permitted by POSIX for the maximum number of simultaneous processes per real user ID. Its value is 6.

_POSIX_NGROUPS_MAX

> The value of this macro is the most restrictive limit permitted by POSIX for the maximum number of supplementary group IDs per process. Its value is 0.

_POSIX_OPEN_MAX

> The value of this macro is the most restrictive limit permitted by POSIX for the maximum number of files that a single process can have open simultaneously. Its value is 16.

_POSIX_SSIZE_MAX

> The value of this macro is the most restrictive limit permitted by POSIX for the maximum value that can be stored in an object of type **ssize_t**. Its value is 32767.

_POSIX_STREAM_MAX

> The value of this macro is the most restrictive limit permitted by POSIX for the maximum number of streams that a single process can have open simultaneously. Its value is **8**.

_POSIX_TZNAME_MAX

> The value of this macro is the most restrictive limit permitted by POSIX for the maximum length of a time zone name. Its value is **3**.

_POSIX2_RE_DUP_MAX

> The value of this macro is the most restrictive limit permitted by POSIX for the numbers used in the '\{*min*,*max*\}' construct in a regular expression. Its value is **255**.

32.6 Limits on File System Capacity

The POSIX.1 standard specifies a number of parameters that describe the limitations of the file system. It's possible for the system to have a fixed, uniform limit for a parameter, but this isn't the usual case. On most systems, it's possible for different file systems (and, for some parameters, even different files) to have different maximum limits. For example, this is very likely if you use NFS to mount some of the file systems from other machines.

Each of the following macros is defined in `limits.h` only if the system has a fixed, uniform limit for the parameter in question. If the system allows different file systems or files to have different limits, then the macro is undefined; use `pathconf` or `fpathconf` to find out the limit that applies to a particular file. See Section 32.9 [Using `pathconf`], page 877.

Each parameter also has another macro, with a name starting with '_POSIX', which gives the lowest value that the limit is allowed to have on *any* POSIX system. See Section 32.8 [Minimum Values for File System Limits], page 876.

int LINK_MAX   [Macro]

> The uniform system limit (if any) for the number of names for a given file. See Section 14.4 [Hard Links], page 405.

int MAX_CANON   [Macro]

> The uniform system limit (if any) for the amount of text in a line of input when input editing is enabled. See Section 17.3 [Two Styles of Input: Canonical or Not], page 491.

int MAX_INPUT   [Macro]

> The uniform system limit (if any) for the total number of characters typed ahead as input. See Section 17.2 [I/O Queues], page 491.

int NAME_MAX   [Macro]

> The uniform system limit (if any) for the length of a file name component, not including the terminating null character.
>
> **Portability Note:** On some systems, the GNU C Library defines NAME_MAX, but does not actually enforce this limit.

int PATH_MAX [Macro]

> The uniform system limit (if any) for the length of an entire file name (that is, the argument given to system calls such as **open**), including the terminating null character.
>
> **Portability Note:** The GNU C Library does not enforce this limit even if **PATH_MAX** is defined.

int PIPE_BUF [Macro]

> The uniform system limit (if any) for the number of bytes that can be written atomically to a pipe. If multiple processes are writing to the same pipe simultaneously, output from different processes might be interleaved in chunks of this size. See Chapter 15 [Pipes and FIFOs], page 437.

These are alternative macro names for some of the same information.

int MAXNAMLEN [Macro]

> This is the BSD name for **NAME_MAX**. It is defined in **dirent.h**.

int FILENAME_MAX [Macro]

> The value of this macro is an integer constant expression that represents the maximum length of a file name string. It is defined in **stdio.h**.
>
> Unlike **PATH_MAX**, this macro is defined even if there is no actual limit imposed. In such a case, its value is typically a very large number. **This is always the case on GNU/Hurd systems.**
>
> **Usage Note:** Don't use **FILENAME_MAX** as the size of an array in which to store a file name! You can't possibly make an array that big! Use dynamic allocation (see Section 3.2 [Allocating Storage For Program Data], page 42) instead.

32.7 Optional Features in File Support

POSIX defines certain system-specific options in the system calls for operating on files. Some systems support these options and others do not. Since these options are provided in the kernel, not in the library, simply using the GNU C Library does not guarantee that any of these features is supported; it depends on the system you are using. They can also vary between file systems on a single machine.

This section describes the macros you can test to determine whether a particular option is supported on your machine. If a given macro is defined in **unistd.h**, then its value says whether the corresponding feature is supported. (A value of **-1** indicates no; any other value indicates yes.) If the macro is undefined, it means particular files may or may not support the feature.

Since all the machines that support the GNU C Library also support NFS, one can never make a general statement about whether all file systems support the **_POSIX_CHOWN_RESTRICTED** and **_POSIX_NO_TRUNC** features. So these names are never defined as macros in the GNU C Library.

int _POSIX_CHOWN_RESTRICTED [Macro]

> If this option is in effect, the **chown** function is restricted so that the only changes permitted to nonprivileged processes is to change the group owner of a file to either be the effective group ID of the process, or one of its supplementary group IDs. See Section 14.9.4 [File Owner], page 420.

`int _POSIX_NO_TRUNC` [Macro]

> If this option is in effect, file name components longer than `NAME_MAX` generate an `ENAMETOOLONG` error. Otherwise, file name components that are too long are silently truncated.

`unsigned char _POSIX_VDISABLE` [Macro]

> This option is only meaningful for files that are terminal devices. If it is enabled, then handling for special control characters can be disabled individually. See Section 17.4.9 [Special Characters], page 503.

If one of these macros is undefined, that means that the option might be in effect for some files and not for others. To inquire about a particular file, call `pathconf` or `fpathconf`. See Section 32.9 [Using `pathconf`], page 877.

32.8 Minimum Values for File System Limits

Here are the names for the POSIX minimum upper bounds for some of the above parameters. The significance of these values is that you can safely push to these limits without checking whether the particular system you are using can go that far. In most cases GNU systems do not have these strict limitations. The actual limit should be requested if necessary.

`_POSIX_LINK_MAX`

> The most restrictive limit permitted by POSIX for the maximum value of a file's link count. The value of this constant is 8; thus, you can always make up to eight names for a file without running into a system limit.

`_POSIX_MAX_CANON`

> The most restrictive limit permitted by POSIX for the maximum number of bytes in a canonical input line from a terminal device. The value of this constant is 255.

`_POSIX_MAX_INPUT`

> The most restrictive limit permitted by POSIX for the maximum number of bytes in a terminal device input queue (or typeahead buffer). See Section 17.4.4 [Input Modes], page 495. The value of this constant is 255.

`_POSIX_NAME_MAX`

> The most restrictive limit permitted by POSIX for the maximum number of bytes in a file name component. The value of this constant is 14.

`_POSIX_PATH_MAX`

> The most restrictive limit permitted by POSIX for the maximum number of bytes in a file name. The value of this constant is 256.

`_POSIX_PIPE_BUF`

> The most restrictive limit permitted by POSIX for the maximum number of bytes that can be written atomically to a pipe. The value of this constant is 512.

`SYMLINK_MAX`

> Maximum number of bytes in a symbolic link.

POSIX_REC_INCR_XFER_SIZE

> Recommended increment for file transfer sizes between the POSIX_REC_MIN_XFER_SIZE and POSIX_REC_MAX_XFER_SIZE values.

POSIX_REC_MAX_XFER_SIZE

> Maximum recommended file transfer size.

POSIX_REC_MIN_XFER_SIZE

> Minimum recommended file transfer size.

POSIX_REC_XFER_ALIGN

> Recommended file transfer buffer alignment.

32.9 Using pathconf

When your machine allows different files to have different values for a file system parameter, you can use the functions in this section to find out the value that applies to any particular file.

These functions and the associated constants for the *parameter* argument are declared in the header file **unistd.h**.

long int pathconf (*const char *filename, int parameter*)   [Function]

> Preliminary: | MT-Safe | AS-Unsafe lock heap | AC-Unsafe lock fd mem | See Section 1.2.2.1 [POSIX Safety Concepts], page 2.
>
> This function is used to inquire about the limits that apply to the file named *filename*.
>
> The *parameter* argument should be one of the '_PC_' constants listed below.
>
> The normal return value from **pathconf** is the value you requested. A value of −1 is returned both if the implementation does not impose a limit, and in case of an error. In the former case, **errno** is not set, while in the latter case, **errno** is set to indicate the cause of the problem. So the only way to use this function robustly is to store 0 into **errno** just before calling it.
>
> Besides the usual file name errors (see Section 11.2.3 [File Name Errors], page 255), the following error condition is defined for this function:
>
> EINVAL   The value of *parameter* is invalid, or the implementation doesn't support the *parameter* for the specific file.

long int fpathconf (*int filedes, int parameter*)   [Function]

> Preliminary: | MT-Safe | AS-Unsafe lock heap | AC-Unsafe lock fd mem | See Section 1.2.2.1 [POSIX Safety Concepts], page 2.
>
> This is just like **pathconf** except that an open file descriptor is used to specify the file for which information is requested, instead of a file name.
>
> The following **errno** error conditions are defined for this function:
>
> EBADF   The *filedes* argument is not a valid file descriptor.
>
> EINVAL   The value of *parameter* is invalid, or the implementation doesn't support the *parameter* for the specific file.

Here are the symbolic constants that you can use as the *parameter* argument to `pathconf`
and `fpathconf`. The values are all integer constants.

`_PC_LINK_MAX`
>Inquire about the value of `LINK_MAX`.

`_PC_MAX_CANON`
>Inquire about the value of `MAX_CANON`.

`_PC_MAX_INPUT`
>Inquire about the value of `MAX_INPUT`.

`_PC_NAME_MAX`
>Inquire about the value of `NAME_MAX`.

`_PC_PATH_MAX`
>Inquire about the value of `PATH_MAX`.

`_PC_PIPE_BUF`
>Inquire about the value of `PIPE_BUF`.

`_PC_CHOWN_RESTRICTED`
>Inquire about the value of `_POSIX_CHOWN_RESTRICTED`.

`_PC_NO_TRUNC`
>Inquire about the value of `_POSIX_NO_TRUNC`.

`_PC_VDISABLE`
>Inquire about the value of `_POSIX_VDISABLE`.

`_PC_SYNC_IO`
>Inquire about the value of `_POSIX_SYNC_IO`.

`_PC_ASYNC_IO`
>Inquire about the value of `_POSIX_ASYNC_IO`.

`_PC_PRIO_IO`
>Inquire about the value of `_POSIX_PRIO_IO`.

`_PC_FILESIZEBITS`
>Inquire about the availability of large files on the filesystem.

`_PC_REC_INCR_XFER_SIZE`
>Inquire about the value of `POSIX_REC_INCR_XFER_SIZE`.

`_PC_REC_MAX_XFER_SIZE`
>Inquire about the value of `POSIX_REC_MAX_XFER_SIZE`.

`_PC_REC_MIN_XFER_SIZE`
>Inquire about the value of `POSIX_REC_MIN_XFER_SIZE`.

`_PC_REC_XFER_ALIGN`
>Inquire about the value of `POSIX_REC_XFER_ALIGN`.

Portability Note: On some systems, the GNU C Library does not enforce `_PC_NAME_MAX`
or `_PC_PATH_MAX` limits.

32.10 Utility Program Capacity Limits

The POSIX.2 standard specifies certain system limits that you can access through `sysconf` that apply to utility behavior rather than the behavior of the library or the operating system.

The GNU C Library defines macros for these limits, and `sysconf` returns values for them if you ask; but these values convey no meaningful information. They are simply the smallest values that POSIX.2 permits.

int `BC_BASE_MAX`   [Macro]
    The largest value of `obase` that the `bc` utility is guaranteed to support.

int `BC_DIM_MAX`   [Macro]
    The largest number of elements in one array that the `bc` utility is guaranteed to support.

int `BC_SCALE_MAX`   [Macro]
    The largest value of `scale` that the `bc` utility is guaranteed to support.

int `BC_STRING_MAX`   [Macro]
    The largest number of characters in one string constant that the `bc` utility is guaranteed to support.

int `COLL_WEIGHTS_MAX`   [Macro]
    The largest number of weights that can necessarily be used in defining the collating sequence for a locale.

int `EXPR_NEST_MAX`   [Macro]
    The maximum number of expressions that can be nested within parentheses by the `expr` utility.

int `LINE_MAX`   [Macro]
    The largest text line that the text-oriented POSIX.2 utilities can support. (If you are using the GNU versions of these utilities, then there is no actual limit except that imposed by the available virtual memory, but there is no way that the library can tell you this.)

int `EQUIV_CLASS_MAX`   [Macro]
    The maximum number of weights that can be assigned to an entry of the `LC_COLLATE` category 'order' keyword in a locale definition. The GNU C Library does not presently support locale definitions.

32.11 Minimum Values for Utility Limits

`_POSIX2_BC_BASE_MAX`
    The most restrictive limit permitted by POSIX.2 for the maximum value of `obase` in the `bc` utility. Its value is 99.

`_POSIX2_BC_DIM_MAX`
    The most restrictive limit permitted by POSIX.2 for the maximum size of an array in the `bc` utility. Its value is 2048.

_POSIX2_BC_SCALE_MAX

> The most restrictive limit permitted by POSIX.2 for the maximum value of `scale` in the `bc` utility. Its value is `99`.

_POSIX2_BC_STRING_MAX

> The most restrictive limit permitted by POSIX.2 for the maximum size of a string constant in the `bc` utility. Its value is `1000`.

_POSIX2_COLL_WEIGHTS_MAX

> The most restrictive limit permitted by POSIX.2 for the maximum number of weights that can necessarily be used in defining the collating sequence for a locale. Its value is 2.

_POSIX2_EXPR_NEST_MAX

> The most restrictive limit permitted by POSIX.2 for the maximum number of expressions nested within parenthesis when using the `expr` utility. Its value is 32.

_POSIX2_LINE_MAX

> The most restrictive limit permitted by POSIX.2 for the maximum size of a text line that the text utilities can handle. Its value is `2048`.

_POSIX2_EQUIV_CLASS_MAX

> The most restrictive limit permitted by POSIX.2 for the maximum number of weights that can be assigned to an entry of the `LC_COLLATE` category 'order' keyword in a locale definition. Its value is 2. The GNU C Library does not presently support locale definitions.

32.12 String-Valued Parameters

POSIX.2 defines a way to get string-valued parameters from the operating system with the function `confstr`:

size_t confstr (*int* `parameter`, *char* *`buf`, *size_t* `len`)　　　　　[Function]

> Preliminary: | MT-Safe | AS-Safe | AC-Safe | See Section 1.2.2.1 [POSIX Safety Concepts], page 2.

> This function reads the value of a string-valued system parameter, storing the string into *len* bytes of memory space starting at *buf*. The *parameter* argument should be one of the '`_CS_`' symbols listed below.

> The normal return value from `confstr` is the length of the string value that you asked for. If you supply a null pointer for *buf*, then `confstr` does not try to store the string; it just returns its length. A value of 0 indicates an error.

> If the string you asked for is too long for the buffer (that is, longer than *len* - 1), then `confstr` stores just that much (leaving room for the terminating null character). You can tell that this has happened because `confstr` returns a value greater than or equal to *len*.

> The following `errno` error conditions are defined for this function:

> EINVAL　　The value of the *parameter* is invalid.

Currently there is just one parameter you can read with `confstr`:

_CS_PATH   This parameter's value is the recommended default path for searching for executable files. This is the path that a user has by default just after logging in.

_CS_LFS_CFLAGS

The returned string specifies which additional flags must be given to the C compiler if a source is compiled using the _LARGEFILE_SOURCE feature select macro; see Section 1.3.4 [Feature Test Macros], page 15.

_CS_LFS_LDFLAGS

The returned string specifies which additional flags must be given to the linker if a source is compiled using the _LARGEFILE_SOURCE feature select macro; see Section 1.3.4 [Feature Test Macros], page 15.

_CS_LFS_LIBS

The returned string specifies which additional libraries must be linked to the application if a source is compiled using the _LARGEFILE_SOURCE feature select macro; see Section 1.3.4 [Feature Test Macros], page 15.

_CS_LFS_LINTFLAGS

The returned string specifies which additional flags must be given to the lint tool if a source is compiled using the _LARGEFILE_SOURCE feature select macro; see Section 1.3.4 [Feature Test Macros], page 15.

_CS_LFS64_CFLAGS

The returned string specifies which additional flags must be given to the C compiler if a source is compiled using the _LARGEFILE64_SOURCE feature select macro; see Section 1.3.4 [Feature Test Macros], page 15.

_CS_LFS64_LDFLAGS

The returned string specifies which additional flags must be given to the linker if a source is compiled using the _LARGEFILE64_SOURCE feature select macro; see Section 1.3.4 [Feature Test Macros], page 15.

_CS_LFS64_LIBS

The returned string specifies which additional libraries must be linked to the application if a source is compiled using the _LARGEFILE64_SOURCE feature select macro; see Section 1.3.4 [Feature Test Macros], page 15.

_CS_LFS64_LINTFLAGS

The returned string specifies which additional flags must be given to the lint tool if a source is compiled using the _LARGEFILE64_SOURCE feature select macro; see Section 1.3.4 [Feature Test Macros], page 15.

The way to use `confstr` without any arbitrary limit on string size is to call it twice: first call it to get the length, allocate the buffer accordingly, and then call `confstr` again to fill the buffer, like this:

```
char *
get_default_path (void)
{
  size_t len = confstr (_CS_PATH, NULL, 0);
  char *buffer = (char *) xmalloc (len);

  if (confstr (_CS_PATH, buf, len + 1) == 0)
    {
      free (buffer);
      return NULL;
    }

  return buffer;
}
```

33 DES Encryption and Password Handling

On many systems, it is unnecessary to have any kind of user authentication; for instance, a workstation which is not connected to a network probably does not need any user authentication, because to use the machine an intruder must have physical access.

Sometimes, however, it is necessary to be sure that a user is authorized to use some service a machine provides—for instance, to log in as a particular user id (see Chapter 30 [Users and Groups], page 815). One traditional way of doing this is for each user to choose a secret *password*; then, the system can ask someone claiming to be a user what the user's password is, and if the person gives the correct password then the system can grant the appropriate privileges.

If all the passwords are just stored in a file somewhere, then this file has to be very carefully protected. To avoid this, passwords are run through a *one-way function*, a function which makes it difficult to work out what its input was by looking at its output, before storing in the file.

The GNU C Library provides a one-way function that is compatible with the behavior of the `crypt` function introduced in FreeBSD 2.0. It supports two one-way algorithms: one based on the MD5 message-digest algorithm that is compatible with modern BSD systems, and the other based on the Data Encryption Standard (DES) that is compatible with Unix systems.

It also provides support for Secure RPC, and some library functions that can be used to perform normal DES encryption. The `AUTH_DES` authentication flavor in Secure RPC, as provided by the GNU C Library, uses DES and does not comply with FIPS 140-2 nor does any other use of DES within the GNU C Library. It is recommended that Secure RPC should not be used for systems that need to comply with FIPS 140-2 since all flavors of encrypted authentication use normal DES.

33.1 Legal Problems

Because of the continuously changing state of the law, it's not possible to provide a definitive survey of the laws affecting cryptography. Instead, this section warns you of some of the known trouble spots; this may help you when you try to find out what the laws of your country are.

Some countries require that you have a license to use, possess, or import cryptography. These countries are believed to include Byelorussia, Burma, India, Indonesia, Israel, Kazakhstan, Pakistan, Russia, and Saudi Arabia.

Some countries restrict the transmission of encrypted messages by radio; some telecommunications carriers restrict the transmission of encrypted messages over their network.

Many countries have some form of export control for encryption software. The Wassenaar Arrangement is a multilateral agreement between 33 countries (Argentina, Australia, Austria, Belgium, Bulgaria, Canada, the Czech Republic, Denmark, Finland, France, Germany, Greece, Hungary, Ireland, Italy, Japan, Luxembourg, the Netherlands, New Zealand, Norway, Poland, Portugal, the Republic of Korea, Romania, the Russian Federation, the Slovak Republic, Spain, Sweden, Switzerland, Turkey, Ukraine, the United Kingdom and the United States) which restricts some kinds of encryption exports. Different countries apply the arrangement in different ways; some do not allow the exception for certain kinds of "public domain" software (which would include this library), some only restrict the export of software in tangible form, and others impose significant additional restrictions.

The United States has additional rules. This software would generally be exportable under 15 CFR 740.13(e), which permits exports of "encryption source code" which is "publicly available" and which is "not subject to an express agreement for the payment of a licensing fee or royalty for commercial production or sale of any product developed with the source code" to most countries.

The rules in this area are continuously changing. If you know of any information in this manual that is out-of-date, please report it to the bug database. See Section C.5 [Reporting Bugs], page 1051.

33.2 Reading Passwords

When reading in a password, it is desirable to avoid displaying it on the screen, to help keep it secret. The following function handles this in a convenient way.

char * getpass (*const char *prompt*)   [Function]

> Preliminary: | MT-Unsafe term | AS-Unsafe heap lock corrupt | AC-Unsafe term lock corrupt | See Section 1.2.2.1 [POSIX Safety Concepts], page 2.
>
> getpass outputs *prompt*, then reads a string in from the terminal without echoing it. It tries to connect to the real terminal, /dev/tty, if possible, to encourage users not to put plaintext passwords in files; otherwise, it uses stdin and stderr. getpass also disables the INTR, QUIT, and SUSP characters on the terminal using the ISIG terminal attribute (see Section 17.4.7 [Local Modes], page 499). The terminal is flushed before and after getpass, so that characters of a mistyped password are not accidentally visible.
>
> In other C libraries, getpass may only return the first PASS_MAX bytes of a password. The GNU C Library has no limit, so PASS_MAX is undefined.
>
> The prototype for this function is in unistd.h. PASS_MAX would be defined in limits.h.

This precise set of operations may not suit all possible situations. In this case, it is recommended that users write their own getpass substitute. For instance, a very simple substitute is as follows:

```
#include <termios.h>
#include <stdio.h>

ssize_t
my_getpass (char **lineptr, size_t *n, FILE *stream)
{
  struct termios old, new;
  int nread;

  /* Turn echoing off and fail if we canflt. */
  if (tcgetattr (fileno (stream), &old) != 0)
    return -1;
  new = old;
  new.c_lflag &= ~ECHO;
  if (tcsetattr (fileno (stream), TCSAFLUSH, &new) != 0)
```

```
        return -1;

    /* Read the password. */
    nread = getline (lineptr, n, stream);

    /* Restore terminal. */
    (void) tcsetattr (fileno (stream), TCSAFLUSH, &old);

    return nread;
}
```

The substitute takes the same parameters as `getline` (see Section 12.9 [Line-Oriented Input], page 274); the user must print any prompt desired.

33.3 Encrypting Passwords

`char * crypt` (*const char *key, const char *salt*)   [Function]

Preliminary: | MT-Unsafe race:crypt | AS-Unsafe corrupt lock heap dlopen | AC-Unsafe lock mem | See Section 1.2.2.1 [POSIX Safety Concepts], page 2.

The `crypt` function takes a password, *key*, as a string, and a *salt* character array which is described below, and returns a printable ASCII string which starts with another salt. It is believed that, given the output of the function, the best way to find a *key* that will produce that output is to guess values of *key* until the original value of *key* is found.

The *salt* parameter does two things. Firstly, it selects which algorithm is used, the MD5-based one or the DES-based one. Secondly, it makes life harder for someone trying to guess passwords against a file containing many passwords; without a *salt*, an intruder can make a guess, run `crypt` on it once, and compare the result with all the passwords. With a *salt*, the intruder must run `crypt` once for each different salt.

For the MD5-based algorithm, the *salt* should consist of the string `$1$`, followed by up to 8 characters, terminated by either another `$` or the end of the string. The result of `crypt` will be the *salt*, followed by a `$` if the salt didn't end with one, followed by 22 characters from the alphabet `./0-9A-Za-z`, up to 34 characters total. Every character in the *key* is significant.

For the DES-based algorithm, the *salt* should consist of two characters from the alphabet `./0-9A-Za-z`, and the result of `crypt` will be those two characters followed by 11 more from the same alphabet, 13 in total. Only the first 8 characters in the *key* are significant.

The MD5-based algorithm has no limit on the useful length of the password used, and is slightly more secure. It is therefore preferred over the DES-based algorithm.

When the user enters their password for the first time, the *salt* should be set to a new string which is reasonably random. To verify a password against the result of a previous call to `crypt`, pass the result of the previous call as the *salt*.

The following short program is an example of how to use `crypt` the first time a password is entered. Note that the *salt* generation is just barely acceptable; in particular, it is not unique between machines, and in many applications it would not be acceptable to let an attacker know what time the user's password was last set.

```
#include <stdio.h>
#include <time.h>
#include <unistd.h>
#include <crypt.h>

int
main(void)
{
  unsigned long seed[2];
  char salt[] = "$1$........";
  const char *const seedchars =
    "./0123456789ABCDEFGHIJKLMNOPQRST"
    "UVWXYZabcdefghijklmnopqrstuvwxyz";
  char *password;
  int i;

  /* Generate a (not very) random seed.
   You should do it better than this... */
  seed[0] = time(NULL);
  seed[1] = getpid() ^ (seed[0] >> 14 & 0x30000);

  /* Turn it into printable characters from `seedcharsfl. */
  for (i = 0; i < 8; i++)
    salt[3+i] = seedchars[(seed[i/5] >> (i%5)*6) & 0x3f];

  /* Read in the userfls password and encrypt it. */
  password = crypt(getpass("Password:"), salt);

  /* Print the results. */
  puts(password);
  return 0;
}
```

The next program shows how to verify a password. It prompts the user for a password and prints "Access granted." if the user types GNU libc manual.

```
#include <stdio.h>
#include <string.h>
#include <unistd.h>
#include <crypt.h>

int
main(void)
{
  /* Hashed form of "GNU libc manual". */
  const char *const pass = "$1$/iSaq7rB$EoUw5jPPvAPECNaaWzMK/";

  char *result;
  int ok;

  /* Read in the userfls password and encrypt it,
   passing the expected password in as the salt. */
  result = crypt(getpass("Password:"), pass);

  /* Test the result. */
  ok = strcmp (result, pass) == 0;

  puts(ok ? "Access granted." : "Access denied.");
```

```
        return ok ? 0 : 1;
    }
```

char * crypt_r (*const char *key, const char *salt, struct*   [Function]
        crypt_data * data)
> Preliminary: | MT-Safe | AS-Unsafe corrupt lock heap dlopen | AC-Unsafe lock
> mem | See Section 1.2.2.1 [POSIX Safety Concepts], page 2.

> The `crypt_r` function does the same thing as `crypt`, but takes an extra parame-
> ter which includes space for its result (among other things), so it can be reentrant.
> `data->initialized` must be cleared to zero before the first time `crypt_r` is called.

> The `crypt_r` function is a GNU extension.

The `crypt` and `crypt_r` functions are prototyped in the header `crypt.h`.

33.4 DES Encryption

The Data Encryption Standard is described in the US Government Federal Information
Processing Standards (FIPS) 46-3 published by the National Institute of Standards and
Technology. The DES has been very thoroughly analyzed since it was developed in the late
1970s, and no new significant flaws have been found.

However, the DES uses only a 56-bit key (plus 8 parity bits), and a machine has been
built in 1998 which can search through all possible keys in about 6 days, which cost about
US$200000; faster searches would be possible with more money. This makes simple DES
insecure for most purposes, and NIST no longer permits new US government systems to
use simple DES.

For serious encryption functionality, it is recommended that one of the many free encryption libraries be used instead of these routines.

The DES is a reversible operation which takes a 64-bit block and a 64-bit key, and
produces another 64-bit block. Usually the bits are numbered so that the most-significant
bit, the first bit, of each block is numbered 1.

Under that numbering, every 8th bit of the key (the 8th, 16th, and so on) is not used
by the encryption algorithm itself. But the key must have odd parity; that is, out of bits 1
through 8, and 9 through 16, and so on, there must be an odd number of '1' bits, and this
completely specifies the unused bits.

void setkey (*const char *key*)   [Function]
> Preliminary: | MT-Unsafe race:crypt | AS-Unsafe corrupt lock | AC-Unsafe lock |
> See Section 1.2.2.1 [POSIX Safety Concepts], page 2.

> The `setkey` function sets an internal data structure to be an expanded form of *key*.
> *key* is specified as an array of 64 bits each stored in a `char`, the first bit is `key[0]`
> and the 64th bit is `key[63]`. The *key* should have the correct parity.

void encrypt (*char *block, int edflag*)   [Function]
> Preliminary: | MT-Unsafe race:crypt | AS-Unsafe corrupt lock | AC-Unsafe lock |
> See Section 1.2.2.1 [POSIX Safety Concepts], page 2.

> The `encrypt` function encrypts *block* if *edflag* is 0, otherwise it decrypts *block*, using
> a key previously set by `setkey`. The result is placed in *block*.

Like `setkey`, *block* is specified as an array of 64 bits each stored in a `char`, but there are no parity bits in *block*.

void setkey_r (*const char *key, struct crypt_data * data*) [Function]

void encrypt_r (*char *block, int edflag, struct crypt_data * data*) [Function]
> Preliminary: | MT-Safe | AS-Unsafe corrupt lock | AC-Unsafe lock | See Section 1.2.2.1 [POSIX Safety Concepts], page 2.
>
> These are reentrant versions of `setkey` and `encrypt`. The only difference is the extra parameter, which stores the expanded version of *key*. Before calling `setkey_r` the first time, `data->initialized` must be cleared to zero.

The `setkey_r` and `encrypt_r` functions are GNU extensions. `setkey`, `encrypt`, `setkey_r`, and `encrypt_r` are defined in `crypt.h`.

int ecb_crypt (*char *key, char *blocks, unsigned int len, unsigned* [Function]
    int mode)
> Preliminary: | MT-Safe | AS-Safe | AC-Safe | See Section 1.2.2.1 [POSIX Safety Concepts], page 2.
>
> The function `ecb_crypt` encrypts or decrypts one or more blocks using DES. Each block is encrypted independently.
>
> The *blocks* and the *key* are stored packed in 8-bit bytes, so that the first bit of the key is the most-significant bit of `key[0]` and the 63rd bit of the key is stored as the least-significant bit of `key[7]`. The *key* should have the correct parity.
>
> *len* is the number of bytes in *blocks*. It should be a multiple of 8 (so that there are a whole number of blocks to encrypt). *len* is limited to a maximum of `DES_MAXDATA` bytes.
>
> The result of the encryption replaces the input in *blocks*.
>
> The *mode* parameter is the bitwise OR of two of the following:
>
> `DES_ENCRYPT`
>> This constant, used in the *mode* parameter, specifies that *blocks* is to be encrypted.
>
> `DES_DECRYPT`
>> This constant, used in the *mode* parameter, specifies that *blocks* is to be decrypted.
>
> `DES_HW` This constant, used in the *mode* parameter, asks to use a hardware device. If no hardware device is available, encryption happens anyway, but in software.
>
> `DES_SW` This constant, used in the *mode* parameter, specifies that no hardware device is to be used.
>
> The result of the function will be one of these values:
>
> `DESERR_NONE`
>> The encryption succeeded.
>
> `DESERR_NOHWDEVICE`
>> The encryption succeeded, but there was no hardware device available.

`DESERR_HWERROR`

> The encryption failed because of a hardware problem.

`DESERR_BADPARAM`

> The encryption failed because of a bad parameter, for instance *len* is not a multiple of 8 or *len* is larger than `DES_MAXDATA`.

`int DES_FAILED (int err)` [Function]

Preliminary: | MT-Safe | AS-Safe | AC-Safe | See Section 1.2.2.1 [POSIX Safety Concepts], page 2.

This macro returns 1 if *err* is a 'success' result code from `ecb_crypt` or `cbc_crypt`, and 0 otherwise.

`int cbc_crypt (char *key, char *blocks, unsigned int len, unsigned` [Function]
        `int mode, char *ivec)`

Preliminary: | MT-Safe | AS-Safe | AC-Safe | See Section 1.2.2.1 [POSIX Safety Concepts], page 2.

The function `cbc_crypt` encrypts or decrypts one or more blocks using DES in Cipher Block Chaining mode.

For encryption in CBC mode, each block is exclusive-ored with *ivec* before being encrypted, then *ivec* is replaced with the result of the encryption, then the next block is processed. Decryption is the reverse of this process.

This has the advantage that blocks which are the same before being encrypted are very unlikely to be the same after being encrypted, making it much harder to detect patterns in the data.

Usually, *ivec* is set to 8 random bytes before encryption starts. Then the 8 random bytes are transmitted along with the encrypted data (without themselves being encrypted), and passed back in as *ivec* for decryption. Another possibility is to set *ivec* to 8 zeroes initially, and have the first block encrypted consist of 8 random bytes.

Otherwise, all the parameters are similar to those for `ecb_crypt`.

`void des_setparity (char *key)` [Function]

Preliminary: | MT-Safe | AS-Safe | AC-Safe | See Section 1.2.2.1 [POSIX Safety Concepts], page 2.

The function `des_setparity` changes the 64-bit *key*, stored packed in 8-bit bytes, to have odd parity by altering the low bits of each byte.

The `ecb_crypt`, `cbc_crypt`, and `des_setparity` functions and their accompanying macros are all defined in the header `rpc/des_crypt.h`.

33.5 Generating Unpredictable Bytes

Some cryptographic applications (such as session key generation) need unpredictable bytes.

In general, application code should use a deterministic random bit generator, which could call the `getentropy` function described below internally to obtain randomness to seed the generator. The `getrandom` function is intended for low-level applications which need additional control over the blocking behavior.

int getentropy (*void *buffer*, *size_t length*)   [Function]
| MT-Safe | AS-Safe | AC-Safe | See Section 1.2.2.1 [POSIX Safety Concepts], page 2.

This function writes *length* bytes of random data to the array starting at *buffer*, which must be at most 256 bytes long. The function returns zero on success. On failure, it returns −1 and **errno** is updated accordingly.

The **getentropy** function is declared in the header file **sys/random.h**. It is derived from OpenBSD.

The **getentropy** function is not a cancellation point. A call to **getentropy** can block if the system has just booted and the kernel entropy pool has not yet been initialized. In this case, the function will keep blocking even if a signal arrives, and return only after the entropy pool has been initialized.

The **getentropy** function can fail with several errors, some of which are listed below.

ENOSYS   The kernel does not implement the required system call.

EFAULT   The combination of *buffer* and *length* arguments specifies an invalid memory range.

EIO   More than 256 bytes of randomness have been requested, or the buffer could not be overwritten with random data for an unspecified reason.

ssize_t getrandom (*void *buffer*, *size_t length*, *unsigned int*   [Function]
    flags)
| MT-Safe | AS-Safe | AC-Safe | See Section 1.2.2.1 [POSIX Safety Concepts], page 2.

This function writes *length* bytes of random data to the array starting at *buffer*. On success, this function returns the number of bytes which have been written to the buffer (which can be less than *length*). On error, −1 is returned, and **errno** is updated accordingly.

The **getrandom** function is declared in the header file **sys/random.h**. It is a GNU extension.

The following flags are defined for the *flags* argument:

GRND_RANDOM
            Use the **/dev/random** (blocking) pool instead of the **/dev/urandom** (non-blocking) pool to obtain randomness. If the **GRND_RANDOM** flag is specified, the **getrandom** function can block even after the randomness source has been initialized.

GRND_NONBLOCK
            Instead of blocking, return to the caller immediately if no data is available.

The **getrandom** function is a cancellation point.

Obtaining randomness from the **/dev/urandom** pool (i.e., a call without the **GRND_RANDOM** flag) can block if the system has just booted and the pool has not yet been initialized.

The **getrandom** function can fail with several errors, some of which are listed below. In addition, the function may not fill the buffer completely and return a value less than *length*.

ENOSYS   The kernel does not implement the **getrandom** system call.

EAGAIN   No random data was available and `GRND_NONBLOCK` was specified in *flags*.

EFAULT   The combination of *buffer* and *length* arguments specifies an invalid memory range.

EINTR   The system call was interrupted. During the system boot process, before the kernel randomness pool is initialized, this can happen even if *flags* is zero.

EINVAL   The *flags* argument contains an invalid combination of flags.

34 Debugging support

Applications are usually debugged using dedicated debugger programs. But sometimes this is not possible and, in any case, it is useful to provide the developer with as much information as possible at the time the problems are experienced. For this reason a few functions are provided which a program can use to help the developer more easily locate the problem.

34.1 Backtraces

A *backtrace* is a list of the function calls that are currently active in a thread. The usual way to inspect a backtrace of a program is to use an external debugger such as gdb. However, sometimes it is useful to obtain a backtrace programmatically from within a program, e.g., for the purposes of logging or diagnostics.

The header file `execinfo.h` declares three functions that obtain and manipulate backtraces of the current thread.

int backtrace (*void **buffer*, *int size*)   [Function]
> Preliminary: | MT-Safe | AS-Unsafe init heap dlopen plugin lock | AC-Unsafe init mem lock fd | See Section 1.2.2.1 [POSIX Safety Concepts], page 2.
>
> The `backtrace` function obtains a backtrace for the current thread, as a list of pointers, and places the information into *buffer*. The argument *size* should be the number of `void *` elements that will fit into *buffer*. The return value is the actual number of entries of *buffer* that are obtained, and is at most *size*.
>
> The pointers placed in *buffer* are actually return addresses obtained by inspecting the stack, one return address per stack frame.
>
> Note that certain compiler optimizations may interfere with obtaining a valid backtrace. Function inlining causes the inlined function to not have a stack frame; tail call optimization replaces one stack frame with another; frame pointer elimination will stop `backtrace` from interpreting the stack contents correctly.

char ** backtrace_symbols (*void *const *buffer*, *int size*)   [Function]
> Preliminary: | MT-Safe | AS-Unsafe heap | AC-Unsafe mem lock | See Section 1.2.2.1 [POSIX Safety Concepts], page 2.
>
> The `backtrace_symbols` function translates the information obtained from the `backtrace` function into an array of strings. The argument *buffer* should be a pointer to an array of addresses obtained via the `backtrace` function, and *size* is the number of entries in that array (the return value of `backtrace`).
>
> The return value is a pointer to an array of strings, which has *size* entries just like the array *buffer*. Each string contains a printable representation of the corresponding element of *buffer*. It includes the function name (if this can be determined), an offset into the function, and the actual return address (in hexadecimal).
>
> Currently, the function name and offset can only be obtained on systems that use the ELF binary format for programs and libraries. On other systems, only the hexadecimal return address will be present. Also, you may need to pass additional flags to the linker to make the function names available to the program. (For example, on systems using GNU ld, you must pass `-rdynamic`.)

The return value of `backtrace_symbols` is a pointer obtained via the `malloc` function, and it is the responsibility of the caller to `free` that pointer. Note that only the return value need be freed, not the individual strings.

The return value is `NULL` if sufficient memory for the strings cannot be obtained.

void backtrace_symbols_fd (*void *const *buffer*, *int size*, *int fd*)   [Function]
Preliminary: | MT-Safe | AS-Safe | AC-Unsafe lock | See Section 1.2.2.1 [POSIX Safety Concepts], page 2.

The `backtrace_symbols_fd` function performs the same translation as the function `backtrace_symbols` function. Instead of returning the strings to the caller, it writes the strings to the file descriptor *fd*, one per line. It does not use the `malloc` function, and can therefore be used in situations where that function might fail.

The following program illustrates the use of these functions. Note that the array to contain the return addresses returned by `backtrace` is allocated on the stack. Therefore code like this can be used in situations where the memory handling via `malloc` does not work anymore (in which case the `backtrace_symbols` has to be replaced by a `backtrace_symbols_fd` call as well). The number of return addresses is normally not very large. Even complicated programs rather seldom have a nesting level of more than, say, 50 and with 200 possible entries probably all programs should be covered.

```
#include <execinfo.h>
#include <stdio.h>
#include <stdlib.h>

/* Obtain a backtrace and print it to stdout. */
void
print_trace (void)
{
  void *array[10];
  size_t size;
  char **strings;
  size_t i;

  size = backtrace (array, 10);
  strings = backtrace_symbols (array, size);

  printf ("Obtained %zd stack frames.\n", size);

  for (i = 0; i < size; i++)
     printf ("%s\n", strings[i]);

  free (strings);
}

/* A dummy function to make the backtrace more interesting. */
void
dummy_function (void)
{
  print_trace ();
}

int
main (void)
```

```
{
  dummy_function ();
  return 0;
}
```

35 POSIX Threads

This chapter describes the GNU C Library POSIX Threads implementation.

35.1 Thread-specific Data

The GNU C Library implements functions to allow users to create and manage data specific to a thread. Such data may be destroyed at thread exit, if a destructor is provided. The following functions are defined:

int pthread_key_create (*pthread_key_t *key*, *void*   [Function]
     (**destructor*)(*void**))
> Preliminary: | MT-Safe | AS-Safe | AC-Safe | See Section 1.2.2.1 [POSIX Safety Concepts], page 2.
>
> Create a thread-specific data key for the calling thread, referenced by *key*.
>
> Objects declared with the C++11 `thread_local` keyword are destroyed before thread-specific data, so they should not be used in thread-specific data destructors or even as members of the thread-specific data, since the latter is passed as an argument to the destructor function.

int pthread_key_delete (*pthread_key_t key*)   [Function]
> Preliminary: | MT-Safe | AS-Safe | AC-Safe | See Section 1.2.2.1 [POSIX Safety Concepts], page 2.
>
> Destroy the thread-specific data *key* in the calling thread. The destructor for the thread-specific data is not called during destruction, nor is it called during thread exit.

void *pthread_getspecific (*pthread_key_t key*)   [Function]
> Preliminary: | MT-Safe | AS-Safe | AC-Safe | See Section 1.2.2.1 [POSIX Safety Concepts], page 2.
>
> Return the thread-specific data associated with *key* in the calling thread.

int pthread_setspecific (*pthread_key_t key*, *const void *value*)   [Function]
> Preliminary: | MT-Safe | AS-Unsafe corrupt heap | AC-Unsafe corrupt mem | See Section 1.2.2.1 [POSIX Safety Concepts], page 2.
>
> Associate the thread-specific *value* with *key* in the calling thread.

35.2 Non-POSIX Extensions

In addition to implementing the POSIX API for threads, the GNU C Library provides additional functions and interfaces to provide functionality not specified in the standard.

35.2.1 Setting Process-wide defaults for thread attributes

The GNU C Library provides non-standard API functions to set and get the default attributes used in the creation of threads in a process.

int **pthread_getattr_default_np** (*pthread_attr_t* *attr*)   [Function]
> Preliminary: | MT-Safe | AS-Unsafe lock | AC-Unsafe lock | See Section 1.2.2.1 [POSIX Safety Concepts], page 2.
>
> Get the default attribute values and set *attr* to match. This function returns 0 on success and a non-zero error code on failure.

int **pthread_setattr_default_np** (*pthread_attr_t* *attr*)   [Function]
> Preliminary: | MT-Safe | AS-Unsafe heap lock | AC-Unsafe lock mem | See Section 1.2.2.1 [POSIX Safety Concepts], page 2.
>
> Set the default attribute values to match the values in *attr*. The function returns 0 on success and a non-zero error code on failure. The following error codes are defined for this function:
>
> EINVAL   At least one of the values in *attr* does not qualify as valid for the attributes or the stack address is set in the attribute.
>
> ENOMEM   The system does not have sufficient memory.

36 Internal probes

In order to aid in debugging and monitoring internal behavior, the GNU C Library exposes nearly-zero-overhead SystemTap probes marked with the `libc` provider.

These probes are not part of the GNU C Library stable ABI, and they are subject to change or removal across releases. Our only promise with regard to them is that, if we find a need to remove or modify the arguments of a probe, the modified probe will have a different name, so that program monitors relying on the old probe will not get unexpected arguments.

36.1 Memory Allocation Probes

These probes are designed to signal relatively unusual situations within the virtual memory subsystem of the GNU C Library.

`memory_sbrk_more` (*void *$arg1*, *size_t $arg2*)   [Probe]
> This probe is triggered after the main arena is extended by calling `sbrk`. Argument *$arg1* is the additional size requested to `sbrk`, and *$arg2* is the pointer that marks the end of the `sbrk` area, returned in response to the request.

`memory_sbrk_less` (*void *$arg1*, *size_t $arg2*)   [Probe]
> This probe is triggered after the size of the main arena is decreased by calling `sbrk`. Argument *$arg1* is the size released by `sbrk` (the positive value, rather than the negative value passed to `sbrk`), and *$arg2* is the pointer that marks the end of the `sbrk` area, returned in response to the request.

`memory_heap_new` (*void *$arg1*, *size_t $arg2*)   [Probe]
> This probe is triggered after a new heap is `mmaped`. Argument *$arg1* is a pointer to the base of the memory area, where the `heap_info` data structure is held, and *$arg2* is the size of the heap.

`memory_heap_free` (*void *$arg1*, *size_t $arg2*)   [Probe]
> This probe is triggered *before* (unlike the other sbrk and heap probes) a heap is completely removed via `munmap`. Argument *$arg1* is a pointer to the heap, and *$arg2* is the size of the heap.

`memory_heap_more` (*void *$arg1*, *size_t $arg2*)   [Probe]
> This probe is triggered after a trailing portion of an `mmaped` heap is extended. Argument *$arg1* is a pointer to the heap, and *$arg2* is the new size of the heap.

`memory_heap_less` (*void *$arg1*, *size_t $arg2*)   [Probe]
> This probe is triggered after a trailing portion of an `mmaped` heap is released. Argument *$arg1* is a pointer to the heap, and *$arg2* is the new size of the heap.

`memory_malloc_retry` (*size_t $arg1*)   [Probe]
`memory_realloc_retry` (*size_t $arg1*, *void *$arg2*)   [Probe]
`memory_memalign_retry` (*size_t $arg1*, *size_t $arg2*)   [Probe]
`memory_calloc_retry` (*size_t $arg1*)   [Probe]
> These probes are triggered when the corresponding functions fail to obtain the requested amount of memory from the arena in use, before they call `arena_get_retry`

to select an alternate arena in which to retry the allocation. Argument $arg1 is the amount of memory requested by the user; in the `calloc` case, that is the total size computed from both function arguments. In the `realloc` case, $arg2 is the pointer to the memory area being resized. In the `memalign` case, $arg2 is the alignment to be used for the request, which may be stricter than the value passed to the `memalign` function. A `memalign` probe is also used by functions `posix_memalign, valloc` and `pvalloc`.

Note that the argument order does *not* match that of the corresponding two-argument functions, so that in all of these probes the user-requested allocation size is in $arg1.

memory_arena_retry (*size_t* $arg1, *void *$arg2*)   [Probe]
> This probe is triggered within `arena_get_retry` (the function called to select the alternate arena in which to retry an allocation that failed on the first attempt), before the selection of an alternate arena. This probe is redundant, but much easier to use when it's not important to determine which of the various memory allocation functions is failing to allocate on the first try. Argument $arg1 is the same as in the function-specific probes, except for extra room for padding introduced by functions that have to ensure stricter alignment. Argument $arg2 is the arena in which allocation failed.

memory_arena_new (*void *$arg1*, *size_t* $arg2)   [Probe]
> This probe is triggered when `malloc` allocates and initializes an additional arena (not the main arena), but before the arena is assigned to the running thread or inserted into the internal linked list of arenas. The arena's `malloc_state` internal data structure is located at $arg1, within a newly-allocated heap big enough to hold at least $arg2 bytes.

memory_arena_reuse (*void *$arg1*, *void *$arg2*)   [Probe]
> This probe is triggered when `malloc` has just selected an existing arena to reuse, and (temporarily) reserved it for exclusive use. Argument $arg1 is a pointer to the newly-selected arena, and $arg2 is a pointer to the arena previously used by that thread.
>
> This occurs within `reused_arena`, right after the mutex mentioned in probe `memory_arena_reuse_wait` is acquired; argument $arg1 will point to the same arena. In this configuration, this will usually only occur once per thread. The exception is when a thread first selected the main arena, but a subsequent allocation from it fails: then, and only then, may we switch to another arena to retry that allocation, and for further allocations within that thread.

memory_arena_reuse_wait (*void *$arg1*, *void *$arg2*, *void *$arg3*)   [Probe]
> This probe is triggered when `malloc` is about to wait for an arena to become available for reuse. Argument $arg1 holds a pointer to the mutex the thread is going to wait on, $arg2 is a pointer to a newly-chosen arena to be reused, and $arg3 is a pointer to the arena previously used by that thread.
>
> This occurs within `reused_arena`, when a thread first tries to allocate memory or needs a retry after a failure to allocate from the main arena, there isn't any free arena, the maximum number of arenas has been reached, and an existing arena was chosen for reuse, but its mutex could not be immediately acquired. The mutex in $arg1 is the mutex of the selected arena.

memory_arena_reuse_free_list (*void *$arg1*)   [Probe]

> This probe is triggered when `malloc` has chosen an arena that is in the free list for use by a thread, within the `get_free_list` function. The argument *$arg1* holds a pointer to the selected arena.

memory_mallopt (*int $arg1, int $arg2*)   [Probe]

> This probe is triggered when function `mallopt` is called to change `malloc` internal configuration parameters, before any change to the parameters is made. The arguments *$arg1* and *$arg2* are the ones passed to the `mallopt` function.

memory_mallopt_mxfast (*int $arg1, int $arg2*)   [Probe]

> This probe is triggered shortly after the `memory_mallopt` probe, when the parameter to be changed is `M_MXFAST`, and the requested value is in an acceptable range. Argument *$arg1* is the requested value, and *$arg2* is the previous value of this `malloc` parameter.

memory_mallopt_trim_threshold (*int $arg1, int $arg2, int $arg3*)   [Probe]

> This probe is triggered shortly after the `memory_mallopt` probe, when the parameter to be changed is `M_TRIM_THRESHOLD`. Argument *$arg1* is the requested value, *$arg2* is the previous value of this `malloc` parameter, and *$arg3* is nonzero if dynamic threshold adjustment was already disabled.

memory_mallopt_top_pad (*int $arg1, int $arg2, int $arg3*)   [Probe]

> This probe is triggered shortly after the `memory_mallopt` probe, when the parameter to be changed is `M_TOP_PAD`. Argument *$arg1* is the requested value, *$arg2* is the previous value of this `malloc` parameter, and *$arg3* is nonzero if dynamic threshold adjustment was already disabled.

memory_mallopt_mmap_threshold (*int $arg1, int $arg2, int $arg3*)   [Probe]

> This probe is triggered shortly after the `memory_mallopt` probe, when the parameter to be changed is `M_MMAP_THRESHOLD`, and the requested value is in an acceptable range. Argument *$arg1* is the requested value, *$arg2* is the previous value of this `malloc` parameter, and *$arg3* is nonzero if dynamic threshold adjustment was already disabled.

memory_mallopt_mmap_max (*int $arg1, int $arg2, int $arg3*)   [Probe]

> This probe is triggered shortly after the `memory_mallopt` probe, when the parameter to be changed is `M_MMAP_MAX`. Argument *$arg1* is the requested value, *$arg2* is the previous value of this `malloc` parameter, and *$arg3* is nonzero if dynamic threshold adjustment was already disabled.

memory_mallopt_check_action (*int $arg1, int $arg2*)   [Probe]

> This probe is triggered shortly after the `memory_mallopt` probe, when the parameter to be changed is `M_CHECK_ACTION`. Argument *$arg1* is the requested value, and *$arg2* is the previous value of this `malloc` parameter.

memory_mallopt_perturb (*int $arg1, int $arg2*)   [Probe]

> This probe is triggered shortly after the `memory_mallopt` probe, when the parameter to be changed is `M_PERTURB`. Argument *$arg1* is the requested value, and *$arg2* is the previous value of this `malloc` parameter.

`memory_mallopt_arena_test` (*int $arg1, int $arg2*)   [Probe]
> This probe is triggered shortly after the `memory_mallopt` probe, when the parameter to be changed is `M_ARENA_TEST`, and the requested value is in an acceptable range. Argument *$arg1* is the requested value, and *$arg2* is the previous value of this `malloc` parameter.

`memory_mallopt_arena_max` (*int $arg1, int $arg2*)   [Probe]
> This probe is triggered shortly after the `memory_mallopt` probe, when the parameter to be changed is `M_ARENA_MAX`, and the requested value is in an acceptable range. Argument *$arg1* is the requested value, and *$arg2* is the previous value of this `malloc` parameter.

`memory_mallopt_free_dyn_thresholds` (*int $arg1, int $arg2*)   [Probe]
> This probe is triggered when function `free` decides to adjust the dynamic brk/mmap thresholds. Argument *$arg1* and *$arg2* are the adjusted mmap and trim thresholds, respectively.

`memory_tunable_tcache_max_bytes` (*int $arg1, int $arg2*)   [Probe]
> This probe is triggered when the `glibc.malloc.tcache_max` tunable is set. Argument *$arg1* is the requested value, and *$arg2* is the previous value of this tunable.

`memory_tunable_tcache_count` (*int $arg1, int $arg2*)   [Probe]
> This probe is triggered when the `glibc.malloc.tcache_count` tunable is set. Argument *$arg1* is the requested value, and *$arg2* is the previous value of this tunable.

`memory_tunable_tcache_unsorted_limit` (*int $arg1, int $arg2*)   [Probe]
> This probe is triggered when the `glibc.malloc.tcache_unsorted_limit` tunable is set. Argument *$arg1* is the requested value, and *$arg2* is the previous value of this tunable.

36.2 Mathematical Function Probes

Some mathematical functions fall back to multiple precision arithmetic for some inputs to get last bit precision for their return values. This multiple precision fallback is much slower than the default algorithms and may have a significant impact on application performance. The systemtap probe markers described in this section may help you determine if your application calls mathematical functions with inputs that may result in multiple-precision arithmetic.

Unless explicitly mentioned otherwise, a precision of 1 implies 24 bits of precision in the mantissa of the multiple precision number. Hence, a precision level of 32 implies 768 bits of precision in the mantissa.

`slowexp_p6` (*double $arg1, double $arg2*)   [Probe]
> This probe is triggered when the `exp` function is called with an input that results in multiple precision computation with precision 6. Argument *$arg1* is the input value and *$arg2* is the computed output.

`slowexp_p32` (*double $arg1, double $arg2*)   [Probe]
> This probe is triggered when the `exp` function is called with an input that results in multiple precision computation with precision 32. Argument *$arg1* is the input value and *$arg2* is the computed output.

slowpow_p10 (*double $arg1, double $arg2, double $arg3, double*   [Probe]
        $arg4)

> This probe is triggered when the `pow` function is called with inputs that result in multiple precision computation with precision 10. Arguments $arg1 and $arg2 are the input values, $arg3 is the value computed in the fast phase of the algorithm and $arg4 is the final accurate value.

slowpow_p32 (*double $arg1, double $arg2, double $arg3, double*   [Probe]
        $arg4)

> This probe is triggered when the `pow` function is called with an input that results in multiple precision computation with precision 32. Arguments $arg1 and $arg2 are the input values, $arg3 is the value computed in the fast phase of the algorithm and $arg4 is the final accurate value.

slowlog (*int $arg1, double $arg2, double $arg3*)   [Probe]

> This probe is triggered when the `log` function is called with an input that results in multiple precision computation. Argument $arg1 is the precision with which the computation succeeded. Argument $arg2 is the input and $arg3 is the computed output.

slowlog_inexact (*int $arg1, double $arg2, double $arg3*)   [Probe]

> This probe is triggered when the `log` function is called with an input that results in multiple precision computation and none of the multiple precision computations result in an accurate result. Argument $arg1 is the maximum precision with which computations were performed. Argument $arg2 is the input and $arg3 is the computed output.

slowatan2 (*int $arg1, double $arg2, double $arg3, double $arg4*)   [Probe]

> This probe is triggered when the `atan2` function is called with an input that results in multiple precision computation. Argument $arg1 is the precision with which computation succeeded. Arguments $arg2 and $arg3 are inputs to the `atan2` function and $arg4 is the computed result.

slowatan2_inexact (*int $arg1, double $arg2, double $arg3, double*   [Probe]
        $arg4)

> This probe is triggered when the `atan` function is called with an input that results in multiple precision computation and none of the multiple precision computations result in an accurate result. Argument $arg1 is the maximum precision with which computations were performed. Arguments $arg2 and $arg3 are inputs to the `atan2` function and $arg4 is the computed result.

slowatan (*int $arg1, double $arg2, double $arg3*)   [Probe]

> This probe is triggered when the `atan` function is called with an input that results in multiple precision computation. Argument $arg1 is the precision with which computation succeeded. Argument $arg2 is the input to the `atan` function and $arg3 is the computed result.

slowatan_inexact (*int $arg1, double $arg2, double $arg3*)   [Probe]

> This probe is triggered when the `atan` function is called with an input that results in multiple precision computation and none of the multiple precision computations

result in an accurate result. Argument $arg1$ is the maximum precision with which computations were performed. Argument $arg2$ is the input to the `atan` function and $arg3$ is the computed result.

slowtan (*double $arg1$, double $arg2$*)   [Probe]

This probe is triggered when the `tan` function is called with an input that results in multiple precision computation with precision 32. Argument $arg1$ is the input to the function and $arg2$ is the computed result.

slowasin (*double $arg1$, double $arg2$*)   [Probe]

This probe is triggered when the `asin` function is called with an input that results in multiple precision computation with precision 32. Argument $arg1$ is the input to the function and $arg2$ is the computed result.

slowacos (*double $arg1$, double $arg2$*)   [Probe]

This probe is triggered when the `acos` function is called with an input that results in multiple precision computation with precision 32. Argument $arg1$ is the input to the function and $arg2$ is the computed result.

slowsin (*double $arg1$, double $arg2$*)   [Probe]

This probe is triggered when the `sin` function is called with an input that results in multiple precision computation with precision 32. Argument $arg1$ is the input to the function and $arg2$ is the computed result.

slowcos (*double $arg1$, double $arg2$*)   [Probe]

This probe is triggered when the `cos` function is called with an input that results in multiple precision computation with precision 32. Argument $arg1$ is the input to the function and $arg2$ is the computed result.

slowsin_dx (*double $arg1$, double $arg2$, double $arg3$*)   [Probe]

This probe is triggered when the `sin` function is called with an input that results in multiple precision computation with precision 32. Argument $arg1$ is the input to the function, $arg2$ is the error bound of $arg1$ and $arg3$ is the computed result.

slowcos_dx (*double $arg1$, double $arg2$, double $arg3$*)   [Probe]

This probe is triggered when the `cos` function is called with an input that results in multiple precision computation with precision 32. Argument $arg1$ is the input to the function, $arg2$ is the error bound of $arg1$ and $arg3$ is the computed result.

36.3 Non-local Goto Probes

These probes are used to signal calls to `setjmp`, `sigsetjmp`, `longjmp` or `siglongjmp`.

setjmp (*void *$arg1$, int $arg2$, void *$arg3$*)   [Probe]

This probe is triggered whenever `setjmp` or `sigsetjmp` is called. Argument $arg1$ is a pointer to the `jmp_buf` passed as the first argument of `setjmp` or `sigsetjmp`, $arg2$ is the second argument of `sigsetjmp` or zero if this is a call to `setjmp` and $arg3$ is a pointer to the return address that will be stored in the `jmp_buf`.

longjmp (*void *$arg1, int $arg2, void *$arg3*)   [Probe]

    This probe is triggered whenever `longjmp` or `siglongjmp` is called. Argument *$arg1* is a pointer to the `jmp_buf` passed as the first argument of `longjmp` or `siglongjmp`, *$arg2* is the return value passed as the second argument of `longjmp` or `siglongjmp` and *$arg3* is a pointer to the return address `longjmp` or `siglongjmp` will return to.

    The `longjmp` probe is triggered at a point where the registers have not yet been restored to the values in the `jmp_buf` and unwinding will show a call stack including the caller of `longjmp` or `siglongjmp`.

longjmp_target (*void *$arg1, int $arg2, void *$arg3*)   [Probe]

    This probe is triggered under the same conditions and with the same arguments as the `longjmp` probe.

    The `longjmp_target` probe is triggered at a point where the registers have been restored to the values in the `jmp_buf` and unwinding will show a call stack including the caller of `setjmp` or `sigsetjmp`.

37 Tunables

Tunables are a feature in the GNU C Library that allows application authors and distribution maintainers to alter the runtime library behavior to match their workload. These are implemented as a set of switches that may be modified in different ways. The current default method to do this is via the `GLIBC_TUNABLES` environment variable by setting it to a string of colon-separated *name*=*value* pairs. For example, the following example enables malloc checking and sets the malloc trim threshold to 128 bytes:

```
GLIBC_TUNABLES=glibc.malloc.trim_threshold=128:glibc.malloc.check=3
export GLIBC_TUNABLES
```

Tunables are not part of the GNU C Library stable ABI, and they are subject to change or removal across releases. Additionally, the method to modify tunable values may change between releases and across distributions. It is possible to implement multiple 'frontends' for the tunables allowing distributions to choose their preferred method at build time.

Finally, the set of tunables available may vary between distributions as the tunables feature allows distributions to add their own tunables under their own namespace.

37.1 Tunable names

A tunable name is split into three components, a top namespace, a tunable namespace and the tunable name. The top namespace for tunables implemented in the GNU C Library is `glibc`. Distributions that choose to add custom tunables in their maintained versions of the GNU C Library may choose to do so under their own top namespace.

The tunable namespace is a logical grouping of tunables in a single module. This currently holds no special significance, although that may change in the future.

The tunable name is the actual name of the tunable. It is possible that different tunable namespaces may have tunables within them that have the same name, likewise for top namespaces. Hence, we only support identification of tunables by their full name, i.e. with the top namespace, tunable namespace and tunable name, separated by periods.

37.2 Memory Allocation Tunables

`glibc.malloc`   [Tunable namespace]

> Memory allocation behavior can be modified by setting any of the following tunables in the `malloc` namespace:

`glibc.malloc.check`   [Tunable]

> This tunable supersedes the `MALLOC_CHECK_` environment variable and is identical in features.
>
> Setting this tunable enables a special (less efficient) memory allocator for the malloc family of functions that is designed to be tolerant against simple errors such as double calls of free with the same argument, or overruns of a single byte (off-by-one bugs). Not all such errors can be protected against, however, and memory leaks can result. The following list describes the values that this tunable can take and the effect they have on malloc functionality:
>
> - 0 Ignore all errors. The default allocator continues to be in use, but all errors are silently ignored.

- 1 Report errors. The alternate allocator is selected and heap corruption, if detected, is reported as diagnostic messages to `stderr` and the program continues execution.

- 2 Abort on errors. The alternate allocator is selected and if heap corruption is detected, the program is ended immediately by calling `abort`.

- 3 Fully enabled. The alternate allocator is selected and is fully functional. That is, if heap corruption is detected, a verbose diagnostic message is printed to `stderr` and the program is ended by calling `abort`.

Like `MALLOC_CHECK_`, `glibc.malloc.check` has a problem in that it diverges from normal program behavior by writing to `stderr`, which could by exploited in SUID and SGID binaries. Therefore, `glibc.malloc.check` is disabled by default for SUID and SGID binaries. This can be enabled again by the system administrator by adding a file `/etc/suid-debug`; the content of the file could be anything or even empty.

`glibc.malloc.top_pad`   [Tunable]

This tunable supersedes the `MALLOC_TOP_PAD_` environment variable and is identical in features.

This tunable determines the amount of extra memory in bytes to obtain from the system when any of the arenas need to be extended. It also specifies the number of bytes to retain when shrinking any of the arenas. This provides the necessary hysteresis in heap size such that excessive amounts of system calls can be avoided.

The default value of this tunable is '0'.

`glibc.malloc.perturb`   [Tunable]

This tunable supersedes the `MALLOC_PERTURB_` environment variable and is identical in features.

If set to a non-zero value, memory blocks are initialized with values depending on some low order bits of this tunable when they are allocated (except when allocated by calloc) and freed. This can be used to debug the use of uninitialized or freed heap memory. Note that this option does not guarantee that the freed block will have any specific values. It only guarantees that the content the block had before it was freed will be overwritten.

The default value of this tunable is '0'.

`glibc.malloc.mmap_threshold`   [Tunable]

This tunable supersedes the `MALLOC_MMAP_THRESHOLD_` environment variable and is identical in features.

When this tunable is set, all chunks larger than this value in bytes are allocated outside the normal heap, using the `mmap` system call. This way it is guaranteed that the memory for these chunks can be returned to the system on `free`. Note that requests smaller than this threshold might still be allocated via `mmap`.

If this tunable is not set, the default value is set to '131072' bytes and the threshold is adjusted dynamically to suit the allocation patterns of the program. If the tunable is set, the dynamic adjustment is disabled and the value is set as static.

glibc.malloc.trim_threshold   [Tunable]

> This tunable supersedes the MALLOC_TRIM_THRESHOLD_ environment variable and is identical in features.
>
> The value of this tunable is the minimum size (in bytes) of the top-most, releasable chunk in an arena that will trigger a system call in order to return memory to the system from that arena.
>
> If this tunable is not set, the default value is set as 128 KB and the threshold is adjusted dynamically to suit the allocation patterns of the program. If the tunable is set, the dynamic adjustment is disabled and the value is set as static.

glibc.malloc.mmap_max   [Tunable]

> This tunable supersedes the MALLOC_MMAP_MAX_ environment variable and is identical in features.
>
> The value of this tunable is maximum number of chunks to allocate with mmap. Setting this to zero disables all use of mmap.
>
> The default value of this tunable is '65536'.

glibc.malloc.arena_test   [Tunable]

> This tunable supersedes the MALLOC_ARENA_TEST environment variable and is identical in features.
>
> The glibc.malloc.arena_test tunable specifies the number of arenas that can be created before the test on the limit to the number of arenas is conducted. The value is ignored if glibc.malloc.arena_max is set.
>
> The default value of this tunable is 2 for 32-bit systems and 8 for 64-bit systems.

glibc.malloc.arena_max   [Tunable]

> This tunable supersedes the MALLOC_ARENA_MAX environment variable and is identical in features.
>
> This tunable sets the number of arenas to use in a process regardless of the number of cores in the system.
>
> The default value of this tunable is 0, meaning that the limit on the number of arenas is determined by the number of CPU cores online. For 32-bit systems the limit is twice the number of cores online and on 64-bit systems, it is 8 times the number of cores online.

glibc.malloc.tcache_max   [Tunable]

> The maximum size of a request (in bytes) which may be met via the per-thread cache. The default (and maximum) value is 1032 bytes on 64-bit systems and 516 bytes on 32-bit systems.

glibc.malloc.tcache_count   [Tunable]

> The maximum number of chunks of each size to cache. The default is 7. There is no upper limit, other than available system memory. If set to zero, the per-thread cache is effectively disabled.
>
> The approximate maximum overhead of the per-thread cache is thus equal to the number of bins times the chunk count in each bin times the size of each chunk. With defaults, the approximate maximum overhead of the per-thread cache is approximately 236 KB on 64-bit systems and 118 KB on 32-bit systems.

`glibc.malloc.tcache_unsorted_limit`   [Tunable]

> When the user requests memory and the request cannot be met via the per-thread cache, the arenas are used to meet the request. At this time, additional chunks will be moved from existing arena lists to pre-fill the corresponding cache. While copies from the fastbins, smallbins, and regular bins are bounded and predictable due to the bin sizes, copies from the unsorted bin are not bounded, and incur additional time penalties as they need to be sorted as they're scanned. To make scanning the unsorted list more predictable and bounded, the user may set this tunable to limit the number of chunks that are scanned from the unsorted list while searching for chunks to pre-fill the per-thread cache with. The default, or when set to zero, is no limit.

37.3 Hardware Capability Tunables

`glibc.tune`   [Tunable namespace]

> Behavior of the GNU C Library can be tuned to assume specific hardware capabilities by setting the following tunables in the **tune** namespace:

`glibc.tune.hwcap_mask`   [Tunable]

> This tunable supersedes the `LD_HWCAP_MASK` environment variable and is identical in features.

> The `AT_HWCAP` key in the Auxilliary Vector specifies instruction set extensions available in the processor at runtime for some architectures. The `glibc.tune.hwcap_mask` tunable allows the user to mask out those capabilities at runtime, thus disabling use of those extensions.

`glibc.tune.hwcaps`   [Tunable]

> The `glibc.tune.hwcaps=-xxx,yyy,-zzz...` tunable allows the user to enable CPU/ARCH feature `yyy`, disable CPU/ARCH feature `xxx` and `zzz` where the feature name is case-sensitive and has to match the ones in `sysdeps/x86/cpu-features.h`.

> This tunable is specific to i386 and x86-64.

`glibc.tune.cpu`   [Tunable]

> The `glibc.tune.cpu=xxx` tunable allows the user to tell the GNU C Library to assume that the CPU is `xxx` where `xxx` may have one of these values: `generic`, `thunderxt88`.

> This tunable is specific to aarch64.

`glibc.tune.x86_data_cache_size`   [Tunable]

> The `glibc.tune.x86_data_cache_size` tunable allows the user to set data cache size in bytes for use in memory and string routines.

> This tunable is specific to i386 and x86-64.

`glibc.tune.x86_shared_cache_size`   [Tunable]

> The `glibc.tune.x86_shared_cache_size` tunable allows the user to set shared cache size in bytes for use in memory and string routines.

`glibc.tune.x86_non_temporal_threshold`   [Tunable]

The `glibc.tune.x86_non_temporal_threshold` tunable allows the user to set threshold in bytes for non temporal store.

This tunable is specific to i386 and x86-64.

Appendix A C Language Facilities in the Library

Some of the facilities implemented by the C library really should be thought of as parts of the C language itself. These facilities ought to be documented in the C Language Manual, not in the library manual; but since we don't have the language manual yet, and documentation for these features has been written, we are publishing it here.

A.1 Explicitly Checking Internal Consistency

When you're writing a program, it's often a good idea to put in checks at strategic places for "impossible" errors or violations of basic assumptions. These kinds of checks are helpful in debugging problems with the interfaces between different parts of the program, for example.

The `assert` macro, defined in the header file `assert.h`, provides a convenient way to abort the program while printing a message about where in the program the error was detected.

Once you think your program is debugged, you can disable the error checks performed by the `assert` macro by recompiling with the macro `NDEBUG` defined. This means you don't actually have to change the program source code to disable these checks.

But disabling these consistency checks is undesirable unless they make the program significantly slower. All else being equal, more error checking is good no matter who is running the program. A wise user would rather have a program crash, visibly, than have it return nonsense without indicating anything might be wrong.

`void assert (int expression)`   [Macro]

> Preliminary: | MT-Safe | AS-Unsafe heap corrupt | AC-Unsafe mem lock corrupt | See Section 1.2.2.1 [POSIX Safety Concepts], page 2.
>
> Verify the programmer's belief that *expression* is nonzero at this point in the program.
>
> If `NDEBUG` is not defined, `assert` tests the value of *expression*. If it is false (zero), `assert` aborts the program (see Section 25.7.4 [Aborting a Program], page 771) after printing a message of the form:
>
>   file:linenum: function: Assertion `expression' failed.
>
> on the standard error stream `stderr` (see Section 12.2 [Standard Streams], page 257). The filename and line number are taken from the C preprocessor macros `__FILE__` and `__LINE__` and specify where the call to `assert` was made. When using the GNU C compiler, the name of the function which calls `assert` is taken from the built-in variable `__PRETTY_FUNCTION__`; with older compilers, the function name and following colon are omitted.
>
> If the preprocessor macro `NDEBUG` is defined before `assert.h` is included, the `assert` macro is defined to do absolutely nothing.
>
> **Warning:** Even the argument expression *expression* is not evaluated if `NDEBUG` is in effect. So never use `assert` with arguments that involve side effects. For example, `assert (++i > 0);` is a bad idea, because `i` will not be incremented if `NDEBUG` is defined.

Sometimes the "impossible" condition you want to check for is an error return from an operating system function. Then it is useful to display not only where the program crashes, but also what error was returned. The `assert_perror` macro makes this easy.

void assert_perror (*int errnum*) [Macro]

Preliminary: | MT-Safe | AS-Unsafe heap corrupt | AC-Unsafe mem lock corrupt | See Section 1.2.2.1 [POSIX Safety Concepts], page 2.

Similar to `assert`, but verifies that *errnum* is zero.

If `NDEBUG` is not defined, `assert_perror` tests the value of *errnum*. If it is nonzero, `assert_perror` aborts the program after printing a message of the form:

```
file:linenum: function: error text
```

on the standard error stream. The file name, line number, and function name are as for `assert`. The error text is the result of `strerror (errnum)`. See Section 2.3 [Error Messages], page 35.

Like `assert`, if `NDEBUG` is defined before `assert.h` is included, the `assert_perror` macro does absolutely nothing. It does not evaluate the argument, so *errnum* should not have any side effects. It is best for *errnum* to be just a simple variable reference; often it will be `errno`.

This macro is a GNU extension.

Usage note: The `assert` facility is designed for detecting *internal inconsistency*; it is not suitable for reporting invalid input or improper usage by the *user* of the program.

The information in the diagnostic messages printed by the `assert` and `assert_perror` macro is intended to help you, the programmer, track down the cause of a bug, but is not really useful for telling a user of your program why his or her input was invalid or why a command could not be carried out. What's more, your program should not abort when given invalid input, as `assert` would do—it should exit with nonzero status (see Section 25.7.2 [Exit Status], page 769) after printing its error messages, or perhaps read another command or move on to the next input file.

See Section 2.3 [Error Messages], page 35, for information on printing error messages for problems that *do not* represent bugs in the program.

A.2 Variadic Functions

ISO C defines a syntax for declaring a function to take a variable number or type of arguments. (Such functions are referred to as *varargs functions* or *variadic functions*.) However, the language itself provides no mechanism for such functions to access their non-required arguments; instead, you use the variable arguments macros defined in `stdarg.h`.

This section describes how to declare variadic functions, how to write them, and how to call them properly.

Compatibility Note: Many older C dialects provide a similar, but incompatible, mechanism for defining functions with variable numbers of arguments, using `varargs.h`.

A.2.1 Why Variadic Functions are Used

Ordinary C functions take a fixed number of arguments. When you define a function, you specify the data type for each argument. Every call to the function should supply the expected number of arguments, with types that can be converted to the specified ones. Thus, if the function 'foo' is declared with `int foo (int, char *);` then you must call it with two arguments, a number (any kind will do) and a string pointer.

But some functions perform operations that can meaningfully accept an unlimited number of arguments.

In some cases a function can handle any number of values by operating on all of them as a block. For example, consider a function that allocates a one-dimensional array with `malloc` to hold a specified set of values. This operation makes sense for any number of values, as long as the length of the array corresponds to that number. Without facilities for variable arguments, you would have to define a separate function for each possible array size.

The library function `printf` (see Section 12.12 [Formatted Output], page 279) is an example of another class of function where variable arguments are useful. This function prints its arguments (which can vary in type as well as number) under the control of a format template string.

These are good reasons to define a *variadic* function which can handle as many arguments as the caller chooses to pass.

Some functions such as `open` take a fixed set of arguments, but occasionally ignore the last few. Strict adherence to ISO C requires these functions to be defined as variadic; in practice, however, the GNU C compiler and most other C compilers let you define such a function to take a fixed set of arguments—the most it can ever use—and then only *declare* the function as variadic (or not declare its arguments at all!).

A.2.2 How Variadic Functions are Defined and Used

Defining and using a variadic function involves three steps:

- *Define* the function as variadic, using an ellipsis ('...') in the argument list, and using special macros to access the variable arguments. See Section A.2.2.2 [Receiving the Argument Values], page 912.

- *Declare* the function as variadic, using a prototype with an ellipsis ('...'), in all the files which call it. See Section A.2.2.1 [Syntax for Variable Arguments], page 911.

- *Call* the function by writing the fixed arguments followed by the additional variable arguments. See Section A.2.2.4 [Calling Variadic Functions], page 913.

A.2.2.1 Syntax for Variable Arguments

A function that accepts a variable number of arguments must be declared with a prototype that says so. You write the fixed arguments as usual, and then tack on '...' to indicate the possibility of additional arguments. The syntax of ISO C requires at least one fixed argument before the '...'. For example,

```
int
func (const char *a, int b, ...)
{
  . . .
}
```

defines a function `func` which returns an `int` and takes two required arguments, a `const char *` and an `int`. These are followed by any number of anonymous arguments.

Portability note: For some C compilers, the last required argument must not be declared `register` in the function definition. Furthermore, this argument's type must be *self-promoting*: that is, the default promotions must not change its type. This rules out array and function types, as well as `float`, `char` (whether signed or not) and `short int` (whether signed or not). This is actually an ISO C requirement.

A.2.2.2 Receiving the Argument Values

Ordinary fixed arguments have individual names, and you can use these names to access their values. But optional arguments have no names—nothing but '`...`'. How can you access them?

The only way to access them is sequentially, in the order they were written, and you must use special macros from `stdarg.h` in the following three step process:

1. You initialize an argument pointer variable of type `va_list` using `va_start`. The argument pointer when initialized points to the first optional argument.

2. You access the optional arguments by successive calls to `va_arg`. The first call to `va_arg` gives you the first optional argument, the next call gives you the second, and so on.

   You can stop at any time if you wish to ignore any remaining optional arguments. It is perfectly all right for a function to access fewer arguments than were supplied in the call, but you will get garbage values if you try to access too many arguments.

3. You indicate that you are finished with the argument pointer variable by calling `va_end`.

   (In practice, with most C compilers, calling `va_end` does nothing. This is always true in the GNU C compiler. But you might as well call `va_end` just in case your program is someday compiled with a peculiar compiler.)

See Section A.2.2.5 [Argument Access Macros], page 913, for the full definitions of `va_start`, `va_arg` and `va_end`.

Steps 1 and 3 must be performed in the function that accepts the optional arguments. However, you can pass the `va_list` variable as an argument to another function and perform all or part of step 2 there.

You can perform the entire sequence of three steps multiple times within a single function invocation. If you want to ignore the optional arguments, you can do these steps zero times.

You can have more than one argument pointer variable if you like. You can initialize each variable with `va_start` when you wish, and then you can fetch arguments with each argument pointer as you wish. Each argument pointer variable will sequence through the same set of argument values, but at its own pace.

Portability note: With some compilers, once you pass an argument pointer value to a subroutine, you must not keep using the same argument pointer value after that subroutine returns. For full portability, you should just pass it to `va_end`. This is actually an ISO C requirement, but most ANSI C compilers work happily regardless.

A.2.2.3 How Many Arguments Were Supplied

There is no general way for a function to determine the number and type of the optional arguments it was called with. So whoever designs the function typically designs a convention for the caller to specify the number and type of arguments. It is up to you to define an appropriate calling convention for each variadic function, and write all calls accordingly.

One kind of calling convention is to pass the number of optional arguments as one of the fixed arguments. This convention works provided all of the optional arguments are of the same type.

A similar alternative is to have one of the required arguments be a bit mask, with a bit for each possible purpose for which an optional argument might be supplied. You would test the bits in a predefined sequence; if the bit is set, fetch the value of the next argument, otherwise use a default value.

A required argument can be used as a pattern to specify both the number and types of the optional arguments. The format string argument to `printf` is one example of this (see Section 12.12.7 [Formatted Output Functions], page 287).

Another possibility is to pass an "end marker" value as the last optional argument. For example, for a function that manipulates an arbitrary number of pointer arguments, a null pointer might indicate the end of the argument list. (This assumes that a null pointer isn't otherwise meaningful to the function.) The `execl` function works in just this way; see Section 26.5 [Executing a File], page 776.

A.2.2.4 Calling Variadic Functions

You don't have to do anything special to call a variadic function. Just put the arguments (required arguments, followed by optional ones) inside parentheses, separated by commas, as usual. But you must declare the function with a prototype and know how the argument values are converted.

In principle, functions that are *defined* to be variadic must also be *declared* to be variadic using a function prototype whenever you call them. (See Section A.2.2.1 [Syntax for Variable Arguments], page 911, for how.) This is because some C compilers use a different calling convention to pass the same set of argument values to a function depending on whether that function takes variable arguments or fixed arguments.

In practice, the GNU C compiler always passes a given set of argument types in the same way regardless of whether they are optional or required. So, as long as the argument types are self-promoting, you can safely omit declaring them. Usually it is a good idea to declare the argument types for variadic functions, and indeed for all functions. But there are a few functions which it is extremely convenient not to have to declare as variadic—for example, `open` and `printf`.

Since the prototype doesn't specify types for optional arguments, in a call to a variadic function the *default argument promotions* are performed on the optional argument values. This means the objects of type `char` or `short int` (whether signed or not) are promoted to either `int` or `unsigned int`, as appropriate; and that objects of type `float` are promoted to type `double`. So, if the caller passes a `char` as an optional argument, it is promoted to an `int`, and the function can access it with `va_arg (ap, int)`.

Conversion of the required arguments is controlled by the function prototype in the usual way: the argument expression is converted to the declared argument type as if it were being assigned to a variable of that type.

A.2.2.5 Argument Access Macros

Here are descriptions of the macros used to retrieve variable arguments. These macros are defined in the header file `stdarg.h`.

`va_list`   [Data Type]

      The type `va_list` is used for argument pointer variables.

void va_start (*va_list* **ap**, *last-required*)   [Macro]
>   Preliminary: | MT-Safe | AS-Safe | AC-Safe | See Section 1.2.2.1 [POSIX Safety
>   Concepts], page 2.
>
>   This macro initializes the argument pointer variable *ap* to point to the first of the
>   optional arguments of the current function; *last-required* must be the last required
>   argument to the function.

type **va_arg** (*va_list* **ap**, *type*)   [Macro]
>   Preliminary: | MT-Safe race:ap | AS-Safe | AC-Unsafe corrupt | See Section 1.2.2.1
>   [POSIX Safety Concepts], page 2.
>
>   The **va_arg** macro returns the value of the next optional argument, and modifies the
>   value of *ap* to point to the subsequent argument. Thus, successive uses of **va_arg**
>   return successive optional arguments.
>
>   The type of the value returned by **va_arg** is *type* as specified in the call. *type* must
>   be a self-promoting type (not **char** or **short int** or **float**) that matches the type of
>   the actual argument.

void va_end (*va_list* **ap**)   [Macro]
>   Preliminary: | MT-Safe | AS-Safe | AC-Safe | See Section 1.2.2.1 [POSIX Safety
>   Concepts], page 2.
>
>   This ends the use of *ap*. After a **va_end** call, further **va_arg** calls with the same *ap*
>   may not work. You should invoke **va_end** before returning from the function in which
>   **va_start** was invoked with the same *ap* argument.
>
>   In the GNU C Library, **va_end** does nothing, and you need not ever use it except for
>   reasons of portability.

Sometimes it is necessary to parse the list of parameters more than once or one wants
to remember a certain position in the parameter list. To do this, one will have to make a
copy of the current value of the argument. But **va_list** is an opaque type and one cannot
necessarily assign the value of one variable of type **va_list** to another variable of the same
type.

void va_copy (*va_list* **dest**, *va_list* **src**)   [Macro]
void __va_copy (*va_list* **dest**, *va_list* **src**)   [Macro]
>   Preliminary: | MT-Safe | AS-Safe | AC-Safe | See Section 1.2.2.1 [POSIX Safety
>   Concepts], page 2.
>
>   The **va_copy** macro allows copying of objects of type **va_list** even if this is not
>   an integral type. The argument pointer in *dest* is initialized to point to the same
>   argument as the pointer in *src*.
>
>   This macro was added in ISO C99. When building for strict conformance to ISO
>   C90 ('**gcc -ansi**'), it is not available. The macro **__va_copy** is available as a GNU
>   extension in any standards mode; before GCC 3.0, it was the only macro for this
>   functionality.

If you want to use **va_copy** and be portable to pre-C99 systems, you should always be
prepared for the possibility that this macro will not be available. On architectures where

a simple assignment is invalid, hopefully `va_copy` *will* be available, so one should always write something like this if concerned about pre-C99 portability:

```
{
  va_list ap, save;
  ...
#ifdef va_copy
  va_copy (save, ap);
#else
  save = ap;
#endif
  ...
}
```

A.2.3 Example of a Variadic Function

Here is a complete sample function that accepts a variable number of arguments. The first argument to the function is the count of remaining arguments, which are added up and the result returned. While trivial, this function is sufficient to illustrate how to use the variable arguments facility.

```
#include <stdarg.h>
#include <stdio.h>

int
add_em_up (int count,...)
{
  va_list ap;
  int i, sum;

  va_start (ap, count);          /* Initialize the argument list. */

  sum = 0;
  for (i = 0; i < count; i++)
    sum += va_arg (ap, int);     /* Get the next argument value. */

  va_end (ap);                   /* Clean up. */
  return sum;
}

int
main (void)
{
  /* This call prints 16. */
  printf ("%d\n", add_em_up (3, 5, 5, 6));

  /* This call prints 55. */
  printf ("%d\n", add_em_up (10, 1, 2, 3, 4, 5, 6, 7, 8, 9, 10));

  return 0;
}
```

A.3 Null Pointer Constant

The null pointer constant is guaranteed not to point to any real object. You can assign it to any pointer variable since it has type **void** *. The preferred way to write a null pointer constant is with **NULL**.

void * NULL   [Macro]

This is a null pointer constant.

You can also use 0 or (void *)0 as a null pointer constant, but using NULL is cleaner because it makes the purpose of the constant more evident.

If you use the null pointer constant as a function argument, then for complete portability you should make sure that the function has a prototype declaration. Otherwise, if the target machine has two different pointer representations, the compiler won't know which representation to use for that argument. You can avoid the problem by explicitly casting the constant to the proper pointer type, but we recommend instead adding a prototype for the function you are calling.

A.4 Important Data Types

The result of subtracting two pointers in C is always an integer, but the precise data type varies from C compiler to C compiler. Likewise, the data type of the result of `sizeof` also varies between compilers. ISO C defines standard aliases for these two types, so you can refer to them in a portable fashion. They are defined in the header file `stddef.h`.

ptrdiff_t   [Data Type]

This is the signed integer type of the result of subtracting two pointers. For example, with the declaration `char *p1, *p2;`, the expression `p2 - p1` is of type `ptrdiff_t`. This will probably be one of the standard signed integer types (`short int`, `int` or `long int`), but might be a nonstandard type that exists only for this purpose.

size_t   [Data Type]

This is an unsigned integer type used to represent the sizes of objects. The result of the `sizeof` operator is of this type, and functions such as `malloc` (see Section 3.2.3 [Unconstrained Allocation], page 44) and `memcpy` (see Section 5.4 [Copying Strings and Arrays], page 95) accept arguments of this type to specify object sizes. On systems using the GNU C Library, this will be `unsigned int` or `unsigned long int`.

Usage Note: `size_t` is the preferred way to declare any arguments or variables that hold the size of an object.

Compatibility Note: Implementations of C before the advent of ISO C generally used `unsigned int` for representing object sizes and `int` for pointer subtraction results. They did not necessarily define either `size_t` or `ptrdiff_t`. Unix systems did define `size_t`, in `sys/types.h`, but the definition was usually a signed type.

A.5 Data Type Measurements

Most of the time, if you choose the proper C data type for each object in your program, you need not be concerned with just how it is represented or how many bits it uses. When you do need such information, the C language itself does not provide a way to get it. The header files `limits.h` and `float.h` contain macros which give you this information in full detail.

A.5.1 Computing the Width of an Integer Data Type

The most common reason that a program needs to know how many bits are in an integer type is for using an array of `long int` as a bit vector. You can access the bit at index n with

        vector[n / LONGBITS] & (1 << (n % LONGBITS))

provided you define `LONGBITS` as the number of bits in a `long int`.

There is no operator in the C language that can give you the number of bits in an integer data type. But you can compute it from the macro `CHAR_BIT`, defined in the header file `limits.h`.

`int CHAR_BIT`   [Macro]

>   This is the number of bits in a `char`. POSIX.1-2001 requires this to be 8.

>   You can compute the number of bits in any data type *type* like this:

>   sizeof (type) * CHAR_BIT

That expression includes padding bits as well as value and sign bits. On all systems supported by the GNU C Library, standard integer types other than `_Bool` do not have any padding bits. TS 18661-1:2014 defines additional macros for the width of integer types (the number of value and sign bits); these macros can also be used in `#if` preprocessor directives, whereas `sizeof` cannot. The following macros are defined in `limits.h`.

`CHAR_WIDTH`
`SCHAR_WIDTH`
`UCHAR_WIDTH`
`SHRT_WIDTH`
`USHRT_WIDTH`
`INT_WIDTH`
`UINT_WIDTH`
`LONG_WIDTH`
`ULONG_WIDTH`
`LLONG_WIDTH`
`ULLONG_WIDTH`

>   These are the widths of the types `char`, `signed char`, `unsigned char`, `short int`, `unsigned short int`, `int`, `unsigned int`, `long int`, `unsigned long int`, `long long int` and `unsigned long long int`, respectively.

Further such macros are defined in `stdint.h`. Apart from those for types specified by width (see Section 20.1 [Integers], page 575), the following are defined.

`INTPTR_WIDTH`
`UINTPTR_WIDTH`
`PTRDIFF_WIDTH`
`SIG_ATOMIC_WIDTH`
`SIZE_WIDTH`
`WCHAR_WIDTH`
`WINT_WIDTH`

>   These are the widths of the types `intptr_t`, `uintptr_t`, `ptrdiff_t`, `sig_atomic_t`, `size_t`, `wchar_t` and `wint_t`, respectively.

A.5.2 Range of an Integer Type

Suppose you need to store an integer value which can range from zero to one million. Which is the smallest type you can use? There is no general rule; it depends on the C compiler and target machine. You can use the 'MIN' and 'MAX' macros in `limits.h` to determine which type will work.

Each signed integer type has a pair of macros which give the smallest and largest values that it can hold. Each unsigned integer type has one such macro, for the maximum value; the minimum value is, of course, zero.

The values of these macros are all integer constant expressions. The 'MAX' and 'MIN' macros for `char` and `short int` types have values of type `int`. The 'MAX' and 'MIN' macros for the other types have values of the same type described by the macro—thus, `ULONG_MAX` has type `unsigned long int`.

SCHAR_MIN

> This is the minimum value that can be represented by a `signed char`.

SCHAR_MAX
UCHAR_MAX

> These are the maximum values that can be represented by a `signed char` and `unsigned char`, respectively.

CHAR_MIN

> This is the minimum value that can be represented by a `char`. It's equal to `SCHAR_MIN` if `char` is signed, or zero otherwise.

CHAR_MAX

> This is the maximum value that can be represented by a `char`. It's equal to `SCHAR_MAX` if `char` is signed, or `UCHAR_MAX` otherwise.

SHRT_MIN

> This is the minimum value that can be represented by a `signed short int`. On most machines that the GNU C Library runs on, `short` integers are 16-bit quantities.

SHRT_MAX
USHRT_MAX

> These are the maximum values that can be represented by a `signed short int` and `unsigned short int`, respectively.

INT_MIN

> This is the minimum value that can be represented by a `signed int`. On most machines that the GNU C Library runs on, an `int` is a 32-bit quantity.

INT_MAX
UINT_MAX

> These are the maximum values that can be represented by, respectively, the type `signed int` and the type `unsigned int`.

LONG_MIN

This is the minimum value that can be represented by a **signed long int**. On most machines that the GNU C Library runs on, **long** integers are 32-bit quantities, the same size as **int**.

LONG_MAX
ULONG_MAX

These are the maximum values that can be represented by a **signed long int** and **unsigned long int**, respectively.

LLONG_MIN

This is the minimum value that can be represented by a **signed long long int**. On most machines that the GNU C Library runs on, **long long** integers are 64-bit quantities.

LLONG_MAX
ULLONG_MAX

These are the maximum values that can be represented by a **signed long long int** and **unsigned long long int**, respectively.

LONG_LONG_MIN
LONG_LONG_MAX
ULONG_LONG_MAX

These are obsolete names for **LLONG_MIN**, **LLONG_MAX**, and **ULLONG_MAX**. They are only available if **_GNU_SOURCE** is defined (see Section 1.3.4 [Feature Test Macros], page 15). In GCC versions prior to 3.0, these were the only names available.

WCHAR_MAX

This is the maximum value that can be represented by a **wchar_t**. See Section 6.1 [Introduction to Extended Characters], page 134.

The header file **limits.h** also defines some additional constants that parameterize various operating system and file system limits. These constants are described in Chapter 32 [System Configuration Parameters], page 862.

A.5.3 Floating Type Macros

The specific representation of floating point numbers varies from machine to machine. Because floating point numbers are represented internally as approximate quantities, algorithms for manipulating floating point data often need to take account of the precise details of the machine's floating point representation.

Some of the functions in the C library itself need this information; for example, the algorithms for printing and reading floating point numbers (see Chapter 12 [Input/Output on Streams], page 257) and for calculating trigonometric and irrational functions (see Chapter 19 [Mathematics], page 525) use it to avoid round-off error and loss of accuracy. User programs that implement numerical analysis techniques also often need this information in order to minimize or compute error bounds.

The header file **float.h** describes the format used by your machine.

A.5.3.1 Floating Point Representation Concepts

This section introduces the terminology for describing floating point representations.

You are probably already familiar with most of these concepts in terms of scientific or exponential notation for floating point numbers. For example, the number `123456.0` could be expressed in exponential notation as `1.23456e+05`, a shorthand notation indicating that the mantissa `1.23456` is multiplied by the base 10 raised to power 5.

More formally, the internal representation of a floating point number can be characterized in terms of the following parameters:

- The *sign* is either `-1` or `1`.

- The *base* or *radix* for exponentiation, an integer greater than `1`. This is a constant for a particular representation.

- The *exponent* to which the base is raised. The upper and lower bounds of the exponent value are constants for a particular representation.

  Sometimes, in the actual bits representing the floating point number, the exponent is *biased* by adding a constant to it, to make it always be represented as an unsigned quantity. This is only important if you have some reason to pick apart the bit fields making up the floating point number by hand, which is something for which the GNU C Library provides no support. So this is ignored in the discussion that follows.

- The *mantissa* or *significand* is an unsigned integer which is a part of each floating point number.

- The *precision* of the mantissa. If the base of the representation is b, then the precision is the number of base-b digits in the mantissa. This is a constant for a particular representation.

  Many floating point representations have an implicit *hidden bit* in the mantissa. This is a bit which is present virtually in the mantissa, but not stored in memory because its value is always 1 in a normalized number. The precision figure (see above) includes any hidden bits.

  Again, the GNU C Library provides no facilities for dealing with such low-level aspects of the representation.

The mantissa of a floating point number represents an implicit fraction whose denominator is the base raised to the power of the precision. Since the largest representable mantissa is one less than this denominator, the value of the fraction is always strictly less than 1. The mathematical value of a floating point number is then the product of this fraction, the sign, and the base raised to the exponent.

We say that the floating point number is *normalized* if the fraction is at least `1/b`, where b is the base. In other words, the mantissa would be too large to fit if it were multiplied by the base. Non-normalized numbers are sometimes called *denormal*; they contain less precision than the representation normally can hold.

If the number is not normalized, then you can subtract 1 from the exponent while multiplying the mantissa by the base, and get another floating point number with the same value. *Normalization* consists of doing this repeatedly until the number is normalized. Two distinct normalized floating point numbers cannot be equal in value.

(There is an exception to this rule: if the mantissa is zero, it is considered normalized. Another exception happens on certain machines where the exponent is as small as the representation can hold. Then it is impossible to subtract 1 from the exponent, so a number may be normalized even if its fraction is less than `1/b`.)

A.5.3.2 Floating Point Parameters

These macro definitions can be accessed by including the header file `float.h` in your program.

Macro names starting with 'FLT_' refer to the `float` type, while names beginning with 'DBL_' refer to the `double` type and names beginning with 'LDBL_' refer to the `long double` type. (If GCC does not support `long double` as a distinct data type on a target machine then the values for the 'LDBL_' constants are equal to the corresponding constants for the `double` type.)

Of these macros, only `FLT_RADIX` is guaranteed to be a constant expression. The other macros listed here cannot be reliably used in places that require constant expressions, such as '#if' preprocessing directives or in the dimensions of static arrays.

Although the ISO C standard specifies minimum and maximum values for most of these parameters, the GNU C implementation uses whatever values describe the floating point representation of the target machine. So in principle GNU C actually satisfies the ISO C requirements only if the target machine is suitable. In practice, all the machines currently supported are suitable.

`FLT_ROUNDS`

> This value characterizes the rounding mode for floating point addition. The following values indicate standard rounding modes:
>
> -1   The mode is indeterminable.
>
> 0   Rounding is towards zero.
>
> 1   Rounding is to the nearest number.
>
> 2   Rounding is towards positive infinity.
>
> 3   Rounding is towards negative infinity.
>
> Any other value represents a machine-dependent nonstandard rounding mode.
>
> On most machines, the value is 1, in accordance with the IEEE standard for floating point.
>
> Here is a table showing how certain values round for each possible value of `FLT_ROUNDS`, if the other aspects of the representation match the IEEE single-precision standard.
>
> ```
>                   0       1            2             3
>   1.00000003     1.0     1.0          1.00000012    1.0
>   1.00000007     1.0     1.00000012   1.00000012    1.0
>  -1.00000003    -1.0    -1.0         -1.0          -1.00000012
>  -1.00000007    -1.0    -1.00000012  -1.0          -1.00000012
> ```

`FLT_RADIX`

> This is the value of the base, or radix, of the exponent representation. This is guaranteed to be a constant expression, unlike the other macros described in this section. The value is 2 on all machines we know of except the IBM 360 and derivatives.

`FLT_MANT_DIG`

> This is the number of base-`FLT_RADIX` digits in the floating point mantissa for the `float` data type. The following expression yields 1.0 (even though mathematically it should not) due to the limited number of mantissa digits:

```
float radix = FLT_RADIX;

1.0f + 1.0f / radix / radix / ... / radix
```

where `radix` appears `FLT_MANT_DIG` times.

`DBL_MANT_DIG`
`LDBL_MANT_DIG`

> This is the number of base-`FLT_RADIX` digits in the floating point mantissa for the data types `double` and `long double`, respectively.

`FLT_DIG`

> This is the number of decimal digits of precision for the `float` data type. Technically, if p and b are the precision and base (respectively) for the representation, then the decimal precision q is the maximum number of decimal digits such that any floating point number with q base 10 digits can be rounded to a floating point number with p base b digits and back again, without change to the q decimal digits.
>
> The value of this macro is supposed to be at least 6, to satisfy ISO C.

`DBL_DIG`
`LDBL_DIG`

> These are similar to `FLT_DIG`, but for the data types `double` and `long double`, respectively. The values of these macros are supposed to be at least 10.

`FLT_MIN_EXP`

> This is the smallest possible exponent value for type `float`. More precisely, it is the minimum negative integer such that the value `FLT_RADIX` raised to this power minus 1 can be represented as a normalized floating point number of type `float`.

`DBL_MIN_EXP`
`LDBL_MIN_EXP`

> These are similar to `FLT_MIN_EXP`, but for the data types `double` and `long double`, respectively.

`FLT_MIN_10_EXP`

> This is the minimum negative integer such that 10 raised to this power minus 1 can be represented as a normalized floating point number of type `float`. This is supposed to be −37 or even less.

`DBL_MIN_10_EXP`
`LDBL_MIN_10_EXP`

> These are similar to `FLT_MIN_10_EXP`, but for the data types `double` and `long double`, respectively.

`FLT_MAX_EXP`

> This is the largest possible exponent value for type `float`. More precisely, this is the maximum positive integer such that value `FLT_RADIX` raised to this power minus 1 can be represented as a floating point number of type `float`.

```
DBL_MAX_EXP
LDBL_MAX_EXP
```
These are similar to `FLT_MAX_EXP`, but for the data types `double` and `long double`, respectively.

```
FLT_MAX_10_EXP
```
This is the maximum positive integer such that 10 raised to this power minus 1 can be represented as a normalized floating point number of type `float`. This is supposed to be at least 37.

```
DBL_MAX_10_EXP
LDBL_MAX_10_EXP
```
These are similar to `FLT_MAX_10_EXP`, but for the data types `double` and `long double`, respectively.

```
FLT_MAX
```
The value of this macro is the maximum number representable in type `float`. It is supposed to be at least 1E+37. The value has type `float`.

The smallest representable number is - `FLT_MAX`.

```
DBL_MAX
LDBL_MAX
```
These are similar to `FLT_MAX`, but for the data types `double` and `long double`, respectively. The type of the macro's value is the same as the type it describes.

```
FLT_MIN
```
The value of this macro is the minimum normalized positive floating point number that is representable in type `float`. It is supposed to be no more than 1E-37.

```
DBL_MIN
LDBL_MIN
```
These are similar to `FLT_MIN`, but for the data types `double` and `long double`, respectively. The type of the macro's value is the same as the type it describes.

```
FLT_EPSILON
```
This is the difference between 1 and the smallest floating point number of type `float` that is greater than 1. It's supposed to be no greater than 1E-5.

```
DBL_EPSILON
LDBL_EPSILON
```
These are similar to `FLT_EPSILON`, but for the data types `double` and `long double`, respectively. The type of the macro's value is the same as the type it describes. The values are not supposed to be greater than 1E-9.

A.5.3.3 IEEE Floating Point

Here is an example showing how the floating type measurements come out for the most common floating point representation, specified by the *IEEE Standard for Binary Floating Point Arithmetic (ANSI/IEEE Std 754-1985)*. Nearly all computers designed since the 1980s use this format.

The IEEE single-precision float representation uses a base of 2. There is a sign bit, a mantissa with 23 bits plus one hidden bit (so the total precision is 24 base-2 digits), and an 8-bit exponent that can represent values in the range -125 to 128, inclusive.

So, for an implementation that uses this representation for the `float` data type, appropriate values for the corresponding parameters are:

```
FLT_RADIX                               2
FLT_MANT_DIG                           24
FLT_DIG                                 6
FLT_MIN_EXP                          -125
FLT_MIN_10_EXP                        -37
FLT_MAX_EXP                           128
FLT_MAX_10_EXP                        +38
FLT_MIN                 1.17549435E-38F
FLT_MAX                 3.40282347E+38F
FLT_EPSILON             1.19209290E-07F
```

Here are the values for the `double` data type:

```
DBL_MANT_DIG                           53
DBL_DIG                                15
DBL_MIN_EXP                         -1021
DBL_MIN_10_EXP                       -307
DBL_MAX_EXP                          1024
DBL_MAX_10_EXP                        308
DBL_MAX        1.7976931348623157E+308
DBL_MIN        2.2250738585072014E-308
DBL_EPSILON    2.2204460492503131E-016
```

A.5.4 Structure Field Offset Measurement

You can use `offsetof` to measure the location within a structure type of a particular structure member.

`size_t offsetof (type, member)`   [Macro]

> Preliminary: | MT-Safe | AS-Safe | AC-Safe | See Section 1.2.2.1 [POSIX Safety Concepts], page 2.
>
> This expands to an integer constant expression that is the offset of the structure member named *member* in the structure type *type*. For example, `offsetof (struct s, elem)` is the offset, in bytes, of the member `elem` in a `struct s`.
>
> This macro won't work if *member* is a bit field; you get an error from the C compiler in that case.

Appendix B Summary of Library Facilities

This appendix is a complete list of the facilities declared within the header files supplied with the GNU C Library. Each entry also lists the standard or other source from which each facility is derived, and tells you where in the manual you can find more information about how to use it.

ACCOUNTING

> `utmp.h` (SVID): Section 30.12.1 [Manipulating the User Accounting Database], page 826.

AF_FILE

> `sys/socket.h` (GNU): Section 16.3.1 [Address Formats], page 444.

AF_INET

> `sys/socket.h` (BSD): Section 16.3.1 [Address Formats], page 444.

AF_INET6

> `sys/socket.h` (IPv6 Basic API): Section 16.3.1 [Address Formats], page 444.

AF_LOCAL

> `sys/socket.h` (POSIX): Section 16.3.1 [Address Formats], page 444.

AF_UNIX

> `sys/socket.h` (BSD): Section 16.3.1 [Address Formats], page 444.

> `sys/socket.h` (Unix98): Section 16.3.1 [Address Formats], page 444.

AF_UNSPEC

> `sys/socket.h` (BSD): Section 16.3.1 [Address Formats], page 444.

tcflag_t ALTWERASE

> `termios.h` (BSD): Section 17.4.7 [Local Modes], page 499.

int ARGP_ERR_UNKNOWN

> `argp.h` (GNU): Section 25.3.5 [Argp Parser Functions], page 742.

ARGP_HELP_BUG_ADDR

> `argp.h` (GNU): Section 25.3.10 [Flags for the `argp_help` Function], page 750.

ARGP_HELP_DOC

> `argp.h` (GNU): Section 25.3.10 [Flags for the `argp_help` Function], page 750.

ARGP_HELP_EXIT_ERR

> `argp.h` (GNU): Section 25.3.10 [Flags for the `argp_help` Function], page 750.

ARGP_HELP_EXIT_OK

> `argp.h` (GNU): Section 25.3.10 [Flags for the `argp_help` Function], page 750.

ARGP_HELP_LONG

> `argp.h` (GNU): Section 25.3.10 [Flags for the `argp_help` Function], page 750.

ARGP_HELP_LONG_ONLY

> `argp.h` (GNU): Section 25.3.10 [Flags for the `argp_help` Function], page 750.

ARGP_HELP_POST_DOC

> `argp.h` (GNU): Section 25.3.10 [Flags for the `argp_help` Function], page 750.

ARGP_HELP_PRE_DOC

> `argp.h` (GNU): Section 25.3.10 [Flags for the `argp_help` Function], page 750.

ARGP_HELP_SEE

> `argp.h` (GNU): Section 25.3.10 [Flags for the `argp_help` Function], page 750.

ARGP_HELP_SHORT_USAGE

> `argp.h` (GNU): Section 25.3.10 [Flags for the `argp_help` Function], page 750.

Appendix B: Summary of Library Facilities

ARGP_NO_HELP

        argp.h (GNU): Section 25.3.7 [Flags for `argp_parse`], page 748.

ARGP_PARSE_ARGV0

        argp.h (GNU): Section 25.3.7 [Flags for `argp_parse`], page 748.

ARGP_SILENT

        argp.h (GNU): Section 25.3.7 [Flags for `argp_parse`], page 748.

int ARG_MAX

        limits.h (POSIX.1): Section 32.1 [General Capacity Limits], page 862.

int BC_BASE_MAX

        limits.h (POSIX.2): Section 32.10 [Utility Program Capacity Limits], page 879.

int BC_DIM_MAX

        limits.h (POSIX.2): Section 32.10 [Utility Program Capacity Limits], page 879.

int BC_SCALE_MAX

        limits.h (POSIX.2): Section 32.10 [Utility Program Capacity Limits], page 879.

int BC_STRING_MAX

        limits.h (POSIX.2): Section 32.10 [Utility Program Capacity Limits], page 879.

BOOT_TIME

        utmp.h (SVID): Section 30.12.1 [Manipulating the User Accounting Database], page 826.

        utmpx.h (XPG4.2): Section 30.12.2 [XPG User Accounting Database Functions], page 831.

tcflag_t BRKINT

        termios.h (POSIX.1): Section 17.4.4 [Input Modes], page 495.

int BUFSIZ

        stdio.h (ISO): Section 12.20.3 [Controlling Which Kind of Buffering], page 321.

tcflag_t CCTS_OFLOW

        termios.h (BSD): Section 17.4.6 [Control Modes], page 498.

int CHAR_BIT

        limits.h (C90): Section A.5.1 [Computing the Width of an Integer Data Type], page 917.

CHAR_MAX

        limits.h (ISO): Section A.5.2 [Range of an Integer Type], page 918.

CHAR_MIN

        limits.h (ISO): Section A.5.2 [Range of an Integer Type], page 918.

CHAR_WIDTH

        limits.h (ISO): Section A.5.1 [Computing the Width of an Integer Data Type], page 917.

int CHILD_MAX

        limits.h (POSIX.1): Section 32.1 [General Capacity Limits], page 862.

tcflag_t CIGNORE

        termios.h (BSD): Section 17.4.6 [Control Modes], page 498.

int CLK_TCK

        time.h (POSIX.1): Section 21.3.2 [Processor Time Inquiry], page 622.

tcflag_t CLOCAL

        termios.h (POSIX.1): Section 17.4.6 [Control Modes], page 498.

int CLOCKS_PER_SEC

        time.h (ISO): Section 21.3.1 [CPU Time Inquiry], page 621.

int COLL_WEIGHTS_MAX

        limits.h (POSIX.2): Section 32.10 [Utility Program Capacity Limits], page 879.

void CPU_CLR (int *cpu*, cpu_set_t **set*)
> sched.h (GNU): Section 22.3.5 [Limiting execution to certain CPUs], page 669.

int CPU_ISSET (int *cpu*, const cpu_set_t **set*)
> sched.h (GNU): Section 22.3.5 [Limiting execution to certain CPUs], page 669.

void CPU_SET (int *cpu*, cpu_set_t **set*)
> sched.h (GNU): Section 22.3.5 [Limiting execution to certain CPUs], page 669.

int CPU_SETSIZE
> sched.h (GNU): Section 22.3.5 [Limiting execution to certain CPUs], page 669.

void CPU_ZERO (cpu_set_t **set*)
> sched.h (GNU): Section 22.3.5 [Limiting execution to certain CPUs], page 669.

tcflag_t CREAD
> termios.h (POSIX.1): Section 17.4.6 [Control Modes], page 498.

tcflag_t CRTS_IFLOW
> termios.h (BSD): Section 17.4.6 [Control Modes], page 498.

tcflag_t CS5
> termios.h (POSIX.1): Section 17.4.6 [Control Modes], page 498.

tcflag_t CS6
> termios.h (POSIX.1): Section 17.4.6 [Control Modes], page 498.

tcflag_t CS7
> termios.h (POSIX.1): Section 17.4.6 [Control Modes], page 498.

tcflag_t CS8
> termios.h (POSIX.1): Section 17.4.6 [Control Modes], page 498.

tcflag_t CSIZE
> termios.h (POSIX.1): Section 17.4.6 [Control Modes], page 498.

tcflag_t CSTOPB
> termios.h (POSIX.1): Section 17.4.6 [Control Modes], page 498.

DBL_DIG
> float.h (C90): Section A.5.3.2 [Floating Point Parameters], page 921.

DBL_EPSILON
> float.h (C90): Section A.5.3.2 [Floating Point Parameters], page 921.

DBL_MANT_DIG
> float.h (C90): Section A.5.3.2 [Floating Point Parameters], page 921.

DBL_MAX
> float.h (C90): Section A.5.3.2 [Floating Point Parameters], page 921.

DBL_MAX_10_EXP
> float.h (C90): Section A.5.3.2 [Floating Point Parameters], page 921.

DBL_MAX_EXP
> float.h (C90): Section A.5.3.2 [Floating Point Parameters], page 921.

DBL_MIN
> float.h (C90): Section A.5.3.2 [Floating Point Parameters], page 921.

DBL_MIN_10_EXP
> float.h (C90): Section A.5.3.2 [Floating Point Parameters], page 921.

DBL_MIN_EXP
> float.h (C90): Section A.5.3.2 [Floating Point Parameters], page 921.

DEAD_PROCESS
> utmp.h (SVID): Section 30.12.1 [Manipulating the User Accounting Database], page 826.
>
> utmpx.h (XPG4.2): Section 30.12.2 [XPG User Accounting Database Functions], page 831.

`DESERR_BADPARAM`

       `rpc/des_crypt.h` (SUNRPC): Section 33.4 [DES Encryption], page 887.

`DESERR_HWERROR`

       `rpc/des_crypt.h` (SUNRPC): Section 33.4 [DES Encryption], page 887.

`DESERR_NOHWDEVICE`

       `rpc/des_crypt.h` (SUNRPC): Section 33.4 [DES Encryption], page 887.

`DESERR_NONE`

       `rpc/des_crypt.h` (SUNRPC): Section 33.4 [DES Encryption], page 887.

`DES_DECRYPT`

       `rpc/des_crypt.h` (SUNRPC): Section 33.4 [DES Encryption], page 887.

`DES_ENCRYPT`

       `rpc/des_crypt.h` (SUNRPC): Section 33.4 [DES Encryption], page 887.

`int DES_FAILED (int err)`

       `rpc/des_crypt.h` (SUNRPC): Section 33.4 [DES Encryption], page 887.

`DES_HW`

       `rpc/des_crypt.h` (SUNRPC): Section 33.4 [DES Encryption], page 887.

`DES_SW`

       `rpc/des_crypt.h` (SUNRPC): Section 33.4 [DES Encryption], page 887.

`DIR`

       `dirent.h` (POSIX.1): Section 14.2.2 [Opening a Directory Stream], page 394.

`mode_t DTTOIF (int dtype)`

       `dirent.h` (BSD): Section 14.2.1 [Format of a Directory Entry], page 392.

`int E2BIG`

       `errno.h` (POSIX.1): Section 2.2 [Error Codes], page 23.

`int EACCES`

       `errno.h` (POSIX.1): Section 2.2 [Error Codes], page 23.

`int EADDRINUSE`

       `errno.h` (BSD): Section 2.2 [Error Codes], page 23.

`int EADDRNOTAVAIL`

       `errno.h` (BSD): Section 2.2 [Error Codes], page 23.

`int EADV`

       `errno.h` (Linux???): Section 2.2 [Error Codes], page 23.

`int EAFNOSUPPORT`

       `errno.h` (BSD): Section 2.2 [Error Codes], page 23.

`int EAGAIN`

       `errno.h` (POSIX.1): Section 2.2 [Error Codes], page 23.

`int EALREADY`

       `errno.h` (BSD): Section 2.2 [Error Codes], page 23.

`int EAUTH`

       `errno.h` (BSD): Section 2.2 [Error Codes], page 23.

`int EBACKGROUND`

       `errno.h` (GNU): Section 2.2 [Error Codes], page 23.

`int EBADE`

       `errno.h` (Linux???): Section 2.2 [Error Codes], page 23.

int EBADF

> `errno.h` (POSIX.1): Section 2.2 [Error Codes], page 23.

int EBADFD

> `errno.h` (Linux???): Section 2.2 [Error Codes], page 23.

int EBADMSG

> `errno.h` (XOPEN): Section 2.2 [Error Codes], page 23.

int EBADR

> `errno.h` (Linux???): Section 2.2 [Error Codes], page 23.

int EBADRPC

> `errno.h` (BSD): Section 2.2 [Error Codes], page 23.

int EBADRQC

> `errno.h` (Linux???): Section 2.2 [Error Codes], page 23.

int EBADSLT

> `errno.h` (Linux???): Section 2.2 [Error Codes], page 23.

int EBFONT

> `errno.h` (Linux???): Section 2.2 [Error Codes], page 23.

int EBUSY

> `errno.h` (POSIX.1): Section 2.2 [Error Codes], page 23.

int ECANCELED

> `errno.h` (POSIX.1): Section 2.2 [Error Codes], page 23.

int ECHILD

> `errno.h` (POSIX.1): Section 2.2 [Error Codes], page 23.

tcflag_t ECHO

> `termios.h` (POSIX.1): Section 17.4.7 [Local Modes], page 499.

tcflag_t ECHOCTL

> `termios.h` (BSD): Section 17.4.7 [Local Modes], page 499.

tcflag_t ECHOE

> `termios.h` (POSIX.1): Section 17.4.7 [Local Modes], page 499.

tcflag_t ECHOK

> `termios.h` (POSIX.1): Section 17.4.7 [Local Modes], page 499.

tcflag_t ECHOKE

> `termios.h` (BSD): Section 17.4.7 [Local Modes], page 499.

tcflag_t ECHONL

> `termios.h` (POSIX.1): Section 17.4.7 [Local Modes], page 499.

tcflag_t ECHOPRT

> `termios.h` (BSD): Section 17.4.7 [Local Modes], page 499.

int ECHRNG

> `errno.h` (Linux???): Section 2.2 [Error Codes], page 23.

int ECOMM

> `errno.h` (Linux???): Section 2.2 [Error Codes], page 23.

int ECONNABORTED

> `errno.h` (BSD): Section 2.2 [Error Codes], page 23.

int ECONNREFUSED

> `errno.h` (BSD): Section 2.2 [Error Codes], page 23.

`int ECONNRESET`

        `errno.h` (BSD): Section 2.2 [Error Codes], page 23.

`int ED`

        `errno.h` (GNU): Section 2.2 [Error Codes], page 23.

`int EDEADLK`

        `errno.h` (POSIX.1): Section 2.2 [Error Codes], page 23.

`int EDEADLOCK`

        `errno.h` (Linux???): Section 2.2 [Error Codes], page 23.

`int EDESTADDRREQ`

        `errno.h` (BSD): Section 2.2 [Error Codes], page 23.

`int EDIED`

        `errno.h` (GNU): Section 2.2 [Error Codes], page 23.

`int EDOM`

        `errno.h` (ISO): Section 2.2 [Error Codes], page 23.

`int EDOTDOT`

        `errno.h` (Linux???): Section 2.2 [Error Codes], page 23.

`int EDQUOT`

        `errno.h` (BSD): Section 2.2 [Error Codes], page 23.

`int EEXIST`

        `errno.h` (POSIX.1): Section 2.2 [Error Codes], page 23.

`int EFAULT`

        `errno.h` (POSIX.1): Section 2.2 [Error Codes], page 23.

`int EFBIG`

        `errno.h` (POSIX.1): Section 2.2 [Error Codes], page 23.

`int EFTYPE`

        `errno.h` (BSD): Section 2.2 [Error Codes], page 23.

`int EGRATUITOUS`

        `errno.h` (GNU): Section 2.2 [Error Codes], page 23.

`int EGREGIOUS`

        `errno.h` (GNU): Section 2.2 [Error Codes], page 23.

`int EHOSTDOWN`

        `errno.h` (BSD): Section 2.2 [Error Codes], page 23.

`int EHOSTUNREACH`

        `errno.h` (BSD): Section 2.2 [Error Codes], page 23.

`int EHWPOISON`

        `errno.h` (Linux): Section 2.2 [Error Codes], page 23.

`int EIDRM`

        `errno.h` (XOPEN): Section 2.2 [Error Codes], page 23.

`int EIEIO`

        `errno.h` (GNU): Section 2.2 [Error Codes], page 23.

`int EILSEQ`

        `errno.h` (ISO): Section 2.2 [Error Codes], page 23.

`int EINPROGRESS`

        `errno.h` (BSD): Section 2.2 [Error Codes], page 23.

`int EINTR`

> `errno.h` (POSIX.1): Section 2.2 [Error Codes], page 23.

`int EINVAL`

> `errno.h` (POSIX.1): Section 2.2 [Error Codes], page 23.

`int EIO`

> `errno.h` (POSIX.1): Section 2.2 [Error Codes], page 23.

`int EISCONN`

> `errno.h` (BSD): Section 2.2 [Error Codes], page 23.

`int EISDIR`

> `errno.h` (POSIX.1): Section 2.2 [Error Codes], page 23.

`int EISNAM`

> `errno.h` (Linux???): Section 2.2 [Error Codes], page 23.

`int EKEYEXPIRED`

> `errno.h` (Linux): Section 2.2 [Error Codes], page 23.

`int EKEYREJECTED`

> `errno.h` (Linux): Section 2.2 [Error Codes], page 23.

`int EKEYREVOKED`

> `errno.h` (Linux): Section 2.2 [Error Codes], page 23.

`int EL2HLT`

> `errno.h` (Obsolete): Section 2.2 [Error Codes], page 23.

`int EL2NSYNC`

> `errno.h` (Obsolete): Section 2.2 [Error Codes], page 23.

`int EL3HLT`

> `errno.h` (Obsolete): Section 2.2 [Error Codes], page 23.

`int EL3RST`

> `errno.h` (Obsolete): Section 2.2 [Error Codes], page 23.

`int ELIBACC`

> `errno.h` (Linux???): Section 2.2 [Error Codes], page 23.

`int ELIBBAD`

> `errno.h` (Linux???): Section 2.2 [Error Codes], page 23.

`int ELIBEXEC`

> `errno.h` (Linux???): Section 2.2 [Error Codes], page 23.

`int ELIBMAX`

> `errno.h` (Linux???): Section 2.2 [Error Codes], page 23.

`int ELIBSCN`

> `errno.h` (Linux???): Section 2.2 [Error Codes], page 23.

`int ELNRNG`

> `errno.h` (Linux???): Section 2.2 [Error Codes], page 23.

`int ELOOP`

> `errno.h` (BSD): Section 2.2 [Error Codes], page 23.

`int EMEDIUMTYPE`

> `errno.h` (Linux???): Section 2.2 [Error Codes], page 23.

`int EMFILE`

> `errno.h` (POSIX.1): Section 2.2 [Error Codes], page 23.

`int EMLINK`

> `errno.h` (POSIX.1): Section 2.2 [Error Codes], page 23.

`EMPTY`

> `utmp.h` (SVID): Section 30.12.1 [Manipulating the User Accounting Database], page 826.
>
> `utmpx.h` (XPG4.2): Section 30.12.2 [XPG User Accounting Database Functions], page 831.

`int EMSGSIZE`

> `errno.h` (BSD): Section 2.2 [Error Codes], page 23.

`int EMULTIHOP`

> `errno.h` (XOPEN): Section 2.2 [Error Codes], page 23.

`int ENAMETOOLONG`

> `errno.h` (POSIX.1): Section 2.2 [Error Codes], page 23.

`int ENAVAIL`

> `errno.h` (Linux???): Section 2.2 [Error Codes], page 23.

`int ENEEDAUTH`

> `errno.h` (BSD): Section 2.2 [Error Codes], page 23.

`int ENETDOWN`

> `errno.h` (BSD): Section 2.2 [Error Codes], page 23.

`int ENETRESET`

> `errno.h` (BSD): Section 2.2 [Error Codes], page 23.

`int ENETUNREACH`

> `errno.h` (BSD): Section 2.2 [Error Codes], page 23.

`int ENFILE`

> `errno.h` (POSIX.1): Section 2.2 [Error Codes], page 23.

`int ENOANO`

> `errno.h` (Linux???): Section 2.2 [Error Codes], page 23.

`int ENOBUFS`

> `errno.h` (BSD): Section 2.2 [Error Codes], page 23.

`int ENOCSI`

> `errno.h` (Linux???): Section 2.2 [Error Codes], page 23.

`int ENODATA`

> `errno.h` (XOPEN): Section 2.2 [Error Codes], page 23.

`int ENODEV`

> `errno.h` (POSIX.1): Section 2.2 [Error Codes], page 23.

`int ENOENT`

> `errno.h` (POSIX.1): Section 2.2 [Error Codes], page 23.

`int ENOEXEC`

> `errno.h` (POSIX.1): Section 2.2 [Error Codes], page 23.

`int ENOKEY`

> `errno.h` (Linux): Section 2.2 [Error Codes], page 23.

`int ENOLCK`

> `errno.h` (POSIX.1): Section 2.2 [Error Codes], page 23.

`int ENOLINK`

> `errno.h` (XOPEN): Section 2.2 [Error Codes], page 23.

`int ENOMEDIUM`

> `errno.h` (Linux???): Section 2.2 [Error Codes], page 23.

`int ENOMEM`

> `errno.h` (POSIX.1): Section 2.2 [Error Codes], page 23.

`int ENOMSG`

> `errno.h` (XOPEN): Section 2.2 [Error Codes], page 23.

`int ENONET`

> `errno.h` (Linux???): Section 2.2 [Error Codes], page 23.

`int ENOPKG`

> `errno.h` (Linux???): Section 2.2 [Error Codes], page 23.

`int ENOPROTOOPT`

> `errno.h` (BSD): Section 2.2 [Error Codes], page 23.

`int ENOSPC`

> `errno.h` (POSIX.1): Section 2.2 [Error Codes], page 23.

`int ENOSR`

> `errno.h` (XOPEN): Section 2.2 [Error Codes], page 23.

`int ENOSTR`

> `errno.h` (XOPEN): Section 2.2 [Error Codes], page 23.

`int ENOSYS`

> `errno.h` (POSIX.1): Section 2.2 [Error Codes], page 23.

`int ENOTBLK`

> `errno.h` (BSD): Section 2.2 [Error Codes], page 23.

`int ENOTCONN`

> `errno.h` (BSD): Section 2.2 [Error Codes], page 23.

`int ENOTDIR`

> `errno.h` (POSIX.1): Section 2.2 [Error Codes], page 23.

`int ENOTEMPTY`

> `errno.h` (POSIX.1): Section 2.2 [Error Codes], page 23.

`int ENOTNAM`

> `errno.h` (Linux???): Section 2.2 [Error Codes], page 23.

`int ENOTRECOVERABLE`

> `errno.h` (Linux): Section 2.2 [Error Codes], page 23.

`int ENOTSOCK`

> `errno.h` (BSD): Section 2.2 [Error Codes], page 23.

`int ENOTSUP`

> `errno.h` (POSIX.1): Section 2.2 [Error Codes], page 23.

`int ENOTTY`

> `errno.h` (POSIX.1): Section 2.2 [Error Codes], page 23.

`int ENOTUNIQ`

> `errno.h` (Linux???): Section 2.2 [Error Codes], page 23.

`int ENXIO`

> `errno.h` (POSIX.1): Section 2.2 [Error Codes], page 23.

`int EOF`

>> `stdio.h` (ISO): Section 12.15 [End-Of-File and Errors], page 311.

`int EOPNOTSUPP`

>> `errno.h` (BSD): Section 2.2 [Error Codes], page 23.

`int EOVERFLOW`

>> `errno.h` (XOPEN): Section 2.2 [Error Codes], page 23.

`int EOWNERDEAD`

>> `errno.h` (Linux): Section 2.2 [Error Codes], page 23.

`int EPERM`

>> `errno.h` (POSIX.1): Section 2.2 [Error Codes], page 23.

`int EPFNOSUPPORT`

>> `errno.h` (BSD): Section 2.2 [Error Codes], page 23.

`int EPIPE`

>> `errno.h` (POSIX.1): Section 2.2 [Error Codes], page 23.

`int EPROCLIM`

>> `errno.h` (BSD): Section 2.2 [Error Codes], page 23.

`int EPROCUNAVAIL`

>> `errno.h` (BSD): Section 2.2 [Error Codes], page 23.

`int EPROGMISMATCH`

>> `errno.h` (BSD): Section 2.2 [Error Codes], page 23.

`int EPROGUNAVAIL`

>> `errno.h` (BSD): Section 2.2 [Error Codes], page 23.

`int EPROTO`

>> `errno.h` (XOPEN): Section 2.2 [Error Codes], page 23.

`int EPROTONOSUPPORT`

>> `errno.h` (BSD): Section 2.2 [Error Codes], page 23.

`int EPROTOTYPE`

>> `errno.h` (BSD): Section 2.2 [Error Codes], page 23.

`int EQUIV_CLASS_MAX`

>> `limits.h` (POSIX.2): Section 32.10 [Utility Program Capacity Limits], page 879.

`int ERANGE`

>> `errno.h` (ISO): Section 2.2 [Error Codes], page 23.

`int EREMCHG`

>> `errno.h` (Linux???): Section 2.2 [Error Codes], page 23.

`int EREMOTE`

>> `errno.h` (BSD): Section 2.2 [Error Codes], page 23.

`int EREMOTEIO`

>> `errno.h` (Linux???): Section 2.2 [Error Codes], page 23.

`int ERESTART`

>> `errno.h` (Linux???): Section 2.2 [Error Codes], page 23.

`int ERFKILL`

>> `errno.h` (Linux): Section 2.2 [Error Codes], page 23.

`int EROFS`

>> `errno.h` (POSIX.1): Section 2.2 [Error Codes], page 23.

`int ERPCMISMATCH`

> `errno.h` (BSD): Section 2.2 [Error Codes], page 23.

`int ESHUTDOWN`

> `errno.h` (BSD): Section 2.2 [Error Codes], page 23.

`int ESOCKTNOSUPPORT`

> `errno.h` (BSD): Section 2.2 [Error Codes], page 23.

`int ESPIPE`

> `errno.h` (POSIX.1): Section 2.2 [Error Codes], page 23.

`int ESRCH`

> `errno.h` (POSIX.1): Section 2.2 [Error Codes], page 23.

`int ESRMNT`

> `errno.h` (Linux???): Section 2.2 [Error Codes], page 23.

`int ESTALE`

> `errno.h` (BSD): Section 2.2 [Error Codes], page 23.

`int ESTRPIPE`

> `errno.h` (Linux???): Section 2.2 [Error Codes], page 23.

`int ETIME`

> `errno.h` (XOPEN): Section 2.2 [Error Codes], page 23.

`int ETIMEDOUT`

> `errno.h` (BSD): Section 2.2 [Error Codes], page 23.

`int ETOOMANYREFS`

> `errno.h` (BSD): Section 2.2 [Error Codes], page 23.

`int ETXTBSY`

> `errno.h` (BSD): Section 2.2 [Error Codes], page 23.

`int EUCLEAN`

> `errno.h` (Linux???): Section 2.2 [Error Codes], page 23.

`int EUNATCH`

> `errno.h` (Linux???): Section 2.2 [Error Codes], page 23.

`int EUSERS`

> `errno.h` (BSD): Section 2.2 [Error Codes], page 23.

`int EWOULDBLOCK`

> `errno.h` (BSD): Section 2.2 [Error Codes], page 23.

`int EXDEV`

> `errno.h` (POSIX.1): Section 2.2 [Error Codes], page 23.

`int EXFULL`

> `errno.h` (Linux???): Section 2.2 [Error Codes], page 23.

`int EXIT_FAILURE`

> `stdlib.h` (ISO): Section 25.7.2 [Exit Status], page 769.

`int EXIT_SUCCESS`

> `stdlib.h` (ISO): Section 25.7.2 [Exit Status], page 769.

`int EXPR_NEST_MAX`

> `limits.h` (POSIX.2): Section 32.10 [Utility Program Capacity Limits], page 879.

`int FD_CLOEXEC`

> `fcntl.h` (POSIX.1): Section 13.13 [File Descriptor Flags], page 374.

void FD_CLR (int *filedes*, fd_set **set*)
> sys/types.h (BSD): Section 13.8 [Waiting for Input or Output], page 355.

int FD_ISSET (int *filedes*, const fd_set **set*)
> sys/types.h (BSD): Section 13.8 [Waiting for Input or Output], page 355.

void FD_SET (int *filedes*, fd_set **set*)
> sys/types.h (BSD): Section 13.8 [Waiting for Input or Output], page 355.

int FD_SETSIZE
> sys/types.h (BSD): Section 13.8 [Waiting for Input or Output], page 355.

void FD_ZERO (fd_set **set*)
> sys/types.h (BSD): Section 13.8 [Waiting for Input or Output], page 355.

FE_DIVBYZERO
> fenv.h (ISO): Section 20.5.3 [Examining the FPU status word], page 584.

FE_DOWNWARD
> fenv.h (ISO): Section 20.6 [Rounding Modes], page 587.

FE_INEXACT
> fenv.h (ISO): Section 20.5.3 [Examining the FPU status word], page 584.

FE_INVALID
> fenv.h (ISO): Section 20.5.3 [Examining the FPU status word], page 584.

FE_OVERFLOW
> fenv.h (ISO): Section 20.5.3 [Examining the FPU status word], page 584.

int FE_SNANS_ALWAYS_SIGNAL
> fenv.h (ISO): Section 20.5.2 [Infinity and NaN], page 583.

FE_TONEAREST
> fenv.h (ISO): Section 20.6 [Rounding Modes], page 587.

FE_TOWARDZERO
> fenv.h (ISO): Section 20.6 [Rounding Modes], page 587.

FE_UNDERFLOW
> fenv.h (ISO): Section 20.5.3 [Examining the FPU status word], page 584.

FE_UPWARD
> fenv.h (ISO): Section 20.6 [Rounding Modes], page 587.

FILE
> stdio.h (ISO): Section 12.1 [Streams], page 257.

int FILENAME_MAX
> stdio.h (ISO): Section 32.6 [Limits on File System Capacity], page 874.

FLT_DIG
> float.h (C90): Section A.5.3.2 [Floating Point Parameters], page 921.

FLT_EPSILON
> float.h (C90): Section A.5.3.2 [Floating Point Parameters], page 921.

FLT_MANT_DIG
> float.h (C90): Section A.5.3.2 [Floating Point Parameters], page 921.

FLT_MAX
> float.h (C90): Section A.5.3.2 [Floating Point Parameters], page 921.

FLT_MAX_10_EXP
> float.h (C90): Section A.5.3.2 [Floating Point Parameters], page 921.

FLT_MAX_EXP

> `float.h` (C90): Section A.5.3.2 [Floating Point Parameters], page 921.

FLT_MIN

> `float.h` (C90): Section A.5.3.2 [Floating Point Parameters], page 921.

FLT_MIN_10_EXP

> `float.h` (C90): Section A.5.3.2 [Floating Point Parameters], page 921.

FLT_MIN_EXP

> `float.h` (C90): Section A.5.3.2 [Floating Point Parameters], page 921.

FLT_RADIX

> `float.h` (C90): Section A.5.3.2 [Floating Point Parameters], page 921.

FLT_ROUNDS

> `float.h` (C90): Section A.5.3.2 [Floating Point Parameters], page 921.

tcflag_t FLUSHO

> `termios.h` (BSD): Section 17.4.7 [Local Modes], page 499.

FNM_CASEFOLD

> `fnmatch.h` (GNU): Section 10.1 [Wildcard Matching], page 230.

FNM_EXTMATCH

> `fnmatch.h` (GNU): Section 10.1 [Wildcard Matching], page 230.

FNM_FILE_NAME

> `fnmatch.h` (GNU): Section 10.1 [Wildcard Matching], page 230.

FNM_LEADING_DIR

> `fnmatch.h` (GNU): Section 10.1 [Wildcard Matching], page 230.

FNM_NOESCAPE

> `fnmatch.h` (POSIX.2): Section 10.1 [Wildcard Matching], page 230.

FNM_PATHNAME

> `fnmatch.h` (POSIX.2): Section 10.1 [Wildcard Matching], page 230.

FNM_PERIOD

> `fnmatch.h` (POSIX.2): Section 10.1 [Wildcard Matching], page 230.

int FOPEN_MAX

> `stdio.h` (ISO): Section 12.3 [Opening Streams], page 258.

FPE_DECOVF_TRAP

> `signal.h` (BSD): Section 24.2.1 [Program Error Signals], page 687.

FPE_FLTDIV_FAULT

> `signal.h` (BSD): Section 24.2.1 [Program Error Signals], page 687.

FPE_FLTDIV_TRAP

> `signal.h` (BSD): Section 24.2.1 [Program Error Signals], page 687.

FPE_FLTOVF_FAULT

> `signal.h` (BSD): Section 24.2.1 [Program Error Signals], page 687.

FPE_FLTOVF_TRAP

> `signal.h` (BSD): Section 24.2.1 [Program Error Signals], page 687.

FPE_FLTUND_FAULT

> `signal.h` (BSD): Section 24.2.1 [Program Error Signals], page 687.

FPE_FLTUND_TRAP

> `signal.h` (BSD): Section 24.2.1 [Program Error Signals], page 687.

FPE_INTDIV_TRAP

> `signal.h` (BSD): Section 24.2.1 [Program Error Signals], page 687.

`int F_OFD_SETLK`

        `fcntl.h` (POSIX.1): Section 13.16 [Open File Description Locks], page 384.

`int F_OFD_SETLKW`

        `fcntl.h` (POSIX.1): Section 13.16 [Open File Description Locks], page 384.

`int F_OK`

        `unistd.h` (POSIX.1): Section 14.9.8 [Testing Permission to Access a File], page 425.

`F_RDLCK`

        `fcntl.h` (POSIX.1): Section 13.15 [File Locks], page 380.

`int F_SETFD`

        `fcntl.h` (POSIX.1): Section 13.13 [File Descriptor Flags], page 374.

`int F_SETFL`

        `fcntl.h` (POSIX.1): Section 13.14.4 [Getting and Setting File Status Flags], page 379.

`int F_SETLK`

        `fcntl.h` (POSIX.1): Section 13.15 [File Locks], page 380.

`int F_SETLKW`

        `fcntl.h` (POSIX.1): Section 13.15 [File Locks], page 380.

`int F_SETOWN`

        `fcntl.h` (BSD): Section 13.18 [Interrupt-Driven Input], page 387.

`F_UNLCK`

        `fcntl.h` (POSIX.1): Section 13.15 [File Locks], page 380.

`F_WRLCK`

        `fcntl.h` (POSIX.1): Section 13.15 [File Locks], page 380.

`GLOB_ABORTED`

        `glob.h` (POSIX.2): Section 10.2.1 [Calling `glob`], page 231.

`GLOB_ALTDIRFUNC`

        `glob.h` (GNU): Section 10.2.3 [More Flags for Globbing], page 237.

`GLOB_APPEND`

        `glob.h` (POSIX.2): Section 10.2.2 [Flags for Globbing], page 236.

`GLOB_BRACE`

        `glob.h` (GNU): Section 10.2.3 [More Flags for Globbing], page 237.

`GLOB_DOOFFS`

        `glob.h` (POSIX.2): Section 10.2.2 [Flags for Globbing], page 236.

`GLOB_ERR`

        `glob.h` (POSIX.2): Section 10.2.2 [Flags for Globbing], page 236.

`GLOB_MAGCHAR`

        `glob.h` (GNU): Section 10.2.3 [More Flags for Globbing], page 237.

`GLOB_MARK`

        `glob.h` (POSIX.2): Section 10.2.2 [Flags for Globbing], page 236.

`GLOB_NOCHECK`

        `glob.h` (POSIX.2): Section 10.2.2 [Flags for Globbing], page 236.

`GLOB_NOESCAPE`

        `glob.h` (POSIX.2): Section 10.2.2 [Flags for Globbing], page 236.

`GLOB_NOMAGIC`

        `glob.h` (GNU): Section 10.2.3 [More Flags for Globbing], page 237.

GLOB_NOMATCH

> glob.h (POSIX.2): Section 10.2.1 [Calling glob], page 231.

GLOB_NOSORT

> glob.h (POSIX.2): Section 10.2.2 [Flags for Globbing], page 236.

GLOB_NOSPACE

> glob.h (POSIX.2): Section 10.2.1 [Calling glob], page 231.

GLOB_ONLYDIR

> glob.h (GNU): Section 10.2.3 [More Flags for Globbing], page 237.

GLOB_PERIOD

> glob.h (GNU): Section 10.2.3 [More Flags for Globbing], page 237.

GLOB_TILDE

> glob.h (GNU): Section 10.2.3 [More Flags for Globbing], page 237.

GLOB_TILDE_CHECK

> glob.h (GNU): Section 10.2.3 [More Flags for Globbing], page 237.

HOST_NOT_FOUND

> netdb.h (BSD): Section 16.6.2.4 [Host Names], page 456.

double HUGE_VAL

> math.h (ISO): Section 20.5.4 [Error Reporting by Mathematical Functions], page 586.

float HUGE_VALF

> math.h (ISO): Section 20.5.4 [Error Reporting by Mathematical Functions], page 586.

long double HUGE_VALL

> math.h (ISO): Section 20.5.4 [Error Reporting by Mathematical Functions], page 586.

_FloatN HUGE_VAL_FN

> math.h (TS 18661-3:2015): Section 20.5.4 [Error Reporting by Mathematical Functions], page 586.

_FloatNx HUGE_VAL_FNx

> math.h (TS 18661-3:2015): Section 20.5.4 [Error Reporting by Mathematical Functions], page 586.

tcflag_t HUPCL

> termios.h (POSIX.1): Section 17.4.6 [Control Modes], page 498.

const float complex I

> complex.h (C99): Section 20.9 [Complex Numbers], page 606.

tcflag_t ICANON

> termios.h (POSIX.1): Section 17.4.7 [Local Modes], page 499.

tcflag_t ICRNL

> termios.h (POSIX.1): Section 17.4.4 [Input Modes], page 495.

tcflag_t IEXTEN

> termios.h (POSIX.1): Section 17.4.7 [Local Modes], page 499.

size_t IFNAMSIZ

> net/if.h (???): Section 16.4 [Interface Naming], page 447.

int IFTODT (mode_t mode)

> dirent.h (BSD): Section 14.2.1 [Format of a Directory Entry], page 392.

tcflag_t IGNBRK

> termios.h (POSIX.1): Section 17.4.4 [Input Modes], page 495.

tcflag_t IGNCR

> termios.h (POSIX.1): Section 17.4.4 [Input Modes], page 495.

`tcflag_t IGNPAR`
> `termios.h` (POSIX.1): Section 17.4.4 [Input Modes], page 495.

`tcflag_t IMAXBEL`
> `termios.h` (BSD): Section 17.4.4 [Input Modes], page 495.

`uint32_t INADDR_ANY`
> `netinet/in.h` (BSD): Section 16.6.2.2 [Host Address Data Type], page 453.

`uint32_t INADDR_BROADCAST`
> `netinet/in.h` (BSD): Section 16.6.2.2 [Host Address Data Type], page 453.

`uint32_t INADDR_LOOPBACK`
> `netinet/in.h` (BSD): Section 16.6.2.2 [Host Address Data Type], page 453.

`uint32_t INADDR_NONE`
> `netinet/in.h` (BSD): Section 16.6.2.2 [Host Address Data Type], page 453.

`float INFINITY`
> `math.h` (ISO): Section 20.5.2 [Infinity and NaN], page 583.

`INIT_PROCESS`
> `utmp.h` (SVID): Section 30.12.1 [Manipulating the User Accounting Database], page 826.
>
> `utmpx.h` (XPG4.2): Section 30.12.2 [XPG User Accounting Database Functions], page 831.

`tcflag_t INLCR`
> `termios.h` (POSIX.1): Section 17.4.4 [Input Modes], page 495.

`tcflag_t INPCK`
> `termios.h` (POSIX.1): Section 17.4.4 [Input Modes], page 495.

`INTPTR_WIDTH`
> `stdint.h` (ISO): Section A.5.1 [Computing the Width of an Integer Data Type], page 917.

`INT_MAX`
> `limits.h` (ISO): Section A.5.2 [Range of an Integer Type], page 918.

`INT_MIN`
> `limits.h` (ISO): Section A.5.2 [Range of an Integer Type], page 918.

`INT_WIDTH`
> `limits.h` (ISO): Section A.5.1 [Computing the Width of an Integer Data Type], page 917.

`int IPPORT_RESERVED`
> `netinet/in.h` (BSD): Section 16.6.3 [Internet Ports], page 460.

`int IPPORT_USERRESERVED`
> `netinet/in.h` (BSD): Section 16.6.3 [Internet Ports], page 460.

`tcflag_t ISIG`
> `termios.h` (POSIX.1): Section 17.4.7 [Local Modes], page 499.

`tcflag_t ISTRIP`
> `termios.h` (POSIX.1): Section 17.4.4 [Input Modes], page 495.

`ITIMER_PROF`
> `sys/time.h` (BSD): Section 21.5 [Setting an Alarm], page 649.

`ITIMER_REAL`
> `sys/time.h` (BSD): Section 21.5 [Setting an Alarm], page 649.

`ITIMER_VIRTUAL`
> `sys/time.h` (BSD): Section 21.5 [Setting an Alarm], page 649.

`tcflag_t IXANY`
> `termios.h` (BSD): Section 17.4.4 [Input Modes], page 495.

`tcflag_t IXOFF`

> `termios.h` (POSIX.1): Section 17.4.4 [Input Modes], page 495.

`tcflag_t IXON`

> `termios.h` (POSIX.1): Section 17.4.4 [Input Modes], page 495.

`LANG`

> `locale.h` (ISO): Section 7.3 [Locale Categories], page 177.

`LC_ALL`

> `locale.h` (ISO): Section 7.3 [Locale Categories], page 177.

`LC_COLLATE`

> `locale.h` (ISO): Section 7.3 [Locale Categories], page 177.

`LC_CTYPE`

> `locale.h` (ISO): Section 7.3 [Locale Categories], page 177.

`LC_MESSAGES`

> `locale.h` (XOPEN): Section 7.3 [Locale Categories], page 177.

`LC_MONETARY`

> `locale.h` (ISO): Section 7.3 [Locale Categories], page 177.

`LC_NUMERIC`

> `locale.h` (ISO): Section 7.3 [Locale Categories], page 177.

`LC_TIME`

> `locale.h` (ISO): Section 7.3 [Locale Categories], page 177.

`LDBL_DIG`

> `float.h` (C90): Section A.5.3.2 [Floating Point Parameters], page 921.

`LDBL_EPSILON`

> `float.h` (C90): Section A.5.3.2 [Floating Point Parameters], page 921.

`LDBL_MANT_DIG`

> `float.h` (C90): Section A.5.3.2 [Floating Point Parameters], page 921.

`LDBL_MAX`

> `float.h` (C90): Section A.5.3.2 [Floating Point Parameters], page 921.

`LDBL_MAX_10_EXP`

> `float.h` (C90): Section A.5.3.2 [Floating Point Parameters], page 921.

`LDBL_MAX_EXP`

> `float.h` (C90): Section A.5.3.2 [Floating Point Parameters], page 921.

`LDBL_MIN`

> `float.h` (C90): Section A.5.3.2 [Floating Point Parameters], page 921.

`LDBL_MIN_10_EXP`

> `float.h` (C90): Section A.5.3.2 [Floating Point Parameters], page 921.

`LDBL_MIN_EXP`

> `float.h` (C90): Section A.5.3.2 [Floating Point Parameters], page 921.

`int LINE_MAX`

> `limits.h` (POSIX.2): Section 32.10 [Utility Program Capacity Limits], page 879.

`int LINK_MAX`

> `limits.h` *optional* (POSIX.1): Section 32.6 [Limits on File System Capacity], page 874.

`LLONG_MAX`

> `limits.h` (ISO): Section A.5.2 [Range of an Integer Type], page 918.

`LLONG_MIN`

> `limits.h` (ISO): Section A.5.2 [Range of an Integer Type], page 918.

`LLONG_WIDTH`

> `limits.h` (ISO): Section A.5.1 [Computing the Width of an Integer Data Type], page 917.

`LOGIN_PROCESS`

> `utmp.h` (SVID): Section 30.12.1 [Manipulating the User Accounting Database], page 826.

> `utmpx.h` (XPG4.2): Section 30.12.2 [XPG User Accounting Database Functions], page 831.

`LONG_LONG_MAX`

> `limits.h` (GNU): Section A.5.2 [Range of an Integer Type], page 918.

`LONG_LONG_MIN`

> `limits.h` (GNU): Section A.5.2 [Range of an Integer Type], page 918.

`LONG_MAX`

> `limits.h` (ISO): Section A.5.2 [Range of an Integer Type], page 918.

`LONG_MIN`

> `limits.h` (ISO): Section A.5.2 [Range of an Integer Type], page 918.

`LONG_WIDTH`

> `limits.h` (ISO): Section A.5.1 [Computing the Width of an Integer Data Type], page 917.

`L_INCR`

> `sys/file.h` (BSD): Section 12.18 [File Positioning], page 314.

`L_SET`

> `sys/file.h` (BSD): Section 12.18 [File Positioning], page 314.

`L_XTND`

> `sys/file.h` (BSD): Section 12.18 [File Positioning], page 314.

int `L_ctermid`

> `stdio.h` (POSIX.1): Section 28.7.1 [Identifying the Controlling Terminal], page 801.

int `L_cuserid`

> `stdio.h` (POSIX.1): Section 30.11 [Identifying Who Logged In], page 825.

int `L_tmpnam`

> `stdio.h` (ISO): Section 14.11 [Temporary Files], page 433.

int `MAXNAMLEN`

> `dirent.h` (BSD): Section 32.6 [Limits on File System Capacity], page 874.

int `MAXSYMLINKS`

> `sys/param.h` (BSD): Section 14.5 [Symbolic Links], page 406.

int `MAX_CANON`

> `limits.h` (POSIX.1): Section 32.6 [Limits on File System Capacity], page 874.

int `MAX_INPUT`

> `limits.h` (POSIX.1): Section 32.6 [Limits on File System Capacity], page 874.

int `MB_CUR_MAX`

> `stdlib.h` (ISO): Section 6.3.1 [Selecting the conversion and its properties], page 138.

int `MB_LEN_MAX`

> `limits.h` (ISO): Section 6.3.1 [Selecting the conversion and its properties], page 138.

tcflag_t `MDMBUF`

> `termios.h` (BSD): Section 17.4.6 [Control Modes], page 498.

int `MSG_DONTROUTE`

> `sys/socket.h` (BSD): Section 16.9.5.3 [Socket Data Options], page 474.

`int MSG_OOB`

> `sys/socket.h` (BSD): Section 16.9.5.3 [Socket Data Options], page 474.

`int MSG_PEEK`

> `sys/socket.h` (BSD): Section 16.9.5.3 [Socket Data Options], page 474.

`int NAME_MAX`

> `limits.h` (POSIX.1): Section 32.6 [Limits on File System Capacity], page 874.

`float NAN`

> `math.h` (GNU): Section 20.5.2 [Infinity and NaN], page 583.

`int NCCS`

> `termios.h` (POSIX.1): Section 17.4.1 [Terminal Mode Data Types], page 492.

`NEW_TIME`

> `utmp.h` (SVID): Section 30.12.1 [Manipulating the User Accounting Database], page 826.
>
> `utmpx.h` (XPG4.2): Section 30.12.2 [XPG User Accounting Database Functions], page 831.

`int NGROUPS_MAX`

> `limits.h` (POSIX.1): Section 32.1 [General Capacity Limits], page 862.

`tcflag_t NOFLSH`

> `termios.h` (POSIX.1): Section 17.4.7 [Local Modes], page 499.

`tcflag_t NOKERNINFO`

> `termios.h` *optional* (BSD): Section 17.4.7 [Local Modes], page 499.

`NO_ADDRESS`

> `netdb.h` (BSD): Section 16.6.2.4 [Host Names], page 456.

`NO_RECOVERY`

> `netdb.h` (BSD): Section 16.6.2.4 [Host Names], page 456.

`int NSIG`

> `signal.h` (BSD): Section 24.2 [Standard Signals], page 687.

`void * NULL`

> `stddef.h` (ISO): Section A.3 [Null Pointer Constant], page 915.

`OLD_TIME`

> `utmp.h` (SVID): Section 30.12.1 [Manipulating the User Accounting Database], page 826.
>
> `utmpx.h` (XPG4.2): Section 30.12.2 [XPG User Accounting Database Functions], page 831.

`tcflag_t ONLCR`

> `termios.h` (POSIX.1): Section 17.4.5 [Output Modes], page 497.

`tcflag_t ONOEOT`

> `termios.h` *optional* (BSD): Section 17.4.5 [Output Modes], page 497.

`int OPEN_MAX`

> `limits.h` (POSIX.1): Section 32.1 [General Capacity Limits], page 862.

`tcflag_t OPOST`

> `termios.h` (POSIX.1): Section 17.4.5 [Output Modes], page 497.

`OPTION_ALIAS`

> `argp.h` (GNU): Section 25.3.4.1 [Flags for Argp Options], page 741.

`OPTION_ARG_OPTIONAL`

> `argp.h` (GNU): Section 25.3.4.1 [Flags for Argp Options], page 741.

`OPTION_DOC`

> `argp.h` (GNU): Section 25.3.4.1 [Flags for Argp Options], page 741.

`OPTION_HIDDEN`

>   `argp.h` (GNU): Section 25.3.4.1 [Flags for Argp Options], page 741.

`OPTION_NO_USAGE`

>   `argp.h` (GNU): Section 25.3.4.1 [Flags for Argp Options], page 741.

`tcflag_t OXTABS`

>   `termios.h` *optional* (BSD): Section 17.4.5 [Output Modes], page 497.

`int O_ACCMODE`

>   `fcntl.h` (POSIX.1): Section 13.14.1 [File Access Modes], page 376.

`int O_APPEND`

>   `fcntl.h` (POSIX.1): Section 13.14.3 [I/O Operating Modes], page 378.

`int O_ASYNC`

>   `fcntl.h` (BSD): Section 13.14.3 [I/O Operating Modes], page 378.

`int O_CREAT`

>   `fcntl.h` (POSIX.1): Section 13.14.2 [Open-time Flags], page 377.

`int O_EXCL`

>   `fcntl.h` (POSIX.1): Section 13.14.2 [Open-time Flags], page 377.

`int O_EXEC`

>   `fcntl.h` *optional* (GNU): Section 13.14.1 [File Access Modes], page 376.

`int O_EXLOCK`

>   `fcntl.h` *optional* (BSD): Section 13.14.2 [Open-time Flags], page 377.

`int O_FSYNC`

>   `fcntl.h` (BSD): Section 13.14.3 [I/O Operating Modes], page 378.

`int O_IGNORE_CTTY`

>   `fcntl.h` *optional* (GNU): Section 13.14.2 [Open-time Flags], page 377.

`int O_NDELAY`

>   `fcntl.h` (BSD): Section 13.14.3 [I/O Operating Modes], page 378.

`int O_NOATIME`

>   `fcntl.h` (GNU): Section 13.14.3 [I/O Operating Modes], page 378.

`int O_NOCTTY`

>   `fcntl.h` (POSIX.1): Section 13.14.2 [Open-time Flags], page 377.

`int O_NOLINK`

>   `fcntl.h` *optional* (GNU): Section 13.14.2 [Open-time Flags], page 377.

`int O_NONBLOCK`

>   `fcntl.h` (POSIX.1): Section 13.14.2 [Open-time Flags], page 377.
>
>   `fcntl.h` (POSIX.1): Section 13.14.3 [I/O Operating Modes], page 378.

`int O_NOTRANS`

>   `fcntl.h` *optional* (GNU): Section 13.14.2 [Open-time Flags], page 377.

`int O_RDONLY`

>   `fcntl.h` (POSIX.1): Section 13.14.1 [File Access Modes], page 376.

`int O_RDWR`

>   `fcntl.h` (POSIX.1): Section 13.14.1 [File Access Modes], page 376.

`int O_READ`

>   `fcntl.h` *optional* (GNU): Section 13.14.1 [File Access Modes], page 376.

`int O_SHLOCK`

>   `fcntl.h` *optional* (BSD): Section 13.14.2 [Open-time Flags], page 377.

int O_SYNC

> `fcntl.h` (BSD): Section 13.14.3 [I/O Operating Modes], page 378.

int O_TRUNC

> `fcntl.h` (POSIX.1): Section 13.14.2 [Open-time Flags], page 377.

int O_WRITE

> `fcntl.h` *optional* (GNU): Section 13.14.1 [File Access Modes], page 376.

int O_WRONLY

> `fcntl.h` (POSIX.1): Section 13.14.1 [File Access Modes], page 376.

tcflag_t PARENB

> `termios.h` (POSIX.1): Section 17.4.6 [Control Modes], page 498.

tcflag_t PARMRK

> `termios.h` (POSIX.1): Section 17.4.4 [Input Modes], page 495.

tcflag_t PARODD

> `termios.h` (POSIX.1): Section 17.4.6 [Control Modes], page 498.

int PATH_MAX

> `limits.h` (POSIX.1): Section 32.6 [Limits on File System Capacity], page 874.

PA_CHAR

> `printf.h` (GNU): Section 12.12.10 [Parsing a Template String], page 293.

PA_DOUBLE

> `printf.h` (GNU): Section 12.12.10 [Parsing a Template String], page 293.

PA_FLAG_LONG

> `printf.h` (GNU): Section 12.12.10 [Parsing a Template String], page 293.

PA_FLAG_LONG_DOUBLE

> `printf.h` (GNU): Section 12.12.10 [Parsing a Template String], page 293.

PA_FLAG_LONG_LONG

> `printf.h` (GNU): Section 12.12.10 [Parsing a Template String], page 293.

int PA_FLAG_MASK

> `printf.h` (GNU): Section 12.12.10 [Parsing a Template String], page 293.

PA_FLAG_PTR

> `printf.h` (GNU): Section 12.12.10 [Parsing a Template String], page 293.

PA_FLAG_SHORT

> `printf.h` (GNU): Section 12.12.10 [Parsing a Template String], page 293.

PA_FLOAT

> `printf.h` (GNU): Section 12.12.10 [Parsing a Template String], page 293.

PA_INT

> `printf.h` (GNU): Section 12.12.10 [Parsing a Template String], page 293.

PA_LAST

> `printf.h` (GNU): Section 12.12.10 [Parsing a Template String], page 293.

PA_POINTER

> `printf.h` (GNU): Section 12.12.10 [Parsing a Template String], page 293.

PA_STRING

> `printf.h` (GNU): Section 12.12.10 [Parsing a Template String], page 293.

tcflag_t PENDIN

> `termios.h` (BSD): Section 17.4.7 [Local Modes], page 499.

`int PF_FILE`

> `sys/socket.h` (GNU): Section 16.5.2 [Details of Local Namespace], page 448.

`int PF_INET`

> `sys/socket.h` (BSD): Section 16.6 [The Internet Namespace], page 450.

`int PF_INET6`

> `sys/socket.h` (X/Open): Section 16.6 [The Internet Namespace], page 450.

`int PF_LOCAL`

> `sys/socket.h` (POSIX): Section 16.5.2 [Details of Local Namespace], page 448.

`int PF_UNIX`

> `sys/socket.h` (BSD): Section 16.5.2 [Details of Local Namespace], page 448.

`int PIPE_BUF`

> `limits.h` (POSIX.1): Section 32.6 [Limits on File System Capacity], page 874.

`POSIX_REC_INCR_XFER_SIZE`

> `limits.h` (POSIX.1): Section 32.8 [Minimum Values for File System Limits], page 876.

`POSIX_REC_MAX_XFER_SIZE`

> `limits.h` (POSIX.1): Section 32.8 [Minimum Values for File System Limits], page 876.

`POSIX_REC_MIN_XFER_SIZE`

> `limits.h` (POSIX.1): Section 32.8 [Minimum Values for File System Limits], page 876.

`POSIX_REC_XFER_ALIGN`

> `limits.h` (POSIX.1): Section 32.8 [Minimum Values for File System Limits], page 876.

`PRIO_MAX`

> `sys/resource.h` (BSD): Section 22.3.4.2 [Functions For Traditional Scheduling], page 668.

`PRIO_MIN`

> `sys/resource.h` (BSD): Section 22.3.4.2 [Functions For Traditional Scheduling], page 668.

`PRIO_PGRP`

> `sys/resource.h` (BSD): Section 22.3.4.2 [Functions For Traditional Scheduling], page 668.

`PRIO_PROCESS`

> `sys/resource.h` (BSD): Section 22.3.4.2 [Functions For Traditional Scheduling], page 668.

`PRIO_USER`

> `sys/resource.h` (BSD): Section 22.3.4.2 [Functions For Traditional Scheduling], page 668.

`PTRDIFF_WIDTH`

> `stdint.h` (ISO): Section A.5.1 [Computing the Width of an Integer Data Type], page 917.

`char * P_tmpdir`

> `stdio.h` (SVID): Section 14.11 [Temporary Files], page 433.

`int RAND_MAX`

> `stdlib.h` (ISO): Section 19.8.1 [ISO C Random Number Functions], page 565.

`REG_BADBR`

> `regex.h` (POSIX.2): Section 10.3.1 [POSIX Regular Expression Compilation], page 240.

`REG_BADPAT`

> `regex.h` (POSIX.2): Section 10.3.1 [POSIX Regular Expression Compilation], page 240.

`REG_BADRPT`

> `regex.h` (POSIX.2): Section 10.3.1 [POSIX Regular Expression Compilation], page 240.

`REG_EBRACE`

> `regex.h` (POSIX.2): Section 10.3.1 [POSIX Regular Expression Compilation], page 240.

`RLIMIT_FSIZE`

> `sys/resource.h` (BSD): Section 22.2 [Limiting Resource Usage], page 656.

`RLIMIT_MEMLOCK`

> `sys/resource.h` (BSD): Section 22.2 [Limiting Resource Usage], page 656.

`RLIMIT_NOFILE`

> `sys/resource.h` (BSD): Section 22.2 [Limiting Resource Usage], page 656.

`RLIMIT_NPROC`

> `sys/resource.h` (BSD): Section 22.2 [Limiting Resource Usage], page 656.

`RLIMIT_RSS`

> `sys/resource.h` (BSD): Section 22.2 [Limiting Resource Usage], page 656.

`RLIMIT_STACK`

> `sys/resource.h` (BSD): Section 22.2 [Limiting Resource Usage], page 656.

`rlim_t RLIM_INFINITY`

> `sys/resource.h` (BSD): Section 22.2 [Limiting Resource Usage], page 656.

`RLIM_NLIMITS`

> `sys/resource.h` (BSD): Section 22.2 [Limiting Resource Usage], page 656.

`RUN_LVL`

> `utmp.h` (SVID): Section 30.12.1 [Manipulating the User Accounting Database], page 826.
>
> `utmpx.h` (XPG4.2): Section 30.12.2 [XPG User Accounting Database Functions], page 831.

`RUSAGE_CHILDREN`

> `sys/resource.h` (BSD): Section 22.1 [Resource Usage], page 654.

`RUSAGE_SELF`

> `sys/resource.h` (BSD): Section 22.1 [Resource Usage], page 654.

`int R_OK`

> `unistd.h` (POSIX.1): Section 14.9.8 [Testing Permission to Access a File], page 425.

`int SA_NOCLDSTOP`

> `signal.h` (POSIX.1): Section 24.3.5 [Flags for `sigaction`], page 700.

`int SA_ONSTACK`

> `signal.h` (BSD): Section 24.3.5 [Flags for `sigaction`], page 700.

`int SA_RESTART`

> `signal.h` (BSD): Section 24.3.5 [Flags for `sigaction`], page 700.

`SCHAR_MAX`

> `limits.h` (ISO): Section A.5.2 [Range of an Integer Type], page 918.

`SCHAR_MIN`

> `limits.h` (ISO): Section A.5.2 [Range of an Integer Type], page 918.

`SCHAR_WIDTH`

> `limits.h` (ISO): Section A.5.1 [Computing the Width of an Integer Data Type], page 917.

`SC_SSIZE_MAX`

> `unistd.h` (X/Open): Section 32.4.2 [Constants for `sysconf` Parameters], page 865.

`int SEEK_CUR`

> `stdio.h` (ISO): Section 12.18 [File Positioning], page 314.

`int SEEK_END`

> `stdio.h` (ISO): Section 12.18 [File Positioning], page 314.

`int SEEK_SET`

> `stdio.h` (ISO): Section 12.18 [File Positioning], page 314.

SHRT_MAX

> `limits.h` (ISO): Section A.5.2 [Range of an Integer Type], page 918.

SHRT_MIN

> `limits.h` (ISO): Section A.5.2 [Range of an Integer Type], page 918.

SHRT_WIDTH

> `limits.h` (ISO): Section A.5.1 [Computing the Width of an Integer Data Type], page 917.

int SIGABRT

> `signal.h` (ISO): Section 24.2.1 [Program Error Signals], page 687.

int SIGALRM

> `signal.h` (POSIX.1): Section 24.2.3 [Alarm Signals], page 691.

int SIGBUS

> `signal.h` (BSD): Section 24.2.1 [Program Error Signals], page 687.

int SIGCHLD

> `signal.h` (POSIX.1): Section 24.2.5 [Job Control Signals], page 692.

int SIGCLD

> `signal.h` (SVID): Section 24.2.5 [Job Control Signals], page 692.

int SIGCONT

> `signal.h` (POSIX.1): Section 24.2.5 [Job Control Signals], page 692.

int SIGEMT

> `signal.h` (BSD): Section 24.2.1 [Program Error Signals], page 687.

int SIGFPE

> `signal.h` (ISO): Section 24.2.1 [Program Error Signals], page 687.

int SIGHUP

> `signal.h` (POSIX.1): Section 24.2.2 [Termination Signals], page 690.

int SIGILL

> `signal.h` (ISO): Section 24.2.1 [Program Error Signals], page 687.

int SIGINFO

> `signal.h` (BSD): Section 24.2.7 [Miscellaneous Signals], page 694.

int SIGINT

> `signal.h` (ISO): Section 24.2.2 [Termination Signals], page 690.

int SIGIO

> `signal.h` (BSD): Section 24.2.4 [Asynchronous I/O Signals], page 691.

int SIGIOT

> `signal.h` (Unix): Section 24.2.1 [Program Error Signals], page 687.

int SIGKILL

> `signal.h` (POSIX.1): Section 24.2.2 [Termination Signals], page 690.

int SIGLOST

> `signal.h` (GNU): Section 24.2.6 [Operation Error Signals], page 693.

int SIGPIPE

> `signal.h` (POSIX.1): Section 24.2.6 [Operation Error Signals], page 693.

int SIGPOLL

> `signal.h` (SVID): Section 24.2.4 [Asynchronous I/O Signals], page 691.

int SIGPROF

> `signal.h` (BSD): Section 24.2.3 [Alarm Signals], page 691.

int SIGQUIT

> `signal.h` (POSIX.1): Section 24.2.2 [Termination Signals], page 690.

int SIGSEGV

> `signal.h` (ISO): Section 24.2.1 [Program Error Signals], page 687.

int SIGSTOP

> `signal.h` (POSIX.1): Section 24.2.5 [Job Control Signals], page 692.

int SIGSYS

> `signal.h` (Unix): Section 24.2.1 [Program Error Signals], page 687.

int SIGTERM

> `signal.h` (ISO): Section 24.2.2 [Termination Signals], page 690.

int SIGTRAP

> `signal.h` (BSD): Section 24.2.1 [Program Error Signals], page 687.

int SIGTSTP

> `signal.h` (POSIX.1): Section 24.2.5 [Job Control Signals], page 692.

int SIGTTIN

> `signal.h` (POSIX.1): Section 24.2.5 [Job Control Signals], page 692.

int SIGTTOU

> `signal.h` (POSIX.1): Section 24.2.5 [Job Control Signals], page 692.

int SIGURG

> `signal.h` (BSD): Section 24.2.4 [Asynchronous I/O Signals], page 691.

int SIGUSR1

> `signal.h` (POSIX.1): Section 24.2.7 [Miscellaneous Signals], page 694.

int SIGUSR2

> `signal.h` (POSIX.1): Section 24.2.7 [Miscellaneous Signals], page 694.

int SIGVTALRM

> `signal.h` (BSD): Section 24.2.3 [Alarm Signals], page 691.

int SIGWINCH

> `signal.h` (BSD): Section 24.2.7 [Miscellaneous Signals], page 694.

int SIGXCPU

> `signal.h` (BSD): Section 24.2.6 [Operation Error Signals], page 693.

int SIGXFSZ

> `signal.h` (BSD): Section 24.2.6 [Operation Error Signals], page 693.

SIG_ATOMIC_WIDTH

> `stdint.h` (ISO): Section A.5.1 [Computing the Width of an Integer Data Type], page 917.

SIG_BLOCK

> `signal.h` (POSIX.1): Section 24.7.3 [Process Signal Mask], page 718.

sighandler_t SIG_ERR

> `signal.h` (ISO): Section 24.3.1 [Basic Signal Handling], page 696.

SIG_SETMASK

> `signal.h` (POSIX.1): Section 24.7.3 [Process Signal Mask], page 718.

Appendix B: Summary of Library Facilities

SIG_UNBLOCK
 signal.h (POSIX.1): Section 24.7.3 [Process Signal Mask], page 718.

SIZE_WIDTH
 stdint.h (ISO): Section A.5.1 [Computing the Width of an Integer Data Type], page 917.

double SNAN
 math.h (TS 18661-1:2014): Section 20.5.2 [Infinity and NaN], page 583.

float SNANF
 math.h (TS 18661-1:2014): Section 20.5.2 [Infinity and NaN], page 583.

_FloatN SNANFN
 math.h (TS 18661-3:2015): Section 20.5.2 [Infinity and NaN], page 583.

_FloatNx SNANFNx
 math.h (TS 18661-3:2015): Section 20.5.2 [Infinity and NaN], page 583.

long double SNANL
 math.h (TS 18661-1:2014): Section 20.5.2 [Infinity and NaN], page 583.

int SOCK_DGRAM
 sys/socket.h (BSD): Section 16.2 [Communication Styles], page 443.

int SOCK_RAW
 sys/socket.h (BSD): Section 16.2 [Communication Styles], page 443.

int SOCK_STREAM
 sys/socket.h (BSD): Section 16.2 [Communication Styles], page 443.

int SOL_SOCKET
 sys/socket.h (BSD): Section 16.12.2 [Socket-Level Options], page 486.

SO_BROADCAST
 sys/socket.h (BSD): Section 16.12.2 [Socket-Level Options], page 486.

SO_DEBUG
 sys/socket.h (BSD): Section 16.12.2 [Socket-Level Options], page 486.

SO_DONTROUTE
 sys/socket.h (BSD): Section 16.12.2 [Socket-Level Options], page 486.

SO_ERROR
 sys/socket.h (BSD): Section 16.12.2 [Socket-Level Options], page 486.

SO_KEEPALIVE
 sys/socket.h (BSD): Section 16.12.2 [Socket-Level Options], page 486.

SO_LINGER
 sys/socket.h (BSD): Section 16.12.2 [Socket-Level Options], page 486.

SO_OOBINLINE
 sys/socket.h (BSD): Section 16.12.2 [Socket-Level Options], page 486.

SO_RCVBUF
 sys/socket.h (BSD): Section 16.12.2 [Socket-Level Options], page 486.

SO_REUSEADDR
 sys/socket.h (BSD): Section 16.12.2 [Socket-Level Options], page 486.

SO_SNDBUF
 sys/socket.h (BSD): Section 16.12.2 [Socket-Level Options], page 486.

SO_STYLE
 sys/socket.h (GNU): Section 16.12.2 [Socket-Level Options], page 486.

SO_TYPE

        sys/socket.h (BSD): Section 16.12.2 [Socket-Level Options], page 486.

ssize_t SSIZE_MAX

        limits.h (POSIX.1): Section 32.1 [General Capacity Limits], page 862.

STDERR_FILENO

        unistd.h (POSIX.1): Section 13.4 [Descriptors and Streams], page 346.

STDIN_FILENO

        unistd.h (POSIX.1): Section 13.4 [Descriptors and Streams], page 346.

STDOUT_FILENO

        unistd.h (POSIX.1): Section 13.4 [Descriptors and Streams], page 346.

int STREAM_MAX

        limits.h (POSIX.1): Section 32.1 [General Capacity Limits], page 862.

int SUN_LEN (struct sockaddr_un * ptr)

        sys/un.h (BSD): Section 16.5.2 [Details of Local Namespace], page 448.

SYMLINK_MAX

        limits.h (POSIX.1): Section 32.8 [Minimum Values for File System Limits], page 876.

S_IEXEC

        sys/stat.h (BSD): Section 14.9.5 [The Mode Bits for Access Permission], page 421.

S_IFBLK

        sys/stat.h (BSD): Section 14.9.3 [Testing the Type of a File], page 417.

S_IFCHR

        sys/stat.h (BSD): Section 14.9.3 [Testing the Type of a File], page 417.

S_IFDIR

        sys/stat.h (BSD): Section 14.9.3 [Testing the Type of a File], page 417.

S_IFIFO

        sys/stat.h (BSD): Section 14.9.3 [Testing the Type of a File], page 417.

S_IFLNK

        sys/stat.h (BSD): Section 14.9.3 [Testing the Type of a File], page 417.

int S_IFMT

        sys/stat.h (BSD): Section 14.9.3 [Testing the Type of a File], page 417.

S_IFREG

        sys/stat.h (BSD): Section 14.9.3 [Testing the Type of a File], page 417.

S_IFSOCK

        sys/stat.h (BSD): Section 14.9.3 [Testing the Type of a File], page 417.

S_IREAD

        sys/stat.h (BSD): Section 14.9.5 [The Mode Bits for Access Permission], page 421.

S_IRGRP

        sys/stat.h (POSIX.1): Section 14.9.5 [The Mode Bits for Access Permission], page 421.

S_IROTH

        sys/stat.h (POSIX.1): Section 14.9.5 [The Mode Bits for Access Permission], page 421.

S_IRUSR

        sys/stat.h (POSIX.1): Section 14.9.5 [The Mode Bits for Access Permission], page 421.

S_IRWXG

        sys/stat.h (POSIX.1): Section 14.9.5 [The Mode Bits for Access Permission], page 421.

S_IRWXO

      sys/stat.h (POSIX.1): Section 14.9.5 [The Mode Bits for Access Permission], page 421.

S_IRWXU

      sys/stat.h (POSIX.1): Section 14.9.5 [The Mode Bits for Access Permission], page 421.

int S_ISBLK (mode_t *m*)
      sys/stat.h (POSIX): Section 14.9.3 [Testing the Type of a File], page 417.

int S_ISCHR (mode_t *m*)
      sys/stat.h (POSIX): Section 14.9.3 [Testing the Type of a File], page 417.

int S_ISDIR (mode_t *m*)
      sys/stat.h (POSIX): Section 14.9.3 [Testing the Type of a File], page 417.

int S_ISFIFO (mode_t *m*)
      sys/stat.h (POSIX): Section 14.9.3 [Testing the Type of a File], page 417.

S_ISGID

      sys/stat.h (POSIX): Section 14.9.5 [The Mode Bits for Access Permission], page 421.

int S_ISLNK (mode_t *m*)
      sys/stat.h (GNU): Section 14.9.3 [Testing the Type of a File], page 417.

int S_ISREG (mode_t *m*)
      sys/stat.h (POSIX): Section 14.9.3 [Testing the Type of a File], page 417.

int S_ISSOCK (mode_t *m*)
      sys/stat.h (GNU): Section 14.9.3 [Testing the Type of a File], page 417.

S_ISUID

      sys/stat.h (POSIX): Section 14.9.5 [The Mode Bits for Access Permission], page 421.

S_ISVTX

      sys/stat.h (BSD): Section 14.9.5 [The Mode Bits for Access Permission], page 421.

S_IWGRP

      sys/stat.h (POSIX.1): Section 14.9.5 [The Mode Bits for Access Permission], page 421.

S_IWOTH

      sys/stat.h (POSIX.1): Section 14.9.5 [The Mode Bits for Access Permission], page 421.

S_IWRITE

      sys/stat.h (BSD): Section 14.9.5 [The Mode Bits for Access Permission], page 421.

S_IWUSR

      sys/stat.h (POSIX.1): Section 14.9.5 [The Mode Bits for Access Permission], page 421.

S_IXGRP

      sys/stat.h (POSIX.1): Section 14.9.5 [The Mode Bits for Access Permission], page 421.

S_IXOTH

      sys/stat.h (POSIX.1): Section 14.9.5 [The Mode Bits for Access Permission], page 421.

S_IXUSR

      sys/stat.h (POSIX.1): Section 14.9.5 [The Mode Bits for Access Permission], page 421.

int S_TYPEISMQ (struct stat *s*)
      sys/stat.h (POSIX): Section 14.9.3 [Testing the Type of a File], page 417.

int S_TYPEISSEM (struct stat *s*)
      sys/stat.h (POSIX): Section 14.9.3 [Testing the Type of a File], page 417.

int S_TYPEISSHM (struct stat *s*)
      sys/stat.h (POSIX): Section 14.9.3 [Testing the Type of a File], page 417.

TCSADRAIN

termios.h (POSIX.1): Section 17.4.2 [Terminal Mode Functions], page 493.

TCSAFLUSH

termios.h (POSIX.1): Section 17.4.2 [Terminal Mode Functions], page 493.

TCSANOW

termios.h (POSIX.1): Section 17.4.2 [Terminal Mode Functions], page 493.

TCSASOFT

termios.h (BSD): Section 17.4.2 [Terminal Mode Functions], page 493.

TEMP_FAILURE_RETRY (*expression*)

unistd.h (GNU): Section 24.5 [Primitives Interrupted by Signals], page 711.

int TMP_MAX

stdio.h (ISO): Section 14.11 [Temporary Files], page 433.

tcflag_t TOSTOP

termios.h (POSIX.1): Section 17.4.7 [Local Modes], page 499.

TRY_AGAIN

netdb.h (BSD): Section 16.6.2.4 [Host Names], page 456.

int TZNAME_MAX

limits.h (POSIX.1): Section 32.1 [General Capacity Limits], page 862.

UCHAR_MAX

limits.h (ISO): Section A.5.2 [Range of an Integer Type], page 918.

UCHAR_WIDTH

limits.h (ISO): Section A.5.1 [Computing the Width of an Integer Data Type], page 917.

UINTPTR_WIDTH

stdint.h (ISO): Section A.5.1 [Computing the Width of an Integer Data Type], page 917.

UINT_MAX

limits.h (ISO): Section A.5.2 [Range of an Integer Type], page 918.

UINT_WIDTH

limits.h (ISO): Section A.5.1 [Computing the Width of an Integer Data Type], page 917.

ULLONG_MAX

limits.h (ISO): Section A.5.2 [Range of an Integer Type], page 918.

ULLONG_WIDTH

limits.h (ISO): Section A.5.1 [Computing the Width of an Integer Data Type], page 917.

ULONG_LONG_MAX

limits.h (GNU): Section A.5.2 [Range of an Integer Type], page 918.

ULONG_MAX

limits.h (ISO): Section A.5.2 [Range of an Integer Type], page 918.

ULONG_WIDTH

limits.h (ISO): Section A.5.1 [Computing the Width of an Integer Data Type], page 917.

USER_PROCESS

utmp.h (SVID): Section 30.12.1 [Manipulating the User Accounting Database], page 826.

utmpx.h (XPG4.2): Section 30.12.2 [XPG User Accounting Database Functions], page 831.

USHRT_MAX

limits.h (ISO): Section A.5.2 [Range of an Integer Type], page 918.

USHRT_WIDTH

        `limits.h` (ISO): Section A.5.1 [Computing the Width of an Integer Data Type], page 917.

int VDISCARD

        `termios.h` (BSD): Section 17.4.9.4 [Other Special Characters], page 507.

int VDSUSP

        `termios.h` (BSD): Section 17.4.9.2 [Characters that Cause Signals], page 505.

int VEOF

        `termios.h` (POSIX.1): Section 17.4.9.1 [Characters for Input Editing], page 503.

int VEOL

        `termios.h` (POSIX.1): Section 17.4.9.1 [Characters for Input Editing], page 503.

int VEOL2

        `termios.h` (BSD): Section 17.4.9.1 [Characters for Input Editing], page 503.

int VERASE

        `termios.h` (POSIX.1): Section 17.4.9.1 [Characters for Input Editing], page 503.

int VINTR

        `termios.h` (POSIX.1): Section 17.4.9.2 [Characters that Cause Signals], page 505.

int VKILL

        `termios.h` (POSIX.1): Section 17.4.9.1 [Characters for Input Editing], page 503.

int VLNEXT

        `termios.h` (BSD): Section 17.4.9.4 [Other Special Characters], page 507.

int VMIN

        `termios.h` (POSIX.1): Section 17.4.10 [Noncanonical Input], page 507.

int VQUIT

        `termios.h` (POSIX.1): Section 17.4.9.2 [Characters that Cause Signals], page 505.

int VREPRINT

        `termios.h` (BSD): Section 17.4.9.1 [Characters for Input Editing], page 503.

int VSTART

        `termios.h` (POSIX.1): Section 17.4.9.3 [Special Characters for Flow Control], page 506.

int VSTATUS

        `termios.h` (BSD): Section 17.4.9.4 [Other Special Characters], page 507.

int VSTOP

        `termios.h` (POSIX.1): Section 17.4.9.3 [Special Characters for Flow Control], page 506.

int VSUSP

        `termios.h` (POSIX.1): Section 17.4.9.2 [Characters that Cause Signals], page 505.

int VTIME

        `termios.h` (POSIX.1): Section 17.4.10 [Noncanonical Input], page 507.

int VWERASE

        `termios.h` (BSD): Section 17.4.9.1 [Characters for Input Editing], page 503.

WCHAR_MAX

        `limits.h` (GNU): Section A.5.2 [Range of an Integer Type], page 918.

wint_t WCHAR_MAX

        `wchar.h` (ISO): Section 6.1 [Introduction to Extended Characters], page 134.

`wint_t WCHAR_MIN`

> `wchar.h` (ISO): Section 6.1 [Introduction to Extended Characters], page 134.

`WCHAR_WIDTH`

> `stdint.h` (ISO): Section A.5.1 [Computing the Width of an Integer Data Type], page 917.

`int WCOREDUMP (int status)`

> `sys/wait.h` (BSD): Section 26.7 [Process Completion Status], page 781.

`int WEOF`

> `wchar.h` (ISO): Section 12.15 [End-Of-File and Errors], page 311.

`wint_t WEOF`

> `wchar.h` (ISO): Section 6.1 [Introduction to Extended Characters], page 134.

`int WEXITSTATUS (int status)`

> `sys/wait.h` (POSIX.1): Section 26.7 [Process Completion Status], page 781.

`int WIFEXITED (int status)`

> `sys/wait.h` (POSIX.1): Section 26.7 [Process Completion Status], page 781.

`int WIFSIGNALED (int status)`

> `sys/wait.h` (POSIX.1): Section 26.7 [Process Completion Status], page 781.

`int WIFSTOPPED (int status)`

> `sys/wait.h` (POSIX.1): Section 26.7 [Process Completion Status], page 781.

`WINT_WIDTH`

> `stdint.h` (ISO): Section A.5.1 [Computing the Width of an Integer Data Type], page 917.

`WRDE_APPEND`

> `wordexp.h` (POSIX.2): Section 10.4.3 [Flags for Word Expansion], page 247.

`WRDE_BADCHAR`

> `wordexp.h` (POSIX.2): Section 10.4.2 [Calling `wordexp`], page 246.

`WRDE_BADVAL`

> `wordexp.h` (POSIX.2): Section 10.4.2 [Calling `wordexp`], page 246.

`WRDE_CMDSUB`

> `wordexp.h` (POSIX.2): Section 10.4.2 [Calling `wordexp`], page 246.

`WRDE_DOOFFS`

> `wordexp.h` (POSIX.2): Section 10.4.3 [Flags for Word Expansion], page 247.

`WRDE_NOCMD`

> `wordexp.h` (POSIX.2): Section 10.4.3 [Flags for Word Expansion], page 247.

`WRDE_NOSPACE`

> `wordexp.h` (POSIX.2): Section 10.4.2 [Calling `wordexp`], page 246.

`WRDE_REUSE`

> `wordexp.h` (POSIX.2): Section 10.4.3 [Flags for Word Expansion], page 247.

`WRDE_SHOWERR`

> `wordexp.h` (POSIX.2): Section 10.4.3 [Flags for Word Expansion], page 247.

`WRDE_SYNTAX`

> `wordexp.h` (POSIX.2): Section 10.4.2 [Calling `wordexp`], page 246.

`WRDE_UNDEF`

> `wordexp.h` (POSIX.2): Section 10.4.3 [Flags for Word Expansion], page 247.

`int WSTOPSIG (int status)`

> `sys/wait.h` (POSIX.1): Section 26.7 [Process Completion Status], page 781.

int WTERMSIG (int *status*)
> sys/wait.h (POSIX.1): Section 26.7 [Process Completion Status], page 781.

int W_OK
> unistd.h (POSIX.1): Section 14.9.8 [Testing Permission to Access a File], page 425.

int X_OK
> unistd.h (POSIX.1): Section 14.9.8 [Testing Permission to Access a File], page 425.

_CS_LFS64_CFLAGS
> unistd.h (Unix98): Section 32.12 [String-Valued Parameters], page 880.

_CS_LFS64_LDFLAGS
> unistd.h (Unix98): Section 32.12 [String-Valued Parameters], page 880.

_CS_LFS64_LIBS
> unistd.h (Unix98): Section 32.12 [String-Valued Parameters], page 880.

_CS_LFS64_LINTFLAGS
> unistd.h (Unix98): Section 32.12 [String-Valued Parameters], page 880.

_CS_LFS_CFLAGS
> unistd.h (Unix98): Section 32.12 [String-Valued Parameters], page 880.

_CS_LFS_LDFLAGS
> unistd.h (Unix98): Section 32.12 [String-Valued Parameters], page 880.

_CS_LFS_LIBS
> unistd.h (Unix98): Section 32.12 [String-Valued Parameters], page 880.

_CS_LFS_LINTFLAGS
> unistd.h (Unix98): Section 32.12 [String-Valued Parameters], page 880.

_CS_PATH
> unistd.h (POSIX.2): Section 32.12 [String-Valued Parameters], page 880.

const float complex _Complex_I
> complex.h (C99): Section 20.9 [Complex Numbers], page 606.

_DEFAULT_SOURCE
> *no header* (GNU): Section 1.3.4 [Feature Test Macros], page 15.

void _Exit (int *status*)
> stdlib.h (ISO): Section 25.7.5 [Termination Internals], page 771.

_FILE_OFFSET_BITS
> *no header* (X/Open): Section 1.3.4 [Feature Test Macros], page 15.

_GNU_SOURCE
> *no header* (GNU): Section 1.3.4 [Feature Test Macros], page 15.

int _IOFBF
> stdio.h (ISO): Section 12.20.3 [Controlling Which Kind of Buffering], page 321.

int _IOLBF
> stdio.h (ISO): Section 12.20.3 [Controlling Which Kind of Buffering], page 321.

int _IONBF
> stdio.h (ISO): Section 12.20.3 [Controlling Which Kind of Buffering], page 321.

_ISOC99_SOURCE
> *no header* (GNU): Section 1.3.4 [Feature Test Macros], page 15.

_LARGEFILE64_SOURCE
> *no header* (X/Open): Section 1.3.4 [Feature Test Macros], page 15.

_LARGEFILE_SOURCE

> *no header* (X/Open): Section 1.3.4 [Feature Test Macros], page 15.

_PC_ASYNC_IO

> unistd.h (POSIX.1): Section 32.9 [Using **pathconf**], page 877.

_PC_CHOWN_RESTRICTED

> unistd.h (POSIX.1): Section 32.9 [Using **pathconf**], page 877.

_PC_FILESIZEBITS

> unistd.h (LFS): Section 32.9 [Using **pathconf**], page 877.

_PC_LINK_MAX

> unistd.h (POSIX.1): Section 32.9 [Using **pathconf**], page 877.

_PC_MAX_CANON

> unistd.h (POSIX.1): Section 32.9 [Using **pathconf**], page 877.

_PC_MAX_INPUT

> unistd.h (POSIX.1): Section 32.9 [Using **pathconf**], page 877.

_PC_NAME_MAX

> unistd.h (POSIX.1): Section 32.9 [Using **pathconf**], page 877.

_PC_NO_TRUNC

> unistd.h (POSIX.1): Section 32.9 [Using **pathconf**], page 877.

_PC_PATH_MAX

> unistd.h (POSIX.1): Section 32.9 [Using **pathconf**], page 877.

_PC_PIPE_BUF

> unistd.h (POSIX.1): Section 32.9 [Using **pathconf**], page 877.

_PC_PRIO_IO

> unistd.h (POSIX.1): Section 32.9 [Using **pathconf**], page 877.

_PC_REC_INCR_XFER_SIZE

> unistd.h (POSIX.1): Section 32.9 [Using **pathconf**], page 877.

_PC_REC_MAX_XFER_SIZE

> unistd.h (POSIX.1): Section 32.9 [Using **pathconf**], page 877.

_PC_REC_MIN_XFER_SIZE

> unistd.h (POSIX.1): Section 32.9 [Using **pathconf**], page 877.

_PC_REC_XFER_ALIGN

> unistd.h (POSIX.1): Section 32.9 [Using **pathconf**], page 877.

_PC_SYNC_IO

> unistd.h (POSIX.1): Section 32.9 [Using **pathconf**], page 877.

_PC_VDISABLE

> unistd.h (POSIX.1): Section 32.9 [Using **pathconf**], page 877.

_POSIX2_BC_BASE_MAX

> limits.h (POSIX.2): Section 32.11 [Minimum Values for Utility Limits], page 879.

_POSIX2_BC_DIM_MAX

> limits.h (POSIX.2): Section 32.11 [Minimum Values for Utility Limits], page 879.

_POSIX2_BC_SCALE_MAX

> limits.h (POSIX.2): Section 32.11 [Minimum Values for Utility Limits], page 879.

_POSIX2_BC_STRING_MAX

> limits.h (POSIX.2): Section 32.11 [Minimum Values for Utility Limits], page 879.

_POSIX2_COLL_WEIGHTS_MAX

> limits.h (POSIX.2): Section 32.11 [Minimum Values for Utility Limits], page 879.

`int _POSIX2_C_DEV`

> `unistd.h` (POSIX.2): Section 32.2 [Overall System Options], page 863.

`long int _POSIX2_C_VERSION`

> `unistd.h` (POSIX.2): Section 32.3 [Which Version of POSIX is Supported], page 864.

`_POSIX2_EQUIV_CLASS_MAX`

> `limits.h` (POSIX.2): Section 32.11 [Minimum Values for Utility Limits], page 879.

`_POSIX2_EXPR_NEST_MAX`

> `limits.h` (POSIX.2): Section 32.11 [Minimum Values for Utility Limits], page 879.

`int _POSIX2_FORT_DEV`

> `unistd.h` (POSIX.2): Section 32.2 [Overall System Options], page 863.

`int _POSIX2_FORT_RUN`

> `unistd.h` (POSIX.2): Section 32.2 [Overall System Options], page 863.

`_POSIX2_LINE_MAX`

> `limits.h` (POSIX.2): Section 32.11 [Minimum Values for Utility Limits], page 879.

`int _POSIX2_LOCALEDEF`

> `unistd.h` (POSIX.2): Section 32.2 [Overall System Options], page 863.

`_POSIX2_RE_DUP_MAX`

> `limits.h` (POSIX.2): Section 32.5 [Minimum Values for General Capacity Limits], page 873.

`int _POSIX2_SW_DEV`

> `unistd.h` (POSIX.2): Section 32.2 [Overall System Options], page 863.

`_POSIX_AIO_LISTIO_MAX`

> `limits.h` (POSIX.1): Section 32.5 [Minimum Values for General Capacity Limits], page 873.

`_POSIX_AIO_MAX`

> `limits.h` (POSIX.1): Section 32.5 [Minimum Values for General Capacity Limits], page 873.

`_POSIX_ARG_MAX`

> `limits.h` (POSIX.1): Section 32.5 [Minimum Values for General Capacity Limits], page 873.

`_POSIX_CHILD_MAX`

> `limits.h` (POSIX.1): Section 32.5 [Minimum Values for General Capacity Limits], page 873.

`int _POSIX_CHOWN_RESTRICTED`

> `unistd.h` (POSIX.1): Section 32.7 [Optional Features in File Support], page 875.

`_POSIX_C_SOURCE`

> *no header* (POSIX.2): Section 1.3.4 [Feature Test Macros], page 15.

`int _POSIX_JOB_CONTROL`

> `unistd.h` (POSIX.1): Section 32.2 [Overall System Options], page 863.

`_POSIX_LINK_MAX`

> `limits.h` (POSIX.1): Section 32.8 [Minimum Values for File System Limits], page 876.

`_POSIX_MAX_CANON`

> `limits.h` (POSIX.1): Section 32.8 [Minimum Values for File System Limits], page 876.

`_POSIX_MAX_INPUT`

> `limits.h` (POSIX.1): Section 32.8 [Minimum Values for File System Limits], page 876.

`_POSIX_NAME_MAX`

> `limits.h` (POSIX.1): Section 32.8 [Minimum Values for File System Limits], page 876.

`_POSIX_NGROUPS_MAX`

> `limits.h` (POSIX.1): Section 32.5 [Minimum Values for General Capacity Limits], page 873.

`int _POSIX_NO_TRUNC`

> `unistd.h` (POSIX.1): Section 32.7 [Optional Features in File Support], page 875.

_POSIX_OPEN_MAX
> `limits.h` (POSIX.1): Section 32.5 [Minimum Values for General Capacity Limits], page 873.

_POSIX_PATH_MAX
> `limits.h` (POSIX.1): Section 32.8 [Minimum Values for File System Limits], page 876.

_POSIX_PIPE_BUF
> `limits.h` (POSIX.1): Section 32.8 [Minimum Values for File System Limits], page 876.

int _POSIX_SAVED_IDS
> `unistd.h` (POSIX.1): Section 32.2 [Overall System Options], page 863.

_POSIX_SOURCE
> *no header* (POSIX.1): Section 1.3.4 [Feature Test Macros], page 15.

_POSIX_SSIZE_MAX
> `limits.h` (POSIX.1): Section 32.5 [Minimum Values for General Capacity Limits], page 873.

_POSIX_STREAM_MAX
> `limits.h` (POSIX.1): Section 32.5 [Minimum Values for General Capacity Limits], page 873.

_POSIX_TZNAME_MAX
> `limits.h` (POSIX.1): Section 32.5 [Minimum Values for General Capacity Limits], page 873.

unsigned char _POSIX_VDISABLE
> `unistd.h` (POSIX.1): Section 32.7 [Optional Features in File Support], page 875.

long int _POSIX_VERSION
> `unistd.h` (POSIX.1): Section 32.3 [Which Version of POSIX is Supported], page 864.

_REENTRANT
> *no header* (Obsolete): Section 1.3.4 [Feature Test Macros], page 15.

_SC_2_C_DEV
> `unistd.h` (POSIX.2): Section 32.4.2 [Constants for `sysconf` Parameters], page 865.

_SC_2_FORT_DEV
> `unistd.h` (POSIX.2): Section 32.4.2 [Constants for `sysconf` Parameters], page 865.

_SC_2_FORT_RUN
> `unistd.h` (POSIX.2): Section 32.4.2 [Constants for `sysconf` Parameters], page 865.

_SC_2_LOCALEDEF
> `unistd.h` (POSIX.2): Section 32.4.2 [Constants for `sysconf` Parameters], page 865.

_SC_2_SW_DEV
> `unistd.h` (POSIX.2): Section 32.4.2 [Constants for `sysconf` Parameters], page 865.

_SC_2_VERSION
> `unistd.h` (POSIX.2): Section 32.4.2 [Constants for `sysconf` Parameters], page 865.

_SC_AIO_LISTIO_MAX
> `unistd.h` (POSIX.1): Section 32.4.2 [Constants for `sysconf` Parameters], page 865.

_SC_AIO_MAX
> `unistd.h` (POSIX.1): Section 32.4.2 [Constants for `sysconf` Parameters], page 865.

_SC_AIO_PRIO_DELTA_MAX
> `unistd.h` (POSIX.1): Section 32.4.2 [Constants for `sysconf` Parameters], page 865.

_SC_ARG_MAX
> `unistd.h` (POSIX.1): Section 32.4.2 [Constants for `sysconf` Parameters], page 865.

_SC_ASYNCHRONOUS_IO
> `unistd.h` (POSIX.1): Section 32.4.2 [Constants for `sysconf` Parameters], page 865.

_SC_ATEXIT_MAX
> `unistd.h` (GNU): Section 32.4.2 [Constants for `sysconf` Parameters], page 865.

_SC_AVPHYS_PAGES
    unistd.h (GNU): Section 32.4.2 [Constants for sysconf Parameters], page 865.

_SC_BC_BASE_MAX
    unistd.h (POSIX.2): Section 32.4.2 [Constants for sysconf Parameters], page 865.

_SC_BC_DIM_MAX
    unistd.h (POSIX.2): Section 32.4.2 [Constants for sysconf Parameters], page 865.

_SC_BC_SCALE_MAX
    unistd.h (POSIX.2): Section 32.4.2 [Constants for sysconf Parameters], page 865.

_SC_BC_STRING_MAX
    unistd.h (POSIX.2): Section 32.4.2 [Constants for sysconf Parameters], page 865.

_SC_CHARCLASS_NAME_MAX
    unistd.h (GNU): Section 32.4.2 [Constants for sysconf Parameters], page 865.

_SC_CHAR_BIT
    unistd.h (X/Open): Section 32.4.2 [Constants for sysconf Parameters], page 865.

_SC_CHAR_MAX
    unistd.h (X/Open): Section 32.4.2 [Constants for sysconf Parameters], page 865.

_SC_CHAR_MIN
    unistd.h (X/Open): Section 32.4.2 [Constants for sysconf Parameters], page 865.

_SC_CHILD_MAX
    unistd.h (POSIX.1): Section 32.4.2 [Constants for sysconf Parameters], page 865.

_SC_CLK_TCK
    unistd.h (POSIX.1): Section 32.4.2 [Constants for sysconf Parameters], page 865.

_SC_COLL_WEIGHTS_MAX
    unistd.h (POSIX.2): Section 32.4.2 [Constants for sysconf Parameters], page 865.

_SC_DELAYTIMER_MAX
    unistd.h (POSIX.1): Section 32.4.2 [Constants for sysconf Parameters], page 865.

_SC_EQUIV_CLASS_MAX
    unistd.h (POSIX.2): Section 32.4.2 [Constants for sysconf Parameters], page 865.

_SC_EXPR_NEST_MAX
    unistd.h (POSIX.2): Section 32.4.2 [Constants for sysconf Parameters], page 865.

_SC_FSYNC
    unistd.h (POSIX.1): Section 32.4.2 [Constants for sysconf Parameters], page 865.

_SC_GETGR_R_SIZE_MAX
    unistd.h (POSIX.1): Section 32.4.2 [Constants for sysconf Parameters], page 865.

_SC_GETPW_R_SIZE_MAX
    unistd.h (POSIX.1): Section 32.4.2 [Constants for sysconf Parameters], page 865.

_SC_INT_MAX
    unistd.h (X/Open): Section 32.4.2 [Constants for sysconf Parameters], page 865.

_SC_INT_MIN
    unistd.h (X/Open): Section 32.4.2 [Constants for sysconf Parameters], page 865.

_SC_JOB_CONTROL
    unistd.h (POSIX.1): Section 32.4.2 [Constants for sysconf Parameters], page 865.

_SC_LINE_MAX
    unistd.h (POSIX.2): Section 32.4.2 [Constants for sysconf Parameters], page 865.

_SC_LOGIN_NAME_MAX
    unistd.h (POSIX.1): Section 32.4.2 [Constants for sysconf Parameters], page 865.

_SC_LONG_BIT
>   unistd.h (X/Open): Section 32.4.2 [Constants for sysconf Parameters], page 865.

_SC_MAPPED_FILES
>   unistd.h (POSIX.1): Section 32.4.2 [Constants for sysconf Parameters], page 865.

_SC_MB_LEN_MAX
>   unistd.h (X/Open): Section 32.4.2 [Constants for sysconf Parameters], page 865.

_SC_MEMLOCK
>   unistd.h (POSIX.1): Section 32.4.2 [Constants for sysconf Parameters], page 865.

_SC_MEMLOCK_RANGE
>   unistd.h (POSIX.1): Section 32.4.2 [Constants for sysconf Parameters], page 865.

_SC_MEMORY_PROTECTION
>   unistd.h (POSIX.1): Section 32.4.2 [Constants for sysconf Parameters], page 865.

_SC_MESSAGE_PASSING
>   unistd.h (POSIX.1): Section 32.4.2 [Constants for sysconf Parameters], page 865.

_SC_MQ_OPEN_MAX
>   unistd.h (POSIX.1): Section 32.4.2 [Constants for sysconf Parameters], page 865.

_SC_MQ_PRIO_MAX
>   unistd.h (POSIX.1): Section 32.4.2 [Constants for sysconf Parameters], page 865.

_SC_NGROUPS_MAX
>   unistd.h (POSIX.1): Section 32.4.2 [Constants for sysconf Parameters], page 865.

_SC_NL_ARGMAX
>   unistd.h (X/Open): Section 32.4.2 [Constants for sysconf Parameters], page 865.

_SC_NL_LANGMAX
>   unistd.h (X/Open): Section 32.4.2 [Constants for sysconf Parameters], page 865.

_SC_NL_MSGMAX
>   unistd.h (X/Open): Section 32.4.2 [Constants for sysconf Parameters], page 865.

_SC_NL_NMAX
>   unistd.h (X/Open): Section 32.4.2 [Constants for sysconf Parameters], page 865.

_SC_NL_SETMAX
>   unistd.h (X/Open): Section 32.4.2 [Constants for sysconf Parameters], page 865.

_SC_NL_TEXTMAX
>   unistd.h (X/Open): Section 32.4.2 [Constants for sysconf Parameters], page 865.

_SC_NPROCESSORS_CONF
>   unistd.h (GNU): Section 32.4.2 [Constants for sysconf Parameters], page 865.

_SC_NPROCESSORS_ONLN
>   unistd.h (GNU): Section 32.4.2 [Constants for sysconf Parameters], page 865.

_SC_NZERO
>   unistd.h (X/Open): Section 32.4.2 [Constants for sysconf Parameters], page 865.

_SC_OPEN_MAX
>   unistd.h (POSIX.1): Section 32.4.2 [Constants for sysconf Parameters], page 865.

_SC_PAGESIZE
>   unistd.h (GNU): Section 32.4.2 [Constants for sysconf Parameters], page 865.

_SC_PHYS_PAGES
>   unistd.h (GNU): Section 32.4.2 [Constants for sysconf Parameters], page 865.

_SC_PII
>   unistd.h (POSIX.1g): Section 32.4.2 [Constants for sysconf Parameters], page 865.

`_SC_PII_INTERNET`
>   unistd.h (POSIX.1g): Section 32.4.2 [Constants for sysconf Parameters], page 865.

`_SC_PII_INTERNET_DGRAM`
>   unistd.h (POSIX.1g): Section 32.4.2 [Constants for sysconf Parameters], page 865.

`_SC_PII_INTERNET_STREAM`
>   unistd.h (POSIX.1g): Section 32.4.2 [Constants for sysconf Parameters], page 865.

`_SC_PII_OSI`
>   unistd.h (POSIX.1g): Section 32.4.2 [Constants for sysconf Parameters], page 865.

`_SC_PII_OSI_CLTS`
>   unistd.h (POSIX.1g): Section 32.4.2 [Constants for sysconf Parameters], page 865.

`_SC_PII_OSI_COTS`
>   unistd.h (POSIX.1g): Section 32.4.2 [Constants for sysconf Parameters], page 865.

`_SC_PII_OSI_M`
>   unistd.h (POSIX.1g): Section 32.4.2 [Constants for sysconf Parameters], page 865.

`_SC_PII_SOCKET`
>   unistd.h (POSIX.1g): Section 32.4.2 [Constants for sysconf Parameters], page 865.

`_SC_PII_XTI`
>   unistd.h (POSIX.1g): Section 32.4.2 [Constants for sysconf Parameters], page 865.

`_SC_PRIORITIZED_IO`
>   unistd.h (POSIX.1): Section 32.4.2 [Constants for sysconf Parameters], page 865.

`_SC_PRIORITY_SCHEDULING`
>   unistd.h (POSIX.1): Section 32.4.2 [Constants for sysconf Parameters], page 865.

`_SC_REALTIME_SIGNALS`
>   unistdh.h (POSIX.1): Section 32.4.2 [Constants for sysconf Parameters], page 865.

`_SC_RTSIG_MAX`
>   unistd.h (POSIX.1): Section 32.4.2 [Constants for sysconf Parameters], page 865.

`_SC_SAVED_IDS`
>   unistd.h (POSIX.1): Section 32.4.2 [Constants for sysconf Parameters], page 865.

`_SC_SCHAR_MAX`
>   unistd.h (X/Open): Section 32.4.2 [Constants for sysconf Parameters], page 865.

`_SC_SCHAR_MIN`
>   unistd.h (X/Open): Section 32.4.2 [Constants for sysconf Parameters], page 865.

`_SC_SELECT`
>   unistd.h (POSIX.1g): Section 32.4.2 [Constants for sysconf Parameters], page 865.

`_SC_SEMAPHORES`
>   unistd.h (POSIX.1): Section 32.4.2 [Constants for sysconf Parameters], page 865.

`_SC_SEM_NSEMS_MAX`
>   unistd.h (POSIX.1): Section 32.4.2 [Constants for sysconf Parameters], page 865.

`_SC_SEM_VALUE_MAX`
>   unistd.h (POSIX.1): Section 32.4.2 [Constants for sysconf Parameters], page 865.

`_SC_SHARED_MEMORY_OBJECTS`
>   unistd.h (POSIX.1): Section 32.4.2 [Constants for sysconf Parameters], page 865.

`_SC_SHRT_MAX`
>   unistd.h (X/Open): Section 32.4.2 [Constants for sysconf Parameters], page 865.

`_SC_SHRT_MIN`
>   unistd.h (X/Open): Section 32.4.2 [Constants for sysconf Parameters], page 865.

_SC_SIGQUEUE_MAX

> unistd.h (POSIX.1): Section 32.4.2 [Constants for sysconf Parameters], page 865.

_SC_STREAM_MAX

> unistd.h (POSIX.1): Section 32.4.2 [Constants for sysconf Parameters], page 865.

_SC_SYNCHRONIZED_IO

> unistd.h (POSIX.1): Section 32.4.2 [Constants for sysconf Parameters], page 865.

_SC_THREADS

> unistd.h (POSIX.1): Section 32.4.2 [Constants for sysconf Parameters], page 865.

_SC_THREAD_ATTR_STACKADDR

> unistd.h (POSIX.1): Section 32.4.2 [Constants for sysconf Parameters], page 865.

_SC_THREAD_ATTR_STACKSIZE

> unistd.h (POSIX.1): Section 32.4.2 [Constants for sysconf Parameters], page 865.

_SC_THREAD_DESTRUCTOR_ITERATIONS

> unistd.h (POSIX.1): Section 32.4.2 [Constants for sysconf Parameters], page 865.

_SC_THREAD_KEYS_MAX

> unistd.h (POSIX.1): Section 32.4.2 [Constants for sysconf Parameters], page 865.

_SC_THREAD_PRIORITY_SCHEDULING

> unistd.h (POSIX.1): Section 32.4.2 [Constants for sysconf Parameters], page 865.

_SC_THREAD_PRIO_INHERIT

> unistd.h (POSIX.1): Section 32.4.2 [Constants for sysconf Parameters], page 865.

_SC_THREAD_PRIO_PROTECT

> unistd.h (POSIX.1): Section 32.4.2 [Constants for sysconf Parameters], page 865.

_SC_THREAD_PROCESS_SHARED

> unistd.h (POSIX.1): Section 32.4.2 [Constants for sysconf Parameters], page 865.

_SC_THREAD_SAFE_FUNCTIONS

> unistd.h (POSIX.1): Section 32.4.2 [Constants for sysconf Parameters], page 865.

_SC_THREAD_STACK_MIN

> unistd.h (POSIX.1): Section 32.4.2 [Constants for sysconf Parameters], page 865.

_SC_THREAD_THREADS_MAX

> unistd.h (POSIX.1): Section 32.4.2 [Constants for sysconf Parameters], page 865.

_SC_TIMERS

> unistd.h (POSIX.1): Section 32.4.2 [Constants for sysconf Parameters], page 865.

_SC_TIMER_MAX

> unistd.h (POSIX.1): Section 32.4.2 [Constants for sysconf Parameters], page 865.

_SC_TTY_NAME_MAX

> unistd.h (POSIX.1): Section 32.4.2 [Constants for sysconf Parameters], page 865.

_SC_TZNAME_MAX

> unistd.h (POSIX.1): Section 32.4.2 [Constants for sysconf Parameters], page 865.

_SC_T_IOV_MAX

> unistd.h (POSIX.1g): Section 32.4.2 [Constants for sysconf Parameters], page 865.

_SC_UCHAR_MAX

> unistd.h (X/Open): Section 32.4.2 [Constants for sysconf Parameters], page 865.

_SC_UINT_MAX

> unistd.h (X/Open): Section 32.4.2 [Constants for sysconf Parameters], page 865.

_SC_UIO_MAXIOV

> unistd.h (POSIX.1g): Section 32.4.2 [Constants for sysconf Parameters], page 865.

`_SC_ULONG_MAX`

> `unistd.h` (X/Open): Section 32.4.2 [Constants for `sysconf` Parameters], page 865.

`_SC_USHRT_MAX`

> `unistd.h` (X/Open): Section 32.4.2 [Constants for `sysconf` Parameters], page 865.

`_SC_VERSION`

> `unistd.h` (POSIX.1): Section 32.4.2 [Constants for `sysconf` Parameters], page 865.

> `unistd.h` (POSIX.2): Section 32.4.2 [Constants for `sysconf` Parameters], page 865.

`_SC_WORD_BIT`

> `unistd.h` (X/Open): Section 32.4.2 [Constants for `sysconf` Parameters], page 865.

`_SC_XOPEN_CRYPT`

> `unistd.h` (X/Open): Section 32.4.2 [Constants for `sysconf` Parameters], page 865.

`_SC_XOPEN_ENH_I18N`

> `unistd.h` (X/Open): Section 32.4.2 [Constants for `sysconf` Parameters], page 865.

`_SC_XOPEN_LEGACY`

> `unistd.h` (X/Open): Section 32.4.2 [Constants for `sysconf` Parameters], page 865.

`_SC_XOPEN_REALTIME`

> `unistd.h` (X/Open): Section 32.4.2 [Constants for `sysconf` Parameters], page 865.

`_SC_XOPEN_REALTIME_THREADS`

> `unistd.h` (X/Open): Section 32.4.2 [Constants for `sysconf` Parameters], page 865.

`_SC_XOPEN_SHM`

> `unistd.h` (X/Open): Section 32.4.2 [Constants for `sysconf` Parameters], page 865.

`_SC_XOPEN_UNIX`

> `unistd.h` (X/Open): Section 32.4.2 [Constants for `sysconf` Parameters], page 865.

`_SC_XOPEN_VERSION`

> `unistd.h` (X/Open): Section 32.4.2 [Constants for `sysconf` Parameters], page 865.

`_SC_XOPEN_XCU_VERSION`

> `unistd.h` (X/Open): Section 32.4.2 [Constants for `sysconf` Parameters], page 865.

`_SC_XOPEN_XPG2`

> `unistd.h` (X/Open): Section 32.4.2 [Constants for `sysconf` Parameters], page 865.

`_SC_XOPEN_XPG3`

> `unistd.h` (X/Open): Section 32.4.2 [Constants for `sysconf` Parameters], page 865.

`_SC_XOPEN_XPG4`

> `unistd.h` (X/Open): Section 32.4.2 [Constants for `sysconf` Parameters], page 865.

`_THREAD_SAFE`

> *no header* (Obsolete): Section 1.3.4 [Feature Test Macros], page 15.

`_XOPEN_SOURCE`

> *no header* (X/Open): Section 1.3.4 [Feature Test Macros], page 15.

`_XOPEN_SOURCE_EXTENDED`

> *no header* (X/Open): Section 1.3.4 [Feature Test Macros], page 15.

`__STDC_WANT_IEC_60559_BFP_EXT__`

> *no header* (ISO): Section 1.3.4 [Feature Test Macros], page 15.

`__STDC_WANT_IEC_60559_FUNCS_EXT__`

> *no header* (ISO): Section 1.3.4 [Feature Test Macros], page 15.

`__STDC_WANT_IEC_60559_TYPES_EXT__`

> *no header* (ISO): Section 1.3.4 [Feature Test Macros], page 15.

`__STDC_WANT_LIB_EXT2__`

> *no header* (ISO): Section 1.3.4 [Feature Test Macros], page 15.

`size_t __fbufsize (FILE *stream)`

        `stdio_ext.h` (GNU): Section 12.20.3 [Controlling Which Kind of Buffering], page 321.

`int __flbf (FILE *stream)`

        `stdio_ext.h` (GNU): Section 12.20.3 [Controlling Which Kind of Buffering], page 321.

`size_t __fpending (FILE *stream)`

        `stdio_ext.h` (GNU): Section 12.20.3 [Controlling Which Kind of Buffering], page 321.

`void __fpurge (FILE *stream)`

        `stdio_ext.h` (GNU): Section 12.20.2 [Flushing Buffers], page 320.

`int __freadable (FILE *stream)`

        `stdio_ext.h` (GNU): Section 12.3 [Opening Streams], page 258.

`int __freading (FILE *stream)`

        `stdio_ext.h` (GNU): Section 12.3 [Opening Streams], page 258.

`__free_hook`

        `malloc.h` (GNU): Section 3.2.3.9 [Memory Allocation Hooks], page 53.

`int __fsetlocking (FILE *stream, int type)`

        `stdio_ext.h` (GNU): Section 12.5 [Streams and Threads], page 263.

`__ftw64_func_t`

        `ftw.h` (GNU): Section 14.3 [Working with Directory Trees], page 401.

`__ftw_func_t`

        `ftw.h` (GNU): Section 14.3 [Working with Directory Trees], page 401.

`int __fwritable (FILE *stream)`

        `stdio_ext.h` (GNU): Section 12.3 [Opening Streams], page 258.

`int __fwriting (FILE *stream)`

        `stdio_ext.h` (GNU): Section 12.3 [Opening Streams], page 258.

`void (*__gconv_end_fct) (struct gconv_step *)`

        `gconv.h` (GNU): Section 6.5.4 [The `iconv` Implementation in the GNU C Library], page 162.

`int (*__gconv_fct) (struct __gconv_step *, struct __gconv_step_data *, const char **, const char *, size_t *, int)`

        `gconv.h` (GNU): Section 6.5.4 [The `iconv` Implementation in the GNU C Library], page 162.

`int (*__gconv_init_fct) (struct __gconv_step *)`

        `gconv.h` (GNU): Section 6.5.4 [The `iconv` Implementation in the GNU C Library], page 162.

`struct __gconv_step`

        `gconv.h` (GNU): Section 6.5.4 [The `iconv` Implementation in the GNU C Library], page 162.

`struct __gconv_step_data`

        `gconv.h` (GNU): Section 6.5.4 [The `iconv` Implementation in the GNU C Library], page 162.

`__malloc_hook`

        `malloc.h` (GNU): Section 3.2.3.9 [Memory Allocation Hooks], page 53.

`__memalign_hook`

        `malloc.h` (GNU): Section 3.2.3.9 [Memory Allocation Hooks], page 53.

`__nftw64_func_t`

        `ftw.h` (GNU): Section 14.3 [Working with Directory Trees], page 401.

`__nftw_func_t`

        `ftw.h` (GNU): Section 14.3 [Working with Directory Trees], page 401.

`__realloc_hook`

        `malloc.h` (GNU): Section 3.2.3.9 [Memory Allocation Hooks], page 53.

`void _exit (int status)`

        `unistd.h` (POSIX.1): Section 25.7.5 [Termination Internals], page 771.

Appendix B: Summary of Library Facilities

void _flushlbf (void)
: stdio_ext.h (GNU): Section 12.20.2 [Flushing Buffers], page 320.

int _tolower (int *c*)
: ctype.h (SVID): Section 4.2 [Case Conversion], page 83.

int _toupper (int *c*)
: ctype.h (SVID): Section 4.2 [Case Conversion], page 83.

long int a64l (const char *string*)
: stdlib.h (XPG): Section 5.14 [Encode Binary Data], page 127.

void abort (void)
: stdlib.h (ISO): Section 25.7.4 [Aborting a Program], page 771.

int abs (int *number*)
: stdlib.h (ISO): Section 20.8.1 [Absolute Value], page 591.

int accept (int *socket*, struct sockaddr *addr*, socklen_t *length_ptr*)
: sys/socket.h (BSD): Section 16.9.3 [Accepting Connections], page 470.

int access (const char *filename*, int *how*)
: unistd.h (POSIX.1): Section 14.9.8 [Testing Permission to Access a File], page 425.

double acos (double *x*)
: math.h (ISO): Section 19.3 [Inverse Trigonometric Functions], page 528.

float acosf (float *x*)
: math.h (ISO): Section 19.3 [Inverse Trigonometric Functions], page 528.

_FloatN acosfN (_Float*N* *x*)
: math.h (TS 18661-3:2015): Section 19.3 [Inverse Trigonometric Functions], page 528.

_FloatNx acosfNx (_Float*Nx* *x*)
: math.h (TS 18661-3:2015): Section 19.3 [Inverse Trigonometric Functions], page 528.

double acosh (double *x*)
: math.h (ISO): Section 19.5 [Hyperbolic Functions], page 536.

float acoshf (float *x*)
: math.h (ISO): Section 19.5 [Hyperbolic Functions], page 536.

_FloatN acoshfN (_Float*N* *x*)
: math.h (TS 18661-3:2015): Section 19.5 [Hyperbolic Functions], page 536.

_FloatNx acoshfNx (_Float*Nx* *x*)
: math.h (TS 18661-3:2015): Section 19.5 [Hyperbolic Functions], page 536.

long double acoshl (long double *x*)
: math.h (ISO): Section 19.5 [Hyperbolic Functions], page 536.

long double acosl (long double *x*)
: math.h (ISO): Section 19.3 [Inverse Trigonometric Functions], page 528.

int addmntent (FILE *stream*, const struct mntent *mnt*)
: mntent.h (BSD): Section 31.3.1.2 [The mtab file], page 852.

int adjtime (const struct timeval *delta*, struct timeval *olddelta*)
: sys/time.h (BSD): Section 21.4.2 [High-Resolution Calendar], page 624.

int adjtimex (struct timex *timex*)
: sys/timex.h (GNU): Section 21.4.2 [High-Resolution Calendar], page 624.

int aio_cancel (int *fildes*, struct aiocb *aiocbp*)
: aio.h (POSIX.1b): Section 13.10.4 [Cancellation of AIO Operations], page 369.

int aio_cancel64 (int *fildes*, struct aiocb64 *aiocbp*)
: aio.h (Unix98): Section 13.10.4 [Cancellation of AIO Operations], page 369.

`int aio_error (const struct aiocb *aiocbp)`

> `aio.h` (POSIX.1b): Section 13.10.2 [Getting the Status of AIO Operations], page 366.

`int aio_error64 (const struct aiocb64 *aiocbp)`

> `aio.h` (Unix98): Section 13.10.2 [Getting the Status of AIO Operations], page 366.

`int aio_fsync (int op, struct aiocb *aiocbp)`

> `aio.h` (POSIX.1b): Section 13.10.3 [Getting into a Consistent State], page 367.

`int aio_fsync64 (int op, struct aiocb64 *aiocbp)`

> `aio.h` (Unix98): Section 13.10.3 [Getting into a Consistent State], page 367.

`void aio_init (const struct aioinit *init)`

> `aio.h` (GNU): Section 13.10.5 [How to optimize the AIO implementation], page 370.

`int aio_read (struct aiocb *aiocbp)`

> `aio.h` (POSIX.1b): Section 13.10.1 [Asynchronous Read and Write Operations], page 362.

`int aio_read64 (struct aiocb64 *aiocbp)`

> `aio.h` (Unix98): Section 13.10.1 [Asynchronous Read and Write Operations], page 362.

`ssize_t aio_return (struct aiocb *aiocbp)`

> `aio.h` (POSIX.1b): Section 13.10.2 [Getting the Status of AIO Operations], page 366.

`ssize_t aio_return64 (struct aiocb64 *aiocbp)`

> `aio.h` (Unix98): Section 13.10.2 [Getting the Status of AIO Operations], page 366.

`int aio_suspend (const struct aiocb *const list[], int nent, const struct timespec *timeout)`

> `aio.h` (POSIX.1b): Section 13.10.3 [Getting into a Consistent State], page 367.

`int aio_suspend64 (const struct aiocb64 *const list[], int nent, const struct timespec *timeout)`

> `aio.h` (Unix98): Section 13.10.3 [Getting into a Consistent State], page 367.

`int aio_write (struct aiocb *aiocbp)`

> `aio.h` (POSIX.1b): Section 13.10.1 [Asynchronous Read and Write Operations], page 362.

`int aio_write64 (struct aiocb64 *aiocbp)`

> `aio.h` (Unix98): Section 13.10.1 [Asynchronous Read and Write Operations], page 362.

`struct aiocb`

> `aio.h` (POSIX.1b): Section 13.10 [Perform I/O Operations in Parallel], page 359.

`struct aiocb64`

> `aio.h` (POSIX.1b): Section 13.10 [Perform I/O Operations in Parallel], page 359.

`struct aioinit`

> `aio.h` (GNU): Section 13.10.5 [How to optimize the AIO implementation], page 370.

`unsigned int alarm (unsigned int seconds)`

> `unistd.h` (POSIX.1): Section 21.5 [Setting an Alarm], page 649.

`void * aligned_alloc (size_t alignment, size_t size)`

> `stdlib.h` (???): Section 3.2.3.6 [Allocating Aligned Memory Blocks], page 48.

`void * alloca (size_t size)`

> `stdlib.h` (GNU): Section 3.2.7 [Automatic Storage with Variable Size], page 73.

> `stdlib.h` (BSD): Section 3.2.7 [Automatic Storage with Variable Size], page 73.

`int alphasort (const struct dirent **a, const struct dirent **b)`

> `dirent.h` (BSD): Section 14.2.6 [Scanning the Content of a Directory], page 399.

> `dirent.h` (SVID): Section 14.2.6 [Scanning the Content of a Directory], page 399.

`int alphasort64 (const struct dirent64 **a, const struct dirent **b)`

> `dirent.h` (GNU): Section 14.2.6 [Scanning the Content of a Directory], page 399.

`struct argp`

> `argp.h` (GNU): Section 25.3.3 [Specifying Argp Parsers], page 739.

struct `argp_child`
> `argp.h` (GNU): Section 25.3.6 [Combining Multiple Argp Parsers], page 748.

`error_t argp_err_exit_status`
> `argp.h` (GNU): Section 25.3.2 [Argp Global Variables], page 739.

`void argp_error (const struct argp_state *state, const char *fmt, ...)`
> `argp.h` (GNU): Section 25.3.5.3 [Functions For Use in Argp Parsers], page 746.

`void argp_failure (const struct argp_state *state, int status, int errnum, const char *fmt, ...)`
> `argp.h` (GNU): Section 25.3.5.3 [Functions For Use in Argp Parsers], page 746.

`void argp_help (const struct argp *argp, FILE *stream, unsigned flags, char *name)`
> `argp.h` (GNU): Section 25.3.9 [The `argp_help` Function], page 750.

struct `argp_option`
> `argp.h` (GNU): Section 25.3.4 [Specifying Options in an Argp Parser], page 740.

`error_t argp_parse (const struct argp *argp, int argc, char **argv, unsigned flags, int *arg_index, void *input)`
> `argp.h` (GNU): Section 25.3 [Parsing Program Options with Argp], page 738.

`const char * argp_program_bug_address`
> `argp.h` (GNU): Section 25.3.2 [Argp Global Variables], page 739.

`const char * argp_program_version`
> `argp.h` (GNU): Section 25.3.2 [Argp Global Variables], page 739.

`argp_program_version_hook`
> `argp.h` (GNU): Section 25.3.2 [Argp Global Variables], page 739.

struct `argp_state`
> `argp.h` (GNU): Section 25.3.5.2 [Argp Parsing State], page 745.

`void argp_state_help (const struct argp_state *state, FILE *stream, unsigned flags)`
> `argp.h` (GNU): Section 25.3.5.3 [Functions For Use in Argp Parsers], page 746.

`void argp_usage (const struct argp_state *state)`
> `argp.h` (GNU): Section 25.3.5.3 [Functions For Use in Argp Parsers], page 746.

`error_t argz_add (char **argz, size_t *argz_len, const char *str)`
> `argz.h` (GNU): Section 5.15.1 [Argz Functions], page 129.

`error_t argz_add_sep (char **argz, size_t *argz_len, const char *str, int delim)`
> `argz.h` (GNU): Section 5.15.1 [Argz Functions], page 129.

`error_t argz_append (char **argz, size_t *argz_len, const char *buf, size_t buf_len)`
> `argz.h` (GNU): Section 5.15.1 [Argz Functions], page 129.

`size_t argz_count (const char *argz, size_t argz_len)`
> `argz.h` (GNU): Section 5.15.1 [Argz Functions], page 129.

`error_t argz_create (char *const argv[], char **argz, size_t *argz_len)`
> `argz.h` (GNU): Section 5.15.1 [Argz Functions], page 129.

`error_t argz_create_sep (const char *string, int sep, char **argz, size_t *argz_len)`
> `argz.h` (GNU): Section 5.15.1 [Argz Functions], page 129.

`void argz_delete (char **argz, size_t *argz_len, char *entry)`
> `argz.h` (GNU): Section 5.15.1 [Argz Functions], page 129.

`void argz_extract (const char *argz, size_t argz_len, char **argv)`
> `argz.h` (GNU): Section 5.15.1 [Argz Functions], page 129.

`error_t argz_insert (char **argz, size_t *argz_len, char *before, const char *entry)`
> `argz.h` (GNU): Section 5.15.1 [Argz Functions], page 129.

`char * argz_next (const char *argz, size_t argz_len, const char *entry)`
> `argz.h` (GNU): Section 5.15.1 [Argz Functions], page 129.

`error_t argz_replace (char **argz, size_t *argz_len, const char *str, const char *with, unsigned *replace_count)`
> `argz.h` (GNU): Section 5.15.1 [Argz Functions], page 129.

`void argz_stringify (char *argz, size_t len, int sep)`
> `argz.h` (GNU): Section 5.15.1 [Argz Functions], page 129.

`char * asctime (const struct tm *brokentime)`
> `time.h` (ISO): Section 21.4.5 [Formatting Calendar Time], page 632.

`char * asctime_r (const struct tm *brokentime, char *buffer)`
> `time.h` (POSIX.1c): Section 21.4.5 [Formatting Calendar Time], page 632.

`double asin (double x)`
> `math.h` (ISO): Section 19.3 [Inverse Trigonometric Functions], page 528.

`float asinf (float x)`
> `math.h` (ISO): Section 19.3 [Inverse Trigonometric Functions], page 528.

`_FloatN asinfN (_FloatN x)`
> `math.h` (TS 18661-3:2015): Section 19.3 [Inverse Trigonometric Functions], page 528.

`_FloatNx asinfNx (_FloatNx x)`
> `math.h` (TS 18661-3:2015): Section 19.3 [Inverse Trigonometric Functions], page 528.

`double asinh (double x)`
> `math.h` (ISO): Section 19.5 [Hyperbolic Functions], page 536.

`float asinhf (float x)`
> `math.h` (ISO): Section 19.5 [Hyperbolic Functions], page 536.

`_FloatN asinhfN (_FloatN x)`
> `math.h` (TS 18661-3:2015): Section 19.5 [Hyperbolic Functions], page 536.

`_FloatNx asinhfNx (_FloatNx x)`
> `math.h` (TS 18661-3:2015): Section 19.5 [Hyperbolic Functions], page 536.

`long double asinhl (long double x)`
> `math.h` (ISO): Section 19.5 [Hyperbolic Functions], page 536.

`long double asinl (long double x)`
> `math.h` (ISO): Section 19.3 [Inverse Trigonometric Functions], page 528.

`int asprintf (char **ptr, const char *template, ...)`
> `stdio.h` (GNU): Section 12.12.8 [Dynamically Allocating Formatted Output], page 290.

`void assert (int expression)`
> `assert.h` (ISO): Section A.1 [Explicitly Checking Internal Consistency], page 909.

`void assert_perror (int errnum)`
> `assert.h` (GNU): Section A.1 [Explicitly Checking Internal Consistency], page 909.

`double atan (double x)`
> `math.h` (ISO): Section 19.3 [Inverse Trigonometric Functions], page 528.

`double atan2 (double y, double x)`
> `math.h` (ISO): Section 19.3 [Inverse Trigonometric Functions], page 528.

`float atan2f (float y, float x)`
> `math.h` (ISO): Section 19.3 [Inverse Trigonometric Functions], page 528.

`_FloatN atan2fN (_FloatN y, _FloatN x)`
> `math.h` (TS 18661-3:2015): Section 19.3 [Inverse Trigonometric Functions], page 528.

`_FloatNx atan2fNx (_FloatNx y, _FloatNx x)`
> `math.h` (TS 18661-3:2015): Section 19.3 [Inverse Trigonometric Functions], page 528.

`long double atan2l (long double y, long double x)`
> `math.h` (ISO): Section 19.3 [Inverse Trigonometric Functions], page 528.

float atanf (float *x*)
> math.h (ISO): Section 19.3 [Inverse Trigonometric Functions], page 528.

_FloatN atanfN (_Float*N x*)
> math.h (TS 18661-3:2015): Section 19.3 [Inverse Trigonometric Functions], page 528.

_FloatNx atanfNx (_Float*Nx x*)
> math.h (TS 18661-3:2015): Section 19.3 [Inverse Trigonometric Functions], page 528.

double atanh (double *x*)
> math.h (ISO): Section 19.5 [Hyperbolic Functions], page 536.

float atanhf (float *x*)
> math.h (ISO): Section 19.5 [Hyperbolic Functions], page 536.

_FloatN atanhfN (_Float*N x*)
> math.h (TS 18661-3:2015): Section 19.5 [Hyperbolic Functions], page 536.

_FloatNx atanhfNx (_Float*Nx x*)
> math.h (TS 18661-3:2015): Section 19.5 [Hyperbolic Functions], page 536.

long double atanhl (long double *x*)
> math.h (ISO): Section 19.5 [Hyperbolic Functions], page 536.

long double atanl (long double *x*)
> math.h (ISO): Section 19.3 [Inverse Trigonometric Functions], page 528.

int atexit (void (**function*) (void))
> stdlib.h (ISO): Section 25.7.3 [Cleanups on Exit], page 770.

double atof (const char **string*)
> stdlib.h (ISO): Section 20.11.2 [Parsing of Floats], page 613.

int atoi (const char **string*)
> stdlib.h (ISO): Section 20.11.1 [Parsing of Integers], page 608.

long int atol (const char **string*)
> stdlib.h (ISO): Section 20.11.1 [Parsing of Integers], page 608.

long long int atoll (const char **string*)
> stdlib.h (ISO): Section 20.11.1 [Parsing of Integers], page 608.

int backtrace (void **buffer*, int *size*)
> execinfo.h (GNU): Section 34.1 [Backtraces], page 892.

char ** backtrace_symbols (void *const **buffer*, int *size*)
> execinfo.h (GNU): Section 34.1 [Backtraces], page 892.

void backtrace_symbols_fd (void *const **buffer*, int *size*, int *fd*)
> execinfo.h (GNU): Section 34.1 [Backtraces], page 892.

char * basename (char **path*)
> libgen.h (XPG): Section 5.10 [Finding Tokens in a String], page 120.

char * basename (const char **filename*)
> string.h (GNU): Section 5.10 [Finding Tokens in a String], page 120.

int bcmp (const void **a1*, const void **a2*, size_t *size*)
> string.h (BSD): Section 5.7 [String/Array Comparison], page 107.

void bcopy (const void **from*, void **to*, size_t *size*)
> string.h (BSD): Section 5.4 [Copying Strings and Arrays], page 95.

int bind (int *socket*, struct sockaddr **addr*, socklen_t *length*)
> sys/socket.h (BSD): Section 16.3.2 [Setting the Address of a Socket], page 446.

char * bind_textdomain_codeset (const char **domainname*, const char **codeset*)
> libintl.h (GNU): Section 8.2.1.4 [How to specify the output character set **gettext** uses], page 213.

`char * bindtextdomain (const char *domainname, const char *dirname)`
       `libintl.h` (GNU): Section 8.2.1.2 [How to determine which catalog to be used], page 207.

`blkcnt64_t`
       `sys/types.h` (Unix98): Section 14.9.1 [The meaning of the File Attributes], page 412.

`blkcnt_t`
       `sys/types.h` (Unix98): Section 14.9.1 [The meaning of the File Attributes], page 412.

`int brk (void *addr)`
       `unistd.h` (BSD): Section 3.3 [Resizing the Data Segment], page 76.

`void * bsearch (const void *key, const void *array, size_t count, size_t size, comparison_fn_t compare)`
       `stdlib.h` (ISO): Section 9.2 [Array Search Function], page 220.

`wint_t btowc (int c)`
       `wchar.h` (ISO): Section 6.3.3 [Converting Single Characters], page 140.

`void bzero (void *block, size_t size)`
       `string.h` (BSD): Section 5.4 [Copying Strings and Arrays], page 95.

`double cabs (complex double z)`
       `complex.h` (ISO): Section 20.8.1 [Absolute Value], page 591.

`float cabsf (complex float z)`
       `complex.h` (ISO): Section 20.8.1 [Absolute Value], page 591.

`_FloatN cabsfN (complex _FloatN z)`
       `complex.h` (TS 18661-3:2015): Section 20.8.1 [Absolute Value], page 591.

`_FloatNx cabsfNx (complex _FloatNx z)`
       `complex.h` (TS 18661-3:2015): Section 20.8.1 [Absolute Value], page 591.

`long double cabsl (complex long double z)`
       `complex.h` (ISO): Section 20.8.1 [Absolute Value], page 591.

`complex double cacos (complex double z)`
       `complex.h` (ISO): Section 19.3 [Inverse Trigonometric Functions], page 528.

`complex float cacosf (complex float z)`
       `complex.h` (ISO): Section 19.3 [Inverse Trigonometric Functions], page 528.

`complex _FloatN cacosfN (complex _FloatN z)`
       `complex.h` (TS 18661-3:2015): Section 19.3 [Inverse Trigonometric Functions], page 528.

`complex _FloatNx cacosfNx (complex _FloatNx z)`
       `complex.h` (TS 18661-3:2015): Section 19.3 [Inverse Trigonometric Functions], page 528.

`complex double cacosh (complex double z)`
       `complex.h` (ISO): Section 19.5 [Hyperbolic Functions], page 536.

`complex float cacoshf (complex float z)`
       `complex.h` (ISO): Section 19.5 [Hyperbolic Functions], page 536.

`complex _FloatN cacoshfN (complex _FloatN z)`
       `complex.h` (TS 18661-3:2015): Section 19.5 [Hyperbolic Functions], page 536.

`complex _FloatNx cacoshfNx (complex _FloatNx z)`
       `complex.h` (TS 18661-3:2015): Section 19.5 [Hyperbolic Functions], page 536.

`complex long double cacoshl (complex long double z)`
       `complex.h` (ISO): Section 19.5 [Hyperbolic Functions], page 536.

`complex long double cacosl (complex long double z)`
       `complex.h` (ISO): Section 19.3 [Inverse Trigonometric Functions], page 528.

`void * calloc (size_t count, size_t eltsize)`
> `malloc.h` (ISO): Section 3.2.3.5 [Allocating Cleared Space], page 48.
>
> `stdlib.h` (ISO): Section 3.2.3.5 [Allocating Cleared Space], page 48.

`int canonicalize (double *cx, const double *x)`
> `math.h` (ISO): Section 20.8.5 [Setting and modifying single bits of FP values], page 599.

`char * canonicalize_file_name (const char *name)`
> `stdlib.h` (GNU): Section 14.5 [Symbolic Links], page 406.

`int canonicalizef (float *cx, const float *x)`
> `math.h` (ISO): Section 20.8.5 [Setting and modifying single bits of FP values], page 599.

`int canonicalizefN (_FloatN *cx, const _FloatN *x)`
> `math.h` (TS 18661-3:2015): Section 20.8.5 [Setting and modifying single bits of FP values], page 599.

`int canonicalizefNx (_FloatNx *cx, const _FloatNx *x)`
> `math.h` (TS 18661-3:2015): Section 20.8.5 [Setting and modifying single bits of FP values], page 599.

`int canonicalizel (long double *cx, const long double *x)`
> `math.h` (ISO): Section 20.8.5 [Setting and modifying single bits of FP values], page 599.

`double carg (complex double z)`
> `complex.h` (ISO): Section 20.10 [Projections, Conjugates, and Decomposing of Complex Numbers], page 607.

`float cargf (complex float z)`
> `complex.h` (ISO): Section 20.10 [Projections, Conjugates, and Decomposing of Complex Numbers], page 607.

`_FloatN cargfN (complex _FloatN z)`
> `complex.h` (TS 18661-3:2015): Section 20.10 [Projections, Conjugates, and Decomposing of Complex Numbers], page 607.

`_FloatNx cargfNx (complex _FloatNx z)`
> `complex.h` (TS 18661-3:2015): Section 20.10 [Projections, Conjugates, and Decomposing of Complex Numbers], page 607.

`long double cargl (complex long double z)`
> `complex.h` (ISO): Section 20.10 [Projections, Conjugates, and Decomposing of Complex Numbers], page 607.

`complex double casin (complex double z)`
> `complex.h` (ISO): Section 19.3 [Inverse Trigonometric Functions], page 528.

`complex float casinf (complex float z)`
> `complex.h` (ISO): Section 19.3 [Inverse Trigonometric Functions], page 528.

`complex _FloatN casinfN (complex _FloatN z)`
> `complex.h` (TS 18661-3:2015): Section 19.3 [Inverse Trigonometric Functions], page 528.

`complex _FloatNx casinfNx (complex _FloatNx z)`
> `complex.h` (TS 18661-3:2015): Section 19.3 [Inverse Trigonometric Functions], page 528.

`complex double casinh (complex double z)`
> `complex.h` (ISO): Section 19.5 [Hyperbolic Functions], page 536.

`complex float casinhf (complex float z)`
> `complex.h` (ISO): Section 19.5 [Hyperbolic Functions], page 536.

`complex _FloatN casinhfN (complex _FloatN z)`
> `complex.h` (TS 18661-3:2015): Section 19.5 [Hyperbolic Functions], page 536.

`complex _FloatNx casinhfNx (complex _FloatNx z)`
> `complex.h` (TS 18661-3:2015): Section 19.5 [Hyperbolic Functions], page 536.

`complex long double casinhl (complex long double z)`
> complex.h (ISO): Section 19.5 [Hyperbolic Functions], page 536.

`complex long double casinl (complex long double z)`
> complex.h (ISO): Section 19.3 [Inverse Trigonometric Functions], page 528.

`complex double catan (complex double z)`
> complex.h (ISO): Section 19.3 [Inverse Trigonometric Functions], page 528.

`complex float catanf (complex float z)`
> complex.h (ISO): Section 19.3 [Inverse Trigonometric Functions], page 528.

`complex _FloatN catanfN (complex _FloatN z)`
> complex.h (TS 18661-3:2015): Section 19.3 [Inverse Trigonometric Functions], page 528.

`complex _FloatNx catanfNx (complex _FloatNx z)`
> complex.h (TS 18661-3:2015): Section 19.3 [Inverse Trigonometric Functions], page 528.

`complex double catanh (complex double z)`
> complex.h (ISO): Section 19.5 [Hyperbolic Functions], page 536.

`complex float catanhf (complex float z)`
> complex.h (ISO): Section 19.5 [Hyperbolic Functions], page 536.

`complex _FloatN catanhfN (complex _FloatN z)`
> complex.h (TS 18661-3:2015): Section 19.5 [Hyperbolic Functions], page 536.

`complex _FloatNx catanhfNx (complex _FloatNx z)`
> complex.h (TS 18661-3:2015): Section 19.5 [Hyperbolic Functions], page 536.

`complex long double catanhl (complex long double z)`
> complex.h (ISO): Section 19.5 [Hyperbolic Functions], page 536.

`complex long double catanl (complex long double z)`
> complex.h (ISO): Section 19.3 [Inverse Trigonometric Functions], page 528.

`nl_catd catopen (const char *cat_name, int flag)`
> nl_types.h (X/Open): Section 8.1.1 [The `catgets` function family], page 195.

`int cbc_crypt (char *key, char *blocks, unsigned int len, unsigned int mode, char *ivec)`
> rpc/des_crypt.h (SUNRPC): Section 33.4 [DES Encryption], page 887.

`double cbrt (double x)`
> math.h (BSD): Section 19.4 [Exponentiation and Logarithms], page 530.

`float cbrtf (float x)`
> math.h (BSD): Section 19.4 [Exponentiation and Logarithms], page 530.

`_FloatN cbrtfN (_FloatN x)`
> math.h (TS 18661-3:2015): Section 19.4 [Exponentiation and Logarithms], page 530.

`_FloatNx cbrtfNx (_FloatNx x)`
> math.h (TS 18661-3:2015): Section 19.4 [Exponentiation and Logarithms], page 530.

`long double cbrtl (long double x)`
> math.h (BSD): Section 19.4 [Exponentiation and Logarithms], page 530.

`cc_t`
> termios.h (POSIX.1): Section 17.4.1 [Terminal Mode Data Types], page 492.

`complex double ccos (complex double z)`
> complex.h (ISO): Section 19.2 [Trigonometric Functions], page 526.

`complex float ccosf (complex float z)`
> complex.h (ISO): Section 19.2 [Trigonometric Functions], page 526.

`complex _FloatN ccosfN (complex _FloatN z)`
> complex.h (TS 18661-3:2015): Section 19.2 [Trigonometric Functions], page 526.

complex _FloatNx ccosfNx (complex _FloatNx z)
> complex.h (TS 18661-3:2015): Section 19.2 [Trigonometric Functions], page 526.

complex double ccosh (complex double z)
> complex.h (ISO): Section 19.5 [Hyperbolic Functions], page 536.

complex float ccoshf (complex float z)
> complex.h (ISO): Section 19.5 [Hyperbolic Functions], page 536.

complex _FloatN ccoshfN (complex _FloatN z)
> complex.h (TS 18661-3:2015): Section 19.5 [Hyperbolic Functions], page 536.

complex _FloatNx ccoshfNx (complex _FloatNx z)
> complex.h (TS 18661-3:2015): Section 19.5 [Hyperbolic Functions], page 536.

complex long double ccoshl (complex long double z)
> complex.h (ISO): Section 19.5 [Hyperbolic Functions], page 536.

complex long double ccosl (complex long double z)
> complex.h (ISO): Section 19.2 [Trigonometric Functions], page 526.

double ceil (double x)
> math.h (ISO): Section 20.8.3 [Rounding Functions], page 594.

float ceilf (float x)
> math.h (ISO): Section 20.8.3 [Rounding Functions], page 594.

_FloatN ceilfN (_FloatN x)
> math.h (TS 18661-3:2015): Section 20.8.3 [Rounding Functions], page 594.

_FloatNx ceilfNx (_FloatNx x)
> math.h (TS 18661-3:2015): Section 20.8.3 [Rounding Functions], page 594.

long double ceill (long double x)
> math.h (ISO): Section 20.8.3 [Rounding Functions], page 594.

complex double cexp (complex double z)
> complex.h (ISO): Section 19.4 [Exponentiation and Logarithms], page 530.

complex float cexpf (complex float z)
> complex.h (ISO): Section 19.4 [Exponentiation and Logarithms], page 530.

complex _FloatN cexpfN (complex _FloatN z)
> complex.h (TS 18661-3:2015): Section 19.4 [Exponentiation and Logarithms], page 530.

complex _FloatNx cexpfNx (complex _FloatNx z)
> complex.h (TS 18661-3:2015): Section 19.4 [Exponentiation and Logarithms], page 530.

complex long double cexpl (complex long double z)
> complex.h (ISO): Section 19.4 [Exponentiation and Logarithms], page 530.

speed_t cfgetispeed (const struct termios *termios-p)
> termios.h (POSIX.1): Section 17.4.8 [Line Speed], page 502.

speed_t cfgetospeed (const struct termios *termios-p)
> termios.h (POSIX.1): Section 17.4.8 [Line Speed], page 502.

void cfmakeraw (struct termios *termios-p)
> termios.h (BSD): Section 17.4.10 [Noncanonical Input], page 507.

int cfsetispeed (struct termios *termios-p, speed_t speed)
> termios.h (POSIX.1): Section 17.4.8 [Line Speed], page 502.

int cfsetospeed (struct termios *termios-p, speed_t speed)
> termios.h (POSIX.1): Section 17.4.8 [Line Speed], page 502.

int cfsetspeed (struct termios *termios-p, speed_t speed)
> termios.h (BSD): Section 17.4.8 [Line Speed], page 502.

`int chdir (const char *filename)`
> `unistd.h` (POSIX.1): Section 14.1 [Working Directory], page 390.

`int chmod (const char *filename, mode_t mode)`
> `sys/stat.h` (POSIX.1): Section 14.9.7 [Assigning File Permissions], page 423.

`int chown (const char *filename, uid_t owner, gid_t group)`
> `unistd.h` (POSIX.1): Section 14.9.4 [File Owner], page 420.

`double cimag (complex double z)`
> `complex.h` (ISO): Section 20.10 [Projections, Conjugates, and Decomposing of Complex Numbers], page 607.

`float cimagf (complex float z)`
> `complex.h` (ISO): Section 20.10 [Projections, Conjugates, and Decomposing of Complex Numbers], page 607.

`_FloatN cimagfN (complex _FloatN z)`
> `complex.h` (TS 18661-3:2015): Section 20.10 [Projections, Conjugates, and Decomposing of Complex Numbers], page 607.

`_FloatNx cimagfNx (complex _FloatNx z)`
> `complex.h` (TS 18661-3:2015): Section 20.10 [Projections, Conjugates, and Decomposing of Complex Numbers], page 607.

`long double cimagl (complex long double z)`
> `complex.h` (ISO): Section 20.10 [Projections, Conjugates, and Decomposing of Complex Numbers], page 607.

`int clearenv (void)`
> `stdlib.h` (GNU): Section 25.4.1 [Environment Access], page 763.

`void clearerr (FILE *stream)`
> `stdio.h` (ISO): Section 12.16 [Recovering from errors], page 313.

`void clearerr_unlocked (FILE *stream)`
> `stdio.h` (GNU): Section 12.16 [Recovering from errors], page 313.

`clock_t clock (void)`
> `time.h` (ISO): Section 21.3.1 [CPU Time Inquiry], page 621.

`clock_t`
> `time.h` (ISO): Section 21.3.1 [CPU Time Inquiry], page 621.

`complex double clog (complex double z)`
> `complex.h` (ISO): Section 19.4 [Exponentiation and Logarithms], page 530.

`complex double clog10 (complex double z)`
> `complex.h` (GNU): Section 19.4 [Exponentiation and Logarithms], page 530.

`complex float clog10f (complex float z)`
> `complex.h` (GNU): Section 19.4 [Exponentiation and Logarithms], page 530.

`complex _FloatN clog10fN (complex _FloatN z)`
> `complex.h` (GNU): Section 19.4 [Exponentiation and Logarithms], page 530.

`complex _FloatNx clog10fNx (complex _FloatNx z)`
> `complex.h` (GNU): Section 19.4 [Exponentiation and Logarithms], page 530.

`complex long double clog10l (complex long double z)`
> `complex.h` (GNU): Section 19.4 [Exponentiation and Logarithms], page 530.

`complex float clogf (complex float z)`
> `complex.h` (ISO): Section 19.4 [Exponentiation and Logarithms], page 530.

`complex _FloatN clogfN (complex _FloatN z)`
> `complex.h` (TS 18661-3:2015): Section 19.4 [Exponentiation and Logarithms], page 530.

`complex _FloatNx clogfNx (complex _FloatNx z)`
> complex.h (TS 18661-3:2015): Section 19.4 [Exponentiation and Logarithms], page 530.

`complex long double clogl (complex long double z)`
> complex.h (ISO): Section 19.4 [Exponentiation and Logarithms], page 530.

`int close (int filedes)`
> unistd.h (POSIX.1): Section 13.1 [Opening and Closing Files], page 333.

`int closedir (DIR *dirstream)`
> dirent.h (POSIX.1): Section 14.2.3 [Reading and Closing a Directory Stream], page 395.

`void closelog (void)`
> syslog.h (BSD): Section 18.2.3 [closelog], page 522.

`size_t confstr (int parameter, char *buf, size_t len)`
> unistd.h (POSIX.2): Section 32.12 [String-Valued Parameters], page 880.

`complex double conj (complex double z)`
> complex.h (ISO): Section 20.10 [Projections, Conjugates, and Decomposing of Complex Numbers], page 607.

`complex float conjf (complex float z)`
> complex.h (ISO): Section 20.10 [Projections, Conjugates, and Decomposing of Complex Numbers], page 607.

`complex _FloatN conjfN (complex _FloatN z)`
> complex.h (TS 18661-3:2015): Section 20.10 [Projections, Conjugates, and Decomposing of Complex Numbers], page 607.

`complex _FloatNx conjfNx (complex _FloatNx z)`
> complex.h (TS 18661-3:2015): Section 20.10 [Projections, Conjugates, and Decomposing of Complex Numbers], page 607.

`complex long double conjl (complex long double z)`
> complex.h (ISO): Section 20.10 [Projections, Conjugates, and Decomposing of Complex Numbers], page 607.

`int connect (int socket, struct sockaddr *addr, socklen_t length)`
> sys/socket.h (BSD): Section 16.9.1 [Making a Connection], page 469.

`cookie_close_function_t`
> stdio.h (GNU): Section 12.21.2.2 [Custom Stream Hook Functions], page 327.

`cookie_io_functions_t`
> stdio.h (GNU): Section 12.21.2.1 [Custom Streams and Cookies], page 326.

`cookie_read_function_t`
> stdio.h (GNU): Section 12.21.2.2 [Custom Stream Hook Functions], page 327.

`cookie_seek_function_t`
> stdio.h (GNU): Section 12.21.2.2 [Custom Stream Hook Functions], page 327.

`cookie_write_function_t`
> stdio.h (GNU): Section 12.21.2.2 [Custom Stream Hook Functions], page 327.

`double copysign (double x, double y)`
> math.h (ISO): Section 20.8.5 [Setting and modifying single bits of FP values], page 599.

`float copysignf (float x, float y)`
> math.h (ISO): Section 20.8.5 [Setting and modifying single bits of FP values], page 599.

`_FloatN copysignfN (_FloatN x, _FloatN y)`
> math.h (TS 18661-3:2015): Section 20.8.5 [Setting and modifying single bits of FP values], page 599.

`_FloatNx copysignfNx (_FloatNx x, _FloatNx y)`
> math.h (TS 18661-3:2015): Section 20.8.5 [Setting and modifying single bits of FP values], page 599.

`long double copysignl (long double x, long double y)`
> `math.h` (ISO): Section 20.8.5 [Setting and modifying single bits of FP values], page 599.

`double cos (double x)`
> `math.h` (ISO): Section 19.2 [Trigonometric Functions], page 526.

`float cosf (float x)`
> `math.h` (ISO): Section 19.2 [Trigonometric Functions], page 526.

`_FloatN cosfN (_FloatN x)`
> `math.h` (TS 18661-3:2015): Section 19.2 [Trigonometric Functions], page 526.

`_FloatNx cosfNx (_FloatNx x)`
> `math.h` (TS 18661-3:2015): Section 19.2 [Trigonometric Functions], page 526.

`double cosh (double x)`
> `math.h` (ISO): Section 19.5 [Hyperbolic Functions], page 536.

`float coshf (float x)`
> `math.h` (ISO): Section 19.5 [Hyperbolic Functions], page 536.

`_FloatN coshfN (_FloatN x)`
> `math.h` (TS 18661-3:2015): Section 19.5 [Hyperbolic Functions], page 536.

`_FloatNx coshfNx (_FloatNx x)`
> `math.h` (TS 18661-3:2015): Section 19.5 [Hyperbolic Functions], page 536.

`long double coshl (long double x)`
> `math.h` (ISO): Section 19.5 [Hyperbolic Functions], page 536.

`long double cosl (long double x)`
> `math.h` (ISO): Section 19.2 [Trigonometric Functions], page 526.

`complex double cpow (complex double base, complex double power)`
> `complex.h` (ISO): Section 19.4 [Exponentiation and Logarithms], page 530.

`complex float cpowf (complex float base, complex float power)`
> `complex.h` (ISO): Section 19.4 [Exponentiation and Logarithms], page 530.

`complex _FloatN cpowfN (complex _FloatN base, complex _FloatN power)`
> `complex.h` (TS 18661-3:2015): Section 19.4 [Exponentiation and Logarithms], page 530.

`complex _FloatNx cpowfNx (complex _FloatNx base, complex _FloatNx power)`
> `complex.h` (TS 18661-3:2015): Section 19.4 [Exponentiation and Logarithms], page 530.

`complex long double cpowl (complex long double base, complex long double power)`
> `complex.h` (ISO): Section 19.4 [Exponentiation and Logarithms], page 530.

`complex double cproj (complex double z)`
> `complex.h` (ISO): Section 20.10 [Projections, Conjugates, and Decomposing of Complex Numbers], page 607.

`complex float cprojf (complex float z)`
> `complex.h` (ISO): Section 20.10 [Projections, Conjugates, and Decomposing of Complex Numbers], page 607.

`complex _FloatN cprojfN (complex _FloatN z)`
> `complex.h` (TS 18661-3:2015): Section 20.10 [Projections, Conjugates, and Decomposing of Complex Numbers], page 607.

`complex _FloatNx cprojfNx (complex _FloatNx z)`
> `complex.h` (TS 18661-3:2015): Section 20.10 [Projections, Conjugates, and Decomposing of Complex Numbers], page 607.

`complex long double cprojl (complex long double z)`
> `complex.h` (ISO): Section 20.10 [Projections, Conjugates, and Decomposing of Complex Numbers], page 607.

`cpu_set_t`

> `sched.h` (GNU): Section 22.3.5 [Limiting execution to certain CPUs], page 669.

`double creal (complex double z)`

> `complex.h` (ISO): Section 20.10 [Projections, Conjugates, and Decomposing of Complex Numbers], page 607.

`float crealf (complex float z)`

> `complex.h` (ISO): Section 20.10 [Projections, Conjugates, and Decomposing of Complex Numbers], page 607.

`_FloatN crealfN (complex _FloatN z)`

> `complex.h` (TS 18661-3:2015): Section 20.10 [Projections, Conjugates, and Decomposing of Complex Numbers], page 607.

`_FloatNx crealfNx (complex _FloatNx z)`

> `complex.h` (TS 18661-3:2015): Section 20.10 [Projections, Conjugates, and Decomposing of Complex Numbers], page 607.

`long double creall (complex long double z)`

> `complex.h` (ISO): Section 20.10 [Projections, Conjugates, and Decomposing of Complex Numbers], page 607.

`int creat (const char *filename, mode_t mode)`

> `fcntl.h` (POSIX.1): Section 13.1 [Opening and Closing Files], page 333.

`int creat64 (const char *filename, mode_t mode)`

> `fcntl.h` (Unix98): Section 13.1 [Opening and Closing Files], page 333.

`char * crypt (const char *key, const char *salt)`

> `crypt.h` (BSD): Section 33.3 [Encrypting Passwords], page 885.
>
> `crypt.h` (SVID): Section 33.3 [Encrypting Passwords], page 885.

`char * crypt_r (const char *key, const char *salt, struct crypt_data * data)`

> `crypt.h` (GNU): Section 33.3 [Encrypting Passwords], page 885.

`complex double csin (complex double z)`

> `complex.h` (ISO): Section 19.2 [Trigonometric Functions], page 526.

`complex float csinf (complex float z)`

> `complex.h` (ISO): Section 19.2 [Trigonometric Functions], page 526.

`complex _FloatN csinfN (complex _FloatN z)`

> `complex.h` (TS 18661-3:2015): Section 19.2 [Trigonometric Functions], page 526.

`complex _FloatNx csinfNx (complex _FloatNx z)`

> `complex.h` (TS 18661-3:2015): Section 19.2 [Trigonometric Functions], page 526.

`complex double csinh (complex double z)`

> `complex.h` (ISO): Section 19.5 [Hyperbolic Functions], page 536.

`complex float csinhf (complex float z)`

> `complex.h` (ISO): Section 19.5 [Hyperbolic Functions], page 536.

`complex _FloatN csinhfN (complex _FloatN z)`

> `complex.h` (TS 18661-3:2015): Section 19.5 [Hyperbolic Functions], page 536.

`complex _FloatNx csinhfNx (complex _FloatNx z)`

> `complex.h` (TS 18661-3:2015): Section 19.5 [Hyperbolic Functions], page 536.

`complex long double csinhl (complex long double z)`

> `complex.h` (ISO): Section 19.5 [Hyperbolic Functions], page 536.

`complex long double csinl (complex long double z)`

> `complex.h` (ISO): Section 19.2 [Trigonometric Functions], page 526.

`complex double csqrt (complex double z)`

> `complex.h` (ISO): Section 19.4 [Exponentiation and Logarithms], page 530.

```
complex float csqrtf (complex float z)
```
        `complex.h` (ISO): Section 19.4 [Exponentiation and Logarithms], page 530.

```
complex _FloatN csqrtfN (_FloatN z)
```
        `complex.h` (TS 18661-3:2015): Section 19.4 [Exponentiation and Logarithms], page 530.

```
complex _FloatNx csqrtfNx (complex _FloatNx z)
```
        `complex.h` (TS 18661-3:2015): Section 19.4 [Exponentiation and Logarithms], page 530.

```
complex long double csqrtl (complex long double z)
```
        `complex.h` (ISO): Section 19.4 [Exponentiation and Logarithms], page 530.

```
complex double ctan (complex double z)
```
        `complex.h` (ISO): Section 19.2 [Trigonometric Functions], page 526.

```
complex float ctanf (complex float z)
```
        `complex.h` (ISO): Section 19.2 [Trigonometric Functions], page 526.

```
complex _FloatN ctanfN (complex _FloatN z)
```
        `complex.h` (TS 18661-3:2015): Section 19.2 [Trigonometric Functions], page 526.

```
complex _FloatNx ctanfNx (complex _FloatNx z)
```
        `complex.h` (TS 18661-3:2015): Section 19.2 [Trigonometric Functions], page 526.

```
complex double ctanh (complex double z)
```
        `complex.h` (ISO): Section 19.5 [Hyperbolic Functions], page 536.

```
complex float ctanhf (complex float z)
```
        `complex.h` (ISO): Section 19.5 [Hyperbolic Functions], page 536.

```
complex _FloatN ctanhfN (complex _FloatN z)
```
        `complex.h` (TS 18661-3:2015): Section 19.5 [Hyperbolic Functions], page 536.

```
complex _FloatNx ctanhfNx (complex _FloatNx z)
```
        `complex.h` (TS 18661-3:2015): Section 19.5 [Hyperbolic Functions], page 536.

```
complex long double ctanhl (complex long double z)
```
        `complex.h` (ISO): Section 19.5 [Hyperbolic Functions], page 536.

```
complex long double ctanl (complex long double z)
```
        `complex.h` (ISO): Section 19.2 [Trigonometric Functions], page 526.

```
char * ctermid (char *string)
```
        `stdio.h` (POSIX.1): Section 28.7.1 [Identifying the Controlling Terminal], page 801.

```
char * ctime (const time_t *time)
```
        `time.h` (ISO): Section 21.4.5 [Formatting Calendar Time], page 632.

```
char * ctime_r (const time_t *time, char *buffer)
```
        `time.h` (POSIX.1c): Section 21.4.5 [Formatting Calendar Time], page 632.

```
char * cuserid (char *string)
```
        `stdio.h` (POSIX.1): Section 30.11 [Identifying Who Logged In], page 825.

```
int daylight
```
        `time.h` (SVID): Section 21.4.8 [Functions and Variables for Time Zones], page 648.

```
char * dcgettext (const char *domainname, const char *msgid, int category)
```
        `libintl.h` (GNU): Section 8.2.1.1 [What has to be done to translate a message?], page 205.

```
char * dcngettext (const char *domain, const char *msgid1, const char *msgid2, unsigned long int
n, int category)
```
        `libintl.h` (GNU): Section 8.2.1.3 [Additional functions for more complicated situations], page 209.

```
void des_setparity (char *key)
```
        `rpc/des_crypt.h` (SUNRPC): Section 33.4 [DES Encryption], page 887.

dev_t
> sys/types.h (POSIX.1): Section 14.9.1 [The meaning of the File Attributes], page 412.

char * dgettext (const char *domainname, const char *msgid)
> libintl.h (GNU): Section 8.2.1.1 [What has to be done to translate a message?], page 205.

double difftime (time_t time1, time_t time0)
> time.h (ISO): Section 21.2 [Elapsed Time], page 619.

struct dirent
> dirent.h (POSIX.1): Section 14.2.1 [Format of a Directory Entry], page 392.

int dirfd (DIR *dirstream)
> dirent.h (GNU): Section 14.2.2 [Opening a Directory Stream], page 394.

char * dirname (char *path)
> libgen.h (XPG): Section 5.10 [Finding Tokens in a String], page 120.

div_t div (int numerator, int denominator)
> stdlib.h (ISO): Section 20.2 [Integer Division], page 576.

div_t
> stdlib.h (ISO): Section 20.2 [Integer Division], page 576.

char * dngettext (const char *domain, const char *msgid1, const char *msgid2, unsigned long int n)
> libintl.h (GNU): Section 8.2.1.3 [Additional functions for more complicated situations], page 209.

double drand48 (void)
> stdlib.h (SVID): Section 19.8.3 [SVID Random Number Function], page 568.

int drand48_r (struct drand48_data *buffer, double *result)
> stdlib.h (GNU): Section 19.8.3 [SVID Random Number Function], page 568.

double drem (double numerator, double denominator)
> math.h (BSD): Section 20.8.4 [Remainder Functions], page 598.

float dremf (float numerator, float denominator)
> math.h (BSD): Section 20.8.4 [Remainder Functions], page 598.

long double dreml (long double numerator, long double denominator)
> math.h (BSD): Section 20.8.4 [Remainder Functions], page 598.

int dup (int old)
> unistd.h (POSIX.1): Section 13.12 [Duplicating Descriptors], page 373.

int dup2 (int old, int new)
> unistd.h (POSIX.1): Section 13.12 [Duplicating Descriptors], page 373.

int ecb_crypt (char *key, char *blocks, unsigned int len, unsigned int mode)
> rpc/des_crypt.h (SUNRPC): Section 33.4 [DES Encryption], page 887.

char * ecvt (double value, int ndigit, int *decpt, int *neg)
> stdlib.h (SVID): Section 20.13 [Old-fashioned System V number-to-string functions], page 616.
>
> stdlib.h (Unix98): Section 20.13 [Old-fashioned System V number-to-string functions], page 616.

int ecvt_r (double value, int ndigit, int *decpt, int *neg, char *buf, size_t len)
> stdlib.h (GNU): Section 20.13 [Old-fashioned System V number-to-string functions], page 616.

void encrypt (char *block, int edflag)
> crypt.h (BSD): Section 33.4 [DES Encryption], page 887.
>
> crypt.h (SVID): Section 33.4 [DES Encryption], page 887.

`void encrypt_r (char *block, int edflag, struct crypt_data * data)`
> `crypt.h` (GNU): Section 33.4 [DES Encryption], page 887.

`void endfsent (void)`
> `fstab.h` (BSD): Section 31.3.1.1 [The `fstab` file], page 849.

`void endgrent (void)`
> `grp.h` (SVID): Section 30.14.3 [Scanning the List of All Groups], page 839.

> `grp.h` (BSD): Section 30.14.3 [Scanning the List of All Groups], page 839.

`void endhostent (void)`
> `netdb.h` (BSD): Section 16.6.2.4 [Host Names], page 456.

`int endmntent (FILE *stream)`
> `mntent.h` (BSD): Section 31.3.1.2 [The `mtab` file], page 852.

`void endnetent (void)`
> `netdb.h` (BSD): Section 16.13 [Networks Database], page 488.

`void endnetgrent (void)`
> `netdb.h` (BSD): Section 30.16.2 [Looking up one Netgroup], page 842.

`void endprotoent (void)`
> `netdb.h` (BSD): Section 16.6.6 [Protocols Database], page 463.

`void endpwent (void)`
> `pwd.h` (SVID): Section 30.13.3 [Scanning the List of All Users], page 836.

> `pwd.h` (BSD): Section 30.13.3 [Scanning the List of All Users], page 836.

`void endservent (void)`
> `netdb.h` (BSD): Section 16.6.4 [The Services Database], page 461.

`void endutent (void)`
> `utmp.h` (SVID): Section 30.12.1 [Manipulating the User Accounting Database], page 826.

`void endutxent (void)`
> `utmpx.h` (XPG4.2): Section 30.12.2 [XPG User Accounting Database Functions], page 831.

`char ** environ`
> `unistd.h` (POSIX.1): Section 25.4.1 [Environment Access], page 763.

`error_t envz_add (char **envz, size_t *envz_len, const char *name, const char *value)`
> `envz.h` (GNU): Section 5.15.2 [Envz Functions], page 132.

`char * envz_entry (const char *envz, size_t envz_len, const char *name)`
> `envz.h` (GNU): Section 5.15.2 [Envz Functions], page 132.

`char * envz_get (const char *envz, size_t envz_len, const char *name)`
> `envz.h` (GNU): Section 5.15.2 [Envz Functions], page 132.

`error_t envz_merge (char **envz, size_t *envz_len, const char *envz2, size_t envz2_len, int override)`
> `envz.h` (GNU): Section 5.15.2 [Envz Functions], page 132.

`void envz_remove (char **envz, size_t *envz_len, const char *name)`
> `envz.h` (GNU): Section 5.15.2 [Envz Functions], page 132.

`void envz_strip (char **envz, size_t *envz_len)`
> `envz.h` (GNU): Section 5.15.2 [Envz Functions], page 132.

`double erand48 (unsigned short int xsubi[3])`
> `stdlib.h` (SVID): Section 19.8.3 [SVID Random Number Function], page 568.

`int erand48_r (unsigned short int xsubi[3], struct drand48_data *buffer, double *result)`
> `stdlib.h` (GNU): Section 19.8.3 [SVID Random Number Function], page 568.

`double erf (double x)`
> `math.h` (SVID): Section 19.6 [Special Functions], page 539.

```
double erfc (double x)
```
math.h (SVID): Section 19.6 [Special Functions], page 539.

```
float erfcf (float x)
```
math.h (SVID): Section 19.6 [Special Functions], page 539.

```
_FloatN erfcfN (_FloatN x)
```
math.h (TS 18661-3:2015): Section 19.6 [Special Functions], page 539.

```
_FloatNx erfcfNx (_FloatNx x)
```
math.h (TS 18661-3:2015): Section 19.6 [Special Functions], page 539.

```
long double erfcl (long double x)
```
math.h (SVID): Section 19.6 [Special Functions], page 539.

```
float erff (float x)
```
math.h (SVID): Section 19.6 [Special Functions], page 539.

```
_FloatN erffN (_FloatN x)
```
math.h (TS 18661-3:2015): Section 19.6 [Special Functions], page 539.

```
_FloatNx erffNx (_FloatNx x)
```
math.h (TS 18661-3:2015): Section 19.6 [Special Functions], page 539.

```
long double erfl (long double x)
```
math.h (SVID): Section 19.6 [Special Functions], page 539.

```
void err (int status, const char *format, ...)
```
err.h (BSD): Section 2.3 [Error Messages], page 35.

```
volatile int errno
```
errno.h (ISO): Section 2.1 [Checking for Errors], page 22.

```
void error (int status, int errnum, const char *format, ...)
```
error.h (GNU): Section 2.3 [Error Messages], page 35.

```
void error_at_line (int status, int errnum, const char *fname, unsigned int lineno, const char
*format, ...)
```
error.h (GNU): Section 2.3 [Error Messages], page 35.

```
unsigned int error_message_count
```
error.h (GNU): Section 2.3 [Error Messages], page 35.

```
int error_one_per_line
```
error.h (GNU): Section 2.3 [Error Messages], page 35.

```
void (*error_print_progname) (void)
```
error.h (GNU): Section 2.3 [Error Messages], page 35.

```
void errx (int status, const char *format, ...)
```
err.h (BSD): Section 2.3 [Error Messages], page 35.

```
int execl (const char *filename, const char *arg0, ...)
```
unistd.h (POSIX.1): Section 26.5 [Executing a File], page 776.

```
int execle (const char *filename, const char *arg0, ..., char *const env[])
```
unistd.h (POSIX.1): Section 26.5 [Executing a File], page 776.

```
int execlp (const char *filename, const char *arg0, ...)
```
unistd.h (POSIX.1): Section 26.5 [Executing a File], page 776.

```
int execv (const char *filename, char *const argv[])
```
unistd.h (POSIX.1): Section 26.5 [Executing a File], page 776.

```
int execve (const char *filename, char *const argv[], char *const env[])
```
unistd.h (POSIX.1): Section 26.5 [Executing a File], page 776.

```
int execvp (const char *filename, char *const argv[])
```
unistd.h (POSIX.1): Section 26.5 [Executing a File], page 776.

`void exit (int status)`
> `stdlib.h` (ISO): Section 25.7.1 [Normal Termination], page 769.

`struct exit_status`
> `utmp.h` (SVID): Section 30.12.1 [Manipulating the User Accounting Database], page 826.

`double exp (double x)`
> `math.h` (ISO): Section 19.4 [Exponentiation and Logarithms], page 530.

`double exp10 (double x)`
> `math.h` (ISO): Section 19.4 [Exponentiation and Logarithms], page 530.

`float exp10f (float x)`
> `math.h` (ISO): Section 19.4 [Exponentiation and Logarithms], page 530.

`_FloatN exp10fN (_FloatN x)`
> `math.h` (TS 18661-4:2015): Section 19.4 [Exponentiation and Logarithms], page 530.

`_FloatNx exp10fNx (_FloatNx x)`
> `math.h` (TS 18661-4:2015): Section 19.4 [Exponentiation and Logarithms], page 530.

`long double exp10l (long double x)`
> `math.h` (ISO): Section 19.4 [Exponentiation and Logarithms], page 530.

`double exp2 (double x)`
> `math.h` (ISO): Section 19.4 [Exponentiation and Logarithms], page 530.

`float exp2f (float x)`
> `math.h` (ISO): Section 19.4 [Exponentiation and Logarithms], page 530.

`_FloatN exp2fN (_FloatN x)`
> `math.h` (TS 18661-3:2015): Section 19.4 [Exponentiation and Logarithms], page 530.

`_FloatNx exp2fNx (_FloatNx x)`
> `math.h` (TS 18661-3:2015): Section 19.4 [Exponentiation and Logarithms], page 530.

`long double exp2l (long double x)`
> `math.h` (ISO): Section 19.4 [Exponentiation and Logarithms], page 530.

`float expf (float x)`
> `math.h` (ISO): Section 19.4 [Exponentiation and Logarithms], page 530.

`_FloatN expfN (_FloatN x)`
> `math.h` (TS 18661-3:2015): Section 19.4 [Exponentiation and Logarithms], page 530.

`_FloatNx expfNx (_FloatNx x)`
> `math.h` (TS 18661-3:2015): Section 19.4 [Exponentiation and Logarithms], page 530.

`long double expl (long double x)`
> `math.h` (ISO): Section 19.4 [Exponentiation and Logarithms], page 530.

`void explicit_bzero (void *block, size_t len)`
> `string.h` (BSD): Section 5.11 [Erasing Sensitive Data], page 125.

`double expm1 (double x)`
> `math.h` (ISO): Section 19.4 [Exponentiation and Logarithms], page 530.

`float expm1f (float x)`
> `math.h` (ISO): Section 19.4 [Exponentiation and Logarithms], page 530.

`_FloatN expm1fN (_FloatN x)`
> `math.h` (TS 18661-3:2015): Section 19.4 [Exponentiation and Logarithms], page 530.

`_FloatNx expm1fNx (_FloatNx x)`
> `math.h` (TS 18661-3:2015): Section 19.4 [Exponentiation and Logarithms], page 530.

`long double expm1l (long double x)`
> `math.h` (ISO): Section 19.4 [Exponentiation and Logarithms], page 530.

`double fabs (double number)`
> `math.h` (ISO): Section 20.8.1 [Absolute Value], page 591.

`float fabsf (float number)`
> `math.h` (ISO): Section 20.8.1 [Absolute Value], page 591.

`_FloatN fabsfN (_FloatN number)`
> `math.h` (TS 18661-3:2015): Section 20.8.1 [Absolute Value], page 591.

`_FloatNx fabsfNx (_FloatNx number)`
> `math.h` (TS 18661-3:2015): Section 20.8.1 [Absolute Value], page 591.

`long double fabsl (long double number)`
> `math.h` (ISO): Section 20.8.1 [Absolute Value], page 591.

`int fchdir (int filedes)`
> `unistd.h` (XPG): Section 14.1 [Working Directory], page 390.

`int fchmod (int filedes, mode_t mode)`
> `sys/stat.h` (BSD): Section 14.9.7 [Assigning File Permissions], page 423.

`int fchown (int filedes, uid_t owner, gid_t group)`
> `unistd.h` (BSD): Section 14.9.4 [File Owner], page 420.

`int fclose (FILE *stream)`
> `stdio.h` (ISO): Section 12.4 [Closing Streams], page 262.

`int fcloseall (void)`
> `stdio.h` (GNU): Section 12.4 [Closing Streams], page 262.

`int fcntl (int filedes, int command, ...)`
> `fcntl.h` (POSIX.1): Section 13.11 [Control Operations on Files], page 371.

`char * fcvt (double value, int ndigit, int *decpt, int *neg)`
> `stdlib.h` (SVID): Section 20.13 [Old-fashioned System V number-to-string functions], page 616.
>
> `stdlib.h` (Unix98): Section 20.13 [Old-fashioned System V number-to-string functions], page 616.

`int fcvt_r (double value, int ndigit, int *decpt, int *neg, char *buf, size_t len)`
> `stdlib.h` (SVID): Section 20.13 [Old-fashioned System V number-to-string functions], page 616.
>
> `stdlib.h` (Unix98): Section 20.13 [Old-fashioned System V number-to-string functions], page 616.

`fd_set`
> `sys/types.h` (BSD): Section 13.8 [Waiting for Input or Output], page 355.

`int fdatasync (int fildes)`
> `unistd.h` (POSIX): Section 13.9 [Synchronizing I/O operations], page 358.

`double fdim (double x, double y)`
> `math.h` (ISO): Section 20.8.7 [Miscellaneous FP arithmetic functions], page 604.

`float fdimf (float x, float y)`
> `math.h` (ISO): Section 20.8.7 [Miscellaneous FP arithmetic functions], page 604.

`_FloatN fdimfN (_FloatN x, _FloatN y)`
> `math.h` (TS 18661-3:2015): Section 20.8.7 [Miscellaneous FP arithmetic functions], page 604.

`_FloatNx fdimfNx (_FloatNx x, _FloatNx y)`
> `math.h` (TS 18661-3:2015): Section 20.8.7 [Miscellaneous FP arithmetic functions], page 604.

`long double fdiml (long double x, long double y)`
> `math.h` (ISO): Section 20.8.7 [Miscellaneous FP arithmetic functions], page 604.

FILE * fdopen (int *filedes*, const char **opentype*)
        stdio.h (POSIX.1): Section 13.4 [Descriptors and Streams], page 346.

DIR * fdopendir (int *fd*)
        dirent.h (GNU): Section 14.2.2 [Opening a Directory Stream], page 394.

int feclearexcept (int *excepts*)
        fenv.h (ISO): Section 20.5.3 [Examining the FPU status word], page 584.

int fedisableexcept (int *excepts*)
        fenv.h (GNU): Section 20.7 [Floating-Point Control Functions], page 589.

int feenableexcept (int *excepts*)
        fenv.h (GNU): Section 20.7 [Floating-Point Control Functions], page 589.

int fegetenv (fenv_t **envp*)
        fenv.h (ISO): Section 20.7 [Floating-Point Control Functions], page 589.

int fegetexcept (void)
        fenv.h (GNU): Section 20.7 [Floating-Point Control Functions], page 589.

int fegetexceptflag (fexcept_t **flagp*, int *excepts*)
        fenv.h (ISO): Section 20.5.3 [Examining the FPU status word], page 584.

int fegetmode (femode_t **modep*)
        fenv.h (ISO): Section 20.7 [Floating-Point Control Functions], page 589.

int fegetround (void)
        fenv.h (ISO): Section 20.6 [Rounding Modes], page 587.

int feholdexcept (fenv_t **envp*)
        fenv.h (ISO): Section 20.7 [Floating-Point Control Functions], page 589.

int feof (FILE **stream*)
        stdio.h (ISO): Section 12.15 [End-Of-File and Errors], page 311.

int feof_unlocked (FILE **stream*)
        stdio.h (GNU): Section 12.15 [End-Of-File and Errors], page 311.

int feraiseexcept (int *excepts*)
        fenv.h (ISO): Section 20.5.3 [Examining the FPU status word], page 584.

int ferror (FILE **stream*)
        stdio.h (ISO): Section 12.15 [End-Of-File and Errors], page 311.

int ferror_unlocked (FILE **stream*)
        stdio.h (GNU): Section 12.15 [End-Of-File and Errors], page 311.

int fesetenv (const fenv_t **envp*)
        fenv.h (ISO): Section 20.7 [Floating-Point Control Functions], page 589.

int fesetexcept (int *excepts*)
        fenv.h (ISO): Section 20.5.3 [Examining the FPU status word], page 584.

int fesetexceptflag (const fexcept_t **flagp*, int *excepts*)
        fenv.h (ISO): Section 20.5.3 [Examining the FPU status word], page 584.

int fesetmode (const femode_t **modep*)
        fenv.h (ISO): Section 20.7 [Floating-Point Control Functions], page 589.

int fesetround (int *round*)
        fenv.h (ISO): Section 20.6 [Rounding Modes], page 587.

int fetestexcept (int *excepts*)
        fenv.h (ISO): Section 20.5.3 [Examining the FPU status word], page 584.

int fetestexceptflag (const fexcept_t **flagp*, int *excepts*)
        fenv.h (ISO): Section 20.5.3 [Examining the FPU status word], page 584.

`int feupdateenv (const fenv_t *envp)`
> `fenv.h` (ISO): Section 20.7 [Floating-Point Control Functions], page 589.

`int fflush (FILE *stream)`
> `stdio.h` (ISO): Section 12.20.2 [Flushing Buffers], page 320.

`int fflush_unlocked (FILE *stream)`
> `stdio.h` (POSIX): Section 12.20.2 [Flushing Buffers], page 320.

`int fgetc (FILE *stream)`
> `stdio.h` (ISO): Section 12.8 [Character Input], page 271.

`int fgetc_unlocked (FILE *stream)`
> `stdio.h` (POSIX): Section 12.8 [Character Input], page 271.

`struct group * fgetgrent (FILE *stream)`
> `grp.h` (SVID): Section 30.14.3 [Scanning the List of All Groups], page 839.

`int fgetgrent_r (FILE *stream, struct group *result_buf, char *buffer, size_t buflen, struct group **result)`
> `grp.h` (GNU): Section 30.14.3 [Scanning the List of All Groups], page 839.

`int fgetpos (FILE *stream, fpos_t *position)`
> `stdio.h` (ISO): Section 12.19 [Portable File-Position Functions], page 317.

`int fgetpos64 (FILE *stream, fpos64_t *position)`
> `stdio.h` (Unix98): Section 12.19 [Portable File-Position Functions], page 317.

`struct passwd * fgetpwent (FILE *stream)`
> `pwd.h` (SVID): Section 30.13.3 [Scanning the List of All Users], page 836.

`int fgetpwent_r (FILE *stream, struct passwd *result_buf, char *buffer, size_t buflen, struct passwd **result)`
> `pwd.h` (GNU): Section 30.13.3 [Scanning the List of All Users], page 836.

`char * fgets (char *s, int count, FILE *stream)`
> `stdio.h` (ISO): Section 12.9 [Line-Oriented Input], page 274.

`char * fgets_unlocked (char *s, int count, FILE *stream)`
> `stdio.h` (GNU): Section 12.9 [Line-Oriented Input], page 274.

`wint_t fgetwc (FILE *stream)`
> `wchar.h` (ISO): Section 12.8 [Character Input], page 271.

`wint_t fgetwc_unlocked (FILE *stream)`
> `wchar.h` (GNU): Section 12.8 [Character Input], page 271.

`wchar_t * fgetws (wchar_t *ws, int count, FILE *stream)`
> `wchar.h` (ISO): Section 12.9 [Line-Oriented Input], page 274.

`wchar_t * fgetws_unlocked (wchar_t *ws, int count, FILE *stream)`
> `wchar.h` (GNU): Section 12.9 [Line-Oriented Input], page 274.

`int fileno (FILE *stream)`
> `stdio.h` (POSIX.1): Section 13.4 [Descriptors and Streams], page 346.

`int fileno_unlocked (FILE *stream)`
> `stdio.h` (GNU): Section 13.4 [Descriptors and Streams], page 346.

`int finite (double x)`
> `math.h` (BSD): Section 20.4 [Floating-Point Number Classification Functions], page 579.

`int finitef (float x)`
> `math.h` (BSD): Section 20.4 [Floating-Point Number Classification Functions], page 579.

`int finitel (long double x)`
> `math.h` (BSD): Section 20.4 [Floating-Point Number Classification Functions], page 579.

struct flock

> fcntl.h (POSIX.1): Section 13.15 [File Locks], page 380.

void flockfile (FILE *stream)

> stdio.h (POSIX): Section 12.5 [Streams and Threads], page 263.

double floor (double x)

> math.h (ISO): Section 20.8.3 [Rounding Functions], page 594.

float floorf (float x)

> math.h (ISO): Section 20.8.3 [Rounding Functions], page 594.

_FloatN floorfN (_FloatN x)

> math.h (TS 18661-3:2015): Section 20.8.3 [Rounding Functions], page 594.

_FloatNx floorfNx (_FloatNx x)

> math.h (TS 18661-3:2015): Section 20.8.3 [Rounding Functions], page 594.

long double floorl (long double x)

> math.h (ISO): Section 20.8.3 [Rounding Functions], page 594.

double fma (double x, double y, double z)

> math.h (ISO): Section 20.8.7 [Miscellaneous FP arithmetic functions], page 604.

float fmaf (float x, float y, float z)

> math.h (ISO): Section 20.8.7 [Miscellaneous FP arithmetic functions], page 604.

_FloatN fmafN (_FloatN x, _FloatN y, _FloatN z)

> math.h (TS 18661-3:2015): Section 20.8.7 [Miscellaneous FP arithmetic functions], page 604.

_FloatNx fmafNx (_FloatNx x, _FloatNx y, _FloatNx z)

> math.h (TS 18661-3:2015): Section 20.8.7 [Miscellaneous FP arithmetic functions], page 604.

long double fmal (long double x, long double y, long double z)

> math.h (ISO): Section 20.8.7 [Miscellaneous FP arithmetic functions], page 604.

double fmax (double x, double y)

> math.h (ISO): Section 20.8.7 [Miscellaneous FP arithmetic functions], page 604.

float fmaxf (float x, float y)

> math.h (ISO): Section 20.8.7 [Miscellaneous FP arithmetic functions], page 604.

_FloatN fmaxfN (_FloatN x, _FloatN y)

> math.h (TS 18661-3:2015): Section 20.8.7 [Miscellaneous FP arithmetic functions], page 604.

_FloatNx fmaxfNx (_FloatNx x, _FloatNx y)

> math.h (TS 18661-3:2015): Section 20.8.7 [Miscellaneous FP arithmetic functions], page 604.

long double fmaxl (long double x, long double y)

> math.h (ISO): Section 20.8.7 [Miscellaneous FP arithmetic functions], page 604.

double fmaxmag (double x, double y)

> math.h (ISO): Section 20.8.7 [Miscellaneous FP arithmetic functions], page 604.

float fmaxmagf (float x, float y)

> math.h (ISO): Section 20.8.7 [Miscellaneous FP arithmetic functions], page 604.

_FloatN fmaxmagfN (_FloatN x, _FloatN y)

> math.h (TS 18661-3:2015): Section 20.8.7 [Miscellaneous FP arithmetic functions], page 604.

_FloatNx fmaxmagfNx (_FloatNx x, _FloatNx y)

> math.h (TS 18661-3:2015): Section 20.8.7 [Miscellaneous FP arithmetic functions], page 604.

long double fmaxmagl (long double x, long double y)

> math.h (ISO): Section 20.8.7 [Miscellaneous FP arithmetic functions], page 604.

FILE * fmemopen (void *buf, size_t size, const char *opentype)

> stdio.h (GNU): Section 12.21.1 [String Streams], page 324.

`double fmin (double x, double y)`
> `math.h` (ISO): Section 20.8.7 [Miscellaneous FP arithmetic functions], page 604.

`float fminf (float x, float y)`
> `math.h` (ISO): Section 20.8.7 [Miscellaneous FP arithmetic functions], page 604.

`_FloatN fminfN (_FloatN x, _FloatN y)`
> `math.h` (TS 18661-3:2015): Section 20.8.7 [Miscellaneous FP arithmetic functions], page 604.

`_FloatNx fminfNx (_FloatNx x, _FloatNx y)`
> `math.h` (TS 18661-3:2015): Section 20.8.7 [Miscellaneous FP arithmetic functions], page 604.

`long double fminl (long double x, long double y)`
> `math.h` (ISO): Section 20.8.7 [Miscellaneous FP arithmetic functions], page 604.

`double fminmag (double x, double y)`
> `math.h` (ISO): Section 20.8.7 [Miscellaneous FP arithmetic functions], page 604.

`float fminmagf (float x, float y)`
> `math.h` (ISO): Section 20.8.7 [Miscellaneous FP arithmetic functions], page 604.

`_FloatN fminmagfN (_FloatN x, _FloatN y)`
> `math.h` (TS 18661-3:2015): Section 20.8.7 [Miscellaneous FP arithmetic functions], page 604.

`_FloatNx fminmagfNx (_FloatNx x, _FloatNx y)`
> `math.h` (TS 18661-3:2015): Section 20.8.7 [Miscellaneous FP arithmetic functions], page 604.

`long double fminmagl (long double x, long double y)`
> `math.h` (ISO): Section 20.8.7 [Miscellaneous FP arithmetic functions], page 604.

`double fmod (double numerator, double denominator)`
> `math.h` (ISO): Section 20.8.4 [Remainder Functions], page 598.

`float fmodf (float numerator, float denominator)`
> `math.h` (ISO): Section 20.8.4 [Remainder Functions], page 598.

`_FloatN fmodfN (_FloatN numerator, _FloatN denominator)`
> `math.h` (TS 18661-3:2015): Section 20.8.4 [Remainder Functions], page 598.

`_FloatNx fmodfNx (_FloatNx numerator, _FloatNx denominator)`
> `math.h` (TS 18661-3:2015): Section 20.8.4 [Remainder Functions], page 598.

`long double fmodl (long double numerator, long double denominator)`
> `math.h` (ISO): Section 20.8.4 [Remainder Functions], page 598.

`int fmtmsg (long int classification, const char *label, int severity, const char *text, const char *action, const char *tag)`
> `fmtmsg.h` (XPG): Section 12.22.1 [Printing Formatted Messages], page 328.

`int fnmatch (const char *pattern, const char *string, int flags)`
> `fnmatch.h` (POSIX.2): Section 10.1 [Wildcard Matching], page 230.

`FILE * fopen (const char *filename, const char *opentype)`
> `stdio.h` (ISO): Section 12.3 [Opening Streams], page 258.

`FILE * fopen64 (const char *filename, const char *opentype)`
> `stdio.h` (Unix98): Section 12.3 [Opening Streams], page 258.

`FILE * fopencookie (void *cookie, const char *opentype, cookie_io_functions_t io-functions)`
> `stdio.h` (GNU): Section 12.21.2.1 [Custom Streams and Cookies], page 326.

`pid_t fork (void)`
> `unistd.h` (POSIX.1): Section 26.4 [Creating a Process], page 775.

`int forkpty (int *amaster, char *name, const struct termios *termp, const struct winsize *winp)`
> `pty.h` (BSD): Section 17.8.2 [Opening a Pseudo-Terminal Pair], page 515.

`long int fpathconf (int filedes, int parameter)`
> `unistd.h` (POSIX.1): Section 32.9 [Using `pathconf`], page 877.

`int fpclassify (`*`float-type x`*`)`
> `math.h` (ISO): Section 20.4 [Floating-Point Number Classification Functions], page 579.

`fpos64_t`
> `stdio.h` (Unix98): Section 12.19 [Portable File-Position Functions], page 317.

`fpos_t`
> `stdio.h` (ISO): Section 12.19 [Portable File-Position Functions], page 317.

`int fprintf (FILE *`*`stream`*`, const char *`*`template`*`, ...)`
> `stdio.h` (ISO): Section 12.12.7 [Formatted Output Functions], page 287.

`int fputc (int `*`c`*`, FILE *`*`stream`*`)`
> `stdio.h` (ISO): Section 12.7 [Simple Output by Characters or Lines], page 268.

`int fputc_unlocked (int `*`c`*`, FILE *`*`stream`*`)`
> `stdio.h` (POSIX): Section 12.7 [Simple Output by Characters or Lines], page 268.

`int fputs (const char *`*`s`*`, FILE *`*`stream`*`)`
> `stdio.h` (ISO): Section 12.7 [Simple Output by Characters or Lines], page 268.

`int fputs_unlocked (const char *`*`s`*`, FILE *`*`stream`*`)`
> `stdio.h` (GNU): Section 12.7 [Simple Output by Characters or Lines], page 268.

`wint_t fputwc (wchar_t `*`wc`*`, FILE *`*`stream`*`)`
> `wchar.h` (ISO): Section 12.7 [Simple Output by Characters or Lines], page 268.

`wint_t fputwc_unlocked (wchar_t `*`wc`*`, FILE *`*`stream`*`)`
> `wchar.h` (POSIX): Section 12.7 [Simple Output by Characters or Lines], page 268.

`int fputws (const wchar_t *`*`ws`*`, FILE *`*`stream`*`)`
> `wchar.h` (ISO): Section 12.7 [Simple Output by Characters or Lines], page 268.

`int fputws_unlocked (const wchar_t *`*`ws`*`, FILE *`*`stream`*`)`
> `wchar.h` (GNU): Section 12.7 [Simple Output by Characters or Lines], page 268.

`size_t fread (void *`*`data`*`, size_t `*`size`*`, size_t `*`count`*`, FILE *`*`stream`*`)`
> `stdio.h` (ISO): Section 12.11 [Block Input/Output], page 278.

`size_t fread_unlocked (void *`*`data`*`, size_t `*`size`*`, size_t `*`count`*`, FILE *`*`stream`*`)`
> `stdio.h` (GNU): Section 12.11 [Block Input/Output], page 278.

`void free (void *`*`ptr`*`)`
> `malloc.h` (ISO): Section 3.2.3.3 [Freeing Memory Allocated with `malloc`], page 46.
> `stdlib.h` (ISO): Section 3.2.3.3 [Freeing Memory Allocated with `malloc`], page 46.

`FILE * freopen (const char *`*`filename`*`, const char *`*`opentype`*`, FILE *`*`stream`*`)`
> `stdio.h` (ISO): Section 12.3 [Opening Streams], page 258.

`FILE * freopen64 (const char *`*`filename`*`, const char *`*`opentype`*`, FILE *`*`stream`*`)`
> `stdio.h` (Unix98): Section 12.3 [Opening Streams], page 258.

`double frexp (double `*`value`*`, int *`*`exponent`*`)`
> `math.h` (ISO): Section 20.8.2 [Normalization Functions], page 592.

`float frexpf (float `*`value`*`, int *`*`exponent`*`)`
> `math.h` (ISO): Section 20.8.2 [Normalization Functions], page 592.

`_FloatN frexpfN (_Float`*`N`* `value`*``*`, int *`*`exponent`*`)`
> `math.h` (TS 18661-3:2015): Section 20.8.2 [Normalization Functions], page 592.

`_FloatNx frexpfNx (_Float`*`Nx`* `value`*``*`, int *`*`exponent`*`)`
> `math.h` (TS 18661-3:2015): Section 20.8.2 [Normalization Functions], page 592.

`long double frexpl (long double `*`value`*`, int *`*`exponent`*`)`
> `math.h` (ISO): Section 20.8.2 [Normalization Functions], page 592.

`intmax_t fromfp (double x, int round, unsigned int width)`
> math.h (ISO): Section 20.8.3 [Rounding Functions], page 594.

`intmax_t fromfpf (float x, int round, unsigned int width)`
> math.h (ISO): Section 20.8.3 [Rounding Functions], page 594.

`intmax_t fromfpfN (_FloatN x, int round, unsigned int width)`
> math.h (TS 18661-3:2015): Section 20.8.3 [Rounding Functions], page 594.

`intmax_t fromfpfNx (_FloatNx x, int round, unsigned int width)`
> math.h (TS 18661-3:2015): Section 20.8.3 [Rounding Functions], page 594.

`intmax_t fromfpl (long double x, int round, unsigned int width)`
> math.h (ISO): Section 20.8.3 [Rounding Functions], page 594.

`intmax_t fromfpx (double x, int round, unsigned int width)`
> math.h (ISO): Section 20.8.3 [Rounding Functions], page 594.

`intmax_t fromfpxf (float x, int round, unsigned int width)`
> math.h (ISO): Section 20.8.3 [Rounding Functions], page 594.

`intmax_t fromfpxfN (_FloatN x, int round, unsigned int width)`
> math.h (TS 18661-3:2015): Section 20.8.3 [Rounding Functions], page 594.

`intmax_t fromfpxfNx (_FloatNx x, int round, unsigned int width)`
> math.h (TS 18661-3:2015): Section 20.8.3 [Rounding Functions], page 594.

`intmax_t fromfpxl (long double x, int round, unsigned int width)`
> math.h (ISO): Section 20.8.3 [Rounding Functions], page 594.

`int fscanf (FILE *stream, const char *template, ...)`
> stdio.h (ISO): Section 12.14.8 [Formatted Input Functions], page 309.

`int fseek (FILE *stream, long int offset, int whence)`
> stdio.h (ISO): Section 12.18 [File Positioning], page 314.

`int fseeko (FILE *stream, off_t offset, int whence)`
> stdio.h (Unix98): Section 12.18 [File Positioning], page 314.

`int fseeko64 (FILE *stream, off64_t offset, int whence)`
> stdio.h (Unix98): Section 12.18 [File Positioning], page 314.

`int fsetpos (FILE *stream, const fpos_t *position)`
> stdio.h (ISO): Section 12.19 [Portable File-Position Functions], page 317.

`int fsetpos64 (FILE *stream, const fpos64_t *position)`
> stdio.h (Unix98): Section 12.19 [Portable File-Position Functions], page 317.

`struct fstab`
> fstab.h (BSD): Section 31.3.1.1 [The `fstab` file], page 849.

`int fstat (int filedes, struct stat *buf)`
> sys/stat.h (POSIX.1): Section 14.9.2 [Reading the Attributes of a File], page 416.

`int fstat64 (int filedes, struct stat64 *buf)`
> sys/stat.h (Unix98): Section 14.9.2 [Reading the Attributes of a File], page 416.

`int fsync (int fildes)`
> unistd.h (POSIX): Section 13.9 [Synchronizing I/O operations], page 358.

`long int ftell (FILE *stream)`
> stdio.h (ISO): Section 12.18 [File Positioning], page 314.

`off_t ftello (FILE *stream)`
> stdio.h (Unix98): Section 12.18 [File Positioning], page 314.

`off64_t ftello64 (FILE *stream)`
> stdio.h (Unix98): Section 12.18 [File Positioning], page 314.

```
int ftruncate (int fd, off_t length)
```
> unistd.h (POSIX): Section 14.9.10 [File Size], page 428.

```
int ftruncate64 (int id, off64_t length)
```
> unistd.h (Unix98): Section 14.9.10 [File Size], page 428.

```
int ftrylockfile (FILE *stream)
```
> stdio.h (POSIX): Section 12.5 [Streams and Threads], page 263.

```
int ftw (const char *filename, __ftw_func_t func, int descriptors)
```
> ftw.h (SVID): Section 14.3 [Working with Directory Trees], page 401.

```
int ftw64 (const char *filename, __ftw64_func_t func, int descriptors)
```
> ftw.h (Unix98): Section 14.3 [Working with Directory Trees], page 401.

```
void funlockfile (FILE *stream)
```
> stdio.h (POSIX): Section 12.5 [Streams and Threads], page 263.

```
int futimes (int fd, const struct timeval tvp[2])
```
> sys/time.h (BSD): Section 14.9.9 [File Times], page 426.

```
int fwide (FILE *stream, int mode)
```
> wchar.h (ISO): Section 12.6 [Streams in Internationalized Applications], page 266.

```
int fwprintf (FILE *stream, const wchar_t *template, ...)
```
> wchar.h (ISO): Section 12.12.7 [Formatted Output Functions], page 287.

```
size_t fwrite (const void *data, size_t size, size_t count, FILE *stream)
```
> stdio.h (ISO): Section 12.11 [Block Input/Output], page 278.

```
size_t fwrite_unlocked (const void *data, size_t size, size_t count, FILE *stream)
```
> stdio.h (GNU): Section 12.11 [Block Input/Output], page 278.

```
int fwscanf (FILE *stream, const wchar_t *template, ...)
```
> wchar.h (ISO): Section 12.14.8 [Formatted Input Functions], page 309.

```
double gamma (double x)
```
> math.h (SVID): Section 19.6 [Special Functions], page 539.

```
float gammaf (float x)
```
> math.h (SVID): Section 19.6 [Special Functions], page 539.

```
long double gammal (long double x)
```
> math.h (SVID): Section 19.6 [Special Functions], page 539.

```
char * gcvt (double value, int ndigit, char *buf)
```
> stdlib.h (SVID): Section 20.13 [Old-fashioned System V number-to-string functions], page 616.
>
> stdlib.h (Unix98): Section 20.13 [Old-fashioned System V number-to-string functions], page 616.

```
long int get_avphys_pages (void)
```
> sys/sysinfo.h (GNU): Section 22.4.2 [How to get information about the memory subsystem?], page 672.

```
char * get_current_dir_name (void)
```
> unistd.h (GNU): Section 14.1 [Working Directory], page 390.

```
int get_nprocs (void)
```
> sys/sysinfo.h (GNU): Section 22.5 [Learn about the processors available], page 674.

```
int get_nprocs_conf (void)
```
> sys/sysinfo.h (GNU): Section 22.5 [Learn about the processors available], page 674.

```
long int get_phys_pages (void)
```
> sys/sysinfo.h (GNU): Section 22.4.2 [How to get information about the memory subsystem?], page 672.

`unsigned long int getauxval (unsigned long int type)`
> `sys/auxv.h` (???): Section 25.5 [Auxiliary Vector], page 766.

`int getc (FILE *stream)`
> `stdio.h` (ISO): Section 12.8 [Character Input], page 271.

`int getc_unlocked (FILE *stream)`
> `stdio.h` (POSIX): Section 12.8 [Character Input], page 271.

`int getchar (void)`
> `stdio.h` (ISO): Section 12.8 [Character Input], page 271.

`int getchar_unlocked (void)`
> `stdio.h` (POSIX): Section 12.8 [Character Input], page 271.

`int getcontext (ucontext_t *ucp)`
> `ucontext.h` (SVID): Section 23.4 [Complete Context Control], page 679.

`char * getcwd (char *buffer, size_t size)`
> `unistd.h` (POSIX.1): Section 14.1 [Working Directory], page 390.

`struct tm * getdate (const char *string)`
> `time.h` (Unix98): Section 21.4.6.2 [A More User-friendly Way to Parse Times and Dates], page 643.

`getdate_err`
> `time.h` (Unix98): Section 21.4.6.2 [A More User-friendly Way to Parse Times and Dates], page 643.

`int getdate_r (const char *string, struct tm *tp)`
> `time.h` (GNU): Section 21.4.6.2 [A More User-friendly Way to Parse Times and Dates], page 643.

`ssize_t getdelim (char **lineptr, size_t *n, int delimiter, FILE *stream)`
> `stdio.h` (GNU): Section 12.9 [Line-Oriented Input], page 274.

`int getdomainnname (char *name, size_t length)`
> `unistd.h` (???): Section 31.1 [Host Identification], page 845.

`gid_t getegid (void)`
> `unistd.h` (POSIX.1): Section 30.5 [Reading the Persona of a Process], page 817.

`int getentropy (void *buffer, size_t length)`
> `sys/random.h` (GNU): Section 33.5 [Generating Unpredictable Bytes], page 889.

`char * getenv (const char *name)`
> `stdlib.h` (ISO): Section 25.4.1 [Environment Access], page 763.

`uid_t geteuid (void)`
> `unistd.h` (POSIX.1): Section 30.5 [Reading the Persona of a Process], page 817.

`struct fstab * getfsent (void)`
> `fstab.h` (BSD): Section 31.3.1.1 [The `fstab` file], page 849.

`struct fstab * getfsfile (const char *name)`
> `fstab.h` (BSD): Section 31.3.1.1 [The `fstab` file], page 849.

`struct fstab * getfsspec (const char *name)`
> `fstab.h` (BSD): Section 31.3.1.1 [The `fstab` file], page 849.

`gid_t getgid (void)`
> `unistd.h` (POSIX.1): Section 30.5 [Reading the Persona of a Process], page 817.

`struct group * getgrent (void)`
> `grp.h` (SVID): Section 30.14.3 [Scanning the List of All Groups], page 839.
>
> `grp.h` (BSD): Section 30.14.3 [Scanning the List of All Groups], page 839.

`int getgrent_r (struct group *result_buf, char *buffer, size_t buflen, struct group **result)`
> `grp.h` (GNU): Section 30.14.3 [Scanning the List of All Groups], page 839.

`struct group * getgrgid (gid_t gid)`
> `grp.h` (POSIX.1): Section 30.14.2 [Looking Up One Group], page 838.

`int getgrgid_r (gid_t gid, struct group *result_buf, char *buffer, size_t buflen, struct group **result)`
> `grp.h` (POSIX.1c): Section 30.14.2 [Looking Up One Group], page 838.

`struct group * getgrnam (const char *name)`
> `grp.h` (SVID): Section 30.14.2 [Looking Up One Group], page 838.
> `grp.h` (BSD): Section 30.14.2 [Looking Up One Group], page 838.

`int getgrnam_r (const char *name, struct group *result_buf, char *buffer, size_t buflen, struct group **result)`
> `grp.h` (POSIX.1c): Section 30.14.2 [Looking Up One Group], page 838.

`int getgrouplist (const char *user, gid_t group, gid_t *groups, int *ngroups)`
> `grp.h` (BSD): Section 30.7 [Setting the Group IDs], page 819.

`int getgroups (int count, gid_t *groups)`
> `unistd.h` (POSIX.1): Section 30.5 [Reading the Persona of a Process], page 817.

`struct hostent * gethostbyaddr (const void *addr, socklen_t length, int format)`
> `netdb.h` (BSD): Section 16.6.2.4 [Host Names], page 456.

`int gethostbyaddr_r (const void *addr, socklen_t length, int format, struct hostent *restrict result_buf, char *restrict buf, size_t buflen, struct hostent **restrict result, int *restrict h_errnop)`
> `netdb.h` (GNU): Section 16.6.2.4 [Host Names], page 456.

`struct hostent * gethostbyname (const char *name)`
> `netdb.h` (BSD): Section 16.6.2.4 [Host Names], page 456.

`struct hostent * gethostbyname2 (const char *name, int af)`
> `netdb.h` (IPv6 Basic API): Section 16.6.2.4 [Host Names], page 456.

`int gethostbyname2_r (const char *name, int af, struct hostent *restrict result_buf, char *restrict buf, size_t buflen, struct hostent **restrict result, int *restrict h_errnop)`
> `netdb.h` (GNU): Section 16.6.2.4 [Host Names], page 456.

`int gethostbyname_r (const char *restrict name, struct hostent *restrict result_buf, char *restrict buf, size_t buflen, struct hostent **restrict result, int *restrict h_errnop)`
> `netdb.h` (GNU): Section 16.6.2.4 [Host Names], page 456.

`struct hostent * gethostent (void)`
> `netdb.h` (BSD): Section 16.6.2.4 [Host Names], page 456.

`long int gethostid (void)`
> `unistd.h` (BSD): Section 31.1 [Host Identification], page 845.

`int gethostname (char *name, size_t size)`
> `unistd.h` (BSD): Section 31.1 [Host Identification], page 845.

`int getitimer (int which, struct itimerval *old)`
> `sys/time.h` (BSD): Section 21.5 [Setting an Alarm], page 649.

`ssize_t getline (char **lineptr, size_t *n, FILE *stream)`
> `stdio.h` (GNU): Section 12.9 [Line-Oriented Input], page 274.

`int getloadavg (double loadavg[], int nelem)`
> `stdlib.h` (BSD): Section 22.5 [Learn about the processors available], page 674.

`char * getlogin (void)`
> `unistd.h` (POSIX.1): Section 30.11 [Identifying Who Logged In], page 825.

struct mntent * getmntent (FILE *stream)
>   mntent.h (BSD): Section 31.3.1.2 [The mtab file], page 852.

struct mntent * getmntent_r (FILE *stream, struct mntent *result, char *buffer, int bufsize)
>   mntent.h (BSD): Section 31.3.1.2 [The mtab file], page 852.

struct netent * getnetbyaddr (uint32_t net, int type)
>   netdb.h (BSD): Section 16.13 [Networks Database], page 488.

struct netent * getnetbyname (const char *name)
>   netdb.h (BSD): Section 16.13 [Networks Database], page 488.

struct netent * getnetent (void)
>   netdb.h (BSD): Section 16.13 [Networks Database], page 488.

int getnetgrent (char **hostp, char **userp, char **domainp)
>   netdb.h (BSD): Section 30.16.2 [Looking up one Netgroup], page 842.

int getnetgrent_r (char **hostp, char **userp, char **domainp, char *buffer, size_t buflen)
>   netdb.h (GNU): Section 30.16.2 [Looking up one Netgroup], page 842.

int getopt (int argc, char *const *argv, const char *options)
>   unistd.h (POSIX.2): Section 25.2.1 [Using the getopt function], page 731.

int getopt_long (int argc, char *const *argv, const char *shortopts, const struct option *longopts, int *indexptr)
>   getopt.h (GNU): Section 25.2.3 [Parsing Long Options with getopt_long], page 734.

int getopt_long_only (int argc, char *const *argv, const char *shortopts, const struct option *longopts, int *indexptr)
>   getopt.h (GNU): Section 25.2.3 [Parsing Long Options with getopt_long], page 734.

int getpagesize (void)
>   unistd.h (BSD): Section 22.4.2 [How to get information about the memory subsystem?], page 672.

char * getpass (const char *prompt)
>   unistd.h (BSD): Section 33.2 [Reading Passwords], page 884.

double getpayload (const double *x)
>   math.h (ISO): Section 20.8.5 [Setting and modifying single bits of FP values], page 599.

float getpayloadf (const float *x)
>   math.h (ISO): Section 20.8.5 [Setting and modifying single bits of FP values], page 599.

_FloatN getpayloadfN (const _FloatN *x)
>   math.h (TS 18661-3:2015): Section 20.8.5 [Setting and modifying single bits of FP values], page 599.

_FloatNx getpayloadfNx (const _FloatNx *x)
>   math.h (TS 18661-3:2015): Section 20.8.5 [Setting and modifying single bits of FP values], page 599.

long double getpayloadl (const long double *x)
>   math.h (ISO): Section 20.8.5 [Setting and modifying single bits of FP values], page 599.

int getpeername (int socket, struct sockaddr *addr, socklen_t *length-ptr)
>   sys/socket.h (BSD): Section 16.9.4 [Who is Connected to Me?], page 472.

int getpgid (pid_t pid)
>   unistd.h (POSIX.1): Section 28.7.2 [Process Group Functions], page 801.

pid_t getpgrp (void)
>   unistd.h (POSIX.1): Section 28.7.2 [Process Group Functions], page 801.

pid_t getpid (void)
>   unistd.h (POSIX.1): Section 26.3 [Process Identification], page 774.

`pid_t getppid (void)`
> `unistd.h` (POSIX.1): Section 26.3 [Process Identification], page 774.

`int getpriority (int class, int id)`
> `sys/resource.h` (BSD): Section 22.3.4.2 [Functions For Traditional Scheduling], page 668.

> `sys/resource.h` (POSIX): Section 22.3.4.2 [Functions For Traditional Scheduling], page 668.

`struct protoent * getprotobyname (const char *name)`
> `netdb.h` (BSD): Section 16.6.6 [Protocols Database], page 463.

`struct protoent * getprotobynumber (int protocol)`
> `netdb.h` (BSD): Section 16.6.6 [Protocols Database], page 463.

`struct protoent * getprotoent (void)`
> `netdb.h` (BSD): Section 16.6.6 [Protocols Database], page 463.

`int getpt (void)`
> `stdlib.h` (GNU): Section 17.8.1 [Allocating Pseudo-Terminals], page 513.

`struct passwd * getpwent (void)`
> `pwd.h` (POSIX.1): Section 30.13.3 [Scanning the List of All Users], page 836.

`int getpwent_r (struct passwd *result_buf, char *buffer, size_t buflen, struct passwd **result)`
> `pwd.h` (GNU): Section 30.13.3 [Scanning the List of All Users], page 836.

`struct passwd * getpwnam (const char *name)`
> `pwd.h` (POSIX.1): Section 30.13.2 [Looking Up One User], page 835.

`int getpwnam_r (const char *name, struct passwd *result_buf, char *buffer, size_t buflen, struct passwd **result)`
> `pwd.h` (POSIX.1c): Section 30.13.2 [Looking Up One User], page 835.

`struct passwd * getpwuid (uid_t uid)`
> `pwd.h` (POSIX.1): Section 30.13.2 [Looking Up One User], page 835.

`int getpwuid_r (uid_t uid, struct passwd *result_buf, char *buffer, size_t buflen, struct passwd **result)`
> `pwd.h` (POSIX.1c): Section 30.13.2 [Looking Up One User], page 835.

`ssize_t getrandom (void *buffer, size_t length, unsigned int flags)`
> `sys/random.h` (GNU): Section 33.5 [Generating Unpredictable Bytes], page 889.

`int getrlimit (int resource, struct rlimit *rlp)`
> `sys/resource.h` (BSD): Section 22.2 [Limiting Resource Usage], page 656.

`int getrlimit64 (int resource, struct rlimit64 *rlp)`
> `sys/resource.h` (Unix98): Section 22.2 [Limiting Resource Usage], page 656.

`int getrusage (int processes, struct rusage *rusage)`
> `sys/resource.h` (BSD): Section 22.1 [Resource Usage], page 654.

`char * gets (char *s)`
> `stdio.h` (ISO): Section 12.9 [Line-Oriented Input], page 274.

`struct servent * getservbyname (const char *name, const char *proto)`
> `netdb.h` (BSD): Section 16.6.4 [The Services Database], page 461.

`struct servent * getservbyport (int port, const char *proto)`
> `netdb.h` (BSD): Section 16.6.4 [The Services Database], page 461.

`struct servent * getservent (void)`
> `netdb.h` (BSD): Section 16.6.4 [The Services Database], page 461.

`pid_t getsid (pid_t pid)`
> `unistd.h` (SVID): Section 28.7.2 [Process Group Functions], page 801.

`int getsockname (int socket, struct sockaddr *addr, socklen_t *length-ptr)`
> `sys/socket.h` (BSD): Section 16.3.3 [Reading the Address of a Socket], page 446.

int getsockopt (int *socket*, int *level*, int *optname*, void *optval*, socklen_t *optlen-ptr*)
sys/socket.h (BSD): Section 16.12.1 [Socket Option Functions], page 485.

int getsubopt (char **optionp*, char *const **tokens*, char **valuep*)
stdlib.h (???): Section 25.3.12.1 [Parsing of Suboptions], page 760.

char * gettext (const char *msgid*)
libintl.h (GNU): Section 8.2.1.1 [What has to be done to translate a message?], page 205.

int gettimeofday (struct timeval *tp*, struct timezone *tzp*)
sys/time.h (BSD): Section 21.4.2 [High-Resolution Calendar], page 624.

uid_t getuid (void)
unistd.h (POSIX.1): Section 30.5 [Reading the Persona of a Process], page 817.

mode_t getumask (void)
sys/stat.h (GNU): Section 14.9.7 [Assigning File Permissions], page 423.

struct utmp * getutent (void)
utmp.h (SVID): Section 30.12.1 [Manipulating the User Accounting Database], page 826.

int getutent_r (struct utmp *buffer*, struct utmp **result*)
utmp.h (GNU): Section 30.12.1 [Manipulating the User Accounting Database], page 826.

struct utmp * getutid (const struct utmp *id*)
utmp.h (SVID): Section 30.12.1 [Manipulating the User Accounting Database], page 826.

int getutid_r (const struct utmp *id*, struct utmp *buffer*, struct utmp **result*)
utmp.h (GNU): Section 30.12.1 [Manipulating the User Accounting Database], page 826.

struct utmp * getutline (const struct utmp *line*)
utmp.h (SVID): Section 30.12.1 [Manipulating the User Accounting Database], page 826.

int getutline_r (const struct utmp *line*, struct utmp *buffer*, struct utmp **result*)
utmp.h (GNU): Section 30.12.1 [Manipulating the User Accounting Database], page 826.

int getutmp (const struct utmpx *utmpx*, struct utmp *utmp*)
utmp.h (GNU): Section 30.12.2 [XPG User Accounting Database Functions], page 831.
utmpx.h (GNU): Section 30.12.2 [XPG User Accounting Database Functions], page 831.

int getutmpx (const struct utmp *utmp*, struct utmpx *utmpx*)
utmp.h (GNU): Section 30.12.2 [XPG User Accounting Database Functions], page 831.
utmpx.h (GNU): Section 30.12.2 [XPG User Accounting Database Functions], page 831.

struct utmpx * getutxent (void)
utmpx.h (XPG4.2): Section 30.12.2 [XPG User Accounting Database Functions], page 831.

struct utmpx * getutxid (const struct utmpx *id*)
utmpx.h (XPG4.2): Section 30.12.2 [XPG User Accounting Database Functions], page 831.

struct utmpx * getutxline (const struct utmpx *line*)
utmpx.h (XPG4.2): Section 30.12.2 [XPG User Accounting Database Functions], page 831.

int getw (FILE *stream*)
stdio.h (SVID): Section 12.8 [Character Input], page 271.

wint_t getwc (FILE *stream*)
wchar.h (ISO): Section 12.8 [Character Input], page 271.

wint_t getwc_unlocked (FILE *stream*)
wchar.h (GNU): Section 12.8 [Character Input], page 271.

wint_t getwchar (void)
wchar.h (ISO): Section 12.8 [Character Input], page 271.

wint_t getwchar_unlocked (void)
wchar.h (GNU): Section 12.8 [Character Input], page 271.

char * getwd (char *buffer)
> unistd.h (BSD): Section 14.1 [Working Directory], page 390.

gid_t
> sys/types.h (POSIX.1): Section 30.5 [Reading the Persona of a Process], page 817.

int glob (const char *pattern, int flags, int (*errfunc) (const char *filename, int error-code), glob_t *vector-ptr)
> glob.h (POSIX.2): Section 10.2.1 [Calling glob], page 231.

int glob64 (const char *pattern, int flags, int (*errfunc) (const char *filename, int error-code), glob64_t *vector-ptr)
> glob.h (GNU): Section 10.2.1 [Calling glob], page 231.

glob64_t
> glob.h (GNU): Section 10.2.1 [Calling glob], page 231.

glob_t
> glob.h (POSIX.2): Section 10.2.1 [Calling glob], page 231.

void globfree (glob_t *pglob)
> glob.h (POSIX.2): Section 10.2.3 [More Flags for Globbing], page 237.

void globfree64 (glob64_t *pglob)
> glob.h (GNU): Section 10.2.3 [More Flags for Globbing], page 237.

struct tm * gmtime (const time_t *time)
> time.h (ISO): Section 21.4.3 [Broken-down Time], page 626.

struct tm * gmtime_r (const time_t *time, struct tm *resultp)
> time.h (POSIX.1c): Section 21.4.3 [Broken-down Time], page 626.

int grantpt (int filedes)
> stdlib.h (SVID): Section 17.8.1 [Allocating Pseudo-Terminals], page 513.
> stdlib.h (XPG4.2): Section 17.8.1 [Allocating Pseudo-Terminals], page 513.

struct group
> grp.h (POSIX.1): Section 30.14.1 [The Data Structure for a Group], page 838.

int gsignal (int signum)
> signal.h (SVID): Section 24.6.1 [Signaling Yourself], page 712.

int gtty (int filedes, struct sgttyb *attributes)
> sgtty.h (BSD): Section 17.5 [BSD Terminal Modes], page 509.

char * hasmntopt (const struct mntent *mnt, const char *opt)
> mntent.h (BSD): Section 31.3.1.2 [The mtab file], page 852.

int hcreate (size_t nel)
> search.h (SVID): Section 9.5 [The hsearch function.], page 224.

int hcreate_r (size_t nel, struct hsearch_data *htab)
> search.h (GNU): Section 9.5 [The hsearch function.], page 224.

void hdestroy (void)
> search.h (SVID): Section 9.5 [The hsearch function.], page 224.

void hdestroy_r (struct hsearch_data *htab)
> search.h (GNU): Section 9.5 [The hsearch function.], page 224.

struct hostent
> netdb.h (BSD): Section 16.6.2.4 [Host Names], page 456.

ENTRY * hsearch (ENTRY item, ACTION action)
> search.h (SVID): Section 9.5 [The hsearch function.], page 224.

int hsearch_r (ENTRY item, ACTION action, ENTRY **retval, struct hsearch_data *htab)
> search.h (GNU): Section 9.5 [The hsearch function.], page 224.

`uint32_t htonl (uint32_t `*`hostlong`*`)`
> `netinet/in.h` (BSD): Section 16.6.5 [Byte Order Conversion], page 462.

`uint16_t htons (uint16_t `*`hostshort`*`)`
> `netinet/in.h` (BSD): Section 16.6.5 [Byte Order Conversion], page 462.

`double hypot (double `*`x`*`, double `*`y`*`)`
> `math.h` (ISO): Section 19.4 [Exponentiation and Logarithms], page 530.

`float hypotf (float `*`x`*`, float `*`y`*`)`
> `math.h` (ISO): Section 19.4 [Exponentiation and Logarithms], page 530.

`_FloatN hypotfN (_Float`*`N`*` `*`x`*`, _Float`*`N`*` `*`y`*`)`
> `math.h` (TS 18661-3:2015): Section 19.4 [Exponentiation and Logarithms], page 530.

`_FloatNx hypotfNx (_Float`*`Nx`*` `*`x`*`, _Float`*`Nx`*` `*`y`*`)`
> `math.h` (TS 18661-3:2015): Section 19.4 [Exponentiation and Logarithms], page 530.

`long double hypotl (long double `*`x`*`, long double `*`y`*`)`
> `math.h` (ISO): Section 19.4 [Exponentiation and Logarithms], page 530.

`size_t iconv (iconv_t `*`cd`*`, char **`*`inbuf`*`, size_t *`*`inbytesleft`*`, char **`*`outbuf`*`, size_t *`*`outbytesleft`*`)`
> `iconv.h` (XPG2): Section 6.5.1 [Generic Character Set Conversion Interface], page 156.

`int iconv_close (iconv_t `*`cd`*`)`
> `iconv.h` (XPG2): Section 6.5.1 [Generic Character Set Conversion Interface], page 156.

`iconv_t iconv_open (const char *`*`tocode`*`, const char *`*`fromcode`*`)`
> `iconv.h` (XPG2): Section 6.5.1 [Generic Character Set Conversion Interface], page 156.

`iconv_t`
> `iconv.h` (XPG2): Section 6.5.1 [Generic Character Set Conversion Interface], page 156.

`void if_freenameindex (struct if_nameindex *`*`ptr`*`)`
> `net/if.h` (IPv6 basic API): Section 16.4 [Interface Naming], page 447.

`char * if_indextoname (unsigned int `*`ifindex`*`, char *`*`ifname`*`)`
> `net/if.h` (IPv6 basic API): Section 16.4 [Interface Naming], page 447.

`struct if_nameindex`
> `net/if.h` (IPv6 basic API): Section 16.4 [Interface Naming], page 447.

`struct if_nameindex * if_nameindex (void)`
> `net/if.h` (IPv6 basic API): Section 16.4 [Interface Naming], page 447.

`unsigned int if_nametoindex (const char *`*`ifname`*`)`
> `net/if.h` (IPv6 basic API): Section 16.4 [Interface Naming], page 447.

`int ilogb (double `*`x`*`)`
> `math.h` (ISO): Section 19.4 [Exponentiation and Logarithms], page 530.

`int ilogbf (float `*`x`*`)`
> `math.h` (ISO): Section 19.4 [Exponentiation and Logarithms], page 530.

`int ilogbfN (_Float`*`N`*` `*`x`*`)`
> `math.h` (TS 18661-3:2015): Section 19.4 [Exponentiation and Logarithms], page 530.

`int ilogbfNx (_Float`*`Nx`*` `*`x`*`)`
> `math.h` (TS 18661-3:2015): Section 19.4 [Exponentiation and Logarithms], page 530.

`int ilogbl (long double `*`x`*`)`
> `math.h` (ISO): Section 19.4 [Exponentiation and Logarithms], page 530.

`intmax_t imaxabs (intmax_t `*`number`*`)`
> `inttypes.h` (ISO): Section 20.8.1 [Absolute Value], page 591.

`imaxdiv_t imaxdiv (intmax_t `*`numerator`*`, intmax_t `*`denominator`*`)`
> `inttypes.h` (ISO): Section 20.2 [Integer Division], page 576.

`imaxdiv_t`

> `inttypes.h` (ISO): Section 20.2 [Integer Division], page 576.

`struct in6_addr`

> `netinet/in.h` (IPv6 basic API): Section 16.6.2.2 [Host Address Data Type], page 453.

`struct in6_addr in6addr_any`

> `netinet/in.h` (IPv6 basic API): Section 16.6.2.2 [Host Address Data Type], page 453.

`struct in6_addr in6addr_loopback`

> `netinet/in.h` (IPv6 basic API): Section 16.6.2.2 [Host Address Data Type], page 453.

`struct in_addr`

> `netinet/in.h` (BSD): Section 16.6.2.2 [Host Address Data Type], page 453.

`char * index (const char *string, int c)`

> `string.h` (BSD): Section 5.9 [Search Functions], page 115.

`uint32_t inet_addr (const char *name)`

> `arpa/inet.h` (BSD): Section 16.6.2.3 [Host Address Functions], page 454.

`int inet_aton (const char *name, struct in_addr *addr)`

> `arpa/inet.h` (BSD): Section 16.6.2.3 [Host Address Functions], page 454.

`uint32_t inet_lnaof (struct in_addr addr)`

> `arpa/inet.h` (BSD): Section 16.6.2.3 [Host Address Functions], page 454.

`struct in_addr inet_makeaddr (uint32_t net, uint32_t local)`

> `arpa/inet.h` (BSD): Section 16.6.2.3 [Host Address Functions], page 454.

`uint32_t inet_netof (struct in_addr addr)`

> `arpa/inet.h` (BSD): Section 16.6.2.3 [Host Address Functions], page 454.

`uint32_t inet_network (const char *name)`

> `arpa/inet.h` (BSD): Section 16.6.2.3 [Host Address Functions], page 454.

`char * inet_ntoa (struct in_addr addr)`

> `arpa/inet.h` (BSD): Section 16.6.2.3 [Host Address Functions], page 454.

`const char * inet_ntop (int af, const void *cp, char *buf, socklen_t len)`

> `arpa/inet.h` (IPv6 basic API): Section 16.6.2.3 [Host Address Functions], page 454.

`int inet_pton (int af, const char *cp, void *buf)`

> `arpa/inet.h` (IPv6 basic API): Section 16.6.2.3 [Host Address Functions], page 454.

`int initgroups (const char *user, gid_t group)`

> `grp.h` (BSD): Section 30.7 [Setting the Group IDs], page 819.

`char * initstate (unsigned int seed, char *state, size_t size)`

> `stdlib.h` (BSD): Section 19.8.2 [BSD Random Number Functions], page 566.

`int initstate_r (unsigned int seed, char *restrict statebuf, size_t statelen, struct random_data *restrict buf)`

> `stdlib.h` (GNU): Section 19.8.2 [BSD Random Number Functions], page 566.

`int innetgr (const char *netgroup, const char *host, const char *user, const char *domain)`

> `netdb.h` (BSD): Section 30.16.3 [Testing for Netgroup Membership], page 843.

`ino64_t`

> `sys/types.h` (Unix98): Section 14.9.1 [The meaning of the File Attributes], page 412.

`ino_t`

> `sys/types.h` (POSIX.1): Section 14.9.1 [The meaning of the File Attributes], page 412.

`int ioctl (int filedes, int command, ...)`

> `sys/ioctl.h` (BSD): Section 13.19 [Generic I/O Control operations], page 388.

`struct iovec`
> `sys/uio.h` (BSD): Section 13.6 [Fast Scatter-Gather I/O], page 349.

`int isalnum (int c)`
> `ctype.h` (ISO): Section 4.1 [Classification of Characters], page 81.

`int isalpha (int c)`
> `ctype.h` (ISO): Section 4.1 [Classification of Characters], page 81.

`int isascii (int c)`
> `ctype.h` (SVID): Section 4.1 [Classification of Characters], page 81.
>
> `ctype.h` (BSD): Section 4.1 [Classification of Characters], page 81.

`int isatty (int filedes)`
> `unistd.h` (POSIX.1): Section 17.1 [Identifying Terminals], page 490.

`int isblank (int c)`
> `ctype.h` (ISO): Section 4.1 [Classification of Characters], page 81.

`int iscanonical (float-type x)`
> `math.h` (ISO): Section 20.4 [Floating-Point Number Classification Functions], page 579.

`int iscntrl (int c)`
> `ctype.h` (ISO): Section 4.1 [Classification of Characters], page 81.

`int isdigit (int c)`
> `ctype.h` (ISO): Section 4.1 [Classification of Characters], page 81.

`int iseqsig (real-floating x, real-floating y)`
> `math.h` (ISO): Section 20.8.6 [Floating-Point Comparison Functions], page 602.

`int isfinite (float-type x)`
> `math.h` (ISO): Section 20.4 [Floating-Point Number Classification Functions], page 579.

`int isgraph (int c)`
> `ctype.h` (ISO): Section 4.1 [Classification of Characters], page 81.

`int isgreater (real-floating x, real-floating y)`
> `math.h` (ISO): Section 20.8.6 [Floating-Point Comparison Functions], page 602.

`int isgreaterequal (real-floating x, real-floating y)`
> `math.h` (ISO): Section 20.8.6 [Floating-Point Comparison Functions], page 602.

`int isinf (double x)`
> `math.h` (BSD): Section 20.4 [Floating-Point Number Classification Functions], page 579.

`int isinff (float x)`
> `math.h` (BSD): Section 20.4 [Floating-Point Number Classification Functions], page 579.

`int isinfl (long double x)`
> `math.h` (BSD): Section 20.4 [Floating-Point Number Classification Functions], page 579.

`int isless (real-floating x, real-floating y)`
> `math.h` (ISO): Section 20.8.6 [Floating-Point Comparison Functions], page 602.

`int islessequal (real-floating x, real-floating y)`
> `math.h` (ISO): Section 20.8.6 [Floating-Point Comparison Functions], page 602.

`int islessgreater (real-floating x, real-floating y)`
> `math.h` (ISO): Section 20.8.6 [Floating-Point Comparison Functions], page 602.

`int islower (int c)`
> `ctype.h` (ISO): Section 4.1 [Classification of Characters], page 81.

`int isnan (float-type x)`
> `math.h` (ISO): Section 20.4 [Floating-Point Number Classification Functions], page 579.

`int isnan (double x)`
> `math.h` (BSD): Section 20.4 [Floating-Point Number Classification Functions], page 579.

`int isnanf (float x)`
> `math.h` (BSD): Section 20.4 [Floating-Point Number Classification Functions], page 579.

`int isnanl (long double x)`
> `math.h` (BSD): Section 20.4 [Floating-Point Number Classification Functions], page 579.

`int isnormal (float-type x)`
> `math.h` (ISO): Section 20.4 [Floating-Point Number Classification Functions], page 579.

`int isprint (int c)`
> `ctype.h` (ISO): Section 4.1 [Classification of Characters], page 81.

`int ispunct (int c)`
> `ctype.h` (ISO): Section 4.1 [Classification of Characters], page 81.

`int issignaling (float-type x)`
> `math.h` (ISO): Section 20.4 [Floating-Point Number Classification Functions], page 579.

`int isspace (int c)`
> `ctype.h` (ISO): Section 4.1 [Classification of Characters], page 81.

`int issubnormal (float-type x)`
> `math.h` (ISO): Section 20.4 [Floating-Point Number Classification Functions], page 579.

`int isunordered (real-floating x, real-floating y)`
> `math.h` (ISO): Section 20.8.6 [Floating-Point Comparison Functions], page 602.

`int isupper (int c)`
> `ctype.h` (ISO): Section 4.1 [Classification of Characters], page 81.

`int iswalnum (wint_t wc)`
> `wctype.h` (ISO): Section 4.3 [Character class determination for wide characters], page 84.

`int iswalpha (wint_t wc)`
> `wctype.h` (ISO): Section 4.3 [Character class determination for wide characters], page 84.

`int iswblank (wint_t wc)`
> `wctype.h` (ISO): Section 4.3 [Character class determination for wide characters], page 84.

`int iswcntrl (wint_t wc)`
> `wctype.h` (ISO): Section 4.3 [Character class determination for wide characters], page 84.

`int iswctype (wint_t wc, wctype_t desc)`
> `wctype.h` (ISO): Section 4.3 [Character class determination for wide characters], page 84.

`int iswdigit (wint_t wc)`
> `wctype.h` (ISO): Section 4.3 [Character class determination for wide characters], page 84.

`int iswgraph (wint_t wc)`
> `wctype.h` (ISO): Section 4.3 [Character class determination for wide characters], page 84.

`int iswlower (wint_t wc)`
> `ctype.h` (ISO): Section 4.3 [Character class determination for wide characters], page 84.

`int iswprint (wint_t wc)`
> `wctype.h` (ISO): Section 4.3 [Character class determination for wide characters], page 84.

`int iswpunct (wint_t wc)`
> `wctype.h` (ISO): Section 4.3 [Character class determination for wide characters], page 84.

`int iswspace (wint_t wc)`
> `wctype.h` (ISO): Section 4.3 [Character class determination for wide characters], page 84.

`int iswupper (wint_t wc)`
> `wctype.h` (ISO): Section 4.3 [Character class determination for wide characters], page 84.

`int iswxdigit (wint_t wc)`
> `wctype.h` (ISO): Section 4.3 [Character class determination for wide characters], page 84.

int isxdigit (int *c*)
> ctype.h (ISO): Section 4.1 [Classification of Characters], page 81.

int iszero (*float-type x*)
> math.h (ISO): Section 20.4 [Floating-Point Number Classification Functions], page 579.

struct itimerval
> sys/time.h (BSD): Section 21.5 [Setting an Alarm], page 649.

double j0 (double *x*)
> math.h (SVID): Section 19.6 [Special Functions], page 539.

float j0f (float *x*)
> math.h (SVID): Section 19.6 [Special Functions], page 539.

_FloatN j0fN (_Float*N x*)
> math.h (GNU): Section 19.6 [Special Functions], page 539.

_FloatNx j0fNx (_Float*Nx x*)
> math.h (GNU): Section 19.6 [Special Functions], page 539.

long double j0l (long double *x*)
> math.h (SVID): Section 19.6 [Special Functions], page 539.

double j1 (double *x*)
> math.h (SVID): Section 19.6 [Special Functions], page 539.

float j1f (float *x*)
> math.h (SVID): Section 19.6 [Special Functions], page 539.

_FloatN j1fN (_Float*N x*)
> math.h (GNU): Section 19.6 [Special Functions], page 539.

_FloatNx j1fNx (_Float*Nx x*)
> math.h (GNU): Section 19.6 [Special Functions], page 539.

long double j1l (long double *x*)
> math.h (SVID): Section 19.6 [Special Functions], page 539.

jmp_buf
> setjmp.h (ISO): Section 23.2 [Details of Non-Local Exits], page 677.

double jn (int *n*, double *x*)
> math.h (SVID): Section 19.6 [Special Functions], page 539.

float jnf (int *n*, float *x*)
> math.h (SVID): Section 19.6 [Special Functions], page 539.

_FloatN jnfN (int *n*, _Float*N x*)
> math.h (GNU): Section 19.6 [Special Functions], page 539.

_FloatNx jnfNx (int *n*, _Float*Nx x*)
> math.h (GNU): Section 19.6 [Special Functions], page 539.

long double jnl (int *n*, long double *x*)
> math.h (SVID): Section 19.6 [Special Functions], page 539.

long int jrand48 (unsigned short int *xsubi*[3])
> stdlib.h (SVID): Section 19.8.3 [SVID Random Number Function], page 568.

int jrand48_r (unsigned short int *xsubi*[3], struct drand48_data **buffer*, long int **result*)
> stdlib.h (GNU): Section 19.8.3 [SVID Random Number Function], page 568.

int kill (pid_t *pid*, int *signum*)
> signal.h (POSIX.1): Section 24.6.2 [Signaling Another Process], page 713.

int killpg (int *pgid*, int *signum*)
> signal.h (BSD): Section 24.6.2 [Signaling Another Process], page 713.

`char * l64a (long int n)`
>> `stdlib.h` (XPG): Section 5.14 [Encode Binary Data], page 127.

`long int labs (long int number)`
>> `stdlib.h` (ISO): Section 20.8.1 [Absolute Value], page 591.

`void lcong48 (unsigned short int param[7])`
>> `stdlib.h` (SVID): Section 19.8.3 [SVID Random Number Function], page 568.

`int lcong48_r (unsigned short int param[7], struct drand48_data *buffer)`
>> `stdlib.h` (GNU): Section 19.8.3 [SVID Random Number Function], page 568.

`struct lconv`
>> `locale.h` (ISO): Section 7.7.1 [`localeconv`: It is portable but . . .], page 182.

`double ldexp (double value, int exponent)`
>> `math.h` (ISO): Section 20.8.2 [Normalization Functions], page 592.

`float ldexpf (float value, int exponent)`
>> `math.h` (ISO): Section 20.8.2 [Normalization Functions], page 592.

`_FloatN ldexpfN (_FloatN value, int exponent)`
>> `math.h` (TS 18661-3:2015): Section 20.8.2 [Normalization Functions], page 592.

`_FloatNx ldexpfNx (_FloatNx value, int exponent)`
>> `math.h` (TS 18661-3:2015): Section 20.8.2 [Normalization Functions], page 592.

`long double ldexpl (long double value, int exponent)`
>> `math.h` (ISO): Section 20.8.2 [Normalization Functions], page 592.

`ldiv_t ldiv (long int numerator, long int denominator)`
>> `stdlib.h` (ISO): Section 20.2 [Integer Division], page 576.

`ldiv_t`
>> `stdlib.h` (ISO): Section 20.2 [Integer Division], page 576.

`void * lfind (const void *key, const void *base, size_t *nmemb, size_t size, comparison_fn_t compar)`
>> `search.h` (SVID): Section 9.2 [Array Search Function], page 220.

`double lgamma (double x)`
>> `math.h` (SVID): Section 19.6 [Special Functions], page 539.

`double lgamma_r (double x, int *signp)`
>> `math.h` (XPG): Section 19.6 [Special Functions], page 539.

`float lgammaf (float x)`
>> `math.h` (SVID): Section 19.6 [Special Functions], page 539.

`_FloatN lgammafN (_FloatN x)`
>> `math.h` (TS 18661-3:2015): Section 19.6 [Special Functions], page 539.

`_FloatN lgammafN_r (_FloatN x, int *signp)`
>> `math.h` (GNU): Section 19.6 [Special Functions], page 539.

`_FloatNx lgammafNx (_FloatNx x)`
>> `math.h` (TS 18661-3:2015): Section 19.6 [Special Functions], page 539.

`_FloatNx lgammafNx_r (_FloatNx x, int *signp)`
>> `math.h` (GNU): Section 19.6 [Special Functions], page 539.

`float lgammaf_r (float x, int *signp)`
>> `math.h` (XPG): Section 19.6 [Special Functions], page 539.

`long double lgammal (long double x)`
>> `math.h` (SVID): Section 19.6 [Special Functions], page 539.

`long double lgammal_r (long double x, int *signp)`
>> `math.h` (XPG): Section 19.6 [Special Functions], page 539.

`struct linger`

> sys/socket.h (BSD): Section 16.12.2 [Socket-Level Options], page 486.

`int link (const char *oldname, const char *newname)`

> unistd.h (POSIX.1): Section 14.4 [Hard Links], page 405.

`int lio_listio (int mode, struct aiocb *const list[], int nent, struct sigevent *sig)`

> aio.h (POSIX.1b): Section 13.10.1 [Asynchronous Read and Write Operations], page 362.

`int lio_listio64 (int mode, struct aiocb64 *const list[], int nent, struct sigevent *sig)`

> aio.h (Unix98): Section 13.10.1 [Asynchronous Read and Write Operations], page 362.

`int listen (int socket, int n)`

> sys/socket.h (BSD): Section 16.9.2 [Listening for Connections], page 470.

`long long int llabs (long long int number)`

> stdlib.h (ISO): Section 20.8.1 [Absolute Value], page 591.

`lldiv_t lldiv (long long int numerator, long long int denominator)`

> stdlib.h (ISO): Section 20.2 [Integer Division], page 576.

`lldiv_t`

> stdlib.h (ISO): Section 20.2 [Integer Division], page 576.

`long int llogb (double x)`

> math.h (ISO): Section 19.4 [Exponentiation and Logarithms], page 530.

`long int llogbf (float x)`

> math.h (ISO): Section 19.4 [Exponentiation and Logarithms], page 530.

`long int llogbfN (_FloatN x)`

> math.h (TS 18661-3:2015): Section 19.4 [Exponentiation and Logarithms], page 530.

`long int llogbfNx (_FloatNx x)`

> math.h (TS 18661-3:2015): Section 19.4 [Exponentiation and Logarithms], page 530.

`long int llogbl (long double x)`

> math.h (ISO): Section 19.4 [Exponentiation and Logarithms], page 530.

`long long int llrint (double x)`

> math.h (ISO): Section 20.8.3 [Rounding Functions], page 594.

`long long int llrintf (float x)`

> math.h (ISO): Section 20.8.3 [Rounding Functions], page 594.

`long long int llrintfN (_FloatN x)`

> math.h (TS 18661-3:2015): Section 20.8.3 [Rounding Functions], page 594.

`long long int llrintfNx (_FloatNx x)`

> math.h (TS 18661-3:2015): Section 20.8.3 [Rounding Functions], page 594.

`long long int llrintl (long double x)`

> math.h (ISO): Section 20.8.3 [Rounding Functions], page 594.

`long long int llround (double x)`

> math.h (ISO): Section 20.8.3 [Rounding Functions], page 594.

`long long int llroundf (float x)`

> math.h (ISO): Section 20.8.3 [Rounding Functions], page 594.

`long long int llroundfN (_FloatN x)`

> math.h (TS 18661-3:2015): Section 20.8.3 [Rounding Functions], page 594.

`long long int llroundfNx (_FloatNx x)`

> math.h (TS 18661-3:2015): Section 20.8.3 [Rounding Functions], page 594.

`long long int llroundl (long double x)`

> math.h (ISO): Section 20.8.3 [Rounding Functions], page 594.

```
struct lconv * localeconv (void)
```
> `locale.h` (ISO): Section 7.7.1 [`localeconv`: It is portable but ...], page 182.

```
struct tm * localtime (const time_t *time)
```
> `time.h` (ISO): Section 21.4.3 [Broken-down Time], page 626.

```
struct tm * localtime_r (const time_t *time, struct tm *resultp)
```
> `time.h` (POSIX.1c): Section 21.4.3 [Broken-down Time], page 626.

```
double log (double x)
```
> `math.h` (ISO): Section 19.4 [Exponentiation and Logarithms], page 530.

```
double log10 (double x)
```
> `math.h` (ISO): Section 19.4 [Exponentiation and Logarithms], page 530.

```
float log10f (float x)
```
> `math.h` (ISO): Section 19.4 [Exponentiation and Logarithms], page 530.

```
_FloatN log10fN (_FloatN x)
```
> `math.h` (TS 18661-3:2015): Section 19.4 [Exponentiation and Logarithms], page 530.

```
_FloatNx log10fNx (_FloatNx x)
```
> `math.h` (TS 18661-3:2015): Section 19.4 [Exponentiation and Logarithms], page 530.

```
long double log10l (long double x)
```
> `math.h` (ISO): Section 19.4 [Exponentiation and Logarithms], page 530.

```
double log1p (double x)
```
> `math.h` (ISO): Section 19.4 [Exponentiation and Logarithms], page 530.

```
float log1pf (float x)
```
> `math.h` (ISO): Section 19.4 [Exponentiation and Logarithms], page 530.

```
_FloatN log1pfN (_FloatN x)
```
> `math.h` (TS 18661-3:2015): Section 19.4 [Exponentiation and Logarithms], page 530.

```
_FloatNx log1pfNx (_FloatNx x)
```
> `math.h` (TS 18661-3:2015): Section 19.4 [Exponentiation and Logarithms], page 530.

```
long double log1pl (long double x)
```
> `math.h` (ISO): Section 19.4 [Exponentiation and Logarithms], page 530.

```
double log2 (double x)
```
> `math.h` (ISO): Section 19.4 [Exponentiation and Logarithms], page 530.

```
float log2f (float x)
```
> `math.h` (ISO): Section 19.4 [Exponentiation and Logarithms], page 530.

```
_FloatN log2fN (_FloatN x)
```
> `math.h` (TS 18661-3:2015): Section 19.4 [Exponentiation and Logarithms], page 530.

```
_FloatNx log2fNx (_FloatNx x)
```
> `math.h` (TS 18661-3:2015): Section 19.4 [Exponentiation and Logarithms], page 530.

```
long double log2l (long double x)
```
> `math.h` (ISO): Section 19.4 [Exponentiation and Logarithms], page 530.

```
double logb (double x)
```
> `math.h` (ISO): Section 19.4 [Exponentiation and Logarithms], page 530.

```
float logbf (float x)
```
> `math.h` (ISO): Section 19.4 [Exponentiation and Logarithms], page 530.

```
_FloatN logbfN (_FloatN x)
```
> `math.h` (TS 18661-3:2015): Section 19.4 [Exponentiation and Logarithms], page 530.

```
_FloatNx logbfNx (_FloatNx x)
```
> `math.h` (TS 18661-3:2015): Section 19.4 [Exponentiation and Logarithms], page 530.

long double logbl (long double *x*)
> math.h (ISO): Section 19.4 [Exponentiation and Logarithms], page 530.

float logf (float *x*)
> math.h (ISO): Section 19.4 [Exponentiation and Logarithms], page 530.

_FloatN logfN (_Float*N x*)
> math.h (TS 18661-3:2015): Section 19.4 [Exponentiation and Logarithms], page 530.

_FloatNx logfNx (_Float*Nx x*)
> math.h (TS 18661-3:2015): Section 19.4 [Exponentiation and Logarithms], page 530.

void login (const struct utmp *entry*)
> utmp.h (BSD): Section 30.12.3 [Logging In and Out], page 833.

int login_tty (int *filedes*)
> utmp.h (BSD): Section 30.12.3 [Logging In and Out], page 833.

long double logl (long double *x*)
> math.h (ISO): Section 19.4 [Exponentiation and Logarithms], page 530.

int logout (const char *ut_line*)
> utmp.h (BSD): Section 30.12.3 [Logging In and Out], page 833.

void logwtmp (const char *ut_line*, const char *ut_name*, const char *ut_host*)
> utmp.h (BSD): Section 30.12.3 [Logging In and Out], page 833.

void longjmp (jmp_buf *state*, int *value*)
> setjmp.h (ISO): Section 23.2 [Details of Non-Local Exits], page 677.

long int lrand48 (void)
> stdlib.h (SVID): Section 19.8.3 [SVID Random Number Function], page 568.

int lrand48_r (struct drand48_data *buffer*, long int *result*)
> stdlib.h (GNU): Section 19.8.3 [SVID Random Number Function], page 568.

long int lrint (double *x*)
> math.h (ISO): Section 20.8.3 [Rounding Functions], page 594.

long int lrintf (float *x*)
> math.h (ISO): Section 20.8.3 [Rounding Functions], page 594.

long int lrintfN (_Float*N x*)
> math.h (TS 18661-3:2015): Section 20.8.3 [Rounding Functions], page 594.

long int lrintfNx (_Float*Nx x*)
> math.h (TS 18661-3:2015): Section 20.8.3 [Rounding Functions], page 594.

long int lrintl (long double *x*)
> math.h (ISO): Section 20.8.3 [Rounding Functions], page 594.

long int lround (double *x*)
> math.h (ISO): Section 20.8.3 [Rounding Functions], page 594.

long int lroundf (float *x*)
> math.h (ISO): Section 20.8.3 [Rounding Functions], page 594.

long int lroundfN (_Float*N x*)
> math.h (TS 18661-3:2015): Section 20.8.3 [Rounding Functions], page 594.

long int lroundfNx (_Float*Nx x*)
> math.h (TS 18661-3:2015): Section 20.8.3 [Rounding Functions], page 594.

long int lroundl (long double *x*)
> math.h (ISO): Section 20.8.3 [Rounding Functions], page 594.

void * lsearch (const void *key*, void *base*, size_t *nmemb*, size_t *size*, comparison_fn_t *compar*)
> search.h (SVID): Section 9.2 [Array Search Function], page 220.

`off_t lseek (int` *filedes*`, off_t` *offset*`, int` *whence*`)`
> `unistd.h` (POSIX.1): Section 13.3 [Setting the File Position of a Descriptor], page 343.

`off64_t lseek64 (int` *filedes*`, off64_t` *offset*`, int` *whence*`)`
> `unistd.h` (Unix98): Section 13.3 [Setting the File Position of a Descriptor], page 343.

`int lstat (const char *`*filename*`, struct stat *`*buf*`)`
> `sys/stat.h` (BSD): Section 14.9.2 [Reading the Attributes of a File], page 416.

`int lstat64 (const char *`*filename*`, struct stat64 *`*buf*`)`
> `sys/stat.h` (Unix98): Section 14.9.2 [Reading the Attributes of a File], page 416.

`int lutimes (const char *`*filename*`, const struct timeval` *tvp*`[2])`
> `sys/time.h` (BSD): Section 14.9.9 [File Times], page 426.

`int madvise (void *`*addr*`, size_t` *length*`, int` *advice*`)`
> `sys/mman.h` (POSIX): Section 13.7 [Memory-mapped I/O], page 350.

`void makecontext (ucontext_t *`*ucp*`, void (*`*func*`) (void), int` *argc*`, ...)`
> `ucontext.h` (SVID): Section 23.4 [Complete Context Control], page 679.

`struct mallinfo`
> `malloc.h` (GNU): Section 3.2.3.10 [Statistics for Memory Allocation with `malloc`], page 55.

`struct mallinfo mallinfo (void)`
> `malloc.h` (SVID): Section 3.2.3.10 [Statistics for Memory Allocation with `malloc`], page 55.

`void * malloc (size_t` *size*`)`
> `malloc.h` (ISO): Section 3.2.3.1 [Basic Memory Allocation], page 44.
>
> `stdlib.h` (ISO): Section 3.2.3.1 [Basic Memory Allocation], page 44.

`int mblen (const char *`*string*`, size_t` *size*`)`
> `stdlib.h` (ISO): Section 6.4.1 [Non-reentrant Conversion of Single Characters], page 151.

`size_t mbrlen (const char *restrict` *s*`, size_t` *n*`, mbstate_t *`*ps*`)`
> `wchar.h` (ISO): Section 6.3.3 [Converting Single Characters], page 140.

`size_t mbrtowc (wchar_t *restrict` *pwc*`, const char *restrict` *s*`, size_t` *n*`, mbstate_t *restrict` *ps*`)`
> `wchar.h` (ISO): Section 6.3.3 [Converting Single Characters], page 140.

`int mbsinit (const mbstate_t *`*ps*`)`
> `wchar.h` (ISO): Section 6.3.2 [Representing the state of the conversion], page 139.

`size_t mbsnrtowcs (wchar_t *restrict` *dst*`, const char **restrict` *src*`, size_t` *nmc*`, size_t` *len*`, mbstate_t *restrict` *ps*`)`
> `wchar.h` (GNU): Section 6.3.4 [Converting Multibyte and Wide Character Strings], page 146.

`size_t mbsrtowcs (wchar_t *restrict` *dst*`, const char **restrict` *src*`, size_t` *len*`, mbstate_t *restrict` *ps*`)`
> `wchar.h` (ISO): Section 6.3.4 [Converting Multibyte and Wide Character Strings], page 146.

`mbstate_t`
> `wchar.h` (ISO): Section 6.3.2 [Representing the state of the conversion], page 139.

`size_t mbstowcs (wchar_t *`*wstring*`, const char *`*string*`, size_t` *size*`)`
> `stdlib.h` (ISO): Section 6.4.2 [Non-reentrant Conversion of Strings], page 153.

`int mbtowc (wchar_t *restrict` *result*`, const char *restrict` *string*`, size_t` *size*`)`
> `stdlib.h` (ISO): Section 6.4.1 [Non-reentrant Conversion of Single Characters], page 151.

`int mcheck (void (*`*abortfn*`) (enum mcheck_status` *status*`))`
> `mcheck.h` (GNU): Section 3.2.3.8 [Heap Consistency Checking], page 51.

`void * memalign (size_t` *boundary*`, size_t` *size*`)`
> `malloc.h` (BSD): Section 3.2.3.6 [Allocating Aligned Memory Blocks], page 48.

`void * memccpy (void *restrict` *to*`, const void *restrict` *from*`, int` *c*`, size_t` *size*`)`
> `string.h` (SVID): Section 5.4 [Copying Strings and Arrays], page 95.

void * memchr (const void *block, int c, size_t size)
> string.h (ISO): Section 5.9 [Search Functions], page 115.

int memcmp (const void *a1, const void *a2, size_t size)
> string.h (ISO): Section 5.7 [String/Array Comparison], page 107.

void * memcpy (void *restrict to, const void *restrict from, size_t size)
> string.h (ISO): Section 5.4 [Copying Strings and Arrays], page 95.

void * memfrob (void *mem, size_t length)
> string.h (GNU): Section 5.13 [Trivial Encryption], page 126.

void * memmem (const void *haystack, size_t haystack-len,
const void *needle, size_t needle-len)
> string.h (GNU): Section 5.9 [Search Functions], page 115.

void * memmove (void *to, const void *from, size_t size)
> string.h (ISO): Section 5.4 [Copying Strings and Arrays], page 95.

void * mempcpy (void *restrict to, const void *restrict from, size_t size)
> string.h (GNU): Section 5.4 [Copying Strings and Arrays], page 95.

void * memrchr (const void *block, int c, size_t size)
> string.h (GNU): Section 5.9 [Search Functions], page 115.

void * memset (void *block, int c, size_t size)
> string.h (ISO): Section 5.4 [Copying Strings and Arrays], page 95.

int mkdir (const char *filename, mode_t mode)
> sys/stat.h (POSIX.1): Section 14.8 [Creating Directories], page 411.

char * mkdtemp (char *template)
> stdlib.h (BSD): Section 14.11 [Temporary Files], page 433.

int mkfifo (const char *filename, mode_t mode)
> sys/stat.h (POSIX.1): Section 15.3 [FIFO Special Files], page 440.

int mknod (const char *filename, mode_t mode, dev_t dev)
> sys/stat.h (BSD): Section 14.10 [Making Special Files], page 432.

int mkstemp (char *template)
> stdlib.h (BSD): Section 14.11 [Temporary Files], page 433.

char * mktemp (char *template)
> stdlib.h (Unix): Section 14.11 [Temporary Files], page 433.

time_t mktime (struct tm *brokentime)
> time.h (ISO): Section 21.4.3 [Broken-down Time], page 626.

int mlock (const void *addr, size_t len)
> sys/mman.h (POSIX.1b): Section 3.4.3 [Functions To Lock And Unlock Pages], page 78.

int mlockall (int flags)
> sys/mman.h (POSIX.1b): Section 3.4.3 [Functions To Lock And Unlock Pages], page 78.

void * mmap (void *address, size_t length, int protect, int flags, int filedes, off_t offset)
> sys/mman.h (POSIX): Section 13.7 [Memory-mapped I/O], page 350.

void * mmap64 (void *address, size_t length, int protect, int flags, int filedes, off64_t offset)
> sys/mman.h (LFS): Section 13.7 [Memory-mapped I/O], page 350.

struct mntent
> mntent.h (BSD): Section 31.3.1.2 [The mtab file], page 852.

mode_t
> sys/types.h (POSIX.1): Section 14.9.1 [The meaning of the File Attributes], page 412.

`double modf (double value, double *integer-part)`
> `math.h` (ISO): Section 20.8.3 [Rounding Functions], page 594.

`float modff (float value, float *integer-part)`
> `math.h` (ISO): Section 20.8.3 [Rounding Functions], page 594.

`_FloatN modffN (_FloatN value, _FloatN *integer-part)`
> `math.h` (TS 18661-3:2015): Section 20.8.3 [Rounding Functions], page 594.

`_FloatNx modffNx (_FloatNx value, _FloatNx *integer-part)`
> `math.h` (TS 18661-3:2015): Section 20.8.3 [Rounding Functions], page 594.

`long double modfl (long double value, long double *integer-part)`
> `math.h` (ISO): Section 20.8.3 [Rounding Functions], page 594.

`int mount (const char *special_file, const char *dir, const char *fstype, unsigned long int options, const void *data)`
> `sys/mount.h` (SVID): Section 31.3.2 [Mount, Unmount, Remount], page 855.
>
> `sys/mount.h` (BSD): Section 31.3.2 [Mount, Unmount, Remount], page 855.

`long int mrand48 (void)`
> `stdlib.h` (SVID): Section 19.8.3 [SVID Random Number Function], page 568.

`int mrand48_r (struct drand48_data *buffer, long int *result)`
> `stdlib.h` (GNU): Section 19.8.3 [SVID Random Number Function], page 568.

`void * mremap (void *address, size_t length, size_t new_length, int flag)`
> `sys/mman.h` (GNU): Section 13.7 [Memory-mapped I/O], page 350.

`int msync (void *address, size_t length, int flags)`
> `sys/mman.h` (POSIX): Section 13.7 [Memory-mapped I/O], page 350.

`void mtrace (void)`
> `mcheck.h` (GNU): Section 3.2.4.1 [How to install the tracing functionality], page 58.

`int munlock (const void *addr, size_t len)`
> `sys/mman.h` (POSIX.1b): Section 3.4.3 [Functions To Lock And Unlock Pages], page 78.

`int munlockall (void)`
> `sys/mman.h` (POSIX.1b): Section 3.4.3 [Functions To Lock And Unlock Pages], page 78.

`int munmap (void *addr, size_t length)`
> `sys/mman.h` (POSIX): Section 13.7 [Memory-mapped I/O], page 350.

`void muntrace (void)`
> `mcheck.h` (GNU): Section 3.2.4.1 [How to install the tracing functionality], page 58.

`double nan (const char *tagp)`
> `math.h` (ISO): Section 20.8.5 [Setting and modifying single bits of FP values], page 599.

`float nanf (const char *tagp)`
> `math.h` (ISO): Section 20.8.5 [Setting and modifying single bits of FP values], page 599.

`_FloatN nanfN (const char *tagp)`
> `math.h` (TS 18661-3:2015): Section 20.8.5 [Setting and modifying single bits of FP values], page 599.

`_FloatNx nanfNx (const char *tagp)`
> `math.h` (TS 18661-3:2015): Section 20.8.5 [Setting and modifying single bits of FP values], page 599.

`long double nanl (const char *tagp)`
> `math.h` (ISO): Section 20.8.5 [Setting and modifying single bits of FP values], page 599.

`int nanosleep (const struct timespec *requested_time, struct timespec *remaining)`
> `time.h` (POSIX.1): Section 21.6 [Sleeping], page 652.

`double nearbyint (double x)`
> `math.h` (ISO): Section 20.8.3 [Rounding Functions], page 594.

`float nearbyintf (float x)`
> `math.h` (ISO): Section 20.8.3 [Rounding Functions], page 594.

`_FloatN nearbyintfN (_FloatN x)`
> `math.h` (TS 18661-3:2015): Section 20.8.3 [Rounding Functions], page 594.

`_FloatNx nearbyintfNx (_FloatNx x)`
> `math.h` (TS 18661-3:2015): Section 20.8.3 [Rounding Functions], page 594.

`long double nearbyintl (long double x)`
> `math.h` (ISO): Section 20.8.3 [Rounding Functions], page 594.

`struct netent`
> `netdb.h` (BSD): Section 16.13 [Networks Database], page 488.

`double nextafter (double x, double y)`
> `math.h` (ISO): Section 20.8.5 [Setting and modifying single bits of FP values], page 599.

`float nextafterf (float x, float y)`
> `math.h` (ISO): Section 20.8.5 [Setting and modifying single bits of FP values], page 599.

`_FloatN nextafterfN (_FloatN x, _FloatN y)`
> `math.h` (TS 18661-3:2015): Section 20.8.5 [Setting and modifying single bits of FP values], page 599.

`_FloatNx nextafterfNx (_FloatNx x, _FloatNx y)`
> `math.h` (TS 18661-3:2015): Section 20.8.5 [Setting and modifying single bits of FP values], page 599.

`long double nextafterl (long double x, long double y)`
> `math.h` (ISO): Section 20.8.5 [Setting and modifying single bits of FP values], page 599.

`double nextdown (double x)`
> `math.h` (ISO): Section 20.8.5 [Setting and modifying single bits of FP values], page 599.

`float nextdownf (float x)`
> `math.h` (ISO): Section 20.8.5 [Setting and modifying single bits of FP values], page 599.

`_FloatN nextdownfN (_FloatN x)`
> `math.h` (TS 18661-3:2015): Section 20.8.5 [Setting and modifying single bits of FP values], page 599.

`_FloatNx nextdownfNx (_FloatNx x)`
> `math.h` (TS 18661-3:2015): Section 20.8.5 [Setting and modifying single bits of FP values], page 599.

`long double nextdownl (long double x)`
> `math.h` (ISO): Section 20.8.5 [Setting and modifying single bits of FP values], page 599.

`double nexttoward (double x, long double y)`
> `math.h` (ISO): Section 20.8.5 [Setting and modifying single bits of FP values], page 599.

`float nexttowardf (float x, long double y)`
> `math.h` (ISO): Section 20.8.5 [Setting and modifying single bits of FP values], page 599.

`long double nexttowardl (long double x, long double y)`
> `math.h` (ISO): Section 20.8.5 [Setting and modifying single bits of FP values], page 599.

`double nextup (double x)`
> `math.h` (ISO): Section 20.8.5 [Setting and modifying single bits of FP values], page 599.

`float nextupf (float x)`
> `math.h` (ISO): Section 20.8.5 [Setting and modifying single bits of FP values], page 599.

`_FloatN nextupfN (_FloatN x)`
> `math.h` (TS 18661-3:2015): Section 20.8.5 [Setting and modifying single bits of FP values], page 599.

`_FloatNx nextupfNx (_FloatNx x)`
> `math.h` (TS 18661-3:2015): Section 20.8.5 [Setting and modifying single bits of FP values], page 599.

`long double nextupl (long double x)`
> `math.h` (ISO): Section 20.8.5 [Setting and modifying single bits of FP values], page 599.

`int nftw (const char *filename, __nftw_func_t func, int descriptors, int flag)`
> `ftw.h` (XPG4.2): Section 14.3 [Working with Directory Trees], page 401.

`int nftw64 (const char *filename, __nftw64_func_t func, int descriptors, int flag)`
> `ftw.h` (Unix98): Section 14.3 [Working with Directory Trees], page 401.

`char * ngettext (const char *msgid1, const char *msgid2, unsigned long int n)`
> `libintl.h` (GNU): Section 8.2.1.3 [Additional functions for more complicated situations], page 209.

`int nice (int increment)`
> `unistd.h` (BSD): Section 22.3.4.2 [Functions For Traditional Scheduling], page 668.

`char * nl_langinfo (nl_item item)`
> `langinfo.h` (XOPEN): Section 7.7.2 [Pinpoint Access to Locale Data], page 185.

`nlink_t`
> `sys/types.h` (POSIX.1): Section 14.9.1 [The meaning of the File Attributes], page 412.

`long int nrand48 (unsigned short int xsubi[3])`
> `stdlib.h` (SVID): Section 19.8.3 [SVID Random Number Function], page 568.

`int nrand48_r (unsigned short int xsubi[3], struct drand48_data *buffer, long int *result)`
> `stdlib.h` (GNU): Section 19.8.3 [SVID Random Number Function], page 568.

`uint32_t ntohl (uint32_t netlong)`
> `netinet/in.h` (BSD): Section 16.6.5 [Byte Order Conversion], page 462.

`uint16_t ntohs (uint16_t netshort)`
> `netinet/in.h` (BSD): Section 16.6.5 [Byte Order Conversion], page 462.

`int ntp_adjtime (struct timex *tptr)`
> `sys/timex.h` (GNU): Section 21.4.4 [High Accuracy Clock], page 629.

`int ntp_gettime (struct ntptimeval *tptr)`
> `sys/timex.h` (GNU): Section 21.4.4 [High Accuracy Clock], page 629.

`struct obstack`
> `obstack.h` (GNU): Section 3.2.6.1 [Creating Obstacks], page 62.

`void obstack_1grow (struct obstack *obstack-ptr, char c)`
> `obstack.h` (GNU): Section 3.2.6.6 [Growing Objects], page 66.

`void obstack_1grow_fast (struct obstack *obstack-ptr, char c)`
> `obstack.h` (GNU): Section 3.2.6.7 [Extra Fast Growing Objects], page 68.

`int obstack_alignment_mask (struct obstack *obstack-ptr)`
> `obstack.h` (GNU): Section 3.2.6.9 [Alignment of Data in Obstacks], page 71.

`void * obstack_alloc (struct obstack *obstack-ptr, int size)`
> `obstack.h` (GNU): Section 3.2.6.3 [Allocation in an Obstack], page 64.

`obstack_alloc_failed_handler`
> `obstack.h` (GNU): Section 3.2.6.2 [Preparing for Using Obstacks], page 63.

`void * obstack_base (struct obstack *obstack-ptr)`
> `obstack.h` (GNU): Section 3.2.6.8 [Status of an Obstack], page 70.

void obstack_blank (struct obstack *obstack-ptr, int size)
          obstack.h (GNU): Section 3.2.6.6 [Growing Objects], page 66.

void obstack_blank_fast (struct obstack *obstack-ptr, int size)
          obstack.h (GNU): Section 3.2.6.7 [Extra Fast Growing Objects], page 68.

int obstack_chunk_size (struct obstack *obstack-ptr)
          obstack.h (GNU): Section 3.2.6.10 [Obstack Chunks], page 71.

void * obstack_copy (struct obstack *obstack-ptr, void *address, int size)
          obstack.h (GNU): Section 3.2.6.3 [Allocation in an Obstack], page 64.

void * obstack_copy0 (struct obstack *obstack-ptr, void *address, int size)
          obstack.h (GNU): Section 3.2.6.3 [Allocation in an Obstack], page 64.

void * obstack_finish (struct obstack *obstack-ptr)
          obstack.h (GNU): Section 3.2.6.6 [Growing Objects], page 66.

void obstack_free (struct obstack *obstack-ptr, void *object)
          obstack.h (GNU): Section 3.2.6.4 [Freeing Objects in an Obstack], page 65.

void obstack_grow (struct obstack *obstack-ptr, void *data, int size)
          obstack.h (GNU): Section 3.2.6.6 [Growing Objects], page 66.

void obstack_grow0 (struct obstack *obstack-ptr, void *data, int size)
          obstack.h (GNU): Section 3.2.6.6 [Growing Objects], page 66.

int obstack_init (struct obstack *obstack-ptr)
          obstack.h (GNU): Section 3.2.6.2 [Preparing for Using Obstacks], page 63.

void obstack_int_grow (struct obstack *obstack-ptr, int data)
          obstack.h (GNU): Section 3.2.6.6 [Growing Objects], page 66.

void obstack_int_grow_fast (struct obstack *obstack-ptr, int data)
          obstack.h (GNU): Section 3.2.6.7 [Extra Fast Growing Objects], page 68.

void * obstack_next_free (struct obstack *obstack-ptr)
          obstack.h (GNU): Section 3.2.6.8 [Status of an Obstack], page 70.

int obstack_object_size (struct obstack *obstack-ptr)
          obstack.h (GNU): Section 3.2.6.6 [Growing Objects], page 66.

          obstack.h (GNU): Section 3.2.6.8 [Status of an Obstack], page 70.

int obstack_printf (struct obstack *obstack, const char *template, ...)
          stdio.h (GNU): Section 12.12.8 [Dynamically Allocating Formatted Output], page 290.

void obstack_ptr_grow (struct obstack *obstack-ptr, void *data)
          obstack.h (GNU): Section 3.2.6.6 [Growing Objects], page 66.

void obstack_ptr_grow_fast (struct obstack *obstack-ptr, void *data)
          obstack.h (GNU): Section 3.2.6.7 [Extra Fast Growing Objects], page 68.

int obstack_room (struct obstack *obstack-ptr)
          obstack.h (GNU): Section 3.2.6.7 [Extra Fast Growing Objects], page 68.

int obstack_vprintf (struct obstack *obstack, const char *template, va_list ap)
          stdio.h (GNU): Section 12.12.9 [Variable Arguments Output Functions], page 290.

off64_t
          sys/types.h (Unix98): Section 13.3 [Setting the File Position of a Descriptor], page 343.

off_t
          sys/types.h (POSIX.1): Section 13.3 [Setting the File Position of a Descriptor], page 343.

size_t offsetof (type, member)
          stddef.h (ISO): Section A.5.4 [Structure Field Offset Measurement], page 924.

```
int on_exit (void (*function)(int status, void *arg), void *arg)
```
stdlib.h (SunOS): Section 25.7.3 [Cleanups on Exit], page 770.

```
int open (const char *filename, int flags[, mode_t mode])
```
fcntl.h (POSIX.1): Section 13.1 [Opening and Closing Files], page 333.

```
int open64 (const char *filename, int flags[, mode_t mode])
```
fcntl.h (Unix98): Section 13.1 [Opening and Closing Files], page 333.

```
FILE * open_memstream (char **ptr, size_t *sizeloc)
```
stdio.h (GNU): Section 12.21.1 [String Streams], page 324.

```
DIR * opendir (const char *dirname)
```
dirent.h (POSIX.1): Section 14.2.2 [Opening a Directory Stream], page 394.

```
void openlog (const char *ident, int option, int facility)
```
syslog.h (BSD): Section 18.2.1 [openlog], page 518.

```
int openpty (int *amaster, int *aslave, char *name, const struct termios *termp, const struct
winsize *winp)
```
pty.h (BSD): Section 17.8.2 [Opening a Pseudo-Terminal Pair], page 515.

```
char * optarg
```
unistd.h (POSIX.2): Section 25.2.1 [Using the **getopt** function], page 731.

```
int opterr
```
unistd.h (POSIX.2): Section 25.2.1 [Using the **getopt** function], page 731.

```
int optind
```
unistd.h (POSIX.2): Section 25.2.1 [Using the **getopt** function], page 731.

```
struct option
```
getopt.h (GNU): Section 25.2.3 [Parsing Long Options with **getopt_long**], page 734.

```
int optopt
```
unistd.h (POSIX.2): Section 25.2.1 [Using the **getopt** function], page 731.

```
size_t parse_printf_format (const char *template, size_t n, int *argtypes)
```
printf.h (GNU): Section 12.12.10 [Parsing a Template String], page 293.

```
struct passwd
```
pwd.h (POSIX.1): Section 30.13.1 [The Data Structure that Describes a User], page 834.

```
long int pathconf (const char *filename, int parameter)
```
unistd.h (POSIX.1): Section 32.9 [Using **pathconf**], page 877.

```
int pause (void)
```
unistd.h (POSIX.1): Section 24.8.1 [Using **pause**], page 723.

```
int pclose (FILE *stream)
```
stdio.h (POSIX.2): Section 15.2 [Pipe to a Subprocess], page 439.

stdio.h (SVID): Section 15.2 [Pipe to a Subprocess], page 439.

stdio.h (BSD): Section 15.2 [Pipe to a Subprocess], page 439.

```
void perror (const char *message)
```
stdio.h (ISO): Section 2.3 [Error Messages], page 35.

```
pid_t
```
sys/types.h (POSIX.1): Section 26.3 [Process Identification], page 774.

```
int pipe (int filedes[2])
```
unistd.h (POSIX.1): Section 15.1 [Creating a Pipe], page 437.

```
FILE * popen (const char *command, const char *mode)
```
stdio.h (POSIX.2): Section 15.2 [Pipe to a Subprocess], page 439.

stdio.h (SVID): Section 15.2 [Pipe to a Subprocess], page 439.

stdio.h (BSD): Section 15.2 [Pipe to a Subprocess], page 439.

int posix_memalign (void **memptr, size_t alignment, size_t size)
> stdlib.h (POSIX): Section 3.2.3.6 [Allocating Aligned Memory Blocks], page 48.

double pow (double base, double power)
> math.h (ISO): Section 19.4 [Exponentiation and Logarithms], page 530.

double pow10 (double x)
> math.h (GNU): Section 19.4 [Exponentiation and Logarithms], page 530.

float pow10f (float x)
> math.h (GNU): Section 19.4 [Exponentiation and Logarithms], page 530.

long double pow10l (long double x)
> math.h (GNU): Section 19.4 [Exponentiation and Logarithms], page 530.

float powf (float base, float power)
> math.h (ISO): Section 19.4 [Exponentiation and Logarithms], page 530.

_FloatN powfN (_FloatN base, _FloatN power)
> math.h (TS 18661-3:2015): Section 19.4 [Exponentiation and Logarithms], page 530.

_FloatNx powfNx (_FloatNx base, _FloatNx power)
> math.h (TS 18661-3:2015): Section 19.4 [Exponentiation and Logarithms], page 530.

long double powl (long double base, long double power)
> math.h (ISO): Section 19.4 [Exponentiation and Logarithms], page 530.

ssize_t pread (int filedes, void *buffer, size_t size, off_t offset)
> unistd.h (Unix98): Section 13.2 [Input and Output Primitives], page 336.

ssize_t pread64 (int filedes, void *buffer, size_t size, off64_t offset)
> unistd.h (Unix98): Section 13.2 [Input and Output Primitives], page 336.

ssize_t preadv (int fd, const struct iovec *iov, int iovcnt, off_t offset)
> sys/uio.h (BSD): Section 13.2 [Input and Output Primitives], page 336.

ssize_t preadv2 (int fd, const struct iovec *iov, int iovcnt, off_t offset, int flags)
> sys/uio.h (GNU): Section 13.2 [Input and Output Primitives], page 336.

ssize_t preadv64 (int fd, const struct iovec *iov, int iovcnt, off64_t offset)
> unistd.h (BSD): Section 13.2 [Input and Output Primitives], page 336.

ssize_t preadv64v2 (int fd, const struct iovec *iov, int iovcnt, off64_t offset, int flags)
> unistd.h (GNU): Section 13.2 [Input and Output Primitives], page 336.

int printf (const char *template, ...)
> stdio.h (ISO): Section 12.12.7 [Formatted Output Functions], page 287.

printf_arginfo_function
> printf.h (GNU): Section 12.13.3 [Defining the Output Handler], page 298.

printf_function
> printf.h (GNU): Section 12.13.3 [Defining the Output Handler], page 298.

struct printf_info
> printf.h (GNU): Section 12.13.2 [Conversion Specifier Options], page 297.

int printf_size (FILE *fp, const struct printf_info *info, const void *const *args)
> printf.h (GNU): Section 12.13.5 [Predefined printf Handlers], page 300.

int printf_size_info (const struct printf_info *info, size_t n, int *argtypes)
> printf.h (GNU): Section 12.13.5 [Predefined printf Handlers], page 300.

char * program_invocation_name
> errno.h (GNU): Section 2.3 [Error Messages], page 35.

char * program_invocation_short_name
> errno.h (GNU): Section 2.3 [Error Messages], page 35.

`struct protoent`

> `netdb.h` (BSD): Section 16.6.6 [Protocols Database], page 463.

`void psignal (int signum, const char *message)`

> `signal.h` (BSD): Section 24.2.8 [Signal Messages], page 695.

`int pthread_getattr_default_np (pthread_attr_t *attr)`

> `pthread.h` (GNU): Section 35.2.1 [Setting Process-wide defaults for thread attributes], page 895.

`void *pthread_getspecific (pthread_key_t key)`

> `pthread.h` (POSIX): Section 35.1 [Thread-specific Data], page 895.

`int pthread_key_create (pthread_key_t *key, void (*destructor)(void*))`

> `pthread.h` (POSIX): Section 35.1 [Thread-specific Data], page 895.

`int pthread_key_delete (pthread_key_t key)`

> `pthread.h` (POSIX): Section 35.1 [Thread-specific Data], page 895.

`int pthread_setattr_default_np (pthread_attr_t *attr)`

> `pthread.h` (GNU): Section 35.2.1 [Setting Process-wide defaults for thread attributes], page 895.

`int pthread_setspecific (pthread_key_t key, const void *value)`

> `pthread.h` (POSIX): Section 35.1 [Thread-specific Data], page 895.

`ptrdiff_t`

> `stddef.h` (ISO): Section A.4 [Important Data Types], page 916.

`char * ptsname (int filedes)`

> `stdlib.h` (SVID): Section 17.8.1 [Allocating Pseudo-Terminals], page 513.

> `stdlib.h` (XPG4.2): Section 17.8.1 [Allocating Pseudo-Terminals], page 513.

`int ptsname_r (int filedes, char *buf, size_t len)`

> `stdlib.h` (GNU): Section 17.8.1 [Allocating Pseudo-Terminals], page 513.

`int putc (int c, FILE *stream)`

> `stdio.h` (ISO): Section 12.7 [Simple Output by Characters or Lines], page 268.

`int putc_unlocked (int c, FILE *stream)`

> `stdio.h` (POSIX): Section 12.7 [Simple Output by Characters or Lines], page 268.

`int putchar (int c)`

> `stdio.h` (ISO): Section 12.7 [Simple Output by Characters or Lines], page 268.

`int putchar_unlocked (int c)`

> `stdio.h` (POSIX): Section 12.7 [Simple Output by Characters or Lines], page 268.

`int putenv (char *string)`

> `stdlib.h` (SVID): Section 25.4.1 [Environment Access], page 763.

`int putpwent (const struct passwd *p, FILE *stream)`

> `pwd.h` (SVID): Section 30.13.4 [Writing a User Entry], page 837.

`int puts (const char *s)`

> `stdio.h` (ISO): Section 12.7 [Simple Output by Characters or Lines], page 268.

`struct utmp * pututline (const struct utmp *utmp)`

> `utmp.h` (SVID): Section 30.12.1 [Manipulating the User Accounting Database], page 826.

`struct utmpx * pututxline (const struct utmpx *utmp)`

> `utmpx.h` (XPG4.2): Section 30.12.2 [XPG User Accounting Database Functions], page 831.

`int putw (int w, FILE *stream)`

> `stdio.h` (SVID): Section 12.7 [Simple Output by Characters or Lines], page 268.

`wint_t putwc (wchar_t wc, FILE *stream)`

> `wchar.h` (ISO): Section 12.7 [Simple Output by Characters or Lines], page 268.

`wint_t putwc_unlocked (wchar_t wc, FILE *stream)`
> wchar.h (GNU): Section 12.7 [Simple Output by Characters or Lines], page 268.

`wint_t putwchar (wchar_t wc)`
> wchar.h (ISO): Section 12.7 [Simple Output by Characters or Lines], page 268.

`wint_t putwchar_unlocked (wchar_t wc)`
> wchar.h (GNU): Section 12.7 [Simple Output by Characters or Lines], page 268.

`ssize_t pwrite (int filedes, const void *buffer, size_t size, off_t offset)`
> unistd.h (Unix98): Section 13.2 [Input and Output Primitives], page 336.

`ssize_t pwrite64 (int filedes, const void *buffer, size_t size, off64_t offset)`
> unistd.h (Unix98): Section 13.2 [Input and Output Primitives], page 336.

`ssize_t pwritev (int fd, const struct iovec *iov, int iovcnt, off_t offset)`
> sys/uio.h (BSD): Section 13.2 [Input and Output Primitives], page 336.

`ssize_t pwritev2 (int fd, const struct iovec *iov, int iovcnt, off_t offset, int flags)`
> sys/uio.h (GNU): Section 13.2 [Input and Output Primitives], page 336.

`ssize_t pwritev64 (int fd, const struct iovec *iov, int iovcnt, off64_t offset)`
> unistd.h (BSD): Section 13.2 [Input and Output Primitives], page 336.

`ssize_t pwritev64v2 (int fd, const struct iovec *iov, int iovcnt, off64_t offset, int flags)`
> unistd.h (GNU): Section 13.2 [Input and Output Primitives], page 336.

`char * qecvt (long double value, int ndigit, int *decpt, int *neg)`
> stdlib.h (GNU): Section 20.13 [Old-fashioned System V number-to-string functions], page 616.

`int qecvt_r (long double value, int ndigit, int *decpt, int *neg, char *buf, size_t len)`
> stdlib.h (GNU): Section 20.13 [Old-fashioned System V number-to-string functions], page 616.

`char * qfcvt (long double value, int ndigit, int *decpt, int *neg)`
> stdlib.h (GNU): Section 20.13 [Old-fashioned System V number-to-string functions], page 616.

`int qfcvt_r (long double value, int ndigit, int *decpt, int *neg, char *buf, size_t len)`
> stdlib.h (GNU): Section 20.13 [Old-fashioned System V number-to-string functions], page 616.

`char * qgcvt (long double value, int ndigit, char *buf)`
> stdlib.h (GNU): Section 20.13 [Old-fashioned System V number-to-string functions], page 616.

`void qsort (void *array, size_t count, size_t size, comparison_fn_t compare)`
> stdlib.h (ISO): Section 9.3 [Array Sort Function], page 221.

`int raise (int signum)`
> signal.h (ISO): Section 24.6.1 [Signaling Yourself], page 712.

`int rand (void)`
> stdlib.h (ISO): Section 19.8.1 [ISO C Random Number Functions], page 565.

`int rand_r (unsigned int *seed)`
> stdlib.h (POSIX.1): Section 19.8.1 [ISO C Random Number Functions], page 565.

`long int random (void)`
> stdlib.h (BSD): Section 19.8.2 [BSD Random Number Functions], page 566.

`struct random_data`
> stdlib.h (GNU): Section 19.8.2 [BSD Random Number Functions], page 566.

`int random_r (struct random_data *restrict buf, int32_t *restrict result)`
> stdlib.h (GNU): Section 19.8.2 [BSD Random Number Functions], page 566.

void * rawmemchr (const void *block, int c)
>   string.h (GNU): Section 5.9 [Search Functions], page 115.

ssize_t read (int filedes, void *buffer, size_t size)
>   unistd.h (POSIX.1): Section 13.2 [Input and Output Primitives], page 336.

struct dirent * readdir (DIR *dirstream)
>   dirent.h (POSIX.1): Section 14.2.3 [Reading and Closing a Directory Stream], page 395.

struct dirent64 * readdir64 (DIR *dirstream)
>   dirent.h (LFS): Section 14.2.3 [Reading and Closing a Directory Stream], page 395.

int readdir64_r (DIR *dirstream, struct dirent64 *entry, struct dirent64 **result)
>   dirent.h (LFS): Section 14.2.3 [Reading and Closing a Directory Stream], page 395.

int readdir_r (DIR *dirstream, struct dirent *entry, struct dirent **result)
>   dirent.h (GNU): Section 14.2.3 [Reading and Closing a Directory Stream], page 395.

ssize_t readlink (const char *filename, char *buffer, size_t size)
>   unistd.h (BSD): Section 14.5 [Symbolic Links], page 406.

ssize_t readv (int filedes, const struct iovec *vector, int count)
>   sys/uio.h (BSD): Section 13.6 [Fast Scatter-Gather I/O], page 349.

void * realloc (void *ptr, size_t newsize)
>   malloc.h (ISO): Section 3.2.3.4 [Changing the Size of a Block], page 47.
>   stdlib.h (ISO): Section 3.2.3.4 [Changing the Size of a Block], page 47.

void * reallocarray (void *ptr, size_t nmemb, size_t size)
>   malloc.h (BSD): Section 3.2.3.4 [Changing the Size of a Block], page 47.
>   stdlib.h (BSD): Section 3.2.3.4 [Changing the Size of a Block], page 47.

char * realpath (const char *restrict name, char *restrict resolved)
>   stdlib.h (XPG): Section 14.5 [Symbolic Links], page 406.

ssize_t recv (int socket, void *buffer, size_t size, int flags)
>   sys/socket.h (BSD): Section 16.9.5.2 [Receiving Data], page 473.

ssize_t recvfrom (int socket, void *buffer, size_t size, int flags, struct sockaddr *addr,
socklen_t *length-ptr)
>   sys/socket.h (BSD): Section 16.10.2 [Receiving Datagrams], page 481.

int regcomp (regex_t *restrict compiled, const char *restrict pattern, int cflags)
>   regex.h (POSIX.2): Section 10.3.1 [POSIX Regular Expression Compilation], page 240.

size_t regerror (int errcode, const regex_t *restrict compiled, char *restrict buffer, size_t
length)
>   regex.h (POSIX.2): Section 10.3.6 [POSIX Regexp Matching Cleanup], page 244.

regex_t
>   regex.h (POSIX.2): Section 10.3.1 [POSIX Regular Expression Compilation], page 240.

int regexec (const regex_t *restrict compiled, const char *restrict string, size_t nmatch,
regmatch_t matchptr[restrict], int eflags)
>   regex.h (POSIX.2): Section 10.3.3 [Matching a Compiled POSIX Regular Expression],
>   page 242.

void regfree (regex_t *compiled)
>   regex.h (POSIX.2): Section 10.3.6 [POSIX Regexp Matching Cleanup], page 244.

int register_printf_function (int spec, printf_function handler-function,
printf_arginfo_function arginfo-function)
>   printf.h (GNU): Section 12.13.1 [Registering New Conversions], page 296.

regmatch_t
>   regex.h (POSIX.2): Section 10.3.4 [Match Results with Subexpressions], page 243.

`regoff_t`

> `regex.h` (POSIX.2): Section 10.3.4 [Match Results with Subexpressions], page 243.

`double remainder (double numerator, double denominator)`

> `math.h` (ISO): Section 20.8.4 [Remainder Functions], page 598.

`float remainderf (float numerator, float denominator)`

> `math.h` (ISO): Section 20.8.4 [Remainder Functions], page 598.

`_FloatN remainderfN (_FloatN numerator, _FloatN denominator)`

> `math.h` (TS 18661-3:2015): Section 20.8.4 [Remainder Functions], page 598.

`_FloatNx remainderfNx (_FloatNx numerator, _FloatNx denominator)`

> `math.h` (TS 18661-3:2015): Section 20.8.4 [Remainder Functions], page 598.

`long double remainderl (long double numerator, long double denominator)`

> `math.h` (ISO): Section 20.8.4 [Remainder Functions], page 598.

`int remove (const char *filename)`

> `stdio.h` (ISO): Section 14.6 [Deleting Files], page 409.

`int rename (const char *oldname, const char *newname)`

> `stdio.h` (ISO): Section 14.7 [Renaming Files], page 410.

`void rewind (FILE *stream)`

> `stdio.h` (ISO): Section 12.18 [File Positioning], page 314.

`void rewinddir (DIR *dirstream)`

> `dirent.h` (POSIX.1): Section 14.2.5 [Random Access in a Directory Stream], page 398.

`char * rindex (const char *string, int c)`

> `string.h` (BSD): Section 5.9 [Search Functions], page 115.

`double rint (double x)`

> `math.h` (ISO): Section 20.8.3 [Rounding Functions], page 594.

`float rintf (float x)`

> `math.h` (ISO): Section 20.8.3 [Rounding Functions], page 594.

`_FloatN rintfN (_FloatN x)`

> `math.h` (TS 18661-3:2015): Section 20.8.3 [Rounding Functions], page 594.

`_FloatNx rintfNx (_FloatNx x)`

> `math.h` (TS 18661-3:2015): Section 20.8.3 [Rounding Functions], page 594.

`long double rintl (long double x)`

> `math.h` (ISO): Section 20.8.3 [Rounding Functions], page 594.

`struct rlimit`

> `sys/resource.h` (BSD): Section 22.2 [Limiting Resource Usage], page 656.

`struct rlimit64`

> `sys/resource.h` (Unix98): Section 22.2 [Limiting Resource Usage], page 656.

`int rmdir (const char *filename)`

> `unistd.h` (POSIX.1): Section 14.6 [Deleting Files], page 409.

`double round (double x)`

> `math.h` (ISO): Section 20.8.3 [Rounding Functions], page 594.

`double roundeven (double x)`

> `math.h` (ISO): Section 20.8.3 [Rounding Functions], page 594.

`float roundevenf (float x)`

> `math.h` (ISO): Section 20.8.3 [Rounding Functions], page 594.

`_FloatN roundevenfN (_FloatN x)`

> `math.h` (TS 18661-3:2015): Section 20.8.3 [Rounding Functions], page 594.

_FloatNx roundevenfNx (_FloatNx x)
> math.h (TS 18661-3:2015): Section 20.8.3 [Rounding Functions], page 594.

long double roundevenl (long double x)
> math.h (ISO): Section 20.8.3 [Rounding Functions], page 594.

float roundf (float x)
> math.h (ISO): Section 20.8.3 [Rounding Functions], page 594.

_FloatN roundfN (_FloatN x)
> math.h (TS 18661-3:2015): Section 20.8.3 [Rounding Functions], page 594.

_FloatNx roundfNx (_FloatNx x)
> math.h (TS 18661-3:2015): Section 20.8.3 [Rounding Functions], page 594.

long double roundl (long double x)
> math.h (ISO): Section 20.8.3 [Rounding Functions], page 594.

int rpmatch (const char *response)
> stdlib.h (GNU): Section 7.9 [Yes-or-No Questions], page 194.

struct rusage
> sys/resource.h (BSD): Section 22.1 [Resource Usage], page 654.

void *sbrk (ptrdiff_t delta)
> unistd.h (BSD): Section 3.3 [Resizing the Data Segment], page 76.

double scalb (double value, double exponent)
> math.h (BSD): Section 20.8.2 [Normalization Functions], page 592.

float scalbf (float value, float exponent)
> math.h (BSD): Section 20.8.2 [Normalization Functions], page 592.

long double scalbl (long double value, long double exponent)
> math.h (BSD): Section 20.8.2 [Normalization Functions], page 592.

double scalbln (double x, long int n)
> math.h (BSD): Section 20.8.2 [Normalization Functions], page 592.

float scalblnf (float x, long int n)
> math.h (BSD): Section 20.8.2 [Normalization Functions], page 592.

_FloatN scalblnfN (_FloatN x, long int n)
> math.h (TS 18661-3:2015): Section 20.8.2 [Normalization Functions], page 592.

_FloatNx scalblnfNx (_FloatNx x, long int n)
> math.h (TS 18661-3:2015): Section 20.8.2 [Normalization Functions], page 592.

long double scalblnl (long double x, long int n)
> math.h (BSD): Section 20.8.2 [Normalization Functions], page 592.

double scalbn (double x, int n)
> math.h (BSD): Section 20.8.2 [Normalization Functions], page 592.

float scalbnf (float x, int n)
> math.h (BSD): Section 20.8.2 [Normalization Functions], page 592.

_FloatN scalbnfN (_FloatN x, int n)
> math.h (TS 18661-3:2015): Section 20.8.2 [Normalization Functions], page 592.

_FloatNx scalbnfNx (_FloatNx x, int n)
> math.h (TS 18661-3:2015): Section 20.8.2 [Normalization Functions], page 592.

long double scalbnl (long double x, int n)
> math.h (BSD): Section 20.8.2 [Normalization Functions], page 592.

int scandir (const char *dir, struct dirent ***namelist, int (*selector) (const struct dirent *), int (*cmp) (const struct dirent **, const struct dirent **))
> dirent.h (BSD): Section 14.2.6 [Scanning the Content of a Directory], page 399.
> dirent.h (SVID): Section 14.2.6 [Scanning the Content of a Directory], page 399.

`int scandir64 (const char *dir, struct dirent64 ***namelist, int (*selector) (const struct dirent64 *), int (*cmp) (const struct dirent64 **, const struct dirent64 **))`
        `dirent.h` (GNU): Section 14.2.6 [Scanning the Content of a Directory], page 399.

`int scanf (const char *template, ...)`
        `stdio.h` (ISO): Section 12.14.8 [Formatted Input Functions], page 309.

`int sched_get_priority_max (int policy)`
        `sched.h` (POSIX): Section 22.3.3 [Basic Scheduling Functions], page 663.

`int sched_get_priority_min (int policy)`
        `sched.h` (POSIX): Section 22.3.3 [Basic Scheduling Functions], page 663.

`int sched_getaffinity (pid_t pid, size_t cpusetsize, cpu_set_t *cpuset)`
        `sched.h` (GNU): Section 22.3.5 [Limiting execution to certain CPUs], page 669.

`int sched_getparam (pid_t pid, struct sched_param *param)`
        `sched.h` (POSIX): Section 22.3.3 [Basic Scheduling Functions], page 663.

`int sched_getscheduler (pid_t pid)`
        `sched.h` (POSIX): Section 22.3.3 [Basic Scheduling Functions], page 663.

`struct sched_param`
        `sched.h` (POSIX): Section 22.3.3 [Basic Scheduling Functions], page 663.

`int sched_rr_get_interval (pid_t pid, struct timespec *interval)`
        `sched.h` (POSIX): Section 22.3.3 [Basic Scheduling Functions], page 663.

`int sched_setaffinity (pid_t pid, size_t cpusetsize, const cpu_set_t *cpuset)`
        `sched.h` (GNU): Section 22.3.5 [Limiting execution to certain CPUs], page 669.

`int sched_setparam (pid_t pid, const struct sched_param *param)`
        `sched.h` (POSIX): Section 22.3.3 [Basic Scheduling Functions], page 663.

`int sched_setscheduler (pid_t pid, int policy, const struct sched_param *param)`
        `sched.h` (POSIX): Section 22.3.3 [Basic Scheduling Functions], page 663.

`int sched_yield (void)`
        `sched.h` (POSIX): Section 22.3.3 [Basic Scheduling Functions], page 663.

`char * secure_getenv (const char *name)`
        `stdlib.h` (GNU): Section 25.4.1 [Environment Access], page 763.

`unsigned short int * seed48 (unsigned short int seed16v[3])`
        `stdlib.h` (SVID): Section 19.8.3 [SVID Random Number Function], page 568.

`int seed48_r (unsigned short int seed16v[3], struct drand48_data *buffer)`
        `stdlib.h` (GNU): Section 19.8.3 [SVID Random Number Function], page 568.

`void seekdir (DIR *dirstream, long int pos)`
        `dirent.h` (BSD): Section 14.2.5 [Random Access in a Directory Stream], page 398.

`int select (int nfds, fd_set *read-fds, fd_set *write-fds, fd_set *except-fds, struct timeval *timeout)`
        `sys/types.h` (BSD): Section 13.8 [Waiting for Input or Output], page 355.

`ssize_t send (int socket, const void *buffer, size_t size, int flags)`
        `sys/socket.h` (BSD): Section 16.9.5.1 [Sending Data], page 472.

`ssize_t sendto (int socket, const void *buffer, size_t size, int flags, struct sockaddr *addr, socklen_t length)`
        `sys/socket.h` (BSD): Section 16.10.1 [Sending Datagrams], page 480.

`struct servent`
        `netdb.h` (BSD): Section 16.6.4 [The Services Database], page 461.

`void setbuf (FILE *stream, char *buf)`
        `stdio.h` (ISO): Section 12.20.3 [Controlling Which Kind of Buffering], page 321.

```
void setbuffer (FILE *stream, char *buf, size_t size)
```
stdio.h (BSD): Section 12.20.3 [Controlling Which Kind of Buffering], page 321.

```
int setcontext (const ucontext_t *ucp)
```
ucontext.h (SVID): Section 23.4 [Complete Context Control], page 679.

```
int setdomainname (const char *name, size_t length)
```
unistd.h (???): Section 31.1 [Host Identification], page 845.

```
int setegid (gid_t newgid)
```
unistd.h (POSIX.1): Section 30.7 [Setting the Group IDs], page 819.

```
int setenv (const char *name, const char *value, int replace)
```
stdlib.h (BSD): Section 25.4.1 [Environment Access], page 763.

```
int seteuid (uid_t neweuid)
```
unistd.h (POSIX.1): Section 30.6 [Setting the User ID], page 818.

```
int setfsent (void)
```
fstab.h (BSD): Section 31.3.1.1 [The fstab file], page 849.

```
int setgid (gid_t newgid)
```
unistd.h (POSIX.1): Section 30.7 [Setting the Group IDs], page 819.

```
void setgrent (void)
```
grp.h (SVID): Section 30.14.3 [Scanning the List of All Groups], page 839.

grp.h (BSD): Section 30.14.3 [Scanning the List of All Groups], page 839.

```
int setgroups (size_t count, const gid_t *groups)
```
grp.h (BSD): Section 30.7 [Setting the Group IDs], page 819.

```
void sethostent (int stayopen)
```
netdb.h (BSD): Section 16.6.2.4 [Host Names], page 456.

```
int sethostid (long int id)
```
unistd.h (BSD): Section 31.1 [Host Identification], page 845.

```
int sethostname (const char *name, size_t length)
```
unistd.h (BSD): Section 31.1 [Host Identification], page 845.

```
int setitimer (int which, const struct itimerval *new, struct itimerval *old)
```
sys/time.h (BSD): Section 21.5 [Setting an Alarm], page 649.

```
int setjmp (jmp_buf state)
```
setjmp.h (ISO): Section 23.2 [Details of Non-Local Exits], page 677.

```
void setkey (const char *key)
```
crypt.h (BSD): Section 33.4 [DES Encryption], page 887.

crypt.h (SVID): Section 33.4 [DES Encryption], page 887.

```
void setkey_r (const char *key, struct crypt_data * data)
```
crypt.h (GNU): Section 33.4 [DES Encryption], page 887.

```
void setlinebuf (FILE *stream)
```
stdio.h (BSD): Section 12.20.3 [Controlling Which Kind of Buffering], page 321.

```
char * setlocale (int category, const char *locale)
```
locale.h (ISO): Section 7.4 [How Programs Set the Locale], page 178.

```
int setlogmask (int mask)
```
syslog.h (BSD): Section 18.2.4 [setlogmask], page 523.

```
FILE * setmntent (const char *file, const char *mode)
```
mntent.h (BSD): Section 31.3.1.2 [The mtab file], page 852.

```
void setnetent (int stayopen)
```
netdb.h (BSD): Section 16.13 [Networks Database], page 488.

`int setnetgrent (const char *netgroup)`
> netdb.h (BSD): Section 30.16.2 [Looking up one Netgroup], page 842.

`int setpayload (double *x, double payload)`
> math.h (ISO): Section 20.8.5 [Setting and modifying single bits of FP values], page 599.

`int setpayloadf (float *x, float payload)`
> math.h (ISO): Section 20.8.5 [Setting and modifying single bits of FP values], page 599.

`int setpayloadfN (_FloatN *x, _FloatN payload)`
> math.h (TS 18661-3:2015): Section 20.8.5 [Setting and modifying single bits of FP values], page 599.

`int setpayloadfNx (_FloatNx *x, _FloatNx payload)`
> math.h (TS 18661-3:2015): Section 20.8.5 [Setting and modifying single bits of FP values], page 599.

`int setpayloadl (long double *x, long double payload)`
> math.h (ISO): Section 20.8.5 [Setting and modifying single bits of FP values], page 599.

`int setpayloadsig (double *x, double payload)`
> math.h (ISO): Section 20.8.5 [Setting and modifying single bits of FP values], page 599.

`int setpayloadsigf (float *x, float payload)`
> math.h (ISO): Section 20.8.5 [Setting and modifying single bits of FP values], page 599.

`int setpayloadsigfN (_FloatN *x, _FloatN payload)`
> math.h (TS 18661-3:2015): Section 20.8.5 [Setting and modifying single bits of FP values], page 599.

`int setpayloadsigfNx (_FloatNx *x, _FloatNx payload)`
> math.h (TS 18661-3:2015): Section 20.8.5 [Setting and modifying single bits of FP values], page 599.

`int setpayloadsigl (long double *x, long double payload)`
> math.h (ISO): Section 20.8.5 [Setting and modifying single bits of FP values], page 599.

`int setpgid (pid_t pid, pid_t pgid)`
> unistd.h (POSIX.1): Section 28.7.2 [Process Group Functions], page 801.

`int setpgrp (pid_t pid, pid_t pgid)`
> unistd.h (BSD): Section 28.7.2 [Process Group Functions], page 801.

`int setpriority (int class, int id, int niceval)`
> sys/resource.h (BSD): Section 22.3.4.2 [Functions For Traditional Scheduling], page 668.
>
> sys/resource.h (POSIX): Section 22.3.4.2 [Functions For Traditional Scheduling], page 668.

`void setprotoent (int stayopen)`
> netdb.h (BSD): Section 16.6.6 [Protocols Database], page 463.

`void setpwent (void)`
> pwd.h (SVID): Section 30.13.3 [Scanning the List of All Users], page 836.
>
> pwd.h (BSD): Section 30.13.3 [Scanning the List of All Users], page 836.

`int setregid (gid_t rgid, gid_t egid)`
> unistd.h (BSD): Section 30.7 [Setting the Group IDs], page 819.

`int setreuid (uid_t ruid, uid_t euid)`
> unistd.h (BSD): Section 30.6 [Setting the User ID], page 818.

`int setrlimit (int resource, const struct rlimit *rlp)`
> sys/resource.h (BSD): Section 22.2 [Limiting Resource Usage], page 656.

`int setrlimit64 (int resource, const struct rlimit64 *rlp)`
> sys/resource.h (Unix98): Section 22.2 [Limiting Resource Usage], page 656.

`void setservent (int stayopen)`
> netdb.h (BSD): Section 16.6.4 [The Services Database], page 461.

`pid_t setsid (void)`
> `unistd.h` (POSIX.1): Section 28.7.2 [Process Group Functions], page 801.

`int setsockopt (int socket, int level, int optname, const void *optval, socklen_t optlen)`
> `sys/socket.h` (BSD): Section 16.12.1 [Socket Option Functions], page 485.

`char * setstate (char *state)`
> `stdlib.h` (BSD): Section 19.8.2 [BSD Random Number Functions], page 566.

`int setstate_r (char *restrict statebuf, struct random_data *restrict buf)`
> `stdlib.h` (GNU): Section 19.8.2 [BSD Random Number Functions], page 566.

`int settimeofday (const struct timeval *tp, const struct timezone *tzp)`
> `sys/time.h` (BSD): Section 21.4.2 [High-Resolution Calendar], page 624.

`int setuid (uid_t newuid)`
> `unistd.h` (POSIX.1): Section 30.6 [Setting the User ID], page 818.

`void setutent (void)`
> `utmp.h` (SVID): Section 30.12.1 [Manipulating the User Accounting Database], page 826.

`void setutxent (void)`
> `utmpx.h` (XPG4.2): Section 30.12.2 [XPG User Accounting Database Functions], page 831.

`int setvbuf (FILE *stream, char *buf, int mode, size_t size)`
> `stdio.h` (ISO): Section 12.20.3 [Controlling Which Kind of Buffering], page 321.

`struct sgttyb`
> `termios.h` (BSD): Section 17.5 [BSD Terminal Modes], page 509.

`int shm_open (const char *name, int oflag, mode_t mode)`
> `sys/mman.h` (POSIX): Section 13.7 [Memory-mapped I/O], page 350.

`int shutdown (int socket, int how)`
> `sys/socket.h` (BSD): Section 16.8.2 [Closing a Socket], page 467.

`sig_atomic_t`
> `signal.h` (ISO): Section 24.4.7.2 [Atomic Types], page 710.

`int sigaction (int signum, const struct sigaction *restrict action, struct sigaction *restrict old-action)`
> `signal.h` (POSIX.1): Section 24.3.2 [Advanced Signal Handling], page 698.

`struct sigaction`
> `signal.h` (POSIX.1): Section 24.3.2 [Advanced Signal Handling], page 698.

`int sigaddset (sigset_t *set, int signum)`
> `signal.h` (POSIX.1): Section 24.7.2 [Signal Sets], page 717.

`int sigaltstack (const stack_t *restrict stack, stack_t *restrict oldstack)`
> `signal.h` (XPG): Section 24.9 [Using a Separate Signal Stack], page 725.

`int sigblock (int mask)`
> `signal.h` (BSD): Section 24.10 [BSD Signal Handling], page 727.

`int sigdelset (sigset_t *set, int signum)`
> `signal.h` (POSIX.1): Section 24.7.2 [Signal Sets], page 717.

`int sigemptyset (sigset_t *set)`
> `signal.h` (POSIX.1): Section 24.7.2 [Signal Sets], page 717.

`int sigfillset (sigset_t *set)`
> `signal.h` (POSIX.1): Section 24.7.2 [Signal Sets], page 717.

`sighandler_t`
> `signal.h` (GNU): Section 24.3.1 [Basic Signal Handling], page 696.

`int siginterrupt (int signum, int failflag)`
> `signal.h` (XPG): Section 24.10 [BSD Signal Handling], page 727.

Appendix B: Summary of Library Facilities

int sigismember (const sigset_t *set, int signum)
        signal.h (POSIX.1): Section 24.7.2 [Signal Sets], page 717.

sigjmp_buf
        setjmp.h (POSIX.1): Section 23.3 [Non-Local Exits and Signals], page 678.

void siglongjmp (sigjmp_buf state, int value)
        setjmp.h (POSIX.1): Section 23.3 [Non-Local Exits and Signals], page 678.

int sigmask (int signum)
        signal.h (BSD): Section 24.10 [BSD Signal Handling], page 727.

sighandler_t signal (int signum, sighandler_t action)
        signal.h (ISO): Section 24.3.1 [Basic Signal Handling], page 696.

int signbit (float-type x)
        math.h (ISO): Section 20.8.5 [Setting and modifying single bits of FP values], page 599.

double significand (double x)
        math.h (BSD): Section 20.8.2 [Normalization Functions], page 592.

float significandf (float x)
        math.h (BSD): Section 20.8.2 [Normalization Functions], page 592.

long double significandl (long double x)
        math.h (BSD): Section 20.8.2 [Normalization Functions], page 592.

int sigpause (int mask)
        signal.h (BSD): Section 24.10 [BSD Signal Handling], page 727.

int sigpending (sigset_t *set)
        signal.h (POSIX.1): Section 24.7.6 [Checking for Pending Signals], page 721.

int sigprocmask (int how, const sigset_t *restrict set, sigset_t *restrict oldset)
        signal.h (POSIX.1): Section 24.7.3 [Process Signal Mask], page 718.

sigset_t
        signal.h (POSIX.1): Section 24.7.2 [Signal Sets], page 717.

int sigsetjmp (sigjmp_buf state, int savesigs)
        setjmp.h (POSIX.1): Section 23.3 [Non-Local Exits and Signals], page 678.

int sigsetmask (int mask)
        signal.h (BSD): Section 24.10 [BSD Signal Handling], page 727.

int sigstack (struct sigstack *stack, struct sigstack *oldstack)
        signal.h (BSD): Section 24.9 [Using a Separate Signal Stack], page 725.

struct sigstack
        signal.h (BSD): Section 24.9 [Using a Separate Signal Stack], page 725.

int sigsuspend (const sigset_t *set)
        signal.h (POSIX.1): Section 24.8.3 [Using sigsuspend], page 724.

double sin (double x)
        math.h (ISO): Section 19.2 [Trigonometric Functions], page 526.

void sincos (double x, double *sinx, double *cosx)
        math.h (GNU): Section 19.2 [Trigonometric Functions], page 526.

void sincosf (float x, float *sinx, float *cosx)
        math.h (GNU): Section 19.2 [Trigonometric Functions], page 526.

_FloatN sincosfN (_FloatN x, _FloatN *sinx, _FloatN *cosx)
        math.h (GNU): Section 19.2 [Trigonometric Functions], page 526.

_FloatNx sincosfNx (_FloatNx x, _FloatNx *sinx, _FloatNx *cosx)
        math.h (GNU): Section 19.2 [Trigonometric Functions], page 526.

`void sincosl (long double x, long double *sinx, long double *cosx)`
> `math.h` (GNU): Section 19.2 [Trigonometric Functions], page 526.

`float sinf (float x)`
> `math.h` (ISO): Section 19.2 [Trigonometric Functions], page 526.

`_FloatN sinfN (_FloatN x)`
> `math.h` (TS 18661-3:2015): Section 19.2 [Trigonometric Functions], page 526.

`_FloatNx sinfNx (_FloatNx x)`
> `math.h` (TS 18661-3:2015): Section 19.2 [Trigonometric Functions], page 526.

`double sinh (double x)`
> `math.h` (ISO): Section 19.5 [Hyperbolic Functions], page 536.

`float sinhf (float x)`
> `math.h` (ISO): Section 19.5 [Hyperbolic Functions], page 536.

`_FloatN sinhfN (_FloatN x)`
> `math.h` (TS 18661-3:2015): Section 19.5 [Hyperbolic Functions], page 536.

`_FloatNx sinhfNx (_FloatNx x)`
> `math.h` (TS 18661-3:2015): Section 19.5 [Hyperbolic Functions], page 536.

`long double sinhl (long double x)`
> `math.h` (ISO): Section 19.5 [Hyperbolic Functions], page 536.

`long double sinl (long double x)`
> `math.h` (ISO): Section 19.2 [Trigonometric Functions], page 526.

`size_t`
> `stddef.h` (ISO): Section A.4 [Important Data Types], page 916.

`unsigned int sleep (unsigned int seconds)`
> `unistd.h` (POSIX.1): Section 21.6 [Sleeping], page 652.

`int snprintf (char *s, size_t size, const char *template, ...)`
> `stdio.h` (GNU): Section 12.12.7 [Formatted Output Functions], page 287.

`struct sockaddr`
> `sys/socket.h` (BSD): Section 16.3.1 [Address Formats], page 444.

`struct sockaddr_in`
> `netinet/in.h` (BSD): Section 16.6.1 [Internet Socket Address Formats], page 451.

`struct sockaddr_un`
> `sys/un.h` (BSD): Section 16.5.2 [Details of Local Namespace], page 448.

`int socket (int namespace, int style, int protocol)`
> `sys/socket.h` (BSD): Section 16.8.1 [Creating a Socket], page 466.

`int socketpair (int namespace, int style, int protocol, int filedes[2])`
> `sys/socket.h` (BSD): Section 16.8.3 [Socket Pairs], page 468.

`speed_t`
> `termios.h` (POSIX.1): Section 17.4.8 [Line Speed], page 502.

`int sprintf (char *s, const char *template, ...)`
> `stdio.h` (ISO): Section 12.12.7 [Formatted Output Functions], page 287.

`double sqrt (double x)`
> `math.h` (ISO): Section 19.4 [Exponentiation and Logarithms], page 530.

`float sqrtf (float x)`
> `math.h` (ISO): Section 19.4 [Exponentiation and Logarithms], page 530.

`_FloatN sqrtfN (_FloatN x)`
> `math.h` (TS 18661-3:2015): Section 19.4 [Exponentiation and Logarithms], page 530.

`_FloatNx sqrtfNx (_FloatNx x)`
> `math.h` (TS 18661-3:2015): Section 19.4 [Exponentiation and Logarithms], page 530.

`long double sqrtl (long double x)`
> `math.h` (ISO): Section 19.4 [Exponentiation and Logarithms], page 530.

`void srand (unsigned int seed)`
> `stdlib.h` (ISO): Section 19.8.1 [ISO C Random Number Functions], page 565.

`void srand48 (long int seedval)`
> `stdlib.h` (SVID): Section 19.8.3 [SVID Random Number Function], page 568.

`int srand48_r (long int seedval, struct drand48_data *buffer)`
> `stdlib.h` (GNU): Section 19.8.3 [SVID Random Number Function], page 568.

`void srandom (unsigned int seed)`
> `stdlib.h` (BSD): Section 19.8.2 [BSD Random Number Functions], page 566.

`int srandom_r (unsigned int seed, struct random_data *buf)`
> `stdlib.h` (GNU): Section 19.8.2 [BSD Random Number Functions], page 566.

`int sscanf (const char *s, const char *template, ...)`
> `stdio.h` (ISO): Section 12.14.8 [Formatted Input Functions], page 309.

`sighandler_t ssignal (int signum, sighandler_t action)`
> `signal.h` (SVID): Section 24.3.1 [Basic Signal Handling], page 696.

`ssize_t`
> `unistd.h` (POSIX.1): Section 13.2 [Input and Output Primitives], page 336.

`stack_t`
> `signal.h` (XPG): Section 24.9 [Using a Separate Signal Stack], page 725.

`int stat (const char *filename, struct stat *buf)`
> `sys/stat.h` (POSIX.1): Section 14.9.2 [Reading the Attributes of a File], page 416.

`struct stat`
> `sys/stat.h` (POSIX.1): Section 14.9.1 [The meaning of the File Attributes], page 412.

`int stat64 (const char *filename, struct stat64 *buf)`
> `sys/stat.h` (Unix98): Section 14.9.2 [Reading the Attributes of a File], page 416.

`struct stat64`
> `sys/stat.h` (LFS): Section 14.9.1 [The meaning of the File Attributes], page 412.

`FILE * stderr`
> `stdio.h` (ISO): Section 12.2 [Standard Streams], page 257.

`FILE * stdin`
> `stdio.h` (ISO): Section 12.2 [Standard Streams], page 257.

`FILE * stdout`
> `stdio.h` (ISO): Section 12.2 [Standard Streams], page 257.

`int stime (const time_t *newtime)`
> `time.h` (SVID): Section 21.4.1 [Simple Calendar Time], page 623.
>
> `time.h` (XPG): Section 21.4.1 [Simple Calendar Time], page 623.

`char * stpcpy (char *restrict to, const char *restrict from)`
> `string.h` (Unknown origin): Section 5.4 [Copying Strings and Arrays], page 95.

`char * stpncpy (char *restrict to, const char *restrict from, size_t size)`
> `string.h` (GNU): Section 5.6 [Truncating Strings while Copying], page 103.

`int strcasecmp (const char *s1, const char *s2)`
> `string.h` (BSD): Section 5.7 [String/Array Comparison], page 107.

char * strcasestr (const char *haystack, const char *needle)
>   string.h (GNU): Section 5.9 [Search Functions], page 115.

char * strcat (char *restrict to, const char *restrict from)
>   string.h (ISO): Section 5.5 [Concatenating Strings], page 100.

char * strchr (const char *string, int c)
>   string.h (ISO): Section 5.9 [Search Functions], page 115.

char * strchrnul (const char *string, int c)
>   string.h (GNU): Section 5.9 [Search Functions], page 115.

int strcmp (const char *s1, const char *s2)
>   string.h (ISO): Section 5.7 [String/Array Comparison], page 107.

int strcoll (const char *s1, const char *s2)
>   string.h (ISO): Section 5.8 [Collation Functions], page 111.

char * strcpy (char *restrict to, const char *restrict from)
>   string.h (ISO): Section 5.4 [Copying Strings and Arrays], page 95.

size_t strcspn (const char *string, const char *stopset)
>   string.h (ISO): Section 5.9 [Search Functions], page 115.

char * strdup (const char *s)
>   string.h (SVID): Section 5.4 [Copying Strings and Arrays], page 95.

char * strdupa (const char *s)
>   string.h (GNU): Section 5.4 [Copying Strings and Arrays], page 95.

char * strerror (int errnum)
>   string.h (ISO): Section 2.3 [Error Messages], page 35.

char * strerror_r (int errnum, char *buf, size_t n)
>   string.h (GNU): Section 2.3 [Error Messages], page 35.

int strfromd (char *restrict string, size_t size, const char *restrict format, double value)
>   stdlib.h (ISO/IEC TS 18661-1): Section 20.12 [Printing of Floats], page 615.

int strfromf (char *restrict string, size_t size, const char *restrict format, float value)
>   stdlib.h (ISO/IEC TS 18661-1): Section 20.12 [Printing of Floats], page 615.

int strfromfN (char *restrict string, size_t size, const char *restrict format, _FloatN value)
>   stdlib.h (ISO/IEC TS 18661-3): Section 20.12 [Printing of Floats], page 615.

int strfromfNx (char *restrict string, size_t size, const char *restrict format, _FloatNx value)
>   stdlib.h (ISO/IEC TS 18661-3): Section 20.12 [Printing of Floats], page 615.

int strfroml (char *restrict string, size_t size, const char *restrict format, long double value)
>   stdlib.h (ISO/IEC TS 18661-1): Section 20.12 [Printing of Floats], page 615.

char * strfry (char *string)
>   string.h (GNU): Section 5.12 [strfry], page 126.

size_t strftime (char *s, size_t size, const char *template, const struct tm *brokentime)
>   time.h (ISO): Section 21.4.5 [Formatting Calendar Time], page 632.

size_t strlen (const char *s)
>   string.h (ISO): Section 5.3 [String Length], page 93.

int strncasecmp (const char *s1, const char *s2, size_t n)
>   string.h (BSD): Section 5.7 [String/Array Comparison], page 107.

char * strncat (char *restrict to, const char *restrict from, size_t size)
>   string.h (ISO): Section 5.6 [Truncating Strings while Copying], page 103.

int strncmp (const char *s1, const char *s2, size_t size)
   string.h (ISO): Section 5.7 [String/Array Comparison], page 107.

char * strncpy (char *restrict to, const char *restrict from, size_t size)
   string.h (C90): Section 5.6 [Truncating Strings while Copying], page 103.

char * strndup (const char *s, size_t size)
   string.h (GNU): Section 5.6 [Truncating Strings while Copying], page 103.

char * strndupa (const char *s, size_t size)
   string.h (GNU): Section 5.6 [Truncating Strings while Copying], page 103.

size_t strnlen (const char *s, size_t maxlen)
   string.h (GNU): Section 5.3 [String Length], page 93.

char * strpbrk (const char *string, const char *stopset)
   string.h (ISO): Section 5.9 [Search Functions], page 115.

char * strptime (const char *s, const char *fmt, struct tm *tp)
   time.h (XPG4): Section 21.4.6.1 [Interpret string according to given format], page 638.

char * strrchr (const char *string, int c)
   string.h (ISO): Section 5.9 [Search Functions], page 115.

char * strsep (char **string_ptr, const char *delimiter)
   string.h (BSD): Section 5.10 [Finding Tokens in a String], page 120.

char * strsignal (int signum)
   string.h (GNU): Section 24.2.8 [Signal Messages], page 695.

size_t strspn (const char *string, const char *skipset)
   string.h (ISO): Section 5.9 [Search Functions], page 115.

char * strstr (const char *haystack, const char *needle)
   string.h (ISO): Section 5.9 [Search Functions], page 115.

double strtod (const char *restrict string, char **restrict tailptr)
   stdlib.h (ISO): Section 20.11.2 [Parsing of Floats], page 613.

float strtof (const char *string, char **tailptr)
   stdlib.h (ISO): Section 20.11.2 [Parsing of Floats], page 613.

_FloatN strtofN (const char *string, char **tailptr)
   stdlib.h (ISO/IEC TS 18661-3): Section 20.11.2 [Parsing of Floats], page 613.

_FloatNx strtofNx (const char *string, char **tailptr)
   stdlib.h (ISO/IEC TS 18661-3): Section 20.11.2 [Parsing of Floats], page 613.

intmax_t strtoimax (const char *restrict string, char **restrict tailptr, int base)
   inttypes.h (ISO): Section 20.11.1 [Parsing of Integers], page 608.

char * strtok (char *restrict newstring, const char *restrict delimiters)
   string.h (ISO): Section 5.10 [Finding Tokens in a String], page 120.

char * strtok_r (char *newstring, const char *delimiters, char **save_ptr)
   string.h (POSIX): Section 5.10 [Finding Tokens in a String], page 120.

long int strtol (const char *restrict string, char **restrict tailptr, int base)
   stdlib.h (ISO): Section 20.11.1 [Parsing of Integers], page 608.

long double strtold (const char *string, char **tailptr)
   stdlib.h (ISO): Section 20.11.2 [Parsing of Floats], page 613.

long long int strtoll (const char *restrict string, char **restrict tailptr, int base)
   stdlib.h (ISO): Section 20.11.1 [Parsing of Integers], page 608.

long long int strtoq (const char *restrict string, char **restrict tailptr, int base)
   stdlib.h (BSD): Section 20.11.1 [Parsing of Integers], page 608.

`unsigned long int strtoul (const char *retrict string, char **restrict tailptr, int base)`
> stdlib.h (ISO): Section 20.11.1 [Parsing of Integers], page 608.

`unsigned long long int strtoull (const char *restrict string, char **restrict tailptr, int base)`
> stdlib.h (ISO): Section 20.11.1 [Parsing of Integers], page 608.

`uintmax_t strtoumax (const char *restrict string, char **restrict tailptr, int base)`
> inttypes.h (ISO): Section 20.11.1 [Parsing of Integers], page 608.

`unsigned long long int strtouq (const char *restrict string, char **restrict tailptr, int base)`
> stdlib.h (BSD): Section 20.11.1 [Parsing of Integers], page 608.

`int strverscmp (const char *s1, const char *s2)`
> string.h (GNU): Section 5.7 [String/Array Comparison], page 107.

`size_t strxfrm (char *restrict to, const char *restrict from, size_t size)`
> string.h (ISO): Section 5.8 [Collation Functions], page 111.

`int stty (int filedes, const struct sgttyb *attributes)`
> sgtty.h (BSD): Section 17.5 [BSD Terminal Modes], page 509.

`int swapcontext (ucontext_t *restrict oucp, const ucontext_t *restrict ucp)`
> ucontext.h (SVID): Section 23.4 [Complete Context Control], page 679.

`int swprintf (wchar_t *ws, size_t size, const wchar_t *template, ...)`
> wchar.h (GNU): Section 12.12.7 [Formatted Output Functions], page 287.

`int swscanf (const wchar_t *ws, const wchar_t *template, ...)`
> wchar.h (ISO): Section 12.14.8 [Formatted Input Functions], page 309.

`int symlink (const char *oldname, const char *newname)`
> unistd.h (BSD): Section 14.5 [Symbolic Links], page 406.

`void sync (void)`
> unistd.h (X/Open): Section 13.9 [Synchronizing I/O operations], page 358.

`long int syscall (long int sysno, ...)`
> unistd.h (???): Section 25.6 [System Calls], page 767.

`long int sysconf (int parameter)`
> unistd.h (POSIX.1): Section 32.4.1 [Definition of sysconf], page 865.

`int sysctl (int *names, int nlen, void *oldval, size_t *oldlenp, void *newval, size_t newlen)`
> sys/sysctl.h (BSD): Section 31.4 [System Parameters], page 859.

`void syslog (int facility_priority, const char *format, ...)`
> syslog.h (BSD): Section 18.2.2 [syslog, vsyslog], page 520.

`int system (const char *command)`
> stdlib.h (ISO): Section 26.1 [Running a Command], page 773.

`sighandler_t sysv_signal (int signum, sighandler_t action)`
> signal.h (GNU): Section 24.3.1 [Basic Signal Handling], page 696.

`double tan (double x)`
> math.h (ISO): Section 19.2 [Trigonometric Functions], page 526.

`float tanf (float x)`
> math.h (ISO): Section 19.2 [Trigonometric Functions], page 526.

`_FloatN tanfN (_FloatN x)`
> math.h (TS 18661-3:2015): Section 19.2 [Trigonometric Functions], page 526.

`_FloatNx tanfNx (_FloatNx x)`
> math.h (TS 18661-3:2015): Section 19.2 [Trigonometric Functions], page 526.

`double tanh (double x)`
> math.h (ISO): Section 19.5 [Hyperbolic Functions], page 536.

float tanhf (float *x*)

      math.h (ISO): Section 19.5 [Hyperbolic Functions], page 536.

_FloatN tanhfN (_Float*N* *x*)

      math.h (TS 18661-3:2015): Section 19.5 [Hyperbolic Functions], page 536.

_FloatNx tanhfNx (_Float*Nx* *x*)

      math.h (TS 18661-3:2015): Section 19.5 [Hyperbolic Functions], page 536.

long double tanhl (long double *x*)

      math.h (ISO): Section 19.5 [Hyperbolic Functions], page 536.

long double tanl (long double *x*)

      math.h (ISO): Section 19.2 [Trigonometric Functions], page 526.

int tcdrain (int *filedes*)

      termios.h (POSIX.1): Section 17.6 [Line Control Functions], page 510.

tcflag_t

      termios.h (POSIX.1): Section 17.4.1 [Terminal Mode Data Types], page 492.

int tcflow (int *filedes*, int *action*)

      termios.h (POSIX.1): Section 17.6 [Line Control Functions], page 510.

int tcflush (int *filedes*, int *queue*)

      termios.h (POSIX.1): Section 17.6 [Line Control Functions], page 510.

int tcgetattr (int *filedes*, struct termios *termios-p*)

      termios.h (POSIX.1): Section 17.4.2 [Terminal Mode Functions], page 493.

pid_t tcgetpgrp (int *filedes*)

      unistd.h (POSIX.1): Section 28.7.3 [Functions for Controlling Terminal Access], page 803.

pid_t tcgetsid (int *fildes*)

      termios.h (Unix98): Section 28.7.3 [Functions for Controlling Terminal Access], page 803.

int tcsendbreak (int *filedes*, int *duration*)

      termios.h (POSIX.1): Section 17.6 [Line Control Functions], page 510.

int tcsetattr (int *filedes*, int *when*, const struct termios *termios-p*)

      termios.h (POSIX.1): Section 17.4.2 [Terminal Mode Functions], page 493.

int tcsetpgrp (int *filedes*, pid_t *pgid*)

      unistd.h (POSIX.1): Section 28.7.3 [Functions for Controlling Terminal Access], page 803.

void * tdelete (const void *key*, void **rootp*, comparison_fn_t *compar*)

      search.h (SVID): Section 9.6 [The tsearch function.], page 227.

void tdestroy (void *vroot*, __free_fn_t *freefct*)

      search.h (GNU): Section 9.6 [The tsearch function.], page 227.

long int telldir (DIR *dirstream*)

      dirent.h (BSD): Section 14.2.5 [Random Access in a Directory Stream], page 398.

char * tempnam (const char *dir*, const char *prefix*)

      stdio.h (SVID): Section 14.11 [Temporary Files], page 433.

struct termios

      termios.h (POSIX.1): Section 17.4.1 [Terminal Mode Data Types], page 492.

char * textdomain (const char *domainname*)

      libintl.h (GNU): Section 8.2.1.2 [How to determine which catalog to be used], page 207.

void * tfind (const void *key*, void *const *rootp*, comparison_fn_t *compar*)

      search.h (SVID): Section 9.6 [The tsearch function.], page 227.

double tgamma (double *x*)

      math.h (XPG): Section 19.6 [Special Functions], page 539.

      math.h (ISO): Section 19.6 [Special Functions], page 539.

`float tgammaf (float x)`
> `math.h` (XPG): Section 19.6 [Special Functions], page 539.

> `math.h` (ISO): Section 19.6 [Special Functions], page 539.

`_FloatN tgammafN (_FloatN x)`
> `math.h` (TS 18661-3:2015): Section 19.6 [Special Functions], page 539.

`_FloatNx tgammafNx (_FloatNx x)`
> `math.h` (TS 18661-3:2015): Section 19.6 [Special Functions], page 539.

`long double tgammal (long double x)`
> `math.h` (XPG): Section 19.6 [Special Functions], page 539.

> `math.h` (ISO): Section 19.6 [Special Functions], page 539.

`time_t time (time_t *result)`
> `time.h` (ISO): Section 21.4.1 [Simple Calendar Time], page 623.

`time_t`
> `time.h` (ISO): Section 21.4.1 [Simple Calendar Time], page 623.

`time_t timegm (struct tm *brokentime)`
> `time.h` (???): Section 21.4.3 [Broken-down Time], page 626.

`time_t timelocal (struct tm *brokentime)`
> `time.h` (???): Section 21.4.3 [Broken-down Time], page 626.

`clock_t times (struct tms *buffer)`
> `sys/times.h` (POSIX.1): Section 21.3.2 [Processor Time Inquiry], page 622.

`struct timespec`
> `sys/time.h` (POSIX.1): Section 21.2 [Elapsed Time], page 619.

`struct timeval`
> `sys/time.h` (BSD): Section 21.2 [Elapsed Time], page 619.

`long int timezone`
> `time.h` (SVID): Section 21.4.8 [Functions and Variables for Time Zones], page 648.

`struct timezone`
> `sys/time.h` (BSD): Section 21.4.2 [High-Resolution Calendar], page 624.

`struct tm`
> `time.h` (ISO): Section 21.4.3 [Broken-down Time], page 626.

`FILE * tmpfile (void)`
> `stdio.h` (ISO): Section 14.11 [Temporary Files], page 433.

`FILE * tmpfile64 (void)`
> `stdio.h` (Unix98): Section 14.11 [Temporary Files], page 433.

`char * tmpnam (char *result)`
> `stdio.h` (ISO): Section 14.11 [Temporary Files], page 433.

`char * tmpnam_r (char *result)`
> `stdio.h` (GNU): Section 14.11 [Temporary Files], page 433.

`struct tms`
> `sys/times.h` (POSIX.1): Section 21.3.2 [Processor Time Inquiry], page 622.

`int toascii (int c)`
> `ctype.h` (SVID): Section 4.2 [Case Conversion], page 83.

> `ctype.h` (BSD): Section 4.2 [Case Conversion], page 83.

`int tolower (int c)`
> `ctype.h` (ISO): Section 4.2 [Case Conversion], page 83.

int totalorder (double *x*, double *y*)
    math.h (TS 18661-1:2014): Section 20.8.6 [Floating-Point Comparison Functions], page 602.

int totalorderf (float *x*, float *y*)
    math.h (TS 18661-1:2014): Section 20.8.6 [Floating-Point Comparison Functions], page 602.

int totalorderfN (_Float*N x*, _Float*N y*)
    math.h (TS 18661-3:2015): Section 20.8.6 [Floating-Point Comparison Functions], page 602.

int totalorderfNx (_Float*N*x *x*, _Float*N*x *y*)
    math.h (TS 18661-3:2015): Section 20.8.6 [Floating-Point Comparison Functions], page 602.

int totalorderl (long double *x*, long double *y*)
    math.h (TS 18661-1:2014): Section 20.8.6 [Floating-Point Comparison Functions], page 602.

int totalordermag (double *x*, double *y*)
    math.h (TS 18661-1:2014): Section 20.8.6 [Floating-Point Comparison Functions], page 602.

int totalordermagf (float *x*, float *y*)
    math.h (TS 18661-1:2014): Section 20.8.6 [Floating-Point Comparison Functions], page 602.

int totalordermagfN (_Float*N x*, _Float*N y*)
    math.h (TS 18661-3:2015): Section 20.8.6 [Floating-Point Comparison Functions], page 602.

int totalordermagfNx (_Float*N*x *x*, _Float*N*x *y*)
    math.h (TS 18661-3:2015): Section 20.8.6 [Floating-Point Comparison Functions], page 602.

int totalordermagl (long double *x*, long double *y*)
    math.h (TS 18661-1:2014): Section 20.8.6 [Floating-Point Comparison Functions], page 602.

int toupper (int *c*)
    ctype.h (ISO): Section 4.2 [Case Conversion], page 83.

wint_t towctrans (wint_t *wc*, wctrans_t *desc*)
    wctype.h (ISO): Section 4.5 [Mapping of wide characters.], page 89.

wint_t towlower (wint_t *wc*)
    wctype.h (ISO): Section 4.5 [Mapping of wide characters.], page 89.

wint_t towupper (wint_t *wc*)
    wctype.h (ISO): Section 4.5 [Mapping of wide characters.], page 89.

double trunc (double *x*)
    math.h (ISO): Section 20.8.3 [Rounding Functions], page 594.

int truncate (const char **filename*, off_t *length*)
    unistd.h (X/Open): Section 14.9.10 [File Size], page 428.

int truncate64 (const char **name*, off64_t *length*)
    unistd.h (Unix98): Section 14.9.10 [File Size], page 428.

float truncf (float *x*)
    math.h (ISO): Section 20.8.3 [Rounding Functions], page 594.

_FloatN truncfN (_Float*N x*)
    math.h (TS 18661-3:2015): Section 20.8.3 [Rounding Functions], page 594.

_FloatNx truncfNx (_Float*N*x *x*)
    math.h (TS 18661-3:2015): Section 20.8.3 [Rounding Functions], page 594.

long double truncl (long double *x*)
    math.h (ISO): Section 20.8.3 [Rounding Functions], page 594.

void * tsearch (const void **key*, void ***rootp*, comparison_fn_t *compar*)
    search.h (SVID): Section 9.6 [The tsearch function.], page 227.

char * ttyname (int *filedes*)
    unistd.h (POSIX.1): Section 17.1 [Identifying Terminals], page 490.

`int ttyname_r (int `*`filedes`*`, char *`*`buf`*`, size_t `*`len`*`)`
> `unistd.h` (POSIX.1): Section 17.1 [Identifying Terminals], page 490.

`void twalk (const void *`*`root`*`, __action_fn_t `*`action`*`)`
> `search.h` (SVID): Section 9.6 [The `tsearch` function.], page 227.

`char * tzname [2]`
> `time.h` (POSIX.1): Section 21.4.8 [Functions and Variables for Time Zones], page 648.

`void tzset (void)`
> `time.h` (POSIX.1): Section 21.4.8 [Functions and Variables for Time Zones], page 648.

`ucontext_t`
> `ucontext.h` (SVID): Section 23.4 [Complete Context Control], page 679.

`uintmax_t ufromfp (double `*`x`*`, int `*`round`*`, unsigned int `*`width`*`)`
> `math.h` (ISO): Section 20.8.3 [Rounding Functions], page 594.

`uintmax_t ufromfpf (float `*`x`*`, int `*`round`*`, unsigned int `*`width`*`)`
> `math.h` (ISO): Section 20.8.3 [Rounding Functions], page 594.

`uintmax_t ufromfpfN (_Float`*`N`*` `*`x`*`, int `*`round`*`, unsigned int `*`width`*`)`
> `math.h` (TS 18661-3:2015): Section 20.8.3 [Rounding Functions], page 594.

`uintmax_t ufromfpfNx (_Float`*`Nx`*` `*`x`*`, int `*`round`*`, unsigned int `*`width`*`)`
> `math.h` (TS 18661-3:2015): Section 20.8.3 [Rounding Functions], page 594.

`uintmax_t ufromfpl (long double `*`x`*`, int `*`round`*`, unsigned int `*`width`*`)`
> `math.h` (ISO): Section 20.8.3 [Rounding Functions], page 594.

`uintmax_t ufromfpx (double `*`x`*`, int `*`round`*`, unsigned int `*`width`*`)`
> `math.h` (ISO): Section 20.8.3 [Rounding Functions], page 594.

`uintmax_t ufromfpxf (float `*`x`*`, int `*`round`*`, unsigned int `*`width`*`)`
> `math.h` (ISO): Section 20.8.3 [Rounding Functions], page 594.

`uintmax_t ufromfpxfN (_Float`*`N`*` `*`x`*`, int `*`round`*`, unsigned int `*`width`*`)`
> `math.h` (TS 18661-3:2015): Section 20.8.3 [Rounding Functions], page 594.

`uintmax_t ufromfpxfNx (_Float`*`Nx`*` `*`x`*`, int `*`round`*`, unsigned int `*`width`*`)`
> `math.h` (TS 18661-3:2015): Section 20.8.3 [Rounding Functions], page 594.

`uintmax_t ufromfpxl (long double `*`x`*`, int `*`round`*`, unsigned int `*`width`*`)`
> `math.h` (ISO): Section 20.8.3 [Rounding Functions], page 594.

`uid_t`
> `sys/types.h` (POSIX.1): Section 30.5 [Reading the Persona of a Process], page 817.

`long int ulimit (int `*`cmd`*`, ...)`
> `ulimit.h` (BSD): Section 22.2 [Limiting Resource Usage], page 656.

`mode_t umask (mode_t `*`mask`*`)`
> `sys/stat.h` (POSIX.1): Section 14.9.7 [Assigning File Permissions], page 423.

`int umount (const char *`*`file`*`)`
> `sys/mount.h` (SVID): Section 31.3.2 [Mount, Unmount, Remount], page 855.
> `sys/mount.h` (GNU): Section 31.3.2 [Mount, Unmount, Remount], page 855.

`int umount2 (const char *`*`file`*`, int `*`flags`*`)`
> `sys/mount.h` (GNU): Section 31.3.2 [Mount, Unmount, Remount], page 855.

`int uname (struct utsname *`*`info`*`)`
> `sys/utsname.h` (POSIX.1): Section 31.2 [Platform Type Identification], page 847.

`int ungetc (int `*`c`*`, FILE *`*`stream`*`)`
> `stdio.h` (ISO): Section 12.10.2 [Using `ungetc` To Do Unreading], page 277.

`wint_t ungetwc (wint_t wc, FILE *stream)`
> wchar.h (ISO): Section 12.10.2 [Using ungetc To Do Unreading], page 277.

`int unlink (const char *filename)`
> unistd.h (POSIX.1): Section 14.6 [Deleting Files], page 409.

`int unlockpt (int filedes)`
> stdlib.h (SVID): Section 17.8.1 [Allocating Pseudo-Terminals], page 513.
> stdlib.h (XPG4.2): Section 17.8.1 [Allocating Pseudo-Terminals], page 513.

`int unsetenv (const char *name)`
> stdlib.h (BSD): Section 25.4.1 [Environment Access], page 763.

`void updwtmp (const char *wtmp_file, const struct utmp *utmp)`
> utmp.h (SVID): Section 30.12.1 [Manipulating the User Accounting Database], page 826.

`struct utimbuf`
> utime.h (POSIX.1): Section 14.9.9 [File Times], page 426.

`int utime (const char *filename, const struct utimbuf *times)`
> utime.h (POSIX.1): Section 14.9.9 [File Times], page 426.

`int utimes (const char *filename, const struct timeval tvp[2])`
> sys/time.h (BSD): Section 14.9.9 [File Times], page 426.

`int utmpname (const char *file)`
> utmp.h (SVID): Section 30.12.1 [Manipulating the User Accounting Database], page 826.

`int utmpxname (const char *file)`
> utmpx.h (XPG4.2): Section 30.12.2 [XPG User Accounting Database Functions], page 831.

`struct utsname`
> sys/utsname.h (POSIX.1): Section 31.2 [Platform Type Identification], page 847.

`type va_arg (va_list ap, type)`
> stdarg.h (ISO): Section A.2.2.5 [Argument Access Macros], page 913.

`void va_copy (va_list dest, va_list src)`
> stdarg.h (ISO): Section A.2.2.5 [Argument Access Macros], page 913.

`void va_end (va_list ap)`
> stdarg.h (ISO): Section A.2.2.5 [Argument Access Macros], page 913.

`va_list`
> stdarg.h (ISO): Section A.2.2.5 [Argument Access Macros], page 913.

`void va_start (va_list ap, last-required)`
> stdarg.h (ISO): Section A.2.2.5 [Argument Access Macros], page 913.

`void * valloc (size_t size)`
> malloc.h (BSD): Section 3.2.3.6 [Allocating Aligned Memory Blocks], page 48.
> stdlib.h (BSD): Section 3.2.3.6 [Allocating Aligned Memory Blocks], page 48.

`int vasprintf (char **ptr, const char *template, va_list ap)`
> stdio.h (GNU): Section 12.12.9 [Variable Arguments Output Functions], page 290.

`void verr (int status, const char *format, va_list ap)`
> err.h (BSD): Section 2.3 [Error Messages], page 35.

`void verrx (int status, const char *format, va_list ap)`
> err.h (BSD): Section 2.3 [Error Messages], page 35.

`int versionsort (const struct dirent **a, const struct dirent **b)`
> dirent.h (GNU): Section 14.2.6 [Scanning the Content of a Directory], page 399.

`int versionsort64 (const struct dirent64 **a, const struct dirent64 **b)`
> dirent.h (GNU): Section 14.2.6 [Scanning the Content of a Directory], page 399.

`pid_t vfork (void)`
> `unistd.h` (BSD): Section 26.4 [Creating a Process], page 775.

`int vfprintf (FILE *stream, const char *template, va_list ap)`
> `stdio.h` (ISO): Section 12.12.9 [Variable Arguments Output Functions], page 290.

`int vfscanf (FILE *stream, const char *template, va_list ap)`
> `stdio.h` (ISO): Section 12.14.9 [Variable Arguments Input Functions], page 310.

`int vfwprintf (FILE *stream, const wchar_t *template, va_list ap)`
> `wchar.h` (ISO): Section 12.12.9 [Variable Arguments Output Functions], page 290.

`int vfwscanf (FILE *stream, const wchar_t *template, va_list ap)`
> `wchar.h` (ISO): Section 12.14.9 [Variable Arguments Input Functions], page 310.

`int vlimit (int resource, int limit)`
> `sys/vlimit.h` (BSD): Section 22.2 [Limiting Resource Usage], page 656.

`int vprintf (const char *template, va_list ap)`
> `stdio.h` (ISO): Section 12.12.9 [Variable Arguments Output Functions], page 290.

`int vscanf (const char *template, va_list ap)`
> `stdio.h` (ISO): Section 12.14.9 [Variable Arguments Input Functions], page 310.

`int vsnprintf (char *s, size_t size, const char *template, va_list ap)`
> `stdio.h` (GNU): Section 12.12.9 [Variable Arguments Output Functions], page 290.

`int vsprintf (char *s, const char *template, va_list ap)`
> `stdio.h` (ISO): Section 12.12.9 [Variable Arguments Output Functions], page 290.

`int vsscanf (const char *s, const char *template, va_list ap)`
> `stdio.h` (ISO): Section 12.14.9 [Variable Arguments Input Functions], page 310.

`int vswprintf (wchar_t *ws, size_t size, const wchar_t *template, va_list ap)`
> `wchar.h` (GNU): Section 12.12.9 [Variable Arguments Output Functions], page 290.

`int vswscanf (const wchar_t *s, const wchar_t *template, va_list ap)`
> `wchar.h` (ISO): Section 12.14.9 [Variable Arguments Input Functions], page 310.

`void vsyslog (int facility_priority, const char *format, va_list arglist)`
> `syslog.h` (BSD): Section 18.2.2 [syslog, vsyslog], page 520.

`int vtimes (struct vtimes *current, struct vtimes *child)`
> `sys/vtimes.h` (???): Section 22.1 [Resource Usage], page 654.

`void vwarn (const char *format, va_list ap)`
> `err.h` (BSD): Section 2.3 [Error Messages], page 35.

`void vwarnx (const char *format, va_list ap)`
> `err.h` (BSD): Section 2.3 [Error Messages], page 35.

`int vwprintf (const wchar_t *template, va_list ap)`
> `wchar.h` (ISO): Section 12.12.9 [Variable Arguments Output Functions], page 290.

`int vwscanf (const wchar_t *template, va_list ap)`
> `wchar.h` (ISO): Section 12.14.9 [Variable Arguments Input Functions], page 310.

`pid_t wait (int *status-ptr)`
> `sys/wait.h` (POSIX.1): Section 26.6 [Process Completion], page 779.

`pid_t wait3 (int *status-ptr, int options, struct rusage *usage)`
> `sys/wait.h` (BSD): Section 26.8 [BSD Process Wait Function], page 782.

`pid_t wait4 (pid_t pid, int *status-ptr, int options, struct rusage *usage)`
> `sys/wait.h` (BSD): Section 26.6 [Process Completion], page 779.

`pid_t waitpid (pid_t pid, int *status-ptr, int options)`
> `sys/wait.h` (POSIX.1): Section 26.6 [Process Completion], page 779.

void warn (const char *format, ...)
    err.h (BSD): Section 2.3 [Error Messages], page 35.

void warnx (const char *format, ...)
    err.h (BSD): Section 2.3 [Error Messages], page 35.

wchar_t
    stddef.h (ISO): Section 6.1 [Introduction to Extended Characters], page 134.

wchar_t * wcpcpy (wchar_t *restrict wto, const wchar_t *restrict wfrom)
    wchar.h (GNU): Section 5.4 [Copying Strings and Arrays], page 95.

wchar_t * wcpncpy (wchar_t *restrict wto, const wchar_t *restrict wfrom, size_t size)
    wchar.h (GNU): Section 5.6 [Truncating Strings while Copying], page 103.

size_t wcrtomb (char *restrict s, wchar_t wc, mbstate_t *restrict ps)
    wchar.h (ISO): Section 6.3.3 [Converting Single Characters], page 140.

int wcscasecmp (const wchar_t *ws1, const wchar_t *ws2)
    wchar.h (GNU): Section 5.7 [String/Array Comparison], page 107.

wchar_t * wcscat (wchar_t *restrict wto, const wchar_t *restrict wfrom)
    wchar.h (ISO): Section 5.5 [Concatenating Strings], page 100.

wchar_t * wcschr (const wchar_t *wstring, int wc)
    wchar.h (ISO): Section 5.9 [Search Functions], page 115.

wchar_t * wcschrnul (const wchar_t *wstring, wchar_t wc)
    wchar.h (GNU): Section 5.9 [Search Functions], page 115.

int wcscmp (const wchar_t *ws1, const wchar_t *ws2)
    wchar.h (ISO): Section 5.7 [String/Array Comparison], page 107.

int wcscoll (const wchar_t *ws1, const wchar_t *ws2)
    wchar.h (ISO): Section 5.8 [Collation Functions], page 111.

wchar_t * wcscpy (wchar_t *restrict wto, const wchar_t *restrict wfrom)
    wchar.h (ISO): Section 5.4 [Copying Strings and Arrays], page 95.

size_t wcscspn (const wchar_t *wstring, const wchar_t *stopset)
    wchar.h (ISO): Section 5.9 [Search Functions], page 115.

wchar_t * wcsdup (const wchar_t *ws)
    wchar.h (GNU): Section 5.4 [Copying Strings and Arrays], page 95.

size_t wcsftime (wchar_t *s, size_t size, const wchar_t *template, const struct tm *brokentime)
    time.h (ISO/Amend1): Section 21.4.5 [Formatting Calendar Time], page 632.

size_t wcslen (const wchar_t *ws)
    wchar.h (ISO): Section 5.3 [String Length], page 93.

int wcsncasecmp (const wchar_t *ws1, const wchar_t *s2, size_t n)
    wchar.h (GNU): Section 5.7 [String/Array Comparison], page 107.

wchar_t * wcsncat (wchar_t *restrict wto, const wchar_t *restrict wfrom, size_t size)
    wchar.h (ISO): Section 5.6 [Truncating Strings while Copying], page 103.

int wcsncmp (const wchar_t *ws1, const wchar_t *ws2, size_t size)
    wchar.h (ISO): Section 5.7 [String/Array Comparison], page 107.

wchar_t * wcsncpy (wchar_t *restrict wto, const wchar_t *restrict wfrom, size_t size)
    wchar.h (ISO): Section 5.6 [Truncating Strings while Copying], page 103.

size_t wcsnlen (const wchar_t *ws, size_t maxlen)
    wchar.h (GNU): Section 5.3 [String Length], page 93.

size_t wcsnrtombs (char *restrict dst, const wchar_t **restrict src, size_t nwc, size_t len,
mbstate_t *restrict ps)
    wchar.h (GNU): Section 6.3.4 [Converting Multibyte and Wide Character Strings], page 146.

wchar_t * wcspbrk (const wchar_t *wstring, const wchar_t *stopset)
        wchar.h (ISO): Section 5.9 [Search Functions], page 115.

wchar_t * wcsrchr (const wchar_t *wstring, wchar_t c)
        wchar.h (ISO): Section 5.9 [Search Functions], page 115.

size_t wcsrtombs (char *restrict dst, const wchar_t **restrict src, size_t len, mbstate_t *restrict ps)
        wchar.h (ISO): Section 6.3.4 [Converting Multibyte and Wide Character Strings], page 146.

size_t wcsspn (const wchar_t *wstring, const wchar_t *skipset)
        wchar.h (ISO): Section 5.9 [Search Functions], page 115.

wchar_t * wcsstr (const wchar_t *haystack, const wchar_t *needle)
        wchar.h (ISO): Section 5.9 [Search Functions], page 115.

double wcstod (const wchar_t *restrict string, wchar_t **restrict tailptr)
        wchar.h (ISO): Section 20.11.2 [Parsing of Floats], page 613.

float wcstof (const wchar_t *string, wchar_t **tailptr)
        wchar.h (ISO): Section 20.11.2 [Parsing of Floats], page 613.

_FloatN wcstofN (const wchar_t *string, wchar_t **tailptr)
        wchar.h (GNU): Section 20.11.2 [Parsing of Floats], page 613.

_FloatNx wcstofNx (const wchar_t *string, wchar_t **tailptr)
        wchar.h (GNU): Section 20.11.2 [Parsing of Floats], page 613.

intmax_t wcstoimax (const wchar_t *restrict string, wchar_t **restrict tailptr, int base)
        wchar.h (ISO): Section 20.11.1 [Parsing of Integers], page 608.

wchar_t * wcstok (wchar_t *newstring, const wchar_t *delimiters, wchar_t **save_ptr)
        wchar.h (ISO): Section 5.10 [Finding Tokens in a String], page 120.

long int wcstol (const wchar_t *restrict string, wchar_t **restrict tailptr, int base)
        wchar.h (ISO): Section 20.11.1 [Parsing of Integers], page 608.

long double wcstold (const wchar_t *string, wchar_t **tailptr)
        wchar.h (ISO): Section 20.11.2 [Parsing of Floats], page 613.

long long int wcstoll (const wchar_t *restrict string, wchar_t **restrict tailptr, int base)
        wchar.h (ISO): Section 20.11.1 [Parsing of Integers], page 608.

size_t wcstombs (char *string, const wchar_t *wstring, size_t size)
        stdlib.h (ISO): Section 6.4.2 [Non-reentrant Conversion of Strings], page 153.

long long int wcstoq (const wchar_t *restrict string, wchar_t **restrict tailptr, int base)
        wchar.h (GNU): Section 20.11.1 [Parsing of Integers], page 608.

unsigned long int wcstoul (const wchar_t *restrict string, wchar_t **restrict tailptr, int base)
        wchar.h (ISO): Section 20.11.1 [Parsing of Integers], page 608.

unsigned long long int wcstoull (const wchar_t *restrict string, wchar_t **restrict tailptr, int base)
        wchar.h (ISO): Section 20.11.1 [Parsing of Integers], page 608.

uintmax_t wcstoumax (const wchar_t *restrict string, wchar_t **restrict tailptr, int base)
        wchar.h (ISO): Section 20.11.1 [Parsing of Integers], page 608.

unsigned long long int wcstouq (const wchar_t *restrict string, wchar_t **restrict tailptr, int base)
        wchar.h (GNU): Section 20.11.1 [Parsing of Integers], page 608.

wchar_t * wcswcs (const wchar_t *haystack, const wchar_t *needle)
        wchar.h (XPG): Section 5.9 [Search Functions], page 115.

size_t wcsxfrm (wchar_t *restrict wto, const wchar_t *wfrom, size_t size)
        wchar.h (ISO): Section 5.8 [Collation Functions], page 111.

int wctob (wint_t c)

>   wchar.h (ISO): Section 6.3.3 [Converting Single Characters], page 140.

int wctomb (char *string, wchar_t wchar)

>   stdlib.h (ISO): Section 6.4.1 [Non-reentrant Conversion of Single Characters], page 151.

wctrans_t wctrans (const char *property)

>   wctype.h (ISO): Section 4.5 [Mapping of wide characters.], page 89.

wctrans_t

>   wctype.h (ISO): Section 4.5 [Mapping of wide characters.], page 89.

wctype_t wctype (const char *property)

>   wctype.h (ISO): Section 4.3 [Character class determination for wide characters], page 84.

wctype_t

>   wctype.h (ISO): Section 4.3 [Character class determination for wide characters], page 84.

wint_t

>   wchar.h (ISO): Section 6.1 [Introduction to Extended Characters], page 134.

wchar_t * wmemchr (const wchar_t *block, wchar_t wc, size_t size)

>   wchar.h (ISO): Section 5.9 [Search Functions], page 115.

int wmemcmp (const wchar_t *a1, const wchar_t *a2, size_t size)

>   wchar.h (ISO): Section 5.7 [String/Array Comparison], page 107.

wchar_t * wmemcpy (wchar_t *restrict wto, const wchar_t *restrict wfrom, size_t size)

>   wchar.h (ISO): Section 5.4 [Copying Strings and Arrays], page 95.

wchar_t * wmemmove (wchar_t *wto, const wchar_t *wfrom, size_t size)

>   wchar.h (ISO): Section 5.4 [Copying Strings and Arrays], page 95.

wchar_t * wmempcpy (wchar_t *restrict wto, const wchar_t *restrict wfrom, size_t size)

>   wchar.h (GNU): Section 5.4 [Copying Strings and Arrays], page 95.

wchar_t * wmemset (wchar_t *block, wchar_t wc, size_t size)

>   wchar.h (ISO): Section 5.4 [Copying Strings and Arrays], page 95.

int wordexp (const char *words, wordexp_t *word-vector-ptr, int flags)

>   wordexp.h (POSIX.2): Section 10.4.2 [Calling wordexp], page 246.

wordexp_t

>   wordexp.h (POSIX.2): Section 10.4.2 [Calling wordexp], page 246.

void wordfree (wordexp_t *word-vector-ptr)

>   wordexp.h (POSIX.2): Section 10.4.2 [Calling wordexp], page 246.

int wprintf (const wchar_t *template, ...)

>   wchar.h (ISO): Section 12.12.7 [Formatted Output Functions], page 287.

ssize_t write (int filedes, const void *buffer, size_t size)

>   unistd.h (POSIX.1): Section 13.2 [Input and Output Primitives], page 336.

ssize_t writev (int filedes, const struct iovec *vector, int count)

>   sys/uio.h (BSD): Section 13.6 [Fast Scatter-Gather I/O], page 349.

int wscanf (const wchar_t *template, ...)

>   wchar.h (ISO): Section 12.14.8 [Formatted Input Functions], page 309.

double y0 (double x)

>   math.h (SVID): Section 19.6 [Special Functions], page 539.

float y0f (float x)

>   math.h (SVID): Section 19.6 [Special Functions], page 539.

_FloatN y0fN (_FloatN x)

>   math.h (GNU): Section 19.6 [Special Functions], page 539.

`_FloatNx y0fNx (_FloatNx x)`
> `math.h` (GNU): Section 19.6 [Special Functions], page 539.

`long double y0l (long double x)`
> `math.h` (SVID): Section 19.6 [Special Functions], page 539.

`double y1 (double x)`
> `math.h` (SVID): Section 19.6 [Special Functions], page 539.

`float y1f (float x)`
> `math.h` (SVID): Section 19.6 [Special Functions], page 539.

`_FloatN y1fN (_FloatN x)`
> `math.h` (GNU): Section 19.6 [Special Functions], page 539.

`_FloatNx y1fNx (_FloatNx x)`
> `math.h` (GNU): Section 19.6 [Special Functions], page 539.

`long double y1l (long double x)`
> `math.h` (SVID): Section 19.6 [Special Functions], page 539.

`double yn (int n, double x)`
> `math.h` (SVID): Section 19.6 [Special Functions], page 539.

`float ynf (int n, float x)`
> `math.h` (SVID): Section 19.6 [Special Functions], page 539.

`_FloatN ynfN (int n, _FloatN x)`
> `math.h` (GNU): Section 19.6 [Special Functions], page 539.

`_FloatNx ynfNx (int n, _FloatNx x)`
> `math.h` (GNU): Section 19.6 [Special Functions], page 539.

`long double ynl (int n, long double x)`
> `math.h` (SVID): Section 19.6 [Special Functions], page 539.

Appendix C Installing the GNU C Library

Before you do anything else, you should read the FAQ at `http://sourceware.org/glibc/wiki/FAQ`. It answers common questions and describes problems you may experience with compilation and installation.

Features can be added to the GNU C Library via *add-on* bundles. These are separate tar files, which you unpack into the top level of the source tree. Then you give `configure` the '`--enable-add-ons`' option to activate them, and they will be compiled into the library.

You will need recent versions of several GNU tools: definitely GCC and GNU Make, and possibly others. See Section C.3 [Recommended Tools for Compilation], page 1049, below.

C.1 Configuring and compiling the GNU C Library

The GNU C Library cannot be compiled in the source directory. You must build it in a separate build directory. For example, if you have unpacked the GNU C Library sources in `/src/gnu/glibc-version`, create a directory `/src/gnu/glibc-build` to put the object files in. This allows removing the whole build directory in case an error occurs, which is the safest way to get a fresh start and should always be done.

From your object directory, run the shell script `configure` located at the top level of the source tree. In the scenario above, you'd type

```
$ ../glibc-version/configure args...
```

Please note that even though you're building in a separate build directory, the compilation may need to create or modify files and directories in the source directory.

`configure` takes many options, but the only one that is usually mandatory is '`--prefix`'. This option tells `configure` where you want the GNU C Library installed. This defaults to `/usr/local`, but the normal setting to install as the standard system library is '`--prefix=/usr`' for GNU/Linux systems and '`--prefix=`' (an empty prefix) for GNU/Hurd systems.

It may also be useful to set the *CC* and *CFLAGS* variables in the environment when running `configure`. *CC* selects the C compiler that will be used, and *CFLAGS* sets optimization options for the compiler.

The following list describes all of the available options for `configure`:

'`--prefix=directory`'

> Install machine-independent data files in subdirectories of *directory*. The default is to install in `/usr/local`.

'`--exec-prefix=directory`'

> Install the library and other machine-dependent files in subdirectories of *directory*. The default is to the '`--prefix`' directory if that option is specified, or `/usr/local` otherwise.

'`--with-headers=directory`'

> Look for kernel header files in *directory*, not `/usr/include`. The GNU C Library needs information from the kernel's header files describing the interface to the kernel. The GNU C Library will normally look in `/usr/include` for them, but if you specify this option, it will look in *DIRECTORY* instead.

This option is primarily of use on a system where the headers in `/usr/include` come from an older version of the GNU C Library. Conflicts can occasionally happen in this case. You can also use this option if you want to compile the GNU C Library with a newer set of kernel headers than the ones found in `/usr/include`.

‘`--enable-add-ons[=list]`’
> Specify add-on packages to include in the build. If this option is specified with no list, it enables all the add-on packages it finds in the main source directory; this is the default behavior. You may specify an explicit list of add-ons to use in *list*, separated by spaces or commas (if you use spaces, remember to quote them from the shell). Each add-on in *list* can be an absolute directory name or can be a directory name relative to the main source directory, or relative to the build directory (that is, the current working directory). For example, ‘`--enable-add-ons=nptl,../glibc-libidn-version`’.

‘`--enable-kernel=version`’
> This option is currently only useful on GNU/Linux systems. The *version* parameter should have the form X.Y.Z and describes the smallest version of the Linux kernel the generated library is expected to support. The higher the *version* number is, the less compatibility code is added, and the faster the code gets.

‘`--with-binutils=directory`’
> Use the binutils (assembler and linker) in `directory`, not the ones the C compiler would default to. You can use this option if the default binutils on your system cannot deal with all the constructs in the GNU C Library. In that case, `configure` will detect the problem and suppress these constructs, so that the library will still be usable, but functionality may be lost—for example, you can't build a shared libc with old binutils.

‘`--without-fp`’
> Use this option if your computer lacks hardware floating-point support and your operating system does not emulate an FPU.

‘`--disable-shared`’
> Don't build shared libraries even if it is possible. Not all systems support shared libraries; you need ELF support and (currently) the GNU linker.

‘`--disable-profile`’
> Don't build libraries with profiling information. You may want to use this option if you don't plan to do profiling.

‘`--enable-static-nss`’
> Compile static versions of the NSS (Name Service Switch) libraries. This is not recommended because it defeats the purpose of NSS; a program linked statically with the NSS libraries cannot be dynamically reconfigured to use a different name database.

'`--enable-hardcoded-path-in-tests`'

> By default, dynamic tests are linked to run with the installed C library. This option hardcodes the newly built C library path in dynamic tests so that they can be invoked directly.

'`--disable-timezone-tools`'

> By default, timezone related utilities (`zic`, `zdump`, and `tzselect`) are installed with the GNU C Library. If you are building these independently (e.g. by using the '`tzcode`' package), then this option will allow disabling the install of these.

> Note that you need to make sure the external tools are kept in sync with the versions that the GNU C Library expects as the data formats may change over time. Consult the `timezone` subdirectory for more details.

'`--enable-lock-elision=yes`'

> Enable lock elision for pthread mutexes by default.

'`--enable-stack-protector`'
'`--enable-stack-protector=strong`'
'`--enable-stack-protector=all`'

> Compile the C library and all other parts of the glibc package (including the threading and math libraries, NSS modules, and transliteration modules) using the GCC `-fstack-protector`, `-fstack-protector-strong` or `-fstack-protector-all` options to detect stack overruns. Only the dynamic linker and a small number of routines called directly from assembler are excluded from this protection.

'`--enable-bind-now`'

> Disable lazy binding for installed shared objects. This provides additional security hardening because it enables full RELRO and a read-only global offset table (GOT), at the cost of slightly increased program load times.

'`--enable-pt_chown`'

> The file `pt_chown` is a helper binary for `grantpt` (see Section 17.8.1 [Allocating Pseudo-Terminals], page 513) that is installed setuid root to fix up pseudo-terminal ownership. It is not built by default because systems using the Linux kernel are commonly built with the `devpts` filesystem enabled and mounted at `/dev/pts`, which manages pseudo-terminal ownership automatically. By using '`--enable-pt_chown`', you may build `pt_chown` and install it setuid and owned by `root`. The use of `pt_chown` introduces additional security risks to the system and you should enable it only if you understand and accept those risks.

'`--disable-werror`'

> By default, the GNU C Library is built with `-Werror`. If you wish to build without this option (for example, if building with a newer version of GCC than this version of the GNU C Library was tested with, so new warnings cause the build with `-Werror` to fail), you can configure with `--disable-werror`.

'`--disable-mathvec`'

> By default for x86_64, the GNU C Library is built with the vector math library. Use this option to disable the vector math library.

'`--enable-tunables`'

> Tunables support allows additional library parameters to be customized at runtime. This feature is enabled by default. This option can take the following values:

> yes   This is the default if no option is passed to configure. This enables tunables and selects the default frontend (currently '`valstring`').

> no   This option disables tunables.

> valstring

> > This enables tunables and selects the '`valstring`' frontend for tunables. This frontend allows users to specify tunables as a colon-separated list in a single environment variable `GLIBC_TUNABLES`.

'`--enable-obsolete-nsl`'

> By default, libnsl is only built as shared library for backward compatibility and the NSS modules libnss_compat, libnss_nis and libnss_nisplus are not built at all. Use this option to enable libnsl with all depending NSS modules and header files.

'`--disable-experimental-malloc`'

> By default, a per-thread cache is enabled in `malloc`. While this cache can be disabled on a per-application basis using tunables (set glibc.malloc.tcache_count to zero), this option can be used to remove it from the build completely.

'`--build=build-system`'
'`--host=host-system`'

> These options are for cross-compiling. If you specify both options and *build-system* is different from *host-system*, `configure` will prepare to cross-compile the GNU C Library from *build-system* to be used on *host-system*. You'll probably need the '`--with-headers`' option too, and you may have to override *configure*'s selection of the compiler and/or binutils.

> If you only specify '`--host`', `configure` will prepare for a native compile but use what you specify instead of guessing what your system is. This is most useful to change the CPU submodel. For example, if `configure` guesses your machine as `i686-pc-linux-gnu` but you want to compile a library for 586es, give '`--host=i586-pc-linux-gnu`' or just '`--host=i586-linux`' and add the appropriate compiler flags ('`-mcpu=i586`' will do the trick) to *CFLAGS*.

> If you specify just '`--build`', `configure` will get confused.

'`--with-pkgversion=version`'

> Specify a description, possibly including a build number or build date, of the binaries being built, to be included in `--version` output from programs installed with the GNU C Library. For example, `--with-pkgversion='FooBar GNU/Linux glibc build 123'`. The default value is '`GNU libc`'.

'`--with-bugurl=url`'

> Specify the URL that users should visit if they wish to report a bug, to be included in `--help` output from programs installed with the GNU C Library. The default value refers to the main bug-reporting information for the GNU C Library.

To build the library and related programs, type `make`. This will produce a lot of output, some of which may look like errors from `make` but aren't. Look for error messages from `make` containing '***'. Those indicate that something is seriously wrong.

The compilation process can take a long time, depending on the configuration and the speed of your machine. Some complex modules may take a very long time to compile, as much as several minutes on slower machines. Do not panic if the compiler appears to hang.

If you want to run a parallel make, simply pass the '`-j`' option with an appropriate numeric parameter to `make`. You need a recent GNU `make` version, though.

To build and run test programs which exercise some of the library facilities, type `make check`. If it does not complete successfully, do not use the built library, and report a bug after verifying that the problem is not already known. See Section C.5 [Reporting Bugs], page 1051, for instructions on reporting bugs. Note that some of the tests assume they are not being run by `root`. We recommend you compile and test the GNU C Library as an unprivileged user.

Before reporting bugs make sure there is no problem with your system. The tests (and later installation) use some pre-existing files of the system such as `/etc/passwd`, `/etc/nsswitch.conf` and others. These files must all contain correct and sensible content.

Normally, `make check` will run all the tests before reporting all problems found and exiting with error status if any problems occurred. You can specify '`stop-on-test-failure=y`' when running `make check` to make the test run stop and exit with an error status immediately when a failure occurs.

The GNU C Library pretty printers come with their own set of scripts for testing, which run together with the rest of the testsuite through `make check`. These scripts require the following tools to run successfully:

- Python 2.7.6/3.4.3 or later

  Python is required for running the printers' test scripts.

- PExpect 4.0

  The printer tests drive GDB through test programs and compare its output to the printers'. PExpect is used to capture the output of GDB, and should be compatible with the Python version in your system.

- GDB 7.8 or later with support for Python 2.7.6/3.4.3 or later

  GDB itself needs to be configured with Python support in order to use the pretty printers. Notice that your system having Python available doesn't imply that GDB supports it, nor that your system's Python and GDB's have the same version.

If these tools are absent, the printer tests will report themselves as `UNSUPPORTED`. Notice that some of the printer tests require the GNU C Library to be compiled with debugging symbols.

To format the *GNU C Library Reference Manual* for printing, type `make dvi`. You need a working TEX installation to do this. The distribution builds the on-line formatted version of the manual, as Info files, as part of the build process. You can build them manually with `make info`.

The library has a number of special-purpose configuration parameters which you can find in `Makeconfig`. These can be overwritten with the file `configparms`. To change them, create a `configparms` in your build directory and add values as appropriate for your system. The file is included and parsed by `make` and has to follow the conventions for makefiles.

It is easy to configure the GNU C Library for cross-compilation by setting a few variables in `configparms`. Set `CC` to the cross-compiler for the target you configured the library for; it is important to use this same `CC` value when running `configure`, like this: '`CC=target-gcc configure target`'. Set `BUILD_CC` to the compiler to use for programs run on the build system as part of compiling the library. You may need to set `AR` to cross-compiling versions of `ar` if the native tools are not configured to work with object files for the target you configured for. When cross-compiling the GNU C Library, it may be tested using '`make check test-wrapper="srcdir/scripts/cross-test-ssh.sh hostname"`', where *srcdir* is the absolute directory name for the main source directory and *hostname* is the host name of a system that can run the newly built binaries of the GNU C Library. The source and build directories must be visible at the same locations on both the build system and *hostname*.

In general, when testing the GNU C Library, '`test-wrapper`' may be set to the name and arguments of any program to run newly built binaries. This program must preserve the arguments to the binary being run, its working directory and the standard input, output and error file descriptors. If '`test-wrapper env`' will not work to run a program with environment variables set, then '`test-wrapper-env`' must be set to a program that runs a newly built program with environment variable assignments in effect, those assignments being specified as '`var=value`' before the name of the program to be run. If multiple assignments to the same variable are specified, the last assignment specified must take precedence. Similarly, if '`test-wrapper env -i`' will not work to run a program with an environment completely empty of variables except those directly assigned, then '`test-wrapper-env-only`' must be set; its use has the same syntax as '`test-wrapper-env`', the only difference in its semantics being starting with an empty set of environment variables rather than the ambient set.

C.2 Installing the C Library

To install the library and its header files, and the Info files of the manual, type `make install`. This will build things, if necessary, before installing them; however, you should still compile everything first. If you are installing the GNU C Library as your primary C library, we recommend that you shut the system down to single-user mode first, and reboot afterward. This minimizes the risk of breaking things when the library changes out from underneath.

'`make install`' will do the entire job of upgrading from a previous installation of the GNU C Library version 2.x. There may sometimes be headers left behind from the previous installation, but those are generally harmless. If you want to avoid leaving headers behind you can do things in the following order.

You must first build the library ('`make`'), optionally check it ('`make check`'), switch the include directories and then install ('`make install`'). The steps must be done in this order. Not moving the directory before install will result in an unusable mixture of header files from both libraries, but configuring, building, and checking the library requires the ability to compile and run programs against the old library. The new `/usr/include`, after switching the include directories and before installing the library should contain the Linux headers, but nothing else. If you do this, you will need to restore any headers from libraries other than the GNU C Library yourself after installing the library.

You can install the GNU C Library somewhere other than where you configured it to go by setting the `DESTDIR` GNU standard make variable on the command line for 'make install'. The value of this variable is prepended to all the paths for installation. This is useful when setting up a chroot environment or preparing a binary distribution. The directory should be specified with an absolute file name. Installing with the `prefix` and `exec_prefix` GNU standard make variables set is not supported.

The GNU C Library includes a daemon called `nscd`, which you may or may not want to run. `nscd` caches name service lookups; it can dramatically improve performance with NIS+, and may help with DNS as well.

One auxiliary program, `/usr/libexec/pt_chown`, is installed setuid `root` if the '--enable-pt_chown' configuration option is used. This program is invoked by the `grantpt` function; it sets the permissions on a pseudoterminal so it can be used by the calling process. If you are using a Linux kernel with the `devpts` filesystem enabled and mounted at `/dev/pts`, you don't need this program.

After installation you might want to configure the timezone and locale installation of your system. The GNU C Library comes with a locale database which gets configured with `localedef`. For example, to set up a German locale with name `de_DE`, simply issue the command 'localedef -i de_DE -f ISO-8859-1 de_DE'. To configure all locales that are supported by the GNU C Library, you can issue from your build directory the command 'make localedata/install-locales'.

To configure the locally used timezone, set the `TZ` environment variable. The script `tzselect` helps you to select the right value. As an example, for Germany, `tzselect` would tell you to use 'TZ='Europe/Berlin''. For a system wide installation (the given paths are for an installation with '--prefix=/usr'), link the timezone file which is in `/usr/share/zoneinfo` to the file `/etc/localtime`. For Germany, you might execute 'ln -s /usr/share/zoneinfo/Europe/Berlin /etc/localtime'.

C.3 Recommended Tools for Compilation

We recommend installing the following GNU tools before attempting to build the GNU C Library:

- GNU `make` 3.79 or newer

  You need the latest version of GNU `make`. Modifying the GNU C Library to work with other `make` programs would be so difficult that we recommend you port GNU `make` instead. **Really.** We recommend GNU `make` version 3.79. All earlier versions have severe bugs or lack features.

- GCC 4.9 or newer

  GCC 4.9 or higher is required. In general it is recommended to use the newest version of the compiler that is known to work for building the GNU C Library, as newer compilers usually produce better code. As of release time, GCC 7.1 is the newest compiler verified to work to build the GNU C Library.

For PowerPC 64-bits little-endian (powerpc64le), GCC 6.2 or higher is required. This compiler version is the first to provide the features required for building the GNU C Library with support for `_Float128`. .

For multi-arch support it is recommended to use a GCC which has been built with support for GNU indirect functions. This ensures that correct debugging information is generated for functions selected by IFUNC resolvers. This support can either be enabled by configuring GCC with '`--enable-gnu-indirect-function`', or by enabling it by default by setting '`default_gnu_indirect_function`' variable for a particular architecture in the GCC source file `gcc/config.gcc`.

You can use whatever compiler you like to compile programs that use the GNU C Library.

Check the FAQ for any special compiler issues on particular platforms.

- GNU `binutils` 2.25 or later

  You must use GNU `binutils` (as and ld) to build the GNU C Library. No other assembler or linker has the necessary functionality at the moment. As of release time, GNU `binutils` 2.27 is the newest verified to work to build the GNU C Library.

- GNU `texinfo` 4.7 or later

  To correctly translate and install the Texinfo documentation you need this version of the `texinfo` package. Earlier versions do not understand all the tags used in the document, and the installation mechanism for the info files is not present or works differently. As of release time, `texinfo` 6.0 is the newest verified to work to build the GNU C Library.

- GNU `awk` 3.1.2, or higher

  `awk` is used in several places to generate files. Some `gawk` extensions are used, including the `asorti` function, which was introduced in version 3.1.2 of `gawk`. As of release time, `gawk` version 4.1.3 is the newest verified to work to build the GNU C Library.

- Perl 5

  Perl is not required, but it is used if present to test the installation. We may decide to use it elsewhere in the future.

- GNU `sed` 3.02 or newer

  `Sed` is used in several places to generate files. Most scripts work with any version of `sed`. As of release time, `sed` version 4.2.2 is the newest verified to work to build the GNU C Library.

If you change any of the `configure.ac` files you will also need

- GNU `autoconf` 2.69 (exactly)

and if you change any of the message translation files you will need

- GNU `gettext` 0.10.36 or later

If you wish to regenerate the `yacc` parser code in the `intl` subdirectory you will need

- GNU `bison` 2.7 or later

You may also need these packages if you upgrade your source tree using patches, although we try to avoid this.

C.4 Specific advice for GNU/Linux systems

If you are installing the GNU C Library on GNU/Linux systems, you need to have the header files from a 3.2 or newer kernel around for reference. (For the ia64 architecture, you need version 3.2.18 or newer because this is the first version with support for the `accept4` system call.) These headers must be installed using 'make headers_install'; the headers present in the kernel source directory are not suitable for direct use by the GNU C Library. You do not need to use that kernel, just have its headers installed where the GNU C Library can access them, referred to here as *install-directory*. The easiest way to do this is to unpack it in a directory such as `/usr/src/linux-version`. In that directory, run 'make headers_install INSTALL_HDR_PATH=*install-directory*'. Finally, configure the GNU C Library with the option '--with-headers=*install-directory*/include'. Use the most recent kernel you can get your hands on. (If you are cross-compiling the GNU C Library, you need to specify 'ARCH=*architecture*' in the 'make headers_install' command, where *architecture* is the architecture name used by the Linux kernel, such as 'x86' or 'powerpc'.)

After installing the GNU C Library, you may need to remove or rename directories such as `/usr/include/linux` and `/usr/include/asm`, and replace them with copies of directories such as `linux` and `asm` from *install-directory*/include. All directories present in *install-directory*/include should be copied, except that the GNU C Library provides its own version of `/usr/include/scsi`; the files provided by the kernel should be copied without replacing those provided by the GNU C Library. The `linux`, `asm` and `asm-generic` directories are required to compile programs using the GNU C Library; the other directories describe interfaces to the kernel but are not required if not compiling programs using those interfaces. You do not need to copy kernel headers if you did not specify an alternate kernel header source using '--with-headers'.

The Filesystem Hierarchy Standard for GNU/Linux systems expects some components of the GNU C Library installation to be in `/lib` and some in `/usr/lib`. This is handled automatically if you configure the GNU C Library with '--prefix=/usr'. If you set some other prefix or allow it to default to `/usr/local`, then all the components are installed there.

C.5 Reporting Bugs

There are probably bugs in the GNU C Library. There are certainly errors and omissions in this manual. If you report them, they will get fixed. If you don't, no one will ever know about them and they will remain unfixed for all eternity, if not longer.

It is a good idea to verify that the problem has not already been reported. Bugs are documented in two places: The file `BUGS` describes a number of well known bugs and the central GNU C Library bug tracking system has a WWW interface at `http://sourceware.org/bugzilla/`. The WWW interface gives you access to open and closed reports. A closed report normally includes a patch or a hint on solving the problem.

To report a bug, first you must find it. With any luck, this will be the hard part. Once you've found a bug, make sure it's really a bug. A good way to do this is to see if the GNU C Library behaves the same way some other C library does. If so, probably you are wrong and the libraries are right (but not necessarily). If not, one of the libraries is probably wrong. It might not be the GNU C Library. Many historical Unix C libraries permit things that we don't, such as closing a file twice.

If you think you have found some way in which the GNU C Library does not conform to the ISO and POSIX standards (see Section 1.2 [Standards and Portability], page 1), that is definitely a bug. Report it!

Once you're sure you've found a bug, try to narrow it down to the smallest test case that reproduces the problem. In the case of a C library, you really only need to narrow it down to one library function call, if possible. This should not be too difficult.

The final step when you have a simple test case is to report the bug. Do this at `http://www.gnu.org/software/libc/bugs.html`.

If you are not sure how a function should behave, and this manual doesn't tell you, that's a bug in the manual. Report that too! If the function's behavior disagrees with the manual, then either the library or the manual has a bug, so report the disagreement. If you find any errors or omissions in this manual, please report them to the bug database. If you refer to specific sections of the manual, please include the section names for easier identification.

Appendix D Library Maintenance

D.1 Adding New Functions

The process of building the library is driven by the makefiles, which make heavy use of special features of GNU `make`. The makefiles are very complex, and you probably don't want to try to understand them. But what they do is fairly straightforward, and only requires that you define a few variables in the right places.

The library sources are divided into subdirectories, grouped by topic.

The `string` subdirectory has all the string-manipulation functions, `math` has all the mathematical functions, etc.

Each subdirectory contains a simple makefile, called `Makefile`, which defines a few `make` variables and then includes the global makefile `Rules` with a line like:

```
include ../Rules
```

The basic variables that a subdirectory makefile defines are:

`subdir`   The name of the subdirectory, for example `stdio`. This variable **must** be defined.

`headers`   The names of the header files in this section of the library, such as `stdio.h`.

`routines`
`aux`   The names of the modules (source files) in this section of the library. These should be simple names, such as 'strlen' (rather than complete file names, such as `strlen.c`). Use `routines` for modules that define functions in the library, and `aux` for auxiliary modules containing things like data definitions. But the values of `routines` and `aux` are just concatenated, so there really is no practical difference.

`tests`   The names of test programs for this section of the library. These should be simple names, such as 'tester' (rather than complete file names, such as `tester.c`). 'make tests' will build and run all the test programs. If a test program needs input, put the test data in a file called *test-program*.input; it will be given to the test program on its standard input. If a test program wants to be run with arguments, put the arguments (all on a single line) in a file called *test-program*.args. Test programs should exit with zero status when the test passes, and nonzero status when the test indicates a bug in the library or error in building.

`others`   The names of "other" programs associated with this section of the library. These are programs which are not tests per se, but are other small programs included with the library. They are built by 'make others'.

`install-lib`
`install-data`
`install`   Files to be installed by 'make install'. Files listed in 'install-lib' are installed in the directory specified by 'libdir' in `configparms` or `Makeconfig` (see Appendix C [Installing the GNU C Library], page 1043). Files listed in `install-data` are installed in the directory specified by 'datadir' in

configparms or Makeconfig. Files listed in **install** are installed in the directory specified by 'bindir' in configparms or Makeconfig.

distribute

> Other files from this subdirectory which should be put into a distribution tar file. You need not list here the makefile itself or the source and header files listed in the other standard variables. Only define **distribute** if there are files used in an unusual way that should go into the distribution.

generated

> Files which are generated by **Makefile** in this subdirectory. These files will be removed by '**make clean**', and they will never go into a distribution.

extra-objs

> Extra object files which are built by **Makefile** in this subdirectory. This should be a list of file names like **foo.o**; the files will actually be found in whatever directory object files are being built in. These files will be removed by '**make clean**'. This variable is used for secondary object files needed to build **others** or **tests**.

D.1.1 Platform-specific types, macros and functions

It's sometimes necessary to provide nonstandard, platform-specific features to developers. The C library is traditionally the lowest library layer, so it makes sense for it to provide these low-level features. However, including these features in the C library may be a disadvantage if another package provides them as well as there will be two conflicting versions of them. Also, the features won't be available to projects that do not use the GNU C Library but use other GNU tools, like GCC.

The current guidelines are:

- If the header file provides features that only make sense on a particular machine architecture and have nothing to do with an operating system, then the features should ultimately be provided as GCC built-in functions. Until then, the GNU C Library may provide them in the header file. When the GCC built-in functions become available, those provided in the header file should be made conditionally available prior to the GCC version in which the built-in function was made available.

- If the header file provides features that are specific to an operating system, both GCC and the GNU C Library could provide it, but the GNU C Library is preferred as it already has a lot of information about the operating system.

- If the header file provides features that are specific to an operating system but used by the GNU C Library, then the GNU C Library should provide them.

The general solution for providing low-level features is to export them as follows:

- A nonstandard, low-level header file that defines macros and inline functions should be called **sys/platform/*name*.h**.

- Each header file's name should include the platform name, to avoid users thinking there is anything in common between the different header files for different platforms. For example, a **sys/platform/*arch*.h** name such as **sys/platform/ppc.h** is better than **sys/platform.h**.

- A platform-specific header file provided by the GNU C Library should coordinate with GCC such that compiler built-in versions of the functions and macros are preferred if available. This means that user programs will only ever need to include sys/platform/arch.h, keeping the same names of types, macros, and functions for convenience and portability.

- Each included symbol must have the prefix __arch_, such as __ppc_get_timebase.

The easiest way to provide a header file is to add it to the sysdep_headers variable. For example, the combination of Linux-specific header files on PowerPC could be provided like this:

```
sysdep_headers += sys/platform/ppc.h
```

Then ensure that you have added a sys/platform/ppc.h header file in the machine-specific directory, e.g., sysdeps/powerpc/sys/platform/ppc.h.

D.2 Porting the GNU C Library

The GNU C Library is written to be easily portable to a variety of machines and operating systems. Machine- and operating system-dependent functions are well separated to make it easy to add implementations for new machines or operating systems. This section describes the layout of the library source tree and explains the mechanisms used to select machine-dependent code to use.

All the machine-dependent and operating system-dependent files in the library are in the subdirectory sysdeps under the top-level library source directory. This directory contains a hierarchy of subdirectories (see Section D.2.1 [Layout of the sysdeps Directory Hierarchy], page 1057).

Each subdirectory of sysdeps contains source files for a particular machine or operating system, or for a class of machine or operating system (for example, systems by a particular vendor, or all machines that use IEEE 754 floating-point format). A configuration specifies an ordered list of these subdirectories. Each subdirectory implicitly appends its parent directory to the list. For example, specifying the list unix/bsd/vax is equivalent to specifying the list unix/bsd/vax unix/bsd unix. A subdirectory can also specify that it implies other subdirectories which are not directly above it in the directory hierarchy. If the file Implies exists in a subdirectory, it lists other subdirectories of sysdeps which are appended to the list, appearing after the subdirectory containing the Implies file. Lines in an Implies file that begin with a '#' character are ignored as comments. For example, unix/bsd/Implies contains:

```
# BSD has Internet-related things.
unix/inet
```

and unix/Implies contains:

```
posix
```

So the final list is unix/bsd/vax unix/bsd unix/inet unix posix.

sysdeps has a "special" subdirectory called generic. It is always implicitly appended to the list of subdirectories, so you needn't put it in an Implies file, and you should not create any subdirectories under it intended to be new specific categories. generic serves two purposes. First, the makefiles do not bother to look for a system-dependent version of a file that's not in generic. This means that any system-dependent source file must have an analogue in generic, even if the routines defined by that file are not implemented on other platforms. Second, the `generic` version of a system-dependent file is used if the makefiles do not find a version specific to the system you're compiling for.

If it is possible to implement the routines in a `generic` file in machine-independent C, using only other machine-independent functions in the C library, then you should do so. Otherwise, make them stubs. A *stub* function is a function which cannot be implemented on a particular machine or operating system. Stub functions always return an error, and set `errno` to `ENOSYS` (Function not implemented). See Chapter 2 [Error Reporting], page 22. If you define a stub function, you must place the statement `stub_warning(function)`, where *function* is the name of your function, after its definition. This causes the function to be listed in the installed `<gnu/stubs.h>`, and makes GNU ld warn when the function is used.

Some rare functions are only useful on specific systems and aren't defined at all on others; these do not appear anywhere in the system-independent source code or makefiles (including the `generic` directory), only in the system-dependent `Makefile` in the specific system's subdirectory.

If you come across a file that is in one of the main source directories (`string`, `stdio`, etc.), and you want to write a machine- or operating system-dependent version of it, move the file into `sysdeps/generic` and write your new implementation in the appropriate system-specific subdirectory. Note that if a file is to be system-dependent, it **must not** appear in one of the main source directories.

There are a few special files that may exist in each subdirectory of `sysdeps`:

`Makefile`

> A makefile for this machine or operating system, or class of machine or operating system. This file is included by the library makefile `Makerules`, which is used by the top-level makefile and the subdirectory makefiles. It can change the variables set in the including makefile or add new rules. It can use GNU `make` conditional directives based on the variable '`subdir`' (see above) to select different sets of variables and rules for different sections of the library. It can also set the `make` variable '`sysdep-routines`', to specify extra modules to be included in the library. You should use '`sysdep-routines`' rather than adding modules to '`routines`' because the latter is used in determining what to distribute for each subdirectory of the main source tree.
>
> Each makefile in a subdirectory in the ordered list of subdirectories to be searched is included in order. Since several system-dependent makefiles may be included, each should append to '`sysdep-routines`' rather than simply setting it:
>
> ```
> sysdep-routines := $(sysdep-routines) foo bar
> ```

`Subdirs`

> This file contains the names of new whole subdirectories under the top-level library source tree that should be included for this system. These subdirectories are treated just like the system-independent subdirectories in the library source tree, such as `stdio` and `math`.
>
> Use this when there are completely new sets of functions and header files that should go into the library for the system this subdirectory of `sysdeps` implements. For example, `sysdeps/unix/inet/Subdirs` contains `inet`; the `inet`

directory contains various network-oriented operations which only make sense to put in the library on systems that support the Internet.

configure

> This file is a shell script fragment to be run at configuration time. The top-level `configure` script uses the shell . command to read the `configure` file in each system-dependent directory chosen, in order. The `configure` files are often generated from `configure.ac` files using Autoconf.
>
> A system-dependent `configure` script will usually add things to the shell variables 'DEFS' and 'config_vars'; see the top-level `configure` script for details. The script can check for '--with-*package*' options that were passed to the top-level `configure`. For an option '--with-*package*=*value*' configure sets the shell variable 'with_*package*' (with any dashes in *package* converted to underscores) to *value*; if the option is just '--with-*package*' (no argument), then it sets 'with_*package*' to 'yes'.

configure.ac

> This file is an Autoconf input fragment to be processed into the file `configure` in this subdirectory. See Section "Introduction" in *Autoconf: Generating Automatic Configuration Scripts*, for a description of Autoconf. You should write either `configure` or `configure.ac`, but not both. The first line of `configure.ac` should invoke the m4 macro 'GLIBC_PROVIDES'. This macro does several AC_PROVIDE calls for Autoconf macros which are used by the top-level `configure` script; without this, those macros might be invoked again unnecessarily by Autoconf.

That is the general system for how system-dependencies are isolated. The next section explains how to decide what directories in **sysdeps** to use. Section D.2.2 [Porting the GNU C Library to Unix Systems], page 1059, has some tips on porting the library to Unix variants.

D.2.1 Layout of the sysdeps Directory Hierarchy

A GNU configuration name has three parts: the CPU type, the manufacturer's name, and the operating system. `configure` uses these to pick the list of system-dependent directories to look for. If the '--nfp' option is *not* passed to `configure`, the directory *machine*/fpu is also used. The operating system often has a *base operating system*; for example, if the operating system is 'Linux', the base operating system is 'unix/sysv'. The algorithm used to pick the list of directories is simple: `configure` makes a list of the base operating system, manufacturer, CPU type, and operating system, in that order. It then concatenates all these together with slashes in between, to produce a directory name; for example, the configuration 'i686-linux-gnu' results in unix/sysv/linux/i386/i686. `configure` then tries removing each element of the list in turn, so unix/sysv/linux and unix/sysv are also tried, among others. Since the precise version number of the operating system is often not important, and it would be very inconvenient, for example, to have identical irix6.2 and irix6.3 directories, `configure` tries successively less specific operating system names by removing trailing suffixes starting with a period.

As an example, here is the complete list of directories that would be tried for the configuration 'i686-linux-gnu' (with the **crypt** and **linuxthreads** add-on):

```
sysdeps/i386/elf
crypt/sysdeps/unix
linuxthreads/sysdeps/unix/sysv/linux
linuxthreads/sysdeps/pthread
linuxthreads/sysdeps/unix/sysv
linuxthreads/sysdeps/unix
linuxthreads/sysdeps/i386/i686
linuxthreads/sysdeps/i386
linuxthreads/sysdeps/pthread/no-cmpxchg
sysdeps/unix/sysv/linux/i386
sysdeps/unix/sysv/linux
sysdeps/gnu
sysdeps/unix/common
sysdeps/unix/mman
sysdeps/unix/inet
sysdeps/unix/sysv/i386/i686
sysdeps/unix/sysv/i386
sysdeps/unix/sysv
sysdeps/unix/i386
sysdeps/unix
sysdeps/posix
sysdeps/i386/i686
sysdeps/i386/i486
sysdeps/libm-i387/i686
sysdeps/i386/fpu
sysdeps/libm-i387
sysdeps/i386
sysdeps/wordsize-32
sysdeps/ieee754
sysdeps/libm-ieee754
sysdeps/generic
```

Different machine architectures are conventionally subdirectories at the top level of the sysdeps directory tree. For example, sysdeps/sparc and sysdeps/m68k. These contain files specific to those machine architectures, but not specific to any particular operating system. There might be subdirectories for specializations of those architectures, such as sysdeps/m68k/68020. Code which is specific to the floating-point coprocessor used with a particular machine should go in sysdeps/*machine*/fpu.

There are a few directories at the top level of the sysdeps hierarchy that are not for particular machine architectures.

generic   As described above (see Section D.2 [Porting the GNU C Library], page 1055), this is the subdirectory that every configuration implicitly uses after all others.

ieee754   This directory is for code using the IEEE 754 floating-point format, where the C type float is IEEE 754 single-precision format, and double is IEEE 754 double-precision format. Usually this directory is referred to in the Implies file in a machine architecture-specific directory, such as m68k/Implies.

libm-ieee754
           This directory contains an implementation of a mathematical library usable on platforms which use IEEE 754 conformant floating-point arithmetic.

libm-i387
           This is a special case. Ideally the code should be in sysdeps/i386/fpu but for various reasons it is kept aside.

posix   This directory contains implementations of things in the library in terms of POSIX.1 functions. This includes some of the POSIX.1 functions themselves. Of course, POSIX.1 cannot be completely implemented in terms of itself, so a configuration using just `posix` cannot be complete.

unix   This is the directory for Unix-like things. See Section D.2.2 [Porting the GNU C Library to Unix Systems], page 1059. `unix` implies `posix`. There are some special-purpose subdirectories of `unix`:

unix/common

        This directory is for things common to both BSD and System V release 4. Both `unix/bsd` and `unix/sysv/sysv4` imply `unix/common`.

unix/inet

        This directory is for `socket` and related functions on Unix systems. `unix/inet/Subdirs` enables the `inet` top-level subdirectory. `unix/common` implies `unix/inet`.

mach   This is the directory for things based on the Mach microkernel from CMU (including GNU/Hurd systems). Other basic operating systems (VMS, for example) would have their own directories at the top level of the `sysdeps` hierarchy, parallel to `unix` and `mach`.

D.2.2 Porting the GNU C Library to Unix Systems

Most Unix systems are fundamentally very similar. There are variations between different machines, and variations in what facilities are provided by the kernel. But the interface to the operating system facilities is, for the most part, pretty uniform and simple.

The code for Unix systems is in the directory `unix`, at the top level of the `sysdeps` hierarchy. This directory contains subdirectories (and subdirectory trees) for various Unix variants.

The functions which are system calls in most Unix systems are implemented in assembly code, which is generated automatically from specifications in files named `syscalls.list`. There are several such files, one in `sysdeps/unix` and others in its subdirectories. Some special system calls are implemented in files that are named with a suffix of '`.S`'; for example, `_exit.S`. Files ending in '`.S`' are run through the C preprocessor before being fed to the assembler.

These files all use a set of macros that should be defined in `sysdep.h`. The `sysdep.h` file in `sysdeps/unix` partially defines them; a `sysdep.h` file in another directory must finish defining them for the particular machine and operating system variant. See `sysdeps/unix/sysdep.h` and the machine-specific `sysdep.h` implementations to see what these macros are and what they should do.

The system-specific makefile for the `unix` directory (`sysdeps/unix/Makefile`) gives rules to generate several files from the Unix system you are building the library on (which is assumed to be the target system you are building the library *for*). All the generated files are put in the directory where the object files are kept; they should not affect the source tree itself. The files generated are `ioctls.h`, `errnos.h`, `sys/param.h`, and `errlist.c` (for the `stdio` section of the library).

Appendix E Platform-specific facilities

The GNU C Library can provide machine-specific functionality.

E.1 PowerPC-specific Facilities

Facilities specific to PowerPC that are not specific to a particular operating system are declared in `sys/platform/ppc.h`.

`uint64_t __ppc_get_timebase` (*void*)   [Function]
    Preliminary: | MT-Safe | AS-Safe | AC-Safe | See Section 1.2.2.1 [POSIX Safety Concepts], page 2.

    Read the current value of the Time Base Register.

    The *Time Base Register* is a 64-bit register that stores a monotonically incremented value updated at a system-dependent frequency that may be different from the processor frequency. More information is available in *Power ISA 2.06b - Book II - Section 5.2*.

    `__ppc_get_timebase` uses the processor's time base facility directly without requiring assistance from the operating system, so it is very efficient.

`uint64_t __ppc_get_timebase_freq` (*void*)   [Function]
    Preliminary: | MT-Unsafe init | AS-Unsafe corrupt:init | AC-Unsafe corrupt:init | See Section 1.2.2.1 [POSIX Safety Concepts], page 2.

    Read the current frequency at which the Time Base Register is updated.

    This frequency is not related to the processor clock or the bus clock. It is also possible that this frequency is not constant. More information is available in *Power ISA 2.06b - Book II - Section 5.2*.

The following functions provide hints about the usage of resources that are shared with other processors. They can be used, for example, if a program waiting on a lock intends to divert the shared resources to be used by other processors. More information is available in *Power ISA 2.06b - Book II - Section 3.2*.

`void __ppc_yield` (*void*)   [Function]
    Preliminary: | MT-Safe | AS-Safe | AC-Safe | See Section 1.2.2.1 [POSIX Safety Concepts], page 2.

    Provide a hint that performance will probably be improved if shared resources dedicated to the executing processor are released for use by other processors.

`void __ppc_mdoio` (*void*)   [Function]
    Preliminary: | MT-Safe | AS-Safe | AC-Safe | See Section 1.2.2.1 [POSIX Safety Concepts], page 2.

    Provide a hint that performance will probably be improved if shared resources dedicated to the executing processor are released until all outstanding storage accesses to caching-inhibited storage have been completed.

void __ppc_mdoom (*void*)   [Function]
>   Preliminary: | MT-Safe | AS-Safe | AC-Safe | See Section 1.2.2.1 [POSIX Safety
>   Concepts], page 2.
>
>   Provide a hint that performance will probably be improved if shared resources dedi-
>   cated to the executing processor are released until all outstanding storage accesses to
>   cacheable storage for which the data is not in the cache have been completed.

void __ppc_set_ppr_med (*void*)   [Function]
>   Preliminary: | MT-Safe | AS-Safe | AC-Safe | See Section 1.2.2.1 [POSIX Safety
>   Concepts], page 2.
>
>   Set the Program Priority Register to medium value (default).
>
>   The *Program Priority Register* (PPR) is a 64-bit register that controls the program's
>   priority. By adjusting the PPR value the programmer may improve system through-
>   put by causing the system resources to be used more efficiently, especially in con-
>   tention situations. The three unprivileged states available are covered by the functions
>   __ppc_set_ppr_med (medium – default), __ppc_set_ppc_low (low) and __ppc_set_
>   ppc_med_low (medium low). More information available in *Power ISA 2.06b - Book
>   II - Section 3.1*.

void __ppc_set_ppr_low (*void*)   [Function]
>   Preliminary: | MT-Safe | AS-Safe | AC-Safe | See Section 1.2.2.1 [POSIX Safety
>   Concepts], page 2.
>
>   Set the Program Priority Register to low value.

void __ppc_set_ppr_med_low (*void*)   [Function]
>   Preliminary: | MT-Safe | AS-Safe | AC-Safe | See Section 1.2.2.1 [POSIX Safety
>   Concepts], page 2.
>
>   Set the Program Priority Register to medium low value.

Power ISA 2.07 extends the priorities that can be set to the Program Priority Register
(PPR). The following functions implement the new priority levels: very low and medium
high.

void __ppc_set_ppr_very_low (*void*)   [Function]
>   Preliminary: | MT-Safe | AS-Safe | AC-Safe | See Section 1.2.2.1 [POSIX Safety
>   Concepts], page 2.
>
>   Set the Program Priority Register to very low value.

void __ppc_set_ppr_med_high (*void*)   [Function]
>   Preliminary: | MT-Safe | AS-Safe | AC-Safe | See Section 1.2.2.1 [POSIX Safety
>   Concepts], page 2.
>
>   Set the Program Priority Register to medium high value. The medium high priority
>   is privileged and may only be set during certain time intervals by problem-state
>   programs. If the program priority is medium high when the time interval expires or
>   if an attempt is made to set the priority to medium high when it is not allowed, the
>   priority is set to medium.

Appendix F Contributors to the GNU C Library

The GNU C Library project would like to thank its many contributors. Without them the project would not have been nearly as successful as it has been. Any omissions in this list are accidental. Feel free to file a bug in bugzilla if you have been left out or some of your contributions are not listed. Please keep this list in alphabetical order.

- Nick Alcock for contributing fixes to allow the GNU C Library to be built with the stack smashing protector enabled.
- John David Anglin for various fixes to the hppa port.
- Ryan S. Arnold for his improvements for Linux on PowerPC and his direction as FSF Project Steward for the GNU C Library.
- Miles Bader for writing the `argp` argument-parsing package, and the `argz`/`envz` interfaces.
- Jeff Bailey for his maintainership of the HPPA architecture.
- Petr Baudis for bug fixes and testing.
- Stephen R. van den Berg for contributing a highly-optimized `strstr` function.
- Ondrej Bilka for contributing optimized string routines for x64 and various fixes.
- Eric Blake for adding $O(n)$ implementations of `memmem`, `strstr` and `strcasestr`.
- Philip Blundell for the ports to Linux/ARM (`arm-ANYTHING-linuxaout`) and ARM standalone (`arm-ANYTHING-none`), as well as for parts of the IPv6 support code.
- Per Bothner for the implementation of the `libio` library which is used to implement `stdio` functions.
- Mark Brown for his direction as part of the GNU C Library steering committee.
- Thomas Bushnell for his contributions to Hurd.
- DJ Delorie for various fixes.
- Wilco Dijkstra for various fixes.
- Liubov Dmitrieva for optimized string and math functions on x86-64 and x86.
- Ulrich Drepper for his many contributions in almost all parts of the GNU C Library, including:
  - internationalization support, including the `locale` and `localedef` utilities.
  - Linux i386/ELF support
  - the `hsearch` and `drand48` families of functions, reentrant '`..._r`' versions of the `random` family; System V shared memory and IPC support code
  - several highly-optimized string functions for ix86 processors
  - many math functions
  - the character conversion functions (`iconv`)
  - the `ftw` and `nftw` functions
  - the floating-point printing function used by `printf` and friends and the floating-point reading function used by `scanf`, `strtod` and friends
  - the `catgets` support and the entire suite of multi-byte and wide-character support functions (`wctype.h`, `wchar.h`, etc.).

- versioning of objects on the symbol level
- Wilco Dijkstra for various fixes.
- Richard Earnshaw for continued support and fixes to the various ARM machine files.
- Paul Eggert for the `mktime` function and for his direction as part of the GNU C Library steering committee.
- Steve Ellcey for various fixes.
-
  Mike FABIAN for various fixes to locales.
- Tulio Magno Quites Machado Filho for adding a new class of installed headers for low-level platform-specific functionality and one such for PowerPC and various fixes.
- Mike Frysinger for his maintaining of the IA64 architecture and for testing and bug fixing.
- Martin Galvan for contributing gdb pretty printer support to glibc and adding an initial set of pretty printers for structures in the POSIX Threads library.
- Michael Glad for the DES encryption function `crypt` and related functions.
- Wolfram Gloger for contributing the memory allocation functions functions `malloc`, `realloc` and `free` and related code.
- Torbjörn Granlund for fast implementations of many of the string functions (`memcpy`, `strlen`, etc.).
- Michael J. Haertel for writing the merge sort function `qsort` and malloc checking functions like `mcheck`.
- Bruno Haible for his improvements to the `iconv` and locale implementations.
- Richard Henderson for the port to Linux on Alpha (`alpha-anything-linux`).
- David Holsgrove for the port to Linux on MicroBlaze.
- Daniel Jacobowitz for various fixes and enhancements.
- Andreas Jaeger for the port to Linux on x86-64 (`x86_64-anything-linux` and his work on Linux for MIPS (`mips-anything-linux`), implementing the `ldconfig` program, providing a test suite for the math library and for his direction as part of the GNU C Library steering committee.
- Aurelien Jarno for various fixes.
- Rical Jasan for contributing various fixes in the GNU C Library manual.
- Jakub Jelinek for implementing a number of checking functions and for his direction as part of the GNU C Library steering committee.
- Geoffrey Keating for the port to Linux on PowerPC (`powerpc-anything-linux`).
- Brendan Kehoe for contributing the port to the MIPS DECStation running Ultrix 4 (`mips-dec-ultrix4`) and the port to the DEC Alpha running OSF/1 (`alpha-dec-osf1`).
- Mark Kettenis for implementing the `utmpx` interface and a utmp daemon, and for a Hesiod NSS module.
- Andi Kleen for implementing pthreads lock elision with TSX.
- Kazumoto Kojima for the port of the Mach and Hurd code to the MIPS architecture (`mips-anything-gnu`) and for his work on the SH architecture.

- Maxim Kuvyrkov for various fixes.

- Andreas Krebbel for his work on Linux for s390 and s390x.

- Thorsten Kukuk for providing an implementation for NIS (YP) and NIS+, securelevel 0, 1 and 2 and for the implementation for a caching daemon for NSS (`nscd`).

- Akhilesh Kumar for various fixes to locales.

- Jeff Law for various fixes.

- Doug Lea for contributing the memory allocation functions `malloc`, `realloc` and `free` and related code.

- Chris Leonard for various fixes and enhancements to localedata.

- Stefan Liebler for various fixes.

- Hongjiu Lu for providing the support for a Linux 32-bit runtime environment under x86-64 (x32), for porting to Linux on IA64, for improved string functions, a framework for testing IFUNC implementations, and many bug fixes.

- Rafal Luzynski for various fixes to locales.

- Luis Machado for optimized functions on PowerPC.

- David J. MacKenzie for his contribution to the `getopt` function and writing the `tar.h` header.

- Greg McGary for adding runtime support for bounds checking.

- Roland McGrath for writing most of the GNU C Library originally, for his work on the Hurd port, his direction as part of the GNU C Library steering committee and as FSF Project Steward for the GNU C Library, and for many bug fixes and reviewing of contributions.

- Allan McRae for various fixes.

- Jason Merrill for the port to the Sequent Symmetry running Dynix version 3 (`i386-sequent-bsd`).

- Chris Metcalf for the port to Linux/Tile (`tilegx-anything-linux` and `tilepro-anything-linux`).

- David Miller for contributing the port to Linux/Sparc (`sparc*-anything-linux`).

- Alan Modra for his improvements for Linux on PowerPC.

- David Mosberger-Tang for contributing the port to Linux/Alpha (`alpha-anything-linux`).

- Wainer dos Santos Moschetta for various fixes to powerpc.

- Stephen Moshier for implementing some 128-bit long double format math functions.

- Stephen Munroe for his port to Linux on PowerPC64 (`powerpc64-anything-linux`) and for adding optimized implementations for PowerPC.

- Paul E. Murphy for various fixes on PowerPC.

- Joseph S. Myers for numerous bug fixes for the libm functions, for his maintainership of the ARM and MIPS architectures, improving cross-compilation and cross-testing of the GNU C Library, expanded coverage of conformtest, merging the ports/ subdirectory into the GNU C Library main repository and his direction as FSF Project Steward for the GNU C Library.

- Marko Myllynen for various fixes.
- Szabolcs Nagy for various fixes.
- Will Newton for contributing some optimized string functions and pointer encryption support for ARM and various fixes.
- Carlos O'Donell for his maintainership of the HPPA architecture, for maintaining the GNU C Library web pages and wiki, for his direction as FSF Project Steward for the GNU C Library and various bug fixes.
- Alexandre Oliva for adding TLS descriptors for LD and GD on x86 and x86-64, for the am33 port, for completing the MIPS n64/n32/o32 multilib port, for thread-safety, async-signal safety and async-cancellation safety documentation in the manual, for his direction as FSF Project Maintainer and for various fixes.
- Paul Pluzhnikov for various fixes.
- Marek Polacek for various fixes.
- Siddhesh Poyarekar for various fixes, an implementation of a framework for performance benchmarking of functions and implementing the tunables infrastructure.
- Tom Quinn for contributing the startup code to support SunOS shared libraries and the port to SGI machines running Irix 4 (`mips-sgi-irix4`).
- Torvald Riegel for the implementation of new algorithms for semaphores, pthread_rwlock and condition variables.
- Maciej W. Rozycki for various fixes.
- Pravin Satpute for writing sorting rules for some Indian languages.
- Douglas C. Schmidt for writing the quick sort function used as a fallback by `qsort`.
- Will Schmidt for optimized string functions on PowerPC.
- Andreas Schwab for the port to Linux/m68k (`m68k-anything-linux`) and for his direction as part of the GNU C Library steering committee.
- Martin Schwidefsky for porting to Linux on s390 (`s390-anything-linux`) and s390x (`s390x-anything-linux`).
- Thomas Schwinge for his contribution to Hurd and the SH architecture.
- Andrew Senkevich for contributing vector math function implementations for x86.
- Carlos Eduardo Seo for optimized functions on PowerPC.
- Marcus Shawcroft for contributing the AArch64 port.
- Franz Sirl for various fixes.
- Jes Sorensen for porting to Linux on IA64 (`ia64-anything-linux`).
- Rajalakshmi Srinivasaraghavan for various fixes and optimizations on PowerPC.
- Richard Stallman for his contribution to the `getopt` function.
- Alfred M. Szmidt for various fixes.
- Chung-Lin Tang for contributing the Nios II port.
- Ian Lance Taylor for contributing the port to the MIPS DECStation running Ultrix 4 (`mips-dec-ultrix4`).
- Samuel Thibault for improving the Hurd port.
- Pino Toscano for various fixes.

- Tim Waugh for the implementation of the POSIX.2 `wordexp` function family.
- Zack Weinberg for the `explicit_bzero` implementation and for various fixes.
- Eric Youngdale for implementing versioning of objects on the symbol level.
- Adhemerval Zanella for optimized functions on PowerPC and various fixes.

Some code in the GNU C Library comes from other projects and might be under a different license:

- The timezone support code is derived from the public-domain timezone package by Arthur David Olson and his many contributors.
- Some of the support code for Mach is taken from Mach 3.0 by CMU; the file `if_ppp.h` is also copyright by CMU, but under a different license; see the file `LICENSES` for the text of the licenses.
- The random number generation functions `random`, `srandom`, `setstate` and `initstate`, which are also the basis for the `rand` and `srand` functions, were written by Earl T. Cohen for the University of California at Berkeley and are copyrighted by the Regents of the University of California. They have undergone minor changes to fit into the GNU C Library and to fit the ISO C standard, but the functional code is Berkeley's.
- The Internet-related code (most of the `inet` subdirectory) and several other miscellaneous functions and header files have been included from 4.4 BSD with little or no modification. The copying permission notice for this code can be found in the file `LICENSES` in the source distribution.
- The `getaddrinfo` and `getnameinfo` functions and supporting code were written by Craig Metz; see the file `LICENSES` for details on their licensing.
- The DNS resolver code is taken directly from BIND 4.9.5, which includes copyrighted code from UC Berkeley and from Digital Equipment Corporation. See the file `LICENSES` for the text of the DEC license.
- The code to support Sun RPC is taken verbatim from Sun's RPCSRC-4.0 distribution; see the file `LICENSES` for the text of the license.
- The math functions are taken from `fdlibm-5.1` by Sun Microsystems, as modified by J.T. Conklin, Ian Lance Taylor, Ulrich Drepper, Andreas Schwab, and Roland McGrath.
- Many of the IEEE 64-bit double precision math functions (in the `sysdeps/ieee754/dbl-64` subdirectory) come from the IBM Accurate Mathematical Library, contributed by IBM.
- Many of the IA64 math functions are taken from a collection of "Highly Optimized Mathematical Functions for Itanium" that Intel makes available under a free license; see the file `LICENSES` for details.

Appendix G Free Software Needs Free Documentation

The biggest deficiency in the free software community today is not in the software—it is the lack of good free documentation that we can include with the free software. Many of our most important programs do not come with free reference manuals and free introductory texts. Documentation is an essential part of any software package; when an important free software package does not come with a free manual and a free tutorial, that is a major gap. We have many such gaps today.

Consider Perl, for instance. The tutorial manuals that people normally use are non-free. How did this come about? Because the authors of those manuals published them with restrictive terms—no copying, no modification, source files not available—which exclude them from the free software world.

That wasn't the first time this sort of thing happened, and it was far from the last. Many times we have heard a GNU user eagerly describe a manual that he is writing, his intended contribution to the community, only to learn that he had ruined everything by signing a publication contract to make it non-free.

Free documentation, like free software, is a matter of freedom, not price. The problem with the non-free manual is not that publishers charge a price for printed copies—that in itself is fine. (The Free Software Foundation sells printed copies of manuals, too.) The problem is the restrictions on the use of the manual. Free manuals are available in source code form, and give you permission to copy and modify. Non-free manuals do not allow this.

The criteria of freedom for a free manual are roughly the same as for free software. Redistribution (including the normal kinds of commercial redistribution) must be permitted, so that the manual can accompany every copy of the program, both on-line and on paper.

Permission for modification of the technical content is crucial too. When people modify the software, adding or changing features, if they are conscientious they will change the manual too—so they can provide accurate and clear documentation for the modified program. A manual that leaves you no choice but to write a new manual to document a changed version of the program is not really available to our community.

Some kinds of limits on the way modification is handled are acceptable. For example, requirements to preserve the original author's copyright notice, the distribution terms, or the list of authors, are ok. It is also no problem to require modified versions to include notice that they were modified. Even entire sections that may not be deleted or changed are acceptable, as long as they deal with nontechnical topics (like this one). These kinds of restrictions are acceptable because they don't obstruct the community's normal use of the manual.

However, it must be possible to modify all the *technical* content of the manual, and then distribute the result in all the usual media, through all the usual channels. Otherwise, the restrictions obstruct the use of the manual, it is not free, and we need another manual to replace it.

Please spread the word about this issue. Our community continues to lose manuals to proprietary publishing. If we spread the word that free software needs free reference manuals and free tutorials, perhaps the next person who wants to contribute by writing documentation will realize, before it is too late, that only free manuals contribute to the free software community.

If you are writing documentation, please insist on publishing it under the GNU Free Documentation License or another free documentation license. Remember that this decision requires your approval—you don't have to let the publisher decide. Some commercial publishers will use a free license if you insist, but they will not propose the option; it is up to you to raise the issue and say firmly that this is what you want. If the publisher you are dealing with refuses, please try other publishers. If you're not sure whether a proposed license is free, write to `licensing@gnu.org`.

You can encourage commercial publishers to sell more free, copylefted manuals and tutorials by buying them, and particularly by buying copies from the publishers that paid for their writing or for major improvements. Meanwhile, try to avoid buying non-free documentation at all. Check the distribution terms of a manual before you buy it, and insist that whoever seeks your business must respect your freedom. Check the history of the book, and try reward the publishers that have paid or pay the authors to work on it.

The Free Software Foundation maintains a list of free documentation published by other publishers, at `http://www.fsf.org/doc/other-free-books.html`.

Appendix H GNU Lesser General Public License

Version 2.1, February 1999

Copyright © 1991, 1999 Free Software Foundation, Inc.
51 Franklin Street, Fifth Floor, Boston, MA 02110-1301, USA

Everyone is permitted to copy and distribute verbatim copies
of this license document, but changing it is not allowed.

[This is the first released version of the Lesser GPL. It also counts
as the successor of the GNU Library Public License, version 2, hence the
version number 2.1.]

Preamble

The licenses for most software are designed to take away your freedom to share and change it. By contrast, the GNU General Public Licenses are intended to guarantee your freedom to share and change free software—to make sure the software is free for all its users.

This license, the Lesser General Public License, applies to some specially designated software—typically libraries—of the Free Software Foundation and other authors who decide to use it. You can use it too, but we suggest you first think carefully about whether this license or the ordinary General Public License is the better strategy to use in any particular case, based on the explanations below.

When we speak of free software, we are referring to freedom of use, not price. Our General Public Licenses are designed to make sure that you have the freedom to distribute copies of free software (and charge for this service if you wish); that you receive source code or can get it if you want it; that you can change the software and use pieces of it in new free programs; and that you are informed that you can do these things.

To protect your rights, we need to make restrictions that forbid distributors to deny you these rights or to ask you to surrender these rights. These restrictions translate to certain responsibilities for you if you distribute copies of the library or if you modify it.

For example, if you distribute copies of the library, whether gratis or for a fee, you must give the recipients all the rights that we gave you. You must make sure that they, too, receive or can get the source code. If you link other code with the library, you must provide complete object files to the recipients, so that they can relink them with the library after making changes to the library and recompiling it. And you must show them these terms so they know their rights.

We protect your rights with a two-step method: (1) we copyright the library, and (2) we offer you this license, which gives you legal permission to copy, distribute and/or modify the library.

To protect each distributor, we want to make it very clear that there is no warranty for the free library. Also, if the library is modified by someone else and passed on, the recipients should know that what they have is not the original version, so that the original author's reputation will not be affected by problems that might be introduced by others.

Finally, software patents pose a constant threat to the existence of any free program. We wish to make sure that a company cannot effectively restrict the users of a free program by obtaining a restrictive license from a patent holder. Therefore, we insist that any patent license obtained for a version of the library must be consistent with the full freedom of use specified in this license.

Most GNU software, including some libraries, is covered by the ordinary GNU General Public License. This license, the GNU Lesser General Public License, applies to certain designated libraries, and is quite different from the ordinary General Public License. We use this license for certain libraries in order to permit linking those libraries into non-free programs.

When a program is linked with a library, whether statically or using a shared library, the combination of the two is legally speaking a combined work, a derivative of the original library. The ordinary General Public License therefore permits such linking only if the entire combination fits its criteria of freedom. The Lesser General Public License permits more lax criteria for linking other code with the library.

We call this license the *Lesser* General Public License because it does *Less* to protect the user's freedom than the ordinary General Public License. It also provides other free software developers Less of an advantage over competing non-free programs. These disadvantages are the reason we use the ordinary General Public License for many libraries. However, the Lesser license provides advantages in certain special circumstances.

For example, on rare occasions, there may be a special need to encourage the widest possible use of a certain library, so that it becomes a de-facto standard. To achieve this, non-free programs must be allowed to use the library. A more frequent case is that a free library does the same job as widely used non-free libraries. In this case, there is little to gain by limiting the free library to free software only, so we use the Lesser General Public License.

In other cases, permission to use a particular library in non-free programs enables a greater number of people to use a large body of free software. For example, permission to use the GNU C Library in non-free programs enables many more people to use the whole GNU operating system, as well as its variant, the GNU/Linux operating system.

Although the Lesser General Public License is Less protective of the users' freedom, it does ensure that the user of a program that is linked with the Library has the freedom and the wherewithal to run that program using a modified version of the Library.

The precise terms and conditions for copying, distribution and modification follow. Pay close attention to the difference between a "work based on the library" and a "work that uses the library". The former contains code derived from the library, whereas the latter must be combined with the library in order to run.

TERMS AND CONDITIONS FOR COPYING, DISTRIBUTION AND MODIFICATION

0. This License Agreement applies to any software library or other program which contains a notice placed by the copyright holder or other authorized party saying it may be distributed under the terms of this Lesser General Public License (also called "this License"). Each licensee is addressed as "you".

    A "library" means a collection of software functions and/or data prepared so as to be conveniently linked with application programs (which use some of those functions and data) to form executables.

The "Library", below, refers to any such software library or work which has been distributed under these terms. A "work based on the Library" means either the Library or any derivative work under copyright law: that is to say, a work containing the Library or a portion of it, either verbatim or with modifications and/or translated straightforwardly into another language. (Hereinafter, translation is included without limitation in the term "modification".)

"Source code" for a work means the preferred form of the work for making modifications to it. For a library, complete source code means all the source code for all modules it contains, plus any associated interface definition files, plus the scripts used to control compilation and installation of the library.

Activities other than copying, distribution and modification are not covered by this License; they are outside its scope. The act of running a program using the Library is not restricted, and output from such a program is covered only if its contents constitute a work based on the Library (independent of the use of the Library in a tool for writing it). Whether that is true depends on what the Library does and what the program that uses the Library does.

1. You may copy and distribute verbatim copies of the Library's complete source code as you receive it, in any medium, provided that you conspicuously and appropriately publish on each copy an appropriate copyright notice and disclaimer of warranty; keep intact all the notices that refer to this License and to the absence of any warranty; and distribute a copy of this License along with the Library.

   You may charge a fee for the physical act of transferring a copy, and you may at your option offer warranty protection in exchange for a fee.

2. You may modify your copy or copies of the Library or any portion of it, thus forming a work based on the Library, and copy and distribute such modifications or work under the terms of Section 1 above, provided that you also meet all of these conditions:

   a. The modified work must itself be a software library.

   b. You must cause the files modified to carry prominent notices stating that you changed the files and the date of any change.

   c. You must cause the whole of the work to be licensed at no charge to all third parties under the terms of this License.

   d. If a facility in the modified Library refers to a function or a table of data to be supplied by an application program that uses the facility, other than as an argument passed when the facility is invoked, then you must make a good faith effort to ensure that, in the event an application does not supply such function or table, the facility still operates, and performs whatever part of its purpose remains meaningful.

      (For example, a function in a library to compute square roots has a purpose that is entirely well-defined independent of the application. Therefore, Subsection 2d requires that any application-supplied function or table used by this function must be optional: if the application does not supply it, the square root function must still compute square roots.)

   These requirements apply to the modified work as a whole. If identifiable sections of that work are not derived from the Library, and can be reasonably considered independent and separate works in themselves, then this License, and its terms, do not apply to those sections when you distribute them as separate works. But when you distribute the same sections as part of a whole which is a work based on the Library, the distribution of the whole must be on the terms of this License, whose permissions for other licensees extend to the entire whole, and thus to each and every part regardless of who wrote it.

Thus, it is not the intent of this section to claim rights or contest your rights to work written entirely by you; rather, the intent is to exercise the right to control the distribution of derivative or collective works based on the Library.

In addition, mere aggregation of another work not based on the Library with the Library (or with a work based on the Library) on a volume of a storage or distribution medium does not bring the other work under the scope of this License.

3. You may opt to apply the terms of the ordinary GNU General Public License instead of this License to a given copy of the Library. To do this, you must alter all the notices that refer to this License, so that they refer to the ordinary GNU General Public License, version 2, instead of to this License. (If a newer version than version 2 of the ordinary GNU General Public License has appeared, then you can specify that version instead if you wish.) Do not make any other change in these notices.

   Once this change is made in a given copy, it is irreversible for that copy, so the ordinary GNU General Public License applies to all subsequent copies and derivative works made from that copy.

   This option is useful when you wish to copy part of the code of the Library into a program that is not a library.

4. You may copy and distribute the Library (or a portion or derivative of it, under Section 2) in object code or executable form under the terms of Sections 1 and 2 above provided that you accompany it with the complete corresponding machine-readable source code, which must be distributed under the terms of Sections 1 and 2 above on a medium customarily used for software interchange.

   If distribution of object code is made by offering access to copy from a designated place, then offering equivalent access to copy the source code from the same place satisfies the requirement to distribute the source code, even though third parties are not compelled to copy the source along with the object code.

5. A program that contains no derivative of any portion of the Library, but is designed to work with the Library by being compiled or linked with it, is called a "work that uses the Library". Such a work, in isolation, is not a derivative work of the Library, and therefore falls outside the scope of this License.

   However, linking a "work that uses the Library" with the Library creates an executable that is a derivative of the Library (because it contains portions of the Library), rather than a "work that uses the library". The executable is therefore covered by this License. Section 6 states terms for distribution of such executables.

   When a "work that uses the Library" uses material from a header file that is part of the Library, the object code for the work may be a derivative work of the Library even though the source code is not. Whether this is true is especially significant if the work can be linked without the Library, or if the work is itself a library. The threshold for this to be true is not precisely defined by law.

If such an object file uses only numerical parameters, data structure layouts and accessors, and small macros and small inline functions (ten lines or less in length), then the use of the object file is unrestricted, regardless of whether it is legally a derivative work. (Executables containing this object code plus portions of the Library will still fall under Section 6.)

Otherwise, if the work is a derivative of the Library, you may distribute the object code for the work under the terms of Section 6. Any executables containing that work also fall under Section 6, whether or not they are linked directly with the Library itself.

6. As an exception to the Sections above, you may also combine or link a "work that uses the Library" with the Library to produce a work containing portions of the Library, and distribute that work under terms of your choice, provided that the terms permit modification of the work for the customer's own use and reverse engineering for debugging such modifications.

   You must give prominent notice with each copy of the work that the Library is used in it and that the Library and its use are covered by this License. You must supply a copy of this License. If the work during execution displays copyright notices, you must include the copyright notice for the Library among them, as well as a reference directing the user to the copy of this License. Also, you must do one of these things:

   a. Accompany the work with the complete corresponding machine-readable source code for the Library including whatever changes were used in the work (which must be distributed under Sections 1 and 2 above); and, if the work is an executable linked with the Library, with the complete machine-readable "work that uses the Library", as object code and/or source code, so that the user can modify the Library and then relink to produce a modified executable containing the modified Library. (It is understood that the user who changes the contents of definitions files in the Library will not necessarily be able to recompile the application to use the modified definitions.)

   b. Use a suitable shared library mechanism for linking with the Library. A suitable mechanism is one that (1) uses at run time a copy of the library already present on the user's computer system, rather than copying library functions into the executable, and (2) will operate properly with a modified version of the library, if the user installs one, as long as the modified version is interface-compatible with the version that the work was made with.

   c. Accompany the work with a written offer, valid for at least three years, to give the same user the materials specified in Subsection 6a, above, for a charge no more than the cost of performing this distribution.

   d. If distribution of the work is made by offering access to copy from a designated place, offer equivalent access to copy the above specified materials from the same place.

   e. Verify that the user has already received a copy of these materials or that you have already sent this user a copy.

For an executable, the required form of the "work that uses the Library" must include any data and utility programs needed for reproducing the executable from it. However, as a special exception, the materials to be distributed need not include anything that is normally distributed (in either source or binary form) with the major components (compiler, kernel, and so on) of the operating system on which the executable runs, unless that component itself accompanies the executable.

It may happen that this requirement contradicts the license restrictions of other proprietary libraries that do not normally accompany the operating system. Such a contradiction means you cannot use both them and the Library together in an executable that you distribute.

7. You may place library facilities that are a work based on the Library side-by-side in a single library together with other library facilities not covered by this License, and distribute such a combined library, provided that the separate distribution of the work based on the Library and of the other library facilities is otherwise permitted, and provided that you do these two things:

   a. Accompany the combined library with a copy of the same work based on the Library, uncombined with any other library facilities. This must be distributed under the terms of the Sections above.

   b. Give prominent notice with the combined library of the fact that part of it is a work based on the Library, and explaining where to find the accompanying uncombined form of the same work.

8. You may not copy, modify, sublicense, link with, or distribute the Library except as expressly provided under this License. Any attempt otherwise to copy, modify, sublicense, link with, or distribute the Library is void, and will automatically terminate your rights under this License. However, parties who have received copies, or rights, from you under this License will not have their licenses terminated so long as such parties remain in full compliance.

9. You are not required to accept this License, since you have not signed it. However, nothing else grants you permission to modify or distribute the Library or its derivative works. These actions are prohibited by law if you do not accept this License. Therefore, by modifying or distributing the Library (or any work based on the Library), you indicate your acceptance of this License to do so, and all its terms and conditions for copying, distributing or modifying the Library or works based on it.

10. Each time you redistribute the Library (or any work based on the Library), the recipient automatically receives a license from the original licensor to copy, distribute, link with or modify the Library subject to these terms and conditions. You may not impose any further restrictions on the recipients' exercise of the rights granted herein. You are not responsible for enforcing compliance by third parties with this License.

11. If, as a consequence of a court judgment or allegation of patent infringement or for any other reason (not limited to patent issues), conditions are imposed on you (whether by court order, agreement or otherwise) that contradict the conditions of this License, they do not excuse you from the conditions of this License. If you cannot distribute so as to satisfy simultaneously your obligations under this License and any other pertinent obligations, then as a consequence you may not distribute the Library at all. For example, if a patent license would not permit royalty-free redistribution of the Library by all those who receive copies directly or indirectly through you, then the only way you could satisfy both it and this License would be to refrain entirely from distribution of the Library.

If any portion of this section is held invalid or unenforceable under any particular circumstance, the balance of the section is intended to apply, and the section as a whole is intended to apply in other circumstances.

It is not the purpose of this section to induce you to infringe any patents or other property right claims or to contest validity of any such claims; this section has the sole purpose of protecting the integrity of the free software distribution system which is implemented by public license practices. Many people have made generous contributions to the wide range of software distributed through that system in reliance on consistent application of that system; it is up to the author/donor to decide if he or she is willing to distribute software through any other system and a licensee cannot impose that choice.

This section is intended to make thoroughly clear what is believed to be a consequence of the rest of this License.

12. If the distribution and/or use of the Library is restricted in certain countries either by patents or by copyrighted interfaces, the original copyright holder who places the Library under this License may add an explicit geographical distribution limitation excluding those countries, so that distribution is permitted only in or among countries not thus excluded. In such case, this License incorporates the limitation as if written in the body of this License.

13. The Free Software Foundation may publish revised and/or new versions of the Lesser General Public License from time to time. Such new versions will be similar in spirit to the present version, but may differ in detail to address new problems or concerns.

Each version is given a distinguishing version number. If the Library specifies a version number of this License which applies to it and "any later version", you have the option of following the terms and conditions either of that version or of any later version published by the Free Software Foundation. If the Library does not specify a license version number, you may choose any version ever published by the Free Software Foundation.

14. If you wish to incorporate parts of the Library into other free programs whose distribution conditions are incompatible with these, write to the author to ask for permission. For software which is copyrighted by the Free Software Foundation, write to the Free Software Foundation; we sometimes make exceptions for this. Our decision will be guided by the two goals of preserving the free status of all derivatives of our free software and of promoting the sharing and reuse of software generally.

NO WARRANTY

15. BECAUSE THE LIBRARY IS LICENSED FREE OF CHARGE, THERE IS NO WARRANTY FOR THE LIBRARY, TO THE EXTENT PERMITTED BY APPLICABLE LAW. EXCEPT WHEN OTHERWISE STATED IN WRITING THE COPYRIGHT HOLDERS AND/OR OTHER PARTIES PROVIDE THE LIBRARY "AS IS" WITHOUT WARRANTY OF ANY KIND, EITHER EXPRESSED OR IMPLIED, INCLUDING, BUT NOT LIMITED TO, THE IMPLIED WARRANTIES OF MERCHANTABILITY AND FITNESS FOR A PARTICULAR PURPOSE. THE ENTIRE RISK AS TO THE QUALITY AND PERFORMANCE OF THE LIBRARY IS WITH YOU. SHOULD THE LIBRARY PROVE DEFECTIVE, YOU ASSUME THE COST OF ALL NECESSARY SERVICING, REPAIR OR CORRECTION.

16. IN NO EVENT UNLESS REQUIRED BY APPLICABLE LAW OR AGREED TO IN

WRITING WILL ANY COPYRIGHT HOLDER, OR ANY OTHER PARTY WHO MAY MODIFY AND/OR REDISTRIBUTE THE LIBRARY AS PERMITTED ABOVE, BE LIABLE TO YOU FOR DAMAGES, INCLUDING ANY GENERAL, SPECIAL, INCIDENTAL OR CONSEQUENTIAL DAMAGES ARISING OUT OF THE USE OR INABILITY TO USE THE LIBRARY (INCLUDING BUT NOT LIMITED TO LOSS OF DATA OR DATA BEING RENDERED INACCURATE OR LOSSES SUSTAINED BY YOU OR THIRD PARTIES OR A FAILURE OF THE LIBRARY TO OPERATE WITH ANY OTHER SOFTWARE), EVEN IF SUCH HOLDER OR OTHER PARTY HAS BEEN ADVISED OF THE POSSIBILITY OF SUCH DAMAGES.

END OF TERMS AND CONDITIONS

How to Apply These Terms to Your New Libraries

If you develop a new library, and you want it to be of the greatest possible use to the public, we recommend making it free software that everyone can redistribute and change. You can do so by permitting redistribution under these terms (or, alternatively, under the terms of the ordinary General Public License).

To apply these terms, attach the following notices to the library. It is safest to attach them to the start of each source file to most effectively convey the exclusion of warranty; and each file should have at least the "copyright" line and a pointer to where the full notice is found.

```
one line to give the library's name and an idea of what it does.
Copyright (C) year  name of author

This library is free software; you can redistribute it and/or modify it
under the terms of the GNU Lesser General Public License as published by
the Free Software Foundation; either version 2.1 of the License, or (at
your option) any later version.

This library is distributed in the hope that it will be useful, but
WITHOUT ANY WARRANTY; without even the implied warranty of
MERCHANTABILITY or FITNESS FOR A PARTICULAR PURPOSE.  See the GNU
Lesser General Public License for more details.

You should have received a copy of the GNU Lesser General Public
License along with this library; if not, write to the Free Software
Foundation, Inc., 51 Franklin Street, Fifth Floor, Boston, MA 02110-1301,
USA.
```

Also add information on how to contact you by electronic and paper mail.

You should also get your employer (if you work as a programmer) or your school, if any, to sign a "copyright disclaimer" for the library, if necessary. Here is a sample; alter the names:

```
Yoyodyne, Inc., hereby disclaims all copyright interest in the library
`Frob' (a library for tweaking knobs) written by James Random Hacker.

signature of Ty Coon, 1 April 1990
Ty Coon, President of Vice
```

That's all there is to it!

Appendix I GNU Free Documentation License

Version 1.3, 3 November 2008

Copyright © 2000, 2001, 2002, 2007, 2008 Free Software Foundation, Inc.
`http://fsf.org/`

Everyone is permitted to copy and distribute verbatim copies
of this license document, but changing it is not allowed.

0. PREAMBLE

The purpose of this License is to make a manual, textbook, or other functional and useful document *free* in the sense of freedom: to assure everyone the effective freedom to copy and redistribute it, with or without modifying it, either commercially or non-commercially. Secondarily, this License preserves for the author and publisher a way to get credit for their work, while not being considered responsible for modifications made by others.

This License is a kind of "copyleft", which means that derivative works of the document must themselves be free in the same sense. It complements the GNU General Public License, which is a copyleft license designed for free software.

We have designed this License in order to use it for manuals for free software, because free software needs free documentation: a free program should come with manuals providing the same freedoms that the software does. But this License is not limited to software manuals; it can be used for any textual work, regardless of subject matter or whether it is published as a printed book. We recommend this License principally for works whose purpose is instruction or reference.

1. APPLICABILITY AND DEFINITIONS

This License applies to any manual or other work, in any medium, that contains a notice placed by the copyright holder saying it can be distributed under the terms of this License. Such a notice grants a world-wide, royalty-free license, unlimited in duration, to use that work under the conditions stated herein. The "Document", below, refers to any such manual or work. Any member of the public is a licensee, and is addressed as "you". You accept the license if you copy, modify or distribute the work in a way requiring permission under copyright law.

A "Modified Version" of the Document means any work containing the Document or a portion of it, either copied verbatim, or with modifications and/or translated into another language.

A "Secondary Section" is a named appendix or a front-matter section of the Document that deals exclusively with the relationship of the publishers or authors of the Document to the Document's overall subject (or to related matters) and contains nothing that could fall directly within that overall subject. (Thus, if the Document is in part a textbook of mathematics, a Secondary Section may not explain any mathematics.) The relationship could be a matter of historical connection with the subject or with related matters, or of legal, commercial, philosophical, ethical or political position regarding them.

The "Invariant Sections" are certain Secondary Sections whose titles are designated, as being those of Invariant Sections, in the notice that says that the Document is released under this License. If a section does not fit the above definition of Secondary then it is not allowed to be designated as Invariant. The Document may contain zero Invariant Sections. If the Document does not identify any Invariant Sections then there are none.

The "Cover Texts" are certain short passages of text that are listed, as Front-Cover Texts or Back-Cover Texts, in the notice that says that the Document is released under this License. A Front-Cover Text may be at most 5 words, and a Back-Cover Text may be at most 25 words.

A "Transparent" copy of the Document means a machine-readable copy, represented in a format whose specification is available to the general public, that is suitable for revising the document straightforwardly with generic text editors or (for images composed of pixels) generic paint programs or (for drawings) some widely available drawing editor, and that is suitable for input to text formatters or for automatic translation to a variety of formats suitable for input to text formatters. A copy made in an otherwise Transparent file format whose markup, or absence of markup, has been arranged to thwart or discourage subsequent modification by readers is not Transparent. An image format is not Transparent if used for any substantial amount of text. A copy that is not "Transparent" is called "Opaque".

Examples of suitable formats for Transparent copies include plain ASCII without markup, Texinfo input format, LaTeX input format, SGML or XML using a publicly available DTD, and standard-conforming simple HTML, PostScript or PDF designed for human modification. Examples of transparent image formats include PNG, XCF and JPG. Opaque formats include proprietary formats that can be read and edited only by proprietary word processors, SGML or XML for which the DTD and/or processing tools are not generally available, and the machine-generated HTML, PostScript or PDF produced by some word processors for output purposes only.

The "Title Page" means, for a printed book, the title page itself, plus such following pages as are needed to hold, legibly, the material this License requires to appear in the title page. For works in formats which do not have any title page as such, "Title Page" means the text near the most prominent appearance of the work's title, preceding the beginning of the body of the text.

The "publisher" means any person or entity that distributes copies of the Document to the public.

A section "Entitled XYZ" means a named subunit of the Document whose title either is precisely XYZ or contains XYZ in parentheses following text that translates XYZ in another language. (Here XYZ stands for a specific section name mentioned below, such as "Acknowledgements", "Dedications", "Endorsements", or "History".) To "Preserve the Title" of such a section when you modify the Document means that it remains a section "Entitled XYZ" according to this definition.

The Document may include Warranty Disclaimers next to the notice which states that this License applies to the Document. These Warranty Disclaimers are considered to be included by reference in this License, but only as regards disclaiming warranties: any other implication that these Warranty Disclaimers may have is void and has no effect on the meaning of this License.

2. VERBATIM COPYING

You may copy and distribute the Document in any medium, either commercially or noncommercially, provided that this License, the copyright notices, and the license notice saying this License applies to the Document are reproduced in all copies, and that you add no other conditions whatsoever to those of this License. You may not use technical measures to obstruct or control the reading or further copying of the copies you make or distribute. However, you may accept compensation in exchange for copies. If you distribute a large enough number of copies you must also follow the conditions in section 3.

You may also lend copies, under the same conditions stated above, and you may publicly display copies.

3. COPYING IN QUANTITY

If you publish printed copies (or copies in media that commonly have printed covers) of the Document, numbering more than 100, and the Document's license notice requires Cover Texts, you must enclose the copies in covers that carry, clearly and legibly, all these Cover Texts: Front-Cover Texts on the front cover, and Back-Cover Texts on the back cover. Both covers must also clearly and legibly identify you as the publisher of these copies. The front cover must present the full title with all words of the title equally prominent and visible. You may add other material on the covers in addition. Copying with changes limited to the covers, as long as they preserve the title of the Document and satisfy these conditions, can be treated as verbatim copying in other respects.

If the required texts for either cover are too voluminous to fit legibly, you should put the first ones listed (as many as fit reasonably) on the actual cover, and continue the rest onto adjacent pages.

If you publish or distribute Opaque copies of the Document numbering more than 100, you must either include a machine-readable Transparent copy along with each Opaque copy, or state in or with each Opaque copy a computer-network location from which the general network-using public has access to download using public-standard network protocols a complete Transparent copy of the Document, free of added material. If you use the latter option, you must take reasonably prudent steps, when you begin distribution of Opaque copies in quantity, to ensure that this Transparent copy will remain thus accessible at the stated location until at least one year after the last time you distribute an Opaque copy (directly or through your agents or retailers) of that edition to the public.

It is requested, but not required, that you contact the authors of the Document well before redistributing any large number of copies, to give them a chance to provide you with an updated version of the Document.

4. MODIFICATIONS

You may copy and distribute a Modified Version of the Document under the conditions of sections 2 and 3 above, provided that you release the Modified Version under precisely this License, with the Modified Version filling the role of the Document, thus licensing distribution and modification of the Modified Version to whoever possesses a copy of it. In addition, you must do these things in the Modified Version:

A. Use in the Title Page (and on the covers, if any) a title distinct from that of the Document, and from those of previous versions (which should, if there were any, be listed in the History section of the Document). You may use the same title as a previous version if the original publisher of that version gives permission.

B. List on the Title Page, as authors, one or more persons or entities responsible for authorship of the modifications in the Modified Version, together with at least five of the principal authors of the Document (all of its principal authors, if it has fewer than five), unless they release you from this requirement.

C. State on the Title page the name of the publisher of the Modified Version, as the publisher.

D. Preserve all the copyright notices of the Document.

E. Add an appropriate copyright notice for your modifications adjacent to the other copyright notices.

F. Include, immediately after the copyright notices, a license notice giving the public permission to use the Modified Version under the terms of this License, in the form shown in the Addendum below.

G. Preserve in that license notice the full lists of Invariant Sections and required Cover Texts given in the Document's license notice.

H. Include an unaltered copy of this License.

I. Preserve the section Entitled "History", Preserve its Title, and add to it an item stating at least the title, year, new authors, and publisher of the Modified Version as given on the Title Page. If there is no section Entitled "History" in the Document, create one stating the title, year, authors, and publisher of the Document as given on its Title Page, then add an item describing the Modified Version as stated in the previous sentence.

J. Preserve the network location, if any, given in the Document for public access to a Transparent copy of the Document, and likewise the network locations given in the Document for previous versions it was based on. These may be placed in the "History" section. You may omit a network location for a work that was published at least four years before the Document itself, or if the original publisher of the version it refers to gives permission.

K. For any section Entitled "Acknowledgements" or "Dedications", Preserve the Title of the section, and preserve in the section all the substance and tone of each of the contributor acknowledgements and/or dedications given therein.

L. Preserve all the Invariant Sections of the Document, unaltered in their text and in their titles. Section numbers or the equivalent are not considered part of the section titles.

M. Delete any section Entitled "Endorsements". Such a section may not be included in the Modified Version.

N. Do not retitle any existing section to be Entitled "Endorsements" or to conflict in title with any Invariant Section.

O. Preserve any Warranty Disclaimers.

If the Modified Version includes new front-matter sections or appendices that qualify as Secondary Sections and contain no material copied from the Document, you may at your option designate some or all of these sections as invariant. To do this, add their titles to the list of Invariant Sections in the Modified Version's license notice. These titles must be distinct from any other section titles.

You may add a section Entitled "Endorsements", provided it contains nothing but endorsements of your Modified Version by various parties—for example, statements of peer review or that the text has been approved by an organization as the authoritative definition of a standard.

You may add a passage of up to five words as a Front-Cover Text, and a passage of up to 25 words as a Back-Cover Text, to the end of the list of Cover Texts in the Modified Version. Only one passage of Front-Cover Text and one of Back-Cover Text may be added by (or through arrangements made by) any one entity. If the Document already includes a cover text for the same cover, previously added by you or by arrangement made by the same entity you are acting on behalf of, you may not add another; but you may replace the old one, on explicit permission from the previous publisher that added the old one.

The author(s) and publisher(s) of the Document do not by this License give permission to use their names for publicity for or to assert or imply endorsement of any Modified Version.

5. COMBINING DOCUMENTS

You may combine the Document with other documents released under this License, under the terms defined in section 4 above for modified versions, provided that you include in the combination all of the Invariant Sections of all of the original documents, unmodified, and list them all as Invariant Sections of your combined work in its license notice, and that you preserve all their Warranty Disclaimers.

The combined work need only contain one copy of this License, and multiple identical Invariant Sections may be replaced with a single copy. If there are multiple Invariant Sections with the same name but different contents, make the title of each such section unique by adding at the end of it, in parentheses, the name of the original author or publisher of that section if known, or else a unique number. Make the same adjustment to the section titles in the list of Invariant Sections in the license notice of the combined work.

In the combination, you must combine any sections Entitled "History" in the various original documents, forming one section Entitled "History"; likewise combine any sections Entitled "Acknowledgements", and any sections Entitled "Dedications". You must delete all sections Entitled "Endorsements."

6. COLLECTIONS OF DOCUMENTS

You may make a collection consisting of the Document and other documents released under this License, and replace the individual copies of this License in the various documents with a single copy that is included in the collection, provided that you follow the rules of this License for verbatim copying of each of the documents in all other respects.

You may extract a single document from such a collection, and distribute it individually under this License, provided you insert a copy of this License into the extracted document, and follow this License in all other respects regarding verbatim copying of that document.

7. AGGREGATION WITH INDEPENDENT WORKS

A compilation of the Document or its derivatives with other separate and independent documents or works, in or on a volume of a storage or distribution medium, is called an "aggregate" if the copyright resulting from the compilation is not used to limit the legal rights of the compilation's users beyond what the individual works permit. When the Document is included in an aggregate, this License does not apply to the other works in the aggregate which are not themselves derivative works of the Document.

If the Cover Text requirement of section 3 is applicable to these copies of the Document, then if the Document is less than one half of the entire aggregate, the Document's Cover Texts may be placed on covers that bracket the Document within the aggregate, or the electronic equivalent of covers if the Document is in electronic form. Otherwise they must appear on printed covers that bracket the whole aggregate.

8. TRANSLATION

Translation is considered a kind of modification, so you may distribute translations of the Document under the terms of section 4. Replacing Invariant Sections with translations requires special permission from their copyright holders, but you may include translations of some or all Invariant Sections in addition to the original versions of these Invariant Sections. You may include a translation of this License, and all the license notices in the Document, and any Warranty Disclaimers, provided that you also include the original English version of this License and the original versions of those notices and disclaimers. In case of a disagreement between the translation and the original version of this License or a notice or disclaimer, the original version will prevail.

If a section in the Document is Entitled "Acknowledgements", "Dedications", or "History", the requirement (section 4) to Preserve its Title (section 1) will typically require changing the actual title.

9. TERMINATION

You may not copy, modify, sublicense, or distribute the Document except as expressly provided under this License. Any attempt otherwise to copy, modify, sublicense, or distribute it is void, and will automatically terminate your rights under this License.

However, if you cease all violation of this License, then your license from a particular copyright holder is reinstated (a) provisionally, unless and until the copyright holder explicitly and finally terminates your license, and (b) permanently, if the copyright holder fails to notify you of the violation by some reasonable means prior to 60 days after the cessation.

Moreover, your license from a particular copyright holder is reinstated permanently if the copyright holder notifies you of the violation by some reasonable means, this is the first time you have received notice of violation of this License (for any work) from that copyright holder, and you cure the violation prior to 30 days after your receipt of the notice.

Termination of your rights under this section does not terminate the licenses of parties who have received copies or rights from you under this License. If your rights have been terminated and not permanently reinstated, receipt of a copy of some or all of the same material does not give you any rights to use it.

10. FUTURE REVISIONS OF THIS LICENSE

The Free Software Foundation may publish new, revised versions of the GNU Free Documentation License from time to time. Such new versions will be similar in spirit to the present version, but may differ in detail to address new problems or concerns. See `http://www.gnu.org/copyleft/`.

Each version of the License is given a distinguishing version number. If the Document specifies that a particular numbered version of this License "or any later version" applies to it, you have the option of following the terms and conditions either of that specified version or of any later version that has been published (not as a draft) by the Free Software Foundation. If the Document does not specify a version number of this License, you may choose any version ever published (not as a draft) by the Free Software Foundation. If the Document specifies that a proxy can decide which future versions of this License can be used, that proxy's public statement of acceptance of a version permanently authorizes you to choose that version for the Document.

11. RELICENSING

"Massive Multiauthor Collaboration Site" (or "MMC Site") means any World Wide Web server that publishes copyrightable works and also provides prominent facilities for anybody to edit those works. A public wiki that anybody can edit is an example of such a server. A "Massive Multiauthor Collaboration" (or "MMC") contained in the site means any set of copyrightable works thus published on the MMC site.

"CC-BY-SA" means the Creative Commons Attribution-Share Alike 3.0 license published by Creative Commons Corporation, a not-for-profit corporation with a principal place of business in San Francisco, California, as well as future copyleft versions of that license published by that same organization.

"Incorporate" means to publish or republish a Document, in whole or in part, as part of another Document.

An MMC is "eligible for relicensing" if it is licensed under this License, and if all works that were first published under this License somewhere other than this MMC, and subsequently incorporated in whole or in part into the MMC, (1) had no cover texts or invariant sections, and (2) were thus incorporated prior to November 1, 2008.

The operator of an MMC Site may republish an MMC contained in the site under CC-BY-SA on the same site at any time before August 1, 2009, provided the MMC is eligible for relicensing.

ADDENDUM: How to use this License for your documents

To use this License in a document you have written, include a copy of the License in the document and put the following copyright and license notices just after the title page:

```
Copyright (C)  year  your name.
Permission is granted to copy, distribute and/or modify this document
under the terms of the GNU Free Documentation License, Version 1.3
or any later version published by the Free Software Foundation;
with no Invariant Sections, no Front-Cover Texts, and no Back-Cover
Texts.  A copy of the license is included in the section entitled ``GNU
Free Documentation License''.
```

If you have Invariant Sections, Front-Cover Texts and Back-Cover Texts, replace the "with...Texts." line with this:

```
with the Invariant Sections being list their titles, with
the Front-Cover Texts being list, and with the Back-Cover Texts
being list.
```

If you have Invariant Sections without Cover Texts, or some other combination of the three, merge those two alternatives to suit the situation.

If your document contains nontrivial examples of program code, we recommend releasing these examples in parallel under your choice of free software license, such as the GNU General Public License, to permit their use in free software.

Concept Index

Concept Index

G

H

I

Concept Index

M

N

T

Type Index

M

N

O

P

R

S

T

U

V

W

Function and Macro Index

D

G

H

I

M

N

O

P

Q

R

S

T

Y

Variable and Constant Macro Index

A

B

C

M

Program and File Index